Software Engineering for Embedded Systems

Software Engineering for Embedded Systems

Methods, Practical Techniques, and Applications

Robert Oshana
Mark Kraeling

AMSTERDAM • BOSTON • HEIDELBERG • LONDON
NEW YORK • OXFORD • PARIS • SAN DIEGO
SAN FRANCISCO • SINGAPORE • SYDNEY • TOKYO
Newnes is an imprint of Elsevier

Newnes is an imprint of Elsevier
225 Wyman Street, Waltham, MA 02451, USA

First edition 2013

Copyright © 2013 Elsevier Inc. All rights reserved.

No part of this publication may be reproduced, stored in a retrieval system, or transmitted in any form or by any means, electronic, mechanical, photocopying, recording, or otherwise, without the prior written permission of the publisher.

Permissions may be sought directly from Elsevier's Science & Technology Rights Department in Oxford, UK: phone (+44) (0) 1865 843830; fax (+44) (0) 1865 853333; email: permissions@elsevier.com. Alternatively you can submit your request online by visiting the Elsevier web site at http://elsevier.com/locate/permissions, and selecting Obtaining permission to use Elsevier material.

Notice
No responsibility is assumed by the publisher for any injury and/or damage to persons or property as a matter of products liability, negligence or otherwise, or from any use or operation of any methods, products, instructions or ideas contained in the material herein. Because of rapid advances in the medical sciences, in particular, independent verification of diagnoses and drug dosages should be made.

British Library Cataloguing-in-Publication Data
A catalogue record for this book is available from the British Library.

Library of Congress Cataloging-in-Publication Data
A catalog record for this book is availabe from the Library of Congress.

ISBN: 978-0-12-415917-4

For information on all Newnes publications
visit our Web site at www.books.elsevier.com

Printed in the United States of America

13 14 15 16 17   10 9 8 7 6 8 4 3 2 1

Contents

Software Engineering for Embedded Systems: A Roadmap

Over the past ten years or so, the world of computing has moved from large, static, desktop machines to small, mobile, and embedded devices. The methods, techniques, and tools for developing software systems that were successfully applied in desktop systems are not as readily applicable to embedded applications. Software systems running on mobile, embedded devices must exhibit properties that are not always required of more traditional systems:

- near-optimal performance
- robustness
- distribution
- dynamism
- mobility

This book will examine the key properties of software systems in the embedded, resource constrained, mobile, and networked world. We will assess the applicability of mainstream software engineering methods and techniques (e.g., software design, component-based development, software architecture, system integration and test) to this domain.

Embedded systems can be conceptualized as a layered structure of software enablement and management as shown in Figure 1. There are five horizontal areas of consideration in this embedded systems discussion;

1. Process layer
2. Hardware layer
3. Platform layer
4. Middleware layer
5. Application layer

There are three vertical focus areas discussed in this book;

1. Automotive applications
2. Networking application
3. Storage and I/O applications

There are many other vertical application areas that can be discussed but these three are representative of many embedded systems.

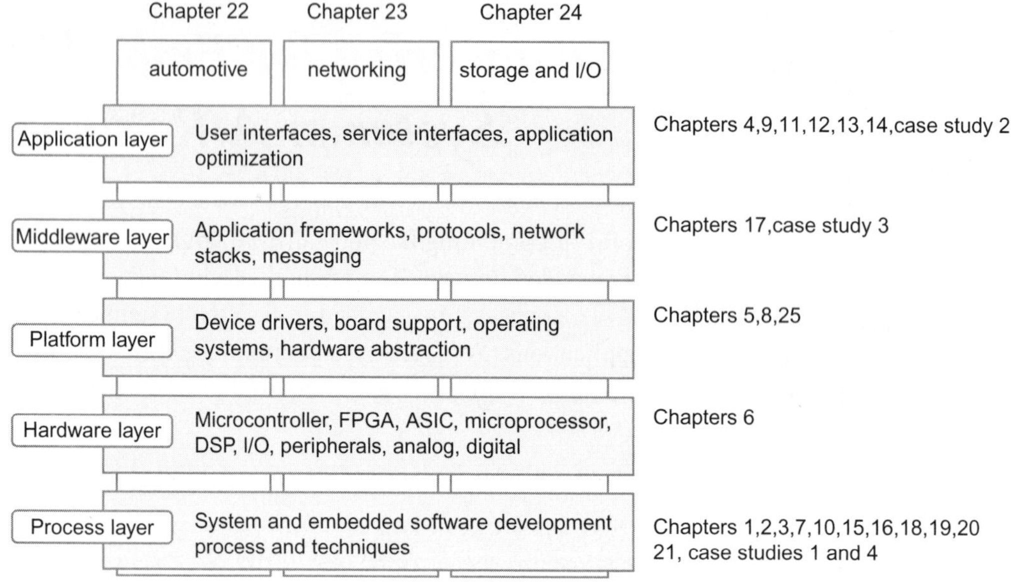

Figure 1:
Layered Hierarchy for Embedded Systems Development.

This book is structured to address this layered hierarchy of embedded system development as shown in this model. Each of the chapters and case studies are mapped to this model;

- Chapter 1; Overview of Embedded and Real-Time Systems
- Chapter 2; Embedded Systems Hardware/Software Co-design
- Chapter 3; Specification and Modeling Techniques
- Chapter 4; Architecture and Design Patterns
- Chapter 5; Real-Time Building Blocks
- Chapter 6; The Hardware Interface to Embedded Software
- Chapter 7; Embedded Software Programming and Implementation Guidelines
- Chapter 8; Embedded Operating systems
- Chapter 9; Software Reuse in Embedded Systems
- Chapter 10; Software Performance Engineering
- Chapter 11; Optimizing Embedded Software for Performance
- Chapter 12; Optimizing Embedded Software for Memory
- Chapter 13; Optimizing Embedded Software for Power
- Chapter 14; Human Factors and User Interface Design for embedded systems
- Chapter 15; Integration and Testing techniques and Quality for Embedded Software
- Chapter 16; Software Development Tools for Embedded Systems
- Chapter 17; Multicore Software Development for Embedded Systems

- Chapter 18; Safety-Critical Software Development for Embedded Systems
- Chapter 19; Intellectual Property Issues with Embedded Software
- Chapter 20; Managing Embedded Software Development
- Chapter 21; Agile Development for Embedded Systems
- Chapter 22; Embedded Software Development for Storage and I/O
- Chapter 23; Embedded Software for Automotive Applications
- Chapter 24; Embedded Software Development for Embedded Networking
- Chapter 25; Linux and Open Source Software for Embedded Systems
- Performance Engineering Case Study 1
- User Interface Design Case Study 2
- Multicore Software Development Case Study 3
- Software Measurement and Metrics Case Study 4
- Appendix A; C Syntax Coding Standards

The embedded system hardware/software co-design life cycle model is shown in Figure 2. The chapters in this book can also be mapped to this embedded system lifecycle as shown in this figure.

This book contains 25 chapters of practical and up to date information on many of the topical areas shown in Figures 1 and 2. These chapter by chapter details are summarized below.

Chapter 1; Introduction to embedded and real time systems; An embedded system is a computer system designed for a specific function within a larger system, and often has one or more real-time computing constraints. It is *embedded* as part of a larger device which can include hardware and mechanical parts. This is in stark contrast to a general-purpose computer, which is designed to be flexible and meet a wide range of end-user needs. The methods, techniques, and tools for developing software systems that were successfully applied in the former scenario are not as readily applicable in the latter. Software systems running on networks of mobile, embedded devices must exhibit properties that are not always required of more traditional systems such as near-optimal performance, robustness, distribution, dynamism, and mobility. This chapter will examine the key properties of software systems in the embedded, resource constrained, mobile, and highly distributed world. The applicability of mainstream software engineering methods is assessed and techniques (e.g., software design, component-based development, software architecture, system integration and test) are also discussed in the context of this domain. This chapter will overview embedded and real-time systems.

Chapter 2; Embedded Systems hardware/software co-design; When planning the development of modern embedded systems, hardware and software cannot be considered independently. Over the last two decades, chip and system complexity have seen an enormous amount of growth, while more and more system functionality has moved from dedicated hardware implementation into software executing on general purposed embedded

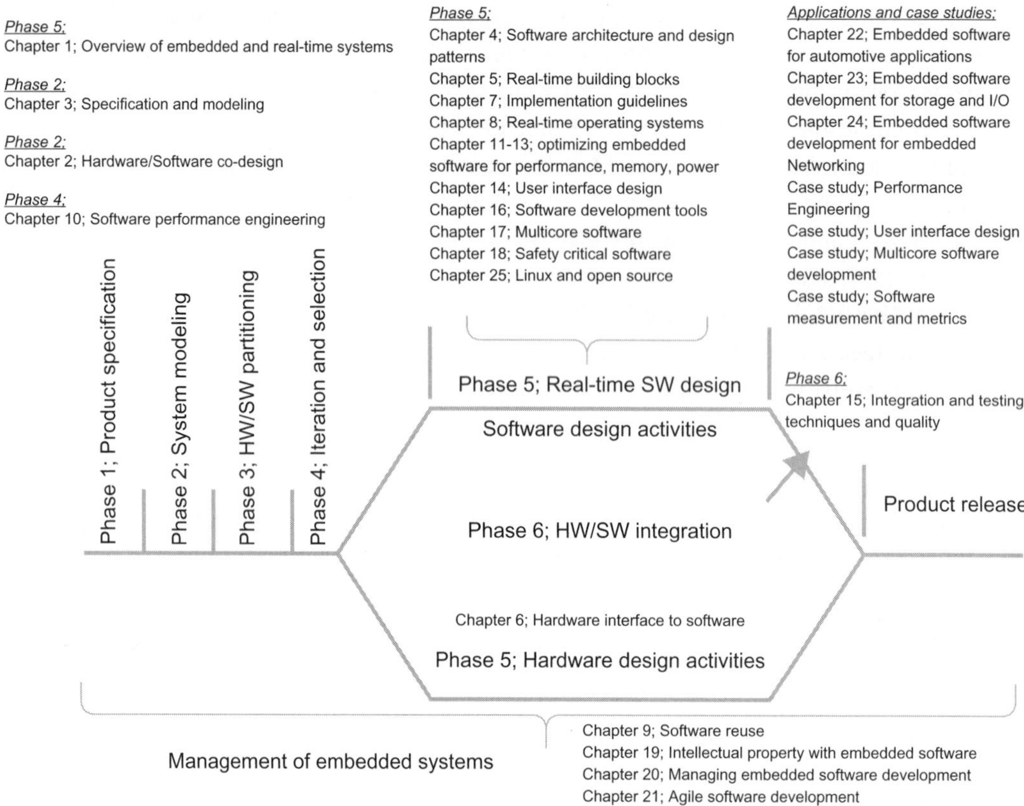

Figure 2:
Embedded Systems Hardware/Software Co-design Model.

processors. By 2010 the development effort for software had outgrown the development efforts for hardware, and the complexity trend continues in favor of software. Traditional design techniques such as independent hardware and software design are being challenged due to heterogeneous models and applications gettinging integrated to create a complex system on chip. Using proper techniques of hardware-software codesign, designers consider the trade-offs in the way hardware and software components of a system work together to exhibit a specified behavior, given a set of performance goals and technology. This chapter will cover these topics.

Chapter 3; Specification and Modeling techniques; Creating a model for your embedded system provides a time and cost-effective approach to the development of simple or incredibly complex dynamic control systems, all based on a single model maintained in a tightly integrated software suite. Using modern modeling software tools you can design and perform initial validation in off-line simulation. These models then form the basis for all subsequent development stages. Creating models for your embedded design provides numerous advantages over the traditional design approach. Using this approach – combined with hardware prototyping - you reduce the risk of mistakes and shorten the development cycle by performing verification and validation testing throughout the development instead of only during the final testing stage. Design evaluations and predictions can be made much more quickly and reliably with a system model as a basis. This iterative approach results in improved designs, both in terms of performance and reliability. The cost of resources is reduced, because of reusability of models between design teams, design stages, and various projects and the reduced dependency on physical prototypes. Development errors and overhead can be reduced through the use of automatic code generation techniques. These advantages translate to more accurate and robust control designs, shorter time to market, and reduced design cost.

Chapter 4; Architecture and software design patterns; The software architecture of embedded computing system is a depiction of the system as a set of structures that aids in the reasoning and understanding of how the system will behave. Software architecture acts as the blueprint for the system as well as the project developing it. The architecture is the primary framework of important embedded system qualities such as performance, modifiability, and security, none of which can be achieved without a unifying architectural vision. Architecture is an artifact for early analysis to ensure that a design approach will lead to an acceptable system. This chapter will discuss the details of these aspects of embedded software architectures.

Chapter 5; Embedded Building Blocks; The previous chapter approaches embedded systems from a higher level of abstraction; from the system design architecture and how to apply design patterns for the implementation. This chapter introduces two fundamental concepts and design patterns in real time systems; a) the ability to set asynchronous event flags (*Events*) and b) to have things triggered in a timely fashion (*Triggers*). These two concepts are both used in systems with a real time operating system (RTOS) and as well in system not using an RTOS. The chapter starts with use cases and then develops different ways to implement *Events* and *Triggers*. It presents different implementation details and discusses the advantages and disadvantages. The sources both for Event and Trigger implementation is provided at the end of the chapter.

Chapter 6; Hardware Interface to Software; This chapter discusses the interface that hardware provides for the embedded software. It discusses the registers and interrupts that provides that interface. But there is more; there is the human aspects of getting the hardware team and the embedded software team to collaborate on the project. Collaboration is needed during the design phase, the co-development phase, the integration phase, and the debugging phase and this chapter discusses those concepts. Several hardware design aspects are discussed that improve the quality of the product and software design aspects are discussed to help support hardware versions.

Chapter 7; Embedded Software Programming and Implementation Guidelines. This chapter provides some guidelines that are commonly used in embedded software development. It starts with principles of programming, including readability, testability, and maintainability. The chapter then proceeds with discussing how to start an embedded software project, including considerations for hardware, file organization, and development guidelines. The focus then shifts to programming guidelines that are important to any software development project, which includes the importance of a syntax coding standard. The chapter concludes with descriptions of variables and definitions and how they are typically used in an embedded software project.

Chapter 8; Embedded Operating systems; Real-Time Operating Systems (RTOS) are ubiquitous in embedded systems This chapter explains what a real-time kernel is, what services it provides the product developer and explains some of the internals of a kernel. A kernel is a component of an RTOS. In this chapter, we'll look at task management, interrupt handling, scheduling, context switching, time management, resource management, message passing, priority inversions and much more.

Chapter 9; Software Reuse in Embedded Systems; This chapter explores the unique challenges that limit reuse in embedded systems, and strategies to overcome them. It explores what limits reuse, and traditional approaches to overcome the limitations such as a hardware abstraction layer or an RTOS porting layer. It does not stop there. The shortcomings of layered software drive a desire for highly-optimized reusable software components. This chapter introduces the Component Factory concept: a mechanism that creates reconfigurable and reusable hardware- and RTOS-agnostic components generated by an expert system.

Chapter 10; Software Performance Engineering; Embedded systems often have one or more real-time requirements. The complexity of modern embedded software systems requires a systematic approach for achieving these performance targets. An ad hoc process can lead to missed deadlines, poor performing systems and cancelled projects. There is a maturity required to define, manage, and deliver on multiple real time performance requirements. Software Performance Engineering (SPE) is a discipline within the broader systems engineering area that can improve the maturity of the performance engineering process. SPE is a systematic, quantitative approach to constructing software systems that meet performance objectives. SPE is a software oriented approach; focuses on architecture, design, and implementation choices. It focuses on the activities, techniques, and deliverables that are applied at every phase of the embedded software development lifecycle, especially responsiveness and scalability, to ensure software is being architected and implemented to meet the performance related requirements for the system.

Chapter 11; Optimizing Embedded Software for Performance; Code optimization is a critical step in the development process as it directly impacts the ability of the system to do its intended job. Code that executes faster means more channels, more work performed and competitive advantage. Code that executes in less memory enables more application features to fit into the cell phone. Code that executes with less overall power consumption increases battery life or reduces money spent on powering a basestation. This chapter is intended to help programmers write the most efficient code possible, whether that is measured in processor cycles, memory, or power. It starts with an introduction to using the tool chain, covers the importance of knowing the embedded architecture before optimization, then moves on to cover wide range of optimization techniques. Techniques are presented which are valid on all programmable architectures – C-language optimization techniques and general loop transformations. Real-world examples are presented throughout.

Chapter 12; Optimizing Embedded Software for Memory; Optimization metrics for compiled code are not always measured in resulting execution clock cycles on the target architecture. Consider modern cellular telephone or wireless device which may download executables over a wireless network connection or backhaul infrastructure. In such cases, it is often advantageous or the compiler to reduce the size of the compiled code which must be downloaded to the wireless device. By reducing the size of the code needed to be downloaded, savings are achieved in terms of bandwidth required for each wireless point of download. Optimization metrics such as the memory system performance of compiled code are another metric which are often important to developers. These are metrics correlated to the dynamic runtime behavior of not only the compiled code on the target processor, but also the underlying memory system, caches, DRAM and busses etc. By efficiently arranging the data within the application, or more specifically, the order in which data and corresponding data structures are accessed by the application dynamically at runtime, significant performance improvements can be gained at the memory system level. In addition, vectorizing compilers can also improve performance due to spatial locality of data when SIMD instruction sets are present and varying memory system alignment conditions are met.

Chapter 13; Optimizing Embedded Software for Power; One of the most important considerations in the product lifecycle of an embedded project is to understand and optimize the power consumption of the device. Power consumption is highly visible for handheld devices which require battery power to be able to guarantee certain minimum usage / idle times between recharging. Other main embedded applications: medical equipment, test, measurement, media, and wireless base station, are very sensitive to power as well - due to the need to manage heat dissipation of increasingly powerful processors, power supply cost, and energy consumption cost, so the fact is that power consumption cannot be overlooked. The responsibility of setting and keeping power requirements often falls on the shoulders of hardware designers, but the software programmer has the ability to provide a large contribution to power optimization. Often, the impact that the software engineer has to influence the power consumption of a device is overlooked or underestimated. The goal of this chapter is to discuss how software can be used to optimize power consumption, starting with the basics of what power consumption consists of, how to properly measure power consumption, and then moving on to techniques for minimizing power consumption in software at the algorithmic level, hardware level, and data flow. This will include demonstrations of the various techniques and explanations of both how and why certain methods are effective at reducing power so the reader can take and apply this work to their application immediately.

Chapter 14; Human Factors and User Interface Design for embedded systems. When designing an embedded system, special care must be taken when you design the user interface. For simple devices, simple text, command buttons, and LEDs are adequate. For more complex systems, full graphical user interfaces and touch panels are required. User interface design focuses on the following key areas; a) the design of interfaces between different software components, b) the design of interfaces between the software and other nonhuman producers and consumers of information, and c) the design of the interface between a human and the computer. This chapter will focus on the process, guidelines, human factors and techniques required to design an effective user interface.

Chapter 15; Integration and Testing Techniques and Quality for Embedded Software; State of the art techniques and best practices in the development of embedded software apply not only to high integrity devices (such as those for safety critical applications like aircraft flight controllers, car braking systems or medical devices), but also to lesser integrity applications when the need to optimize the effectiveness of the available test time and budget demands that pragmatic decisions should be made. To complement this multitude of software test techniques there is a similar plethora of test tools available to automate them. These tools are commonplace in the development of safety critical applications, but elsewhere not everyone has the budget to buy all, or indeed any, of them. Of course, the providers of these tools would advocate the purchase of each and every one of them, so how can a limited budget best be allocated? And where no budget exists, how can similar principles be applied without such tools to provide confidence that the finished item is of adequate quality? In addressing these issues in this chapter, not only are the concepts behind the techniques presented but also some "case study" software code examples illustrate how some of them are implemented in practice.

Chapter 16; Software Development Tools for Embedded Systems; This chapter focuses on the software development tools for embedded systems, especially on the debugging and investigation tools. The chapter starts by presenting the capabilities of a source code debugger – a tool that allows the developer to see what is inside his program in the current execution point or in the moment when that program crashed. The debugger features are described using as example one of the most popular and used debuggers, GDB – GNU

Debugger provided by Free Software Foundation. In order to cover all the requirements of an embedded system, the chapter presents in the following how to design a debug agent that fits into our special target requirements starting from a simple debug routine and evolving to a fully featured debugger. It also presents the typical use cases and the key points of the design like context switch, position independent executable, debug event handling and multi-core. It then presents the benefits of using the JTAG, an external device used to connect the debugger directly to the target, allowing the debugger to have full control of the target and its resources. By the end of the chapter it presents other tools that may help in the debugging process like integrated development tools based on free open-source software (Eclipse, GDB), instrumented code and analysis tools.

Chapter 17; Multicore software development for Embedded Systems; Multicore software development is growing in importance and applicability in many areas of embedded systems from automotive to networking, to wireless basestations. This chapter is a summary of key sections of the recently released Multicore Programming Practices (MPP) from the Multicore Association (MCA). The MPP standardized "best practices" guide is written specifically for engineers and engineering managers of companies considering or implementing a development project involving multicore processors and favoring use of existing multicore technology. There is an important need to better understand how today's C/C++ code may be written to be "multicore ready", and this was accomplished under the influence of the MPP working group. The guide will enable you to a) produce higher performing software; b) reduce bug rate due to multicore software issues; c) develop portable multicore code which can be targeted at multiple platforms; d) reduce the multicore programming learning curve and speed up development time; and e) tie into the current structure and roadmap of the Multicore Association's API infrastructure.

Chapter 18; Safety-Critical Software Development for Embedded Systems. In this chapter, we cover the aspects of developing safety-critical software. The first part of the chapter covers project planning, and the crucial steps that are needed to scope the effort and getting started. It offers insights into managing safety-critical requirements and how to meet them during the development. Key strategies for project management are also provided. The second part of the chapter goes through an analysis of faults, failures, and hazards. It includes a description of risk analysis. The next part of the chapter covers a few safety-critical architectures that could be used for an embedded system. The final part of the chapter covers software implementation guidelines for safety-critical software development.

Chapter 19; Intellectual Property Issues with Embedded Software; Intellectual property normally means one of two things - the patents or other legal protections you have accumulated to protect your inventions, or the inventions and designs themselves. So we may talk about "licensing one's intellectual property", and mean either selling a license to someone to make use of your patented ideas, or selling a license to build, distribute or use a product, as ARM does with its processor and other designs or a tools company does with its compiler and OS products. In this chapter, we will be concentrating more on the first meaning - dealing with the legal protections around your work, and we will be covering the basics in two major sections, one covering the issues surrounding what you need to do to be sure that you actually do own that software that you wrote or bought, what you need to do when selling it or licensing it to others, including the role of 'open software'; and the other covering the various protections you can obtain for your software and any valuable inventions in it.

Chapter 20; Managing Embedded Software Development; The chapter, Managing Embedded Software Development, provides information to successfully organize and manage any embedded software project or program. It introduces quality systems, the OSI model of architecting software into stacks, several software development models, ways in which teams may be organized, and overviews communications. Managing the constraints of scope, schedule, costs including resources, quality, and customer satisfaction fully addresses all the work and activities of any project or program. The natural progression of software development from its concept through its lifecycle until release is discussed. Tools are presented for successful planning and execution of resource management, risk management, problem solving, and the traceability of work extending from requirements to respective engineering responses to testing against those software specifications.

Chapter 21; Agile Software Development for Embedded Systems; Agile software development is a set of software development techniques based on iterative development. Requirements and software systems evolve through collaboration between self-organizing, cross-functional teams. Agile development supports adaptive planning, evolutionary development and delivery, and a time-boxed iterative approach. The goal of Agile is rapid and flexible response to change. Agile is a conceptual framework which promotes interactions throughout the development cyçle. Applying Agile to embedded software projects introduces some unique challenges, such as more difficulty effectively testing evolving software features, because the corresponding hardware may not be available in time, less freedom to make changes, due to the fact that the corresponding hardware change may have an unacceptably high cost, and less ability for "learn as you go" approaches, considering the hardware construction may demand a more upfront style of planning and design. This chapter will introduce Agile software development and show how to apply these techniques to an embedded system.

Chapter 22; Embedded Software for Automotive Applications; The Embedded Software for Automotive Applications chapter introduces the automotive system which is unlike any other, characterized by its rigorous planning, architecting, development, testing, validation and verification. The physical task of writing embedded software for automotive applications versus other application areas is not significantly different from other embedded systems, but the key differences are the quality standards which must be followed for any development and test project. To write automotive software the engineer needs to understand: how and why the systems have evolved in to the complex environment it is today. They must be aware of the differences and commonalties between the automotive submarkets. They must be familiar with the applicable quality standards and why such strict quality controls exist, along with how quality is tested and measured, all of which are described in this chapter with examples of the most common practices. This chapter introduces various processes to help software engineers write high quality, fault tolerant, interoperable code such as modeling, autocoding and advanced trace and debug assisted by the emergence of the latest AUTOSAR and ISO26262 standards, as well as more traditional standards such as AEC, OBD-II and MISRA.

Chapter 23; Embedded Software Development for Storage and I/O; Input and Output (I/O) devices are very important components in embedded systema. I/O diversity makes I/O management in embedded systems a very complicated process. One of the basic functions of an embedded operating system is to control and manage all of the I/O devices, and to coordinate multiple processes accessing I/O devices simultaneously. The key function for device management is to control I/O implementation between the CPU and the devices. The operating system must send commands to the devices, respond to the interrupt and handle the exception of the devices. It should also provide a simple and easily to use interface between the devices and other parts of the system. Therefore, the I/O management module needs to improve parallel processing capabilities between the CPU and I/O devices as well between I/O devices. Therefore, to get the best utilization efficiency of the system resources, I/O management modules should provide a unified, transparent, independent and scalable I/O interface. The storage in this book refers to the external storage devices such as NOR/NAND Flash, eSDHC, U-Disk, HDD and SSD, which are commonly used in embedded system. With the recent development of cloud computing, storage technology plays as increasingly important role in the system. This chapter will discuss data transfer modes between CPU and I/O devices, interrupt technology, I/O control processes and the corresponding device driver implementation process. The programming model of storage devices is also discussed, including feature support and performance optimization.

Chapter 24; Software Development for Embedded Networking Applications; Embedded networking applications are changing and evolving quickly. Embedded multicore technology, for example, is appearing not only in high end networking applications, but even mid and low end networking applications. Achieving networking performance is only possible if software takes advantage of multiple cores. Multicore programming is not as simple as single core programming. New mindset is required from architecting, designing to coding. Networking application development in multicore SoCs not only should concentrate on achieving scalable performance, but also should ease the development and be maintainable for a long time. Some of the programming techniques listed in this chapter should help in achieving this goal.

Chapter 25; Linux and Open Source Software for Embedded Systems; Linux continues to grow as an operating system of choice in many embedded systems such as networking, wireless, and base stations. In this chapter we look at possible uses of Linux in embedded systems. The chapter covers getting a Linux Kernel setup, getting started with creating your Linux baseline, and the initial steps of getting an application running on the platform. If you haven't used Linux for an embedded system before, this chapter will cover all of the basic steps to get you going!

Case Study 1; Multicore Software development; In this case study, Multicore programming practices will be applied to a real-world industry application. The migration of an embedded software application from a single core application to a Multicore application requires changing the software programming model, software scheduling system, system partitioning approaches, and optimization strategies. Knowledge of the application domain, the SoC details including the core, offload blocks, peripherals, and interconnect details, as well as the software optimization alternatives will determine how effectively this transition will be. This case study will walk through the steps involved to migrate a networking software application from a single core implementation to a highly optimized Multicore implementation.

Case Study 2; Software Measurement and Metrics; This case study will look at software development and system integration metrics for a Femto embedded system. Femtocell is a low-power, short range, self-contained basestation. Femtocells are essentially mini basestations for the home and small offices. The key attributes of Femtocells include IP backhaul (voice traffic is sent of the internet), self-optimization, low power consumption and ease of deployment. Actual industry data is used to reinforce many of the techniques discussed in the case study.

Case Study 3; Performance Engineering; This case study will look at the application of Software Performance Engineering (SPE) to a real industry project. SPE is a set of techniques for gathering data, constructing a system performance model, evaluating the performance model, managing risk of uncertainty, evaluating alternatives, and verifying the models and results. SPE also includes strategies for the effective use of these techniques. Expensive disasters can be avoided when system performance evaluation takes place relatively early in the software development lifecycle. Applications will generally have better performance when alternative designs are evaluated prior to implementation.

Case Study 4; User Interface Design; This case study is a user interface prototype of a Police Command and Control System which will incorporate user interface development techniques to the development of a low fidelity prototype for this system. This case study will incorporate the processes and techniques outlined in Chapter 10 on Human Factors and User Interface Design. User interface design focuses on the following key areas; the design of interfaces between different software components, the design of interfaces between the software and other nonhuman producers and consumers of information, and the design of the interface between a human and the computer.

C Syntax Coding Standard Appendix; This section includes a syntax standard which could be considered for an embedded project. It includes a style guide and naming conventions for variables and declarations. It can be used as is, or modified to fit the particular application being developed. Using a standard for coding can help with providing uniformity in the code baseline, which helps with readability and maintainability among all of the developers. It also suggests practices that help reduce bugs in the code, such as initialization order and conventions that should be avoided.

Foreword to Software Engineering for Embedded Systems

This is a monumental work. It's probably the most comprehensive book about embedded systems to date. And it is desperately needed.

Firmware is getting big. Some estimates peg firmware at 80% of the development cost of modern products. Whereas a few years ago a system with a few hundred thousand lines of code was considered huge, today it's common to find multi-megaline code bases. Smart phones use tens of millions of lines and are spectacularly complex. Consumers figure 70% of the value of an automobile comes from the electronics – they're buying code more than engines and wheels.

Since the introduction of the first microprocessor forty years ago the standard way to build firmware was heroics. Smart people, way too much overtime, and a lot of yelling from drill sergeant bosses got products out the door. But that approach just does not scale and simply can't cope with today's huge systems. A more disciplined approach is needed. And this book does an awesome job of conveying that information.

Chapter 15 on integration and testing, for instance, covers those subjects in exactly the right way. It all starts from the requirements, and ends with tests mapped back to those requirements. Mark shows how one can use control-flow graphs to insure the tests are complete. Today most developers have no idea if their test suite covers 10% of possible flows, or 90% or 100%. As engineers we need to do the analysis he outlines to prove our product is correct. And – mirabile dictu! – there are plenty of tools from a variety of vendors that will construct test cases, manage requirements, and ensure complete testing coverage.

Chapter 4 covers design patterns for embedded systems. Patterns are reuse in a disciplined way and is common in IT projects. It is only now finding a place in the embedded world. Chapter 9 covering software reuse gives insight into more traditional (and all-too-rarely practiced) aspects of recycling software components.

Lest one thinks that this means big-up-front design, the authors also address agile programming and the special challenges presented with embedded systems.

But it also deals with the ugly realities of engineering. Chapter 2 on hardware/software co-design shows the reader how to bring both hardware and software up in parallel, despite the obvious problem that with neither complete, neither can be tested using conventional strategies.

What makes embedded so unique? A big reason is scarce resources. Limited memory and CPU cycles sorely test the developer; today power consumption is a big concern since so many systems are expected to run from batteries. A number of chapters address all of these issues, even showing software techniques to squeeze every microwatt from a battery.

Another aspect unique to firmware is its close integration with the hardware. That, too, gets treated in-depth in several chapters.

Other topics include the special needs of automotive code. Linux and Android, of course. Building safety-critical systems (and more of us do this than we might expect; change "safety-critical" to "mission-critical" and you may be surprised at how your product should be embracing the concerns of the safety community).

It's hard to think of any aspect of embedded software that this book doesn't cover.

The only constant in this field is change. A November, 2012 article in India Times claims software developers are obsolete by age 40. That's a tough age to start a new career. Read this book and learn more effective ways to get your projects out the door. It'll help you stay relevant and avoid becoming one of those doomed over 40 engineers.

Jack Ganssle

Acknowledgments

As part of the compilation of this embedded software engineering book, we asked many of the leading engineers in the embedded space to contribute according to their area of expertise. The outcome of this decision is the chapters themselves become more self-inclusive; where the author has put together the information necessary to complete the purpose for that singular chapter. In some cases, this may cause duplication of information across chapters – but this is done on purpose.

The goal is to have a software engineering handbook that can be consulted on various topics without having to flip between multiple areas in the book. The authors of each chapter were given the freedom and flexibility to place their respective knowledge on the subject into the chapter. The chapters were designed to be practical and based on real-world experiences from the authors. This book contains over 300 years of combined embedded systems experience!

A website dedicated for information about the book as well as useful references and support material can be found at www.elsevierstore.com/companions/9780124159174. Feel free to download the tools and peruse this additional information. It's a valuable part of the overall experience.

Shifting gears, the editors would like to thank each of the authors for their contribution to this book. We would also like to thank the Production Project Manager at Elsevier Pauline Wilkinson and copy-editor Roger Borthwick, and the Elsevier staff including Tim Pitts and Charlie Kent. Thanks for all of your help!

We hope that the book is a useful reference to the readers, and can be used to gain insight into the various areas of embedded systems.

Rob would like to thank his lovely wife Susan and his sons Sam and Noah for their patience during this project!

Mark would like to thank his wonderful wife Shannon, and also Brad, Spencer, Chandra, Glen, Jeff, RJ, Shelly, Todd, Mom, and Dad.

We hope you enjoy the book.

Rob and Mark

About the Editors

Robert Oshana
Email: robert.oshana@freescale.com

Robert Oshana has over 30 years of experience in the embedded software industry, primarily focused on embedded and real-time systems for the defense industry and semiconductor industries. Rob has extensive experience in embedded systems, software engineering, software quality and process, and leading global development teams. He has BSEE, MSEE, MSCS, and MBA degrees and is a Senior Member of IEEE. Rob is an international speaker and has over 100 presentations and publications in various technology fields and has written several books on embedded software technology. Rob is an adjunct professor at Southern Methodist University where he teaches graduate software engineering and embedded systems courses. and is a Distinguished Member of Technical Staff and Director of Global Software R&D for Networking and Multimedia at Freescale Semiconductor.

Mark Kraeling
Email: markfl04@yahoo.com

Mark Kraeling has over 20 years of experience in the embedded software industry, primarily focused on embedded real-time systems for the automotive and transportation industries. He has a BSEE, MSEE, and MBA degrees. Mark is a regular speaker at embedded conferences worldwide, and has various papers and articles focused on embedded development that have been published over the course of his career. Mark actively participates in industry development, including presenting embedded systems papers at Embedded Systems and Design Conferences, as well as developing standards with various subcommittees of the Association of American Railroads (AAR). Mark started his career at Cummins, Inc. developing real-time engine controls. Mark is currently a Product Manager at GE Transportation, developing real-time and safety-critical railway systems.

About the Authors

Srini Addepalli

Email: addepalli.srinivasa@gmail.com

Srini Addepalli is a Fellow and chief software architect at Freescale Semiconductor. In this role he focuses on architecture of network software technologies and acceleration engines from a software perspective. Srini previously served as Chief Architect at Intoto and was responsible for the architecture of their Unified Threat Management software products for single and multicore processors. He is a 22-year veteran in networking and data communications and has worked at Intoto, Holontech, NEC and HP. His experience spans a range of areas from routing, switching and mobility technologies to network security technologies, including firewall, VPN, intrusion detection and anti-virus technologies.

Michael C Brogioli

Dr. Michael C. Brogioli is currently a Principal and Founder at Polymathic Consulting in Austin, TX, an Adjunct Professor of Computer Engineering at Rice University in Houston, TX, and an avid entrepreneur/advisor in the Central Texas, USA, area. Prior to his time at Polymathic, Dr. Brogioli was a Senior Member of the Technical Staff and Chief Architect at Freescale Semiconductor in Austin, TX, USA. In addition to his tenure at Freescale, he has served roles at Texas Instruments' Advanced Architecture and Chip Technology Research, as well as Intel Corporation's Advanced Microprocessor Research Labs under the leadership of Dr. Jesse Fang. Dr. Brogioli holds a PhD/MSc in Electrical and Computer Engineering from Rice University, as well as a BSc in Electrical Engineering from Rensselaer Polytechnic Institute.

Bruce Powel Douglass
Email: bruce.douglass@us.ibm.com

Bruce Powel Douglass, who has a doctorate in neurocybernetics from the USD Medical School, has over 30 years experience designing safety-critical real-time applications in a variety of hard real-time environments. He has designed and taught courses in agile methods, object orientation, MDA, real-time systems, and safety-critical systems development, and is the author of over 5000 book pages from a number of technical books including *Real-Time UML*, *Real-Time UML Workshop for Embedded Systems*, *Real-Time Design Patterns*, *Doing Hard Time*, *Real-Time Agility*, and *Design Patterns for Embedded Systems in C*. He is the Chief Evangelist at IBM Rational, where he is a thought leader in the systems space, consulting with and mentoring IBM customers all over the world, represents IBM at many different conferences, and authors tools and processes for the embedded real-time industry. He can be followed on Twitter @BruceDouglass. Papers and presentations are available at his Real-Time UML Yahoo technical group (http://tech.groups.yahoo.com/group/RT-UML) and from his IBM page (www-01.ibm.com/software/rational/leadership/thought/brucedouglass.html).

Shelley Gretlein
Email: Shelley.gretlein@ni.com

Shelley Gretlein is the Director of Software Product Marketing at National Instruments. Currently focused on growing the application and success of graphical system design globally, Gretlein is responsible for the development strategy and worldwide evangelism of the LabVIEW software platform including LabVIEW Real-Time and LabVIEW FPGA. Recently she was also actively involved in working with lead users to enhance robotics and autonomous system design applications. She is also involved in industry consortia on robotics, industrial control and embedded forums, including as a graphical system and embedded design consultant for various publications. She joined National Instruments in 2000 and holds a bachelor's degree in computer science and management systems as well as minors in Mathematics and French from the Missouri University of Science and Technology.

Inga Harris
Email: inga.harris@freescale.com

Inga Harris is a Senior Applications Engineer at Freescale, a leading international semiconductor company, with extensive experience in embedded industrial, consumer and automotive systems. Freescale is the global leader in embedded processing solutions, advancing the automotive, consumer, industrial and networking markets. As a Senior Applications Engineer she is responsible for the testing, development and support of 32-bit microcontroller products for the Powertrain applications area. Inga has a BEng with Honors in Electronic and Electrical Engineering with Business Studies from the University of Strathclyde in Scotland, has been published numerous times in industry publications all over the world was granted her first patent in early 2013.

Jean J. Labrosse
Email: jean.labrosse@micrium.com

Jean J. Labrosse, Founder, CEO and President. Jean Labrosse founded Micrium in 1999 and continues to maintain an active role in product development, ensuring that the company adheres to the strict policies and standards that make it strong. Labrosse is a regular speaker at the Embedded Systems Conference in Boston and Silicon Valley, and other industry conferences. He is the author of three definitive books on embedded design: *MicroC/OS-II, The Real-Time Kernel*, *Embedded Systems Building Blocks*, *Complete and Ready-to-Use Modules in C*, and *μC/OS-III, The Real-Time Kernel*, and has published numerous articles and appeared on industry panels on the subject of embedded design. He holds BSEE and MSEE degrees from the University of Sherbrooke, Quebec, Canada.

Frank Schirrmeister
Email: frank@schirrmeister.com

Frank Schirrmeister currently works as Senior Director for Product Management of the System Development Suite at Cadence Design Systems. He has 20 + years of experience in IP and semiconductor design, embedded software development, hardware/software co-development and electronic design automation. He holds an MSEE (Dipl.-Ing.) from the Technical University of Berlin, Germany.

Gary Stringham
Email: gary@garystringham.com

Gary Stringham is an embedded systems expert with a specialization in writing firmware and in hardware/firmware integration. He is the founder of Gary Stringham & Associates, LLC (www.garystringham.com). With over 25 years of industry experience, Gary focuses on diagnosing and resolving difficult system integration issues and produces solid solutions to prevent future occurrences of those issues. He is an expert witness, a frequent presenter, and is the author of the book *Hardware/Firmware Interface Design: Best Practices for Improving Embedded Systems Development*. Previous to founding the company, Gary was a technical lead at HP establishing standards in firmware and ASIC designs. His efforts have saved HP more than $100 million in development costs across several projects. He holds a BSEE from Brigham Young University and an MSEE from Utah State University. Gary holds 12 patents in the area of printer hardware and firmware.

Erich Styger
Email: Erich.styger@freescale.com

Erich Styger is Professor at Lucerne University of Applied Sciences and Arts and Distinguished Member of Technical Staff at Freescale Semiconductor. Erich has an MsCS degree and 18 + years of experience in the embedded software and tools world. He created many embedded cross C/C + + compilers and debuggers. Additionally he is researching in the domain of programming languages, real time and mechatronic systems.

Jim Trudeau
Email: jamesedwardtrudeau@gmail.com

Jim Trudeau majored in international relations at Georgetown University, Washington DC, and the Institute for American Universities, Avignon, France. He subsequently pursued mentored education in three distinct and successful careers, the most recent of which is software development and technical communication. He is currently a technical writer and trainer focusing on learning management systems with 42 Lines Inc. He is the author of *Programming Starter Kit for Macintosh* (Hayden Books, 1995) and *Mastering CodeWarrior* (Sybex, 1997), as well as numerous articles and training courses on various aspects of software development.

Catalin Udma
Email: catalin.udma@freescale.com

Catalin Udma joined Freescale Semiconductor in 2010 focusing on software development tools for embedded systems including Linux kernel debugging, trace and performance evaluation Linux tools. Prior to joining Freescale, he spent more than 10 years working in various embedded software development projects including Linux kernel development, device drivers, board bring-up, carrier-grade network management, real-time data-plane software, and T1/E1 and voice over IP. He has been also involved in several research projects in domains like wireless network design, multimedia communications in WiMax networks, resource management, quality of service and clock recovery algorithms. He characterizes himself as a Linux enthusiast and he loves to seek and enjoy challenges when being a code warrior or when not sitting in front of a computer screen.

Whitson Gamaliel Waldo, III

Whitson Gamaliel Waldo, III has a broad background in the semiconductor industry with experience in business operations, volume manufacturing, engineering, and research and development. Whit has worked for Freescale Semiconductor, Texas Instruments, and Motorola, and has participated in corporate and university joint ventures with IBM and the University of Wisconsin, respectively. He has experience in program management, project management, and engineering management. Whit's program and project management experience is in new product introductions for SoC, software, and SoC platform products. Whit is the author of the books *Program Management for System on Chip Platforms* and *Classic Leadership Principles* and has numerous technical publications. A Master of Science degree was earned from Clemson University in Chemical Engineering. His undergraduate studies were completed at the University of Florida. A Master's Certificate in Project Management was earned from George Washington University. Whit is certified as a Project Management Professional through the Project Management Institute. He earned certification as a Motorola Six Sigma Black Belt for accomplishments in applied statistics. He was recognized by Motorola as a Distinguished Innovator for 13 issued patents.

Pete Wilson
Email: pete@kivadesigngroupe.com

Pete Wilson has a degree in Physics and Pure and Applied Mathematics from Sheffield University, England. He spent some time at Ferranti's Digital Systems Division in Bracknell, England, writing the software for the radar autotracking portion of CAAIS, a real-time embedded system for British Navy warships. He also worked on and prototyped the kernel of a small-domain capability system's RTOS for the FM1600E computer. Later, he wrote the software for the printer in the ICL 7500 series intelligent mainframe terminal, and provided a new processor architecture for a next-generation engine. At Inmos, he investigated intelligent peripherals, and then took up the position of Transputer Applications Manager in Colorado Springs. After that, he architected the processor for Prisma, a GaAs real-time supercomputer startup, and eventually joined Groupe Bull in Billerica, MA, where he was Director, Design Validation. Later he moved to work with Bull's PowerPC partners in Austin, TX. He was appointed Director, Microsystems Architecture, and worked on the verification of the PowerPC 620. Joining Motorola Semiconductor Products Sector in 1997, he contributed to advanced systems architecture, initiating the RapidIO interconnect, the e500 processor, the e200 series, the ADL architecture description language and Plasma, a concurrency-support extension to C++. In 2008, he became a member of the Freescale Intellectual Property Licensing group.

Dr. Xin-Xin Yang

Dr. Xin-Xin Yang is the senior engineering manager of the Beijing software R&D team, Networking & Multimedia Solutions Group, Freescale Inc. He is leading an engineering team focusing on the development of Linux SDK (Software Development Kit) and related software running on Power, ColdFire and ARM architectures. He is a Senior Member of Technical Staff in Freescale. Prior to moving to Freescale, Xin-Xin had been working as a senior engineer, senior staff engineer and engineering manager in the Networking & Computing System Group, Semiconductor Products Sector, Motorola Electronics China Ltd. He is a member of the patent committee of Motorola China R&D Institute. Xin-Xin holds a PhD degree in Computer Science & Technology from Tsinghua University, China.

Mark Pitchford

Mark Pitchford has over 25 years' experience in software development for engineering applications on a variety of platforms, including safety critical developments. Many such applications have involved the extension of existing code bases. He has worked on many significant industrial and commercial projects in development and management, both in the UK and internationally including extended periods in Canada and Australia. For the past 12 years, he has specialized in software testing and now works throughout Europe and beyond as a Field Applications Engineer with LDRA.

Andrew McKay

Andrew McKay is currently an Embedded Systems Architect at Iders Inc, developing industrial rated networking and communications equipment. He joined Iders Inc in July 2002 after graduating from Computer Engineering at the University of Manitoba.

CHAPTER 1

Software Engineering of Embedded and Real-Time Systems

Robert Oshana

Chapter Outline

Software engineering

Over the past ten years or so, the world of computing has moved from large, static, desktop machines to small, mobile, and embedded devices. The methods, techniques, and tools

Software Engineering for Embedded Systems.
DOI: http://dx.doi.org/10.1016/B978-0-12-415917-4.00001-3
© 2013 Elsevier Inc. All rights reserved.

for developing software systems that were successfully applied in the former scenario are not as readily applicable in the latter. Software systems running on networks of mobile, embedded devices must exhibit properties that are not always required of more traditional systems:

- near-optimal performance
- robustness
- distribution
- dynamism
- mobility.

This book will examine the key properties of software systems in the embedded, resource-constrained, mobile, and highly distributed world. We will assess the applicability of mainstream software engineering methods and techniques (e.g., software design, component-based development, software architecture, system integration and test) to this domain.

One of the differences in software engineering for embedded systems is the additional knowledge the engineer has of electrical power and electronics; physical interfacing of digital and analog electronics with the computer; and software design for embedded systems and digital signal processors (DSP).

Over 95% of software systems are actually embedded. Consider the devices you use at home on a daily basis;

- cell phone, iPod, microwave
- satellite receiver, cable box
- car engine control unit
- DVD player.

So what do we mean by software engineering for embedded systems? Let's look at this in the context of engineering in general. Engineering is defined as the application of scientific principles and methods to the construction of useful structures and machines. This includes disciplines such as:

- mechanical engineering
- civil engineering
- chemical engineering
- electrical engineering
- nuclear engineering
- aeronautical engineering.

Software engineering is a term that is 35 years old, originating at a NATO conference in Garmisch, Germany, October 7–11, 1968. Computer science is the scientific basis and many aspects have been made systematic in software engineering:

- methods/methodologies/techniques
- languages
- tools
- processes.

We will explore all of these in this book.

The basic tenets of software engineering include:

- development of software systems whose size/complexity warrants team(s) of engineers (or as David Parnas puts it, "multi-person construction of multi-version software");
- scope, which we will focus on the study of software process, development principles, techniques, and notations;
- goal, in our case the production of quality software, delivered on time, within budget, satisfying customers' requirements and users' needs.

With this come the ever-present difficulties of software engineering that still exist today:

- there are relatively few guiding scientific principles;
- there are few universally applicable methods;
- software engineering is as much managerial/psychological/sociological as it is technological.

There difficulties exist because software engineering is a unique form of engineering:

- software is malleable;
- software construction is human-intensive;
- software is intangible;
- software problems are unprecedentedly complex;
- software directly depends upon the hardware;
- software solutions require unusual rigor;
- software has discontinuous operational nature.

Software engineering is not the same as software programming. Software programming usually involves a single developer developing "toy" applications and involves a relatively short lifespan. With programming, there is a single or few stakeholders and the project is mostly one-of-a-kind systems built from scratch with minimal maintenance.

Software engineering on the other hand involves teams of developers with multiple roles building complex systems with an indefinite lifespan. There are numerous stakeholders, families of systems, a heavy emphasis on reuse to amortize costs and a maintenance phase that accounts for over 60% of overall development costs.

There are economic and management aspects of software engineering. Software production includes the development and maintenance (evolution) of the system. Maintenance costs are the majority of all development costs. Quicker development is not always preferable. In other words, higher up-front costs may defray downstream costs. Poorly designed and implemented software is a critical cost factor. In this book we will focus on software engineering of embedded systems, not programming embedded systems.

Embedded software development uses the same software development models as other forms of software development, including the Waterfall model (Figure 1.1), the Spiral model (Figure 1.2) and the Agile model (Figure 1.3). The benefits and limitations of each of these models are well documented so we will review these here. We will, however, spend more time later in this book on Agile development, as this approach is well suited to the changing, dynamic nature of embedded systems.

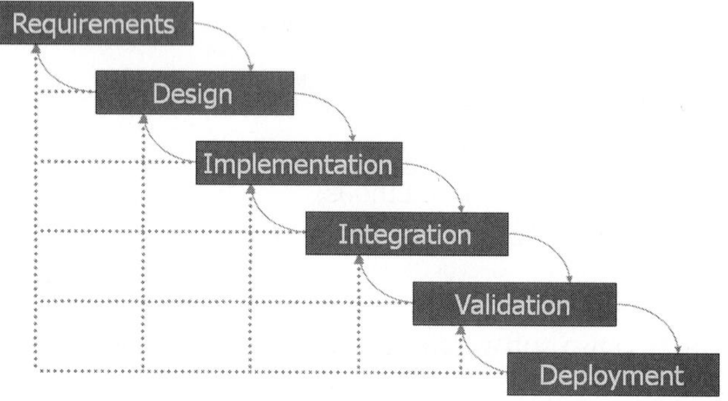

Figure 1.1:
Waterfall software development model.

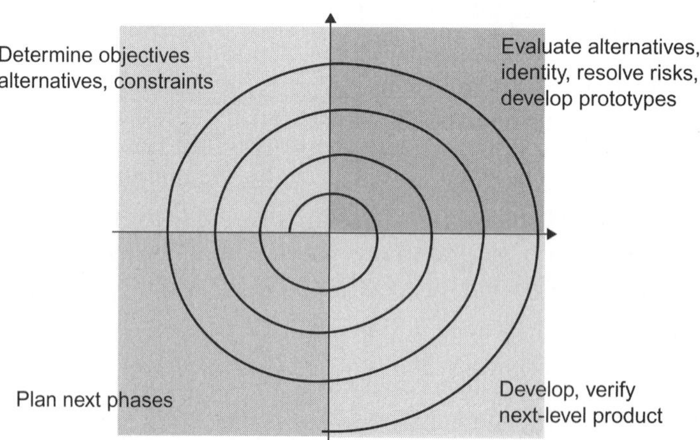

Figure 1.2:
Spiral software development model.

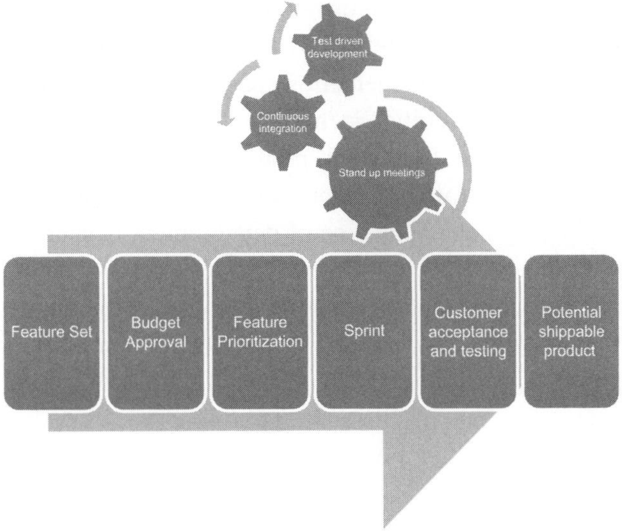

Figure 1.3:
Agile software development model.

The key software development phases for embedded systems are briefly summarized below.

1. Problem definition: in this phase we determine exactly what the customer and user want. This may include the development of a contract with the customer, depending on what type of product is being developed. This goal of this phase is to specify what the software product is to do. Difficulties include the client asking for the wrong product, the client being computer/software illiterate, which limits the effectiveness of this phase, and specifications that are ambiguous, inconsistent, and incomplete.
2. Architecture/design: architecture is concerned with the selection of architectural elements, their interactions, and the constraints on those elements and their interactions necessary to provide a framework in which to satisfy the requirements and serve as a basis for the design. Design is concerned with the modularization and detailed interfaces of the design elements, their algorithms and procedures, and the data types needed to support the architecture and to satisfy the requirements. During the architecture and design phases, the system is decomposed into software modules with interfaces. During design the software team develops module specifications (algorithms, data types), maintains a record of design decisions and traceability, and specifies how the software product is to do its tasks. The primary difficulties during this phase include miscommunication between module designers and developing a design that may be inconsistent, incomplete, ambiguous.

3. Implementation: during this phase the development team implements the modules and components and verify that they meet their specifications. Modules are combined according to the design. The implementation specifies how the software product does its tasks. Some of the key difficulties include module interaction errors and the order of integration that may influence quality and productivity.

   More and more development of software for embedded systems is moving towards component-based development. This type of development is generally applicable for components of a reasonable size and reuse across systems, which is a growing trend in embedded systems. Developers ensure these components are adaptable to varying contexts and extend the idea beyond code to other development artifacts as well. This approach changes the equation from "Integration, Then Deployment" to "Deployment, Then Integration".

   There are different makes and models of software components:
   - third-party software components
   - plug-ins / add-ins
   - frameworks
   - open systems
   - distributed object infrastructures
   - compound documents
   - legacy systems.
4. Verification and validation (V&V): there are several forms of V&V and there is a dedicated chapter on this topic. One form is "analysis". Analysis can be in the form of static, scientific, formal verification, and informal reviews and walkthroughs. Testing is a more dynamic form of V&V. This form of testing comes in the form of white box (we have access to the code) and black box (no access to the source code). Testing can be structural as well as behavioral. There are the standard issues of test adequacy but we will defer this discussion to later when we dedicate a chapter to this topic.

As we progress through this book, we will continue to focus on the foundational software engineering principles (Figure 1.4);

- rigor and formality
- separation of concerns
  - modularity and decomposition
  - abstraction
- anticipation of change
- generality
- incrementality
- scalability
- compositionality

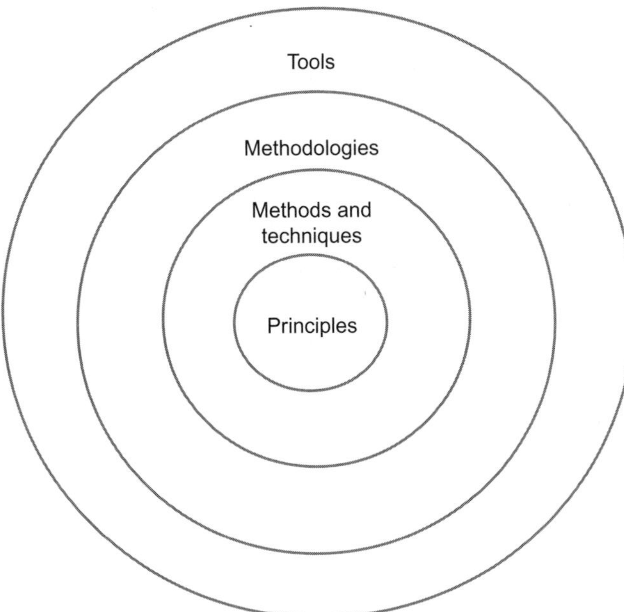

Figure 1.4:
Software engineering principles.

- heterogeneity
- from principles to tools.

Embedded systems

So what is an embedded system? There are many answers to this question. Some define an embedded system simply as "a computer whose end function is not to be a computer". If we follow this definition, then automobile anti-lock braking systems, digital cameras, household appliances, and televisions are embedded systems because they contain computers but aren't intended to be computers. Conversely, the laptop computer I'm using to write this chapter is not an embedded system because it contains a computer that is intended to be a computer (see Bill Gatliff's article "There's no such thing as an Embedded System" on embedded.com).

Jack Ganssle and Mike Barr, in their book *Embedded Systems Dictionary*, define an embedded system as "A combination of computer hardware and software, and perhaps additional mechanical or other parts, designed to perform a dedicated function. In some cases, embedded systems are part of a larger system or product, as in the case of an antilock braking system in a car".

There are many definitions but in this book we will proceed as follows.

An embedded system is a specialized computer system that is usually integrated as part of a larger system. An embedded system consists of a combination of hardware and software components to form a computational engine that will perform a specific function. Unlike desktop systems which are designed to perform a general function, embedded systems are constrained in their application.

Embedded systems often perform in reactive and time-constrained environments. A rough partitioning of an embedded system consists of the hardware which provides the performance necessary for the application (and other system properties like security) and the software which provides a majority of the features and flexibility in the system. A typical embedded system is shown in Figure 1.5.

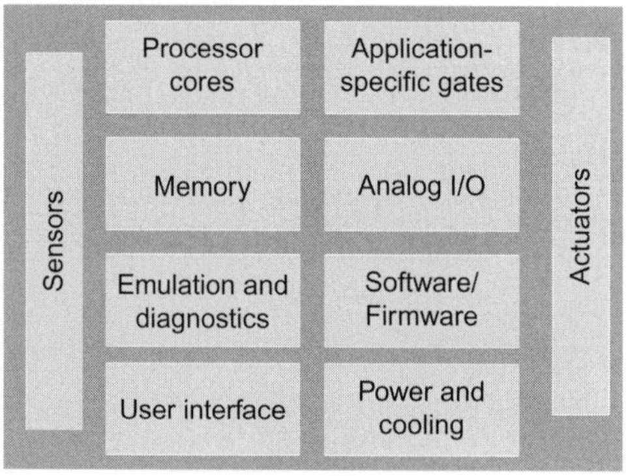

Figure 1.5:
Typical embedded system components.

- Processor core: at the heart of the embedded system is the processor core(s). This can range from a simple inexpensive 8-bit microcontroller to a more complex 32- or 64-bit microprocessor or even multiple processors. The embedded designer must select the most cost-sensitive device for the application that can meet all of the functional and non-functional (timing) requirements.
- Analog I/O: D/A and A/D converters are used to get data from the environment and back out to the environment. The embedded designer must understand the type of data required from the environment, the accuracy requirements for that data, and the input/output data rates in order to select the right converters for the application. The external environment drives the reactive nature of the embedded system. Embedded systems have to be at least fast enough to keep up with the environment. This is where the analog information such as light or sound pressure or acceleration is sensed and input into the embedded system.

- Sensors and actuators: sensors are used to sense analog information from the environment. Actuators are used to control the environment in some way.
- User interfaces: these interfaces may be as simple as a flashing LED or as complex as a sophisticated cell phone or digital still camera interface.
- Application-specific gates: hardware acceleration such as ASIC or FPGA is used for accelerating specific functions in the application that have high-performance requirements. The embedded designer must be able to map or partition the application appropriately using available accelerators to gain maximum application performance.
- Software: software is a significant part of embedded system development. Over the last several years the amount of embedded software has grown faster than Moore's law, with the amount doubling approximately every 10 months. Embedded software is usually optimized in some way (performance, memory, or power). More and more embedded software is written in a high-level language such as C/C++, with some of the more performance-critical pieces of code still written in assembly language.
- Memory is an important part of an embedded system and embedded applications can run out of either RAM or ROM depending on the application. There are many types of volatile and non-volatile memory used for embedded systems and we will talk more about this later.
- Emulation and diagnostics: many embedded systems are hard to see or get to. There needs to be a way to interface to embedded systems to debug them. Diagnostic ports such as a JTAG (Joint Test Action Group) are used to debug embedded systems. On-chip emulation is used to provide visibility into the behavior of the application. These emulation modules provide sophisticated visibility into the run-time behavior and performance, in effect replacing external logic analyzer functions with on-board diagnostic capability.

Embedded systems are reactive systems

A typical embedded system responds to the environment via sensors and controls the environment using actuators (Figure 1.6). This imposes a requirement on embedded systems to achieve performance consistent with that of the environment. This is why embedded systems are often referred to as reactive systems. A reactive system must use a combination of hardware and software to respond to events in the environment within defined constraints. Complicating the matter is the fact that these external events can be periodic and predictable or aperiodic and hard to predict. When scheduling events for processing in an embedded system, both periodic and aperiodic events must be considered and performance must be guaranteed for worst-case rates of execution.

An example of an embedded sensor system is a tire pressure monitoring system (TPMS). This is a sensor chipset designed to enable a timely warning to the driver in the case of under-inflated or over-inflated tires on cars, trucks or buses – even while in motion. These

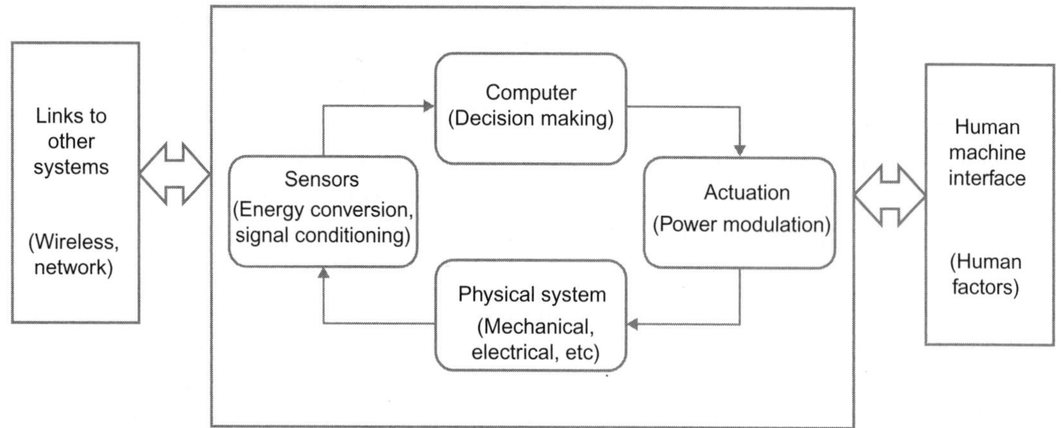

Figure 1.6:
A model of sensors and actuators in embedded systems.

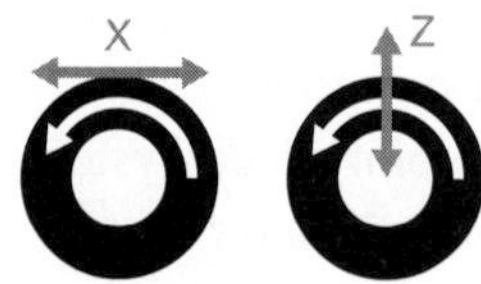

Figure 1.7:
X- and *Z*-axis sensing direction.

sensor systems are a full integration of a pressure sensor, an 8-bit microcontroller (MCU), a radio-frequency (RF) transmitter and *X*- and *Z*-axis accelerometers in one package. A key to this sensor technology is acceleration *X* and *Z* acquisition (Figure 1.7). The purpose of the X and Z-axis g cells is to allow tire recognition using the appropriate embedded algorithms that analyze the rotating signal caused by the Earth's gravitational field. Motion will use either the *Z*-axis *g*-cell to detect acceleration level or use the *X*-axis *g*-cell to detect a $\pm 1\ g$ signal caused by the Earth's gravitational field.

There are several key characteristics of embedded systems;

a. Monitoring and reacting to the environment: embedded systems typically get input by reading data from input sensors. There are many different types of sensors that monitor various analog signals in the environment including temperature, sound pressure, and vibration. This data is processed using embedded system algorithms. The results may be displayed in some format to a user or simply used to control actuators (like deploying the airbags and calling the police).
b. Controlling the environment: embedded systems may generate and transmit commands that control actuators such as airbags, motors, etc.

c. Processing of information: embedded systems process the data collected from the sensors in some meaningful way, such as data compression/decompression, side impact detection, etc.
d. Application-specific: embedded systems are often designed for applications such as airbag deployment, digital still cameras or cell phones. Embedded systems may also be designed for processing control laws, finite-state machines, and signal-processing algorithms. Embedded systems must also be able to detect and react appropriately to faults in both the internal computing environment as well as the surrounding systems.
e. Optimized for the application: embedded systems are all about performing the desired computations with as few resources as possible in order to reduce cost, power, size, etc. This means that embedded systems need to be optimized for the application. This requires software as well as hardware optimization. Hardware needs to be able to perform operations in as few gates as possible, and software must be optimized to perform operations using the least cycles, memory, or power possible depending on the application.
f. Resource constrained: embedded systems are optimized for the application, which means that many of the precious resources of an embedded system, processor cycles, memory, power, are in scarce supply in a relative sense in order to reduce cost, size, weight, etc.
g. Real-time: embedded systems must react to the real-time changing nature of the environment in which they operate; more on real-time systems below.
h. Multi-rate: embedded systems must be able to handle multiple rates of processing requirements simultaneously, for example video processing at 30 frames per second (30 Hz) and audio processing at 20 kHz rates.

Figure 1.8 shows a simple embedded system that demonstrates these key characteristics.

1. Monitor and control environment: the embedded system monitors the fluid flow sensor in the environment and then controls the value (actuator) in that same environment.
2. Perform meaningful operations: the computation task would compute the desired algorithms to control the value in a safe way.
3. Application-specific: this embedded system would be designed for this particular application.
4. Optimized for application: the embedded system computation and algorithms would be designed for this particular system.
5. Resource-constrained: the embedded system will execute on a small inexpensive microcontroller with a small amount of memory and operating at lower power for cost savings.
6. Real-time: this system has to be able to respond to the flow sensor in real time; any delays in processing could lead to failure of the system.

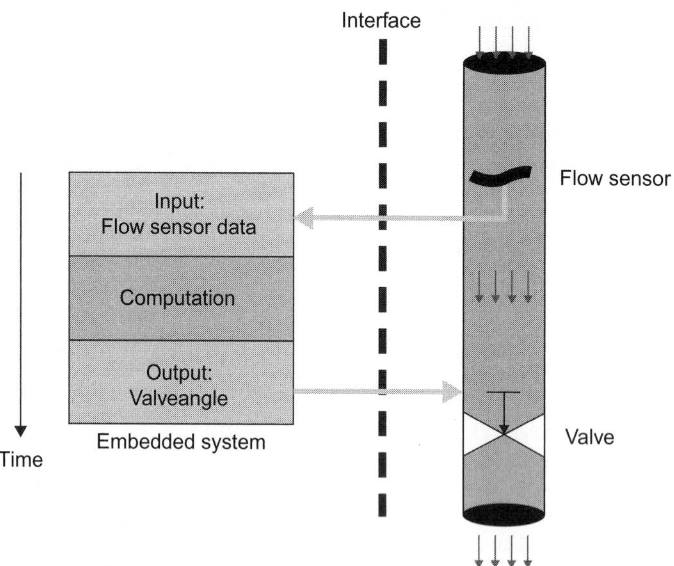

Figure 1.8:
Example embedded system.

7. Multi-rate: there may be the need to respond to the flow sensor as well as a user interface, so multiple input rates to the embedded system are possible.

Real-time systems

A real-time system is any information-processing activity or system which has to respond to externally generated input stimuli within a finite and specified period. Real-time systems must process information and produce a response within a specified time. Failure to do so will risk severe consequences, including failure. In a system with a real-time constraint, it is unacceptable to have the correct action or the correct answer *after* a certain deadline: the result must be produced by the deadline or the system will degrade or fail completely. Generally, real-time systems maintain a *continuous timely* interaction with its environment (Figure 1.9).

Types of real-time systems – soft and hard

In real-time systems, the correctness of the computation depends not only upon its results but also upon the time at which its outputs are generated. A real-time system must satisfy response time constraints or suffer significant system consequences. If the consequences consist of a degradation of performance, but not failure, the system is referred to as a soft

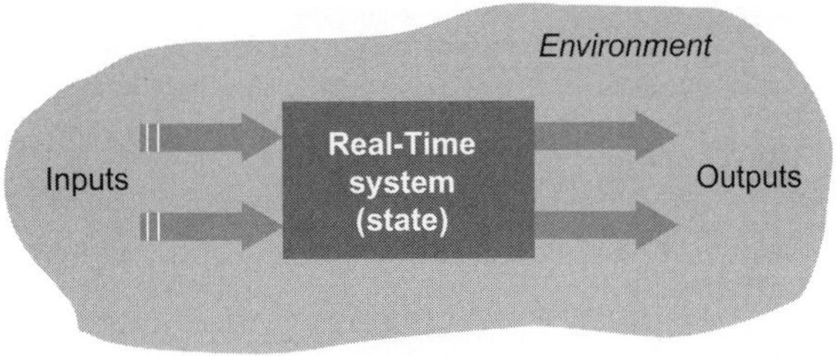

Figure 1.9:
A real-time system reacts to inputs from the environment and produces outputs that affect the environment.

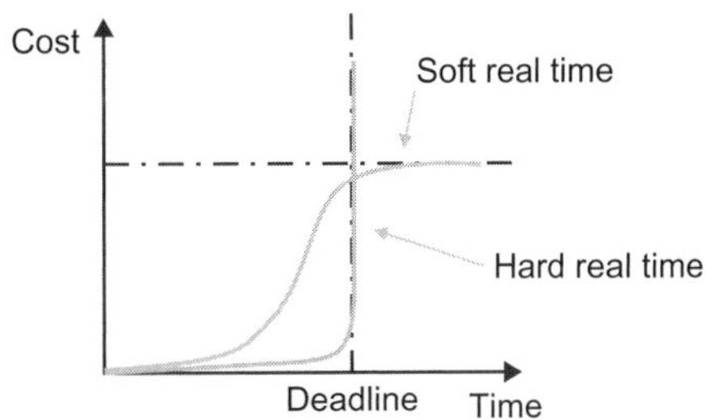

Figure 1.10:
A comparison between hard and soft real time.

real-time system. If the consequences are system failure, the system is referred to as a hard real-time system (e.g., an anti-lock braking system in an automobile). See Figure 1.10.

We can also think of this in terms of the real-time interval, which is defined as how quickly the system has to respond. In this context, the Windows operating system is soft real-time because it is relatively slow and cannot handle shorter time constraints. In this case, the system does not "fail" but is degraded.

The objective of an embedded system is to execute as fast as necessary in an asynchronous world using the smallest amount of code and with the highest level of predictability. (Note: predictability is the embedded world's term for reliability.)

Figure 1.11 shows some examples of hard and soft real-time systems. As shown in this list of examples, many embedded systems also have a criticality to the computation in the sense that a failure to meet real-time deadlines can have disastrous consequences. For example determining drivers' intentions and driving conditions in real time (see Figure 1.12) is an example of a hard real-time safety-critical application.

System type	Hard or soft real time?
Traffic light control	Hard RT – Critical
Automated teller machine	Soft RT – Non-Critical
Controller for radiation therapy machine	Hard RT – Critical
Car simulator for driver training	Hard RT – Non Critical
Highway car counter	Soft RT – Non-Critical
Missile control	Hard RT – Critical
Video games	Hard RT – Non Critical
Network chat	Soft RT – Non-Critical

Figure 1.11:
Examples of hard and soft real-time systems.

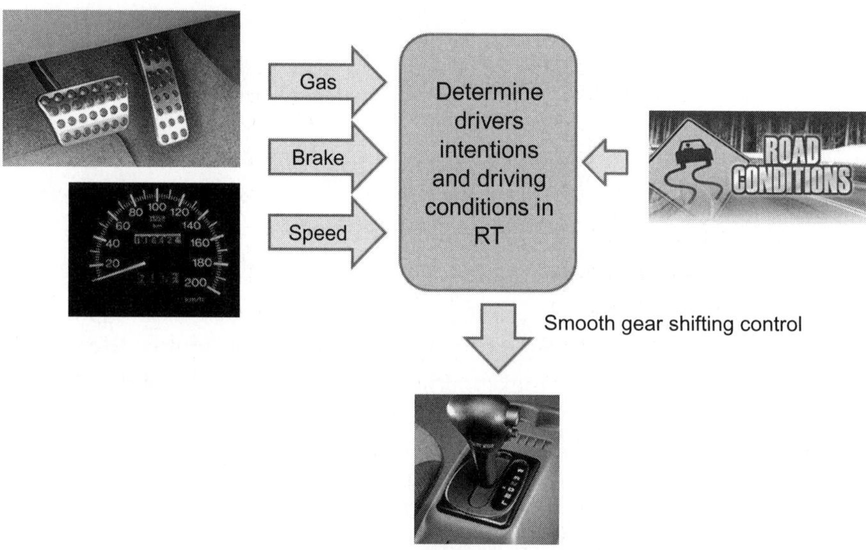

Figure 1.12:
An automobile shift control system is an example of a hard real-time safety-critical system.

Differences between real-time and time-shared systems

Real-time systems are different from time shared systems in the three fundamental areas (Table 1.1). These include:

- High degree of schedulability: timing requirements of the system must be satisfied at high degrees of resource usage, and predictably fast response to urgent events;
- Worst case latency: ensuring the system still operates under worst case response time to events;

Table 1.1: Real-time systems are fundamentally different from time shared systems.

Characteristic	Time-Shared Systems	Real-Time Systems
System capacity	High throughput	Schedulability and the ability of system tasks to meet all deadlines
Responsiveness	Fast average response time	Ensured worst case latency which is the worst-case response time to events
Overload	Fairness to all	Stability; when the system is overloaded important tasks must meet deadlines while others may be starved

- Stability under transient overload: when the system is overloaded by events and it is impossible to meet all deadlines, the deadlines of selected critical tasks must still be guaranteed.

Examples of hard real-time

Many embedded systems are real-time systems. As an example, assume that an analog signal is to be processed digitally. The first question to consider is how often to *sample* or measure the analog signal in order to represent that signal accurately in the digital domain. The sample rate is the number of samples of an analog event (like sound) that are taken per second to represent the event in the digital domain. Based on a signal-processing rule called the Nyquist rule, the signal must be sampled at a rate at least equal to twice the highest frequency that we wish to preserve. For example, if the signal contains important components at 4 kHz, then the sampling frequency would need to be at least 8 kHz. The sampling period would then be:

$$T = 1/8000 = 125 \text{ microseconds} = 0.000125 \text{ seconds}$$

Based on signal sample, time to perform actions before next sample arrives

This tells us that, for this signal being sampled at this rate, we would have 0.000125 seconds to perform *all* the processing necessary before the next sample arrived. Samples are arriving on a continuous basis and if the system falls behind in processing these samples, the system will degrade. This is an example of a soft real-time embedded system.

Hard real-time systems

The collective timeliness of the hard real-time tasks is binary – i.e., either they all will always meet their deadlines (in a correctly functioning system), or they will not (the system is infeasible). In all hard real-time systems, collective timeliness is deterministic. This determinism does not imply that the actual individual task completion times, or the task execution ordering, are necessarily known in advance.

A computing system being hard real-time says nothing about the magnitudes of the deadlines. They may be microseconds or weeks. There is a bit of confusion with regard to the usage of the term "hard real-time". Some relate hard real-time to response time magnitudes below some arbitrary threshold, such as 1 msec. This is not the case. Many of these systems actually happen to be soft real-time. These systems would be more accurately termed "real fast" or perhaps "real predictable"; but certainly not hard real-time.

The feasibility and costs (e.g., in terms of system resources) of hard real-time computing depend on how well known a priori are the relevant future behavioral characteristics of the tasks and execution environment. These task characteristics include:

- timeliness parameters, such as arrival periods or upper bounds
- deadlines
- worst case execution times
- ready and suspension times
- resource utilization profiles
- precedence and exclusion constraints
- relative importance, etc.

There are also important characteristics relating to the system itself, some of which include:

- system loading
- resource interactions
- queuing disciplines
- arbitration mechanisms
- service latencies
- interrupt priorities and timing
- caching.

Deterministic collective task timeliness in hard (and soft) real-time computing requires that the future characteristics of the relevant tasks and execution environment be deterministic – i.e., known absolutely in advance. The knowledge of these characteristics must then be used to pre-allocate resources so that hard deadlines, such as motor control, will be met and soft deadlines such as responding to a key press can be delayed.

A real-time system task and execution environment must be adjusted to enable a schedule and resource allocation which meets all deadlines. Different algorithms or schedules which meet all deadlines are evaluated with respect to other factors. In many real-time computing applications getting the job done at the lowest cost is usually more important than simply maximizing the processor utilization (if this was true, we would all still be writing assembly language). Time to market, for example, may be more important than maximizing utilization due to the cost of squeezing the last 5% of efficiency out of a processor.

Allocation for hard real-time computing has been performed using various techniques. Some of these techniques involve conducting an off-line enumerative search for a static schedule which will deterministically always meet all deadlines. Scheduling algorithms include the use of priorities that are assigned to the various system tasks. These priorities can be assigned either off-line by application programmers, or on-line by the application or operating system software. The task priority assignments may either be static (fixed), as with rate monotonic algorithms, or dynamic (changeable), as with the earliest-deadline-first algorithm.

Real-time event characteristics

Real-time event categories

Real-time events fall into one of the three categories: asynchronous, synchronous, or isochronous.

- Asynchronous events are entirely unpredictable. An example of this is a cell phone call arriving at a cellular base station. As far as the base station is concerned, the action of making a phone call cannot be predicted.
- Synchronous events are predictable events and occur with precise regularity. For example, the audio and video in a camcorder take place in synchronous fashion.
- Isochronous events occur with regularity within a given window of time. For example, audio data in a networked multimedia application must appear within a window of time when the corresponding video stream arrives. Isochronous is a sub-class of asynchronous.

In many real-time systems, task and execution environment characteristics may be hard to predict. This makes true hard real-time scheduling infeasible. In hard real-time computing, deterministic satisfaction of the collective timeliness criterion is the driving requirement. The necessary approach to meeting that requirement is static (i.e., a priori) scheduling of deterministic task and execution environment characteristic cases. The requirement for advance knowledge about each of the system tasks and their future execution environment to enable off-line scheduling and resource allocation significantly restricts the applicability of hard real-time computing.

Efficient execution and the execution environment

Efficiency overview

Real-time systems are time-critical and the efficiency of their implementation is more important than in other systems. Efficiency can be categorized in terms of processor cycles, memory, or power. This constraint may drive everything from the choice of processor to the choice of the programming language. One of the main benefits of using a higher-level language is to allow the programmer to abstract away implementation details and concentrate on solving the problem. This is not always true in the embedded-system world. Some higher-level languages have instructions that can be an order of magnitude slower than assembly language. However, higher-level languages can be used in real-time systems effectively using the right techniques. We will be discussing much more about this topic in the chapter on optimizing source code for DSPs.

Resource management

A system operates in real time as long as it completes the time-critical processes with acceptable timeliness. "Acceptable timeliness" is defined as part of the behavioral or "non-functional" requirements for the system. These requirements must be objectively quantifiable and measureable (stating that the system must be "fast", for example, is not quantifiable). A system is said to be real-time if it contains some model of real-time resource management (these resources must be explicitly managed for the purpose of operating in real time). As mentioned earlier, resource management may be performed statically off-line or dynamically on-line.

Real-time resource management comes at a cost. The degree to which a system is required to operate in real time cannot necessarily be attained solely by hardware over-capacity (e.g., high processor performance using a faster CPU).

There must exist some form of real-time resource management to be cost-effective. Systems which must operate in real time consist of both real-time resource management and hardware resource capacity. Systems which have interactions with physical devices may require higher degrees of real-time resource management. One resource management approach that is used is static and requires analysis of the system prior to it executing in its environment. In a real-time system, physical time (as opposed to logical time) is necessary for real-time resource management in order to relate events to the precise moments of occurrence. Physical time is also important for action time constraints as well as measuring costs incurred as processes progress to completion. Physical time can also be used for logging history data.

All real-time systems make trade-offs of scheduling costs vs. performance in order to reach an appropriate balance for attaining acceptable timeliness between the real-time portion of the scheduling optimization rules and the off-line scheduling performance evaluation and analysis.

Challenges in real-time system design

Designing real-time systems poses significant challenges to the designer. One of the significant challenges comes from the fact that real-time systems must interact with the environment. The environment is complex and changing and these interactions can become very complex. Many real-time systems don't just interact with one, but many different entities in the environment, with different characteristics and rates of interaction. A cell-phone base station, for example, must be able to handle calls from literally thousands of cell-phone subscribers at the same time. Each call may have different requirements for processing and in different sequences of processing. All of this complexity must be managed and coordinated.

Response time

Real-time systems must respond to external interactions in the environment within a predetermined amount of time. Real-time systems must produce the correct result and produce it in a timely way. The response time is as important as producing correct results. Real-time systems must be engineered to meet these response times. Hardware and software must be designed to support response time requirements for these systems. Optimal partitioning of the system requirements into hardware and software is also important.

Real-time systems must be architected to meet system response time requirements. Using combinations of hardware and software components, engineering makes architecture decisions such as interconnectivity of the system processors, system link speeds, processor speeds, memory size, I/O bandwidth, etc. Key questions to be answered include:

- Is the architecture suitable? To meet the system response time requirements, the system can be architected using one powerful processor or several smaller processors. Can the application be partitioned among the several smaller processors without imposing large communication bottlenecks throughout the system? If the designer decides to use one powerful processor, will the system meet its power requirements? Sometimes a simpler architecture may be the better approach – more complexity can lead to unnecessary bottlenecks which cause response time issues.
- Are the processing elements powerful enough? A processing element with high utilization (greater than 90%) will lead to unpredictable run-time behavior. At this utilization level lower-priority tasks in the system may get starved. As a general rule, real-time systems that are loaded at 90% take approximately twice as long to develop due to the cycles of optimization and integration issues with the system at these utilization rates. At 95% utilization, systems can take three times longer to develop due to these same issues. Using multiple processors will help but the inter-processor communication must be managed.
- Are the communication speeds adequate? Communication and I/O is a common bottleneck in real-time embedded systems. Many response time problems come not from the processor being overloaded but in latencies in getting data into and out of the

system. In other cases, overloading a communication port (greater than 75%) can cause unnecessary queuing in different system nodes and this causes delays in message-passing throughout the rest of the system.

- Is the right scheduling system available? In real-time systems tasks that are processing real-time events must take higher priority. But how do you schedule multiple tasks that are all processing real-time events? There are several scheduling approaches available and the engineer must design the scheduling algorithm to accommodate the system priorities in order to meet all real-time deadlines. Because external events may occur at any time, the scheduling system must be able to preempt currently running tasks to allow higher-priority tasks to run. The scheduling system (or real-time operating system) must not introduce a significant amount of overhead into the real-time system.

Recovering from failures

Real-time systems interact with the environment, which is inherently unreliable. Therefore real-time systems must be able to detect and overcome failures in the environment. Also, since real-time systems are also embedded into other systems and may be hard to get at (such as a space craft or satellite) these systems must also be able to detect and overcome internal failures as well (there is no "reset" button in easy reach of the user!). Also since events in the environment are unpredictable, it is almost impossible to test for every possible combination and sequence of events in the environment. This is a characteristic of real-time software that makes it somewhat non-deterministic in the sense that it is almost impossible in some real-time systems to predict the multiple paths of execution based on the non-deterministic behavior of the environment. Examples of internal and external failures that must be detected and managed by real-time systems include:

- processor failures
- board failures
- link failures
- invalid behavior of external environment
- inter connectivity failure.

Many real-time systems are embedded systems with multiple inputs and outputs and multiple events occurring independently. Separating these tasks simplifies programming, but requires switching back and forth among the multiple tasks. This is referred to as multi-tasking. Concurrency in embedded systems is the appearance of multiple tasks executing simultaneously. For example, the three tasks listed in Figure 1.13 will execute on a single embedded processor and the scheduling algorithm is responsible for defining the priority of execution of these three tasks.

```
/*  Monitor Room_Temperature */
do forever {
     measure temperature;
     if (temperature < temperature_setting)
          start furnace_heater;
     else if (temperature > temperature_setting + delta)
          stop furnace_heater;

}

/* Monitor Time of Day */
do forever {
     measure time_of_day;
          if (7:00am)
               setting = 72_degrees_F;
          else if (10:00pm)
               setting = 60_degrees_F;
}

/* Monitor Thermostat Keypad */
do forever {
     check thermostat_keypad;
     if (raise temperature)
          setting++;
     else if (lower temperature)
          setting--;
}
```

Figure 1.13:
Multiple tasks execute simultaneously on embedded systems.

The embedded system software build process

Another difference in embedded systems is the software system build process, as shown in Figure 1.14.

Embedded system programming is not substantially different from ordinary programming. The main difference is that each target hardware platform is unique. The process of converting the source code representation of embedded software into an executable binary image involves several distinct steps:

- compiling/assembling using an optimizing compiler;
- linking using a linker;
- relocating using a locator.

In the first step, each of the source files must be compiled or assembled into object code. The job of a compiler is mainly to translate programs written in some human-readable format into the equivalent set of opcodes for a particular processor. The use of the cross compiler is one of the defining features of embedded software development.

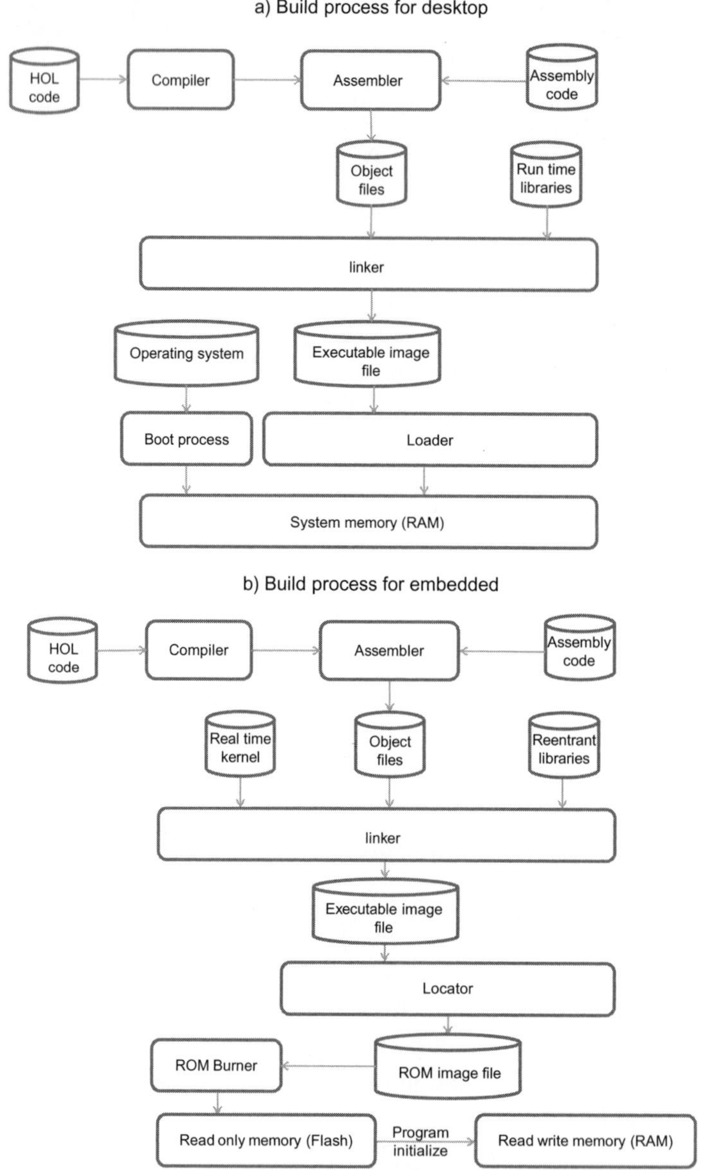

Figure 1.14:
Embedded system software build process is different from non-embedded system build process.

In the second step all of the object files that result from the first step must be linked together to produce a single object file, called the relocatable program. Finally, physical memory addresses must be assigned to the relative offsets within the relocatable program in a process called relocation. The tool that performs the conversion from relocatable to executable binary image is called a locator. The result of the final step of the build process is an absolute binary image that can be directly programmed into a ROM or FLASH device.

We have covered several areas where embedded systems differ from other desktop-like systems. Some other differences that make embedded systems unique are:

1. Energy efficiency (embedded systems, in general, consume minimum power for the purpose).
2. Custom voltage/power requirements.
3. Security (need to be hacker-proof; for example a Femto base station needs IP Security when sending phone calls over an internet backhaul).
4. Reliability (embedded systems need to work without failure for days, months, and years).
5. Environment (embedded systems need to support a broad temperature range, sealed from chemicals, and radiation tolerant).
6. Efficient interaction with user (fewer buttons, touchscreen, etc.).
7. Integrated with design in a HW/SW co-design approach.

The chapters in this book will touch on many of these topics as they relate to software engineering for embedded systems.

Distributed and multi-processor architectures

Some real-time systems are becoming so complex that applications are executed on multi-processor systems that are distributed across some communication system. This poses challenges to the designer that relate to the partitioning of the application in a multi-processor system. These systems will involve processing on several different nodes. One node may be a DSP, another node a more general-purpose processor, some specialized hardware processing elements, etc. This leads to several design challenges for the engineering team:

- Initialization of the system: initializing a multi-processor system can be complicated. In most multi-processor systems the software load file resides on the general-purpose processing node. Nodes that are directly connected to the general purpose processor, for example a DSP, will initialize first. After these nodes complete loading and initialization, other nodes connected to them may then go through this same process until the system completes initialization.
- Processor interfaces: when multiple processors must communicate with each other, care must be taken to ensure that messages sent along interfaces between the processors are well defined and consistent with the processing elements. Differences in message protocol including endianness, byte ordering and other padding rules can complicate

system integration, especially if there is a system requirement for backwards compatibility.

- Load distribution: as mentioned earlier, multiple processors lead to the challenge of distributing the application, and possibly developing the application to support efficient partitioning of the application among the processing elements. Mistakes in partitioning the application can lead to bottlenecks in the system and this degrades the full capability of the system by overloading certain processing elements and leaving others under-utilized. Application developers must design the application to be efficiently partitioned across the processing elements.
- Centralized resource allocation and management: in a system of multiple processing elements, there is still a common set of resources including peripherals, cross bar switches, memory, etc., that must be managed. In some cases the operating system can provide mechanisms such as semaphores to manage these shared resources. In other cases there may be dedicated hardware to manage the resources. Either way, important shared resources in the system must be managed in order to prevent more system bottlenecks.

Software for embedded systems

This book will spend a considerable amount of time covering each phase of software development for embedded systems. Software for embedded systems is also different from other "run to completion" or other desktop software applications. So we will introduce the concepts here and go into more detail in later chapters.

Super loop architecture

The most straightforward software architecture for embedded systems is "super loop architecture". This approach is used because when programming embedded systems, it is frequently very important to meet the deadlines of the system, and to complete all the key tasks of the system in a reasonable amount of time, and in the right order. Super loop architecture is a common program architecture that is very useful in fulfilling these requirements. This approach is a program structure composed of an infinite loop, with all the tasks of the system contained in that loop structure. An example is shown in Figure 1.15.

The initialization routines are completed before entering the super loop because the system only needs to be initialized once. Once the infinite loop begins, the valves are not reset because of the need to maintain persistent state in the embedded system.

The loop is a variant of "batch processing" control flow: read input, calculate some values, write out values. Embedded systems software is not the only type of software which uses

```
Function Main_Function()
{
        Initialization();
        Do_Forever
        {
                Check_Status_of_Task();
                Perform_Calculations();
                Output_Result();
        }
}
```

Figure 1.15:
Template of a super loop architecture.

this kind of architecture. Computer games often use a similar loop. There the loop is called *(tight) (main) game loop*. The steps that are followed in this type of gaming technology are:

```
Function Main_Game_Function()
{
   Initialization();
   Do_Forever
   {
        Game_AI();
        Move_Objects();
        Scoring();
        Draw_Objects();
   }
   Cleanup();
}
```

Power-save super loop

The super loop discussed previously works fine unless the scheduling requirements are not consistent with the loop execution time. For example, assume an embedded system with average loop time of 1 ms, which needs to check a certain input only once per second. Does it really make sense to continue looping the program every 1 ms? If we let the loop continue to execute, the program will loop 1000 times before it needs to read the input again; 999 loops of the program will effectively countdown to the next read. In situations like this an expanded super loop can be used to build in a delay as shown in Figure 1.16.

Let's assume a microcontroller that uses 20 mA of current in "normal mode", but only needs 5 mA of power in "low-power mode". Assume using the example super loop above,

```
Function Main_Function()
{
    Initialization();
    Do_Forever
    {
            Check_Status_of_Task();
            Perform_Calculations();
            Output_Result();
            Delay_Before_Starting_Next_Loop();
    }
}
```

Figure 1.16:
Template of a power-saving super loop architecture.

which is in "low-power mode" 99.9% of the time (1 ms of calculations every second), and is only in normal mode 0.1% of the time. An example of this is an LCD communication protocol used in alphanumeric LCD modules. The components provide methods to wait for a specified time. The foundation of waiting for a given time is to wait for a number of CPU or bus cycles. As a result, the component implements the two methods Wait10Cycles() and Wait100Cycles(). Both are implemented in assembly code as they are heavily CPU dependent.

Window lift embedded design

Lets look at an example of a slightly more advanced software architecture. Figure 1.17 shows a simplified diagram of a window lift. In some countries, it is a requirement to have

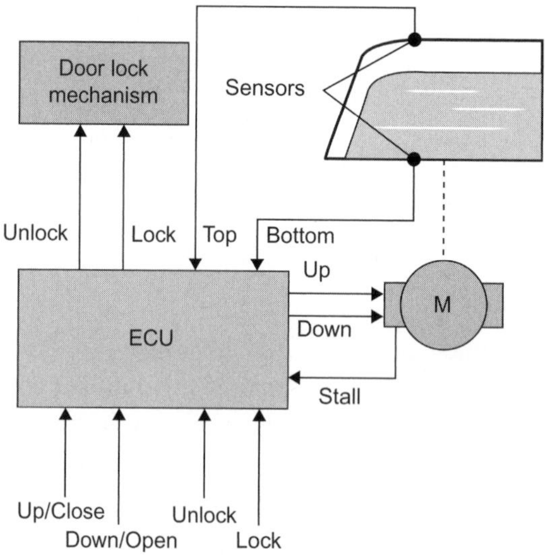

Figure 1.17:
Example – window lift hardware design.

mechanisms to detect fingers in window areas to prevent injury. In some cases, window cranks are now outlawed for this reason. Adding a capability like this after the system has already been deployed could result in difficult changes to the software. The two options would be to add this event and task to the control loop or add a task.

When embedded software systems get complex, we need to move away from simple looping structures and migrate to more complex tasking models. Figure 1.18 is an example

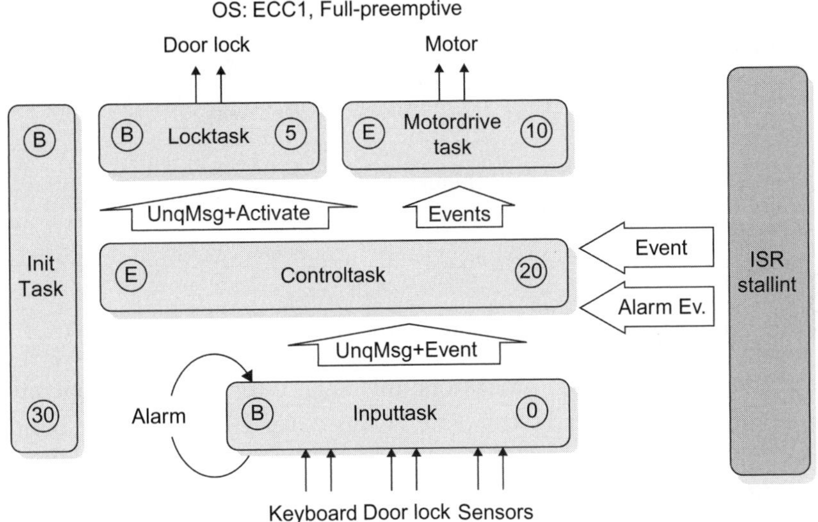

Figure 1.18:
Example – window lift software design.

of what a tasking model would look like for the window lift example. As a general guideline, when the control loop gets ugly then go to multitasking and when you have too many tasks then go to Linux, Windows, or some other similar type of operating system. We'll cover all of these alternatives in more detail in later chapters.

Hardware abstraction layers (HAL) for embedded systems

Embedded system development is about programming at the hardware level. But hardware abstraction layers are a way to provide an interface between hardware and software so applications can be device independent. This is becoming more common in embedded systems. Basically, embedded applications access hardware through the hardware abstraction layer. The HAL encapsulates peripherals of a microcontroller and several API implementations can be provided at different levels of abstraction. An example HAL for an automotive application is shown in Figure 1.19.

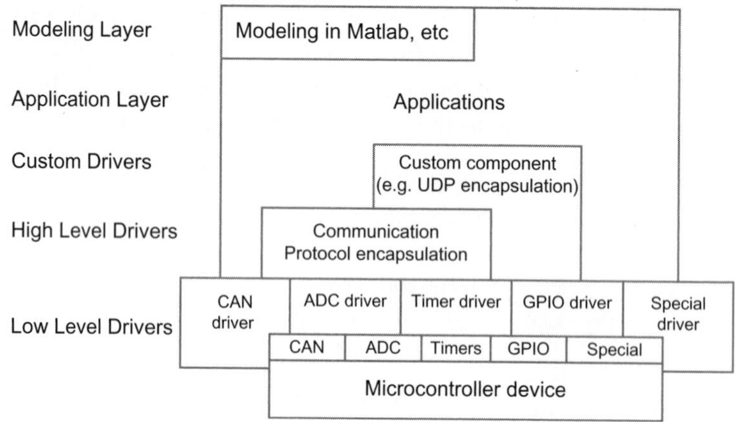

Figure 1.19:
Hardware abstraction layer.

There are a few problems that a HAL attempts to address:

- Complexity of peripherals and processors: this is hard for a real-time operating system (RTOS) to support out of the box; most RTOSes cover 20–30% of the peripherals out of the box.
- Packaging of chip muxing function: how does the RTOS work as you move from standard device to custom device?
- The RTOS is basically the lowest common denominator; a HAL can support the largest number of processors. But some peripherals, such as an analog to digital converter (ADC), require custom support (peripherals work in either DMA mode or direct mode, and we need to support both).

The benefits of a HAL include:

- it allows easy migration between embedded processors;
- it leverages existing processor knowledge base;
- it creates code compliant with a defined programming interface such as a standard application programming interface (API) such as a CAN driver source code, or an extension to a standard API such as a higher protocol over SCI communication (such as UDP), or even your own API.

As an example of this more advanced software architecture and a precursor to more detailed material to follow later, consider the case of an automobile front light management system as shown in Figure 1.20. In this system, what happens if software components are running on different processors? Keep in mind that this automobile system must be a

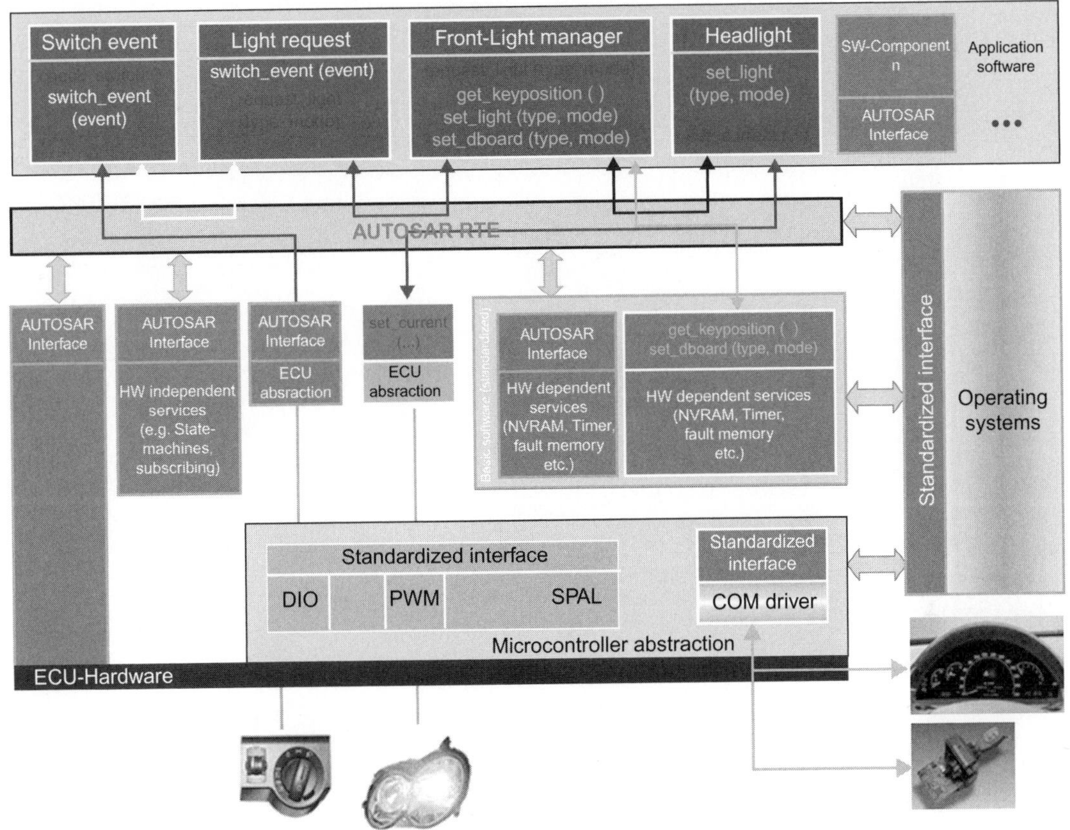

Figure 1.20:
Use case example: front light management.

deterministic network environment. The CAN bus inside the car is not necessarily all the same CPU.

As shown in Figure 1.21, we would like to minimize the changes to the software architecture if we need to make a small change such as replacing a headlight type. We want to be able to change the peripheral (like changing the headlight or offering optional components like those shown in Figure 1.22) but not have to change anything else.

Finally, embedded systems development flow follows a model similar to that shown in Figure 1.23. Research is performed early in the process followed by a proof of concept and hardware and software co-design and test. System integration follows this phase, where all of the hardware and software components are integrated together. This leads to a prototype system that is iterated until eventually a production system is deployed. We look into the

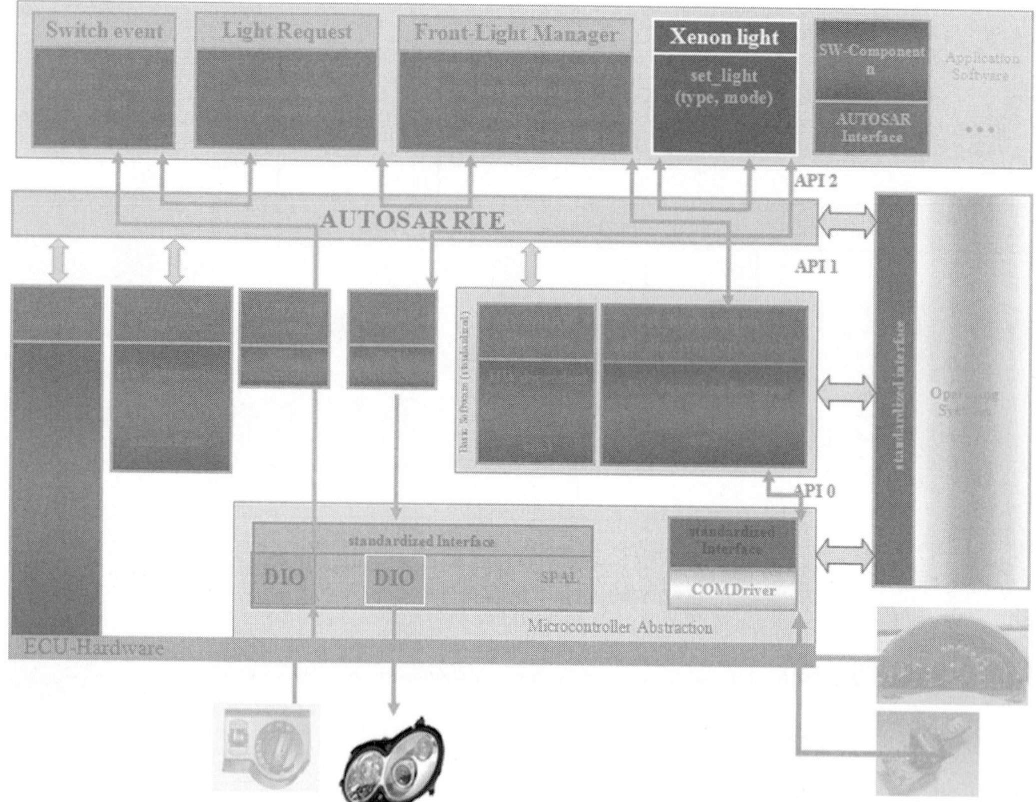

Figure 1.21:
Use case example: front light management.

details of this flow as we begin to dive deeper into the important phases of software engineering for embedded systems.

Summary

Many of the items that we interface with or use on a daily basis contain an embedded system. An embedded system is a system that is "hidden" inside the item we interface with. Systems such as cell phones, answering machines, microwave ovens, VCRs, DVD players, video game consoles, digital cameras, music synthesizers, and cars all contain embedded processors. A late-model automobile can contain up to 80 embedded microprocessors. These embedded processors keep us safe and comfortable by controlling such tasks as antilock braking, climate control, engine control, audio system control, and airbag deployment.

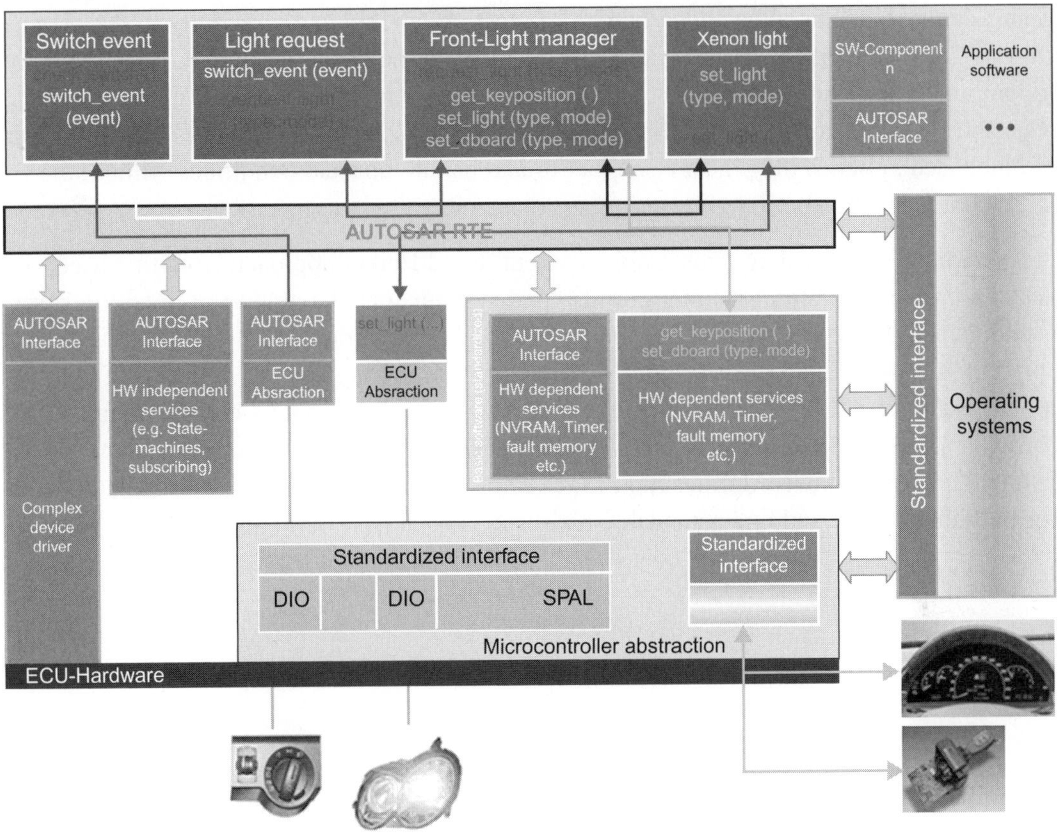

Figure 1.22:
Use case example: front light management.

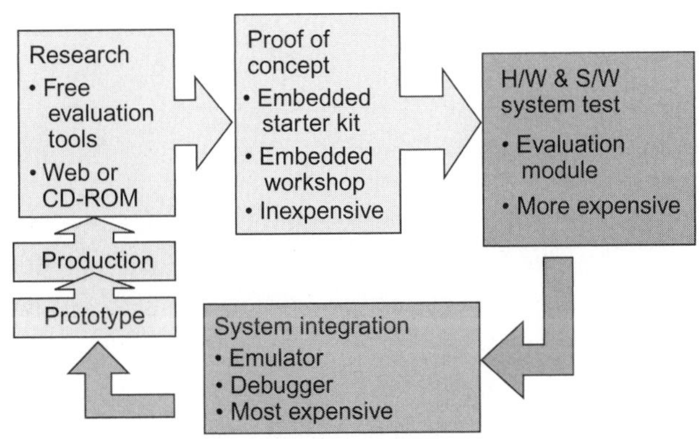

Figure 1.23:
Embedded system development flow.

Embedded systems have the added burden of reacting quickly and efficiently to the external "analog" environment. That may include responding to the push of a button, or a sensor to trigger an air bag during a collision, or the arrival of a phone call on a cell phone. Simply put, embedded systems have deadlines which can be hard or soft. Given the "hidden" nature of embedded systems, they must also react to and handle unusual conditions without the intervention of a human.

Programming embedded systems requires an entirely different approach from that used in desktop or mainframe programming. Embedded systems must be able to respond to external events in a very predictable and reliable way. Real-time programs must not only execute correctly, they must execute on time. A late answer is a wrong answer. Because of this requirement, we will be looking at issues such as concurrency, mutual exclusion, interrupts, hardware control and processing, etc., later in the book because these topics become the dominant considerations. Multitasking, for example, has proven to be a powerful paradigm for building reliable and understandable real-time programs.

CHAPTER 2

Embedded Systems Hardware/Software Co-Development

Frank Schirrmeister

Chapter Outline

Today's embedded systems – an example

When planning the development of modern embedded systems, hardware and software cannot be considered independently. Over the last two decades chip and system complexity have seen an enormous amount of growth, while more and more system functionality has moved from dedicated hardware implementation into software executing on general purposed embedded processors. By 2010 the development effort for software had outgrown the development efforts for hardware, and the complexity trend continues in favor of software.

What does such an embedded system look like today and what are its development challenges? Figure 2.1 shows an example of the hardware/software portion of an embedded

Software Engineering for Embedded Systems.
DOI: http://dx.doi.org/10.1016/B978-0-12-415917-4.00002-5
© 2013 Elsevier Inc. All rights reserved.

system. The system on chip (SoC) on the left hand side is a typical ARM® core-based SoC with a processor subsystem containing various processors with a coherent fabric connection to the rest of the chip. The SoC also contains custom application-specific components for 3D graphics, digital signal processing, dedicated application-specific hardware accelerators, low-speed peripherals, and high-speed interfaces. One of the main development challenges of such an SoC is to ensure that the integration of all the pre-defined silicon IP blocks works correctly across complex interconnects together with newly developed blocks of hardware functionality. Various interconnect protocols in sub-systems and across the chip need to be validated for correctness, all of it in the context of the software executing on the processors.

The right hand side of Figure 2.1 shows this same SoC in its system context. Connections between the SoCs and the actual system peripherals are established on the PCB and are

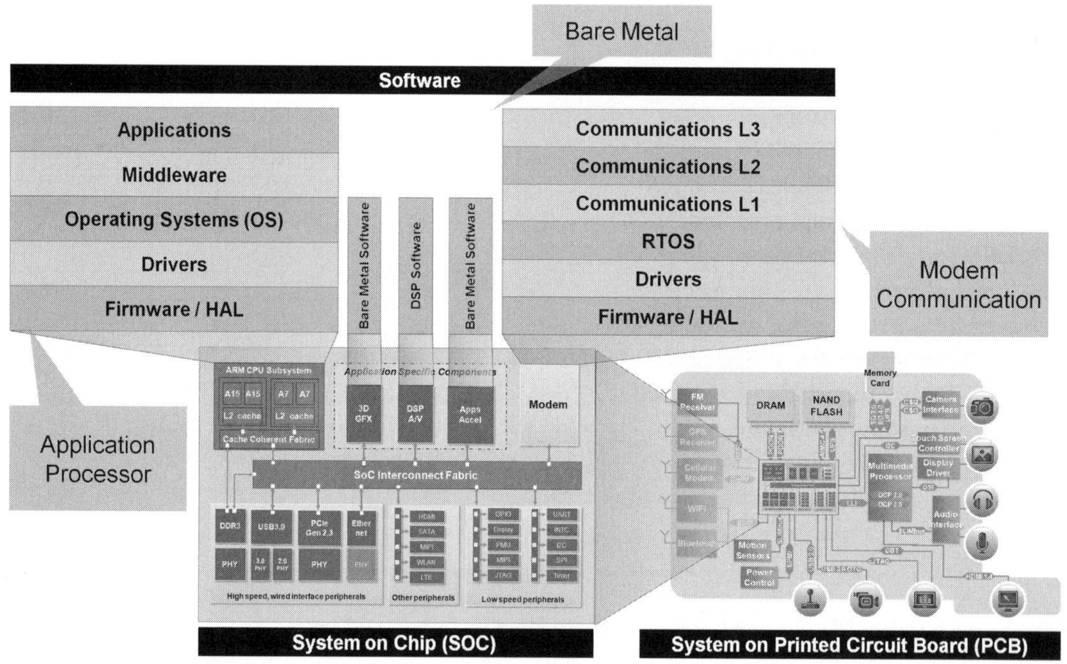

Figure 2.1:
An ARM® core-based system on chip in its system context.

often based on standards like DIGRF, MIPI, and USB. Now the verification challenge shifts from the on-chip areas to how the chip behaves in its environment. For instance, are the frames generated by the graphics engine correctly displayed by the external display? Various off-chip and in-system effects need to be considered together with on-chip effects, as they often drive the graphics content and control. Figure 2.1 outlines different types of software stacks, from the application software stack running on the application processor,

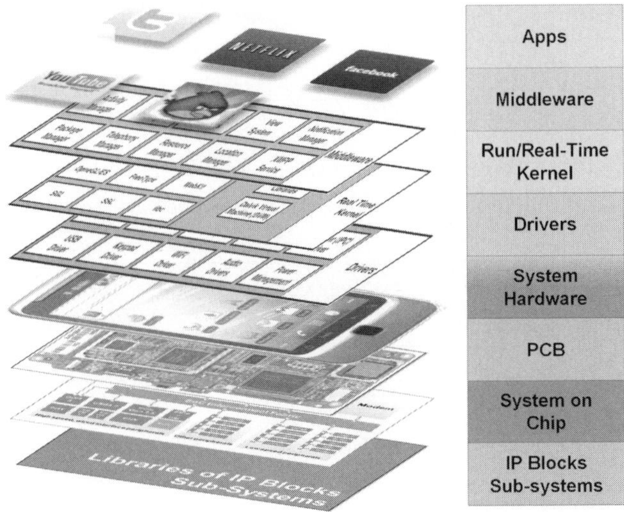

Figure 2.2:
Layers of hardware and software in an embedded system.

the OSI communication layers enabling the modem to communicate as well as bare metal software directly executing on the processor.

Both hardware and software are developed in layers, as indicated in Figure 2.2. The complex hardware portion at the chip level is largely assembled from pre-defined hardware blocks and sub-systems. The SoC itself is integrated together with other chips and passive components on printed circuit boards and then integrated into the actual product packaging of the system hardware the end consumer will use. Various layers of software enable the applications which at the end define the end-user experience. The applications are enabled by at times complex middleware, which in turn executes on operating systems. Depending on the application the operating systems may have to be real-time capable. Software drivers connect the software to specific hardware components.

In order to further understand the challenges for hardware/software co-development, one needs to consider a typical project flow and the dependencies between hardware and software.

Figure 2.3 shows a typical embedded system design flow for hardware and software, as well as the effort of the different phases. The height of the blocks along the *Y* axis indicates the percentage of effort each of the tasks takes on average as measured over a set of 12 example projects. For instance, of the combined hardware/software (HW/SW) development effort, application software development consumes about 30% of the effort. The width of the blocks along the *X* axis indicates the time each of the tasks took as part of the overall project, measured as a percentage of the time from RTL development to silicon tape out, which it was necessary to normalize to the different project lengths. For example,

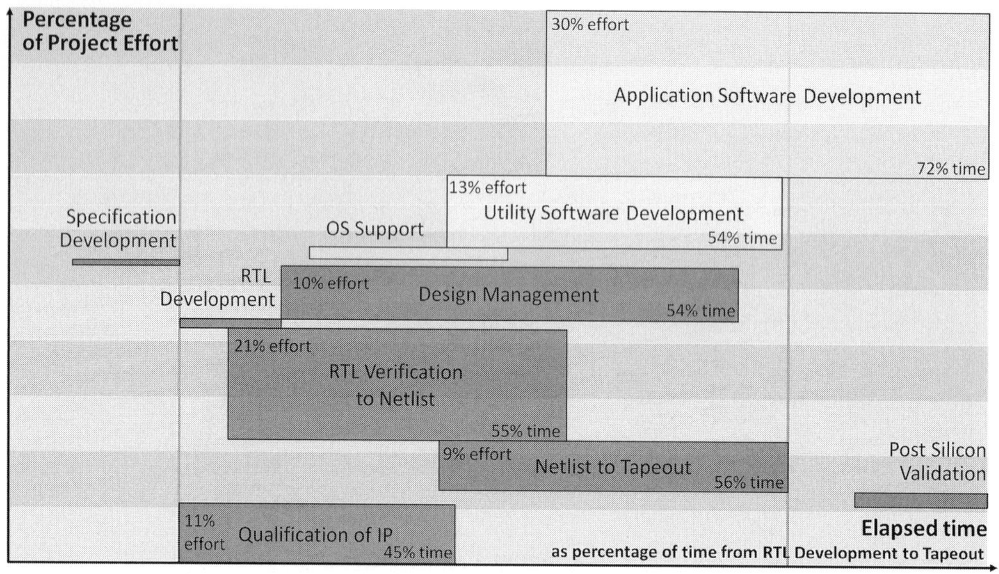

Figure 2.3:
Typical embedded system design flow and percentage of project effort.

application software development took on average 72% of the time it took to get from RTL to tape out.

This classic waterfall flow starts with specification development executed by architects, followed by RTL development and verification performed by hardware verification engineers. Compared to register-transfer level (RTL) development and verification, development of blocks at the TLM level takes less effort because less detail is put in, resulting in less accurate models. Designs at the RT-level become executable in simulation first, and once RTL is reasonably stable, sub-systems or full SoCs can be brought up in emulation or acceleration engines. Once the RTL is very stable, it can be brought up in FPGA-based prototyping as well. Finally, once the first silicon samples are available, prototype boards can be made available for software development. Software development happens in two main categories: hardware-aware software development for OS porting and utility development as required in the lower layers of the software stack as shown in Figure 2.2, and application software development. While not clearly defined as an independent step, the integration of hardware and software needs to be validated by HW/SW validation engineers prior to chip tape out and then on silicon once actual chip samples are available.

Figure 2.3 makes it clear that starting software development as early as possible greatly contributes to schedule improvements for the overall embedded system.

Recognizing this dependency, the electronics industry is today using several types of prototypes during the design flow. Due to the high NRE cost of mask sets for chip development and the significant impact a product delay can have on the return on investment (ROI) for a project, most companies demand the use of prototyping prior to silicon tape-out to ensure first-time-right silicon development. Assume a complex project taking 15 months from RTL to tapeout and requiring 3 more months for silicon availability. Virtual prototypes can be available 12–15 months prior to silicon. The elapsed time for development and verification of RTL would be about 10 months, so emulation and acceleration can become available 6–9 months prior to silicon, and FPGA prototypes can become available 3–6 months prior to silicon. This clearly illustrates that time of availability during a project is a clear difference between the software development engines.

Several different types of prototypes allow hardware/software integration and debugging before the actual silicon and embedded system are available. In addition, different users within a design team have potentially different needs for prototype capabilities. Just exactly what type of prototype to choose is not always 100% clear, and the multitude of choices can make it hard for design teams to find the right combination of prototypes to support their needs.

HW/SW prototyping users

Different users with a development team have different requirements for prototypes.

Application software developers need a representation of the hardware as early as possible and ideally as independent from the hardware as possible. It needs to execute as fast as possible and needs to be functionally accurate. In wireless and consumer application domains, the application software development can be done without full timing detail of the hardware. For example, detailed memory latency and bus delays are generally not of concern when developing applications running on a cell phone. In contrast, applications in military/aeronautic and automotive may need very detailed understanding of the underlying hardware to work correctly.

Similarly, hardware-aware software developers would also like representations of the hardware to be available as early as possible. However, they need to see the details of the register interfaces and they expect the prototype to look exactly as the target hardware will look. While for application software development cross compilation of software originally executed on the host may be an option, for hardware-aware software development users will want to execute the same binary which eventually will be brought up in the hardware. Depending on their task, timing information may be required. In exchange, this type of developer is likely to compromise on speed to gain the appropriate accuracy.

System architects care about early availability of the prototype, as they have to make decisions even before all the characteristics of the hardware are defined. They need to be able to trade off hardware versus software and make decisions about resource usage. For them, the actual functionality counts less than some of the details – which makes it very difficult to provide appropriate prototypes for example for designs with a completely new interconnect structure. For example, functionality can be abstracted into representations of the traffic it creates, but for items like the interconnect fabric and the memory architecture, very accurate models are desirable. In exchange, this type of user is willing to compromise on speed and does not typically require complete functionality as the decisions are often made at a sub-system level.

Hardware verification engineers do need precise timing accuracy of the hardware, at least on a clock cycle basis for the digital domain. Depending on the scope of their verification assignment, they need to be able to model the impact of software as it interacts with the hardware, and often make the software part of their test infrastructure. Given the growing number of processors per chip, it becomes more and more common that some of the software executing on the processors is dedicated to hardware testing and verification. For hardware verification engineers, accuracy definitely trumps speed, but the faster the prototype executes, the better the verification efficiency will be. This type of user also cares about being able to reuse test benches once they have been developed. The reuse happens across different prototypes using software- or hardware-based execution.

Finally, HW/SW validation engineers make sure the integration of hardware and software works as specified, and they need a balance of speed and accuracy to execute tests of significant length to pinpoint defects if they occur. This type of user especially needs to be able to connect to the environment of the chip and system to verify functionality in the system context. For that purpose prototype speed and sufficient accuracy of environment models are important.

HW/SW prototyping options

During an embedded systems development, different prototypes are available at different stages of the project. A summary overview of all the platforms is shown in Figure 2.4.

Software development kits (SDKs) like the Android and Apple iPhone SDK typically do not run the actual software binary but require re-compilation of the software before

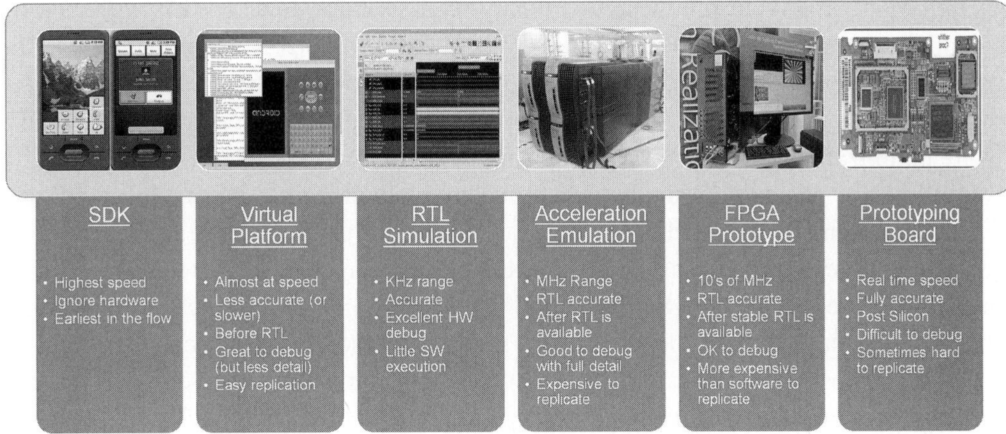

Figure 2.4:
Prototyping options – there is no "one fits all".

executing on the target. The main users are application software developers who require only minimal awareness of hardware details. SDKs offer high speed but lack hardware accuracy. The software executing on the processors runs natively on the host first or executes on abstraction layers like Java. Complex computation, as used in graphics and video engines, is abstracted using high-level APIs that map those functions to the capabilities of the development workstation. For instance, calls to OpenGL can be intercepted and are executed in the native environment of the workstation which runs the SDK. As a result for this type of user and use model the details of how the hardware performs its task are not important enough to warrant more detailed models.

Architectural virtual prototypes based on transaction-level models are mixed-accuracy models that enable architecture decision-making and validation of performance. The items in question – bus latency and contention, memory delays, etc. – are described with high fidelity maybe even as small portions of RTL. Because it may not be available in implementation yet, the rest of the system is abstracted into statistic traffic generators or use traces captured in real environments. The main target users are system architects and system validation engineers. Specifically, the hardware effects of the interconnect fabric of the examples given earlier will be modeled in full detail, but the analysis will be done per sub-system. Execution speed may vary greatly depending on the amount of timing accuracy, but normally will be limited to 10 s to low-100 s of kHz.

Software virtual prototypes run the actual binary on transaction-level models without re-compilation at speeds close to real time – 50s of MHz to 100s of MHz. Target users are software developers, both apps developers and "hardware-aware software developers", for the use of models of software development, bring-up, debug, validation and test, as well as software optimization. With software increasingly determining product functionality, software-driven verification of the hardware under development has become adopted more recently. Depending on the need of the developer, some of the hardware timing may be more accurately represented. This type of prototype can also be used by HW/SW validation engineers who need to see both hardware and software details. Due to the nature of "just-in-time binary translation", the code stream of a given processor can be executed very fast natively on the host. This makes virtual prototypes great for software development, but modeling other components of the example systems – like the 3D engines or other parallel hardware – would result in significant speed degradation. The hardware is just modeled with enough detail to represent all registers accurately and provide proper functionality – even if abstracted.

Once the RTL for the hardware has been developed, RTL-based prototypes offer more accuracy. RTL simulation is the standard simulation vehicle for hardware verification engineers. Given its execution in software, it executes equally slowly – in the range of 100s of Hz – for all components in the system to be prototyped. The hardware is modeled in full detail (at least for the digital side); RTL becomes the golden reference model for hardware development.

Acceleration is a mix of software-based and hardware-based execution. When RTL simulation becomes too slow, acceleration allows users to bring performance to the next orders of magnitude – 200 kHz to 500 kHz. Interfaces to the real world are added, but selectively.

Using in-circuit emulation all components of the design are put into a dedicated verification computing engine – an emulator. With synthesizable test benches users get even more speed – 1 to 2 MHz. Emulation offers great debug insight, especially for hardware, but also for software in debuggers attached using direct proprietary or JTAG interfaces. Given the higher speed, more interfaces to the real world are added. For both in-circuit emulation and acceleration, the speed is much faster than basic RTL simulation. However, when it comes to pure software execution on a processor, transaction-level models (TLMs) of a processor on a PC will execute faster.

FPGA-based prototyping: when the RTL is pretty stable after a fair amount of verification has progressed, users can utilize an even faster hardware-based execution environment. This works especially well for IP that already exists in RTL form. Real-world interfaces are now getting to even higher speeds of 10s of MHz. Similar to acceleration and in-circuit emulation, when it comes to pure software execution on a processor, TLMs of a processor on a PC will still execute faster.

Silicon-based prototypes use either the chip from a previous-generation project or the silicon samples once they become available. The actual silicon-based prototype can be used once the chip is back from fabrication. Now users can run at real speeds, with all connections, but debug becomes harder as execution control is not trivial. Starting, stopping, and pausing execution at specific breakpoints is not as easy as in software-based execution, FPGA-based prototyping, and acceleration and emulation. For instance, in a heterogeneous multicore system, a breakpoint may stop one of the processors, but the other parts of the hardware will continue to execute.

Chips from the last project can still be used, especially for application development. However, the latest features of the development for the new chip are not available until the appropriate drivers, OS ports, and middleware become available.

Prototyping decision criteria

To understand the benefits associated with each type of prototype, it is important to summarize the actual concerns derived from the different users and use models:

- Time of availability during a project: when can I get it after project start? Software virtual prototypes win here as the loosely timed transaction-level model (TLM) development effort is much lower than RTL development. Hybrid execution with a hardware-based engine alleviates re-modeling concerns for legacy IP that does not exist yet as a TLM.
- Speed: how fast does the prototype execute? Previous-generation chips and actual samples are executing at actual target speed. Software virtual prototypes without timing annotation are next in line, followed by FPGA-based prototypes and in-circuit emulation and acceleration.
- Accuracy: how detailed is the hardware that is represented compared to the actual implementation? Software virtual prototypes based on TLMs, with their register accuracy, are sufficient for a number of software development tasks including driver development. However, with significant timing annotation, speed slows down so much that RTL in hardware-based prototypes is often actually faster.
- Capacity: how big can the executed design be? Here the different hardware-based execution engines differ greatly. Emulation is available in standard configurations of up to 2 billion gates, and standard products for FPGA-based prototyping are in the range of 18 to 30 million gates, although multiple boards can be connected for higher capacity. Software-based techniques for RTL simulation and virtual prototypes are only limited

by the capabilities of the executing host. Hybrid connections to software-based virtual prototypes allow additional capacity extensions.

- Development cost and bring-up time: how much effort needs to be spent to build the prototype on top of the traditional development flow? Here virtual prototypes are still expensive because they are not yet part of the standard flow. Emulation is well understood and bring-up is very predictable, of the order of weeks. FPGA-based prototyping from scratch is still a much bigger effort, often taking 3 to 6 months. Significant acceleration is possible when the software front-end of emulation can be shared.
- Replication cost: how much does it cost to replicate the prototype? This is the actual cost of the execution vehicle, not counting the bring-up cost and time. Pricing for RTL simulation has been under competitive pressure and is well understood. TLM execution is in a similar price range, but the hardware-based techniques of emulation and FPGA-based prototyping require more significant capital investment and can be measured in dollars per executed gate.
- Software debug, hardware debug, and execution control: how easily can software debuggers be attached for HW/SW analysis and how easily can the execution be controlled? Debugger attachment to software-based techniques is straightforward and execution control is excellent. The lack of speed in RTL simulation makes software debug feasible only for niche applications. For hardware debug, the different hardware-based engines differ – hardware debug in emulation is very powerful and comparable to RTL simulation, while in FPGA-based prototyping it is very limited. Hardware insight into software-based techniques is great, but the lack of accuracy in TLMs limits what can be observed. With respect to execution control, software-based execution allows users to efficiently start and stop the design, and users can selectively run only a subset of processors, enabling unique multi-core debug capabilities.
- System connections: how can the environment be included? In hardware, rate adapters enable speed conversions and a large number of connections are available as standard add-ons. RTL simulation is typically too slow to connect to the actual environment. TLM-based virtual prototypes execute fast enough and have virtual I/O to connect to real-world interfaces like USB, Ethernet, and PCI. This has become a standard feature of commercial virtual prototyping environments.
- Power analysis: can users run power analysis on the prototype? How accurate is the power analysis? With accurate switching information at the RTL level, power consumption can be analyzed fairly accurately. Emulation adds the appropriate speed to execute long enough sequences to understand the impact of software. At the TLM level, annotation of power information allows early power-aware software development, but the results are by far not as accurate as at the RTL level.
- Environment complexity: how complex are the connections between the different engines? As more hardware and software engines are connected (like in acceleration),

the complexity can become significant and hard to handle, and this needs to be weighed against the value.

Choosing the right prototype

Figure 2.5 attempts to put user needs and prototyping capabilities in context in one capability/need matrix. Given that no prototype by itself fulfills all criteria, hybrid combinations are increasingly getting more demand.

	Virtual Prototyping	RTL Simulation	Acceleration Emulation	FPGA Based Prototyping	Silicon
Early Availability	++	+		-	--
Speed	++	--	-	+	++
HW Accuracy	--	++	++	++	++
HW Debug	--	++	+	-	--
SW Debug	++	--		+	++
Execution Control	++	++	+		--
Effort of Extra Development	--	++	+		++
Cost of Replication	++	++	--	-	+

Figure 2.5:
Prototyping user needs vs. prototyping capabilities.

First, the combination of RTL simulation and virtual prototyping is attractive for verification engineers who care about speed and accuracy in combination. Software debug may be prohibitively slow on RTL simulation itself, but when key blocks including the processor can be moved into virtual prototyping, the software development advantages can be utilized and the higher speed also improves verification efficiency.

Also, the combination of emulation/acceleration and virtual prototyping is attractive for software developers and HW/SW validation engineers when processors, which would be limited to the execution speed of emulation or FPGA-based prototyping when mapped into hardware-based execution, can be executed on a virtual prototype. Equally, massively parallel hardware execution – as is used in video and graphics engines central to the examples referred to above – is executed faster in hardware-based execution than in a virtual prototype.

Given that hardware-based prototypes for hardware/software co-development have been available for years, the rest of this chapter will concentrate on virtual prototypes.

Industry design chain

Prototypes of all forms can be used to interact more efficiently between design teams – within and between companies. For the latter, relationships between stake holders in the SoC design chain can be quite complex. Figure 2.6 illustrates a simplified design chain for the wireless handset segment including some company examples and the relationship to the basic user types.

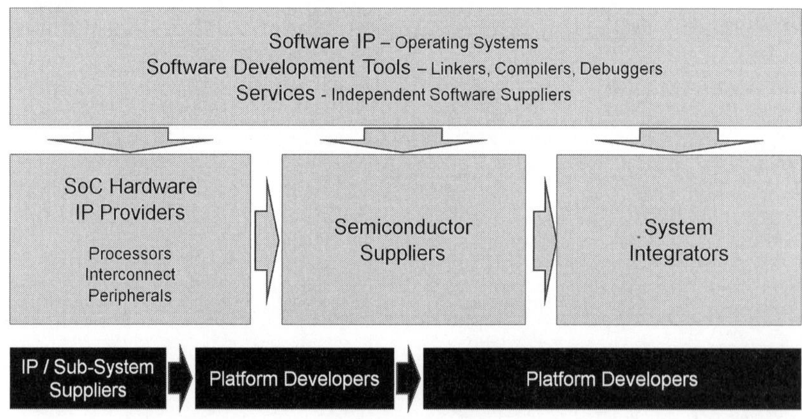

Figure 2.6:
Wireless design chain and users.

System OEMs are the actual interface to the consumer, using the network providers like Vodafone and T-Mobile as their channel. Semiconductor houses provide the silicon, including reference design kits, to the system houses. Given the significant amount of IP reuse in today's chip designs, the semiconductor vendors often license IP from external hardware IP providers. Semiconductor and system houses interact with software IP providers – the independent software vendors (ISVs), which include both operating systems (e.g., Symbian, WinCE, Android and Linux) and application software developers like those who develop multimedia and game applications.

With respect to users, the software programmers are split among semiconductor houses, system houses and ISVs. Programmers in the semiconductor houses and IP providers are traditionally more focused on lower-level drivers and kernel, while the ISVs and system houses actively use middleware and application software as their differentiator.

For the interaction between the different stakeholders within the design chain different use models apply. Enabling software development early is one of the most pressing requirements, but enabling proper hardware verification and validation of performance become equally important. Often the prototype becomes an early demonstration vehicle actually showing the desired functionality in an executable fashion as well.

The need to change the design flow

The objectives for a virtual prototype-based design flow in combination with other prototypes are indicated as overlay in Figure 2.3.

As indicated above, traditional product development approaches led to a sequential process which ended with a "big bang" integration of hardware and software, after hardware prototypes or development boards became available. A virtual prototype approach allows delivery of a software development prototype much earlier, as part of the architecture design phase. A staged delivery allows instruction accurate models in as little as a few weeks, which enables firmware, OS and driver development often before the first line of RTL is coded or reused IP is qualified. Pre-silicon software development is the main use model for virtual prototypes today. However, timing approximation can be added with reasonable incremental effort to the virtual prototype models in later pre-implementation stages, which in turn allows feedback on the actual chip design, often for the same revision of the design still in development.

Different types of virtual prototypes

Virtual prototypes were introduced earlier as one potential form of prototyping. The rest of this chapter will outline different forms and use models of virtual prototypes in more detail.

A software virtual prototype is a fully functional software representation of a hardware design that encompasses a single- or multi-core SoC, peripheral devices, I/O and even the user interface. The virtual prototype runs on a general-purpose PC or workstation and is detailed enough to execute unmodified production code, including drivers, the OS and applications at reasonable simulation speed. Users have articulated the need for virtual prototypes to not be more than ten times slower than real time to be effective for embedded software development. The achievable simulation speed depends on the level of model abstraction, which also determines the prototype's accuracy.

To be most effective at improving productivity, a virtual prototype is available as early as possible, sometimes within weeks of the architecture being specified. Even at the beginning of an SoC design flow, the system architecture can be defined to a level of detail that enables an unambiguous executable specification – a virtual prototype of the system or virtual prototype. This prototype can be used to develop and integrate the software, which can in turn be used to refine the hardware architecture in an iterative process. It is sufficient to allow a "just-in-time" delivery in phases, i.e., starting with an instruction-accurate version and delivering timed versions later in time.

For hardware designers, virtual prototypes support the SoC design flow with mixed-mode simulation and a path to RTL design and verification. A virtual prototype can integrate with simulation acceleration technologies and even actual hardware in the loop. Virtual prototypes can be particularly useful for refining high-level power-reduction strategies, because these strategies depend on architectural choices and the evaluation of software effects on the chip's power consumption.

Rather than creating an entirely new methodology, a virtual prototype supports existing best-practice design, debug and verification processes for both hardware and software developers. The prototype interfaces with a range of hardware and software tools, including standard languages for hardware and software development. For software engineers, for example, the virtual prototype enables the use of development environments such as Texas Instruments' Code Composer Studio, ARM's RealView, the GNU tool chain and debug environments from other vendors.

Most importantly, the prototype ensures full binary compatibility with production software. To get this level of compatibility, it is not necessary to use cycle-accurate models. Such models provide a high level of detail and timing metrics, but are more difficult to validate, require additional development effort and typically execute software at only about 500 kilo-instructions per second. This performance level is too slow for porting an operating system, integrating middleware and developing applications.

A brief history of virtual prototypes

Several companies formed about 10 years ago to deliver the virtualization of embedded hardware for pre-silicon software development to the market.

From the start, all of these virtual prototype vendors addressed two key SoC trends – the escalating cost of software, and the fact that to avoid finding bugs late, the software development would have to start earlier. The relative costs to repair embedded software defects increases the later during the development phase they are found. Analyses of embedded software development show that bugs that originate in the requirements phase are five times as expensive to repair during design, 10 times as expensive during coding and more than 350 times as expensive when a device is delivered and in operation (Source: NASA) as indicated in Figure 2.7. Pre-silicon embedded software development advances the integration phase, which was traditionally done after silicon became available, to an earlier project phase, thus allowing bugs to be found earlier and the overall cost of repairing them to be reduced.

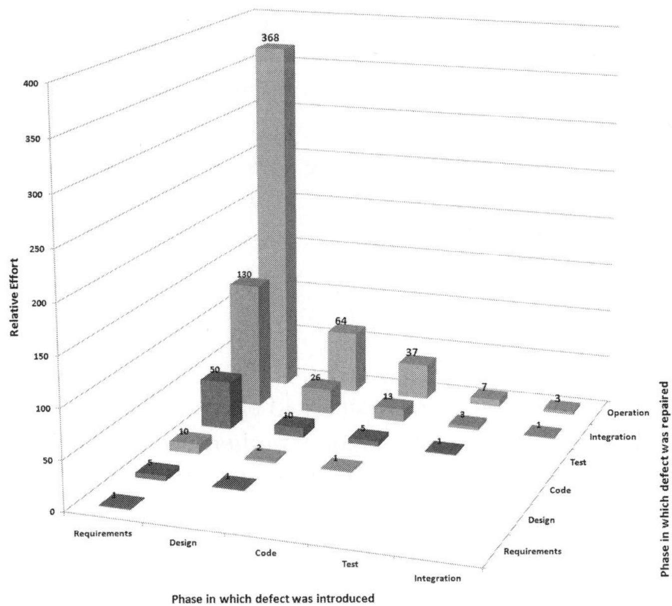

Figure 2.7:
Bug propagation.

The limits of proprietary offerings

In the absence of a pre-existing standard, all early providers of virtual prototype technology developed proprietary modeling solutions. Among these were AXYS Design Automation and VaST Systems Technology, formed in 1997, Virtutech, formed in 1998, and Virtio, formed in 1999. Several in-house solutions from system OEMs also enabled similar virtualization, a prominent example of which is the Motorola Objected Oriented Simulation Environment (MOOSE).

At that time, traditional EDA companies, such as CoWare, Synopsys, Mentor and Cadence, were still more focused on architecture exploration, hardware/software co-design and verification. This was directly reflected in the early days of SystemC and limited its applicability to provide SystemC-based offerings for embedded software development. Within OSCI's transaction-level modeling (TLM) working group, several different abstraction levels were introduced to address the speed versus accuracy of the models. The varying abstraction levels left some users confused, forcing them to create custom derivatives to address specific needs. In addition, processor models often included more detail than the majority of software programmers really needed. In turn, execution speeds were in the single-MIPS or even sub-MIPS range, which is far too slow for most software programmers.

In 2006, the paths of proprietary virtual prototype solutions and OSCI SystemC met. ARM had acquired AXYS Design Automation in 2004, Synopsys had acquired Virtio in 2006 and CoWare had also added virtual prototypes to complement its architecture exploration product lines. The proprietary offerings for virtual prototypes had saturated the market of early adopters, who were willing to sacrifice flexibility, model interoperability and standards compliance to get a working solution. The requirements of mainstream users are different, however. The fact that TLMs created in one proprietary tool would not work in any other meant that a user's investment in modeling was not paying off. As a result, market adoption was slower than anticipated.

Standardization to ensure model interoperability had become the key requirement for interoperability and has today become an important criterion when choosing a virtual prototype. While some of the proprietary offerings are still around and in use, standards-based interoperability can today no longer be ignored.

What makes virtual prototypes fast

Besides the inherent speed of the models for processors, peripherals and busses, there are three interface-related attributes of virtual prototypes that make them fast enough for pre-silicon software development.

First of all, the components in a virtual prototype need to be decoupled temporally. Older technologies required all components to advance one clock cycle and then return to a master scheduler. The resulting overhead significantly limited the execution. In contrast, today's virtual prototypes with temporally decoupled components allow "quantum-based" simulation. They create a set of free running models, which "check-in" after a defined quantum time, e.g., the time it takes to execute 1000 instructions. Using temporal decoupling, the overhead becomes negligible, resulting in execution speed fast enough to satisfy software programmers' requirements. Today's virtual prototypes allow, for instance, operating systems like Android to boot within seconds as opposed to days in traditional solutions. A significant portion of software development tasks, including driver development, can be performed this way.

Secondly, the access to memories needs to be fast. Traditional techniques required traversing the design hierarchy through bridges, busses and their arbiters for every memory access to fetch instructions and data into processor models. This process required a lot of simulation events and context switches, significantly limiting execution speed. In today's virtual prototypes, "back doors" for direct memory accesses significantly speed up simulation, especially for compute-bound tasks in which a lot of the actual computation happens within the processor model from data stored in caches.

Thirdly, low-overhead timing annotation needs to be supported in virtual prototypes. It is important to be able to flexibly annotate timing to the execution of processors, memory accesses and peripheral operations. Traditional techniques often would block simulation progress while they execute the peripheral operation. A significant percentage of cases, however, can be dealt with using an immediate return to the master scheduler, while still notifying the master scheduler how much time has to be consumed.

Standardization: the era of SystemC TLM-2.0

By 2006, proprietary virtual prototype offerings had developed individual, proprietary solutions for these three key technologies. In early 2007 key technologies were donated to the OSCI TLM working group. Since then, the APIs for TLM-2.0 have been standardized and ratified. The new TLM-2.0 API standard now offers standard techniques for temporal decoupling, direct memory interfaces and timing annotation, introducing the loosely timed (LT) and approximately timed (AT) modeling styles.

Specifically, the blocking interface for LT modeling supports temporal decoupling. Models can block, or may return immediately with optional timing annotation. The LT modeling API had been designed for ease of use and doesn't require a backward path. For virtual prototypes, an estimated 90% of all cases can be dealt with by a combination of immediate return with timing annotation.

SystemC TLM-2 abstraction levels

As indicated above, the value of virtual prototypes within the design flow is tightly linked to two main aspects: first, the early availability to enable software development long before first silicon is available, and second, high simulation performance to allow the execution of software with almost real-time performance. Both aspects call for abstracting from unnecessary details. Abstraction allows for faster model creation, and achieves higher simulation performance.

The need for abstraction results in the concept of transaction-level modeling, making transaction level models the building blocks of virtual prototypes. TLMs come in different flavors, categorized by the timing accuracy: these range from cycle-accurate to approximately timed (AT) to loosely timed (LT). What is common to all of them is the way to model the communication among them: representing transactions flowing within the system instead of individual bus cycles, or specific pins and wires, and thus achieving higher simulation speeds.

Figure 2.8 illustrates the different abstraction levels at which SystemC TLM 2.0 virtual prototypes can be used. While actual application development often can be done even without instruction, accurate representation of the processor models (using what is indicated

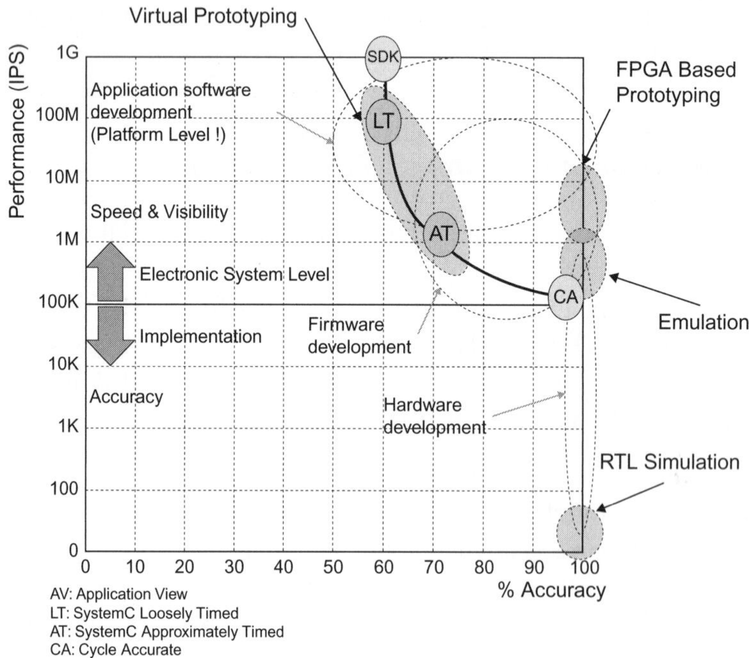

Figure 2.8:
TLM abstraction levels and use models.

as Application View), the pre-silicon integration of firmware, OS and drivers at least requires instruction and register accurate representation of the hardware. Loosely timed virtual prototypes focus on the hardware details that are exposed to software running on the systems. Processors in a virtual prototype execute target program binaries on an instruction-by-instruction basis and are thus binary compatible with the actual hardware. Functional models of the memory management unit (MMU) and caches provide run-time statistics on cache hits and misses. To maximize speed, however, the prototype avoids processor details that are not exposed to the programming model, such as the processor's pipeline.

Bus models in loosely timed prototypes use a similar approach, reducing complex bus traffic to simple read and write transactions. These transactions include representations of address decoding and control registers for elements such as bus bridges and arbiters. However, the bus models avoid detailed bus phasing, arbitration and timing beyond simple access delays.

This abstraction level is the most commonly used one and ideal for early embedded software development of drivers, kernel and OS bring-up.

The next level of abstraction, adding yet more accuracy, is the approximately timed (AT) view, which is used for architectural exploration and real-time software development. Approximately timed virtual prototypes offer more timing detail. For example, these prototypes might include cycle-approximate bus models that add arbitration, pipelining and concurrency details. Access timing for on- and off-chip peripherals can also be included. This additional timing information allows the prototype to better support detailed software partitioning, performance tradeoffs and debugging of time-dependent problems such as race conditions. This is the level of abstraction at which annotation of timing and power to the virtual prototype real hardware software trade-offs can be performed.

The remaining stages indicated in Figure 2.8 – C-translated RTL models, co-emulation and RTL co-verification – are often not only too slow for real hardware/software trade-offs, they also require the actual implementation to have progressed to a stage at which changes to the current design are often no longer feasible. They are, however, useful for verification of low-level software in the context of hardware simulation.As described earlier, virtual prototypes can be separated into architectural virtual prototypes for architectural analysis and performance validation and software virtual prototypes for software development, debug, bring-up, validation and test, software optimization and software driven verification.

Architecture virtual prototypes

Used earliest in the design flow, architecture virtual prototypes have to balance early availability in order to allow decisions impacting the design partitioning with the appropriate accuracy of information about the hardware/software system. Important performance parameters needed to base decisions on are sometimes not available until the actual implementation is done.

Depending on the characteristics of the hardware/software system to be optimized, different accuracy for the individual components will be used and the system may not even be modeled in its entirety. For example, to optimize a complex on-chip interconnect like the ARM NIC and ACE protocols, which have 100s of parameters for configuration, the interconnect itself needs to be modeled accurately while the components it is connecting can be abstracted into traffic models representing transaction sequences or even stochastic models.

To optimize the blocks in the system themselves – like processor pipelines or caches – again the component itself needs to be represented accurately, while its environment can be abstracted into less accurate representations.

As a result, architecture vurtual platforms will seldom be a complete representation of the system's functionality but will instead be modeled in a very specific fashion, designd to answer very specific questions like "will this cache be big enough" or "will this interconnect provide enough bandwidth for a specific traffic scenario".

Software virtual prototypes

Especially for any software debug, bring-up, validation and test, a software virtual prototype provides superb visibility and control. In addition to virtually unlimited signal trace and logging capability, the system exposes details such as memory management states and the intermediate states of specialized accelerators – in contrast to a hardware-based method in which a user has to wait for a JTAG dump.

Because virtual prototypes are simulation-based, any debugger can freeze all system clocks at a breakpoint – a capability that is especially useful for multicore SoCs. In fact, virtual prototypes solve a major problem with debugging software on the actual multicore hardware, where some clocks continue to run after a breakpoint, and some system states may be altered. By stopping all activity simultaneously, including interprocessor-communication hardware and peripheral clocks, a virtual prototype preserves all the system states that led to the breakpoint and allows analysis not possible in real hardware-based prototypes.

With this visibility and the ability to run software long before actual hardware becomes available, virtual prototypes have fundamentally changed the way software is ported to SoCs, beginning with OS boot-up and continuing to the porting of application software. To see how this process works, it is useful to consider the example of an SoC whose main processor runs Linux. To offer this SoC with a development board, the software team must create sample applications for the board as well as the basic software for the chip. When working with a new physical processor, one of the first tasks is to develop a boot-loading routine that installs Linux in memory so that the OS can begin executing. At this point, dealing with problems is difficult because the OS resources needed to resolve problems are not yet in place.

A virtual prototype bypasses this difficulty by providing direct access to the model's memory. The OS can be loaded directly into the model, and the boot sequence can be verified when the processor's basic operations have been proven. By allowing developers to work with the OS using only minimal processor resources, the virtual prototype limits the number of variables that have to be considered when debugging.

For any test run, developers can load the OS instantly, rather than waiting for the simulation model to boot each time. Similarly, flash and ROM contents can be updated instantaneously, rather than waiting the several minutes required to flash a physical development board. A virtual prototype also saves time by allowing other system states to be set as desired through back-door access.

After verifying that the OS and the core processor work together, developers can add additional hardware, and debug in manageable steps. When creating peripheral drivers, for example, developers can enable the peripherals as needed, making sure each peripheral works before adding another.

With the SoC's drivers and basic software in place, the development team can work on board-level drivers and application examples. The development board may not be as clearly defined as the SoC, but the team can still make headway by verifying software against different prototype variants. If the choice between NAND and NOR flash memory has not been made, for example, the software team can use models for each memory type to make sure that the software works with both.

In any development project using a virtual prototype, the software team will probably have to deal with uncertainties about details such as flash memory types, the address mapping of peripheral registers, and interrupt assignments. Some rework is inevitable as these details are resolved, and good regression testing is needed to ensure that the software stays in sync with the actual silicon. Still, it is reasonable to expect that about 85% of the software will run unchanged on the final hardware.

A great example of a virtual platform focused for software development and Linux bring-up can be found in my colleague Jason Andrew's Blog series "Exploring the Virtual Platform" (http://www.cadence.com/Community/blogs/sd/archive/2009/01/16/welcome-to-quot-understanding-the-virtual-platform-quot-series.aspx). In five posts related to virtual prototypes many aspects of how to create an embedded system with Linux are explored and a solid background to understand how to construct all of the needed software from scratch is provided. Today electronic systems have to be optimized for power, performance and area. Software has a great deal to do with how much power an SoC consumes, how fast it runs and how much area is consumed (directly translating into cost). For example, hardware designers cannot know a design's actual power consumption until the software is available to drive the hardware in realistic usage scenarios.

Since virtual prototypes enable early software development, they can also provide early insight into power consumption at a system level. With information about power consumption on an application-by-application basis, system architects can make realistic trade-offs. For example, looking at execution frequency versus application run-time allows architects to make intelligent choices that can achieve significant power savings.

Further, some power management schemes use a software management layer or power-aware OS to manage a hardware controller that handles settings for frequency scaling and various power domains. A virtual prototype enables validation and refinement of this interlocking hardware/software scheme. Using a virtual prototype that includes an ARM1136 processor core, for example, a system architect can get immediate visual feedback about the results of frequency scaling applied to the processor while running actual applications. The system can then be optimized accordingly.

Power consumption has become a key issue in the design of SoCs, whether the chips are battery-powered or not, and power management is just one of the ways in which hardware and software are interdependent. By enabling early software development and hardware/software co-design, virtual prototypes supply a critical part of the SoC puzzle that has been missing. As SoC complexity continues to grow, this solution will become increasingly vital for meeting both schedule and functionality goals.

While the main use model for virtual prototypes is pre-silicon software development, as the SoC design cycle progresses a virtual prototype can evolve to meet different needs. There are three main use models of "software-driven verification", which utilize the integration of virtual prototypes with signal level simulation at the register transfer level:

- When an RTL block becomes available, for example, it can be substituted for its transaction-level model in the virtual prototype. Software can then be verified on this version of the prototype as a way to validate both hardware and software.
- The virtual prototype can also provide a head start towards test-bench development and post-silicon validation tests by acting as a test-bench component running actual system software. The virtual prototype can be used to generate system stimuli to test RTL, and then verify that the virtual prototype and RTL function in the same way.
- Additionally, as portions of the virtual prototype are verified as equivalent to their corresponding RTL, the virtual prototype can become a golden or reference executable specification.

Figures 2.9, 2.10 and 2.11 illustrate these three use models bridging the TLM abstraction level to signal-level RTL simulation.

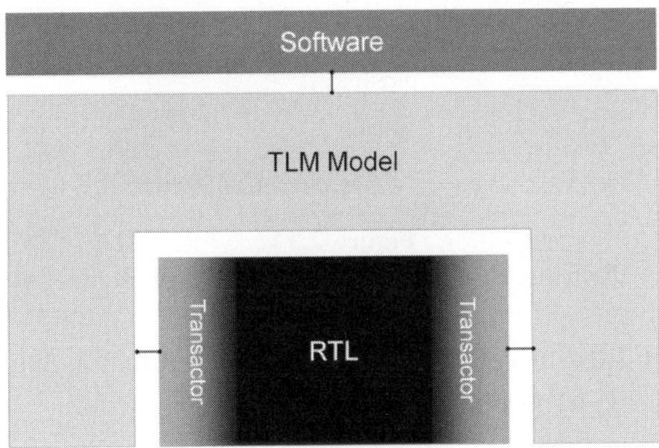

Figure 2.9:
Using the TLM model to generate stimulus for RTL verification.

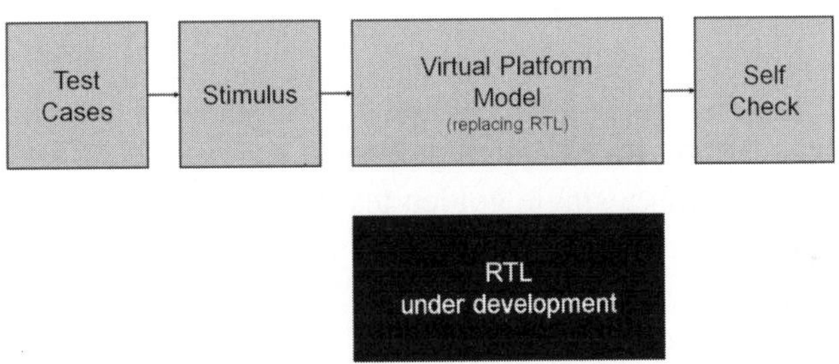

Figure 2.10:
Early test-bench creation and post-silicon validation test development.

The interface from virtual prototypes to traditional RTL simulation can be done using transaction-level interfaces, allowing the actual transactor to be written in SystemVerilog and the bus functional model to be synthesizable in order to allow co-execution with hardware-based environments. Alternatively, the transactor can be written in SystemC and the interface to RTL simulation can be at the signal level.

The first use model – using TLM models to generate stimulus for RTL verification – allows early software validation on the actual hardware implementation, as well as efficient scalable system validation, for which software becomes part of the verification setup. Knowing that real system scenarios are used does increase verification confidence.

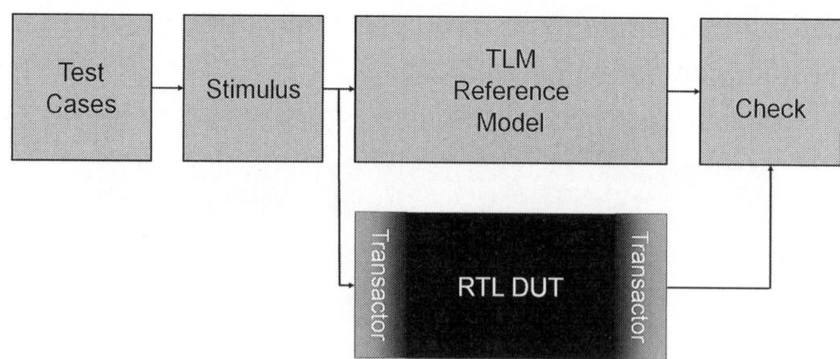

Figure 2.11:
Verifying TLM prototype and RTL equivalence.

Furthermore, simulation used in verification is faster, given that as much of the system as possible is simulated at the transaction level.

The second use model – early test-bench creation and development of post-silicon validation tests on a virtual prototype – allows development of all test bench and validation infrastructure on a virtual prototype, as well as early scenario and test-case creation. Users can efficiently develop on the TLM model "embedded directed software" tests, which can be used for system integration testing. As a result productivity of verification test-case development increases.

The third use model – verifying TLM prototype and RTL equivalence – helps to validate the correctness of the software development prototype against the RTL once it becomes available. As a result users gain a single golden test bench for the transaction level and the RT level.

Summary – the growing importance of virtualization

Given the growing importance of software, virtual prototypes are a key component for reducing time to market in high-software-content chip designs. The most cleverly architected chip will not sell if the associated software is not ready. Hence the main use model for virtual prototypes is the enablement of pre-silicon software development to allow as much software development as possible to happen pre-silicon. Once virtual prototypes are available, they can be used as part of the verification flows as well.

The return on investment into virtual prototypes has several components:

- By using a virtual prototype based on the architecture specification, the actual implementation cost for the phase from specification to RTL and net list can be reduced using early design validation. An executable reference virtual prototype especially helps to avoid communication issues when implementing the RTL from specification.

- Getting a virtual prototype into the hand of software developers early avoids "lost integration days" by virtually advancing the integration phase to a much earlier time in the project. No hardware development kits need to be shared; every software developer can be equipped with a virtual prototype exactly when needed.
- Virtual prototypes help augment hardware-based verification based on FPGA prototypes, emulation or hardware acceleration. Only the absolutely essential tests need to be executed on hardware and co-execution with virtual prototypes increases the utilization of hardware-based verification.
- Given the "electronic" nature of virtual prototypes they can be distributed to users easily and at low cost. In some instances and for some use models they can replace hardware development kits, which significantly reduces cost.
- Finally, given the parallel software development virtual prototypes enable, users completely avoid the penalties of arriving late at market.

In summary however, while virtualization is certainly a key trend to further accelerate hardware-software co-development, during a project flow users have to consider all options to provide prototypes of the hardware early. As outlined earlier in Figure 2.4, there is no one-fits-all solution and different prototypes will be applicable for different use models and may be more often used in conjunction to enable the advantages of the different prototypes in combination.

CHAPTER 3

Software Modeling for Embedded Systems

Shelley Gretlein

Chapter Outline

When and why should you model your embedded system?

Creating a model for your embedded system provides a time- and cost-effective approach to the development of simple or incredibly complex dynamic control systems, all based on a

Software Engineering for Embedded Systems.
DOI: http://dx.doi.org/10.1016/B978-0-12-415917-4.00003-7
© 2013 Elsevier Inc. All rights reserved.

single model maintained in a tightly integrated software suite. Throughout this chapter, you will discover:

- By using modern modeling software tools you can design and perform initial validation in off-line simulation.
- You can then use models to form the basis for all subsequent development stages.
- Modeling – combined with hardware prototyping – will reduce the risk of mistakes and shorten the development cycle by performing verification and validation testing throughout the development.
- Design evaluations and predictions can be made much more quickly and reliably with a system model as a basis.
- This iterative approach results in improved designs, in terms of both performance and reliability.
- The cost of resources is reduced, because of reusability of models between design teams, design stages, and various projects and the reduced dependency on physical prototypes.
- Development errors and overhead can be reduced through the use of automatic code-generation techniques.

These advantages translate to more accurate and robust control designs, shorter time to market, and reduced design cost.

Modeling

Modeling is a broadly used term casually applied to disparate concepts ranging from behavioral and structural models to more simulation-centric methodologies. The challenge with broad terms or broad concepts of course is knowing when, where, and how they apply to your own application.

What then is the appropriate definition of modeling as it pertains to embedded system design?

Modeling, in its most abstract sense, is a methodology in which some representation is created to describe and/or communicate an aspect of the system not easily, naturally or sufficiently captured through system implementation. We will loosely refer to the domain of modeling focused on describing actors or functions and entities, their states, inputs, structure, and views of these over time as "architectural modeling". We will refer to the domain of modeling focused on simulating the behavior of any given system entity as "simulation modeling".

Figure 3.1 below shows the classic statechart diagram invented by David Harel of the Weizmann Institute of Science in the 1980s. By adding hierarchy, concurrency, and communication to state diagrams, Harel created a more expressive form of the state

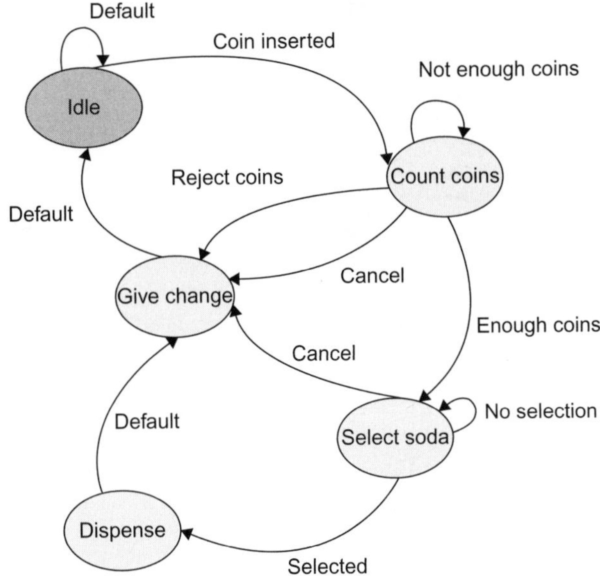

Figure 3.1:
The classic statechart diagram represents a behavioral diagram.

diagram. He invented the diagram while he helped design a complex avionics system, presumably finding the existing tools for such a system lacking. In the 1990s, statecharts were adopted as a behavioral diagram within the Unified Modeling Language (UML) specification.

The classic state diagram consists of two main constructs: states and transitions. In Figure 3.1, the state diagram describes a simple vending machine with five states and seven transitions to illustrate how the machine operates. The machine starts in the "idle" state and transitions to the "count coins" state when coins are inserted. The state diagram shows additional states and transitions when the machine waits for a selection, dispenses a soda, and gives change.

In addition to hierarchy and concurrency, statecharts have features that make them valuable for complex embedded systems as shown in Figure 3.2. Statecharts have a concept of history, allowing a superstate to "remember" which substate within it was previously active. For example, consider a superstate that describes a machine that pours a substance and then heats it. A halt event may pause the execution of the machine while it is pouring. When a resume event occurs, the machine remembers to resume pouring.

Both of these diagram types provide expressions of overall system behavior while also visually describing key states and behaviors within the overall system.

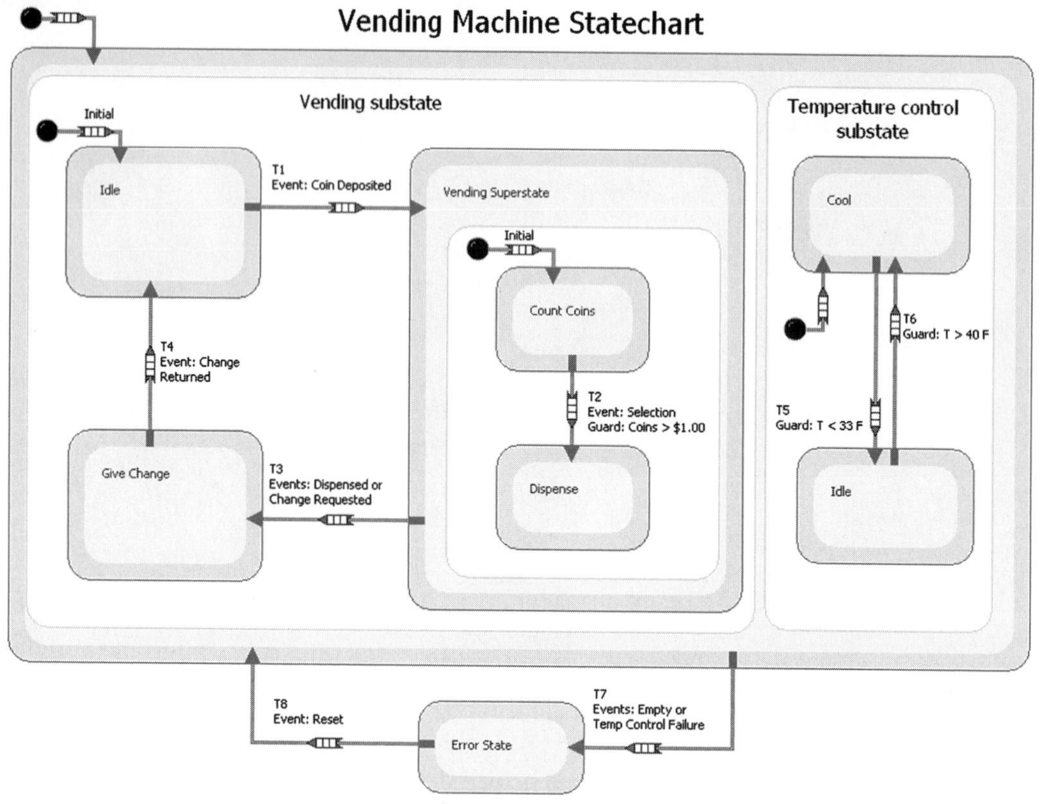

Figure 3.2:
A statechart diagram which also present a concept of "history".

Figure 3.3, by way of contrast, represents a simulation model for a FIFO element within a system. A FIFO – or first in, first out – software element is a way to organize and manipulate your data relative to time in terms of when you acquire it. In the case above, the FIFO might be used to model communication between two hardware devices via a bus. The FIFO definition provides a basic abstraction and interfaces to the notion of a FIFO supplying basic read and write operations, FIFO count and so on. Presumably, VHDL (VHSIC hardware description language) could be re-used either in the actual system or for system modeling via a VHDL simulator. Designers and implementers would agree on this interface definition and then provide implementations to provide data that emulates expected data transmissions through the FIFO over time.

It's important to note that while the code snippet does not visually convey a tremendous amount of architectural information about the system, it does represent a critical abstraction of an element and its interface which then allows for both unit testing at the API boundary

```
entity NiFpgaSimSingleClkFifo is
  generic (
    kAddressWidth : positive;
    kRamReadLatency : natural;|
    kFifoAdditiveLatency : natural := 1
  );
  port (
    aReset : in boolean;
    Clk : in std_logic;

    cReset : in boolean := false;
    cClkEn : in boolean := true;

    -- FIFO Interface
    cWrite : in boolean;
    cDataIn : in std_logic_vector ( kFiDataWidth - 1 downto 0 );

    cRead : in boolean;
    cDataOut : out std_logic_vector ( kFiDataWidth - 1 downto 0 );

    cFullCount,
    cEmptyCount : out unsigned(kAddressWidth downto 0);

    cDataValid : out boolean

  );
end entity NiFpgaSimSingleClkFifo;
```

Figure 3.3:
Simple FIFO simulation entity.

and building systems that switch between a simulatable instance of the FIFO and a real-world bus with FIFO mechanics and constraints.

Ideally, both the architectural and simulation aspects of your modeling should deliver better design insights, more reuse of design, test, and implementation artifacts, earlier and more tight integration of the test and debug phases and more rapid iteration between design and implementation.

Very importantly, simulation modeling enables earlier and in-parallel execution of development phases, which is in stark contrast with traditional methodologies, particularly waterfall approaches, which are by design highly sequential.

For engineering and design tasks, especially related to embedded systems, you typically use some form of software modeling as the initial approach to roughing-in or framing your overall application design. Software models vary greatly in terms of format, level of detail and functionality – so much so that some embedded engineers do not realize they are even modeling. Some software models are behavioral; some are simply visual aids for understanding and architecting, while others are used more as frameworks for ensuring consistency among similar applications or for facilitating communication among teams of

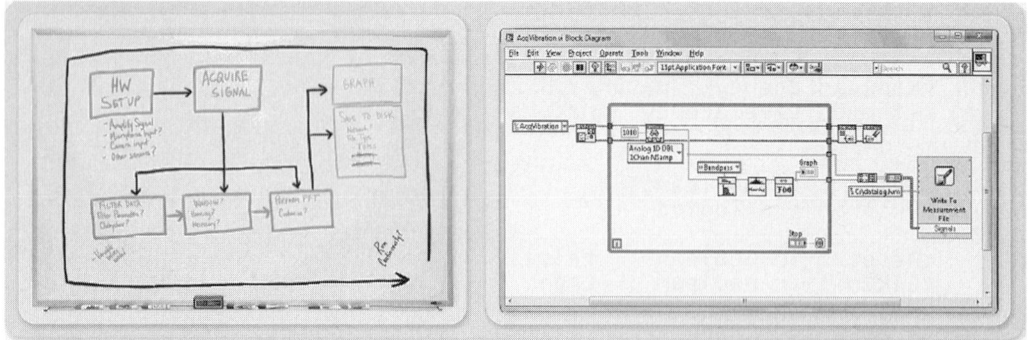

Figure 3.4:
Software modeling ranges from sketches on a whiteboard to far more complex and rigorous activities, languages, and frameworks.

engineers. In essence, software modeling ranges from sketches on a whiteboard showing functional elements and their relationships to far more complex and rigorous modeling activities and frameworks like UML (Figure 3.4). Unified Modeling Language (UML) is an object modeling and specification language most often used in software engineering-related applications.

The challenge for the embedded system designer is to know what type and level of modeling are most appropriate for their unique situation and the problem at hand. In effect, it is about the age-old art of selecting the right tool for the right job. For large, complex, multi-team efforts, formal specification of systems via UML may increase design correctness and the efficiency of communication between teams. On the other hand, for a single developer or small team working on a fairly simple embedded system, it may prove to be overly heavyweight and generally a drag on team efficiency. The same trade-offs hold true for simulation modeling. Whether a system needs simulation or not is highly dependent on the nature of the embedded system itself and the nature of the real-world elements with which the embedded system interacts.

For example, if the embedded system was a widely available and simple processor-based system with simple digital control of a relay or switch, then developing simulation models for the processor and relay would not really add much benefit beyond direct implementation on the processor and a simple test harness to exercise the digital control. On the other hand, if the embedded system included a field programmable gate array (FPGA) and was controlling an expensive and complex real-world device, then it might make sense to both simulate the control logic on the FPGA to avoid the time-intensive FPGA synthesis as well as simulate the expensive real-world device to avoid damaging or destroying it.

What is a modeling language?

Modeling languages, like programming languages, are well-defined and standard language grammars used to express structural and functional actors and their key relationships over time. Different forms of modeling languages have evolved over time and for specific domains. One key concept to keep in mind when evaluating modeling languages is the specific domain for which the language is best suited. The University of California at Berkeley has defined the term "model of computation" to capture the general idea of domain-specific modeling languages, which defines the critical notion that modeling languages provide the most productivity benefit to a designer when they cater specifically to a given problem domain. This is both intuitive and true from observed practice, but designers and modelers as we know, like programmers, can have a healthy bias for their language preference even when it is ill-suited for the actual task at hand.

Modeling languages take many forms and are often either graphical or textual.

Graphical modeling languages use a diagram technique with named symbols that represent concepts and lines that connect the symbols and represent relationships and various other graphical notations to represent constraints.

Textual modeling languages typically use standardized keywords accompanied by parameters to make computer-interpretable expressions.

There are several key aspects of modeling languages to evaluate; graphical versus textual; documentation, simulation, or execution oriented, and focused on architectural-level content or implementation-level content. Figure 3.5 captures these dimensions and overlays several standard modeling techniques and approaches. UML and its subsequent diagrams dominate the landscape of documentation and architectural-oriented modeling diagrams. The standard implementation languages of C, C# and hundreds of other programming languages fit in the implementation and execution-oriented cell represented in the diagram. One of the more prominent hybrid or dual-purpose models are statecharts and their more prohibitive sibling finite state machines (FSMs). These modeling languages are useful at capturing a higher-level architectural view and are able to run in simulation with a high-fidelity and natural mapping to native execution – or the ability to easily map the language to the compiler/execution engine. Models like time-based simulation can specify algorithmic simulation, but then require a code-generation step into one of the execution-dominant programming languages like C, VHDL or G. The quality of the code generation, the naturalness with which the model can map to execution, and the breadth of expressiveness of the model all dictate the quality of the simulation-based approach. Dataflow modeling spans implementation simulations and execution implementations. Most dataflow languages are very visual (typically graphical) and also do an inherently good job at expressing the architecture of your design – certainly more than traditional text-based modeling software packages.

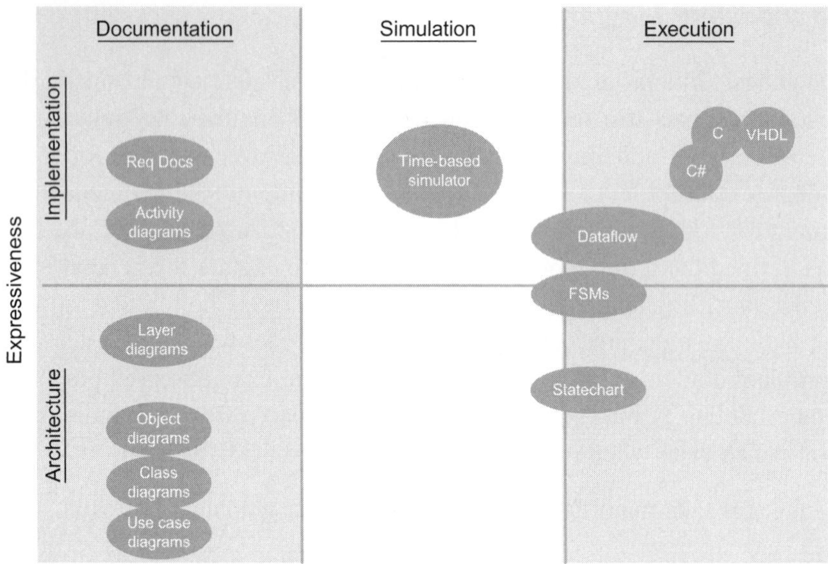

Figure 3.5:
There are several key aspects of modeling languages to evaluate; graphical versus textual; documentation, simulation, or execution oriented, and focused on architectural-level content or implementation-level content.

When delving into the simulation-oriented models as applied to a typical embedded control application, it's interesting to note key touch points in a particular implementation. These points often serve as useful locations to define abstractions such that any one part of the system can be swapped in and out between a simulated system element and a real system element. Figure 3.6 shows a typical embedded control system pattern in which there is some notion of a plant, real or simulated, a controller, real or simulated, and a supervisory control system which can also be real or simulated. Between each of these main system elements, you can identify critical communication paths (network and I/O) as key points to abstract within a design. The discipline to do this well (documented, consistently) allows you to switch between the real and simulated components as you refine your design.

In the rest of this chapter, we will be discussing how designing your embedded system with well-defined structure, clear visualization of relationships between components, with well-defined abstractions enables very productive and efficient embedded designs.

Examples of modeling languages

Moving out of the abstract view of modeling, we can see what it looks like in practice with a few different software approaches. Below we use a PID control algorithm (a common

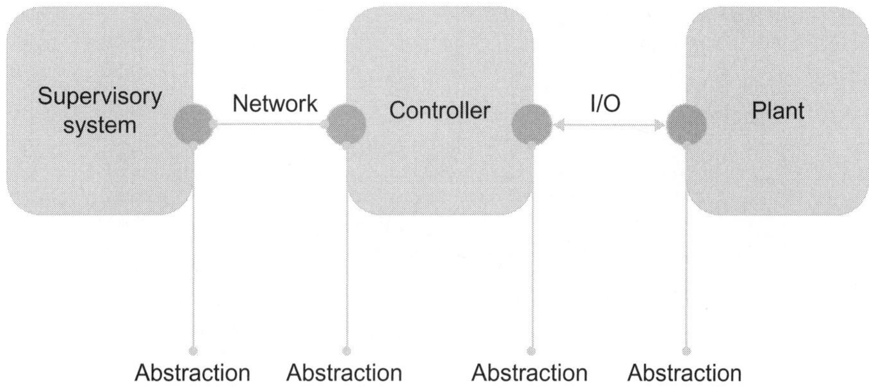

Figure 3.6:
A typical embedded control system pattern in which there is some notion of a plant, real or simulated, a controller, real or simulated, and a supervisory control system which can also be real or simulated.

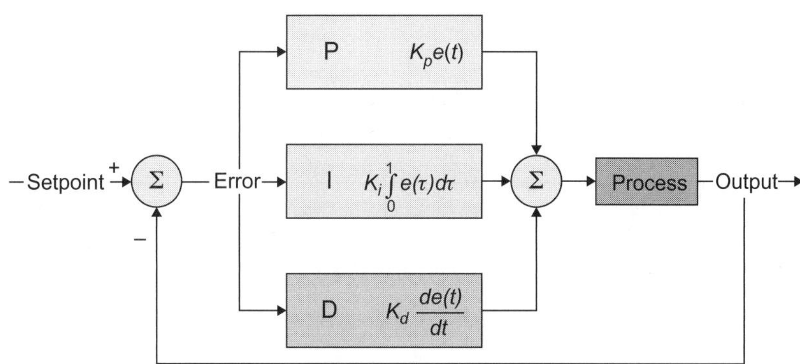

Figure 3.7:
Documentation of a PID control algorithm. A common algorithm used in control applications based on a generic feedback loop based on a proportional-integral-derivative or PID controller – represented in a graphical software view.

algorithm used in control applications based on a generic feedback loop based on a proportional-integral-derivative or PID controller) to help you see a documentation lens as well as the varied visuals and implementation capabilities (Figures 3.7 to 3.12). As you scan these code snippets, note the value and differences in creating those abstraction boundaries – some are clear, some are non-existent.

Not all modeling languages are executable, and for those that are, the use of them doesn't necessarily mean that programmers are no longer required. On the contrary, executable modeling languages are intended to amplify the productivity of skilled

```
previous_error = setpoint - process_feedback
integral = 0
start:

        wait(dt)
        error = setpoint - process_feedback
        integral = integral + (error*dt)
        derivative = (error - previous_error)/dt
        output = (Kp*error) + (Ki*integral) + (Kd*derivative)
        previous_error = error

goto start
```

Figure 3.8:
C code: textual, execution, implementation language.

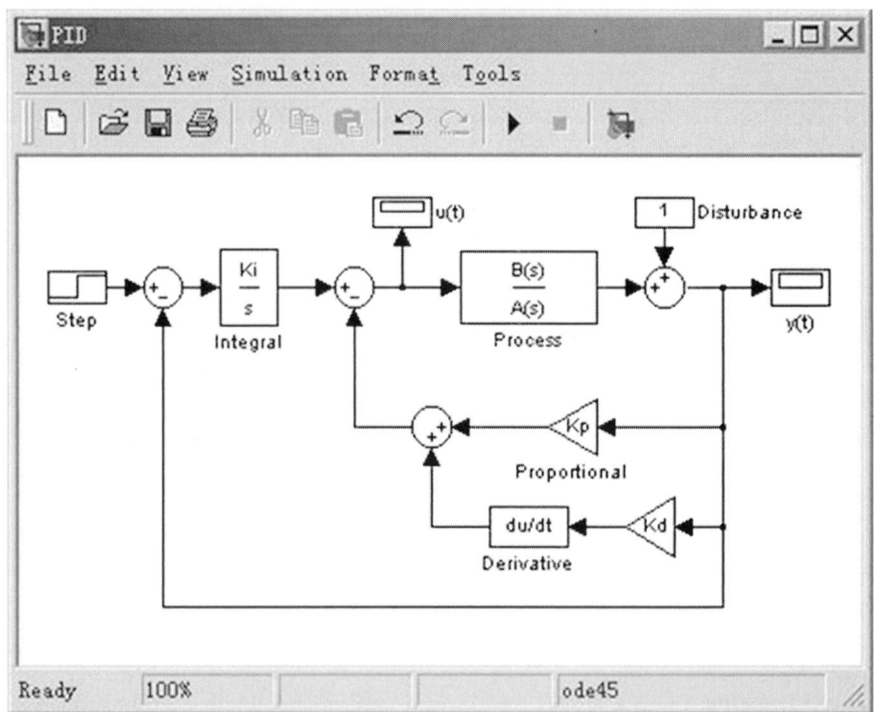

Figure 3.9:
Time-based simulation: graphical, implementation, simulation tool.

programmers, so that they can address more challenging problems, such as distributed systems and parallel computing.

Some modeling languages combine the characteristics of providing a high-level architectural model as well as reasonable amounts of expressiveness and can also easily

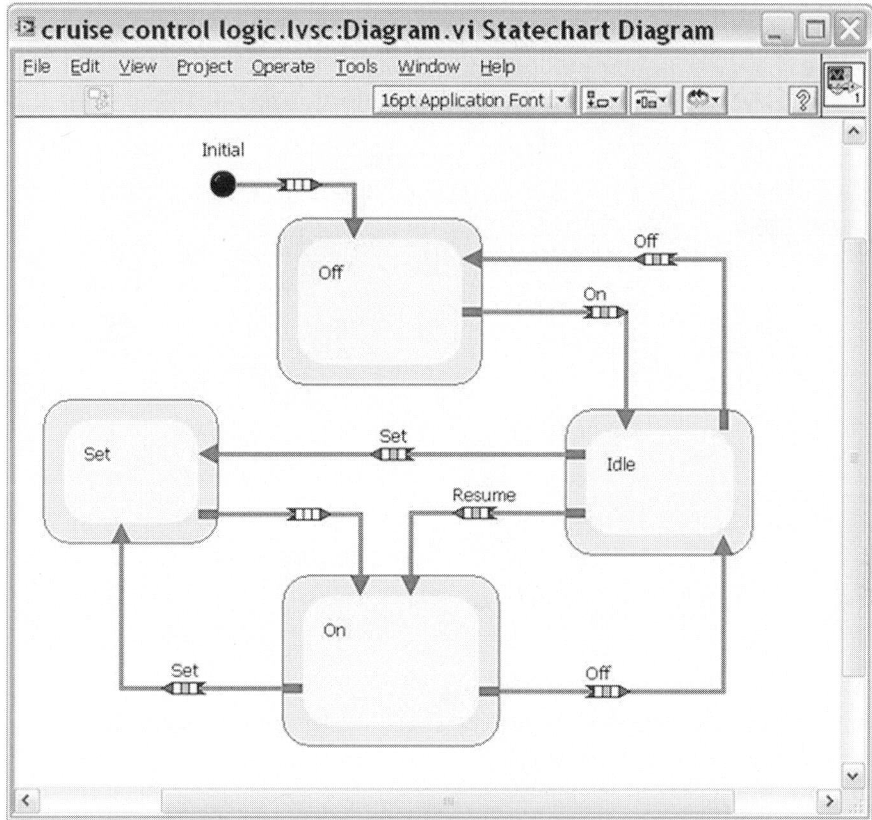

Figure 3.10:
Statechart: graphical, architectural and implementation tool.

map to an implementation. Statecharts, specifically finite state machines, combine these characteristics well. The ideal modeling language would express clearly architectural aspects of code, be as expressive as fully open programming languages and map simply to execution.

The V diagram promise

Let's look at a common visual in the embedded space – Figure 3.13, which illustrates the embedded control "V diagram", is often used to describe an embedded modeling development cycle. The V was originally developed to encapsulate the design process of many different software applications. Several versions of this diagram can be found to describe a variety of product design cycles. Figure 3.13 shows one example of such a diagram representing the design cycle of embedded control applications common to automotive, aerospace, and defense applications.

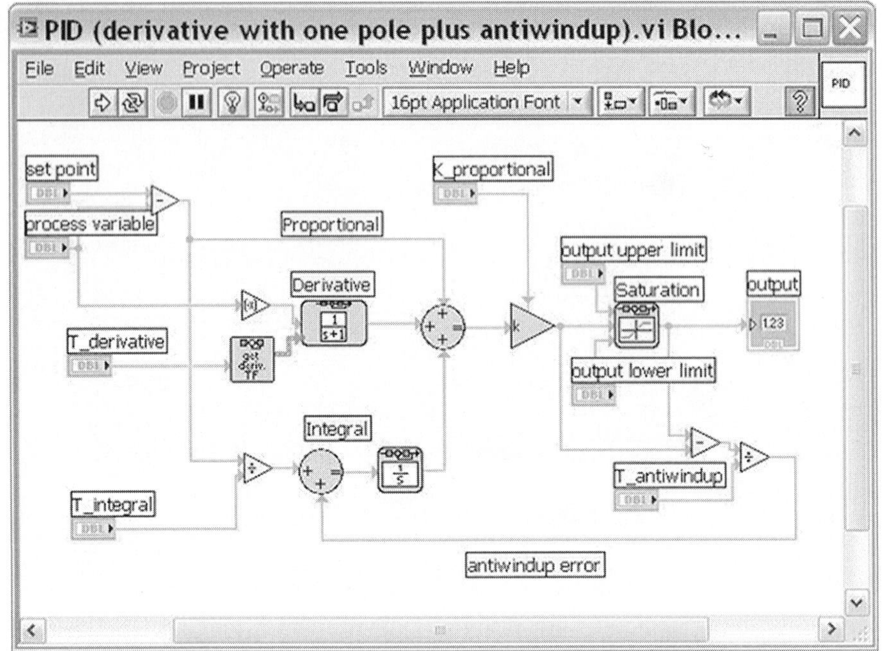

Figure 3.11:
Dataflow: graphical, architectural and implementation software.

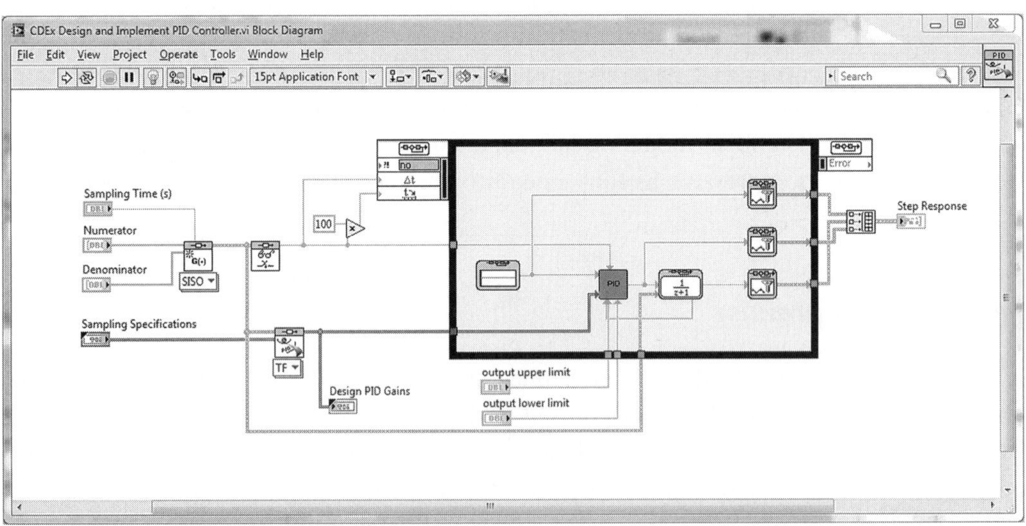

Figure 3.12:
A zoomed-out view of the same dataflow diagram in Figure 3.11.

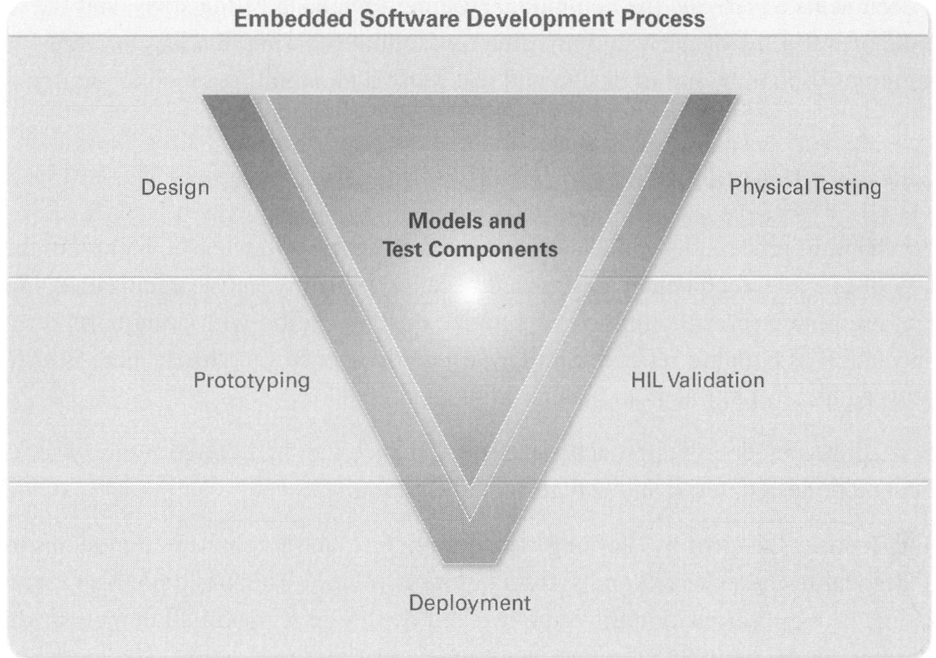

Figure 3.13:
The "V" diagram. Often used to describe an embedded software development process.

In the V diagram, the general progression of the development stages in time is shown from left to right. Note, however, that this is often an iterative process and the actual development will not proceed linearly through these steps. The goal of rapid development is to make this cycle as efficient as possible by minimizing the iterations required for a design. If the *x*-axis of the diagram is thought of as time, the goal is to narrow the "V" as much as possible by drawing the two legs of the diagram closer, thereby reducing development time. The *y*-axis of this diagram can be thought of as the level at which the system components are considered.

Early in development, overall system requirements must be considered. As the system is divided into subsystems and components, we find very low-level processes, down to the point of mapping implementation to hardware architectures.

Afterwards components are integrated and tested together until such time that the entire system can enter final production testing. Therefore the top of the diagram represents the high-level system view and the bottom of the diagram represents a very low-level implementation and mapping view.

Traditionally, engineers involved with each stage of the process have observed strict boundaries between the specification, design, coding, and testing activities, relying on design documents to provide the communication between each of the steps, and the tools within the overall flow of the V did not directly facilitate sharing, leading to large discontinuities in tooling and in design and test reuse and overall team collaboration.

So, why would you want to model your embedded system?

The "V" diagram process described suffers from a variety of drawbacks, including the difficulty of keeping documentation updated because, typically, most organizations do not have the discipline and/or tooling to synchronize documentation with design and implementation as both are refined. Similar to the documentation "drift", there is also often drift between the design intent and actual implementation.

A well-integrated modeling approach can greatly reduce the drift between the system documentation, design, tests, and actual implementation.

Modeling reduces this drift by "forcing" the design, test, and implementation teams to design a model of the expected end system before it is built. This basic premise forces a key distinguishing discipline that is often skipped by design teams in all domains, which is a functioning model or simulation that is not the actual implementation. The model is thus used to vet early design considerations, elaborate system requirements, and can facilitate early development of tests that run against the nascent model. Most of these benefits could be derived through carefully managed organizational discipline without a modeling software approach, but practice has proven that very few teams have the discipline to use a model-centric view and or tooling that facilitates it.

In addition to the key benefits listed above, for some class of embedded systems problems, modeling approaches lead directly to additional efficiency and accuracy gains.

Efficiency can be defined in this sense as efficient time and/or efficiency in terms of cost. As you will see in the "cost of getting it wrong" table, it is undeniably more cost and time efficient to find design issues early in your embedded design cycle. Modeling, using the right techniques and the right tools, will help teams find issues early. Modeling often saves further development time by reducing the number of compiles and iterations on the final embedded target since more time can be spent working through issues at the top of the V rather than in final deployment to hardware. For example, if you're designing an FPGA-based embedded application, the synthesis and deployment can take hours or days per iteration depending on the complexity of your design. By modeling the system properly ahead of time, you directly reduce the required number of design/debug iterations saving development time.

Modeling often results in a more accurate and more precise solution by increasing the rate of iterating on different design options. By reducing the cycle time of tweaking the algorithm, teams are far more likely to experiment with many different combinations of inputs, outputs and algorithm combinations. Another way that your system can be more accurate is the built-in commonality it provides between the design and test teams in your organization.

By designing a model of your embedded system, you have created a common tool that the embedded designers can use to optimize the design and then the test team can turn around and use to validate the design during testing. The model is versatile and applicable to both teams – often enabling the convergence of design and test as expressed in the central idea of the V diagram.

When should you model your embedded system?

Even though there are numerous general benefits to modeling, you shouldn't always model every embedded system. Certainly simple systems or prototypes don't require this level of formality. However, modeling is very useful, if not required, in the following systems:

- mission- and safety-critical applications
- highly complex applications and systems
- large development teams
- no other choice – when prototyping isn't an option.

Mission- and safety-critical applications

Software as percentage of the overall system is growing rapidly in all embedded systems, but particularly in mission-critical and safety-critical applications. The definition of "mission critical" may vary depending upon whom you talk to, but generally speaking this refers to any application whose failure could potentially cost large amounts of money, cause injury or seriously damage the reputation of a company. For mission- and safety-critical systems, software modeling, best practices in software engineering and formal industry standards such as DO-254B all combine to facilitate and guarantee safe and reliable embedded systems.

As we see more software content in embedded systems, governments and industry are evolving the required provisions in the overall design process. Typically, these start with formal requirements tracking with documented paper trails, clear correlation of the design requirements to code and very clear correlation of tests validating each of the design requirements. In the most idealistic sense, we seek a design tool and modeling language that create correct-by-design solutions or provably correct systems, but in the absence of these theoretically attainable systems, most 'real' embedded systems especially safety-critical can derive great benefit from the union of software engineering best practices with software modeling approaches.

Highly complex applications and systems

Every embedded system report or embedded community survey speaks to the skyrocketing complexity of our designs combined with shrinking timelines.

As an example to highlight the evolution of complexity in embedded design, the list below shows a few facts about different hardware capabilities and software content in different hardware and software systems:

- Apollo Guidance Computer (AGC) <64 kilowords, 1.024 MHz
- 1960s jet fighter $\sim$ 50 thousand lines
- JSF $\sim$ 50 million lines
- F-22 Raptor uses 2.5 million lines while the F-35 uses 5.6 million lines
- 100 million lines of code in a modern vehicle (Figure 3.14).

Embedded control systems for the automotive space are good examples to examine as complex and critical designs. Specifically, modern automotive powertrain control systems benefit from modeling techniques as they must continue to evolve to satisfy requirements including regulating exhaust emissions to meet increasingly stringent standards, providing improved fuel economy to comply with corporate average fuel economy (CAFE) regulations, and meeting customer demands for performance and comfort. These objectives are interrelated and often

Figure 3.14:
Modern embedded systems have grown exponentially in complexity.

conflict. For example, lean-burn technology can reduce fuel consumption significantly, but it also reduces the three-way catalytic conversion efficiency, causing additional air pollution. Because of this complexity, modeling can be an efficient way to optimize your design.

Using software modeling for automotive designs, you can much more easily understand the impact of the overall design while tweaking the numerous parameters. One automotive design house in the United Kingdom – Visteon – had this challenge. They used software-modeling techniques (Figure 3.15) to simulate multiple variables to validate complex automotive engine designs in order to achieve the best fuel economy, engine performance, and emission control. One project was to design a twin-independent variable camshaft-timing engine where both the intake and exhaust camshafts are adjusted independently. The variation is a function of throttle position and engine speed. Because the system offered a large number of degrees of freedom for obtaining engine performance, they needed a method to optimize the valve-timing parameters for the best fuel economy, engine performance, and emission control while understanding and implementing the highly complex real-time control algorithm that results from this design.

In order to manipulate this challenge, the embedded engineers chose a real-time control and analysis approach for their design. The purpose of their control strategy was to provide the

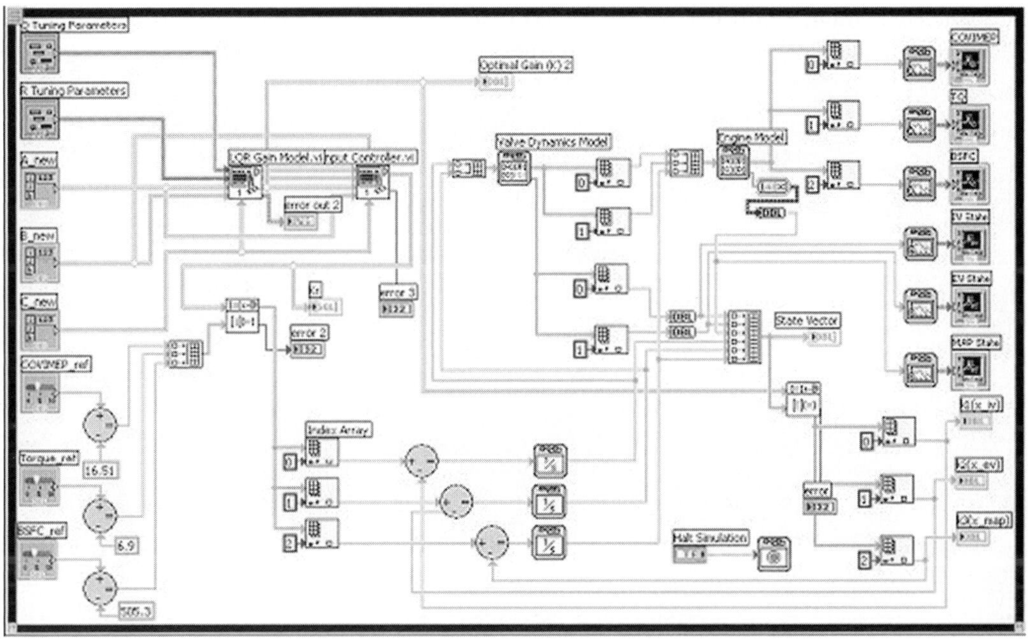

Figure 3.15:
Using NI LabVIEW as a modeling tool, this automotive embedded design engineering team was able to create interactive simulation for modeling their real-time control system.

engine with torque reference tracking while minimizing brake-specific fuel consumption and optimizing combustion stability. They chose to do their modeling and simulation with a graphical system design tool that not only could perform the modeling and simulation, but was also tightly integrated with the real-time hardware they needed for the prototype and deployment of their design.

For the engine model, the main manipulated variables for the control system include mass airflow into the intake manifold, and independent camshaft positioning of the inlet and exhaust valve timing with respect to the crankshaft. The controlled outputs are the engine torque, brake-specific fuel consumption, and the coefficient of variance of indicated mean effective pressure. Other variables influencing the system such as engine speed and engine coolant temperature are treated as external parameters and are used as scheduling variables for control.

Using the graphical modeling software, they were able to ensure the continuous time engine model combined a static characteristic of the combustion process with differential equations describing actuators and the intake manifold to obtain a dynamic model. The resulting nonlinear engine model (Figure 3.16) with multiple input, multiple output (MIMO) properties was analyzed by manipulating each input variable and exhibited strong cross-interaction between inputs and outputs. A local model was developed for the control application by linearizing the nonlinear model at fixed operating points.

An advanced optimal controller was designed using the LQR technique. The controller in this design had two objectives – offset minimization and regulator action. These objectives

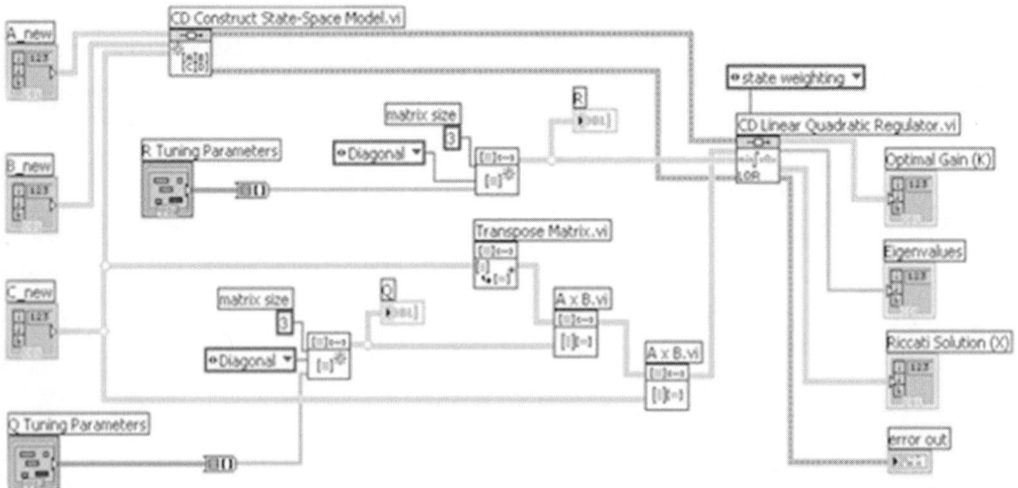

Figure 3.16:
A screenshot demonstrating the MIMO (multiple input, multiple output) control design approach used in this design.

were achieved by introducing integral action within the loop to remove steady-state errors in the presence of disturbances. To define the performance index and to minimize the output error and rate of change in the output, the gain was obtained using the modeling software for the engine-state feedback and reference tracking using the optimal theory of continuous time systems.

The local controller and linearized model were also built and simulated in their software. The system tracked the engine torque with an accurate steady-state value corresponding to the set point while simultaneously minimizing brake-specific fuel consumption and the coefficient of variation in indicated mean effective pressure. To ensure online response tuning by visual inspection, the Q and R tuning parameters were made available on the front panel, which optimized the interactive simulation capabilities of the embedded application.

These embedded engineers chose to implement the structure of the model and controller in discrete time so it could easily be transferred to computer hardware for final implementation. The discrete controller can either be derived from the designed continuous controller or designed directly in discrete time using the same LQR application. A local model was developed for the control application by linearizing (Figure 3.17) the nonlinear model at fixed operating points.

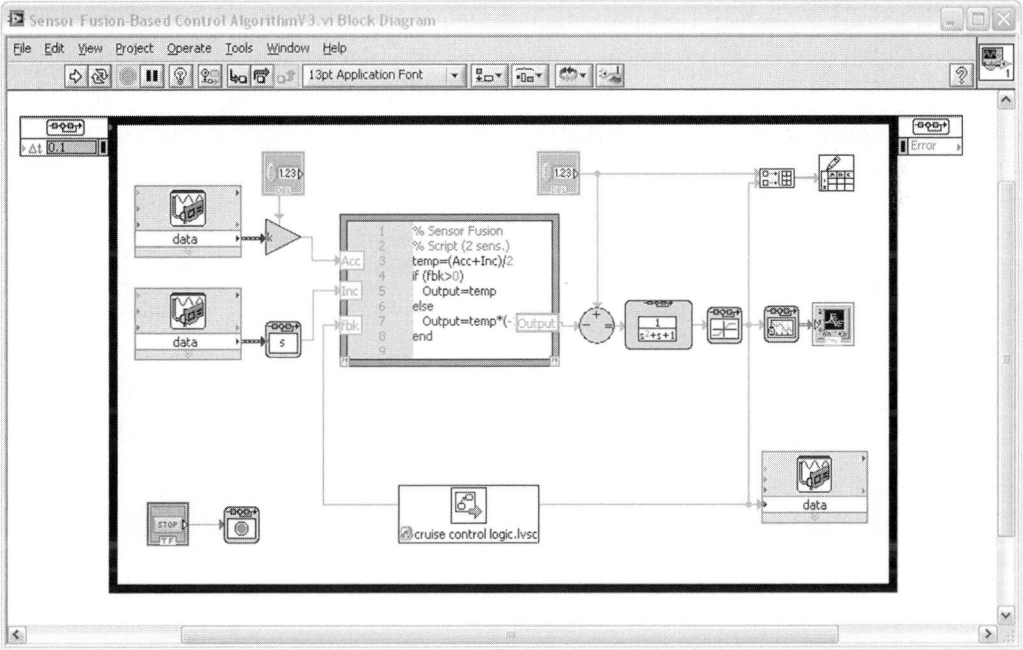

Figure 3.17:
Many control design and simulation software tools are designed for linear and nonlinear systems.

Since their model was nonlinear, the optimal gain parameters that produce the desired response at one operating point might not produce a satisfactory response at another operating point. Therefore, gain scheduling can be applied using different sets of optimal gain parameters for different regions of operation of the nonlinear model. The process of gain tuning was streamlined using interactive adjustment of parameters through the graphical user interface.

This automotive example demonstrates how valuable modeling and simulation can be in an embedded application with many different design parameters. Without these powerful software tools, this application could have easily taken twice as long to design and may have never been able to result in such an optimal design.

Operational complexity

Complexity can also be in the form of operational complexity as in the case of Agworks, Inc. (Ontario, Canada). They needed to develop an embedded control system capable of automating a large soybean processing plant with multiple concurrent processes and provide a software architecture that was both scalable and maintainable.

Developing and integrating a state-based application with so many concurrent processes presented a unique challenge. Because much of their equipment is not directly viewable, developers had to rely on development tools to aid in the integration and debugging of the code. A statechart implementation was ideal for this application. During the design phase, the abstraction provided by the NI LabVIEW Statechart Module made it much easier to visualize how all the separate processes would work together (Figure 3.18). The

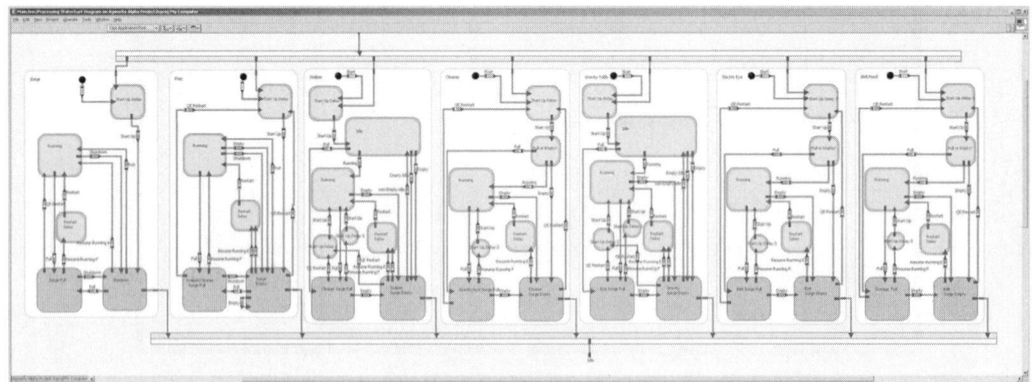

Figure 3.18:
The abstraction that the statechart software provided made it much easier to visualize how the complex network of systems would work together.

self-documenting nature of statechart diagrams also saved valuable time during the design phase of the project.

As development progressed, extensive use of the statechart tool helped keep the code organized and readable. When integration began, the utility for debugging the statecharts was crucial. With highlight execution enabled, the developers were able to monitor many concurrent processes very closely. They could tell exactly when a transition was triggered and exactly which state it went into. This saved a great deal of time during the debugging process.

After several months of operation, Agworks needed some additional features. The upfront software design, modeling and documentation made a very complex application much easier to understand and much faster to learn. The statechart diagrams provided a clearer overall picture of the embedded system. Not only was it clear, but the statechart in this complex situation was also effective in explaining the architecture and self-documenting, demonstrated by the fact that the new developer on the Agworks team was able to quickly get up to speed with this large project and edit the application, adding capabilities to satisfy the customer's request.

For these types of complex applications, using the right software tool and modeling approach can be beneficial in every step of the development life-cycle, and continue to benefit you and your customers throughout the life-cycle of the product.

Cost of defect versus when detected

Ensuring you employ proper modeling and simulation techniques isn't just about getting a better design; it is also about cost savings and getting it right sooner. After an analysis [1] of more than 60 software development projects at companies such as IBM, GTE, and TRW, we can clearly see in Figure 3.19 that the cost of finding a problem early in the process is far less expensive.

Modeling combined with software engineering best practices will help address most, if not all, of the common pitfalls in poor embedded system design programming.

Development Phase	Cost Ratio
Requirements	1
Design	3 – 6x
Implementation	10x
Development Testing	15 – 40x
Acceptance Testing	30 – 70x
Post Release	40 – 1000x

Figure 3.19:
The cost of a defect is significantly impacted by when the defect is found.

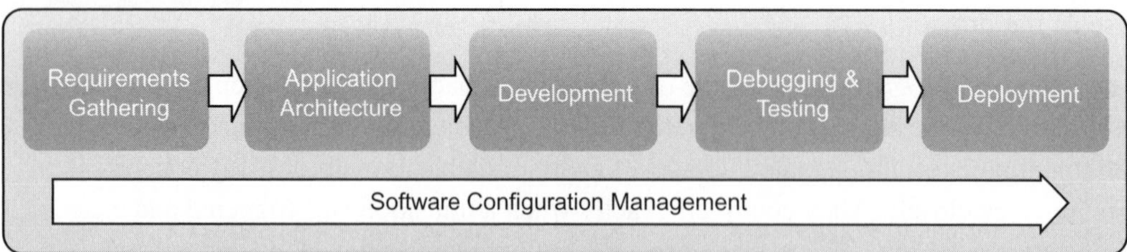

Figure 3.20:
The software engineering process is independent of programming language but can be applied throughout your embedded design practices.

Figure 3.20 is a simple way of viewing the software engineering process. It reflects what is typically referred to as the waterfall method of development. While great in principle, most software engineers accept that the waterfall method is impractical and that reality requires significant overlap between these various phases. In other words, it's almost impossible to avoid changes to requirements later in development. The key is to have tools and practices to mitigate the risks caused by these last-minute changes and to understand how these changes will impact other aspects of your application. You can apply software engineering and modeling techniques throughout this development.

Large development teams require modeling

Even though the modern trend is to create small, agile development teams, we know that certain complex embedded projects require larger teams. Large teams suffer from a few critical challenges:

- communication challenges
- geographic and language distribution
- tool differences.

Modeling can help address some of these issues.

First, and perhaps most impactful, modeling can facilitate clear communication among different teams on one embedded project. Project requirements can only look to serve as a project calibration device to a point, and then the engineers must get into the actual application. If the team can design a useful system model, it is a dynamic, accurate representation of the project that can ease cross-team communication.

Related to this, this type of project communication can easily span multiple speaking languages as well as geographic locations. Instead of relying on either written documentation that would need to be translated, an embedded model can be the consistent "voice" of the project. While physical prototypes are very capable of demonstrating the concepts and goals of a project, they are limited to being in a single location.

When you have a large team you are also bound to have developers with differing tool preferences. This means you need to keep your model in software that can be shared between tools – something open and viewable by anyone on the team.

Just employing modeling of course doesn't solve large development team issues; you still must develop readable (and therefore maintainable) code, documenting your code, employing source code control and change management, utilizing unit testing and getting as much standardization and code reuse as possible.

Modeling is often the only choice

Sometimes you must model, you simply can't prototype or iterate on your design. Have you ever had a situation when you couldn't prototype? Consider a project when perhaps the embedded system doesn't exist – when you are designing for hardware that is not yet complete or ready like the latest chip, where you are designing to specifications instead of silicon. This is a great example where modeling, simulation, emulation and later prototyping is a valuable approach.

One example is at National Instruments (NI), where they were designing for unreleased hardware. The embedded team needed to move a significant amount of their core product designs to a new MPU + FPGA + I/O architecture before the integrated silicon was on the market. They saw the value of this new technology early through confidential interactions with the silicon vendor. This early access allowed them to plan for the new technology upgrade in the embedded system. The engineers worked closely with the vendor throughout the entire process – an important point if you are in a similar situation.

Throughout these discussions, the vendor did an excellent job of setting up a development platform for the NI embedded team to use as an emulation of what the final architecture would look like – including a fixed-personality FPGA that would represent or behave like the final FPGA fabric in the eventual design. This development platform (Figure 3.21) was a valuable board used for early prototyping, design, and test. However, it was certainly not an exact stand-in for the final product. There were several subtle and a few substantial differences. These discrepancies were well documented by the vendor so there were no surprises, but the engineers needed to optimize for and understand the substantial differences as they were developing, so there was still a bit of work to do.

The most important shortcoming of the given development board was the fact that instead of a single, high-performance FPGA fabric like the final design, the engineers at NI were designing for a system with multiple FPGAs, and the communication delay between silicon

Figure 3.21:
Example of a silicon prototype board (courtesy of LogicBricks) versus a final hardware design (NI CompactRIO courtesy of National Instruments).

caused a significant performance degradation. The development board couldn't replicate an entire system running say at 40 MHz, but instead could only reach 10 MHz, making it unusable for timing and testing accurate application performance. This is a good example where all models, even physical emulation platforms, aren't 100% accurate, but when you understand the shortcomings, they are still very useful. To compensate for the shortcomings of the model, the team chose to also include a software-based design in the development. They first found off-the-shelf boards, which had similar CPU characteristics in terms of performance and architectures (multicore ARM designs that were close to the final design), that provided performance comparable to the final product as development platforms for more performance-based designs and testing. This hybrid design approach was helpful in getting them up and running and provided a closer system in terms of floating-point performance.

To accommodate the FPGA design aspects, the team designed a software-based environment on the real-time CPU that allowed the deployment of FPGA code to a real-time target and have it behave similarly in terms of timing to the final FPGA fabric that was then cross-referenced with the slower, more accurate FPGA combination board from the vendor.

Of important note, the team specifically chose not to simulate the entire hardware platform using cycle- or even instruction-accurate simulation tools. They deemed "stand-in" hardware platforms with sufficiently similar characteristics as "good enough" and the most efficient approach for development. The team was confident in this approach because they knew once real silicon materialized that the final implementation could leverage the early design and full test frameworks as developed on the hardware stand-ins.

If you find yourself in a similar situation, designing for a target that isn't in the market yet, you can approach your design in a similar fashion.

1. Work closely with your vendor to understand what features and capabilities the future platform will have and understand the differences in performance and hardware architecture.
2. Select an existing, off-the-shelf or similar platform for early design and development.

3. Once you run into the performance or feature limitations of that existing platform (the areas where the new design will differ and add more value) then select a surrogate hardware and software emulation platform for designing to those new, unreleased capabilities. This step requires additional software work to create the simulated or emulated environment.

Even with these well-planned steps, you note there will be differences, there will be additional development once you get your final hardware device – but if you focus on proper design techniques and clear abstraction boundaries, you can protect large portions of your algorithms and focus on optimizing timing and specific I/O features once you get your first prototypes up and running.

Related to the silicon being unreleased, perhaps you can't prototype because of the size or cost of the project. If you are creating a new control system for a new light rail system, you can't work on the prototypes until late in the game – and you certainly don't want to experiment on the real thing. These are situations where software models can be very helpful.

So – modeling is great, but aren't all models wrong?

"All models are wrong, some are just useful" is a phrase generally attributed to statistician George Box [2]. Whether you are new to modeling or have been expertly designing embedded systems for decades, this warning pertains to us all. No matter how carefully or completely you might model a system; the model will always be less than the reality that is actually modeled.

You may remember when Boeing's 787 Dreamliner was introduced – this aerospace innovation is one of the most exciting technology introductions in modern times (Figure 3.22). The mid-sized, twin-engine jet airliner developed by Boeing Commercial Airplanes is composed of 50% composite (carbon fiber), 20% aluminum, 15% titanium, 10% steel and 5% other but in terms of volume, the aircraft is 80% composite. Each 787 contains approximately 35 tons of carbon fiber reinforced plastic. What does this have to do with modeling? Paolo Feraboli, an assistant professor at the University of Washington School's Automobili Lamborghini Advanced Composite Structures Laboratory, was extensively involved in the Dreamliner design and had this to say about modeling the 787: "Unlike homogeneous metals, multi-layered composites are very difficult to simulate accurately on a computer. We don't currently have the knowledge and the computational power to do a prediction based on purely mathematical models" [3]. New, innovative materials require modeling *and* prototyping in order to be designed and tested.

Figure 3.22:
Boeing's 787 Dreamliner was so innovative in terms of material, the embedded designers needed to model and prototype to truly understand the behavior of the design.

This doesn't mean models are useless. If done well, you can use models to help in all of the situations covered in this chapter. You just don't *only* want to use models for your embedded system design.

From the examples, you understand how useful models are and then we tell you they are all wrong – what are you to do? You embrace another useful quote from author Jim Collins, embrace "the genius of the and". You must model your system *and* combine it with the "real world". Often the best way to combine your theories and requirements with the real world is to create a prototype.

This approach – modeling, simulation and prototyping – is also critical in complex mechatronics systems such as robotics. Fred Nikgohar, CEO of Robodynamics, points out the value of the real world. Since building robots is about managing a multi-disciplinary project, it involves not just software but mechanics, electronics, and integration. Nikgohar believes "Integration is often the after-thought in building robots. It is that final step in the design process where all the disciplines come together and create a robot greater than the sum of its engineered parts. It is also the step where things that worked in isolation often fail. And worse, troubleshooting becomes enormously more difficult because if the robot doesn't behave as planned, you have to troubleshoot throughout the engineered chain ...". He points out that the challenge in robotics is that a lot of ideas never come to fruition. "The real world is ... very real! Wires come loose, mechanical parts bend, even firmware uploads fail sometimes. By sheer necessity to create robot engineering efficiencies, we have developed testing plans, troubleshooting plans, and even simulation runs to make things go further and smoother. But nothing has been more valuable than the actual experience of building robots." This applies to all of our embedded system design – nothing is more valuable than experiencing your design with real-world constraints and real-world situations. You must model and prototype to perfect your design.

To model and create a prototype, you need a hardware prototyping platform. Prototyping platforms are typically composed primarily of commercial off-the-shelf components configured to meet the I/O specifications of the system, and provide a quick, seamless way to connect the control model with real-world I/O, making it easier to test and iterate the design. As shown in Figure 3.23, the controller design is tested in a real-time environment

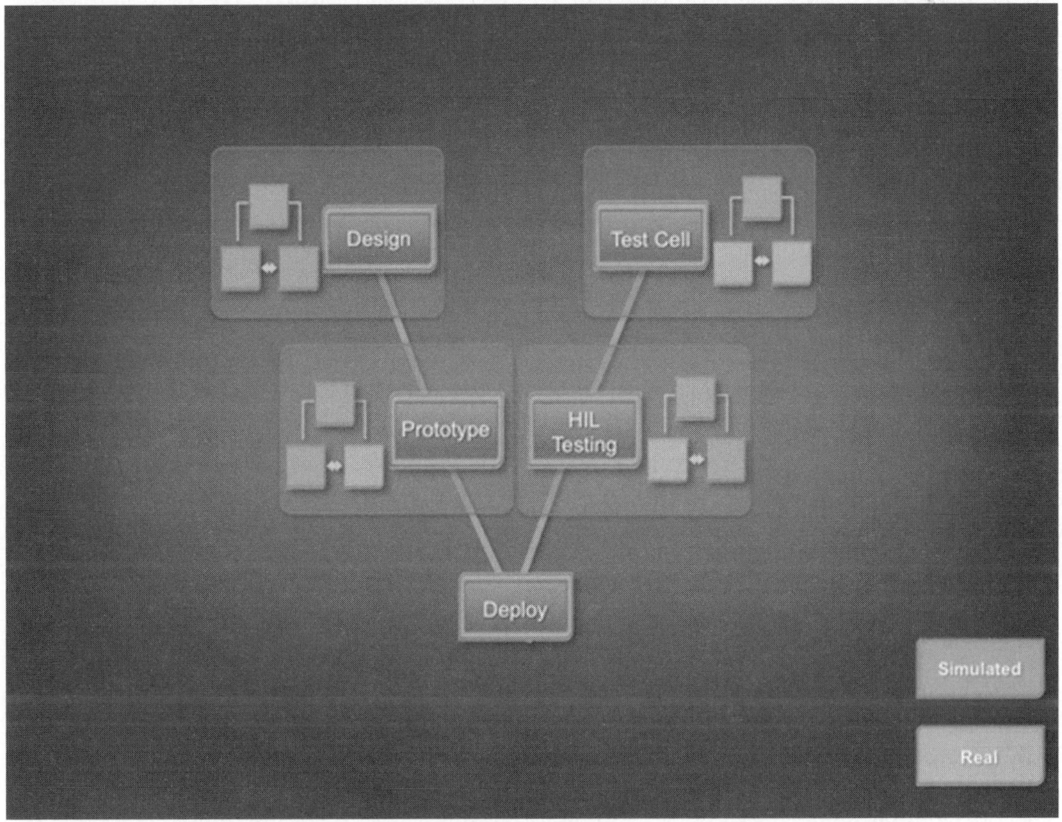

Figure 3.23:
The design V integrates simulated and real-world I/O to be most effective.

and connected to actual hardware. This provides excellent verification and validation feedback on the fidelity of the modeling effort and the resulting control design early in the design flow. Further refinements to the controller and hardware designs and requirements can be made prior to finishing the design of the production systems.

Beyond getting your system up and running before you have your final hardware, there are other reasons you should focus on getting to your prototype quickly. If you're in an innovative space, prototypes allow you to fail early and inexpensively. Real innovation always includes a risk of failure. Thomas Edison once joked, "We now know a thousand ways not to build a light bulb". By building a prototype, you can quickly weed out the approaches that don't work to focus on the ones that do.

Prototypes also help you to technically understand the problem. By developing a functional prototype sooner rather than later, you are forced to address both the foreseen and the unforeseen technical challenges of a device's design. Then, you can apply those solutions to a more elegant system design and model as you move to developing the final deployed solution. Related to this, the prototype can also help resolve conflicts. The best engineers have strong opinions about how a given feature should be implemented. Inevitably, differences of opinion result in conflicts, and these conflicts can be difficult to resolve because both sides have only opinions, experience, and conjecture to refer to as evidence. By taking advantage of a prototyping platform, you can quickly conduct several different implementations of the feature and benchmark the resulting performance to analyze the trade-offs of each approach. This can save time, but it also ensures that you make the correct design decisions.

Finally, prototypes can help you file patents more easily. Before 1880, all inventors had to present working models or prototypes of their inventions to the patent office as part of the patent application process. Today, the patent office uses the "first to invent rule", which grants a patent to the first inventor who conceives and reduces the technology or invention to practice. Though no longer required, a prototype is still the best and safest way to demonstrate "reduction to practice".

You have your prototype – now what?

If you can demonstrate or, better yet, put a prototype into the customer's hands and get real feedback on the value of your innovation, the probability of business success greatly increases. This is especially important when you are working in an extremely innovative area where "proving it" means progressing in your project.

The Loccioni Group in Italy is one example of an innovative team that employs modeling, simulation and iterative prototypes. Loccioni Group is considered a flag-bearer for Italian innovation because of its reputation for developing custom technical solutions to ensure quality, comfort, and safety in many areas. They focus primarily on two industries: automotive and electrical appliances.

Loccionio Group embraced "the genius of the and" in a recent embedded test system – the Mexus project – for measuring and charting the flow rate of diesel engine nozzles (Figure 3.24). This project originated from the need to measure the flow rate of diesel engine nozzles with a detailed quantification of the fuel injected during a single injection. The final product is an instrument used worldwide by injector manufacturers for end-of-line production tests. The goal was to provide a low-cost embedded product with better performance than any other instrument on the market.

Loccionio Group designed a reliable product capable of accurately determining the two fundamental parameters characterizing injectors: the flow rate injected for each shot and the chart of the instantaneous flow rate. The instrument provides the measurement of the fuel quantity injected in each single shot event up to a maximum of 10 events per revolution (also known as multi-injection). By simulating the engine operation at 3,000 rpm, the

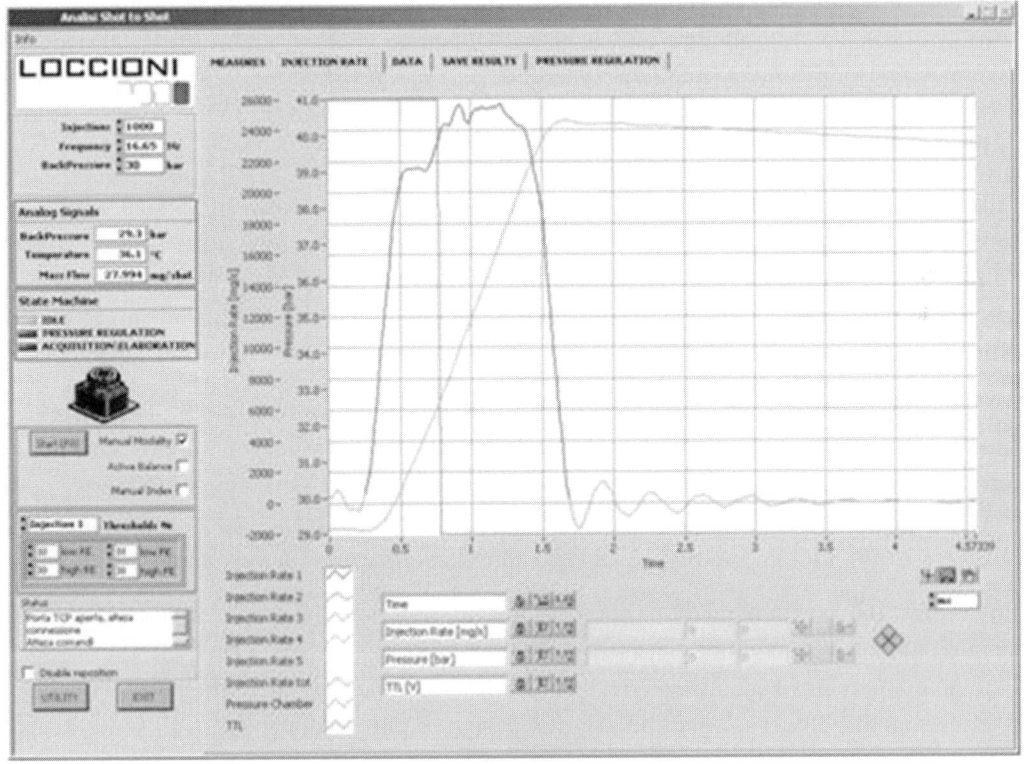

Figure 3.24:
The injection chamber and its control system were modeled using modern graphical design tools.

readout value injection for each revolution can be easily detected by the system, which provides the quantity of each fuel injection in real time. The innovative aspect of this project is the calculus algorithm used in the solution. The system acquires different analog signals and processes them in real time, providing the user with reliable test results up to the injector functioning rate of 50 instantaneous values per second. The system is also able to determine how much fuel is dispensed in each injection. This information is significant for injector characterization because emissions regulations are becoming more restrictive. Consequently, it is important to provide manufacturers with more detailed information to gain high-level combustion, reducing either fuel consumption or the quantity of pollutant gas within the environment.

One critical element of the Mexus system is the injection chamber, the cylinder fitted with control sensors and valves where the fuel is injected and the specific measurements are performed. The injection chamber and its control system were modeled with graphical design and simulation software. In this stage, simulations were also performed using the same graphical system design environment. During prototyping, the same computer was maintained through a data-acquisition board that performed functional characterization and validation. This important development stage of the project highlighted the need for a more refined chamber injection model. This was determined by using system identification software as part of the same graphical system design tools, which made it possible to obtain the transfer function of the injection chamber and consequently to design a suitable control algorithm.

To enable a large-scale deployment, Loccionio Group needed a hardware device with failure-free technology that was capable of operating around the clock, offered a compact form factor, and was suitable for an industrial environment. They chose hardware that helped them make a quick shift from prototyping to deployment as well as ensuring they met the sampling rate requirements and the real-time, deterministic control of the process.

The Mexus final product guarantees the highest reliability in test operations. The accuracy of the measurements is due to the introduction of innovative working methodologies that ensure test compliance with the most restrictive regulations. By employing modeling, simulation, prototyping and deployment techniques, Loccioni Group has provided the automotive world with an innovative product that delivers excellent test standards.

Following similar recommendations for your design, you now have your prototype and your embedded model, you can then optimize, refine and test the system. When all your individual components and subsystems have been tested and validated, they are combined and tested together to ensure that the original design requirements are met. In some cases, parameters in your controller are finely tuned during this phase to meet original design requirements. Although creating embedded models in your design process does not completely eliminate the need for testing, it offers several opportunities to reduce the amount of test that will be required prior to the release of the production system. Additionally, modeling design technology is currently evolving to aid in automating the final testing process. Early tool-providers in this space automatically generate test vectors and execute scripted sequences to verify both models and automatically generated code. Soon, these capabilities will extend to physical tests, scripting test sequences, including real-world I/O connections, needed to verify all behaviors of the control system.

Conclusion

Creating a model for your embedded system provides a time and cost-effective approach to the development of simple or incredibly complex dynamic control systems, all based on a single model maintained in a tightly integrated software suite. Using modern modeling software tools you can design and perform initial validation in off-line simulation. These models then form the basis for all subsequent development stages. As we have seen, creating models for your embedded design provides numerous advantages over the traditional design approach. Using this approach – combined with hardware prototyping – you reduce the risk of mistakes and shorten the development cycle by performing verification and validation testing throughout the development instead of only during the final testing stage. Design evaluations and predictions can be made much more quickly and reliably with a system model as a basis. This iterative approach results in improved designs, in terms of both performance and reliability. The cost of resources is reduced, because of the reusability of models between design teams, design stages, and various projects and the reduced dependency on physical prototypes. Development errors and overhead can be reduced through the use of automatic code-generation techniques. These advantages translate to more accurate and robust control designs, shorter time to market, and reduced design cost.

Next steps – try it!

As part of this book, you have access to a free trial of several modeling packages including National Instruments LabVIEW and open-source Modelica. Here are a few embedded tutorials and code snippets to get you up and running quickly with your next embedded system design.

Download a 3-hour short course to learn how to use the control and modeling tools described in this chapter.

National Instruments offers several tools for engineers and researchers to analyze and simulate dynamic systems and design and deploy control systems. These tools help you gain a better understanding of linear systems and control design concepts by facilitating a hands-on, experiential learning environment that is flexible and interactive in nature.

This 3-hour short course is designed as an instructor-led and self-study introduction to the control design process. This includes modeling, designing a controller, simulating the controller, and deploying a controller using LabVIEW, the Control Design Toolkit and the Simulation Module. The course includes a presentation, manual, exercises, and solutions.

Closed-loop control with a DC motor

The concepts of control are essential for understanding natural and man-made systems. Since control is a systems field, to get a full appreciation of control it is necessary to cover both theory and applications. The skill base required in control includes modeling, control design, simulation, implementation, tuning, and operation of a control system. This tutorial shows how these concepts can be taught through use of a Quanser DC Motor plug-in board for the NI LabVIEW Control Design and Simulation with LabVIEW MathScript RT software. Traditionally, tuning a controller requires multiple iterations and trial and error to perfect. However, LabVIEW allows you to tune your controller in real time and then move directly into verification with a seamless integration with hardware.

Learn more about prototyping with a downloadable kit

The flexibility and productivity of NI tools have proven useful in getting a prototype working quickly – from medical devices, to industrial machinery, to automated test systems. The NI graphical system design platform, including NI LabVIEW and flexible off-the-shelf hardware, provides one of the quickest paths to a working prototype for any engineer, scientist, or academician. This resource kit contains a variety of online resources for prototyping with NI tools.

Designing applications with the NI Statechart Module

With the NI LabVIEW Statechart Module, you can create statecharts in LabVIEW software for developing event-based control and test systems. The statechart programming model complements the LabVIEW models for data flow, textual math, dynamic system modeling, and configuration-based development. You can choose the right model or combination of models to develop your system based on your application requirements.

Design and simulate a brushed dc motor h-bridge circuit

With NI Multisim, you can implement the desktop simulation of your entire analog and digital system before prototyping. Digital FPGA controller logic and closed-loop simulation of transistor-level power electronics components are now possible using the Multisim/LabVIEW cosimulation feature. This tutorial shows how you can use Multisim and LabVIEW to develop the analog circuit design and digital control blocks of a brushed

DC motor H-bridge circuit. In this article, learn how to use the electromechanical, power electronics, and sensor feedback blocks to create a closed-loop control system. LabVIEW FPGA IP core development and debugging are briefly described as well. Cosimulation enables codesign of an entire system to ensure algorithms and code simulated for the FPGA in LabVIEW are verified for performance with analog circuitry and can be directly implemented in hardware with minimal changes. With the improved Multisim design approach powered by simulation, you can obtain a more accurate understanding of performance earlier in the design flow. The result of this is a reduction in prototype iterations (up to three saved PCB turns) and accurate embedded code with fewer compiles (saving as much as 4 hours per compile).

Multi-domain physical modeling with open-source Modelica models

Modelica is an open, object-oriented, equation-based language to conveniently model complex physical systems containing, e.g., mechanical, electrical, electronic, hydraulic, thermal, control, electric power or process-oriented subcomponents. In order for the Modelica modeling language to solve actual problems, a modeling and simulation environment is needed:

- to conveniently define a Modelica model with a graphical user interface (composition diagram/schematic editor) such that the result of the graphical editing is a (internal) textual description of the model in Modelica format;
- to translate the defined Modelica model into a form which can be efficiently simulated in an appropriate simulation environment. This requires especially sophisticated symbolic transformation techniques;
- to simulate the translated model with standard numerical integration methods and visualize the result.

References

[1] Available from: http://www.irma-international.org/proceeding-paper/gathering-user-needs/32282/.
[2] Available from: http://www.wired.com/science/discoveries/magazine/16-07/pb_theory.
[3] Available from: http://www.carbonfibergear.com/is-the-carbon-fiber-787-dreamliner-safe-enough-to-fly/.

CHAPTER 4

Software Design Architecture and Patterns for Embedded Systems

Bruce Douglass

Chapter Outline

Overview of architecture and design

It is interesting that there are probably more definitions of the term "architecture" than there are architects. The term is constantly being redefined to be more (or less) inclusive and for more (or fewer) contexts. For the purpose of this discussion, we will heavily rely on the definition from IEEE 1472000, "IEEE Recommended Practice for

Software Engineering for Embedded Systems.
DOI: http://dx.doi.org/10.1016/B978-0-12-415917-4.00004-9

© 2013 Elsevier Inc. All rights reserved.

Architectural Description of Software-Intensive Systems" (IEEE Computer Society, IEEE 1472000, 2000):

> *Architecture is the fundamental organization of a system embodied in its components, their relationships to each other, and to the environment, and the principles guiding its design and evolution.*

The definition is perhaps a bit vague and broad, so to understand what it *is*, let's first discuss why we need it. After all, the "real work" done by the software is embedded in the individual lines of code so why do we need larger-scale organization?

Architecture is about system-wide optimization

One key to a good architecture is the organization of the semantic elements into organizational units that optimize properties of the overall system. The semantic elements are low-level primitive things such as software functions, lines of code, data structures, and classes while the organizational units are things like subsystems, components, tasks, channels, and disciplines. These optimization properties, known as *design constraints*, are not really about meeting the functional needs of the system; these are, after all, met by the semantic elements. These properties are about maximizing some aspect(s) of the system at the expense of others, which are considered less valuable in the specific context of concern.

Generally speaking, embedded systems have an enhanced requirement for optimization. Some optimization concerns are:

- Performance
  - Worst case
  - Average case
  - Average throughput
  - Burst throughput
  - Bandwidth
  - Predictability
- Capacity
- Schedulability
- Distributability
- Flexibility
- Scalability
- Adaptability
- Robustness
- Reusability
- Maintainability

- Development (non-recurring) cost
- Manufacturing (recurring) cost
- Ease of use
- Dependability
  - Safety
  - Reliability
  - Security
- Accuracy and fidelity

Collectively, these design constraints are often referred to as *Qualities of Service* (QoS).

Architecture seeks to identify units that organize the software semantic elements to optimize the design constraints of importance to a specific system executing in its operational context. Note that implicit in the term "optimization" is the notion that you cannot maximize the values of all these concerns simultaneously. In fact, maximization of some aspects *always* minimizes others; that is, optimization of some system features deoptimizes others.

For example, consider the following system description:

> *The system reads data from a sensor and performs some complex mathematical computations and then returns the results of the computation to the client software. The algorithm requires the storage of a significant amount of data when complete.*

If the system samples the data infrequently (with respect to how often the clients need the data), overall performance can be improved by precomputing the value passed to the client. This optimizes performance because the computation is performed only once to handle many client requests. On the other hand, if the data arrives at the sensor much more frequently than it is used by the client, the system loses performance if it precomputes the client values.

Even in the case where it makes sense (in terms of improved performance) to precompute the client value, we are likely to require more memory to store intermediate and final results since they must be retained between client requests. If performance optimization is more important than space optimization, then precomputation makes sense; if space optimization is more important, then it does not.

Trade-offs are not limited to just performance and space. Some other common trade-off pairs are shown in Table 4.1.

We will talk more about making design trade-offs in the next section on design patterns.

Table 4.1: Common design trade-offs.

Design Property	Design Property	Trade-off Considerations
Usability	Security	To make a system more secure usually requires authentication and management of protective barriers. These often reduce the perceived ease of use of the system.
Robustness	Time to market, run-time performance	To make a system more robust requires the creation of additional run-time tests and checks of preconditions and other invariants. Creating this additional software requires more development and testing time and effort.
Performance	Accuracy	Simple but less accurate algorithms can be executed in less time than more complex, but more accurate ones. Often more accurate algorithms require computation of additional corrective terms requiring more time.
Reliability	Safety	If a system has a fail-safe state, then the safest thing to do when an error is detected is to enter that state. Since this is usually less functional, then the reliability of the system (as measured by the availability of services) decreases.
Predictability	Performance	A cyclic execution scheduling algorithm is highly predictable in terms of which lines of code execute when and in what order. However, a cyclic executive is demonstrably suboptimal to a far less predictable rate monotonic priority-based schedule algorithm in terms of responsiveness to incoming events.

In light of this discussion, we can characterize a good architecture in the following way:

> *A good architecture is an architecture in which important system properties are acceptably optimized at the expense of properties which are less important.*

Three levels of design

This optimization of design constraints really takes place at three levels in most systems. Architectural designs are system-wide optimization decisions that maximize a set of overall system properties. Architectural design decisions may be categorized into subject areas, as will be done later in this chapter. Architectural optimizations must optimize the design properties of the system as a whole and may, in fact, be suboptimal for performance within a given architectural unit. For example, an object broker architecture might be selected for a system as a whole, meaning that this mechanism provides the primary means by which distributed software elements collaborate. But this decision may result in unacceptable performance overhead in some specific high-bandwidth channel even though the overall system design optimizes its performance-space-costs attributes. In this case, the system may either live with the poor performance for some of the data or may construct a specialized transport for just that data path.

In contrast, collaboration-level design (known as *mechanistic design* in the Harmony process; see ref. [1] for a more detailed description of the process) optimizes software collaborating within the architectural units. This allows different collaborations to be optimized for different properties and gives a great deal of flexibility with respect to meeting design constraints effectively. Although there are few books on patterns at this level for embedded systems (see ref. [2] for some patterns at this scope) the major work for collaboration-level patterns is the book by Gamma *et al.* [3]. While not specific to embedded systems, many of these patterns may be applied in that context.

Finally, detailed design focuses on optimizing primitive software units such as data structures, functions, and individual classes. Although this is the most common area of design optimization, in general it has the least impact on overall system performance. In any event, in all cases, the focus is not really on achieving correct functionality, but rather on achieving that functionality well. Design patterns exist at all three levels of abstraction and bring value to the designer by providing reusable solutions with known optimization properties.

What are design patterns?

Design patterns aren't magic, and they aren't all that difficult. Applying design patterns is what good designers (including architects) do everyday anyway – even if they don't recognize that is what they are doing. Good designers examine their new design problems and try to reason about what they've done or seen done in the past that solved similar problems. That's nothing more or less than apply design patterns, even though it is implicit rather than explicit. What a design-pattern-centric design approach does is formalize this a bit to simplify both the capture of good design solutions and their application to specific design contexts.

A design pattern is a "generalized solution to a commonly occurring problem". If a design solution addresses a problem very specific to a particular system, there is no value in abstracting it into a reusable design pattern. Similarly, a design pattern must abstract away the specifics of a particular system so that it may be easily applied to other systems operating in other contexts.

Each design pattern has a number of fundamental aspects that must be considered in order to effectively use it. First, the pattern must have a *name* that conveys its essential application. The name "Broker Architecture Pattern" tells us that a broker is involved somehow in the identification and delivery of services or data while the name "Observer

Pattern" tells us that there are software elements being observed (called "Subjects" in the pattern) and elements that are doing the observers (known as "Clients"). "Data Bus Pattern" brings up images of a central repository ("bus") for shared data.

Many patterns provide a brief *abstract* of what they are trying to accomplish and the mechanism by which they operate. This brief description allows the designer to peruse a large number of patterns quickly to find the best one for his or her problem.

The next aspect of pattern is the *problem context* – properties required for its proper application. That is, what must be true of the system for the appropriate application of the pattern.

The *pattern structure and behavior* describes in detail the elements of the pattern (classes, functions, and data with various relations) and a description of how these elements interact to achieve the intent of the pattern.

The *consequences* of the pattern are probably most important – at least in terms of pattern selection. The consequences include both the benefits and the costs of using the pattern. This is best described as a set of system or project optimizations and deoptimizations. Does the pattern optimize worst-case performance at the expense of additional space complexity, such as memory usage? Does it improve safety at the expense of additional recurring cost due to additional sensors? Given a set of patterns that serve a common purpose, the consequences allow us to select the best choice for our particular system.

Lastly, an *example* is often provided to illustrate the use and application of the pattern. While not strictly required, such examples can greatly aid the designer in understanding the subtle details of a patterns use.

Must I use object-oriented techniques to use design patterns?

If you read that pattern literature, you might come away with the opinion that design patterns are only available/appropriate/useful for object-oriented systems. As we have discussed, design patterns are simply generalized design solutions that optimize certain aspects of systems. While object-oriented design and programming has much to recommend it, most embedded systems are still written in the C language. There are many reasons for this, ranging from availability of target compilers and compiler efficiency to conservatism on the part of developers. Nevertheless, design patterns apply to systems implemented in C as much as they do to ones implemented in object-oriented languages (see, for example, ref. [2]).

Having said that, some patterns are clearly object-oriented in their *orientation*. With respect to programming style, patterns may be grouped into three distinct styles – structured, object-based, and object-oriented. All of these styles may be implemented in C but structured and object-based approaches are more obvious.

Structured programming style patterns use C in a standard way. Basic elements are header and implementation files, which contain types, constants, variables, functions, and compiler directives. The system software is the object code compiled and linked from the set of such files. All very "standard C" in appearance. Patterns applied in the structured style just add these simple programmatic elements together to implement the design optimization. This simple form of coding is shown in Code Listing 4.1.

```
#ifndefine Motor_H
#define Motor_H


typedef enum Motorstate {MOFF, MSLOW, MFAST, MERROR} Motorstate;


/* variables */
int motorspeed;
int updateFrequency;
MotorState ms;


/* functions */
void setMotorSpeed(int s, Motorstate m);
int getMotorSpeed(void);
void init(void);
#endif
```

Code Listing 4.1:
Structured code.

An object-based programming style merges data and functionality together. This is pretty straightforward with C structs and typedefs.

With these structs, we can create "objects" – variables (instances) of these struct types. Stylistically, there are three primary differences between structured and object-based code. First, we typically create multiple instances of these structs while in structured code we usually have only single instances ("singletons"). Secondly, we typically manually munge the data of the struct (now often referred to as the "class") into the function name to identify the data that the functions are managing. Lastly, we add a `me` pointer to the function's argument list to identify on which instance we want the function to operate. Sample code equivalent to that in Code Listing 4.1 is shown in Code Listing 4.2.

```
#ifndefine Motor_H
#define Motor_H


typedef enum Motorstate {MOFF, MSLOW, MFAST, MERROR} Motorstate;
typedef struct Motor {  /* class Motor */
      int motorspeed;                /* attributes */
      int updateFrequency;
      MotorState ms;
      };


/* functions */
void Motor_setMotorSpeed(const Motor* me, int s, Motorstate m);
int Motor_getMotorSpeed(const Motor* me);
void Motor_init(const Motor* me);
#endif
```

Code Listing 4.2:
Structured code.

An object-based approach allows us to design data and the functions that manipulate them more easily. The object-based approach extends this by adding the notion of subclassing. A subclass is a class that inherits all the properties of another but then specializes and/or extends the latter. This is done by not directly referring to the functions in a static way but rather by using pointers-to-functions to abstract the invocation of these functions. This enables us to override the original class functions by replacing them, as desired, with pointers to new functions. This allows us to scope the functions within the struct, leading to simplified naming (no munging) and allows us to replace the pointer in a subclass to point to a different function with the same signature (specialization). We can also add new attributes and functions in the subclass (extension). This is illustrated in Code Listing 4.3. Further information on how to do object-oriented programming in C can be found elsewhere.

Some patterns are easier to implement in one programming style than another, but ultimately any pattern can be implemented in whichever programming language you select.

An architectural example

Let's consider the following system design problem:

> *Large architectural units (subsystems) must be connected to enable communication by sending events and data. Several middleware solutions support this, including CORBA*

```
#ifndefine Motor_H
#define Motor_H


typedef enum Motorstate {MOFF, MSLOW, MFAST, MERROR} Motorstate;
typedef struct Motor {   /* class Motor */
      int motorspeed;                /* attributes */
      int updateFrequency;
      MotorState ms;
      /* member functions */
      void (*setMotorSpeed)(const Motor* me, int s, Motorstate m);
      int (*getMotorSpeed)(const Motor* me);
      void (*init)(const Motor* me);
      };
#endif
```

Code Listing 4.3:
Object-oriented code.

and DDS. However, there is a need to support the same subsystems on different middleware platforms as well as hosted within the same address space (i.e., without middleware). The design should allow changing the middleware with a minimum of work – ideally without having to rewrite a single line of code within the subsystems themselves. That is to say, reusability and portability are very important design criteria to optimize for the success of this project.

A key problem faced by designers is that the most common way to implement such middleware solutions is to write lots of code in a middleware-specific IDL (interface definition language). This results in software embedded in the various subsystems but the code is inherently middleware-specific.

This problem can be addressed in any number of ways. One way is to create a *new* IDL that can be compiled into different target middlewares. Another solution is to somehow "tag" the various relations between distributed elements and create IDL for just those links. A third solution is to create "interface connector objects" that sit between the subsystems and have them translate communication requests at run-time into appropriate middleware services. This last pattern has been helpful for this kind of problem in systems as diverse as avionics FMS (flight management systems) and medical tomography scanners. It is the Port Proxy Pattern (adapted from ref. [4]).

Name: port proxy pattern

Abstract

This pattern specializes the connection points between architectural units to incorporate and encapsulate all distribution knowledge.

Problem context

A set of architectural units (subsystems or components) are connected via a set of discrete connection points (ports). However, there is a strong desire for independence of communication infrastructure to support portability and reusability of the architectural units.

Pattern structure and behavior

The mechanism of action of the pattern is to create proxy objects that sit "between" the architectural units and translated messages and services from "application" services to "network" services and vice versa. To deploy the architectural units to a different communication infrastructure requires only the recreation of the proxy objects, not of the architectural units themselves.

The basic pattern structure is shown in Figure 4.1.

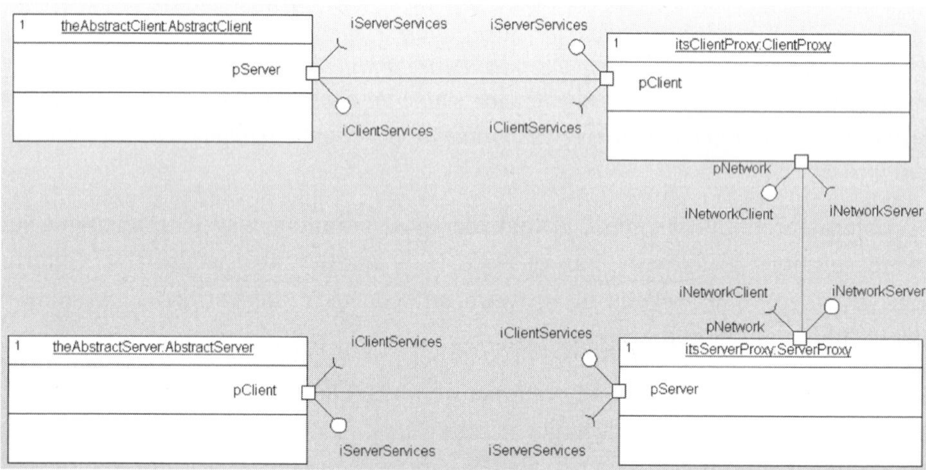

Figure 4.1:
Port proxy pattern structure.

The AbstractClient and AbstractServer classes both support only "semantic" (application service) interfaces. They may be connected together directly, if a middleware-free solution is desired. If they connect across a communication infrastructure such as TCP/IP, CORBA, or DDS, then the proxies perform a bi-directional conversion between the semantic interfaces and the network-specific interfaces. This is illustrated in Figure 4.2.

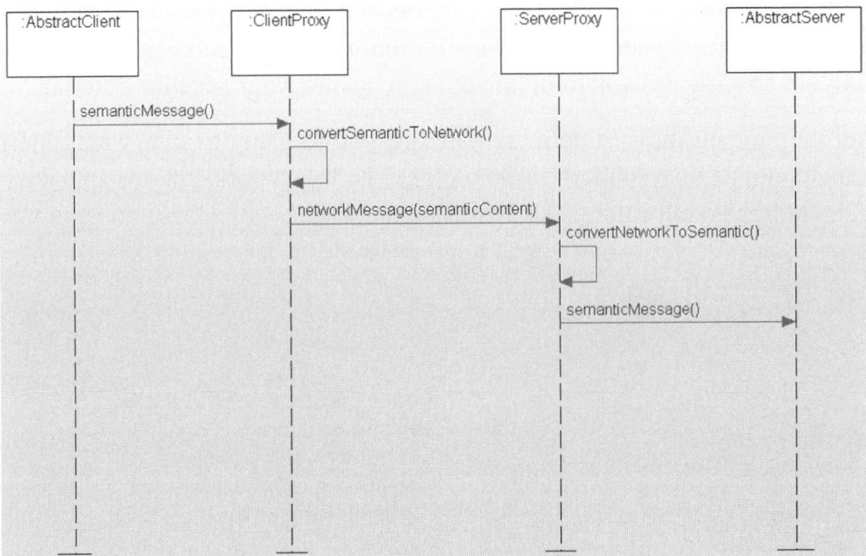

Figure 4.2:
Port proxy interactive behavior.

Consequences

This is a straightforward combination of the Port and Proxy patterns. It isolates the semantic elements of the software from the details of the communication infrastructure including network characteristics and middleware IDL. The proxies can be written to support various kinds of qualities of service (at most once, at least once, or exactly once) and both synchronous and asynchronous communication. To deploy the client and service architectural elements on a different communication infrastructure requires no modifications whatsoever to the elements themselves.

Disadvantages of the pattern include the writing of sets of proxies for each communication infrastructure to be supported. These proxies may be themselves quite complex and require significant work. In addition, the use of generalized proxies may introduce communications delays.

Using patterns

There are three primary ways of using patterns. *Pattern mining* refers to the creation of patterns. This is most often done by looking at a set of similar specific solutions and abstracting the commonalities into a pattern. *Pattern hatching* describes the selection of relevant patterns from a pattern library. A recent Google™ search found 7,000,000 hits for the term "design pattern". A search on Amazon™ finds just under 2000 book titles.

There is a lot of active work available on patterns and literally thousands from which to choose. The last usage of patterns is *pattern instantiation*. This activity focuses on applying patterns in your specific designs to optimize them against your specific criteria.

Unless you're in the business of defining patterns, you're likely to start with pattern hatching and continue on to pattern instantiation. The basic workflow for applying patterns in design, including architecture, is shown in Figure 4.3.

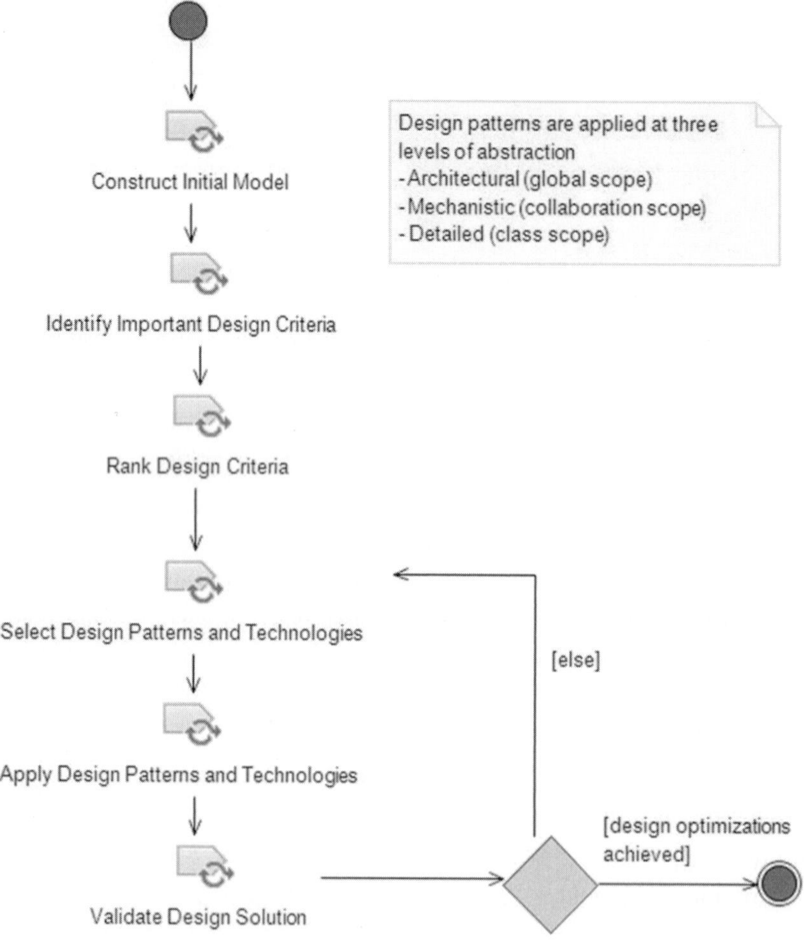

Figure 4.3:
Basic design workflow.

The first step is to construct the initial model. By that, we mean that we develop software that is functionally correct. A common problem is optimization of the system too early in development and our recommendation is that you defer optimization until after the software is demonstrated to be functionally correct. Having said that, it can be profitable to identify some aspects of architecture near the beginning of the project (such as the subsystems, their responsibilities and interfaces), particularly when a large team is involved. The architectural units can then serve not only as run-time organizational units but also as a means of dividing up the work among your development teams. We will discuss the different categories and views of architecture later in this chapter.

The next step is to identify the important design criteria. This is a step often ignored but this results in systems that do not meet their responsibilities as well as they could. Remember, when you optimize some aspects of the system you always deoptimize others. Only by clearly identifying the relevant design constraints can you create a good architecture that meets the system needs.

Of course, it isn't enough to merely identify the design criteria – they must also be ranked in order of criticality. A good design is one in which we optimize the most critical aspects of the system at the expense of deoptimizing the least. A list of design criteria weighted with their criticality enables us to perform a trade-off analysis of different alternatives.

The next step is to evaluate different potential solutions (patterns) against the weighted design criteria. This is typically known as a trade-off analysis, or simply a "trade study". The trade-off analysis can be done informally (e.g., in your head) or more formally using spreadsheets or other tools. A semi-formal way to perform trade-off analysis is described in the next section.

Following the selection of the patterns you want to use, they must be applied to your design. A design pattern has two kinds of elements. *Pattern elements* provide the functionality of the pattern and the glue that allows the pattern as a whole to provide its benefits. *Formal parameters* of the pattern are elements that will be replaced by elements in your functional software to provide the application behavior needed. This usually requires a small amount of reorganization of your software, an activity known as *refactoring*. Together, the pattern elements and the *actual parameters* (provided by your software) form the design solution.

Once the design optimization is in place, it must be tested. First, since the software was functionally correct before the addition of the pattern, it should be retested to ensure that the work refactoring the software and instantiating the patterns didn't break the software. Secondly, the pattern was added to optimize one or more properties of the system. The resulting design solution should be tested to ensure that the desired optimization was achieved. If the pattern was meant to improve performance, is it now (sufficiently) better? If the pattern was meant to save memory, how much memory did it free up? If the pattern was intended to improve reusability, the reusability of the software should be assessed.

While this workflow looks linear, the fact remains that this can be done both iteratively and continuously. We recommend that the software be developed and tested in small cycles lasting no more than an hour. (In the Harmony™ process, this is known as the *nanocycle.* See *ref.* [1] as well as later in this book: Chapter 22 – Agile development for embedded systems.) Once that software meets its functional requirements, we can begin to optimize it using the workflow described in Figure 4.3. We might end up instantiating four distinct patterns for the software but we can do this not only one pattern at a time, but also a piece of a pattern at a time.

Making trade-off decisions

In order to make good optimization decisions, the design criteria must be identified and ranked according to the criticality of the criterion. Next, a set of possible solutions are identified. Each of these solutions must then be assessed against each criterion. The degree to which a given solution optimizes a design criterion is known as its *score* for that criterion. By summing up the cross product of the criticality of the criteria and the related scores, the overall effectiveness of the pattern is computed; this is a value called the *total weighted score.* The solution with the highest score is the winner and is instantiated in the design solution.

Spreadsheets provide a simple tool for the computation of the total weighted score for a set of pattern alternatives. Table 4.2 shows how such a table might look.

Table 4.2: Design trade-off spreadsheet.

	Design Criteria					
	Criterion 1	Criterion 2	Criterion 3	Criterion 4	Criterion 5	
	Weight = 7	Weight = 5	Weight = 3	Weight = 2	Weight = 1.5	
Design Solution	Score	Score	Score	Score	Score	Total Weighted Score
Alternative 1	7	3	6	9	4	106
Alternative 2	4	8	5	3	4	95
Alternative 3	10	2	4	8	8	**120**
Alternative 4	2	4	9	7	6	84

In this case, there are five different criteria. The weight is a value representing the criticality of the criterion. In this table, the weights are normalized to be in the range of 0 to 10. These are the central columns in the spreadsheet.

The rows show the scores of the different alternative pattern solutions – these are our assessments of degree of the optimization for each aspect with this pattern. Alternative 1, for example, does a pretty good job on Criterion 1 (7) and a less good job on Criterion 2. The total weighted score is simply the cross product of the scores and the weights. For Alternative 1, this is 7*7 + 3*5 + 6*3 + 9*2 + 4*15 = 106. The best solution appears to be Alternative 3, which has a total weighted score of 120. This is the pattern that will be instantiated.

Patterns are a key approach to making design optimizations effectively. First, construct a functional model of the system that is demonstrably correct. Second, identify and rank the design criteria you want to optimize. Then, select design patterns that optimize the aspects you have deemed most important. Lastly, verify that you've done a good job.

Architecture is the highest level of design. Architectural design patterns optimize the system at a gross, overall level. Using design patterns will optimize your system structure, make it more understandable, and provide a context in which more detailed design optimizations can take place.

Software architecture categories and views

Architecture is not a single, primitive thing. It is a set of design patterns that integrate together to organize, orchestrate, and optimize the important aspects of the system as a whole. Because of the complexity and breadth of a system architecture, we define categories that focus on related aspects. These categories may also be considered viewpoints of the architect in that they bring to the fore these design decisions around these related aspects.

Primary architectural views

The primary views of the architecture are considered key for a couple of reasons. First, they are generally important in most systems in the embedded space. Almost all embedded systems must define some optimizations within these areas of concern. Secondly, they have a profound impact on the overall structure, behavior, or performance of the system. Other architectural categories may be very important for your specific system but may be less universal or have less overall impact on system structure or behavior.

In the Harmony process mentioned earlier, there are five important categories of the architecture, as shown in Figure 4.4. Each of these viewpoints is represented in most or all systems in the embedded space and has a profound impact on the structure, behavior and performance of the delivered system. Each of these viewpoints is a relatively independent subject matter with a rich vocabulary, conceptual ontology, and set of patterns. A system architecture is (mostly) composed of one or more patterns in each of these subject areas.

Table 4.3 describes these viewpoints.

Let's briefly discuss each of these areas of architectural interest.

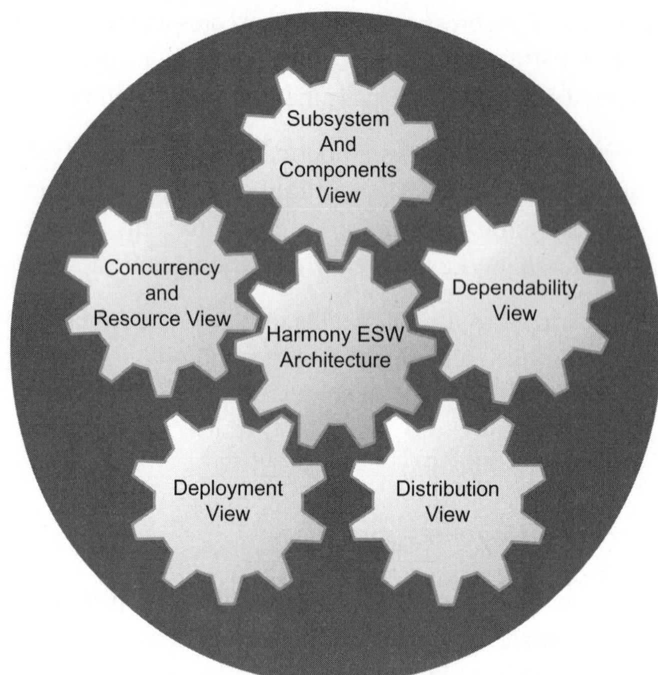

Figure 4.4:
Primary architectural viewpoints.

Subsystem and component view

This category of architectural decisions identifies the largest-scale pieces of the system, assigns them responsibilities, characterizes their interfaces, and allocates any existing software elements to those structures. In UML 2, components and subsystem are just structured classes – elements that delegate their responsibilities and behaviors to internal parts (each of which is typically typed by other classes). Because of this, we'll just refer to such elements as subsystems, knowing that components are included in that description as well. The UML standard is pretty flexible on how subsystems and components are used. We recommend that subsystems are the largest pieces, components the next, followed by tasks that execute within the components, then by other structured classes and finally by simple (unstructured) classes (Figure 4.5).

Robust subsystems contain parts which are relatively tightly coupled to each other (good cohesion), provide a coherent set of services (coherence) and hide the implementation details from other subsystems (encapsulation). Subsystems serve not only as run-time organizational units but also as a means to distribute work to teams. Each subsystem is often constructed as a set of components, such as math libraries, middleware, and

Table 4.3: Primary architectural viewpoints.

Viewpoint	Description	Example Patterns*
Subsystem and component view	This view identifies the largest scale organizational units of the system and details their responsibilities and allocation of services and data and characterizes their interfaces, both offered and required.	Layered pattern Microkernel pattern Recursive containment pattern Hierarchical control pattern Port pattern
Concurrency and resource view	This view identifies the concurrency units and related concurrency metadata, scheduling policies, and resource sharing policies.	Cyclic executive pattern Static priority pattern Dynamic priority pattern Interrupt pattern Guarded call pattern Message queue pattern Rendezvous pattern
Deployment View	This view identifies the different engineering disciplines involved (such as software, electronic, hydraulic, pneumatic, optical, and so on), the responsibilities of each, and the interfaces between these disciplines.	Static allocation pattern Hardware proxy pattern Hardware adapter pattern Mediator pattern Debouncing pattern
Distribution view	This view identifies the policies for distributing software across multiple address spaces (single or multicore), how elements discover services and collaborate over the communication infrastructure, including network topology, middleware and communication protocols.	Shared memory pattern Observer pattern Proxy pattern Port proxy pattern Data bus pattern Broker pattern
Dependability view	This view addresses the integrated concerns of safety, reliability, and security and how normal and exceptional functionality must deal with these issues.	Protected single channel pattern Homogeneous redundancy pattern Heterogeneous redundancy pattern CRC pattern Smart data pattern Proxy-based firewall pattern Secure channel Pattern

*Details of these patterns can be found in the author's *Real-Time Design Patterns* [5] and *Design Patterns for Embedded Systems in C* [2] books, or in other references.

application components. Each component may have multiple threads of internal execution. The real work is done ultimately by the primitive classes, functions, and variables – for this reason, these small elements are often called the "semantic elements" of the system.

Subsystem patterns vary how the system functionality and knowledge is divided and connected. For example, a *Layered Pattern* sets up subsystems as a set of layers of abstraction or control. For many systems, this is a useful way to partition in the system. One layer might deal with application concepts, which are in turn implemented using the facilities of a lower layer containing middleware, UI, and physics models, which are ultimately implemented at the lowest layer in terms of hardware. This pattern optimizes the

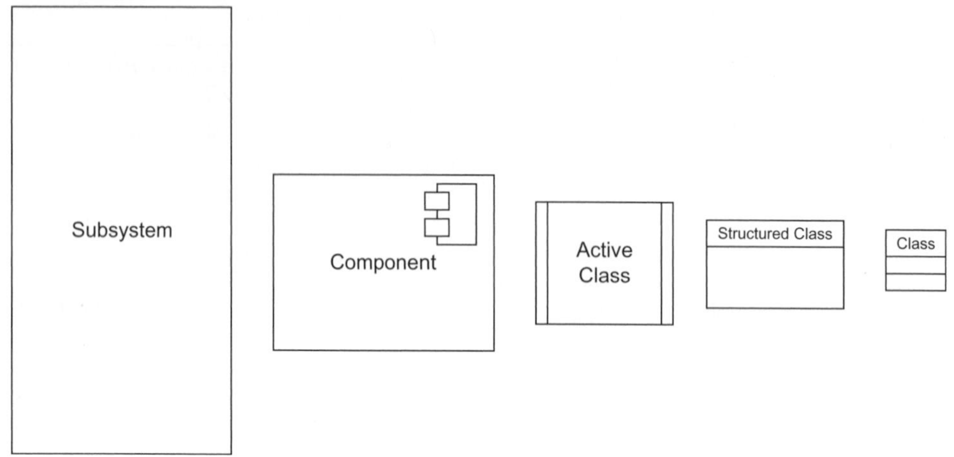

Figure 4.5:
Recommend size taxonomy.

reusability of the software for different hardware platforms (by replacing the lower layer), middlewares or UIs (by replacing the middle layers) or by providing a platform environment (by replacing the upper application layer). Layered patterns often add performance overhead because requests must be delegated through the layers.

Alternatively, while the *Microkernel Architecture* also structures the system into a set of layers, these layers are organized into more and less critical features. Such a structure is more like an onion than a stack. At the core is the kernel – a set of critical features. Outside that is the set of next most important features. Outside that is the set of slightly less important features. And so on. This allows for the creation of different product variants of differing capabilities with different footprints.

A *Channel Pattern* organizes the system into a set of units, each of which acquires raw sensor data and controls some physical output. Internally, the subsystem (known as a *channel*) performs a series of data transformations in order to compute the correct actuation signals. Such a structure is very helpful for safety-critical and high-reliability systems because it is a simple matter to create multiple parallel channels that act in concert to deliver services even if one of the channels fails. The channel pattern usually has a higher recurring cost (cost per shipped system) because of the need to replicate hardware and increased memory requirements.

The *Port Pattern* is a simple pattern for the connection of different subsystems based on interface compatibility. A port is simply a named connection point that supports one or more interfaces. Two ports may be connected if they are port conjugates – that is, if one offers the services needed by the other, and vice versa. The pattern allows systems to be connected together not on the basis of the *type* (class) of the subsystem, but rather on the compliance to the specified interfaces. However, ports also add some delegation overhead. Sometimes this overhead can be optimized away but not always.

All of these patterns (and more) provide benefits – that is, they optimize some aspect of the system. They also provide costs – they deoptimize other aspects. Figure 4.6 graphically shows the differences in three of these patterns.

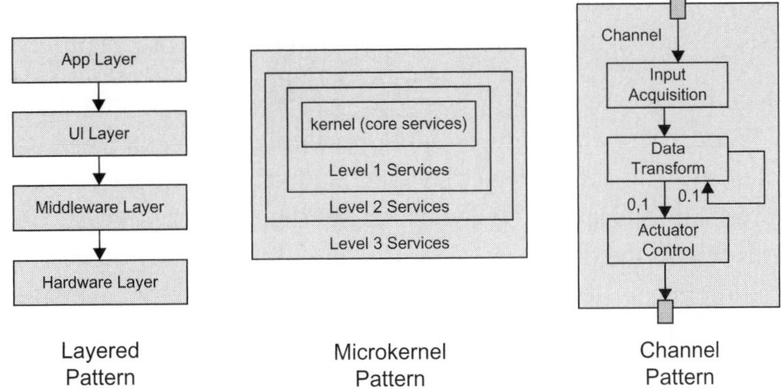

Figure 4.6:
Comparison of three subsystem patterns.

Concurrency and resource view

The concurrency and resource view is another of the key architectural perspectives. Concurrency refers to the simultaneous execution of concurrency units, such as tasks, threads, and processes. Each concurrency unit contains a sequence of action executions with a known execution sequence (including branching). But the order of executions of actions between concurrency units is generally unknown, except at explicit synchronization points. True concurrency occurs when the concurrency units can actually execute in parallel, such as on different CPUs and on different cores of a multicore processor. This architectural view must also concern itself with pseudoconcurrency in which concurrency units must be executed one-at-a-time because they share a common computational resource but for the most part appear concurrent. Task- or context-switching is an important consideration in embedded systems because too much of it (known as “thrashing”) leads to loss of performance and too little of it (known as “starvation”) leads to work not getting done in the right time frame.

If the execution of concurrency units is truly independent, then design is very straightforward, although there are design optimization decisions to be made. When the concurrency units interact – either directly (e.g., with asynchronous events or function calls) or indirectly (e.g., through sharing data or other resources), then designs become much more complex.

The primary areas of design concern for the concurrency and resource architecture category are:

- scheduling – defines when tasks run, both in isolation and with respect to each other;
- "thread-safe" sharing of resources – defines the means by which resources may be used by multiple concurrency units;
- deadlock avoidance – specifies how deadlock is avoided.

Performance issues appear in all of these areas of design concern, including worst-case and average-case execution time, bandwidth, throughput, and predictability.

In the UML, concurrency units are represented as «active» classes and running tasks are instances of them. These classes have the responsibility to create the thread in which their semantic elements run and manage the event and message queue for those semantic elements. Resources are typically modeled as classes that provide services or data to the semantic elements within the concurrency units. Care must be taken to avoid getting bad results or even corrupting system data. A class diagram that presents the concurrency architecture is commonly known as a *task diagram.* An example is shown in Figure 4.7.

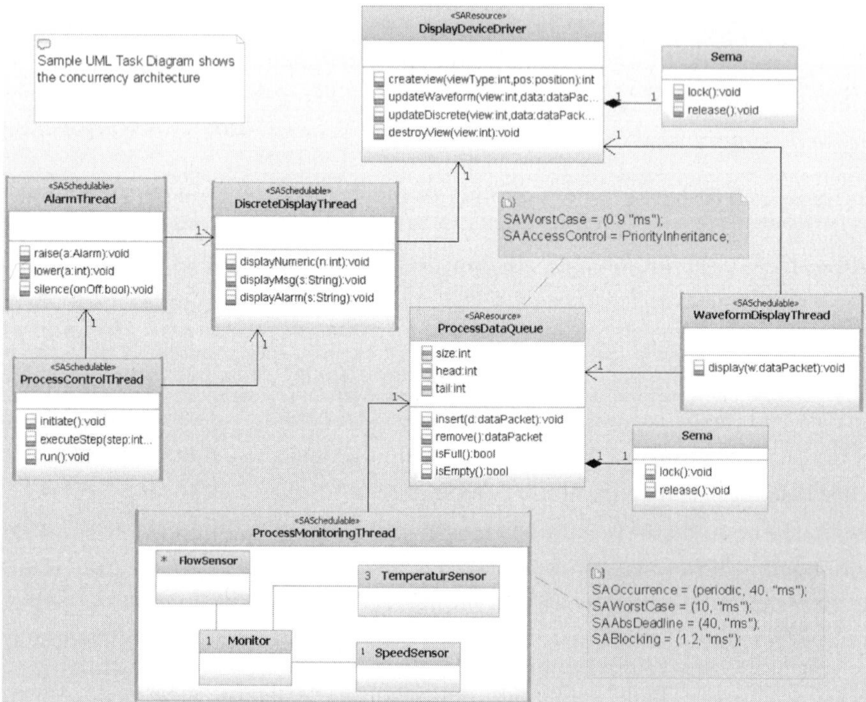

Figure 4.7:
UML task diagram.

In this example, «active» classes are shown with heavy side borders, and stereotypes identify the «active» and resources as well. Semaphores and the data queue are explicitly shown. In addition, concurrency metadata, describing the task execution characteristics, is given in constraints.

Scheduling policies are design patterns that focus on when and how tasks are scheduled. This is particularly important for pseudoconcurrent systems in which concurrency units must share common single-threaded computational hardware. (True concurrency means that the objects execute simultaneously. Pseudoconcurrent objects give the appearance of executing concurrently but since they execute on a single-threaded computational resource (CPU), the resource switches focus among concurrency units, so that only one is actually executing at any point in time.) Different scheduling patterns provide different benefits. Some of the common scheduling design patterns are shown in Table 4.4.

Table 4.4: Some scheduling design patterns.

Pattern	Description	Benefits	Costs
Cyclic executive	The scheduler runs a list of tasks (each to completion) in the same order in a repetitive cycle.	Simple Fair Highly predictable	Low responsiveness Unstable Suboptimal performance Requires tuning
Time-triggered cyclic executive	Same as cyclic executive except that each cycle begins on a time-based epoch.	Simple Fair Highly predictable Synchronizes with reference clock	Low responsiveness Unstable Suboptimal performance Requires tuning
Rate monotonic scheduling (RMS)	All tasks are assumed to be periodic with the deadline at the end of the period. Priorities are assigned at design time on the basis of period – the shorter the period, the higher the priority. Highest priority task always runs.	Stable Optimal Robust	Unfair May not scale to very complex systems More complex Less predictable
Earliest deadline first (EDF)	Priorities are assigned at run-time based on the nearness of the deadline (i.e., its urgency). Highest priority waiting task always runs.	Optimal Robust	Unfair Naive implementation leads to thrashing Unstable More complex Less predictable

Deployment view

In the development of embedded systems, not all of the implementation is represented in the software. It is, in fact, the collaboration of elements from a number of different engineering disciplines that fully realizes the system functionality. Such disciplines might include:

- Software
- Electronics
  - Analog
  - Digital
- Mechanical
  - Hydraulics
  - Pneumatics
  - Structural
- Optical
- Nuclear
- Chemical
- Biological.

The deployment view is important for a couple of reasons. First, it is important to understand the allocation of requirements and functionality to the elements of the different disciplines. That makes the scope and content clear to the different engineering teams. Secondly, it is crucial to have well-defined interfaces between adjacent disciplines. (An *adjacent discipline* is one that contains design elements that connect directly to elements of another; for example software often controls electronics, so software and electronics are adjacent. To control a pneumatic pump, however, software needs to control electronics that in turn control the mechanical parts, so software is not adjacent to mechanical engineering.) A common problem is that these inter-disciplinary interfaces are poorly defined, leading to long integration times and late, expensive rework.

Although UML defines a kind of diagram called a "deployment diagram", it is very limited in expressiveness. When we defined the SysML specification (Systems Modeling Language, a profile of the UML standard [6]), we rejected the use of the deployment diagram to represent the deployment view but instead relied on block diagrams (i.e., class diagrams) to depict the deployment architecture. An example, part of a medical gas delivery system, is shown in Figure 4.8. Stereotypes identify the different disciplines to which the elements belong. Although usually software elements remain unstereotyped, explicit stereotypes were added in the example figure for clarity.

The interfaces for such elements can be identified in UML tags associated with the stereotype and filled in for each separate model element. For example, the

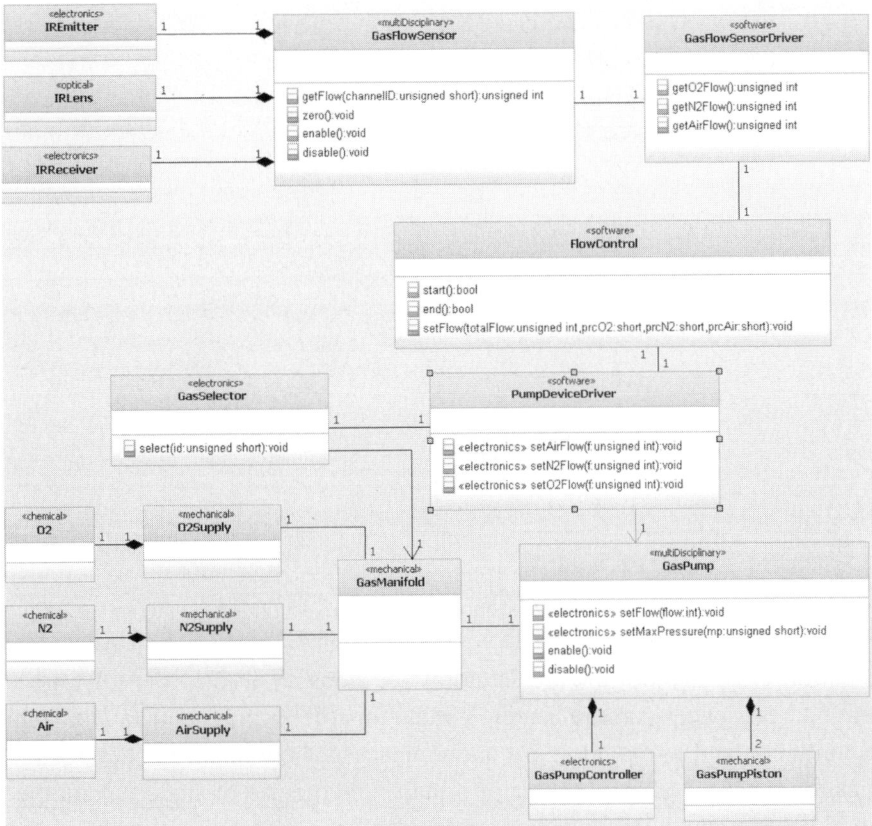

Figure 4.8:
Deployment architecture diagram.

electronic-software interface details of the `setAirflow(flow)` operation is provided by the tags defined for that element, shown in Figure 4.9. These details show that it is a memory-mapped interface located at address.

The published pattern literature for this view focus primarily on the software-electronic allocation and interfaces (See Table 4.5).

Distribution view

Many, if not most, embedded systems have multiple processing units, whether they are different cores of a multi-core CPU or different CPUs altogether, each of which runs software. One of the challenges of modern-day embedded systems is getting the software distributed across different address spaces to communicate and collaborate effectively and efficiently. We call this view of the architecture the "distribution view".

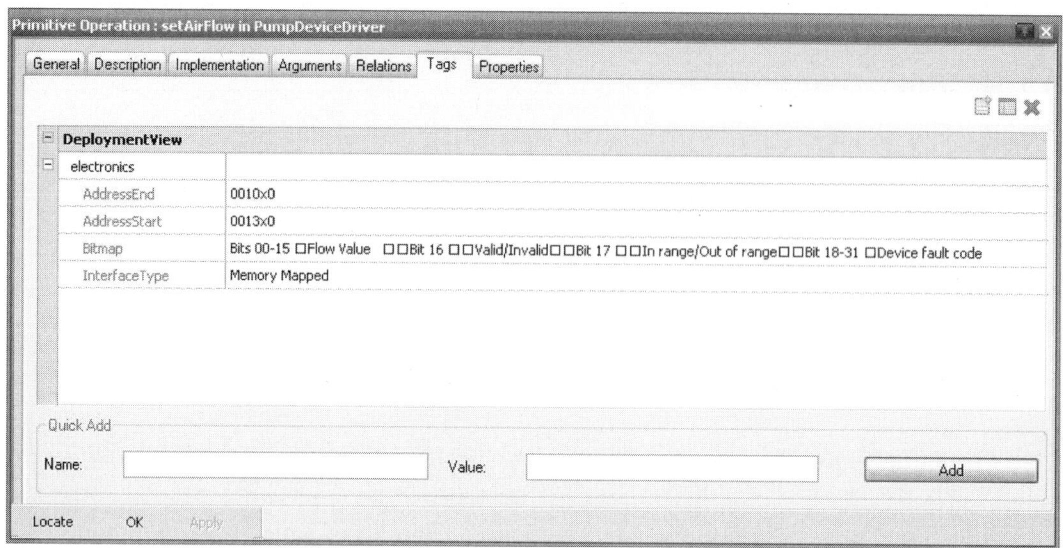

Figure 4.9:
Electronics interface details for `setAirFlow()` operation.

The distribution view includes the architectural decisions about how the software in different address spaces communicates – including the sharing of data and control messages, initiation and termination of communications, how quality of service for the communication is managed, network data formats, and the use of shared memory, sockets, middleware and communication protocols.

This is such an important topic that there are many books that focus exclusively on it.

Table 4.6 shows some common patterns in this architectural viewpoint.

Dependability view

Dependability refers to our ability to depend on the systems we construct. Dependability has three primary aspects. The first is *safety*, which may be defined as "freedom from harm". The second, *reliability*, is a stochastic measure of the availability of services of the system. The last aspect is *security*, or "freedom from outside influence, intrusion, or theft". The importance of the dependability view of architecture continues to increase as we make our systems both smarter (for some definition of the term) and give them roles in which their misadventures can have huge negative impact on the lives of people around them.

Sometimes the concerns of the different aspects are independent and sometimes they are coincident. A few examples:

- Making the car media player more secure (so that user credit card information used to download media to the player isn't stolen) doesn't affect the safety of the car.

Table 4.5: Some deployment patterns.

Pattern	Description	Benefits	Costs
Static allocation	The functionality of a hardware-software interface is defined at design time.	Simple	Doesn't provide robustness in the presence of faults Lack of flexibility of use
Symmetric allocation	The functionality of a hardware-software interface is dynamically configurable.	Provides flexibility for different loads and conditions Can dynamically reconfigure in the presence of faults	More complex Typically requires more hardware and recurring cost
Hardware proxy	The proxy publishes services that allow values to be read from and written to the device, as well as initialize, configure, and shut down the device as appropriate. The proxy provides an encoding and connection-independent interface for clients and so promotes easy modification should the nature of the device interface or connection change.	Simplified maintenance	May have run-time performance overhead
Hardware adapter	This pattern provides an adapter for mismatched hardware-software interfaces. Useful when existing hardware and software are brought together in a new system context.	Improves portability Improves reusability	Adds a level of indirection and may negatively impact performance
Mediator	The Mediator pattern is particularly useful for managing different hardware elements when their behavior must be coordinated in well-defined but complex ways. It is particularly useful for C applications because it doesn't require a lot of specialization (subclassing), which can introduce its own complexities into the implementation.	Simplifies coupling of many elements in complex control systems Especially valuable in C^2 (command and control) applications	May negatively affect performance Complicates bi-directional communication among elements

- Adding an air bag power-on safety check makes the car safer but reduces its reliability since there are now more components that can fail.
- Requiring the user to log in with a long password before allowing brake, acceleration, and steering functionality makes the car more difficult to steal but reduces safety in emergency conditions.
- Adding additional brake pedal position sensors improves the reliability of the brake pedal assembly and makes the car safer at the same time.

Every system is different and the dependability needs of those affected by the system in the specific context of its intended use must be considered. If an automobile is only used to play a radio (and not to drive) then most safety concerns go away. A cardiac assist device in an attended environment (meaning that medical personnel are nearby and monitoring

Table 4.6: Some distribution patterns.

Pattern	Description	Benefits	Costs
Shared memory	Uses multi-ported (often dual-ported) memory to share global data and events.	Large data sets may be efficiently shared Low run-time performance overhead	Requires special hardware to manage synchronization Doesn't scale well to large number of interconnections
Observer	Instruments servers with subscribe/unsubscribe functionality to decouple from clients.	Maintains proper client-server knowledge Good run-time performance Easy to implement different notification policies	Complicates the server somewhat
Proxy	Implements an observer pattern across different address spaces.	Isolates details of communications means away from application semantics Minimizes network traffic	Proxies may themselves become quite complex
Port proxy	Encapsulates all communication media details into connective objects (ports) that manage marshalling, transmission, and unmarshalling of messages.	Isolates application semantics from communication semantics Network protocols can be changed with no change to application software Aids portability and reusability	Requires writing of multiple sets of proxies Port proxies may be complex
Data bus	Virtualizes data into a common repository "bus" to add distribution and decouple clients and servers. Comes in both "push" and "pull" variants.	Localizes data into a single location Manages large data sets well Scales to many clients well Simplifies linkage topologies	Vulnerable to single point faults Data bus itself may be complex
Broker	Provides a repository of clients and servers making connections flexible and robust	Easy to implement fault-tolerant systems Supports symmetric multiprocessing well	Brokers may be complex (although commercial solutions are available) Brokers often have a large memory footprint and significant performance overhead

the system) has a very different set of requirements than one that is used "unattended". In general, safety analysis and assessment must take into account many factors to make the "safety case" for the system.

A "dependable" systems employ redundancy in various ways to provide safety, security, and reliability. The different patterns implement this redundancy to optimize different specific concerns at varying degrees of cost. Table 4.7 shows a few of these patterns.

Table 4.7: Some dependability patterns.

Pattern	Description	Benefits	Costs
Protected single channel	The protected single channel Pattern is a simple pattern in which data checks are added at one or more concrete data transformation steps. It provides lightweight redundancy but typically cannot continue to provide service if a fault is discovered.	Low design cost Low recurring cost Straightforward means for checking correctness of input and/or computation	Can't continue in the presence of a fault (requires fail-safe state)
Homogeneous redundancy	Uses multiple instances of identical channels that operate in either parallel or backup fashion, so that if one channel fails, the system can continue to provide service.	Low design cost Identifies random faults Can continue in the presence of a fault	High recurring cost Cannot identify systematic faults (i.e., design or implementation errors)
Heterogeneous redundancy	Uses multiple instances of differently designed or implemented channels that operate either in parallel or backup fashion so that if one channel fails, the system can continue to provide service.	Can continue in the presence of a faultIdentifies random and systematic faults	High design cost High recurring cost
CRC	The Cyclic Redundancy Check (CRC) pattern computes a fixed-length binary code, called a CRC value, on your data to detect whether or not it has been corrupted. This code is stored in addition to the data values and is set when the data is updated and checked when the data is read.	Identifies single with absolute confidence and multiple bit errors with high confidence	Some computational overhead for checking the data on every access Cannot continue if fault is detected Tabular implementation uses more memory Algorithmic implementation uses more time
Smart data	Encapsulates data into classes and access required accessors that check pre- and post-conditional invariants, throwing exceptions when they are violated.	Widely applicable and different kinds of invariant checking can be easily added	Performance suffers since invariants must be verified on each access Some additional memory required for range and limit data, if necessary
Proxy-based firewall*	Application-specific proxies filter and screen incoming and outgoing network traffic.	Identifies application-specific threats addresses the primary threat vector for networked systems May be set to allow only specifically expected traffic and reject all other messages	Additional development costs not adaptable to changing environments
Secure channel	Sensitive communications transmitted across public media are sent via channel in which all data is encrypted.	Security is improved; even captured data cannot be interpreted Middleware solutions commonly available	Additional design cost There may be performance overhead for encryption and decryption May decrease the ability to perform symmetric processing since server affinity may result

*Proxy-based firewall and secure channel patterns can be found in ref. [7].

LIVERPOOL JO... ...NIVERSITY
LEARN... SERVICES

Figure 4.10 shows the basic structure of the protected single channel pattern. The SensorDeviceDriver acquires the data. A linked set of ConcreteDataTransforms process the data in a series of steps until the outcome of the computation is used to drive some actuator via the AcutatorDeviceDriver. The "protected" part comes in by attaching data verifiers, known in the pattern as AbstractTransformCheckers, to check the intermediate processing of the data. This might be done by ensuring the data is within some range limit, or that backwards computation might recreate the original sensor value. If a problem is identified, then the appropriate safety mechanism is invoked.

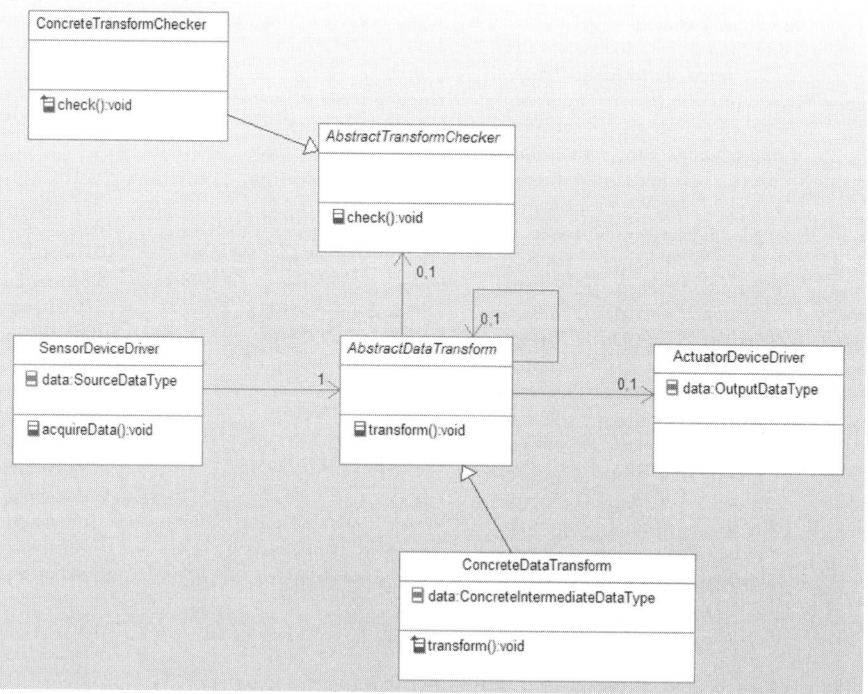

Figure 4.10:
Structure of the protected single channel pattern.

An example use of this pattern is shown in Figure 4.11. In this case, data comes from two sensor classes – the Thermometer and FanSpeedSensor – plus a device for setting the desired temperature (Thermostat). The temperature data is checked by the CheckTemperature class. The ComputeHeatFlow classes use the data from the two sensors to calculate the actual heat flow. The desired heat flow is calculated by the ComputeReqHeatFlow class. Both of these values are checked by the HeatFlowLimits class to ensure that both the actual and the requested heat flow are within appropriate limits. The difference between actual and desired is used to calculate the parameters to

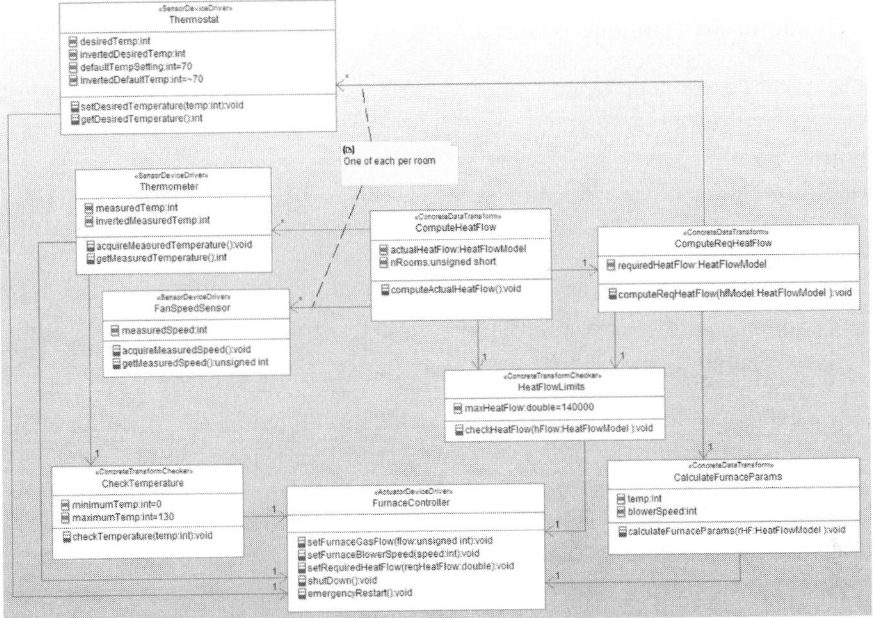

Figure 4.11:
Example of the protected single channel pattern.

drive the furnace, which is the actuator in this system. The intermediate checks of the system improve safety by ensure pre- and post-conditional invariants are true.

Secondary viewpoints

The five primary views certainly do not cover all aspects of architecture. The ones covered by the primary views generally have the greatest impact on the structure and behavior of the system overall. Nevertheless, other architectural optimizations must be made as well. Other architectural viewpoints that might be important include data management, exception handling and reporting, and system maintenance support. The overall architecture is the sum of all the architectural decisions, both primary and secondary.

Summary

Architecture is the collection of organization and optimization design decisions at the highest level. Different architectural decisions can result in significantly different performance properties despite identical functionality. Architecture is important because it allows us to optimize the product for technological, contextual, economic and deployment advantages.

A valuable approach to developing architectures is to understand the fundamental grouping of design criteria. In the Harmony process, these are

- subsystem and component view
- concurrency and resource view
- distribution view
- dependability view
- deployment view.

Each of these viewpoints has different sets of criteria and a different literature that defines core concepts and needs. The overall architecture is the collection of design optimizations in each of these separate aspects.

For each one of these viewpoints, the recommended architectural optimization approach is similar:

1. Identify and characterize the important optimization criteria.
2. Rank the criteria in order of criticality or importance.
3. Identify design solutions (patterns) that optimize the most important criteria at the expense of the least.
4. Apply the design solutions.
5. Verify that the functionality is properly maintained and the desired optimizations are achieved.

This design pattern workflow has been used to successfully architect a great many systems, ranging from small hand-held sensors to large interconnected avionics systems. The wide availability of patterns, both in books and on the web, has further enhanced this approach.

References

[1] B.P. Douglass, Real-Time Agility, Addison-Wesley, 2009.
[2] B.P. Douglass, Design Patterns for Embedded Systems in C by Bruce Powel Douglass, Elsevier Press, 2010.
[3] E. Gamma, R. Helm, R. Johnson, J. Vlissides, Design patterns: Elements of Reusable Object-Oriented Software, Addison-Wesley, 1994.
[4] B.P. Douglass, Real-Time UML Workshop for Embedded Systems, Newnes, 2006.
[5] B.P. Douglass, Real-Time Design Patterns, Addison-Wesley, 2003.
[6] Available from: http://www.omg.org/spec/SysML/1.2/PDF.
[7] M. Schumacher, E. Fernandez-Buglioni, D. Hybertson, F. Buschmann, P. Sommerlad, Security Patterns: Integrating Security and Systems Engineering, John Wiley, 2006.

CHAPTER 5

Real-Time Building Blocks: Events and Triggers

Erich Styger

Chapter Outline

Software Engineering for Embedded Systems.
DOI: http://dx.doi.org/10.1016/B978-0-12-415917-4.00005-0
© 2013 Elsevier Inc. All rights reserved.

Events and triggers

A key element of a real-time system is the interaction with the real world: this means with the *real time* of the *real world.* An embedded system needs to synchronize with the events from the outside world, and the system itself can create events. Events are things like a button pressed, a sensor reaching a certain value, or the system flagging a status to another part of the system. Such an infrastructure you might find in a real-time operating system (RTOS). However, you want to use that functionality in a context where an operating system is either not desired or not needed.

The other element in real-time systems is *real time*: once there is an event, the system has to react in a timely manner. Not only has the system to produce the correct result, it has to produce the correct result at the right time. For this, we need a mechanism to perform an action at a guaranteed time. In this chapter we are using a *trigger* for this: a way to do something at a given (relative) time.

Room temperature unit

To illustrate the need for events, we are going to use a simple example. A typical asynchronous event is the handling of a key or switch pressed.

Imagine an air-conditioning system (Figure 5.1) which uses a remote device. The remote device in the room has buttons and a display: using the *up* or *down* button the user

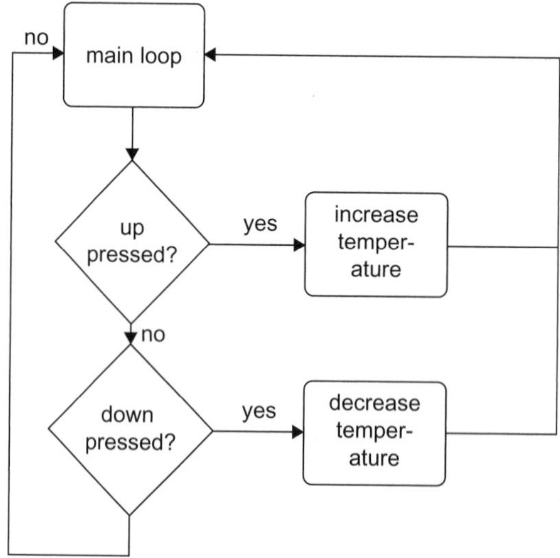

Figure 5.1:
Example system.

can increase or decrease the desired room temperature. If the application detects a key pressed, then it will update the display with the new desired temperature and transmit the new desired value to the heating system (e.g., through a wireless communication channel). In many cases you might have an interrupt raised to detect the switch pressed.

One approach to deal with this use case is to handle everything directly in the interrupt service routine (Figure 5.2).

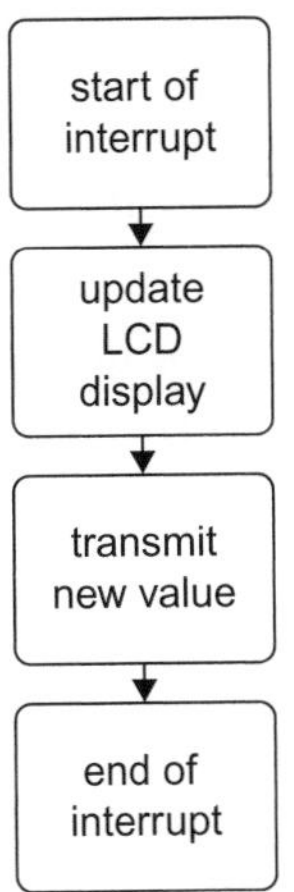

Figure 5.2:
AC room unit ISR.

This approach is simple, but has one problem: updating the display and transmitting the new value might take some time, up to several hundreds of milliseconds. Depending on your microcontroller and interrupt system, all other interrupts might be holding off during the interrupt execution. So this will greatly increase the interrupt latency time unless your system allows nested interrupts.

Additionally it violates a fundamental design rule for interrupt service routines:

1. Keep interrupt handlers as small and fast as possible.
2. Only do things in the interrupt handler which cannot wait.

The first rule is about latency and performance for the main program. The longer an interrupt handler takes to execute, the longer the main program will be interrupted and cannot perform its normal work. Additionally it impacts the latency of other interrupts. The latency is defined by the time it takes from the occurrence of the interrupt (e.g., a switch pressed) upon entry of the corresponding interrupt (e.g., keyboard interrupt). Some systems have non-nested interrupts: if during execution of an interrupt service routine another interrupt happens, it needs to wait until the currently executed interrupt service routine finishes. If the system allows nested interrupts (an interrupt routine can be executed while another interrupt is already served), this still means that lower-priority interrupts still have to wait.

Updating a display and doing a wireless transmission is typically *not* simple and fast. On the other hand: the display has *not* been updated at the same microsecond as the button is pressed: for the user it should be acceptable if this happens in the next 100 to 200 milliseconds. Even more, the wireless transmission of the new desired room temperature can happen a few seconds later. An AC system cannot react very fast and is a rather slow system.

The second rule is a consequence of the first rule: to keep things fast, only do things which are really needed and cannot wait. What we *do* need to do fast is to recognize the key press. So we want a mechanism to recognize something fast, which can set a flag to do the things which are not urgent. Such a flag we name Event here. And this is what we are going to implement.

Event system

We are going to implement a system which helps us to handle quickly things which need to be fast, and postponing things which can wait. For this we are going to implement an *Event* module. I'm going to describe first the interface and the high-level concept, and then go into the implementation details later.

The Event module proposed here follows the idea that the interrupt service routine only sets an event flag. That flag is processed asynchronously by the event handler loop (Figure 5.3).

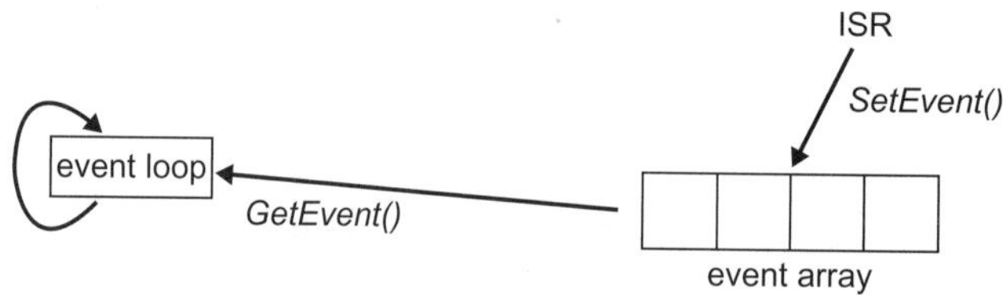

Figure 5.3:
Event ISR system.

That way the main loop or event handler does the heavy work, while the interrupt service routine only sets a notification of the event. This approach is not limited only to interrupts, it can be used for polled keys (Figure 5.4) or other cases. It is possible that a single event can cause multiple actions, or that an event can cause the creation of additional events. That way a sequence of events and actions can be created, or actions and events can be nested.

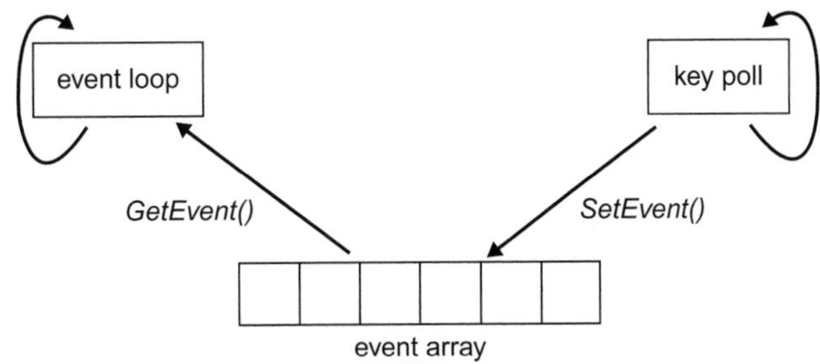

Figure 5.4:
Event polling system.

With this in mind, we can start defining the interface for our Event module:

- Static number of events: the number and kind of events are known at compilation time.
- Singularity: an event of a kind can only exist once. It is not possible to have multiple events of the same kind.
- Static memory: as the number of events is known, we are using an array of event descriptors. We are not using lists or dynamic memory for efficiency reasons.
- Event handle: we are using numbers as an event handle or identifier. As using an array of event descriptors, this event handle is an index into the event array.

Event handle

First, we declare a type for the event handle:

```
typedef uint8_t EVNT_Handle;

 /*!< We support up to 256 different events */
```

Using an 8-bit type allows us to use up to 256 different events, which will be sufficient for most applications. If you are wondering about the comments starting with `/*!`: these are normal comments, but treated in a special way by the doxygen (www.doxygen.org) compiler which can generate documentation based on source files.

Next we list the different events we are going to use:

```
#define EVNT_INIT          0

 /*!< System Initialization Event */

#define EVNT_SW1_PRESSED 1

 /*!< SW1 pressed */
```

```
#define EVNT_SW2_PRESSED 2
  /*!< SW2 pressed */
#define EVNT_SW3_PRESSED 3
  /*!< SW3 pressed */
#define EVNT_SW4_PRESSED 4
  /*!< SW4 pressed */
#define EVNT_NOF_EVENTS  5
  /*!< Must be last one! */
```

The first event handle number starts with zero. We define an initialization event which will be set at application startup. Additionally we define events for the number of switches we are going to support. Additionally there is a sentinel event number (`EVNT_NOF_EVENTS`) at the end which gives us the number of different events. Alternatively we could use an enumeration type:

```
typedef enum {
  EVNT_INIT, /*!< System Initialization Event */
  EVNT_SW1_PRESSED, /*!< SW1 pressed */
  EVNT_SW2_PRESSED, /*!< SW2 pressed */
  EVNT_SW3_PRESSED, /*!< SW3 pressed */
  EVNT_SW4_PRESSED, /*!< SW4 pressed */
  EVNT_NOF_EVENTS, /*!< Must be last one! */
} EVNT_Handle;
```

Using an enumeration is a more elegant way. However, as `enum` is defined as `int` in ANSI-C, the code might not be as efficient. It depends on the microcontroller and compiler used. An 8-bit microcontroller will handle an 8-bit type more efficiently, while a 32-bit (or even 16-bit) controller might handle an `int` better. Additionally there are many compilers for which you can set the enumeration standard type to a user-defined type (e.g., to an `unsigned` 8-bit type).

With the fact that our events are numbered, we could use the numbering as well with a prioritization scheme: depending on your implementation, the lower the event number, the higher the priority of the event could be (or the other way around).

Event methods

The interface for our event module is straightforward: methods to set, clear and check events. Additionally there is a method which checks whether there are any pending events and which calls a provided callback:

```
/*!

 * \brief Sets an event.

 * \param[in] event The handle of the event to set.

 */

void EVNT_SetEvent(EVNT_Handle event);
/*!

 * \brief Clears an event.

 * \param[in] event The event handle of the event to clear.

 */

void EVNT_ClearEvent(EVNT_Handle event);
/*!

 * \brief Returns the status of an event.

 * \param[in] event The event handler of the event to check.

 * \return TRUE if the event is set, FALSE otherwise.

 */

bool EVNT_GetEvent(EVNT_Handle event);
/*!

 * \brief Routine to check if an event is pending.

 *  If an event is pending, the event is cleared

 *  and the callback is called.

 * \param[in] callback Callback routine to be called.

 *  The event handle is passed as argument to the callback.

 */

void EVNT_HandleEvent(void (*callback)(EVNT_Handle));
/*! \brief Event module initialization */
void EVNT_Init(void);
```

Event data structure

With the high-level interface set, it is time to get into the details of the implementation. As previously mentioned, we are going to implement the events with an array of event descriptors. We do have a type to be used as event handle (`EVNT_Handle`), and an event can be either set or not set (cleared). As such, all that we need is an array of bits. The number of bits needed is defined by `EVNT_NOF_EVENTS`. With this, we can come up with the following implementation for the event array which packs the event bits into an array of bytes:

```
static uint8_t EVNT_Events[((EVNT_NOF_EVENTS-1)/8)+1];

  /*!< Bit set of events */
```

This implementation has the advantage of using minimal memory. But as we see later on, this comes with additional costs for accessing the events. If performance is a concern, you might trade in memory for additional run-time performance. An alternative implementation would use a byte for each event, which will simplify access to the event array. As long as you do have enough RAM available and not too many events, that might be a valuable alternative implementation. The interface proposed for our module allows one to change the implementation without impacting the application.

Figure 5.5 shows how the event handle numbers are mapped to bit numbers in the array of bytes. Figure 5.5 shows the first byte of the array.

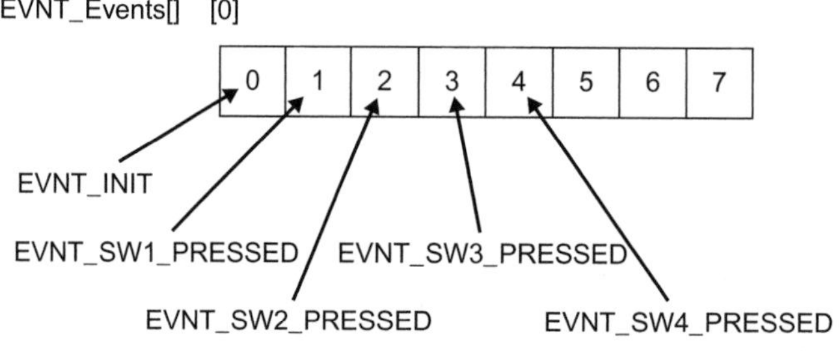

Figure 5.5:
Event to bit mapping.

To set an event, we need to access and set the corresponding bit number in the array, based on the event handle. This can be accomplished with a combination of division, shift and modulo operations on the event array:

```
EVNT_Events[event/8] |= 0x80>>(event%8);

  /*!< Set the event */
```

Clearing an event bit is accomplished in a similar way:

```
EVNT_Events[(event)/8] &= ~(0x80>>((event)%8))

 /*!< Clear the event */
```

And finally the implementation to determine whether an event is set or not:

```
(bool)(EVNT_Events[(event)/8]&(0x80>>((event)%8)))

 /*!< Return TRUE if event is set */
```

With this we are now able to implement the methods for our module:

```
void EVNT_SetEvent(EVNT_Handle event) {

 SET_EVENT(event);

}
void EVNT_ClearEvent(EVNT_Handle event) {

 CLR_EVENT(event);

}
bool EVNT_GetEvent(EVNT_Handle event) {

 return GET_EVENT(event);

}
```

Reentrancy

One problem remains: as shown in Figure 5.3 it is possible that our event array data structure is accessed both by our main program and by an ISR. As a consequence, we need to protect access to the event array. Or in other words: we need to have a way to grant mutual exclusive access to the data structure. What we need is a mutex. Basically the mutex can be something like:

1. Disable/Enable Interrupts
2. EnterCritical and ExitCritical
3. SemaphoreTake and SemaphoreGive

Disabling and enabling interrupts is simple, but does not preserve the interrupt state (whether interrupts are enabled or not). EnterCritical and ExitCritical exist as macros for many microprocessors: they preserve the state of the interrupts. Semaphores are something provided by an operating system and might not always be available.

Disable and enable interrupts

As we need to protect access to the common data from any other routines, and as such other routines could access the data from an ISR, the easiest way is to simply disable all interrupts before accessing the data, and enable the interrupts afterwards again. For an HCS08 microcontroller this could look like this:

```
#define EnableInterrupts() asm("cli")
#define DisableInterrupts() asm("sei")

DisableInterrupts();
/* critical section here */
EnableInterrupts();
```

This approach works fine and is very efficient. However, if interrupts were already disabled, they will always be enabled after the critical section.

EnterCritical and ExitCritical

To solve the previous problem, another approach is to save and restore the current interrupt status. For the HCS08 microcontroller this would look like this:

```
#define EnterCritical() \

  { asm PSHA; asm TPA; asm SEI; asm STA savedReg; asm PULA; }

#define ExitCritical() \

  { asm PSHA; asm LDA savedReg; asm TAP; asm PULA; }

EnterCritical();
/* critical section */
ExitCritical();
```

The difference is that the macros now save the previous condition register content (which contains the interrupt mask bit) and restore it at the end of the critical section. Still, you need to be careful about where the register content is stored: if this is a global variable, then you need to make sure that you do not nest multiple `EnterCritical()` and `ExitCritical()`. You might consider an implementation which stores the register value on the stack instead in global memory.

Semaphores

Last but not least, if you are using an operating system, you could use the mutual exclusion and critical section protection methods offered by the operating system. Mutual exclusion refers to the problem of ensuring that multiple threads/processes/interrupts have exclusive access to a piece of code or data at the same time. A "critical section" is a piece of code that accesses a shared resource. Normally every operating system offers some means of protecting critical sections using semaphores or similar means. Compared with previous methods they are more powerful and flexible, but they use more system resources too. As a general guidelines use them wisely, and keep the critical sections to a minimum.

Implementation with Enter/ExitCritical

As we want to be independent of an RTOS, we are using `EnterCritical()` and `ExitCritcal()` to protect our critical sections:

```
void EVNT_SetEvent(EVNT_Handle event) {

 EnterCritical();

 SET_EVENT(event);

 ExitCritical();

}
void EVNT_ClearEvent(EVNT_Handle event) {

 EnterCritical();

 CLR_EVENT(event);

 ExitCritical();

}
bool EVNT_GetEvent(EVNT_Handle event) {

 bool isSet;

 EnterCritical();

 isSet = GET_EVENT(event);

 ExitCritical();

 return isSet;

}
```

Event processing

We can now set, clear and check events. Typically we will set events in the interrupt service routine, and our main program will handle them. So what we need is an easy way to check whether there are any pending events from the main application loop. For this we are going to implement the function `EVNT_HandleEvent()`. This function goes through the event array and checks whether there are any events set. If there is an event set, it clears the event and calls a callback.

```
void EVNT_HandleEvent(void (*callback)(EVNT_Handle)) {
  /* Handle the one with the highest priority.
   Zero is the event with the highest priority. */
  uint8_t event;
  EnterCritical();
  /* do a test on every event: */
  for (event=0; event<EVNT_NOF_EVENTS; event++) {
    if (GET_EVENT(event)) { /* event present? */
      CLR_EVENT(event); /* clear event */
      break; /* get out of loop */
    }
  }
  ExitCritical();
  if (event != EVNT_NOF_EVENTS) {
    callback(event);
  }
}
```

The method iterates through the array of event bits. For the first event bit set, it clears the bit and breaks out of the loop. As it is accessing shared data, the routine needs to protect the critical section. If an event has been found as set, it will call the provided callback.

Integration

Now it is time to see how everything fits together. Below is an example where a keyboard interrupt sets an event flag, which then is processed by the main application loop. In our example below, the `main()` routine sets an initial event itself, followed by an endless loop to handle and process the events:

```
void main(void) {
 EVNT_SetEvent(EVNT_INIT);
 for(;;) {
  EVNT_HandleEvent(APP_HandleEvent);
 }
}
```

With `EVNT_HandleEvent()` we pass an additional callback function pointer `APP_HandleEvent`.

```
void APP_HandleEvent(EVNT_Handle event) {
 switch(event) {
  case EVNT_INIT:
   /* write welcome message */
   LCD_WriteString("System startup...");
  case EVNT_SW1_PRESSED:
   SND_Beep(300); /* beep for 300 ms */
   /* changes desired temperature */
   ChangeTemperature(1); /* increase temperature */
   SendTemperature(); /* use transceiver */
   break;
  case EVNT_SW2_PRESSED:
   SND_Beep(300); /* beep for 300 ms */
   /* changes desired temperature */
   ChangeTemperature(-1); /* decrease temperature */
   SendTemperature(); /*  use transceiver */
   break;
 } /* switch */
}
```

What is missing is where we set the event. In our AC system an interrupt will be raised for a key pressed. In our ISR we simply can set the event:

```
void interrupt KeyISR(void) {
 ACK_KBI_INTERRUPT(); /* acknowledge interrupt */
 if (Key1Pressed()) {
  EVNT_SetEvent(EVNT_SW1_PRESSED);
 } else if (Key2Pressed()) {
  EVNT_SetEvent(EVNT_SW2_PRESSED);
 }
}
```

With our Event module now we have a way to set flags which are processed asynchronously in the main loop. It helps us to keep the interrupt service routines small and efficient.

Triggers

So far we have the ability and infrastructure to flag an event and to process it in the main loop. What is missing is a way to do something in a time-triggered fashion: for example to blink an LED every second, or to turn on an LED 500 ms after a button has been pressed.

For this we are going to introduce the concept of a *trigger*. Triggers are sometimes also used to denote a hardware functionality: for example a microcontroller hardware is set up to *trigger* on a read or write access to halt the processor in order to implement what is also known as *watchpoint*. We are using triggers here in a slightly different way. We want the application to trigger at a given time in the future.

Blinking LED

A common thing used in embedded applications is blinking an LED with a given period. For example you might want an LED blink every 500 ms to indicate that your application is still running. Such a blinking LED is often called a *heartbeat*. An easy way to do this would be to set up a periodic timer which is then triggered every 500 ms:

```
interrupt void Timer500 ms(void) {
 LED_Neg(); /* toggle the LED */
}
```

That works fine, but wastes a timer just blinking an LED. So it might be much better to reuse one of your existing periodic timers to avoid this. For example, if you already have a 10 ms periodic tick timer, then you could reuse that timer to blink the LED:

```
interrupt void Timer10ms(void) {
 static uint8_t cnt = 0;
 /* blinking LED */
 cnt++; /* increment counter */
 if (cnt==500/10) { /* 500 ms reached */
  LED_Neg(); /* toggle the LED */
  cnt = 0; /* restart counter */
 }
 /* other things to do every 10 ms follows here...*/
}
```

We are using a `static` local variable as a counter: Technically this is like a normal global variable, but visible only inside the function where we have defined that `cnt` variable. This solution is fine as it only adds a little overhead to our 10 ms interrupt routine. But we need to keep in mind that adding more and more to our interrupt service routine will increase latency for other things in the system.

While our approach sounds fine, it might get a little bit complicated, once you start to extend it. Having a second LED blinking with another frequency? Flash an LED for 250 ms after a button has been pressed? Or turn on a sounder for 500 ms? Things might get more and more complicated with some additional `if` and `else if` in our interrupt routine. So we need to have something implemented which is more versatile.

Design idea

First, it would be good to collect what we need:

- An infrastructure to do things in a periodic way.
- Suitable for "fire and forget": you should be able to specify things like "do this in 850 ms" and it will take care of it.
- It should be suitable for rather small things, like blinking an LED. For more heavyweight stuff, it would be better to use something different or even an RTOS.
- It should be lightweight: use few resources on the microcontroller.

- It is for only a few such things we want to do: around ten or a few more, but not hundreds of things.
- It should be easy to use and to understand.
- It should be suitable both with and without using an RTOS.

Having this in mind, we could maybe base our design on the `Timer10 ms()` periodic interrupt. This would give us a periodic interrupt and time base. The idea is that instead of implementing things directly in the interrupt routine, we implement a "trigger" module which maintains the jobs or "triggers" we want to perform. The application could add or set such triggers, and the periodic timer interrupt routine simply would check whether there is any pending "trigger" to execute.

What we need to keep in mind is the impact on the rest of our system: as we would when executing via an interrupt, we need to be careful not to increase the latency for the rest of the system. So again we need to do things as fast and as efficiently as possible. And we always need to keep in mind that the "triggers" are executed in the context of an interrupt.

Tick timer

So the basic idea is to have a periodic tick timer which is fired say every 10 ms. This would give us a time base: the *tick counter*. Then we could compare that tick counter against the tick counter of the trigger we want to execute: if this matches, we execute that trigger and continue with the rest of the ISR (Figure 5.6).

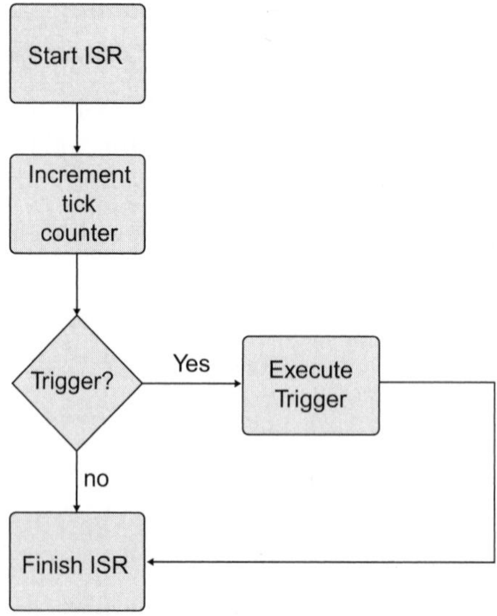

Figure 5.6:
Tick timer ISR control flow.

So it is now a good time to think about the interface. First, we want to keep track with the number of ticks, so we define a method to count the ticks:

```
void TRG_IncTicks(void);
```

This method then would be called from our periodic timer interrupt:

```
interrupt void Timer10ms(void) {

  TRG_IncTicks(); /* inform about the new time */

  /* other things to do every 10 ms follows here...*/

}
```

So the idea is that from the tick interrupt we call the `TRG_IncTicks()` function, and this would check whether there are any triggers: if the time is up to do something, it would execute it. One question remains: what should happen with the trigger once it has been executed? Basically there are two options:

1. Keep the trigger so it triggers again. This is handy for periodic triggers like flashing the LED: you set the trigger say to execute in 100 ms, it will trigger in 100 ms and then again the next 100 ms.
2. Clear the trigger. This means that once it has been executed, it will not trigger again. If the trigger is to be executed again, then it needs to be activated again.

In our approach we are using the clearing approach: it should make the implementation simpler (we will see this later on), plus if the trigger needs to be re-installed, the trigger could do this itself too.

Trigger interface

As we have a pretty good idea how things should work, we could come up with the following interface:

```
/*!

 * \brief Initializes the trigger module

 */

void TRG_Init(void);
/*!

 * \brief Increments the tick counter,

 *  called from an interrupt service routine.
```

```
 * Executes any pending triggers.

 */

void TRG_IncTicks(void);
/*!

 * \brief sets a trigger to be executed.

 */

void TRG_SetTrigger(uint16_t ticktime, callbackType callback);
```

This is just an initial draft, and we need to refine it later on.

Trigger descriptor

With this, we could start defining the data structure needed. What we need is:

- the time when the trigger shall be executed; it makes sense to use the tick counter as the entity as we measure the time with ticks;
- the information of what to execute: the usual way to implement this is to use a function pointer;
- any optional arguments for the function pointer; to make it generic, we could use a `void` data pointer to pass any kind of parameters.

```
typedef struct TriggerDesc {

  uint16_t triggerTicks; /* time to trigger */

  void (*callback)(void); /* callback function */

  void *data; /* parameter for callback */

} TriggerDesc;
```

That already looks good, but is maybe not very generic. For example, we might use a 32-bit trigger counter later on. Then using `uint16_t` for the `triggerTicks` is not a flexible solution. Instead, we could come up with our own types so they can be changed easily later:

```
typedef void *TRG_CallBackDataPtr;
typedef void (*TRG_Callback)(TRG_CallBackDataPtr);
typedef uint16_t TRG_TriggerTime;
typedef struct TriggerDesc {

  TRG_TriggerTime ticks;
```

```
  TRG_Callback callback;

  TRG_CallBackDataPtr data;

} TriggerDesc;
```

Data allocation

We now have a descriptor for a single trigger. Now we have to decide how we want to store the triggers. Basically there are several ways:

- dynamic: allocate the trigger descriptor on the heap using `malloc()` or something similar;
- static: using a fixed array of descriptors.

Using a *dynamic* approach would allow a dynamic number of triggers. On the other hand the performance impact of the allocation and de-allocation is a concern. Additionally memory fragmentation and possible memory leaks are a concern.

The *static* approach is simple but is less flexible. But probably this is enough for our use cases. So we are going to implement it as a static array.

Consequently, we need to know the number of triggers in advance to define our array. For our application we want to implement the following three functions:

1. Blink an LED with a given frequency.
2. Turn off the LED (after a given time) that has been turned on by pressing a button.
3. Turn off the buzzer after a given time.

This could be implemented by using an *enumeration* type to identify the triggers:

```
typedef enum {

  TRG_LED_BLINK,  /*!< LED blinking */

  TRG_BTNLED_OFF, /*!< Turn LED off */

  TRG_BTNSND_OFF, /*!< Switch sounder off  */

  TRG_LAST   /*!< Must be last! */

} TRG_TriggerKind;
static TRG_TriggerDesc TRG_Triggers[TRG_LAST];

  /*!< trigger array */
```

SetTrigger

It is time to implement the code to set a trigger. What we need is the trigger to set, specifying the time and what callback has to be called with the optional data. So this would give us the following interface:

```
TRG_SetTrigger(TRG_TriggerKind kind, TRG_TriggerTime ticks,
  TRG_Callback callback, TRG_CallBackDataPtr data);
```

The question is whether the parameter `ticks` should be relative to the current tick time or absolute. I think it makes sense to use it as a `relative` time, as this is how triggers are used in many cases:

- Turn the LED off for the next 30 ms.
- Disable buzzer in 60 ms.
- After button has been pressed, check status again in 100 ms.

Using a relative notion is natural for the above use cases. It would be different if you need something like

- Sound an alarm at 6:35 pm.
- Turn off water irrigation at 3:00 am.

Assuming a 16-bit unsigned parameter and a 10 ms tick counter, this would still allow us to specify a time of 65535*0.01 s = 655.35 s or about 11 minutes, which should suitable for most systems.

The other question is whether the `ticks` counter in our data structure should be relative or absolute. If we store the relative `ticks` parameter as well as relative `ticks` inside the `TRG_Triggers` array, the implementation would look like this

```
void TRG_SetTrigger(TRG_TriggerKind kind,
  TRG_TriggerTime ticks,
  TRG_Callback callback,
  TRG_CallBackDataPtr data)
{
  TRG_Triggers[trigger].ticks = ticks; /* relative */
  TRG_Triggers[trigger].callback = callback;
```

```
  TRG_Triggers[trigger].data = data;
}
```

If you store it as absolute, you would need to change it to

```
void TRG_SetTrigger(TRG_TriggerKind kind,
  TRG_TriggerTime ticks,
  TRG_Callback callback,
  TRG_CallBackDataPtr data)
{
  TRG_Triggers[trigger].ticks = TRG_CurrTicks + ticks;
  TRG_Triggers[trigger].callback = callback;
  TRG_Triggers[trigger].data = data;
}
```

That way we need to add the current tick counter to the parameter: doable, but comes with some overhead. To keep things simple, we rather stick with using the relative tick counter in the data structure. One thing we have missed so far: our implementation needs to protect a *critical section*, as both the application code and interrupt code through `TRG_IncTick()` will access the shared data.

```
void TRG_SetTrigger(TRG_TriggerKind kind,
  TRG_TriggerTime ticks,
  TRG_Callback callback,
  TRG_CallBackDataPtr data)
{
  EnterCritical();
  TRG_Triggers[trigger].ticks = ticks;
  TRG_Triggers[trigger].callback = callback;
  TRG_Triggers[trigger].data = data;
  ExitCritical();
}
```

And to make things prepared for future extensions and error handling, we extend our interface and implementation to return an error code:

```
uint8_t TRG_SetTrigger(TRG_TriggerKind kind,
  TRG_TriggerTime ticks,
  TRG_Callback callback,
  TRG_CallBackDataPtr data)
{
  EnterCritical();
  TRG_Triggers[trigger].ticks = ticks;
  TRG_Triggers[trigger].callback = callback;
  TRG_Triggers[trigger].data = data;
  ExitCritical();
  return ERR_OK;
}
```

IncTicks

Now we get to the implementation of `TRG_IncTick()`, which could look like this in pseudocode:

```
void TRG_IncTick(void) {
  Increment Tick Counter;
  if HasTriggerForThisTickCount then
    removeTrigger;
    call callback with parameter;
  end if
}
```

First, we increment the tick counter by one. As we have implemented the data structure as an array, we need to iterate through the array:

```
void TRG_IncTick(void) {
 CurrentTickCounter++
 for all elements in array
  if ElementTickCount == CurrentTickCounter then
   CallCallbackWithParameter
  end if
 end for
}
```

Then we check the condition *HasTriggerForThisTickCount*. Now we see another advantage of using a relative tick counter in our data structure. If we had used an absolute tick counter, then we could compare that value with the current tick counter. But what happens if our application had just called `TRG_SetTrigger` with a zero tick count?

```
TRG_SetTrigger(TRG_BTNLED_OFF, 0, MyLEDOff, NULL);
```

As we increment the tick counter at the beginning of `TRG_IncTick()` we might miss that trigger until our tick counter makes a wrap over. To catch this case, a solution would be to postpone the counter increment to the end of `TRG_IncTick()`.

As we are using a *relative* tick counter in our data structure, we could simply count down the tick counter for each trigger. If the count is zero we call the callback. Additionally, as we do not need to compare against the `CurrentTickCounter`, we can have it removed:

```
void TRG_IncTick(void) {
 for all Elements in array
  ElementTickCount--
  if ElementTickCount is 0 then
   CallCallbackWithParameter
```

```
  end if
 end for
}
```

The only remaining problem we have is how to know whether a trigger is still active or not. We could add an `enabled` flag to the data structure, but this would consume additional memory. Instead, we find out from the callback function pointer: if it is NULL, we don't have to call it. With this in mind, we can finally come up with the following implementation:

```
 TRG_Callback callback;
 TRG_CallBackDataPtr data;
 TRG_TriggerKind i;
 for(i=(TRG_TriggerKind)0;i<TRG_LAST;i++) {
  if (TRG_Triggers[i].ticks!=0) {
   TRG_Triggers[i].ticks--;
  }
  if ( TRG_Triggers[i].ticks==0
    && TRG_Triggers[i].callback != NULL)
  {
   callback = TRG_Triggers[i].callback;
   data = TRG_Triggers[i].data;
   TRG_Triggers[i].callback = NULL;
   callback(data);
  }
 } /* for */
}
```

This implementation iterates the array and decrements the tick counter. If the counter is zero and a valid callback, it resets the function pointer and calls the callback with the parameter. But two problems still remain: if the callback sets a trigger again for the relative time zero (at the current time), we might miss it. With following implementation we can catch this case: we call a separate function as long there are callbacks:

```
static bool CheckCallbacks(void) {
 TRG_TriggerKind i;
 TRG_Callback callback;
 TRG_CallBackDataPtr data;
 bool calledCallBack = FALSE;
 for(i = (TRG_TriggerKind)0;i<TRG_LAST;i++) {
  if ( TRG_Triggers[i].ticks == 0
     && TRG_Triggers[i].callback != NULL)
  {
   callback = TRG_Triggers[i].callback;
   data = TRG_Triggers[i].data;
   TRG_Triggers[i].callback = NULL;
   callback(data);
   calledCallBack = TRUE;
  }
 } /* for */
 return calledCallBack;
}
void TRG_IncTick(void) {
 TRG_TriggerKind i;
 for(i = 0;i<TRG_LAST;i++) {
  if (TRG_Triggers[i].ticks!=0) {
   TRG_Triggers[i].ticks--;
  }
 } /* for */
```

```
  while(CheckCallbacks()) {}
}
```

Making it reentrant

One thing is missing: in the case of nested interrupts and if other interrupts can set triggers, you need to insert code for critical section protection as well. First we need to add `EnterCritical()` and `ExitCritical()` in `TRG_IncTick()`:

```
void TRG_IncTick(void) {
  TRG_TriggerKind i;
  EnterCritical();
  for(i=(TRG_TriggerKind)0;i<TRG_LAST;i++) {
    if (TRG_Triggers[i].ticks!=0) {
      TRG_Triggers[i].ticks--;
    }
  } /* for */
  ExitCritical();
  while(CheckCallbacks()) {}
}
```

What remains is to protect the data access with `EnterCritical()` and `ExitCritical()` in `CheckCallbacks()`:

```
static bool CheckCallbacks(void) {
  TRG_TriggerKind i;
  TRG_Callback callback;
  TRG_CallBackDataPtr data;
  bool calledCallBack = FALSE;
  for(i=(TRG_TriggerKind)0;i<TRG_LAST;i++) {
    EnterCritical();
    if ( TRG_Triggers[i].ticks == 0
```

```
      && TRG_Triggers[i].callback != NULL)
    {
      callback = TRG_Triggers[i].callback;
      data = TRG_Triggers[i].data;
      TRG_Triggers[i].callback = NULL;
      ExitCritical();
      callback(data);
      calledCallBack = TRUE;
    } else {
    ExitCritical();
    }
  } /* for */
  return calledCallBack;
}
```

Initialization

What is missing is the initialization of our trigger module.

```
void TRG_Init(void) {
  TRG_TriggerKind i;
  for(i=(TRG_TriggerKind)0;i<TRG_LAST;i++) {
    TRG_Triggers[i].ticks = 0;
    TRG_Triggers[i].callback = NULL;
    TRG_Triggers[i].data = NULL;
  }
}
```

Alternatively `TRG_Init()` could also set up the periodic interrupt which calls `TRG_IncTick()`. In our application this will be implemented in a `TMR_Init()` function which is called as part of our application startup.

Blink!

With this we are ready to use our triggers to blink the LED:

```
void main(void) {

  TMR_Init(); /* initialize periodic tick timer */

  TRG_Init(); /* initialize module */

  EnableInterrupts();

  /* install trigger to blink LED */

  TRG_SetTrigger(TRG_LED_BLINK, 0, LED_HeartBeat, NULL);

  for(;;) {} /* let the trigger do the work */

}
```

After initializing the hardware and software module, we set a trigger to blink our LED. We set the next trigger to trigger immediately at the next tick interrupt. `LED_HeartBeat()` is our callback. As we do not need an additional data parameter, we pass NULL for it.

The `LED_Heartbeat()` function is implemented as:

```
static void LED_HeartBeat(void *p) {

  (void)p; /* unused parameter */

  LED1_Neg();

  TRG_SetTrigger(TRG_LED_BLINK,

    1000/TRG_TICKS_MS, LED_HeartBeat, NULL);

}
```

At the next tick timer interrupt, `TRG_IncTick()` will go through our trigger list. It will find that `TRG_LED_BLINK` is due and will call our `LED_HeartBeat()` method. This will turn off the LED and set the trigger again to be called in 1000 milliseconds.

But what if you want to blink different LEDs? Here you could use an additional parameter: the parameter `ledP` tells the trigger which LED has to be used:

```
static void LED_Blink (void *ledP) {

  if (*((uint8_t*)ledP) = =1) {
```

```
    LED1_Neg();
    (*(uint8_t*)ledP)++;
  } else if (*((uint8_t*)ledP)==2) {
    LED2_Neg();
    (*(uint8_t*)ledP)=1;
  }
  TRG_SetTrigger(TRG_LED_BLINK,
    1000/TRG_TICKS_MS, LED_Blink, ledP);
}
```

We are passing a data pointer to our trigger. Special care needs to be taken that the data is valid at all times. The following example will not work:

```
void foo(void) {
  uint8_t led = 1;
  TRG_SetTrigger(TRG_LED_BLINK, 0, LED_Blink, &led);
}
```

Here the address of a local variable is passed, and the variable `led` is only available as long as we stay in the function `foo()`. To solve this problem we can use a `static` local variable instead:

```
void foo(void) {
  static uint8_t led = 1;
  TRG_SetTrigger(TRG_LED_BLINK, 0, LED_Blink, &led);
}
```

Beep!

While our LED Heartbeat is a periodic trigger, we can use our infrastructure for non-periodic triggers too. For this we are using a buzzer which we want to turn on for a given time, and then it will be turned off automatically with a trigger.

```
static void Sounder(void *data) {
  uint16_t duration = *((uint16_t*)data);
```

```
  if (duration= =0) { /* off */
   BUZZER_Off();
  } else {
   BUZZER_On();
   *((uint16_t*)data) = 0;
   TRG_SetTrigger(TRG_SOUNDER, duration, Sounder, data);
  }
}
void SND_Beep(uint16_t ms) {
  static uint16_t time = ms/TRG_TICK_MS;
  TRG_SetTrigger(TRG_SOUNDER, 0, Sounder, &time);
}
```

In our examples we used a `static` local variable to ensure that the memory address we pass to the trigger is always valid. This increases the amount of RAM used. If we just want to pass a value as a parameter, it would be possible to pass that value directly, instead of using its address.

```
static void Sounder(void *data) {
  /* sizeof(int) = =sizeof(void*) */
  uint16_t duration = (int)data;
  if (duration= =0) { /* off */
   BUZZER_Off(); /* stop sounder */
  } else {
   BUZZER_On(); /* start sounder */
   TRG_SetTrigger(TRG_SOUNDER,
    duration, Sounder, 0);
  }
}
void foo(void) {
```

```
 Sounder((void*)200/TRG_TICK_MS);

}
```

With this we can come up with a simple `Beep()` function. `Beep()` accepts an argument for how long the buzzer will be on. It simply enables the buzzer and sets up a trigger which will turn it off using a trigger.

```
static void SoundOff(void *p) {

 BUZZER_Off(); /* turn buzzer off */

}
void Beep(uint16_t ms) {

 BUZZER_On(); /* turn buzzer on */

 TRG_SetTrigger(TRG_BTNSND_OFF,

    ms/TRG_TICKS_MS, SoundOff, 0);

}
```

Real-time aspects

With our triggers in place, it is worth looking at some real-time aspects of it. One thing to consider is the frequency and period of the tick timer used for our trigger module. As with the tick timer used in an RTOS, the tick timer used for the triggers define the resolution: if you have a tick timer with a period of 100 ms, then you have triggers with an accuracy of 100 ms as well. Everything will be synchronized at the tick interrupt time.

The other thing to consider: our triggers are executed in the context of an interrupt service routine. The interrupt service routine of the tick timer calls our trigger module, which then will execute any pending trigger. With this in mind, you should:

- Keep the number of triggers as small as possible. The more triggers you have, the longer it will take for the trigger module to go through the list. If you have many triggers, but only a few active at a time, then consider for example a linked list.
- Whatever you do in a trigger, it should be something small that you would otherwise do in an interrupt service routine; things like toggling a pin. It is not designed to do complicated things which consume a lot of time as this would increase the interrupt latency time. Instead consider just setting an event flag and do the heavy lifting outside the interrupt service routine.

- As triggers are executed from an interrupt service routine, every shared code between interrupt service routine and main application needs to be reentrant. If you have shared data, you need to ensure with critical sections that things are properly guarded against mutual access.

The core requirement for a real-time system is to produce the *correct result* at the *correct time*. The *events* and *triggers* presented here help us to achieve this. The *triggers* help us to do things at a given deadline or within the boundaries of a deadline. As the triggers are executed from a periodic timer interrupt, that timer needs to be carefully configured to meet the required timing. This includes the priority of the timer, but also the latency introduced by our implementation.

The *events* help us to reduce the latency time in interrupt service routines. They can improve the responsiveness and timeliness of the system, as they provide a way to postpone things from an interrupt service routine if they can wait. If things are triggered by an interrupt, we can delay things outside the actual interrupt routine, reducing the load on the interrupt service routine. Still we need to ensure that the events are handled in a timely fashion too.

Keeping this in mind, you should be able to apply both the events and the triggers module successfully.

Summary and source code

In summary, we have implemented two modules: *events* and *triggers*.

Events allows the application to set flags which then can be handled later on in the main program. This can greatly reduce the work load in interrupt service routines. Additionally the events can be used for interprocess communication if an RTOS does not offer a similar functionality.

Triggers can be used to have things done in a timely fashion: you can create periodic tasks or you can do things one off.

The combination of *events* and *triggers* gives you important building blocks for real-time systems.

The full source code of the *events* and *triggers* software is available from the link provided in the book.

CHAPTER 6

Hardware's Interface to Embedded Software

Gary Stringham

Chapter Outline

Software Engineering for Embedded Systems.
DOI: http://dx.doi.org/10.1016/B978-0-12-415917-4.00006-2
© 2013 Elsevier Inc. All rights reserved.

Introduction

Most of the other parts of this book discuss embedded software with very little need to refer to the hardware it is running on. Discussions on co-development and microprocessors talk to some degree about hardware. If a compiler is used, the processor's details are mostly hidden from the embedded software engineer. But at some point, embedded software has to be written that will directly interface with hardware. This chapter focuses on that interface between hardware and embedded software.

In the ideal world, hardware can be changed and modified up to the last minute just like software can. But that is obviously not reality. Co-development tools and techniques allow embedded software to run on simulated hardware (either simulated in software on a computer or simulated on FPGAs) before it is locked in; eventually the embedded software must run on actual hardware. When problems occur on real hardware, the challenge then becomes how to determine whether the problem is in hardware or software, and then how to resolve the problem. At that point, the pressure is on the embedded software engineers to generate a fix or workaround in embedded software. As Jack Ganssle humorously stated, "Quality is firmware's fault – because it is too late to fix it in hardware". ("Firmware" and "embedded software" are generally the same thing and can be used interchangeably.)

This chapter will discuss ways to eliminate defects and to mitigate the errors that do creep in. It will call out potential problems that the embedded software engineer needs to be aware of when accessing hardware.

Occasionally the design of the hardware is such that it is cumbersome for the embedded software to interface with. Most of the time, the embedded software engineer is stuck with that design because the hardware is an off-the-shelf part or is already cast in silicon. But if there is an opportunity for the software team to make design recommendations to the hardware team, do it. This chapter will discuss some of those recommended hardware design practices in the form of Hardware Best Practices. These are part of a collection of 300 best practices published in *Hardware/Firmware Interface Design: Best Practices for Improving Embedded Systems Development*, written by Gary Stringham and published by Elsevier. Those 300 best practices are available as a spreadsheet to purchasers of this software engineering book. In this chapter, references to "Hardware Best Practice *x.y.z*" refers to one of those 300 best practices where *x.y.z* is the number of that best practice in the spreadsheet and in the *Hardware/Firmware Interface Design* book.

I will follow the same pattern for "Embedded Software Best Practices" though I won't number them.

This chapter will cover the following topics:

- Collaborating with the hardware team

- Useful hardware design aspects
- Supporting multiple versions of hardware
- Difficult hardware interactions
- Testing and troubleshooting.

Collaborate with the hardware team

A successful embedded systems product requires the successful collaboration of different teams, including the hardware team and the embedded software team. However, collaboration between those two teams does not come naturally.

The two teams have different tool sets, life-cycles, cultures, and vocabularies. They may be in different buildings, different geographical locations, or even different companies. But I have also heard from engineers that even in a small company, where the few hardware and software engineers are in the same room, even they don't collaborate very well.

Because of the lead times required to build hardware, collaboration is further complicated by the different timing. The hardware team often has their design frozen before the software team starts up. In order for the software team to have an influence on the hardware design, they must start early, even before they really have much to do yet.

Proactive collaboration

Early in my time as an embedded software engineer in Hewlett-Packard's LaserJet design lab, we, the embedded software team, would be developing device drivers for one ASIC while the hardware team was designing the next-generation ASIC. We were on the same floor, just a few hundred feet from each other. But we didn't talk to each other very much back then. Those of us on the embedded software team would occasionally complain to the hardware team for the lousy hardware design we were forced to work with. But then the hardware team would complain that we were too busy to talk to them back when they were designing that ASIC. We were too busy writing the device drivers for the previous-generation ASIC.

I quickly learned to make regular visits to my counterparts in the hardware team. I found out where they were in their design cycle and asked them for copies of their register documentation when it became available. I took the time to read it, mark it up, and then go back with questions, comments, and recommendations for changes in the hardware design. But this was not in my job description – I was busy enough with my work writing device drivers for the current ASIC that I was not supposed to take time to work with the hardware team on the next ASIC. But I did it anyway. And it paid off. A year later, when that new

ASIC landed on my desk, I knew it and I had some of its problems corrected. I was then able to produce my device drivers in less time.

> **Embedded Software Best Practice:** Initiate contact with the hardware engineer early in the design of the block to discuss the block, its device driver, and their interactions.

I championed this approach and, as a result, changes were made to the development process and embedded software became a required signoff item in the various checkpoints of the hardware design life-cycle. For example, a milestone required that the embedded software team sign off on the register documentations for all the blocks. This formality then required those embedded software engineers who write device drivers to read their respective documentation – it became part of their job description.

> **Embedded Software Best Practice:** Review hardware design documents.
> **Hardware Best Practice 3.2.5:** Make sure that the firmware team is represented in reviews and signoffs of hardware checkpoints throughout the life-cycle.

The success of adding that formality to the hardware development life-cycle was evident when a hardware team called a meeting with the embedded software engineers to review the high-level design of a new ASIC. It resulted in a very productive discussion because the embedded software engineers knew of necessary ASIC changes that were required that the hardware team didn't know of. Since this was very early in the development of the ASIC, the changes were able to be accommodated.

Ambassadors

In addition to the checkpoints, the LaserJet lab management assigned ambassadors to each team (though that title was not used). Someone from the software team was assigned to be the ambassador to the hardware team, to sit in on their meetings, to note any schedule updates, and to answer any questions they might have. And the same with someone from the hardware team as ambassador to the software team. This gave each team a point of contact to the other side and significantly helped the collaborative efforts.

> **Embedded Software Best Practice:** Designate a member of the embedded software team as ambassador to the hardware team.
> **Hardware Best Practice 3.1.2:** Designate a member of the hardware team as ambassador to the embedded software team.

Register design tools

One of the biggest challenges in getting hardware and software to work together is making sure that both sides are working off the same specifications.

Typically, a hardware engineer writes the documentation that specifies what registers are at what addresses and contain what bits in what location. The hardware engineer then enters that same information again in the hardware design files. The software engineer reads the documentation and enters the register and bit information into software files.

That is three times that the register and bit information is entered into something. That gives three chances for human errors to be entered. Plus there is the chance that the hardware design changes but the documentation or the software do not. Then when software is loaded on hardware, things don't work and time must be spent to figure out why.

Many design teams tried to solve the problem by using automated scripts to keep hardware and software files in sync. But as is common with in-house tools, it lacked sufficient support to maintain it, keep it current, and add necessary features.

A few years ago, such tools became available commercially and open source. I call this niche Register Design Tools. Engineers enter register and bit information into an input file which is then processed to generate hardware include files, software include files, and documentation files. If a change is needed, the input file is modified and reprocessed, then the new output files are deployed. This keeps everybody in sync. Figure 6.1 illustrates this process.

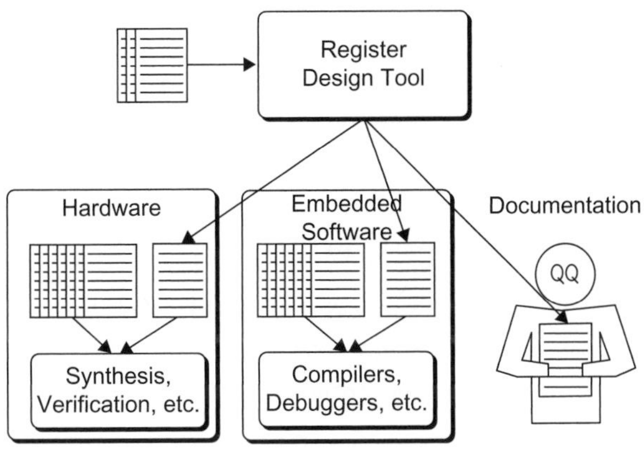

Figure 6.1:
Register design tools generate hardware, embedded software, and documentation files.

As stated earlier, this is a new market niche that is still evolving and it is still relatively unknown. So to promote this niche, I have provided a list of commercial and open-source products. However, products come and go, or are purchased by other companies. So the following is the list of products that is correct that time of going to press:

- CSRCompiler™ by Semifore, Inc, commercial, http://www.semifore.com.
- csrGen by Chuck Benz ASIC and FPGA Design, open source, http://asics.chuckbenz.com/#csrGen_-_generate_verilog_RTL_code_for.

- IDesignSpec™ by Agnisys Inc, commercial, http://agnisys.com/products/ids.
- MRV – Magillem Register View by Magillem, commercial, http://www.magillem.com/eda/mrv-magillem-register-view.
- Socrates Bitwise™ by Duolog Technologies, commercial, http://www.duolog.com/products/bitwise/.
- SpectaReg™ by PDTi, commercial, http://www.productive-eda.com/register-management/.
- Vregs by Veripool, open source, http://www.veripool.org/wiki/vregs.

If you are working with your hardware teams on the design of ASICs, SoCs, FPGAs, etc., encourage them to use one of these tools if they are not currently doing so. It will improve collaboration efforts.

> **Hardware Best Practice 5.5.2:** Use automated register design tools to generate register and bit documentation from block design files.

Co-development activities

In contrast to register design tools, co-development tools are very well known and have several product offerings from several companies. Co-development tools come in a variety of platforms and features. But the main purpose is to allow embedded software to execute on simulated hardware. The hardware may be simulated in software, FPGAs, or some other method. It may be simulated slowly in great detail or faster at a high level. This has the advantage of allowing software to run before final hardware is made, and even to be able to find and fix hardware problems before it is too late.

While some of these tools are lacking support and features and are still maturing, using them judiciously can boost co-development activities. Don't make major changes all at once – start with one piece with good potential then test it, deploy it, and add from there.

> **Hardware Best Practice 3.2.6:** Use co-development activities, such as virtual prototypes, FPGAs, co-simulation, and old hardware to get firmware engineers involved in developing code and finding and resolving problems before the physical chips arrive.

Chapter 2, Embedded Systems Hardware/Software Co-development. discusses this topic in more detail.

System integration

When hardware and embedded software are being integrated together as a complete system, there will be problems. Problems will occur immediately in bringing up the system.

And problems will occur during final test when something goes wrong after a 20-hour test under specific conditions.

Hardware engineers need to make themselves available as needed to help the software engineers with system-level integration and testing. Finding the root cause is only half of the effort. Coming up with a fix or workaround is the other half. If the root cause is in hardware, then hardware engineers may need to assist in determining a software workaround to avoid respinning the chip at a cost of a million dollars and a three-month delay.

> **Hardware Best Practice 3.3.6:** Involve both hardware and firmware engineers to determine the root cause of complicated defects and to then design a firmware workaround.

Useful hardware design aspects

In this section I will discuss a few hardware design aspects that make programming easier for the embedded software engineers. When you read the hardware documentation, look for these aspects and ask for them if they are not there.

Notification of hardware events

Events occur in hardware that the embedded software needs to be made aware of. Events can be grouped into two general categories:

1. Software-initiated events: events that are the result of having completed hardware tasks launched by the embedded software, such as completing the transmission of an outgoing I/O packet.
2. External events: events that are the result of external triggers, such as an asynchronous incoming I/O packet.

In either case, the hardware needs to notify the software so that software can take appropriate action. The following are different ways that hardware can notify embedded software of an event:

- No notification: this is the worst kind. Software has to guess when it can take the next step.
- Timed delay: with software-initiated events, software can set a timer to wait a specific amount of time before taking the next step. If the delay is long (seconds or more) and response does not need to be precise, software can use the OS timeout support. But if the timed delay is short, it is very difficult for software to know how much time has elapsed without hardware support.

- Status bit: hardware sets a status bit when an event occurs. Software has to check the bit, polling if necessary, until the event has occurred. A status bit is good if it is a software-initiated event that is going to occur soon. If not, then software must poll, tying up bandwidth, until the event occurs.
- Interrupt bit: this is the best way for hardware to notify software of events. This allows software to tend to other tasks until an event occurs. This works well for external events and for software-initiated events that will take some time to complete.

In one ASIC block I had to wait a short amount of time after hitting a reset bit before I could do the next step. There was no status or interrupt bit to let me know when it was done. I figured out that three times through a busy loop generated enough of a delay.

About three years later on a new-generation product, there was a problem and the engineer assigned to that printer was trying to figure out why it was not behaving well. He spent a few months but could not figure out what was causing it. Management finally had to bring me back to work on it. After two weeks of investigation, I noticed the delay loop and remembered why I had that. The new generation product had a different CPU resulting in a faster delay loop – three passes was no longer enough.

Even if I had documented that section of code well (which I hadn't) it still would have taken a long time to determine that the symptom was due to the insufficient delay loop. Had there been a status bit in the hardware, months of engineering effort could have been averted.

> **Hardware Best Practice 7.1.1:** Always provide an indicator to firmware of any event or condition that firmware needs to know about.

If you have to deal with non-indicative hardware events, do your best with timing delays but be sure to clearly comment in the code what the issue is to alert future maintainers of that code.

Launching tasks in hardware

Preferably when software needs to launch a task in hardware, software writes a 1 to a queue bit which hardware clears when done. (The technical description of a queue bit is R/W1S, Read/Write 1 Set, in which software must write a 1 to set the bit but cannot clear the bit.) This is how it is done most of the time. But in some designs, the software sets the bit and then later software has to clear the bit (an R/W, Read/Write bit). This is dangerous for two reasons.

If the software can clear the bit before hardware has a chance to see it, hardware will not know to run the task. But hardware is faster than software, right? So it should be able to see it no matter how fast software is, right? Wrong. I had a case where a state machine in hardware would occasionally look to see whether the bit was set when it went through that state. Occasionally that state machine has to service an external event. We discovered that if that state machine was busy handling that external event, software could set then clear that bit before the state machine came back. I had to put in a short delay in my code to ensure that the bit stayed set long enough for hardware to see it under all conditions.

The other danger is software leaves the bit set too long. When the hardware is done with the task and it sees the bit is set, is it still set from the past time and so it shouldn't run the task again? Or has it been cleared and then set again so it should run the task again? Software could get delayed because of higher-priority tasks causing it to not clear that bit in a timely fashion.

Because of these potential problems, a queue bit should be used to launch a hardware task, not a read/write bit. A queue bit provides a good handshake between software and hardware.

- Software reads the queue bit.
- If it is zero, software knows it can set the bit to tell the hardware to do the task.
- Once set, software can poll the hardware bit until it clears. Once cleared, software knows that hardware saw the bit and is executing the task.
- Hardware checks the bit occasionally.
- Once the hardware sees the bit is set, hardware can start executing the task.
- When hardware starts the task, it clears the queue bit.

Hardware Best Practice 8.5.3: Provide a queue bit that firmware must set – and only hardware can clear – to initiate a task in the block.

If you have a situation where hardware tasks are launched with R/W bits, examine the situation very carefully for any too short or too long problems that may occur and document what the software is doing to address them.

Bit field alignment

From the perspective of software and hardware, the position and locations of bit fields (groups of two or more consecutive bits) in a register usually don't matter. But since human beings are involved, it does. It is because we human beings need help in reading and interpreting bits. By convention, we read and write the contents of registers as a series of hexadecimal numbers with each character representing four bits.

The following is a 32-bit register with five bit fields, A, B, C, D, and E. Each bit field has three bits. The contents of this register are also shown.

Bits	31 30 29 28	27 26 25 24	23 22 21 20	19 18 17 16	15 14 13 12	11 10 9 8	7 6 5 4	3 2 1 0
R/W	– – – –	– – – –	– – – –	– – – –	– E E E	D D D C	C C B B	B A A A
Contents	0 0 0 0	0 0 0 0	0 0 0 0	0 0 0 0	0 0 0 1	0 1 0 0	1 1 1 0	0 1 0 1
Hex	0	0	0	0	1	4	E	5

For the purposes of readability by humans, this will be written as an 8-character hexadecimal number, 0x000014E5. But it is hard to determine from that the contents of bit field C. However, by adding unused spacing to fill in partial nibble fields, the five fields can look like this.

Bits	31 30 29 28	27 26 25 24	23 22 21 20	19 18 17 16	15 14 13 12	11 10 9 8	7 6 5 4	3 2 1 0
R/W	– – – –	– – – –	– – – –	– E E E	– D D D	– C C C	– B B B	– A A A
Contents	0 0 0 0	0 0 0 0	0 0 0 0	0 0 0 1	0 0 1 0	0 0 1 1	0 1 0 0	0 1 0 1
Hex	0	0	0	1	2	3	4	5

The hex number for this register is now 0x00012345, making it much easier to see that field C, located in the third nibble from the right, contains a 3. In this example, the 3-bit fields are nibble-aligned. If the bit field is 5 or more bits, it should be byte aligned.

> **Hardware Best Practice 8.2.5:** Place bit fields of 3 to 4 bits nibble-aligned, of 5 to 8 bits byte-aligned, of 9 to 16 bits 16-bit aligned, and so on.

If you are stuck with an alignment like in the first example, maybe you can modify the print routine to break out the fields for you, such as like this: "E = 1, D = 2, C = 3, B = 4, A = 5".

Fixed bit positions

To help software access different versions of hardware with changes in bits in registers, the hardware design team should follow these best practices:

> **Hardware Best Practice 8.2.9:** Avoid changing bit assignments from one version of the block to the next.
> **Hardware Best Practice 8.2.10:** Avoid reusing bit positions of deleted bits in an existing register.

To illustrate, supposed block version A defines bits T, A, and H in bits 0, 1, and 2, respectively. But for block version B, the H bit is dropped and the C bit is added. Following the above best practice 8.2.10, the C bit is not put in the same place where H was. The C bit is put in a previously unused position, bit 3. The software can be set up to support all four bits, T, A, H, and C, as illustrated in this diagram.

Bits	. . .	5	4	3	2	1	0
Block version A	. . .	–	–	–	H	A	T
Block version B	. . .	–	–	C	–	A	T
Software Supports	. . .	–	–	C	H	A	T

In block version A, the software will never read a 1 in position 3 so it won't ever invoke the C action. If the software tries to write a 1 in that position in block version A, it is ignored.

If C had been placed in position 2, software would first have to determine which block version it is, then switch on whether to handle position 2 as an H or as a C.

Block version number

Chips that have multiple blocks, such as ASICs, SoCs, and FPGAs, typically have a register that contains the chip version number. This helps software identify which version of chip is installed so that it can handle any differences between the versions. Differences may include new features, deleted features, or defects fixed.

These chips often consist of several blocks, such as a USB host block or an MP3 decoder. When a new version of the chip is released, the chip-level version number changes, even though some of the blocks did not change. This forces all device drivers to update their database, even if their respective block didn't change.

A better solution is to give each block its own version register. Then only those device drivers for blocks that changed need to be updated.

For example, suppose the USB block changed but the MP3 block did not. A new chip with the new USB version would have a new chip version number because something on the chip is different. The USB block version number would change but the MP3 block would not change. No change is necessary for the MP3 driver because it already recognizes the MP3 version number.

This is especially beneficial in FPGA environments when the contents of the FPGA can change frequently. The overall FPGA version number will keep changing for each new mix but those blocks that have not changed don't need their device drivers updated.

> **Hardware Best Practice 8.4.6:** Provide block-level ID and version registers for each block on a chip.

Debug hooks

As is well known, it is difficult to make perfect designs. When trying to integrate embedded software with hardware, it can be challenging to know if the root cause of a problem is located in hardware or software. When trying to locate the root cause, software has the advantage. Debuggers can be attached to monitor internal variables and execution paths. Debug statements can be added to the code, which is then re-compiled and re-run on the hardware to get more information.

Hardware does not have that luxury. Once cast in silicon, it cannot be changed nor can internal signals be probed, making it a black box that forces engineers to intuit what might be going on. It is especially difficult for software engineers since they know very little of how things are supposed to work inside the hardware. (This is where collaboration with the hardware engineers is helpful.)

Debug hooks built into the hardware and left there can become very useful to help diagnose problems. Hooks consist of extra bits and registers solely for the purpose of providing additional support to software. But some will raise the issue that these hooks take up silicon space. That is true, though generally very, very little space. Plus, adding hooks is like buying insurance for your car. You don't plan on getting into an accident just so you can collect on the insurance. But if you do get into one, you will be glad you have insurance. Same with debug hooks. If there are problems, you will be glad you have them.

> **Hardware Best Practice 11.1.1:** Allocate silicon space for test and debug hooks.

The following are just a few possible hooks:

- Internal registers: provide read access to many key registers (or any bank of flip-flops).
- State machine state: provides read access to the current state of state machines. Reading the state machine register multiple times can reveal if the state machine is stuck or moving along fine.
- Signals: provide read access to key internal signals. Several signals could be grouped into one register.
- I/O signals: provide read access to I/O signals. This helps diagnose discreet signals and communication protocols.
- DMA controller registers: provide read access to the address and byte-count registers of DMA controllers. Multiple successive reads can reveal if data is flowing or if data is stuck somehow.

Think about past challenges you have had in trying to integrate software with hardware. Ask yourself what information from within the hardware would have been helpful during the integration. Then talk to the hardware engineers about adding those as debug hooks.

Another very useful debugging hook is to have one or more GPIO pins available for debugging purposes. They come in handy to look for timing problems, activity levels, occurrences of rare events, and other uses.

> **Hardware Best Practice 11.5.2:** Provide extra unassigned GPIO pins to permit debugging and last-minute fixes.

Again, these hooks are not only for finding problems in hardware, but also for finding problems in software. Reading the DMA registers will help ensure that the software wrote the correct values to them.

Supporting multiple versions of hardware

I worked on the LaserJet printer product line for many years and my software code had to support many different versions of hardware. I had to support large, medium, and small LaserJet printers, color and monochrome printers, and single-function and multi-function printers. In addition, I had to support old and new printers. It would have been prohibitive to support a different version of the embedded software code for each and every product that we sold.

I strived to have one version of the software code support multiple versions of printers. This has the advantage in that if a defect is found and fixed in the code, it is fixed for all products using that code. If a new feature is added for one product, it is then available for all products that need that new feature. And it was easy to see where differences exist between hardware versions.

Eventually, I was able to get to the point where an easy port to a new LaserJet printer only took one hour.

> **Embedded Software Best Practice:** Maintain a common firmware code base that supports multiple versions of hardware platforms.

Code that supports multiple hardware versions uses switches to handle differences between versions. I will be discussing four types of switches:

- Compile-time switches
- Build-time switches
- Run-time switches
- Self-adapting switches.

Compile-time switches

Compile time switches uses the C Preprocessor (CPP) directives, #define, #undef, #if, #endif, etc. This can be used if the code does not need to switch at run time. And it should only be used if the differences are small.

Note: there are those who strongly favor avoiding CPP directives in favor of alternative methods, such as using const var instead of #define VAR to define constants. Both methods have pros and cons which I will not get into here.

Use #define to specify constants values that apply to one particular model. The #define directive is often used when a constant is needed in more than one location in the code. But it can also be used if it is only needed once. Even though it is used only once, using #define allows consolidation of all version-specific constants in one place, simplifying the porting effort.

In this discussion, I will use as an example a hypothetical automobile dashboard controller module. The software in this module needs to work with a few different SoCs, a few different types of display panels, and be used in a few different models of automobiles that the company produces. Ideally the same software will work in all cases and be able to handle the differences as necessary.

Suppose the display panels use stepper motors to position the needle for the speedometer. The software positions the needle by giving the stepper motor a value and the stepper motor moves to that location. But it is not as simple as telling the stepper motor to position the needle at 55 mph. Maybe it needs to tell the stepper motor to move to position number 220. In other words, the unit of the stepper motor is not necessarily 1 unit per mph unit. And one type of display might differ from another in the stepper motor units. Figure 6.2 shows a speedometer and calls out two important numbers, Units At Zero (what value to give to the stepper motor to put the needle at 0) and Units Per Ten (how many stepper motor units it takes to move the needle for every 10 mph).

Table 6.1 shows two hypothetical speedometers with their respective values, along with the calculated values for 55 and 88.

The formula for calculating the stepper motor value is as follows:

$$Stepper = \frac{Speed^{*}UPT}{10} + UAZ$$

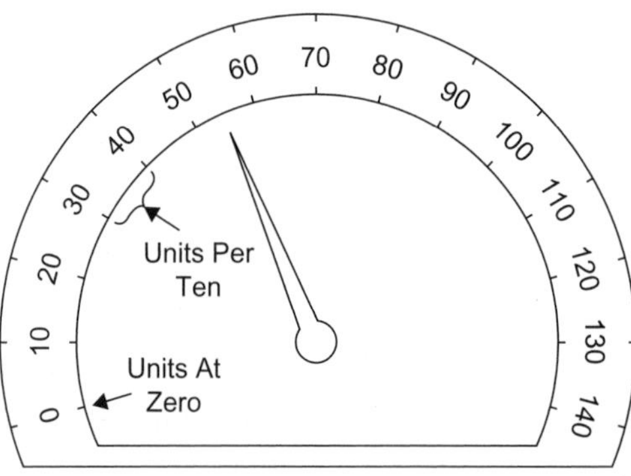

Figure 6.2:
A hypothetical speedometer with constants to position the needle.

Table 6.1: Values for two speedometer models.

	Speedometer	
Details	**ABC**	**VRM**
Units at zero (UAZ)	65	450
Units per ten (UPT)	100	− 75
Stepper for 55 (to show mph)	615	38
Stepper for 88 (to show kph)	945	− 210

If the vehicle is traveling at 55 mph, then the controller module would want to move the needle to 55. It uses the right UAZ and UPT values for whichever model is being used and comes up with either 615 or 38 and instructs the stepper motor to move the needle to that position. If, however, the driver had put the dashboard into metric units, then the speed would be 88 kph; 88 would be plugged into the formula and either 945 or −210 would be the value to give to the stepper motor.

Listing 6.1 shows how a speedometer switch can be used to have one version of the software code support these variations.

```
#if defined(SPEEDOMETER_ABC)
#  define UNITS_AT_ZERO 65
#  define UNITS_PER_TEN 100
#elif defined(SPEEDOMETER_VRM)
#  define UNITS_AT_ZERO 450
#  define UNITS_PER_TEN -75
#else
#  error Unknown speedometer model
#endif
```

Listing 6.1:
Speedometer switch: set-up constants based on speedometer model used.

Notice the #else clause that will cause a compiler warning if neither speedometer model is specified. This technique is very useful when porting code to a new product to ensure that a speedometer is specified. It may be that the engineer forgot to specify whether it was the ABC or the VRM speedometer, or it may be that a new speedometer is now being used and constants need to be defined for it.

> **Embedded Software Best Practice:** When using #if switches in the C Preprocessor, use #elif to test for all known cases then include a #else case with a #error to catch unexpected or incomplete switch branches.

Now suppose there are three cars, with the codenames Potato, Corn, and Carrot, that use these two speedometer models. Listing 6.2 shows how a car switch is used to keep straight which car uses which speedometer.

Again notice the #else clause to catch if a car is not specified.

The speedometer stepper motor is not the only aspect that would be different. Suppose that the VRM speedometer also supports a tachometer. But the ABC speedometer does not. Any tachometer-specific code would then need to be compiled in for VRM. But rather than using #ifdef SPEEDOMETER_VRM around tachometer code, it is better to use something

```
#if defined(CAR_POTATO)
#  define SPEEDOMETER_ABC
#elif defined(CAR_CORN)
#  define SPEEDOMETER_VRM
#elif defined(CAR_CARROT)
#  define SPEEDOMETER_VRM
#else
#  error Unknown car
#endif
```

Listing 6.2:
Car switch: specify speedometer model used by each car.

like #ifdef TACHOMETER. The #define TACHOMETER would then be placed in the #if SPEEDOMETER_VRM switch of the speedometer switch section. This allows a new speedometer type that also supports a tachometer to simply turn that on.

Suppose also that a fuel computer is a feature on some models but not all. Marketing would determine whether a car should have the fuel computer feature. Somewhere on the dashboard is support for the fuel computer if enabled. Another #define in the car switch would be used to specify if the fuel computer feature should be turned on. Listing 6.3 now shows the tachometer and fuel computer aspects added in.

```
/*** List of cars ***/
#if defined(CAR_POTATO)
#  define SPEEDOMETER_ABC
#elif defined(CAR_CORN)
#  define SPEEDOMETER_VRM
#elif defined(CAR_CARROT)
#  define SPEEDOMETER_VRM
#  define FUEL_COMPUTER  // Only the Carrot gets the fuel computer
#else
#  error Unknown car
#endif
/*** List of speedometers ***/
#if defined(SPEEDOMETER_ABC)
#  define UNITS_AT_ZERO 65
#  define UNITS_PER_TEN 100
#elif defined(SPEEDOMETER_VRM)
#  define UNITS_AT_ZERO 450
#  define UNITS_PER_TEN -75
#  define TACHOMETER     // Only VRM can support tachometer feature
#else
#  error Unknown speedometer model
#endif
```

Listing 6.3:
Car and speedometer switch with tachometer and fuel computer added.

Any references to a car or speedometer are only mentioned here in this section of code. This section makes necessary #defines that are used elsewhere in the code as needed. This is important to keep the code clean. For example, it gets cumbersome to have #ifdef CAR_ <car_model> around the tachometer code. This is what will happen:

```
#if defined(CAR_CORN) || defined(CAR_CARROT) || <...list of all cars...>
 tachometer code...
#endif
```

The problem is that as new cars are added, the list gets long and difficult to keep straight.

Now, let's add a new car, Peas. Peas comes with a new speedometer model, the XLS, but no new features beyond that. In other words, all necessary code support is in place. The code section containing the car and speedometer switches is the only place that needs to be changed to support a Peas, as shown in Listing 6.4.

This is all the changes needed to now add support for Peas. It uses the XLS speedometer which supports the tachometer, and the fuel computer is enabled. No other changes are necessary elsewhere in the code.

Tables 6.2 and 6.3 give a clearer picture of the details for the above car and speedometer switches.

One piece remains, and that is to specify which car to build the code for. One option is on the command line for the compiler.

```
cc ... –DCAR_PEAS ...
```

Another option is pointing to a #include file located in the Peas directory, and the file contains #define CAR_PEAS.

```
Cc ... –I/products/peas/inc ...
```

Again, this technique should not be used to control large chunks of source code – build-time switches would handle that better.

Build-time switches

Suppose that the differences between the above-mentioned speedometers are not as simple as a few constants and features, and that the software code required to access them is quite different. What is needed are separate subroutines to handle the differences. Subroutines

```
/*** List of cars ***/
#if defined(CAR_POTATO)
#  define SPEEDOMETER_ABC

#elif defined(CAR_CORN)
#  define SPEEDOMETER_VRM

#elif defined(CAR_CARROT)
#  define SPEEDOMETER_VRM
#  define FUEL_COMPUTER

#elif defined(CAR_PEAS)      // New car
#  define SPEEDOMETER_VRM    // Uses new speedometer
#  define FUEL_COMPUTER      // And gets the fuel computer

#else
#  error Unknown car
#endif

/*** List of speedometers ***/
#if defined(SPEEDOMETER_ABC)
#  define UNITS_AT_ZERO 65
#  define UNITS_PER_TEN 100

#elif defined(SPEEDOMETER_VRM)
#  define UNITS_AT_ZERO 450
#  define UNITS_PER_TEN -75
#  define TACHOMETER

#elif defined(SPEEDOMETER_XLS) // New speedometer
#  define UNITS_AT_ZERO 32      // With its constants
#  define UNITS_PER_TEN 80
#  define TACHOMETER            // It supports the tachometer

#else
#  error Unknown speedometer model
#endif
```

Listing 6.4:
Adding support for the Peas and its new XLS speedometer.

Table 6.2: Car details.

Details	Car			
	Potato	**Corn**	**Carrot**	**Peas**
Speedometer	ABC	VRM	VRM	XLS
Fuel computer	No	No	Yes	Yes

Table 6.3: Speedometer details.

Details	Speedometer		
	ABC	VRM	XLS
Units at zero (UAZ)	65	450	32
Units per ten (UPT)	100	−75	80
Tachometer	No	Yes	Yes

can be large and it is not a good idea to use #ifdef/#endif to switch them in and out. Instead, let's create three files, one for each speedometer:

- speedometer_abc.c
- speedometer_vrm.c
- speedometer_xls.c

Each file will have at least these two functions:

- DisplaySpeed (int speed)
- DisplayTachometer (int rpm).

The main code, when the car is traveling at 55 mph, will call DisplaySpeed (55). Or if it is in metric mode, and thus going 88 kph, it will call DisplaySpeed (88). Then whichever function is built into the code, ABC, VRM, or XLS, it will do whatever is necessary to move the needle to the desired position.

To display 2700 rpm (revolutions per minute) on the tachometer, the main code will call DisplayTachometer (2700). For VRM and XLS, they will respond appropriately and display it. For ABC, which does not support a tachometer, it simply returns to the main code saying "Done" even though it really didn't do anything.

The main code does not need to worry about which speedometer is attached. It simply makes the call and whichever code is linked in will be the one to respond.

To handle the fuel computer feature if needed, a separate source code file, fuel_computer.c, would be linked into the code.

Listing 6.5 shows how the code for the four cars could be built.

Note that the appropriate speedometer is listed and that fuel computer support is included only when needed.

Of course there are other ways to accomplish this build-time switching, depending on your build environment. But the point is that code that is only needed some of the time is contained in separate files that are included in the build only when needed.

```
potato:
        cc main.c speedometer_abc.c -o potato.exe

corn:
        cc main.c speedometer_vrm.c -o corn.exe

carrot:
        cc main.c speedometer_vrm.c fuel_computer.c -o carrot.exe

peas:
        cc main.c speedometer_xls.c fuel_computer.c -o peas.exe
```

Listing 6.5:
Portions of the makefile for car code.

Run-time switches

Now let's suppose that the dashboard controller module, including its embedded software, needs to be identical for all cars. In other words, run-time switching is necessary to accommodate the different speedometers and other optional components. This requires that the necessary information about all supported devices must be included in the code.

Listing 6.6 shows how this is to be done. Section 1 contains two enum specifications, one for cars and one for speedometers. Section 2 contains the car and speedometer tables with the pertinent details. Section 3 makes a function call to get the car model and, using the structs, gets the necessary constants. Section 4 makes a function call to get the current speed and, using the constants, calculates the necessary stepper motor value.

Using arrays as above is not necessarily the best way to write the code. Using pointers is a more common way of doing it. The following shows section 3 rewritten to use pointers. The necessary struct and table changes are not shown.

```
/* Section 3: Get specific details for this car model */
carStruct *pCar = getCarStruct(); /* Get pointer for this car */
int uaz = pCar->pSpeedometer->units_at_zero;
int upt = pCar->pSpeedometer->units_per_ten;
```

If separate functions are needed, then appropriate functions would be selected, as illustrated here.

```
pCar->pSpeedometer->DisplaySpeed(55);
```

Self-adapting switches

In the previous examples, human beings have to write the necessary constants into the code. That is prone to errors. Another approach is to build the constants into the speedometer and

```
/* Section 1: Set up enums */
enum cars {potato,
           corn,
           carrot,
           peas};

enum speedometers {abc,
                   vrm,
                   xls};

/* Section 2: Set up tables */
struct speedometerStruct {int units_at_zero;
                          int units_per_ten;
                          boolean support_tach;
                         } speedometerStructs [] =
                       {{ 65, 100, false},  /* ABC */
                        {450, -75,  true},  /* VRM */
                        { 32,  80,  true}}; /* XLS */

struct carStruct {enum speedometers speedometer;
                  boolean fuelComputer;
                 } carStructs [] =
               {{abc, false},  /* Potato */
                {vrm, false},  /* Corn */
                {vrm,  true},  /* Carrot */
                {xls,  true}}; /* Peas */

/* Section 3: Get specific details for this car model */
enum cars car = getCarModel(); /* What car is this controller installed on? */
int uaz = speedometerStructs[carStructs[car].speedometer].units_at_zero;
int upt = speedometerStructs[carStructs[car].speedometer].units_per_ten;

/* Section 4: Get the current speed, calculate the stepper motor value,
   and set the stepper motor */
int speed = getCurrentSpeed();
stepperValue = speed * upt / 10 + uaz;
setSpeedometerStepper (stepperValue);
```

Listing 6.6:
Run-time support for dashboard.

have the code query the speedometer to get the values. This way, no matter which (old or new) speedometer is plugged in, the code can adapt.

While it might not be needed in this speedometer example, it might be useful in situations where there might be slight variations from unit to unit. Instead of it being 65 for units at zero for the ABC speedometer, a calibration might put one unit at 64 and another one at 66. A more precise display of the speed is then available by having hardware provide these constants.

```
int uaz = GetSpeedometerUnitsAtZero();
int upt = GetSpeedometerUnitsPerTen();
stepperValue = speed * upt / 10 + uaz;
setSpeedometerStepper (stepperValue);
```

As can be seen, there are several different ways that one code base can support multiple products and components. They each have their pros and cons. Use the approach that makes the code more maintainable.

> **Embedded Software Best Practice:** use switches so that one embedded software code base can support multiple types and versions of hardware.

The hard part may be to determine what should or should not be a switch. This is something that requires looking back at previous products and/or waiting to see what future products look like. But as support for more products is added, it will be fairly easy to make that determination.

Difficult hardware interactions

This next section will go over some common interactions with hardware that have the potential to be dangerous if not carefully handled. Problems in these areas could result in some very tedious debugging sessions.

Atomic register access

Most registers in a chip are accessed by only one device driver or one thread of execution. A few registers, such as GPIO and global interrupt enable registers, are likely to be modified by more than one thread. Registers, especially those shared by multiple threads, are modified by first reading the current contents of the register, modifying the desired bit, then writing the modified contents back out to the register.

Problems occur when one thread modifying the contents of the register is interrupted by another that also wants to modify the register. Figure 6.3 illustrates this. Thread A reads the register which has 0xBED. Thread A ORs it with 0 × 400, which yields 0xFED. But, before Thread A can write it back out to the register, Thread B interrupts. It reads the register and gets 0xBED. It then ANDs it with ~0 × 040 to get 0xBAD, which it then writes out to the register and then exits. Thread A is allowed to resume; however, its copy of the register is now out of date but it doesn't know that. Its next step is to write its modified, out-of-date copy to the register, which results in overwriting the changes that Thread B made.

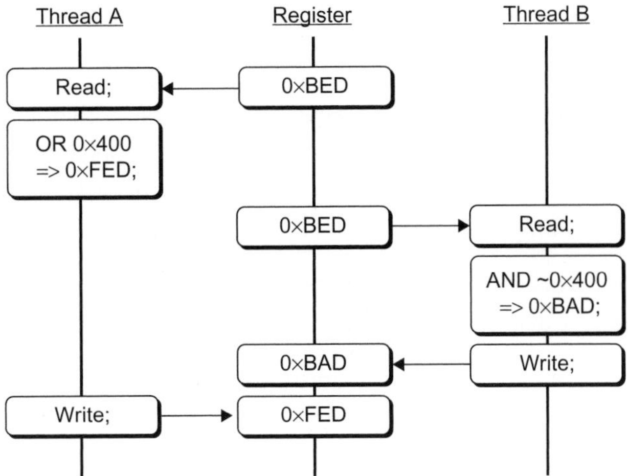

Figure 6.3:
Driver B's changes will be overwritten if it interrupts Thread A mid-task.

This nasty condition is rare. The timing has to be just right for it to happen. But it will happen – eventually. And when it does, the side effect of overwriting the interrupting thread's changes could be widely varied, making it difficult to identify this problem.

There is no safe way to resolve this problem in software. The best way is to temporarily disable interrupts around the read-modify-write portion of the code as seen in Listing 6.7.

Sometimes registers, such as memory-mapped registers, are accessed using pointers as if they were pointing to a regular memory location. The three-line code can then be written as one line, as seen in Listing 6.8.

```
disableInterrupts ();
value = readReg (reg);  // Get the current register settings
value |= 0x400;         // Set the desired bit
writeReg (regA, value); // Write it back out
enableInterrupts ();
```

Listing 6.7:
The best (though not perfect) way software can avoid register overwrites.

```
disableInterrupts ();
*pReg |= 0x400;         // Set the desired bit
enableInterrupts ();
```

Listing 6.8:
Even this one-liner needs to have interrupts disabled.

It is only one line in C but it translates into several assembly language steps, leaving it exposed to being interrupted mid-task.

The problem with this approach is that engineers need to ensure that each and every read-modify-write code for that register has the disable interrupts around it. If one section does not, the system is still exposed, since any other higher-priority section can still interrupt it and make a change that will be overwritten when the first thread resumes.

Semaphores would not work if interrupt service routines are involved because they cannot risk being blocked by a semaphore get() call while servicing the interrupt.

The only foolproof system is to have hardware implement atomic registers. The following is an example of one. Actually it is two register addresses; one (shown as being at address 0x6000) is used to set desired bits and the other (at address 0x6004) is used to clear desired bits. Bits can be set and cleared as desired without having to first read the existing contents or without having to coordinate with any other thread. Either address can be used to read, if desired, to determine what the current contents are.

	MSB	GPIO Output Register – **R/W1S 0x6000, R/W1C 0x6004**						LSB
Bits	31 30 29 28	27 26 25 24	23 22 21 20	19 18 17 16	15 14 13 12	11 10 9 8	7 6 5 4	3 2 1 0
R/W1S	– – – –	– – – –	– – – –	– – – –	– – – –	– – – –	H G F E	D C B A
R/W1C	– – – –	– – – –	– – – –	– – – –	– – – –	– – – –	H G F E	D C B A
Reset	0 0 0 0	0 0 0 0	0 0 0 0	0 0 0 0	0 0 0 0	0 0 0 0	0 0 0 0	0 0 0 0

Hardware Best Practice 8.5.9: Provide atomic access to registers that more than one device driver will access.

Mixed bit types in the same register

There are five types of bits that are commonly used in hardware registers:

- **Read/Write (R/W):** these are common. Software sets and clears the bits by writing 1 s and 0 s to configure the hardware as desired. Software can read these bits to determine their current setting.
- **Read-only (RO):** these are also common. Hardware reports conditions and status. Software can only read these bits, not change them. Writes to them are ignored.
- **Write-only (WO):** these are not common but hardware engineers should avoid implementing them if possible. It is hard for software to verify what it wrote out if it can't read it back. Preferably, hardware engineers should make them R/W bits instead.
- **Interrupt (R/W1C):** hardware sets the bit and software clears it by writing a 1 (W1C = Write 1 Clear). This is commonly used for hardware to report interrupt conditions. Software reads the register to determine which interrupts are pending, then

writes a 1 in one or more of the pending positions to acknowledge (ack) the interrupt. Writing a 0 does nothing. Software can only clear this bit, not set it.

- **Queue (R/W1S):** software sets this bit by writing a 1 (W1S = Write 1 Set). Software uses queue bits to invoke a task in hardware. Hardware will clear the bit at some time before its task is done. Software can read the bit to see if it is still set. Writing a 0 does nothing. Software can only set this bit, not clear it.

A register should only have bits of one type. Mixing types in the same register could create problems for the software engineer if not careful. For example, for R/W bits, software often reads it, modifies the desired bits leaving the other bits unchanged, then writes it back out. For interrupt bits, software often reads it then writes one 1 to ack one interrupt but leaves any other pending bits pending by writing 0 s in all other bit positions.

If R/W bits and interrupt bits are in the same register, then the following could occur. The R/W operation of read-modify-write is dangerous because any pending interrupts (which returned a 1 when read) will be erroneously acked (when writing that 1 back out), thereby losing interrupts. Responding to interrupts will have the software write a 1 in one pending bit position but then writing 0 everywhere else, which would reset any bits in the R/W locations.

Listing 6.9 shows the extra steps necessary to avoid problems with both R/W and Interrupt bits in the same register.

Similar steps are required for other combinations of writeable (not read-only) bits.

```
#define READ_WRITE_BITS 0x0000007F // Which bits are R/W bits
#define INTERRUPT_BITS  0x001F0000 // Which bits are interrupt bits

// Turn on bit 3 in regA
value = readReg (regA);             // Get the current register settings
value &= ~REG_A_INTERRUPT_BITS;     // Ignore any pending interrupts
value |= 0x8;                       // Set bit 3
writeReg (regA, value);             // Write it back out

// Look for any interrupts
value = readReg (regA);             // Get the current register settings
value &= ~REG_A_READ_WRITE_BITS;    // Ignore read/write bits

// Look at value and discover that interrupt 18 is pending
// Ack interrupt 18 but no other interrupt that may be pending while
// leaving the read/write bits unchanged
value = readReg (regA);             // Get the current register settings
value &= ~REG_A_INTERRUPT_BITS;     // Ignore any pending interrupts
value |= 0x40000;                   // Put in a 1 to ack interrupt 18
writeReg (regA, value);             // Ack intr 18, leaving r/w bits the same
```

Listing 6.9:
Extra steps required to handle a register with both R/W bits and interrupt bits.

Hardware Best Practice 8.2.13: Do not mix different writeable bit types in any combination in the same register.

Edge vs. level interrupts

Interrupt modules trigger interrupts in one of two ways, edge or level.

Edge-triggered interrupts are triggered when the interrupt module sees an edge on the incoming signal line, a change from deasserted to the asserted level. Once pending, software can ack the interrupt, making the interrupt no longer pending, even if the incoming signal line is still asserted.

Level-triggered interrupts are those where the interrupt module will trigger an interrupt whenever the incoming signal is asserted. As long as the signal is still asserted, the interrupt cannot be acked. Attempts to do so will simply re-trigger the interrupt. The software must first get the incoming signal to clear before it can ack the interrupt. Some incoming signals last very briefly so that no additional action is required by the software before it acks the interrupt. But others might require software to take some additional action, such as clear a buffer or an error condition, before the interrupt can be acked.

Level-triggered interrupts are more difficult to deal with because of the requirement to clear the incoming signal first. So, ideally, hardware does not implement level-triggered interrupts, only edge-triggered interrupts.

Hardware Best Practice 9.1.9: Make the interrupt module edge triggered.

Testing and troubleshooting

Most of the time during development is spent on the assumption that things will work. Just some of the time is spent in handling error conditions. Testing that is done early will only be on simulated or incomplete platforms. But when near-final embedded software is put on near-final hardware, the tough stuff starts because it is hard to ensure that every aspect gets tested.

An important part of embedded software is to have the ability to conduct some tests and do some troubleshooting in a system with very little debugging hardware attached. The most we had attached during this stage on our LaserJet printers was an RS-232 port. But it gave us a view into the inner activities of the printer. We used this extensively.

Temporary hooks

Ideally the embedded software should be tested for proper handling of any of hardware's possible behavior. Testing normal behavior is easy. But getting the hardware to pretend that some anomaly has occurred can be tricky if not impossible.

In order to test for proper response by the embedded software, add a temporary hook to simulate unusual hardware conditions. For example, in the routine that reads hardware's current status, do so normally but then on the tenth time through the loop, modify the value returned from hardware by turning on some error bits, or, in other words, add a temporary hook which will replace hardware's real response with a pretend response that indicates the rare condition. Then you can observe whether the software is responding properly.
The following is a list of potential things to test for with temporary hooks:

- Overflow and underflow conditions by incrementing or decrementing counts by one.
- Put the block in an illegal configuration and test for proper response.
- Replace incoming data packets with bad ones to simulate various error conditions.
- Artificially insert delays to add stress to the system.

Embedded Software Best Practice: Put in temporary test hooks to unit test the device driver for difficult test cases, such as rare error conditions reported by the block.

It is okay that temporary hooks mess up the system and maybe even crash it. The object is to test something for proper behavior. Once the section being tested has passed, then it does not matter what happens to the system. For example, testing for stack underflow conditions may result in hanging the system because it was shorted something and it is still waiting.

Be careful, though, to ensure that all temporary hooks added that cause bad behavior to occur get removed before shipping the final product. Using techniques such as `#if TEMPORARY_CODE` or `/* TEMPORARY CODE Please Remove */` will help make the temporary code easy to find.

Embedded Software Best Practice: Mark all temporary hooks in code so that it can be easily found for removal.

Permanent hooks

Temporary hooks that perturb the system should come out. But there are some testing and debugging hooks that should stay in permanently. Probably the most powerful tool I had for troubleshooting LaserJet problems was the permanent hooks in the code.

Permanent hooks should be very light on resources and unobtrusive while running in normal operation. But if invoked, the permanent hooks could put a load on the system, potentially causing it to fail. The following are some ideas for permanent hooks:

- Log the last few data packets in a ring buffer that can be dumped to the debugger.
- Log the last few interrupts in a ring buffer.
- Log the order of events from the block, the application, and any other sources.

- Break into and dump any ring buffers, the software's variables and structures, and the current state of the registers in that respective block.
- Ability to poke values in hardware registers.

My permanent hooks were used extensively even months after my device driver was stable because they kept catching other system-level problems from other modules in the system.

> **Embedded Software Best Practice:** Design debugging hooks into the device driver, such as an interrupt and event log, an ability to query software variables, and to peek and poke hardware registers.

Conclusion

The most important concept from this chapter is collaboration with the hardware team. If you remember nothing else from this chapter work closely with the hardware team and many of these issues will be addressed.

I outlined a few hardware design concepts that help the embedded software engineers in their coding and encouraged the software engineers to visit with their respective hardware engineers about adding these features. I gave examples on how one version of embedded software could support multiple versions of hardware and components, and how that makes the code easier to keep current with new features and bug fixes. I also discussed difficult hardware interactions to watch out for and some tips on testing and troubleshooting problems.

Best practices

Again, the Hardware Best Practices listed in this chapter are some of 300 best practices that come from the book *Hardware/Firmware Interface Design: Best Practices for Improving Embedded Systems Development*. Many concepts in this chapter are discussed at length in that book. A spreadsheet of the 300 best practices from the Hardware/Firmware Interface book is available to purchasers of this software engineering book.

CHAPTER 7

Embedded Software Programming and Implementation Guidelines

Mark Kraeling

Chapter Outline

Software Engineering for Embedded Systems.
DOI: http://dx.doi.org/10.1016/B978-0-12-415917-4.00007-4
© 2013 Elsevier Inc. All rights reserved.

Introduction

For software programming and implementation guidelines, many things come to mind. The first could be syntax-oriented; how the code looks and is written. The second could be rules that programmers must follow, in order to keep the code "cleaner". The ways that software is written and how it is formatted can bring about heated arguments between developers. This chapter is not written to provide a specific way of implementing software, but instead focuses on recommendations – so that a determination can be made on whether they are incorporated or not. There isn't a single answer to how software is implemented, because of the many factors involved.

The first factor is project size. Time and time again there are arguments around project structure, use of global variables, and other factors. There are a lot of implementation guidelines that are largely dependent on how large (in source lines of code, for instance) the project is. Having 30 software engineers embark on an activity to use nothing but assembly language, using cryptic variable names, all in the same 8-bit processor space doesn't seem fruitful. Take that same project, and have two software engineers working on it seems a little more reasonable! Keeping project size in mind is important when reading over these guidelines.

The second factor is programmers' experience and background. Hopefully there is a degree of freedom to tailor some of the implementation guidelines based on what the members of the team can do well, and not so well. It's quite possible that your team may be made up of people who moved over from another project, or even another company/division. There may be implementation guidelines and standards that that group is comfortable doing – and provide benefit to the rest of the team. Don't fall into the trap of believing "that is the way it has always been done, keep doing it". An assessment of the way programming and implementation is being done is healthy – if it is done at the right time. Trying to change course in the middle of a project delivery isn't that time – at the beginning or in between major releases may be more appropriate.

The third factor is future maintainability and project length. The shorter the duration of the project, or if maintainability is not a key factor, then maybe a great deal of effort isn't put into project structure and commenting. Don't misunderstand – having useful comments in code is always good for reviewers and even to jog your own memory after a weekend! But after reading some of the guidelines that are suggested here – temper some of them if the project is one programmer putting together code for a project that lasts a month.

There are other factors as well, including safety-critical code development, software that is being sold as software for others to use in their product, and industry regulations for your product or market segment. All of these influence (or even can dictate) the implementation of software for your product.

Principles of high-quality programming

The implementation guidelines in this chapter are derived to drive higher-quality programming on embedded systems. Embedded systems by their very nature are products or systems where the computer processing portion isn't necessarily evident to the user. Because of this, end-customer quality assessment is not directly software, but could be the performance characteristics of the system itself. In this way, quality can be measured in a variety of different ways.

Readability

Readability in software programming can be defined by the ease with which the software is read and understood. Readability of software can be somewhat objective. Programmers who are "journeymen" and move from one project to another throughout their career tend to have an easier time reading a variety of software code. However, making software more readable helps in reviewing and maintaining it over the course of its life. Simplicity in logic, conditional statements, and the structure of the code all help with readability.

The following is an example of a proper "C" code segment, that isn't entirely readable:

```
// Check for stuff to proceed
if((!((Engine_Speed!=0)||(Vehicle_Speed!=0))) ||
SecureTest!=FALSE ){

  // ABC...

}
```

With a little better readability, the same conditional can be written as:

```
// Check for secure testing to be running, or if vehicle is stopped
//  along with the engine not running. Then we can execute <ABC>
if (( Secure_Test == TRUE ) ||    \

   (( Vehicle_Speed == 0 ) && ( Engine_Speed == 0 )))

{

  // ABC...

}
```

Maintainability

Maintaining the code after it is written is a task that can become extremely difficult. Often, the code just doesn't make sense to others who look at it. This can lead to incorrect interpretation, so even though a new feature goes into the code the existing code around it breaks. Another thing that can happen is if someone besides the author comes into the code to make a change; if he doesn't understand the existing structure then another "if" condition could get placed at the bottom of the code just to avoid making any changes to the top part of the code.

Consider using descriptive comments in the code for the "intent" of what is being done. Much later when the code is being updated, where the maintainer doesn't have a solid reference of the structure of the code, the comments can help clarify its overall purpose. For example, a comment of "Reset timer because if we are here we have received a properly formatted, CRC-checked, ping request message" is much better than "Set timer to 10 seconds".

Testability

One of the key components for writing good software components is writing software with testability in mind. For unit testing, or debugging of code, it is important to be able to test each executable line or test each path the software could take. Combining executable lines within conditional statements is not a good idea. If an equate or math operation occurs within an if evaluation, portions of it will not be testable. It is better to do that operation before the evaluation. This allows a programmer to set up a unit test case or modify memory while stepping through to allow a variety of options in choosing with path to take.

Consider the following code segment:

```
if ( GetEngineSpeed()>700 )
{

   // Execute All Speed Governor code

}
```

For high-level source code debugging, it would not be immediately clear what the engine speed was while debugging. The tester could analyze the particular register being used for the return value, but it certainly is not readily apparent. Re-writing the code to use a local variable allows the variable to be placed into a watch window or other source analysis window. The code could be re-written as follows:

```
current_engine_speed = GetEngineSpeed();
if ( current_engine_speed>700 )
{

   // Execute All Speed Governor code

}
```

One argument for this could be program efficiency. This was certainly true years ago when embedded compilers were not very efficient in taking high-level source code and translating it to machine instructions. Now, with compiler optimizers written to look for optimizations through multiple passes through the code, most of these opportunities have been taken care of.

What sets embedded apart from general programming

The easiest way to evaluate what sets embedded apart from general programming is to look at the characteristics of an embedded programmer. The better embedded programmers tend to have a good working knowledge of hardware. They also are very aware of resources they have, where bottlenecks could be in their system, and the speed associated with the various functions they need to perform.

There are varying definitions of what an embedded system is, but my favorite definition is "a system where the presence of a processor is not readily apparent to the user". Because the processor itself is "hidden", an embedded programmer concentrates on a set of performance and system requirements to complete specific tasks. As such, the software itself is just a part of the system, and the rest of the embedded platform around it is important as well.

An embedded software programmer keeps the following items in mind:

1. Resources: every line of code and module that is written is scrutinized for the processing time it takes to execute as well as the amount of other resources (such as memory) that is being used. It becomes more difficult writing a tight embedded system using dynamic allocation languages such as C++ and Java, versus programming languages like C and assembly.
2. Hardware features: software is split between the hardware pieces of the embedded system that can execute them more efficiently as opposed to separating software by a software-only architecture. Interrupts, DMAs, and hardware coprocessors are key components in software design.
3. Performance: an embedded programmer has a keen sense of what the hardware can and cannot do. For processors that do not have floating-point units, mathematical equations and calculations are done using fixed-point math. The programmer also focuses on performing calculations that are native to the atomic size of the processor, so they shy away from doing 32-bit calcuations on a 16-bit processor, for instance.

Starting the embedded software project

One of the easier things to do is actually starting an embedded project, as opposed to inheriting a project that was written a long time ago. Starting a new project is typically an exciting time and programmers are looking forward to starting something new. Promises to not repeat previous evils are recited by the programmers. The software will be done correctly the first time! Depending on how many projects exist or are being kicked off at a particular company, this event may not happen very often.

It is also the easiest and best time to get organized and determine how the software team should develop embedded software. No new source code has been written yet – though there may be libraries or core modules that are going to be pulled into the software baseline. This is the best time to determine how the project is going to be handled, and get buy-in from all of the programmers that this will be the development cycle that will be followed.

It is a lot more difficult to institute new standards or development practices in the middle of a project. If faced with that situation, the best time to make any changes is after some incremental delivery has been made. Changes to standards that try to take place "weeks before software delivery" typically add more confusion and make things worse. Unless there is total anarchy going on, and the project can afford to have everyone stop, come together, and agree upon a new direction, wait until after a major release delivery of some kind before making changes.

The following subsections discuss software items that are discussed and agreed upon as a team (and written down!).

Hardware platform input

Although this particular chapter is dedicated to software programming and implementation guidelines, it is worth mentioning that there should have already been an opportunity to provide input to the hardware developers on software aspects. Items like hardware interrupt request lines, and what they are tied to, to play a key role in the organization and the performance of the embedded software. Also other resource input such as memory size, on-chip vs. off-chip resources, processor being used, and other hardware I/O interfaces are critical to embedded development.

Another key aspect is the debugging interface that the particular processor has. An interface like JTAG may be perfect for hardware checking, but may not have all of the functionality that is available for a software programmer. Many processors (like those based on ARM™ cores) have a JTAG interface but also have a software-centric type of debugging interface using additional lines on the same chip. Bringing those out to a header for software development boards makes debugging and insight into the operation of the software much easier.

Because this chapter focuses on the software programming guidelines, there won't be any more particular discussion on this topic. But make sure that the connection with the hardware developers is made early, or it could be very difficult to follow software implementation guidelines!

Project files/organization

There are three key components that go into project file organization. The first is any dependencies that the project has on the configuration management system being used. Some CM tools prefer directory structures to look a particular way, or make it so the tool can interface better with existing systems. The second component is the compiler/debugger/linker suite that is being used for the project. The directory structure for some of the files (such as libraries) may need to be organized a particular way. The third is the project file organization that the team prefers, or a file organization that is the same as other embedded projects done by the same group or at the same company.

To make things easier for development, there should be a separation between the following items listed here. The most common way to have these separated is by using subdirectories, or separate folders depending on the development environment.

Source files written locally

This directory would contain all of the source files that have been written by your development team. Depending on the number of modules being written or the size of the overall code base, consider further subdividing this into more subdirectories and folders. For multiple processor systems, it may make sense to separate by processor (such as "1" and "2") and then have another directory at the same level that contains files common to both.

An additional way to further subdivide a large source file directory is to subdivide it by functionality. Maybe dividing into major feature groupings such as "display", "serial comm", and "user IO" would make sense. The mark of a good project and directory organization for your source files is the fact that your software falls into a particular category easily without a lot of searching around for it or arguments on whether it belongs one place or another.

Source files from company libraries

This directory would contain either the software or links to the general repository where your company keeps libraries of source files useable by all projects. When doing links, it is important that some sort of control be in place so that new files don't just show up every time the software is built. Version control needs to be kept tight, so there is no unexpected change between the tested and released baseline. Links to a specific version of a file work best. If the files must be physically copied into this directory with no links, it is very important to remember (and have written down) exactly which version was copied. Periodic checking back to the library should be done as well for newer updates or bug fix releases.

The same thing applies with this directory or folder – depending on the number of files being used it may make sense to further break it down into subdirectories or subfolders as well.

Libraries from third parties

There may be libraries that are used by third parties as well. It could also be source code – maybe an operating system or network stack that has been provided for you. It is critically important to have these files in a separate directory from the other source files! Programmers need to know that these files probably shouldn't just be changed, but there could be a tie-off that needs to happen with the software provider. If these are mixed in with the general population of the source files that are written by the software team, there is a larger risk that these could be changed inadvertantly.

There are typically files that are provided by the third parties that are supposed to be changed. These may include definitions or links to pieces in the embedded system. For instance, one common entry is defining the number of tasks for an RTOS. Files that are supposed to be changed should either go in their own subdirectory in this group, or be pulled over into a folder in the source files that your group is writing. Then privileges like "no modify / no write" could possibly be applied to the folder, to make sure that they are not changed.

Libraries from compiler/linker toolset

There may be restrictions on where the libraries that the compiler and linker toolset provider can be located. Typically, these can just be left alone. It needs to be agreed upon by all of the developers which libraries are going to be used up front. The toolset company may include a full C stdlib available for use, or other alternatives like a smaller "micro" library that can be used instead. Tradeoffs between the various libraries should be done, like whether the library allows re-entrant library use, the functionality that is available, and the size of the library when linked in your embedded system.

There also may be options to remove libraries entirely from being used. A common library that we often remove is the floating-point link library. So library functions like a floating-point multiply (fmul) cannot be linked into the system. So if a programmer has a link to this library, it won't link and the mistake can be corrected.

Team programming guidelines

How a team agrees to program the system and the criteria they will use for evaluating other programmers' source code is important to decide up front. If a programmer holds to a higher standard of software development, but it only becomes clear in the first code review after that programmer has already designed and written the code, it is too late. The criteria for how a programmer can successfully pass a code review should be understood up front, so time isn't wasted re-writing and re-unit-testing code.

Guidelines could include a variety of rules or recommendations. The more the guidelines are measureable, the more successful they will be. For example, if there is a guideline for the programmer that "the code is not complex" as one of the criteria, it could be largely subjective to a group of programmers. One may feel it is too complex, another may not. This particular measurement could actually be measureable.

In this example, the group could decide to use a cyclomatic complexity measurement to evaluate a software module. The software is run through a tool, and it produces a complexity number for the module. Higher numbers represent more complex code according to the formula, where lower ones are simpler. With a complexity formula that measures the number of "edges" and "nodes" in your software program, the simplest complexity represented by a value of "1" is a program that contains no "if" or "for" conditions, and has a single entry and exit point. As the number of conditions and flows goes up, the complexity goes up. So the evaluation criteria could change to "the code is not complex, cyclomatic complexity <= 18". This way it is not subjective.

What this is hinting at is a "checklist" of sorts that a programmer could use when writing and preparing his software code for review. Having the list of accepted programming guidelines up front that everyone follows makes expectations clear. The following are examples of items that could be on a "Software Guidelines Checklist" that would be evaluated for each module reviewed:

- Conformance to syntax standard
- Cyclomatic complexity calculation
- Number of source lines per function / per file
- Number of comments
- Ratio of number of source lines per number of comments
- Run through code formatter
- Comment and design document understandability / matches code
- Code under CM control / linked to "change request"
- No compiler warnings
- Rule exceptions properly documented (if warnings ignored or doesn't match standard)
- #pragma directives documented clearly in source code
- Non-constant pointers to functions are not present
- All members of union or struct are fully specified
- Data representation (scale, bits, bit assignments) clearly documented
- Data defined and initialized before being used
- Loop bounds and terminations are correct

- Mathematical operations correct (no divide-by-zero, overflows)
- No deadlocks, priority inversions, re-entrant faults.

Syntax standard

There are a variety of ways that a coding syntax standard can look. A syntax standard defines the way code is spaced, capitalized, and formatted when written into source code. There is a lot of personal preference that can come into using a particular syntax standard for the group. There may also be a mix of syntax rules that a group could incorporate for a project where others are not mandatory, but recommended. This section contains some ideas on how it could look. The most important thing is getting the developers to agree on a given standard and sticking to it throughout. If the project is reusing quite a bit of code, preference should be given to the standard that the existing code uses.

This section has some ideas for how the syntax standard could be developed. There isn't a right or wrong – unless all the developers on a team are all doing something different. This impacts the ability to review the code, or to be able to go in and easily make changes. If the code is developed by all team members using the same syntax, it makes it much easier to change and understand when reviewing.

A full coding syntax standard is available as an appendix in this book. A lot of iteration has gone into this particular standard. The original author, Daniel Moone, specialized in embedded software for control systems and medical devices throughout his career. Others have picked it up and made various changes as well.

The following sections are just some of the syntax-oriented coding standard items that are found in this standard.

Code white space

The following are examples on how various software lines could add white space to increase the readability of the code itself. All of these examples are operationally equivalent – they produce the same machine code. They are listed in order of increasing amounts of white space:

```
int i;
for(i=0;i<20;i++)
{

  printf("%02u",i*2);

}
int i;
for ( i=0; i<20; i++ )
```

```
{
   printf( "%02u", i*2 );
}
int i;
for ( i = 0; i<20; i++ )
{
   printf( "%02u", i * 2 );
}
```

The examples above concern themselves with the white space that is between the various operators and numbers on a given line of source code. Numerous studies indicate that more white space increases readability in software code. This would support using the third example outlined above. However, if the increased amount of whitespace could cause the software to wrap to the next line, then it is clearly too much white space because wrapping is very unreadable.

Tabs in source files

Most syntax standards indicate that tab characters should not be used in source files when writing code. This is because the tab character could be interpreted differently by source editing tools, file viewers, or when it is printed. They are also not readily visible when editing. Source code editors typically provide a way to substitute spaces with the tab character. So while programming, when the tab key is hit, it automatically fills it the tab with x number of spaces.

This brings about an important point. How many spaces should represent a tab key press or a normal indent in source code? Most editors have a substitution for either "3" or "4" spaces per tab. Either is fine – it will be based on some personal preference and also how the rest of the code is formatted. Depending on the spacing that is used for other things, like the "for" loop spacing above, the amount of indent space may align better with what is chosen.

Alignment within source

How things are aligned in source code makes an impact on readability as well. Take into consideration the following two operationally equivalent sections of code:

```
int incubator = RED_MAX; /* Setup for Red Zone */
char marker = '\0'; /* Marker code for zone */

int incubator = RED_MAX /* Setup for Red Zone  */
char marker   = '\0';   /* Marker code for zone */
```

White space is used on the second example, lining up the variable names, initialization values, and comments on the same column for the code block.

The examples above were quick examples on how various code syntaxes with white space could be done. Consistency and readability are key components for writing good embedded software source code.

Safety requirements in source code

When writing safety-critical software, the implementation guidelines for software source code change. Many considerations need to be made when developing this code.

Is all of the code in your system safety-critical? If a system is safety-critical, it may not actually rely on *all* of the code to be safety critical. The system itself needs to have fail-safe operations in place so that things fail to the least permissive case as defined by the system FMEA analysis. There may be operations like logging that are not required to be safety-critical unto themselves, but they cannot cause the safety-critical code in the system to act in an unsafe manner.

Documentation of safety-critical sections of code is important. Special care and consideration should be made to mark these sections differently, or even have comments that refer directly to the safety case or documentation that the code adheres to. Using all capitals such as "SAFETY-CRITICAL CODE SECTION START" in a comment section certainly alerts programmers who may come in to change code later or add new requirements that they should tread lightly in these sections.

Development standards such as "MISRA C" (Motor Industry Software Reliability Association) and "MISRA C++" can also help facilitate writing code that operates in a safe manner. There are many users of the standard outside the automotive and transportation industries, including medical and defense. There are many tools that can check source code for MISRA compliance as well, and can be included as part of the overall software build process. More information on the MISRA standard can be found at http://www.misra.org.uk.

There may be special programming requirements for safety-critical sections of code. There may be a separate development guideline list, which includes things like performing a software FMEA on the safety-critical code section being implemented. There also may be additional reviewers in the code review itself, such as representatives from a safety team or a software engineer who specializes in safety-critical code development.

The following are additional factors or checklist items that could be considered as part of safety-critical code development:

- Adherence and checking to a standard, such as MISRA C or C++
- Safety sections clearly marked to standard
- Data that is safety-critical is marked that way in the variable name
- All safety-critical variables are initialized to the least permissive state
- Any safety-critical data is clearly marked as stale and/or deleted after use
- Comparisons between safety-critical data are handled correctly
- All paths are covered when variables are used for path decision-making
- Checks are in place to make sure safety-critical code is executed on-time
- Periodic flash and RAM checks are done to check hardware correctness
- Safety-critical data is protected by regular CRC or data integrity checks
- "Voting" mechanisms between software and processors is done correctly
- Safety dependencies on functions (like watchdog timer) are checked periodically for correct operation.

More details on safety-critical software development are outlined in Chapter 19, Safety-critical software development.

Variable structure

Variable declarations

One of the key components for developing an embedded software system is determining how the data in the system will be declared and used. In order to discuss each type of variable declaration, it is probably best to break it down by type. The three primary types of variables in a system are global variables, file-scope variables, and function-scope variables.

Global variables

Global variables are variables that are visible to any linked component of the system in a single build. They could be declared at the top of a source file, but could also be present in header files where the variable is declared in one spot, and then made available as an extern to any other file that includes that header file. There certainly is an entire philosophy with global variables – some programmers hate them and software leads can ban them.

There are differing opinions on the usage of global variables. Programmers can define a correct and "right" way to use them, as long as they don't help foster the creation of unorganized (spaghetti) code. There are a couple of guidelines that could be used to allow global variables into your system, as it will typically help increase the performance of the system without using access functions to modify encapsulated local data.

The first is to declare the variable in a header file. Anyone who includes the header file would then have access to the variable, but it also helps make sure that if the global was declared as an unsigned integer then all of the extern references match. The header file (ip.h) would look something like this:

```
#ifdef IP_C
  #define EXT
#else
  #define EXT extern
#endif

EXT uint16_t IP_Movement_En
EXT uint16_t IP_Direction_Ctrl
#undef EXT
```

The example above would need each of the source files to declare a definition of their "filename_C" in order for the variable to be declared. The source file (ip.c) would look like this:

```
#define IP_C
#include "ip.h"
#undef IP_C
#include ... /* Rest of the include files needed by the source file */
```

By declaring the variable in a header file, the type will be correct and there will also be a good start in who might be looking at this variable by seeing who is including the header file. Using this type of method could also allow the team to dictate that no global variables are declared in source files – they would only be declared in this manner.

The second recommendation for using global variables is to always prefix the name with the "owner" of the variable itself. In the example above, IP stands for "Input Processing". So any variable used with global scope of IP_xxx is a variable declared in the input processing header. That helps by not having a bunch of random names floating around for variables.

The third recommendation that would help make global variable usage easier links nicely with the second recommendation above. After a global variable is declared in a header file, the only program that could modify that variable would be an input processing source file, such as "ip.c". Other source files would have "read" access to that variable, but not be allowed to change the value. Of course the compiler would allow the programmer to change it – but if this was a rule the project team wanted to use it would be easy to find in a code review. Any instance of a variable prefixed with the "ownership" shouldn't be modified by another program. Consider the source lines below in output processing (op.c):

```
if ( IP_Movement_En = = TRUE )
{
  if (( IP_Direction_Ctrl = = IP_FORWARD ) ||
    ( IP_Direction_Ctrl = = IP_REVERSE ))
  {
  OP_Display_Movement = TRUE;
  IP_Display_Shown = TRUE;  /* Unacceptable... */
  }
  else
  {
    OP_Display_Movement = FALSE;
  }
}
```

In the example above, we definitely do not want to be modifying an input processing variable following the third recommendation. This hopefully would be easy to see during a code inspection or review. Instead, consider having input processing figure this out by looking at the variable OP_Display_Movement. If this cannot be done, then a function call from here to an input processing function and having that function change IP_Display_Shown could work. For debugging purposes, and to try and keep the code organized, having a rule like this in place can make global variables a lot cleaner.

The final recommendation for global variables, in addition to showing "ownership" of the variable by prefixing the source file indicator, is to capitalize each letter in the variable name. This would be further indication that the variable is a global variable, and could be getting read multiple places so changes to meaning, scaling, or size could have a ripple effect throughout the system.

File scope variables

File scope variables are used to share data between multiple functions in a single source file. They are definitely easier to use than global variables, because typically there is a single owner in a particular source file, at least when it is initially written. File scope variables make it easy to share data between functions, without having to pass them as arguments between them on the stack.

A key recommendation is to keep the keyword "static" in front of each of the file scope variable being declared. This keeps them from being used by other files, and keeps it local. One particular issue with this is visibility into the map (or possibly even debugger) file. For compilers, if a variable is declared in a file without visibility to other files, there isn't a need to put a reference to it for linking. Sometimes it is nice to be able to see that variable during source line debugging or peeking at memory while the system is running.

In order to give that variable visibility during debugging, consider declaring the file scope variables in the following way in a source file:

```
STATIC uint32_t IP_time_count;
STATIC uint16_t IP_direction_override;
```

This "STATIC" definition would then reside in one of the "master" header files in your system. Further discussion of this type of header file is under Data Types on the next page. When compiling the debugger version of your code, the programmer can define a keyword "DEBUG" for those source files, and when it is time to release the code the keyword "DEBUG" is not defined. This is particularly useful if there are special setup steps that need to be done (like turning on a debug function on the microcontroller at initialization). With this type of setup, the following lines would appear in the common header file:

```
#ifdef DEBUG PROBABLY WANT TO CHECK FOR NOT STATIC TOO, CHECK

  #define STATIC

#else

  #define STATIC static

#endif
```

Another recommendation for file scope variables is also use of capitalization and lower case. Consider prefixing all of the file scope variables with the same "filename" or feature set indicator on the front, and then make all of the other letters lower case. In this way, it will be easy to discern between a global variable and a file scope variable.

Local variables

Local variables have the easiest recommendations of all types. The first recommendation is to drop the prefix mentioned in the previous two sections, because it is clear that it is just a variable for the function. Second, with the use of decent comments, the variable names for local variables really do not need to be overly descriptive. In my opinion, it is all right to have variable names of n, i, j, etc., when using them to index arrays and loop variables. Even a simple variable like "count" is OK – again if there are comments to let an observer know what the function is trying to do.

The other type of local variable in a function is one with the keyword "static" in front of it. These are used when a variable needs to retain the data through multiple calls of the function, but it is not shared by any of the other functions in a file.

For local variables, consider keeping them as all lower case. In the case of a "static" variable declared in a function, consider capitalizing the first character. In that way, when looking through the function or maintaining it later, it is clear that the variable retains its value. The following is an example of how function local variables could look:

```
static void ip_count_iterations( void )
{

   uint16_t     i, j, n;

   static uint16_t Error_count_exec = 0;

   uint32_t     *reference_ptr;

   ...
```

Data types

One of the key attributes for embedded systems is resource management. In the preceding sections, the declarations that were made were using type definitions. In order to keep an embedded system portable to other processors, and to keep resources in check, type definitions could be used for the various data types. The following is a list of type definitions that could be declared in a master header file, which would be included by all source files.

Consider a file called "portable.h" which is included by the source files:

```
typedef unsigned char      uint8_t;
typedef unsigned short int uint16_t;
typedef unsigned long int  uint32_t;
typedef signed char        int8_t;
typedef signed short int   int16_t;
typedef signed long int    int32_t;
```

Because an "integer" size is dependent on the microcontroller architecture size, the programmer can use the type definitions above and then only change this file if porting to a different platform. Library templates could also be written using the type definitions above, so that when they are pulled in and used on any platform they work correctly.

Another variation of the same concept above is to shorten the type definitions, to save some white space when writing the source files. A variation of the definitions above is shown below:

```
typedef unsigned char       UINT8;
typedef unsigned short int UINT16;
typedef unsigned long int UINT32;
typedef signed char        INT8;
typedef signed short int  INT16;
typedef signed long int  INT32;
```

Building on the same naming convention, when structures are declared consider adding a suffix of "_t" to show it is a type definition. An example of a structure declaration is shown below:

```
#define DIO_MEM_DATA_BLOCKS 64
typedef struct
{

  UINT16 block_write_id;

  UINT16 block_write_words;

  UINT16 data[DIO_MEM_DATA_BLOCKS];

  UINT16 block_read_id;

  UINT16 startup_sync1;

  UINT16 startup_sync2;

} DIO_Mem_Block_t;
```

Following the same convention, a union type definition is shown below:

```
typedef union
{

  UINT16 value;

  struct

  {

    UINT16  data:15;

    UINT16  header_flag :1;

  } bits;

} DIO_FIFO_Data;
```

For the struct and union examples above, type definitions are used for the data sizes as discussed above. Spacing and white space are really up to the programmers, but having them maintained uniformly across all source files adds to the maintainability.

Another thing to notice is that the type definitions above are prefixed with "DIO_" and then contain a mix of capital and lowercase letters. This is definitely a stylistic choice, but one thought process is to have type definitions in header files be declared this way, and then have file scope type definitions be all lower case, without the need for the prefix. As discussed in Section 3.2, this can help a reviewer understand if the structure is something that may be global in scope or just local.

Definitions

Conditional compilation

Another topic of developing embedded software is the use of conditional compiles in the source code. Conditional compiles allow a compiler to dictate which code is compiled and which code is skipped. There are many books written for software engineering that suggest that conditional compiles should not be used in the code.

For hardware-oriented code that is written to work on multiple processors in a system, there may be conditional compiles to specify "Processor A" vs. "Processor B". For software source code, if more than 15% of the source code has conditional compiles in it, consideration should be given to splitting the code up, keeping the common code in one file and separating the reason for the conditional compiles between two (or more) files. As the

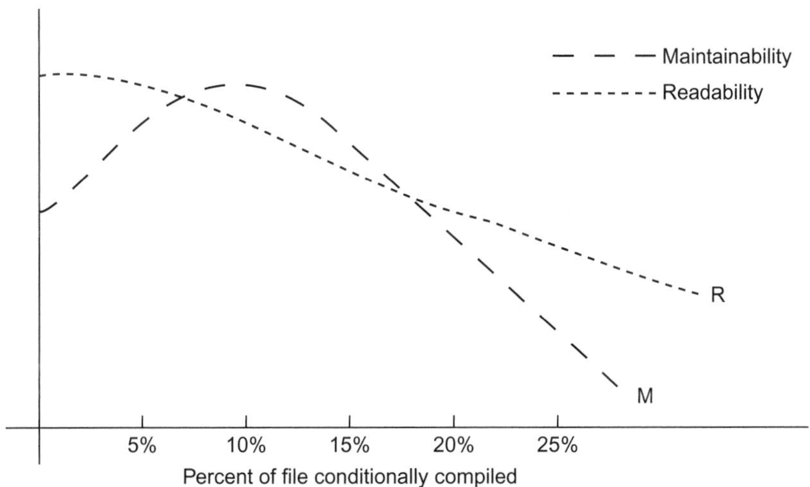

Figure 7.1:
Conditional Compilation Graph.

number of conditional compiles increases the readability decreases. Files with minimal conditional compiles are likely easier to maintain than a file that has been branched or separated, but again as the number of conditional compiles increases past 15% the maintainability drops as well. Consider the following graph for conditional compiles.

Consider the following source code section for a module written to run on two processors specified as PROCA and PROCB. Depending on which makefile is selected, the compiler defines one of these two values depending on the processor target.

```
  frame_idle_usec = API_Get_Time();

#ifdef PROCA

  /* Only send data when running on processor B */

  ICH_Send_Data( ICH_DATA_CHK_SIZE, (uint32_t *)&frame_idle_usec );

#else
#ifdef PROCB

  /* Nothing to send with processor B in this situation */

#else

  /* Let's make sure if we ever add a PROCC, that we get error */

  DoNotLink();

#endif /* PROCA */
#endif /* PROCB */
```

There is one additional thing to note with the code above. In this example, we simply did not just look for processor A and then do nothing if we weren't processor A. There is an else condition, so that if we ever run on a processor besides A or B a made-up function "DoNotLink()" will be called, which will result in a compiler warning and a linker error (the function doesn't exist). In this way, if another processor is added in the future it will force the software engineer to take a look at this code to see if a special case should be added for this new processor. It is simply a defensive technique to catch the various conditional compiles that may exist in the source code baseline.

#define

A commonly used symbolic constant or preprocessor macro in C or C++ coding is implemented using the `#define`.

Symbolic constants allow the programmer to use a particular naming convention for values. When used as a constant, it can allow better definition, as opposed to "magic numbers" that are placed throughout the code. It allows the programmer either to create a common set of frequently used definitions in a single location, or to create more singular instances to help code readability.

Consider the following code segment:

```
// Check for engine speed above 700 RPM
if ( engine_speed > 5600 )
{
```

The code segment checks for a value of 5600. But where does this come from? The following is a slightly more readable version of this code segment:

```
// Check for engine speed above 700 RPM
if ( engine_speed > (700 * ENG_SPD_SCALE ))
{
```

This is a little better as it uses a symbolic constant for the fixed-point scaling of engine speed, which is used throughout the software code baseline. There certainly should not be multiple definitions of this particular value, such as having ENGINE_SPEED_SCALE and ENG_SPD_SCALE both used in the same code baseline. This can lead to confusion, or incompatibility if only one of these scalar values is changed. The code segment above also has "700" being used. What if there are other places in the code where this value is used? What is this value? The following code segment is more maintainable and readable:

```
// Check for speed where we need to transition from low-speed to all-//  speed governor
if ( engine_speed > LSG_TO_ASG_TRANS_RPM )
{
```

A `#define` would be placed in a header file for engine speed for visibility to multiple files, or in the header of this source file if it is only used in a file-scope scenario. The `#define` would appear as:

```
// Transition from low-speed to all-speed governor in RPM
#define LSG_TO_ASG_TRANS_RPM (UINT16)( 700 * ENG_SPD_SCALE )
```

This has the additional cast of UINT16 to make sure that the symbolic constant is a fixed-point value so floating-point evaluations are not made in the code. This would be important if the transition speed was defined as 700.5 RPM, or even if a value of 700.0 was used as the transitional speed. Once floating-point values appear in the code, the compiler tends to keep any comparisons or evaluation using floating-point operations.

Preprocessor macros allow the programmer to develop formulas commonly used throughout the code and define them in a single location. Consider the following code segment:

```
Area1 = 3.14159 * radius1 * radius1;
Area2 = 3.14159 * (diameter2 / 2) * (diameter2 / 2);
```

The code listed above can be improved by creating a preprocessor macro that calculates the circular area as opposed to listing it in the code. Another improvement is using a symbolic constant for PI so that the code can use the same value throughout. That way if additional decimal places are used, it can be changed in one location. The following could be defined at the top of the source file, or in a common header file:

```
#define PI 3.14159
#define AREA_OF_CIRCLE(x)   PI*(x)*(x)
```

The code could then use this preprocessor macro as follows:

```
Area1 = AREA_OF_CIRCLE(radius1);
Area2 = AREA_OF_CIRCLE(diameter2 / 2);
```

The code segments shown above could be used for a higher-end microcontroller that has floating-point hardware, or for a processor where floating-point libraries are acceptable. Another implementation could be in fixed-point, where tables would approximate PI values so that native fixed-point code could speed up processing times.

CHAPTER 8

Embedded Operating Systems

Jean J. Labrosse

Chapter Outline

Software Engineering for Embedded Systems.
DOI: http://dx.doi.org/10.1016/B978-0-12-415917-4.00008-6
© 2013 Elsevier Inc. All rights reserved.

Real-time systems are systems whereby the correctness of the computed values and their timeliness are at the forefront. There are two types of real-time systems, hard and soft real time.

What differentiates hard and soft real-time systems is their tolerance to missing deadlines and the consequences associated with those misses. Correctly computed values after a deadline has passed are often useless.

For hard real-time systems, missing deadlines is not an option. In fact, in many cases, missing a deadline often results in loss of assets and worse yet, loss of lives. For soft real-time systems, however, missing deadlines is generally not as critical. For example, updating a display every 200 ms might not be critical (i.e., whether it's 200 ms or 250 ms may not matter).

Real-time applications cover a wide range, but many real-time systems are embedded. An embedded system is a computer built into a system and typically dedicated to a single use; in other words, systems that are designed to perform a dedicated function. The following list shows just a few examples of embedded systems:

- Audio
  - MP3 players
  - Amplifiers and tuners
- Automotive
  - Antilock braking systems
  - Climate control
  - Engine controls
  - Navigation systems (GPS)
- Avionics
  - Flight management systems
  - Jet engine controls
  - Weapons systems
- Office automation
  - FAX machines / copiers

- Home automation
  - Air conditioning units
  - Thermostats
  - White goods
- Communications
  - Routers
  - Switches
  - Cell phones
- Process control
  - Chemical plants
  - Factory automation
  - Food processing
- Agriculture
  - Round balers
  - Square balers
  - Windrowers
  - Combines
- Video
  - Broadcasting equipment
  - HD televisions.

Real-time systems are typically more complicated to design, debug, and deploy than non-real-time systems.

Foreground/background systems

Small systems of low complexity are typically designed as foreground/background systems or super-loops as shown in Figure 8.1. An application consists of an infinite loop that calls modules (i.e., tasks) to perform the desired operations (background). Interrupt service routines (ISRs) handle asynchronous events (foreground). Foreground is also called interrupt level; background is called task level. Interrupts allow a microprocessor to process events when they occur (i.e., asynchronously), which prevents the microprocessor from continuously *polling* (looking at) an event to see if it occurred.

Critical operations that should be performed at the task level must unfortunately be handled by the ISRs to ensure that they are dealt with in a timely fashion. This causes ISRs to take longer than they should. Will that affect the responsiveness of other ISRs? How much work must the ISR do? Will this make the ISR more difficult to debug?

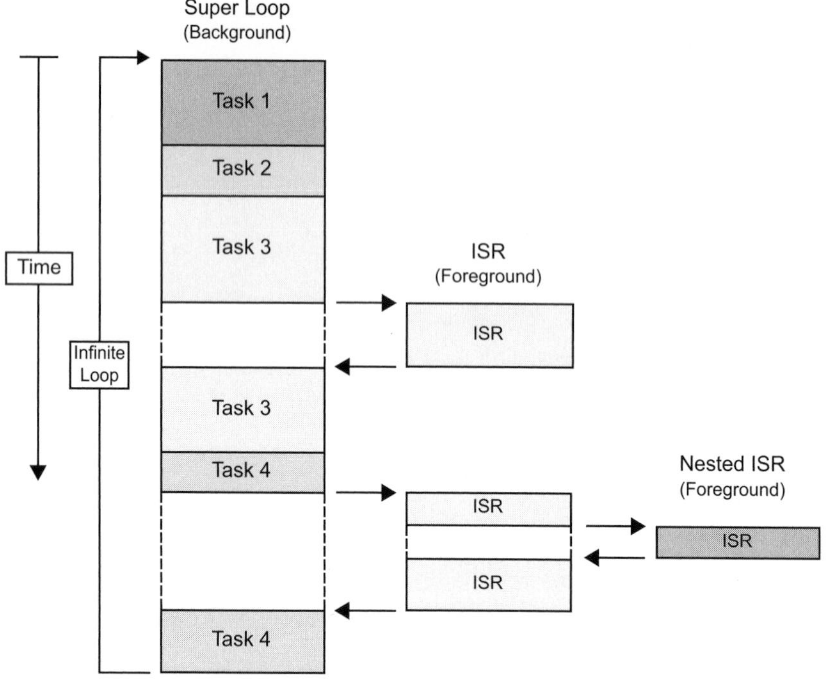

Figure 8.1:
Foreground/background systems.

However, if you defer the work to be done to the background, that work will not be processed until the background routine gets its turn to execute, which is called the task-level response. The worst-case task-level response time depends on how long a background loop takes to execute and, since the execution time of typical code is not constant, the time for successive passes through a portion of the loop is nondeterministic. Furthermore, if a code change is made, the timing of the loop is affected.

Most high-volume and low-cost microcontroller-based applications (e.g., microwave ovens, telephones, toys, etc.) are designed as foreground/background systems.

Real-time kernels

A real-time kernel (or simply kernel) is software (potentially with hardware privileges) that manages the time and resources of a microprocessor, microcontroller or digital signal processor (DSP). Through functions provided by the kernel, you basically split the work of the processor into tasks, each responsible for a portion of the job. A task (also called a thread) is a simple program that thinks it has the central processing unit (CPU) completely to itself. On a single CPU, only one task can execute at any given time.

The main function of the kernel is the management of tasks and is called *multitasking*. Multitasking is the process of scheduling and switching the CPU between several tasks. The CPU switches its attention between several sequential tasks. Multitasking provides the illusion of having multiple CPUs and maximizes the use of the CPU. Multitasking also helps in the creation of modular applications. One of the most important aspects of multitasking is that it allows the application programmer to manage the complexity inherent in real-time applications. Application programs are easier to design and maintain when multitasking is used.

Most real-time kernels are preemptive, which means that the kernel always runs the most important task that is ready-to-run as shown in Figure 8.2.

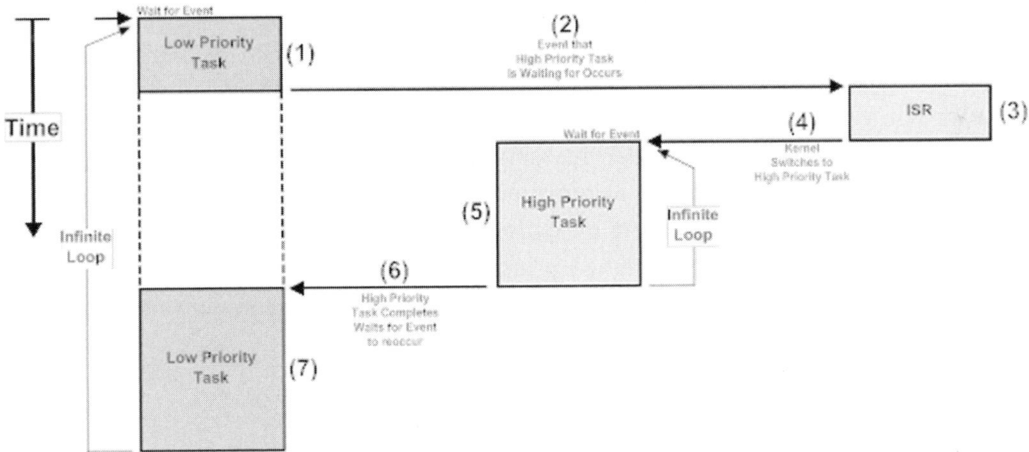

Figure 8.2:
Preemptive kernels.

1. A low-priority task is executing.
2. An interrupt occurs, and the CPU vectors to the ISR responsible for servicing the interrupting device.
3. The ISR services the interrupt device, but actually does very little work. The ISR will typically signal or send a message to a higher-priority task that will be responsible for most of the processing of the interrupting device. For example, if the interrupt comes from an Ethernet controller, the ISR simply signals a task, which will process the received packet.
4. When the ISR finishes, the kernel notices that a more important task has been made ready-to-run by the ISR and will not return to the interrupted task, but instead context switch to the more important task.

5. The higher-priority task executes and performs the necessary processing in response to the interrupt device.
6. When the higher-priority task completes its work, it loops back to the beginning of the task code and makes a kernel function call to wait for the next interrupt from the device.
7. The low-priority task resumes exactly at the point where it was interrupted, not knowing what happened.

Kernels are also responsible for managing communication between tasks, and managing system resources (memory and I/O devices).

A kernel adds overhead to a system because the services provided by the kernel require time to execute. The amount of overhead depends on how often these services are invoked. In a well-designed application, a kernel uses between 2% and 4% of a CPU's time. And, since a kernel is software that is added to an application, it requires extra ROM (code space) and RAM (data space). However, in return for this small amount of overhead, you get better determinism, you can break you application into smaller, more manageable pieces, it's a lot easier to reassign priorities in software than in hardware (even dynamically adjust priorities at run-time), your code is much more portable, you gain better control of the application by letting the kernel dynamically decide when each task should run (based on assigned priorities), and more. In fact, adding low-priority tasks will generally not affect the responsiveness of your system to high-priority ones.

RTOS (real-time operating system)

A real-time operating system generally contains a real-time kernel and other higher-level services such as file management, protocol stacks, a graphical user interface (GUI), and other components. Most of the additional services revolve around I/O devices.

Critical sections

A critical section of code, also called a *critical region*, is code that needs to be treated indivisibly. For example, modifying a software time-of-day clock requires that you update seconds, minutes, hours without interruption by ISRs or other tasks. There are many critical sections of code contained in typical kernels. If a critical section is accessible by an interrupt service routine (ISR) and a task, then disabling interrupts is necessary to protect the critical region. If the critical section is only accessible by task-level code, the critical section may be protected through the use of a *preemption lock*.

Task management

The design process of a real-time application generally involves splitting the work to be completed into tasks, each responsible for a portion of the problem. Kernels make it easy for an application programmer to adopt this paradigm. A task (also called a *thread*) is a program that thinks it has the central processing unit (CPU) all to itself. On a single CPU, only one task can execute at any given time.

Most kernels support multitasking and allow the application to have any number of tasks. The maximum number of tasks is actually only limited by the amount of memory (both code and data space) available to the processor. Of course, there is potentially a limit to just how much work can be accomplished by the selected processor and it's possible that an underpowered processor could prevent your lowest-priority tasks to run. This is called *starvation*. Multitasking is the process of *scheduling* and *switching* the CPU between several tasks (this will be expanded upon later). The CPU switches its attention between several *sequential* tasks. Multitasking provides the illusion of having multiple CPUs and actually maximizes the use of the CPU. Multitasking also helps in the creation of modular applications. One of the most important aspects of multitasking is that it allows the application programmer to manage the complexity inherent in real-time applications. Application programs are typically easier to design and maintain when multitasking is used.

Tasks must be created in order for the kernel to know about your tasks. You create a task by calling one of the kernel's services (something like `OSTaskCreate()`) and you specify as arguments to the function call:

1. The start address of the task. In C, this is the name of the function that makes up the task code.
2. The priority of the task based on the relative importance of the task.
3. The stack space and its size that will be used by the task. In a multitasking environment, each task requires its own stack space.
4. There are possibly other parameters specific to the task that could be specified. These greatly depend on the kernel implementation but the above three elements are a minimum.

When a task is created, it is assigned what's called a *Task Control Block* or *TCB*. The TCB is used to hold run-time information about your task. The TCB is managed by the kernel and the user of the kernel generally doesn't need to worry about this data structure.

A task can access variables, data structures or tables that it either owns or shares with other tasks. If these are shared then the application programmer needs to ensure that the task has exclusive access to these variables, data structures or tables. Fortunately, the kernel provides services that allow you to protect such shared resources. These are discussed later.

A task can also access I/O devices which, again, it can own or share with other tasks. As expected, services are available from the kernel to ensure exclusive access to these I/O devices.

Figure 8.3 shows the elements that a task can interact with. You should note that the stack is managed by the compiler (function calls, local variables, etc.) and the TCB is managed by the kernel.

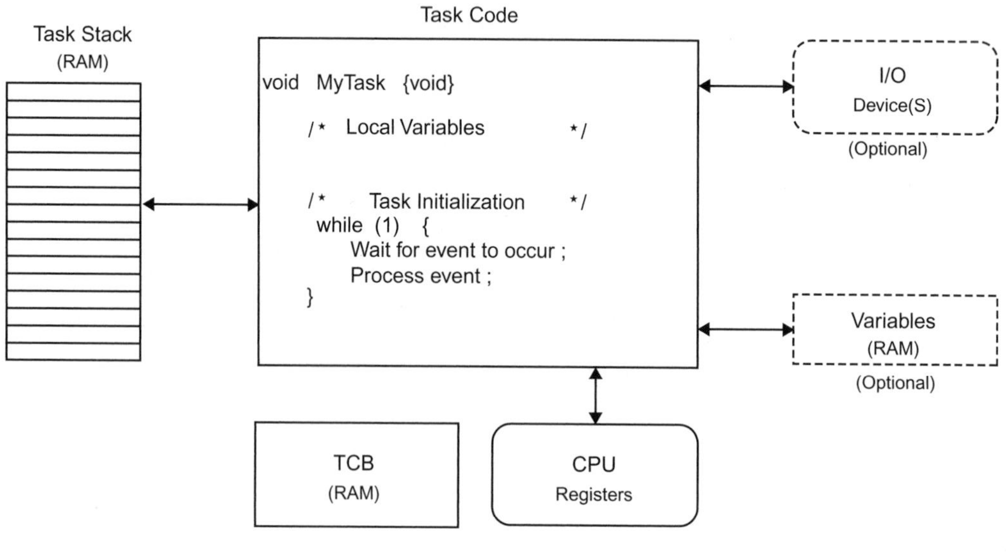

Figure 8.3:
Task resources.

Tasks are used for such chores as monitoring inputs, updating outputs, performing computations, controls, updating one or more displays, reading buttons and keyboards, communicating with other systems, and more. A task might own or share I/O devices and RAM with other tasks. However, when shared, the application code must use services provided by the kernel to protect each task from concurrently accessing the I/O device or RAM (more on this in later sections). An application may contain a handful of tasks while another application may require hundreds. The number of tasks does not establish how good or effective a design may be; it really depends on what the application (or product) needs to do. The amount of work a task performs also depends on the application. One task may have a few microseconds worth of work to perform while another task may require tens of milliseconds.

Tasks look like just any other C function except for a few small differences. There are typically two types of tasks: run-to-completion (Listing 8.1) and infinite loop (Listing 8.2).

```
void  MyRunToCompletionTask (void)
{
    /* Local variables                                                      */


    /* Task initialization                                                  */
    /* Task body ... do work!                                               */
    /* Task calls a service provided by the kernel to 'terminate self'      */
}
```

Listing 8.1:
Run-to-completion task.

```
void  MyInfiniteLoopTask (void)
{
    /* Local variables                                                 */


    /* Task initialization                                             */
    while (1) {            /* Task body, as an infinite loop.          */
        :
        /* Task body ... do work!                                      */
        :
        /* Must call a service to 'wait for an event'                  */
        :
        /* Task body ... do work!                                      */
        :
    }
}
```

Listing 8.2:
Infinite loop task.

In most embedded systems, tasks typically take the form of an infinite loop. Also, no task is allowed to return as other C functions can because these are "special" functions (they just look like regular functions) that are managed by the kernel. Given that a task is a regular C function, it can declare local variables.

A run-to-completion task must delete itself by calling on the services provided by the kernel. In other words, the task starts, performs its function, and terminates. There would typically not be too many such tasks in the embedded system because of the generally high overhead associated with "creating" and "deleting" tasks at run-time.

The body of the task can invoke other services provided by the kernel. Specifically, a task can create another task, suspend and resume other tasks, send signals or messages to other tasks, share resources with other tasks, and more. In other words, tasks are not limited to only make "wait for an event" function calls.

You can call either C or assembly language functions from a task. In fact, it is possible to call the same C function from different tasks as long as the functions are reentrant. A *reentrant* function is a function that does not use static or otherwise global variables unless they are protected (kernels provide mechanisms for this) from multiple access. If shared C functions only use local variables, they are generally reentrant (assuming that the compiler generates reentrant code). An example of a non-reentrant function is the popular `strtok()` provided by most C compilers as part of the standard library. This function is used to parse an ASCII string for "tokens". The first time you call this function, you specify the ASCII string to parse and a list of token delimiters. As soon as the function finds the first token, it returns. The function "remembers" where it was last so, when called again, it can extract additional tokens. Two tasks cannot use `strtok()` at the same time because which of the two string position will `strtok()` remember? `strtok()` is thus non-reentrant.

The use of an infinite loop is more common in embedded systems because of the repetitive work needed in such systems (reading inputs, updating displays, performing control operations, etc.). This is one aspect that makes a task different than a regular C function. Note that you could use a "`while (1)`" or "`for (;;)`" to implement the infinite loop, since both behave the same. The one used is simply a matter of personal preference. The infinite loop must call a service provided by the kernel (i.e., function) that will cause the task to wait for an event to occur. It is important that each task wait for an event to occur, otherwise the task would be a true infinite loop and there would be no easy way for other, lower-priority tasks to execute.

The event the task is waiting for may simply be the passage of time. Kernels provide "sleep" or "time delay" services. For example, a design may need to scan a keyboard every 50 milliseconds as shown in the pseudocode of Listing 8.3. In this case, you would simply delay the task for 100 milliseconds then see if a key was pressed on the keyboard and possibly perform some action based on which key was pressed. Typically, however, a

```
void  KeyboardScanningTask (void)
{
    Setup the I/O devices needed for the keyboard scanning;
    while (1) {
        Call kernel to delay task 50 ms;         /* Suspend task execution for 50 ms */
        if (a key was pressed) {
            Determine which key it was;
            Place the scan-code of the key into a buffer;
        }
    }
}
```

Listing 8.3:
Scanning a keyboard.

keyboard scanning task should just buffer an "identifier" unique to the key pressed and use another task to decide what to do with the key(s) pressed.

Similarly, the event the task is waiting for could be the arrival of a packet from an Ethernet controller. The task will have nothing to do until the packet is received. Once the packet is received, the task processes the contents of the packet, and possibly moves the packet along a network stack. Kernels provide signaling and message-passing mechanisms.

It is important to note that when a task waits for an event, it does not consume any CPU time because the kernel places the task in a special *wait list* until the event occurs, and selects and runs the next most important task that is *ready-to-run* (i.e., not waiting for any event).

Assigning task priorities

Sometimes determining the priority of a task is both obvious and intuitive. For example, if the most important aspect of the embedded system is to perform some type of control and it is known that the control algorithm must be responsive then it is best to assign the control task a high priority while display and operator interface tasks are assigned low priority. However, most of the time, assigning task priorities is not so cut and dried because of the complex nature of real-time systems. In most systems, not all tasks are considered critical, and non-critical tasks should obviously be given low priorities.

An interesting technique called rate monotonic scheduling (RMS) assigns task priorities based on how often tasks execute. Simply put, tasks with the highest rate of execution are given the highest priority. However, RMS makes a number of assumptions, including:

- all tasks are periodic (they occur at regular intervals);
- tasks do not synchronize with one another, share resources, or exchange data;
- the CPU must always execute the highest-priority task that is ready-to-run. In other words, preemptive scheduling must be used.

Given a set of n tasks that are assigned RMS priorities, the basic RMS theorem states that all task hard real-time deadlines are always met if the following inequality holds true:

$$\sum_i \frac{E_i}{T_i} \leq n\left(2^{1/n} - 1\right)$$

where E_i corresponds to the maximum execution time of task i, and T_i corresponds to the execution period of task i. In other words, E_i/T_i corresponds to the fraction of CPU time required to execute task i.

Table 8.1 shows the value for size $n(2^{1/n} - 1)$ based on the number of tasks. The upper bound for an infinite number of tasks is given by ln(2), or 0.693, which means that you meet all hard real-time deadlines based on RMS.

Table 8.1: Allowable CPU usage based on the number of tasks.

Number of Tasks	$n(2^{1/n} - 1)$
1	1.000
2	0.828
3	0.779
4	0.756
5	0.743
:	:
Infinite	0.693

Note that you can still have non-time-critical tasks in a system and thus use close to 100% of the CPU's time. However, using 100% of your CPU's time is not a desirable goal as it does not allow for code changes and added features. As a rule of thumb, you should always design a system to use less than 60 to 70% of the CPU.

RMS says that the highest-rate task has the highest priority. In some cases, the highest-rate task might not be the most important task. The application should dictate how to assign priorities. Also, RMS assumes that you know ahead of time the execution of your tasks, which might not be necessarily the case when you start your design. However, RMS is an interesting starting point.

Determining the size of a stack

The size of the stack required by the task is application specific. When sizing the stack, however, you must account for the nesting of all the functions called by the task, the number of local variables to be allocated by all functions called by the task, and the stack requirements for all nested interrupt service routines (if the ISR uses the task's stack). In addition, the stack must be able to store all CPU registers and possibly floating-point unit (FPU) registers if the processor has an FPU. In addition, as a general rule in embedded systems, avoid writing recursive code.

It is possible to manually figure out the stack space needed by adding all the memory required by all function call nesting (1 pointer for each function call for the return address), plus all the memory required by all the arguments passed in those function calls, plus storage for a full CPU context (depends on the CPU), plus another full CPU context for each nested ISRs (if the CPU doesn't have a separate stack to handle ISRs), plus whatever stack space is needed by those ISRs. Adding all this up is a tedious chore and the resulting number is a minimum requirement. Most likely you would not make the stack size that precise in order to account for "surprises". The number arrived at should probably be multiplied by some safety factor, possibly 1.25 to 3.0. This calculation assumes that the exact path of the code is known at all times, which is not always possible. Specifically, when calling a function such as `printf()` or some other library function, it might be difficult or nearly impossible to even guess just how much stack space `printf()` will require. In this case, start with a fairly large stack space and monitor the stack usage at run-time to see just how much stack space is actually used after the application runs for a while.

There are really cool and clever compilers/linkers that provide this information in a link map. For each function, the link map indicates the worst-case stack usage. This feature clearly enables you to better evaluate stack usage for each task. It is still necessary to add the stack space for a full CPU context, plus another full CPU context for each nested ISR (if the CPU does not have a separate stack to handle ISRs), plus whatever stack space is needed by those ISRs. Again, allow for a safety net and multiply this value by some factor. The factor depends on the type of product. Safety-critical systems may allocate 3 × the needed stack space, industrial controls 2 ×, etc. A lot depends on how well you can predict your application's worst-case stack requirements.

Always monitor stack usage at run-time while developing and testing the product as stack overflows occur often and can lead to some curious behaviors. In fact, whenever someone mentions that his or her application behaves "strangely", insufficient stack size should be one of the first thing that comes to mind.

A task can be in any one of five states, as shown in Figure 8.4.

1. The *Dormant* state corresponds to a task that resides in memory but has not been made available to the kernel. A task is made available to the kernel by calling a function to create the task. The task code actually resides in code space but the kernel needs to be informed about it. When the task is no longer needed, your code can call the kernel's task delete function. The code is not actually deleted, it is simply not eligible to access the CPU.
2. A task is in the *Ready* state when it is ready-to-run. There can be any number of tasks ready and the kernel keeps track of all ready tasks in a ready list (discussed later). This list is sorted by priority.
3. The most important ready-to-run task is placed in the *Running* state. On a single CPU, only one task can be running at any given time. The task selected to run on the CPU is *switched in* by the kernel when it determines that it's the highest-priority task that is ready-to-run. As previously discussed, tasks must wait for an event to occur. A task waits for an event by calling one of the functions that brings the task to the pending state if the event has not occurred.

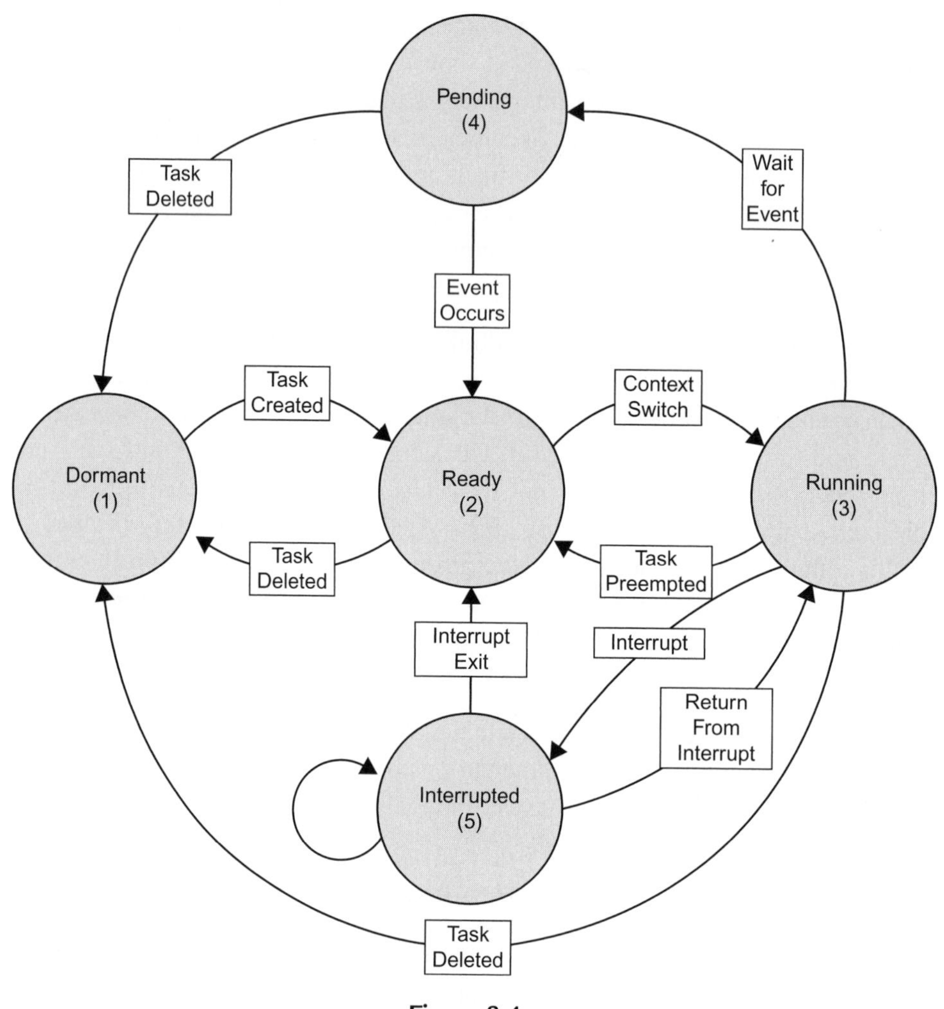

Figure 8.4:
Task states.

4. Tasks in the *Pending* state are placed in a special list called a *pend-list* (or wait list) associated with the event the task is waiting for. When waiting for the event to occur, the task does not consume CPU time. When the event occurs, the task is placed back into the ready list and the kernel decides whether the newly readied task is the most important ready-to-run task. If this is the case, the currently running task will be preempted (placed back in the ready list) and the newly readied task is given control of the CPU. In other words, the newly readied task will run immediately if it is the most important task.

5. Assuming that CPU interrupts are enabled, an interrupting device will suspend execution of a task and execute an interrupt service routine (ISR). ISRs are typically events that tasks wait for. Generally speaking, an ISR should simply notify a task that an event occurred and let the task process the event. ISRs should be as short as possible and most of the work of handling the interrupting devices should be done at the task level where it can be managed by the kernel. As the state diagram indicates, an interrupt can interrupt another interrupt. This is called interrupt nesting and most processors allow this. However, interrupt nesting easily leads to stack overflow if not managed properly.

The idle task

Most kernels create an internal task called the *idle task*. The idle task basically runs when no other application task is able to run because none of the events these tasks are waiting for have occurred. The idle task is the lowest-priority task in the application and is a "true" infinite loop that never calls functions to "wait for an event". This is because, on most processors, when there is "nothing to do", the processor still executes instructions.

A hook function (also known as a *callback*) is generally available to the application programmer and can be used to place the CPU in low-power mode for battery-powered applications and thus avoid wasting energy. Typically, most processors exit low-power mode when an interrupt occurs. Depending on the processor, however, the ISR may have to write to "special" registers to return the CPU to its full or desired speed. If the ISR wakes up a high-priority task (every task is higher in priority than the idle task) then the ISR will not immediately return to the interrupted idle task, but instead switch to the higher-priority task. Power management is very chip specific and is beyond the scope of this chapter.

Priority levels

All kernels allow you to assign priorities to tasks based on their importance in your application. Typically, a low priority number means a high priority. In other words, "priority 1" is more important than "priority 10". The number of different priority levels greatly depends on the implementation of the kernel. It's not uncommon to have up to 256 different priority levels and thus the kernel can use an 8-bit variable to represent the priority of a task. Most kernels allow the priority of tasks to be changed dynamically at run-time through a "change a task's priority" service (i.e., function).

On most kernels, an application can have multiple tasks assigned to the same priority. When this priority becomes the highest priority, the kernel generally executes each task at that priority in a *round-robin* fashion. In other words, each task gets to execute for up to a configurable amount of time.

The ready list

Tasks that are ready-to-run are placed in the *ready list*. The ready list is ordered by priority. The highest-priority task is at the beginning of the list and the lowest-priority task is placed at the end. There are techniques that allow inserting and removing tasks from the ready list. However, this is beyond the scope of this chapter.

Preemptive scheduling

The *scheduler*, also called the *dispatcher*, is a part of the kernel responsible for determining which task runs next. Most kernels are implemented using a *preemptive* scheme. The word preemptive means that when an event occurs, and that event makes a more important task ready-to-run, then the kernel will immediately give control of the CPU to that task. Thus, when a task signals or sends a message to a higher-priority task, the current task is suspended and the higher-priority task is given control of the CPU. Similarly, if an ISR signals or sends a message to a higher-priority task, when the message has been sent the interrupted task remains suspended, and the new higher-priority task resumes. Preemptive scheduling is illustrated in Figure 8.5.

1. A low-priority task is executing, and an interrupt occurs.
2. If interrupts are enabled, the CPU vectors (i.e., jumps) to the ISR that is responsible for servicing the interrupting device.
3. The ISR services the device and signals or sends a message to a higher-priority task waiting to service this device. This task is thus ready-to-run.
4. When the ISR completes its work it makes a service call to the kernel.
5. Since there is a more important ready-to-run task, the kernel decides to not return to the interrupted task but switches to the more important task. This is called a *context switch*.

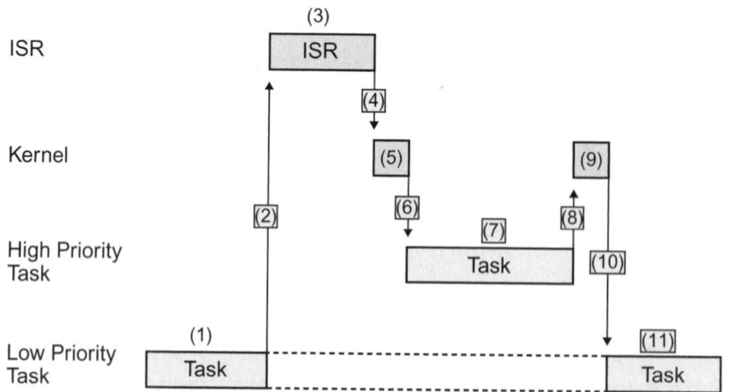

Figure 8.5:
Preemptive scheduling.

6. The higher-priority task services the interrupting device and, when finished, calls the kernel, asking it to wait for another interrupt from the device.
7. The kernel blocks the high-priority task until the next time the device needs servicing. Since the device has not interrupted a second time, the kernel switches back to the original task (the one that was interrupted).
8. The interrupted task resumes execution, exactly at the point where it was interrupted.

Scheduling points

Scheduling occurs at *scheduling points* and nothing special must be done in the application code since scheduling occurs automatically based some conditions as described below. Scheduling occurs within kernel services (i.e., API calls). This is a partial list for brevity.

- A task signals or sends a message to another task:
  This occurs when the task signals or sends a message to another task.
- A task 'sleeps' for a certain amount of time:
  Scheduling always occurs since the calling task is placed in a list waiting for time to expire. Scheduling occurs as soon as the task is inserted in the wait list and this call will always result in a context switch to the next task that is ready-to-run at the same or lower priority than the task that is placed to sleep.
- A task waits for an event to occur and the event has not yet occurred:
  The task is placed in the wait list for the event and, if a non-zero timeout is specified, the task is also inserted in the list of tasks waiting to timeout. The scheduler is then called to select the next most important task to run.
- If a task is created:
  The newly created task may have a higher priority than the task's creator. In this case, the scheduler is called.
- If a task is deleted:
  When terminating a task, the scheduler is called if the current task is deleted.
- A task changes the priority of itself or another task:
  The scheduler is called when a task changes the priority of another task (or itself) and the new priority of that task is higher than the task that changed the priority.
- At the end of all nested ISRs:
  The scheduler is called at the end of all nested ISRs to determine whether a more important task is made ready-to-run by one of the ISRs.
- A task gives up its time quanta by voluntarily relinquishing the CPU through a kernel call:
  This assumes that the task is running alongside with other tasks at the same priority and the currently running task decides that it can give up its time quanta and let another task run.

Round-robin scheduling

When two or more tasks have the same priority, most kernels allow one task to run for a predetermined amount of time (called a *time quantum*) before selecting another task. This process is called *round-robin scheduling* or *time slicing*. If a task does not need to use its full time quantum it can voluntarily give up the CPU so that the next task can execute. This is called *yielding* and the task must call a special function (provided by the kernel) that tells the kernel: "I'm done with the work I need to do, give the CPU to another task".

Context switching

When the kernel decides to run a different task, it saves the current task's context, which typically consists of the CPU registers, onto the current task's stack and restores the context of the new task and resumes execution of that task. This process is called a *context switch*.

Context switching adds overhead and the more registers a CPU has, the higher the overhead. The time required to perform a context switch is generally determined by how many registers must be saved and restored by the CPU.

The context switch code is generally part of a processor's *port* which adapts the kernel (typically written in C or other higher-level languages) to the processor architecture. The latter is typically written in assembly language.

Here, we will discuss the context switching process in generic terms using a fictitious CPU as shown in Figure 8.6. Our fictitious CPU contains 16 integer registers (`R0` to `R15`), a separate ISR stack pointer, and a separate status register (`SR`). Every register is 32 bits wide and each of the 16 integer registers can hold either data or an address. The program counter (or instruction pointer) is `R15` and there are two separate stack pointers labeled `R14` and `R14'`. `R14` represents a task stack pointer (`TSP`), and `R14'` represents an ISR stack pointer (`ISP`). The CPU automatically switches to the ISR stack when servicing an exception or interrupt. The task stack is accessible from an ISR (i.e., we can push and pop elements onto the task stack when in an ISR), and the interrupt stack is also accessible from a task.

The task initialization code (i.e., task create function) for a kernel generally sets up the stack frame for a ready task to look as if an interrupt has just occurred and all processor registers were saved onto it. Tasks enter the ready state upon creation and thus their stack frames are pre-initialized by software in a similar manner. Using our fictitious CPU, we'll assume that a stack frame for a task that is ready to be restored is shown in Figure 8.7.

The task stack pointer points to the last register saved onto the task's stack. The program counter (`PC` or `R15`) and status register (`SR`) are the first registers saved onto the stack. In

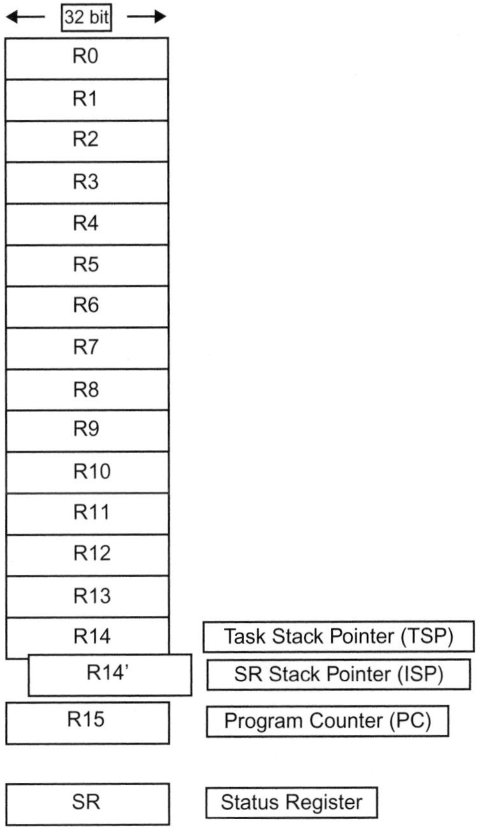

Figure 8.6:
Fictitious CPU.

fact, these are saved automatically by the CPU when an exception or interrupt occurs (assuming interrupts are enabled) while the other registers are pushed onto the stack by software in the exception handler. The stack pointer (`SP` or `R14`) is not actually saved on the stack but instead is saved in the task's control block (`TCB`).

The interrupt stack pointer points to the current top-of-stack for the interrupt stack, which is a different memory area. When an ISR executes, the processor uses `R14'` as the stack pointer for function calls and local arguments.

Figure 8.8 shows what happens during a context switch.

1. The kernel maintains a pointer to the current task's TCB (task control block).
2. Through scheduling, the kernel determined the address of the new task's TCB.
3. The processor's stack pointer points to the current top-of-stack of the task being switched out.

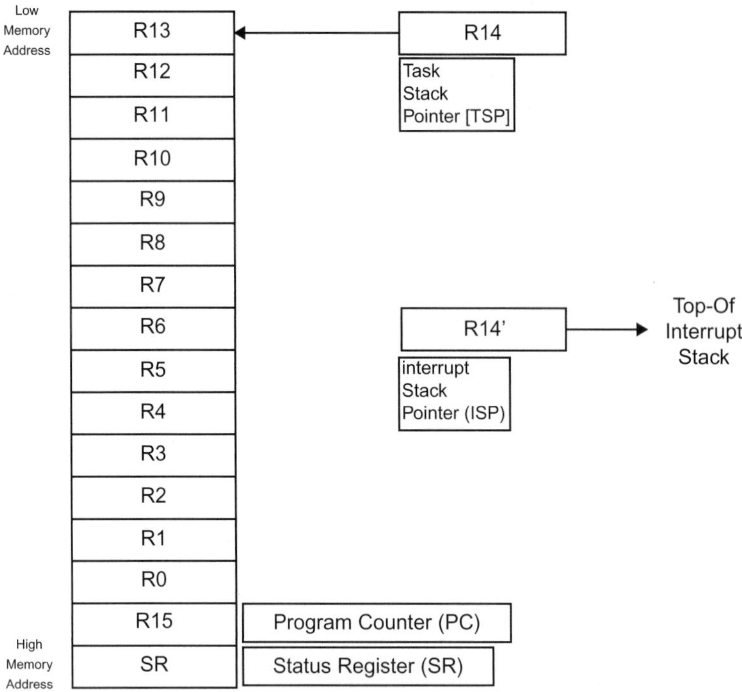

Figure 8.7:
CPU register stacking order for a ready task.

4. The kernel saves all the CPU registers (except the stack pointer itself) onto the current task's stack.
5. The kernel then saves the current value of the CPU's stack pointer into the TCB of the current task. At this point, the "context" of the CPU of the task being suspended has been completely saved.
6. The new task's TCB contains the value of the top-of-stack of the new task to run.
7. The kernel loads the pointer to the new task's top-of-stack into the CPU's stack pointer register from the new task's TCB.
8. Finally, the CPU registers are loaded from the stack frame of the new task and, once the PC is loaded into the CPU, the CPU executes the code of the new task.

The execution time of the above process greatly depends on the number of CPU registers to save and restore and, in fact, should be about the same from one kernel to another. Also, a context switch is normally performed with interrupts disabled so that the whole process is treated atomically. A CPU that has many registers (integer, floating-point, DSP and other special registers) could offer benefits from a code efficiency point-of-view but could impact responsiveness.

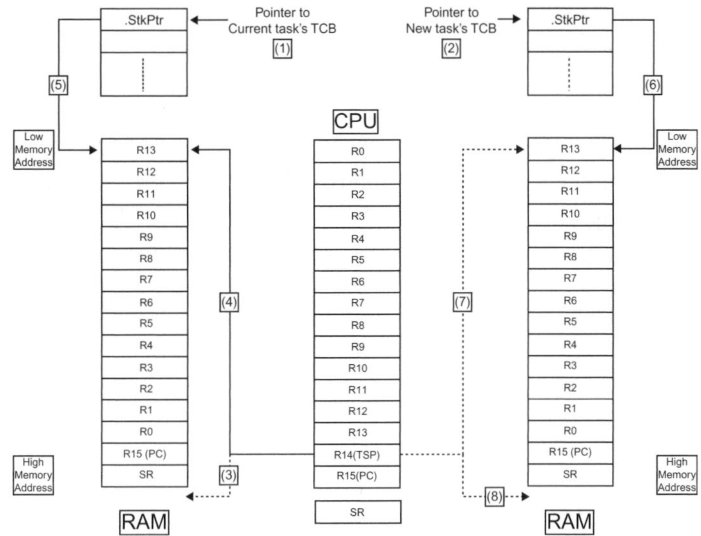

Figure 8.8:
Context switch.

Interrupt management

An *interrupt* is a hardware mechanism used to inform the CPU that an asynchronous event occurred. When an interrupt is recognized, the CPU saves part (or all) of its context (i.e., registers) and jumps to a special subroutine called an *interrupt service routine* (ISR). The ISR processes the event, and – upon completion of the ISR – the program returns to either the interrupted task or the highest-priority task, if the ISR made a higher-priority task ready-to-run.

As previously mentioned, interrupts allow a microprocessor to process events when they occur (i.e., asynchronously), which prevents the microprocessor from continuously *polling* (looking at) an event to see if it occurred. Task-level response to events is typically better using interrupt mode as opposed to polling mode. Microprocessors allow interrupts to be ignored or recognized through the use of two special instructions: disable interrupts and enable interrupts, respectively.

In a real-time environment, interrupts should be disabled as little as possible. Disabling interrupts affects interrupt latency, possibly causing interrupts to be missed.

Processors generally allow interrupts to be nested, which means that while servicing an interrupt, the processor recognizes and services other (more important) interrupts.

All real-time systems disable interrupts to manipulate critical sections of code and re-enable interrupts when critical sections are completed. The longer interrupts are disabled, the higher the interrupt latency.

Interrupt response is defined as the time between the reception of the interrupt and the start of the user code that handles the interrupt. Interrupt response time accounts for the entire overhead involved in handling an interrupt. Typically, the processor's context (CPU registers) is saved on the stack before the user code is executed.

Interrupt recovery is defined as the time required for the processor to return to the interrupted code or to a higher-priority task if the ISR made such a task ready-to-run.

Task latency is defined as the time it takes from the time the interrupt occurs to the time task-level code resumes.

Handling CPU interrupts

There are many popular CPU architectures on the market today, and most processors typically handle interrupts from a multitude of sources. For example, a UART receives a character, an Ethernet controller receives a packet, a DMA controller completes a data transfer, an analog-to-digital converter (ADC) completes an analog conversion, a timer expires, etc.

In most cases, an *interrupt controller* captures all of the different interrupts presented to the processor, as shown in Figure 8.9 (note that the "CPU Interrupt Enable/Disable" is typically part of the CPU, but is shown here separately for the sake of the illustration).

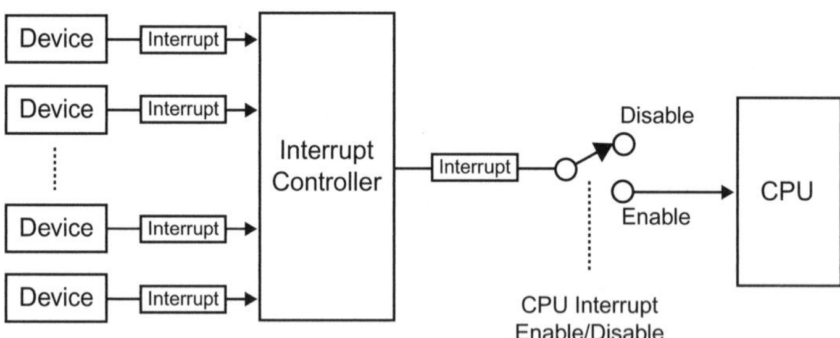

Figure 8.9:
Interrupt controllers.

Interrupting devices signal the interrupt controller, which then prioritizes the interrupts and presents the highest-priority interrupt to the CPU.

Modern interrupt controllers have built-in intelligence that enable the user to prioritize interrupts, remember which interrupts are still pending and, in many cases, have the interrupt controller provide the address of the ISR (also called the vector address) directly to the CPU.

If "global" interrupts (i.e., the switch in Figure 8.9) are disabled, then the CPU will ignore requests from the interrupt controller. However, interrupts will be held pending by the interrupt controller until the CPU re-enables interrupts.

CPUs deal with interrupts using one of two models:

1. All interrupts vector to a single interrupt handler.
2. Each interrupt vectors directly to an interrupt handler.

Before discussing these two methods, it is important to understand how a kernel handles CPU interrupts.

In most cases, interrupt service routines are written in assembly language. However, if a C compiler supports in-line assembly language, the ISR code can be placed directly into a C source file. The pseudocode for a typical ISR when using a kernel is shown in Listing 8.4.

```
MyKernelAwareISR:                                                            (1)
    ; ISR Prologue
    Disable all interrupts;                                                  (2)
    Save the CPU registers;                                                  (3)
    Increment ISR nesting counter;                                           (4)
    Save the CPU's stack pointer register value into the TCB of the current task; (5)
    Clear interrupting device;                                               (6)
    Re-enable interrupts (optional);                                         (7)
    Call user ISR;                                                           (8)
    ; ISR Epilogue
    Notify the kernel that the ISR has completed;                            (9)
    Restore the CPU registers;                                               (10)
    Return from interrupt;                                                   (11)
```

Listing 8.4:
Kernel aware interrupt service routine.

1. As mentioned above, an ISR is typically written in assembly language. `MyKernelAwareISR()` corresponds to the name of the handler that will handle the interrupting device.
2. It is important that all interrupts are disabled before going any further. Some processors have interrupts disabled whenever an interrupt handler starts. Others require the user to explicitly disable interrupts as shown here. This step may be tricky if a processor supports different interrupt priority levels. However, there is always a way to solve the problem.

3. The first thing the interrupt handler must do is save the context of the CPU onto the interrupted task's stack. On some processors, this occurs automatically. However, on most processors it is important to know how to save the CPU registers onto the task's stack. You should save the full "context" of the CPU, which may also include floating-point unit (FPU) registers if the CPU used is equipped with an FPU. However, it's possible that some tasks may not do any floating-point calculations and it would be a waste of CPU cycles to save the FPU registers. Luckily, you can tell some kernels (through task create options) that a task will not require floating-point capabilities.

   Certain CPUs also automatically switch to a special stack just to process interrupts (i.e., an interrupt stack). This is generally beneficial as it avoids using up valuable task stack space. However, for most kernels, the context of the interrupted task needs to be saved onto that task's stack.

   If the processor does not have a dedicated stack pointer to handle ISRs then it is possible to implement one in software. Specifically, upon entering the ISR, you would simply save the current task stack, switch to a dedicated ISR stack and, when done with the ISR, switch back to the task stack. Of course, this means that there would be additional code to write; however, the benefits are enormous since it is not necessary to allocate extra space on the task stacks to accommodate for worst-case interrupt stack usage including interrupt nesting.
4. Next, the ISR would increment a nesting counter to keep track of interrupt nesting. This is done because upon completing the ISR, the kernel needs to know whether it will return to a task or a previous ISR.
5. If this is the first nested interrupt, you need to save the current value of the stack pointer of the interrupted task into its TCB.

   The previous four steps are called the *ISR prologue*.
6. At this point, the ISR needs to clear the interrupting device so that it does not generate the same interrupt. However, most people defer the clearing of the interrupting device within the user ISR handler, which can be written in C.
7. If the interrupting source has been cleared, it is safe to re-enable interrupts if you want to support nested interrupts. This step is optional.
8. At this point, further processing can be deferred to a C function called from assembly language. This is especially useful if there is a large amount of processing to do in the ISR handler. However, as a general rule, keep the ISRs as short as possible. In fact, it is best to simply signal or send a message to a task and let the task handle the details of servicing the interrupting device.

   The ISR must call a kernel function to signal or send a message to a task that is waiting for this event. In other words, most likely you would have designed your task to wait for ISRs to notify them. If the ISR does not need to signal or send a message to a task then you might consider writing the ISR as a "non-kernel-aware interrupt service routine", as described in the next section.

9. When the ISR completes, the kernel is notified once more. The kernel simply decrements the nesting counter and if all interrupts have nested (i.e., the counter reaches 0) then the kernel will need to determine whether the task that was signaled or sent a message is now the most important task because it has a higher priority than the interrupted task, or not.

   If the task that was waiting for this signal or message has a higher priority than the interrupted task then the kernel will context switch to this higher-priority task instead of returning to the interrupted task. In this latter case, the kernel doesn't return from the ISR but takes a different path.
10. If the ISR signaled or sent a message to a lower-priority task than the interrupted task, then the kernel code returns to the ISR and the ISR restores the previously saved registers.
11. Finally, the ISR performs a return from interrupts to resume the interrupted task.

These last three steps are called the *ISR epilogue*.

Non-kernel-aware interrupt service routine (ISR)

The above sequence assumes that the ISR signals or sends a message to a task. However, in many cases, the ISR may not need to notify a task and can simply perform all of its work within the ISR (assuming it can be done quickly). In this case, the ISR will appear as shown in Listing 8.5.

```
MyNonKernelAwareISR:                                        (1)
    Save enough registers as needed by the ISR;             (2)
    Clear interrupting device;                              (3)
    DO NOT re-enable interrupts;                            (4)
    Call user ISR;                                          (5)
    Restore the saved CPU registers;                        (6)
    Return from interrupt;                                  (7)
```

Listing 8.5:
Non-kernel-aware interrupt service routine.

1. As mentioned above, an ISR is typically written in assembly language. `MyNonKernelAwareISR()` corresponds to the name of the handler that will handle the interrupting device.
2. Here, you save sufficient registers as required to handle the ISR.
3. The user probably needs to clear the interrupting device to prevent it from generating the same interrupt once the ISR returns.
4. You should not re-enable interrupts at this point since another interrupt could be kernel aware, thus forcing a context switch to a higher-priority task. This means that the above ISR would complete, but at a much later time.

5. Now you can take care of the interrupting device in assembly language or call a C function, if necessary.
6. Once finished, simply restore the saved CPU registers.
7. The ISR completes by performing a return from interrupt to resume the interrupted task.

Processors with multiple interrupt priorities

There are some processors that actually support multiple interrupt levels as shown in Figure 8.10.

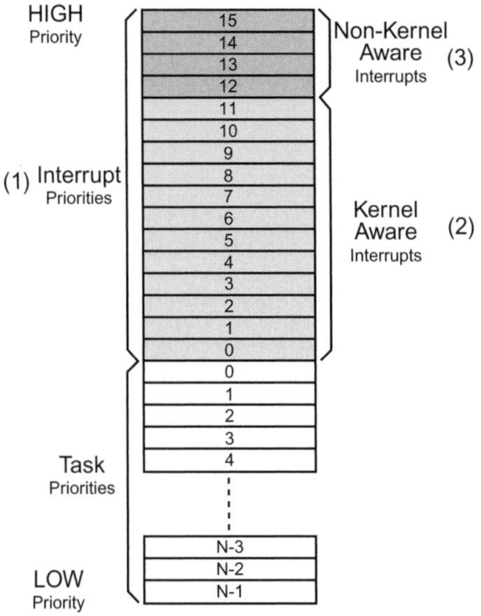

Figure 8.10:
Processors supporting multiple interrupt priorities.

1. Here, we are assuming that the processor supports 16 different interrupt priority levels. Priority 0 is the lowest priority while 15 is the highest. As shown, interrupts are always higher in priority than tasks (assuming interrupts are enabled).
2. The designer of the product decided that interrupt levels 0 through 12 will be "kernel aware" and thus will be able to notify tasks that are assigned to service these interrupts. It's important to note that disabling interrupts (when entering critical sections) for task-aware interrupts means raising the interrupt mask to level 12. In other words, interrupt levels 0 through 11 would be disabled but, levels 12 and above would be allowed.
3. Interrupt levels 12 through 15 are "non-kernel-aware" and thus are not allowed to make any kernel calls and are thus implemented as shown in Listing 8.5. It's important to note that since the kernel cannot disable these interrupts, interrupt latency for these interrupts is very short.

```
MyNonKernelAwareISR:
    Save enough registers as needed by the ISR;
    Clear interrupting device;
    Call user ISR;
    Restore the saved CPU registers;
    Return from interrupt;
```

Listing 8.6:
Non-kernel-aware ISR with processors supporting multiple interrupt priorities.

Listing 8.6 shows how to implement non-kernel-aware ISRs when the processor supports multiple interrupt priorities.

All interrupts vector to a common location

Even though an interrupt controller is present in most designs, some CPUs still vector to a common interrupt handler, and the ISR needs to query the interrupt controller to determine the source of the interrupt. At first glance, this might seem silly since most interrupt controllers are able to force the CPU to jump directly to the proper interrupt handler. It turns out, however, that for some kernels it is easier to have the interrupt controller vector to a single ISR handler than to vector to a unique ISR handler for each source. Listing 8.7 describes the sequence of events to be performed when the interrupt controller forces the CPU to vector to a single location.

```
An interrupt occurs;                                      (1)
The CPU vectors to a common location;                     (2)
ISR Prologue;                                             (3)

The C handler performs the following:                     (4)
    while (there are still interrupts to process) {       (5)
        Get vector address from interrupt controller;
        Call interrupt handler;
    }

ISR Epilogue;                                             (6)
```

Listing 8.7:
Single interrupt vector for all interrupts.

1. An interrupt occurs from any device. The interrupt controller activates the interrupt pin on the CPU. If there are other interrupts that occur after the first one, the interrupt controller will latch them and properly prioritize the interrupts.

2. The CPU vectors to a single interrupt handler address. In other words, all interrupts are to be handled by this one interrupt handler.
3. The ISR executes the "ISR prologue" (see Listing 8.4) code needed by the kernel.
4. The ISR calls a special handler which is typically written in C. This handler will continue processing the ISR. This makes the code easier to write (and read). Notice that interrupts are not re-enabled at this point.
5. The kernel handler then interrogates the interrupt controller and asks it: "Who caused the interrupt?" The interrupt controller will respond either with a number (0 to $N-1$) or with the address of the interrupt handler of the highest-priority interrupting device. Of course, the handler will know how to handle the specific interrupt controller since the C handler is written specifically for that controller.

   If the interrupt controller provides a number between 0 and $N-1$, the C handler simply uses this number as an index into a table (in ROM or RAM) containing the address of the interrupt service routine associated with the interrupting device. A RAM table is handy to change interrupt handlers at run-time. For many embedded systems, however, the table may also reside in ROM.

   If the interrupt controller responds with the address of the interrupt service routine, the C handler only needs to call this function.

   In both of the above cases, the ISRs for all of the interrupting devices need to be declared as follows:

   ```
   void MyISRHandler (void);
   ```

   There is one such handler for each possible interrupt source (obviously, each having a unique name).

   The "`while`" loop terminates when there are no other interrupting devices to service.
6. Finally, the ISR executes the "ISR epilogue" (see Listing 8.4) code.

A couple of interesting points to note:

- If another device caused an interrupt before the C handler had a chance to query the interrupt controller, most likely the interrupt controller will capture that interrupt. In fact, if that second device happens to be a higher-priority interrupting device, it will most likely be serviced first, as the interrupt controller will prioritize the interrupts.
- The loop will not terminate until all pending interrupts are serviced. This is similar to allowing nested interrupts, but better, since it is not necessary to redo the ISR prologue and epilogue.

The disadvantage of this method is that a high-priority interrupt that occurs after the servicing of another interrupt that has already started must wait for that interrupt to complete before it will be serviced. So, the latency of any interrupt, regardless of priority, can be as long as it takes to process the longest interrupt.

Every interrupt vectors to a unique location

If the interrupt controller vectors directly to the appropriate interrupt handler, each of the ISRs must be written in assembly language as described in "Handling CPU interrupts" and shown in Listing 8.4. This, of course, slightly complicates the design. However, a good portion of the code is the same and can be hidden in assembly language macros and just change what is specific to the actual device.

If the interrupt controller allows the user to query it for the source of the interrupt, it may be possible to simulate the mode in which all interrupts vector to the same location by simply setting all vectors to point to the same location. Most interrupt controllers that vector to a unique location, however, do not allow users to query it for the source of the interrupt since, by definition, having a unique vector for all interrupting devices should not be necessary.

The clock tick (or system tick)

Kernel-based systems generally require the presence of a periodic time source called the clock tick or system tick.

A hardware timer configured to generate an interrupt at a rate between 10 and 1000 Hz provides the clock tick. A tick source may also be obtained by generating an interrupt from an AC power line (typically 50 or 60 Hz). In fact, you can easily derive 100 or 120 Hz by detecting zero crossings of the power line. That being said, if your product is subject to being used in regions that use both power line frequencies then you may need to have the user specify which frequency to use or have the product automatically detect which region it's in.

The clock tick interrupt can be viewed as the system's heartbeat. The rate is application specific and depends on the desired resolution of this time source. However, the faster the tick rate, the higher is the overhead imposed on the system.

The clock tick interrupt allows the kernel to delay (also called sleep) tasks for an integral number of clock ticks and provide timeouts when tasks are waiting for events to occur.

A common misconception is that a system tick is always needed with a kernel. In fact, many low-power applications may not implement the system tick because of the power required to maintain the tick list. In other words, it is not reasonable to continuously power down and power up the product just to maintain the system tick. Since most kernels are preemptive, an event other than a tick interrupt can wake up a system placed in low-power mode by either a keystroke from a keypad or other means. Not having a system tick means that the user is not allowed to use time delays and timeouts on system calls. This is a decision required to be made by the designer of the low-power product.

Alternatively, you can disable the system tick when the application doesn't need it and bring it back when it does.

Wait lists

A task is placed in a *wait list* (also called a *pend list*) when it is waiting on a *kernel object*. A kernel object is generally a data structure that provides an abstraction of a concept such as a semaphore, mailbox, message queue or other. Tasks will generally be waiting on these objects to be *signaled* or *posted* by other tasks or ISRs.

A wait list is similar to the *Ready List*, except that instead of keeping track of tasks that are ready-to-run, the wait list keeps track of tasks waiting for an object to be signaled or posted. In addition, the wait list is sorted by priority; the highest-priority task waiting on the object is placed at the head of the list, and the lowest-priority task waiting on the object is placed at the end of the list. A kernel object along with tasks waiting for this object to be signaled or posted to is shown in Figure 8.11. We will be looking at different types of kernel objects in upcoming sections.

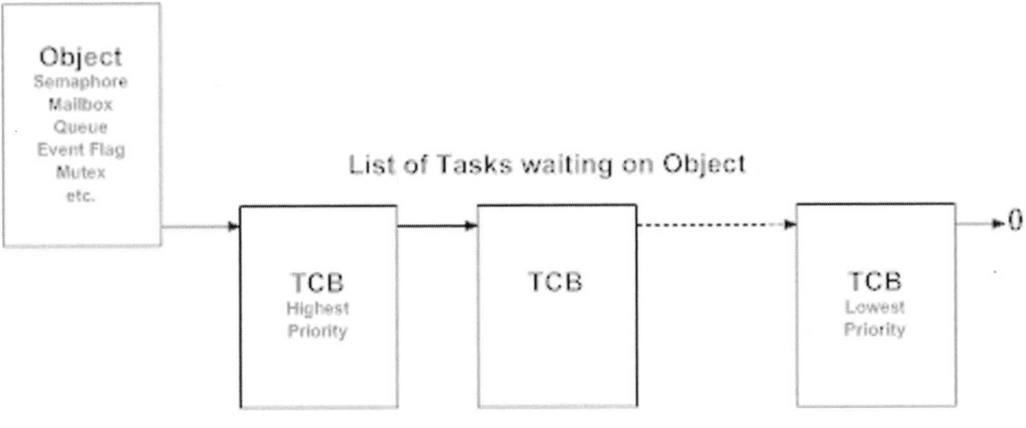

Figure 8.11:
Kernel object with tasks waiting for object to be signaled or posted.

Time management

Kernels typically provide time-related services to the application programmer.

As previously discussed, kernels require that the user provide a periodic interrupt to keep track of time delays and timeouts. This periodic time source is called a clock tick and should occur between 10 and 1000 times per second, or hertz. The actual frequency of the clock tick depends on the desired tick resolution of the application.

A kernel provides a number of services to manage time: delay (or sleep) for "*N*" ticks, delay for a user-specified amount of time in seconds and milliseconds, get the current tick count, set the current tick count and more. Example kernel APIs for these functions could be:

> `OSTimeDly()` or `OSTaskSleep()`
> `OSTimeDlySecMilli()` or `OSTaskSleepSecMilli()`
> `OSTimeGet()` or `OSTickCntGet()`
> `OSTimeSet()` or `OSTickCntSet()`

A task can call `OSTimeDly()` to suspend execution until some amount of time expires. The calling function will not execute until the specified time expires. Listing 8.8 shows a typical use of this function.

```
void  MyTask (void)
{
    :
    :
    while (1) {
      :
      :
      OSTimeDly(2);             /* Suspend execution of this task until 2 tick passes by */
      :
      :
    }
}
```

Listing 8.8:
Delaying (i.e., sleeping) a task for some period of time.

The actual delay is not exact, as described in Figure 8.12.

1. We get a tick interrupt and the kernel services the ISR.
2. At the end of the ISR, all higher-priority tasks (HPTs) execute. The execution time of HPTs is unknown and can vary.
3. Once all HPTs have executed, the kernel runs the task that has called `OSTimeDly()` as shown in Listing 8.8. For the sake of discussion, it is assumed that this task is a lower-priority task (LPT).
4. The task calls `OSTimeDly()` and specifies to delay for two ticks. At this point, the kernel places the current task in the tick list where it will wait for two ticks to expire. The delayed task consumes zero CPU time while waiting for the time to expire.

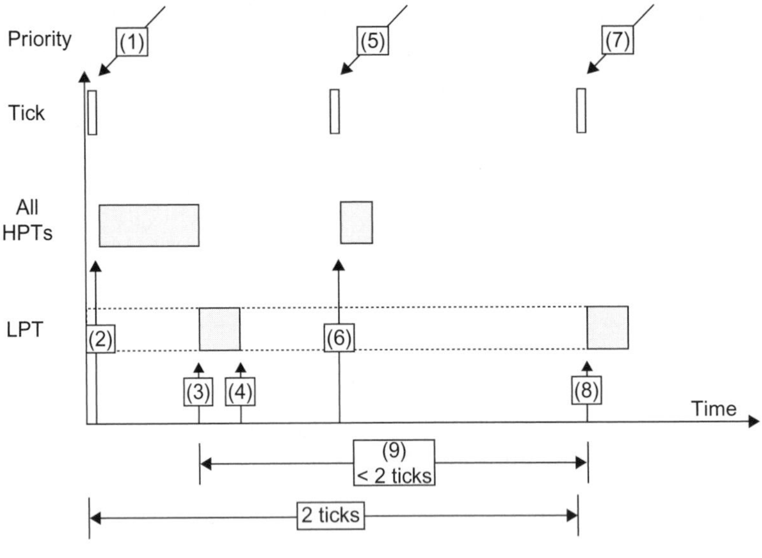

Figure 8.12:
Time delays are not exact.

5. The next tick occurs. If there are HPTs waiting for this particular tick, the kernel will schedule them to run at the end of the ISR.
6. The HPTs execute.
7. The next tick interrupt occurs. This is the tick that the LPT was waiting for and will now be made ready-to-run by the kernel.
8. Since there are no HPTs to execute on this tick, the kernel switches to the LPT.

Given the execution time of the HPTs, the time delay is not exactly two ticks, as requested. In fact, it is virtually impossible to obtain a delay of exactly the desired number of ticks. You might ask for a delay of two ticks, but the very next tick could occur almost immediately after calling `OSTimeDly()`! In fact, imagine what might happen if all HPTs took longer to execute and pushed (3) and (4) further to the right. In this case, the delay would actually appear as one tick instead of two.

Resource management

Kernels provide services to manage shared resources. A shared resource is typically a variable (static or global), a data structure, table (in RAM), or registers in an I/O device.

When protecting a shared resource it is preferred to use mutual-exclusion semaphores, as will be described later in this chapter. Other methods are also presented.

Tasks can easily share data when all tasks exist in a single address space and can reference global variables, pointers, buffers, linked lists, ring buffers, etc. Although sharing data simplifies the exchange of information between tasks, it is important to ensure that each task has exclusive access to the data to avoid contention and data corruption.

For example, when implementing a module that performs a simple time-of-day algorithm in software, the module obviously keeps track of hours, minutes and seconds. The `TimeOfDay()` task may appear as shown in Listing 8.9.

```
int  Hours;
int  Minutes;
int  Seconds;


void  TimeOfDay (void)
{
    while (1) {
        OSTimeDlySecMilli(1, 0);          /* Suspend execution of task for 1 second */
        Seconds++;
        if (Seconds > 59) {
            Seconds = 0;
            Minutes++;
            if (Minutes > 59) {
                Minutes = 0;
                Hours++;
                if (Hours > 23) {
                    Hours = 0;
                }
            }
        }
    }
}
```

Listing 8.9:
Time of day task.

Imagine if this task was preempted by another task because an interrupt occurred, and, the other task was more important than the `TimeOfDay()`. Let's suppose the interrupt occurred after setting the `Minutes` to 0. Now imagine what will happen if this higher-priority task wants to know the current time from the time-of-day module. Since the `Hours` were not incremented prior to the interrupt, the higher-priority task will read the time incorrectly and, in this case, it will be incorrect by a whole hour.

The code that updates variables for the `TimeOfDay()` task must treat all of the variables indivisibly (or atomically) whenever there is possible preemption. Time-of-day variables are considered shared resources and any code that accesses those variables must have exclusive access through what is called a *critical section*. All kernels provide services to protect shared resources and enable the easy creation of critical sections. Unfortunately, the responsibility of knowing which variable(s) or I/O device(s) need to be treated as shared resources rests upon your shoulders. However, you can reduce that dependency by having tasks "own" the I/O device(s) or memory location(s) and offer "services" to other tasks. In other words, implement tasks as *clients* and other tasks as *servers*.

The most common methods of obtaining exclusive access to shared resources and to create critical sections are:

- disabling interrupts
- disabling the scheduler
- using semaphores
- using mutual-exclusion semaphores (a.k.a. a mutex).

The mutual-exclusion mechanism used depends on how fast the code will access a shared resource, as shown in Table 8.2.

Table 8.2: Mutual-exclusion mechanisms.

Resource-Sharing Method	When Should You Use?
Disable/enable interrupts	When access to shared resource is very quick (reading from or writing to few variables) and access is faster than the kernel's interrupt disable time. It is highly recommended to not use this method as it impacts interrupt latency.
Semaphores	When all tasks that need to access a shared resource do not have deadlines. This is because semaphores may cause unbounded priority inversions (described later). However, semaphore services are slightly faster (in execution time) than mutual-exclusion semaphores.
Mutual-exclusion semaphores	This is the preferred method for accessing shared resources, especially if the tasks that need to access a shared resource have deadlines. µC/OS-III's mutual-exclusion semaphores have a built-in priority inheritance mechanism, which avoids unbounded priority inversions. However, mutual-exclusion semaphore services are slightly slower (in execution time) than semaphores since the priority of the owner may need to be changed, which requires CPU processing.

Resource management, disable/enable interrupts

The easiest and fastest way to gain exclusive access to a shared resource is by disabling and enabling interrupts, as shown in the pseudocode in Listing 8.10.

Most kernels use this technique to access certain internal variables and data structures, ensuring that these variables and data structures are manipulated atomically. Note that this

```
Disable interrupts;
Access the resource;
Enable interrupts;
```

Listing 8.10:
Disabling and enabling interrupts to access a shared resource.

is the only way that a task can share variables or data structures with an ISR. Although this method works, you should avoid disabling interrupts as it affects the responsiveness of the system to real-time events.

Resource management, semaphores

A semaphore was originally a mechanical signaling mechanism. The railroad industry used the device to provide a form of mutual exclusion for railroads tracks shared by more than one train. In this form, the semaphore signaled trains by closing a set of mechanical arms to block a train from a section of track that was currently in use. When the track became available, the arm would swing up and the waiting train would then proceed.

The notion of using a semaphore in software as a means of mutual exclusion was invented by the Dutch computer scientist Edsger Dijkstra in 1959. In computer software, a semaphore is a protocol mechanism offered by most multitasking kernels. Semaphores were originally used to control access to shared resources, but now they are used for synchronization, as described later. However, it is useful to describe how semaphores can be used to share resources. The pitfalls of semaphores will be discussed in a later section.

A semaphore was originally a "lock mechanism" and code acquired the "key" to this lock to continue execution. Acquiring the key means that the executing task has permission to enter the section of otherwise locked code. Entering a section of locked code causes the task to wait until the key becomes available.

Typically, two types of semaphores exist: binary semaphores and counting semaphores. As its name implies, a binary semaphore can only take two values: 0 or 1. A counting semaphore allows for values between 0 and 255, 65,535, or 4,294,967,295, depending on whether the semaphore mechanism is implemented using 8, 16, or 32 bits, respectively. Along with the semaphore's value, the kernel contains a list of tasks waiting for the semaphore's availability. Only tasks are allowed to use semaphores when semaphores are used for sharing resources; ISRs are not allowed.

Listing 8.11 shows how semaphores are typically used. As you will see, semaphore management is a service provide by kernel implementers but you need to know how to use this service and when. Your application needs to *create* all the semaphores it needs and

```
OS_SEM  MySem;                          (1)


void  main (void)
{
    :
    OSInit();
    :
    :
    OSSemCreate(&MySem, 1);            (2)
    :
    :
    OSStart();
}


void MyTask (void)
{
    while (1) {
            :
            :
        OSSemWait(&MySem);             (3)
        Access the resource;
        OSSemRelease(&MySem);          (4)
            :
            :
    }
}
```

Listing 8.11:
Using a binary semaphore to access a shared resource.

wrap shared resources around a *wait* and *release* function. An application can have many semaphores, one to protect access to a shared time-of-day clock, another to share access to a display, another to access a pool of buffers, etc.

1. A semaphore is a kernel object and the application can have any number of semaphores (limited only by the amount of RAM available). The semaphore object must be globally accessible to all tasks that will be sharing the resources guarded by the semaphore.
2. A semaphore must be created before it can be used. Creating a semaphore is done by calling a function provided by the kernel. When you create a semaphore, you need to specify its maximum value, which represents the number of resources the semaphore is *guarding*. In other words, if you are protecting a single variable or data structure, you would create a semaphore with a count of 1. If you are protecting a pool of 100 identical buffers then you'd initialize the semaphore to 100. In the code of Listing 8.11,

the semaphore was initialized to 1 and this type of semaphore is typically called a *binary semaphore.*

Kernel objects are typically created prior to the start of multitasking.

3. A task that wants to acquire a resource must perform a *wait* (or *pend*) operation. If the semaphore is available (the semaphore value is greater than 0), the semaphore value is decremented, and the task continues execution (owning the resource). If the semaphore's value is 0, the task performing a wait on the semaphore is placed in a waiting list.
4. A task releases a semaphore by performing a *release* (or *post*) operation. If no task is waiting for the semaphore, the semaphore value is simply incremented. If there is at least one task waiting for the semaphore, the highest-priority task waiting on the semaphore is made ready-to-run, and the semaphore value is not incremented. If the readied task has a higher priority than the current task (the task releasing the semaphore), a context switch occurs and the higher-priority task resumes execution. The current task is suspended until it again becomes the highest-priority task that is ready-to-run.

The application must declare a semaphore as a variable of type OS_SEM. This variable will be referenced by other semaphore services.

You create a semaphore by calling OSSemCreate() and pass the address to the semaphore allocated in (1). The semaphore must be created before it can be used by other tasks. Here, the semaphore is initialized in startup code (i.e., main ()); however, it could also be initialized by a task (but it must be initialized before it is used).

You can assign an ASCII name to the semaphore, which can be used by debuggers or µC/Probe to easily identify the semaphore. Storage for the ASCII characters is typically in ROM, which is typically more plentiful than RAM. If it is necessary to change the name of the semaphore at run-time, you can store the characters in an array in RAM and simply pass the address of the array to OSSemCreate(). Of course, the array must be NUL terminated.

Semaphores are especially useful when tasks share I/O devices. Imagine what would happen if two tasks were allowed to send characters to a printer at the same time. The printer would contain interleaved data from each task. For instance, the printout from Task 1 printing "I am Task 1" and Task 2 printing "I am Task 2" could result in "I Ia amm T Tasask k1 2". In this case, you can use a semaphore and initialize it to 1. The rule is simple: to access the printer each task must first obtain the resource's semaphore. Figure 8.13 shows tasks competing for a semaphore to gain exclusive access to the printer. Note that a key, indicating that each task must obtain this key to use the printer, represents the semaphore symbolically.

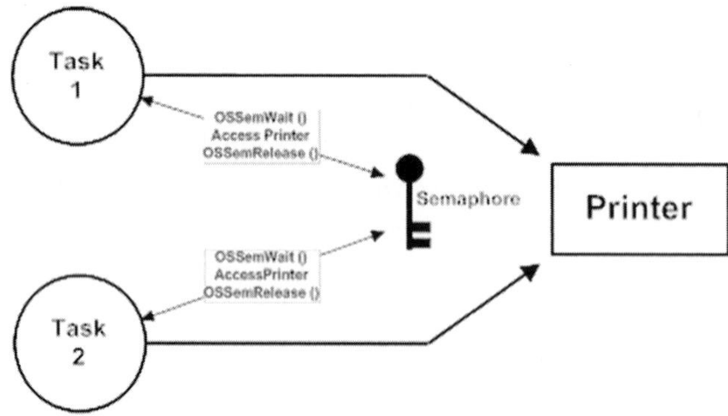

Figure 8.13:
Accessing a shared peripheral device.

The above example implies that each task knows about the existence of the semaphore to access the resource. It is almost always better to encapsulate the critical section and its protection mechanism. Each task would therefore not know that it is acquiring a semaphore when accessing the resource. For example, you could write a module that offers printer services to your application like `Print_Char()`, `Print_Line()`, `Print_FF()`, `Print_Acquire()`, `Print_Release()`, `Print_File()`, etc. These functions would know when they would need to access the semaphore and thus hide those details from the user of these services.

A counting semaphore is used when elements of a resource can be used by more than one task at the same time. For example, a counting semaphore is used in the management of a buffer pool, as shown in Figure 8.14.

Let's assume that the buffer pool initially contains 10 buffers. A task obtains a buffer from the buffer manager by calling `BufReq()`. When the buffer is no longer needed, the task returns the buffer to the buffer manager by calling `BufRel()`. The buffer manager satisfies the first 10 buffer requests because the semaphore was initialized to 10. When all buffers are used, a task requesting a buffer is suspended (placed in the semaphore wait list) until a buffer becomes available. When a task is done with the buffer it acquired, the task calls `BufRel()` to return the buffer to the buffer manager and the buffer is inserted into the linked list before the semaphore is signaled. If there are tasks in the wait list then the buffer is allocated to the highest-priority task waiting for a buffer. By encapsulating the interface to the buffer manager in `BufReq()` and `BufRel()`, the caller does not need to be concerned with actual implementation details.

Resource management, notes on semaphores

Using a semaphore to access a shared resource does not increase interrupt latency. If an ISR or the current task makes a higher-priority task ready-to-run while accessing shared data, the higher-priority task executes immediately.

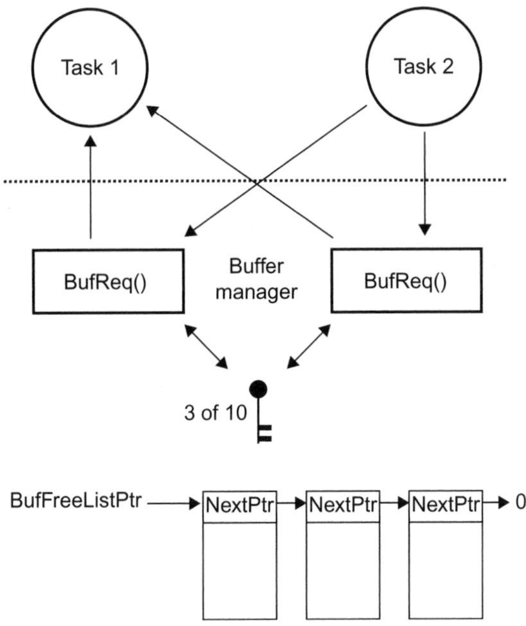

Figure 8.14:
Using counting a semaphore to access a pool of identical buffers.

An application may have as many semaphores as required to protect a variety of different resources. For example, one semaphore may be used to access a shared display, another to access a shared printer, another for shared data structures, and another to protect a pool of buffers, etc. However, it is preferable to use semaphores to protect access to I/O devices rather than memory locations because in the latter case you should use mutual-exclusion semaphores, which are described in the next section.

Semaphores are often overused. The use of a semaphore to access a simple shared variable is overkill in most situations. The overhead involved in acquiring and releasing the semaphore consumes valuable CPU time. You can perform the job more efficiently by disabling and enabling interrupts; however, there is an indirect cost to disabling interrupts: even higher-priority tasks that do not share the specific resource are blocked from using the CPU. Suppose, for instance, that two tasks share a 32-bit integer variable. The first task increments the variable, while the second task clears it. When considering how long a processor takes to perform either operation, it is easy to see that a semaphore is not required to gain exclusive access to the variable. Each task simply needs to disable interrupts before performing its operation on the variable and enable interrupts when the operation is complete. A semaphore should be used if the variable is a floating-point variable and the microprocessor does not support hardware floating-point operations. In this case, the time involved in processing the floating-point variable may affect interrupt latency if interrupts are disabled.

Semaphores are subject to a serious problem in real-time systems called priority inversion, which is described next.

Resource management, priority inversions

Priority inversion is a problem in real-time systems, and occurs only when using a priority-based preemptive kernel. Figure 8.15 illustrates a priority-inversion scenario. Task H (high priority) has a higher priority than Task M (medium priority), which in turn has a higher priority than Task L (low priority).

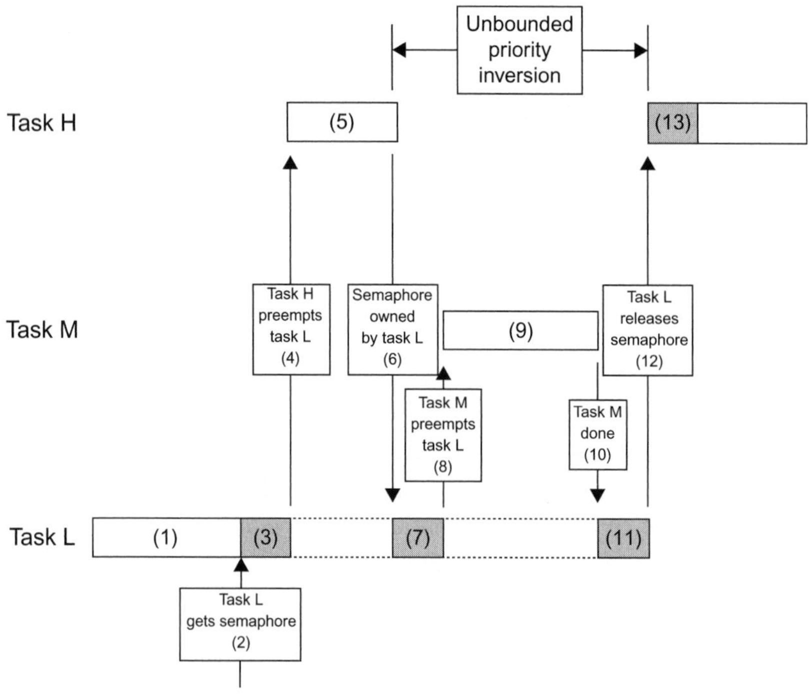

Figure 8.15:
Unbounded priority inversion.

1. Task H and Task M are both waiting for an event to occur and Task L is executing.
2. At some point, Task L acquires a semaphore, which it needs before it can access a shared resource.
3. Task L performs operations on the acquired resource.
4. The event that Task H was waiting for occurs, and the kernel suspends Task L and starts executing Task H since Task H has a higher priority.
5. Task H performs computations based on the event it just received.

6. Task H now wants to access the resource that Task L currently owns (i.e., it attempts to get the semaphore that Task L owns). Because Task L owns the resource, Task H is placed in a list of tasks waiting for the semaphore to be available.
7. Task L is resumed and continues to access the shared resource.
8. Task L is preempted by Task M since the event that Task M was waiting for occurred.
9. Task M handles the event.
10. When Task M completes, the kernel relinquishes the CPU back to Task L.
11. Task L continues accessing the resource.
12. Task L finally finishes working with the resource and releases the semaphore. At this point, the kernel knows that a higher-priority task is waiting for the semaphore, and a context switch takes place to resume Task H.
13. Task H has the semaphore and can access the shared resource.

So, what happened here is that the priority of Task H has been reduced to that of Task L since it waited for the resource that Task L owned. The trouble begins when Task M preempted Task L, further delaying the execution of Task H. This is called an *unbounded priority inversion*. It is unbounded because any medium priority can extend the time Task H has to wait for the resource. Technically, if all medium-priority tasks have known worst-case periodic behavior and bounded execution times, the priority inversion time is computable. This process, however, may be tedious and would need to be revised every time the medium-priority tasks change.

This situation can be corrected by raising the priority of Task L, only during the time it takes to access the resource, and restore the original priority level when the task is finished. The priority of Task L should be raised up to the priority of Task H. In fact, many kernels contain a special type of semaphore that does just that and is called a *mutual-exclusion semaphore*.

Resource management, mutual-exclusion semaphores (mutex)

Some kernels support a special type of binary semaphore called a mutual-exclusion semaphore (also known as a *mutex*) which eliminates unbounded priority inversions. Figure 8.16 shows how priority inversions are bounded using a mutex.

1. Task H and Task M are both waiting for an event to occur and Task L is executing.
2. At some point, Task L acquires a mutex, which it needs before it is able to access a shared resource.
3. Task L performs operations on the acquired resource.
4. The event that Task H waited for occurs and the kernel suspends Task L and begins executing Task H since Task H has a higher priority.
5. Task H performs computations based on the event it just received.

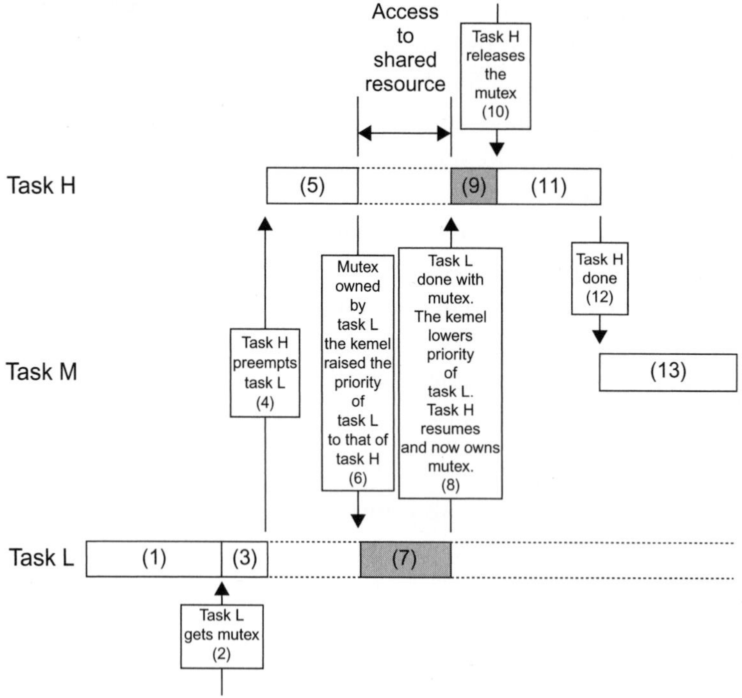

Figure 8.16:
Eliminating unbounded priority inversions with mutexes.

6. Task H now wants to access the resource that Task L currently owns (i.e., it attempts to get the mutex from Task L). Given that Task L owns the resource, the kernel raises the priority of Task L to the same priority as Task H to allow Task L to finish with the resource and prevent Task L from being preempted by medium-priority tasks.
7. Task L continues accessing the resource; however, it now does so while it is running at the same priority as Task H. Note that Task H is not actually running since it is waiting for Task L to release the mutex. In other words, Task H is in the mutex wait list.
8. Task L finishes working with the resource and releases the mutex. The kernel notices that Task L was raised in priority and thus lowers Task L to its original priority. After doing so, the kernel gives the mutex to Task H, which was waiting for the mutex to be released.
9. Task H now has the mutex and can access the shared resource.
10. Task H is finished accessing the shared resource, and frees up the mutex.
11. There are no higher-priority tasks to execute, therefore Task H continues execution.
12. Task H completes and decides to wait for an event to occur. At this point, µC/OS-III resumes Task M, which was made ready-to-run while Task H or Task L were

executing. Task M was made ready-to-run because an interrupt (not shown in Figure 8.16) occurred which Task M was waiting for.

13. Task M executes.

Note that there is no priority inversion, only resource sharing. Of course, the faster that Task L accesses the shared resource and frees up the mutex, the better.

Kernels should implement full-priority inheritance and therefore if a higher priority requests the resource, the priority of the owner task will be raised to the priority of the new requestor.

Only tasks are allowed to use mutual-exclusion semaphores (ISRs are not allowed). You as the programmer have to define what resource is assigned to what mutex (you can have as many mutexes as needed). As with semaphores, you can have a mutex to protect a time-of-day clock (YYYY-MM-DD HH:MM:SS.T), another for an array, another for a pool of buffers, etc.

Resource management, deadlocks (or deadly embrace)

A deadlock, also called a deadly embrace, is a situation in which two tasks are each unknowingly waiting for resources held by the other.

Assume Task T1 has exclusive access to Resource R1 and Task T2 has exclusive access to Resource R2 as shown in the pseudocode of Listing 8.12.

1. Assume that the event that task T1 is waiting for occurs and T1 is now the highest-priority task that must execute.
2. Task T1 executes and acquires Mutex M1.
3. Resource R1 is accessed.
4. An interrupt occurs causing the CPU to switch to task T2 since T2 has a higher priority than task T1.
5. The ISR is the event that task T2 was waiting for and therefore T2 resumes execution.
6. Task T2 acquires mutex M2 and is able to access resource R2.
7. Task T2 tries to acquire mutex M1, but the kernel knows that mutex M1 is owned by another task.
8. The kernel switches back to task T1 because Task T2 can no longer continue. It needs mutex M1 to access resource R1.
9. Task T1 now tries to access mutex M2 but, unfortunately, mutex M2 is owned by task T2. At this point, the two tasks are deadlocked, neither one can continue because each owns a resource that the other one wants.

```
void  T1 (void)
{
    while (1) {
        Wait for event to occur;              (1)
        Acquire M1;                           (2)
        Access  R1;                           (3)
        :
        :
        \-------  Interrupt!                  (4)
        :
        :                                     (8)
        Acquire M2;                           (9)
        Access  R2;
    }
}


void  T2 (void)
{
    while (1) {
        Wait for event to occur;              (5)
        Acquire M2;                           (6)
        Access  R2;
        :
        :
        Acquire M1;                           (7)
        Access  R1;
    }
}
```

Listing 8.12:
Deadlocks.

Some techniques used to avoid deadlocks are for tasks to:

- acquire all resources before proceeding;
- always acquire resources in the same order;
- use timeouts on wait calls (the kernel must provide timeouts on wait calls).

Synchronization

This section focuses on how tasks can synchronize their activities with interrupt service routines (ISRs), or other tasks.

When an ISR executes, it can signal a task telling the task that an event of interest has occurred. After signaling the task, the ISR exits and, depending on the signaled task priority, the scheduler is run.

The signaled task may then service the interrupting device, or otherwise react to the event. Servicing interrupting devices from task level is preferred whenever possible, since it reduces the amount of time that interrupts are disabled and the code is easier to debug.

Synchronization, semaphores

As previously described, a semaphore is a protocol mechanism offered by most multitasking kernels. Semaphores were originally used to control access to shared resources. However, a mutex is a better mechanism to protect access to shared resources, as previously described.

Semaphores are best used to synchronize an ISR to a task, or synchronize a task with another task, as shown in Figure 8.17, and this is called a *unilateral rendez-vous*.

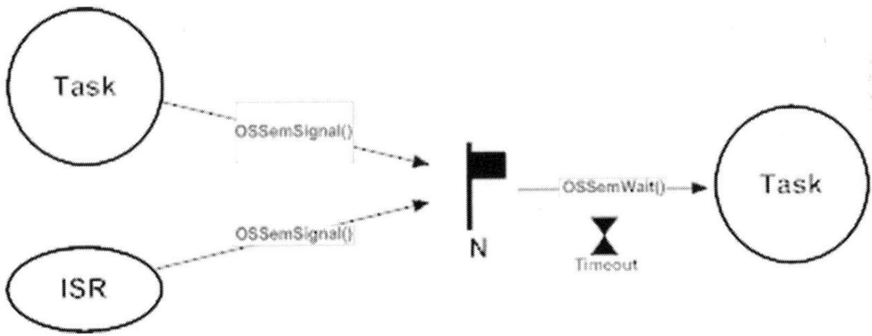

Figure 8.17:
Semaphore used as a signaling mechanism for synchronization.

Note that the semaphore is drawn as a flag to indicate that it is used to signal the occurrence of an event. The initial value for the semaphore is typically zero (0), indicating the event has not yet occurred.

The value "N" next to the flag indicates that the semaphore can accumulate events or *credits*. An ISR (or a task) can signal a semaphore multiple times and the semaphore will remember how many times it was signaled. It is possible to initialize the semaphore with a value other than zero, indicating that the semaphore initially contains that number of events.

Also, the small hourglass close to the receiving task indicates that the task has an option to specify a timeout. This timeout indicates that the task is willing to wait for the semaphore to be signaled within a certain amount of time. If the semaphore is not signaled within that time, the kernel will resume the task and return an error code indicating that the task was made ready-to-run because of a timeout and not because the semaphore was signaled.

A few interesting things are worth noting Figure 8.17. First, the task that calls `OSSemWait()` will not consume any CPU time until it is signaled and becomes the highest-priority task ready-to-run. In other words, as far as the task is concerned, it called a function (`OSSemWait()`) that will return when the event it is waiting for occurs. Second, if the signal did not occur, the kernel maximizes the use of the CPU by selecting the next most important task to run. In fact, the signal may not occur for many milliseconds and, during that time, the CPU will work on other tasks.

Again, semaphores must be created before they can be signaled or waited on.

Synchronization, credit tracking

As previously mentioned, a semaphore "remembers" how many times it was signaled. In other words, if an ISR occurs multiple times before the task waiting for the event becomes the highest-priority task, the semaphore will keep count of the number of times it was signaled. When the task becomes the highest-priority ready-to-run task, it will execute without blocking as many times as there were ISR signals. This is called *credit tracking* and is illustrated in Figure 8.18 and described below.

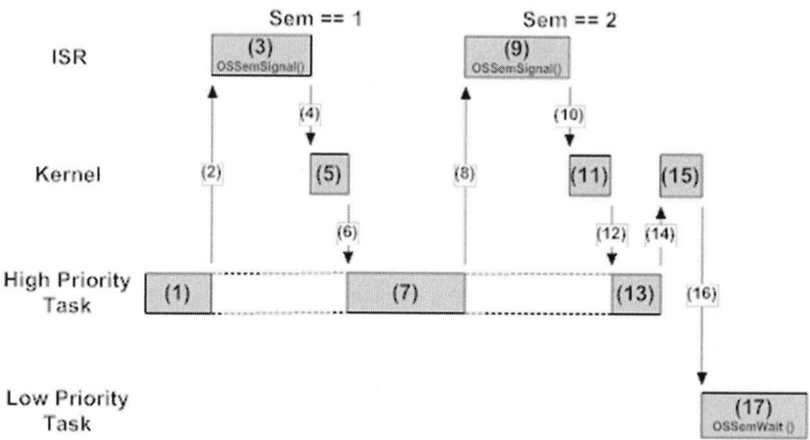

Figure 8.18:
Semaphore and credit tracking.

1. A high-priority task is executing.
2. An event meant for a lower-priority task occurs which preempts the task (assuming interrupts are enabled). The ISR executes and posts the semaphore. At this point the semaphore count is 1.

3. A kernel API is called at the end of the ISR to see whether the ISR caused a higher-priority task to be ready-to-run. Since the ISR was an event that a lower-priority task was waiting for, the kernel will resume execution of the higher-priority task at the exact point where it was interrupted.
4. The high-priority task is resumed and continues execution.
5. The interrupt occurs a second time. The ISR executes and posts the semaphore. At this point the semaphore count is 2.
6. The kernel is called at the end of the ISR to see whether the ISR caused a higher-priority task to be ready-to-run. Since the ISR was an event that a lower-priority task was waiting for, the kernel resumes execution of the higher-priority task at the exact point where it was interrupted.
7. The high-priority task resumes execution and actually terminates the work it was doing. This task will then call one of the kernel services to wait for "its" event to occur.
8. The kernel will then select the next most important task, which happens to be the task waiting for the event, and will context switch to that task.
9. The new task executes and will know that the ISR occurred twice since the semaphore count is two. The task will handle this accordingly.

Bilateral rendez-vous

Two tasks can synchronize their activities by using two semaphores, as shown in Figure 8.19, and this is called a *bilateral rendez-vous*. A bilateral rendez-vous is similar to a unilateral rendez-vous, except that both tasks must synchronize with one another before

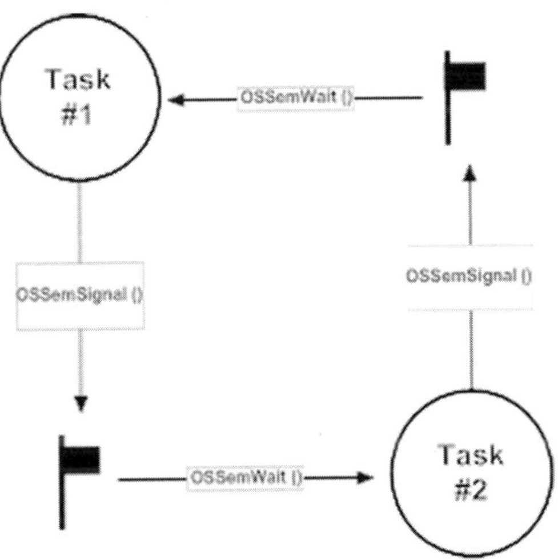

Figure 8.19:
Bilateral rendez-vous.

proceeding. A bilateral rendez-vous cannot be performed between a task and an ISR because an ISR cannot wait on a semaphore.

The code for a bilateral rendez-vous is shown in Listing 8.13.

```
OS_SEM  MySem1;
OS_SEM  MySem2;


void Task1 (void)
{
    while (1) {
        :
        OSSemSignal(&MySem2);                    (1)
        OSSemWait(&MySem1);                      (2)
        :
    }
}


void Task2 (void)
{
    while (1) {
        :
        OSSemSignal(&MySem1);                    (3)
        OSSemWait(&MySem2);                      (4)
        :
    }
}
```

Listing 8.13:
Implementing a bilateral rendez-vous.

1. Task 1 is executing and signals semaphore 2.
2. Task 1 waits on semaphore 1. Because Task 2 has not executed yet, Task 1 is blocked waiting for its semaphore to be signaled. The kernel context switches to Task 2.
3. Task 2 executes, and signals semaphore 1.
4. Since it has already been signaled, Task 2 is now synchronized to Task 1. If Task 1 is higher in priority than Task 2, the kernel will switch back to Task 1. If not, Task 2 continues execution.

Message passing

It is sometimes necessary for a task or an ISR to communicate information to another task. This information transfer is called *inter-task communication*. Information can be communicated between tasks in two ways: through global data, or by sending messages.

As discussed in the resource management section, when using global variables each task or ISR must ensure that it has exclusive access to variables. If an ISR is involved, the only way to ensure exclusive access to common variables is to disable interrupts. If two tasks share data, each can gain exclusive access to variables either by disabling interrupts, using a semaphore, or, preferably, by using a mutual-exclusion semaphore. Note that a task can only communicate information to an ISR by using global variables. A task is not aware when a global variable is changed by an ISR, unless the ISR signals the task, or the task polls the contents of a variable periodically.

Messages can be sent to an intermediate object called a *message queue*. Multiple tasks can wait for messages to arrive in a message queue and the kernel generally gives the received message to the highest-priority task waiting for a message for that queue. When a task waits for a message to arrive, it does not consume CPU time.

Messages

A message generally consists of a pointer to data instead of copying the actual data. The pointer can point to a data area or even a function. Obviously, the sender and the receiver must agree as to the contents and the meaning of the message. In other words, the receiver of the message will need to know the meaning of the message received to be able to process it. For example, an Ethernet controller receives a packet and sends a pointer to this packet to a task that knows how to handle the packet.

The message contents must always remain in scope since the data is actually sent by reference (i.e., a pointer to the data) instead of by value. In other words, data sent is not copied. You might consider using dynamically allocated memory for the actual message content but you should avoid allocating memory from the heap because your heap will eventually before so fragmented that your request for memory might not be satisfied. Alternatively, you can pass a pointer to a global variable, a global data structure, a global array, or a function, etc.

Message queues

A message queue is a kernel object allocated by the application. In fact, you can allocate any number of message queues. The only limit is the amount of RAM available. There are a number of operations that the user can perform on message queues but the most typical ones are "create a queue", "send a message through a queue" and "wait for a message to arrive on a queue". An ISR can only send a message to a queue; it cannot wait for a message. A message queue must be created before sending messages through it.

Message queues are drawn as a first-in, first-out pipe (FIFO). However, some kernels allow messages to be sent in last-in, first-out order (LIFO). The LIFO mechanism is useful when a task or an ISR must send an "urgent" message to a task. In this case, the message bypasses all other messages already in the message queue. The size of the message queue (i.e., the number of messages that can be held in a queue waiting for processing) is typically configurable either at run-time or at configuration time.

Figure 8.20 shows typical operations performed on a message queue (queue creation is not shown). The small hourglass close to the receiving task indicates that the task has an option to specify a timeout. This timeout indicates that the task is willing to wait for a message to be sent to the message queue within a certain amount of time. If the message is not sent within that time, the kernel resumes the task and returns an error code indicating that the task was made ready-to-run because of a timeout, and not because the message was received. It is possible to specify an infinite timeout and indicate that the task is willing to wait forever for the message to arrive.

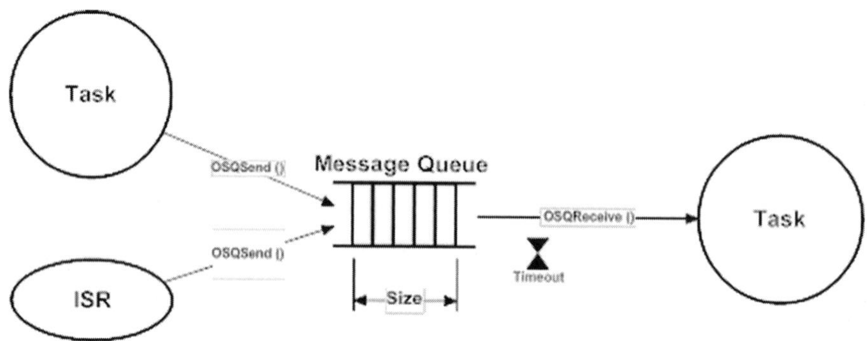

Figure 8.20:
Sending and receiving data through a message queue.

The message queue also contains a list of tasks waiting for messages to be sent to the message queue. Multiple tasks can wait on a message queue as shown in Figure 8.21a. When a message is sent to the message queue, the highest priority task waiting on the message queue receives the message. Optionally, the sender can broadcast a message to all tasks waiting on the message queue. In this case, if any of the tasks receiving the message from the broadcast has a higher priority than the task sending the message (or interrupted task, if the message is sent by an ISR), the kernel will run the highest-priority task that is waiting. Notice that not all tasks must specify a timeout; some tasks may want to wait forever.

Flow control

Task-to-task communication often involves data transfer from one task to another. One task produces data while the other consumes it. However, data processing takes time and

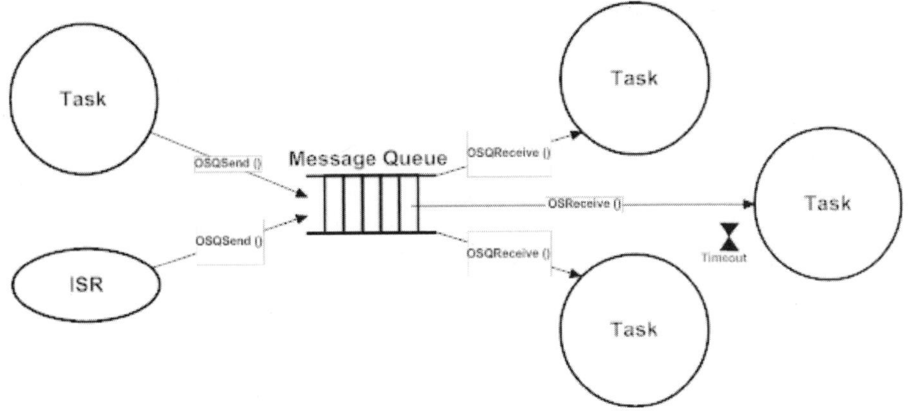

Figure 8.21a:
Multiple tasks waiting for messages.

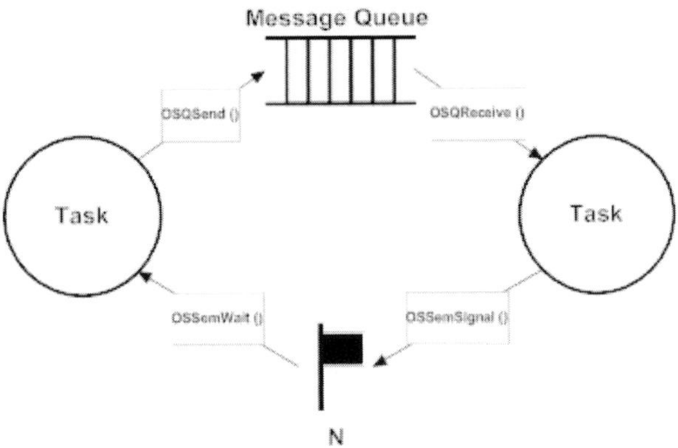

Figure 8.21b:
Multiple tasks waiting for messages.

consumers might not consume data as fast as it is produced. In other words, it is possible for the producer to overflow the message queue if a higher-priority task preempts the consumer. One way to solve this problem is to add flow control in the process as shown in Figure 8.21b.

Here, a counting semaphore is used and initialized with the number of allowable messages that can be received by the consumer. If the consumer cannot queue more than 10 messages, the counting semaphore contains a count of 10.

As shown in the pseudocode of Listing 8.14, the producer must wait for the semaphore before it is allowed to send a message. The consumer waits for messages and, when processed, signals the semaphore.

```
OS_SEM   MySem;
OS_Q     MyQ;
int      Message;

void  MyProducerTask (void)
{
    while (1) {
        :
        OSSemWait(&MySem);
        OSQSend(&MyQ, (void *)&Message);
        :
    }
}


void  MyConsumerTask (void)
{
    void *p_message;

    while (1) {
        :
        p_message = OSQReceive(&MyQ);
        OSSemSignal(&MySem);
        :
    }
```

Listing 8.14:
Message queue flow control.

Clients and servers

Another interesting use of message queues is shown in Figure 8.22. Here, a task (the server) is used to monitor error conditions that are sent to it by other tasks or ISRs (clients). For example, a client detects whether the RPM of a rotating wheel has been exceeded, another client detects whether an over-temperature exists, and yet another client detects that a user pressed a shutdown button. When the clients detect error conditions, they send a message through the message queue. The message sent could indicate the error detected, which threshold was exceeded, the error code that is associated with error conditions, or even suggest the address of a function that will handle the error, and more.

Memory management

An application can allocate and free dynamic memory using any ANSI C compiler's `malloc()` and `free()` functions, respectively. However, using `malloc()` and `free()` in an embedded real-time system may be dangerous. Eventually, it might not be possible to obtain a single contiguous memory area due to fragmentation. Fragmentation is the development of a large number of separate free areas (i.e., the total free memory is fragmented into small, non-contiguous pieces).

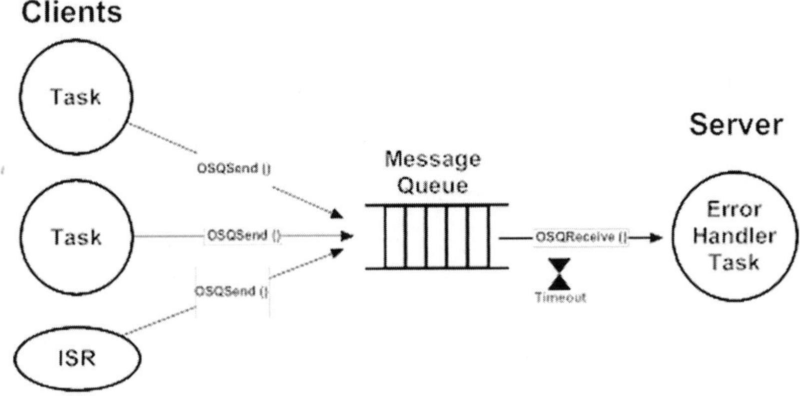

Figure 8.22:
Client/server using message queues.

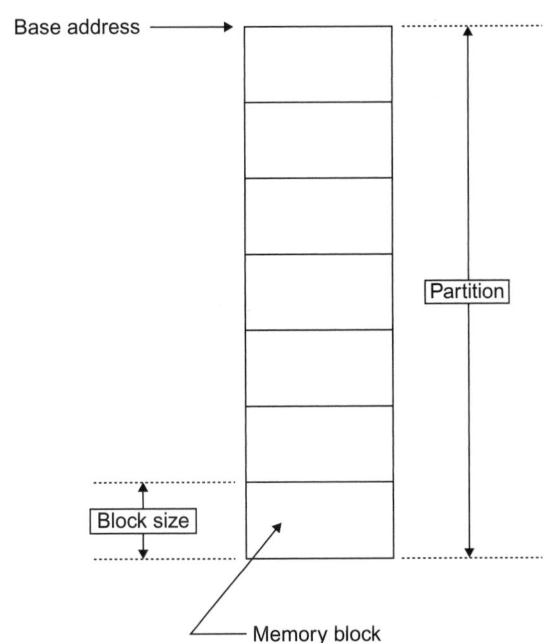

Figure 8.23:
Fixed-size-block memory partition.

Execution time of `malloc()` and `free()` is generally nondeterministic given the algorithms used to locate a contiguous block of free memory large enough to satisfy a `malloc()` request.

Kernels provide alternatives to `malloc()` and `free()` by allowing an application to obtain fixed-sized memory blocks from a partition made from a contiguous memory area, as illustrated in Figure 8.23. All memory blocks are the same size, and the partition

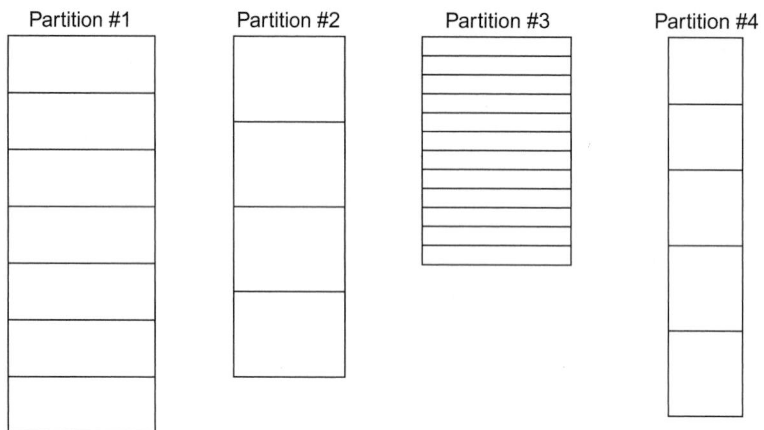

Figure 8.24:
Multiple memory partitions each having different block sizes.

contains an integral number of blocks. Allocation and de-allocation of these memory blocks is performed in constant time and is deterministic. The partition itself is typically allocated statically (as an array), but can also be allocated by using `malloc()` as long as it is never freed.

As indicated in Figure 8.24, more than one memory partition may exist in an application and each one may have a different number of memory blocks and be a different size. An application can obtain memory blocks of different sizes based upon requirements. However, a specific memory block must always be returned to the partition that it came from. This type of memory management is not subject to fragmentation except that it is possible to run out of memory blocks. It is up to the application to decide how many partitions to have and how large each memory block should be within each partition.

Summary

A real-time kernel is software that manages the time and resources of a microprocessor, microcontroller or digital signal processor (DSP). A kernel provides valuable services to your application (product) through a series of application programming interfaces (APIs). Functions are thus available to manage tasks, manage shared resources, notify tasks that events have occurred, send messages to tasks, suspend execution of tasks for a user specified amount of time, and more.

A kernel allows a CPU to multitask. Multitasking is the process of scheduling (determining which task to run next) and context switching (assigning the CPU to a task) the CPU between several tasks. Multitasking provides the illusion of having multiple CPUs and by doing so, maximizes the use of the CPU and helps in the creation of modular applications.

Most real-time kernels are preemptive, meaning that the kernel always runs the highest-priority task that is ready-to-run.

One of the world's most popular real-time kernels is called µC/OS-III (pronounced micro-C-OS-three). µC/OS-III is available from Micrium and its source code has been made *Source Available* by Micrium. Source Available means that the source code can be downloaded from the Micrium website and evaluated for free. However, a license is required if µC/OS-III is used commercially (used with the intent to make a profit).

The internals of µC/OS-III are fully described in the book: *µC/OS-III, The Real-Time Kernel* published by MicriumPress (see www.micrium.com). There are in fact many versions of the µC/OS-III book, each of which provides examples of running µC/OS-III on different popular CPU architectures (see the Micrium website for details).

This chapter was excerpted from sections of the µC/OS-III book.

CHAPTER 9

Software Reuse By Design in Embedded Systems

Jim Trudeau

Chapter Outline

The fundamental premise of this chapter is simple. If you can reliably reuse existing software, you will save time and money. There are significant other advantages, but let's cut to the chase about what really matters to the people running the businesses we work for.

Software reuse is, to put it mildly, a non-trivial problem. Many programmers, and teams of programmers, have picked up existing software thinking "I'll just port this code..." and disappeared into the wilderness never to be heard from again.

In this chapter we will explore the challenges preventing reliable reuse of software for embedded systems. I will explore various historical solutions for surmounting those challenges. This will take us through the world as we know it today.

I will then present the concept of the software component factory. This approach can address software reuse challenges in a hardware-agnostic and operating-system-agnostic manner, especially in the context of embedded systems. We will look at its advantages,

Software Engineering for Embedded Systems.
DOI: http://dx.doi.org/10.1016/B978-0-12-415917-4.00009-8
© 2013 Elsevier Inc. All rights reserved.

disadvantages, and limitations. The component factory represents the leading edge of software tools engineering and development today. Such factories do exist in the real world; this is not just a theory. However, at present they are proprietary and support individual semiconductor manufacturers. There is no open source or general solution at this level of sophistication.

Why does software reuse matter?

Just in case you are not already a believer in the idea that software reuse is mandatory in the modern world, let's take a quick look at the cost of embedded software development. I'm not pretending to do something canonical here. There are many ways to figure out cost estimates. I'm going to use something called the Constructive Cost Model (COCOMO), originally described by Dr. Barry Boehm in his book *Software Engineering Economics* [1]. The model was updated between 1995 and 2000. The revised model is described in *Software Cost Estimation with COCOMO II* [2]. In this model you establish values for many parameters governing various facets of the software project such as:

- How capable are the programmers?
- How experienced is the team with the target platform?
- How much experience does the team have with the programming language and tools?
- Is the team split across multiple sites? Local or international?
- Is the schedule compressed from nominal?
- How much will your software load the CPU?
- What is the consequence of software failure (e.g., loss of human life)?
- Are you writing real-time or reentrant software?
- How would you describe the relationships among the stakeholders in the project?

There are many such parameters, some well-defined and some fuzzy. As an experienced software developer you recognize that these are eminently practical questions about factors that really affect productivity, like whether the bosses get along with each other.

With good estimation software based on this model (or any model of your choosing), you can tweak values and watch the cost of software development vary. Your mileage will vary based on your situation and assumptions. My estimate is captured in Figure 9.1. It is based mostly on "nominal" estimates, adapted for the real word of embedded development. Based on my experience I said that the schedule was compressed to less than nominal, that reliability had to be higher than nominal, testing data was higher than nominal (same reasoning), complexity was very high (the model's definition for reentrant code) and that the code would be reused to some extent. These reasonable middle-of-the-road parameters involving all aspects of the project, including design, implementation, and test, result in a rule of thumb that says 1,500 lines of code require one full-time-equivalent (FTE) of effort,

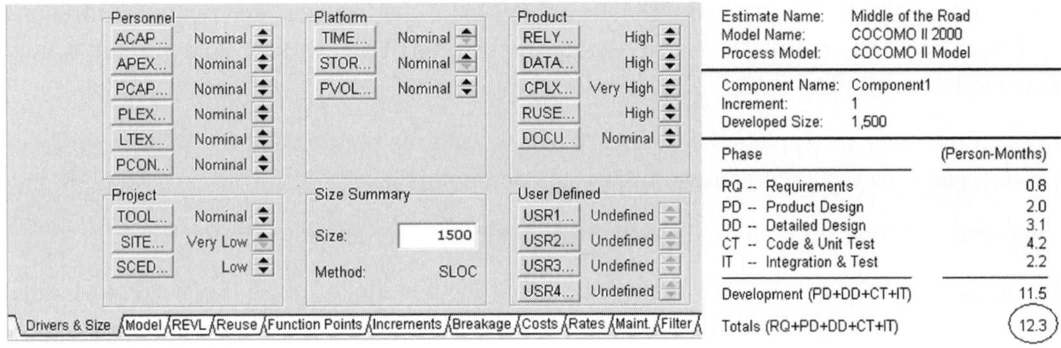

Figure 9.1:
Level of effort estimates based on reasonable embedded software development assumptions.

a year of work. If you have inexperienced programmers, informal production systems, or life-critical code, it gets much worse. Note as well that as a project scales up, the level of effort scales faster: 3,000 lines of code require more than 2 × the time of 1,500 lines of code.

I will be the first person to agree that lines of code are not the ideal measure of productivity. Whatever the value of lines of code as a metric, the underlying principle remains valid. It costs a great deal of money to produce reliable, high-quality software. Assuming you have good software, you can save time and money (probably a lot of both) if you reuse the software. If you can save an FTE per 1,500 lines of code, do the math.

It's more than just saving on the cost of programmers. You also get done faster, and get to market more quickly. I can't tell you what that's worth, seriously, but it has the potential to make all the difference between success and failure in the business world.

But wait, there's more. Let's get a bit less tangible and present a hypothetical. Let's say your code reuse involves the human interface to your software. There is a huge market benefit to reuse: immediate customer recognition of your software (branding!), with resulting reduced learning curve and ready acceptance.

The amount of effort involved in creating a singularly effective human interface is non-trivial. As microcontrollers move up the ladder in capability and out into the world of the consumer, human interaction with the software becomes more and more important.

Let's hypothesize that you design a world-class, simple, clean, intuitive user interface to control a home thermostat, something so simple a child intuitively understands how to use it. It becomes a major differentiator for your company, because you have made programming the HVAC truly simple! Now take that same interface and apply it to lighting systems, irrigation controls, a security system, and so on. You can take your success across new products and platforms.

Look at the reuse of Apple's iOS interface across multiple platforms: MP3 players, mobile phones, and now tablet computers. Clearly it can be done.

There are real, non-trivial hurdles to this feat, which we are about to explore.

Before we do, let me make one more claim about the benefits of reuse. Software you reuse is more likely to be good quality. Once in place, used and reused, it is put through its paces in multiple instances and implementations. Such a known body of code is less likely to harbor defects than new code, if only because it is continually retested in new applications that exercise limits and corner cases.

The other side to that coin is this: reuse of software in a new context certainly involves new scenarios, and defects that were heretofore concealed may be revealed. As well, if you change the code to adjust to the new environment, defects could be introduced. Testing is still required, so this is not an unalloyed benefit, but it is real.

So it is pretty obvious why engineers have pursued the Holy Grail of software reuse for decades:

- cost saving
- time to market advantage
- market acceptance
- code quality.

So, why is it that so much software is still written from scratch?

What limits software reuse?

There are serious problems to that bit of daydreaming above about conquering the home controls market with the world's best HVAC human interface design. Let's look at three of them: assembly language, hardware dependencies, and operating system (software) dependencies.

The first barrier to code reuse is assembly language, the historical ideal for embedded development. Think of "assembly language" here as any hardware-specific language. Assembly language has all the mnemonics for the instruction set for a particular processor. Each processor is different; end of portability. A high-level language like C is portable – a compiler translates the code into assembly for any given processor. Purists still argue that no compiler can write native assembly like a master, that hand-coding will give you code that is faster, smaller, and better. I won't argue the point.

The problem is that there are dozens of microcontroller architectures and instruction sets. If you write assembly for one, you write for one. If you write C code, you write for virtually all of them. You learn the C language once, and you can use it for any platform, albeit with (perhaps) some cost in terms of code size and speed.

The good news is that the historical increase in processor capacity has more than offset any code performance hit. This has allowed *most* developers in *most* cases to move to a high-level language and away from assembly language with no impact to customers. C is platform agnostic, and agnosticism is a good thing when it comes to reusable code.

The second barrier to reuse is hardware dependency. Code, even high-level code, for an embedded system is often written for a particular platform. The code must know something about the hardware it is running on. It will touch registers directly, or make assumptions about peripherals to take advantage of the capabilities of the platform. The code in Example 9.1 is filled with register masks and bit shifting to set up a clock.

```
    while (MCG_S & MCG_S_IREFST_MASK){}; // wait for reference clock status
bit to clear

    while (((MCG_S & MCG_S_CLKST_MASK) >> MCG_S_CLKST_SHIFT) != 0x2){}; //
wait for clock status bits to show clock source is ext ref clk

    // The crystal frequency is used to select the PRDIV value. Only even
frequency crystals are supported
    // This will produce a 2MHz reference clock to the PLL.
    MCG_C5 = MCG_C5_PRDIV(24);

    // Ensure MCG_C6 is at the reset default of 0.
    MCG_C6 = 0;

    // Set system options dividers
    SIM_CLKDIV1 =    SIM_CLKDIV1_OUTDIV1(0) | // core/system clock
                     SIM_CLKDIV1_OUTDIV2(1) | // peripheral clock;
                     SIM_CLKDIV1_OUTDIV3(1) | // FlexBus clock driven to the
external pin (FB_CLK).
                     SIM_CLKDIV1_OUTDIV4(3);  // flash clock
```

Code Example 9.1:
Hardware-specific code is mandatory, even in high-level languages.

These hardware-specific dependencies effectively lock the code to the platform. If you want to move to another platform, this code breaks. Embedded software is filled with such code.

This isn't because the programmers who wrote the code are stupid; quite the opposite. It's quite likely this is an intentional design! For one thing, embedded software runs close to "the metal" and setup code is required. Some software has to set up the hardware; it doesn't run on its own.

There is another compelling market-driven reason our software gets locked to the hardware it runs on.

The product needs to hit performance requirements. Customers demand responsiveness. Designers require minimal code footprint so that production costs can be kept down. The market pressures of the real world demand optimizations that require platform-specific tweaking, and those market pressures override the "theoretical" desire to design a general solution. The potential need to port code next year is far outweighed by the immediate requirement to hit a performance target. This reality isn't going to go away any time soon.

I'm tempted to say "never going to go away", but never is a pretty absolute word. The increasing power of microcontrollers could mean that we'll reach a processor capacity such that performance optimization won't matter anymore. So far, increases in capacity have meant more features to eat the capacity, and optimization has remained a hard requirement. I don't think we'll hit nirvana that soon.

If the second barrier to reuse is hardware locking, the third barrier to reuse is analogous, but at the software level. In the original design of embedded software the analyst/architect will likely choose an operating system. This may be as simple as a home-brew scheduler or a high-end commercial real-time operating system (RTOS). Wherever it is on the spectrum of complexity, the software in the system is written to that operating system. It becomes the lynchpin, and hooks into the RTOS permeating everything about the software.

A typical RTOS will provide a variety of capabilities such as interrupt scheduling, task prioritization using various schemes, messaging (semaphore and mutex perhaps), and so forth. The more your software takes advantage of these services, the more you are locked to the RTOS.

For example, your driver code is about to enter a critical section and must turn off interrupts. In a bare-metal environment, there is typically a register to set. In an RTOS environment you make an API call because there could be a variety of housekeeping steps required. For Micrium's μCOS, you would balance calls to `OS_CRITICAL_ENTER()` and `OS_CRITICAL_EXIT()` macros. If you change your RTOS you must change those calls. For MQX RTOS it's `ENTER_CRITICAL_SECTION()` and `EXIT_CRITICAL_SECTION()`.

Multiply this by the number of RTOS services you use, and you have an understanding of the scale of the problem. When you change, the new RTOS may not have a service you used (perhaps it does not implement mutex) in which case you could be in for serious porting issues.

A solution would be to create an RTOS abstraction layer. All RTOS calls would go to this layer, and then redirect to the actual RTOS. We will discuss this strategy in the next section when we discuss implementing reuse by layers. It has a dual penalty: you have to create it; and it has an indirection performance cost for size and speed.

Given this reality, how do you take software that is, for all practical purposes, custom designed for a particular platform (processor, board, peripherals, drivers, touch-sensing libraries, operating system, and so on), and move that to multiple embedded designs? It may very well be the case that each has a different processor, a different display technology, and perhaps comes in different models with different capabilities. Can it be done?

Kinds of software reuse

The simplest and perhaps first example of software reuse can probably be summed up as "Hey, I've got a really neat algorithm. Here's the code". I call this cut-and-paste programming. It's real, it's valid, and it's valuable. Put a bunch of these together in a single problem domain, and you have a software library. Document it, wrap it up in a neat package, ensure that it will work with multiple compilers, and you are onto something.

The classic example is the standard C library, which in its full implementation has functions for memory allocation, thread manipulation, standard math, floating-point operations, string manipulation, and so on.

A quick search will turn up domain-specific libraries for topics as diverse as user-interface instrumentation, audio and video codecs, and celestial mechanics.

There is a continuum of "polish" to software libraries, from simple collections of somewhat related functions to highly structured frameworks with extensible architectures of abstract classes designed in C++. In the end, they are all, essentially, software libraries and each represents a body of code you can reuse.

For many software libraries there are no hardware dependencies, they are "pure" software. Simply recompile and you should be fine, assuming that the platform has the resources to support the library (for example, if floating point is required, your platform must support it).

If there are hardware dependencies, a well-designed library is factored, and puts all dependencies into a specific location so that you can modify and adapt the library to a particular bit of hardware. Any good RTOS will follow this design, because the range of hardware supported will be broad. One effort currently under way is the Yocto Project, which enables custom Linux-based systems for embedded development. The project defines a common structure for board support packages so that hardware support is standardized and easily understood.

The typical design is to factor the hardware-specific code into separate files, and those files are rewritten every time the OS is ported to a new platform. This is not a hardware abstraction layer. It is simply separating (factoring) the code that touches hardware into a known location so it is easily identified. If you port the code, the hardware touches must be rewritten. By keeping all that software in one place, we keep the areas that have to change controlled. Figure 9.2 shows the concept.

Implementing reuse by layers

A hardware abstraction layer (HAL) implements a reusable hardware interface in software. You can think of this as the "hardware section" of an RTOS or code library generalized into a multi-purpose API to access the hardware layer. The RTOS or application (if necessary) can call the HAL without touching hardware. The HAL acts as a buffer that insulates all the code above it from knowledge of or dependency on any hardware details. Figure 9.3 shows what this looks like as a block diagram.

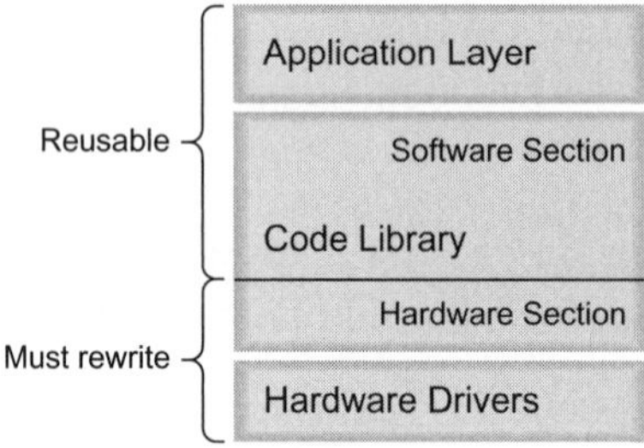

Figure 9.2:
A factored code library helps ease reuse for hardware-independent code.

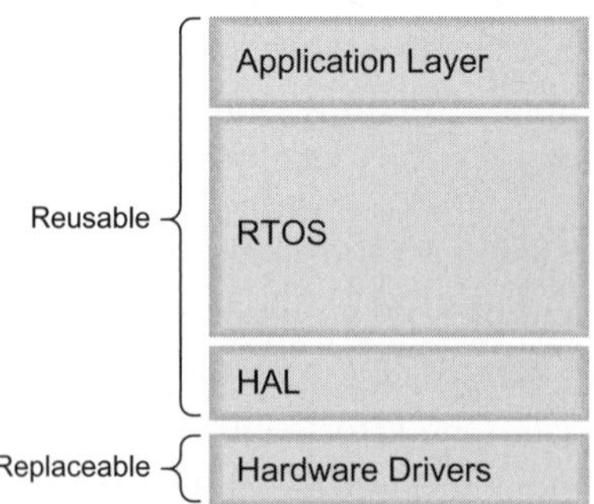

Figure 9.3:
A hardware abstraction layer increases reusability.

The HAL itself, in theory, is fully reusable and does not need rewriting when you port to new hardware. In practice, the HAL typically needs tweaking to accommodate some idiosyncrasy of the new platform, but as a stable API it remains unchanged from the perspective of the higher levels of software. What this means from a software reuse perspective is that, when you port the code to new hardware, all access into and out of the hardware-sensitive code remains unchanged. In *theory*, you can swap in any hardware layer and it still works.

OK, we see that *in theory* using a HAL can help unlock us from hardware. What about our RTOS dependency? Remember that one of the fundamental barriers to reuse at the software level is how code is locked to an RTOS. What can we do about that?

The answer is, it's the same trick: an RTOS abstraction layer. The fundamental technique is indirection. Instead of calling the OS directly, you call a similar function in the abstraction layer (call it the porting layer). The porting layer calls the RTOS (Figure 9.4).

Even if you have not implemented an RTOS porting layer in your software initially, you can still take advantage of this technique after the fact. Like a magician's sleight of hand, you substitute a header file that mimics the RTOS's API. Where your code makes an RTOS call, the new header file redirects the call to your own function. The new function may perform some setup or "wrapper" work if necessary, and then call the new operating system's parallel function to do the work.

This is perhaps the simplest porting and reuse trick in the world. In this way you do not need to substantially rewrite code. Just link in the appropriate header files, provide the necessary glue code, and you get to use a new RTOS.

You probably don't have to invent this from scratch. There are commercial endeavors that follow this strategy. One example is MapuSoft, which provides tools to port from multiple OSes such as VxWorks, pSOS, Nucleus, POSIX, micro-ITRON, and others.

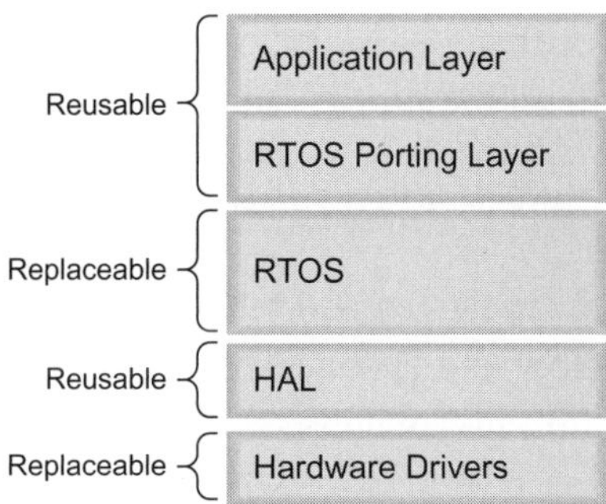

Figure 9.4:
Implementing a porting layer allows RTOS independence.

The advantage is obvious. Suddenly you aren't locked to that RTOS anymore, and you did not have to change a single line of code. Wow, talk about a free lunch!

The disadvantages are perhaps not quite so obvious, but depending on your circumstances may be worth the price of admission.

A porting layer adds a layer of indirection, hence some inefficiency. If nothing else there's a function call jump in between. There may be an increase in code complexity and size. There may be some performance hit as a result. However, a port to a new OS is often happening at the same time as a port to new hardware, and the new processor may accommodate the performance requirements quite nicely. Also, the new RTOS may be inherently more efficient. In fact you may see things get better!

More importantly, all operating systems are not created equal. Functions will not be precisely parallel, so the translation will not be precisely 1:1. For example, the interrupt-handling scheme may be different; how the new RTOS handles priority queues could be subtly changed. You will need to test carefully for functionality and quality.

Nonetheless, this is one strategy for freeing yourself from the tyranny of your code being intricately tied to an operating system. When the only alternative is a complete rewrite, this may have great appeal and could get you to a design goal more quickly.

Going to the next level

What we have discussed so far is embedded software development as we have come to know it. It is a world of practical compromises. To get the code to meet requirements, we squeeze every possible cycle out of the hardware. We optimize the hardware and lock the software to it, thereby condemning ourselves to minimal reuse.

We hate that. We are not stupid; we know the value of reuse. But generic reusable code has always meant "lowest common denominator" and the pressure of performance in embedded systems often does not allow for that. A year or two later when the hardware changes (usually becoming more capable in the process) up go the stakes and down comes the order: move to a new platform. Then we reap what we have sown, and we incur costs because of those hardware and RTOS dependencies.

If you engage in excellent software design and take advantage of the techniques we have discussed, you can soften the blow and enhance the reusability of your software. These tips and tricks have advantages and disadvantages.

You can create a HAL or an RTOS abstraction layer at any time. There is no dependency on any manufacturer, platform, product, or processor. It takes time and engineering effort to be sure.

Also, these techniques involve indirection, a likelihood of code bloat, and difficulties that are always encountered when moving code that is not optimized for a particular platform. Hey, it's a form of job security, but as engineers we know there must be a better way. We are good engineers, we like elegant design. These disadvantages have driven a desire for a better solution. The challenge is straightforward.

How can we create reusable software components that are optimized for hardware but hardware and operating system agnostic?

This is a decidedly non-trivial problem. It has been addressed, but only (to my knowledge) in corporate proprietary tools. Nonetheless, I believe this is worth exploring for two reasons.

First, it is a useful exercise to look at the leading edge of software development. Where we have been so far is the known map. I want to take you a step further into what may be unknown to you. If you understand new concepts, you can advance them in your own world. Ideas may filter down into the public domain and become more generally useful.

Second, the companies who are implementing proprietary solutions (of various flavors and utility) cover a large section of the embedded marketplace. If you become aware of these tools, you may find them useful in your work.

Introducing the component factory

Clearly if you want to create reusable software that is hardware agnostic, you cannot write the software in advance. You define a set of parameters, among which is the hardware description. The hardware can change, in which case the parameters defining your project change. These parameters inform an expert system that generates the code required for your platform. The "magic", if there is such, is that the necessary software is built into the expert system, in all its variants.

The expert system is the component factory. If you change the inputs, the factory changes the output. The output is the software created for the system you have defined. The "system" can be as small as the initialization code for a particular chip, or encapsulate an entire RTOS. Components are and should be modular, to encourage maximum reusability. They are building blocks, bricks out of which you can build larger software structures.

Let's look at the primary features of a component factory, and then at a real-world implementation. In my work at Freescale I am most familiar with Processor Expert Software, so I will use that as a primary exemplar. We'll close with a summary of the advantages and disadvantages of this approach to software reuse.

The factory metaphor is quite apt. A factory has a set of reconfigurable machines. We pull a bunch of levers or push buttons to configure the machines to produce a desired output; then we push a button to set it all running. The component factory matches this general flow. Behind it is an expert system that understands the hardware. Let's go into that in increasing levels of detail.

Factory hardware configuration

The first use case the factory is aimed at is configuring hardware. With growing complexity, silicon reference manuals have grown to thousands of pages. Understanding how to initialize a processor is daunting. Silicon vendors have provided driver libraries or example code for this purpose, but this is often lowest-common-denominator code.

Enter configuration tools, which are often expert systems. Table 9.1 is a non-canonical list of some choices.

Table 9.1: Some component factory tools.

Tool	Provider	Targets	Tools
PSocCreator	Cypress	PSoC3, PSoC5	Keil, Code Sourcery
Grace	TI	MSP430	CodeComposer Studio
DAvE	Infineon	XC800, C500/800, C166/CX166, XE166, XC2000, TriCore	DAvE Bench
Processor Expert Software	Freescale	S08/RS08, S12, DSC, Power Architecture, Coldfire, Coldfire+, Kinetis (ARM Cortex-M4, Cortex-M0+), Vybrid	CodeWarrior, IAR, Kiel, GCC

Each of these is more than simply a hardware configuration tool. I selected these samples because each of these software packages is an expert system and a basic (at least) component factory. Each will generate the source code required to configure the processor to match your configuration choices. The generated code can be quite extensive. Code Example 9.2 shows a small excerpt from generated PWM code from PSoC Creator from Cypress. This is setting various wait cycles depending on chip revisions, precisely the kind of subtle silicon detail that is easy to get wrong when using a reference manual the traditional way.

This is where we diverge from the typical software development process. Classic reusable software, written in advance, must make lowest-common-denominator assumptions about things such as the clock source. If that assumption does not work for you, you need to override it with code you write, typically by defining a term in a header file or setting a value in a register during startup. With a component factory you specify that as an option in

```
{
...
    /* Save current flash wait cycles and set the maximum new one */
    cyPmBackup.flashWaitCycles = (CY_PM_CACHE_CR_CYCLES_MASK &
CY_PM_CACHE_CR_REG);

    /* Device is PSoC 3 and the revision is ES3 or later */
    #if(CY_PM_PSOC3_ES3)

        CyFlash_SetWaitCycles(45u);

    #endif  /* End of (CY_PM_PSOC3_ES3) */

    /* Device is PSoC 3 and the revision is ES2 or earlier */
    #if(CY_PM_PSOC3_ES2)

        CyFlash_SetWaitCycles(49u);

    #endif  /* End of (CY_PM_PSOC3_ES2) */
```

Code Example 9.2:
Expert systems generate code that accounts for subtle differences in technical details.

a configuration utility, and the system will generate the code automatically. Figure 9.5 shows the Processor Expert Software tool from Freescale.

You repeat this process for all the hardware parts you need. It's hardly magic, but the expert system is a phenomenal assistant. It understands every register, every pin on every chip, how every peripheral uses those pins, and every possible conflict. If there are conflicts you are warned as you configure the system, before it generates any software. Once you have made all your configuration choices, you then push a button to generate code. The expert system contains all the variant software required to create the proper code. Based on the configuration choices, the system spits out precisely the right software (like what you see in Code Example 9.2).

Factory software configuration

In a good factory, one size does not fit all. A typical peripheral has a multitude of functions, but your implementation may not need them all. Again we diverge from the standard "driver library" delivery system where every driver has every function, because you never know what someone will want. In a factory system, you configure the factory to produce what you want.

You decide which functions to include. If you don't need it, don't include it, and your code size is minimized. Here's a good, practical example. The Processor Expert factory includes a Timer driver. It has multiple functions, as shown in Figure 9.6.

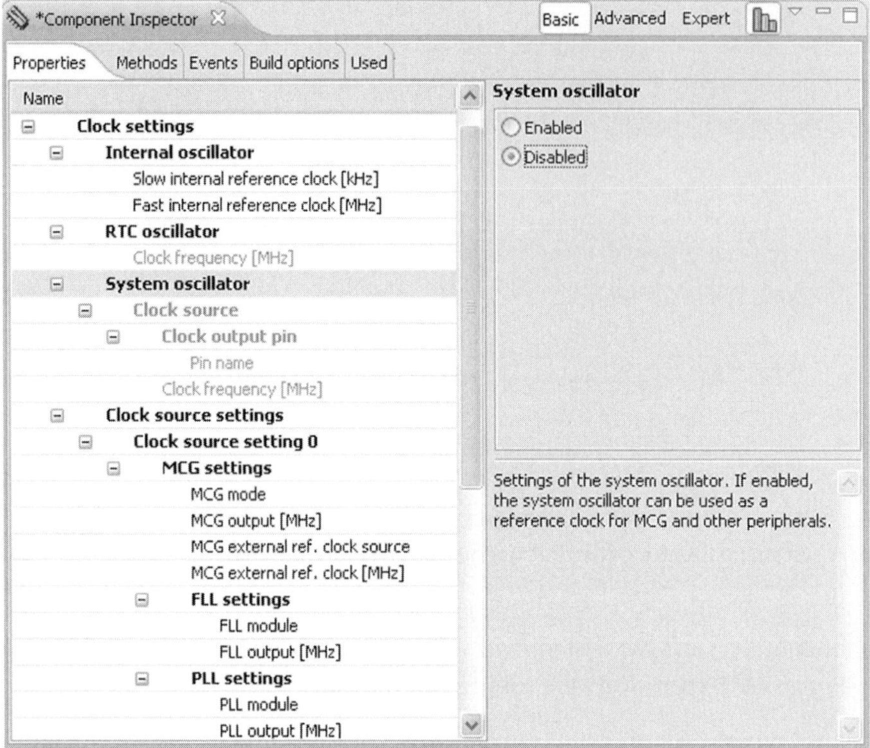

Figure 9.5:
Configuring system clocks in a hardware configuration tool.

If you choose to generate code, the factory will comply. If not, there is no code. (This kind of control is not available in all component factories.) When you push the button the header and source files appear, to match the choices you made to work on the hardware you selected.

The component factory is not a driver library, nor is it a collection of multiple implementations of a driver library, one for every possible configuration.
The factory is:

- a collection of all the things you would use to build a driver library
- an interface so you can choose and configure everything you want, including a way to select particular functions within a driver implementation
- a knowledge base of how they all relate to each other (like pin usage) so it can provide warnings about conflicts
- a button to generate the required code.

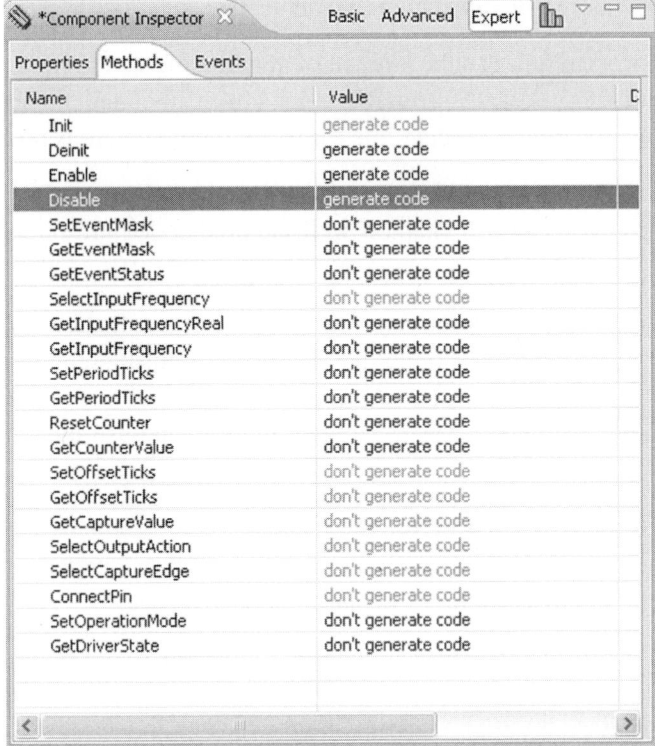

Figure 9.6:
Methods available in a timer driver, which you choose to implement or not.

How the factory aids reusability

When you port to a new platform, you must still adapt your code for all the same changes. "New platform" here could be a different set of I/O peripherals, a different microcontroller derivative, or even a completely different MCU. What is my clock source? What is the bus speed? What pins will I use for the GPIO? What methods do I need in my ADC driver? All the same questions will arise.

How and where you adapt to the changes will be different. Instead of rewriting software, you will reconfigure the factory. With a good factory implementation (good help systems, good UI, a good expert system) it is significantly easier and less error-prone to configure the factory than it is to rewrite software.

Now the real world impinges on our theories. The work required to reconfigure the factory will depend on how different your new platform is from the original. This is where we encounter the principal practical limitation of the factory concept as it exists today.

The target platforms must be included in the expert system, and the systems are vendor specific.

It takes very little effort to imagine the amount of engineering work required to create a component factory. What is available comes from silicon manufacturers, and is limited to that manufacturer's product line (or part thereof). There is no universal solution.

If your new platform is not covered by the vendor's tool, you must rely on the skills and techniques discussed earlier in this chapter: well-factored code built on hardware and/or RTOS abstraction layers.

If the factory covers your new platform, you're in good shape. If the system is similar, reconfiguring may be trivial. If it is quite different, reconfiguring may require some work. A good expert system should alert you to everything that is out of synch with your new platform. Once the new hardware system is reconfigured you push the button, and you have your new code.

I am not trying to trivialize reconfiguring the factory. There is still significant expertise and work required to accommodate a radically new platform. But an expert system built into a factory is going to help prevent a lot of mistakes at design time.

We have discussed hardware and software configuration. There are two more aspects to the component factory that I want to explore: RTOS agnosticism, and arbitrary extensibility. These are genuinely at the leading edge of software development today.

RTOS agnosticism

As noted earlier in this chapter, traditional attempts at creating RTOS agnosticism rely on and require indirection. You can substitute a header file to redirect RTOS calls to a porting layer. This works, but may introduce inefficiencies. The ideal would be to mimic the configurability of the hardware layer. In a truly well-designed component factory, one reconfigurable item should be "I need to use an RTOS service here".

For example, a peripheral driver component may need to allocate memory for a buffer, or enable/disable interrupts. In a "bare metal" environment, it does this directly. If you are using an RTOS, you need to substitute calls to an RTOS, hence the need for an RTOS abstraction layer.

In the ideal factory, the code generation process can do better. An RTOS adapter recognizes all such RTOS dependencies. At code generation time, the RTOS adapter sees that the driver's logic requires an RTOS service at a given point. The code generator automatically substitutes the correct RTOS call at that point.

Code Example 9.3 is a GPIO driver allocating memory "natively", that is, without an RTOS adapter. The call is highlighted.

```
LDD_TDeviceData* GPIO1_Init(LDD_TUserData *UserDataPtr)
{
  /* Allocate LDD device structure */
  GPIO1_TDeviceData *DeviceDataPrv;

  /* {Default RTOS Adapter} Driver memory allocation: Dynamic allocation is
simulated by a pointer to the static object */
  DeviceDataPrv = &DeviceDataPrv__DEFAULT_RTOS_ALLOC;
```

Code Example 9.3:
Memory allocation without an RTOS adapter.

Code Example 9.4 is the same code, generated with an RTOS adapter.

```
LDD_TDeviceData* GPIO1_Init(LDD_TUserData *UserDataPtr)
{
  /* Allocate LDD device structure */
  GPIO1_TDeviceData *DeviceDataPrv;

  /* {MQX RTOS Adapter} Driver memory allocation: RTOS function call is
defined by MQX RTOS Adapter property */
  DeviceDataPrv = (GPIO1_TDeviceData
*)_mem_alloc_system((_mem_size)sizeof(GPIO1_TDeviceData));
  #if MQX_CHECK_MEMORY_ALLOCATION_ERRORS
  if (DeviceDataPrv == NULL) {
    return (NULL);
  }
  #endif
```

Code Example 9.4:
Direct calls to the RTOS are used to allocate memory.

This is not indirection, it is direct substitution. The RTOS adapter is RTOS-specific. So the FreeRTOS adapter puts in calls appropriate for that RTOS. The MQX RTOS adapter puts in its calls. The μCOS adapter puts in its calls. The developer simply says "I'm using this RTOS" and the rest is automatic.

There are no software layers here. There is no call to a method that says "come here for memory allocation, and I'll do the right thing depending on whether you are using an RTOS and what RTOS you are using".

Note that this does not eliminate any direct calls to the RTOS's API from your application software.

Nonetheless this represents the beginning of true RTOS independence in the design of reusable components. This distinction is actually a key point.

The factory concept enables a much greater degree of portability for software that touches hardware: peripheral drivers and processor configuration, what is traditionally called the board support package. It is not aimed at the application software. However, while the focus of the factory is on hardware portability, it can help for pure software as well.

Arbitrary extensibility

A critical element of the factory is its component library. If you have reusable components, you can think of each of them as a brick or module. The software you build is only as good as the collection of components out of which you are able to build. These components typically represent the drivers associated with the IP blocks on the processors, and the peripheral drivers for the boards provided by the manufacturer who built the factory.

The provider will give you a good set of components. The factories listed in this article each come with dozens if not hundreds of components. These may not be sufficient. There is a fair chance that what you need will be missing. In the end, the odds are you are going to build your own board. A good factory should be extensible.

For example, DAvE has an SDK to create plugins to add to the system. Processor Expert has an associated application, the Component Development Environment (CDE), to create arbitrary software components for the system. A software component has no hardware dependency.

Using Infineon's SDK or Freescale's CDE, you can create arbitrary components to encapsulate software modules. The freedom to create software components is enabling. One non-commercial website I am aware of has components that encapsulate: FreeRTOS, a FAT File system, a USB bootloader, text on a graphical display, a universal LED driver, a low-level SD Card driver, an S19 File parser, generic BitIO, and many more.

The ability to create any software functionality as a component encourages more and more reuse. With the proper environment and the proper design, they can be RTOS agnostic as well as hardware agnostic. If you begin to build your application out of such components, the factory begins to have a beneficial impact on the problem of porting an application as well.

Conclusion

The component factory represents a major paradigm shift in software development for embedded systems: you use a machine to generate your code! This is perhaps a greater leap than the one that embedded developers made when shifting from assembly programming to C.

Embedded in the factory is a huge body of code. The factory contains within it all the code that once was the "driver library". Instead of providing one library, lowest-common-denominator style, the factory has a configurable database. It will provide you just what you ask for, a virtual infinity of potential driver libraries. Once you set it up, the factory provides you with a personalized, optimized driver library.

You accomplish changes at design time by making configuration choices, rather than by writing new software. The factory writes the software for you based on its advanced knowledge of the hardware. The beauty of the factory system is that the hardware and RTOS dependencies are abstracted away. You change hardware, you change configuration choices, push a button, and you have new code. Most software engineers no longer need a high degree of hardware expertise, and "porting" becomes much easier.

Also, properly configured hardware-dependent components can be shared across teams, so that a handful of system experts can support a large body of software engineers. Your hardware masters can set things up and handle hardware changes, then share the components across the software development teams.

Finally, you can create well-designed and encapsulated "pure" software components and merge them into the factory. With the ability to enable and disable functions as required, code can be optimized for size without having to rely on dead-stripping linkers. A library of reusable software components can feed into a team's, a company's, or a community's plans and needs.

In the end, components should be as solid, prosaic, and reliable as beams, trusses, and bricks. Out of those, we can build software cathedrals.

Despite the clear advantages of a component factory, the reality is that each comes with proprietary boundaries. You use a factory, you are tied to a particular manufacturer.

There is an obvious market rationale for this limitation. The difficulty of hardware initialization and the need to move software forward across platforms creates a real need. Silicon vendors have a market incentive to fill that need for their products to gain a competitive advantage. This is the force that is driving huge investment, pushing the boundaries of software innovation that has given us the component factory.

Whether the future will see these concepts extend into non-proprietary solutions, only time will tell.

References

[1] B. Boehm, Software Engineering Economics, Prentice-Hall, Englewood Cliffs, NJ, 1981.

[2] B. Boehm, C. Abts, A. Winsor Brown, S. Chulani, B.K. Clark, E. Horowitz, et al., Software Cost Estimation with COCOMO II, Prentice-Hall, Englewood Cliffs, NJ, 2000.

Cost estimations

[3] Personal analysis using CoStar 7.0 from SoftStar Systems to create cost estimates based on COCOMO II. <www.softStarSystems.com>.

[4] Available from: http://en.wikipedia.org/wiki/Barry_Boehm.

[5] Available from: http://en.wikipedia.org/wiki/COCOMO.

[6] Available from: http://sunset.usc.edu/csse/research/COCOMOII/cocomo_main.html.

Defect testing

[7] Available from: http://en.wikipedia.org/wiki/Software_testing.
[8] Available from: http://www.ece.cmu.edu/~koopman/des_s99/sw_reliability/.

Libraries

[9] Available from: http://en.wikipedia.org/wiki/Library_(computing).
[10] Available from: http://en.wikipedia.org/wiki/C_standard_library.

CHAPTER 10

Software Performance Engineering for Embedded Systems

Robert Oshana

Chapter Outline

Embedded systems often have one or more performance-related requirements. The complexity of modern embedded software systems requires a systematic approach for achieving these performance targets. An ad hoc process can lead to missed deadlines, poorly performing systems and cancelled projects. There is a maturity required to define, manage, and deliver on multiple real-time performance requirements.

Performance process maturity can be measured on a scale, similar to the Capability Maturity Model (CMMi) and other related scales. Figure 10.1 shows a similar scale for performance engineering [1].

These maturity levels can be described as follows:

Maturity Level 0: ad hoc fire-fighting. At this level there is little focus given to the operational aspects related to performance. Any requirements that exist related to performance only specify the basic capabilities needed and may not be quantitative. At this level performance issues are found early in the development process, during prototyping or early iterations. These performance issues are addressed by "tuning" the application by optimizing the code. This approach provides only incremental improvement.

Maturity Level 1: systematic performance resolution. At maturity level 1, software teams may have a more systematic performance resolution process that addresses performance bottlenecks using the classic approach of:

- Discover
- Detect

Software Engineering for Embedded Systems.
DOI: http://dx.doi.org/10.1016/B978-0-12-415917-4.00010-4
© 2013 Elsevier Inc. All rights reserved.

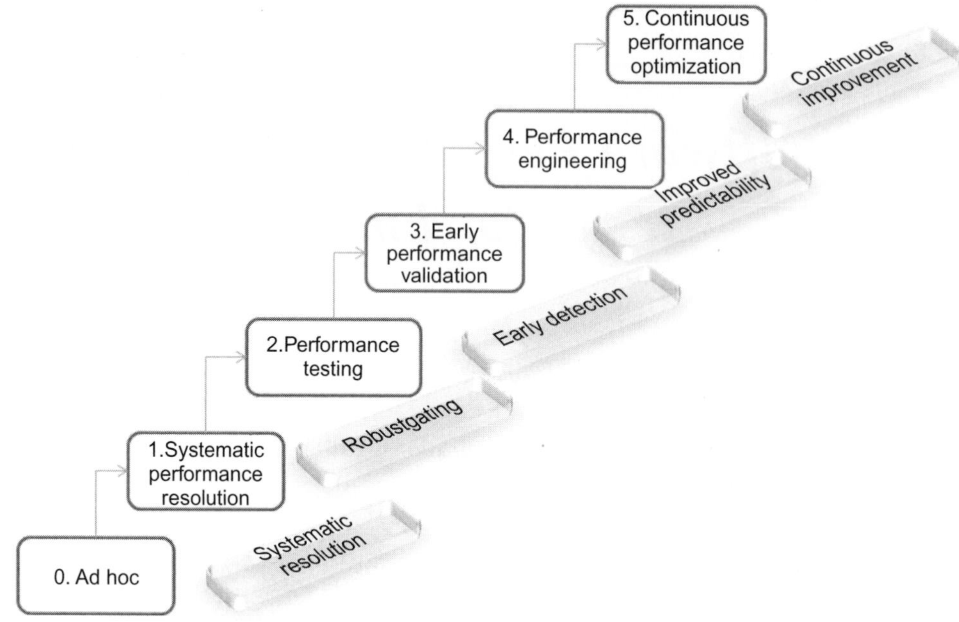

Figure 10.1:
Performance engineering maturity model.

- Isolate
- Resolve.

This approach only focuses on performance resolution by identifying bottlenecks and then tuning appropriately. This approach requires domain experts to help resolve the issues. At this level there is still no process for early identification of performance problems.

Maturity level 2: performance testing. At level 2, the software team may have some level of automation to collect performance data for the embedded system. There is generally a proactive effort to deal systematically with critical resource measurements such as CPU utilization, I/O, memory, and power but until the system is well into development most of the efforts to fix performance defects at this maturity level are limited to operating system or other hardware configuration adjustments.

Maturity Level 3: early performance validation. At this level, performance evaluation and planning is an integral part of the development process. Performance requirements are more aggressively managed using modeling approaches and profiling tools. Performance response time budgets are allocated across the application and managed appropriately.

Maturity level 4: performance engineering. At level 4, the fundamental practices of software performance engineering are practiced and managed throughout the lifecycle.

Maturity Level 5: continuous performance optimization. At this level of process maturity, proposed changes to the system are evaluated for their impact on the end user and there is also an assessment of the impact on relevant and important resource utilizations. Trade-offs are well understood and rationalized. Excessive optimization is prevented by understanding goals and there is no premature optimization. The complete cost of the system is well understood in terms of overall system performance. The team has the discipline to rationalize the benefits for key performance optimizations against the cost of achieving those optimizations in terms of return on investment.

Software performance engineering (SPE) is a discipline within the broader systems engineering area that can improve the maturity of the performance engineering process. SPE is a systematic, quantitative approach to constructing software systems that meet performance objectives. SPE is a software-oriented approach; it focuses on architecture, design, and implementation choices. It focuses on the activities, techniques, and deliverables that are applied at every phase of the embedded software development lifecycle, especially responsiveness and scalability, to ensure software is being architected and implemented to meet the performance-related requirements for the system.

Responsiveness is the ability of a system to meet its objectives for response time or throughput. Defined from a user perspective in end systems this would define the time to complete a task, the number of transactions per unit of time, or how fast to respond to an event. An example would be an embedded networking application which would expect the packet throughput to be roughly at the "line rate" of the peripheral bandwidth such as an Ethernet port.

Scalability is the system ability to continue to meet its response time or throughput objectives as the demand for the software functions increases. For example, as the number of cell phone calls increases in a Femto basestation, the software must scale appropriately to meet the processing requirements for the increased number of users.

Performance failures in systems like this are most often due to fundamental hardware/software architecture or software design factors rather than inefficient coding and implementation. Whether or not a system will be able to exhibit its desired (or required) performance attributes is determined by the time the architecture is chosen.
Ignoring performance-related factors during the early part of the development cycle and tuning performance once the program is running correctly is a "fix it later" attitude that is a primary cause of embedded systems failing to deliver on time and within budget.

Some of the primary objectives of SPE include [3]:

- Eliminating delayed embedded system deployment due to performance issues
- Eliminating avoidable system rework due to performance issues
- Eliminating avoidable system tuning and optimization efforts

- Avoiding additional and unnecessary hardware costs necessary to meet performance objectives
- Reducing increased software maintenance costs due to performance problems in production
- Reducing increased software maintenance costs due to software impacted by ad hoc performance fixes.

The SPE process includes the following steps [3] (see Figure 10.2):

1. Assess performance risk
2. Identify critical use cases

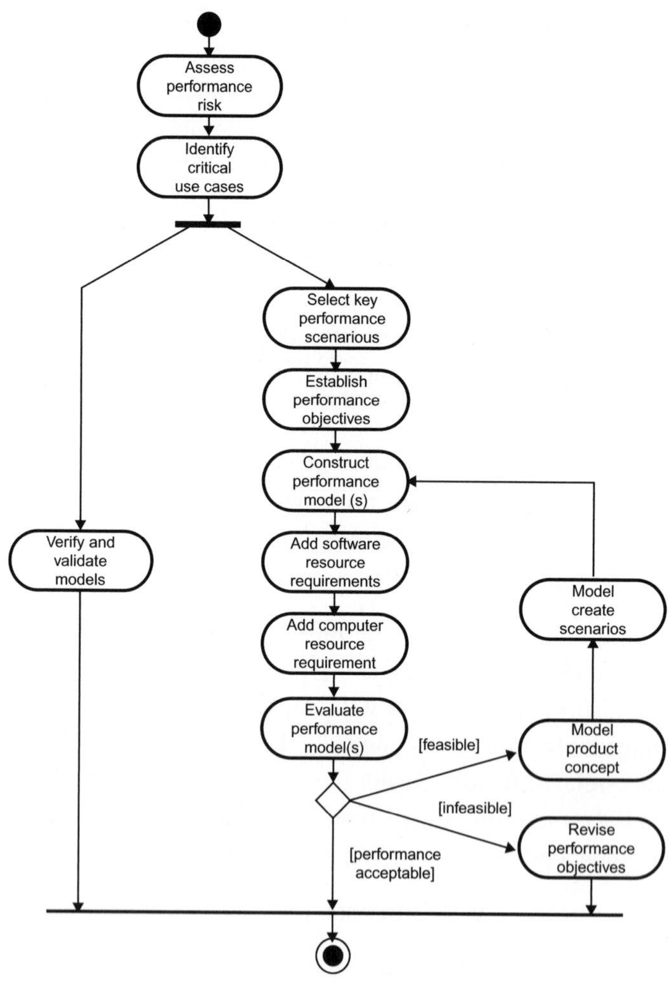

Figure 10.2:
SPE modeling process.

3. Select key performance scenarios
4. Establish performance objectives
5. Construct performance models
6. Determine SW resource requirements
7. Add computer resource requirements
8. Evaluate models
9. Verify and validate models.

The SPE process can be tailored as necessary based on the embedded project and organizational goals. Figure 10.3 shows one such tailored process for a performance

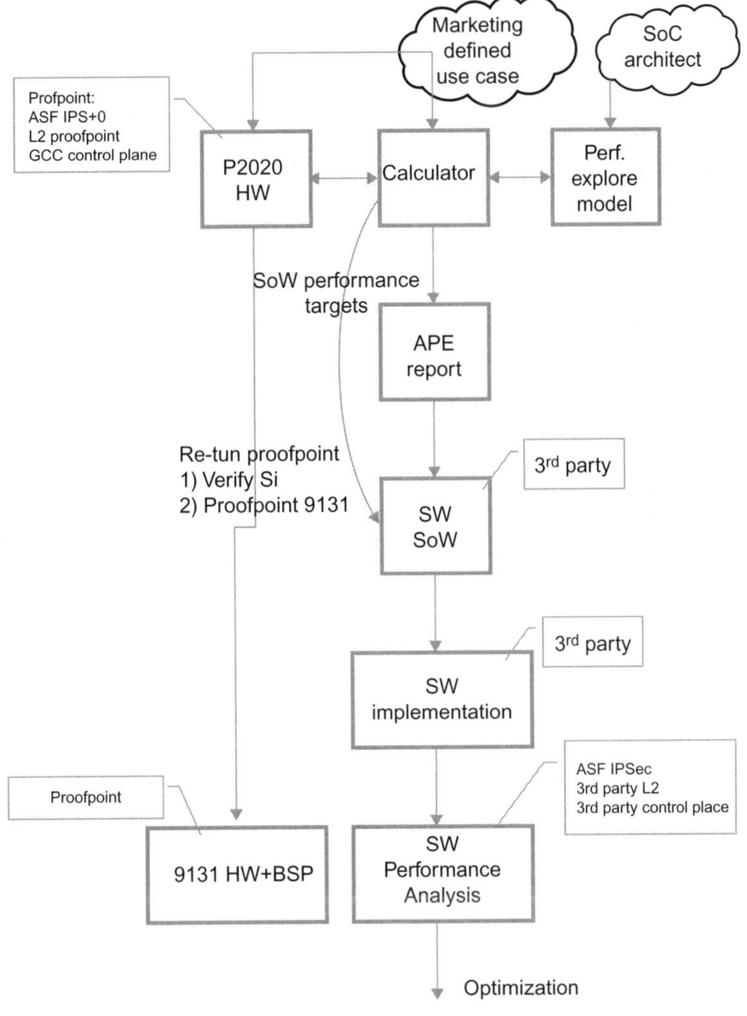

Figure 10.3:
An example process flow for using the performance calculator to manage performance metrics.

engineering activity. In this process, a performance calculator is used to model the important performance use cases for the application. The SoC architecture is also input into this process, as well as data from existing hardware benchmarking (P2020 hardware). Performance targets are used to create a performance report which is used to document in a software statement of work (SOW). This SOW is used for internal development as well as to serve as a requirement document for third-party vendors contributing to the system development process. Software implementation is focused on meeting the performance targets from initial architecture design through the implementation phase. Performance analysis is conducted formally at each major phase of the project to ensure goals are being met. The software architecture for this application is shown in Figure 10.4. The software components within the dotted-line boxes are those developed by the third-party vendor and which are key performance use cases that must be managed to meet performance requirements.

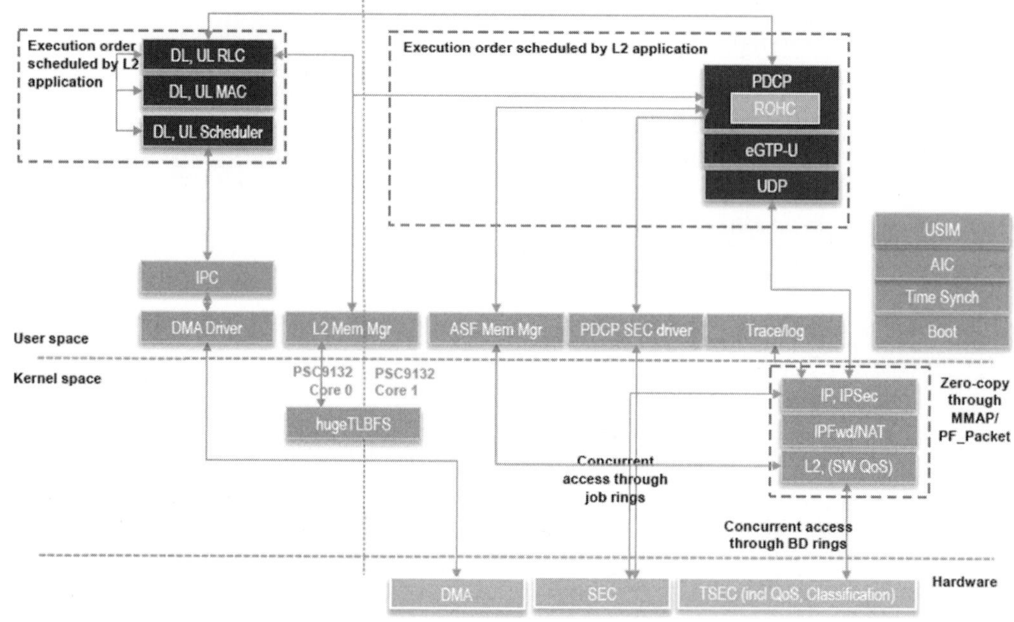

Figure 10.4:
A software architecture partitioning based on results from the performance calculator.

SPE includes best practices in the areas of project management, performance modeling, and performance measurement. Project management best practices include performing early estimates of performance risk, tracking costs and benefits of performance engineering, matching the level of effort for SPE based on the overall system performance risk, integrating SPE into the embedded software development process, establishing quantitative performance objectives and managing the development process to meet these objectives, and identifying critical performance-related use cases that focus on the scenarios that drive worst-case performance.

Modeling is a significant aspect of SPE. Some of the performance-modeling best practices include using performance scenarios to evaluate software architecture and design alternatives before beginning the software coding and implementation phase. SPE starts with the development and analysis of the simplest model that identifies problems with the system architecture, design, or implementation plans. Details are added as more and more details of the software become apparent. Figure 10.5 shows an example of a performance use case used to model expected performance goals for a Femto basestation application. Configuration management practices can be leveraged to create baseline performance models that remain synchronized with changes made to the software. Figure 10.6 shows the CM branching practice established for managing the performance program for a Femto basestation software project. Best and worst case estimates of resource requirement are used to establish bounds on the expected performance.

Use Case Definition

sectors	Band	Frame Config	UL UEs + DL UEs	UL	DL	DL Mbps	UL Mbps	SR/ACK/CQ info (per TTI over PUCCH)	RACH Root seq	Sounding UE (per TTI)	Device	SC3850 Freq.	#Device
1	20	FDD	32+32(6+6 shced per TTI)	1x2	2x2	102	51	1/32/1	1	1 wide band	PSC9131	1000MHz	1

SC3850 Core and MAPLE PE Load

Total MCPS	563
SC3850 Core load	56%
	54%
FTPE	25%
PUPE	5%
eTVPE	54%
DEPE	5%
PDPE	21%

- Projected average core load of 56% at 1GHz core frequency
- Overhead included for scheduling, MAPLE and FAPI control
- Numbers are based on standalone component profiling
- 32 active users are considered, translating into 6 UL + 6 DL scheduled users per TTI

Figure 10.5:
Performance scenarios and use cases used in software performance engineering modeling.

Performance measurement is another important area of SPE. This includes planning measurement experiments to ensure that results are both representative and reproducible. Software also needs to be instrumented to facilitate SPE data collection. Finally, once the performance-critical components of the software are identified, they are measured early and often to validate the models that have been built and also to verify earlier predictions. See Figures 10.7 and 10.8 for an example of the outcome of this process for the Femto basestation project.

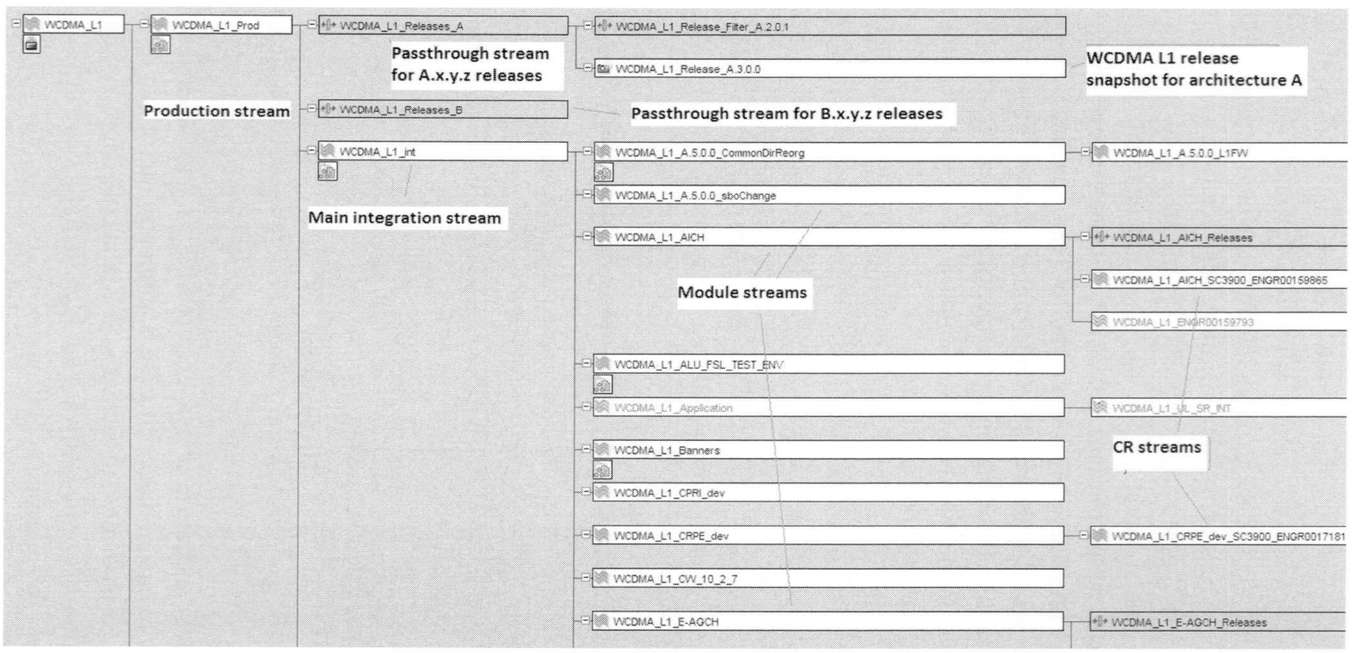

Figure 10.6:
Configuration management streams used to help manage performance improvements of a Femto basestation project.

- Define use-case:

Wireless and stack parameters		DL	UL	
Bitrate (L2/L1 IF) / device		150	75	Mbps
TB/sec (L2/L1 IF)		8000	8000	
Packet payload size (B) - Data		512	512	Byte
Packet payload size (B) - Voice		50		Byte
Number of voice users		16		
Voice activity factor		50		%
Packet rate (PPS) - Voice		400	400	
Packet rate (PPS) - Data		36582	18271	
Total PPS terminated		55654		PPS
L2 overhead (MAC, VLAN, CRC)		22	22	Byte
IPSec overhead (ESP, outer IP)	IPv4	46	46	Byte
	IPv6	66	66	Byte
UDP/GTP overhead		16	16	Byte
IP/TCP overhead	IPv4	40	40	Byte
	IPv6	60	60	Byte
Packet type (choose)	IPv6			Byte
Total packet size S1/X2	IPv4	636	[illegible]4	Byte
Total packet size post-IPSec		568	588	Byte
Total capacity at Ethernet level		186	93	Mbps
Total packet size post-GTP		552	572	Byte
Classification context size		256	256	Byte
QoS shaper context size		128	128	Byte
RoHC context size		1024	1024	Byte
RLC soft queue context size		256	256	Byte
RLC context size		256	256	Byte
MAC context size		256	256	Byte
DSP IO overhead (CQI, MCS, etc) / TB		128	128	Byte
#Connected users			250	users
L3+RRM			60	MCPS
Device parameters				
Core frequency		1200	MHz	

Example

- Define cycle counts
- See remainder slides

Performance/cycle counts	DL estimate pessimist	UL estimate pessimist	DL estimate optimist	UL estimate optimist	DL actual	UL actual
Ethernet/IPSec/UDP	5600	5500	2600	2500	6200	6200
GTP	300	0	300	0		
[illegible]	1000	1000	1250	1250		
[illegible]SEC driver	1000	1000	750	750	711	711
[illegible]oHC	3100	2600	2600	1750		
RLC AM mode, /PDU	3500	2200	1150	2450		
MAC HARQ, /TB	700	1200	550	800		
Rx/Tx (per TTI fixed overh)	10000	10000	10000	10000		

Actual numbers as shown for production code, define optimization targets

Figure 10.7:
Key parameters influencing performance scenarios based on cycle counts.

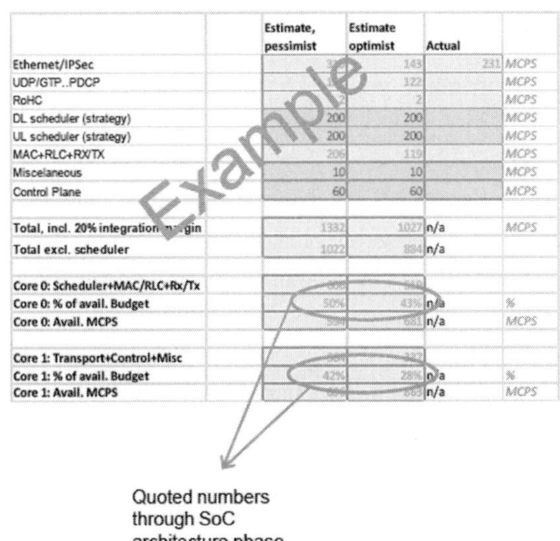

- Calculator output:

		Estimate, pessimist	Estimate optimist	Actual	
Ethernet/IPSec		[illegible]	143	231	MCPS
UDP/GTP..PDCP		[illegible]	122		MCPS
RoHC		[illegible]	2		MCPS
DL scheduler (strategy)		200	200		MCPS
UL scheduler (strategy)		200	200		MCPS
MAC+RLC+RX/TX		206	119		MCPS
Miscelaneous		10	10		MCPS
Control Plane		60	60		MCPS
Total, incl. 20% integration margin		1332	1027	n/a	MCPS
Total excl. scheduler		1022	884	n/a	
Core 0: Scheduler+MAC/RLC+Rx/Tx		[illegible]	[illegible]		
Core 0: % of avail. Budget		50%	43%	n/a	%
Core 0: Avail. MCPS		[illegible]	681	n/a	MCPS
Core 1: Transport+Control+Misc		[illegible]	[illegible]		
Core 1: % of avail. Budget		42%	28%	n/a	%
Core 1: Avail. MCPS		[illegible]	863	n/a	MCPS

Example

Quoted numbers through SoC architecture phase

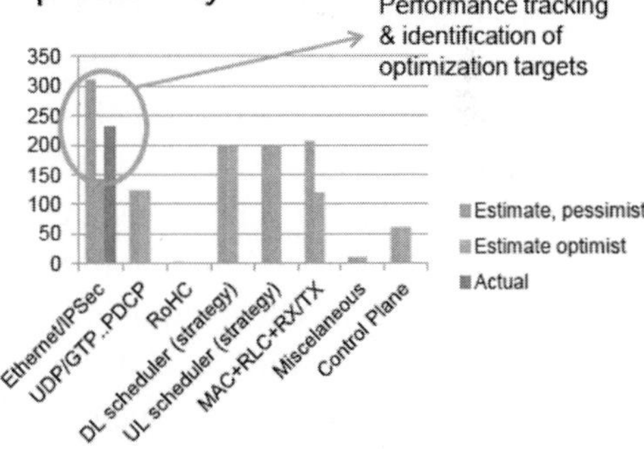

- Track per-component performance using 'actual' cycle counts

Figure 10.8:
Output from a "performance calculator" used to identify and track key performance scenarios.

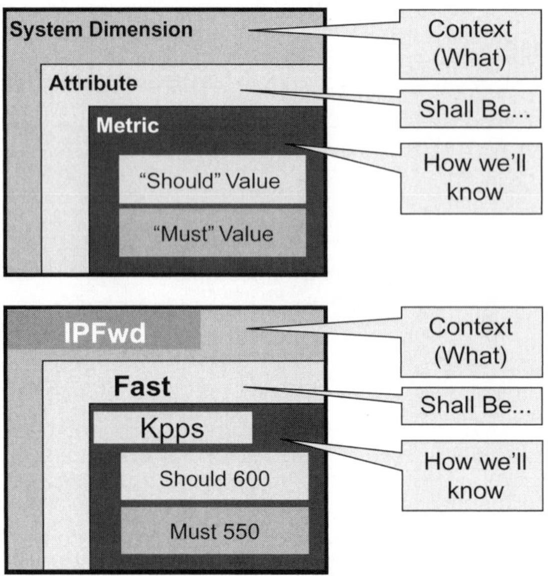

Figure 10.9:
Defining quantitative performance goals.

Lloyd Williams describes five steps to improved performance [2]:

1. Determine where you need to be: reject requirements or demands such as the system should be "As fast as possible". Use quantitative terms such as "Packet throughput must be 600 K packets per second for IP forwarding". Understand potential future use cases of the system and design the necessary scalability to handle these use cases. Figure 10.9 shows an example of how to define these performance goals. To do this properly, the first step is to identify the system dimension. This is the context and establishes the "what". Then the key attributes are identified. This identifies how good the system "shall be". The metrics are then identified that determines "How we'll know". These metrics should include a "Should" value and a "Must" value. In the example in Figure 10.9, IP forwarding is the system dimension. For a networking application, IP forwarding is a key measurement focus for this application area. The key attribute is "fast"; the system is going to be measured based on how many packets can be forwarded through the system. The key metric is thousands of packets per second (Kpps). The system should be able to achieve 600 Kpps and must reach at least 550 Kpps to meet the minimum system requirements.
2. Determine where you are now: understand which system use cases are causing performance problems. Quantify these problems using available tools and measurements. Figure 10.10 shows a debug architecture for a multicore SoC that can provide the visibility "hooks" into the device for performance analysis and tuning.

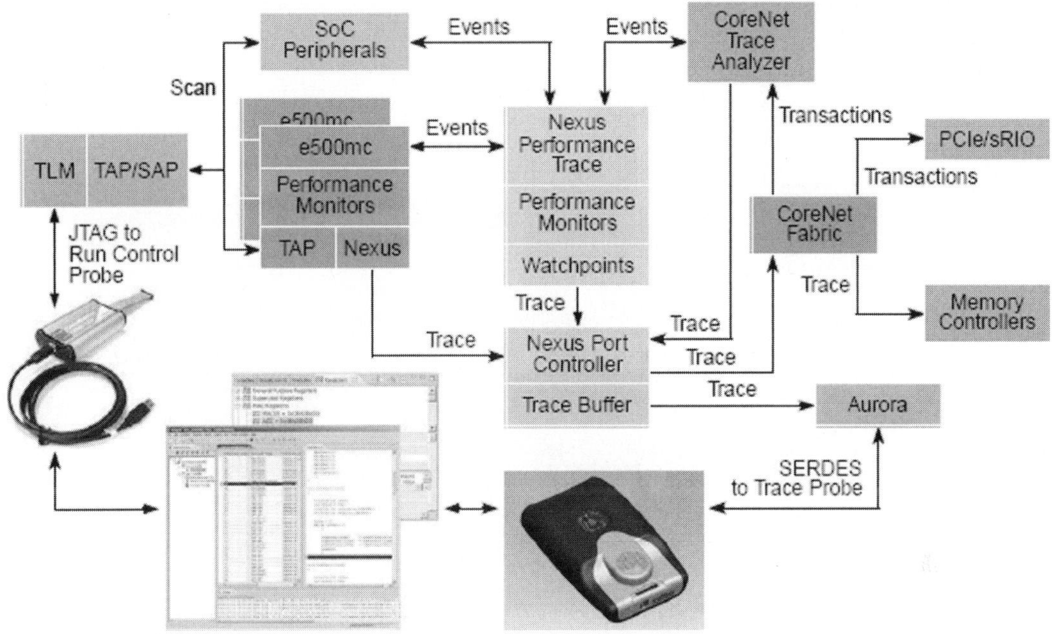

Figure 10.10:
A debug architecture for a multicore SoC that can provide the visibility "hooks" into the device for performance analysis and tuning.

Figure 10.11 shows a strategy for using embedded profiling and analysis tools to provide visibility into an SoC in order to collect the necessary information to quantify performance problems in an embedded system. Perform the appropriate assessment of the system to determine whether the software architecture can support performance objectives. Can the performance issues be solved with standard software tuning and optimization methods? This is important because it is not desirable to spend many months tuning the application only to determine later that the goals cannot be met using these tuning approaches and more fundamental changes are required. Ultimately, this phase needs to determine whether performance improvement requires re-design or if tuning is sufficient.

3. Decide whether you can achieve the objectives: there are several categories of performance optimization ranging from the simple to the more complex.
   - Low-cost/low ROI techniques: usually these techniques involve automatic optimization options. A common approach in embedded systems is the use of compiler options to enable more aggressive optimizations for the embedded software.
   - High-cost/high ROI techniques: re-design or re-factoring the embedded software architecture.

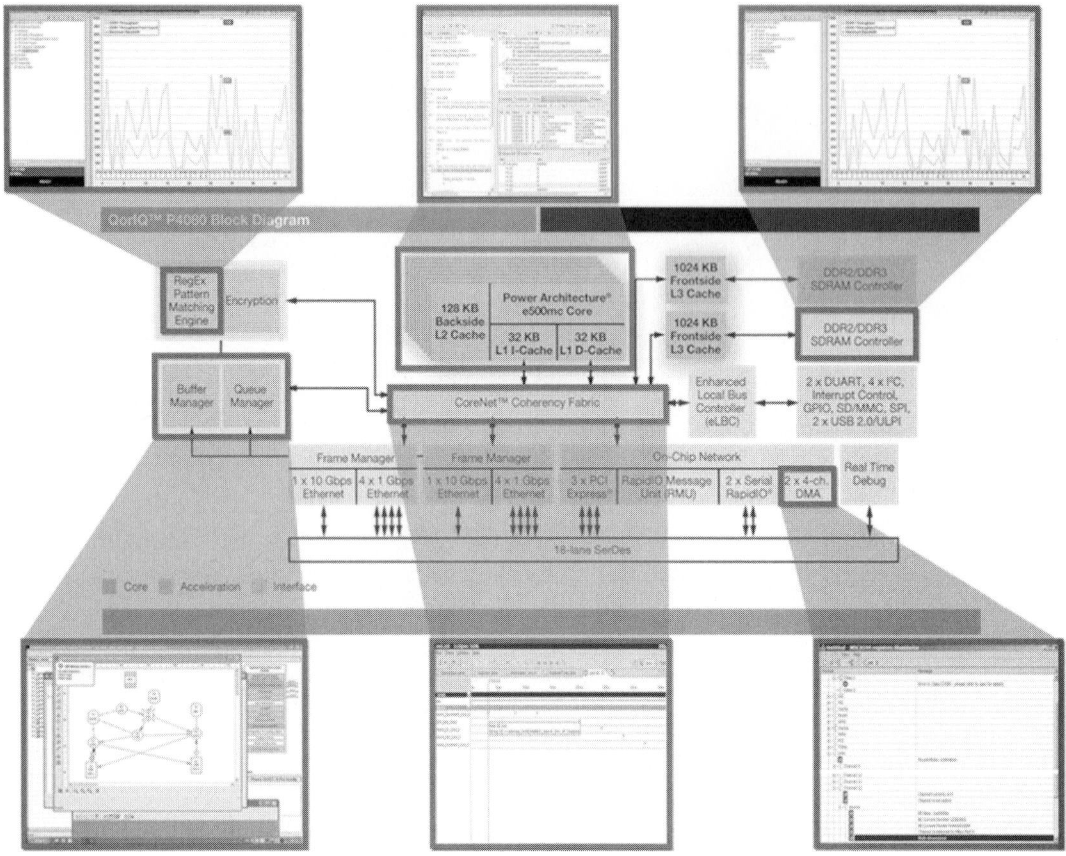

Figure 10.11:
A tools strategy for using embedded profiling and analysis tools to provide visibility into an SoC in order to collect the necessary information to quantify performance problems in an embedded system.

- Intermediate-cost/intermediate ROI techniques: this category includes optimizing algorithms and data structures (for example using a FFT instead of a DFT) as well as approaches like modifying software to use more efficient constructs.

4. Develop a plan for achieving the objectives: the first step is to pareto rank the different proposed solutions based on return on investment. There are various ways to estimate resource requirements including modeling and benchmarking. Once the performance targets have been determined, the tuning phase becomes iterative until the targets have been met. Figure 10.12 shows an example of a process used in optimizing DSP embedded software. As this figure shows, there is a defined process for optimizing the application based on an iterative set of steps:
   - Understand key performance scenarios for the application
   - Set goals for key optimizations for performance, memory, and power

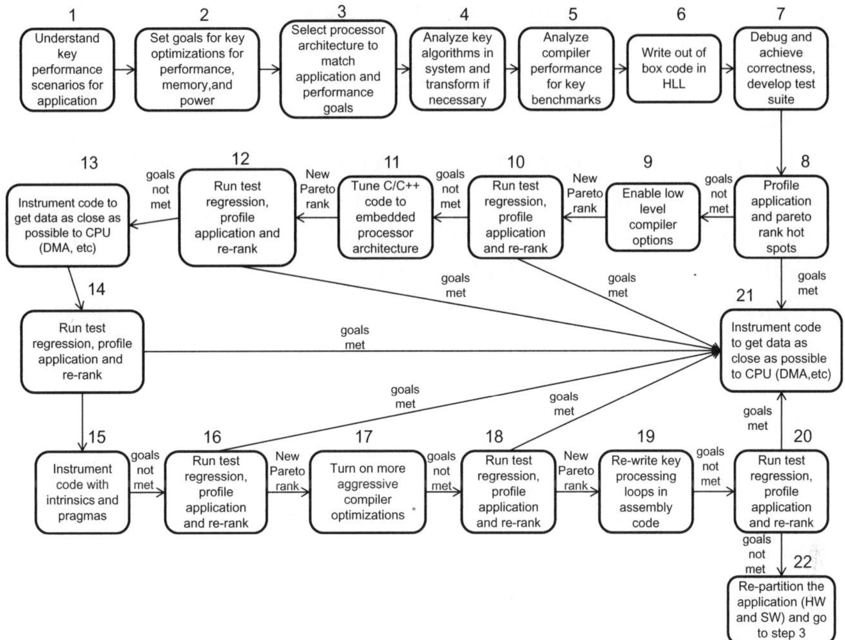

Figure 10.12:
A process for managing the performance of an embedded DSP application.

- Select processor architecture to match the DSP application and performance requirements
- Analyze key algorithms in the system and perform algorithmic transformation if necessary
- Analyze compiler performance and output for key benchmarks
- Write "out of box" code in a high-level language (e.g., C)
- Debug and achieve correctness and develop regression test
- Profile application and pareto rank "hot spots"
- Turn on low-level optimizations with the compiler
- Run test regression, profile application, and re-rank
- Tune C/C++ code to map to the hardware architecture
- Run test regression, profile application, and re-rank
- Instrument code to get data as close as possible to the CPU using DMA and other techniques
- Run test regression, profile application, and re-rank
- Instrument code to provide links to compiler with intrinsics, pragmas, keywords
- Run test regression, profile application, and re-rank
- Turn on higher level of optimizations using compiler directives
- Run test regression, profile application, and re-rank

- Re-write key inner loops using assembly languages
- Run test regression, profile application, and re-rank
- If goals are not met, re-partition the application in hardware and software and start over again
- At each phase, if the goals are met, then document and save code build settings and compiler switch settings.

5. Conduct an economic analysis of the project based on this plan. The first step is to gather data that can be used to support the analysis. This data includes, but is not limited to, time and cost to complete the performance analysis, software changes required, hardware costs if necessary, and software build and distribution costs. The next step is to gather data on the effect of the improvements, which includes things like hardware upgrades that can be deferred, staff cost savings, etc.

Performance engineering can be applied to each phase of the embedded software development process. For example, the rational unified process (RUP) has four key phases as shown below and in Figure 10.13.

- Inception
- Elaboration
- Construction
- Transition.

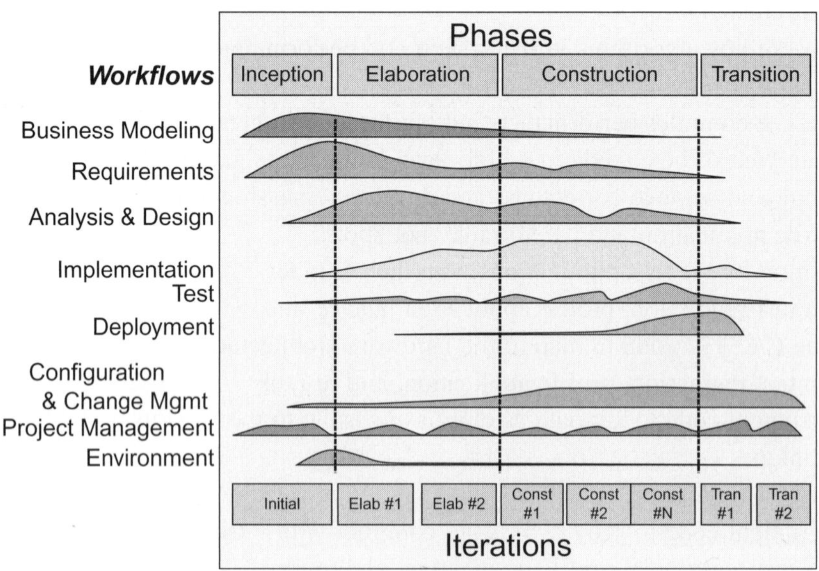

Figure 10.13:
Rational unified process.

RUP is an iterative software development process framework created by the Rational Software Corporation (now IBM). RUP is an adaptable process framework instead of a single concrete prescriptive process. It is intended to be tailored by software development teams that will select the elements of the process that are appropriate for their needs. So adding an SPE component to this process is relatively easy to achieve.

Lloyd Williams has mapped SPE into the RUP process in the following way [4]:

> Inception phase: the primary objective of the inception phase is to scope the system adequately as a basis for validating initial costing and budgets. From an SPE perspective, high-level risks that may impact system performance are identified and described in this phase.
>
> Elaboration phase: in this phase, the main objective is to mitigate the key risk items identified by analysis up to the end of this phase. In this phase the problem domain analysis is done and the architecture of the project gets its basic form. This is where the critical business processes are decomposed to critical use cases. The type of requirements that relate to SPE are the non-functional requirements (NFR) which are not limited to use cases.

The primary difference between functional and non-functional requirements is shown below.

- Functional: "The embedded software ***shall***... (monitor, control, etc.)".
  Functional = what the system should do.
- Non-Functional: "The embedded software ***shall be***... (fast, reliable, scalable, etc.)".
  Non-functional = when and/or how well the system should do it.

One approach to use in attempting for formulate a set of NFRs for an embedded system is to use the acronym "SCRUPLED".

- Security, licensing, installation – access privileges, security requirements, installation and licensing requirements
- Copyright, legal notices and other items – required corporate representations and legal protections
- Reliability – defects, mean time between failures, availability
- Usability – ease of use requirements – presentation design guidelines, UE standards, accessibility standards, training standards, sheets, help systems etc.
- Performance – quantitative performance requirements
- Localization and internationalization – foreign-language operating systems, localization enablement, specific localizations
- Essential standards – industry, regulatory and other externally imposed standards
- Design constraints – other constraints on the system or development technologies; mandated programming languages and standards, platforms, common components, etc.

Initial models are created that describe the overall system load over a specified time period, defining how many of each type of key transaction (networking packets, video frames, etc.) will be executed per unit of time.

Construction: the primary objective of the construction phase is to build the software system. The main focus is on the development of components and other features of the system. This is where the majority of the coding takes place. Several construction iterations may be developed in order to divide the use cases into manageable segments that produce demonstrable prototypes. SPE adds some activities to this phase. Performance-tool-related activities are completed in this phase. For example, specifying a profiling tool for component development and unit testing is necessary. Automated frameworks are needed to drive the components under development and measure performance.

Transition: this is where we "transit" the system from development into production. The activities of this phase include training the end users and maintainers and beta testing the system to validate it against the end-users' expectations. The product is also checked against the quality level set in the Inception phase. From an SPE perspective, this phase is when we configure operating systems, the network, and any message-queuing software and other optimizations identified in the performance test plan. It is important to ensure that all necessary performance monitoring software is developed, deployed and configured.

Example: latency vs. throughput in an eNodeB application

Embedded computer performance is characterized by the amount of useful work accomplished by a computer system compared to the time and resources used. Depending on the context, good computer performance may involve one or more of the following:

- short response time for a given piece of work
- high throughput (rate of processing work)
- low utilization of computing resource(s)
- high availability of the computing system or application.

It can be difficult to design a system that provides both low latency and high performance. However, real-world systems (such as Media, eNodeB, etc.) need both. For example, see Figure 10.14. This eNodeB system must be able to handle two basic NFRs:

- low latency, 1 ms periodic interrupt used for scheduling important calls through the system;
- maximum data throughout of 100 Mbps downlink and 50 Mbps uplink for supporting key customer use cases such as data transfer for web surfing and texting, etc.

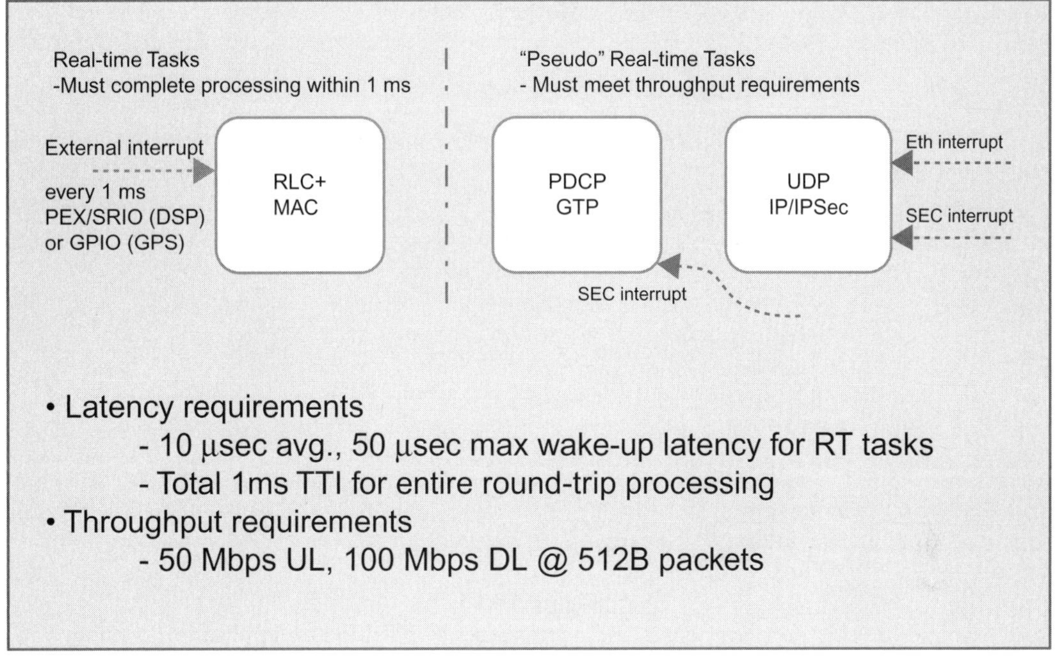

Figure 10.14:
A use case involving both latency and throughput for a Femto application.

This is a case where the designer needs to tune the system for the right balance of latency and performance. This would include the following basic decisions:

- Partitioning the application between hardware cores and hardware acceleration. Embedded systems usually consist of processors that execute domain-specific programs. Much of their functionality is implemented in software, which runs on one or multiple generic processors. High-performance functions may be implemented in hardware. Typical examples include TV sets, cellular phones, eNodeB basestations and printers. Most of these systems run multimedia and/or telecom applications, like video and audio decoders.
- Figure 10.15 shows a table summarizing the key performance-intensive functions required for an eNodeB application, which of those functions are utilizing hardware acceleration, the allocated cycle budget for these functions, and the core loading percentage for each of these functions.
- Partitioning the software application across the programmable cores in order to achieve the NFRs required for the application. Figure 10.14 shows a diagram of how the real-time tasks are allocated to one of the two available cores and the non real-time functions are allocated to the other processing core.

Function	Acceleration	Allocated cycle budget (MHz)	Core loading
Transport, S1/X2	Sec (IPSec) TSEC (Qos)	132	13%
GTP, PDCP	SEC (F8, F9)	58	6%
RLC, MAC		106	11%
Scheduler		200	20%
Misc. + timer handling		12	1%
L3+RRM		72	7%
Total core 0 (1GHz)			56% (1G)

Figure 10.15:
An example of using processor cores and accelerators to partition an application onto an SoC processor.

- Designing the proper software architecture to support the NFRs. Figure 10.16 shows additional software support for performing zero copy transfer of required packets for eNodeB processing around the Linux software stack, avoiding the extra overhead required for unnecessarily going up and down the Linux stack.

If SPE has been properly applied at each iteration and phase of the project, the expectation is that this will be sufficient to enable the system to achieve the required performance goals. If for whatever reason there are use cases that cannot be tuned into compliance, then it will be necessary to consider portions of the system to be re-factored or, in the worse case, re-partitioned between hardware and software. In some cases the problem can be resolved with additional hardware, but adding more hardware leads quickly to diminishing returns, as Amdahl's Law suggests (Figure 10.17).

SPE must be managed throughout the lifecycle. Crawl charts showing actual and target performance targets, like that shown in Figure 10.18, can be used to manage and report on performance status as the project executes. This can be a transparent way of communicating performance to key stakeholders and also a way to measure how well the SPE process is working. Software release iterations are possible with SPE and these iterations can also be tracked using crawl charts showing performance goals for each of the software iterations.

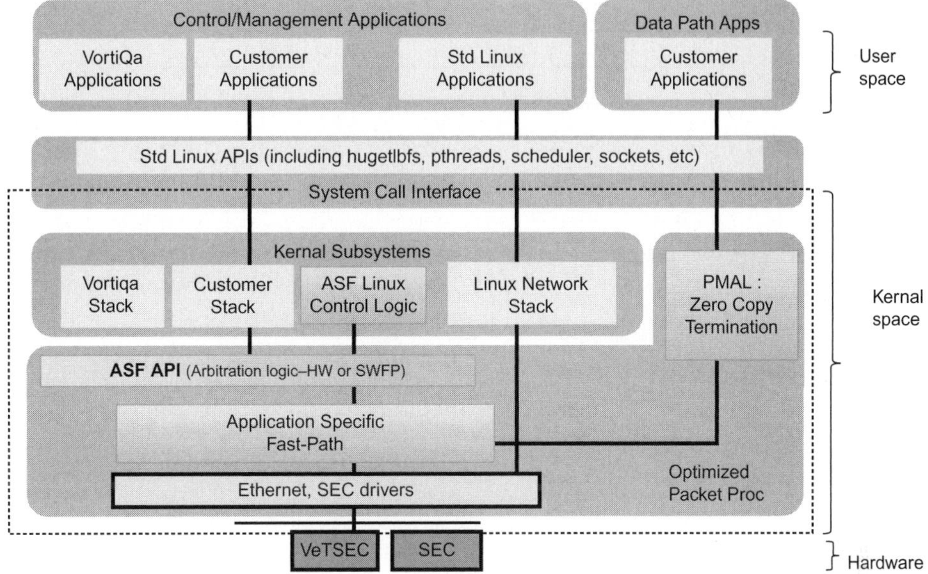

Figure 10.16:
Bypassing the Linux software stack using a "fast-path" software bypass technology.

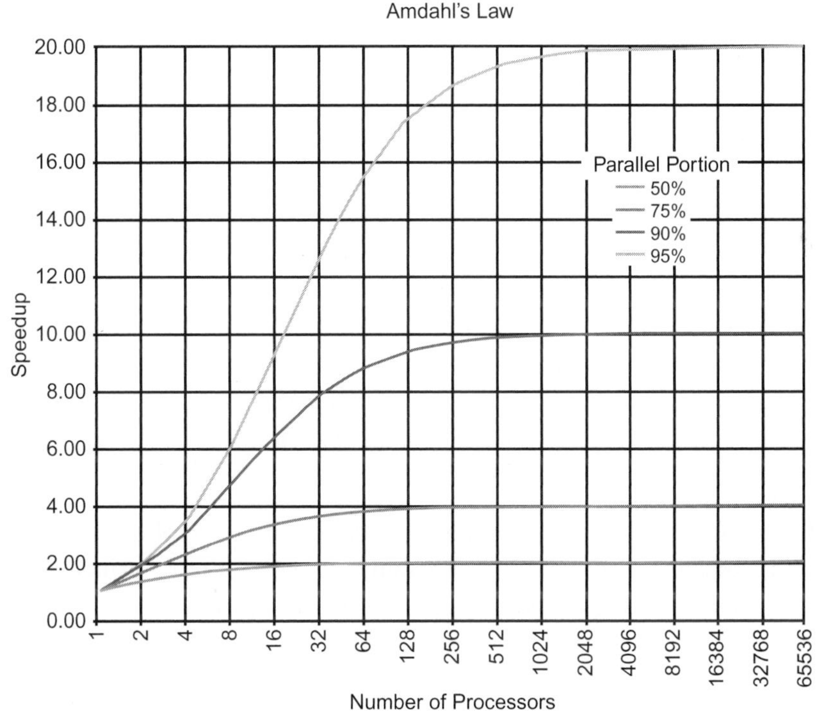

Figure 10.17:
Amdahl's law dictates that more hardware may not necessarily improve performance linearly.

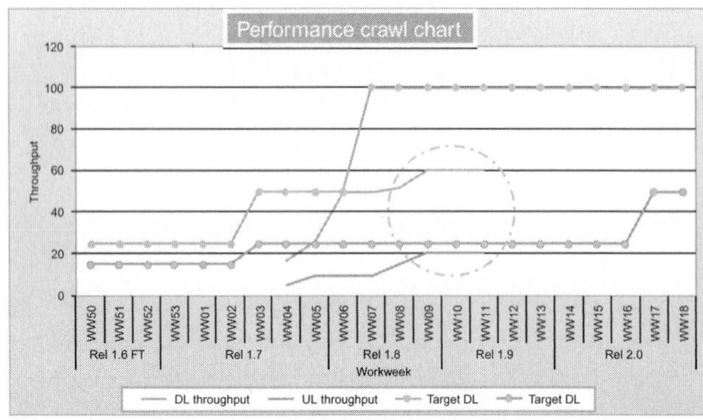

Figure 10.18:
A performance "crawl chart" showing performance improvements over time.

Collecting performance data can be difficult if not planned correctly. There are many factors that may affect the measurement of data including:

- System perturbation
- Capture ratios
- System overhead
- Measurement timing
- Reproducible results
- Representative time periods
- Averages for typical behavior
- Workload generation.

In order to produce accurate well-timed data for analysis, one effective approach is to design probes into the software being developed. It becomes much easier to define measurement requirements and probe points while the software designers are defining the system architecture. Collecting and analyzing data tends to incur less processing overhead if the probes are integrated as the design evolves.

Connie Smith and Lloyd Williams describe a set of analysis principles that are helpful for developing and managing a performance program [4]. Some of these principles that are most relevant for embedded systems development are described below.

Performance control principle**:** using this principle, it is important to define specific, quantitative, measurable performance objectives for the key system performance scenarios**.** Avoid vague or qualitative performance objectives as these are hard to measure and to know when you have met the goal. In Figure 10.19, the "derived from competition" line is essentially the quantitative goal of performance for a key measurement of IP forwarding for this application.

Instrumenting principle: this principle states that engineering should strive to instrument

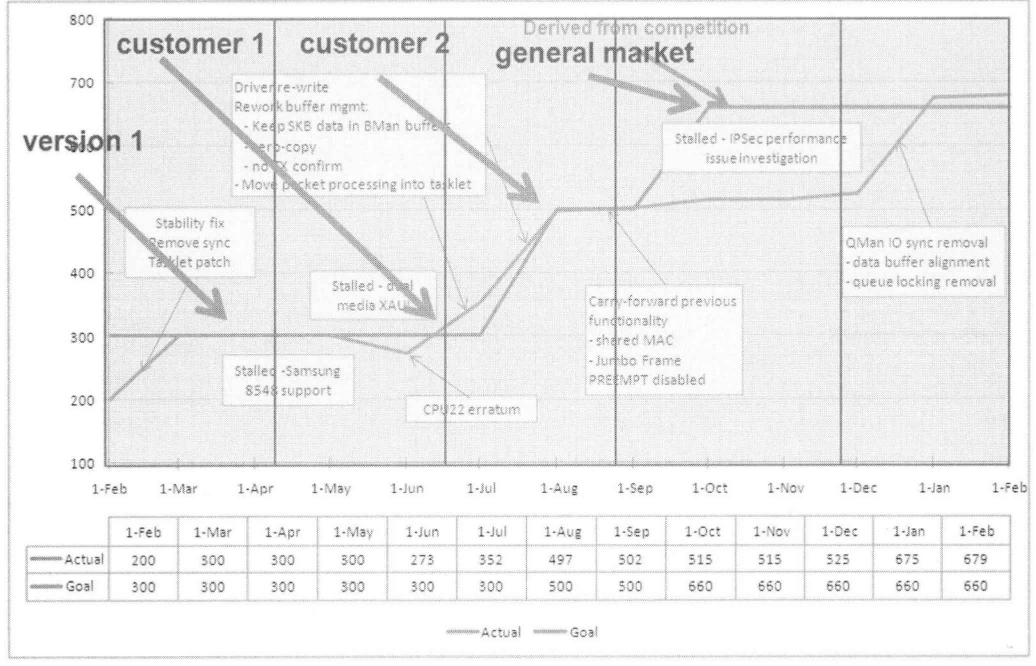

	1-Feb	1-Mar	1-Apr	1-May	1-Jun	1-Jul	1-Aug	1-Sep	1-Oct	1-Nov	1-Dec	1-Jan	1-Feb
Actual	200	300	300	300	273	352	497	502	515	515	525	675	679
Goal	300	300	300	300	300	300	500	500	660	660	660	660	660

Figure 10.19:
A performance crawl chart showing increasing performance improvements supporting an incremental release process.

systems as they build them to enable measurement and analysis of workload scenarios, resource requirements, and performance objective compliance.

Centering principle: this principle focuses on identifying the dominant workload functions (frequently used functions are called "dominant workload functions") and minimizing their processing. The focus and attention should be on those parts of the system with the greatest impact. Generally the 80/20 rule applies to this principle. Figure 10.20 shows a high-level software architecture diagram for an eNodeB application. Layer 1, 2, and 3 software is highlighted in areas where dominant workload functions reside. These areas are where we focus most of our attention.

Locality principle: the locality principle can be used for significant performance improvements by creating actions, functions, and results that are close to physical

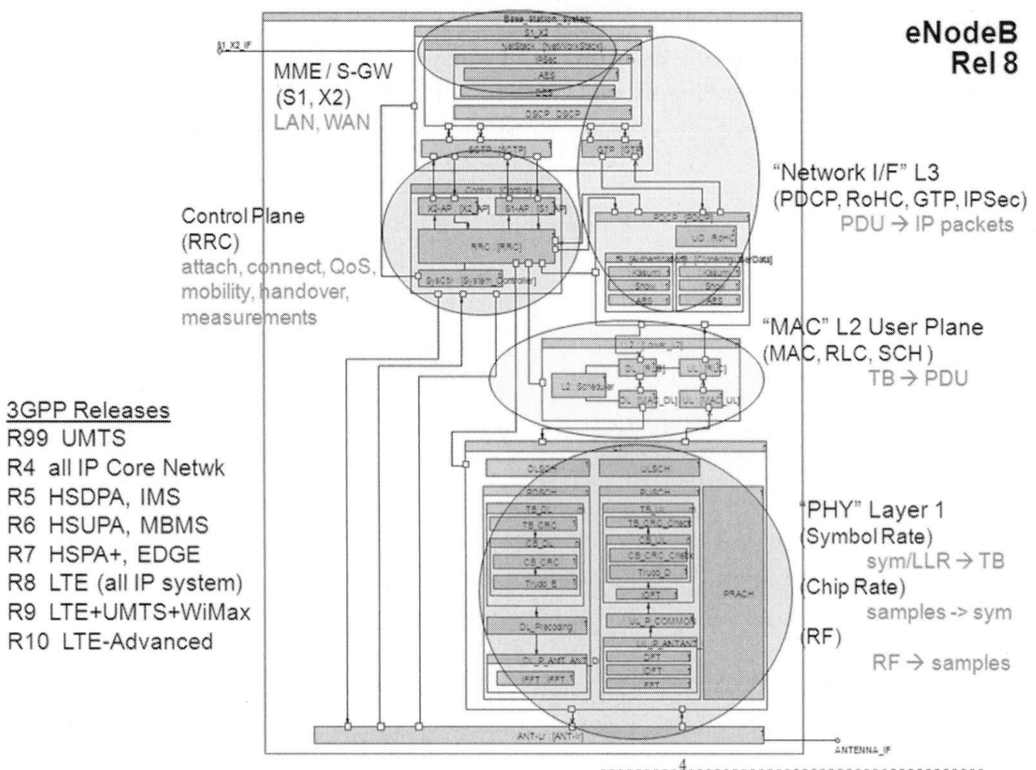

Figure 10.20:
A high-level model of an eNodeB Layer 1/2/3 software architecture identifying the high MIPS functions that need special performance attention.

resources. In this context "closeness" refers to the desired functions and the physical resources that produce them. Some common forms of locality include cache optimizations, where "closeness" can relate to spatial and temporal locality. Other forms include effectual (purpose or intent of a computation) as well as degree. The following chapter on performance optimization will cover this principle in more detail. Shared resources principle: embedded systems are all about the allocation of scarce resources. Scarce resources include the CPU, memory, and peripherals. Using this principle, resources are shared when possible. When exclusive access to a resource is required, the goal should be to minimize the sum of the holding time and the scheduling time. Resources in embedded systems are limited and software processes compete for their use. Sharing is possible and expected, but the sharing must be managed. Semaphores are a common technique used to manage these scarce resources, but these must be used cautiously. The chapter on operating systems will cover semaphores in more detail.

Parallel processing principle: with the parallel processing principle, the goal is to execute processing in parallel only when the processing speed-up offsets communication overhead and resource contention delays. This principle is all about understanding and applying Amdahl's law (Figure 10.17). The chapter on multicore software development will cover this parallel processing principle in more detail.

Spread the load principle: for this principle, spread the load when possible by processing conflicting loads at different times or in different places. The goal is to address resource contention delay and reduce key system delays by reducing the number of processes that need the resource at any given time. Spreading the load principle can be used to help partition a software application across a number of processing elements in an SoC. For example, Figure 10.21 shows an SoC containing several processing elements:

- programmable DSP cores
- a baseband hardware accelerator
- a microcoded network accelerator.

The application can be partitioned according to the "spreading the load principle" by allocating the lower MIPS functions requiring custom software functionality on to the DSP

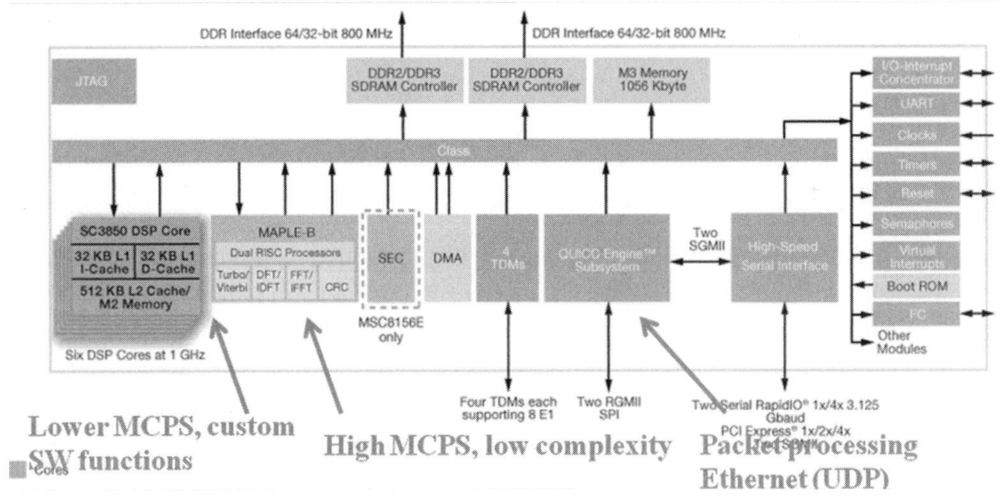

Figure 10.21:
An embedded SoC containing DSP cores, a baseband accelerator, and a network accelerator used to partition a real-time application.

cores, allocating the low-complexity software functions with high MIPS requirements on to the baseband hardware accelerator, and spreading the packet-processing Ethernet processing on to the microcoded network accelerator.

Here are some key guidelines for using these important principles:

1. Apply the principles to software components that are critical to performance.
2. Use performance models or benchmarking to quantify the effect of improvements on the overall performance to ensure that improvements are consistent.
3. Apply the principles until you comply with well-defined performance objectives.
4. Confirm that performance objectives are realistic and that it is cost-effective to achieve them.
5. Create a customized list of examples of each of the principles that is specific to your application domain. Publicize this list so others in your domain may benefit.
6. Document and explain performance improvements using the principles so others on the development team can also gain knowledge in these areas.

Performance patterns and anti-patterns

A software pattern is a common solution to a problem that occurs in many different contexts, a general reusable solution to a commonly occurring problem within a given context in software design. A software pattern is not a completely finished design. Think of it as a description or template for how to solve a problem that can be used in many different situations. Patterns are considered formalized best practices that the programmer must implement themselves in the application. Software patterns draws on best practices in industry.

Performance patterns are at a higher level of abstraction than a design pattern. Here are a few performance patterns proposed by Smith and Williams [4]:

> Fast path pattern: this performance pattern is used to reduce the amount of processing for dominant workloads. The classic example of this is the default withdrawal in an ATM machine. Rather than forcing the user through a number of selections for this common function, just give them an opportunity to go right to the common request. Figure 10.16 shows a software implementation of this pattern. This application-specific fast path (ASF) is a software algorithm that identifies certain packet flows and provides a "fast path" to Linux user space instead of going through the Linux stack (the long way to user space). The centering principle described earlier can be used to minimize the processing for these dominant functions. The example in Figure 10.16 recognizes when important data is needed frequently and minimizes the processing needed to obtain it.
>
> First things first pattern: this performance pattern focuses on prioritizing processing tasks to ensure that important tasks are completed and least important tasks are omitted if necessary. Embedded scheduling techniques include both static and dynamic priorities and the proper scheduling techniques depend on the application. Embedded

systems generally demonstrate bursty behavior that could lead to temporary overload. These overload conditions must be managed properly. One common approach to this is to use rate-monotonic analysis (RMA) and rate-monotonic scheduling (RMS) as a scheduling technique when multiple tasks must be completed. The goal is to gracefully degrade and gracefully improve under overload conditions. Rate-monotonic scheduling is a scheduling algorithm used in real-time systems (usually supported in an RTOS) with a static-priority scheduling algorithm. The static priorities are assigned on the basis of the cycle duration of the job. The shorter the cycle duration is, the higher is the job's priority. The RTOS that incorporates this algorithm is generally preemptive and has deterministic guarantees as it relates to response times. Rate-monotonic analysis is used in conjunction with those systems to provide scheduling guarantees for embedded applications.

Slender cyclic function pattern: this pattern is used for processing that must occur at regular intervals. This type of processing is common in embedded real-time systems (sensor readings) and can be applied to cyclic or periodic functions. The main problem arises when there are concurrent sources of an event or when other processing needs to happen. The key step is to identify the functions that execute repeatedly at regular intervals and minimize those processing requirements. The goal is to reduce queuing delays in the processing chain. For example, see Figure 10.22. This shows two different trade-offs to address the slender cyclic function in this embedded system example. The single-sample approach can reduce latency for incoming data samples but has the

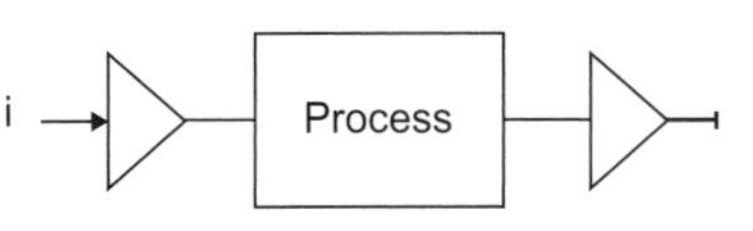

Single-Sample:

- Output result before next input sample
- Minimum latency (in-to-out time)
- Interrupt intensive
- Apps: motor control, noise cancellation

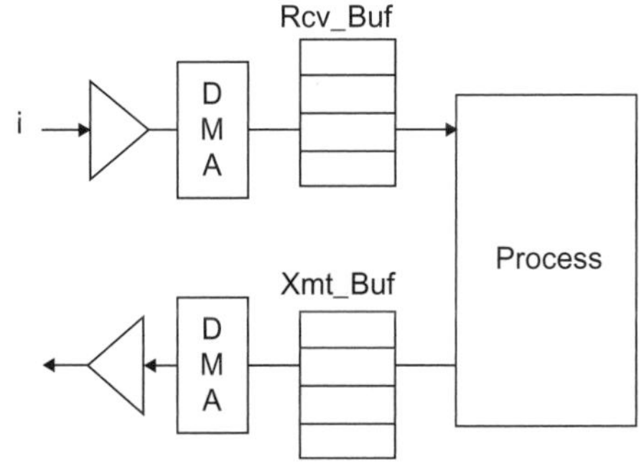

Block Processing

- Output buffer of results before next input buffer fills
- Uses DMA to transfer samples to buffer
- Increased latency
- Computationally efficient
- Apps: cellular telephony, video, telecom infrastructure

Figure 10.22:
Two different approaches to processing input samples with trade-offs of latency and throughput.

disadvantage of being very interrupt-intensive, which can increase processing overhead when handling the interrupts. For certain applications like motor control and noise cancellation, this approach might be the best. For other applications like cell phones and cellular infrastructure, a buffered approach may be better. This approach leads to increased latency due to the buffering but is computationally more efficient.
Anti-patterns: defined as a pattern that may be commonly used but is ineffective and/or counterproductive in practice. Anti-patterns are common mistakes during software development. Anti-patterns are different from a simple oversight or mistake as they represent some repeated pattern of action or a process that initially appears to be beneficial, but ultimately produces more bad consequences than beneficial results, and an alternative solution exists that is clearly documented, proven in actual practice and repeatable (but not being used).

One well known anti-pattern is referred to as the "God" class. Often a God class (GC) is created by accident as functionalities are incrementally added to a central software component over the course of its evolution. This component ends up being the dumping ground for many miscellaneous things. One of the symptoms is using far too many global variables to store state information. The God class is found in designs where one class monopolizes the processing, and other classes primarily encapsulate data. The consequences of this anti-pattern include a component with a large number of methods/attributes or both, a single controller class that performs all or most of the work, maintainability issues, difficult reuse and performance (memory) issues.

"Traffic jam": this type of anti-pattern can occur when there is more traffic than resources, or when this is close to the limit (e.g., highway between Austin and Dallas). Transient behavior produces a wide variability in the response times, taking a long time to return to normal operation. The solution could be to spread the load, or deter some of the load (alternative routes or flex time might help). The developer must know the limits of scalability of the system before building it and plan for handling overload situations smoothly.

Another example of an anti-pattern can be found in the performance engineering area. The "one-lane bridge" is an anti-pattern that requires all processing/data to go through one path (or one-lane bridge), which will decrease performance. This is solved by providing additional paths. Figure 10.23 is an example of this. For cars that have a special access pass or in this case a toll tag, an extra path is provided so that these cars do not have to wait to pay in the "cash" lines. In embedded software we can provide the same solution.
Figure 10.24 is an another example of software that provides a separate path around the Linux kernel so that packets of data that do not need to go through the kernel can be routed around the kernel and directly to user space. This can increase performance up to 7 $\times$ depending on the type of bypass technology that is being used.

Figure 10.23:
A real-life example of a "fast path" for improved performance and latency.

Bart Smaalders [5] does a good job of summarizing some common mistakes in software performance optimization:

1. Fixing performance at the end of the project: failure to formulate performance goals or benchmarks, and waiting until late in the project to measure and address performance issues will almost guarantee project delays or failure.

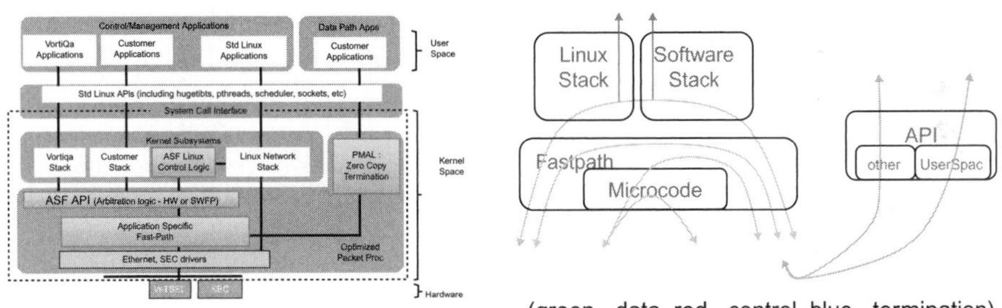

Figure 10.24:
Data flow showing how a fast-path architecture (left) "short circuits" designated data flows and increases performance.

2. Measuring and comparing the wrong things: a common mistake is to benchmark the wrong thing and be surprised later. Don't ignore competitive realities.

   Smaalders defines what a good benchmark is:

   - Repeatable, so experiments of comparison can be conducted relatively easily and with a reasonable degree of precision.

- Observable: if poor performance is observed, the developer has some breadcrumbs to start looking for. A complex benchmark should not deliver a single number, which gives the developer no additional information as to where performance problems might be. The Embedded Microprocessor Benchmark Consortium (EEMBC) does a good job of providing not just benchmark results but also the compiler options used, the version of the software, etc. This additional data is useful when comparing benchmarks.
- Portable: comparisons must be performed with your competitors and even your own previous releases. Maintaining a history of the performance of previous releases is a valuable tool to understanding your own development process.
- Easily understood: all relevant stakeholders should understand the comparisons in a brief presentation.
- Realistic: measurements need to reflect customer-experienced realities and use cases.
- Runnable: all developers must quickly ascertain the effects of their changes. If it takes days to get performance results, it won't happen very often.

  Avoid selecting benchmarks that don't really represent your customer, because your team will end up optimizing for the wrong behavior. Resist the temptation to optimize for the benchmark as this is only a short term "feel good" but will not translate to reality.

3. Algorithmic antipathy: algorithm selection involves having realistic benchmarks and workloads to help make intelligent decisions based on real data rather than intuition or other guesswork. The best time to do performance analysis work is in the earlier phases of the project. This is usually the opposite of what actually happens. Clever compilation options and C-level optimizations are ineffective when dealing with $O(n^2)$ algorithms especially for large values of n. Poor algorithm selection is a primary cause of poor software system performance. Figure 10.25 shows a comparison of a DFT algorithm with algorithm complexity $O(n^{**2})$ and a FFT algorithm with complexity $O(n \log n)$. As the figure shows, the performance of the FFT improves with the number of data points in the transform.
4. Reusing software: software reuse is a noble goal, but the development staff must be cognizant of violating the assumptions made during development of the software being reused. If the software is not designed or optimized for the new use cases in which it will be used, then there will be surprises later in the development process.
5. Iterating because that's what computers do well: if your embedded application is doing unneeded or unappreciated work, for example computing statistics too frequently, etc., then eliminating such waste is a lucrative area for performance work. Keep in mind that what matters most is the end state of the program, not the exact series of steps used to get there. Often a short cut is available that will allow us to reach the goal more quickly. Smaalders describes this as like shortening the race course rather than speeding

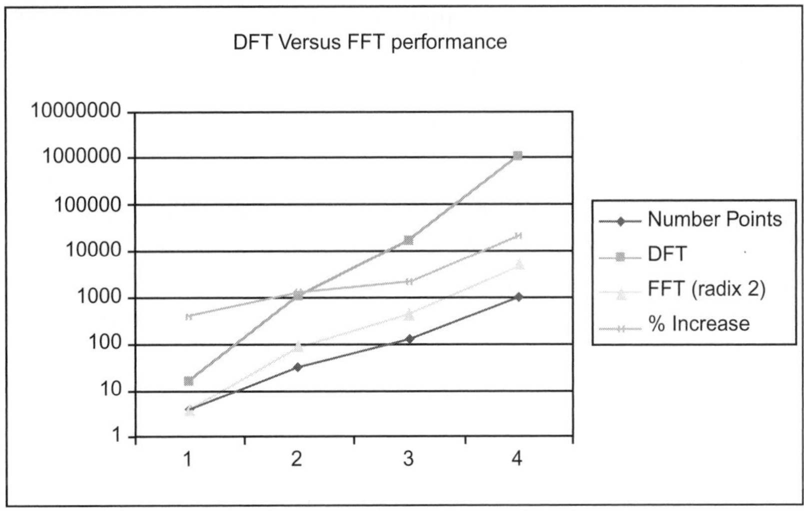

Figure 10.25:
A DFT algorithm versus FFT showing algorithm complexity has a big impact on performance.

up the car: with a few exceptions such as correctly used memory prefetch instructions, the only way to go faster in software is to do less.

6. Premature and excessive optimization: software that is carefully tuned and optimized is fine, but if these hand-unrolled loops, register declarations, inline functions, assembly language inner loops, and other optimizations are only contributing a small overall improvement to the system performance (usually because they are not in a critical path of the software use case) then this is a waste of time and not worth the ROI. It is important to understand where the hot spots are before focusing the tuning effort. Sometimes premature optimization can actually adversely affect performance on benchmarks by increasing the instruction cache footprint enough to cause misses and pipeline stalls, or by confusing the register allocator in the compiler. As Smaalders describes, low-level cycle shaving has its place, but only at the end of the performance effort, not during initial code development. Donald Knuth is quoted as saying "Premature optimization is the root of all evil". Excessive optimizations is just as bad. There are diminishing returns associated with optimization. The developer needs to understand when its time to stop (e.g., when is the goal met and when can we ship?). Figure 10.26 shows an example of this. This algorithm performance benchmark starts at 521 cycles with "out of box" C code, and gets progressively better as the algorithm is further optimized using intrinsic, hand assembly for internal loops and full assembly. Developers need to understand where the curve starts to flatten and further performance becomes harder to obtain.

7. Focusing on what you can see rather than on the problem: each line of code at the top level of the application causes, in general, large amounts of work elsewhere farther down in the software stack. As a result, inefficiencies at the top layer have a large multiplier magnifying their impact, making the top of the stack a good place to look for possible speed-ups.
8. Software layering: software developers use layering to provide various levels of abstraction in their software. This can be useful at times but there are consequences. Improper abstraction can increase the stack data cache footprint, TLB (translation look-aside buffer) misses, as well as function call overhead. Too much data hiding may also

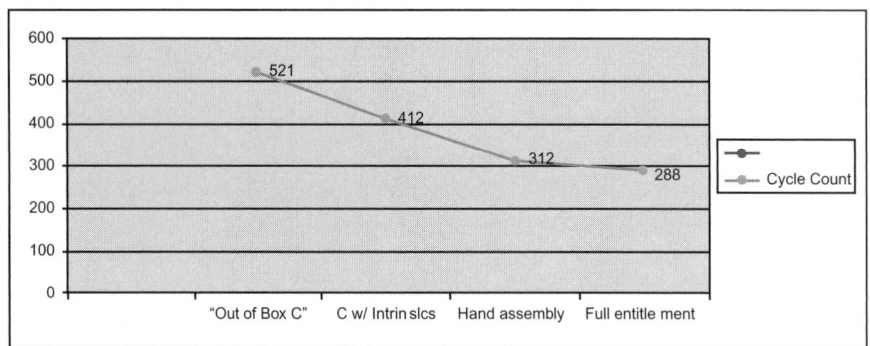

Figure 10.26:
There are diminishing returns on performance optimization.

lead to an excessive number of arguments for function calls as well as the potential creation of new structures to hold additional arguments. This problem becomes exacerbated when it is not fixed and the software is deployed to the field. Once there are multiple users of a new layer of software, modifications become more difficult and the performance trade-offs tend to accumulate over time.
9. Excessive numbers of threads: software threads are familiar to embedded developers. A common mistake is using a different thread for each unit of pending work. Although this can be a simple-to-implement programming model, it can lead to performance problems if taken to an extreme. The goal is to limit the number of threads to a reasonable number (the number of CPUs) and to use some of the programming guidelines mentioned in the chapter on multicore software for embedded systems.
10. Asymmetric hardware utilization: embedded CPUs are much faster than the memory systems connected to them. Embedded processor design these days uses multiple levels of caches to hide the latency of memory accesses, and multilevel TLBs are becoming common in embedded systems as well. These caches and TLBs use varying degrees of associativity to spread the application load across the caches, but this technique is often

accidentally thwarted by other performance optimizations. Iteration and analysis are important to understand these potential side effects of system performance.

11. Not optimizing for the common case: we spoke about this earlier; it is important to identify the performance use cases and focus the optimization efforts on these important performance drivers.

References

[1] S.K. Doddavula, N. Timari, A. Gawande, A maturity model for application performance management process evolution. A model for evolving organization's application performance management process, SOA World Mag. (June 23, 2011).

[2] L.G. Williams, C.U. Smith, Five steps to solving software performance problems, Softw. Eng. Res. Perform Eng. Serv. (2002).

[3] L. Lavagno, G. Martin, B. Selic (Eds.), Software performance engineering, in: UML for Real: Design of Embedded Real-Time Systems, Kluwer, 2003.

[4] L.G. Williams, C.U. Smith, Performance Solutions: A Practical Guide to Creating Responsive, Scalable Software, Addison-Wesley, 2001.

[5] B. Smaalders, Performance Anti-Patterns. Want Your Apps to Run Faster? Here's What not to Do, Sun Microsystems, 2006.

CHAPTER 11

Optimizing Embedded Software for Performance

Robert Oshana

Chapter Outline

Software Engineering for Embedded Systems.
DOI: http://dx.doi.org/10.1016/B978-0-12-415917-4.00011-6
© 2013 Elsevier Inc. All rights reserved.

The code optimization process

Prior to beginning the optimization process, it's important to first confirm functional accuracy. In the case of standards-based code (e.g., voice or video coder), there may be reference vectors already available. If not, then at least some basic tests should be written to ensure that a baseline is obtained before optimization. This enables easy identification that an error has occurred during optimization – incorrect code changes done by the programmer or any overly aggressive optimization by a compiler. Once tests in place, optimization can begin. Figure 11.1 shows the basic optimization process.

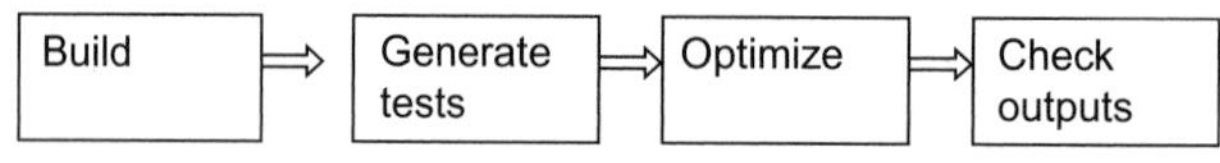

Figure 11.1:
Basic flow of optimization process.

Using the development tools

It's important to understand the features of the development tools as they will provide many useful, time-saving features. Modern compilers are increasingly better performing with embedded software and leading to a reduction in the development time required. Linkers, debuggers and other components of the tool chain will have useful code build and debugging features, but for the purpose of this chapter we will focus only on the compiler.

Compiler optimization

From the compiler perspective, there are two basic ways of compiling an application: traditional compilation or global (cross-file) compilation. In traditional compilation, each source file is compiled separately and then the generated objects are linked together. In global optimization, each C file is preprocessed and passed to the optimizer in the same file. This enables greater optimizations (inter-procedural optimizations) to be made as the compiler has complete visibility of the program and doesn't have to make conservative assumptions about the external functions and references. Global optimization does have some drawbacks, however. Programs compiled this way will take longer to compile and are harder to debug (as the compiler has taken away function boundaries and moved variables). In the event of a compiler bug, it will be more difficult to isolate and work around when built globally. Global or cross-file optimizations result in full visibility into all the functions, enabling much better optimizations for speed and size. The disadvantage is that since the optimizer can remove function boundaries and eliminate variables, the code becomes difficult to debug. Figure 11.2 shows the compilation flow for each.

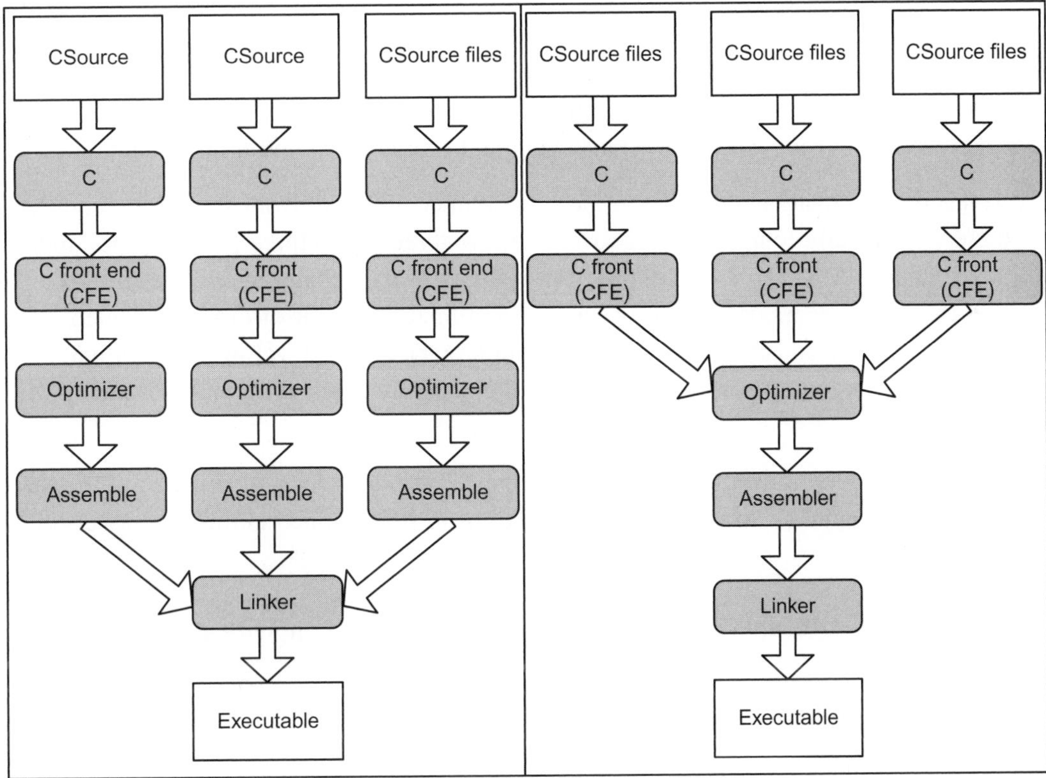

Figure 11.2:
Traditional (on left) versus global (on right) compilation.

Basic compiler configuration

Before building for the first time, some basic configuration will be necessary. Perhaps the development tools come with project stationery which has the basic options configured, but if not, these items should be checked:

- Target architecture: specifying the correct target architecture will allow the best code to be generated.
- Endianness: perhaps the vendor sells silicon with only one edianness, perhaps the silicon can be configured. There will likely be a default option.
- Memory model: different processors may have options for different memory model configurations.
- Initial optimization level: it's best to disable optimizations initially.

Enabling optimizations

Optimizations may be disabled by default when no optimization level is specified and either new project stationery is created or code is built on the command line. Such code is designed for debugging only. With optimizations disabled, all variables are written and read back from the stack, enabling the programmer to modify the value of any variable via the debugger when stopped. The code is inefficient and should not be used in production code.

The levels of optimization available to the programmer will vary from vendor to vendor, but there are typically four levels (e.g., from zero to three), with three producing the most optimized code (Table 11.1). With optimizations turned off, debugging will be simpler because many debuggers have a hard time with optimized and out-of-order scheduled code, but the code will obviously be much slower (and larger). As the level of optimization increases, more and more compiler features will be activated and compilation time will be longer.

Note that typically optimization levels can be applied at the project, module, and function level by using pragmas, allowing different functions to be compiled at different levels of optimization.

Table 11.1: Example optimization levels for an embedded optimizing compiler.

Setting	Description
O0	Optimizations disabled. Outputs un-optimized assembly code.
O1	Performs target-independent high-level optimizations but no target-specific optimizations.
O2	Target independent and target-specific optimizations. Outputs non-linear assembly code.
O3	Target independent and target-specific optimizations, with global register allocation. Outputs non-linear assembly code. Recommended for speed-critical parts of application.

Additional optimization configurations

In addition, there will typically be an option to build for size, which can be specified at any optimization level. In practice, a few optimization levels are most often used: O3 (optimize fully for speed) and O3Os (optimize for size). In a typical application, critical code is optimized for speed and the bulk of the code may be optimized for size.

Using the profiler

Many development environments have a profiler, which enables the programmer to analyze where cycles are spent. These are valuable tools and should be used to find the critical areas. The function profiler works in the IDE and also with the command line simulator.

Background – understanding the embedded architecture

Resources

Before writing code for an embedded processor, it's important to assess the architecture itself and understand the resources and capabilities available. Modern embedded architectures have many features to maximize throughput. Table 11.2 shows some features that should be understood and questions the programmer should ask.

Table 11.2: Embedded architectural features.

Instruction set architecture	Native multiply or multiply followed by add? Is saturation implicit or explicit? Which data types are supported – 8, 16, 32, 40? Fractional and/or floating point will be supported SIMD operations. Present? Does the compiler auto-vectorize? Use via intrinsic functions?
Register file	How many registers are there and what can they be used for? Implication: how many times can a loop be unrolled before performance is worsened due to register pressure?
Predication	How many predicates does the architecture support? Implication: more predicates means better control code performance
Memory system	What kind of memory is available and what are the speed trade-offs between them? How many buses are there? How many reads/writes can be performed in parallel? Can bit-reversed addressing be performed? Is there support for circular buffers in hardware?
Other	Zero-overhead looping

Basic C optimization techniques

This section contains basic C optimization techniques that will benefit code written for all embedded processors. The central ideas are to ensure the compiler is leveraging all features of the architecture and to communicate to the compiler additional information about the program which is not communicated in C.

Choosing the right data types

It's important to learn the sizes of the various types on the core before starting to write code. A compiler is required to support all the required types but there may be performance implications and reasons to choose one type over another.

For example, a processor may not support a 32-bit multiplication. Use of a 32-bit type in a multiply will cause the compiler to generate a sequence of instructions. If 32-bit precision is not needed, it would be better to use 16-bit. Similarly, using a 64-bit type on a processor which does not natively support it will result in a similar construction of 64-bit arithmetic using 32-bit operations.

Use intrinsics to leverage embedded processor features

Intrinsic functions, or intrinsics for short, are a way to express operations not possible or convenient to express in C, or target-specific features (see Table 11.3). Intrinsics in combination with custom data types can allow the use of non-standard data sizes or types. They can also be used to get to application-specific instructions (e.g., viterbi or video instructions) which cannot be automatically generated from ANSI C by the compiler. They are used like function calls but the compiler will replace them with the intended instruction or sequence of instructions. There is no calling overhead.

Some examples of features accessible via intrinsics are:

- saturation
- fractional types
- disabling/enabling interrupts.

For example, an FIR filter can be rewritten to use intrinsics and therefore to specify processor operations natively (Figure 11.3). In this case, simply replacing the multiply and add operations with the intrinsic L_mac (for long multiply-accumulate) replaces two

Table 11.3: Example intrinsic.

Example Intrinsic (C)	Generated Assembly Code
`d = L_add(a,b);`	`iadd d0,d1`

```
short SimpleFir1(
    short *x,
    short *y)
{
   int i;
   long acc;
   short ret;

   acc = 0;
   for(i=0;i<16;i++)
     // multiply, accumulate and saturate
      acc = L_mac(acc,x[i],y[i]);
   ret = acc>>16;

   return(ret);
}
```

Figure 11.3:
Simple FIR filter with intrinsics.

operations with one and adds the saturation function to ensure that DSP arithmetic is handled properly.

Functions calling conventions

Each processor or platform will have different calling conventions. Some will be stack-based, others register-based or a combination of both. Typically, default calling conventions can be overridden though, which is useful. The calling convention should be changed for functions unsuited to the default, such as those with many arguments. In these cases, the calling conventions may be inefficient.

The advantages of changing a calling convention include the ability to pass more arguments in registers rather than on the stack. For example, on some embedded processors, custom calling conventions can be specified for any function through an application configuration file and pragmas. It's a two step process.

Custom calling conventions are defined by using the application configuration file (a file which is included in the compilation) (Figure 11.4).

```
configuration
 call_convention mycall (
  arg [1 : ( * $r9 , $d9),
     2 : ( * $r1 , $d1),
     3 : ( * $r2 , $d2),
     4 : ( * $r3 , $d3),
     5 : ( * $r4 , $d4),
     6 : ( * $r5 , $d5) ];   // argument list
  return $d0;                // return value
  saved_reg  [
         $d6, $d7,        // callee must save and restore
         $d8,
         $d10, $d11,
         $d12, $d13,
         $d14, $d15,
         $r6, $r7,
         $r8,
         $r10, $r11,
         $r12, $r13,
         $r14, $r15,
         $n0, $n1,
         $m0, $m1,
         $n2,$n3,
         $m2, $m3
         ];
  deleted_reg [              // caller must save/restore
         $d0, $d1, $d2, $d3, $d4, $d5,
         $r0, $r1, $r2, $r3, $r4, $r5
         ];
  save = [ ];
)
          view default
          module "main" [
                 opt_level = size
                 function _GoofyBlockChar [
                        opt_level = O3
                 ]
    ]
        end view
        use view default
  end configuration
```

Figure 11.4:
Configuration of calling conventions.

Use case definition

Sectors	Band	Frame config	ULUEs + DLUEs	UL	DL	DL Mbps	UL Mbps	SR/ACK/CQI info (per TTI over PUCCH)	RACH Root seq	Sounding UE (per TTI)	Device	SC3850 freq.	#Device
1	20	FDD	32+32 (6+6 sched per TTI)	1×2	2×2	102	51	1/32/1	1	1 wide band	PSC9131	1000MHz	1

SC3850 core and MAPLW PE load

Total MCPS	563
SC3850 core load	56%
FTPE	25%
PUPE	5%
eTVPE	54%
DEPE	5%
PDPE	21%

- Projected average core load of 56% at 1 GHz core frequency
- Overhead included for scheduling, MAPLE and FAPI control
- Numbers are based on standalone component profiling
- 32 active users are considered, translating into 6 UL + 6 DL scheduled users per TTI

Figure 11.5:
Case Definition for Femto application.

They are invoked via pragma when needed. The rest of the project continues to use the default calling convention. In the example in Figures 11.6 and 11.7, the calling convention is invoked for function TestCallingConvention.

```
char TestCallingConvention (int a, int b, int c, char d, short e)
{
 return a+b+c+d+e;
}
#pragma call_conv TestCallingConvention mycall
```

Figure 11.6:
Invoking calling conventions.

Pointers and memory access

Ensuring alignment

Some embedded processors such as digital signal processors (DSPs) support loading of multiple data values across the busses as this is necessary to keep the arithmetic functional units busy. These moves are called multiple data moves (not to be confused with *packed* or *vector* moves). They move adjacent values in memory to different registers. In addition, many compiler optimizations require these multiple register moves because there is so much data to move to keep all the functional units busy.

Typically, however, a compiler aligns variables in memory to their access width. For example, an array of short (16-bit) data is aligned to 16 bits. However, to leverage multiple

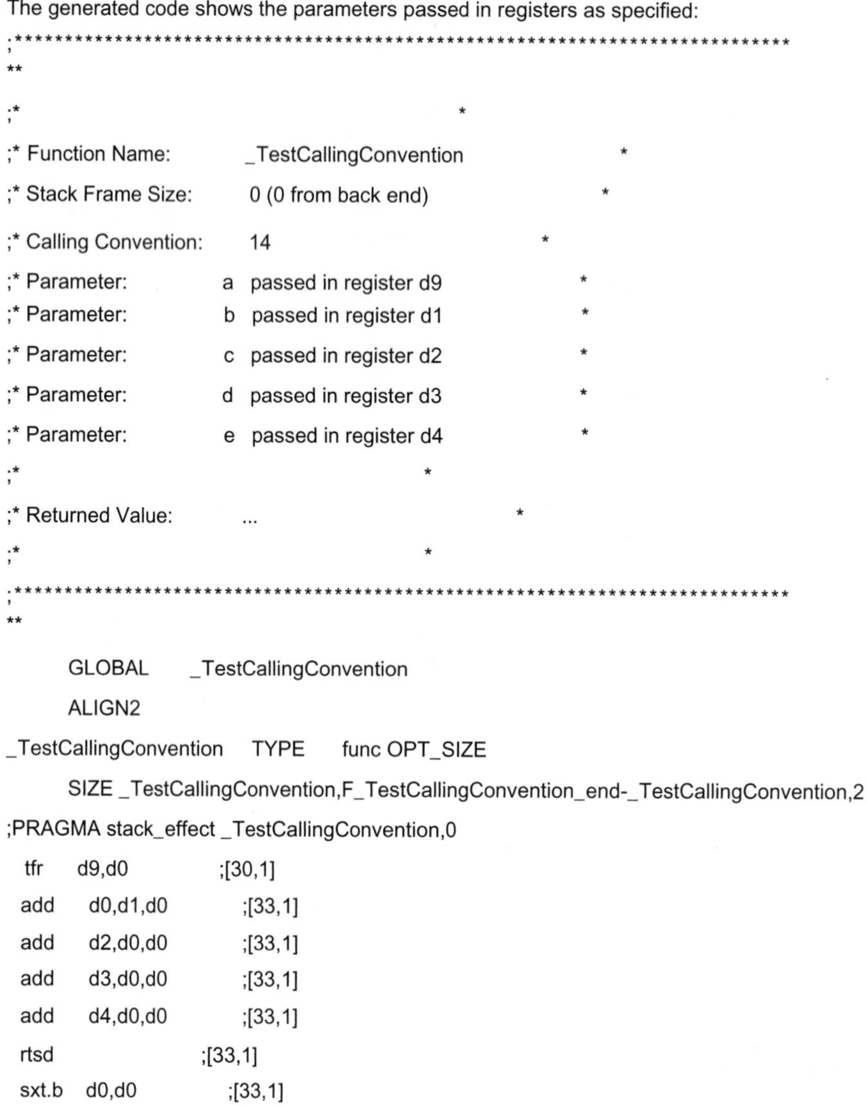
The generated code shows the parameters passed in registers as specified:

```
;**************************************************************************
**

;*                                              *
;* Function Name:        _TestCallingConvention              *
;* Stack Frame Size:     0 (0 from back end)              *
;* Calling Convention:   14                        *
;* Parameter:          a  passed in register d9              *
;* Parameter:          b  passed in register d1              *
;* Parameter:          c  passed in register d2              *
;* Parameter:          d  passed in register d3              *
;* Parameter:          e  passed in register d4              *
;*                                          *
;* Returned Value:       ...                      *
;*                                          *
;**************************************************************************
**

        GLOBAL     _TestCallingConvention
        ALIGN2
_TestCallingConvention    TYPE    func OPT_SIZE
        SIZE _TestCallingConvention,F_TestCallingConvention_end-_TestCallingConvention,2
;PRAGMA stack_effect _TestCallingConvention,0
  tfr    d9,d0           ;[30,1]
  add    d0,d1,d0          ;[33,1]
  add    d2,d0,d0          ;[33,1]
  add    d3,d0,d0          ;[33,1]
  add    d4,d0,d0          ;[33,1]
  rtsd                   ;[33,1]
  sxt.b  d0,d0            ;[33,1]
```

Figure 11.7:
Generated code for function with modified calling conventions.

data moves, the data must be aligned to a higher alignment. For example, to load two 16-bit values at once, the data must be aligned to 32 bits.

Restrict and pointer aliasing

When pointers are used in the same piece of code, make sure that they cannot point to the same memory location (alias). When the compiler knows the pointers do not alias, it can put accesses to memory pointed to by those pointers in parallel, greatly improving performance. Otherwise, the compiler must assume that the pointers could alias. Communicate this to the compiler by one of two methods: using the restrict keyword or by informing the compiler that no pointers alias anywhere in the program (Figure 11.8).

The restrict keyword is a type qualifier that can be applied to pointers, references, and arrays (Tables 11.4 and 11.5). Its use represents a guarantee by the programmer that within the scope of the pointer declaration, the object pointed to can be accessed only by that pointer. A violation of this guarantee can produce undefined results.

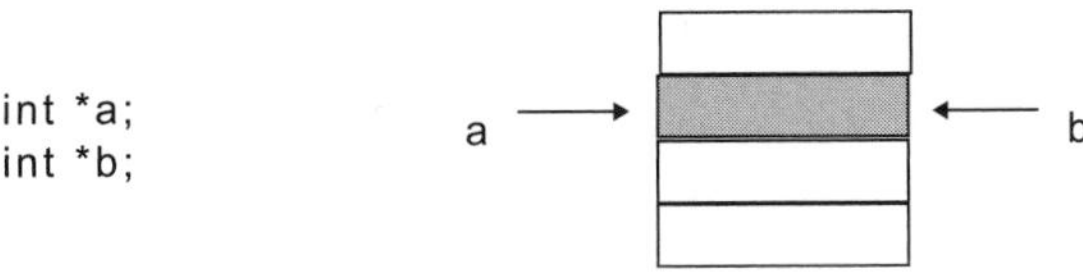

Figure 11.8:
Illustration of pointer aliasing.

Table 11.4: Example loop before restrict added to parameters (DSP code).

Example Loop	Generated Assembly Code

void foo (short * a,short * b,int N) {
int i;
for (i=0;i<N;i++) {
b[i]=shr(a[i],2);
}
return;
}
	doen3 d4
	FALIGN
	LOOPSTART3
	move.w (r0)+,d4
	asrr #<2,d4
	move.w d4,(r1)+
	LOOPEND3

Table 11.5: Example loop after restrict added to parameters.

Example Loop with Restrict Qualifiers Added. Note: Pointers a and b Must not Alias (ensure data is located separately)	Generated Assembly Code. Note: Now Accesses for a and b can be Issued in Parallel

void foo (short * restrict a,short * restrict b,
int N)
int i;
for (i=0;i<N;i++) {
b[i]=shr(a[i],2);
}
return;
}
	move.w (r0)+,d4
	asrr #<2,d4
	doensh3 d2
	FALIGN
	LOOPSTART3
	[move.w d4,(r1)+ ; parallel
	move.w (r0)+,d4 ; accesses
	]
	asrr #<2,d4
	LOOPEND3
	move.w d4,(r1)

Loops

Communicating loop count information

Pragmas can be used to communicate to the compiler information about loop bounds to help loop optimzation. If the loop minimum and maximum are known, for example, the compiler may be able to make more aggressive optimizations.

In the example in Figure 11.9, a pragma is used to specify the loop count bounds to the compiler. In this syntax, the parameters are minimum, maximum and multiple respectively. If a non-zero minimum is specified, the compiler can avoid generation of costly zero-iteration checking code. The compiler can use the maximum and multiple parameters to know how many times to unroll the loop if possible.

```
{
 long int L_tmp = 0;
 int i;

 for (i = 0; i < N; i++)
 #pragma loop_count (4,512,4)
   L_tmp = L_mac (L_tmp, vec1[i], vec2[i]);
 *result = round (L_tmp);
}
```

Figure 11.9:
A pragma used to specify the loop count.

Hardware loops

Hardware loops are mechanisms built into some embedded cores which allow zero-overhead (in most cases) looping by keeping the loop body in a buffer or prefetching. Hardware loops are faster than normal software loops (decrement counter and branch) because they have less change-of-flow overhead. Hardware loops typically use loop registers that start with a count equal to the number of iterations of the loop, decrease by 1 each iteration (step size of -1), and finish when the loop counter is zero (Figure 11.10).

Compilers most often automatically generate hardware loops from C even if the loop counter or loop structure is complex. However, there will be certain criteria under which the compiler will be able to generate a hardware loop (which vary depending on compiler/architecture). In some cases, the loop structure will prohibit generation but if the

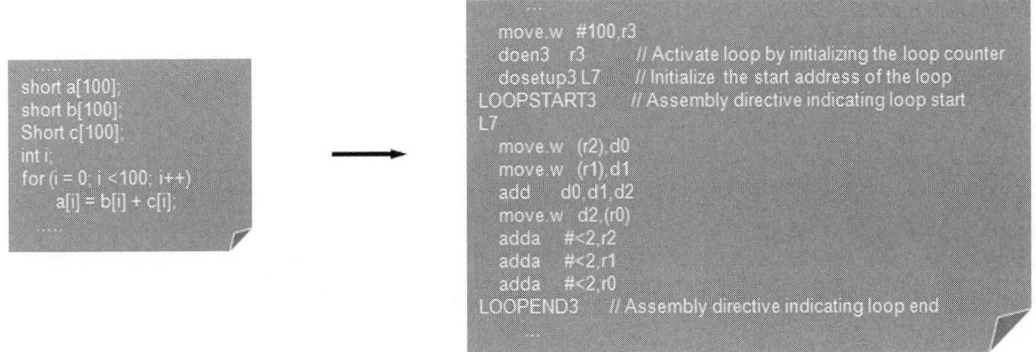

Figure 11.10:
Hardware loop counting in embedded processors.

programmer knows about this, the source can be modified so the compiler can generate the loop using hardware loop functionality. The compiler may have a feature to tell the programmer if a hardware loop was not generated (compiler feedback). Alternatively, the programmer should check the generated code to ensure hardware loops are being generated for critical code.

As an example the StarCore DSP architecture supports four hardware loops. Note the LOOPSTART and LOOPEND markings, which are assembler directives marking the start and end of the loop body, respectively (Figure 11.11).

```
doensh3  #<5
 move.w  #<1,d0
 LOOPSTART3
[ iadd   d2,d1
  iadd   d0,d4
  add    #<2,d0
  add    #<2,d2  ]
 LOOPEND3
```

Figure 11.11:
StarCore DSP architecture.

Additional tips and tricks

The following are some additional tips and tricks to use for further code optimization.

Memory contention

When data is placed in memory, be aware of how the data is accessed. Depending on the memory type, if two buses issue data transactions in a region/bank/etc., they could conflict and cause a penalty. Data should be separated appropriately to avoid this contention. The scenarios that cause contention are device-dependent because memory bank configuration and interleaving differs from device to device.

Use of unaligned accesses

In some embedded processors, devices support unaligned memory access. This is particularly useful for video applications. For example, a programmer might load four byte-values which are offset by one byte from the beginning of an area in memory. Typically there is a performance penalty for doing this.

Cache accesses

In the caches, place data that is used together next to each other in memory so that prefetching the caches is more likely to obtain the data before it is accessed. In addition, ensure that the loading of data for sequential iterations of the loop is in the same dimension as the cache prefetch.

Inline small functions

The compiler normally inlines small functions, but the programmer can force inlining of functions if for some reason it isn't happening (for example if size optimization is activated). For small functions the save, restore, and parameter-passing overhead can be significant relative to the number of cycles of the function itself. Therefore, inlining is beneficial. Also, inlining functions decreases the chance of an instruction cache miss because the function is sequential to the former caller function and is likely to be prefetched. Note that inlining functions increases the size of the code. On some processors, pragma inline forces every call of the function to be inlined (Figure 11.12).

```
int foo () {

#pragma inline

...

}
```

Figure 11.12:
Pragma inline forces.

Use vendor run-time libraries

Embedded processor vendors typically provide optimized library functions for common run-time routines like FFT, FIR, complex operations, etc. Normally, these are hand-written in assembly as it still may be possible to improve performance over C. These can be invoked by the programmer using the published API without the need to write such routines, speeding time to market.

General loop transformations

The optimization techniques described in this section are general in nature. They are critical to taking advantage of modern multi-ALU processors. A modern compiler will perform many of these optimizations, perhaps simultaneously. In addition, they can be applied on all platforms, at the C or assembly level. Therefore, throughout the section, examples are presented in general terms, in C and in assembly.

Loop unrolling

Background

Loop unrolling is a technique whereby a loop body is duplicated one or more times. The loop count is then reduced by the same factor to compensate. Loop unrolling can enable other optimizations such as:

- multisampling
- partial summation
- software pipelining.

Once a loop is unrolled, flexibility in coding is increased. For example, each copy of the original loop can be slightly changed. Different registers could be used in each copy. Moves can be done earlier and multiple register moves can be used.

Unrolling procedure:

Duplicate loop body *N* times

Decrease loop count by factor of *N*

Loop Prior to Unrolling	After Unrolling by Factor of 2

`for (i = 0;i<10;i++)`
`operation();`
	`for (i = 0;i<5;i++) {`
	`operation();`
	`operation(); }`

Implementation

Figure 11.13 is an example of a correlation inner loop which as been unrolled by a factor of two.

```
loopstart1
[ move.f (r0)+,d2 ; Load some data
move.f (r7)+,d4  ; Load some reference
mac d2,d4,d5     ; Do correlation
]
[ move.f (r0)+,d2 ; Load some data
move.f (r7)+,d4  ; Load some reference
mac d2,d4,d5     ; Do correlation
]
loopend1
```

Figure 11.13:
A correlation inner loop.

Multisampling

Background

Multisampling is a technique for maximizing the usage of multiple ALU execution units in parallel for the calculation of independent output values that have an overlap in input source data values. In a multisampling implementation, two or more output values are calculated in parallel by leveraging the commonality of input source data values in calculations. Unlike partial summation, multisampling is not susceptible to output value errors from intermediate calculation steps.

Multisampling can be applied to any signal-processing calculation of the form:

$$y[n] = \sum_{m=0}^{M} x[n+m]h[n]$$

where:

$$y[0] = x[0+0]h[0] + x[1+0]h[1] + x[2+0]h[2] + \ldots + x[M+0]h[M]$$

$$y[1] = x[0+1]h[0] + x[1+1]h[1] + \ldots + x[M-1+1]h[M-1] + x[M+1]h[M]$$

Thus, using C pseudocode, the inner loop for the output value calculation can be written as:

```
tmp1 = x[n];
for(m=0; m<M; m+ =2)
{
tmp2 = x[n+m+1];
y[n] + = tmp1*h[m];
y[n+1] + = tmp2*h[m];
tmp1 = x[k+m+2];
y[n] + = tmp2*h[m+1];
y[n+1] + = tmp1*h[m+1];
}
tmp2 = x[n+m+1];
y[n+1] + = tmp2*h[m];
```

Implementation procedure

The multisampled version works on N output samples at once. Transforming the kernel into a multisample version involves the following changes:

- changing the outer loop counters to reflect the multisampling by N
- use of N registers for accumulation of the output data
- unrolling the inner loop N times to allow for common data elements in the calculation of the N samples to be shared
- reducing the inner loop counter by a factor of N to reflect the unrolling by N.

Implementation

An example implementation on a two-MAC DSP is shown in Figure 11.14.

Partial summation

Background

Partial summation is an optimization technique whereby the computation for one output sum is divided into multiple smaller, or partial, sums. The partial sums are added together at the end of the algorithm. Partial summation allows more use of parallelism since some serial dependency is broken, allowing the operation to complete sooner.

Partial summation can be applied to any signal-processing calculation of the form:

$$y[n] = \sum_{m=0}^{M} x[n+m]h[n]$$

where:

$y[0] = x[0+0]h[0] + x[1+0]h[1] + x[2+0]h[2] + \ldots + x[M+0]h[M]$

```
[ clr d5 ; Clears d5 (accumulator)
clr d6 ; Clears d6 (accumulator)
move.f (r0)+,d2 ; Load data
move.f (r7)+,d4 ; Load some reference
]
move.f (r0)+,d3 ; Load data
InnerLoop:
loopstart1
[ mac d2,d4,d5 ; First output sample
mac d3,d4,d6 ; Second output sample
move.f (r0)+,d2 ; Load some data
move.f (r7)+,d4 ; Load some reference
]
[ mac d3,d4,d5 ; First output sample
mac d2,d4,d6 ; Second output sample
move.f (r0)+,d3 ; Load some data
move.f (r7)+,d4 ; Load some reference
]
loopend1
```

Figure 11.14:
Partial summation.

To do a partial summation, each calculation is simply broken up into multiple sums. For example, for the first output sample, assuming $M = 3$:

$$\text{sum0} = x[0+0]h[0] + x[1+0]h[1]$$

$$\text{sum1} = x[2+0]h[0] + x[3+0]h[1]$$

$$y[0] = \text{sum0} + \text{sum1}$$

Note that the partial sums can be chosen as any part of the total calculation. In this example, the two sums are chosen to be the first + the second, and the third + the fourth calculations.

Note: partial summation can cause saturation arithmetic errors. Saturation is not associative. For example, saturate (a*b) + c may not equal saturate (a*b + c). Care must be taken to ensure that such differences don't affect the program.

Implementation procedure

The partial summed implementation works on *N* partial sums at once. Transforming the kernel involves the following changes:

- use of *N* registers for accumulation of the *N* partial sums;
- unrolling the inner loop will be necessary; the unrolling factor depends on the implementation, how values are reused and how multiple register moves are used;
- changing the inner loop counter to reflect the unrolling.

Implementation

Figure 11.15 shows the implementation on a 2-MAC (multiply/accumulate) DSP.

Software pipelining

Background

Software pipelining is an optimization whereby a sequence of instructions is transformed into a pipeline of several copies of that sequence. The sequences then work in parallel to leverage more of the available parallelism of the architecture. The sequence of instructions can be duplicated as many times as needed, substituting a different set of registers for each sequence. Those sequences of instructions can then be interwoven.

For a given sequence of dependent operations:

```
a = operation();
b = operation(a);
c = operation(b);
```

Software pipelining gives (where operations on the same line can be parallelized):

```
a0 = operation();
b0 = operation(a); a1 = operation();
c0 = operation(b); b1 = operation(a1);
c1 = operation(b1);
```

Implementation

A simple sequence of three dependent instructions can easily be software pipelined, for example the sequence in Figure 11.16. A software pipelining of three sequences is shown. The sequence of code in the beginning where the pipeline is filling up (when there are less than three instructions grouped) is the prologue. Similarly, the end sequence of code with less than three instructions grouped is the epilogue. The grouping

```
[ move.4f (r0)+,d0:d1:d2:d3 ; Load data - x[..]
move.4f (r7)+,d4:d5:d6:d7 ; Load reference - h[..]
]
InnerLoop:
loopstart1
[ mpy d0,d4,d8 ; x[0]*h[0]
mpy d2,d6,d9 ; x[2]*h[2]
]
[ mac d1,d5,d8 ; x[1]*h[1]
mac d3,d7,d9 ; x[3]*h[3]
move.f (r0)+,d0 ; load x[4]
]
add d8,d9,d9 ; y[0]
[ mpy d1,d4,d8 ; x[1]*h[0]
mpy d3,d6,d9 ; x[3]*h[1]
moves.f d9,(r1)+ ; store y[0]
]
[ mac d2,d5,d8 ; x[2]*h[2]
mac d0,d7,d9 ; x[4]*h[3]
move.f (r0)+,d1 ; load x[5]
]
add d8,d9,d9 ; y[1]
[ mpy d2,d4,d8 ; x[2]*h[0]
mpy d0,d6,d9 ; x[4]*h{1]
moves.f d9,(r1)+ ; store y[1]
]
[ mac d3,d5,d8 ; x[3]*h[2]
mac d1,d7,d9 ; x[5]*h[3]
move.f (r0)+,d2 ;load x[6]
]
add d8,d9,d9 ; y[2]
[ mpy d2,d4,d8 ; x[3]*h[0]
mpy d0,d6,d9 ; x[5]*h[1]
moves.f d9,(r1)+ ; store y[2]
]
[ mac d3,d5,d8 ; x[4]*h[2]
mac d1,d7,d9 ; x[6]*h[3]
move.f (r0)+,d3 load x[7]
]
add d8,d9,d9 ; y[3]
moves.f d9,(r1)+ ; store y[3]
loopend1
```

Figure 11.15:
Software pipelined loop prolog.

```
sub d0,d1,d2
impy d2,d2,d2
asr d2,d2
```

Figure 11.16:
Software pipelined loop kernel.

```
sub d0,d1,d2 ; Prologue
[ impy d2,d2,d2 ; Prologue
sub d3,d4,d5
]
[ asr d2,d2 ; Can be transformed into loop
impy d5,d5,d5
sub d6,d7,d8
]
[ asr d5,d5 ; Epilogue
impy d8,d8,d8
]
asr d8,d8 ; Epilogue
```

Figure 11.17:
Software pipelined loop epilogue.

of three instructions in parallel can be transformed into a loop kernel as shown in Figure 11.17.

Note: software pipelining will increase the code size. Ensure that optimizations are worth the increase in size.

Example application of optimization techniques: cross-correlation

A good example for a case study in optimization using the techniques above is the implementation of the cross-correlation algorithm. Cross-correlation is a standard method of estimating the degree to which two series are correlated. It computes the best match for the supplied reference vector within the supplied input vector. The location of the highest cross-correlation (offset) is returned, as shown in Figure 11.18.

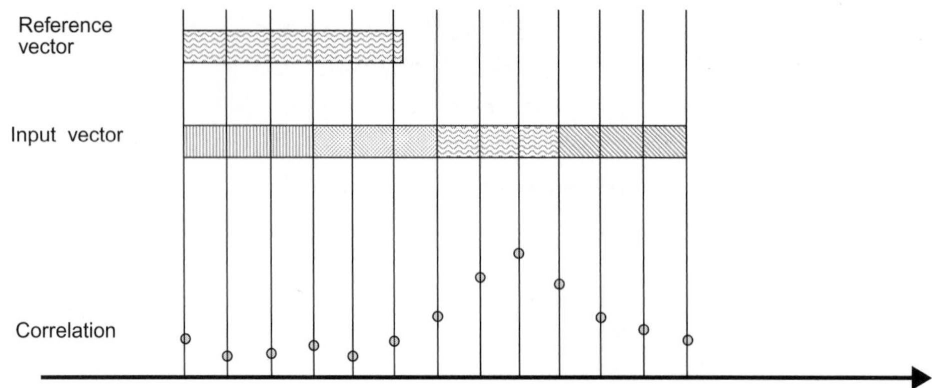

Figure 11.18:
Cross-correlation algorithm.

Setup

The cross-correlation function is set up in a project consisting of a test harness with input vectors and reference output vectors. Testing is done using two different sets of inputs: input vector length 24, reference 4; input size 32, reference 6. For performance measurement, the profiler in the CodeWarrior 10 tool chain for StarCore is used. The minimum and maximum function execution times are measured (corresponding in this case to the shorter and longer vectors respectively). For the purposes of illustration, three different implementations of cross-correlation are presented:

Initial port
Step 1: intrinsics for fractional operations
Step 2: optimized by specifying alignment and using multisampling techniques
Step 3: optimized in assembly

Original implementation

The original implementation is written in ANSI C (Figure 11.19). It consists of two nested loops: the outer loop computes each correlation value (i.e., match) and the inner loop computes each calculation that forms part of that correlation value. So, the outer loop steps through the input vector, while the inner loop steps through the reference vector.

Performance analysis – (example Freescale StarCore SC3850 Core)

Assumptions: zero wait state memory (all in cache). Core only benchmarked.

Test 1 (short vector)	734 cycles
Test 2 (long vector)	1258 cycles

<table>
<tr><th>C Implementation</th><th>Generated Assembly</th></tr>
<tr><td>

```
// Receives pointers to input and reference vectors
short CrossCor(short *iRefPtr, short *iInPtr)
{
  long acc;
  long max = 0;
  int offset = –1;
  int i, j;
// For all values in the input vector
 for(i=0; i<(inSize-refSize+1); i++)
 {
   acc = 0;
// For all values in the reference vector
   for(j=0; j<refSize; j++)
   {
// Cross-correlation operation:
//Multiply integers Shift into fractional representation
//Add to accumulator
     acc += ((int)(iRefPtr[j] * iInPtr[j])) << 1;
   }
   iInPtr++;
   if(acc > max)
   {
// Save location (offset) of maximum correlation result
     max = acc;
     offset = i;
   }
 }
 return offset;
}
```

</td><td>

3 cycle inner loop shown:

```
 FALIGN
  LOOPSTART3
[
  move.w  (r14)+,d4
  move.w  (r4)+,d3
 ]
 [
  impy    d3,d4,d5
  addl1a  r2,r3
 ]
  move.l  d5,r2
  LOOPEND3
```

</td></tr>
</table>

Figure 11.19:
Initial ANSI C implementation.

Step 1: use intrinsics for fractional operations and specify loop counts

In the first step, ensure that intrinsic functions are used to specify fractional operations to ensure the best code is generated. On the Starcore SC3850 core, for example, there is a multiply-accumulate instruction which does the left shift after the multiply and saturates after the addition operation. This combines many operations into one. Replacing the inner loop body with an L_mac intrinsic will ensure that the mac assembly instruction is generated (Figure 11.20).

Performance analysis – (example Freescale StarCore SC3850 Core)

Assumptions: zero wait state memory (all in cache). Core only benchmarked.

Test 1 (short vector)	441 cycles
Test 2 (long vector)	611 cycles

Step 2: specify data alignment and modify for multisampling algorithm

In the final step, multisampling techniques are used to transform the cross-correlation algorithm. The cross-correlation code is modified so that two adjacent correlation samples are calculated simultaneously. This allows data reuse between samples and a reduction in data loaded from memory. In addition, aligning the vectors and using a factor of two for multisampling ensures that when data is loaded, the alignment stays a factor of two, which means multiple-register moves can be used, in this case, two values at once (Figure 11.21). In summary, the changes are:

> Multisampling: perform two correlation calculations each correlation per loop. Zero pad first multiplication of second correlation (then compute the last multiply outside the loop).
> Reuse of data: since two adjacent correlation computations use some of the same values, they can be reused, removing the need to refetch them from memory.
> In addition, the one value reused between iterations is saved in a temporary variable.

Since InSize-refSize + 1 correlations are needed and our vectors are even, there will be one remaining correlation to calculate outside the loop (Figure 11.22).

Leveraging some assumptions made about the data set (even vectors), some more aggressive optimizations could be done at the C level. This optimization means some flexibility is given up for the sake of performance.

Performance analysis – (example Freescale StarCore SC3850 Core)

C Implementation	Generated Assembly

`long acc;`
`long max = 0;`
 	
`int offset = -1;`
 	
`int i, j;`
 	
`for(i=0; i<inSize-refSize+1; i++) {`
`#pragma loop_count (24,32)`
 	
`acc = 0;`
`for (j=0; j <= refSize+1; j++) {`
`#pragma loop_count (4,6)`
 	
`acc = L_mac(acc, iRefPtr[j],`
`iInPtr[j]);`
`}`
`iInPtr++;`
`if(acc > max) {`
`max = acc;`
`offset = i;`
`}`
`}`
`return offset;`
	One Inner Loop Only shown:
	
	`skipls ; note this was added due to`
	`pragma loop count. Now if zero, skips loop`
	
	`FALIGN`
	`LOOPSTART3`
	`DW17 TYPE debugsymbol`
	`[`
	`mac d0,d1,d2`
	`move.f (r2)+,d1`
	`move.f (r10)+,d0`
	`]`
	`LOOPEND3`

Figure 11.20:
Intrinsic functions used to specify fractional operations to ensure the best code is generated.

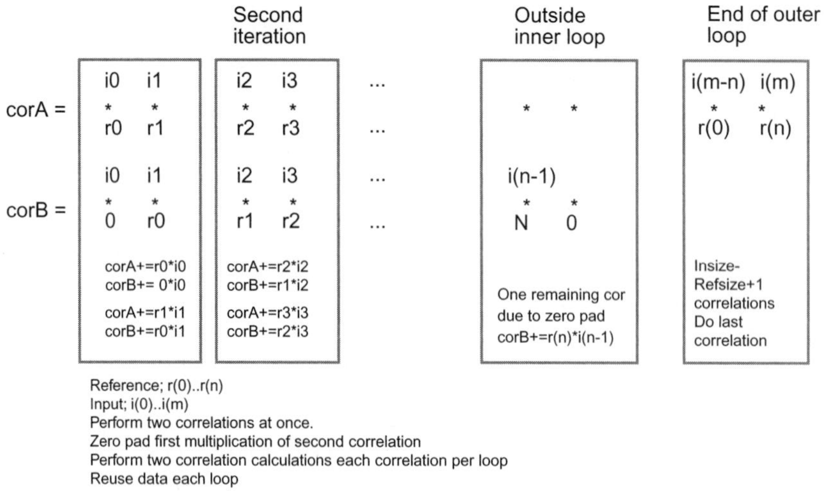

Figure 11.21:
Diagram of multisampling technique.

Assumptions: zero wait state memory (all in cache). Core only benchmarked.

Test 1 (short vector)	227 cycles
Test 2 (long vector)	326 cycles

Step 3: assembly-language optimization

Assembly language is still used in cases where performance is critical. In this example below, we will take the cross-correlation from earlier and write an assembly function, integrate into a C framework then optimize it (Figure 11.23).

Performance analysis – (example Freescale StarCore SC3850 Core)

Assumptions: zero wait state memory (all in cache). Core only benchmarked.

Test 1 (short vector)	296 cycles
Test 2 (long vector)	424 cycles

C Implementation	Generated Assembly

#pragma align *iRefPtr 4
#pragma align *iInPtr 4
long accA, accB;
long max = 0;
short s0,s1,s2,s3,s4;
int offset = -1;
int i, j;
for(i=0; i<inSize-refSize; i+=2) {
#pragma loop_count (4,40,2)
accA = 0;
accB = 0;
s4 = 0;
for(j=0; j<refSize; j+=2) {
#pragma loop_count (4,40,2)
s0 = iInPtr[j];
s1 = iInPtr[j+1];
s2 = iRefPtr[j];
s3 = iRefPtr[j+1];
accA = L_mac(accA, s2, s0);
accB = L_mac(accB, s4, s0);
accA = L_mac(accA, s3, s1);
accB = L_mac(accB, s2, s1);
s4 = s3;
}
s0 = iInPtr[j];
accB = L_mac(accB, s4, s0);
	Both loop bodies shown:
	skipls PL001
	]
	FALIGN
	LOOPSTART3
	FALIGN
	LOOPSTART2
	[
	tstgt d12
	clr d8
	clr d4
	clr d5
	suba r5,r5
	move.l d13,r8
	]
	[
	tfra r1,r2
	jf L5
	]
	[
	tfra r0,r3
	addl1a r4,r2
	]
	[
	move.2f (r2)+,d0:d1
	move.2f (r3)+,d2:d3
	]
	[
	mac d8,d0,d4
	mac d2,d0,d8
	tfr d3,d5
	suba #<1,r8
	tfra r9,r5
	]
	doensh3 r8
	FALIGN
	LOOPSTART3

Figure 11.22:
Since InSize-refSize + 1 correlations are needed and our vectors are even, there will be one remaining correlation to calculate outside the loop.

<pre>   if(accA > max) {
        max = accA;
        offset = i;
    }
    if(accB > max) {
        max = accB;
        offset = i+1;
    }
    iInPtr +=2;
}
  accA = 0;
  accB = 0;
  for(j=0; j<refSize; j+=2) {
#pragma loop_count (4,40,2)
      accA = L_mac(accA, iRefPtr[j],
iInPtr[j]);
      accB = L_mac(accB,
iRefPtr[j+1], iInPtr[j+1]);
  }
  accA = L_add(accA, accB);
  if(accA > max) {
      max = accA;
      offset = i;
  }
  return offset;</pre>
	<pre>[
	  mac d3,d1,d8
	  mac d2,d1,d4
	  move.2f (r2)+,d0:d1 ; packed
	moves
	  move.2f (r3)+,d2:d3
	]
	[
	  mac d2,d0,d8
	  mac d5,d0,d4
	  tfr d3,d5
	]
	  LOOPEND3
	[
	  mac d2,d1,d4
	  mac d3,d1,d8
	]
	[
	  cmpgt d9,d8
	  tfra r1,r2
	  adda r4,r5
	]
	[
	  tfrt d8,d9
	  tfrt d11,d10
	  addl1a r5,r2
	  adda #<2,r4
	]
	  move.f (r2),d1
	  mac d5,d1,d4
	  cmpgt d9,d4
	[
	 IFT addnc.w #<1,d11,d10
	 IFA tfrt d4,d9
	 IFA add #<2,d11
	]
	  LOOPEND2</pre>

Figure 11.22
(Continued)

Example Assembly Integration

```
;
; Function :    CrossCor
;
; Prototype:    extern short CrossCor(short *iRefPtr, short *iInPtr) ;
;
; Description : Cross-correlated input data stream with smaller reference
;           sample stream. Input arguments passed through function
;           global variables.  Return in d0 the offset from the
;           beginning of the input data stream where the highest value
;           was found.
;
; Inputs :      inSize (global variable) -number of samples in input
;                   data stream.
;           refSize (global variable) -number of samples in the
;                   reference stream.
;           refPtr (param 0 -r0) -pointer to the reference
;                   sample stream.  Reference samples are
;                   16-bits.
;           inDataPtr (param 0 -r1) -pointer to the input
;                   sample stream.  Input samples are 16-bits.
;
; Outputs :     d0 -Offset from inDataPtr where the max value can be
;                   found.
;
; Assumptions : Uses stack for temporarily holding cross correlation values.
;
;*************************************************************************
 align $10
 global _CrossCor
_CrossCor: type func
                            ; RefPtr   passed in register r0
 tfra r0,r9                         ; save a copy
                            ; InDataPtr   passed in register r1
 tfra r1,r2                         ; save a copy
 dosetup0 CrossCorTopLoop
 move.w _inSize,d0                  ;  load the data size into d0
 move.w _refSize,d1                 ; load the reference data size into d1
```

Figure 11.23:
Write an assembly function for the cross-correlation from earlier and integrate into a C framework before optimizing.

```
[
  sub d1,d0,d0                ; iterate the loop inSize-refSize+1 times
  clr d11                     ; cor index
  clr d12                     ; current index.
]
[
  clr d10                     ; cor max
  add #1,d0                   ; iterate the loop inSize-refSize+1 times
]
  doen0 d0
  loopstart0
CrossCorTopLoop:
  [
    tfra r9,r0                ; reset refPtr to start
    doensh1 d1                ; do the inner loop refSize times
    clr d2                    ; d2 is the accumulator. clear it.
  ]
  [
    move.f (r1)+,d3           ; load data value before loop
    move.f (r0)+,d4           ; load reference value before loop
  ]
CrossCorInnerLoop:
  loopstart1
  [
    mac d3,d4,d2              ; ref[i]*data[i]
    move.f (r1)+,d3           ; load data value
    move.f (r0)+,d4           ; load reference value
  ]
  loopend1
CrossCorInnerLoopEnd:
  cmpgt d10,d2                ; if d2>d10, SR:T set
  [
      tfrt d2,d10             ;save max corr
      tfrt d12,d11            ; save new max index
    adda #2,r2,r2             ; increment InPtr start by 2 bytes
    adda #2,r2,r1             ; increment InPtr start by 2 bytes
    add #1,d12
  ]
  loopend0
  CrossCorReport:
  tfr d11,d0                  ; save max index
      global F_CrossCor_end
F_CrossCor_end
 rts
```

Figure 11.23
(Continued)

CHAPTER 12

Optimizing Embedded Software for Memory

Mike Brogioli

Chapter Outline

Introduction

Optimization metrics for compiled code are not always measured in resulting execution clock cycles on the target architecture. Consider modern cellular telephone or wireless devices which may download executables over a wireless network connection or backhaul infrastructure. In such cases, it is often advantageous for the compiler to reduce the size of the compiled code which must be downloaded to the wireless device. By reducing the size of the code needed to be downloaded, savings are achieved in terms of bandwidth required for each wireless point of download.

Optimization metrics such as the memory system performance of compiled code are other metrics which are often important to developers. These are metrics correlated to the

Software Engineering for Embedded Systems.
DOI: http://dx.doi.org/10.1016/B978-0-12-415917-4.00012-8
© 2013 Elsevier Inc. All rights reserved.

dynamic run-time behavior of not only the compiled code on the target processor, but also the underlying memory system, caches, DRAM and buses, etc. By efficiently arranging the data within the application or, more specifically, the order in which data and corresponding data structures are accessed by the application dynamically at run-time, significant performance improvements can be gained at the memory-system level. In addition, vectorizing compilers can also improve performance due to spatial locality of data when SIMD instruction sets are present and varying memory-system alignment conditions are met.

The next section illustrates optimization techniques that may be used to improve application code size. The first techniques presented fall under the category of compiler "flag mining", which is the means by which different permutations of compile-time options are used to achieve the desired results on generated code. In addition, lower-level system details are presented such as application binary interfaces and multiple encoding instruction set architectures as vehicles to further reduce code size in the presence of resource-constrained systems.

Code size optimizations

Compiler flags and flag mining

In compiling a source code project for execution on a target architecture, it is often desirable for the resulting code size to be reduced as much as possible. Reasons for this pertain to both the amount of space in memory the code will occupy at program run-time and the potential reduction in the amount of instruction cache needed by the device. In reducing the code size of a given executable, a number of factors can be tweaked during the compilation process to accommodate this.

Typically, users will first begin by configuring the compiler to build the program for size optimization, frequently using a compiler command line option such as −Os, as is available in the GNU GCC compiler as of version 4.5. When building for code size, it is not uncommon for the compiler to disable other optimizations that frequently result in improvements in the run-time performance of the code. Examples of these might be loop optimizations such as loop unrolling, or software pipelining, which typically are performed in an attempt to increase the run-time performance of the code at the cost of increases in the compiled code size. This is due to the fact that the compiler will insert additional code into the optimized loops such as prologue and epilogue code in the case of software pipelining, or additional copies of the loop body in the case of loop unrolling.

In the event that users do not want to disable all optimization or build exclusively at optimization level −O0 with code size optimization enabled, users may also want to disable functionality such as function inlining via either a compiler command line option or compiler pragma, depending on the build tools system and functionality supported. It is often the case that at higher levels of program optimization, specifically when optimizing for program run-time performance, compilers will attempt to inline copies of a function, whereby the body of the function code is inlined into the calling procedure, rather than the calling procedure being required to make a call into a callee procedure, resulting in a change of program flow and obvious system side effects. By specifying either as a command line option or a via a customer compiler pragma, the user can prevent the tools from inadvertently inlining various functions which would result in an increase in the overall code size of the compiled application.

When a development team is building code for a production release, or in a user case scenario when debugging information is no longer needed in the executable, it may also be beneficial to strip out debugging information and symbol table information. In doing this, significant reductions in object file and executable file sizes can be achieved. Furthermore, in stripping out all label information, some level of IP protection may be afforded to the user in that consumers of the executable will have a difficult time reverse engineering the various functions being called within the program.

Target ISA for size and performance tradeoffs

Various target architectures in the embedded space may afford additional degrees of freedom when trying to reduce code size of the input application. Quite often it is advantageous for the system developer to take into consideration not only the algorithmic complexity and software architecture of their code, but also the types of arithmetic required and how well those types of arithmetic and system requirements map to the underlying target architecture. For example, an application that requires heavy use of 32-bit arithmetic may run functionally correctly on an architecture that is primarily tuned for 16-bit arithmetic; however, an architecture tuned for 32-bit arithmetic can provide a number of improvements in terms of both performance, code size, and perhaps power consumption.

Variable-length instruction encoding is one particular technology that a given target architecture may support, which can be effectively exploited by the build tools to reduce overall code size. In variable-length instruction coding schemes, certain instructions within the target processor's ISA may have what is referred to as "premium encodings", whereby those instructions most commonly used can be represented in a reduced binary footprint. One example of this might be a 32-bit embedded Power Architecture device, whereby frequently used instructions such as integer add are also represented with a premium 16-bit encoding. When the source application is compiled for size optimization, the build tools will attempt to map as many instructions as possible to their premium encoding counterpart in an attempt to reduce the overall footprint of the resulting executable.

Freescale Semiconductor supports this feature in the Power Architecture cores for embedded computing, as well as in their StarCore line of DSPs. Other embedded processor designs such as those by ARM Limited and Texas Instruments' DSP have also employed variable encoding formats for premium instructions, in an effort to curb the resulting executable's code size footprint.

In the case of Freescale's Power Architecture, Freescale states that both standard 32-bit code and 16-bit premium-encoded code can be mixed interchangeably within the executable on a flash page size access basis. Other architectures may opt to specify the encoding within some format of prefix bits, allowing an even finer level of code intermingling.

It should be mentioned than the reduced-footprint premium encoding of instructions in a variable-length encoding architecture often comes at the cost of reduced functionality. This is due to the reduction in the number of bits that are afforded in encoding the instruction, often reduced from 32 bits to 16 bits. An example of a non-premium encoding instruction versus a premium encoding instruction might be an integer arithmetic ADD instruction. On a non-premium-encoded variant of the instruction, the source and destination operations of the ADD instruction may be any of the 32 general-purpose integer registers within the target architecture's register file. In the case of a premium-encoded instruction, whereby only 16 bits of encoding space are afforded, the premium-encoded ADD instruction may only be permitted to use R0–R7 as source and destination registers, in an effort to reduce the number of bits used in the source and register destination encodings. Although it may not readily be apparent to the application programmer, this can result in subtle, albeit minor, performance degradations. These are often due to additional copy instructions that may be required to move source and destination operations around to adjacent instructions in the assembly schedule because of restrictions placed on the premium-encoded variants.

As evidence of the benefits and potential drawbacks of using variable-length encoding instruction set architectures as a vehicle for code size reduction, benchmarking of typical embedded codes when targeting Power Architecture devices has shown VLE, or variable-length encoding, enabled code to be approximately 30% smaller in code footprint size than standard Power Architecture code while only exhibiting a 5% reduction in code performance. Resulting minor degradations in code performance are typical, due to limitations in functionality when using a reduced instruction encoding format of an instruction.

Floating-point arithmetic and arithmetic emulation may be another somewhat obfuscated source of code size explosion. Consider the case in which the user's source code contains loops of intensive floating-point arithmetic when targeting an architecture lacking native floating-point functionality in hardware. In order to functionally support the floating-point arithmetic, the build tools will often need to substitute in code to perform floating-point arithmetic emulation at program run-time. This typically entails trapping to a floating-point emulation library that provides the required functionality, such as floating-point division, using the existing non-floating-point instructions natively supported on the target architecture.

As one might predict, it is not uncommon for a given floating-point emulation routine to require hundreds of target processor clock cycles to emulate the floating-point operation, which execute over tens if not hundreds of floating-point emulation instructions. In addition to the obvious performance overhead incurred versus code targeting a processor with native floating-point support in hardware, significant code size increases will occur due to the inclusion of floating-point emulation libraries or inlined floating-point emulation code. By correctly matching the types of arithmetic contained in the source application with the underlying native hardware support of the target architecture, reductions in the overall resulting executable size can be achieved with some effort.

Tuning the ABI for code size

In software engineering, the application binary interface or ABI is the low-level software interface between a given program and the operating system, system libraries, and even inter-module communication within the program itself. The ABI itself is a specification for how a given system represents items such as data types, data sizes, alignment of data elements and structures, calling conventions and related modes of operations. In addition, a given ABI may specify the binary format of object files and program libraries. The calling convention and alignment may be areas of interest to those wishing to reduce the overall code size of their application by using a custom calling convention within their particular application.

A given target processor and related ABI will often specify a calling convention to be used between functions within the application, as well as calls to the underlying operating system, run-time libraries and so forth. It is often desirable for a vendor to specify a default calling convention that affords a reasonable level of performance for the general use case when making calls between caller and callee procedures within an application. At the same time, such a default calling convention may also attempt to make reasonable reductions in the code size generated in both the caller and callee procedures for maintaining machine-level state consistency between both the caller and callee. Often, however, this is not ideal for an application developer who demands either tight restrictions on code size or, in other cases, high levels of compiled code performance in key system kernels of hot paths within the call graph.

Consider for example the function defined in Figure 12.1, which passes a large number of 16-bit integer values from the caller to the callee procedure:

```
void caller_procedure(void)

{

      short tap_00, tap_01, tap_02, tap_03,

            tap_04, tap_05, tap_06, tap_07;

            long callee_result;


      // some computation occurs, setting up taps

      callee_result = callee_procedure(tap_00, tap_01,
                                       tap_02, tap_03,
                                       tap_04, tap_05,
                                       tap_06, tap_07);


      // subsequent computation occurs based on results

}



long callee_procedure(short tap_00, short tap_01,
                      short tap_02, short tap_03,
                      short tap_04, short tap_05,
                      short tap_06, short tap_07)

{

      long result;

      // do computation.

      return result;

}
```

Figure 12.1:
Example C – language caller and callee procedure.

Looking at this example, it can be seen that the caller procedure computes a number of 16-bit values that must be passed as input parameters to the callee procedure. The callee procedure will then use these input values to compute some result that is passed back to the caller procedure to use in subsequent computation.

Let's also assume that we are dealing with a somewhat trivialized ABI that is succinct for this illustrative example. The ABI assumes a 32-bit general purpose embedded architecture that has a 32-bit general purpose register file. The default calling convention for this ABI states that the first two char, short, or integer, values that are passed to a callee procedure get passed in general-purpose registers R00 and R01, with subsequent parameters being passed from the caller to the callee via the stack. This might be typical for a processor targeting a mobile embedded device that was sensitive to both performance and code size. The resulting assembly might look something like Figure 12.2.

We can see here that the default ABI has been used as the vehicle for communications between both the caller and callee procedures named caller_procedure() and callee_procedure() respectively. Looking at the assembly code generated for the caller_procedure, we can see that the local variables computed within caller_procedure, namely tap_00 through tap_07, are loaded from memory within the local procedure, and copied onto the stack for passing to the callee routine, namely callee_procedure. Because the default calling convention as specified by this example ABI states that the first two char, short or integral type parameters may be passed via registers from the caller to the callee procedures, the compiler has taken the liberty of passing tap_00 and tap_01 using target processor registers R00 and R01 respectively.

It is interesting to note that fewer instructions are required for setting up parameters to be passed via registers than for those to be passed via the stack. Additionally, it can be seen from the callee procedure that significantly more instructions must be inserted into the callee procedure by the compiler to restore parameters passed via copy on the stack from the caller function into registers for local computation within the callee routine. While this affords a very nice abstraction of computation between the caller and the callee routines, clearly if the user wishes to reduce the code size of their resulting executable one might consider alternative means of communication between caller and callee routines.

This is where custom calling conventions may be used with a given ABI to further improve performance, or in the case of this example to further reduce the code size and increase performance as well. Suppose that now the user has altered the calling convention within the ABI to be used for these two procedures. Let's call this new calling convention as specified by the user "user_calling_convention". The user has now stated that rather than pass only the first two parameters from the caller function to the callee in registers, with subsequent parameters being passed via the stack, that user_calling_convention may pass up to eight parameters from the caller to the callee function via registers, namely R00–R07. In doing this, the tools will need to account for additional registers being used for parameter passing, and the bookkeeping required on both sides of the caller/callee world; however, for this user's example code which passes large numbers of parameters from caller to callee, a benefit can be gained. Figure 12.3 illustrates what assembly code the user could expect to be generated using this user_calling_convention customization as specified by the developer.

Referring to Figure 12.3, it can be seen that by using the user_calling_convention, the resulting assembly generated by the compiler looks quite different from that of the default calling convention. By permitting the build tools to pass additional parameters between caller and callee functions using registers, a drastic reduction in the number of instructions

```
;*****************************************************************
;* NOTE:  Using default ABI, R00 and R01 can be used to pass
;*        parameters from caller to calle, all other parameters
;*        must be passed via the stack.
;*
;* SP+TAP_00 contains tap_00
;* SP+TAP_01 contains tap_01
;* SP+TAP_02 contains tap_02
;* SP+TAP_03 contains tap_03
;* SP+TAP_04 contains tap_04
;* SP+TAP_05 contains tap_05
;* SP+TAP_06 contains tap_06
;* SP+TAP_07 contains tap_07
;*
;*********************************************************************
__caller_procedure:
      ;* some computation setting tap_00 .. tap_07 in local memory
      ;* and various bookkeeping.

      ;* all parameters that can not be passed via default ABI
      ;* configuration must be pushed onto the stack.
      ;*
      LOAD   R00,(SP+TAP_03);
      PUSH   R00;                          ;* SP+=4
      LOAD   R00,(SP+TAP_04);
      PUSH   R00                           ;* SP+=4
      LOAD   R00,(SP+TAP_05);
      PUSH   R05                           ;* SP+=4
      LOAD   R00,(SP+TAP_06);
      PUSH   R00                           ;* SP+=4
      LOAD   R00,(SP+TAP_07);
      PUSH   R00                           ;* SP+=4
```

Figure 12.2:
Example assembly language based caller procedure (non-optimized).

```
;**********************************************************************
;* R00 contains tap_00
;* R01 contains tap_01;
;* tap_02 through tap_07 have been passed via the stack, as seen
;* previously being setup in caller_procedure via the push operations.
;* Upon entry, callee_procedure must transfer all of the input parameters
;* passed via the stack into registers for local computation.  This
;* requires additional instructions both on the caller side (to put on
;* the stack) as well as the callee size (to restore from the stack).
;*
;* NOTE:  INSERT PROS AND CONS
;*
;*
;*
;**********************************************************************
__callee_procedure:

      ;* ADJUST STACK POINTER TO NOW POINT TO CALLEE'S STACK FRAME
      ;* SO WE CAN ACCESS DATA PASSED STACK IN ABI COMPLIANCE
      ;*
      POP    R07;          ;* tap_07 into R07, SP-=4
      POP    R06;          ;* tap_06 into R06, SP-=4
      POP    R05;          ;* tap_05 into R05, SP-=4
      POP    R04;          ;* tap_04 into R04, SP-=4
      POP    R03;          ;* tap_03 into R03, SP-=4
      POP    R02;          ;* tap_02 into R02, SP-=4

      ;* perform local computation on input paramters now stored
      ;* in registers R00-R07, storing result into
      ;* SP+RESULT_OFFSET
      ;*
```

Figure 12.2
(Continued)

```
;**********************************************************
;* NOTE:  Using default ABI, R00 and R01 can be used to pass
;*        parameters from caller to calle, all other parameters
;*        must be passed via the stack.
;*
;* SP+TAP_00 contains tap_00
;* SP+TAP_01 contains tap_01
;* SP+TAP_02 contains tap_02
;* SP+TAP_03 contains tap_03
;* SP+TAP_04 contains tap_04
;* SP+TAP_05 contains tap_05
;* SP+TAP_06 contains tap_06
;* SP+TAP_07 contains tap_07
;*
;********************************************************************
__caller_procedure:
      ;* some computation setting tap_00 .. tap_07 in local memory
      ;* and various bookkeeping.

      ;* all parameters that can not be passed via default ABI
      ;* configuration must be pushed onto the stack.
      ;*
      LOAD   R00,(SP+TAP_03);
      PUSH   R00;                    ;* SP+=4
      LOAD   R00,(SP+TAP_04);
      PUSH   R00                     ;* SP+=4
      LOAD   R00,(SP+TAP_05);
      PUSH   R05                     ;* SP+=4
      LOAD   R00,(SP+TAP_06);
      PUSH   R00                     ;* SP+=4
      LOAD   R00,(SP+TAP_07);
```

Figure 12.3:
Example assembly language based caller procedure (optimized).

```
;*********************************************************************
;*
;* R00 contains tap_00
;* R01 contains tap_01;
;* tap_02 through tap_07 have been passed via the stack, as seen
;* previously being setup in caller_procedure via the push operations.
;* Upon entry, callee_procedure must transfer all of the input parameters
;* passed via the stack into registers for local computation.  This
;* requires additional instructions both on the caller side (to put on
;* the stack) as well as the callee size (to restore from the stack).
;*
;*
;*
;*
;*
;*********************************************************************
__callee_procedure:

      ;* ADJUST STACK POINTER TO NOW POINT TO CALLEE'S STACK FRAME
      ;* SO WE CAN ACCESS DATA PASSED STACK IN ABI COMPLIANCE
      ;*
      POP    R07;          ;* tap_07 into R07, SP-=4
      POP    R06;          ;* tap_06 into R06, SP-=4
      POP    R05;          ;* tap_05 into R05, SP-=4
      POP    R04;          ;* tap_04 into R04, SP-=4
      POP    R03;          ;* tap_03 into R03, SP-=4
      POP    R02;          ;* tap_02 into R02, SP-=4

      ;* perform local computation on input paramters now stored
      ;* in registers R00-R07, storing result into
      ;* SP+RESULT_OFFSET
      ;*
```

Figure 12.3
(Continued)

generated for each procedure is evident. Specifically, the caller_procedure can be shown to require far fewer moves to the stack before the call to the callee_procedure. This is due to the fact that additional hardware registers are now afforded to the calling convention, whereby values from the caller's memory space may simply be loaded into registers before making the call rather than loading into registers and then copying onto the stack (and possibly adjusting the stack pointer explicitly).

Similarly, referring to the callee_procedure, it can be seen that a number of instructions have been removed from the previous example's generated assembly. Once again, this is due to the fact that parameters are now being passed from the caller to the callee function via the register file, rather than pushing onto and pulling off the stack. As such, the callee does not need the additional instruction overhead to copy local copies from the stack into registers for local computation. In this particular example, not only is it likely that performance improvements will be seen due to fewer instructions being required to execute dynamically at run-time, but code size has also been reduced due to the number of instructions statically reduced in the executable.

While this example has shown how custom calling conventions can be used as part of an embedded system's larger ABI to reduce code size, and tailor memory optimization, there are a number of other concepts that may also play into this. Subjects such as spill code insertion by the compiler, the compiler's ability to compute stack frame sizes to utilize standard MOVE instructions to/from the stack frame rather than PUSH/POP style instructions, and also SIMD-style move operations to the stack whereby increased instruction density is obtained, further increasing performance and reducing code size overhead, are left as further reading and considered beyond the scope of this example.

Caveat emptor: compiler optimization orthogonal to code size!

When compiling code for a production release, developers often want to exploit as much compile-time optimization of their source code as possible in order to achieve the best performance possible. While building projects with −Os as an option will tune the code for optimal code size, it may also restrict the amount of optimization that is performed by the compiler due to such optimizations resulting in increased code size. As such, a user may want to keep an eye out for errant optimizations performed typically around loop nests and selectively disable them on a one-by-one use case rather than disable them for an entire project build. Most compilers support a list of pragmas that can be inserted to control compile-time behavior. Examples of such pragmas can be found with the documentation for your target processors' build tools.

Software pipelining is one optimization that can result in increased code size due to additional instructions that are inserted before and after the loop body of the transformed loop. When the compiler or assembly programmer software pipelines a loop, overlapping iterations of a given loop nest are scheduled concurrently with associated "set up" and "tear down" code inserted before and after the loop body. These additional instructions inserted in the set up and tear down, or prologue and epilogue as they are often referred to in the compiler community, can result in increased instruction counts and code sizes. Typically a compiler will offer a pragma such as "#pragma noswp" to disable software pipelining for a given loop nest, or given loops within a source code file. Users may want to utilize such a pragma on a loop-by-loop basis to reduce increases in code size associated with select loops that may not be performance-critical or on the dominant run-time paths of the application.

Loop unrolling is another fundamental compiler loop optimization that often increases the performance of loop nests at run-time. By unrolling a loop so that multiple iterations of the loop reside in the loop body, additional instruction-level parallelism is exposed for the compiler to schedule on the target processor; in addition fewer branches with branch delay slots must be executed to cover the entire iteration space of the loop nest, potentially increasing the performance of the loop as well. Because multiple iterations of the loop are cloned and inserted into the loop body by the compiler, however, the body of the loop nest typically grows as a multiple of the unroll factor. Users wishing to maintain a modest code size may wish to selectively disable loop unrolling for certain loops within their code production, at the cost of compiled code run-time performance. By selecting those loop nest that may not be on the performance-critical path of the application, savings in code size can be achieved without impacting performance along the dominant run-time path of the application. Typically compilers will support pragmas to control loop unrolling-related behavior, such as the minimum number of iterations a loop will exist or various unroll factors to pass to the compiler. Examples of disabling loop unrolling via a pragma are often of the form "#pragma nounroll". Please refer to your local compiler's documentation for correct syntax on this and related functionality.

Procedure inlining is another optimization that aims to improve the performance of compiled code at the cost of compiled code size. When procedures are inlined, the callee procedure that is the target of a caller procedure's callee invocation site is physically inlined into the body of the caller procedure. Consider the example in Figure 12.4.

Instead of making a call to callee_procedure() every time caller_procedure() is invocated, the compiler may opt to directly substitute the body of callee_procedure into the body of caller_procedure to avoid the overhead associated with the function call. In doing this, the statement a + b will be substituted into the body of caller_procedure in the hope of improving run-time performance by eliminating the function call overhead, and hopefully proving better instruction cache performance. If this inlining is performed for all call sites of callee_procedure within the application, however, one can see how multiple inlinings can

```
int caller_procedure(void)
{
    int result, a, b;

    // intermediate computation
    result = callee_procedure();
    return result;
}

int callee_procedure(void)
{
    return a + b;

}
```

Figure 12.4:
Candidate function inlining use case.

quickly lead to an explosion in the size of the application, especially for examples where callee_procedure contains more than a simple addition statement. As such, users may wish to manually disable function inlining for their entire application or for selective procedures via a compiler-provided pragma. Typical pragmas are of the form "#pragma noinline" and will prevent the tools from inlining the procedure marked at compilation time.

Memory layout optimization

In order to obtain sufficient levels of performance, application developers and software systems architects must not only select the appropriate algorithms to use in their applications, but also the means by which those applications are implemented. Quite often this also crosses the line into data structure design, layout and memory partitioning for optimal system performance. It is true that senior developers often have insight into both algorithms and their complexity, as well as a toolbox of tips and tricks for memory optimization and data structure optimization. At the same time, the scope of most embedded software engineering projects prohibits manual code and data hand optimization due to time, resource and cost constraints. As such, developers must often rely on the tools as much as possible to optimize the general use cases, only resorting to hand-level tuning and analysis to tweak performance on those performance-critical bottlenecks after the initial round of development. This last round of optimization often entails using various system profiling metrics to determine performance-critical bottlenecks, and then optimizing these portions of the application by hand using proprietary intrinsics or assembly code, and in some cases rewriting performance-critical kernel algorithms and/or related data structures. This section details design decisions that may prove useful for embedded system developers concerned with those topics mentioned above.

Overview of memory optimization

Memory optimizations of various types are often beneficial to the run-time performance and even power consumption of a given embedded application. As was mentioned previously, these optimizations can often be performed to varying degrees by the application build tools such as compilers, assemblers, linkers, profilers and so forth. Alternatively, it is often valuable for developers to go into the application and either manually tune the performance or design in consideration of memory system optimization a priori, for either given performance targets or so as to design the software architecture to be amenable to automated-tool optimization in subsequent phases of the development cycle.

In tuning a given application, quite often the baseline or "out of box" version of the application will be developed. Once functionality is brought online, the development team or engineers may select to profile the application for bottlenecks that require further optimization. Often these are known without profiling, if certain kernels within the application must execute within a given number of clock cycles as determined by a spreadsheet or pen and paper exercise during system definition. Once these key kernels are isolated or key data structures are isolated, optimization typically begins by those experts with knowledge of both software optimization techniques, compiler optimizations, the hardware target and perhaps details of the hardware target instruction set.

Focusing optimization efforts

Amdahl's law plays an interesting role in the optimization of full application stacks, however, and is not always appreciated by the software system developer. If only 10% of the dynamic run-time of a given application can benefit from SIMD or instruction-level parallel optimizations versus the 90% of dynamic run-time that must be executed sequentially, then inordinate amounts of effort on parallelizing the 10% portion of the code will still only result in modest performance improvements. Conversely, if 90% of the total application's dynamic run-time is spent in code regions exhibiting large amounts of instruction-level parallelism and data-level parallelism, it may be worthwhile to focus engineering effort on parallelizing these regions to obtain improved dynamic run-time performance.

In determining those portions of the code which dominate the dynamic application run-time, and may be the best candidates for either hand optimization or hand adjustment for applicability to automated-tool optimization, application developers typically use a software profiler in conjunction with either the silicon target or software-based system simulation. Intel's VTUNE is one such example of a profiling framework; alternatively the GNU GCC compiler and GPROF are open-source solutions that provide dynamic run-time information. Many silicon vendors such as Freescale Semiconductor and Texas Instruments also offer their own proprietary solutions for use with their respective silicon targets, allowing for either traces collected on software-based simulation platforms, or alternatively larger application-level traces that can be collected on the native silicon target.

Vectorization and the dynamic code: compute ratio

Vectorization of loops is an optimization whereby computation performed across multiple loop iterations can be combined into single vector instructions, effectively increasing the instruction-to-compute ratio within the application's dynamic run-time behavior. Consider the example in Figure 12.5.

```
short a[16], b[16], c[16];
for(iter=0; iter<16; ++iter)
{
     // results in single 16-bit MPY instruction
     // generated in assembly listing
     //
     a[iter] = b[iter] * c[iter]
}
```

```
short a[16], b[16], c[16];
for(iter=0; iter<16 iter+=4)
{
     // with high level compiler vectorization,
     // results in 4-WAY parallel 4x16-BIT multiply
     // vector instruction, effectively performing the
     // computation of four iterations of the loop in
     // a single atomic SIMD4 instruction.
     //
     a[iter:iter+4] = b[iter:iter+4] * c[iter:iter+4];
}
```

Figure 12.5:
Loop level vectorization example.

In the first loop nest, we can see that each iteration of the loop contains a single 16-bit by 16-bit multiply instruction whose result is written to the a[] array as output. One multiplication instruction is performed for each iteration of the loop, resulting in 16 16-bit multiplications. The second loop, however, shows pseudocode for how the compiler or application developer might vectorize the loop when targeting an architecture that supports a four-way SIMD multiply instruction over 16-bit integer elements. In this case, the compiler has vectorized multiple iterations of the loop together into the multiply instruction, as denoted by the array[start_range:end_range] syntax denoted in the second loop nest. Note that the loop counter is incremented by the vectorized length for each iteration of the loop now. Clearly only four iterations over the loop are now needed to compute the resulting a[]

output array, as each iteration of the loop now contains a single vector multiply instruction that computes four elements of the output vector in parallel.

There are many benefits to vectorizing code in this manner, either by hand if the application developer uses intrinsics that are proprietary with respect to the target architecture, or if the compiler is able to vectorize the code. One such benefit is the increase in performance, as the code now exploits dedicated SIMD hardware, often providing a multiplication in improvement over the vectorized loop on the order of the underlying SIMD vector hardware. Other benefits are the reduction in code size, as loops are no longer unrolled resulting in explosions in the code size, but rather more dense instructions of vector format are used rather than atomic scalar instructions. This may have secondary benefits in reducing the number of instruction fetch transactions that go out to memory as well. Lastly, the overall ratio of dynamically issued instructions to computation performed within the application is increased as well.

There are a number of challenges to both the development tools and the application developers when trying to vectorize code at the loop level. One such challenge is the code shape of loop nests that are candidate for vectorization. Typically, build tools need to understand the loop iteration space of a loop, so using constant loop bounds rather than run-time computed values may be beneficial depending on the advancement of the underlying compiler's vectorization technology. Secondly, the types of computation performed within the loop nest must be amenable to vectorization. For example, in the example above simple 16-bit integer multiplication is performed for a target architecture supporting a supposed 16-bit four-way SIMD multiply instruction. If the underlying target architecture only supports 8-bit SIMD multiplication, it may be advantageous to avoid 16-bit multiplication wherever possible if vectorization is desired.

Loop dependence analysis is another concern when vectorizing or parallelizing loop nests, as the compiler must be able to prove the safety of loop transformations. Loop dependence analysis is the means by which the compiler or dependence analyzer determines whether statements within a loop body form a dependence with respect to array accesses and data modifications, various data reduction patterns, simplification of loop-independent portions of the code and management of various conditional execution statements within the loop body.

As an example, consider the fragment of C-language code in Figure 12.6.

```
for(iter_a=0; iter<LOOP_BOUND_A; ++iter_b)
  for(iter_b=0; iter_b<LOOP_BOUND_B; ++iter_b)
    a[iter_a+4-iter_b] =
         b[2*iter_a-iter_b]+ iter_a*iter_b;
```

Figure 12.6:
Fragment of C-language code.

LIVERPOOL JOHN MOORES UNIVERSITY
LEARNING SERVICES

For the loop above, the compiler's data dependence analyzer will attempt to find all dependences between the statements reading the array b[] and writing to the array a[]. The challenge for the data dependence analyzer is to find all possible dependences between the statements that write to array a[] and read from array b[]. To ensure safety, the data dependence analyzer must ensure that it can explicitly prove safety or, in other words, any dependence that cannot be proven false must be assumed to be true to ensure safety!

The data dependence analysis shows independence between references by proving that no two instances of statements to array a[] and array b[] access or modify the same spot in array a[]. In the event that a possible dependence is found, loop dependence analysis will make an attempt to characterize the dependences, as some types of optimizations over loop nests may still be possible and profitable. It may also be possible to further transform the loop nests so as to remove the dependence.

In summary, writing loop nests so that a minimum of data dependences exists between array references will benefit vectorization and other loop transforms as much as possible. While the compiler technology used in analyzing data dependences and autovectorizing serial code for vector hardware stems from the supercomputing community, improperly written code with troublesome data dependences and loop structure may still thwart the vectorization efforts of the most advanced tool sets. At a high level, simply writing code which is easiest for humans to understand usually produces code that is easiest for the vectorizer to understand as well, as the vectorizer and data dependence analyzers can easily recognize what the programmer intended. In other words, highly hand-tuned code with a priori knowledge of the underlying target architecture is not the best candidate for automated vectorization at the tools level.

There are a number of things that application developers may want to keep an eye out for when developing code with the intent of autovectorization by the build tools.

Pointer aliasing in C

One challenge for vectorizers and data dependence analysis is the user of pointers in the C language. When data is passed to a function via pointers as parameters, it is often difficult or impossible for the data dependence analyzer and subsequent vectorizer to guarantee that the memory regions pointed to by the various pointers do not overlap in the interaction spaces of the loops in which they are computed. As the C standard has evolved over time, support for the "restrict" keyword has been added, as can be seen in the example in Figure 12.7.

By placing the restrict keyword qualifier on the pointers passed to the procedure, this ensures to the compiler that the data accessed by a given pointer with the restrict keyword does not alias with anything else the function may modify using another pointer. Note that

```
void restrict_compute(restrict int *a, restrict int
*b, restrict int *c)
{
     for(int i=0; i<LIMIT; ++i)
          a[i] = b[i] * c[i];
}
```

Figure 12.7:
C Standard "restrict" keyword.

this only applies to the function at hand, not the global scope of the application itself. This permits the data dependence analyzer to recognize that arrays are not aliased or modified by references with other side effects, and allows more aggressive optimization of the loop nest including vectorization amongst other optimizations.

Data structures, arrays of data structures, and adding it all up!

Appropriate selection of data structures, before the design of kernels, which compute over them, can have significant impact when dealing with high-performance embedded DSP codes. This is often especially true for target processors that support SIMD instruction sets and optimizing compiler technology as was detailed previously in this chapter. As an illustrative example, this section details the various trade-offs between using an array-of-structure elements versus a structure-of-array elements for commonly used data structures. As an example data structure, we'll consider a set of six dimensional points that are stored within a given data structure as either an array-of-structures or a structure-of-arrays as detailed in Figure 12.8.

/* array of structures*/	/* structure of arrays */
struct {	struct {
float x_00;	float x_00[SIZE];
float y_00;	float y_00[SIZE];
float z_00;	float z_00[SIZE];
float x_01;	float x_01[SIZE];
float y_01;	float y_01[SIZE];
float z_01;	float z_01[SIZE];
} list[SIZE];	} list;

Figure 12.8:
Structure-of-arrays.

The array of structures, as depicted on the left-hand side of Figure 12.8, details a structure which has six fields of floating-point type, each of which might be the three coordinates of the ends of a line in three-dimensional space. The structures are allocated as an array of SIZE elements. The structure of arrays, which is represented on the right-hand side, creates a single structure which contains six arrays of floating-point data types, each of which is of SIZE elements. It should be noted that all of the data structures above are functionality equivalent, but have varying system side effects with regard to memory system performance and optimization.

Looking at the array-of-structures example above, it can be seen that for a given loop nest that is known to access all of the elements of a given struct element before moving onto the next element in the list, good locality of data will be exhibited. This will be due to the fact that as cache lines of data are fetched from memory into the data caches, adjacent elements within the data structure will be fetched contiguously from memory and exhibit good local reuse.

The downside when using the array-of-structures data structure, however, is that each individual memory reference in a loop that touches all of the field elements of the data structure does not exhibit unit memory stride. For example, consider the illustrative loop in Figure 12.9.

```
for(i=0 i<SIZE; ++i)
{
    local_struct[i].x_00 = 0.00;
    local_struct[i].y_00 = 0.00;
    local_struct[i].z_00 = 0.00;
    local_struct[i].x_01 = 0.00;
    local_struct[i].y_01 = 0.00;
    local_struct[i].z_01 = 0.00;
}
```

Figure 12.9:
Illustrative loop.

Each of the field accesses in the loop above accesses different fields within an instance of the structure, and does not exhibit unit stride memory access patterns which would be conducive to compiler-level autovectorization. In addition, any loop that traverses the list of structures and accesses only one or few fields within a given structure instance will exhibit rather poor spatial locality of data within the cases, due to fetching cache lines from memory that contain data elements which will not be referenced within the loop nest.

We can contrast this rather bleak use case depicted above by migrating the array-of-structures format to the structure-of-arrays format, as depicted in the loop nest in Figure 12.10.

```
for(i=0 i<SIZE; ++i)
{
      local_struct.x_00[i] = 0.00;
      local_struct.y_00[i] = 0.00;
      local_struct.z_00[i] = 0.00;
      local_struct.x_01[i] = 0.00;
      local_struct.y_01[i] = 0.00;
      local_struct.z_01[i] = 0.00;
}
```

Figure 12.10:
Loop nest.

By employing the structure-of-arrays data structure, each field access within the loop nest exhibits unit stride memory references across loop iterations. This is much more conducive to autovectorization by the build tools in most cases. In addition, we still see good locality of data across the multiple array streams within the loop nest. It should also be noted that in contrast to the previous scenario, even if only one field is accessed by a given loop nest, locality within the cache is achieved due to subsequent elements within the array being prefetched for a given cache line load.

While the examples presented previously detail the importance of selecting the data structure that best suits the application developer's needs, it is assumed that the developer or system architect will study the overall application hot spots in driving the selection of appropriate data structures for memory system performance. The result may not be a clear case of black and white, however, and a solution that employs multiple data structure formats may be advised. In these cases, developers may wish to use a hybrid-type approach that mixes and matches between structure-of-array and array-of-structure formats. Furthermore, for legacy code bases which are tightly coupled to their internal data structures for various reasons beyond the scope of this chapter, it may be worthwhile to run-time convert between the various formats as needed. While the computation required to convert from one format to another is non-trivial, there may be use cases where the conversion overhead is dramatically offset by the computational and memory system performance enhancements achieved once the conversion is performed.

Loop optimizations for memory performance

In addition to structuring loops for targetablility by autovectorizing compiler technology, and tailoring data structures over which loops compute, there are loop transformations themselves which may benefit the memory system performance of an application as well. This section details various loop transformations that can be performed either manually by the application developer, or automatically by the development tools to improve system performance.

Data alignment's rippling effects

The alignment of data within the memory system of an embedded target can have rippling effects on the performance of the code, as well as the development tools' ability to optimize certain use cases. On many embedded systems, the underlying memory system does not support unaligned memory accesses, or such accesses are supported with a certain performance penalty. If the user does not take care in aligning data properly within the memory system layout, performance can be lost. In summary, data alignment details the manner in which data is accessed within the computer's memory system. When a processor reads or writes to memory, it will often do this at the resolution of the computer's word size, which might be four bytes on a 32-bit system. Data alignment is the process of putting data elements at offsets that are some multiple of the computer's word size so that various fields may be accessed efficiently. As such, it may be necessary for users to put padding into their data structures or for the tools to automatically pad data structures according to the underlying ABI and data type conventions when aligning data for a given processor target.

Alignment can have an impact on compiler and loop optimizations such as vectorization. For instance, if the compiler is attempting to vectorize computation occurring over multiple arrays within a given loop body, it will need to know whether the data elements are aligned so as to make efficient use of packed SIMD move instructions, and also to know whether certain iterations of the loop nest that execute over non-aligned data elements must be peeled off. If the compiler cannot determine whether or not the data elements are aligned, it may opt to not vectorize the loop at all, thereby leaving the loop body sequential in schedule. Clearly this is not the desired result for the best-performing executable. Alternatively, the compiler may decide to generate multiple versions of the loop nest with a run-time test to determine at loop execution time whether or not the data elements are aligned. In this case the benefits of a vectorized loop version are obtained; however, the cost of a dynamic test at run-time is incurred and the size of the executable will increase due to multiple versions of the loop nest being inserted by the compiler.

Users can often do multiple things to ensure that their data is aligned, for instance padding elements within their data structures and ensuring that various data fields lie on the appropriate word boundaries. Many compilers also support sets of pragmas to denote that a given element is aligned. Alternatively, users can put various asserts within their code to compute at run-time whether or not the data fields are aligned on a given boundary before a particular version of a loop executes.

Selecting data types for big payoffs

It is important that application developers also select the appropriate data types for their performance-critical kernels in addition to the aforementioned strategies of optimization. When the minimal acceptable data type is selected for computation, it may have a number of secondary effects that can be beneficial to the performance of the kernels. Consider, for example, a performance-critical kernel that can be implemented in either 32-bit integral computation or 16-bit integral computation due to the application programmer's knowledge of the data range. If the application developer selects 16-bit computation using one of the built-in C/C++ language data types such as "short int", then the following benefits may be gained at system run-time.

By selecting 16-bit over 32-bit data elements, more data elements can fit into a single data cache line. This allows fewer cache line fetches per unit of computation, and should help alleviate the compute-to-memory bottleneck when fetching data elements. In addition, if the target architecture supports SIMD-style computation, it is highly likely that a given ALU within the processor can support multiple 16-bit computations in parallel versus their 32-bit counterparts. For example, many commercially available DSP architectures support packed 16-bit SIMD operations per ALU, effectively doubling the computational throughput when using 16-bit data elements versus 32-bit data elements. Given the packed nature of the data elements, whereby additional data elements are packed per cache line or can be placed in user-managed scratchpad memory, coupled with the increased computational efficiency, it may also be possible to improve the power efficiency of the system due to the reduced number of data memory fetches required to fill cache lines.

CHAPTER 13

Optimizing Embedded Software for Power

Robert Oshana

Chapter Outline

Software Engineering for Embedded Systems.
DOI: http://dx.doi.org/10.1016/B978-0-12-415917-4.00013-X
© 2013 Elsevier Inc. All rights reserved.

Introduction

One of the most important considerations in the product lifecycle of an embedded project is to understand and optimize the power consumption of the device. Power consumption is highly visible for hand-held devices which require battery power to be able to guarantee certain minimum usage/idle times between recharging. Other embedded applications, such as medical equipment, test, measurement, media, and wireless base stations, are very sensitive to power as well – due to the need to manage the heat dissipation of increasingly powerful processors, power supply cost, and energy consumption cost – so the fact is that power consumption cannot be overlooked.

The responsibility for setting and keeping power requirements often falls on the shoulders of hardware designers, but the software programmer has the ability to provide a large contribution to power optimization. Often, the impact that the software engineer has on influencing the power consumption of a device is overlooked or underestimated.

The goal of this section is to discuss how software can be used to optimize power consumption, starting with the basics of what power consumption consists of, how to properly measure power consumption, and then moving on to techniques for minimizing power consumption in software at the algorithmic level, hardware level, and data-flow level. This will include demonstrations of the various techniques and explanations of both how and why certain methods are effective at reducing power so the reader can take and apply this work to their application right away.

Understanding power consumption

Basics of power consumption

In general, when power consumption is discussed, the four main factors discussed for a device are the application, the frequency, the voltage and the process technology, so we need to understand why exactly it is that these factors are so important.

The application is highly important, so much so that the power profile for two hand-held devices could differ to the point of making power optimization strategies the complete opposite. While we will be explaining more about power optimization strategies later on, the basic idea is clear enough to introduce in this section.

Take for example a portable media player vs. a cellular phone. The portable media player needs to be able to run at 100% usage for a long period of time to display video (full-length movies), audio, etc. We will discuss this later, but the general power-consumption profile for this sort of device would have to focus on algorithmic and data flow power optimization more than on efficient usage of low-power modes.

Compare this to the cellular phone, which spends most of its time in an idle state, and during call time the user only talks for a relatively small percentage of the time. For this small percentage of time, the processor may be heavily loaded, performing encode/decode of voice and transmit/receive data. For the remainder of the call time, the phone is not so heavily tasked, performing procedures such as sending heartbeat packets to the cellular network and providing "comfort noise" to the user to let the user know the phone is still connected during silence. For this sort of profile, power optimization would be focused first on maximizing processor sleep states to save as much power as possible, and then on data flow/algorithmic approaches.

In the case of process technology, the current cutting-edge embedded cores are based on 45 nm and in the near future 28 nm technology, a decrease in size from its predecessor, the 65 nm technology. What this smaller process technology provides is a smaller transistor. Smaller transistors consume less power and produce less heat, so are clearly advantageous compared with their predecessors.

Smaller process technology also generally enables higher clock frequencies, which is clearly a plus, providing more processing capability, but higher frequency, along with higher voltage, comes at the cost of higher power draw. Voltage is the most obvious of these, as we learned in physics (and EE101), power is the product of voltage times current. So if a device requires a large voltage supply, power consumption increase is a fact of life.

While staying on the subject of $P = V^*I$, the frequency is also directly part of this equation because current is a direct result of the clock rate. Another thing we learned in physics and EE101: when voltage is applied across a capacitor, current will flow from the voltage source to the capacitor until the capacitor has reached an equivalent potential. While this is an over-simplification, we can imagine that the clock network in a core consumes power in such a fashion. Thus at every clock edge, when the potential changes, current flows through the device until it reaches the next steady state. The faster the clock is switching, the more current is flowing, therefore faster clocking implies more power consumed by the embedded processor. Depending on the device, the clock circuit is responsible for consuming between 50% and 90% of dynamic device power, so controlling clocks is a theme that will be covered very heavily here.

Static vs. dynamic power consumption

Total power consumption consists of two types of power: dynamic and static (also known as static leakage) consumption, so total device power is calculated as:

$$P_{\text{total}} = P_{\text{Dynamic}} + P_{\text{Static}}$$

As we have just discussed, clock transitions are a large portion of the dynamic consumption, but what is this "dynamic consumption"? Basically, in software we have control over dynamic consumption, but we do not have control over static consumption.

Static power consumption

Leakage consumption is the power that a device consumes independent of any activity or task the core is running, because even in a steady state there is a low "leakage" current path (via transistor tunneling current, reverse diode leakage, etc.) from the device's V_{in} to ground. The only factors that affect the leakage consumption are supply voltage, temperature, and process.

We have already discussed voltage and process in the introduction. In terms of temperature, it is fairly intuitive to understand why heat increases leakage current. Heat increases the mobility of electron carriers, which will lead to an increase in electron flow, causing greater static power consumption. As the focus of this chapter is software, this will be the end of static power consumption theory.

Dynamic power consumption

The dynamic consumption of the embedded processor includes the power consumed by the device actively using the cores, core subsystems, peripherals such as DMA, I/O (radio, Ethernet, PCIe, CMOS camera), memories, and PLLs and clocks. At the low level, this can be translated to say that dynamic power is the power consumed by switching transistors which are charging and discharging capacitances.

Dynamic power increases as we use more elements of the system, more cores, more arithmetic units, more memories, higher clock rates, or anything that could possibly increase the amount of transistors switching, or the speed at which they are switching. The dynamic consumption is independent of temperature, but still depends on voltage supply levels.

Maximum, average, worst-case, and typical power

When measuring power, or determining power usage for a system, there are four main types of power that need to be considered: maximum power, average power, worst-case power consumption, and typical power consumption.

Maximum and average power are general terms, used to describe the power measurement itself more than the effect of software or other variables on a device's power consumption.

Simply stated, maximum power is the highest instantaneous power reading measured over a period of time. This sort of measurement is useful to show the amount of decoupling capacitance required by a device to maintain a decent level of signal integrity (required for reliable operation).

Average power is intuitive at this point: technically the amount of energy consumed in a time period, divided by that time (power readings averaged over time). Engineers do this by calculating the average current consumed over time and use that to find power. Average power readings are what we are focusing on optimizing as this is the determining factor for how much power a battery or power supply must be able to provide for a processor to perform an application over time, and this also used to understand the heat profile of the device.

Both worst case and typical power numbers are based on average power measurement. Worst-case power, or the worst-case power profile, describes the amount of average power a device will consume at 100% usage over a given period. One hundred percent usage refers to the processer utilizing the maximum number of available processing units (data and address generation blocks in the core, accelerators, bit masking, etc.), memories, and peripherals simultaneously. This may be simulated by putting the cores in an infinite loop of performing six or more instructions per cycle (depending on the available processing units in the core) while having multiple DMA channels continuously reading from and writing to memory, and peripherals constantly sending and receiving data. Worst-case power numbers are used by the system architect or board designer in order to provide adequate power supply to guarantee functionality under all worst-case conditions.

In a real system, a device will rarely if ever draw the worst-case power, as applications do not use all the processing elements, memory, and I/O for long periods of time, if at all. In general, a device provides many different I/O peripherals, though only a portion of them are needed, and the device cores may only need to perform heavy computation for small portions of time, accessing just a portion of memory. Typical power consumption then may be based on the assumed "general use case" example application that may use anywhere from 50% to 70% of the processor's available hardware components at a time. This is a major aspect of software applications that we are going to be taking advantage of in order to optimize power consumption.

In this section we have explained the differences of static vs. dynamic power, maximum vs. average power, process effect on power, and core and processing power effect on power. Now that the basics of what makes power consumption are covered, we will discuss power consumption measurement before going into detail about power optimization techniques.

Measuring power consumption

Now that background, theory, and vocabulary have been covered, we will move on to taking power measurements. We will discuss the types of measurements used to get different types of power readings (such as reading static vs. dynamic power), and use these methods in order to test optimization methods used later in the text.

Measuring power is hardware dependent: some embedded processors provide internal measurement capabilities; processor manufacturers may also provide "power calculators" which give some power information; there are a number of power supply controller ICs which provide different forms of power measurement capabilities; some power supply controllers called VRMs (voltage regulator modules) have these capabilities internal to them to be read over peripheral interfaces; and finally, there is the old-fashioned method of connecting an ammeter in series to the core power supply.

Measuring power using an ammeter

The "old-fashioned" method is to measure power via the use of an external power supply connected in series to the positive terminal of an ammeter, which connects via the negative connector to the DSP device power input, as shown in Figure 13.1.

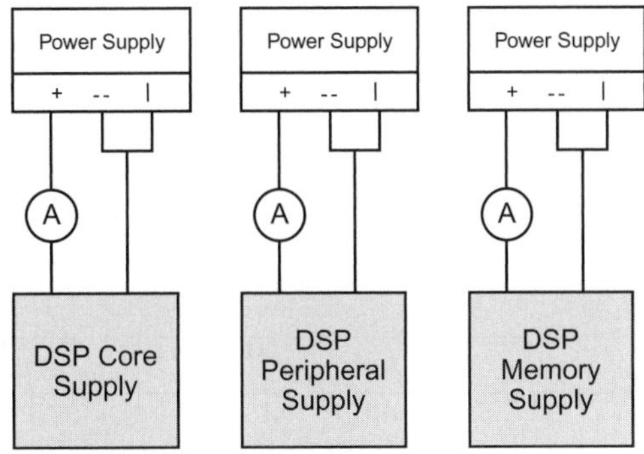

Figure 13.1:
Measuring power via ammeters.

Note that there are three different set-ups shown in Figure 13.1, which are all for a single processor. This is due to the fact that processor power input is isolated, generally between cores (possibly multiple supplies), peripherals, and memories. This is done by design in hardware as different components of a device have different voltage requirements, and this is useful to isolate (and eventually optimize) the power profile of individual components.

In order to properly measure power consumption, the power to each component must be properly isolated, which in some cases may require board modification, specific jumper settings, etc. The most ideal situation is to be able to connect the external supply/ammeter combination as close as possible to the processor power input pins.

Alternatively, one may measure the voltage drop across a (shunt) resister which is in series with the power supply and the processor power pins. By measuring the voltage drop across the resistor, current is found simply by calculating $I = V/R$.

Measuring power using a hall sensor type IC

In order to simplify efficient power measurement, many embedded vendors are building boards that use a Hall-effect-based sensor. When a Hall sensor is placed on a board in the current path to the device's power supply, it generates a voltage equivalent to the current times some coefficient with an offset. In the case of Freescale's MSC8144 DSP Application Development System board, an Allegro ACS0704 Hall sensor is provided on the board, which enables such measurement. With this board, the user can simply place a scope to the board, and view the voltage signal over time, and use this to calculate average power using Allegro's current to voltage graph, shown in Figure 13.2.

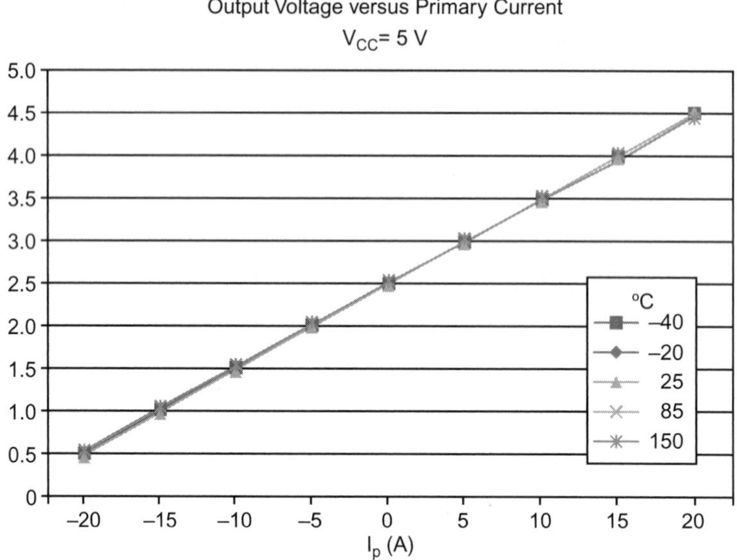

Figure 13.2:
Hall effect IC voltage to current graph (www.allegromicro.com/en/Products/Part.../0704/0704-015.pdf).

Using Figure 13.2, we can calculate input current to a device based on measuring potential across V_{out} as:

$$I = (V_{\text{out}} - 2.5)^{*}10A$$

VRMs (voltage regulator module power supply ICs)

Finally, some VRMs (power supply controller ICs), which are used to split a large input voltage into a number of smaller ones to supply individual sources at varying potentials, measure current/power consumption and store the values in registers to be read by the user. Measuring current via the VRM requires no equipment, but this sometimes comes at the cost of accuracy and real-time measurement. For example, the PowerOne ZM7100 series VRM (also used on the MSC8144ADS) provides current readings for each supply, but the current readings are updated once every 0.5 to 1 seconds, and the reading accuracy is of the order of $\sim$20%, so instantaneous reading for maximum power is not possible, and fine tuning and optimization may not be possible using such devices.

In addition to deciding a specific method for measuring power in general, different methods exist to measure dynamic power versus static leakage consumption. The static leakage consumption data is useful in order to have a floor for our low-power expectations, and to understand how much power the actual application is pulling versus what the device will pull in idle. We can then subtract that from the total power consumption we measure in order to determine the dynamic consumption the processor is pulling, and work to minimize that. There are various tools available in the industry to help in this area.

Static power measurement

Leakage consumption on a processor can usually be measured while the device is placed in a low-power mode, assuming that the mode shuts down clocks to all of the core subsystems and peripherals. If the clocks are not shut down in low-power mode, the PLLs should be bypassed, and then the input clock should be shut down, thus shutting down all clocks and eliminating clock and PLL power consumption from the static leakage measurement.

Additionally, static leakage should be measured at varying temperatures since leakage varies based on temperature. Creating a set of static measurements based on temperature (and voltage) provides valuable reference points for determining how much dynamic power an application is actually consuming at these temperature/voltage points.

Dynamic power measurement

The power measurements should separate the contribution of each major module in the device to give the engineer information about what effect a specific configuration will have on a system's power consumption. As noted above, dynamic power is found simply by measuring the total power (at a given temperature) and then subtracting the leakage consumption for that given temperature using the initial static measurements from above.

Initial dynamic measurement tests include running sleep-state tests, debug-state tests, and a NOP test. Sleep-state and debug-state tests will give the user insight into the cost of enabling certain clocks in the system. A NOP test, as in a loop of NOP commands, will provide a baseline dynamic reading for your core's consumption when mainly using the fetch unit of the device, but no arithmetic units, address generation, bit mask, memory management, etc.

When comparing specific software power optimization techniques, we compare the before and after power consumption numbers of each technique in order to determine the effect of that technique.

Profiling your application's power consumption

Before optimizing an application for power, the programmer should get a baseline power reading of the section of code being optimized. This provides a reference point for measuring optimizations, and also ensures that the alterations to code do in fact decrease total power, and not the opposite. In order to do this, the programmer needs to generate a sample power test which acts as a snapshot of the code segment being tested.

This power test-case generation can be done by profiling code performance using a high-end profiler to gain some base understanding of the percentage of processing elements and memory used. We can demonstrate this by creating a new project in a standard tools IDE (there are many available) with the profiler enabled, then compiling, and running the project. The application will run from start to finish, at which point the user may select a profiler view and get any number of statistics.

Using relevant data such as the percentage of ALUs used, AGUs used, code hot-spots, and knowledge of memories being accessed, we can get a general idea of where our code will spend the most time (and consume the most power). We can use this to generate a basic performance test which runs in an infinite loop, enabling us to profile the average "typical" power of an important code segment.

As an example, using two main functions: func1 and func2. Profiling the example code, we can see from the Figure 13.3 that the vast majority of cycles are consumed by the func1 routine. This routine is located in M2 memory and reads data from cacheable M3 memory (meaning possible causing write back accesses to L2 and L1 cache). By using the profiler (as per Figure 13.4), information regarding the percentage ALU and percentage AGU can be extracted. We can effectively simulate this by turning the code into an infinite loop, adjusting the I/O, and compiling at the same optimization level, and verifying that we see the same performance breakdown. Another option would be to write a sample test in assembly code to force certain ALU/AGU usage models to match our profile, though this is not as precise and makes testing of individual optimizations more difficult.

We can then set a break point, re-run our application, and confirm that the device usage profile is in line with our original code. If not, we can adjust the compiler optimization level or our code until it matches the original application.

This method is quick and effective for measuring core power consumption for various loads and, if we mirrored the original application by properly using the profiler, this should account for stalls and other pipeline issues as the profiler provides information on total cycle count as well as instruction and VLES utilization. By having the infinite loop, testing is much easier as we are simply comparing steady-state current readings of optimized and non-optimized code in the hope of getting lower numbers. We can use this to measure

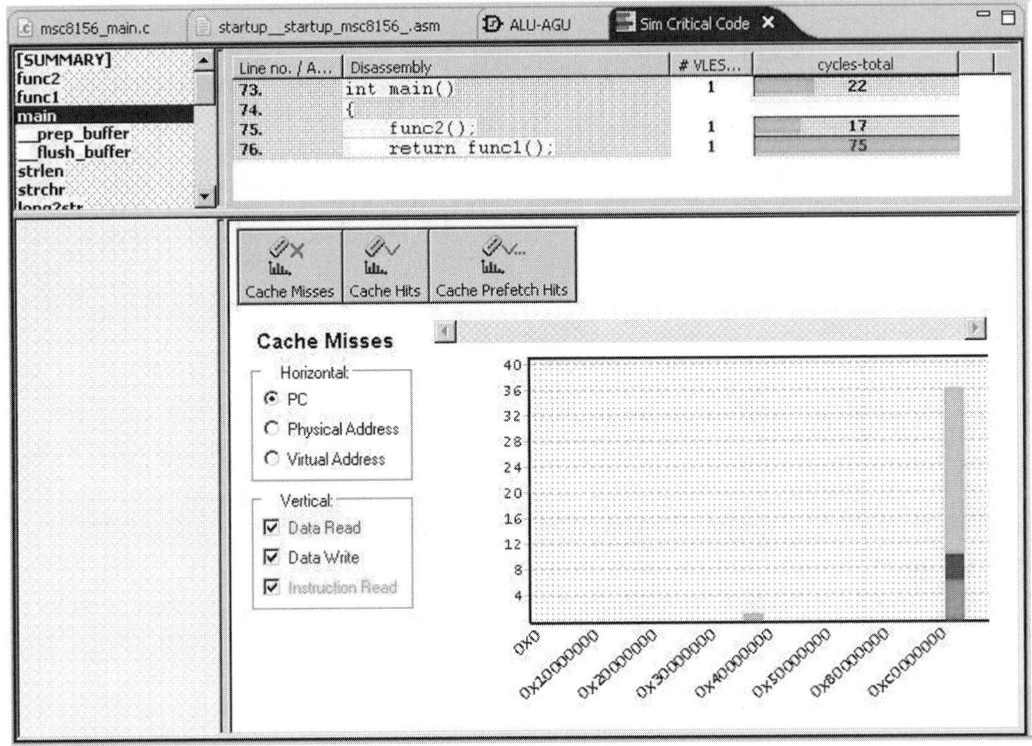

Figure 13.3:
Profiling for hot spots.

numerous metrics such as average power over time, average power per instruction, average power per cycle, and energy (power * time) in joules for some time *t*. For measuring specific algorithms and power-saving techniques, we will form small routines using similar methods and then optimize and measure the power savings over time.

This section has explained a few different methods for measuring static power, dynamic power, and how to profile power for an application. It also covered the availability of power calculators from processor manufacturers, which sometimes may quicken the power estimation process. Using these tools will enable effectively measuring and confirming the knowledge shared in the next section of this text, which covers the software techniques for optimizing power consumption.

Minimizing power consumption

There are three main types of power optimization covered in this text: hardware-supported features, data path optimization, and algorithmic optimization. Algorithmic optimization refers to making changes in code to affect how the cores process data, such as how msc8156_main.c | startup__startup_msc8156_.asm | Simulator Trace [Core 0] | Sim Critical Code | ALU-AGU

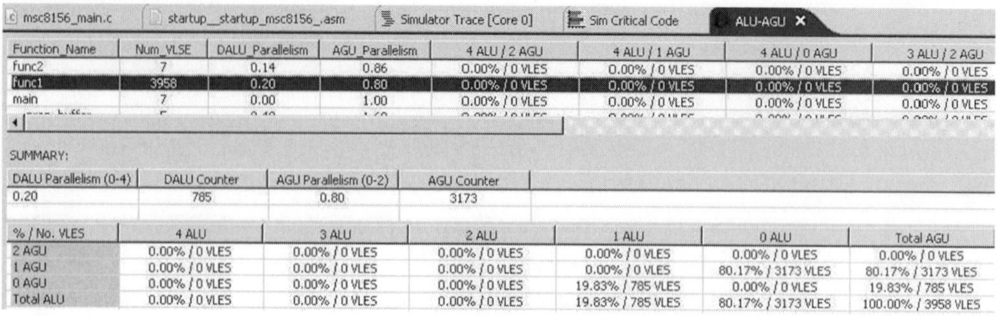

Function_Name	Num_VLSE	DALU_Parallelism	AGU_Parallelism	4 ALU / 2 AGU	4 ALU / 1 AGU	4 ALU / 0 AGU	3 ALU / 2 AGU
func2	7	0.14	0.86	0.00% / 0 VLES	0.00% / 0 VLES	0.00% / 0 VLES	0.00% / 0 VLES
func1	3958	0.20	0.80	0.00% / 0 VLES	0.00% / 0 VLES	0.00% / 0 VLES	0.00% / 0 VLES
main	7	0.00	1.00	0.00% / 0 VLES	0.00% / 0 VLES	0.00% / 0 VLES	0.00% / 0 VLES

SUMMARY:

DALU Parallelism (0-4)	DALU Counter	AGU Parallelism (0-2)	AGU Counter
0.20	785	0.80	3173

% / No. VLES	4 ALU	3 ALU	2 ALU	1 ALU	0 ALU	Total AGU
2 AGU	0.00% / 0 VLES	0.00% / 0 VLES	0.00% / 0 VLES	0.00% / 0 VLES	0.00% / 0 VLES	0.00% / 0 VLES
1 AGU	0.00% / 0 VLES	0.00% / 0 VLES	0.00% / 0 VLES	0.00% / 0 VLES	80.17% / 3173 VLES	80.17% / 3173 VLES
0 AGU	0.00% / 0 VLES	0.00% / 0 VLES	0.00% / 0 VLES	19.83% / 785 VLES	0.00% / 0 VLES	19.83% / 785 VLES
Total ALU	0.00% / 0 VLES	0.00% / 0 VLES	0.00% / 0 VLES	19.83% / 785 VLES	80.17% / 3173 VLES	100.00% / 3958 VLES

Figure 13.4:
Core component (% ALU, % AGU) utilization.

instructions or loops are handled, whereas hardware optimization, as discussed here, focuses more on how to optimize clock control and power features provided in hardware. Data flow optimization focuses on working to minimize the power cost of utilizing different memories, buses, and peripherals where data can be stored or transmitted by taking advantage of relevant features and concepts.

Hardware support

Low-power modes (introduction to devices)

DSP applications normally work on tasks in packets, frames, or chunks. For example, in a media player, frames of video data may come in at 60 frames per second to be decoded, while the actual decoding work may take the processor orders of magnitude less than 1/60th of a second, giving us a chance to utilize sleep modes, shut down peripherals, and organize memory, all to reduce power consumption and maximize efficiency.

We must also keep in mind that the power-consumption profile varies based on application. For instance, two differing hand-held devices, an MP3 player and a cellular phone, will have two very different power profiles.

The cellular phone spends most of its time in an idle state, and when in a call is still not working at full capacity during the entire call duration as speech will commonly contain pauses which are long in terms of the processor's clock cycles.

For both of these power profiles, software-enabled low-power modes (modes/features/controls) are used to save power, and the question for the programmer is how to use them efficiently. A quick note to the reader: different device documents may refer to features discussed in this section such as gating and scaling in various ways, such as low-power modes, power saving modes, power controls, etc. The most common modes available consist of power gating, clock gating, voltage scaling, and clock scaling.

Power gating

This uses a current switch to cut off a circuit from its power supply rails during standby mode, to eliminate static leakage when the circuit is not in use. Using power gating leads to a loss of state and data for a circuit, meaning that using this requires storing necessary context/state data in active memory. As embedded processors are moving more and more towards being full SoC solutions with many peripherals, some peripherals may be unnecessary for certain applications. Power gating may be available to completely shut off such unused peripherals in a system, and the power savings attained from power gating depend on the specific peripheral on the specific device in question.

It is important to note that in some cases, documentation will refer to powering down a peripheral via clock gating, which is different from power gating. It may be possible to gate a peripheral by connecting the power supply of a certain block to ground, depending on device requirements and interdependence on a power supply line. This is possible in software in certain situations, such as when board/system-level power is controlled by an on-board IC, which can be programmed and updated via an I2C bus interface. As an example, the MSC8156 DSP (Figure 13.5) has this option for the MAPLE DSP baseband accelerator peripheral and a portion of M3 memory.

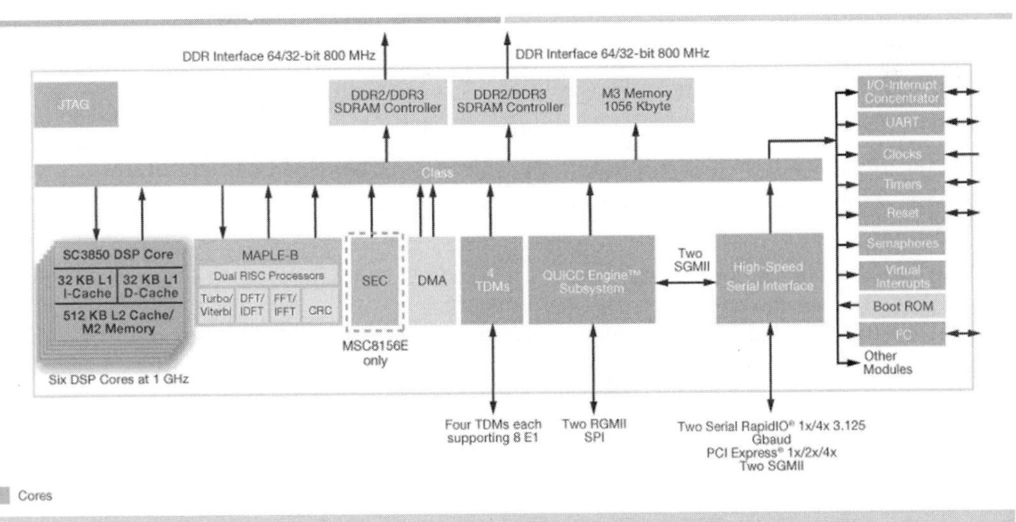

Figure 13.5:
8156 six-core DSP processor.

Clock gating

As the name implies, this shuts down clocks to a circuit or portion of a clock tree in a device. As dynamic power is consumed during state change triggered by clock toggling (as we discussed in the introductory portion of this chapter), clock gating enables the programmer to cut dynamic power through the use of a single (or a few) instructions. Clocking of a processor core like a DSP is generally separated into trees stemming from a main clock PLL into various clock domains as required by design for core, memories, and peripherals, and DSPs generally enable levels of clock gating in order to customize a power-saving solution.

Example low-power modes

As an example, the Freescale MSC815x DSPs provide various levels of clock gating in the core subsystem and peripheral areas. Gating clocks to a core may be done in the form of STOP and WAIT instructions. STOP mode gates clocks to the DSP core and the entire core subsystem (L1 and L2 caches, M2 memory, memory management, debug and profile unit) aside from internal logic used for waking from the STOP state.

In order to safely enter STOP mode, as one may imagine, care must be taken to ensure accesses to memory and cache are all complete, and no fetches/prefetches are under way.

The recommended process is:

Terminate any open L2 prefetch activity.
Stop all internal and external accesses to M2/L2 memory.
Close the subsystem slave port window (peripheral access path to M2 memory) by writing to the core subsystem slave port general configuration register.
Verify slave port is closed by reading the register, and also testing access to the slave port (at this point, any access to the core's slave port will generate an interrupt).
Ensure STOP ACK bit is asserted in General Status Register to show subsystem is in STOP state.
Enter STOP mode.

STOP state can be exited by initiating an interrupt. There are other ways to exit from STOP state, including a reset or debug assertion from external signals.

The WAIT state gates clocks to the core and some of the core subsystem aside from the interrupt controller, debug and profile unit, timer, and M2 memory, which enables faster entering and exiting from WAIT state, but at the cost of greater power consumption. To enter WAIT state, the programmer may simply use the WAIT instruction for a core. Exiting WAIT, like STOP, may also be done via an interrupt.

A particularly nice feature of these low-power states is that both STOP and WAIT mode can be exited via either an enabled or a disabled interrupt. Wake-up via an enabled interrupt follows the standard interrupt handling procedure: the core takes the interrupt, does a full context switch, and then the program counter jumps to the interrupt service routine before returning to the instruction following the segment of code that executed the WAIT (or STOP) instruction. This requires a comparatively large cycle overhead, which is where disabled interrupt waking becomes quite convenient. When using a disabled interrupt to exit from either WAIT or STOP state, the interrupt signals the core using an interrupt priority that is not "enabled" in terms of the core's global interrupt priority level (IPL), and when the core wakes it resumes execution where it left off without executing a context switch or any ISR. An example using a disabled interrupt for waking the MSC8156 is provided at the end of this section.

Clock gating to peripherals is also enabled, where the user may gate specific peripherals individually as needed. This is available for the MSC8156's serial interface, Ethernet controller (QE), DSP accelerators (MAPLE), and DDR. As with STOP mode, when gating clocks to any of these interfaces, the programmer must ensure that all accesses are completed beforehand. Then, via the System Clock Control register, clocks to each of these peripherals may be gated. In order to come out of the clock gated modes, a Power on Reset is required, so this is not something that can be done and undone on the fly in a function, but rather a setting that is decided at system configuration time.

Additionally, partial clock gating is possible on the high-speed serial interface components (SERDES, OCN DMA, SRIO, RMU, PCI Express) and ddr so that they may be temporarily put in a "doze state" in order to save power, but still maintain the functionality of providing an acknowledge to accesses (in order to prevent internal or external bus lockup when accessed by external logic).

Texas Instruments C6000 low-power modes

Another popular DSP family on the market is the C6000 series DSP from Texas Instruments (TI). TI DSPs in the C6000 family provide a few levels of clock gating, depending on the generation of C6000. For example, the previous generation C67x floating-point DSP has low-power modes called "power-down modes". These modes include PD1, PD2, PD3, and "peripheral power down", each of which gates clocking to various components in the silicon.

For example, PD1 mode gates clocks to the C67x CPU (processor core, data registers, control registers, and everything else within the core aside from the interrupt controller). The C67x can wake up from PD1 via an interrupt into the core. Entering power-down mode PD1 (or PD2 / PD3) for the C67x is done via a register write (to CSR). The cost of entering PD1 state is ~9 clock cycles plus the cost of accessing the CSR register. As this power-down state only affects the core (and not cache memories), it is not comparable to the Freescale's STOP or WAIT state.

The two deeper levels of power down, PD2 and PD3, effectively gate clocks to the entire device (all blocks which use an internal clock: internal peripherals, the CPU, cache, etc.). The only way to wake up from PD2 and PD3 clock gating is via a reset, so PD2 and PD3 would not be very convenient or efficient to use mid-application.

Clock and voltage control

Some devices have the ability to scale voltage or clock, which may help optimize the power scheme of a device/application. Voltage scaling, as the name implies, is the process of lowering or raising the power. In the section on measuring current, VRMs were introduced as one method. The main purpose of a VRM (voltage regulator module) is to control the power/voltage supply to a device. Using a VRM, voltage scaling may be done through monitoring and updating voltage ID (VID) parameters.

In general, as voltage is lowered, frequency/processor speed is sacrificed, so generally voltage would be lowered when the demand from a DSP core or a certain peripheral is reduced.

The TI C6000 devices provide a flavor of voltage scaling called SmartReflex®. SmartReflex® enables automatic voltage scaling through a pin interface which provides VID to a VRM. As the pin interface is internally managed, the software engineer does not have much influence over this, so we will not cover any programming examples for this.

Clock control is available in many processors, which allows the changing of the values of various PLLs in runtime. In some cases, updating the internal PLLs requires relocking the PLLs, where some clocks in the system may be stopped, and this must be followed by a soft reset (reset of the internal cores). Because of this inherent latency, clock scaling is not very feasible during normal heavy operation, but may be considered if a processor's requirements over a long period of time are reduced (such as during times of low call volume during the night for processors on a wireless base station).

When considering clock scaling, we must keep the following in mind: during normal operation, running at a lower clock allows for lower dynamic power consumption, assuming clock and power gating are never used. In practice, running a processor at a higher frequency allows for more "free" cycles, which, as previously noted, can be used to hold the device in a low-power/sleep mode – thus offsetting the benefits of such clock scaling.

Additionally, updating the clock for custom cases is time-intensive, and for some processors, not an option at all – meaning clock frequency has to be decided at device reset/power-on time, so the general rule of thumb is to enable enough clock cycles with some additional headroom for the real-time application being run, and to utilize other power optimization techniques. Determining the amount of headroom varies from processor to processor and application to application – at which point it makes sense to profile your application in order to understand the number of cycles required for a packet/frame, and the core utilization during this time period.

Once this is understood, measuring the power consumption for such a profile can be done, as demonstrated earlier in this chapter in the profiling power section. Measure the average power consumption at your main frequency options. (for example this could be 800 MHz and 1 GHz), and then average in idle power over the headroom slots in order to get a head-to-head comparison of the best-case power consumption.

Considerations and usage examples of low-power modes

Here we will summarize the main considerations for low-power mode usage, and then close with a coding example demonstrating low-power mode usage in a real-time multimedia application.

Consider available block functionality when in low-power mode:

- When in low-power modes, we have to remember that certain peripherals will not be available to external peripherals, and peripheral buses may also be affected. As noted earlier in this section, devices may take care of this, but this is not always the case. If power gating a block, special care must be taken regarding shared external buses, clocks, and pins.
- Additionally, memory states and validity of data must be considered. We will cover this when discussing cache and DDR in the next section

Consider the overhead of entering and exiting low-power modes:

- When entering and exiting low -ower modes, in addition to overall power savings, the programmer must ensure the cycle overhead of actually entering and exiting the low power mode does not break real time constraints.
- Cycle overhead may also be affected by the potential difference in initiating a low power mode by register access as opposed to by direct core instructions.

Low-power example

To demonstrate low power usage, we will refer to a Motion JPEG (MJPEG) application. In this application, raw image frames are sent from a PC to an embedded DSP over Ethernet. Each Ethernet packet contains 1 block of an image frame. A full raw QVGA image uses ~396 blocks plus a header. The DSP encodes the image in real time (adjustable from 1 to 30+ frames per second), and sends the encoded Motion JPEG video back over Ethernet to be played on a demo GUI in the PC. The flow and a screenshot of this GUI are shown in Figure 13.6.

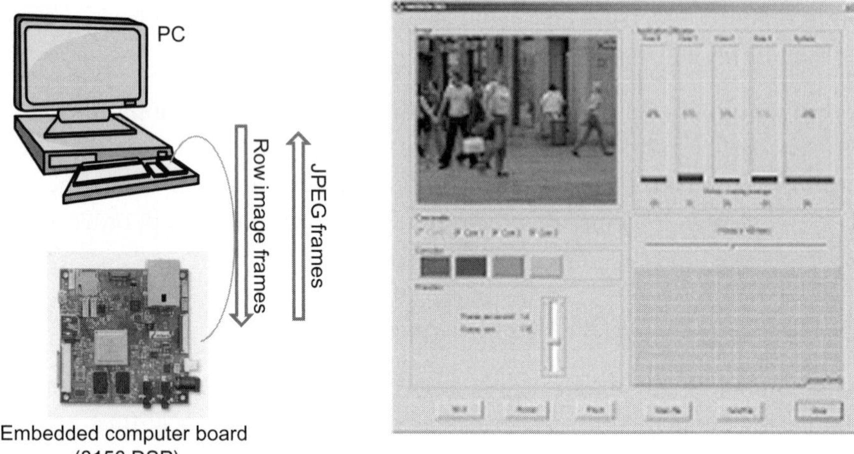

Figure 13.6:
DSP operating system Motion JPEG application.

The GUI will display not only the encoded JPEG image, but also the core utilization (as a percentage of the maximum core cycles available).

For this application, we need to understand how many cycles encoding a frame of JPEG consumes. Using this we can determine the maximum frame rate we can use and, in parallel, also determine the maximum down time we have for low-power mode usage. If we are close to the maximum core utilization for the real-time application, then using low-power modes may not make sense (may break real-time constraints).

As noted in previous chapters, we could simply profile the application to see how many cycles are actually spent per image frame, but this is already handled in the MJPEG demo's code using the core cycle counters in the OCE (on-chip emulator). The OCE is a hardware block on the DSP that the profiler utilizes to get core cycle counts for use in code profiling.

The MJPEG code in this case counts the number of cycles a core spends doing actual work (handling an incoming Ethernet interrupt, dequeueing data, encoding a block of data into JPEG format, enqueueing/sending data back over Ethernet).

The number of core cycles required to process a single block encode of data (and supporting background data movement) is measured to be of the order of 13,000 cycles. For a full JPEG image ($\sim$396 image blocks and Ethernet packets), this is approximately 5 million cycles.

So 1 JPEG frame a second would work out to be 0.5% of a core's potential processing power, assuming a 1 GHz core that is handling all Ethernet I/O, interrupt context switches, etc.

$$Cycles_{Block\ Mgmt\ Encode} = 13,000$$

$$Cycles_{JPEG\ Frame} = Cycles_{Block\ Mgmt\ Encode} \times 396 = 5,148,000$$

$$Core\ Utilization_{30FPS}(\%) = 30 \frac{100 \times OCECount}{1,000,000,000} = 15.4\%$$

In this example the DSP has up to six cores, and only one core would have to manage Ethernet I/O; in a full multicore system, utilization per core drops to a range of 3 to 7%. A master core acts as the manager of the system, managing both Ethernet I/O, intercore communication, and JPEG encoding, while the other slave cores are programmed to solely focus on encoding JPEG frames. Because of this intercore communication and management, the drop in cycle consumption from one core to four or six is not linear.

Based on cycle counts from the OCE, we can run a single core, which is put in a sleep state for 85% of the time, or a multicore system which uses sleep state up to 95% of the time.

This application also uses only a portion of the SoC peripherals (Ethernet, JTAG, a single DDR, and M3 memory). So we can save power by gating the full HSSI System (Serial Rapid IO, PCI Express), the MAPLE accelerator, and the second DDR controller. Additionally, for our GUI demo, we are only showing four cores, so we can gate cores 4 and 5 without affecting this demo as well.

Based on the above, and what we have discussed in this section, here is the plan we want to follow:

- At application start up:
  - Clock gate the unused MAPLE accelerator block (MAPLE described later in this chapter).
  - NOTES:
  - MAPLE power pins share a power supply with core voltage. If the power supply to MAPLE was not shared, we could completely gate power. Due to shared pins on the development board, the most effective choice we have is to gate the MAPLE clock.
  - MAPLE automatically goes into a doze state, which gates part of the clocks to the block when it is not in use. Because of this, power savings from entirely gating MAPLE may not be massive.
  - Clock gate the unused HSSI (high-speed serial interface).

NOTES:
We could also put MAPLE into a doze state, but this gates only part of the clocks. Since we will not be using any portion of these peripherals, complete clock gating is more power efficient.
Clock gate the unused second DDR controller.
NOTES:
When using VTB, the OS places buffer space for VTB in the second DDR memory, so we need to be sure that this is not needed.

- During application runtime:
  At runtime, QE (Ethernet Controller), DDR, interconnect, and cores 1–4 will be active. Things we must consider for these components include:
  The Ethernet Controller cannot be shut down or put into a low power state – as this is the block that receives new packets (JPEG blocks) to encode. Interrupts from the Ethernet controller can be used to wake our master core from low-power mode.
  Active core low-power modes:
  WAIT mode enables core power savings, while allowing the core to be woken up in just a few cycles by using a disabled interrupt to signal exit from WAIT.
  STOP mode enables greater core savings by shutting down more of the subsystem than WAIT (including M2), but requires slightly more time to wake due to more hardware being re-enabled. If data is coming in at high rates, and the wake time is too long, we could get an overflow condition, where packets are lost. This is unlikely here due to the required data rate of the application.
  The first DDR contains sections of program code and data, including parts of the Ethernet handling code. (This can be quickly checked and verified by looking at the program's .map file.) Because the Ethernet controller will be waking the master core from WAIT state, and the first thing the core will need to do out of this state is to run the Ethernet handler, we will not put DDR0 to sleep.

We can use the main background routine for the application to apply these changes without interfering with the RTOS. This code segment is shown in Figure 13.7 with power-down-related code.

Note that the clock gating must be done by only one core as these registers are system level and access is shared by all cores.

This code example demonstrates how a programmer using the OS can make use of the interrupt APIs in order to recover from STOP or wait state without actually requiring a context switch. In the MJPEG player, as noted above, raw image blocks are received via Ethernet (with interrupts), and then shared via shared queues (with interrupts). The master

```
static void appBackground(void)

{

    os_hwi_handle hwi_num;


    if (osGetCoreID() == 0)

    {

        *((unsigned int*)0xfff28014) = 0xF3FCFFFB;//HSSI CR1

        *((unsigned int*)0xfff28018) = 0x0000001F;//HSSI CR2

        *((unsigned int*)0xfff28034) = 0x20000E0E; //GCR5

        *((unsigned int*)0xfff24000) = 0x00001500; //SCCR

    }

    osMessageQueueHwiGet(CORE0_TO_OTHERS_MESSAGE, &hwi_num);

    while(1)

    {

        osHwiSwiftDisable();

        osHwiEnable(OS_HWI_PRIORITY10);

        stop();//wait();

        osHwiEnable(OS_HWI_PRIORITY4);

        osHwiSwiftEnable();

        osHwiPendingClear(hwi_num);

        MessageHandler(CORE0_TO_OTHERS_MESSAGE);


      }
    }
```

Figure 13.7:
Code segment with power-down-related code.

core will have to use context switching to read new Ethernet frames here, but slave cores only need to wake up and go to the MessageHandler function.

We take advantage of this fact by enabling only higher-priority interrupts before going to sleep:

```
osHwiSwiftDisable();
osHwiEnable(OS_HWI_PRIORITY10);
```

Then when a slave core is asleep, if a new queue message arrives on an interrupt, the core will be woken up (on context switch), and standard interrupt priority levels will be restored. The core will then go and manage the new message without context switch overhead by calling the MessageHandler() function. In order to verify our power savings, we will take a baseline power reading before optimizing across the relevant power supplies, and then measure the incremental power savings of each step.

The processor board has power for cores, accelerators, HSSI, and M3 memory connected to the same power supply, simplifying data collection. Since these supplies and DDR are the only blocks we are optimizing, we shall measure improvement based on these supplies alone.

Figure 13.8 provides a visual on the relative power consumed by the relevant power supplies (1V: core, M3, HSSI, MAPLE accelerators, and DDR) across the power-down steps used above. Note that actual power numbers are not provided to avoid any potential non-disclosure issues.

The first two bars provide reference points – indicating the power consumption for these supplies using a standard FIR filter in a loop and the power consumption when the cores are held in debug state (not performing any instructions, but not in a low-power mode). With our steps we can see that there was nearly a 50% reduction in power consumption across the relevant supplies for the Motion JPEG demo with the steps laid out above, with each step providing ~5% reduction in power, with the exception of the STOP and WAIT power modes, which are closer to 15–20% savings.

One thing to keep in mind is that, while the MJPEG demo is the perfect example to demonstrate low-power modes, it is not highly core-intensive, so as we progress through different optimization techniques, we will be using other examples as appropriate.

Optimizing data flow

Reducing power consumption for memory accesses

Because clocks have to be activated not only in the core components, but also in buses, and memory cells, memory-related functionality can be quite power-hungry, but luckily memory

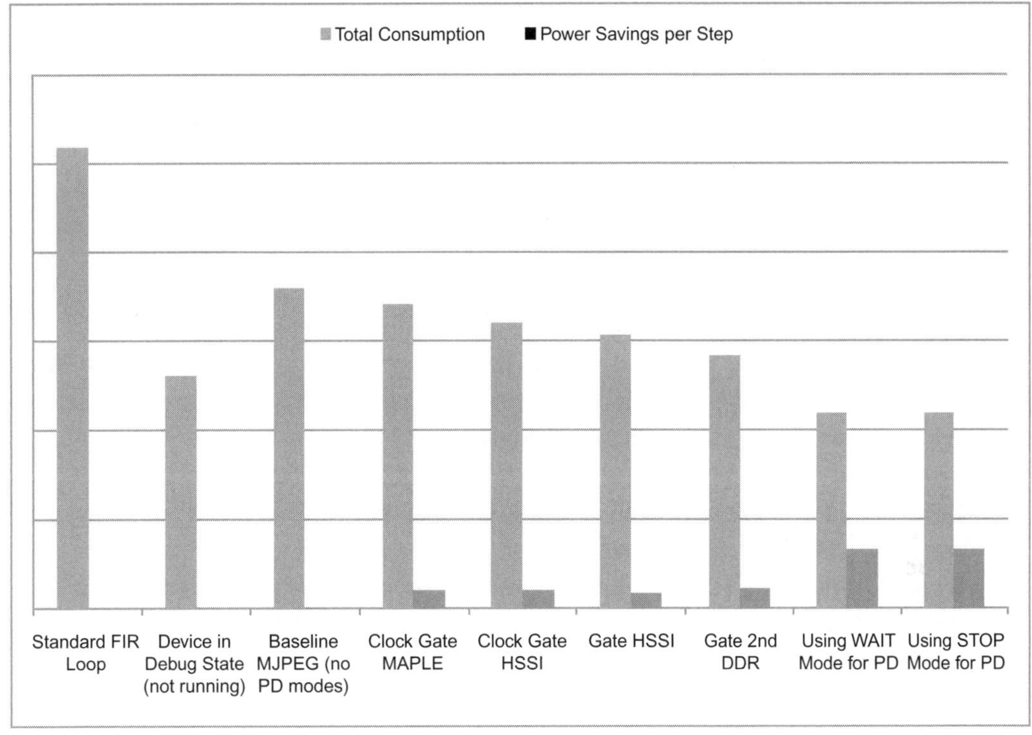

Figure 13.8:
Power consumption savings in PD modes.

access and data paths can also be optimized to reduce power. This section will cover methods to optimize power consumption with regard to memory accesses to DDR and SRAM memories by utilizing knowledge of the hardware design of these memory types. Then we will cover ways to take advantage of other specific memory set-ups at the SoC level. Common practice is to optimize memory in order to maximize the locality of critical or heavily used data and code by placing as much in cache as possible. Cache misses incur not only core stall penalties, but also power penalties as more bus activity is needed, and higher-level memories (internal device SRAM, or external device DDR) are activated and consume power. As a rule, access to higher-level memory such as DDR is not as common as internal memory accesses, so high-level memory accesses are easier to plan, and thus optimize.

DDR overview

The highest level of memory we will discuss here is external DDR memory. To optimize DDR accesses in software, first we need to understand the hardware that the memory consists of. DDR SDRAM, as the DDR (dual data rate) name implies, takes advantage of both edges of the DDR clock source in order to send data, thus doubling the effective data rate at which data reads and writes may occur. DDR provides a number of different types of features which may affect total power utilization, such as EDC (error detection), ECC (error correction), different types of bursting, programmable data refresh rates, programmable memory configuration allowing physical bank interleaving, page management across multiple chip selects, and DDR-specific sleep modes.

- Key DDR vocabulary to be discussed
  - **Chip Select** (also known as **Physical Bank**): selects a set of memory chips (specified as a "rank") connected to the memory controller for accesses.
  - **Rank**: specifies a set of chips on a DIMM to be accessed at once. A **Double Rank** DIMM, for example, would have two sets of chips – differentiated by chip select. When accessed together, each rank allows for a data access width of 64 bits (or 72 with ECC).
  - **Rows** are address bits enabling access to a set of data, known as a "**page**" – so row and page may be used interchangeably.
  - **Logical banks**, like row bits, enable access to a certain segment of memory. By standard practice, the row bits are the MSB address bits of DDR, followed by the bits to select a logical bank, finally followed by column bits.
  - **Column** bits are the bits used to select and access a specific address for reading or writing.

On a typical embedded processor, like a DSP, the DSPs' DDR SDRAM controller is connected to either discrete memory chips or a DIMM (dual inline memory module), which contains multiple memory components (chips). Each discrete component/chip contains multiple logical banks, rows, and columns which provide access for reads and writes to memory. The basic idea of how a discrete DDR3 memory chip's layout is shown in Figure 13.9.

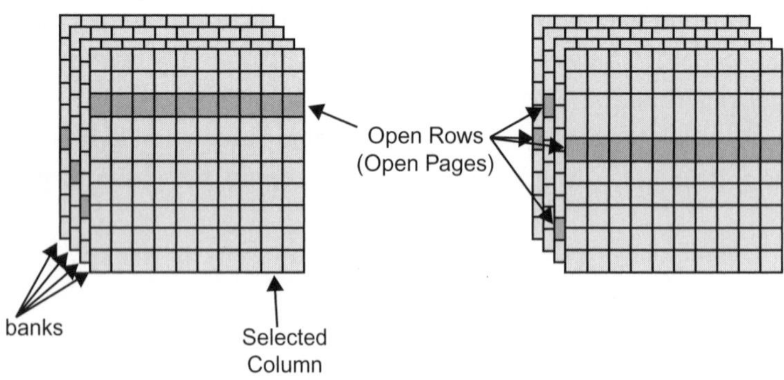

Figure 13.9:
Basic drawing of a discrete DDR3 memory chip's rows/columns.

Standard DDR3 discrete chips are commonly made up of eight logical banks, which provide addressability as shown above. These banks are essentially tables of rows and columns. The action to select a row effectively opens that row (page) for the logical bank being addressed. So different rows can be simultaneously open in different logical banks, as illustrated by the active or open rows highlighted in the picture. A column selection gives access to a portion of the row in the appropriate bank.

When considering sets of memory chips, the concept of chip select is added to the equation. Using chip selects, also known as "physical banks", enables the controller to access a certain set of memory modules (up to 1 GB for the MSC8156, 2 GB for MSC8157 DSPs from Freescale for example) at a time. Once a chip select is enabled, access to the selected memory modules with that chip select are activated, using page selection (rows), banks, and columns. The connection of two chip selects is shown in Figure 13.10.

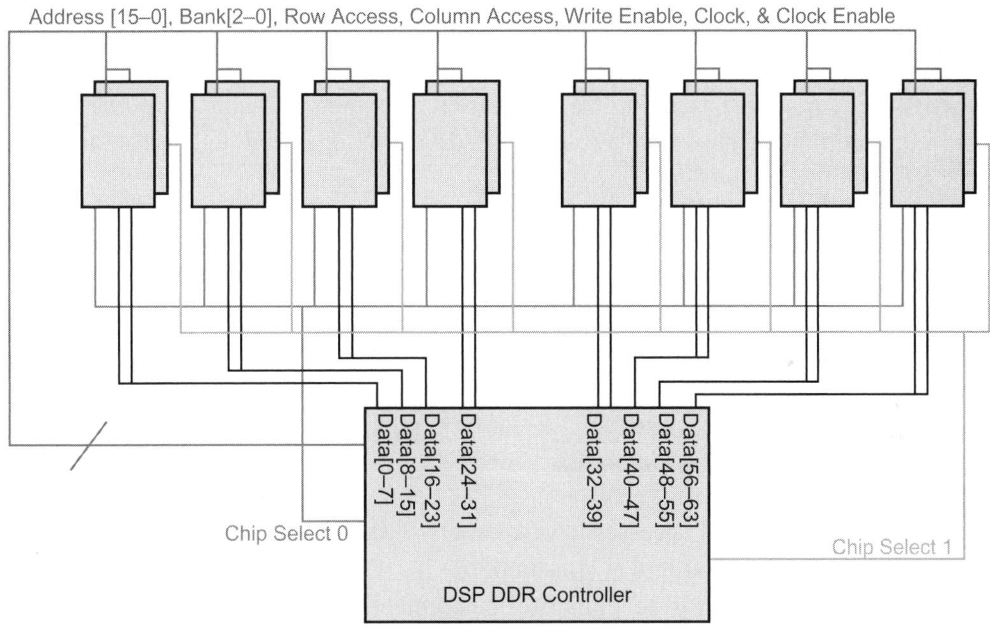

Figure 13.10:
Simplified view: DDR controller to memory connection: two chip selects.

In Figure 13.10 we have our DSP device which is intended to access DDR memory. There are a total of 16 chips connected to two chip selects: chip select 0 on the left in red, and 1 on the right in orange. The 16 discrete chips are paired such that a pair of chips shares all the same signals (Address, bank, data, etc.), except for the chip select pin. (Interesting note: This is basically how a dual rank DDR is organized, except each "pair of chips" exists within a single chip.) There are 64 data bits. So for a single chip select, when we access

DDR and write 64 contiguous bits of data to DDR memory space in our application, the DDR controller does the following:

- Selecting chip select based on your address (0 for example).
- Opening the same page (row) for each bank on all eight chips using the DDR address bits during the Row Access phase.
- New rows are opened via the ACTIVE command, which copies data from the row to a "row buffer" for fast access.
- Rows that were already opened do not require an active command and can skip this step.
- During the next phase, the DDR controller will select the same column on all eight chips. This is the column-access phase.
- Finally, the DDR controller will write the 64 bytes to the now open row buffers for each of the eight separate DDR chips which each input eight bits.

As there is a command to open rows, there is also one to close rows, called PRECHARGE, which tells the DDR modules to store the data from the row buffers back to the actual DDR memory in the chip, thus freeing up the row buffer. So when switching from one row to the next in a single DDR bank, we have to PRECHARGE the open row to close it, and then ACTIVATE the row we wish to start accessing.

A side effect of an ACTIVATE command is that the memory is automatically read and written – thus REFRESHing it. If a row in DDR is PRECHARGED, then it must be periodically refreshed (read/re-written with the same data) to keep data valid. DDR controllers have an autorefresh mechanism that does this for the programmer.

DDR data flow optimization for power

Now that the basics of DDR accesses have been covered, we can cover how DDR accesses can be optimized for minimal power consumption. As is often the case, optimizing for minimal power consumption is beneficial for performance as well.

DDR consumes power in all states, even when the CKE (clock enable – enabling the DDR to perform any operations) is disabled, though this is minimal. One technique to minimize DDR power consumption is made available by some DDR controllers which have a power saving mode that de-asserts the CKE pin – greatly reducing power. In some cases, this is called Dynamic Power Management Mode, which can be enabled via the DDR_SDRAM_CFG[DYN_PWR] register. This feature will de-assert CKE when no memory refreshes or accesses are scheduled. If the DDR memory has self-refresh capabilities, then this power-saving mode can be prolonged as refreshes are not required from the DDR controller.

This power-saving mode does impact performance to some extent, as enabling CKE when a new access is scheduled adds a latency delay.

Tools such as Micron's DDR power calculator can be used to estimate power consumption for DDR. If we choose 1 GB x8 DDR chips with −125 speed grade, we can see estimates for the main power-consuming actions on DDR. Power consumption for non-idle operations is additive, so total power is the idle power plus non-idle operations.

Idle with no rows open and CKE low is shown as: 4.3 mW (IDD2p)
Idle with no rows open and CKE high is shown as: 24.6 mW (IDD2n)
Idle with rows open and no CKE low is shown as: 9.9 mW (IDD3p)
Idle with rows open and CKE high is shown as: 57.3 mW (IDD3n)
ACTIVATE and PRECHARGE is shown as consuming 231.9 mW
REFRESH is shown as 3.9 mW
WRITE is shown as 46.8 mW
READ is shown as 70.9 mW

We can see that using the Dynamic Power Management mode saves up to 32 mW of power, which is quite substantial in the context of DDR usage.

Also, it is clear that the software engineer must do whatever possible to minimize contributions to power from the main power contributors: ACTIVATE, PRECHARGE, READ, and WRITE operations.

The power consumption from row activation/precharge is expected as DDR needs to consume a considerable amount of power in decoding the actual ACTIVATE instruction and address followed by transferring data from the memory array into the row buffer. Likewise, the PRECHARGE command also consumes a significant amount of power in writing data back to the memory array from row buffers.

Optimizing power by timing

One can minimize the maximum "average power" consumed by ACTIVATE commands over time by altering the timing between row activate commands, t_{RC} (a setting the programmer can set at start up for the DDR controller). By extending the time required between DDR row activates, the maximum power spike of activates is spread, so the amount of power pulled by the DDR in a given period of time is lessened, though the total power for a certain number of accesses will remain the same. The important thing to note here is that this can help with limiting the maximum (worst-case) power seen by the device, which can be helpful when having to work within the confines of a certain hardware limitation (power supply, limited decoupling capacitance to DDR supplies on the board, etc.).

Optimizing with interleaving

Now that we understand that our main enemy in power consumption on DDR is the activate/precharge commands (for both power and performance), we can devise plans to minimize the need for such commands. There are a number of things to look at here, the first being address interleaving, which will reduce ACTIVATE/PRECHARGE command pairs via interleaving chip selects (physical banks) and additionally by interleaving logical banks.

In setting up the address space for the DDR controller, the row bits and chip select/bank select bits may be swapped to enable DDR interleaving, whereby changing the higher-order address enables the DDR controller to stay on the same page while changing chip selects (physical banks) and then changing logical banks before changing rows. The software programmer can enable this by register configuration in most cases.

Optimizing memory software data organization

We also need to consider the layout of our memory structures within DDR. If using large ping-pong buffers, for example, the buffers may be organized so that each buffer is in its own logical bank. This way, if DDR is not interleaved, we still can avoid unnecessary ACTIVATE/PRECHARGE pairs if a pair of buffers is larger than a single row (page).

Optimizing general DDR configuration

There are other features available to the programmer which can positively or negatively affect power, including "open/closed" page mode. Closed page mode is a feature available in some controllers which will perform an auto-precharge on a row after each read or write access. This of course unnecessarily increases the power consumption in DDR as a programmer may need to access the same row 10 times, for example; closed page mode would yield at least 9 unneeded PRECHARGE/ACTIVATE command pairs. In the example DDR layout discussed above, this could consume an extra 231.9 mW * 9 = 2087.1 mW.

As you may expect, this has an equally negative effect on performance due to the stall incurred during memory PRECHARGE and ACTIVATE.

Optimizing DDR burst accesses

DDR technology has become more restrictive with each generation: DDR2 allows 4-beat bursts and 8-beat bursts, whereas DDR3 only allows 8. This means that DDR3 will treat all burst lengths as 8-beat (bursts of 8 accesses long). So for the 8-byte (64 bit) wide DDR accesses we have been discussing here, accesses are expected to be 8 beats of 8 bytes, or 64 bytes long.

If accesses are not 64 bytes wide, there will be stalls due to the hardware design. This means that if the DDR memory is accessed only for reading (or writing) 32 bytes of data at a time, DDR will only be running at 50% efficiency, as the hardware will still perform reads/writes for the full 8-beat burst, though only 32 bytes will be used. Because DDR3 operates this way, the same amount of power is consumed whether doing 32-byte or 64-byte-long bursts to our memory here. So for the same amount of data, if doing 4-beat (32 byte) bursts, the DDR3 would consume approximately twice the power.

The recommendation here then is to make all accesses to DDR full 8-beat bursts in order to maximize power efficiency. To do this, the programmer must be sure to pack data in the DDR so that accesses to the DDR are in at least 64-byte-wide chunks. Packing data so it is 64-byte-aligned or any other alignment can be done through the use of pragmas.

The concept of data packing can be used to reduce the amount of used memory as well. For example, packing eight single bit variables into a single character reduces memory footprint and increases the amount of usable data the core or cache can read in with a single burst.

In addition to data packing, accesses need to be 8-byte-aligned (or aligned to the burst length). If an access is not aligned to the burst length, for example, let's assume an 8-byte access starts with a 4-byte offset, both the first and second access will effectively become 4-beat bursts, reducing bandwidth utilization to 50% (instead of aligning to the 64-byte boundary and reading data in with one single burst).

SRAM and cache data flow optimization for power

Another optimization related to the usage of off-chip DDR is avoidance: avoiding using external off-chip memory and maximizing accesses to internal on-chip memory saves the additive power draw that occurs when activating not only internal device buses and clocks, but also off-chip buses, memory arrays, etc.

High-speed memory close to the DSP processor core is typically SRAM memory, whether it functions in the form of cache or as a local on-chip memory. SRAM differs from SDRAM in a number of ways (such as no ACTIVATE/PRECHARGE, and no concept of REFRESH), but some of the principles of saving power still apply, such as pipelining accesses to memory via data packing and memory alignment.

The general rule for SRAM access optimization is that accesses should be optimized for higher performance. The fewer clock cycles the device spends doing a memory operation, the less time that memory, buses, and core are all activated for said memory operation.

SRAM (all memory) and code size

As programmers, we can affect this in both program and data organization. Programs may be optimized for minimal code size (by a compiler, or by hand), in order to consume a minimal amount of space. Smaller programs require less memory to be activated to read the program. This applies not only to SRAM, but also to DDR and any type of memory – less memory having to be accessed implies a lesser amount of power drawn.

Aside from optimizing code using the compiler tools, other techniques such as instruction packing, which are available in some embedded core architectures, enable fitting maximum code into a minimum set of space. The VLES (variable-length execution set) instruction architecture allows the program to pack multiple instructions of varying sizes into a single execution set. As execution sets are not required to be 128-bit-aligned, instructions can be packed tightly, and the prefetch, fetch, and instruction dispatch hardware will handle reading the instructions and identifying the start and end of each instruction set.

Additionally, size can be saved in code by creating functions for common tasks. If tasks are similar, consider using the same function with parameters passed to determine the variation to run instead of duplicating the code in software multiple times.

Be sure to make use of combined functions where available in the hardware. For example, in the Freescale StarCore architecture, using a multiply accumulate (MAC) instruction, which takes one pipelined cycle, saves space and performance in addition to power compared with using separate multiple and add instructions.

Some hardware provides code compression at compile time and decompression on the fly, so this may be an option depending on the hardware the user is dealing with. The problem with this strategy is related to the size of compression blocks. If data is compressed into small blocks, then not as much compression optimization is possible, but this is still more desirable than the alternative. During decompression, if code contains many branches or jumps, the processor will end up wasting bandwidth, cycles, and power decompressing larger blocks that are hardly used.

The problem with the general strategy of minimizing code size is the inherent conflict between optimizing for performance and space. Optimizing for performance generally does not always yield the smallest program, so determining ideal code size vs. cycle performance in order to minimize power consumption requires some balancing and profiling. The general advice here is to use what tricks are available to minimize code size without hurting the performance of a program that meets real-time requirements. The 80/20 rule of applying performance optimization to the 20% of code that performs 80% of the work, while optimizing the remaining 80% of code for size, is a good practice to follow.

SRAM power consumption and parallelization

It is also advisable to optimize data accesses in order to reduce the cycles in which SRAM is activated, pipelining accesses to memory, and organizing data so that it may be accessed consecutively. In systems like the MSC8156, the core/L1 caches connect to the M2 memory via a 128-bit wide bus. If data is organized properly, this means that 128-bit data accesses from M2 SRAM could be performed in one clock cycle each, which would obviously be beneficial when compared to doing 16 independent 8-bit accesses to M2 in terms of performance and power consumption.

An example showing how one may use move instructions to write 128 bits of data back to memory in a single instruction set (VLES) is provided below:

```
[
MOVERH.4F d0:d1:d2:d3,(r4) + n0
MOVERL.4F d4:d5:d6:d7,(r5) + n0
]
```

We can parallelize memory accesses in a single instruction (as with the above where both of the moves are performed in parallel) and, even if the accesses are to separate memories or memory banks, the single-cycle access still consumes less power than doing two independent instructions in two cycles.

Another note: as with DDR, SRAM accesses need to be aligned to the bus width in order to make full use of the bus.

Data transitions and power consumption

SRAM power consumption may also be affected by the type of data used in an application. Power consumption is affected by the number of data transitions (from 0 s to 1 s) in memory as well. This power effect also trickles down to the DSP core processing elements, as found by Kojima *et al.* Processing mathematical instructions using constants consumes less power at the core than with dynamic variables. In many devices, because pre-charging memory to reference voltage is common practice in SRAM memories, power consumption is also proportional to the number of zeros as the memory is pre-charged to a high state.

Using this knowledge, it goes without saying that re-use of constants where possible and avoiding zeroing out memory unnecessarily will, in general, save the programmer some power.

Cache utilization and SoC memory layout

Cache usage can be thought of in the opposite manner to DDR usage when designing a program. An interesting detail about cache is that both dynamic and static power increase with increasing cache sizes; however, the increase in dynamic power is small. The increase in static power is significant, and becomes increasingly relevant for smaller feature sizes. As software programmers, we have no impact on the actual cache size available on a device, but when it is provided, based on the above, it is our duty to use as much of it as possible!

For SoC-level memory configuration and layout, optimizing the most heavily used routines and placing them in the closest cache to the core processors will offer not only the best performance, but also better power consumption.

Explanation of locality

The reason the above is true is thanks to the way caches work. There are a number of different cache architectures, but they all take advantage of the principle of locality. The principle of locality basically states that if one memory address is accessed, the probability of an address nearby being accessed soon is relatively high. Based on this, when a cache miss occurs (when the core tries to access memory that has not been brought into the cache), the cache will read the requested data in from higher-level memory one line at a time. This means that if the core tries to read a 1-byte character from cache, and the data is not in the cache, then there is a miss at this address. When the cache goes to higher-level memory (whether it be on-chip memory or external DDR, etc.), it will not read in an 8-bit character, but rather a full cache line. If our cache uses cache sizes of 256 bytes, then a miss will read in our 1-byte character, along with 255 more bytes that happen to be on the same line in memory.

This is very effective in reducing power if used in the right way. If we are reading an array of characters aligned to the cache line size, once we get a miss on the first element, although we pay a penalty in power and performance for cache to read in the first line of data, the remaining 255 bytes of this array will be in cache. When handling image or video samples, a single frame would typically be stored this way, in a large array of data. When performing compression or decompression on the frame, the entire frame will be accessed in a short period of time, thus it is spatially and temporally local.

Again, let's use the example of the six-core MSC8156 DSP SoC. In this SoC, there are two levels of cache for each of the six DSP processor cores: L1 cache (which consists of 32 KB of instruction and 32 KB of data cache), and a 512 KB L2 memory which can be configured as L2 cache or M2 memory. At the SoC level, there is a 1 MB memory shared by all cores called M3. L1 cache runs at the core processor speed (1 GHz), L2 cache effectively manages data at the same speed (double the bus width, half the frequency), and M3 runs at up to 400 MHz. The easiest way to make use of the memory hierarchy is to enable L2 as cache and make use of data locality. As discussed above, this works when data is stored with high locality. Another option is to DMA data into L2 memory (configured in non-cache mode). We will discuss DMA in a later section.

When we have a large chunk of data stored in M3 or in DDR, the MSC8156 can draw this data in through the caches simultaneously. L1 and L2 caches are linked, so a miss from L1 will pull 256 bytes of data in from L2, and a miss from L2 will pull data in at 64 bytes at a time (64 B line size) from the requested higher-level memory (M3 or DDR). Using L2 cache has two advantages over going directly to M3 or DDR. First, it is running at effectively the same speed as L1 (though there is a slight stall latency here, it is negligible), and second, in addition to being local and fast, it can be up to 16 times larger than L1 cache, allowing us to keep much more data in local memory than just L1 alone would.

Explanation of set-associativity

All caches in the MSC8156 are eight-way set-associative. This means that the caches are split into eight different sections ("ways"). Each section is used to access higher-level memory, meaning that a single address in M3 could be stored in one of eight different sections (ways) of L2 cache, for example. The easiest way to think of this is that the section (way) of cache can be overlaid onto the higher-level memory x times. So so if L2 is set up as all cache, the following equation calculates how many times each set of L2 memory is overlaid onto M3:

$$\begin{aligned}\#\text{ of overlays O} &= \frac{\text{M3size}}{(\text{L2size}/8\text{ways})}\\ &= \frac{1\text{MB}}{(512\text{KB}/8)} = 16384\text{ overlays}\end{aligned}$$

In the MSC8156, a single way of L2 cache is 64 KB in size, so addresses are from $0 \times 0000\_0000$ to $0 \times 0001\_0000$ hexadecimal. If we consider each way of cache individually, we can explain how a single way of L2 is mapped to M3 memory. M3 addresses start at 0xC000_0000. So M3 addresses 0xC000_0000, 0xC001_0000, 0xC002_0000, 0xC003_0000, 0xC004_0000, etc. (up to 16 K times) all map to the same line of a way of cache. So if way #1 of L2 cache has valid data for M3's 0xC000_0000, and the core processor wants to next access 0xC001_0000, what is going to happen?

If the cache has only one way set-associativity, then the line of cache containing 0xC000_0000 will have to be flushed back to cache and re-used in order to cache 0xC001_0000. In an eight-way set-associative cache, however, we can take advantage of the other 7×64 KB sections (ways) of cache. So we can potentially have 0xC000_0000 stored in way #1, and the other seven ways of cache have their first line of cache as empty. In this case, we can store our new memory access to 0xC001_0000 in way #2.

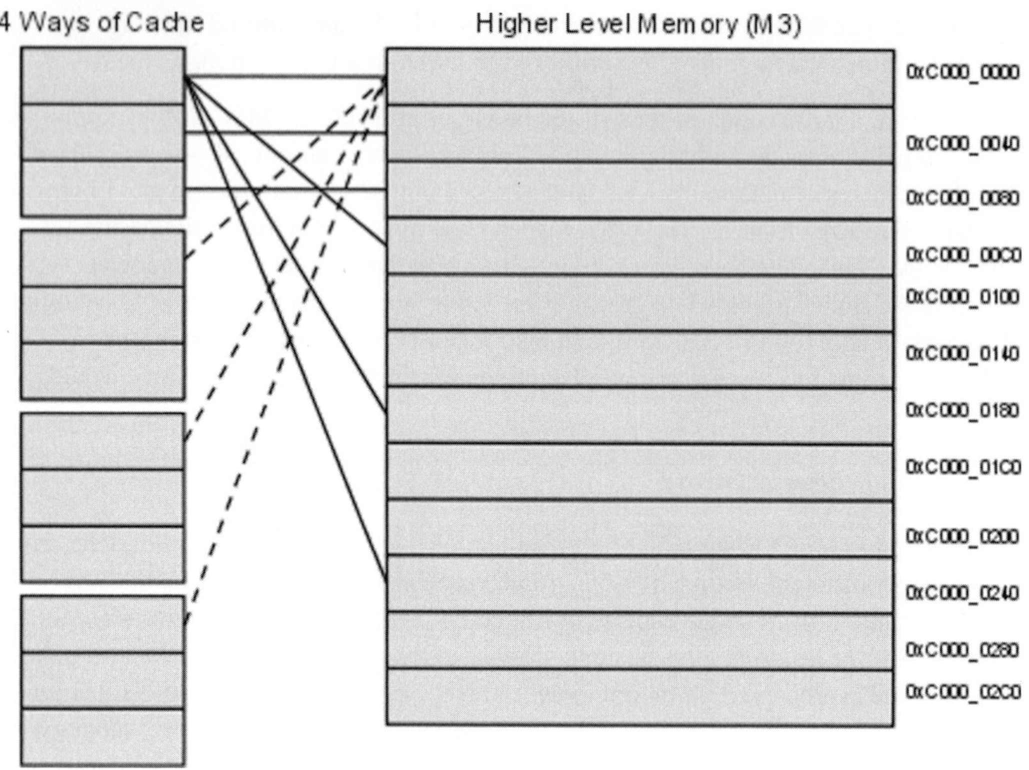

Figure 13.11:
Set-associativity by cache line: four-way set-associative cache.

So, what happens when there is an access to 0xC000_0040? ($0 \times 40 \;=\;= \;64$ B). The answer here is that we have to look at the second cache line in each way of L2 to see if it is empty, as we were only considering the first line of cache in our example above. So here we now have eight more potential places to store a line of data (or program).

Figure 13.11 shows a four-way set-associative cache connecting to M3. In this figure, we can see that every line of M3 maps to four possible lines of the cache (one for each way). So line 0xC000_0040 maps to the second line (second "set") of each way in the cache. So when the core wants to read 0xC000_0040, but the first way has 0xC000_0100 in it, the cache can load the core's request into any of the other three ways if their second lines are empty (invalid).

The reason for discussing set-associativity of caches is that it does have some effect on power consumption (as one might imagine). The goal for optimizing power consumption (and performance) when using cache is to maximize the hit rate in order to minimize accesses to external buses and hardware caused by misses. Set-associativity is normally already determined by hardware, but, if the programmer can change set associativity, set-associative caches maintain a higher hit-rate than directly mapped caches, and thus draw lower power.

Memory layout for cache

While having an eight-way set-associative architecture is statistically beneficial in improving hit ratio and power consumption, the software programmer may also directly improve hit ratio in the cache, and thus lower power by avoiding conflicts in cache. Conflicts in cache occur when the core needs data that will replace cache lines with currently valid data that will be needed again.

We can organize memory in order to avoid these conflicts in a few different ways. For memory segments we need simultaneously, it is important to pay attention to the size of ways in the cache. In our eight-way L2 cache, each way is 64 KB. As we discussed before, we can simultaneously load eight cache lines with the same lower 16 bits of address ($0 \times 0000\_xxxx$).

Another example is if we are working with nine arrays with 64 KB of data simultaneously. If we organize each array contiguously data will be constantly thrashed as all arrays share the same 64 KB offset. If the same indices of each array are being accessed simultaneously, we can offset the start of some of the arrays by inserting buffer, so that each array does not map to the same offset (set) within a cache way.

When data sizes are larger than a single way, the next step is to consider reducing the amount of data that is pulled into the cache at a time – process smaller chunks at a time.

Write-back vs. write-through caches

Some caches are designed as either "write-back" or "write-through" caches, and others, such as the MSC815x series DSPs, are configurable as either. Write-back and write-through buffering differs in how data from the core is managed by the cache in the case of writes.

Write-back is a cache writing scheme in which data is written only to the cache. The main memory is updated when the data in the cache is replaced. In the write-through cache write scheme, data is written simultaneously to the cache and to memory. When setting up cache in software, we have to weigh the benefits of each of these. In a multicore system, coherency is of some concern, but so are performance and power. Coherency refers to how up-to-date data in main memory is compared to the caches. The greatest level of multicore coherency between internal core caches and system level memory is attained by using write-through caching, as every write to cache will immediately be written back to system memory, keeping it up to date. There are a number of down sides to write-through caching including:

- core stalls during writes to higher-level memory;
- increased bus traffic on the system buses (higher chance of contention and system-level stalls);
- increased power consumption as the higher-level memories and buses are activated for every single memory write.

The write-back cache scheme, on the other hand, will avoid all of the above disadvantages at the cost of system-level coherency. For optimal power consumption, a common approach is to use the cache in write-back mode, and strategically flush cache lines/segments when the system needs to be updated with new data.

Cache coherency functions

In addition to write-back and write-through schemes, specific cache commands should also be considered. Commands include:

- invalidation sweep: invalidating a line of data by clearing valid and dirty bits (effectively just re-labeling a line of cache as "empty");
- synchronization sweep: writing any new data back to cache and removing the dirty label;
- flush sweep: writing any new data back to cache and invalidating the line;
- fetch: fetch data into the cache.

Generally these operations can be performed by either cache line, a segment of the cache, or as a global operation. When it is possible to predict that a large chunk of data will be needed in the cache in the near future, performing cache sweep functions on larger segments will make better use of the full bus bandwidths and lead to fewer stalls by the core. As memory accesses all require some initial memory access set-up time, but after set-up bursts will flow at full bandwidth, making use of large prefetches will save power when compared to reading in the same amount of data line by line so long as this is done strategically so as to avoid the data we want from being thrashed before the core actually gets to use it.

When using any of these instructions, we have to be careful about the effect it has on the rest of the cache. For instance, performing a fetch from higher-level memory into cache may require replacing contents currently in the cache. This could result in thrashing data in the cache and invalidating cache in order to make space for the data being fetched.

Compiler cache optimizations

In order to assist with the above, compilers may be used to optimize cache power consumption by reorganizing memory or memory accesses for us. Two main techniques available are array merging and loop interchanging, explained below.

Array merging organizes memory so that arrays accessed simultaneously will be at different offsets (different "sets") from the start of a way. Consider the following two array declarations below:

```
int array1[ array_size ];
int array2[ array_size ];
```

The compiler can merge these two arrays as shown below:

```
struct merged_arrays
  {
  int array1;
  int array2;
  } new_array[ array_ size ]
```

In order to re-order the way that high-level memory is read into cache, reading in smaller chunks to reduce the chance of thrashing loop interchanging can be used. Consider the code below:

```
for (i = 0; i<100; i = i + 1)
 for (j = 0; j<200; j = j + 1)
  for (k = 0; k<10000; k = k + 1)
    z[ k ][ j ] = 10 * z[ k ][ j ];
```

By **interchanging** the second and third nested loops, the compiler can produce the following code, decreasing the likelihood of unnecessary thrashing during the innermost loop.

```
for (i = 0; i<100; i = i + 1)
 for (k = 0; k<10000; k = k + 1)
  for (j = 0; j<200; j = j + 1)
    z[ k ][ j ] = 10 * z[ k ][ j ];
```

Peripheral/communication utilization

When considering reading and writing of data, of course, we cannot just think about memory access: we need to pull data into and out of the device as well. As such, for the final portion of data path optimization we will look at how to minimize power consumption in commonly used embedded processor (I/O) peripherals.

Things to consider include the peripheral's burst size, speed grade, transfer width, and general communication modes. The main standard forms of peripheral communication for embedded processors include DMA (direct memory access), SRIO (serial rapid I/O), Ethernet, PCI Express, and RF antenna interfaces. I2C and UART are also commonly used, though mostly for initialization and debug purposes.

The fact that communication interfaces usually require their own PLLs/clocks increases the individual power consumption impact. The higher-clocked peripherals that we need to consider as the main power consumers are the DMA, SRIO, Ethernet, and PCI Express. Clock gating and peripheral low-power modes for these peripherals were discussed in the low-power modes section of this chapter, so this section will talk about how to optimize actual usage.

Although each protocol is different for the I/O peripherals and the internal DMA, they all share the fact that they are used to read/write data. As such, one basic goal is to maximize the throughput while the peripheral is active in order to maximize efficiency and the time the peripheral/device can be in a low-power state, thus minimizing the active clock times.

The most basic way to do this is to increase transfer/burst size. For DMA, the programmer has control over burst size and transfer size in addition to the start/end address (and can follow the alignment and memory accessing rules we discussed in earlier subsections of data path optimization). Using the DMA, the programmer can decide not only the alignment, but also the transfer "shape", for lack of a better word. What this means is that using the DMA, the programmer can transfer blocks in the form of two-dimensional, three-dimensional, and four-dimensional data chunks, thus transferring data types specific to specific applications on the alignment chosen by the programmer without spending cycles transferring unnecessary data. Figure 13.12 demonstrates the data structure of a three-dimensional DMA.

The user programs the start address for data, the length for the first dimension, the offset for the second dimension, the number of transfers, followed by the offset for the third dimension and the number of transfers. At the end of the all transfers, the programmer may also program the DMA to interrupt the core to signal data transfer completion. Having the DMA intelligently moving the data in the format and organization needed by the user's application helps optimize data flow and core processing by avoiding the need for the core to reorganize data or alter algorithms that are optimized for data in a specific format. This also simplifies the maintaining of certain alignments as the programmer can decide where each dimension of the data structure starts.

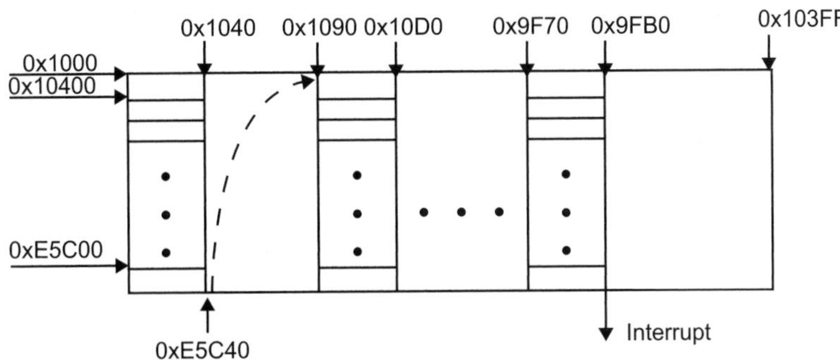

Figure 13.12:
Three-dimensional DMA data format.

Other high-speed peripherals will generally also use a DMA, whether it be the system DMA or the peripheral's own private DMA for data passing. In the case of the MSC8156 discussed earlier, the SRIO, PCI Express, and Ethernet controllers all have their own DMAs separate from the system DMA for data transfers. The basics still apply here: we want data transfers to be long (long bursts), we want bus accesses to be aligned, and, additionally, one more thing we want is optimal access to the system bus! We will discuss system bus optimization later in this section.

DMA of data vs. CPU

While on the topic of DMA, we need to consider whether the core should move data from internal core memory or whether a DMA should be utilized in order to save power. As the DMA hardware is optimized solely for the purpose of moving data, it will move data while consuming less power than the core (which is generally running at much higher frequencies than the DMA). As the core runs at such a higher frequency, not intended solely for data movement, etc., the core utilizes more dynamic power while incurring heavy stall penalties when accessing external memory.

As some external memory access and stalls are incurred for writing to peripheral registers when setting up the DMA, there is a point where data accesses are too small or infrequent to justify DMA usage. In general, when moving larger chunks of data, or data in a predictable manner, for the purpose of optimizing power consumption (and core performance) DMA should be utilized for maximum power savings and application efficiency.

For transactions and I/O that are not large enough to justify DMA we can consider caching, as this assists with stalls and requires virtually no core intervention. Generally speaking, using the cache is much simpler than DMA, so this is the generally accepted solution for unpredictable data I/O, while DMA should be used for larger memory transfers. Due to the overhead of programming the DMA, and the unique properties of data per application, the trade-off between power savings, performance, and program complexity from DMA to cache has to be done on a case-by-case basis. Peripherals with their own DMA generally require the programmer to use that DMA for peripheral interaction, which is a good habit to force the programmer into, as we have just discussed.

Coprocessors

Just as the DMA peripheral is optimized for data movement and can do so more efficiently with less power consumption than the high-frequency embedded core, so are other peripherals acting as coprocessors able to perform special functions more efficiently than the core. In the case of the MSC8156, an on-board baseband coprocessor (accelerator) includes hardware for fast Fourier transforms, discrete Fourier transforms, and turbo Viterbi. When a chain of transforms can be offloaded onto the accelerator, depending on the cost of transferring data and transform sizes, the system is able to save power and cycles by offloading the core and having the coprocessor do this work as the coprocessor is running at a much lower frequency than the core, has fewer processing elements aimed at a single function, and also has automatic lower-power modes that are used when the coprocessor is not processing transforms, etc.

System bus configuration

System bus stalls due to lack of priority on the bus can cause a peripheral to actively wait unnecessarily for extra cycles when not set up properly. These extra active wait cycles mean more wasted power. Generally embedded processors will have system bus configuration registers which allow the programmer to configure the priority and arbitration per bus initiator port. In the case of the MSC8156, the system bus (called the CLASS) has 11 initiator ports and eight target ports (memory and register space). When the programmer understands the I/O needs of the application, it is possible to set up priority appropriately for the initiators that need the extra bandwidth on the bus so they can access memory and register space with minimal stalls.

There is not much of a trick to this; simply set priority based on I/O usage. Some devices such as the MSC815x series DSPs provide bus profiling tools which enable the programmer to count the number of accesses per initiator port to each target. This allows the programmer to see where congestion and bottlenecks are occurring in order to appropriately configure and tune the bus. Profiling tools also allow the programmer to see how many "priority upgrades" are needed per port. This means that the programmer can temporarily assign test priorities to each port, and if some ports constantly require priority upgrades the programmer can decide to set the starting priority of these ports one level up and re-profile.

Peripheral speed grades and bus width

Like with the system bus access, the peripheral's external interface should be set up according to the actual needs of the system. The catch-22 of I/O peripherals is that some peripherals require being powered on all the time (so minimal to no use of low-power modes is available). If a communication port such as SRIO is dedicated to receiving incoming blocks of data to process, when no data is coming in clocks and low-power modes for the SRIO port are not an option. As such, there is a balancing game to be played here.

In testing software and power consumption, we found on the MSC8156 that running four lanes of SRIO at 3.125 GHz with 40% utilization (~4 Gbps of data) consumes a comparable amount of power, or even less, to running four lanes of SRIO at 2.5 GHz with 50% utilization (the same data throughput). So the user needs to test various cases or make use of the device manufacturer's power calculator in order to make an informed decision. In a case like this, peripherals which have an auto-idle feature should make use of the higher-speed bus in order to maximize sleep times.

SRIO, PCI Express, Ethernet over SGMII, and some antenna interfaces make use of the same serial I/O hardware, so similar care should be taken here. All could be required to be held in an active mode as a form of "device wake" or signaling to the DSP core, meaning they may be restricted from going into sleep modes. In the case of antenna signaling, this is especially detrimental as the active antenna's RF interface has to constantly consume power to emit signal. If possible, it is ideal to use an alternative method for waking the core in order to enable idle and sleep modes on the antenna.

Peripheral to core communication

When considering device waking, and general peripheral to core I/O, we have to consider how the peripheral interacts with the core processors. How does the core know that data is available? How often is the core notified that data is available? How does the core know when to send data over the peripheral? There are three main methods for managing this: polling, time-based processing, and interrupt processing.

Polling

This is by far the least efficient method of core-peripheral interaction as it has the core constantly awake and burning through high-frequency clock cycles (consuming active current) just to see if data is ready. The only advantage of using this method happens when the programmer is not concerned about power consumption. In this case, polling enables the core to avoid the context switches that occur during interrupt processing, thus saving some cycles in order to access data faster. Generally this is only used for testing maximum peripheral bandwidth as opposed to being used in a real application.

Time-based processing

This works on the assumption that data will always be available at a certain interval. For example, if a processor is processing a GSM voice codec (AMR, EFR, HR, etc.) the core will know that samples will be arriving every 20 ms, so the core can look for the new audio samples on this time basis and not poll. This process allows the core to sleep, and use a timer for wake functionality, followed by performing data processing. The down side of this is the complexity and inflexibility of this model: set-up and synchronization require a lot of effort on the programmer's side, and the same effect can be reached using simple interrupt processing.

Interrupt processing

The final core-to-peripheral communication mechanism is also the most commonly used one as it allows the benefits of the time-based processing without the complicated software architecture. We also briefly discussed using interrupt processing in the low-power modes section as a method for waking the core from sleep states: when new data samples and packets come in for processing, the core is interrupted by the peripheral (and can be woken if in sleep state) to start processing new data. The peripheral can also be used to interrupt the core when the peripheral is ready to transfer new data, so that the core does not have to constantly poll a heavily loaded peripheral to see when data is ready to send.

Power consumption results for polling vs. interrupt processing were shown in Figure 13.8 when comparing the baseline MJPEG vs. using WAIT for PD and using STOP for PD modes. When not using WAIT and STOP modes, the application would constantly check for new buffers without taking advantage of massive idle times in the application.

Algorithmic

Of the three main areas of power optimization discussed here, algorithmic optimization requires the most work for a given amount of power savings. Algorithmic optimization includes optimization at the core application level, code structuring, data structuring (in some cases, this could be considered as data path optimization), data manipulation, and optimizing instruction selection.

Compiler optimization levels

In the data path section, we briefly discussed how the compiler can be used to optimize code for minimal size. The compiler may also be used to optimize code for maximum performance (utilizing the maximum number of processing units per cycle and minimizing the amount of time code is running). A key question is whether optimizing for performance will reduce power consumption. In general increasing the number of processing units will increase the power consumed per cycle, but the total power to perform a function over time will reduce as the number of cycles to perform the function is reduced. The question of when to optimize for performance versus code size generally still fits with the 80/20 rule (80% of cycle time is spent in 20% of the code), so, as mentioned in the data path section, the general rule here is to optimize the cycle-hungry (20%) portion of code for performance, while focusing on minimizing code size for the rest. Fine tuning this is the job of the programmer and will require power measurement (as discussed earlier). The rest of this section will cover specific algorithmic optimizations, some of which may be performed by the performance optimizer in the compiler.

Instruction packing

Instruction packing was included in the data path optimization section above, but may also be listed as an algorithmic optimization as it involves not only how memory is accessed, but also how code is organized.

Loop unrolling revisited

We briefly discussed using altering loops in code in order to optimize cache utilization before. As we discussed earlier, another method for optimizing both performance and power in embedded processors is via loop unrolling. This method effectively partially unravels a loop, as shown in the code snippets below:

```
Regular loop:
for (i = 0; i<100; i = i + 1)
 for (k = 0; k<10000; k = k + 1)
  a[i] = 10 * b[k];

Loop unrolled by 4x:
for (i = 0; i<100; i = i + 4)
 for (k = 0; k<10000; k = k + 4)
  {
     a[i] = 10 * b[k];
     a[i + 1] = 10 * b[k + 1];
     a[i + 2] = 10 * b[k + 2];
     a[i + 3] = 10 * b[k + 3];
  }
```

Unrolling code in this manner enables the compiler to make use of four MACs (multiply-accumulates) in each loop iteration instead of just one, thus increasing processing parallelization and code efficiency (more processing per cycle means more idle cycles available for sleep and low-power modes). In the above case, we increase the parallelization of the loop by four times, so we perform the same amount of MACs in ¼ the cycle time, thus the effective active clock time needed for this code is reduced by 4×. Measuring the power savings using the MSC8156, we find that the above example optimization (saving 25% cycle time by utilizing four MACs per cycle instead of one) enables the core to have a ~48% total power saving during the time this routine is executed.

Completely unrolling loops is not advisable as it is counterproductive to the code size minimization efforts we discussed in the data path section, which would lead to extra memory accesses and the possibility of increased cache miss penalties.

Software pipelining

Another technique common to both embedded processor performance optimization and embedded processor power optimization is software pipelining. Software pipelining is a technique where the programmer splits up a set of interdependent instructions that would normally have to be performed one at a time so that the DSP core can begin processing multiple instructions in each cycle. Rather than explaining in words, the easiest way to follow this technique is to see an example.

Say we have the following code segment:

```
Regular Loop:
for (i=0; i<100; i=i+1)
{
 a[i]= 10 * b[i];
 b[i]= 10 * c[i];
 c[i]= 10 * d[i];
}
```

Right now, although we have three instructions occurring per loop, the compiler will see that the first instruction depends on the second instruction, and thus could not be pipelined with the second, nor can the second instruction be pipelined with the third due to interdependence: a[i] cannot be set to b[i] as b[i] is simultaneously being set to c[i], and so on. So right now the DSP processor has to execute the above loop 100 times with each iteration performing three individual instructions per cycle (not very efficient), for a total of

300 cycles (best case) performed by MACs in the core of the loop. With software pipelining, we can optimize this in the following way:

First we see where we can parallelize the above code by unrolling the loop to some extent:

```
Unrolled loop
a[i]= 10 * b[i];
b[i]= 10 * c[i];
c[i]= 10 * d[i];
 a[i+1]= 10 * b[i+1];
 b[i+1]= 10 * c[i+1];
 c[i+1]= 10 * d[i+1];
  a[i+2]= 10 * b[i+2];
  b[i+2]= 10 * c[i+2];
  c[i+2]= 10 * d[i+2];
    a[i+3]= 10 * b[i+3];
    b[i+3]= 10 * c[i+3];
    c[i+3]= 10 * d[i+3];
```

Using the above, we can see that certain instructions are not interdependent. The first assignment of array "a" relies on the original array "b", meaning we can potentially assign a entirely before doing any other instructions. If we do this, this means that array "b" would be entirely free of dependence and could be completely assigned to the original array "c". We can abstract this for c as well.

We can use this idea to break the code apart and add parallelism by placing instructions together that can run in parallel when doing some assignment in advance:

First, we have to perform our first instruction (no parallelism):

```
a[i] = 10 * b[i];
```

Then we can have two instructions performed in one cycle:

```
b[i] = 10 * c[i];
a[i + 1] = 10 * b[i + 1];
```

Here we see that the first and second lines do not depend on each other, so there is no problem with running the above in parallel as one execution set.

Finally, we reach the point where three instructions in our loop are all being performed in one cycle:

```
c[i] = 10 * d[i];
b[i + 1] = 10 * c[i + 1];
a[i + 2] = 10 * b[i + 2];
```

Now we see how to parallelize the loop and pipeline, the final software pipelined will first have some "set-up", also known as loading the pipeline. This consists of the first sets of instructions we performed above. After this we have our pipelined loop:

```
//pipeline loading – first stage
a[i]= 10 * b[i];
//pipeline loading – second stage
b[i]= 10 * c[i];
a[i+1]= 10 * b[i+1];
//pipelined loop
for (i=0; i<100-2; i=i+1)
{
c[i]= 10 * d[i];
b[i+1]= 10 * c[i+1];
a[i+2]= 10 * b[i+2];
}
//after this, we still have 2 more partial loops:
c[i+1]= 10 * d[i+1];
b[i+2]= 10 * c[i+2];
//final partial iteration
c[i+2]= 10 * d[i+2];
```

By pipelining the loop, we enabled the compiler to reduce the number of cycles for MACs from 300 to:

3 MACs that can be performed in 2 cycles for pipeline loading
100 cycles (3 MACs each) in the core of our loop
3 MACs that can be performed in 2 cycles for pipeline loading

for a total of 104 cycles or roughly 1/3 of the execution time, thus reducing the amount of time the core clocks must be active by 3× for the same functionality! Similar to the loop unrolling case, the pipelining case has enabled us to save substantially: ~43% total power over the time this routine is executed.

Eliminating recursion

An interesting technique is to eliminate recursive procedure calls in order to reduce function call overhead.

Recursive procedure calls require the function's general context, etc., to be pushed onto the stack with each call. So in the classic case of the factorial example ($n!$), this can be calculated using recursion with a function as follows:

$$fn!(0) = 1 \quad \text{For } n == 0$$
$$fn!(n) = fn!(n-1); \quad \text{For } n > 0$$

If this recursive factorial function is called with $n = 100$, there would be ~100 function calls entailing 100 branches to subroutines (which are change of flow routines which affect the program counter and software stack). Each change of flow instruction takes longer to execute because not only is the core pipeline disrupted during execution, but every branch adds at least a return address to the call stack. Additionally, if multiple variables are being passed, these also must be pushed onto the stack.

This means that this recursive subroutine requires 100× individual writes to physical memory and related stall as writes/reads to memory will not be pipelined and 100× pipeline stalls due to change of flow.

We can optimize this by moving to a simple loop

```
int res = 1;
for(int i = 0; i<n; i++)
{
res* = i;
}
```

This function requires no actual writes to the stack/physical memory as there are no function calls/jumps. As this function only involves a single multiply, it qualifies as a "short loop" on certain devices, whereby the loop is entirely handled in hardware. Thanks to this feature, there are no change of flow penalties, no loop overhead either, so this effectively acts like a completely unrolled loop of multiplies (minus the memory cost).

Compared to the recursive routine, using the loop for *100 factorial* saves approximately:

- 100 changes of flow (pipeline cycle penalties)
- 100+ pushes to the stack (100× memory accesses).

For the above example, avoiding recursion savings can be estimated as follows.

The loop method's change of flow savings from avoiding pipeline disruptions depend on the pipeline length and if there is any branch prediction available in the core hardware. In the case of a 12-stage pipeline, refilling it would potentially be a 12-cycle penalty. As branch target prediction is available on some processors, this may reduce some of this penalty significantly, but not completely. We can multiply the estimated stall penalty by the factorial (iteration), which will indicate the additional active core clock cycles and thus active power consumption from the core due to recursion.

Table 13.1: Summary of power-optimization techniques.

Category	Technique	Impact
Hardware support	Power gating: via a VRM or processor-supported interface, switch off current to specific logic or peripherals of the device	High
Hardware support	Clock gating: often provided as device low-power modes, maximize the amount of clocks that can be shut down for an application	High
Hardware support	Voltage and clock scaling: where available, reduce frequency and voltage.	Processor dependent
Hardware support	Peripheral low-power modes: gating power/clock to peripherals.	Medium-High
Data flow	DDR optimizing timing: increasing timing between ACTIVATE commands	Low
Data flow	DDR interleaving: used to reduce PRECHARGE/ACTIVATE combinations	High
Data flow	DDR optimization of software organization: organizing buffers to fit into logical banks to avoid PRECHARGE/ACTIVATE commands	Medium
Data flow	DDR general configuration: avoid using modes such as open/closed page mode, which would force a PRECHARGE/ACTIVATE after each write	High
Data flow	DDR burst accesses: organize memory to make full use of the DDR burst size. This includes alignment and data packing	Medium
Data flow	Code size: optimize code and data for minimal size via compiler tools	Application dependent
Data flow	Code size: code packing	Medium
Data flow	Code size: creating functions for common tasks	Application dependent
Data flow	Code size: utilized combined function instructions (multiple instructions in one, which save size and cycles)	Processor dependent
Data flow	Code size: use tools for compression on the fly	Processor dependent
Data flow	Parallelize and pipeline accesses to memory	Medium
Data flow	Use constants and avoid zeroing out memory	Processor dependent
Data flow	Cache: layout memory to take advantage of cache set associativity	Application dependent
Data flow	Cache: use write-back model when available and feasible for application	Application dependent
Data flow	Cache: use prefetching to bring data in ahead of time and avoid miss penalties and extra dead clock cycles	Application dependent
Data flow	Cache: array merging	Application dependent
Data flow	Cache: interchanging	Application dependent
Data flow	Take advantage of DMA for memory movement	Medium
Data flow	Coprocessors: use to perform functions instead of core	Medium
Data flow	System bus configuration: configure bus to minimize stalls and bottlenecks	Application dependent
Data flow	Peripheral speed grades and bus width: optimize per usage needs.	Application dependent
Data flow	Peripheral to core flow: use interrupt processing when possible	High
Algorithmic		Medium

(Continued)

Table 13.1: (Continued)

Category	Technique	Impact
	Compiler optimization levels: use compiler optimization tools to optimize for performance to minimize cycle time in critical areas, and optimize for code size elsewhere	
Algorithmic	Instruction packing: maximize code to functionality efficiency	Medium
Algorithmic	Loop unrolling: maximizes parallelism, minimizes active clock time	High
Algorithmic	Software pipelining: another method to maximize parallelism and minimize active clock time	High
Algorithmic	Eliminating recursion: save cycle time from function call overhead	High
Algorithmic	Reducing accuracy: saving cycles by reducing calculations	Application dependent
Algorithmic	Low-power code sequences: using equivalent functions via a lower-power set of instructions	Processor dependent

The cost of recursion causing 100+ individual stack accesses is great, as even in internal device memory there is potentially an initial delay penalty for initial access. As these stack accesses will not be pipelined, initial memory delay is multiplied by the number of recursive calls. If we assume the stack is stored low-latency internal memory running at the core speed, initial latency could still be seen of the order of anywhere from 8 to 20 cycles. A 10-cycle latency for initial access would not be a problem if subsequent accesses were pipelined, meaning 100 reads have a total core stall time of 10 cycles, but in the case of recursion we have non-pipelined accesses and thus 10×100 stalls, or 1000 additional core cycles of active clock-consuming power.

In the above example, removing recursion and moving to loops reduces the total energy (power over time) consumed by the processor to complete the factorial function to less than half.

Reducing accuracy

Often programmers will over-calculate mathematical functions, using too much accuracy (too much precision), which can lead to more complicated programs requiring more functional units and more cycles.

If 16-bit integers could be used as the signal-processing application it is able to tolerate more noise, but if 32-bit integers are used instead, this could cause additional cycles for just a basic multiply. A 16-bit by 16-bit multiply can be completed in one cycle on most architectures, but a 32-bit by 32-bit may require more. Such is the case for the SC3400 DSP core, which requires two cycles instead of one, so the programmer is doubling the cycle time for the operation needlessly (inefficient processing and additional clock cycles where the core is consuming active dynamic power).

Low-power code sequences and data patterns

Another suggestion is to look at the specific instructions used for an operation or algorithm. The programmer may be able to perform exactly the same function with different commands while saving power, though the analysis and work to do this is very time-consuming and detail-oriented.

Different instructions activate different functional units, and thus different power requirements. To accurately use this, it requires the programmer to profile equivalent instructions to understand the power trade-offs.

Obvious examples could be using a MAC when only the multiply functionality is needed. Less obvious comparisons, such as the power consumption difference between using a subtraction to clear a register versus the actual clear instruction, require the programmer to profile power consumption for each instruction, as we may not know internally how the hardware goes about clearing a register.

Summary and closing remarks

In order to provide the reader with tools to optimize software for power, over 30 different optimization techniques in the areas of low power modes, current and voltage controls, memory optimization, data path optimization, and algorithmic strategies have been discussed. A summary of those techniques are provided in Table 13.1.

CHAPTER 14

Human Factors and User Interface Design for Embedded Systems

Robert Oshana

Chapter Outline

User interface design focuses on the following key areas:

- the design of interfaces between different software components;
- the design of interfaces between the software and other nonhuman producers and consumers of information;
- the design of the interface between a human and the computer.

Software Engineering for Embedded Systems.
DOI: http://dx.doi.org/10.1016/B978-0-12-415917-4.00014-1
© 2013 Elsevier Inc. All rights reserved.

Over the years, graphical user interfaces (GUIs) have helped to eliminate many of the worst interface problems. However, many GUIs remain difficult to learn, hard to use, confusing, counterintuitive, unforgiving, and frustrating.

Ben Shneiderman has provided "Eight Golden Rules of Interface Design", which are summarized below [1]:

1. **Strive for consistency:** consistent sequences of actions should be required in similar situations; identical terminology should be used in prompts, menus, and help screens; and consistent commands should be employed throughout.
2. **Enable frequent users to use shortcuts:** as the frequency of use increases, so do the user's desires to reduce the number of interactions and to increase the pace of interaction. Abbreviations, function keys, hidden commands, and macro facilities are very helpful to an expert user.
3. **Offer informative feedback:** for every operator action, there should be some system feedback. For frequent and minor actions, the response can be modest, while for infrequent and major actions, the response should be more substantial.
4. **Design dialog to yield closure:** sequences of actions should be organized into groups with a beginning, middle, and end. The informative feedback at the completion of a group of actions gives the operators the satisfaction of accomplishment, a sense of relief, the signal to drop contingency plans and options from their minds, and an indication that the way is clear to prepare for the next group of actions.
5. **Offer simple error handling:** as much as possible, design the system so the user cannot make a serious error. If an error is made, the system should be able to detect the error and offer simple, comprehensible mechanisms for handling the error.
6. **Permit easy reversal of actions:** this feature relieves anxiety, since the user knows that errors can be undone; it thus encourages exploration of unfamiliar options. The units of reversibility may be a single action, a data entry, or a complete group of actions.
7. **Support internal locus of control:** experienced operators strongly desire the sense that they are in charge of the system and that the system responds to their actions. Design the system to make users the initiators of actions rather than the responders.
8. **Reduce short-term memory load:** the limitation of human information processing in short-term memory requires that displays be kept simple, multiple page displays be consolidated, window-motion frequency be reduced, and sufficient training time be allotted for codes, mnemonics, and sequences of actions.

ISO 9241 describes several principles of the dynamic aspects of a user interface that provide the "feel" of the user interface:

- Suitability for the task; ability to support the user in effective and efficient completion of a given task.

- Self-descriptiveness: the user interface is self-descriptive when each step is immediately comprehensible through feedback from the system or is explained to the user upon request.
- Controllable: the user is able to initiate and control the direction and pace of the interaction until the point at which the goal has been met.
- Conformity with user expectations: the user interface is consistent and corresponds to the user characteristics, such as task knowledge, education, experience, and to commonly accepted conventions.
- Error tolerance: the user interface is error tolerant if, despite errors in input, the intended result may be achieved with either no or minimal action by the user.
- Suitability for individualization: the user interface can be modified to suit the task needs, individual preferences, and skills of the user.
- Suitability for learning: the user interface supports and guides the user in learning to use the system.

The user interface development model is shown in Figure 14.1. There are four main phases;

1. Understand context of use: this phase focuses on the profile of the different users who will interact with the system. The phase concentrates on users, tasks, content and work

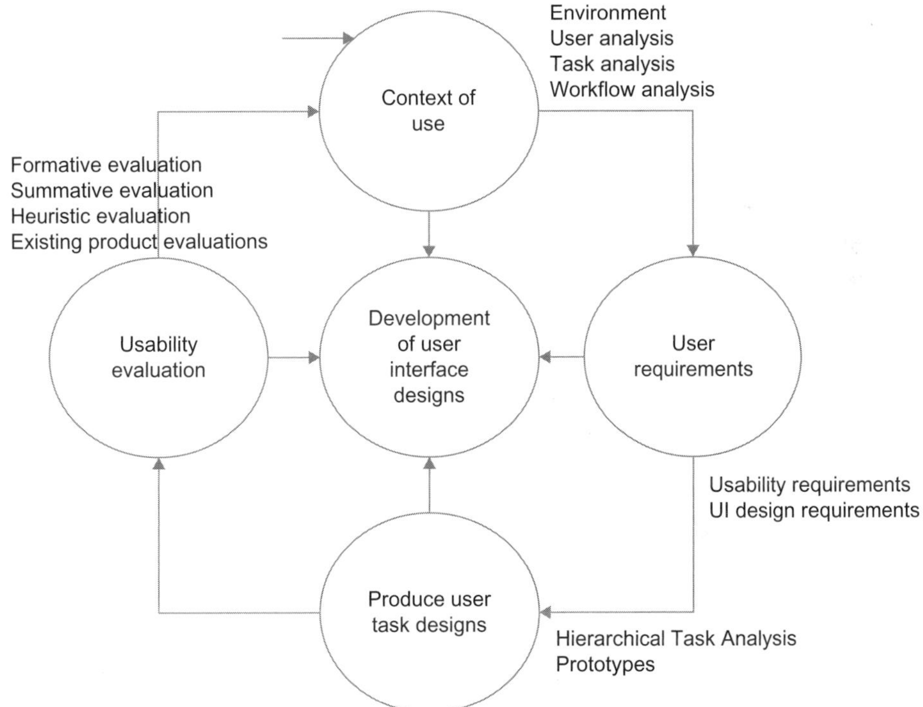

Figure 14.1:
User interface design process.

environment. Engineers study different models of system function as perceived from the outside, and delineate the human- and computer-oriented tasks that are required to achieve system function.

2. Develop user requirements: define the tasks that a user needs to accomplish and the structure of those tasks using techniques such use cases and other requirements-gathering techniques.
3. Perform usability evaluation: evaluate the user interface with representative users to validate the interface. This usually begins with a prototype that can be evaluated by the user.
4. Development of user interface designs; produce user task designs; interface design: this phase defines a set of interface objects and actions as well as the appropriate screen representations that enable a user to perform all defined tasks in a manner that meets every usability goal defined for the system

User interface design follows an iterative process as shown below and in Figure 14.2. The case study on user interface design in this book will follow this high-level flow. These topics will be discussed in more detail throughput the rest of the chapter.

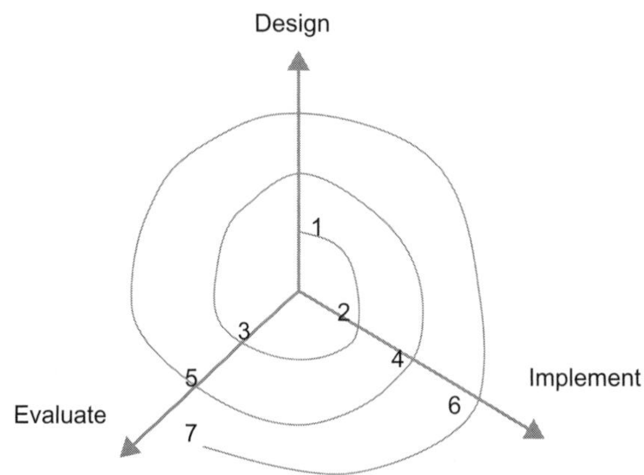

Figure 14.2:
Spiral model of user interface design.

1. Task analysis
2. Paper prototype
3. In-class user testing
4. Computer prototype
5. Heuristic evaluation
6. Implementation
7. User testing.

Four different models come into play when a user interface is analyzed and designed;

1. User profile model: this is established by a human engineer or software engineer
2. Design model: this is created by a software engineer
3. Implementation model: created by the software implementers
4. User's mental model: developed by the user when interacting with the application.

The role of the interface designer is to reconcile these differences and derive a consistent representation of the interface. Below is a discussion of each of these models in more detail.

1. User profile model: this model describes the profile of the end-users of the system. This model is based on user characteristics such as age, gender, physical abilities, education, cultural and ethnic background, motivation, goals, and personality. The user model also focuses on the syntactic knowledge of the user, which describe the mechanics of interaction required to use the interface effectively. The user model also takes into consideration the semantic knowledge of the user. Semantic knowledge focuses on the user's understanding of the functions performed by the application and the overall objectives of the system. The user model generally categorizes users as novices with little syntactic or semantic knowledge of the system, intermittent users with some semantic knowledge but low recall of syntactic information of the system, and frequent users with good semantic and syntactic knowledge (frequent users of short cuts and advanced operations).
2. Design model: this model is derived from the analysis phase of the requirements and takes into consideration the data, and architectural, procedural, and interface aspects of the software. The design model is driven by information in the requirements specification that characterizes the user of the system.
3. Implementation model: this model describes the look and feel of the user interface and supporting information such as help files and tutorials that work together to describe system syntax and semantics. The implementation model should align with the user's mental model so that the user feels comfortable with the user interface and uses it effectively. The implementation model is a translation of the design model and provides the realization of the information contained in the user profile model as well as the user's mental model.
4. Mental model: metaphors involve the use of a concept or word from one setting or environment, usually in the real world, to convey meaning in another environment, such as the digital world. Some of these metaphors are based on physical analogies, such as a spreadsheet or file cabinet. Metaphors can also be based on cultural standards such as color or words. Metaphors help reduce the cognitive load of the user. The use of metaphors in user interface design should be based on an understanding of the user's mental model. Then it's the responsibility of the user interface designer to communicate that metaphor to the user through the user interface (Figure 14.3).

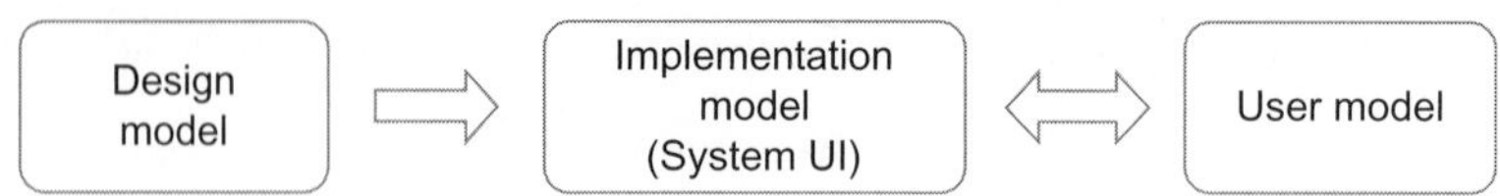

Figure 14.3:
Design model versus user model.

Examples of metaphors include:

- form fill-ins (paper-based forms as a metaphor)
- digital camera software (photo album as a metaphor)
- tabs in a GUI (physical filing system as a metaphor)
- radio buttons (exclusive AM/FM selection as a metaphor)
- play, FF, REW, and Pause symbols (borrowed from electronics)
- input devices (video games – not just buttons and joysticks).

The detailed tasks and deliverables required when developing a user interface design are listed below. The rest of this chapter will discuss each of these steps. The user interface case study shows the details of these steps when applied to an embedded system.

Analysis phase of user interface design

1. Describe the vision.
2. Describe the metaphors and mental models to be used.
3. Elicitation and task analysis
   a. Develop a data model of the system
   b. Develop a task list
   c. Develop the appropriate user profiles
   d. Develop user scenarios
   e. Develop the appropriate use cases and scenarios
   f. Develop a hierarchical task analysis (HTA)
   g. Develop a concur task tree.

First design iteration

- Create a first design using virtual windows
- Develop a CREDO matrix (Create-Read-Edit-Delete-Overview) to verify the virtual windows
- Develop a first prototype using hand sketches (low-fidelity hand-drawn mockup)
- Identify the gestalts being used in the design

- Describe how the gestalts are suitable for the user tasks
- Describe the mental models used for data, functions, and domain
- Perform usability testing on first prototype with prospective users
  - Perform a heuristic evaluation on the prototype
  - Perform a "problem counts" analysis
  - Create a defect list.

Develop a second prototype (high-fidelity tool-drawn mockup)

- Develop a functional prototype (screen prototype)
- Develop the functional design
- Attach semantic and search functions to the virtual windows
- Define undo mechanisms
- Transform virtual windows to real screens
- Add navigation functions to the screens
- Add appropriate color to the prototype
- Choose presentation formats for functions
- Support transition from novice to expert
- Put pieces together into a prototype
- Usability test and defect correction
- Create a test log and test report
- Develop a support plan for the product, including user documentation.

During the user analysis phase, there are several open-ended questions to help drive user analysis.

1. Are the users trained professionals, technicians, clerical or manufacturing workers?
2. What level of formal education does the average user have?
3. Are the users capable of learning on their own from written materials or have they expressed a desire for classroom training?
4. Are the users expert typists or are they keyboard phobic?
5. What is the age range of the user community?
6. Will the users be represented predominantly by one gender?
7. How are users compensated for the work they perform or are they volunteers?
8. Do users work normal office hours, or do they work whenever the job is required?
9. Is the software to be an integral part of the work users do, or will it be used only occasionally?
10. What is the primary spoken language among users?
11. What are the consequences if a user makes a mistake using the system?
12. Are users experts in the subject matter that is addressed by the system?
13. Do users want to know about the technology that sits behind the interface?

Essential use cases

An essential use case is a simplified, abstract, generalized use case that captures the intentions of a user in a technology- and implementation-independent manner. An essential use case is expressed in the language of the application domain and the users. The description, however, is more of an abstract and technology-free (implementation-independent) description of a task or interaction. Essential use cases show user intentions and desire followed by a system response. Essential use cases are at the user/system level only. Essential use cases are used to defer implementation-oriented discussion until later in the design process.

Scenarios for user analysis

Scenarios are built on the information gathered in initial system workflow analysis. Scenarios can focus on the functional level or the task-level detail. High-level scenarios, similar to what are discussed below, are used in the analysis phase for new products. More detailed scenarios are used later in the design phase of new products or when redesigning existing products.

Scenarios are generally individual, fictional accounts of workflow data. They are descriptions of a persona using a product to achieve a particular goal. Scenarios are narratives that tell a story describing one or more tasks in a specific environmental situation.

Scenario development identifies important aspects of using a product in the real world. Scenarios are useful throughout the user interface design process, and can also be useful in developing task descriptions for usability testing.

Hierarchal task analysis

In user interface design, a hierarchy can be thought of as an organization of task-based elements. These task-based elements describe the path of experiences a user takes to accomplish a single behavior that appears higher in the hierarchy. The user interface designer breaks down a task from top to bottom. The result is a hierarchical relationship of the tasks. Instruction is then sequenced bottom up as shown in Figure 14.4.

Design approaches to overcome user limitations of cognition, perception, and learning

The cognitive approach to user interface design takes into cosideration the abilities of the human brain and sensory perception and uses this to develop a user interface that will support the end user.

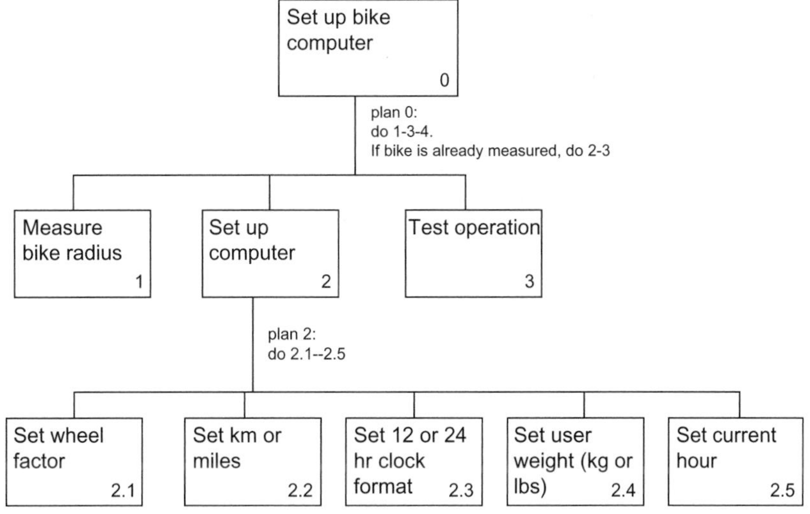

Figure 14.4:
HTA for an embedded bike computer.

Another cognitive issue to consider is the user's attention span. Attention span varies based on environment of use, and the perceived mental workload involved in completing a specific task. Users generally can focus well on only one task at a time.

Workload is measured by the amount of information communicated to each sensory system (visual, auditory, etc.) at a given moment. A good example is Adobe Flash. Some user interfaces incorporate Adobe Flash in the system to impress the user. However, if the Flash presentation does not directly support the user's task, the user's attention may become distracted, or overloaded, by too much auditory and visual information. Overloading the user's memory is a common problem in user interfaces.

Error messages

Errors messages are important in user interface design. The characteristics of good error messages include:

1. A problem: states that a problem occurred.
2. A cause: explains why the problem occurred.
3. A solution: provides a solution so that users can fix the problem.

Additionally, good error messages are presented in a way that is:

- Relevant: the message presents a problem that users care about.
- Actionable: users should either perform an action or change their behavior as the result of the message.

- User-centered: the message describes the problem in terms of target user actions or goals, not in terms of what the code is unhappy with.
- Brief: the message is as short as possible, but no shorter.
- Clear: the message uses plain language so that the target users can easily understand problem and solution.
- Specific: the message describes the problem using specific language, giving specific names, locations, and values of the objects involved.
- Courteous: users shouldn't be blamed or made to feel stupid.
- Rare: displayed infrequently. Frequently displayed error messages are a sign of bad design.

ISO 9241 provides additional guidelines for user feedback and guidance;

- Readily distinguishable from other displayed information.
- Specific for the current context of use.
- Prompts indicating explicitly (specific prompts) or implicitly (generic prompts) that the system is available for input.
- Feedback informing about the user's input timely, perceptible, and non-intrusive.
- Status information indicating the continuing state of the application, the system's hardware and software components, and the user's activities.
- Error management including error prevention, error correction, user support for error management, and error messages.
- On-line help for system-initiated and user-initiated requests with specific information for the current context of use.

Virtual windows

Soren Lauesen [3] describes user interface design as comprising three major activities:

1. organizing data into a set of windows or frames
2. defining functions that let the user control the system
3. designing the graphical appearance of windows and functions.

These three design activities build on previous analysis results such as hierarchical task analysis and data modeling. These activities also include checking activities such as reviews and usability tests. The goal of this process is to create a user interface that is easy to learn, easy to understand, and also supports user tasks efficiently.

The approach uses two systematic approaches that have been used quite extensively.

1. Data-oriented approach: this starts with a description of the data the system must maintain, a data model (entity relationship diagram, ERD) will be used to create this.

Using the ERD, user interface designers define a set of windows such that all data is visible. The functions generally are standard functions for creating, updating, and deleting data.

2. task-oriented approach: the traditional approach used for user interface design discussed in previous sections.

A virtual-windows technique is used to pull these two together. This approach uses data and tasks at the same time. The approach is used to design and test the graphical appearance of the interface before the functions are fully defined.

Lauesen describes a virtual window as a picture on an idealized screen. These idealized screens or windows show data but have no widgets (buttons, menus, etc.). Gestalts are used to format and organize the data in these virtual windows. Complex applications need several virtual windows.

Data models using entity relationship diagrams (ERD)

An ERD is a picture showing the information created, stored, and used by a computer system. The key components are entities, attributes, and relationships.

Entities generally represent similar kinds of information. Attributes describe details about the entities. Lines drawn between entities show relationships among the data.

ERD symbols can show when one instance of an entity can be related to only one or many instances of another entity.

The following steps are used to create an ERD.

Step 1: identify the entities. Identify major categories of information. If available, check the process models for data stores, external entities, and data flows. Check the major inputs and outputs from the use cases. Verify that there is more than one instance of the entity that occurs in the system.

Step 2: add appropriate attributes. Identify attributes of the entity that are relevant to the system under development. Check the process model repository entries for details on data flows and data stores. Check the data requirements of the requirements definition. Interview knowledgeable users. Perform document analysis on existing forms and reports.

Step 3: Draw the relationships. Start with an entity and identify all entities with which it shares relationships. Describe the relationship with the appropriate verb phrase. Determine the cardinality and modality by discussing the business rules with knowledgeable users.

Cardinality refers to the number of times instances in one entity can be related to instances in another entity. There are three types of cardinality:

- **(1:1)** → "one-to-one": one instance in an entity refers to one and only one instance in the related entity;
- **(1:N)** → "one-to-many": one instance in an entity refers to one or more instances in the related entity;
- **(M:N)** → "many-to-many": one or more instances in an entity refer to one or more instances in the related entity.

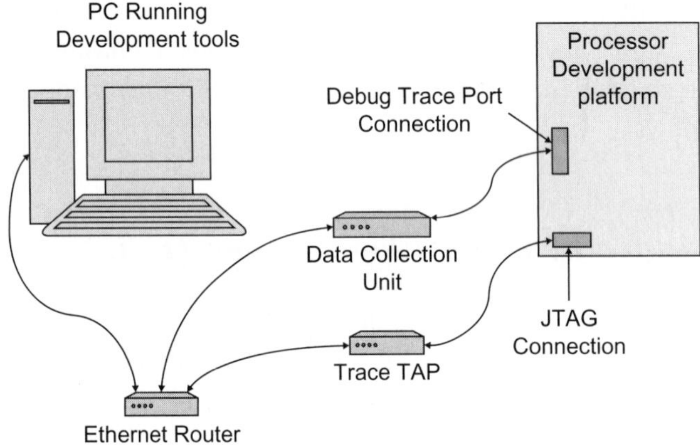

Figure 14.5:
Embedded trace capability.

As an example of creating an ERD for an embedded system, consider the example below for an embedded trace tools capability. This is shown in Figure 14.5. The embedded processor development platform provides a debug trace port connection as well as a standard JTAG connection. The user can extract program counter information as well as debug information while the software application executes on the embedded platform.

The key data required in the user interface is;

- C source code information
- assembly code related to the C code
- debug information from the target device.

This information can be represented using the data model (ERD) shown in Figure 14.6. The key entities are the C source code, the assembly instructions, and the debug messages. There is a relationship between the C source code and the assembly instructions. There can be one or more assembly instructions for each line of C code. This relationship is shown in Figure 14.6. Each assembly line of code can also relate to one of more debug messages. This relationship is also shown in Figure 14.6.

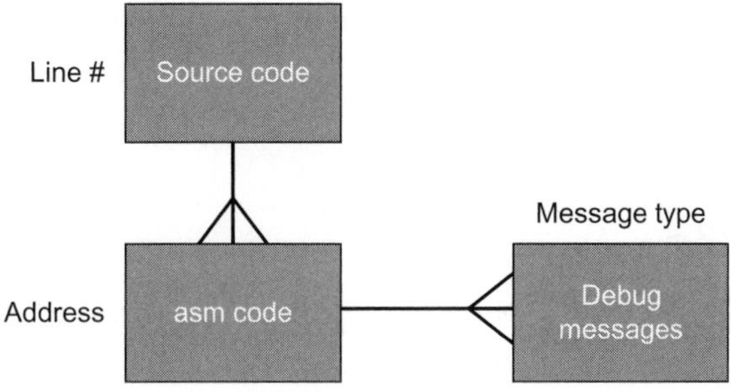

Figure 14.6:
ERD for embedded trace data.

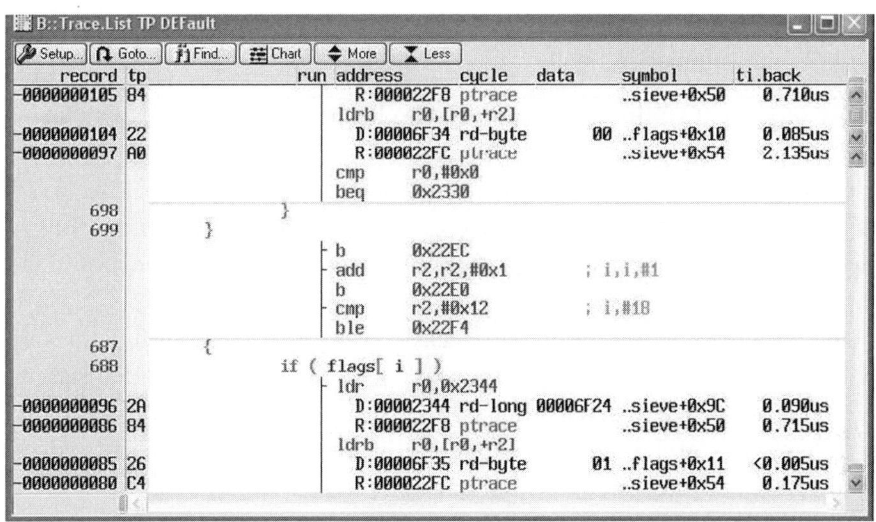

Figure 14.7:
Display for ERD model.

The tight relationship between C source code and assembly code, as well as the relationship between assembly code and debug messages, must be preserved in the user interface. This is shown in Figure 14.7. The C source code, the assembly code, and the debug messages are shown chronologically for a seamless user experience for analyzing this information.

Analysis of virtual windows using a CREDO matrix

CREDO stands for “Create, Read, Edit, Delete, Overview” and represents the different operations on data in a system. We can check whether we have all proper operations on the data in a system by comparing the user interface windows (virtual windows at this point) against the different data types.

Hueristic evaluation

Jakob Nielsen [2] has created ten general principles for assessing user interface design. These are referred to as "heuristics" because they are essentially rules of thumb instead of specific usability guidelines. Heuristic evaluation is a systematic inspection of a user interface design for usability. Heuristic evaluation can help find usability problems in the design so that they can be fixed as part of the iterative design process. A small set of evaluators examine the user interface and assess its compliance with these usability principles.

These heuristics are summarized below:

1. **Visibility of system status**: the system should keep users informed about status using appropriate feedback within reasonable time.
2. **Match between system and the real world**: the system should speak the users' language, with words, phrases and concepts familiar to the user, rather than system-oriented terms. User interface design should follow real-world conventions, and information should appear in a natural and logical order.
3. **User control and freedom**: users will occasionally choose system functions by mistake and will need a clearly marked "emergency exit" to leave the unwanted state without having to go through an extended dialogue.
4. **Consistency and standards**: users should not be burdened with having to determine whether different words, situations, or actions mean the same thing.
5. **Error prevention**: good error messages and careful design preventing problems from occurring in the first place are a primary goal for user interface design. Error-prone conditions should be eliminated, or the system must check for them and present users with a confirmation option before they commit to any action.
6. **Recognition rather than recall**: the user's memory load should be minimized by making objects, actions, and options visible. Users should not have to remember information from one part of the interface to another. Instructions for use of the system should be visible or easily retrievable.
7. **Flexibility and efficiency of use**: accelerators such as hot keys, short cuts, and icons should be used to speed up the interaction for the expert user such that the system can cater to both inexperienced and experienced users. Users should be allowed to tailor frequent actions.
8. **Aesthetic and minimalist design**: dialogs with the user should not contain information which is irrelevant or rarely needed. Eliminate unnecessary dialog "noise".

9. **Help users recognize, diagnose, and recover from errors**: error messages should be easy to understand, conveyed in plain language, accurately indicate the problem, and constructively suggest a solution.
10. **Help and documentation**: help and documentation should be provided when necessary, but not as a crutch for bad design. This information should be easy to search and be focused on the user's task. This information should list concrete steps to be carried out, and not be too large or wordy.

Gestalts

The operational principle of gestalt psychology describes the brain as holistic, parallel, and analog, with self-organizing tendencies. The gestalt principle maintains that the human eye sees objects in their entirety before perceiving their individual parts. The gestalt psychologists believe that perception is the product of complex interactions among various stimuli. This is different from the behaviorist approach, which is based on understanding the elements of cognitive processes. The gestalts, on the other hand, look to understand their organization. This gestalt effect is essentially the form-generating capability of our senses with respect to the visual recognition of figures and whole forms rather than a collection of simple lines and curves.

Three main principles are associated with gestalts:

- Grouping (proximity, similarity, continuity, closure)
- Goodness of figures
- Figure/ground relationships.

The key gestalts used in user interface design are summarized below (Figure 14.8):

- Similarity: designs with similar elements (e.g., color, size and shape) tend to be perceived as a single group. Color results in the strongest grouping effect.
- Proximity: elements placed closely together are perceived to be related.
- Closure: people tend to perceive a set of individual elements as a single, recognizable pattern rather than multiple, individual elements. Used to create interest and emphasize simplicity.
- Good continuation: aligned elements are perceived to be related. Used to indicate related elements.
- Goodness of figure: design elements are perceived to be either figure (objects of focus) or ground (background).
- Common fate: the gestalt law of common fate is a pretty simple concept. It is basically referring to visual directional lines within a design or layout.

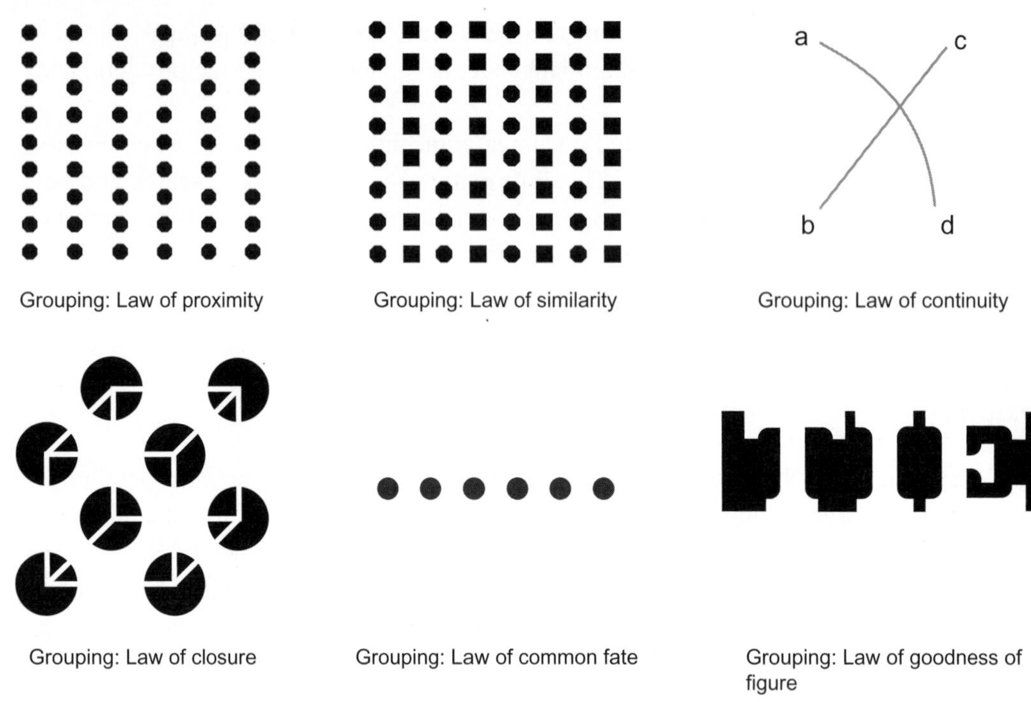

Figure 14.8:
Gestalt laws.

Designing user interfaces with Model View Controller (MVC) architecture

Model View Controller is an architectural pattern used in software engineering. The pattern isolates "domain logic" (the application logic for the user) from the user interface (input and presentation), permitting independent development, testing and maintenance of each (separation of concerns). Key responsibilities of the model include:

- Manage behavior and data of the application domain
- Respond to requests for information about its state (usually from the view)
- Respond to instructions to change state (usually from the controller).

In event-driven systems, the model notifies observers (usually views) when the information changes so that they can react. The view renders the model into a form suitable for interaction, typically a user interface element. Multiple views can exist for a single model for different purposes. A viewport typically has a one-to-one correspondence with a display surface and knows how to render to it.

The controller receives input and initiates a response by making calls on the model object. A controller accepts input from the user and instructs the model and viewport to perform actions based on that input. An MVC application may be a collection of model/view/controller triads, each responsible for a different UI element.

The MVC control flow works as follows:

- The user interacts with the user interface in some way (for example, presses a button).
- The controller handles the input event from the user interface, often via a registered handler or callback, and converts the event into appropriate user action, understandable for the model.
- The controller notifies the model of the user action, possibly resulting in a change in the model's state. (For example, the controller updates the user mode.)
- A view queries the model in order to generate an appropriate user interface.
- The view gets its own data from the model (e.g., the controller may issue a general instruction to the view to render itself). In others, the view is automatically notified by the model of changes in state (Observer) which require a screen update.
- The user interface waits for further user interactions, which restarts the cycle.

Context of the MVC software architecture

The purpose of many computer systems is to retrieve data from a data store and display it for the user. After the user changes the data, the system stores the updates in the data store. Because the key flow of information is between the data store and the user interface, you might be inclined to tie these two pieces together to reduce the amount of coding and to improve application performance. However, this seemingly natural approach has some significant problems. One problem is that the user interface tends to change much more frequently than the data storage system. Another problem with coupling the data and user interface pieces is that business applications tend to incorporate business logic that goes far beyond data transmission.

Problems and forces for the MVC software architecture

Forces act on a system within a context and must be reconciled as you consider a solution to the problem. For the MVC pattern, the user interface logic tends to change more frequently than other parts of the software.

If the presentation code and the application logic are combined in a single object, then it is necessary to modify the object containing application logic every time the user interface changes. This is likely to introduce errors and require the retesting of all application logic after every minimal user interface change.

In some cases, the application displays the same data in different ways; for example, when an analyst prefers a certain view of data whereas another user prefers a different format. In some user interfaces, multiple views of the same data are shown at the same time. If the user changes data in one view, the system must update all other views of the data automatically.

Solution using the MVC

The Model View Controller pattern separates the modeling of the domain, the presentation, and the actions based on user input into three separate classes (Figure 14.9):

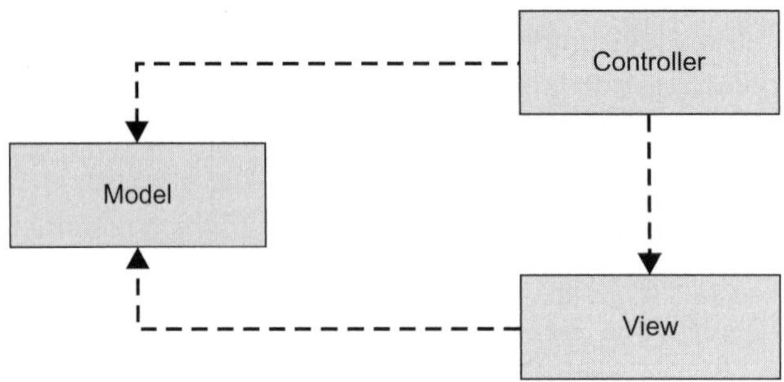

Figure 14.9:
High level context of a Model View Controller architecture.

- **Model**: the model manages the behavior and data of the application domain, responds to requests for information about its state (usually from the view), and responds to instructions to change state (usually from the controller).
- **View**: the view manages the display of information.
- **Controller**: the controller interprets the mouse and keyboard inputs from the user, informing the model and/or the view to change as appropriate

Figure 14.10 shows an example of an application partitioning for an example MVC implementation.

Safety-critical user interfaces

The amount of interaction a user has with the interface can be described using a scale. This scale is summarized below.

- Human does everything
- Computer tells human options available
- Computer tells human options available and suggests one
- Computer suggests an action and implements it if asked
- Computer suggests action, informs human, and implements it if not stopped in time

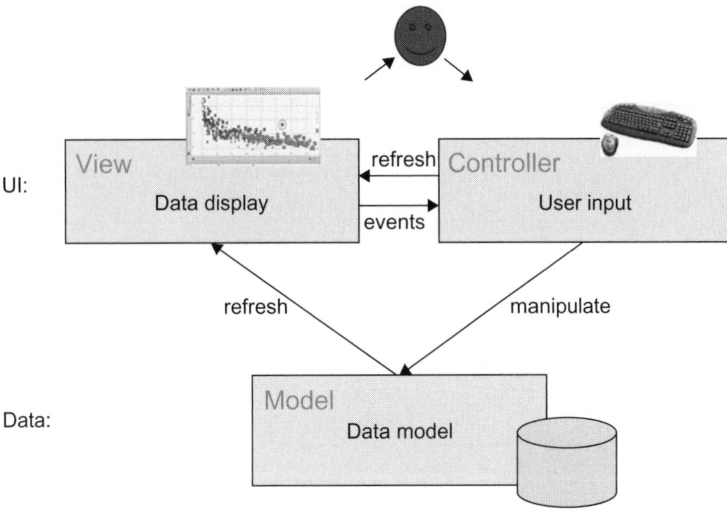

Figure 14.10:
MVC application partitioning.

- Computer selects and implements action if not stopped in time and then informs human
- Computer selects and implements action and tells human if asked
- Computer selects and implements action and tells human if designer decides human should be told
- Computer selects and implements action without any human involvement.

It is possible to reduce error through appropriate design techniques such as:

- Assume the existence of errors
- Continually provide feedback
- Continually interact with the operators in an effective manner
- Allow for the worst situation possible.

Standard process involves task analysis, simulation, design and evaluation. For safety-critical systems, system hazard analysis used to identify high-risk tasks and potentially safety-critical operator errors.

Process for designing a safer HMI

The process for designing a safety-critical user interface is shown in Figure 14.11.

Safety-critical user interfaces should match tasks to human characteristics. They should take account of human characteristics and variability rather than try to change humans. The key goal is to match the task to the human, which means taking advantage of human problem-solving capabilities and reducing the number of human actions that cause accidents. Do not

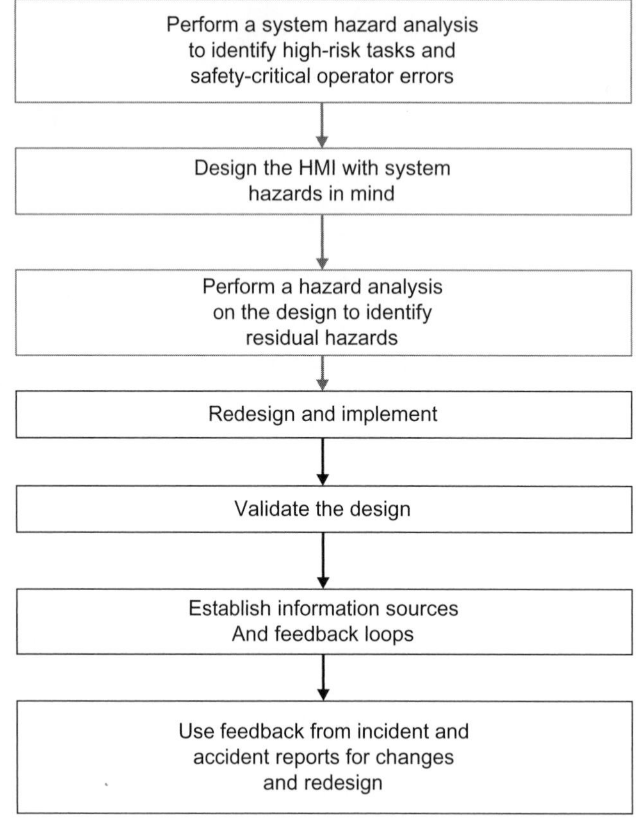

Figure 14.11:
Process flow for safety-critical user interfaces.

assume that systems will be operated by perfect humans who never take short cuts or break the rules. If computers automate too much, the human is left with a set of miscellaneous tasks which will be difficult to execute without error. There are three basic issues in designing safety-critical user interfaces based on human characteristics:

- Alertness: routine tasks tend to degenerate. Automation is not the solution in these cases. It is possible to reduce the quantity of tasks but not their quality. This creates an even more burdensome task of monitoring the system of automatic control. As awareness of the human increases, accident potential decreases. Awareness of the elevated risk associated with an operation provides a better measure of accident potential than the elevation of the risk level itself. Complacency of normal and routine jobs elevates the actual risk. The goal is to introduce a challenge. Introduce a goal or team event. This is good at reducing complacency. Another approach is to provide latitude for making decisions.

- Task allocation: safety-critical user interfaces should be automated for productivity and capacity. If the human is to be included in the safety-critical "control loop" in any capacity, then there must an accurate mental model of the system. The key challenge is how much and what type of involvement should there be. How should tasks be allocated across human and machine?

There exist several design considerations related to task allocation that must be understood when designing safety-critical user interfaces. For example, using a computer to make decisions or to simplify decision-making should be carefully done. Simplifying the decision-making too much may lead to additional errors. Overall performance is dependent on what is currently being done as well as what was done in the past. Human performance varies over time and task demands also change over time. To reduce overall system risk, user decision-making and input are required for hazardous operations such as target selection as well as weapon launch decisions. Total workload must be considered and analyzed when the operator is in the loop.

The type of workload is also important. The intermittency of visual information can impact overall user workload. Whether a user is monitoring a single instrument or many is also important. Humans require longer detection time as well as sufficient practice in controlling safety-critical systems.

When designing a safety-critical system allocation decisions are important. The key question is who does the allocation and when?

Option 1: the user is in charge and requests help when desired. The computer is assigned tasks that the operator chooses not to perform. In this scenario, extra operator workload is required. The user makes the final decisions but the computer makes suggestions to the user.
Option 2: the computer is in charge of task allocation. The user has override capability. This is more of a dynamic allocation scheme, where tasks are allocated according to whether the user or computer has the best resources available to perform the task(s).

- Error tolerance: human error is a necessary condition for successful problem-solving. Humans also use experimentation to solve problems and learn. Because of this, attempt to get rid of routine decision-making since errors are an inevitable result. With manual control, humans obtain enough feedback in a few seconds to correct actions. But irreversible or uncorrectable or nonobservable actions are considered errors.

The goal is to provide feedback about errors. Make errors observable by providing feedback about them, for example echoing characters back to the user. The same feedback principle applied to design of process control applied to human behavior. Task design must take into account the ability of the operator to monitor themselves (for example electronic checklists for pilots).

Feedback should be provided against four error types:

1. Forgetting what the current item is and inadvertently skipping it
2. Skipping items because of interrupts or distractions
3. Intentionally skipping an item and forgetting to get back to it
4. Stating that an item was accomplished when it was not.

Guidelines for safe human-machine interface design

Finally we will summarize a number of guidelines for safe human-machine interface design.

- Design the HMI to augment human abilities, not replace them
- Begin the design process by considering the operator and continue that perspective throughout
- Involve operators in design decisions and safety analysis throughout development
- Allow latitude in how tasks are accomplished
- Distinguish between providing help and taking over; do not oversimplify the operator's task
- Design for error tolerance
    - Make errors observable (provide feedback about actions and the state of a system)
    - Provide time to reverse them
    - Provide compensating (reversing) actions
- Maintain manual involvement or ways to update mental models
- Make safety-enhancing actions easy and robust; stopping an unsafe event should be possible with a single keystroke
- Make potentially dangerous actions difficult or impossible
- Integrate critical actions into the task
- Make safety-critical operational steps incremental
- Design to stereotypes and cultural norms
- Provide adequate feedback to keep operators in the loop
- If the operator is to monitor automatic systems, provide independent information
- Distinguish processing from failure; provide real-time indication that the automated control system is functioning, along with information about its internal state (such as the status of sensors and actuators), its control actions, and its assumptions about the system state
- Provide facilities for operators to experiment, to update their mental models, and to learn about the system; design to enhance the operator's ability to make decisions and to intervene when required emergencies
- Do not overload the operator with too much information; provide ways for the operator to get additional information that the designer did not foresee would be needed in a particular situation

- Allow the operator to maintain manual involvement and to update mental models, maintain skills, and preserve self-confidence
- Design to aid the operator, not take over
- Provide feedback and interaction with the system
- Design tasks to be stimulating and varied, to provide good feedback, and to require active involvement of the operator in most operations
- Minimize activities requiring passive or repetitive action
- Provide multiple ways to change from an unsafe to a safe state
- Provide interlocks to prevent inadvertent, potentially dangerous human actions
- Provide error messages that distinguish safety-critical states or errors from non-safety-critical ones
- Distinguish the override of safety-critical and non-safety-critical error or hazard conditions
- Provide operators with feedback if commands are canceled (not executed) because of timeouts or other reasons
- Flag rather than remove obsolete information from computer displays; require the user to clear it explicitly or implicitly
- If important information changes in a very short interval before or after the operator issues a command, make sure the operator is aware of the changes
- Highlight the status of safety-critical components or variables and present information about the complete state in an unambiguous manner
- For robot systems, signal bystanders when the machine is powered up; provide warnings when a hazardous zone is entered; do not assume that humans will not have to enter the robot's area
- If the automatic system detects an unsafe condition, inform the operator of the anomaly detected, the action taken, and current system configuration
- Do not permit overrides of potentially safety-critical failures or clearing of status data until all data has been displayed and perhaps not until the operator has acknowledged seeing it
- After an emergency stop, require the operator to go through the complete restart sequence
- While safety interlocks are being overridden, their status should be displayed; the design should require confirmation that the interlocks have been restored before allowing resumption of normal operation
- Avoid designs that require or encourage management by exception
- Continually update operators on the current process state
- Provide alternative sources of critical information in case the computer display fails
- Provide independent means for operators to check safety-critical information
- Provide multiple physical devices and logical paths to ensure that a single hardware failure or software error cannot prevent the operator from taking action to maintain a safe system state and avoid hazards

- Instrumentation meant to help operators deal with a malfunction should not be able to be disabled by the malfunction itself
- Minimize spurious signals and alarms; provide operators with straightforward checks to distinguish hazards from faulty instruments
- Safety-critical alarms should be distinguishable from routine alarms; the form of the alarm should indicate the need for urgency
- Clearly indicate which condition is responsible for the alarm display
- Provide the operator with as much temporal information about events and state changes as possible
- Provide scannable displays that allow operators to diagnose using pattern recognition; provide information, if appropriate, in a form in which patterns can be easily recognized
- Use group displays rather than overviews; consider using parallel information presentation on multiple screens
- Make all information needed for a single decision process visible at the same time (for example, put it on one display)
- Avoid displaying absolute values: show changes and use analog instead of digital displays when they are more appropriate; provide references for judgment
- Designs should reflect normal tendencies and expectations; use icons with a standard interpretation; choose icons that are meaningful to users, not necessarily to designers
- Minimize the semantic distance between interface displays and mental models
- Make the physical form of the vocabulary components structurally similar to their meanings (minimize articulatory distance)
- Apply the following precedence: 1, relative position; 2, shape; 3, color; and 4, labels
- Make labels brief, bold, simple, and clear
- Use color coding, highlighting, and other attention-demanding devices for safety-critical information
- Use uniformity when helpful, but don't overuse it
- Place frequently used displays centrally and group displays of information used together
- Make warning displays brief and simple
- Design the control panel to mimic the physical layout of the plant or system.

References

[1] B. Schneiderman, Designing the User Interface: Strategies for Effective Human-Computer Interaction, fifth ed., Addison-Wesley Computing.

[2] J. Nielsen, Usability Engineering.

[3] S. Lauesen, M.B. Harning, Virtual windows: linking user tasks, data models, and interface design, IEEE Softw (July/August 2001).

Bibliography

J. Johnson, Designing with the Mind in Mind: Simple Guide to Understanding User Interface Design Rules.

S. Lauesen, User Interface Design: A Software Engineering Perspective.

CHAPTER 15

Embedded Software Quality, Integration and Testing Techniques

Mark Pitchford

Chapter Outline

Software Engineering for Embedded Systems.
DOI: http://dx.doi.org/10.1016/B978-0-12-415917-4.00015-3
© 2013 Elsevier Inc. All rights reserved.

What is software test?

There is some inconsistency in how the word "test" is used in the context of software development. For some commentators, "software test" implies the execution of software and the resulting confirmation that it performs as was intended by the development team – or not. Such a definition views the inspection or analysis of source code as a different field; that is, one to be contrasted with software test rather than a branch of it.

For the purposes of this chapter, The Oxford English Dictionary's definition of the word "test" is applied: "a procedure intended to establish the quality, performance, or reliability of something, especially before it is taken into widespread use".

Any activity which fits that definition can, therefore, be regarded as software test, whether it involves code execution or not.

The generic term "static analysis" is used to describe a branch of software test involving the analysis of software without the execution of the code. Conversely, "dynamic analysis" describes a branch of software test in which the code is indeed executed.

Why should we test software?

Returning to the definition of "test", software is tested to establish its "quality, performance or reliability". Testing itself only establishes these characteristics; it does not of itself guarantee that software meets any particular criteria for them.

The aim, then, is to quantify the standard of the software. Whether that standard is good enough depends very largely on the context in which it will be deployed.

How much testing is enough?

The checking for adherence to coding rules or the achievement of particular quality metrics is usually easy enough to scope. Either code meets the rules or it doesn't, and if it doesn't it is either justified or corrected.

Dynamic testing is less easy to apply in even fairly trivial applications. The possible combinations and permutations of data values and execution paths can be large enough to make it wholly impractical to prove that all possible scenarios are correctly handled.

This means that almost irrespective of how much time is spent performing software tests of whatever nature, an element of risk will remain with regard to the potential failure of those remaining scenarios which remain unproven. Consequently, the decision on what and how much to test becomes a question of cost versus the impact of the identified risk outcomes. Those risk outcomes include not only the risk of software failure, but also factors such as the risk of delaying the launch of a commercial product and conceding the initiative in the market to a competitor.

Testing is not a cheap activity and there is the cost of both man-hours and associated test tools to take into account. On the opposite side of the equation lies the consequence of flawed software. What is the cost of failure? Will it kill? Maim? Cause temporary discomfort? Or merely become a minor irritation through the need to occasionally restart the application?

Clearly the level of acceptable risk to health and safety in each of these scenarios is significantly different, and the analysis is further complicated if there are also commercial risk factors to be added into that equation.

Some standards such as IEC61508 (see "Setting the standard") define a structured approach to this assessment. In this standard, Software Integrity Level (SIL) 1 is assigned to any parts of a system in continuous use for which a probability of failure on demand of 10^{-5}–10^{-6} is permissible. SILs become less demanding the higher the number assigned, so that SIL2 implies an acceptable probability of failure on demand as 10^{-6}–10^{-7}, SIL 3 as 10^{-7}–10^{-8} and SIL 4 as 10^{-8}–10^{-9}.

The standard recommends many techniques for each of these SILs on the basis that the proficient application of the specified techniques will provide sufficient evidence to suggest that the maximum acceptable risk level will not be exceeded.

Ultimately, then, the decision is about how the software can be proven to be of *adequate* quality. In many cases, this ethos allows different SIL levels to be applied to different elements of a project depending on the criticality of each such element. That principle can, of course, be extended outside the realms of high-integrity applications. It always makes sense to apply more rigorous tests to the most critical parts of an application.

When should testing take place?

To some extent, that depends on the starting point. If there is a suite of legacy code to deal with, then clearly starting at the beginning of development is not an option! However, "the sooner, the better" is a reasonable rule of thumb.

In general terms, the later a defect is found in the product development, the more costly it is to fix – a concept first established in 1975 with the publication of Brooks's *Mythical Man Month* and proven many times since through various studies (Figure 15.1).

The automation of any process changes the dynamic of justification, and that is especially true of test tools given that some are able to make earlier unit test much more feasible.

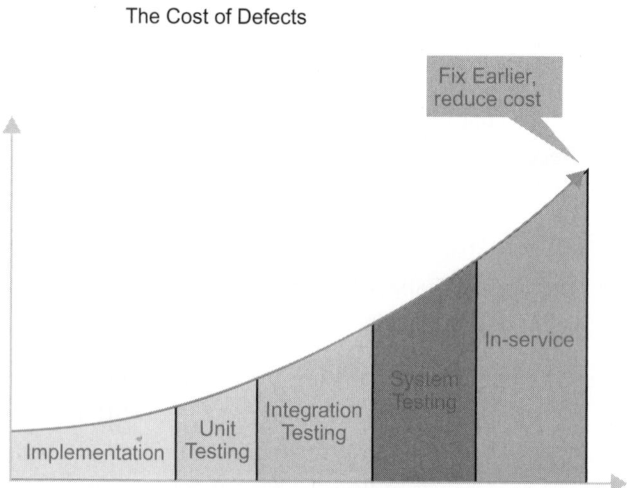

Figure 15.1:
The later a defect is identified, the higher the cost of rectifying it.

Who makes the decisions?

It is clear that the myriad of interrelated decisions on what, when, why, how and how much to test is highly dependent on the reasons for doing so.

The judgments are perhaps relatively straightforward if an outside agency is involved. For instance, the developers of a control system for use in an aircraft will have to adhere to DO-178B (or latterly DO-178C) for their product to become commercially available for use in international airspace. It then becomes clear that if the product is to sell, then a level of test which is appropriate to the standard is unavoidable.

This extends further to the qualification or certification of any tools to be used. That can vary quite significantly from one standard to another, but there are usually guidelines or instructions laid down on what is required.

Conversely, the driver might be an internal one to improve software quality and improve corporate reputation and reduce recall costs. In that case the matter is a decision for management, who will need to make judgments as to how much investment in the associated work and tools is appropriate.

Available techniques

Enter the phrase "software test" in any internet search engine, and the variation in scope of test techniques and test tools is daunting. Static analysis, coding standards, quality metrics, source code coverage, object code coverage, dynamic analysis, memory leak profiling, abstract interpretation . . . the list of buzz words and techniques is seemingly endless.

The confusion generated is compounded by the fact that the boundaries between different techniques and approaches are not as clear cut as they might be. "Static analysis" is a prime example of a term which means different things to different observers.

Static and dynamic analysis

The generic term "static analysis" is used only to indicate that the analysis of the software is performed without executing the code, whereas "dynamic analysis" indicates that the code is indeed executed. So, simple peer review of source code and functional test fit the definitions of "static analysis" and "dynamic analysis" respectively. The boundaries become blurred when it is understood that static analysis can be used to predict dynamic behavior. As a result, it is a precision tool in some contexts and yet in others it harbors approximations.

To cut through this vague terminology, it is useful to consider five key elements of analysis. These are all deployed in one form or another by analysis tools, but many can be and frequently are implemented from first principles, usually in combination to provide a "tool kit" of techniques.

The first three are approaches to static analysis. Note that these attributes do not comprehensively describe the categories of static analysis tools, many tools include more than one of these attributes, and it is possible to approximate each of them without the use of tools at all.

Code review

Code review traditionally takes the form of a peer review process to enforce coding rules dictating coding style and naming conventions and often restrict commands available for developers to a safe subset. Peer review of software source code was established to achieve effective code review long before any tools automated it, and is still effective today. The key to effective peer reviews is to establish a mutually supportive environment so that the raising of non-conformities is not interpreted as negative criticism.

If manual peer review is to be adopted with such as the MISRA standards in mind, then a subset of the rules considered most important to the developing organization is likely to yield the best results.

Many software test tools automate this approach to provide a similar function with benefits in terms of the number and complexity of rules to be checked, and in terms of speed and repeatability.

Code review does not predict dynamic behavior. However, code written in accordance with coding standards can be expected to include fewer flaws that might lead to dynamic failure, and an assurance of a consistent approach from individuals brings its own benefits in terms of readability and maintainability.

It can be applied whether the code under development is for a new project, an enhancement, or a new application using existing code. With legacy applications, automated code review is particularly strong for presenting the logic and layout of such code in order to establish an understanding of how it works with a view to further development. On the other hand, with new development the analysis can begin as soon as any code is written – no need to wait for a compilable code set, let alone a complete system.

Theorem proving

Theorem proving defines desired component behavior and individual run-time requirements.

The use of assertions within source code offers some of the benefits of the theorem-proving tools. Assertions placed before and after algorithms can be used to check that the data passing through them meets particular criteria, or is within particular bounds.

These assertions can take the form of calls to an "assert" function as provided in languages such as C++, or the form of a user-defined mechanism to perhaps raise an error message or set a system to a safe state.

Automated theorem-proof tools often use specially formatted comments (or "annotations") in the native language. These comments can be statically analyzed to confirm that the code accurately reflects these definitions, which are ignored by a standard compiler. Because of these annotations, verification can concentrate on verification conditions: that is, checking that when one starts under some preconditions and executes such a code fragment, the post condition will be met.

The writing of the annotations can be labor-intensive and so these tools tend to be limited to highly safety-critical applications where functional integrity is absolutely paramount over any financial consideration (e.g., flight control systems).

Unlike the prediction of dynamic behavior through static analysis, the use of "design by contract" principles, often in the form of specially formatted comments in the high-level code, can accurately formalize and validate expected run-time behavior of source code.

Such an approach requires a formal and structured development process, text-book style and uncompromising precision. Consequently, retrospective application of such an approach to legacy code would involve a complete rewrite of it.

Prediction of dynamic behavior through static analysis

The prediction of dynamic behavior through static analysis mathematically models the high-level code to predict the probable behavior of the executable that would be generated from it. All possible execution paths through that mathematical model are then simulated, mapping the flow of logic on those paths coupled with how and where data objects are created, used, and destroyed.

The net result consists of predictions of anomalous dynamic behavior that could possibly result in vulnerabilities, execution failure, or data corruption at run-time.

Although there is no practical way of performing exactly this technique manually, the use of assertions within source code again offers some of the benefits. Assertions placed before and after algorithms can be used to check that the data passing through them meets particular criteria, or is within particular bounds – and that includes checking for the circumstances which may cause run-time errors of the type generally sought out by tools of this nature.

As before, these assertions can take the form of calls to an "assert" function as provided in languages such as C++ or the form of a user-defined mechanism, and it is most pragmatic to use assertions in the most difficult and complex algorithms where failures are most likely to occur.

When tools are available, the static prediction of dynamic behavior works well for existing code or less rigorously developed applications. It does not rely on a formal development approach and can simply be applied to the source code as it stands, even when there is no in-depth knowledge of it. That ability makes this methodology very appealing for a development team in a fix – perhaps when timescales are short, but catastrophic and unpredictable run-time errors keep coming up during system test.

There is, however, a downside. The code itself is not executing, but instead is being used as the basis for a mathematical model. As proven by the works of Church, Gödel and Turing in the 1930s, a precise representation of the code is mathematically insoluble for all but the most trivial examples. In other words, the goal of finding every defect in a nontrivial program is unreachable unless approximations are included, which by definition will lead to "false positive" warnings.

The complexity of the mathematical model also increases disproportionately to the size of the code sample under analysis. This is often addressed by the application of simpler mathematical modeling for larger code samples, which keeps the processing time within reasonable bounds. But the increases in the number of these "false positives", which has a significant impact on the time required to interpret results, can make this approach unusable for complex applications.

The last two of the "key attributes" concern dynamic analysis. Note that these attributes do not comprehensively describe the categories of dynamic analysis, and that many tools include more than one of these attributes

An overlap between static and dynamic analysis appears when there is a requirement to consider dynamic behavior. At that point, the dynamic analysis of code which has been compiled, linked and executed offers an alternative to the prediction of dynamic behavior through Static analysis.

Dynamic analysis involves the compilation and execution of the source code either in its entirety or on a piecemeal basis. Again, while many different approaches can be included, these characteristics complete the list of the five key attributes that form the fundamental "toolbox of techniques".

Structural coverage analysis

Structural coverage analysis (SCA) details which parts of compiled and linked code have been executed, often by means of code instrumentation "probes".

In its simplest form, these probes can be implemented with manually inserted print statements as appropriate for the programming language of choice. Although such an approach demands an in-depth knowledge of the code under test and carries the potential for human error, it does have a place in smaller projects or where only practiced on a critical subset of an application.

Automated test tools automatically add probes to the high-level source code before compilation.

Adding instrumentation probes obviously changes the code under test, making it both bigger and slower. There are therefore limitations to what it can achieve, and to the circumstances under which it can be used, especially when timing errors are a concern. However, within appropriate bounds it has been highly successful and in particular has made a major contribution to the sound safety record of software in commercial aircraft.

The more sophisticated test tools on the market can perform SCA in isolation or in combination with unit, module and/or integration testing.

Unit, module and integration testing

Unit, module and integration testing (referred to as "unit testing" hereafter) all describe an approach in which snippets of software code are compiled, linked and built in order that test data (or "vectors") can be specified and checked against expectations.

Traditionally, unit testing involves the development of a "harness" to provide an environment where the subset of code under test can be exposed to the desired parameters in order for the tester to ensure that it behaves as specified. More often than not in modern development environments the application of such techniques is achieved through the use of automated or semi-automated tools. However, a manual approach can still have a place in smaller projects or where only practiced on a critical subset of an application.

Some of the leading automated unit test tools can be extended to include the automatic definition of test vectors by the unit test tool itself.

Unit testing and SCA focus on the behavior of an executing application and so are aspects of dynamic analysis. Unit, integration and system tests use code compiled and executed in a similar environment to that which is being used by the application under development.

Unit testing traditionally employs a bottom-up testing strategy in which units are tested and then integrated with other test units. In the course of such testing, individual test paths can be examined by means of SCA. There is clearly no need to have a complete code set to hand to initiate tests such as these.

Unit testing is complemented by functional testing, a form of top-down testing. Functional testing executes functional test cases, perhaps in a simulator or in a target environment, at system or subsystem level.

Clearly, these dynamic approaches test not only the source code, but also the compiler, linker, development environment, and potentially even target hardware. Static analysis techniques help to produce high-quality code which is less prone to error, but when it comes to proving correct functionality there is little alternative but to deploy dynamic analysis. Unit test or system test must deploy dynamic analysis to prove that the software actually does what it is meant to do.

Perhaps the most telling point with regard to the testing of dynamic behavior – whether by static or dynamic analysis – is precisely what is being tested. Intuitively, a mathematical model with inherent approximations compared with code being compiled and executed in its native target environment suggests far more room for uncertainty.

If the requirement is for a quick-fix solution for some legacy code which will find most problems without involving a deep understanding of the code, then the prediction of dynamic behavior via static analysis has merit. Similarly, this approach offers quick results for completed code which is subject to occasional dynamic failure in the field.

However, if there is a need to not only prove the functionality and robustness of the code, but also provide a logical and coherent development environment and integrated and progressive development process, then it makes more sense to use dynamic unit and system testing. This approach provides proof that the code is robust and that it does what it should do in the environment where it will ultimately operate.

Requirements traceability

As a basis for all validation and verification tasks, all high-quality software must start with a definition of requirements. It means that each high-level software requirement must map to a lower-level requirement, design and implementation. The objective is to ensure that the complete system has been implemented as defined. This is a fundamental element of sound software engineering practice.

Simply ensuring that high-level requirements map to something tangible in the requirements decomposition tree, design and implementation is not enough. The complete set of system requirements comes from multiple sources, including high-level requirements, low-level requirements and derived requirements. As illustrated in Figure 15.2, there is seldom a 1:1 mapping from high-level requirements to source code, so a traceability mechanism is required to map and record the dependency relationships of requirements throughout the requirements decomposition tree.

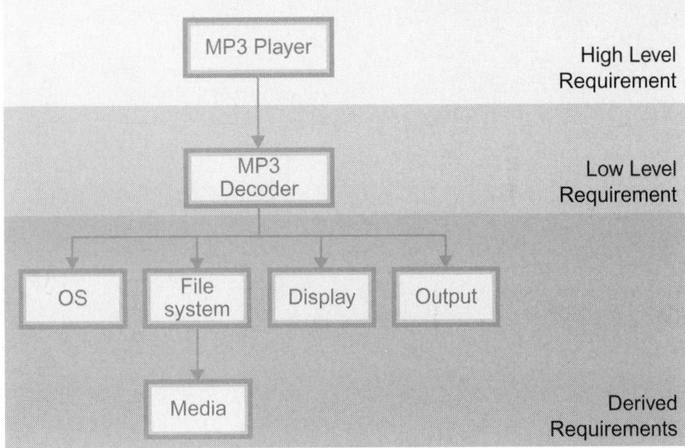

Figure 15.2:
Example of "1:many" mapping from high-level requirement through to requirements decomposition tree.

To complicate matters further, each level of requirements might be captured using a different mechanism. For instance, a formal requirements capture tool might be used for the high-level requirements while the low-level requirements are captured in PDF and the derived requirements captured in a spreadsheet.

Modern requirements traceability solutions enable mapping throughout these levels right down to the verification tasks associated with the source code. The screenshot in Figure 15.3 shows one such example of this. Using this type of requirements traceability tool, the 100% requirements coverage metric objective can be clearly measured, no matter how many layers of requirements, design and implementation decomposition are used. This makes monitoring system completion progress an extremely straightforward activity.

Most test tools ignore the requirements element of software development but the fact is that even the best static and dynamic analysis alone does not prove that the software fulfils its requirements.

Widely accepted as a development best practice, requirements traceability ensures that all requirements are implemented and that all development artifacts can be traced back to one or more requirements. With modern standards such as the automotive ISO 26262 or medical IEC 62304 requiring bidirectional traceability there is constant emphasis on the need for the derivation of one development tier from the one above it.

The ISO 26262 standard states: "The intent of this [bidirectional traceability] is to maintain the bidirectional traceability of requirements for each level of product decomposition. When the requirements are managed well, traceability can be established from the source

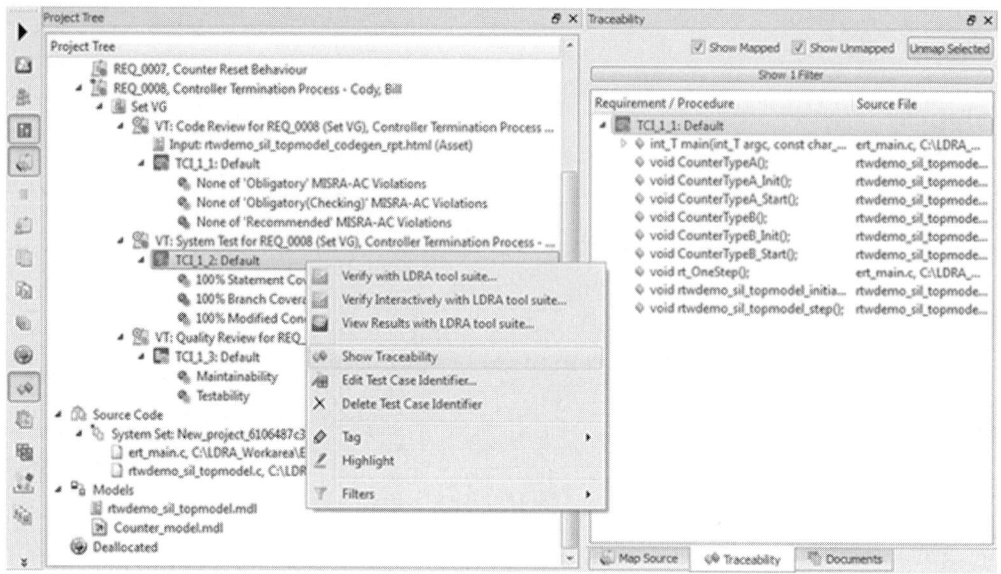

Figure 15.3:
Traceability from high-level requirements down to source code and verification tasks.

requirement to its lower-level requirements and from the lower-level requirements back to their source. Such bidirectional traceability helps determine that all source requirements have been completely addressed and that all lower-level requirements can be traced to a valid source. Requirements traceability can also cover the relationships to other entities such as intermediate and final work products, changes in design documentation, and test plans."

Such an approach lends itself to the model of a continuous and progressive use first of automated code review, followed by unit test and subsequently system test with its execution tracing capability to ensure that all code functions just as the requirements dictate, even on the target hardware itself – a requirement for the more stringent levels of most such standards.

While this is and always has been a laudable principle, last-minute changes of requirements or code made to correct problems identified during test tend to put such ideals in disarray.

Despite good intentions, many projects fall into a pattern of disjointed software development in which requirements, design, implementation, and testing artifacts are produced from isolated development phases. Such isolation results in tenuous links between requirements, the development stages, and/or the development teams.

The traditional view of software development shows each phase flowing into the next, perhaps with feedback to earlier phases, and a surrounding framework of configuration management and process (e.g., Agile, RUP). Traceability is assumed to be part of the relationships between phases. However, the reality is that while each individual phase may be conducted efficiently, the links between development tiers become increasingly poorly maintained over the duration of projects.

The answer to this conundrum lies in the requirements traceability matrix (RTM) which sits at the heart of any project even if it is not identified as such (see Figure 15.4). Whether the links are physically recorded and managed, they still exist. For example, a developer creates a link simply by reading a design specification and using that to drive the implementation.

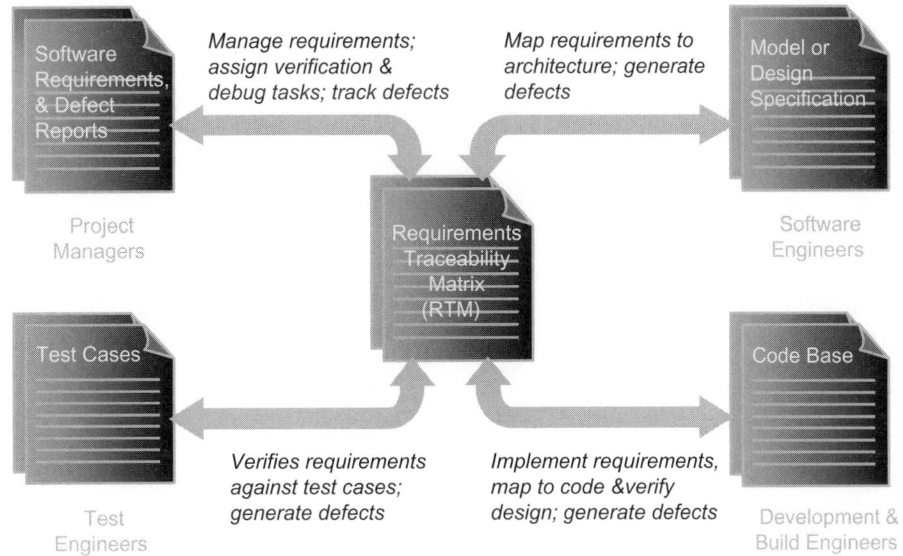

Figure 15.4:
RTM sits at the heart of the project defining and describing the interaction between the design, code, test and verification stages of development.

Safety-critical standards dictate that requirements should be traceable down to high-level code and in some cases object code, but usually more pragmatism is required. A similar approach can be taken for any project with varying levels of detail depending on criticality both of the project as a whole and within an individual project. The important factor is to provide a level of traceability which is adequate for the circumstance.

This alternative view of the development landscape illustrates the importance that should be attached to the RTM. Due to this fundamental centrality, it is vital that project managers place sufficient priority on investing in tooling for RTM construction. The RTM must also be represented explicitly in any lifecycle model to emphasize its importance, as Figure 15.5

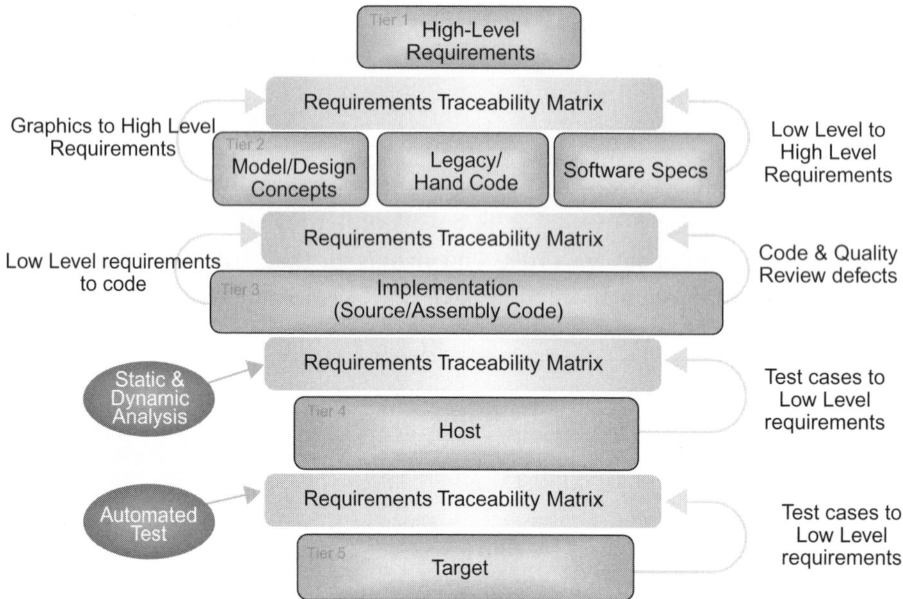

Figure 15.5:
The requirements traceability matrix (RTM) plays a central role in a development life-cycle model. Artifacts at all stages of development are linked directly to requirements matrix and changes within each phase automatically update the RTM so that overall development progress is evident from design through coding and test.

illustrates. With this elevated focus, the RTM is constructed and maintained efficiently and accurately.

When the RTM becomes the centre of the development process, it impacts on all stages of design from high-level requirements through to target-based deployment Where an application is safety-critical, each tier is likely to be implemented in full but, once again, a pragmatic interpretation of the principles can be applied to any project.

The Tier 1 high-level requirements might consist of a definitive statement of the system to be developed. This tier may be subdivided depending on the scale and complexity of the system.

Tier 2 describes the design of the system level defined by Tier 1. Above all, this level must establish links or traceability with Level 1 and begin the process of constructing the RTM. It involves the capture of low-level requirements which are specific to the design and implementation and have no impact on the functional criteria of the system.

Tier 3's implementation refers to the source/assembly code developed in accordance with Tier 2. Verification activities include code rule checking and quality analysis.

Maintenance of the RTM presents many challenges at this level as tracing requirements to source code files may not be specific enough and developers may need to link to individual functions.

In many cases, the system is likely to involve several functions. Traceability of those functions back to Tier 2 requirements includes many-to-few relationships. It is very easy to overlook one or more of these relationships in a manually managed matrix.

In Tier 4, formal host-based verification begins. Once code has been proven to meet the relevant coding standards using automated code review, unit, integration and system tests may be included in a test strategy that may be top-down, bottom-up or a combination of both. Software simulation techniques help create automated test harnesses and test case generators as necessary, and execution histories provide evidence of the degree to which the code has been tested.

Such testing could be supplemented with robustness testing if required, perhaps by means of the automatic definition of unit test vectors or through the use of the static prediction of dynamic behavior.

Test cases from Tier 4 should be repeatable at Tier 5 if required.

At this stage, we confirm that the software is functioning as intended within its development environment, even though there is no guarantee it will work when in its target environment. However, testing in the host environment first allows the time-consuming target test to merely confirm that the tests remain sound in the target environment.

Tier 5's target-based verification represents the on-target testing element of formal verification. This frequently consists of a simple confirmation that the host-based verification performed previously can be duplicated in the target environment, although some tests may only be applicable in that environment itself.

Where reliability is paramount and budgets permit, the static analysis of dynamic behavior with its "full range" data sets would undoubtedly provide a complementary tool for such an approach. However, dynamic analysis would remain key to the process.

Static analysis – adherence to a coding standard

One of the most basic attributes of code that affects quality is readability. The more readable a piece of code is, the more testable it is. The more testable a piece of code is, then the more likely it will have been tested to a reasonable level of completion. Unfortunately, as The International Obfuscated C Code Contest has demonstrated, there are many ways to create complex and unreadable code for the simplest of applications. This metric is about adopting even a basic coding standard to help enhance code quality by establishing the rules for a minimum level of readability for all of the code created within a project.

Modern coding standards go way beyond just addressing readability, however. Encapsulating the wisdom and experience of their creators, coding standards such as the Motor Industry Software Reliability Association (MISRA) C and C++ coding standards, the JSF Airborne Vehicle C++ standard or the Netrino Embedded C Coding standard also identify specific code constructs that can affect overall code quality and reliability, such as areas of C or C++ that the ISO standards states are either undefined or implementation-specific.

Coding standards such as the CERT-C or C++ Secure Coding Standards and the Common Weakness Enumeration list (CWE) also help to identify code constructs that can lead to potentially exploitable vulnerabilities in code.

The optimum coding standard for a project will depend on the project objectives. The table in Figure 15.6 provides a simple outline of the objectives for several coding standards.

Coding Standard	Language	Objective/Application
MISRA	C & C++	High reliability software
JSF Airborne Vehicle C++ Standard	C++	High reliability software
Netrino Embedded C Standard	C	Defect free Embedded C Code
CERT Secure C Coding Standard	C	Secure software

Figure 15.6:
Outline of objectives for several popular coding standards.

In practice, most projects will create their own custom standard that uses one or more of these as a baseline, and modifying the standard to suit their particular needs. Clearly, software which is highly reliable *and* secure is often desirable!

One area in particular where these reliability and security-oriented coding standards excel is in identifying code constructs that lead to latent defects, which are defects that are not normally detected during the normal software verification process yet reveal themselves once the product is released. Consider the following code:

```
#include<stdio.h>
#include<stdint.h>

#define MAX_SIZE 16U
```

```
5
6 int32_t main(void)
7 {
8 uint16_t theArray[MAX_SIZE];
9 uint16_t idx;
10 uint16_t *p_var;
11 uint16_t UR_var;
12
13 p_var = &UR_var;
14
15 for(idx = 0U; idx<= MAX_SIZE; idx + = *p_var;)
16 {
17 theArray[idx] = 1U;
18 }
19
20 for(idx = 0U; idx<MAX_SIZE; idx++)
21 {
22 printf(" %d", theArray[idx]);
23 }
24
25 return(0);
26 }
```

The above code compiles without warnings on GCC and Microsoft Visual Studio (the latter requires the user to provide a stdint.h implementation for versions earlier than 2010). By inspection an experienced programmer can find the errors in this fairly simple code that contains both an array out of bounds error (an off by one error on line 15 when variable idx == MAX_SIZE) and referencing an uninitialized variable (on line 13 as the for loop counter increment operator). Although real code is never as straightforward as this, even in this example there is some isolation from the latter issue as pointer aliasing is used to reference the UR_var variable.

At its most basic, an array out of bounds error is a buffer overflow, even though it is legal C and/or C++ code. For secure code, buffer overflow is one of the most commonly exploited vulnerabilities leading to the worst possible type of exploit: the execution of arbitrary code.

Non-determinism is also the problem with the uninitialized variable. It is impossible to predict the behavior of an algorithm when the value of its variables cannot be guaranteed. What makes this issue even worse is that some compilers will actually assign default values to uninitialized variables! For example, the Microsoft Visual Studio compiler assigns the value 0xCCCC to the variable UR_var by default in debug mode. While this value is meaningless in the context of the algorithm above, it is deterministic, so the code will always behave in the same way. Switch to release mode, however, and the value will be undefined, resulting in non-deterministic behavior (Figure 15.7).

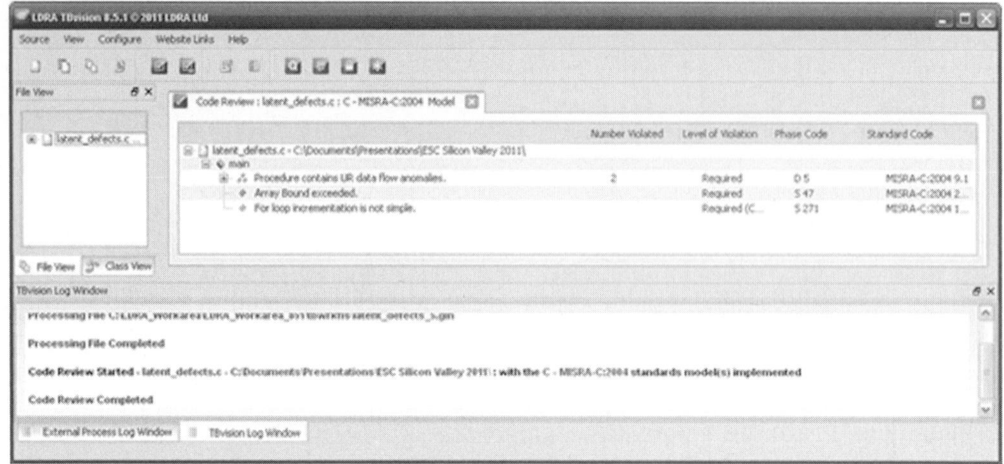

Figure 15.7:
Static analysis results showing the enforcement of the MISRA-C: 2004 coding standard for the above code, revealing 2 latent defects.

In addition to the obvious benefits of identifying and eliminating latent defects, the most significant additional benefit of using static analysis tools for coding standards enforcement is that it helps peer review productivity. By ensuring that a piece of code submitted for peer review has no code standard violations indicated as being mandatory (i.e., no violations of this type must exist in released code), the peer review team can get away from focusing on minutiae and on to what they do best; ensuring that the implementations under inspection are fit for purpose and the best that they can be.

Another area where static analysis enforcement of coding standards really excels is in the identification of areas of unnecessary code complexity.

One of the most common sources of defects in code is areas that are not practically testable due to unnecessary complexity. Complexity is not in and of itself a bad thing; complex problems require complex solutions. However, the problem arises when complex code is used where it is not necessary. This leads to sections of code that are unnecessarily difficult to read, even more difficult to test, and as a result have higher defect rates than a more straightforward equivalent implementation. Hence it follows that unnecessary complexity is to be avoided.

Several coding standards incorporate maximum code complexity limits as a measure for improving overall code quality. The following case study explains the cyclomatic complexity and knots metrics, and how they may be utilized to show how complex a function is. The case study goes on to explain how essential cyclomatic complexity and essential knots metrics may then be utilized to indicate whether or not a function has been written in a structured manner and therefore may be used to provide an indication of unnecessary complexity.

Essential knots & essential cyclomatic complexity – case study

Basic blocks and control flow branches

It is initially useful to consider how the construction of high-level software code can be described.

A basic block is a sequence of one or more consecutive, executable statements in a source program such that the sequence has a start point, an end point and no internal branches.

In other words, once the first executable statement in a basic block is executed, then all subsequent statements in that basic block can be assumed to be executed in sequence.

Control flow branches and natural succession provide the links between basic blocks.

Control flow graphs

During the static analysis of source code, it is possible to detect and understand the structure of the logic associated with that source code.

This logic can be represented by a graphical diagram, a flow graph, showing a number of basic blocks (represented by "nodes") interconnected with arrowed lines to represent the decision paths (called "links") to form a control flow graph (Figure 15.8).

Such a control flow graph forms the basis of a static flow graph when used only to show code structure, and a dynamic flow graph when superimposed with execution history information to show which parts of the source code have been executed.

In languages such as C and C++, it is often necessary to reformat the code to show only one instruction per line. This circumvents the problem of nomenclature for identifying decision points and instructions which occur within a single line of source code.

Calculating a knots value

A knot is a point where two control flows cross (Figure 15.9). A knot is not a "bad thing" per se; in fact knots are inevitable and appear in many perfectly acceptable constructs such as for, while, if/else, switch and exception.

Because they are a function of the chosen programming style and high-level language, the number of knots in a function gives an indication of the complexity added to it as a result of the program implementation.

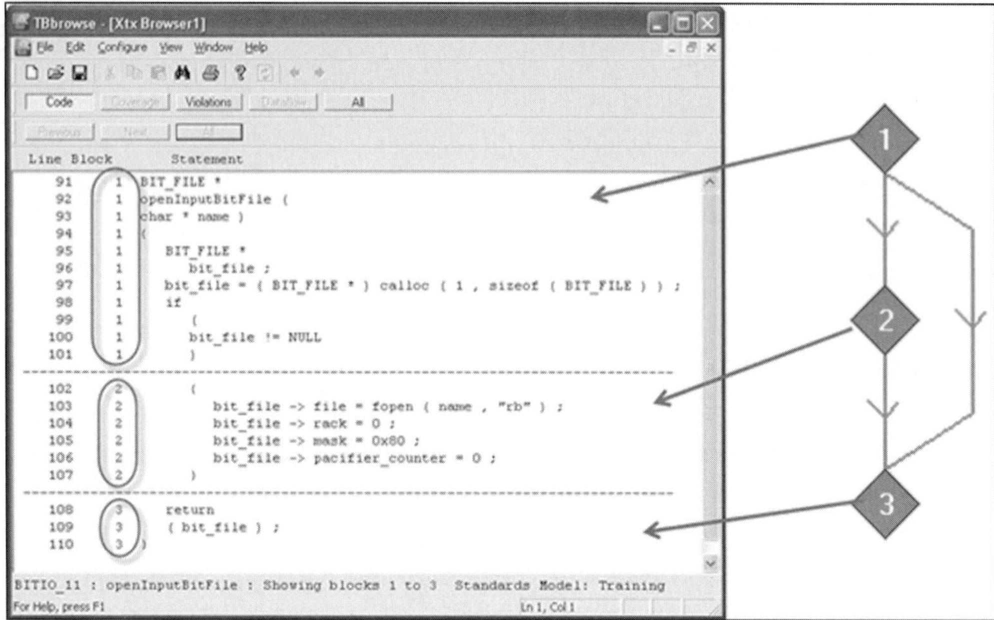

Figure 15.8:
Reformatted code shows the basic blocks ("Nodes") connected by branches ("Links")

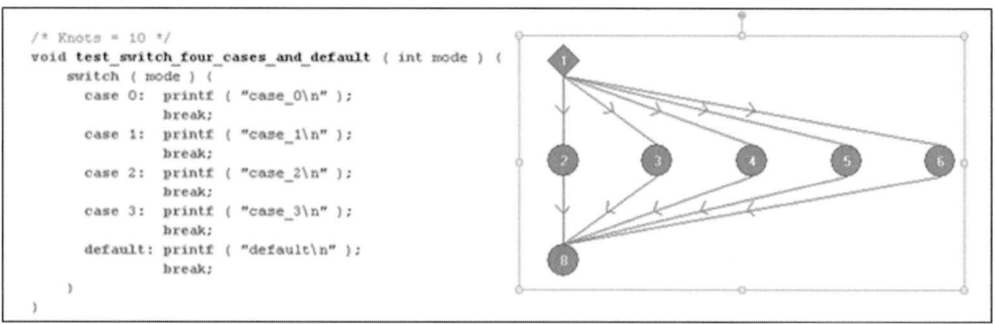

Figure 15.9:
A switch statement generally generates a high number of knots.

Calculating a cyclomatic complexity value.

Cyclomatic complexity is another measurement of how complex a function is. It is a value derived from the geometry of the static flow graph for the function. The absolute value itself is, therefore, a little abstract and meaningless in isolation, but it provides a comparator to show the relative complexity of the problem addressed by one function versus another.

Cyclomatic complexity is represented algebraically by the nomenclature V(G) and can be derived in a number of ways, the simplest perhaps being a count of the number of "regions" separated by the links and nodes of the static flow graph (Figure 15.10).

Identifying structured programming templates – structured analysis

The concept of "structured" programming has been around since the 1960s, derived particularly from work by Böhm and Jacopini, and Edger Dijkstra. In its modern implementation, "structured elements" are defined as those constructs within the code that adhere to one of six "structured programming templates" as illustrated in Figure 15.11.

Structured analysis is an iterative process, where the static flow graph is assessed to see whether it is possible to apply one of the structured programming templates to the original static flow graph. If so, the part of the graph matching that template is 'collapsed' to a single node as illustrated in Figure 15.12.

The same process of matching a template to the resulting modified static flow graph is then applied, and so on repeatedly until no more templates can be matched and structured analysis is complete.

Essential knots and essential cyclomatic complexity

When the knots and cyclomatic complexity calculations are applied to the modified static flow graph that is the product of the structured analysis, the resulting metrics are known as essential knots and essential cyclomatic complexity respectively.

If there is only one node on any static flow graph it will exhibit no knots and only one region, meaning that a perfectly structured function will always have no essential knots, and a cyclomatic complexity of 1.

The converse of this "perfect" result is that the essential measures will be greater than 0 and 1 respectively, which immediately indicates that the code is unstructured and hence may be unnecessarily complex.

Understanding dynamic analysis

As we have discussed before, broadly speaking dynamic analysis involves the execution of some or all of the application source code. In the following section we will introduce and discuss some of the more widely used techniques which fall within this domain.

One such technique is system-level functional test, which defines perhaps the oldest test genre of them all. Simply described, when the code is written and completed, the application is exercised using sample data and the tester confirms that all works as it should.

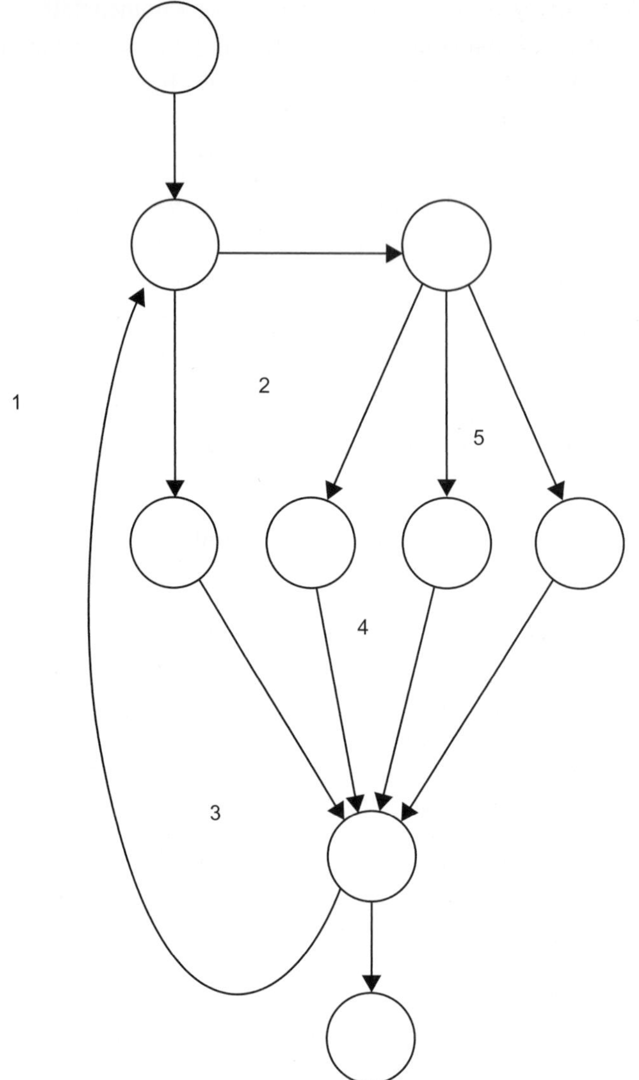

Figure 15.10:
An example of cyclomatic complexity derivation from a static flow graph. here, the cyclomatic complexity value V(G) = 5.

The problem with applying this approach in isolation is that there is no way of knowing how much of the code has actually been exercised. Structural coverage analysis (SCA) addresses this problem by reporting which areas of the application source code have been exercised by the test data and, more importantly, which areas have not. In its simplest form SCA is reported in the form of statement coverage. More sophisticated reporting

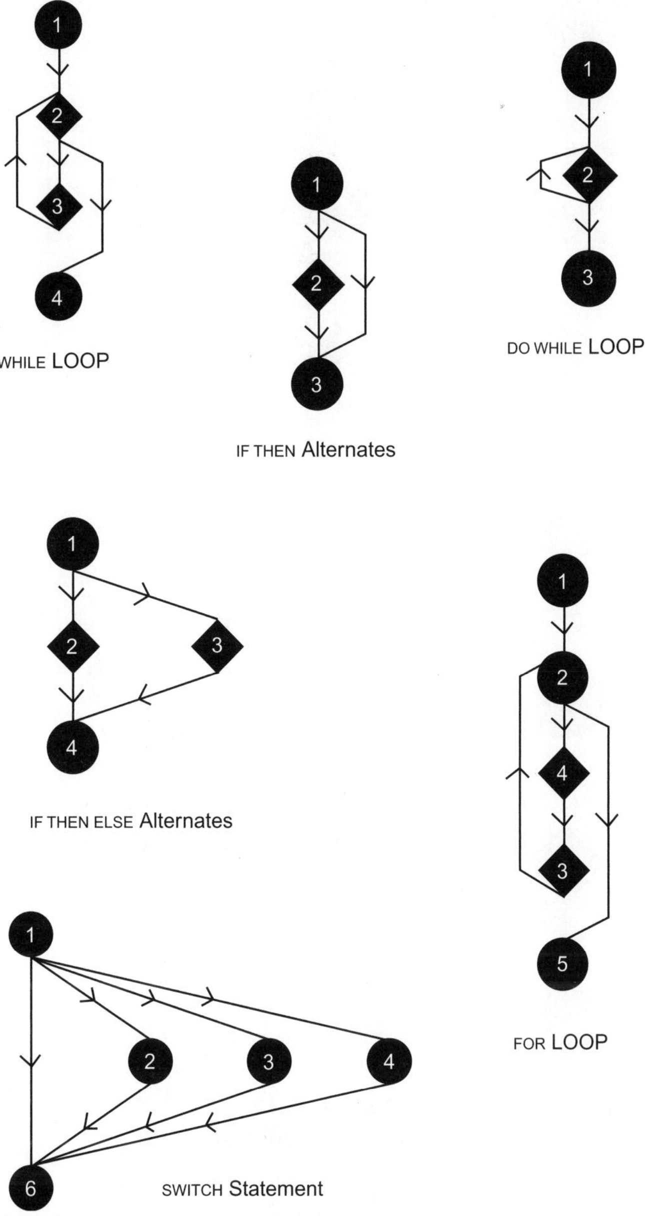

Figure 15.11:
The six structured programming templates.

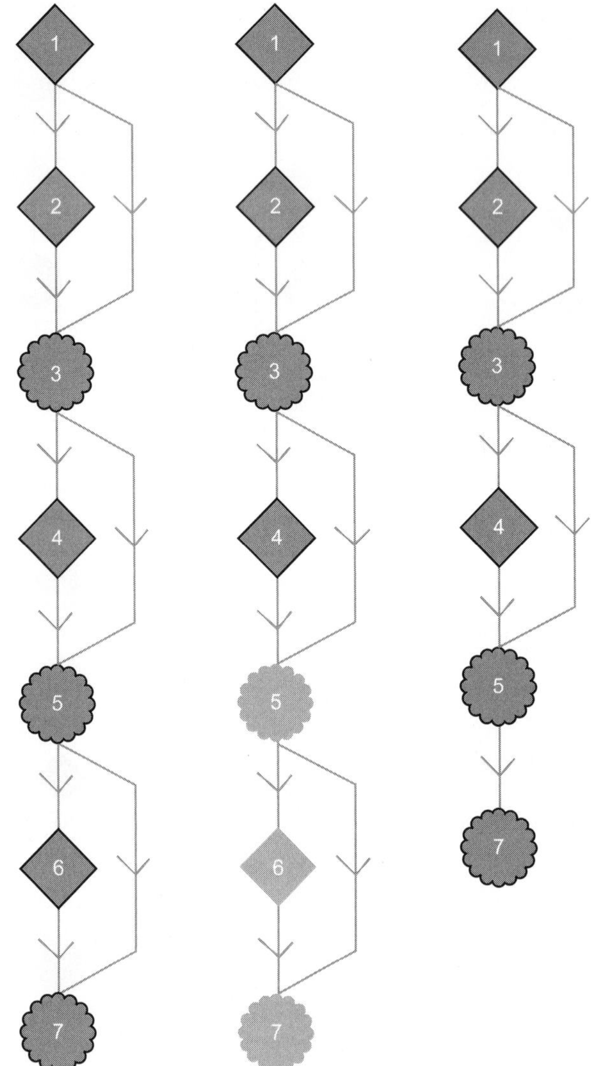

Figure 15.12:
Performing structured analysis.

mechanisms can then build upon this to report coverage of decision points and perhaps even control-flow paths.

Unit test is another widely used dynamic analysis technique and has been around almost as long as software development itself. The cornerstone of this technique at its most basic is that each application building block (unit) – an individual procedure, function or class – is built and executed in isolation with test data to make sure that it does just what it should do without any confusing input from the remainder of the application.

To support the necessary isolation of this process there needs to be a harness program to act as a holding mechanism that calls the unit, details any included files, "stubs" any procedure called by the unit, and prepares data structures for the unit under test to act upon.

Not only is creating that harness from first principles a laborious task, but it takes a lot of skill. More often than not, the harness program requires at least as much testing as the unit under test.

Perhaps more importantly, a fundamental requirement of software testing is to provide an objective, independent view of the software. The very intimate code knowledge required to manually construct a harness compromises the independence of the test process, undermining the legitimacy of the exercise.

The legacy from high-integrity systems

In developing applications for the medical, railway, aerospace and defense industries, unit test is a mandatory part of a software development cycle – a necessary evil. For these high-integrity systems, unit test is compulsory and the only question is how it might be completed in the most efficient manner possible. It is therefore no coincidence that many of the companies developing tools to provide such efficiency have grown from this niche market.

In non-safety-critical environments, perceived wisdom is that unit testing is a nice idea in principle, but commercially unjustifiable. A significant factor in that stance is the natural optimism which abounds at the beginning of any project. At that stage, why would anyone spend money on careful unit testing? There are great engineers in the team, the design is solid and sound management is in place. What could possibly go wrong?

However, things can and do go wrong and while unit test cannot guarantee success, it can certainly help to minimize failure. So, if we look at the tools designed and proven to provide quick and easy unit tests in high-integrity systems, it makes sense that the same unit tests would provide a solid solution for those working on other software as well.

Defining unit, module and integration tests

For some, the terms "unit test" and "module test" are synonymous. For others, the term "unit" implies the testing of a single procedure, whereas "module" suggests a collection of related procedures, perhaps designed to perform some particular purpose within the application.

Using the latter definitions, manually developed module tests are likely to be easier to construct than unit tests, especially if the module represents a functional aspect of the application itself. In this case, most of the calls to procedures are related and the code accesses related data structures, which makes the preparation of the harness code more straightforward.

Test tools render the distinction between unit and module tests redundant. It is perfectly possible to test a single procedure in isolation and equally possible to use exactly the same processes to test multiple procedures, a file or multiple files of procedures, a class (where appropriate), or a functional subset of an entire system. As a result, the distinction between unit and module test is one which has become increasingly irrelevant to the extent that the term "unit test" has come to include both concepts.

Such flexibility facilitates progressive integration testing. Procedures are first unit-tested and then collated as part of the subsystems, which in turn are brought together to perform system tests.

It also provides options when a pragmatic approach is required for less critical applications. A single set of test cases can exercise a specified procedure, all procedures called as a result of exercising the single procedure as illustrated in Figure 15.13, or anything in between. The use of test cases which prove the functionality of the whole call chain are easily constructed. Again, it is easy to "mix and match" the processes depending on the criticality of the code under review.

Defining structural coverage analysis

The structural coverage analysis (SCA) approach is all about ensuring that enough testing is performed on a system to meet its quality objectives.

For the most complete testing possible, it is necessary to ensure that every possible execution path through the code under test is executed at least once. In practice, this is an unachievable aim. An observation made by G.J. Myers in 1976 explains why this is so; Myers described a 100-line program that had 10^{18} unique paths. For comparative purposes, he noted that the universe is only about 4×10^{17} seconds old. With this observation, Myers concluded that complete software execution path testing is impossible, so an approximation alternative and another metric are required to assess testing completeness.

SCA has proven to be an excellent technique for assessing testing effectiveness.

The closest SCA metric to the 100% execution path ideal is based on the linear code sequence and jump (LCSAJ) software analysis technique, or jump-to-jump path (JJ-path) coverage as it is sometimes described. LCSAJ analysis identifies sections of code that have a single input path and a single output path, referred to as an interval. Within each interval, each possible

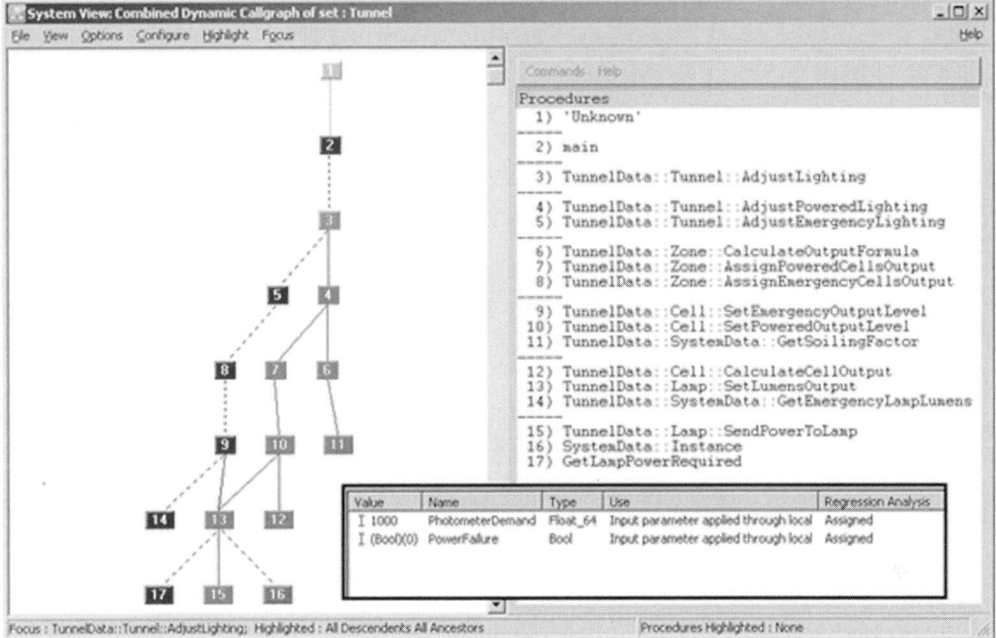

Figure 15.13:
A single test case (inset) can exercise some or all of the call chain associated with it. In this example, "AdjustLighting", note the red coloring highlights exercised code.

execution path is then identified. An SCA metric is then determined by measuring which of these possible execution paths within an interval have been executed.

As with all of these metrics, the use of tools for measuring SCA greatly increases measurement efficiency, effectiveness and accuracy. In addition, the visualization of results provides excellent feedback on what additional test cases are required to improve the overall coverage measurements. For example, Figures 15.14 and 15.15 both represent the same coverage information, with the red used to indicate code that has been executed (i.e., "hot" paths) and blue used to indicate code yet to be executed (i.e., "cold" paths).

From these results, it is a straightforward exercise to determine which test data needs to be generated to exercise the remaining "cold" paths, making the ability to generate the quality-oriented reports required for certification extremely straightforward.

Achieving code coverage with unit test and system test in tandem

Traditionally, many applications have been tested by functional means only – and no matter how carefully the test data is chosen, the percentage of code actually exercised can be very limited.

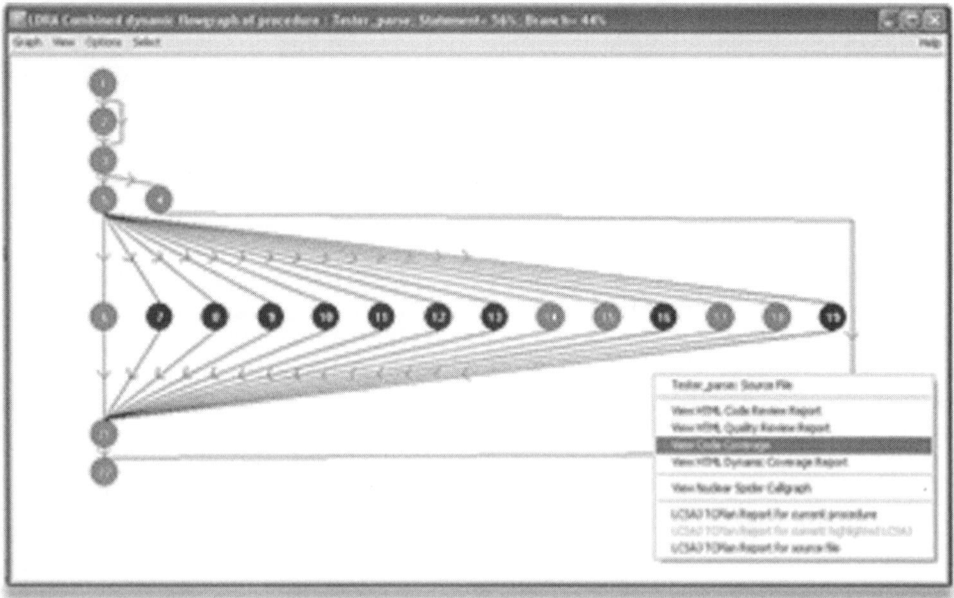

Figure 15.14:
Example coverage analysis results presented against a control flow graph, with the executed paths highlighted in red, and the non-executed paths highlighted in blue.

That issue is compounded by the fact that the procedures tested in this way are only likely to handle data within the range of the current application and test environment. If anything changes a little – perhaps in the way the application is used, or perhaps as a result of slight modifications to the code – the application could be running to an entirely untested execution in the field.

Of course, if all parts of the system are unit-tested and collated on a piecemeal basis through integration testing, then this will not happen. But what if timescales and resources do not permit such an exercise?

The more sophisticated unit test tools provide the facility to instrument code. This instrumented code is equipped to "track" execution paths, providing evidence of the parts of the application which have been exercised during execution. Such an approach provides the information to produce data such as that depicted in Figure 15.16.

Code coverage is an important part of the testing process in that it shows the percentage of the code that has been exercised and proven during test. Proof that all code has been exercised correctly need not be based on unit tests alone. To that end, some unit tests can be used in combination with system test to provide a required level of execution coverage for a system as a whole.

```
case 'w' :
  BarcodeReader_barcode ( 12350U ) ;
  break ;
case 'c' :
  Keyboard_cancel () ;
  break ;
case 'e' :
  Keyboard_end () ;
  break ;
case 's' :
  Keyboard_start () ;
  break ;
case 'r' :

  randomShopping () ;
  break ;
case 'q' :

  goodbye () ;
  break ;
case '\n' :
        /* ignore crlf */
case '\r' :
        /* ignore crlf */
  break ;
  /* For any other character, display the help message */
default :

  Tester_help () ;
  break ;
```

Figure 15.15:
Example coverage analysis results presented against source code, with the executed code highlighted in red, and the non-executed code highlighted in blue.

This means that the system testing of an application can be complemented by unit tests to exercise code which would not normally be exercised in the running of the application. Examples include defensive code (e.g., to prevent crashes due to inadvertent division by zero), exception handlers and interrupt handlers.

Unit test and system test in tandem — case study

Consider the following function, taken from a lighting system written in C++. Line 7 includes defensive code, designed to ensure that a divide by zero error cannot occur.

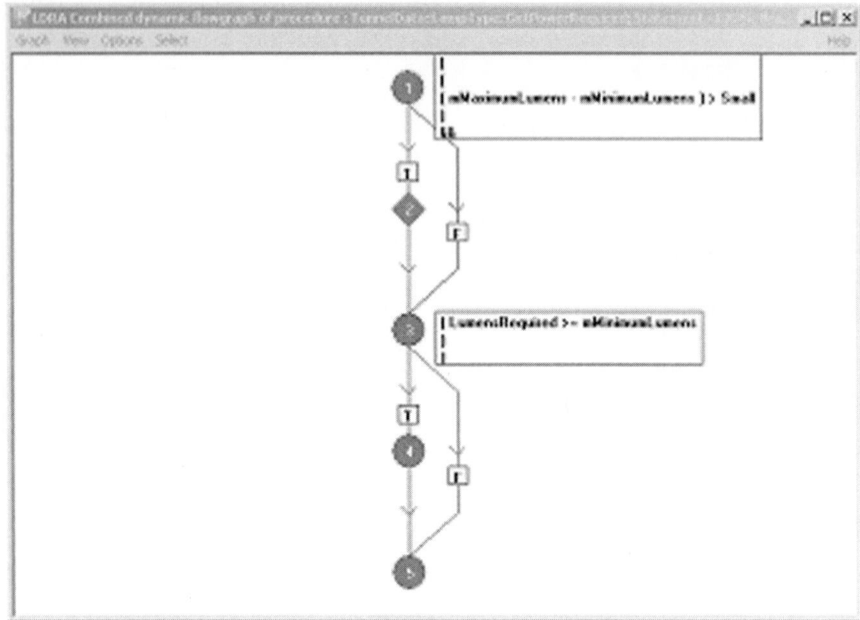

Figure 15.16:
After system test, most of the function has been exercised but a branch associated with defensive programming remains.

```
Sint_32 LampType::GetPowerRequired(const Float_64 LumensRequired) const
/* Assume a linear deterioration of efficiency from HighestPercentOutput lm/W output from
each lamp at
maximum output, down to LowestPercentOutput lm/W at 20% output. Calculate power required
based on
the resulting interpolation. */
{
  Sint_32 Power = 0;
  if (((mMaximumLumens-mMinimumLumens)>Small) && LumensRequired> = mMinimumLumens))
   {
    Power = (Sint_32)(mMinimumPower + (mMaximumPower-mMinimumPower)*
            ((LumensRequired-mMinimumLumens)/(mMaximumLumens-mMinimumLumens)));
   }
  return Power;
}
```

The dynamic flow graph for this function after system test shows that most of the statements and control-flow decisions have been exercised as part of system test. However, in a correctly configured system the values of "mMaximumLumens" and "mMinimumLumens" will never be similar enough to force the defensive aspect of the code to be exercised.

Unit test can be used to complement the code coverage achieved during system test, which forces the defensive branch to be taken (Figure 15.17).

The coverage from the unit test and system test can then be combined so that full coverage is demonstrated (Figure 15.18).

Retaining the functionality through regression test

During the course of development, all too often ongoing development compromises the functionality of software which is considered complete.

Hence as software evolves it is, therefore, essential to keep reapplying existing tests and monitor the subsequent test outcomes against previously determined expected results. This is a process known as regression testing. Often this is achieved by using test case files to store sequences of tests, and it is then possible to recall and reapply them to any revised code to prove that none of the original functionality has been compromised.

Once configured, more sophisticated regression test processes can be initiated as a background task and run perhaps every evening. Reports can highlight any changes to the output generated by earlier test runs. In this way, any code modifications leading to unintentional changes in application behavior can be identified and rectified immediately and the impact of regression tests against other, concurrent, test processes can be kept to a minimum.

Modern unit test tools come equipped with user-friendly, point-and-click graphical user interfaces, which are easy and intuitive to use. However, a GUI interface is not always the most efficient way to implement the thousands of test cases likely to be required in a full-scale development. In recognition of this, the more sophisticated test tools are designed to allow these test case files to be directly developed from applications such as Microsoft Excel. As before, the "regression test" mechanism can then be used to run the test cases held in these files.

Unit test and test-driven development

In addition to using unit test tools to prove developed code, they can also be used to develop test cases for code which is still in the conception phase – an approach known as

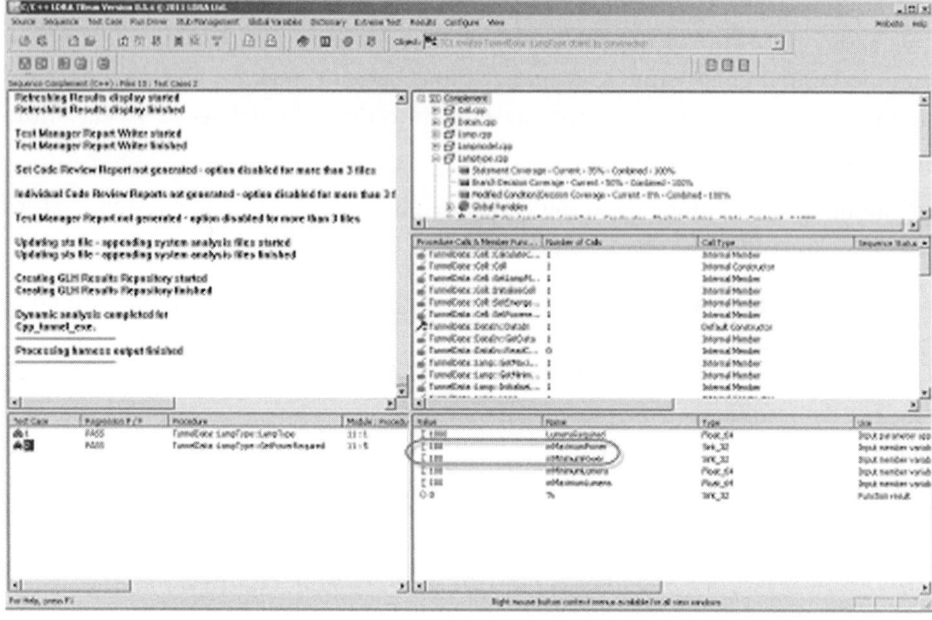

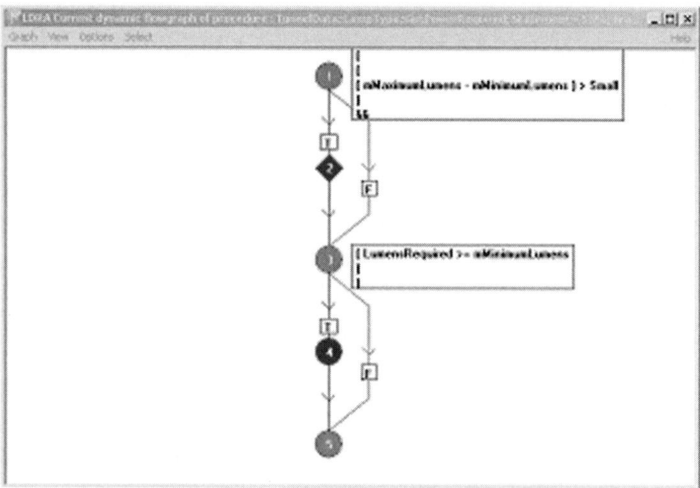

Figure 15.17:
Unit test exercises the defensive branch left untouched by system test remains.

test-driven development (TDD). As illustrated in Figure 15.19, TDD is a software development technique that uses short development iterations based on pre-written unit test cases that define desired improvements or new functions. Each iteration produces code necessary to pass the set of tests that are specific to it. The programmer or team re-factors the code to accommodate changes.

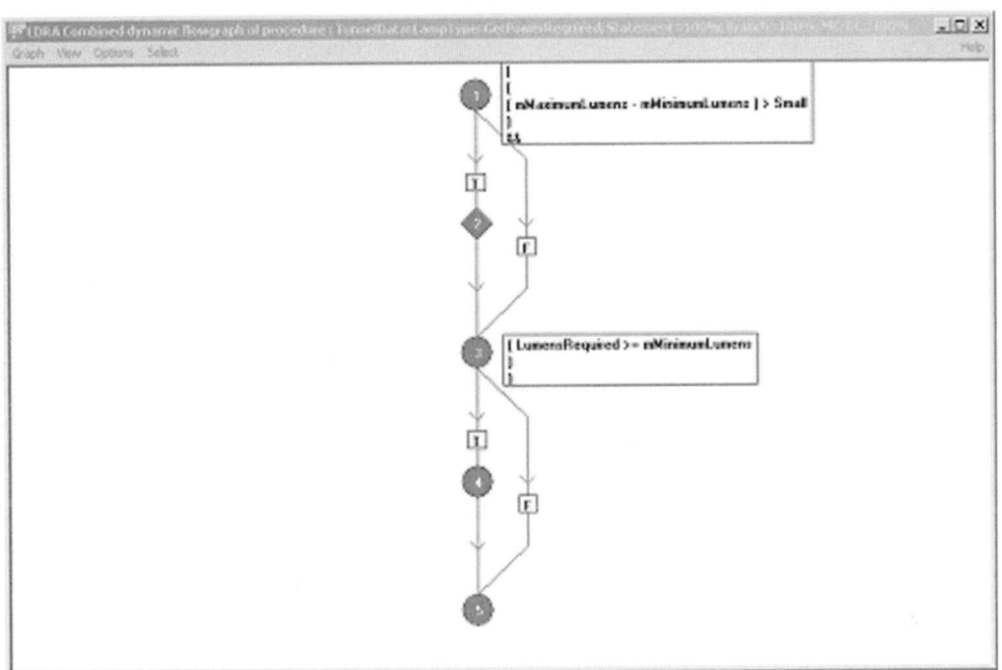

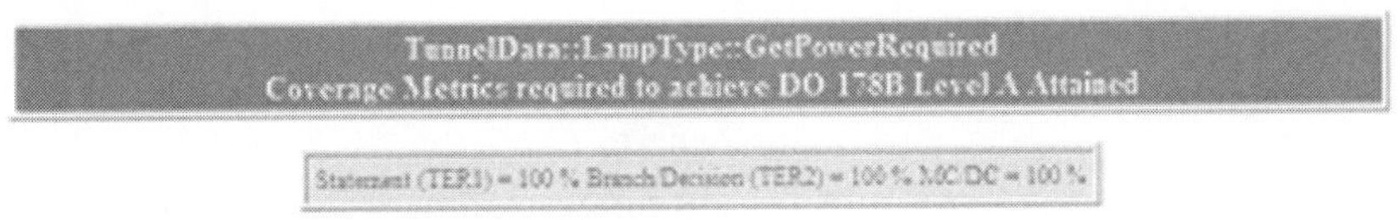

Figure 15.18:
Full coverage is demonstrated by combining the system test and unit test.

Automatically generating test cases

Unit tests are usually performed to demonstrate the adherence to requirements; to show that elements of the code perform the function they were designed to perform.

Generally, then, the output data generated through unit tests is an important end in itself, but this is not necessarily always the case.

There may be occasions when the fact that the unit tests have successfully completed is more important than the test data itself. To address these circumstances as efficiently as possible the more sophisticated unit test tools can generate test cases automatically, based on information gleaned by means of the initial static analysis of the software under test. For example:

- source code may be required to pass robustness tests;
- functionality of source code may already be proven but the required level of code coverage unsatisfied;

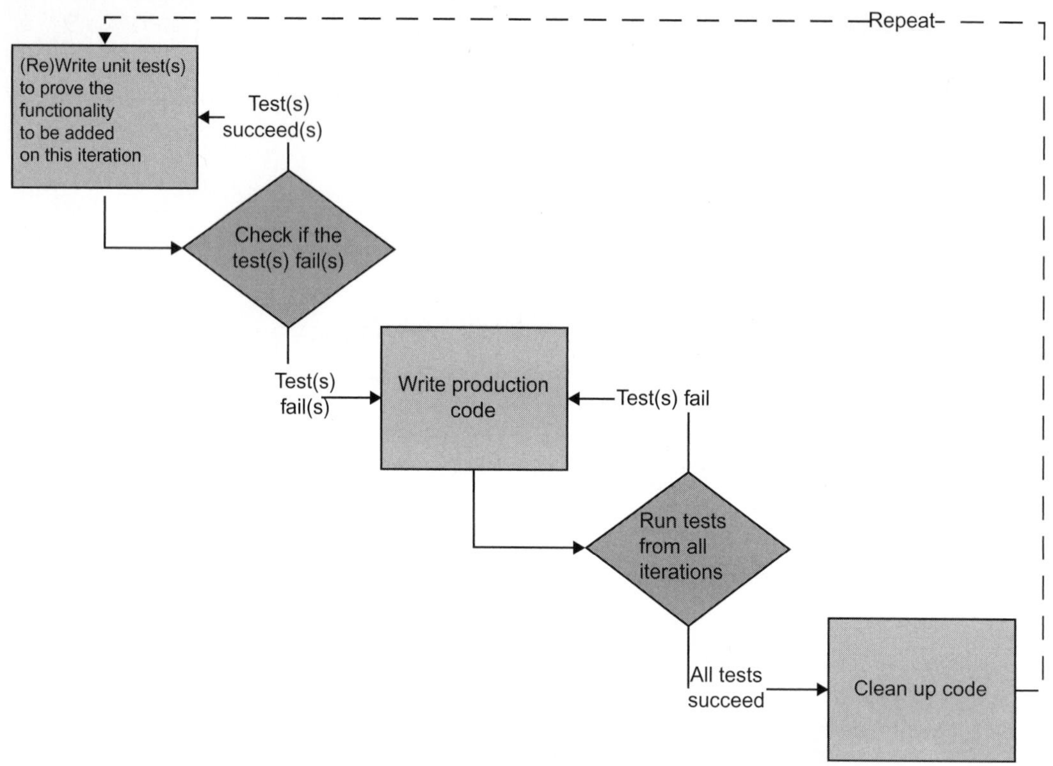

Figure 15.19:
Unit test tools lend themselves admirably to test-driven development by providing a mechanism to write test cases before any source code is available.

- a "personality profile" of source code may be required prior to the modification of source code. Sequences of test cases can be generated based on the unchanged code, and then exercised again when the source has been modified to prove that there has been no inadvertent detrimental effect on existing functionality.

In order to tune the test cases generated in this way, tools provide a range of options to allow different aspects of the code to be considered. For example, options may include

- the generation of test cases to exercise upper and lower boundary values,
- the generation of minimum/mean/maximum values, and
- the generation of the optimal number of test cases in maximizing code coverage.

A word of caution

It would be easy to view the automatic generation of test cases as a potential "silver bullet"; an answer to all possible test questions with the minimum of effort.

It certainly represents an easy way to generate test cases (although it does require caution to ensure (for instance) that test cases do not result in infinite loops or null pointers).

However, there is an intrinsic compromise in the basic premise. The tests themselves are based on the source code – not on any external requirements. Detractors of the technique might argue that automatically generated test cases prove only that the source code does what it was written to do, and that they would prove nothing if the interpretation of the requirements were to be fundamentally flawed.

It is clearly true that such a test process compromises the principle of test independence and it is certainly not being suggested that automatically generated tests can or should replace functional testing, either at system or unit test level.

However, it should be noted that in the leading test tools, once the test cases have been generated the functionality of the test tool is identical to that provided for conventionally defined unit tests. The input and output to each of the test cases is available for inspection, so that the correctness of the response from the software to each generated case can be confirmed if required.

Setting the standard

Recent quality concerns are driving many industries to start looking seriously at ways to improve the quality of software development. Not surprisingly, there are marked differences in the quality of software in the different sectors. The automotive industry does a good job of listing all the requirements in a database and was the original of the MISRA software coding guidelines. However, the railway and process industries have long had standards governing the entire development cycle of electrical, electronic and programmable electronic systems, including the need to track all requirements. The automotive sector has only recently introduced a draft standard for a similarly broad-based approach.

By contrast, medical software guidelines are typically more in line with low-risk applications, even when a software failure could result in serious physical injury or death. Despite this apparent disparity between medical software and other safety-critical standards, the case for software which has been proven to be reliable through standards compliance and requirements traceable process is becoming ever more compelling.

The terminology of standards

In layman's terms there are documents which define how a process should be managed, and standards which dictate the instructions and style to be used by programmers in the process of writing the code itself.

These groups can be further subdivided. For example, there are many collections of these instructions for the use of development teams looking to seek approval for their efforts efficiently. But what are these collections of rules called collectively?

Unfortunately there is little consensus for this terminology amongst the learned committees responsible for what these documents are actually called.

The MISRA C:2004 document, for example, is entitled "Guidelines for the use of the C language in critical systems" and hence each individual coding instruction within the document is a "guideline".

Conversely, the HICC++ document is known as a "coding standards manual" and calls each individual instruction a "rule".

Although the two documents are similar in nature and in order to keep any discussion about any collection of these documents, it is necessary to settle on some terms.

For that reason, this chapter refers to "process standards", "coding standards" and "coding rules" throughout, and distinguishes "internal standards" used within an organization from "recognized standards" such as those established by expert committees.

The evolution of a recognized process standard

It is interesting to consider the evolution of the medical software standard IEC 62304 because it mirrors earlier experience in many other sectors (Figure 15.20).

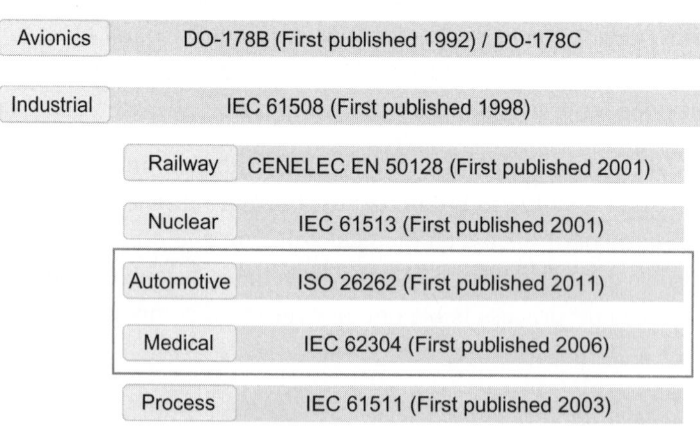

Figure 15.20:
Many safety-critical standards have evolved from the generic standard IEC 61508. Sectors which are relative newcomers to this field (highlighted) are advantaged by the availability of established and proven tools to help them to achieve their goals.

The US government is well aware of the incongruence of the situation and is considering ways to counter it with the Drug and Device Accountability Act (http://www.govtrack.us/congress/bill.xpd?bill = s111-882). Recently, the FDA took punitive action against Baxter Healthcare and their infusion pumps, which the FDA has forced the company to recall: http://www.fda.gov/NewsEvents/Newsroom/PressAnnouncements.

The net result is that many medical device providers are being driven to improve their software development processes as a result of commercial pressures. In short, they are doing so because it affects the "bottom line".

A common concept in the standards applied in the safety-critical sectors is the use of a tiered, risk-based approach for determining the criticality of each function within the system under development. Typically known as "safety integrity levels" (SILs), there are usually four or five grades used to specify the necessary safety measures to avoid an unreasonable residual risk of the whole system or a system component. The SIL is assigned based on the risk of a hazardous event occurring based on the frequency of the situation, the impact of possible damage, and the extent to which the situation can be controlled or managed (Figure 15.21).

For a company to make the transition to certified software, they must integrate the standard's technical safety requirements into their design. To ensure that a design follows the standard, a company must be able to outline the fulfillment of these safety requirements from design through coding, testing and verification.

Figure 15.21:
The standards shown all apply the concept of safety integrity levels, although the terminology used to describe them varies. Again, the principles hold true in the highlighted sectors where standards are newest.

To ease the adoption of this standard and manage the shift in requirements, many companies use gap analysis. Gap analysis begins by gathering and analysing data to gauge the difference between where the business is currently and where it wants to be. Gap analysis examines operating processes and generated artifacts, typically employing a third party for the assessment. The outcome will be notes and findings on which the company or individual project may act.

ISO 26262-recognized process standard – case study

Like IEC 62304 in the medical sector, ISO 26262 is a relatively new standard in the automotive industry. It will therefore serve well as an example of how such a standard might be implemented.

In response to the increased use of electronic systems within the automotive industry and particularly in recognition of their application to safety-critical functions, the ISO 26262 standard has been created in order to comply with needs specific to the application sector of electrical/electronic/programmable electronic (E/E/PE) systems within road vehicles.

In addition to its roots in the IEC 61508 generic standard, it has much in common with the DO-178B/DO-178C standards seen in aerospace applications. In particular, the requirement for MC/DC (modified condition/decision coverage – a technique to dictate the tests required to adequately test lines of code with multiple conditions) and the structural coverage analysis process is very similar.

Safety is already a significant factor in the development of automobile systems. With the ever-increasing use of E/E/PE systems in areas such as driver assistance, braking and steering systems, and safety systems, this significance is set to increase.

The standard provides detailed industry-specific guidelines for the production of all software for automotive systems and equipment, whether it is safety-critical or not. It provides a risk-management approach including the determination of risk classes (automotive safety integrity levels, ASILs).

There are four levels of ASILs (A–D in ISO 26262) to specify the necessary safety measures for avoiding an unreasonable residual risk, with D representing the most stringent level.

The ASIL is a property of a given safety function, not a property of the whole system or a system component. It follows that each safety function in a safety-related system needs to have an appropriate ASIL assigned with the risk of each hazardous event being evaluated based on the following attributes:

- frequency of the situation (or "exposure")
- impact of possible damage (or "severity")
- controllability.

Depending on the values of these three attributes, the appropriate automotive safety integrity level for a given functional defect is evaluated. This determines the overall ASIL for a given safety function.

ISO 26262 translates these safety levels into safety-specific objectives that must be satisfied during the development process. An assigned ASIL therefore determines the level of effort required to show compliance with the standard. This means that the effort and expense of producing a system critical to the continued safe operation of an automobile (e.g., a steer-by-wire system) is necessarily higher than that required to produce a system with only a minor impact in the case of a failure (e.g., the in-car entertainment system).

The standard demands a mature development environment which focuses on requirements that are specified in this standard. In order to claim compliance to ISO 26262, most requirements need to be formally verified aside from exceptional cases where the requirement does not apply or where non-compliance is acceptable.

Part 4 of the standard concerns the product development at the system level and part 6 of the standard concerns the product development at the software level. The scope of these documents may be mapped on to any process diagram, such as the familiar "V" model (Figure 15.22).

Both software analysis and requirements traceability tools are essential for cost-conscious projects. As the application of ISO 26262 becomes more widespread it is equally essential that the choice of tools is based on known expertise.

ISO 26262 process objectives

ISO 26262 recognizes that software safety and security must be addressed in a systematic way throughout the software development life-cycle (SDLC). This includes the safety requirements traceability, software design, coding, and verification processes used to ensure correctness, control and confidence both in the software, and in the E/E/PE systems to which that software contributes.

A key element of ISO 26262 (part 4) is the practice of allocating technical safety requirements in the system design and developing that design further to derive an item integration and testing plan, and subsequently the tests themselves. It implicitly includes software elements of the system, with the explicit subdivision of hardware and software development practices being dealt with further down the "V" model.

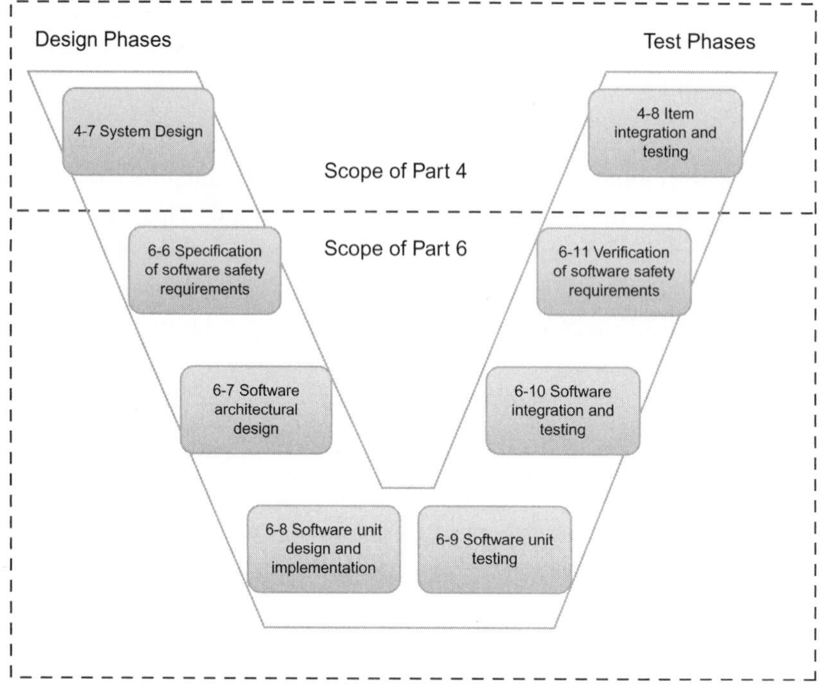

Figure 15.22:
Mapping the scope of the ISO 26262 part 4 and part 6 onto the familiar "V" model.

ISO 26262 (part 6) refers more specifically to the development of the software aspect of the product. It is concerned with:

- the initiation of product development at the software level
- the derivation of software safety requirements from the system level (following from part 4) and their subsequent verification
- the software architectural design
- software unit design and implementation
- software unit testing, and
- software integration and testing.

Traceability (or requirements traceability) refers to the ability to link system requirements to software safety requirements, and then from software safety requirements to design requirements and then to source code and the associated test cases. Although traceability is not explicitly identified as a requirement in the main body of the text, it is certainly desirable in ensuring the verifiability deemed necessary in section 7.4.2. Moreover, the need for "*bi-directional* traceability" (or upstream/downstream traceability) is noted in the same section (and a requirement that would be very difficult to meet without using an automated traceability tool).

Verification tasks

The methods to be deployed in the development of an ISO 26262 system vary depending on the specified ASIL level. This can be illustrated by reference to the verification tasks recommendations as presented in tabular form.

Table 1 in section 5.4.7 of part 6 (Figure 15.23) recommends that design and coding guidelines are used and as an example cites the use of the MISRA C coding standard. It lists a number of topics that are to be covered by modeling and design guidelines. For instance, the enforcement of low complexity is highly recommended for all ASILs.

Modern test tools not only have the potential to cover all of the obligatory elements for each ASIL, but also have the flexibility in configuration to allow less critical code in the same project to be associated with less demanding standards. That principle extends to mixed C and C++ code, where appropriate standards are assigned to each file in accordance with its extension.

Table 12 from section 9 of part 6 (Figure 15.24) shows for instance that measuring statement coverage is highly recommended for all ASILs, and that branch coverage is recommended for ASIL A and highly recommended for the other ASILs. For the highest ASIL D, MC/DC is also highly recommended.

Statement, branch and MC/DC coverage can all be automated through the use of test tools. Some packages can also operate in tandem, so that (for instance) coverage can be generated for most of the source code through a dynamic system test, and that can be complemented using unit tests to exercise defensive code and other aspects which are inaccessible during normal system operation.

Similarly Table 15 in section 10.4.6 shows the structural coverage metrics at the software architectural level (Figure 15.25).

Freedom to choose adequate standards

Not every development organization of every application is obliged to follow a set of process or coding standards which has been laid down by a client or a regulatory body. Indeed, it is probably reasonable to suggest that a majority are not in that position.

However, everyone wants their software to be as sound and as robust as it reasonably can be. Even if it is a trivial application to be used by the writer as a one-off utility, no developer wants their application to crash. As that expands into an application with wider uses, no one wants to have to deal with product recalls. No one wants to deal with irate end-users. And even removing all external factors entirely, most people want the satisfaction of a job well done in an efficient manner.

Topics		ASIL			
		A	B	C	D
1a	Enforcement of low complexity	++ ✓	++✓	++✓	++✓
1b	Use of language subsets	++✓	++✓	++✓	++✓
1c	Enforcement of strong typing	++✓	++✓	++✓	++✓
1d	Use of defensive implementation techniques	O	+✓	++✓	++✓
1e	Use of established design principles	+✓	+✓	+✓	++✓
1f	Use of unambiguous graphical representation	+✓	++✓	++✓	++✓
1g	Use of style guides	+✓	++✓	++✓	++✓
1h	Use of naming conventions	++✓	++✓	++✓	++✓

"++" The method is highly recommended for this ASIL.

"+" The method is recommended for this ASIL.

"o" The method has no recommendation for or against its usage for this ASIL.

✓ Potential for efficiency gains through the use of test tools

Figure 15.23:
Mapping the potential for efficiency gains through the use of test tools to "ISO 26262 Part 6 Table 1: Topics to be covered by modeling and coding guidelines".

So, it follows that if the use of process and coding standards is appropriate when safety or security issues dictate that software must be robust and reliable, then it is sensible to adopt appropriate standards even if an application is not going to threaten anyone's well-being if it fails.

Topics		ASIL			
		A	B	C	D
1a	Statement coverage	++✓	++✓	+✓	+✓
1b	Branch coverage	+✓	++✓	++✓	++✓
1c	MC/DC (Modified Condition/Decision Coverage)	+✓	+✓	+✓	++✓

"++" The method is highly recommended for this ASIL.

"+" The method is recommended for this ASIL.

"o" The method has no recommendation for or against its usage for this ASIL.

✓ Potential for efficiency gains through the use of test tools

Figure 15.24:
Mapping the potential for efficiency gains through the use of test tools to "ISO 26262 Section 9 of Part 6 Table 12: Structural coverage metrics at the software unit level".

Once that is established, a sound pragmatic approach is required to decide what form those standards should take.

Establishing an internal process standard

Many of the recognized standards are most ideally deployed within large organizations. There are many software development teams which consist of two or three people all resident in the same office. It would clearly be overkill to deploy the same tools and techniques here as in a high-integrity team of hundreds of developers spread across the world.

That said, the principles of the requirements traceability matrix (RTM) established earlier in the chapter remain as valid in either case. The difference lies in the scaling of the mechanisms and techniques used to confirm the traceability of requirements. For that reason, an appropriate recognized process standard can prove very useful as a guideline for a pragmatic application of similar principles in a less demanding environment.

Topics		ASIL			
		A	B	C	D
1a	Function coverage	+✓	+✓	++✓	++✓
1b	Call coverage	+✓	+✓	++✓	++✓

"++" The method is highly recommended for this ASIL.

"+" The method is recommended for this ASIL.

"o" The method has no recommendation for or against its usage for this ASIL.

✓ Potential for efficiency gains through the use of test tools

Figure 15.25:
Mapping the potential for efficiency gains through the use of test tools to the "ISO 26262 Section 10.4.6 Table 15: Structural coverage metrics at the software architectural level".

Establishing a common foundation for an internal coding rule set

The principle of using a recognized standard as the basis for an internal one extends to the realm of coding standards.

Even where there is no legacy code to worry about, there is frequently a good deal of inertia within a development team. Even something as simple as agreement over the placement of brackets can become a source of great debate amongst people who prefer one convention over another.

Under these circumstances, the establishment of a common foundation rule set which everyone can agree on is a sound place to begin.

For example, practically no-one would advocate the use of the "goto" statement in C or C++ source code. It is likely that outlawing the use of the "goto" statement by means of a coding rule will achieve support from all interested parties. Consequently it is an uncontentious rule to include as part of a common foundation rule set.

Establishing such a set of rules from nothing is not easy, and given that learned organizations are meeting regularly to do just that, neither is it a sensible use of resources.

It therefore makes sense to derive the internal standard from a recognized standard to which the organization might aspire in an ideal world, This does not necessarily imply an intention on the part of the development organization to ever fully comply with that standard but it does suggest that the rules deployed as part of that subset will be coherent, complementary and chosen with the relevant industry sector in mind.

Dealing with an existing code base

This principle becomes a little more challenging when there is a legacy code base to deal with.

It is likely that the retrospective enforcement of a recognized coding standard such as MISRA C: 2004 to legacy code is too onerous and so a subset compromise is preferred. In that case, it is possible to apply a user-defined set of rules which could simply be less demanding, or which could (say) place particular focus on portability issues.

Where legacy code is subject to continuous development, a progressive transition to a higher ideal may then be made by periodically adding more rules with each new release, so that the impact on incremental functionality improvements is kept to a minimum.

Test tools enable the correction of code to adhere to such rules as efficiently as possible. The more sophisticated tools use a "drill down" approach to provide a link between the description of a violation in a report, and an editor opened on the relevant line of code.

Deriving an internal coding standard for custom software development – case study

In many fields of endeavor for embedded software development – cars, aeroplanes, telephones, medical devices, weapons – the software life-cycle contributes to a product life-cycle of design and development, readying for production, then mass production. In some fields such as control systems for bespoke plant or machinery, duplicates are the exception, not the rule. That brings a unique set of difficulties.

Imagine a situation where there is a software team of three or four developers within a larger engineering company. The actual value of the software within the context of a typical contract might be very small, but even so the software itself is critical to making sure that the client is satisfied when work is completed.

The original code has been designed to be configurable, but as each sale is made by the sales team the functionality is expanded to encompass new features to clinch the deal. The sales team is motivated by the commission derived from the whole of the contract, meaning that a modification to software functionality is not a primary concern for them.

The developers of the software team are tasked with implementing this expanding functionality for each new contract, often under great pressure from other areas of production.

Commercial milestones loom large for these hapless developers because despite their small contribution to the overall value of the project, any failure on their part to meet the milestones could result in the delay of a stage payment, or the triggering of a penalty clause.

To make matters worse, numerous software developers have joined and departed from the team over the years. Each has had their own style and preferences and none has had the time to thoroughly document what they have done.

As a practical example, let us consider that the developers of such a code base designed to control a widget production machine have been tasked with establishing the quality of their software, and improving it on an ongoing basis.

Establishing a common foundation

The first step in establishing an appropriate rules set is to chose a relevant recognized standard as a reference point – perhaps MISRA C++:2008 in this case.

Using a test tool, the code base can be analyzed to discover the parts of the standard where the code base is already adequate. By opting to include information even relating to the rules which pass, a subset of the standard to which the code adheres can immediately be derived (Figure 15.26).

Typically the configuration facilities in the test tool can then be used to map the rules which have not been transgressed into a new subset of the reference standard, and the violated rules disabled as illustrated in Figure 15.27.

Building upon a common foundation

Even if nothing else is achieved beyond checking each future code release against this rule set, it is ensured that the standard of the code in terms of adherence to the chosen reference standard will not deteriorate further.

However, if the aim is to improve the standard of the code then an appropriate strategy is to review the violated rules. It is likely that there are far fewer different rules violated than there are individual violations, and test tools can sometime generate a useful breakdown of this summary information (Figure 15.28).

In some cases, it may be that a decision is reached that some rules are not appropriate, and their exclusion justified.

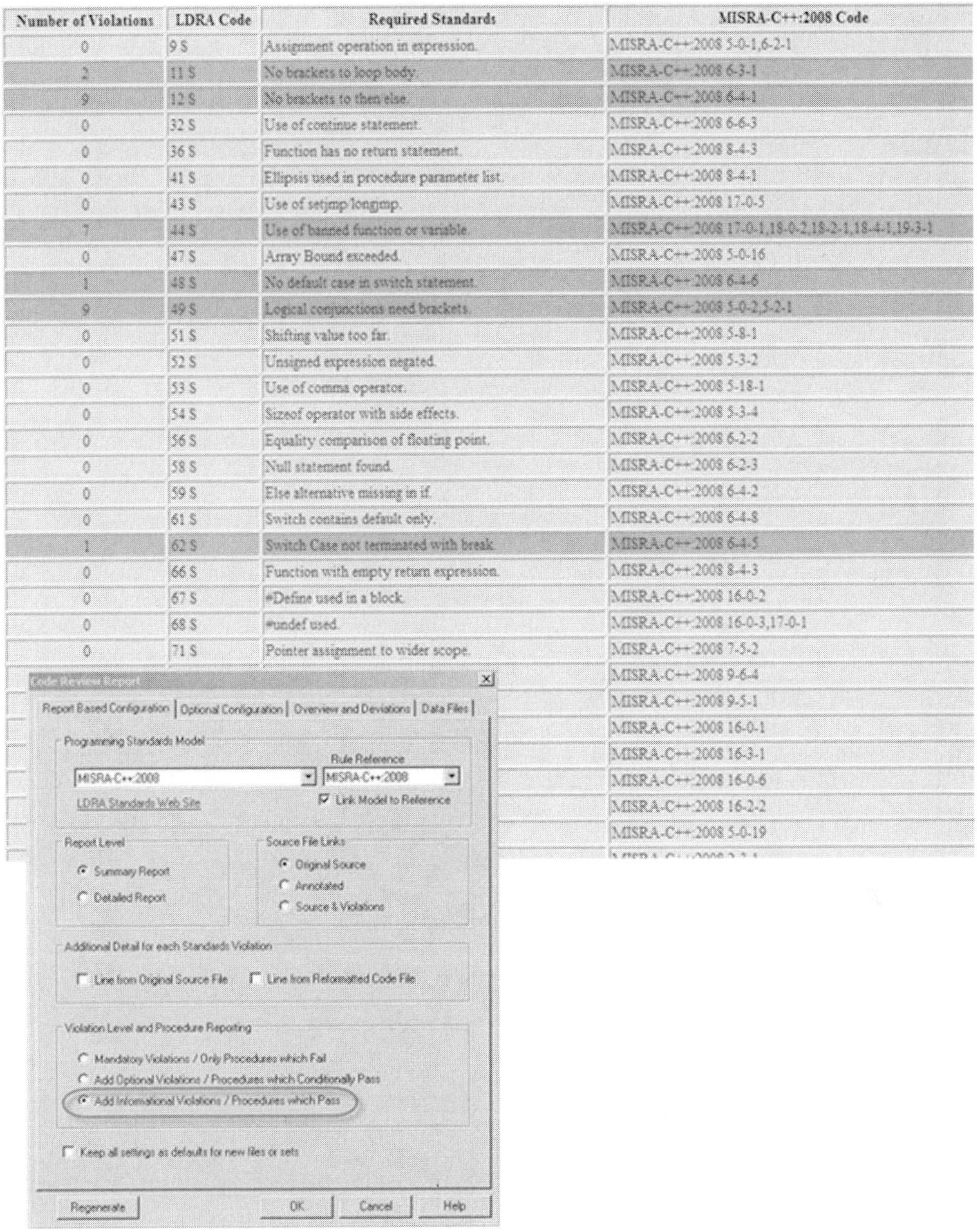

Number of Violations	LDRA Code	Required Standards	MISRA-C++:2008 Code
0	9 S	Assignment operation in expression.	MISRA-C++:2008 5-0-1,6-2-1
2	11 S	No brackets to loop body.	MISRA-C++:2008 6-3-1
9	12 S	No brackets to then/else.	MISRA-C++:2008 6-4-1
0	32 S	Use of continue statement.	MISRA-C++:2008 6-6-3
0	36 S	Function has no return statement.	MISRA-C++:2008 8-4-3
0	41 S	Ellipsis used in procedure parameter list.	MISRA-C++:2008 8-4-1
0	43 S	Use of setjmp/longjmp.	MISRA-C++:2008 17-0-5
7	44 S	Use of banned function or variable.	MISRA-C++:2008 17-0-1,18-0-2,18-2-1,18-4-1,19-3-1
0	47 S	Array Bound exceeded.	MISRA-C++:2008 5-0-16
1	48 S	No default case in switch statement.	MISRA-C++:2008 6-4-6
9	49 S	Logical conjunctions need brackets.	MISRA-C++:2008 5-0-2,5-2-1
0	51 S	Shifting value too far.	MISRA-C++:2008 5-8-1
0	52 S	Unsigned expression negated.	MISRA-C++:2008 5-3-2
0	53 S	Use of comma operator.	MISRA-C++:2008 5-18-1
0	54 S	Sizeof operator with side effects.	MISRA-C++:2008 5-3-4
0	56 S	Equality comparison of floating point.	MISRA-C++:2008 6-2-2
0	58 S	Null statement found.	MISRA-C++:2008 6-2-3
0	59 S	Else alternative missing in if.	MISRA-C++:2008 6-4-2
0	61 S	Switch contains default only.	MISRA-C++:2008 6-4-8
1	62 S	Switch Case not terminated with break.	MISRA-C++:2008 6-4-5
0	66 S	Function with empty return expression.	MISRA-C++:2008 8-4-3
0	67 S	#Define used in a block.	MISRA-C++:2008 16-0-2
0	68 S	#undef used.	MISRA-C++:2008 16-0-3,17-0-1
0	71 S	Pointer assignment to wider scope.	MISRA-C++:2008 7-5-2
			MISRA-C++:2008 9-6-4
			MISRA-C++:2008 9-5-1
			MISRA-C++:2008 16-0-1
			MISRA-C++:2008 16-3-1
			MISRA-C++:2008 16-0-6
			MISRA-C++:2008 16-2-2
			MISRA-C++:2008 5-0-19

Code Review Report

Report Based Configuration | Optional Configuration | Overview and Deviations | Data Files

Programming Standards Model

Rule Reference

MISRA-C++:2008 | MISRA-C++:2008

LDRA Standards Web Site

Link Model to Reference

Report Level

Summary Report

Detailed Report

Source File Links

Original Source

Annotated

Source & Violations

Additional Detail for each Standards Violation

Line from Original Source File

Line from Reformatted Code File

Violation Level and Procedure Reporting

Mandatory Violations / Only Procedures which Fail

Add Optional Violations / Procedures which Conditionally Pass

Add Informational Violations / Procedures which Pass

Keep all settings as defaults for new files or sets

Regenerate | OK | Cancel | Help

Figure 15.26:

Using source code violation reporting to identify rules which are adhered to. In this report subset, only the rules highlighted in red have been violated.

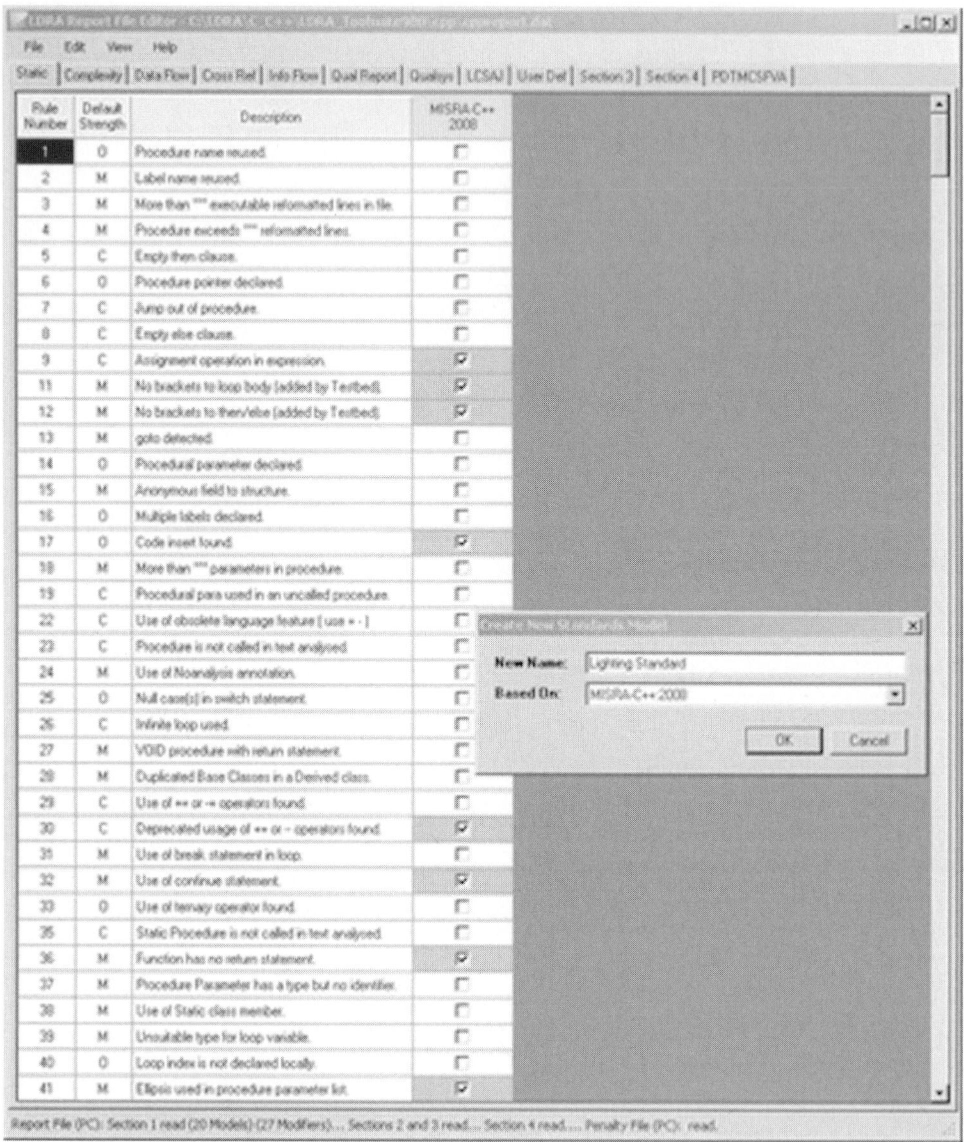

Figure 15.27:
Using unviolated rules from a recognized standard as the basis of an internal standard.

The prioritization of the introduction of the remaining rules can vary depending on the primary motivation. In the example, it is obviously likely to be quicker to address the violations which occur once rather than those which occur 40 or 50 times which will improve the apparent adherence to the standard. However, it makes sense to initially focus

Frequency of Violated Standards - Current Model (MISRA-C++:2008) - Cpp_tunnel_exe	344
Included file not protected with #define.	51
DU anomaly, variable value is not used.	42
Basic type declaration used.	37
Array has decayed to pointer.	18
Declaration does not specify an array.	17
Deprecated usage of ++ or -- operators found.	16
Use of C type cast.	15
Local variable should be declared const.	15
Class data is not explicitly private.	11
Member function should be declared const.	11
Parameter should be declared const.	10
No brackets to then/else.	9
Scope of variable could be reduced.	9
Logical conjunctions need brackets.	9
Expression needs brackets.	8
Comment possibly contains code.	8
Use of banned function or variable.	7
#include preceded by non preproc directives.	5
Expression is not Boolean.	5
Procedure contains UR data flow anomalies.	5
Identifier is typographically ambiguous.	4
Parameter should be declared * const.	4
Type conversion without cast.	4
Pointer Parameter should be declared const	3
Float/integer conversion without cast.	3
Use of mixed mode arithmetic.	3
More than one control variable for loop.	3
Names only differ by case.	2
No brackets to loop body.	2
Array passed as actual parameter.	2
No master exception handler.	1
No default case in switch statement.	1
Use of using directive.	1
Switch Case not terminated with break.	1
Unreachable Code found.	1
Use of underlying enum representation value.	1

Figure 15.28:
Summary showing the breakdown of rule violations in sample code set.

on any particular violations which, if they were to be corrected, would address known issues in the code base.

Whatever the criteria for prioritization, a progressive transition to a higher ideal may then be made by periodically adding more rules with each new release, so that the impact on incremental functionality improvements is kept to a minimum.

Dealing with the unusual

Working with auto-generated code

Many software design tools such as IBM's Rhapsody and MathWork's Matlab (Figure 15.29) have the ability to automatically generate high-level source code from a UML or similar design model.

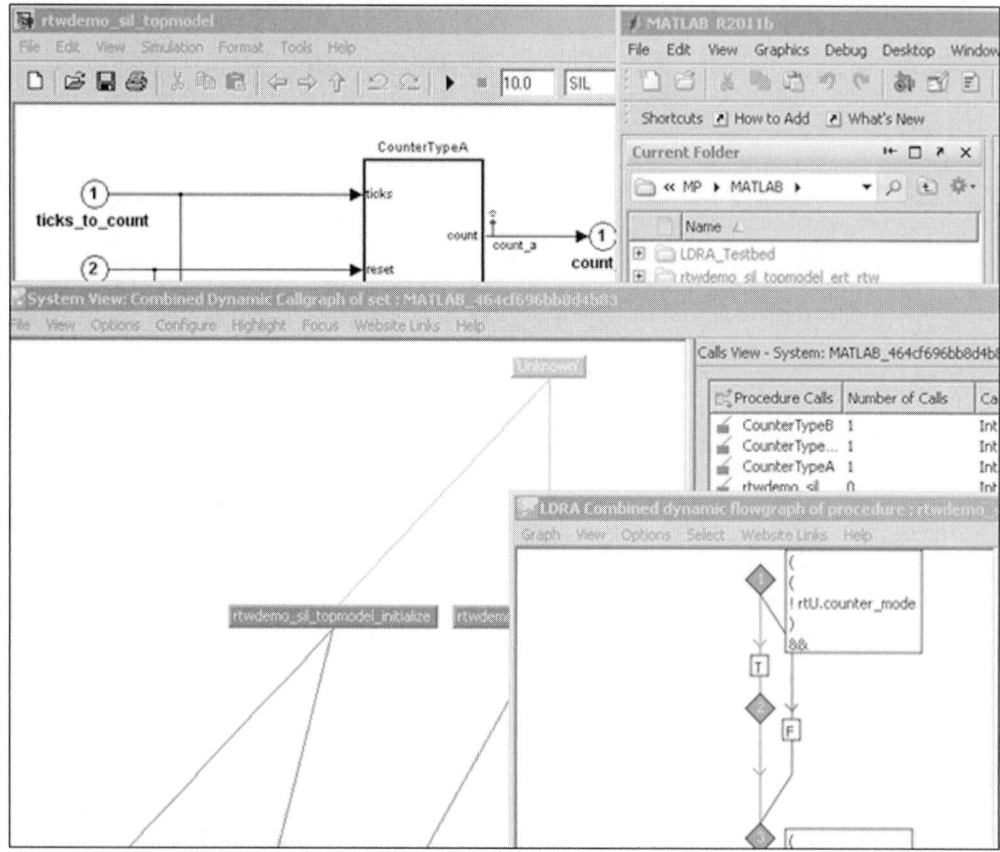

Figure 15.29:
Generating code coverage data in auto-generated code.

At first glance, it may seem pointless testing auto-generated code at source code level. However, this is not the case.

Even assuming that the code is not supplemented by manually generated code, there is a multitude of problems which can exist in auto-generated code. For example, the conversion of the floating-point arithmetic from the model simulation on the PC to floating-point arithmetic on the target may be erroneous and so require testing.

When a standard dictates that a particular level of code coverage is to be achieved, it becomes necessary to demonstrate at source level (and conceivably at system level) that the code has indeed been executed.

It is sometimes in the nature of auto-generated code for redundant code to be generated, and many standards disallow such an inclusion. Static and dynamic analysis of the source code can reveal such superfluous additions and permit their removal.

There are also circumstances where the generated source code is expected to adhere to coding standards, such as MISRA C: 2004. The code generation suite may claim to meet such standards, but independent proof of that is frequently required.

Working with legacy code

Software test tools have been traditionally designed with the expectation that the code has been (or is being) designed and developed following a best practice development process.

Legacy code turns the ideal process on its head. Although such code is a valuable asset, it is likely to have been developed on an experimental, ad hoc basis by a series of "gurus" – experts who prided themselves at getting things done and in knowing the application itself, but not necessarily expert at complying with modern development thinking and bored with providing complete documentation. That does not sit well with the requirements of such standards as DO-178B.

Frequently, this legacy software – software of unknown pedigree (SOUP) – forms the basis of new developments. The resulting challenges do not just come from extended functionality. Such developments may need to meet modern coding standards and deploy updated target hardware and development tool chains, meaning that even unchanged functionality cannot be assumed to be proven.

The need to leverage the value of SOUP presents its own set of unique challenges.

The dangers of SOUP

Many SOUP projects will have initially been subjected only to functional system testing, leaving many code paths unexercised and leading to costly in-service corrections. Even in the field, it is highly likely that the circumstances required to exercise much of the code have never occurred, and such applications have therefore sustained little more than an extension of functional system testing by their in-field use.

When there is a requirement for ongoing development of legacy code, previously unexercised code paths are likely to be called into use by combinations of data never previously encountered (Figure 15.30).

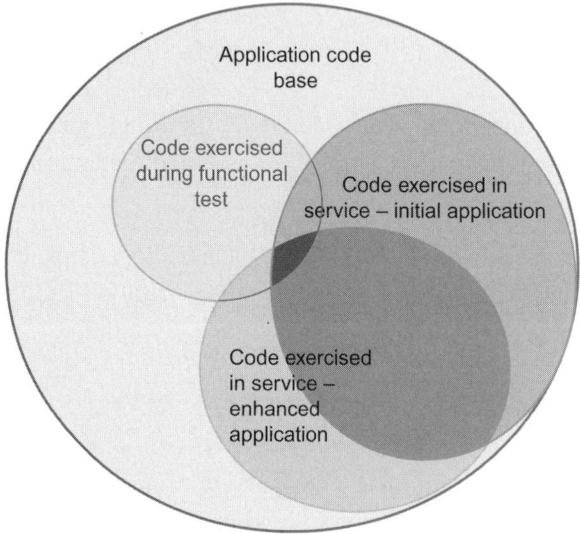

Figure 15.30:
Code exercised both on site and by functional testing is likely to include many unproven execution paths. Code enhancements are prone to call previously unexercised paths into service.

The same commercial pressures which rule out a rewrite are likely to rule out the use of all of the following options. As ever, they can be used selectively depending on the criticality of an application or its subsections.

Static and dynamic analysis of SOUP

In the enhancement of SOUP, the existing code frequently defines the functionality of the system rather than documentation. In enhancing the code, it is therefore vital that the functionality is not unintentionally modified. And, even where all source code remains identical, a new compiler or target hardware can introduce unintentional functionality changes with potentially disastrous results.

The challenge is to identify the building blocks within the test tools which can be used in an appropriate sequence to aid the efficient enhancement of SOUP.

There are five major considerations.

Improving the level of understanding

The system visualization facilities provided by many modern test tools are extremely powerful. Static call graphs provide a hierarchical illustration of the application and system entities, and static flow graphs show the control flow across program blocks.

Such call graphs and flow graphs are just part of the benefit of the comprehensive analysis of all parameters and data objects used in the code. This information is particularly vital to enable the affected procedures and data structures to be isolated and understood when work begins on enhancing functionality.

Enforcing new standards

When new developments are based on existing SOUP, it is likely that standards will have been enhanced in the intervening period. Code review analysis can highlight contravening code.

It may be that the enforcement of an internationally recognized coding standard to SOUP is too onerous and so a subset compromise is preferred. In that case, it is possible to apply a user-defined set of rules which could simply be less demanding, or which could, for instance, place particular focus on portability issues.

The enforcement of new standards to legacy code is covered in more detail in the coding standards case study.

Ensuring adequate code coverage

As established previously, code proven in service has often effectively been subjected only to extensive "functional testing".

Structural coverage analysis addresses this issue by testing equally across the sources, assuming each path through them has an equal chance of being exercised.

Although not offering a complete solution, system-wide functional testing exercises many paths and so provides a logical place to start.

Commonly a test tool may take a copy of the code under test and implant additional procedure calls ("instrumentation") to identify the paths exercised during execution. Textual code coverage reports are then often complemented with colored graphs, such as those illustrated in Figure 15.31, to give an insight into the code tested and into the nature of data required to ensure additional coverage.

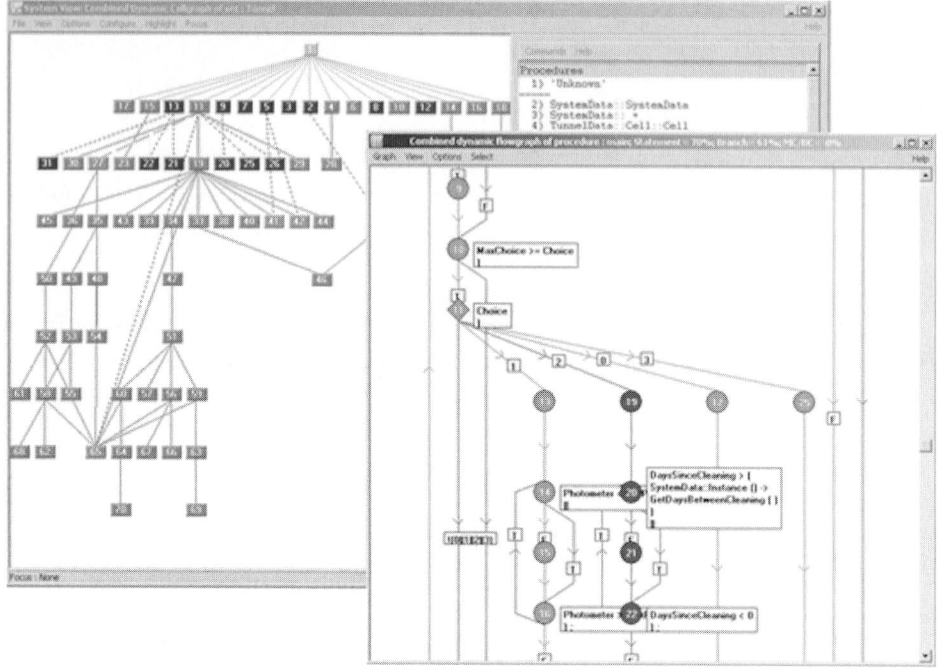

Figure 15.31:
Color-coded graphical information clearly identifies unexercised code.

Manually constructed unit tests can be used to ensure that each part of the code functions correctly in isolation. However, the time and skill involved in constructing a harness to allow the code to compile can be considerable.

Some of the more advanced modern unit test tools minimize that overhead by automatically constructing the harness code within a GUI environment and providing details of the input and output data variables to which the user may assign values. The result can then be exercised on either the host or target machine.

To complement system test, it is possible to apply code instrumentation to unit tests and hence exercise those parts of the code which have yet to be proven. This is equally true of code which is inaccessible under normal circumstances, such as exception handlers.

Sequences of these test cases can be stored, and they can be automatically exercised regularly to ensure that ongoing development does not adversely affect proven functionality.

Dealing with compromised modularity

In some SOUP applications, structure and modularity may have suffered, challenging the notion of testing functional or structural subsections of that code.

However, many unit test tools can be very flexible, and the harness code which is constructed to drive test cases can often be configured to include as much of the source code base as necessary. The ability to do that may be sufficient to suit a purpose.

If a longer-term goal exists to improve overall software quality, then using instrumented code can help to understand which execution paths are taken when different input parameters are passed into a procedure – either in isolation or in the broader context of its calling tree.

Ensuring correct functionality

Perhaps the most important aspect of SOUP-based development is ensuring that all aspects of the software function as expected, despite changes to the code, to the compiler or the target hardware, or to the data handled by the application.

Even with the aid of test tools, generating unit tests for the whole code base may involve more work than the budget will accommodate. However, the primary aim here is not to check that each procedure behaves in a particular way. It is to ensure that there have been no inadvertent changes to functionality.

By statically analyzing the code, test tools provide significant assistance for the generation of test cases and the more sophisticated tools on the market are able to fully automate this process for some test case types. This assistance, whether partially or fully automated, will help to exercise a high percentage of the control-flow paths through the code. Depending on the capabilities of the tool in use, input and output data may also be generated through fully or partially automated means. This data may then be retained for future use.

The most significant future use of this retained data will be in application of regression tests, the primary function of which is to ensure that when those same tests are run on the code under development there are no unexpected changes. These regression tests provide the cross-reference back to the functionality of the original source code and form one of the primary benefits of the unit test process as a whole. As such the more feature-rich of the available unit test tools will often boost the efficiency and through-put of regression tests via the ability to support batch processing.

Tracing requirements through to object code verification (OCV)

With applications whose failure has critical consequences – people's lives could be at risk or significant business impact – there is a growing recognition that most requirements traceability stops short of object code. There is, therefore, an implied reliance on the faithful adherence of compiled object code to the intentions expressed by the author of the source code.

Where an industry standard is enforced, a development team will usually adhere only to the parts of the standard which are relevant to their application – including OCV. On the other hand, it is designed to ensure that critical parts of an application are not compromised by the object code, which in principle is a desirable outcome for any software – whatever its purpose.

Industry standards and software certification

Irrespective of the industry and the maturity of its safety standards, the case for software which has been proven and certified to be reliable through standards compliance and requirements traceable process is becoming ever more compelling.

When the RTM becomes the centre of the development process (Figure 15.32), it impacts on all stages of design from high-level requirements through to target-based deployment and OCV. This tier 6 takes the target-based work a stage further, to tie in the comparison of the object and source code as part of the requirements traceability matrix and an extension to it.

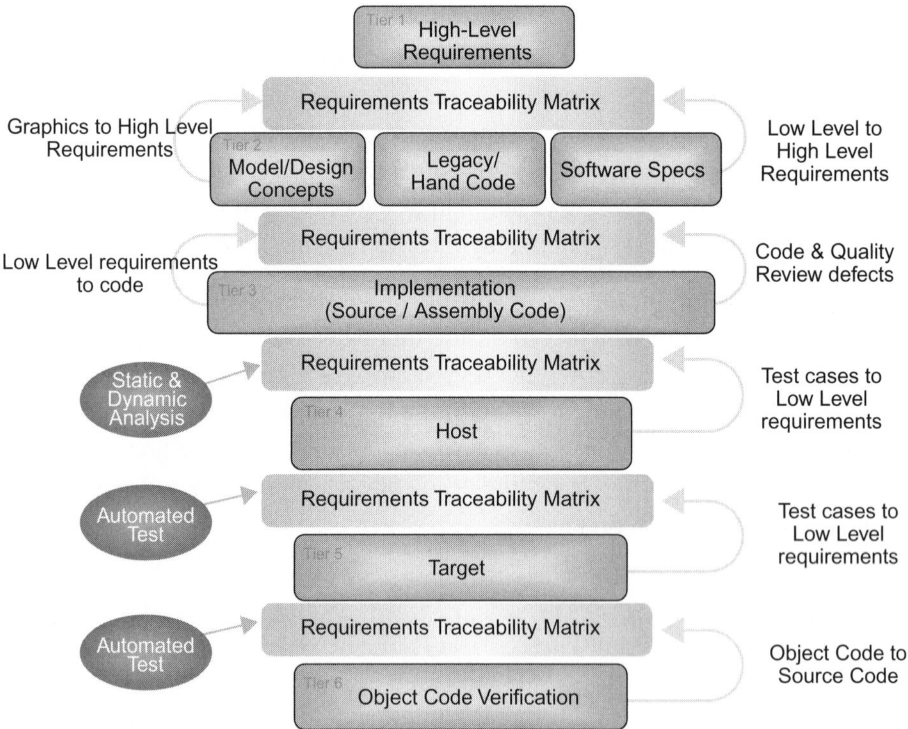

Figure 15.32:
The requirements traceability matrix (RTM) can be extended through to object code verification at the sixth tier.

Object code verification (OCV)

So what is object code verification? The relevant section of the aerospace DO-178B standard describes the technique as follows:

> *The structural coverage analysis may be performed on the source code, unless the software is Level A and the compiler generates object code that is not directly traceable to source code statements. Then, additional verification should be performed on the object code to establish the correctness of such generated code sequences. A compiler-generated array bound check in the object code is an example of object code that is not directly traceable to the source code.*
>
> ***DO-178B standard (6.4.4.2 Structural Coverage Analysis)***

OCV hinges on how much the control flow structure of the compiler-generated object code differs from that of the application source code from which it was derived.

Object code control flow versus source code control flow

It is useful to illustrate this variation. Consider the following very simple source code,

```
void f_while4( int f_while4_input1, int f_while4_input2 )
{

  int f_while4_local1, f_while4_local2 ;

  f_while4_local1 = f_while4_input1 ;

  f_while4_local2 = f_while4_input2 ;

  while( f_while4_local1<1 || f_while4_local2>1 )

   {

     f_while4_local1 ++ ;

     f_while4_local2 - ;

   }

}
```

This C code can be demonstrated to achieve 100% source code coverage by means of a single call thus:

```
f_while4(0,3);
```

and can be reformatted to a single operation per line like so:

```
1 void
1  f_while4 (
```

```
1  int f_while4_input1 ,
1  int f_while4_input2 )
1  {
1   int
1    f_while4_local1 ,
1    f_while4_local2 ;
1   f_while4_local1 = f_while4_input1 ;
1   f_while4_local2 = f_while4_input2 ;
--------------------------------------------
2   while
2    (
2    f_while4_local1<1
2    ||
--------------------------------------------
3    f_while4_local2>1
--------------------------------------------
4    )
--------------------------------------------
5    {
5     f_while4_local1++ ;
5     f_while4_local2-- ;
5    }
--------------------------------------------
6  }
```

The prefix for each of these reformatted lines of code identifies a "basic block" – that is, a sequence of straight line code. The resulting flow graph for the function shows both the structure of the source code, and the coverage attained by such a test case with the basic blocks identified on the flow chart nodes (Figure 15.33).

The object code generated by a compiler will depend on the optimization setting, the compiler vendor, the target and a host of other issues. The following shows just one example of resulting (reformatted) assembler code generated by a widely used commercially available compiler with optimization disabled.

```
_f_while4:

      push    fp

      ldiu    sp,fp

      addi    2,sp

      ldi     *-fp(2),r0      ; |40|

      ldiu    *-fp(3),r1      ; |41|

      sti     r0,*+fp(1)      ; |40|

      sti     r1,*+fp(2)      ; |41|
```

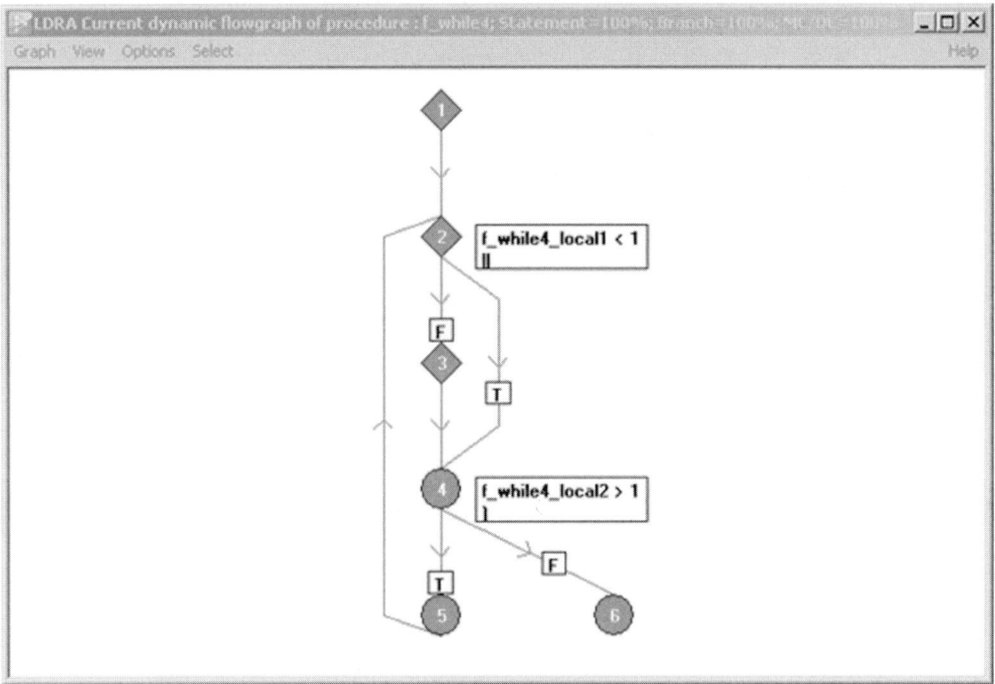

Figure 15.33:
A dynamic flow graph showing the source code exercised through a single function call.

```
      ble    L3                 ; |43|  New test 2
;*    Branch Occurs to L3       ; |43|
      ldiu   r1,r0
      cmpi   1,r0               ; |43|
      ble    L5                 ; |43|
;*    Branch Occurs to L5       ; |43|  New test 3

L3:
      ldiu   1,r0               ; |45|
      ldiu   1,r1               ; |46|
      addi   *+fp(1),r0         ; |45|
      subri  *+fp(2),r1         ; |46|
```

```
59      sti     r0,*+fp(1)     ; |45|
60      cmpi    0,r0           ; |43|
61      sti     r1,*+fp(2)     ; |46|
62      ble     L3             ; |43|  New test 1
63 ;*     Branch Occurs to L3        ; |43|
64      ldiu    r1,r0
65      cmpi    1,r0           ; |43|
66      bgt     L3             ; |43|
67 ;*     Branch Occurs to L3        ; |43|
68
69 L5:
70      ldiu    *-fp(1),r1
71      bud     r1
```

It should be emphasized that there is *nothing wrong* with this compiler or the assembler code it has generated.

However, the flow graph looks quite different for the assembler code – and in particular, using the identical test case generates a quite different flow graph both in terms of appearance and, importantly, in terms of coverage (Figure 15.34).

It is clear from the flow chart and the assembler code that more tests are necessary to achieve 100% code coverage.

- New test 1. Line 62. End of block 3. Branch to L3.
  This blue branch always evaluates to false with the existing test data because it only exercises the loop once, and so only one of the two possible outcomes results from the test to see whether to continue. Adding a new test case to ensure a second pass around that loop exercises both true and false cases. A suitable example can be provided thus:
  `f_while4(-1,3);`
- New test 2. Line 47. End of block 1. Branch to L3.
  This code contains an "or" statement in the while loop conditions. The existing test cases both result in the code
  `f_while4_local1<1`
  returning a "true" value.

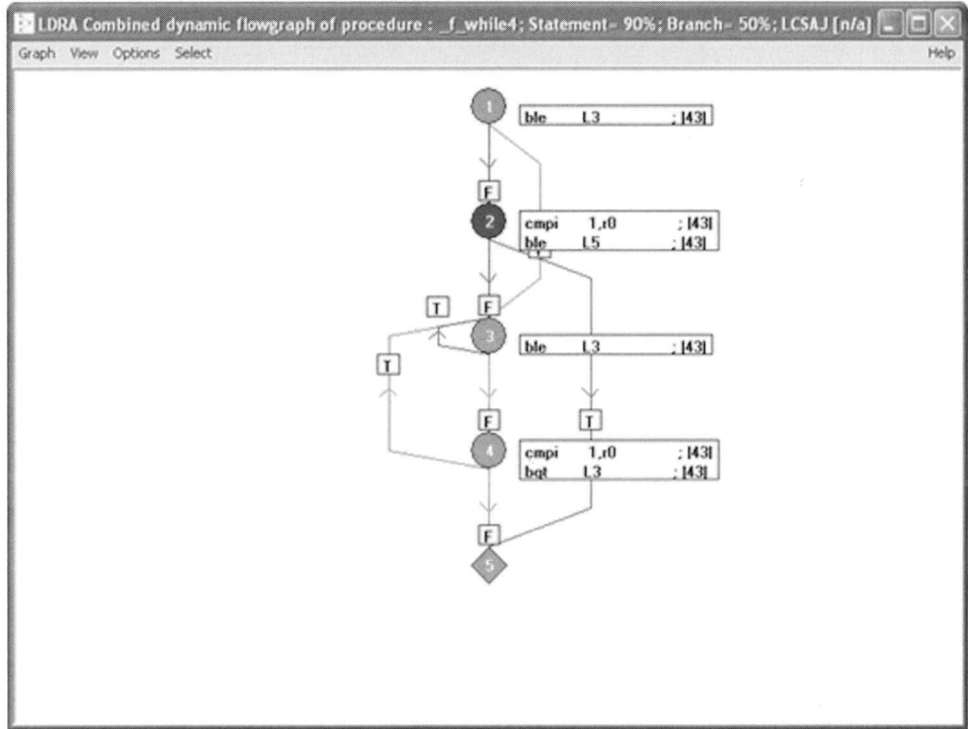

Figure 15.34:
A dynamic flow graph showing the assembler code exercised through a single function call.

The addition of a new test case to return a "false" value will address that.

```
f_while4(3,3);
```

- New test 3. Line 52. End of block 2. Branch to L5.

  The remaining unexercised branch is the result of the fact that if neither of the initial conditions in the "while" statement is satisfied then the code within the loop is bypassed altogether via the ble branch.

  So, the final test is added will provide such a circumstance.

  ```
  f_while4(3,0);
  ```

  These three additional tests result in 100% statement and branch coverage of the assembler code (Figure 15.35).

- So – to achieve 100% coverage of the assembler code, four tests are required:

```
f_while4(0,3);
f_while4(-1,3);
f_while4(3,3);
f_while4(3,0);
```

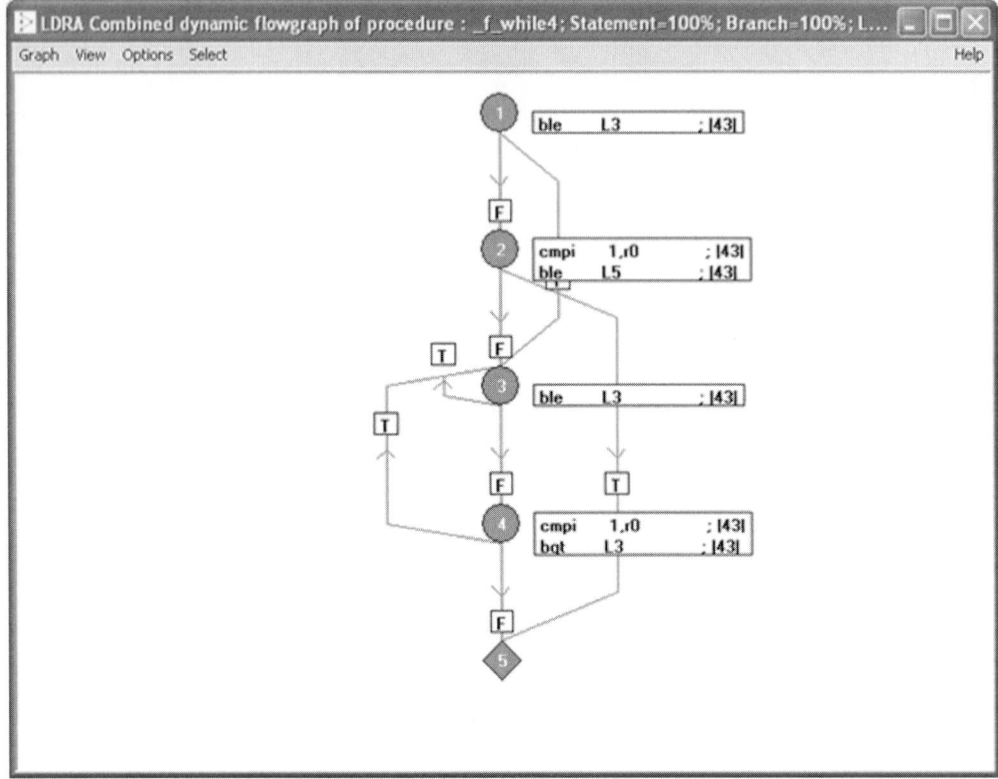

Figure 15.35:
A dynamic flow graph showing 100% assembler code exercised through additional function calls.

Extending source code coverage to object code verification

If structural coverage analysis (SCA) is accepted as significant, then it follows that object code verification (OCV) is also worthy of consideration.

In the general case, SCA provides evidence that *all* of the code base has been exercised. Such an approach has been proven to reduce the risk of failure and consequently is specified in most, if not all, industrial standards concerned with safety.

SCA offers a proven mechanism for ensuring that software is robust and safe. However, we have already established that merely exercising all of the source code does *not* prove that all of the object code has been similarly exercised and proven.

True, it is less likely that an unexercised route through the object code will lead to system failure but even lesser risks can be unacceptable if a system is sufficiently safety, commercially or mission critical.

In short, how big are the risks?

Further, consider the fact that our example mismatch between source and object code flow charts was generated in a compiler with the optimization disabled. Many more differences are likely as the result of compiler interpretation and optimization. While traditional structural coverage techniques are applied at the source code level, the object code executes on the processor – and that is what really matters.

Any differences in control flow structure between the two can make for significant and unacceptable gaps in the testing process.

In some industries, these gaps are acknowledged and accounted for. For example, in aerospace, the DO-178B standard requires developers to implement OCV facilities for those elements of the application that have a Level-A (safety-critical) classification. While this is often a subset of the application as a whole, it has traditionally represented a significant amount of testing effort and hence has always required considerable resources.

Opportunities to implement automated, compiler-independent processes can help to reduce overall development costs by considerable margins, and conversely make the technique of OCV commercially justifiable in other fields.

Automated OCV

Automated OCV solutions can provide a complete SCA solution for both source and object code from unit to system and integration levels (Figure 15.36).

Typical solutions combine both high- and object-level (assembler) code analysis tools, with the object-level tool variant being determined by the target processor that the application is required to run on. A typical example might see C/C++ and PowerPC Assembler analysis tools teamed together to provide the required coverage metrics.

OCV at the unit level

Some automated tools enable users to create test cases for structural coverage of high-level source and apply exactly the same test cases to the structural coverage of the corresponding object code.

A driver program is generated by such a unit test tool which encapsulates the entire test environment, defining, running and monitoring the test cases through initial test verification and then subsequent regression analysis. When used for OCV, this driver may be linked with either the high-level source unit or the associated object code. In so doing, users can apply a uniform test process and compare code in order to determine any discrepancies or deficiencies (Figure 15.37).

If structural coverage discrepancies or deficiencies are identified at the object level, users are then presented with an opportunity to define additional test cases to close any gaps in the test process. The obvious advantage of identifying and applying corrective action at

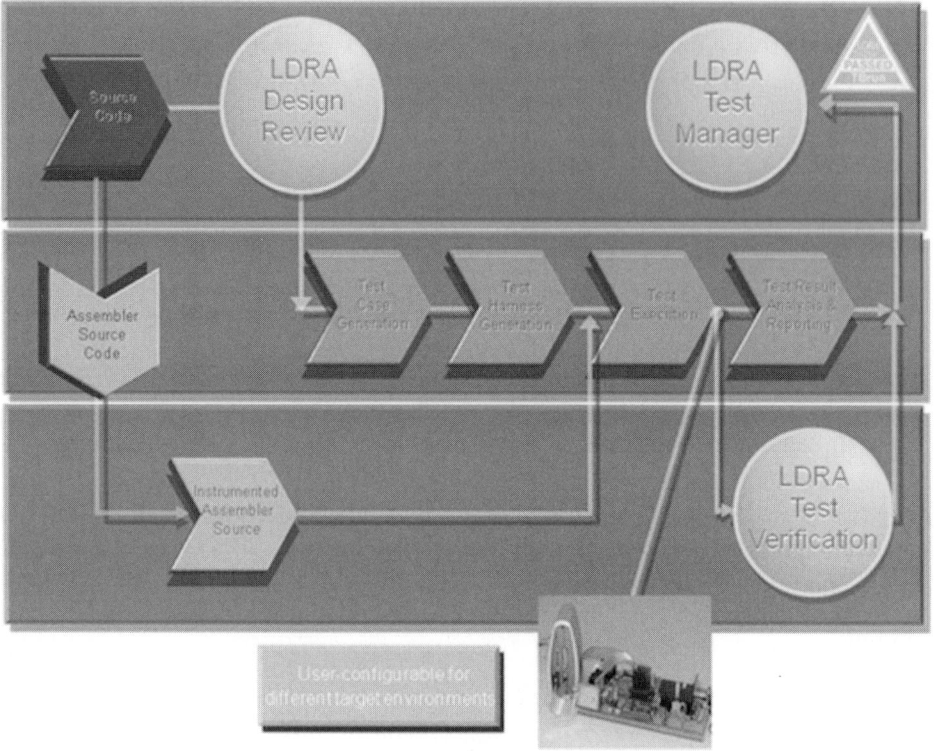

Figure 15.36:
The automation of OCV can reduce the necessary amount of testing effort by a considerable margin.

such an early development stage is that it is much easier and cheaper. It also significantly increases the quality of the code and the overall test process, with the latter reaping benefits at the later stages of integration and system testing and then onward in the form of reduced failure rates/maintenance costs when the application is in the field.

While the code is still under development, together with satisfying the necessary OCV requirements in a highly automated and cost-effective manner, developers can also benefit from the considerable additional test feedback. The results of these analysis facilities can be fed back to the development team with the possibility that further code and design deficiencies may be identified and rectified, further enhancing the quality of the application as a whole.

Justifying the expense

It is clear that OCV has always involved significant overhead and that even in the aerospace sector it is only enforced as a requirement for the most demanding safety

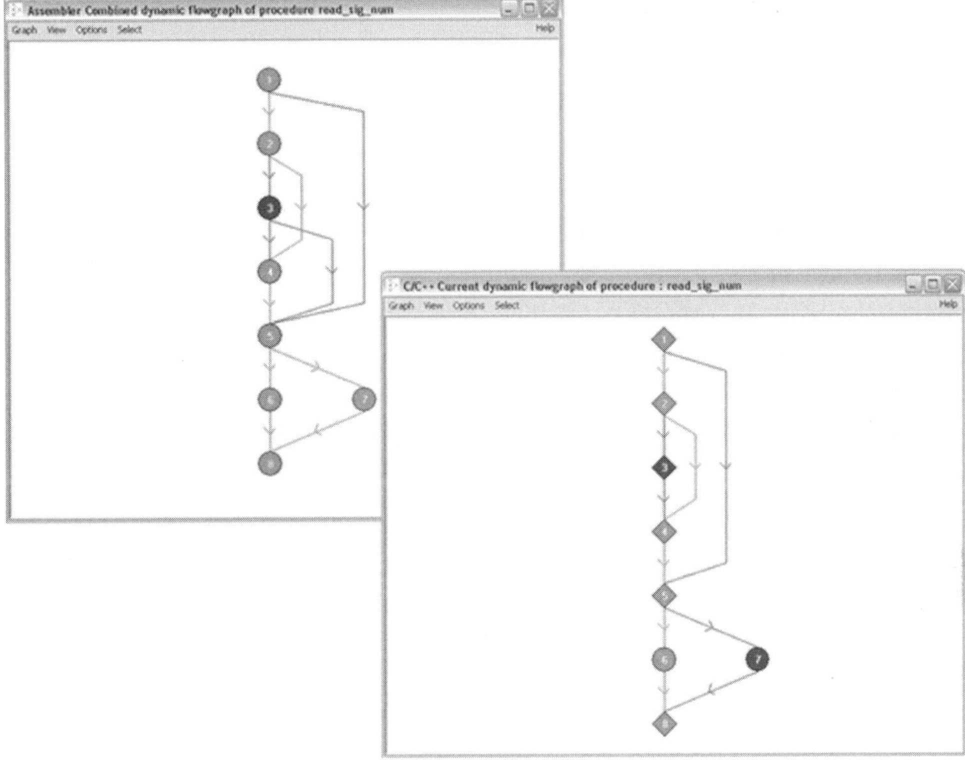

Figure 15.37:
Object code and source code flow graphs illustrate the structure and coverage of the high- and low-level code, and hence any discrepancies between them.

integrity levels. Even then, the elements nominated for object code verification in these applications usually represent a subset of the application as a whole – a specialist niche indeed.

However, there is precedence for this situation. Until quite recently, unit test has been considered by many as a text-book nicety, for the purposes of the aircraft and nuclear industry. More recently, it has found a place in automotive, railway and medical applications, and now the ever-increasing capabilities and ease of use of automated unit test tools have introduced a commercial justification of such techniques even when risks are lower.

Most applications include key elements in the software; a subset of code that is particularly critical to the success of the application and can be identified in the application requirements. The software requiring OCV can be identified and traced through an extension to the requirements traceability matrix.

The advent of tools to automate the whole of that process from requirements traceability right through to OCV challenges the notion that the overhead involved can only justify the technique in very rare circumstances. Just as for unit test before it, perhaps the time has come for OCV to be commercially justifiable in a much broader range of circumstances.

Implementing a test solution environment

Pragmatic considerations

Like so many other things in business life, ultimately the budget which is to be afforded to the test environment depends on commercial justification. If the project under consideration has to be shown to comply with standards in order to sell, then that justification is straightforward. It is much less clear-cut if it is based entirely on cost savings and enhanced reputation resulting from fewer recalls.

Although vendors make presentations assuming developers are to work on a virgin project where they can pick and choose what they like, that is often not the case. Many development projects enhance legacy code, interface to existing applications, are subject to the development methods of client organization's and their contractual obligations, or are restricted by time and budget.

The underlying direction of the organization for future projects also influences choices:

- Is this a quick fix for a problem project in the field? Is the search for a software test tool which will resolve a mystery and occasional run time error crash in final test?
- Maybe there is a development on the order books which involves legacy code requiring a one-off change for an age-old client, but which is unlikely to be used beyond that.
- Perhaps existing legacy code cannot be rewritten, but there is a desire and mandate to raise the quality of software development on an ongoing basis for new developments and/or the existing code base.
- Or perhaps there is a new project to consider, but the lessons of problems in the past suggest that ongoing enhancement of the software development process would be beneficial.

To address a particular situation it is initially useful to consider how each of the five key attributes discussed earlier fit into the development process.

Considering the alternatives

Given that, in general, vendors are not keen to highlight where their own offering falls short, some insight into how to reach such a decision would surely be useful.

The diagram in Figure 15.38 superimposes the different analysis techniques on a traditional "V" development model. Obviously, a particular project may use another development model. In truth, the analysis is model-agnostic and a similar representation could be conceived for any other development process model – waterfall, iterative, agile, etc.

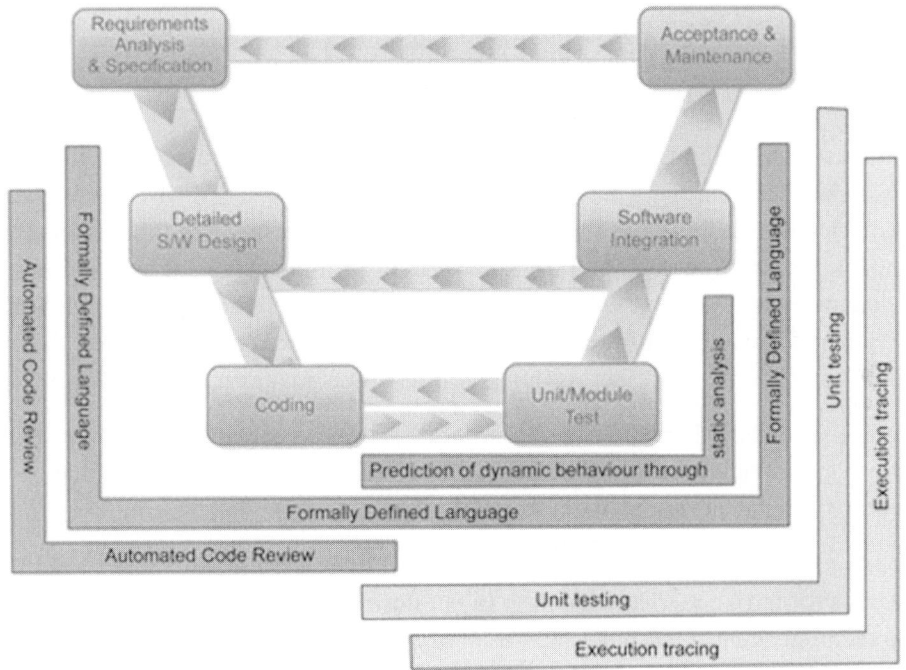

Figure 15.38:
The five fundamental test tool attributes directly relate to the specific development stages of design, code, test and verification, etc.

The extent to which it is desirable to cover all elements of the development cycle depends very much on the initial state of development and the desired outcome.

Each of the five key test tool attributes has merit.

There is a sound argument which supports traditional formal methods, but the development overheads for such an approach and the difficulty involved in applying it retrospectively to existing code limits its usefulness to the highly safety-critical market.

Automated code review checks for the adherence to coding standards, and is likely to be useful in almost all development environments.

Of the remaining approaches, dynamic analysis techniques provide a test environment much more representative of the final application than static predictions of dynamic analysis as well as the means to provide functional testing.

Where requirements traceability is key within a managed and controlled development environment, the progressive nature of automated code review followed by unit, integration and system test aligns well within the overall tiered concept of most modern standards. It also fulfills the frequent requirement or recommendation to exercise the code in its target environment.

Where robustness testing is considered desirable and justified, it can be provided by means of the automatic definition of unit test vectors, or through the use of the static prediction of dynamic behavior. Each of these techniques has its own merits, with the former exercising code in its target environment, and the latter providing a means to exercise the full data set rather than discrete test vectors. Where budgetary constraints permit, these mutually exclusive benefits could justify the application of both techniques. Otherwise, the multi-functional nature of many of the available unit test tools makes it a cost-effective approach.

If there is a secondary desire to evolve corporate processes towards the current best practice, then both automated code review and dynamic analysis techniques have a key role to play in requirements management and traceability, with the latter being essential to show that the code meets its functional objectives.

If the aim is to find a pragmatic solution to cut down on the number of issues displayed by a problem application in the field, then each of the robustness techniques – that is, the static analysis of dynamic behavior or the automatic definition of unit test vectors – have the potential to isolate tricky problems in an efficient manner.

When is unit test justifiable? – case study

It is perhaps useful to consider one of the five attributes to illustrate a possible thought process to be applied when deciding where to invest.

Unit testing cannot always be justified. And sometimes it remains possible to perform unit test from first principles, without the aid of any test tool at all.

There are pragmatic judgments to be made.

Sometimes that judgment is easy. If the software fails, what are the implications? Will anyone be killed, as might be the case in aircraft flight control? Will the commercial implications be disproportionately high, as exemplified by a continuous plastics production plant? Or are the costs of recall extremely high, perhaps in a car's engine controller? In these cases, extensive unit testing is essential and hence any tools that may aid in that purpose make sense.

On the other hand, if software is developed purely for internal use or is perhaps a prototype, then the overhead in unit testing all but the most vital of procedures would be prohibitive.

As might be expected, there is a gray area. Suppose the application software controls a mechanical measuring machine where the quantity of the devices sold is low and the area served is localized. The question becomes: would the occasional failure be more acceptable than the overhead of unit test?

In these circumstances, it is useful to prioritize the parts of the software which are either critical or complex. If a software error leads to a strangely colored display or a need for an occasional reboot, it may be inconvenient but not in itself justification for unit test. On the other hand, the unit test of code which generates reports showing whether machined components are within tolerance may be vital. Hence, as we have already seen advocated by leading standards such as DO-178B, significant benefit may be achieved through a decision to apply the rigor of unit test to a critical sub-set or sub-sets of the application code as a whole.

When are unit test tools justifiable?

Again, it comes down to cost. The later a defect is found in the product development, the more costly it is to fix – a concept first established in 1975 with the publication of Brooks's *Mythical Man Month* and proven many times since through various studies.

The automation of any process changes the dynamic of commercial justification. That is especially true of test tools given that they make earlier unit test much more feasible. Consequently, modern unit test almost implies the use of such a tool unless only a handful of procedures are involved.

The primary function of such unit test tools is to assist with the generation and maintaining of the harness code which provides the main and associated calling functions or procedures (generically "procedures"), with the more sophisticated tools on the market being able to fully automate this process. The harness itself facilitates compilation and allows unit testing to take place.

The tools not only provide the harness itself, but also statically analyse the source code to provide the details of each input and output parameter or global variable in an easily understood form. Where unit testing is performed on an isolated snippet of code, stubbing of called procedures can be an important aspect of unit testing. This can also often be partially or fully automated to further enhance the efficiency of the approach.

High levels of automation afforded by modern unit test tools make the assignment of values to the procedure under test a simple process, and one which demands little knowledge of the code on the part of the test tool operator. This creates that necessary unit test objectivity because it divorces the test process from that of code development where circumstances require it, and from a pragmatic perspective substantially lowers the level of skill required to develop unit tests.

It is this ease of use which means that unit test can now be considered a viable arrow in the development quiver, targeting each procedure at the time of writing. When these early unit tests identify weak code, it can be corrected whilst the original intent remains very fresh in the mind of the developer.

Summary and conclusions

There are hundreds of text books about software testing, and many which deal with only a specialist facet of it. It is therefore clear that a chapter such as this one cannot begin to cover the whole subject in detail.

Some elements of software testing remain unmentioned here. What about testing for stack overflow? Timing considerations? And multithreaded applications, with their potentially problematic race and lethal embrace conditions?

In preference to covering all such matters superficially, the technique demonstrated in this chapter, of “drilling down” into a topic to shed sufficient light on its worth in a particular circumstance, is sound, and will remain so even for test techniques as yet unavailable. It is therefore applicable in those matters not covered in any detail here.

In each case, these are techniques which can be deployed or not as circumstances dictate; the whole genre of software test techniques and tools constitute a tool kit just as surely as a toolbox holding spanners, hammers and screwdrivers.

And just like those handyman’s friends, sometimes it is possible to know from a superficial glance whether a technique or test tool is useful, while at other times it needs more detailed investigation.

The key, then, is to be sure that decisions to follow a particular path are based on sufficient knowledge. Take the time to investigate and be sure that the solution you are considering will prove to be the right one for a particular circumstance.

Consider the option of developing in-house tests and when commercially marketed test tools are considered, be sure to ask for an evaluation copy.

Choosing the wrong technique or the wrong tool can be a very costly and embarrassing mistake indeed.

CHAPTER 16

Software Development Tools for Embedded Systems

Catalin Dan Udma

Chapter Outline

Software Engineering for Embedded Systems.
DOI: http://dx.doi.org/10.1016/B978-0-12-415917-4.00016-5
© 2013 Elsevier Inc. All rights reserved.

Introduction to debugging tools

Debugging is an essential step in the software development process. Before starting the debugging, each developer should have a clear understanding of what the available debugging and analysis tools are and what the hardware and software target platform requirements are. Choosing the right debugging tool is another important step with an impact on the development time, productivity and system performance. Depending on the embedded platform, processor complexity, hardware interfaces, operating system (OS) running on the target and development stage then different tools may bring the best benefits. Here are some quick guidelines for choosing the debugging tools and you can find the details later in this chapter:

- Initial board bring-up, hardware validation, OS development and application development without OS on the target. The first option for debugging is the use of an external device based on JTAG or ARM SWD/SWO interfaces. Typically these devices come with the debugger software bundle – the source-code debugger. Details in section 4.
- High-level application development using the OS services on the target – a typical case is Linux user-space application development. The option would be the debugging tool based on an agent running on the target special designed to handle the target operating system API. The most common example is GDB. Details in section 2.
- Special target requirements need special debugging tools. A standard debugger may not cover all the scenarios and you can design your own debugging tool to fit into your target and application requirements. Details in section 3.
- Improvement, optimization and analysis in software development. While developing or after the software product is completed you can use the memory debuggers, static and dynamic analysis tools to tune the application. Details in sections 6 and 7.
- Finally, sometimes a debugger may be the right tool when the target processor support is provided as an integrated development toolset including compiler, debugger (JTAG or agent-based), target operating system and applications, trace and profiling tools (with hardware and software support).

When talking about software development tools, one of the first things that comes to mind is the source-code debugger – the software tool that allows you to see what is inside your program at the current execution point or at the moment when the program crashed. The debugger can show a lot of information about the current state of the program, such as the location in the program's source code, registers, stack frames, program memory, variables and other factors. In the debugging process, the programmer can step through the code line by line or by assembler instruction, step into or step out of the functions, pause or continue the program, insert and remove breakpoints and detect exceptions or program errors.

The source-code debugger provides the same base capabilities even when the target is accessed through an external debugging device (based on JTAG or ARM SWD/SWO interfaces) or through a debug agent. In the following we will present basic debugger features as they apply to an embedded system using as an example one of the most popular and widely used debuggers, GDB – GNU DeBugger. GDB is free software provided by the Free Software Foundation and protected by the GNU General Public License (GPL).

However, a standard source-code debugger like GDB that has a debug agent running on the target does not cover all the debugging scenarios because the embedded targets may have special requirements and resources may be limited. For these scenarios special debug agents are used. And, more importantly, these debug agents should be designed to fit into the specific target requirements and to provide the necessary tools to improve the debugging process. Such a debug agent does not necessarily have to be a source-code debugger, but it can start as small debug routine and then it can evolve into a fully featured debugger. We will then show how to design a debug agent from scratch, pointing out the key elements of the design.

The limitations of debuggers using debug agent software on the target are resolved using the JTAG interface, an external device used to connect the debugger directly to the target, allowing the debugger to have full control of the target and its resources. Debugging using the JTAG has many benefits, especially for fast initial board bring-up. For each debugging scenario, the debug solutions using debug agents or JTAG have advantages and disadvantages and choosing the right solution is a trade-off of capabilities, flexibility and price.

Open-source free software is today a good alternative for debugging solutions. Using only open-source software we can have an integrated development and debugging tool providing standard debug capabilities. One such solution is to use Eclipse for the graphical user interface, GDB for the debugger and GDBserver or KGDB as debug agents running on target.

No matter how good the debuggers are, a debugger cannot cover the entire investigation for all programming errors. Analysis and trace tools are other development tools that help in finding out other run-time errors by analyzing the program execution on the target. In this category we can talk about memory debuggers, which provide information about incorrect usage of dynamic memory allocation, system call debuggers, or instrumented code. A complete description of analysis tools is outside the scope of this chapter, but a summary of what these tools can provide and how they can be used to complement the investigations done with the debugger is presented.

Overall, when developing software for embedded systems it is always good to know the hardware capabilities of the processor on the target, the available debugging and analysis tools and their capabilities. This way you can choose when and how to use the right tool to obtain the maximum benefits in minimal time.

GDB debugging

GDB is a widely used debugger for embedded software for Linux/Unix systems. At the present time, GDB includes support for a large range of target processors: PowerPC, ARM, MIPS, SPARC, ColdFire are only some of the most used.

The GDB package is open-source software that can be downloaded and configured for a specific architecture. GDB can be used as a single application (*gdb*) – this is most commonly used in the case of debugging host applications, or it can be split into two applications, in *gdb-gdbserver* mode. When debugging embedded applications, the *gdb-gdbserver* mode is what normally should be used: GDB runs on the host computer and GDBserver, the embedded application, runs on the target. GDB and GDBserver communicate using the GDB remote protocol, TCP or serial-based.

Here are some advantages of gdb-gdbserver mode that an embedded programmer should take into consideration when is deciding how to use GDB.

- The GDBserver is a small, lightweight target application that does basic tasks at GDB's request or just sends event notifications to GDB. The GDBserver application's requirements for processing, size and memory are low, as compared to GDB.
- On the other hand, GDB running on the host computer does most of the processing: target application ELF symbol parsing, memory dumps, source file correlation, user interface and other tasks.
- As a source-code debugger, GDB needs access to the target application compiled with debug symbols (un-stripped) and to the application source code. These should be located only on the host computer. The stripped application (Without debug symbols) or the binary file (using the GDB command load) should be transferred to the target.
- On the host computer, a graphical interface can be used together with GDB to provide a more user-friendly debugger.

Configure the GDB debugger

The next step is to configure and install the GDB debugger. Normally, if GDB is already installed on your computer's operating system then it is most probable that it has been configured to debug applications on the host computer.

So you will have to do the configuration for your own target, depending on the processor you have on the target. The configuration and installation steps are the following:

- Download the GDB distribution: (http://www.gnu.org/software/gdb/download/) gdb-x.y.z.tar.gz, where x.y.z is the gdb version (e.g. gdb-7.3.1.tar.gz).
- Unpack the archive and folder gdb-x.y.z will be created.

```
$ tar xvfz gdb-x.y.z.tar.gz
```

- Create the folders for GDB host cross-platform compilation and for GDB target compilation. You should also specify the target type as you may need to use GDB for different platforms. For example <target-type> can be powerpc, arm, or other processor type.

```
$ mkdir gdb-x.y.z-host-<target-type>
$ mkdir gdb-x.y.z-target-<target-type>
```

- Configure the host GDB. The environment variable TARGET should be set before configuration – the value should be taken from the cross-build tool chain you are using for your target. For example TARGET can be powerpc-linux-gnu, powerpc-linux, arm-linux.

```
$ export TARGET=powerpc-linux
$ cd gdb-x.y.z-host-<target-type>
$ /gdb-x.y.z/configure -target=$TARGET -prefix=/usr/local/gdb-x.y.z-<target-type>
```

- Configure the target GDB:

```
$ export TARGET=powerpc-linux
$ cd gdb-x.y.z-target-<target-type>
$ ../gdb-x.y.z/configure -target=$TARGET –host=$TARGET -prefix=<target rootfs>/
usr/local
```

  where <target rootfs> is the target location where the GDB should be installed after compilation. Note that the cross-compile tool location should be added to the paths.
- Compile and install the GDB for target and host by running the following commands in the target and host folders

```
$ make; make install
```

Starting GDB

In the following it is assumed that the target is running the Linux operating system and the target program to be debugged is a user-space target Linux application. The GDBserver is also a Linux user-space application.

To start debugging the target program, the GDBserver and the target program should be available on the target. They could be installed on the target ramdisk or can be copied later on to the target using for example FTP, TFTP, SCP or other file-transfer protocols. The target program can be stripped to save space, as only GDB on the host computer handles the debug symbols.

GDB and GDBserver communicate via a TCP connection or a serial line between the target and the host computer.

There are several ways to start the GDBserver: using a TCP or a serial connection, starting the target program or attaching to a running instance. The general syntax is one of the following:

```
target$ gdbserver COMM PROGRAM [ARGS ...]
target$ gdbserver COMM -attach PID
```

where:

- COMM identifies the connection type to be used for GDB remote serial protocol: serial device (e.g. /dev/ttyS0) or the TCP connection host: < tcp port number > (e.g., host:12345); host is currently ignored;
- PROGRAM is the target program to be debugged;
- ARGS – (optional) are the target program arguments (if they exist);
- PID is the process ID (PID number) of the running process to be debugged.

Here are some examples:

```
target$ gdbserver :12345 myTargetProgram
target$ gdbserver /dev/ttyS0 myTargetProgram
target$ gdbserver :1234 2934
```

where 2934 is the PID number of running myTargetProgram:

```
target$ gdbserver :1234 'pidof myTargetProgram'
```

The next step is to connect from the GDB on the host side to the GDBserver. The un-stripped target application should be passed as a parameter to GDB or can be loaded later on with the GDB command *file*. The target libraries' location, compiled with the cross-build tool, should be set with the command "set sysroot" or the alias "set solib-absolut-prefix". This command is mandatory for debugging an embedded application if the host GDB was not compiled with the "–with-sysroot" option. Otherwise the GDB would use the standard library location, thus using the host libraries instead of the target libraries. The warnings returned in this case may be misleading and sometimes the application (or the core dump) cannot be debugged. The target libraries should also have the debug symbols on the host while on the target they can be stripped. Here is an example of how to run GDB to connect to the GDBserver:

```
$ gdb
(gdb) file myTargetProgram
```

```
(gdb) set sysroot /home/cross-tool/rootfs
(gdb) target remote 192.168.0.1:12345
```

The command "*target remote*" should match the connection parameters used in the GDBserver. In this example the parameter is a TCP connection identified by the IP address of the target where the GDBserver is running and the port number used in the GDBserver.

Compiling the application

The debug process requires the target application to be compiled with debug information. Based on it, the debugger locates the name of the functions and variables and makes the instruction correlation with the line number in the source files. In the simplest scenario when using the GNU-GCC cross-build tool chain, the debug information is added using the "*-g*" option when compiling the application, as in the example below:

```
$ powerpc-linux-gcc -g hello.c -o hello
```

The *-g* option makes the program larger and the debug information supplementary size may be significant for big projects with many source files and libraries. However, this drawback can be avoided for embedded targets: create a copy of the program with debug information (e.g., hello.unstripped) and use it with GDB on the host computer, while on the target use the stripped application – with no debug information. The application can be stripped as in the example:

```
$ powerpc-linux-strip hello
```

But adding the *-g* option does not always do the entire job. It is important to look at other GCC options that may influence the debug process when used with *-g*. These are sometimes overlooked when using Makefile with many flags and configuration options.

- Optimization (*-O, -O2...*): for GCC it is possible use *-g* and *-O* options together. Although it is possible to debug optimized code, through the optimization process the compiler rearranges the program code so the execution path may not follow the same path as in the source files. For example you may see that step-by-step operation does not always go to the next line, or you are not able to see all variables as some were removed by the optimization.
  Overall, it is recommended to do the debugging without optimization when it is possible – optimization may be added later after most of the debug is completed. On the other hand it is worth debugging the optimized code even with the drawbacks described above.
- *-fomit-frame-pointer*: this option avoids the instructions to save, set up and restore frame pointers and it also makes an extra register available in many functions. Same as optimization, it affects the debug process so it is recommended not to use it with *-g*.

- *-s:* this option tells the compiler to remove all symbol table and relocation information from the executable, so all the debug information generated with *-g* is discarded. Therefore if this option is used, the *-g* option has no effect.

For some compilers like GCC, adding the debug information does not change symbol values as compared with compilation without *-g*. This trick can be successfully used in some debugging corner cases. Let us suppose you have a release image, compiled without debug symbols, that is generating a fault: it gets locked or crashes generating a core dump. Without debug symbols you cannot actually use the debugger. The solution is to re-compile the release source files just adding the *-g* option and use the unstripped ELF to debug the fault. Of course, it is assumed that you can re-create exactly the same conditions as for release when you are re-building the project. Source versioning control is a must, the same as adding a tag to each release you deliver. The trick can be used only if your compiler generates the same symbols table after adding the debug information. You can generate the symbols table and check that it remains the same, using the command readelf:

```
$ powerpc-linux-readelf –s targetProgram>symbol_table.txt
```

Debugging the application

Once the previous steps are done, we can start debugging the target application. A full GDB debugging manual is beyond the scope of this chapter – there is a lot of documentation available. We will focus on the most useful set of commands that cover most of a typical debug process. For the purpose of going through the steps of debugging the application, we will use a very simple demo program.

```
#include<stdio.h>
struct data_t {
    int a;
    char b;
};
struct data_t my_data[10];
void compute_data(int number);
struct data_t* get_next_data();

int main() {
   int i;
   for (i = 0; i<100; i++)
        compute_data(i);
   return 1;
```

```
}
void compute_data(int number) {
    struct data_t *p_data = get_next_data();
    p_data->a = number;
    p_data->b = number % 256;
}
struct data_t* get_next_data() {
    static int cnt = 0;
    if (cnt<10)
        return &my_data[cnt++];
    return NULL;
}
```

Running the program generates a segmentation fault so this is what we are going to investigate with GDB in the following. The GDB and GDBserver are started as explained above and after the ***continue*** command, the error is shown in the GDB output:

```
(gdb) c
Continuing.
Program received signal SIGSEGV, Segmentation fault.
0×10000488 in compute_data (number=10) at data.c:18
18   p_data->a = number;
```

On error, the GDB automatically shows the source file and the line number that caused the error. We can continue to do a deeper investigation using the GDB commands.

The ***backtrace*** command displays the stack frames trace or the entire function call tree from main to the current function. You can use the shortcut ***bt.***

```
(gdb) backtrace
#0  0×10000488 in compute_data (number=10) at data.c:18
#1  0×10000424 in main () at data.c:13
```

You can further navigate through the stack frames with the following commands: ***up*** or ***down*** moves the frame to the next up or down position, ***frame <frame_number>*** moves to a specific frame number and ***frame*** shows the current frame location. On each frame you can use the GDB commands to examine the stack, variables, parameters, memory or registers.

Note: while navigating through the stack frames, the content of memory and registers is unique and does not depend on the current position in the stack. The memory and registers content is a snapshot of the moment when the debugger stopped the program execution.

To show the source file content, in the current position in the stack, use the ***list*** command: it displays a pre-configured number of lines from the source file at the current position.

Examining data

Examining data (variables, memory and registers) is essential in the debugging and investigation process and GDB offers a very good set of commands with many configuration options.

To get the values of parameters and variable the command ***print*** is used. Many printing formats are available: decimal, hexadecimal, binary and others. The command can be used for simple types and also for structures and arrays. Some examples are below:

```
(gdb) print /d my_data[0]
$4 = {a = 0, b = 0}
(gdb) print /x i
$5 = 0xa
(gdb)print /x my_data
```

More generally, the ***print*** command allows specifying the variable content as a file or a function: print 'file_name'::varName or print function_name::varName.

```
(gdb) print 'data.c'::my_data[0]
$6 = {a = 0, b = 0 '\000'}
(gdb) print get_next_data::cnt
$7 = 10
```

The commands that display the type information for variables are very useful: you can see the variable type without listing the source code and also the definition of the variable type. This is a very good shortcut especially when debugging a big project with many files. The commands are ***whatis*** and ***ptype***, used as in the examples:

```
(gdb) whatis get_next_data::cnt
type = int
(gdb) whatis my_data
type = struct data_t [10]
(gdb) ptype my_data
type = struct data_t {
   int a;
   char b;
} [10]
```

You can also inspect the memory content. The commands for memory are: ***x*** (examine) – similar to print, ***dump*** or ***restore*** – to copy data between target memory and a file.

```
(gdb) x /4× 0xbfb08e60
0xbfb08e60: 0xbfb08e80   0×10000424   0×0000000a   0×4802f534
(gdb) dump binary memory file_dump.bin 0×170d24f0 0×170d4000
(gdb) restore file_dump.bin binary 0×170d24f0
```

For advanced investigation, the low level details can be examined:

- the registers can be read with the command ***info registers [specific register]***
- the content of the stack: read the value of the stack register and then read the memory from that address
- disassembly: for low level debug use the ***disassembly*** to see the disassembled machine instructions.

Using breakpoints

A debugger provides the ability to suspend the execution of the program using breakpoints. The breakpoints can be set at a specific line number in a file, at the beginning of a function, or at a specific address. The syntax is simple enough: break <functionName>, break <fileName:lineNumber> or break * <address>.

Conditional breakpoints will suspend the execution of the program only if a specific condition is met. The condition can be added when a breakpoint is set: break <functionName> if <condition> or later on with the command <condition> #<breakpoint id> <condition>. Here are some examples:

```
(gdb) break get_next_data
Breakpoint 3 at 0×100004d4: file data.c, line 23.
(gdb) condition 3 cnt = =8
(gdb) break data.c:14 if i = =5
Breakpoint 4 at 0×1000043c: file data.c, line 14.
```

You can show the current breakpoints, delete, enable or disable the breakpoints using the commands:

```
(gdb) info breakpoints [breakpoint id]
(gdb) delete breakpoints [breakpoint id]
(gdb) disable breakpoints [breakpoint id]
(gdb) enable breakpoints [breakpoint id].
```

Stepping

The basic step operations available in any standard debugger are the following:

- step over: executes the next line of code. The GDB command is ***next***.
- step into: if the next line of code is a function, the debugger will stop at the first line in this function, otherwise it executes a step over. The GDB command is ***step***. To execute a single target machine instruction use the GDB command ***stepi***.
- step out: the debugger executes the current function and stops immediately after the line of code where the current function has been called from. The GDB command is ***finish***.

Changing the program

While debugging a program, there are many situations when you observe how to fix the issue, or you just want to modify the program execution. GDB provides the possibility to modify on the fly variables, memory, registers, to call functions, return from functions or to modify the program counter while the program is debugged. This may save some time as compared with the standard solution: modify the code, compile it, run the program on the target, reproduce the same error conditions and test the new program's changes.

Changing the program execution should be done with caution, especially when you directly modify the registers, including the program counter, as it may cause fatal errors in the execution.

The program execution can be changed in the following ways:

- Change the value of a local or global variable: assign 11 to variable "i":
  ```
  (gdb) set variable i = 11
  ```
- Change the memory: set value 37 to the memory 0xbfc45400, converted to int:
  ```
  (gdb) set {int}0xbfc45400 = 37
  ```
- Change the value of a register:
  ```
  (gdb) set $r0 = 0×10
  ```
- Modify the execution address: the program counter is modified. The next run control command (run, continue, step, next) will execute from this new program counter address:
  ```
  (gdb) set $pc = 0×80483a7
  (gdb) set $pc = &compute_data
  ```
- Continue at a different address: resume execution at the specific line or at specific address:
  ```
  (gdb) jump data.c:19
  Continuing at 0×80483a7.
  (gdb) jump *0×80483a7
  Continuing at 0×80483a7.
  ```
- Return from a function: cancel the execution of the current function from the current position. If an argument is passed to the command ***return***, it is used as the return value of the function:
  ```
  (gdb) return 1
  ```
- Execute a function:
  ```
  (gdb) call get_next_data(0)
  $5 = (struct data_t *) 0×8049600
  (gdb) call get_next_data(1)
  $6 = (struct data_t *) 0×8049608
  ```

Analyzing core dumps

What is a core dump? A core dump is a binary file generated by the operating system (e.g., Linux) consisting of the complete status of the application (memory, registers, stack, signals received) when the program terminates abnormally.

How are core dumps enabled? The Linux shell command "ulimit" is used to enable the core dumps if the command is run on the console where the application will be started from.

```
$ ulimit -c unlimited
```

How are core dumps analyzed? GDB can analyze a core dump using the command:

```
$gdb <executable> <core dump>
```

Then you can use all the GDB commands except run control commands (run, continue, stepping, call, return).

Debug agent design

We learned in the previous section how to use a standard debugger to debug and investigate embedded applications. While widely used, a standard debugger does not cover all the debugging scenarios. The GDB-GDBserver is an excellent debugger, but how about the case where GDB cannot run on the target? This is quite usual, as generally the embedded targets have special requirements and resources may be limited. Here are some examples: the target does not run the Linux operating system, it does not have a serial or Ethernet interface or some resource limitation does not allow porting the debug agent. This is true not only for GDB, but for all the debuggers that use a debug agent running on the target.

Bearing in mind these constraints, it is clear that each specific debugging scenario or corner case may need special debugging tools and each programmer can use them to improve and optimize at least some parts of the debugging process. For this purpose we will go through the process of defining a debug agent framework – a generic description of how to start designing a debug agent that fits into our special target requirements.

By definition, a debug agent is a target application. Just like GDBserver, the debug agent is used together with a host debugger that exchanges data with the agent, processes it and displays it in a user-friendly format. Figure 16.1 shows the host debugger, the debug agent and the interaction between them.

The debug agent performs low-level actions on the embedded target, triggered by events like interrupts or requests from the host debugger. It has access to the target resources like

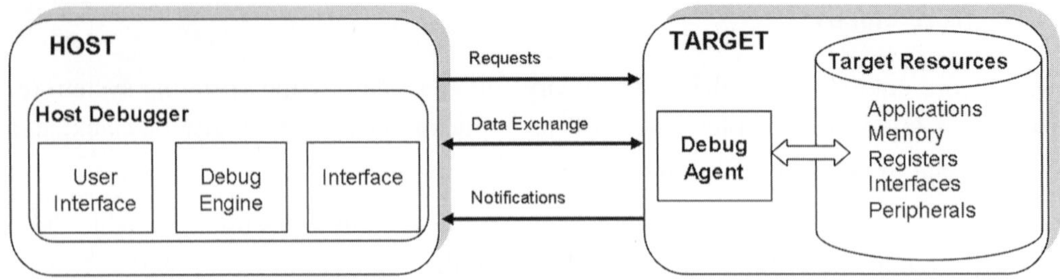

Figure 16.1:
Debug agent.

applications to be debugged, memory (with read and write operations), access to registers and peripherals configuration. A physical target interface or a peripheral should be used for communication with the host debugger. This is not necessarily a serial or Ethernet interface as for the majority of debuggers; for the simplest agents it can also be shared memory or just a GPIO that transmits an event to or from the host debugger.

The host debugger is a host application where most of the processing is done. In the most complex scenario it has an interface module that handles the communication protocol over different interfaces, a core debug engine and a graphical user interface to display the results to the user.

In general, the communication protocol has three types of messages: requests from the host debugger to perform specific actions on the target, data exchange messages where, for example, the memory content can be retrieved from or passed to the target, and notifications from the debug agent to inform the host debugger about asynchronous events on the target.

We will focus in the following on the debug agent use cases and design. For the host debugger an existing host debugger like GDB or a very simple one can be used.

Use cases

A debugger is seen most of the time as a source-code debugger able to provide the current program execution point, to access stack, memory and registers, and to have control of the program using steps, pause, continue, breakpoints and other mechanisms. But on the other hand, the debug agent can be used in different scenarios. It can start as a small debug routine that puts something into the memory and can evolve into a fully featured source-code debugger.

We will provide some practical debug agent use cases where the agent can be directly developed by the programmer, specially designed for his application needs. You can see these use cases as basic stages for developing the debug agent.

Simple debug agent

In a very simple scenario, a basic debug agent runs on the target and there is no host debugger and no communication protocol between host and target. The debug agent is triggered on a debug event, the debug agent code is executed and it performs simple actions such as:

- Save the debugged application context. The current state of the application is saved so that the application execution can be resumed from exactly the same conditions, at a later time. Typically special registers like general-purpose registers, program counter, stack register, and link register are saved. It is mandatory to save the registers that will be modified by the debug agent during this procedure.
- Dump the application context. The context means a set of information, depending on the details of the processor and application design, that is relevant for the person who interprets this information. This includes registers, stack, peripheral or interface status, memory zone, and other application-specific data. The data can be stored in memory or in a file if a file system is available; data can be retrieved and interpreted at a later time.
- Trigger an external event. For a low-level embedded application some information cannot be simply saved into memory. Logical signals between different integrated circuits on the embedded system (microcontrollers, FPGA, ASIC) or target signal outputs (e.g., GPIO) can be read using external devices triggered by the external event (e.g., GPIO) generated in the debug agent routine. For example an oscilloscope or a logical analyzer device can be used to capture signals once it is triggered by the GPIO signal from the debug agent. After triggering the external event, the debug agent can then wait for a specific period of time, as long as the capture needs, before switching back to the application context.
- Restore the application context. The saved application context is restored and the application is resumed from the same conditions.

The debug event – the trigger that invokes the context switch to the debug agent code – is an interrupt, typically a debug interrupt. Depending on the target's processor, the interrupts can be configured to generate debug interrupts on different exceptions. The debug event can be also an external interrupt, triggered by an external signal assertion.

The user can also manually trigger the debug event, for example by pressing a button on the target, or asserting an external signal, which of course generates an external interrupt. This can be seen as a debugger "pause" command, where the application context is dumped and the oscilloscope capture is triggered.

This is a very simple debug agent example which you may think, to some extent, can be integrated into the application code, for example into the debug interrupt handler of the application. While this is possible, it is not recommended. An efficient debug should be done without modifying the application code for debug purposes as this may affect the application functionality. Having the debug agent in a separate application allows updating and improvement of the agent code at any time with no constraints for the application. The debug agent can even be developed by a different team and can be further improved into a more versatile debugger.

Simple communication protocol

For the simple scenario described above we can add a better way to retrieve the debug information and to control the debug agent running on the target.

In the simplest scenario, one can start with a minimal host debugger and a communication protocol that supports very basic commands. The host debugger can be implemented from scratch, based on a very simple communication protocol. For example a request-response based protocol will allow exchange information like:

- Control commands: the host debugger can send requests to the agent code to
  - pause the application: the agent is triggered by receiving this request and makes the context switch from the application code to the agent; the agent then waits for more requests from the host debugger;
  - continue the application: the debug agent switches back to the application context.
- Data exchange commands:
  - retrieve the application context (registers, stack, application specific data);
  - read and write memory.

The debug agent also needs to implement the communication protocol. On the target, a physical interface should be reserved for communication with the host, for example serial, Ethernet, USB or other, and it should be controlled by the debug agent. The debug agent implements the interrupt handler on the receive side of the interface – and this interrupt is used as a debug event trigger.

This solution is very basic in terms of debug capabilities, but has an advantage in development time. The development time to update the simple scenario to this use case with a basic communication protocol is short while the benefits of adding basic control of the debug agent and data exchange capabilities are a significant improvement in the debugging process.

Using GDB

For this use case, a full source-code debugger is needed and this requires a featured host debugger application – which is a complex task if you want to develop it from scratch. But instead of developing a host debugger, sometimes it is worth implementing a standard communication protocol in the debug agent and using the corresponding standard debugger on the host.

The most common example is GDB: in the gdb-gdbserver mode, the host debugger is the GDB, the debug agent is the GDBserver and the communication protocol is GDB remote protocol, TCP or serial-based. For our case we will use the GDB and GDB remote protocol. The debug agent will also implement the GDB remote protocol and in this way, at the interface with the host, it is seen as a GDBserver.

If we look at the implementation requirements for the debug agent, this use case is very similar to the previous one. Of course, developing the full set of features of the communication protocol along with the required low-level implementation is not a small task, but the advantages of having the fully featured GDB debugger make it worthwhile.

Multicore

This is a more complex scenario and it is provided as an example of how to use the previously described scenarios in order to provide an efficient debugging solution.

For this scenario a multicore processor is used with Linux running on the first core while on other cores, named secondary cores, real-time bare-board applications (with no operating system) are running. The goal is to provide a debugging solution for the applications running on the secondary cores.

The main components of the solution based on GDB are presented in Figure 16.2.

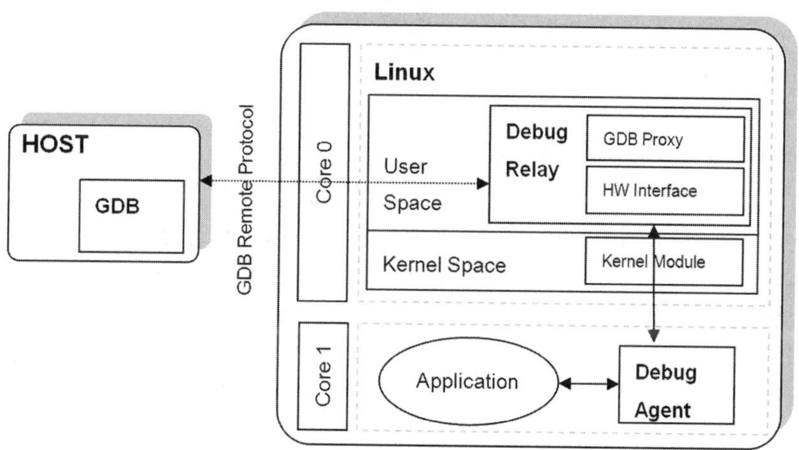

Figure 16.2:
Multicore debugging with GDB.

On the target, a debug agent is running on each secondary core. The agent can be a symmetric multiprocessing (SMP) application – a single ELF running for all secondary cores or, depending on the details of each target, it can be a separate ELF application for each core.

On Linux running on the first core, the debug relay is a Linux user-space application that acts as a relay between the GDB host application and the debug agents running on the secondary cores. The communication between the debug relay and the GDB on the host is GDB remote protocol, TCP-based. Each debug agent is handled on a separate TCP port.

Internally, the debug relay can be based on a GDB proxy – an open-source GDB proxy that allows target-specific interfaces to be added, with proprietary implementation. The GDB proxy implements the communication with the host GDB (GDB remote protocol) and therefore, for our scenario, only the target-specific interface should be implemented from zero. In Figure 16.2, this is represented by the HW Interface module.

The communication between the debug relay and the debug agent is based on the inter-core communication mechanisms available for the target processor. For example a shared memory for data exchange plus an inter-core signaling mechanism (e.g., mailbox or doorbell) can be used.

The host debugger is GDB and if required it can be used as a graphical user interface, GDB compatible. From the host, the debug relay and the debug agents are seen as multiple GDBserver applications running on separate TCP ports, one for each secondary core.

There are some advantages for this scenario, as compared with the previous use cases:

- The solution provides a full-featured GDB debugger, but the development time is reduced by using the GDB on the host and the GDB proxy on the target. Only the target-specific modules are implemented: the debug agent and the communication protocol with the debug relay.
- In the previous use cases, a hardware resource is reserved for the debug agent to be used for communication with the host debugger. In the current solution there is no such restriction as the Ethernet port can be shared with all other Linux applications.

Debug agent overview

As you learned in the previous sections where and how to use the debug agent, in the following we will go deeper into the implementation details of the debug agent and point out the key elements of the design.

The debug agent is a bare-board application running directly on the target with no operating system (OS). It has no knowledge about Linux or any operating system. The application to be debugged is also seen as a bare-board application, with no OS awareness.

The application itself can be an operating system, for example Linux, and the debug agent is able to do a Linux kernel debug, handling Linux as a simple bare-board application.

We will assume in the following that the host debugger is GDB and it communicates with the agent using GDB remote protocol, directly or through a GDB proxy. This allows a complete description of the agent design, based on the features provided by GDB. On the other hand, the debug agent design principles are the same, independent of the host debugger's type.

Figure 16.3 presents how the debug agent interacts with the debugged application on the target.

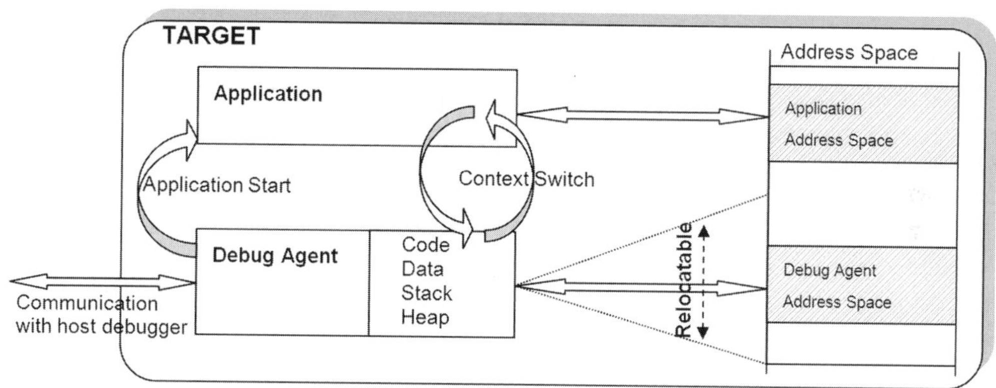

Figure 16.3:
Debug agent overview.

The debug agent is a separate ELF application with its own code, data, stack and heap segments. The application memory space does not overlap with the debug agent memory space. Moreover, as a very valuable feature, the debug agent code should be made position-independent executable; meaning that the memory address from where the agent's code is executed can be changed. This way, the user can configure the run address of the debug agent at the desired location.

Depending on each specific debug scenario, the debug agent can load and start the application or just attach to an already running instance of the application. In any case, the debug agent does not interpret the application ELF; this is done by the host debugger. Application start can be seen as a context switch from debug agent to application, with a clean application context.

The context switch is triggered by a debug event that can be:

- a debug interrupt caused by an exception in the application, in which case the context is switched from the application to the agent, or

- a request from the host debugger that internally generates an interrupt (e.g., a receive data ready interrupt) that, depending on the request, triggers the context switch to the application (e.g., "continue" command) or to the debug agent (e.g., "pause" command).

The debug agent should be able to access the application's address space. It needs read and write access to data, stack and heap so that the host debugger can read and write application variables, read the stack frames and read and write to memory.

These key points will be detailed below.

Starting the application

One possible use case is where the application is loaded and started by the use of the debugger. This way, the application execution can be debugged from the first instruction. Before starting the application, there are some preconditions that have to be met:

- the application is compiled with debug symbols and the ELF file is available in the host debugger;
- the debug agent is running on the target and the connection with the host debugger is up and running;
- the host debugger should support the download capability; for GDB, this is implemented in the command "load".

Through this process, some steps are done by the host debugger and some by the debug agent. To understand the design and implementation requirements for the debug agent we will go step by step through the application download process from the host debugger to the agent.

On the "load" command, the following actions are performed:

- The **binary** image of the application is copied into the target memory. This is done by sending a "write memory" request to the debug agent, containing the binary data and the target memory address where data should be written.
- The program counter register (PC) is set to the application **entry point** – the memory address where the first application instruction should be executed. A "write register" request is sent to the agent, containing the register number and the value to be set.
- The application is now ready to start. It can be started with a different command, "continue".

As you can see, the debug agent performs simple actions like writing memory and assigning a value to a register. The complex tasks are done in the host debugger and we can see again the advantages of using the split solution (debugger host + debug agent).

The other use case is where the application has been started before the debugger connects to it, through the debug agent. On the attach process, the host debugger triggers a debug event to the debug agent and a context switch is started from the application to the debug agent.

Context switch

In the process of a context switch, the execution is changed from the application ELF to the debug agent ELF or vice versa. The context represents the current application states necessary to be able to resume the application from the same point and same conditions at a later time. Typically, in the context general-purpose registers, program counter, stack register, and link register are saved. The application to be debugged has no knowledge about the debug agent and therefore does not handle the context switch. The saving and the restoring of the application context is done in the debug agent code and it is triggered by debug events such as debug interrupts or interrupts triggered by requests from the host debugger.

Generally, the process of a context switch from the application to the debug agent consists of the following steps:

- Triggered by a debug event, the debug event interrupt handler is called.
- Save the application context: general-purpose registers and special registers are saved to the stack. An assembler code sample for a PowerPC architecture looks like this:

  ```
  stwu    r1,-16(r1)d
  stw    r3,4(r1)
  stw    r4,8(r1)
  mflr    r3
  stw    r3,12(r1)
  ```

  The *stwu* (store word and update) instruction allocates space into the stack (r1 register) to save 16 bytes, for four registers: stack, r3, r4 and link register (moved temporarily to r3 before it is saved into the stack). The special link register (LR) holds the address to return to when a function call completes and must be saved into the stack before a branch with LR update instruction (e.g., blrl instruction), for example before jumping to a generic handler routine.
- Save the address of the instruction where the application context should resume. This address is saved in special registers, architecture-dependent. These registers hold the address of the instruction that caused the interrupt or the application program counter at the moment when the debug event interrupt was generated.

  For some architectures, there can be different registers depending on the interrupt type: debug, machine check or critical interrupt. The corresponding status registers should be read to find out what type of interrupt has been called and therefore what register registers should be saved.

- Initialize the stack for the debug agent. The application and the debug agent have separate stacks. In the interrupt handler, the stack register is set to the application stack. For further high-level processing, the debug agent should use its own stack, while the application stack along with the application saved context should be used for the application debugging. The debug agent stack can be initialized as in the example:

```
lis   r1, _stack_addr@ha
addi  r1, r1, _stack_addr@l
```

  If the debug agent is an SMP application running on multiple cores, separate stacks for each core should be used and here the stack initialization should be done accordingly.
- Interrupt handling while the debug agent is running: depending on the application functionality some interrupts should be enabled and some disabled when switching the context to the debug agent. This behavior should be configurable in the debug agent.
- The execution is passed to the main program loop of the debug agent, a C-code high-level handler. The application stack value should be passed as a parameter – for each processor architecture there are specific registers for passing parameters from assembler to C code. A direct branch or an LR instruction can be used (bl, blrl) or a return from interrupt call (rfi) after the corresponding registers have been set (LR or interrupt save/restore registers).

After the high-level handler has been called, the context switch is completed. Now the debug agent is running, it communicates with the host debugger and it is able to do the basic debug functions:

- Read and write registers: on the host debugger request, the debug agent is able to access the registers. The real registers are not actually accessed but the temporary location where the registers values have been retrieved after the application context save. On writing a register, the new value will of course apply after the application context is restored.
- Read and write memory and stack: unlike the registers, the memory, including stack, is directly accessed for read and write operations. The debug agent can have access to the entire memory space. The stack register value is retrieved from the saved application context (e.g., r1 register).
- Breakpoints: in the debug agent implementation, setting software breakpoints means writing the application's code memory zone. Based on the symbolic information in the application ELF, the host debugger finds the address corresponding to the breakpoint location at a specific symbol or at a specific line number. When a breakpoint is set, the host debugger sends this address to the target. The debug agent just replaces the assembler instruction at this address with a special instruction that generates a debug exception.

- Run control: stepping, continue. Stepping can be implemented as a breakpoint to the next instruction and a continue command. The continue command triggers the context switch from the debug agent to the application, where the application context is restored.

On context restore, the debug agent performs steps similar to the context save. The application registers are restored from the temporary location where they may have been modified on user request. The PC is not directly set, but the save/restore registers are restored. The context restore is completed with a return from interrupt call.

Position-independent executables

Position-independent code (PIC) and position-independent executables (PIE) allow an executable to run independently of the position in the memory where it resides. The same code, within the same ELF file, can be copied to any memory address and can run with no changes.

This is very important, as we have seen that the application to be debugged and the debug agent have independent memory address spaces that should not overlap. To give an example, let us assume that the debug agent is compiled to run from a hard-coded memory address (position dependent executable). If the application's memory requirements change and the address space overlaps with the debug agent's memory space, then the debug agent would need to be rebuilt to adjust the run address to the new memory addresses. This is not practical and the programmer that is doing debug of the application would prefer not to rebuild the debug agent every time the memory spaces change. In addition, if the debug agent is provided without source code, it is a problem having a hard-coded run address.

Let us see how the position-independent executable is implemented for our debug agent. First, it is preferable that the compiler has support for position-independent executables. This is not a strict requirement; the code can be specially written to be position-independent without using absolute values for branch and for data section. While possible, this is recommended only for a small number of code lines.

For the GCC build tool chain, a position-independent executable is enabled by adding the options "-fPIE" for compiler and linker. With this option, the function calls and the access to data variables are done through an indirection table, named Global Offset Table (GOT). The GOT table stores the addresses of all functions and global variables. For a position-independent executable, only the addresses from the GOT table have to be updated, at run-time, corresponding to the current load address of the program while the rest of the program remains unchanged.

Along with the build tool chain support at compile time, there are some other requirements for run-time, to be executed from the debug agent code: compute the current load address of the program and update the GOT table accordingly to this value.

The **current load address** is generally different from the link time address. It can be computed, at run time, using for example the sample code below for PowerPC architecture:

```
0x..0100:   bl    __compute_PIC
  __compute_PIC:
0x..0104:   mflr 19
0x..0108:   lis  20,     __compute_PIC@ha
0x..010C:   addi 20, 20, __compute_PIC@l
0x..0110:   sub  19, 19, 20
```

The sample code above computes the offset between the current run address and the link address and places this value in a register, r19. Let us assume that the code has been linked at the address 0x0 and it runs from a different address, 0x0120.0000. The computed offset should be then 0x0120.0000. In this example, the sample code starts at address 0x0000.0100. The label *__compute_PIC* has the value 0x0104 at compile-time and run-time. The steps to compute the offset are the following:

- Do a branch instruction with link register update *bl* (branch then link). The branch address is the sum of the current instruction address and the offset written in the instruction code. You can see that the absolute value of *__compute_PIC* is not used in this instruction. When the branch is executed at run-time, the instruction address would be 0x0120.0100 and the offset has the same value as for compile-time, 0x4 (the relative offset to the label *__compute_PIC*). Therefore, the execution is moved to the next line 0x0120.0104. The LR is also updated so the instruction address following the bl instruction is placed into the link register. Therefore LR is set to 0x0120.0104.
- The LR is read and its value is placed into the register r19 (mflr 19), so r19 = 0x120.0104.
- The *__computer_PIC* symbol value is placed into the r20 register. This is the compile-time value, so r20 = 0x0000.0104.
- The offset value is placed into r19: r19 = r19 − r20. So the offset is r19 = 0x0120.0000.

Update the GOT table. Once the offset has been computed, the GOT table should be updated, at run-time, corresponding to the current load address. Initially, the GOT table contains the compile-time addresses of functions and global variables, as in our example relative to address 0x0. The GOT table update means that each element is updated to the current address by adding the computed offset to the existing value.

The start and end of the GOT table can be identified by defining a symbol at the beginning of the GOT table and at the beginning of the next section. This is done in the linker control file (LCF) as in the following example, where *__got1_start* and *__dynamic_start* identify the GOT table beginning and end:

```
got1      : {
 __got1_start = .;
 *(.got1)
 }
 .got2      : { *(.got2) }
 .dynamic     : {
 __dynamic_start= .;
  *(.dynamic) }
```

The sample code below shows how the addresses are updated in the GOT table. It is assumed that the offset has been previously computed and placed into the r19 register.

```
register int offset = 0;
asm ("mr  %0, 19" : "=r" (offset));

volatile unsigned int* got_start =
(unsigned int*)((unsigned int)&__got1_start + offset);

unsigned int count =
((unsigned int)&__dynamic_start -
(unsigned int)&__got1_start)/sizeof(unsigned int);

for (int i = 0; i<count; ++i)
   got_start[i] += offset;
```

There is a small performance penalty when enabling position-independent code, because of the functions and data variable access through the GOT table. So it is not always a good idea to have this feature, especially for real-time applications. For the debug agent this is not an issue.

Debug event from the application

The debug event from the application is the debug interrupt, triggered whenever an exception occurs (breakpoints or application errors). In the simplest scenario, when the exception occurs, the debug interrupt of the debug agent should be called and, as we learned in the previous sections, the context is switched from the application to the debug agent.

The principle is simple, but putting it into practice can be sometimes a challenge. The design of the debugged application should not consider doing anything special for integration with a debug agent. Therefore the application will do the normal initialization of the interrupt vector table, and the offset for debug interrupt. If a debug exception occurs when running the application without the debug agent, then the debug interrupt handler of the application is called – the handler is therefore in the application code.

When debugging the application with our debug agent, then something should be changed so that, on a debug event, the debug interrupt handler of the agent will be called. The application should be able to use all other interrupts while, for the debug interrupt only, the agent's handler will be called. If it is possible to specify a configurable interrupt vector address only for the debug interrupt, then this can be a very simple solution: when starting, the debug agent would set the debug interrupt address to point to its handler. Unfortunately, this is not possible on many processors: you can only specify a base address for the interrupt table and an offset for each interrupt type.

For these scenarios it is clear that the application debug interrupt is called and the solution is to move the execution, from the application interrupt handler, through a branch instruction, to the debug agent interrupt handler. Of course, this should not add requirements to the application code to hard-code a branch in its debug interrupt handler. Moreover, the load address of the debug agent is not known at compile time. The solution is that the debug agent would overwrite the application's debug interrupt handler, so the desired branch is executed, as described in Figure 16.4.

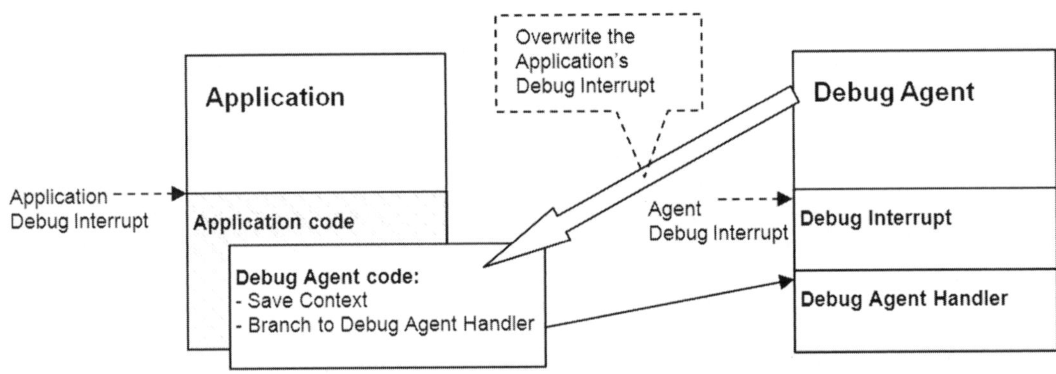

Figure 16.4:
Debug event from the application.

A sample code used to overwrite the application's debug interrupt is presented below, for the PowerPC processor:

```
app_handler_start:
      stwu 1, -16(1)
      stw  3, 4(1)
      stw  4, 8(1)
      mflr 3
```

```
6        stw  3, 12(1)
7        lis  4, debug_agent_handler@h
8        ori  4, 4, debug_agent_handler@l
9        mtlr 4
10       blrl
11 app_handler_end:
12       nop
```

First, the necessary space is allocated in the stack for saving all the registers modified in this routine: stack register, link register, r3 and r4 registers. Then a branch is executed to an absolute address, through LR, to the debug agent interrupt handler address. After the branch, in the *debug_agent_handler* these saved registers must be used in the context save procedure.

The debug agent will copy the above code to the address of the debug interrupt vector of the application. Actually the memory is overwritten with the instruction code resulting after the compilation of these lines. This can be done in the agent code, as in the example below:

```
void* app_handler_start_addr = &&app_handler_start;
void* app_handler_stop_addr = &&app_handler_stop;
int size = app_handler_start_addr - app_handler_start_end;

memcpy((void*)app_debug_int_addr, app_handler_start_addr, size);
```

The variable *app_debug_int_addr* is the debug interrupt address of the application.

Let us consider also the case described above where the debug agent is a position-independent executable. At the debug agent compile-time, the code for the application debug handler is compiled and transformed into instruction code. At this time, the function *debug_agent_handler* has the predefined offset before knowing the application load address. Then when the instruction code is written in the application memory, the instructions at lines 7 and 8 will still contain the compile-time value of the function, so this is not the expected, run-time value.

The correct value of the agent debug handler can be computed based on the following:

- In the agent code, at run time, the address of the debug handler function has the run-time value as the GOT table has been updated with the current load address.
- The assembler instructions that set the address of the debug handler in lines 7 and 8 need to be updated to reflect the run-time address of the handler. Looking at the instruction definition, the address is set in the least-significant 16 bits of the instruction.

Below is the code that updates the address of the debug handler to the correct run time value.

```
unsigned int relocated_addr = (unsigned int)& debug_agent_handler;
unsigned int *instr_addr = ((unsigned int *) app_debug_int_addr + 5);
*instr_addr = ((*instr_addr) & 0xFFFF0000) |
```

```
            ((relocated_addr > 16) & 0xFFFF);

++instr_addr;
*instr_addr = ((*instr_addr) & 0xFFFF0000) |

            ((relocated_addr) & 0xFFFF);
```

There is one more thing to clarify: how to find the address of the debug interrupt vector of the application (*app_debug_int_addr*). There are several ways to obtain this address, depending on each use case scenario:

- In the case where the debug agent attaches to an already running instance of the application, the interrupt vector is assumed to be set in the application. The debug interrupt address can be computed reading some special registers. For example, for PowerPC architecture the address is the sum of values in the registers IVPR (base interrupt address) and IVOR15 (debug interrupt offset).
- The above case cannot be use for early debug of the application before the application sets the interrupt vector. For this case, the debug agent can set the interrupt vector pointing to its address space. The debug interrupt address would in this case be chosen by the debug agent.
- A complete solution is to configure the debug agent with the application's debug interrupt address. This case can be implemented in different ways, for example:
  - Pass the address as start parameter by setting this value into a hardcoded register.
  - Set the parameter from the host debugger. In the case of a GDB host debugger, the *monitor* command allows the sending of a special request to the debug agent. The address can be transmitted for example using the command *monitor debug_addr <address>*.

Multicore

The debug agent can run on single-core or multicore processors. The design principle is the same, but for multi-core there are several things we have to consider. The debug agent can be an SMP executable, a single ELF file, running for all cores, or it can be an individual ELF running on each core. The preferred approach is to have a single SMP executable for all cores, having more flexibility in the debug agent usage: the ELF file is loaded only one time, the code section is reused for all cores, the reserved memory space is compact and the development and build process is simpler. Even in an SMP application, the cores can independently execute the code: some cores can be paused while others are running.

Context switch must be correctly handled for a multicore processor since on each core the debug agent will use its own stack and the application has a different context for each core (stack and registers).

One of the use cases presented in this chapter is the multicore scenario that combines multicore capabilities with the flexibility of having an operating system on one core: the case where Linux runs on the first core while the secondary cores run real-time bare-board applications (with no operating system). For this case, the debug agent should implement communication with the debug relay running on Linux, based on the following:

- Data exchange between the debug agent and debug relay on Linux is done through a shared memory zone. The memory can be accessed with read and write operations by both agent and relay. A simple approach is to use a circular memory buffer, with read and write pointers.
- The access to the shared memory zone from different cores should be protected by a spin lock mechanism. For example, a spin lock test-and-set mechanism should be used to protect common accesses. The implementation depends on the processor's synchronization mechanisms (e.g., memory barrier).
- An inter-core signaling mechanism should be implemented to notify the other core that data is available on the shared memory. This should be an interrupt-based mechanism. Polling would not be a valid solution since the mechanism should be able to trigger, for example, the context switch from the application to the debug agent. And so, while polling can be implemented in the debug agent code, it is not a solution when the application context is running.
- A processor may provide more than one inter-core signaling mechanism. Some mechanisms use a special interrupt to handle an event from the other core. For example, a doorbell inter-core interrupt has a special doorbell interrupt handler. If the debug agent used this interrupt, the doorbell interrupt could no longer be used in the application, which adds some resource limitations when debugging with our debug agent. If it is possible, an inter-core interrupt based on the debug interrupt would be a better choice.

Starting the debug agent

We have seen above how to start the application and debugging it using the debug agent. We will describe below how to start the debug agent.

Some targets may have a boot loader or a monitor program that is able to load other executables using a command-line interface. An example of such a boot loader is u-boot. In this case, the debug agent loading is handled by the boot loader.

If the target does not have a boot loader program, the debug agent binary should be copied into a non-volatile memory; for example, NOR, NAND or SPI flash memory. When booting from the flash memory, the program has to do some supplementary steps as compared to booting from RAM memory: at the reset address, set a jump to the program code in flash, do the relocation of the binary from flash to RAM and run from RAM. This is valid for any executable booting from flash.

For the multicore scenario with Linux running on the first core, we can use a different approach to load and start the debug agent. The process is performed completely from Linux with no other requirements for the debug agent.

The loading of the debug agent program consists of copying the agent binary into the memory, at the desired memory address. A Linux application should be able to access the physical memory location where the debug agent program should be loaded. The binary will be directly copied into the memory. If the debug agent is a position-independent executable, then it can be copied and run from any memory location. The conversion from ELF file to binary can be done using the build tool chain utilities, or the Linux application can handle this conversion.

The starting of the debug agent is a little more complicated than loading. The Linux running on the first core cannot access the other cores' registers and it can only execute instructions on the first core. The execution start can be done similarly to how Linux starts the secondary cores in an SMP scenario. The u-boot boot loader provisions the boot code for the secondary cores so that the secondary cores enter, immediately after they have been enabled, into a spin loop. Each secondary core stays in the spin loop until a specific memory address is written with the address in which to jump out of the loop. Therefore, in order to start the debug agent on a secondary core, the Linux loader application writes into the spin loop jump address the value of the agent's entry point. The secondary core will then exit the spin loop and start executing the debug agent's code.

Another possibility to load and start the debug agent is to use the JTAG probe. We will describe how to use the JTAG in the next section.

Debugging using JTAG

The name JTAG comes from Joint Test Action Group and was standardized later as the IEEE standard 1149.1 – Standard Test Access Port and Boundary-Scan Architecture. It was initially designed and used for testing integrated circuits using a boundary scan. Currently, the JTAG usability extends to a wider scope, including circuits and boundary scan testing, debugging embedded systems including processors and FPGA circuits, data transfer into internal flash memory of circuits, flash programming, trace and analysis.

In the following we will focus on the JTAG usage for debugging embedded systems. The host debugger software uses the JTAG probe for low-level access to the embedded system resources such as read and write registers, read and write memory and complete run control of the target with operations such as run, continue or stepping. Through the use of JTAG, the host debugger provides a featured set of debugging capabilities that allows developers to save development time during target bring-up and debugging. The high-level debugging capabilities such as operating system awareness (e.g., Linux kernel awareness), kernel module drivers, Linux user-space and kernel-space debugging or hypervisor awareness are features provided by the host debugger, while the JTAG executes only basic commands between the host and the target.

Physically, the JTAG is an external device. It connects to the target via a special JTAG pin header connector through a special JTAG cable. For the connection to the host USB, Ethernet or parallel or serial ports can be used.

It is worthwhile mentioning here that along with the JTAG there are also other interfaces available for debugging through an external probe. One example is the ARM Cortex-M debug interface Serial Wire Debug (SWD) – a low-cost interface with only two pins and the single-bit serial wire output (SWO). These interfaces use the ARM debug modules Instrumentation Trace Macrocell (ITM) and Embedded Trace Macrocell (ETM). For full instruction trace, the ETM module provides real-time trace over a 4-bit high-speed port. Overall, this interface provides more powerful debug capabilities with the advantage of lower pin count.

The debugging principles are the same for these debug interfaces and for generality we will refer in the following to the JTAG.

Benefits of using JTAG

When we talk about debugging with JTAG we are referring to a complete debugging solution including featured host debugger software along with the capabilities of controlling the target through the JTAG.

The main advantages of debugging using JTAG are the short development time for embedded system applications and low-level support for initial board bring-up, validation and development.

To better understand the benefits of using JTAG, let us assume an example where the embedded developer receives a new target and is required to do the board validation and to develop an application on the target. How can he start developing and debugging his application? Of course, in the end, these tasks can be done without using a debugger but at a time cost. On the other hand, a debugger would allow a very fast development time. We also learned that the debug agent software can be developed to run on the target, allowing debugging of the user's application. But how long would it take to develop the debug agent itself? And what debugging tools can be used while developing the debug agent? For this case, a debugging solution using the JTAG can be the key: there is no need to develop or to use existing supplementary software (e.g., debug agent) for debugging the application. It provides the complete set of debugging tools to start investigating the application, even for the initial board bring-up.

In addition, debugging with JTAG provides some other capabilities through the host debugger interface, such as the following:

- Initialization files: the debugger provides the possibility of using target initialization files containing the initial settings of the target immediately after power-up. For example, it can contain memory controller set-up, register set-up, RAM memory initialization.
- The target can be completely controlled without running software on the target. The registers and memory can be directly accessed through the special JTAG interface and it is not required that the processor or the core actually execute instruction code. This is important as the registers or memory can be accessed even if the core is not enabled.
- Integrated bare-board application development including target reset, initialization file and application download into the RAM memory.
- Read and write access to the processor's internal flash memory.
- JTAG debugging is non-intrusive in the application to be debugged.

Board bring-up using JTAG

For the initial board bring-up of an embedded system, debugging using JTAG allows a very fast target validation and application development. The bring-up target specific settings are typically done in the initialization file. The debugger allows the reuse of the initialization file every time a new application is downloaded to the target. An advantage of debugging using the JTAG for initial board bring-up is the use of the initialization file. Based on it, the target can be controlled through the JTAG without executing code on the processor. Some examples of target-specific initialization settings are the following:

- memory management unit (MMU) initialization;
- translation lookaside buffer (TLB) initialization – virtual to physical memory address translations are stored in the TLBs; the TLB for DDR memory and for the other memory-mapped peripherals should be defined here;
- local access windows set-up (LAW) (only specific to some processors);
- DDR controller set-up: timing, bus frequency configurations;
- interrupt vector initialization;
- register configuration for peripherals, like flash memory;
- target-specific register initialization;
- debug register settings, like enabling the debug interrupt, enabling the external debug mode (for JTAG);

- core initialization for multicore processors. By default, the secondary cores are disabled. It is the first core that should do the initialization for the secondary core, or, in our case, it can be done by the debugger using the initialization file.

Comparison with the debug agent

Both cases of debugging using JTAG and debugging using a debug agent running on the target are widely used for embedded system development. Each solution has some advantages and, based on this, each solution is more often used in certain circumstances:

- JTAG for initial board bring-up, early application debug and when the debug agent software is not available, typically for bare board applications with no operating system;
- debug agent for high-level debug, typically after some operating system services are available for the debug agent. A common case is Linux user-space application debug using GDB/GDBserver.

In the following we will present some practical use case examples of debugging with JTAG or debug agent.

- For early Linux kernel debug, the better solution is to use JTAG debugging. In this case, the kernel can be debugged from the first instruction, the JTAG is not intrusive in the kernel and the kernel can be completely debugged: kernel core and all drivers. On the other hand, the debug agent solution using KGDB is too limited: the kernel can be debugged only after the KGDB module is loaded and only some parts of the kernel can be debugged. This is an intrusive debugging method where executing the KGDB module may influence the kernel functionality.
- JTAG debugging can provide powerful features like Linux kernel and user-space awareness, allowing debugging at the same time of the Linux user-space applications and kernel. The program execution can be debugged while moving from the user-space application to kernel space through system calls or kernel module functions.
- The bare-board debug agents need a hardware resource (e.g., serial or Ethernet port) reserved for communication with the host debugger. For JTAG debugging there is no restriction as the JTAG interface is dedicated to communication with the host debugger. For some debug agents like GDB/GDBserver, the communication channel (IP interface) to the host debugger can be shared with the other user-space applications.
- For JTAG debugging, the registers and memory can be directly accessed and it is not required for the processor to be enabled or to execute instruction code. This is the main advantage over debug agents for the initial board bring-up.
- Remote access: debug agents generally have support for Ethernet communication and can be accessed remotely. JTAG devices with remote access over Ethernet can be

expensive. For USB JTAG devices a trade-off is to use a computer near the equipment to solve the remote access issue.

- For some scenarios, JTAG debugging is not a practical solution. Let us assume for example we need to debug base station equipment with three or six sector controllers, each running on separate hardware. Having three or six JTAG devices connected to each sector controller is not a practical solution. On the other hand, debug agent software can be embedded in the sector controller, also allowing remote debugging.
- JTAG debugging is most likely to be used in the lab while the software is being developed or investigated. For the final products or equipment installed in the field, connecting the JTAG may be difficult or impossible. The JTAG pin header connector is located on the equipment mother-board and the equipment box has to be opened in order to connect the JTAG device. And of course you cannot have JTAG devices connected to all the equipment in the field.
- For field equipment, debug agents, like GDB, offer reliable solutions: if remote access is available the application can be remotely debugged and without remote access the application's crash dump can be analyzed offline.
- JTAG debugging can only be used if the processor has JTAG support and the JTAG pin header is available on the hardware. For some pieces of equipment, due to constraints of space, power consumption or electromagnetic compliance, the hardware is designed without the JTAG pin header. In this case, development boards with JTAG pin header should be used for the initial board bring-up and, after the software is stable, development can be continued on the final hardware. The debugging can then be continued based on a debug agent solution.
- Some JTAG devices, especially those with remote access (Ethernet, gigabit), can be expensive, especially where a license is needed for debugger software. When one chooses a debugging method it is always based on a trade-off between price and capabilities.

GDB and JTAG

We have seen above the advantages of debugging using JTAG as well as the flexibility of the open-source GDB debugger. For embedded system debugging, GDB is commonly used with a debug agent, like GDBserver, running on the target. However, GDB flexibility allows the integration of GDB and JTAG devices.

One of the commonly used cases is the early Linux kernel debug: as described above, debugging with JTAG would allow a complete and reliable debug, while the KGDB solution is an intrusive solution that covers only some parts of the kernel debugging.

The solution of GDB debugging using JTAG is based on the following.

- There will be no debug agent running on the target. The target will be accessed only through the JTAG.
- On the host, the GDB host debugger will be compiled for cross debugging of the embedded target. Optionally, any available graphical user interfaces can be used, like for a normal GDB debugging. No change is required in GDB for integration with the JTAG device.
- A GDB relay software program will act as a relay between the GDB host debugger and the JTAG. The GDB relay is a host application (e.g., a Linux user-space application) and can run on the same host as GDB or on a different host. The GDB relay implements the GDB remote protocol at the interface with the GDB and, therefore, from the GDB host debugger, the GDB relay is seen as a GDBserver.
- The communication with the JTAG is implemented in GDB relay software. This is specific to each supported JTAG device. The JTAG can be accessed remotely (Ethernet) or locally (USB).
- Internally, the GDB relay can be based on a GDB proxy – an open-source GDB proxy that allows the addition of target-specific interfaces, with proprietary implementation. The GDB proxy implements the communication with the host GDB (GDB remote protocol) and only the interface for the communication with the JTAG should be implemented.

Special JTAG commands can be passed using the GDB "monitor" command. The GDB initialization file (.gdbinit) can be used for the JTAG initialization file.

Currently, many open-source solutions are already available for the integration of GDB and JTAG, for many processors and different JTAG devices.

Debugging tools using Eclipse and GDB

In this section we present an example of how to use free open-source software to obtain an integrated development and debugging tool providing standard debug capabilities for Linux user-space application debug and Linux kernel debug. We will use the following open-source software:

- GDB/GDBserver for low-level support for debugging the applications on the embedded target. We have seen above how to download, compile, configure and use GDB for our target.
- KGDB – this is a kernel functionality that allows the kernel to be debugged over a serial line or Ethernet from a remote host. The remote host uses GDB for connecting to the running kernel on the target through the interface provided by KGDB.
- Eclipse – Eclipse is an open-source community focused on building an open development platform for extensible frameworks, tools and run-times for debugging,

deploying and managing software. Eclipse also provides the graphical user interface for GDB: source view in editor, debug window with stack frames, memory view, register view, variables and many others.

In our example we will use the Eclipse IDE for C/C++ Developers (http://www.eclipse.org/downloads/).

Linux application debug with GDB

In this example we will describe how to set up the debugging environment for Linux user-space application debug. There are some preconditions that have to be met before starting the environment configuration:

- GDB and GDBserver have to be compiled and configured for the embedded target. The GDBserver will be manually started on the target and the GDB will run on the host, compiled for cross-platform debugging.
- Eclipse IDE for C/C++ Developers has to be installed on the host computer.

Eclipse IDE has the necessary support to do the Linux application debug using GDB and GDBserver and we will present how to configure the debug launch of the Eclipse.

The Eclipse project for debugging the Linux application can be created, for example, as in the following examples:

- using the Eclipse wizard for creating a new project: the option "Cross-Compile Project" allows compiling the application using the cross-build tool chain, so that the application is compiled to run on the embedded target;
- importing an already compiled target application.

In the "Debug Configuration" submenu, we will use the "C/C++ Remote Application" launch configuration. The "Debugger" configuration settings are presented in Figure 16.5.

- The preferred launcher should be "GDB (DSF) Manual Remote Debugging Launcher" to debug an application that was manually started on the remote target under control of the GDB debugger integrated using the Debugger Services Framework (DSF).
- In the "Main" tab, the cross-platform GDB debugger is set as the GDB debugger, for example powerpc-linux-gdb or arm-linux-gdb.
- In the same tab, set the location of the GDB command file, or initialization file. The file should contain target-specific settings: for example setting the target root file system.
- In the "Shared Libraries" tab we can add the shared libraries to be debugged along with the application. Load shared library symbols automatically should be enabled.
- In the "Connection" tab set the IP address of the target where the GDBserver has been started and the listening port of the GDBserver.

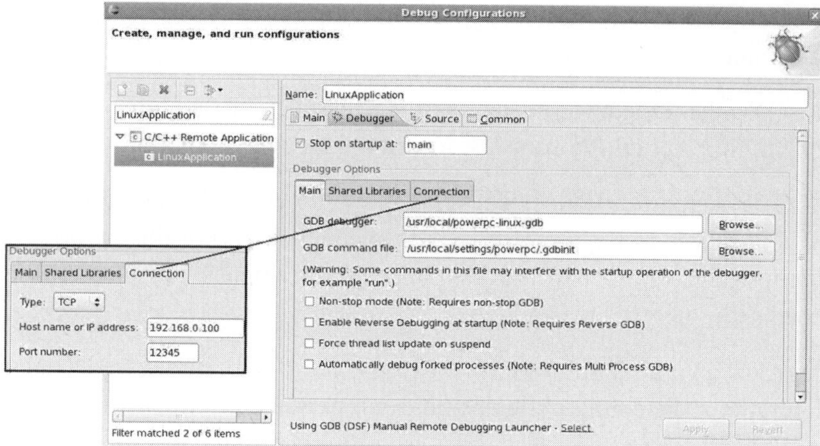

Figure 16.5:
Eclipse Linux application debug.

Linux kernel debug with KGDB

In the same way as for the Linux application debug, for the Linux kernel debug GDB should be configured for cross-platform debugging of the target and the Eclipse IDE for C/C++ Developers should be installed on the host computer.

For kernel debugging, KGDB should be used, instead of GDBserver. Debugging the kernel is not an easy task and it assumes a very good understanding of the kernel. We will present only the configuration steps for getting started with KGDB debugging. KGDB is enabled in the Linux kernel using the standard Linux configuration tool, "make menuconfig". The following items should be enabled in the "Kernel Hacking" submenu:

- kernel debugging
- compile the kernel with debug info
- KGDB – kernel debugging with remote GDB and select one of the options: KGDB over serial or KGDB over Ethernet.

The boot loader (e.g., u-boot) transmits the KGDB parameters to the kernel for serial or Ethernet connection. These parameters can be checked or changed in the running Linux kernel accessing the files:

/sys/module/kgdboc/parameters/kgdboc
/sys/module/kgdboe/parameters/kgdboe

The option kgdbwait causes KGDB to wait for a GDB connection in the early kernel boot stage. The kernel stops in the *kernel_init()* function and waits for the GDB connection from the host computer. For early kernel debug, KGDB support should be compiled inside the kernel, not as a module.

In the Eclipse IDE, the project for debugging the Linux kernel should be created by importing the vmlinux kernel file from the location where the kernel has been compiled.

The standard GDB support in Eclipse does not allow, for example, connection to the target using a UDP connection, as required for KGDB over Ethernet. For this purpose, we propose to use the "Eclipse C/C++ GDB Hardware Debugging" extension available from Indigo – http://download.eclipse.org/releases/indigo.

In the "Debug Configuration" submenu, we will use the "GDB Hardware Debugging" launch configuration. The configuration settings are presented in Figure 16.6.

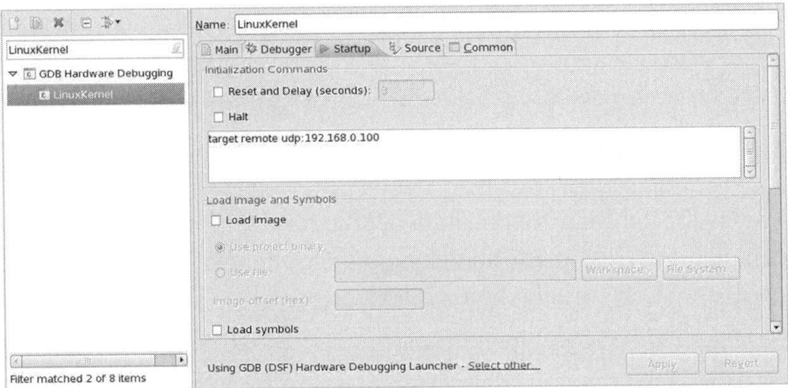

Figure 16.6:
Eclipse Linux kernel debug.

- In the Debugger tab, the settings are similar to the launch used for Linux application debug:
  - the cross-platform GDB tool should be set, for example powerpc-linux-gdb, arm-linux-gdb;
  - the JTAG settings (Use remote target) are disabled. The connection to the target, based on KGDB, is set in the Startup tab.
- In the Startup tab the initialization commands allow connecting to the target using, for example, a UDP connection, using the GDB command *target remote udp: <target IP addr>*.

Instrumented code

In the process of debugging an application, it is not always the best solution to use a source-code debugger, like GDB for example, to investigate and find out information about the issue. One alternative solution to the source-code debugger is to use a trace based on the instrumented code.

GCC provides the instrumented code feature as a compile time option. The compiler option "-finstrument-functions" generates instrumentation calls for entry and exit to functions. The GCC compiler defines two profiling functions to be called just after function entry and just before function exit:

```
void __cyg_profile_func_enter (void *this_fn, void *call_site);
void __cyg_profile_func_exit (void *this_fn, void *call_site);
```

The function arguments represent the address of the current function (function address in the symbol table) and the address where the function has been called from.

When compiled with the "-finstrument-functions" option, it is the user's responsibility to define and implement the above profiling functions. Typically, these functions will log the function call trace into memory or into a file. In projects with multiple files you can pass the instrumented code options only to some of the files. A function may be given the attribute "no_instrument_function", in which case this instrumentation will not be done. This can be used, for example, for the profiling functions listed above, high-priority interrupt routines, and any functions from which the profiling functions cannot safely be called.

Let us see where the instrumented code trace may help in situations where GDB does not provide many clues to fix the problem. When a segmentation fault occurs, the GDB debugger can display the stack and all variables and parameters. But there can be two types of issues:

- The call stack does not provide relevant information about what functions have been called, it just displays information about unfinished functions. Let us consider the following pseudocode:

  ```
  base_function () {
   if (condition1)
    function1();
   if (condition2)
    function2();
   function3();
  }
  ```

  If a crash is generated in the function3, the call stack in GDB looks like the following:

  ```
  #0 function3 () at file.c:xx
  #1 0x... in base_function () at file.c:yy
  ```

There is no information about what happens between the start of base_function() and the call of the function3. The functions that finished the execution (like function1 and function2) are not displayed in the call stack.

- The stack has been corrupted and therefore the GDB can show no information about the call stack. A similar case is where the memory has been corrupted and therefore the GDB can only show the current memory content but not where the corruption has been generated from.

Generally, the issues may be memory or stack corruption and unexpected or incorrect function calls.

The instrumented code options have an important impact on application performance. They should be used with caution for target applications, especially for real-time embedded applications.

Practical example

In the following we will present a practical example with comparison between investigation with instrumented code and GDB.

Let us assume an example where an unexpected function is called that generates a stack corruption, using the following example:

File stack.c

```
#include<stdio.h>
#include<string.h>
struct data_t {
  int a;
  char b;
};
struct data_t my_data[10];
void compute_data(int number);
struct data_t* get_next_data();

int main() {
  int i;
  for (i = 0; i<20; i++)
     compute_data(i);
  return 1;
```

```
16 }
17 void compute_data(int number) {
18   struct data_t *p_data = get_next_data();
19   p_data->a = number;
20 }
21 struct data_t* valid_data(int cnt) {
22   return &my_data[cnt];
23 }
24 struct data_t* invalid_data(int cnt) {
25   memset(&cnt, 2000, 0xAB);
26   return NULL;
27 }
28 struct data_t* get_next_data() {
29   static int cnt = 0;
30   if (cnt<10)
31      return valid_data(cnt++);
32   return invalid_data(cnt++);
33 }
```

In the function invalid_data we generate a stack corruption, in line 25.

GDB investigation

Running the program we obtain a segmentation fault error. The investigation with GDB shows the following:

```
Program received signal SIGSEGV, Segmentation fault.
0×080485ef in get_next_data () at stack.c:33
33    }
(gdb) backtrace
#0  0×080485ef in get_next_data () at stack.c:33
Cannot access memory at address 0xd0d0d0d4
(gdb)
```

The stack cannot be correctly displayed due to the corruption in line 25.

Instrumented code investigation

The instrumented code investigation assumes compilation with option -finstrument-functions and implementation of the profiling functions, in a different file, as in the example:

```
File instr.c
#include<stdio.h>
```

```
#include<time.h>
void __attribute__((no_instrument_function))
__cyg_profile_func_enter (void *this_fn, void *call_site);

void __attribute__((no_instrument_function))
__cyg_profile_func_exit (void *this_fn, void *call_site);

void __cyg_profile_func_enter (void *this_fn, void *call_site) {
  printf("%lu 0 %p %p\n", time(NULL), call_site, this_fn);
}
void __cyg_profile_func_exit (void *this_fn, void *call_site) {
  printf("%lu 1 %p %p\n", time(NULL), call_site, this_fn);
}
```

To simplify things, the implementation of the profiling functions is as simple as possible. In practice, when implementing these functions we must take into consideration the target requirements: printing should be done on console, into a file or into memory, timing information adds a supplementary overhead, the application is multithreading. We minimized the processing as much as possible at run-time while further processing can be done offline, based on the output generated during execution.

The program is compiled with the following command:

```
powerpc-linux-gcc -o stack -Wall -g stack.c instr.c -finstrument-functions
```

The application output can be further processed offline using a simple C program or a bash script, based on:

- the translation from address to function and line number being done using the "addr2line" Linux shell command;
- for a more user-friendly display, the output being displayed as a call stack and increasing indentation for function entry and decreasing indentation for function exit;
- time being displayed in a user-friendly format (hours, minutes, seconds and nanoseconds if required).

The processed log looks like this (-> is function entry, <- is function exit):

```
..............
14:49:18 __<- main (stack.c:13)
14:49:18 ____-> compute_data :called from main (stack.c:13)
14:49:18 ______-> get_next_data :called from compute_data (stack.c:18)
14:49:18 ________-> valid_data :called from get_next_data (stack.c:31)
14:49:18 ______<- get_next_data (stack.c:31)
14:49:18 ____<- compute_data (stack.c:18)
```

```
14:49:18 __<- main (stack.c:13)
14:49:18 ____-> compute_data :called from main (stack.c:13)
14:49:18 ______-> get_next_data :called from compute_data (stack.c:18)
14:49:18 ________-> invalid_data :called from get_next_data (stack.c:32)
14:49:18 ______<- get_next_data (stack.c:32)
14:49:18 ____<- ?? (??:0)
```

The function calls trace shows all the functions and, combined with GDB investigation, may give relevant information for identifying the program errors.

There can be other improvements in the implementation of the profiling functions, for example:

- the functions trace is saved into the memory into a circular buffer with a pre-configurable size;
- the printing on the console or file is done only when a fault (e.g., segmentation fault) occurs; this is done by setting a signal handler for specific Linux signals that will do the printing;
- the functions can be extended to multithreading: the function calls for each thread are saved in separate memory buffers. A mutual exclusion mechanism should be used.

Analysis tools

Analysis tools are other development tools that help in finding out other run-time types of errors that differ from what we can investigate with a source-code debugger. By analyzing the program execution on the target, these run-time tools can provide information about incorrect usage of dynamic memory allocation, system calls from the application or memory leak investigations.

This is not a complete description of analysis tools, but rather a summary of what these tools can provide and how they can be used to complement the investigations done with the debugger. We will present in the following the strace, mtrace and valgrind tools. There are other tools available for both dynamic and static analysis (not run-time) that can reveal some programming errors.

Strace

The strace is a Linux shell command that traces the execution of a program by intercepting and recording the system calls which are called by a process and the signals which are received by a process. A system call is a special function used by a program to request a service from the kernel. On a system call, the kernel takes over the execution of the program, processes the requested task and then transfers back the execution to the application. The strace is a very simple and practical debugging tool that helps to investigate the interface between user space and kernel space.

There are situations where basic investigation is required for a target application. The strace can be used without preparing the set-up for an investigation with a source-code debugger: debugger preparation, connection host to target on serial or Ethernet, source code should be available and the program should have been compiled with debug symbols. Debugging with strace is done by simply calling the strace followed by the name of the program. The strace does not require the application to be compiled with debug symbols. The strace can start the program to be debugged or it can attach to a running process by adding the option "-p <pid>".

Let us analyze with strace a simple program that does an allocation, prints a message and deallocates the pointer. The command is:

```
$ strace ./strace_test
```

Each line of the strace output contains a system call with all its arguments and the return value.

```
execve("./strace_test", ["./strace_test"], [/* 37 vars */]) = 0
brk(0)             = 0×99e7000
access("/etc/ld.so.preload", R_OK)    = -1 ENOENT (No such file or
directory)
open("/etc/ld.so.cache", O_RDONLY)    = 3
fstat64(3, {st_mode=S_IFREG|0644, st_size=46210, ...}) = 0
mmap2(NULL, 46210, PROT_READ, MAP_PRIVATE, 3, 0) = 0xb7f58000
close(3)             = 0
```

The system call arguments are displayed in a user-friendly format: where possible names are displayed instead of numerical values and the structures are expanded so that all the sub-elements are visible. We can check for example that the expected files are open and closed, the correct libraries are loaded, and the system calls have the correct arguments.

The strace tool is recommended when investigating the user-kernel interface, file input/output, kernel module *ioctl* interface, correct arguments and return value of system calls, and memory mapping for the current process. Using the strace is also a good learning exercise to understand how the user-space applications request services from the kernel.

Mtrace

The mtrace tool can be used to investigate dynamic memory allocation: memory allocated that has not been deallocated (so called memory leaks) and deallocating not allocated memory. The mtrace tool is included in the GNU C library.

The mtrace consists of two main parts:

- the runtime routine: when enabled in the application, the mtrace installs handlers for the malloc, realloc and free that will generate a memory allocation log when the application is executed on the target;
- the static routine: this is a simple perl script (mtrace) that is able to parse the log generated by mtrace during the application execution and presents the results in a user-friendly format. It can be run on the target or on the host computer (preferable on host).

At run-time, the mtrace does not use the debug symbols from the application, so the application can be stripped on the target. Only symbol addresses are printed in the log. The static routine requires access to the debug symbols for translation from addresses to file names, function names and line numbers.

The mtrace is enabled by modifying the source code of the application as follows:

- Include the file mcheck.h. The header file is included in the standard GNU C library.
- Call the mtrace() function in the application source code where you want to start the memory trace. The mtrace has the advantage that the trace start can be placed anywhere in your program; it does not necessarily have to be located at the beginning of the main. For big applications you can do memory checking per function or per functional module before doing it for the entire application.
- Call the muntrace() function in the application source code where you want to stop the trace. Same as the mtrace(), the muntrace() can be placed anywhere in the program.

A mandatory step is to specify the log file in which to save the memory trace: the environment variable MALLOC_TRACE should be set to the desired file location. This should be done on the target, on the console where the application is started from. An example is:

```
$ export MALLOC_TRACE=/var/log/my_memory_log.txt
```

After the program is executed, the generated log file is copied to the host computer, where it is analyzed with the mtrace program:

```
$ mtrace <application elf> <memory log file>
```

A simple program is presented the following example:

```
File test_mtrace.c
#include <stdio.h>
#include <stdlib.h>
#include <mcheck.h>
int main() {
```

```
int *a, *b;
char *c;
a = (int *)malloc(sizeof(int));

mtrace();
b = (int *)malloc(sizeof(int));
c = (char *)malloc(100*sizeof(char));
free(a);
muntrace();

free(c);
return 1;
}
```

In the source code, there are several problems we will pay attention to:

- The variable “a” is correctly allocated and deallocated, but the trace is started after its allocation. This is not a real memory allocation problem; it is only reported by the mtrace because the line that is doing the allocation was not included in the trace.
- The variable “b” is never deallocated (memory leak).
- The variable “c” is correctly allocated and deallocated, but the trace is stopped before its deallocation. Same as for the first case, it is only an mtrace reported issue, but not a real issue.

And so, the mtrace output shows all of these issues:

```
$ mtrace test_mtrace malloc_trace.txt
- 0×090fa008 Free 4 was never alloc'd /home/work/test_mtrace.c:13

Memory not freed:
_________________

 Address   Size   Caller

0×090fa388   0×4 at /home/work/test_mtrace.c:10
0×090fa398  0×64 at /home/work/test_mtrace.c:11
```

The mtrace displays also the amount of memory that has been allocated, in bytes, in the column “size”.

A drawback of the mtrace is that for C++ applications it has a very limited usage. In C++ when using “new” and “delete” operators the mtrace will always trace the location of the malloc, realloc and free from the implementation of the “new” and “delete” operators, in the libstdc++ library. Therefore, for C++ application we can see the results, but we will not see the location in the source file where the memory problem was generated.

Valgrind

Valgrind is open-source free software under the GNU General Public License, version 2. Valgrind is an instrumentation framework for dynamic analysis tools providing support for memory management error detection, threading issues, a call-graph generating cache and branch-prediction profiler, and a heap profiler.

Valgrind has support for several embedded platforms. Currently it supports x86, amd64, ppc32, ppc64 and s390x.

We will present below some examples to demonstrate the memory management analysis capabilities of the Valgrind tool. At run-time, Valgrind can detect invalid memory access, uninitialized memory access or memory leaks.

Let us use a simple example with several memory access errors and check the Valgrind log.

```
File test_valgrind.c
#include<stdio.h>
#include<stdlib.h>

int main() {
  int *a, b, *c;

  a = (int *)malloc(sizeof(int));
  *a = b;
  printf("*a = %d\n", *a);
  c = (int *)malloc(10*sizeof(int));
  printf("c[11] = %d\n", c[11]);
  return 1;
}
```

The program is compiled with debug information (*-g*) and the Valgrind tool is started with the following parameters:

```
$ valgrind -tool=memcheck -leak-check=yes ./test_valgrind
```

In the source code we can observe the following errors, also reported by the valgrind.

- The variable "b" is not initialized before accessing it. When the uninitialized value is accessed in the printf through the variable "a", the Valgrind tool reports the access to uninitialized data:

```
==20699== Use of uninitialised value of size 4
==20699==    at 0×2B1BFB: _itoa_word (in /lib/libc-2.5.so)
==20699==    by 0×2B5390: vfprintf (in /lib/libc-2.5.so)
==20699==    by 0×2BCE42: printf (in /lib/libc-2.5.so)
==20699==    by 0×80483F0: main (test_valgrind.c:9)
==20699==
==20699==    Conditional jump or move depends on uninitialised value(s)
==20699==    at 0×2B1C03: _itoa_word (in /lib/libc-2.5.so)
==20699==    by 0×2B5390: vfprintf (in /lib/libc-2.5.so)
==20699==    by 0×2BCE42: printf (in /lib/libc-2.5.so)
==20699==    by 0×80483F0: main (test_valgrind.c:9)
```

- For the variable "c" a memory size of 10 integers is allocated and in the next line the memory is accessed outside the allocated area. The Valgrind reports this error as follows:

```
==20699==    Invalid read of size 4
==20699==    at 0×8048406: main (test_valgrind.c:12)
==20699==    Address 0×401608C is 4 bytes after a block of size 40 alloc'd
==20699==    at 0×40053C0: malloc (vg_replace_malloc.c:149)
==20699==    by 0×80483FC: main (test_valgrind.c:11)
```

- The variable "a" and variable "c" are allocated but are never deallocated. The Valgrind reports the memory leaks:

```
==20699== 4 bytes in 1 blocks are definitely lost in loss record 1 of 2
==20699==    at 0×40053C0: malloc (vg_replace_malloc.c:149)
==20699==    by 0×80483D0: main (test_valgrind.c:7)
==20699==
==20699== 40 bytes in 1 blocks are definitely lost in loss record 2 of 2
==20699==    at 0×40053C0: malloc (vg_replace_malloc.c:149)
==20699==    by 0×80483FC: main (test_valgrind.c:11)
```

These types of errors cannot be detected with a standard debugger, like GDB. Analysis tools should be used together with the debugger to cover a wider scope of typical programming errors.

Hardware capabilities

When debugging embedded systems it is important to understand the hardware capabilities of the processors and to use them to your advantage. That is why it is always a good idea to review the processor architecture, features and capabilities and to keep in mind everything that may help in the debugging process.

Some processors provide a lot of built-in hardware capabilities for debugging, trace and analysis and profiling. We will refer below to some simple capabilities, but also to more general ones like hardware breakpoints and hardware watchpoints. Many debuggers have support for hardware breakpoints or watchpoints. These hardware capabilities do not depend on the physical debug interface and can work for both debug agent and JTAG probe.

Hardware breakpoints

There are two types of breakpoints: hardware breakpoints based on the processor hardware capabilities and software breakpoints. For both types of breakpoints, the debugger apparently takes similar actions. When a breakpoint is added, the debugger needs to know the address in which to insert the breakpoint. At the user interface, the user can directly specify the address, the function name or the line number in a source file and, based on the symbols table, the debugger determines the breakpoint address. When a breakpoint is hit, for both software and hardware breakpoints, a debug interrupt is generated and the debugger stops at the breakpoint address. The difference between them is how the debugger inserts the breakpoint at the required address.

For the software breakpoints, the debugger modifies the program code. The debugger temporarily stores the instruction located at the breakpoint address and overwrites it with a special instruction code, specific for each processor. When the program reaches the breakpoint address, it executes the special instruction that will generate a debug interrupt, then makes the debugger stop at the breakpoint address. When the breakpoint is removed, the debugger restores the temporarily saved instruction at the breakpoint address. To step over a breakpoint, the debugger removes the breakpoint, executes the instruction at the breakpoint address and then re-inserts the breakpoint. There is one more trick the debugger does for software breakpoints. While the breakpoint is enabled, for any read operation through the debugger to the address where the breakpoint has been set it always returns the temporarily saved instruction but not what is currently at the breakpoint address. So reading the memory at the breakpoint address will never return the special breakpoint instruction.

There is no limitation in the number of software breakpoints – it depends only on how many breakpoints are allowed in the debugger software. The software breakpoint is an intrusive method: it always modifies the code and for this purpose the debugger should have write access to the breakpoint address. From this comes the software breakpoint limitation: it cannot be used when the program is running from a read-only location (like ROM or flash).

On the other hand, the hardware breakpoints depend on the hardware capabilities of the processor. In general processors have some dedicated registers for hardware breakpoints. To insert a hardware breakpoint, the debugger writes the breakpoint address in one of these dedicated registers. The rest is done by the processor: when the instruction at that address is executed, a debug interrupt is generated and the control is transferred to the debugger. The number of hardware breakpoints is limited by the number of dedicated registers available in the processor, typically two or four.

Hardware watchpoints

Watchpoints are also named data breakpoints and differ from breakpoints by address use. For breakpoints, the address represents the code address that, when it is executed, triggers the debug interrupt. For watchpoints, the address represents a memory address that, when it is accessed by a read or write operation, triggers the debug interrupt. Therefore, while breakpoints refer to code addresses, functions and line numbers, watchpoints refer to memory or data addresses and variable addresses.

A watchpoint is used to stop the execution of the program whenever the watchpoint address is read from or written to. If the watchpoint is set to a variable, then, the same as for breakpoints, the debugger translates the variable to an address based on the debug symbol table.

Software watchpoints have no hardware support and therefore it is the debugger that does the complete handling. A debugger implements a software watchpoint by single-step running of the program and checking whether the value of the address has been changed after each step. This is extremely inefficient and it has a significant impact on performance. Sometimes it may be worth using software watchpoints just to have an idea about which part of the program corrupts a memory address.

Hardware watchpoints depend on the hardware capabilities of the processor. As for breakpoints, the processors have dedicated registers for hardware watchpoints. When a hardware watchpoint is set, one of these registers is set with the watchpoint address, specifying also the access type: read, write or read-write. For a watchpoint we can specify the memory zone, not only a single address. For this case, the start and the end address of the memory are set in the watchpoint registers. The hardware watchpoints have no impact on performance and therefore it is always recommended to use hardware instead of software watchpoints, if the processor supports it. The number of hardware watchpoints is limited by the number of watchpoint registers of the processor.

Debugging tips and tricks

Debugging is a problem-solving process for which it is required to have knowledge, methodology, intuition, patience and many ideas. Here are some ideas that might help you in the debugging process.

- If the release application has not been compiled with debug information you can still debug it. For some compilers like GCC, adding the debug information does not change symbol values as compared with compilation without *-g*. In the debugger you should load the ELF file with debug symbols while debugging the target with the release application. In the same way you can analyze the core dump created by the release application.
- For the release application it is always a good idea to enable the core dump even when the application is stripped. In the case of an application crash you can get the core and analyze it offline. This is useful especially for applications in the field where you cannot connect directly with the debugger.
- It is not necessary to enable core dump generation for the entire system. You can enable it from the application's source code, as in the example below:

```
struct rlimit set;
set.rlim_cur = 0xFFFFFFFF;
set.rlim_max = 0xFFFFFFFF;
setrlimit(RLIMIT_CORE, &set);
```

- When you want to generate a core dump, make sure you do not have a Linux signal handler defined for the error signals. This will overwrite the default handler so the core dump is not generated.
- To handle an application crash in a reliable way, you can create an application supervisor. The supervisor checks whether the application is still alive, and if it has crashed it will restart it so the down-time will be minimal. You can extend it to watch-dog services to check whether the application is blocked, not just crashed.
- You can save a snapshot of the application state into a core dump. Of course the core dump should be enabled. This is useful when the application is blocked and is not responding (in a deadlock for example) and you cannot connect directly with the debugger (e.g., the application is running in the field). The solution is to restart the application, saving its entire state into a core dump. If you send an error signal to the application, the application will terminate, generating a core dump. You can then get the core dump and analyze it off line with the debugger. The core dump is created with the command:

```
$ kill -SIGSEGV <application pid>
```

- We can extend the previous idea to the following: at any time you can get some status information from the application using the Linux signal. This is useful if the application does not have a management interface (CLI, telnet). In the application, you have to overwrite the default signal handler for a signal (e.g., SIGUSR1) and use this handler to provide some status information. The status is dumped by sending the overwritten signal to the application (kill – SIGUSR1 <application pid>).
- For real-time applications (e.g., bare-board applications with no operating system) the debugger is not always a good solution. Even printf messages on the console can be

time-consuming and may affect the real-time functionality of the program. For these applications it is worth using an oscilloscope. Use the GPIO to trigger different events to the oscilloscope. You can also use it for profiling functions on interrupt routines: a GPIO level is set to high when at routine entry and set to low at routine exit. On the oscilloscope you can see the time duration and the occurrence rate. With more GPIO pins, you can see the distribution in time of different routines.

- For real-time applications, debug information should be captured in some special conditions. If some interrupts occur during the debug information capture, the data may be corrupted or irrelevant. For example, this may happen when you want to correlate some counters (receive and transmit bytes or packets). So before capturing the data, it may be necessary to disable interrupts and to enable them again once the capture is finished.
- Access to memory is the fastest way to store data. For real-time applications, sending the debug data to the host computer while the application is running may affect the application functionality. In this case, the debug data can be stored in memory and then can be retrieved and analyzed later on, offline.
- In the development and debugging process you should pay attention to all of the following: compiler (check all the warnings), static analysis tools, runtime analysis tools (e.g., memory management tools) and the debugger.

CHAPTER 17

Multicore Software Development for Embedded Systems

This Chapter draws on Material from the Multicore Programming Practices Guide (MPP) from the Multicore Association

Dave Stewart, Max Domeika, Scott A. Hissam, Skip Hovsmith, James Ivers, Ross Dickson, Ian Lintault, Stephen Olsen, Hyunki Baik, François Bodin and Robert Oshana

Chapter Outline

Software Engineering for Embedded Systems.
DOI: http://dx.doi.org/10.1016/B978-0-12-415917-4.00017-7
© 2013 Elsevier Inc. All rights reserved.

Part 1: Analysis and high-level design

It is important to understand both the algorithmic intent and the serial implementation of programs being transformed to run in multicore environments. This section discusses program analysis techniques used to uncover opportunities to exploit parallel behavior and the dependencies which constrain that behavior. Analysis results are strongly affected by the use of representative benchmarks and realistic workloads. High-level design decisions, including choice of algorithm, selection of platform architecture, and identification of appropriate parallel design patterns, are then made which will optimize the multicore implementation to meet critical application metrics such as performance, power, footprint, maintainability, and scalability.

Analysis

To effectively exploit multicore resources, you must eventually parallelize your program. There are at least two ways to parallelize. Here are a couple of examples:

- video: it is possible to break one algorithm into pieces based on screen location;
- network processing: these types of applications are parallelized by executing different functions on different processors.

However, there are several steps you should take before introducing parallelism. This section describes two such activities – improving the program's serial performance and understanding the program.

(Throughout this section, we assume that the primary purpose of migrating a program to multicore is to improve its performance (end-to-end time). There are, of course, other reasons to move to multicore, such as improving power consumption. While much of the guidance in this section can be applied with different improvement goals in mind, performance is used in our examples as the primary metric.)

Improving serial performance

The first step in redesigning your program to exploit multicore resources is actually to optimize its serial implementation. This is done first for several reasons – serial performance tuning is typically easier, less time-consuming, and less likely to introduce bugs. Serial improvement will reduce the gap between where you are and your performance goal, which may mean that less parallelization is needed. It also allows parallelization to focus on parallel behavior, rather than a mix of serial and parallel issues.

It is important to remember, though, that serial optimization is *not* the end goal. We want to optimize carefully, applying only changes that will facilitate parallelization and the performance improvements that parallelization can bring. In particular, serial optimizations that interfere with or limit parallelization should be avoided. Examples include introducing unnecessary data dependencies and exploiting details of the single-core hardware architecture (for example, cache capacity).

A disciplined approach to performance tuning

Developers are familiar with lots of tips and tricks that can be used to improve the serial performance of a program; in fact, there is a wealth of public material to help (e.g., articles, books, tools, and accumulated wisdom). But haphazard application of such improvements is generally a bad idea.

> *Programmers waste enormous amounts of time thinking about, or worrying about, the speed of noncritical parts of their programs, and these attempts at efficiency actually have a strong negative impact when debugging and maintenance are considered. We should forget about small efficiencies, say about 97% of the time: premature optimization is the root of all evil [1].*

Instead, the key to effective serial performance tuning is discipline. Use measurements and careful analysis to guide decision-making, change one thing at a time, and meticulously measure again to confirm that changes have been beneficial. The idea is to use an iterative approach based on the steps shown in Figure 17.1.

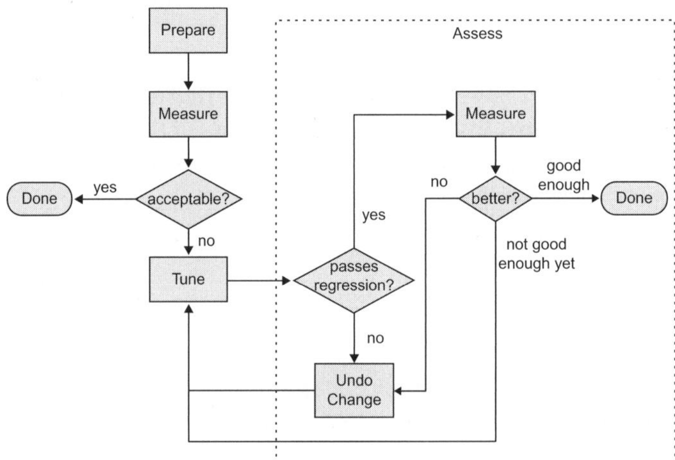

Figure 17.1:
Summary of serial performance tuning approach.

- Prepare: assemble a collection of regression tests and benchmarks against which to improve the program's performance. Carefully consider the data sets used to benchmark the program to ensure it is representative of all cases from best, to average, to worst case.

- Measure: gather performance data through profiling or simulation. If the performance is reasonable, stop.
- Tune: look at the measurements; understand where the program is spending time and whether this is reasonable. Find the biggest bottleneck that you can improve and make a single change.
- Assess: determine whether the change was positive. If the change was negative, then back out the change and improve your understanding before trying again. If the change was positive, but insufficient, return to the tuning step and look for the next bottleneck. Note that some changes may not immediately improve performance, but they enable subsequent changes which lead to further performance improvements.

The following sections provide short elaborations of the steps in this approach. Each topic is richer than can be reasonably covered in this chapter, and the reader is encouraged to do some digging for more information in each area as needed. There has been a great deal of useful work in performance analysis and performance tuning and *most of it* is applicable when preparing for multicore (though the effects of parallelization changes are more sensitive to the order in which the changes are applied).

Prepare

Before even thinking about making changes, think about your objectives and assemble the resources that will help you achieve them efficiently and reliably. Start with the following questions.

- What are your goals? Improving the performance of a program can be a complicated, time-consuming, and error-prone task. You want to stop when you've reached "good enough" results.
- What operational scenarios are most important? Any improvements made will be based on data from observation of the program's execution, but which scenarios are most important? You could focus on steady-state operations, heavy load conditions, error recovery scenarios, or some balance of such scenarios.
- What performance metric makes sense for your program? Perhaps it's the time to process a unit of work, or maybe the number of units of work completed in a unit of time. You need to know what to measure so you can quantize goals or know that you've met them.

Construct a set of benchmarks (uses of the program over specific data and operations) over which you will collect performance data. All optimizations will be relative to the benchmarks, so carefully choose the scenarios for which performance most needs to be improved. It's also a good idea to include cases that vary the workload so that you can see how performance scales (at least three data points are needed to discriminate between linear from non-linear scaling).

(When parallelization begins, it's also important to select a set of machine configurations. It may be a good idea to choose a variety of architectures and different core counts to better understand the effect of changes in different environments. In particular, long-lived programs can be expected to be run in a variety of environments. Understanding a program's behavior across a range of environments helps prevent over-optimization for a particular environment.)

What kinds of changes are unacceptable? Performance optimizations are often trade-offs with some other concern, such as memory consumption, code maintainability, or portability. Know how much you are willing to compromise in any of these areas. Regardless, don't introduce bugs! Faster but wrong is rarely a good choice, so make sure you have a good regression suite available before you start (it should go without saying that the program passes all tests before starting).

Serial performance tuning is an iterative process that involves repeated execution of your program, both to measure performance and ensure that correct functionality is preserved, so make sure you have good automated support for these activities.

Measure

After preparations are complete, the first task is to understand the baseline performance of your program against your benchmarks. To measure performance, you typically make use of development tools called profilers. A profiler is a program that observes the execution of another program and collects measures of its performance. There are several different approaches used for profiling:

- Sampling: a sampling profiler takes measurements at regular intervals. (Grotker, Holtmann, Keding, and Wloka recommend that an area of interest be run often enough that its total runtime is at least two orders of magnitude greater than the sampling interval to compensate for variance in measurement results.)
- Instrumentation: an instrumentation-based profiler typically compiles or links additional instructions into the program for measurement.
- Emulation or simulation: these approaches execute the program in an environment that emulates or simulates (e.g., through interpretation) the execution environment.

The quality of the performance data varies in several ways, two of which are completeness and resemblance to "real performance". Sampling only measures at regular intervals, generating incomplete insight into program behavior. Non-sampling approaches produce complete data, with respect to the measurement granularity. Any profiling approach, however, has some effect on how closely the measurements resemble execution in the absence of measurement. Low-overhead approaches more closely resemble typical execution than those with high overhead, such as instrumentation or interpretation, which may alter the timing properties of the program in significant ways.

Output differs from tool to tool in both granularity and format. Profilers typically measure data relative to functions, with simple measures being the time at which each function call and return occurs. Some profilers capture information at a finer granularity or allow the user add instrumentation points (e.g., around particularly interesting loops).

Profiler output varies considerably, from simple reports to sophisticated GUIs with controls for filtering and sorting. Two common forms of output are:

- flat profile: a flat profile is generally a tabular report of statistics organized by function, such as how much execution time was in a function (by percent and units of time) and how many times the function was called;
- call graph: a call graph shows execution time, again by function, relative to call chains. A call graph will show which functions were called by a given function, how many times, and how much execution time was used.

Typically, you will want to use both forms of output. A flat profile is a good way to quickly find where large portions of time are being spent (e.g., a single function that consumes 60% of the time). A call graph is a good way to see where a function is being used.

Choice of profiler(s) is based on a number of the usual criteria, such as availability/cost, target platform, experience, and so on. You should use at least one profiler that measures how much of your execution time is spent outside your program (e.g., in system calls) to assemble a more complete performance picture. When developing an embedded system, you may need to use an emulation- or simulation-based profiler before target hardware is available or to compensate for lack of a persistent store for measurements in the target device.

Each time you measure the performance of your program, be sure that you use the same tools and the same benchmarks. You want to ensure that performance improvements are real improvements. Gather your first set of measurements before making any changes! This is your baseline; any code changes that you keep should result in better results than your baseline.

Tune

An important rule of thumb in performance tuning is "only change one thing at a time". The definition of "one thing at a time" could be a line of code or a function. It really depends on the application, the amount of code that is changing per iteration, the complexity of the code and other factors. Each tuning iteration, you should use the measurements you gathered through profiling to look for the biggest improvement you can reasonably make. (This is one common approach used in serial performance tuning, but not the only option. In some cases, it is difficult to isolate a single, significant hotspot. In such cases, it may be possible to "polish everywhere" by addressing a large number of smaller inefficiencies throughout a program.)

As always, using common sense should go without saying. If a change would save you 0.5% time but take months of effort, it's probably not a good idea. Remember that you will also be making substantial changes when parallelizing your program, so it's usually a good idea to stick with the "low-hanging fruit" or big wins when improving the performance of your serial program. Changing an algorithm that consumes a large portion of time to scale linearly rather than logarithmically, for instance, would be a good example of a change worth making.

Start by looking through your measurements for hotspots. Hotspots are areas in your program that use disproportionate percentages of your execution time, and can be found using flat profiles. We start with hotspots for a simple reason: a performance improvement in frequently executed code will yield better overall improvement than a similar improvement in infrequently executed code. That is, a 10% improvement in a function using 50% of total execution time is an overall improvement of 5%; a 10% improvement in a function using 5% of total execution time is only an overall improvement of 0.5%. Beware of diminishing returns. After you've improved the program by 30%, this may also reduce all subsequent improvements by 30% as well.

Once you select a hotspot for examination, think about why it is consuming so much time and whether that is reasonable. At a high level, the options are pretty simple – time is spent:

- Computing: executing the instructions is the first thing we tend to think about. Think about whether an appropriate algorithm is used; review the profiling data for different workloads to see if it's scaling as you would expect.
- Think about whether all computations are needed. You may be able to hoist calculations out of a loop or use lookup tables to reduce computation.
- Think about whether you're using the right types and data structures. Moving larger chunks of memory around typically takes longer (e.g., using floats is often faster than using doubles). Consider the impact of different language constructs on your platform (e.g., the overhead that is necessary to support exception handling).
- Think about whether your program decomposition is good. If you have functions whose execution time isn't significantly larger than call/return overhead, inlining or refactoring is a good idea.
- Think about your persistence strategies. Re-initializing and re-using a data structure (or class) can be more efficient than creating a new one.

- Waiting: some operations just have to spend time waiting, which is particularly problematic in serial programs. I/O operations like network or file system access take a long time, as does user interaction. You can examine your caching strategy for some improvements, but using concurrency is the typical solution. Avoid introducing concurrency at this point, but note the dependency. This will factor into your parallelization strategy.
- Moving data: working with large data sets can cause programs to move data in and out of memory frequently. Reducing unnecessary memory moves can be a big help. Memory profilers are good tools for understanding and improving your memory use.
- Though it could improve serial performance, you should avoid reorganizing your data for locality (i.e., keeping data used together close in memory, which could allow a single move instead of several smaller moves). This kind of optimization is better performed as part of parallelization, when factors like cache width and policy are considered.

As you examine each hotspot, use several sources of information. Obviously, there is the code itself. But you can also get a lot of quick information from the call graph generated by a profiler. By looking at calls made by a function and calls made to a function, you gain more insight into how it's used and what it does. In particular, walking back up the call graph (callers of the function) may lead you to a hotspot that is not a leaf node of the call graph.

If the time spent in the hotspot seems reasonable, move on to the next. If it's not, think carefully about a change that will remedy the underlying inefficiency, while changing as little as possible, and which will not hinder parallelization. In general, favor changes that reduce computation over those that minimize data footprint. At this stage, we want to focus on reducing the program to the essential computations needed to function correctly.

Also consider that some changes may temporarily worsen the performance metrics but will enable additional changes which will lead to overall improved performance. See the chapter on performance engineering to get a better feel for some of these software architectures that support this approach. The order of changes may also be significant; some changes introduce constraints to the system which will inhibit additional changes. All things equal, first favor changes which minimally constrain the ability to make additional changes.

Assess

Each time you make a change to your program, you should stop and assess whether it was a good change. Minimally, a "good change" is one that does not introduce bugs and that either directly or indirectly enables additional changes which improve the performance metrics you identified in the Prepare step. To be "good enough", the change has to be significant enough to warrant modifying the program. The maxim of "if it's not broke, don't fix it" comes into play here. For example, assume a change is made that results in a 3% program speed-up. However, this is legacy code that has worked for years. Is exposing the code to new errors worth the 3%? Risk has to be taken into account as well.

You assess these criteria by re-running your regression suite and re-measuring the program using your benchmarks.

If the regression fails or your performance is worse than before the change, then you misunderstood something about the program or your change. Study the program again, before and after the change, to understand why you got the result that you did. If it can be fixed and still seems like a good change, try again. Otherwise, back out the change and return to the Tune step. Look at the hotspot again and think about different changes. If you cannot find another reasonable change, move on to the next hotspot and continue tuning.

If the regression passed and your performance improved, make sure the change is also acceptable with regard to your other concerns of interest. For example, if portability is important, it should preserve the portability properties that your program started with. Such criteria are often more difficult to validate in an automated way, but should be part of your mental checklist.

Understand the application

Regardless of the technique ultimately used to transform the application from one that processes sequentially to one that processes concurrently, having a thorough understanding of the problem being solved cannot be avoided. This understanding can come from a variety of sources, including requirements, documentation, discussions with the application's developers, and profiling data.

As discussed in the following sections, some aspects of an application's behavior are particularly relevant to parallelization, like a thorough understanding of computational and data dependencies. A good application analysis will help to determine which dependencies are inherent in solving the problem and which are artificial, perhaps introduced as part of some serial optimization.

Setting expectations for speed-up

Generally there are two reasons for splitting up and re-architecting an application for parallelization: speed-up and solving large problems. Speed-up is achieved by effectively load-balancing work across the cores to minimize execution time. Solving large problems is achieved not only by distributing the work across cores, but (sometimes) also by distributing the work across processors due to the sheer size of the data which makes the problem too large for a single processor. (This could be true for a multi/many-processor system or a multicore system even though it is not in the traditional HPC realm, which is not the focus of this guide.) Speed-up will be the primary driver for the discussion here.

Setting goals for speed-up is important. Speed-up is achieved by effectively load-balancing work across the cores to minimize execution time, but there are limits to what is reasonable. For example, some segments of code cannot be effectively parallelized. Amdahl's law (see section 6.3) expresses the maximum expected benefit for improving a portion of an application. If the serial execution time of a portion accounts for 80% of the total time and that portion will be spread across eight cores, the result would be at best 3.3 times faster. If that same portion only accounted for 20% of serial execution time, the same parallelization would be at best 1.2 times faster. And these are maximum expected improvements; various overhead factors (e.g., for coordination) will only reduce the benefit further.

The effort to parallelize the application should be justified given an objective analysis of the application, the effort required to make the change, and the realistic expectations from the effort.

Nature of the processing

From a profile of the application it is possible to find parts of the application that are more computationally intensive than in other portions (e.g., hotspots identified from the flat profile generated from measures of the serial application). It is recommended to focus on these portions over other, less intensive portions, as a higher percentage of gain is most likely to be achieved where the greatest amount of computation is performed. The computational nature of these portions of the application will likely fall into one of two general forms of parallel decomposition: function or data parallel.

Function parallel decomposition is a form of decomposition where the solution to a problem could be envisioned as a sequence of steps which could be accomplished concurrently. These steps are absolutely or relatively independent of each another to achieve the same outcome regardless of the order in which those functions are carried out. To be absolutely independent of each other would mean that the functions share no data and that no synchronization between the steps needs to occur (very uncommon). To be relatively independent of each other simply means the more common case that such functions share data and from time to time the functions will need to coordinate their activities in some synchronizing manner. One example of function parallel decomposition is an image-processing and capture application. In this application a bitmap from a camera is received, and the application performs three operations:

- count the number of unique colors in the image
- convert the bitmap to a JPEG
- save the image to disk.

In the serialized application, these activities would occur in sequence, one after the other (see Figure 17.2, left side). In the function parallelized version of this same application, two functions can be done in parallel since there are no dependencies between them (see Figure 17.2, right side), but the third function to save the image can only be done after the bitmap was converted to JPEG – thus requiring synchronization between the function that performs the encoding and the function that saves the image. If the application were only required to save the original bitmap captured from the camera and not the converted JPEG, there would be absolutely no dependencies between the three functions, and all three could be performed in parallel.

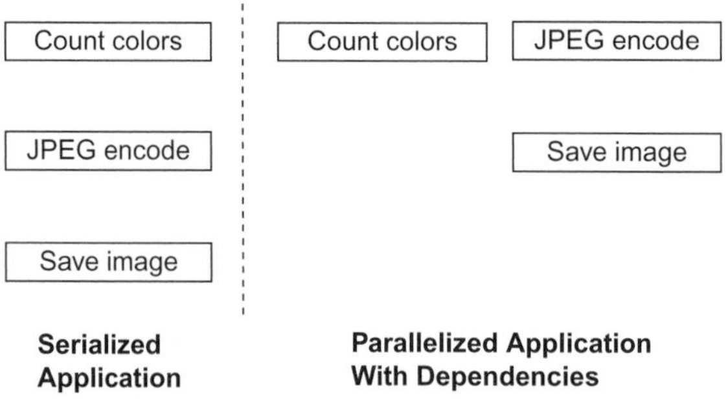

Figure 17.2:
Function parallel decomposition example.

Data parallel decomposition is a form of decomposition where the solution to a problem involves segmenting and decomposing major data structures (e.g., arrays) into smaller, independent chunks of data which can be processed independently of one another and concurrently. One easy example of this form is a scalar multiplication operation on a matrix. In a serialized application, such operations are often performed sequentially through the aid of looping constructs (see Figure 17.3). In this example each cell can be operated on completely independent of other operations on other cells in the matrix. Furthermore, such operations can occur in any order and the resulting matrix from the operation will be the same in any case. The ordering imposed by the serial loop construct is simply artificial given the semantics of the loop construct; a parallelized form of this same matrix operation is not bound by such constraints. As such, each cell of the matrix could be the decomposed form of a parallelization effort. If the matrix is 2×2, then there could be four functions assigned to perform the scalar multiplication to each corresponding cell.

In either form (function or data parallelization) it will often be the case that one form will inform the other. Most problems are amenable to both forms of decomposition – knowing which form is the most appropriate can only be reasoned by thoroughly understanding the problem that is being solved (Alan Kay is quoted as saying "*Point of view is worth 80 IQ*

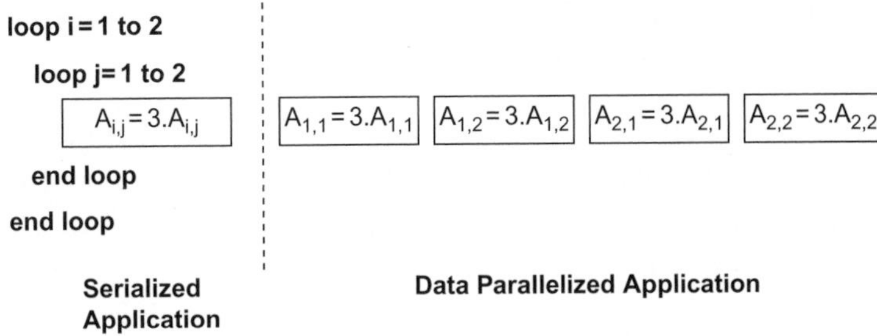

Figure 17.3:
Data parallel decomposition example.

points" [2]). This is because some problems (like the image-processing and capture application problem above) are more amendable to functional decomposition where others (e.g., the scalar multiplication problem) are more amenable to data decomposition. But in either form, data structures will have to be designed so that the tasks from function parallel decomposition can perform their computations and progress to achieve the desired outcome, or tasks will have to be created to manipulate the independent chunks of data resulting from the data parallel decomposition.

Dependencies

Dependencies can be in the form of ordering between operations within the serialized application or data dependencies (e.g., shared memory) between those operations. Some profiling tools are capable of generating call graphs. Such graphs can aid in discovering the ordering and the frequencies of operations and functions evident within the application. The serialized form of the application may yield some insight into what that ordering will be. But recall it is possible that some compromises may have been made to optimize the serialized application for a single-core processor and that the ordering could be artificial to achieve other (prior) objectives. These should be well documented in the code. So having insight and perspective as to the potential for parallelization of the application, separate from the serialized form, may help identify false ordering (ordering which is not required) between operations and present opportunities for parallelization. For example in the image-processing and capture application example above, counting the number of unique colors in the bitmap did not necessarily have to occur first.

Shared data dependencies between different (perhaps large) portions of code may also be discernible from these call graphs, but it is more likely that inspection of the source code will be necessary to either confirm or refute such data dependencies. Static analysis tools and memory profiling tools may be available to aid in the identification of data dependencies for large regions of code (for example, looking for access to global variables, share memory regions, etc. across many lines of code or source code files). Such tools will likely be language-dependent and possibly even platform-dependent – so finding these tools may take some time for a specific target platform.

Understanding the dependencies between delineated operations within the application is important. Just as important when analyzing the serial application are dependencies which may also exist within an operation (for instance a hotspot that is result of a computationally intensive loop). Such hotspots are candidates for parallelization because if the loop can be designed to be executed in parallel some speed-up can be achieved. However, in order to perform this activity the interesting loop has to be analyzed and redesigned so that each iteration of the loop can be made independent – that is, that each iteration of the loop can be safely executed in any order and any dependencies are not carried from each iteration. There are also loops that are used in serialized applications that must have dependencies between iterations, such as performing accumulations or other associative operations which are more difficult to remove.

This section started by identifying speed-up and the primary objective for analysis by effectively and efficiently using all the cores in a manner to get all the work done in a shorter time. To accomplish this, the decomposition, ordering, design, and implementation of the tasks needed to perform the work (be it function parallel or data parallel decomposition) will have to consider the target platform, so that the work created for the tasks will be of sufficient size to keep the cores busy and be correctly balanced between the multiple cores. In the prior scalar multiplication operation, it was illustrated that a task could be created for each element of the matrix to perform the design operation. For this specific example (more a counter-example), this would likely never be done here for various reasons:

- the allocation of a task for each cell of the matrix to one of the cores would simply not scale for a matrix of any practical size (this assumes that a no specialized work queue and thread pool is created to keep processors busy);
- the overhead introduced by parallelization would likely not outperform the original serialized code.

This underscores two important points. The first is that determining the proper sizing (or granularity) of the work itself is non-trivial. For software engineers performing this activity for the first time, this might involve some aspect of trial and error after the parallelization of the application is shown to be correct. There are also heuristics which can aid in estimating granularity which may be available for the target platform, parallelization libraries, or languages used for the parallelization effort. For example, Thread Building Blocks (http://www.threadingbuildingblocks.org/) recommends a "grainsize" (an indicator of granularity for the number of instructions to execute in the body of a task) of 10,000 to 100,000 instructions, but this varies based on the application.

The final point is that after a parallelization exercise is conducted on the source code, revisit the assessment loop in Figure 17.1 to confirm that the expected results for speed-up did indeed occur and that the regression test developed for the application was passed.

High-level design

Once a good understanding of the algorithmic intent and serial implementation of a program is gained, it is appropriate to begin the high-level design for a parallel implementation of the application. The intent of the high-level design phase is to partition the application into separate regions which expose work which can be run in parallel. Dependencies between regions will naturally limit this parallelism. Additionally, characteristics of the target run-time will practically limit the amount of work which can be done in parallel. It is important to choose an appropriate granularity of decomposition which can be efficiently mapped onto the parallel run-time environment.

This section discusses function and data decomposition, data dependency, and run-time characteristics which limit parallelism, and the importance of balancing workloads between parallel resources to maximize execution efficiency. Examples are used to illustrate these concepts for some common high-level design patterns.

Parallel decomposition

The fundamental objective of high-level design is to decompose an application into separate regions which can be run in parallel. Decomposition can expose both function and data parallelism.

Function parallel decomposition

Function parallel decomposition enables different functions to run in parallel. The different functions may read shared data, but they produce independent results. The example depicted in Figure 17.4 shows an image-recognition application.

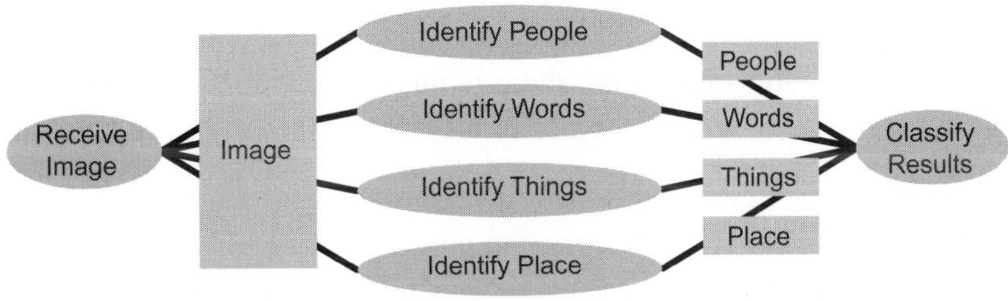

Figure 17.4:
Function parallel image processing.

The four separate identification functions share the same input image data. Each function is specialized to identify different objects in the image. Once all four functions have been completed, the aggregate data may be processed by downstream operations.

Note that for a given processing platform, the different functions may have different execution times. Though the four functions may all be run in parallel, if identifying words, things, and places are each three times faster than identifying people, it may make sense to run the word, thing, and place identification functions one after another in parallel with the slower people-identification task. This type of load balancing is an example of how function parallel decomposition may need to be scheduled properly to most effectively utilize the available processing resources. We also need to understand what mechanisms one needs to use to confirm that all dependencies have been met before beginning the final function.

Data parallel decomposition

Data parallel decomposition focuses on partitioning input data into separate regions. The same function is run in parallel on the different data regions. The example depicted in Figure 17.5 shows an image-recognition application partitioned into separate regions.

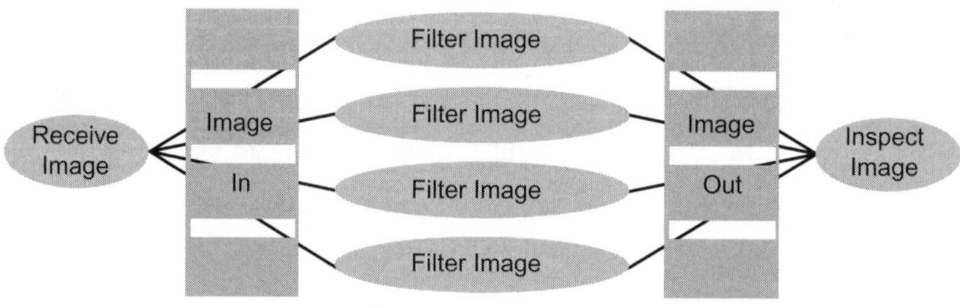

Figure 17.5:
Data parallel image processing.

Each pixel in the output image is calculated using some corresponding combination of input pixels. An output pixel computation may share input pixels with its neighbors, but each output pixel can be computed independently of all others.

Though each pixel may be computed in parallel, again the granularity of decomposition must match the available resources. If, for example, there are eight logical processor cores, it might make sense to slice the image into eight different regions. Within a region the pixels would be computed serially, but the regions themselves would all be computed in parallel.

Note also the natural load balancing of data decomposition. When the function being computed takes the same amount of time per pixel, a static workload, then it is straightforward to divide the data into equal chunks to balance the load.

SIMD processing

Most modern processors include some form of vector operations, termed single instruction, multiple data (SIMD) operations. A SIMD instruction enables the same operation to be applied to multiple data items in parallel. An example instruction might multiply four pairs of 8-bit data values, storing the result as four 16-bit data values. This type of low-level parallelism is often used within loops to do more work per iteration. Where possible, this instruction-level parallelism should be applied first followed by the task-level data decomposition just discussed.

Pipelined decomposition

Pipelined decomposition is a common decomposition which may be considered a hybrid function-data decomposition. Each task may be decomposed into different functional stages. Each stage processes a subset of the overall data and passes its results to the next stage. Though each stage processes its data serially, all stages run in parallel to increase the processing throughput.

Consider an imaging edge-detection application. The application might consist of a number of stages: pixel correction, image smoothing, and Sobel edge detection as shown in Figure 17.6.

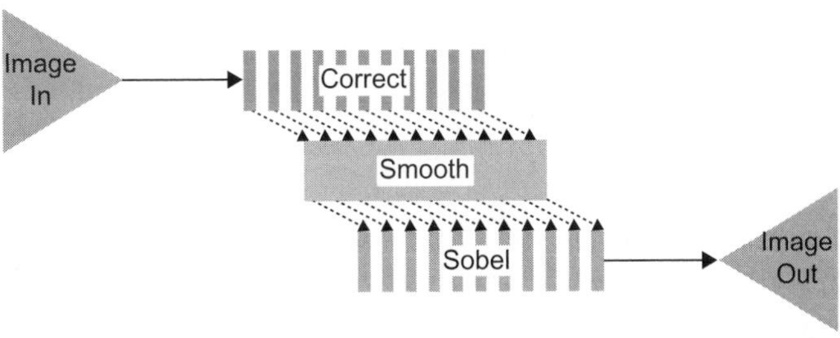

Figure 17.6:
Pipelined edge detection.

With a pipelined decomposition, a block of pixels enter the pipeline at correction and emerge after Sobel. As a data block moves from the first stage to the second, the next data block may enter the first stage. All three stages can run in parallel, each working on a different block of data at a different stage in the algorithm.

This type of decomposition is very sensitive to the available resources. The number of stages should be matched to the available processing resources. The overall throughput of the pipeline is also limited by the slowest stage in the pipeline. In the example above, the smoothing function takes the most amount of work. For each data block, the correction and Sobel functions must idle until the smoothing function has finished. The speed of the smoothing function determines the overall performance of the parallel implementation. Recursively parallelizing the smoothing function may shorten its execution time and better balance the pipeline.

Data dependencies

When algorithms are implemented serially, there is a well-defined order of operations. For some sets of these operations, the order is very important. In the previous edge-detection example, for a given data block, the Sobel cannot be computed until after the smoothing function. For other sets of operations, the order may not matter. For example, within the correction function, the order in which pixels are corrected may not matter at all.

Dependencies between data reads and writes determine the partial order of computation. There are three types of data dependencies which limit the ordering. They are true data dependencies, anti-dependencies, and output dependencies, as shown in Figure 17.7.

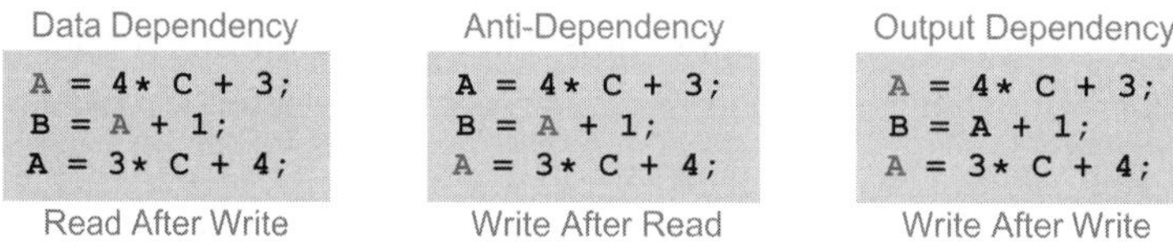

Figure 17.7:
Dependency types.

True data dependencies imply an ordering between operations in which a data value may not be read until after its value has been written. These are fundamental dependencies in an algorithm. Algorithms may be refactored to minimize the impact of this data dependency, but ultimately a data value cannot be used before it has been computed.

Anti-dependencies have the opposite relationship. In an anti-dependency, a data value cannot be written until the previous data value has been read. In the middle example above, the final assignment to A cannot occur before B is assigned, because B needs the previous value of A. This type of dependency can be removed by variable renaming. If, in the final assignment, variable A is renamed to D, then the B and D assignments may be reordered.

Renaming may increase storage requirements when new variables are introduced if the lifetimes of the variables overlap as code is parallelized. Anti-dependencies are common occurrences in sequential code. For example, intermediate variables defined outside the loop may be used within each iteration in a loop. This is fine when operations occur sequentially. The same variable storage may be reused repeatedly. When using shared memory, if all iterations were run in parallel, however, then they would all be competing for the same shared intermediate variable space. One solution would be to have each iteration use its own local intermediate variables. Minimizing variable lifetimes through proper scoping helps to avoid these types of dependencies.

The third type of dependency is an output dependency. In an output dependency, writes to a variable may not be reordered if they change the final value of the variable that remains when the instructions are complete. In the right-hand example in Figure 17.7, the final assignment to A may not be moved above the first assignment, because the remaining value will not be correct.

Communication and synchronization

Data dependencies establish a set of ordering requirements which must be enforced to ensure proper execution. Different parallel programming models use different techniques to ensure proper ordering.

Shared memory

As described earlier, in shared-memory systems, all processing units share the same data memory (Figure 17.8).

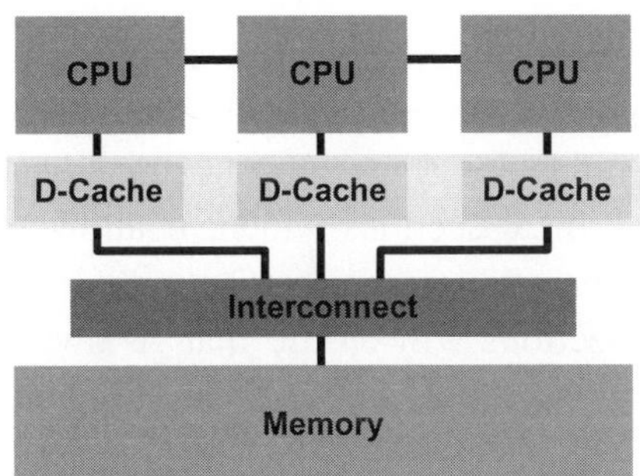

Figure 17.8:
Processing units share the same data memory.

The individual processing units may have local cache memory, but a consistent view of shared memory must be maintained between the processors. With caches, the cost of maintaining a coherent view of memory can become very high if cache lines must be shared between processors. Proper data layout in memory can minimize this penalty.

Multiple threads of execution are used to run multiple tasks simultaneously. Data which is shared between tasks must also be properly synchronized to ensure dependency relationships are properly maintained.

Figure 17.9 shows two threads, T0 and T1, which may both need to read and write variable A. Without synchronization, the order of reads and writes between the two threads is unpredictable, and three different outcomes are possible.

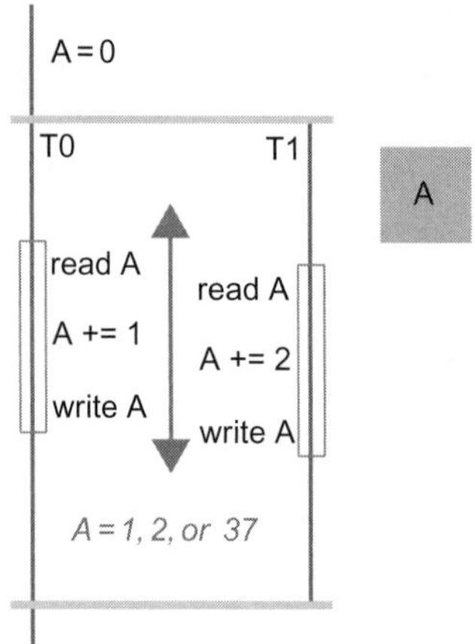

Figure 17.9:
Shared data synchronization.

Mutual exclusion through locks and semaphores is a common technique to ensure that only one thread at a time may execute code which encompasses certain critical dependencies. While one thread holds a lock for a critical section, other threads are blocked from entering other critical sections which, if allowed, could violate dependencies involving data shared between the sections. In the previous example, properly locking the critical sections will ensure that A always receives 3 as a final value.

Generally, each processor runs one thread at a time. More threads may be created across the processors. When one thread blocks waiting for lock, another ready thread may be woken up to take its place.

The cost of acquiring and releasing a lock can be significant. Locks serialize code, so locking large critical sections will inhibit parallelism. On the other hand, using frequent low-level locking may cost a large penalty for synchronization. The cost of creating and destroying completed tasks is also significant, so once again the granularity of tasks and locking should match the available resources.

Distributed memory

With distributed-memory systems, memory is not shared between systems. Each processor manages its own local memory (Figure 17.10).

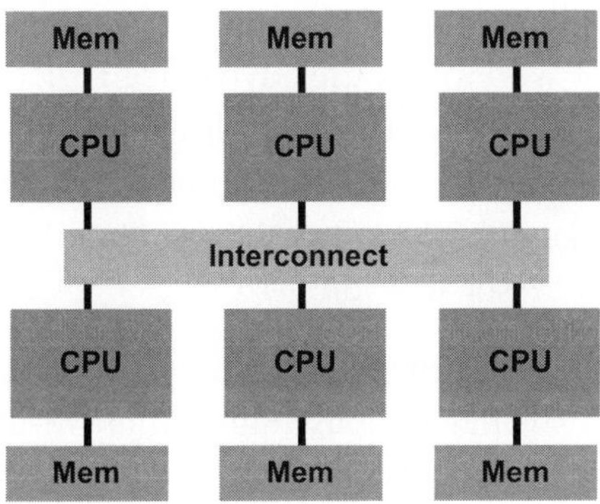

Figure 17.10:
Distributed memory.

Communication of data between tasks running on different processors is accomplished by sending and receiving data between them, often termed message-passing. In this model, data must be *explicitly* shared between tasks. Synchronization between tasks can be achieved by synchronous send-receive semantics. A receiving task will block until the sending data is available. Alternatively, asynchronous send-receive semantics can be used where the receiving task can check or be notified when data is available without blocking. This permits significant overlap of computation and communication, leading to significant performance gains.

Compared to shared memory, there is a higher overhead for communication, both in the set-up and tear-down of a message and in explicit copying of data, so message passing should be optimized for both costs.

While the thread programming model is appropriate for shared memory, the message-passing model may be used with either distributed or shared memory systems.

Load balancing

The amount of work per computation may be fixed or dependent on the input data. Work which is constant, independent of the data values, is termed a static workload, and may be partitioned during design time. Consider the edge-detection example discussed previously.

In data decomposition, the workload is the same for all pixels. Splitting the image into equal-sized areas divides the work evenly. This type of parallelism scales easily across available processors.

Consider what would happen if the run-time of the smoothing function was dependent on the input data. For example, regions with slowly varying pixel values might take fewer compute cycles to smooth while regions with rapidly changing pixel values might require extra processing. This type of workload varies dynamically depending on the pixel values. Now, equal-sized pixel regions may contain very different workloads. Consider an image with widely varying pixels on the top half and a uniform color in the bottom half. If the work is split between two tasks, top and bottom, the bottom half will finish well in advance of the top, and the bottom processor will idle.

With unpredictable workloads, the schedule can only be statistically optimized. In this case, dividing the work into smaller regions might improve the processing efficiency because the differences between neighboring workloads will be less. As the work is divided into smaller tasks, the cost of communication can become a significant portion of the task run-time and must be considered in determining the best task sizes. Run-times using thread pools or work stealing provide built-in support for dynamic load-balancing.

Task, data, and pipeline decompositions should always consider how to balance the workloads between regions. Static workloads are easy to analyze while dynamic workloads will require statistical considerations to find a good level of granularity which both matches the available resources and smooths out the workload mismatches.

Choice of algorithm

Parallelizing an algorithm requires both honoring dependencies and appropriately matching the parallelism to the available resources. Some algorithms with a high amount of data dependencies will not parallelize effectively (it depends on the dependencies; if they can be segmented easily like the MPEG2 algorithm, it's not as big an issue). When all anti-dependencies are removed and still partitioning does not yield acceptable performance, consider changing algorithms to find an equivalent result using an algorithm which is more amenable to parallelism.

This may not be possible when implementing a standard with strictly prescribed algorithms. In other cases, there may be effective ways to achieve similar results.

Decomposition approaches

The high-level design process decomposes the algorithm into separate processing regions considering the data dependencies, communication and synchronization requirements, and load balancing to establish an efficient partitioning for implementation.

There are two main approaches, top-down and bottom-up. In a top-down approach, the algorithm is decomposed into separate regions. Some regions will remain serial, while other regions may be decomposed using function, data, and pipelined decompositions. Profiling information from high-level analysis should be used to identify the most beneficial regions to be decomposed. After each decomposition, the parallel performance can be estimated. If not enough performance is achieved, then regions can be further subdivided to try to find additional parallelism.

Some regions will very easily decompose into very fine-grained regions. Data decomposing an image into pixels might be an extreme example. The number of available cores, overheads of creating and destroying tasks, and communication and synchronization will become a significant cost. The optimal choice will depend on trading-off the granularity of decomposition against these costs.

A bottom-up approach starts with the finest-grained levels of parallelism and moves up. Again, profiling information from high-level analysis identifies the most important hotspot regions to focus on. If the hotspots consume a significant amount of execution time, then parallelizing these first will give the most benefit. A true bottom-up approach will start with the finest-grained partitioning for hotspot regions and move up to encompass larger regions at each step. If the initial partitioning is too fine-grained, then the overhead may not be acceptable. The decomposition would move up a level to start at a coarser level of granularity. Once a suitable starting granularity is established, a larger region can be assembled in parallel from the smaller regions until a satisfactory estimated performance level is achieved.

The generally recommended practice is to partition at as high a level as possible first, decomposing hotspot regions and checking for satisfactory overhead costs and estimated performance. If more performance is needed, next consider finer-grained parallelism which does not cost too much in complexity or overhead costs. Lastly, consider expanding the parallel regions by decomposing less hot areas of the code.

Hybrid decomposition

Decompositions may be applied hierarchically to best match the available processing resources. For example, consider a two-stage pipeline decomposition, and assume that the first stage is 6 times slower than the second. The initial pipeline decomposition will be limited to the slower first stage. The second stage will be idle 5/6th of the time.

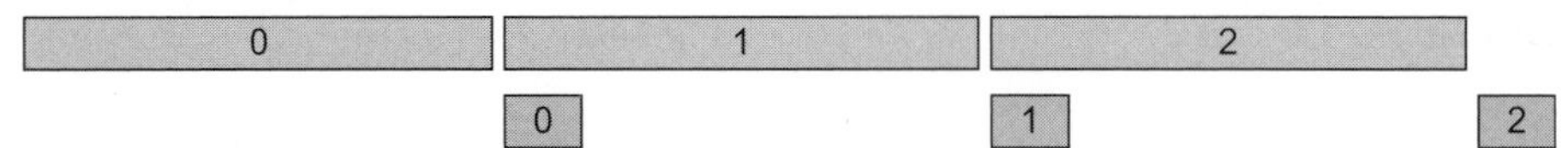

If the first stage can use data decomposition, then it may be possible to run six data blocks in parallel through the first stage. Six data blocks can then run serially through the second stage in the same amount of time, effectively balancing the pipeline and optimizing the throughput. Note, however, that this assumes that there are seven processing resources available to run in parallel (Figure 17.11).

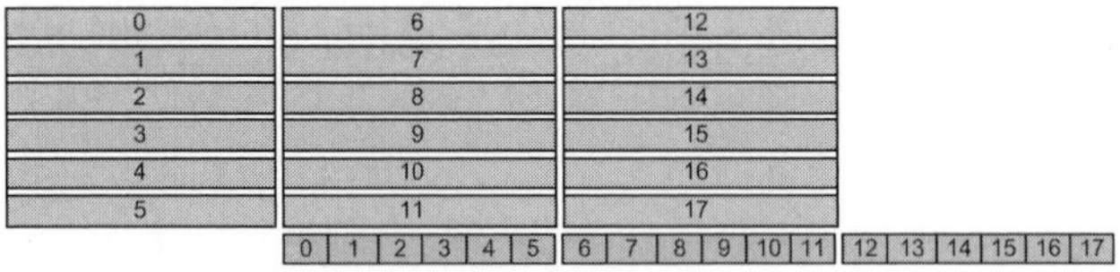

Figure 17.11:
Hybrid decomposition.

Summary of Part 1

It is important to understand both the algorithmic intent and the serial implementation of programs being transformed to run in multicore environments. Profiling techniques should be used to understand the overall structure of the code and the hotspot regions of execution. After optimizing the serial code, the optimized profile information and analysis techniques are used to uncover opportunities to exploit parallel behavior and the dependencies which constrain that behavior. Analysis is mainly dynamic, so best results are achieved by the use of representative benchmarks and realistic workloads. High-level design decisions, including choice of algorithm, overview of platform architectures, and identification of appropriate parallel design patterns, are then made which will optimize the multicore implementation to meet critical application metrics such as performance, power, footprint, and scalability.

Part 2: Implementation and low-level design

Once high-level analysis and design decisions have been made, parallel implementation follows. Implementation is strongly dependent on the platform architecture. For a set of representative architectures, the choice of parallel implementation technology, such as threading or message-passing approaches, and recommended implementation techniques, such as incremental refinement and sequential equivalence, are discussed. Good implementation properly realizes high-level design metrics, eases debugging, and reduces latent bugs.

Thread-based implementations

Threads are a basic means of expressing parallelism in software program. A thread can be thought of as lightweight process that is created, managed, and destroyed via a specific mechanism built into the operating system. Independent of the mechanism, the goal is to improve application responsiveness, use machines with multiple processors more efficiently while improving the program structure and efficiency. Historically there have been many implementations of threading systems usually centered on specific platforms or user requirements. The two basic threading models can be described as user-level threads (ULT) and kernel-level threads (KLT).

User-level threads

- The kernel is managing the process but is unaware of the threads.
- The user is responsible for scheduling and managing the threads.
- If a ULT makes a call into the kernel, the entire process will block.

Kernel-level threads

- The kernel maintains information about each thread.
- The kernel must schedule each thread.
- Process blocking is done per thread.

The hybrid ULT/KLT threading is implemented on platforms such as Linux and Solaris. Figure 17.12 is an illustration of such a mechanism.

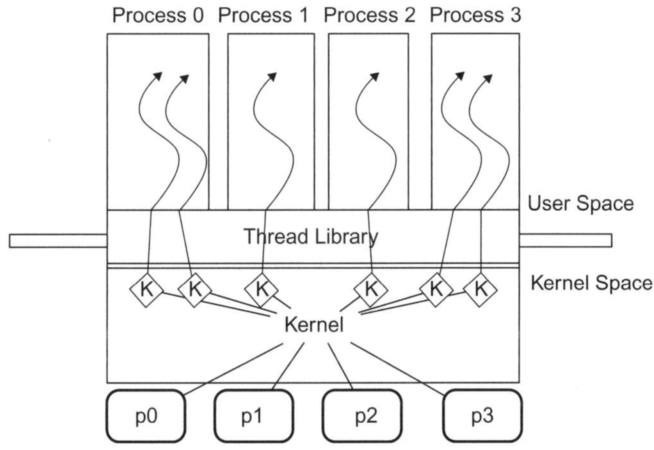

Figure 17.12:
Hybrid threading model.

Threads are created and controlled via function calls for creation, destruction, synchronization, scheduling, and process interaction.

Other basic properties of threads include:

- A thread does not know what thread created it.
- All threads in the same process share the same address space.
- Threads in the same process share instructions, data, file descriptors, signals and signal handlers.
- Each thread has a unique thread ID, set of registers and stack pointer, stack for local variables and return addresses, a signal mask, priority and its return value.

Kernel scheduling

The kernel is programmed to schedule the processes and threads on a machine according to its internal scheduling algorithm. It should be noted that certain effects from the kernel scheduling of threads can be observed:

- The kernel will switch control between threads based on the scheduling algorithm and the state of the machine.
- The kernel will save and restore the context of the thread – known as a context switch. This has a detrimental effect on the performance of the software because of the inherent overhead. As a byproduct of context switching, the underlying microprocessor and cache state are adversely affected.
- Kernel scheduling may be non-deterministic and cannot always be relied upon to schedule threads in any particular order.
- While some scheduling control is granted to the programmer, it's best to design a proper algorithm and verify its performance across a range of input data and execution conditions.

Pthreads

Pthreads is short for the POSIX 1c, Threads extensions (IEEE Std 1003.1c-1995). Pthreads is an application programming interface (API) for creating and manipulating threads. The standard defines roughly 100 primitives with optional components and implementation-dependent semantics. Implementations of this API are available on most POSIX-compliant platforms including Solaris, MAC OS X, HP-UX, FreeBSD, GNU/Linux and others. Windows also benefits from the PPthreads-w32 project, which supports a subset [3] of the API. The API is usually provided as a library that forms a layer between the user and the kernel. Pthreads can be used by many programming languages including C, C++, Fortran and others. This chapter features C++ language examples. However, the Pthreads library can be accessed from other languages such as C and Fortran.

Even though POSIX-compliant platforms feature Pthreads, not all of the implementations are complete or conform to the specification. Some API calls may not have underlying operating system kernel support and do not appear in the library of a given platform. It's wise to check the platform documentation for all Pthreads called used while developing threaded software.

Beyond this chapter there are several classic texts [4,5,6] that cover Pthreads in great depth and even more on-line tutorials.

Using PPthreads

PPthreads programs written in C or C++ must include the Pthreads header file to use any of the API functions.

```
#include<pthread.h>
```

On most Unix like platforms, the library is typically linked with the user binary file with:

```
-lpthread
```

Each PPthreads function call takes an opaque variable (object) as a function parameter. This parameter is used by the thread library to track the state of that object/resource. For instance the `pthread_create` call takes a `pthread_t` type that contains, amongst other things, the ID of the thread. This ID can be retrieved via the `pthread_self` call.

Most Pthreads functions return a value indicating the success, failure or status of the call. It's wise to check these values and deal with them appropriately.

The Pthreads function categories are outlined in Table 17.1. We will introduce most of this API and its applicability later in this chapter.

Table 17.1: Pthreads functions.

Function Prefix	Function
pthread_	Thread management
pthread_attr_	Thread attributes
pthread_mutex_	Mutexes
pthread_mutexattr_	Mutex attributes
pthread_cond_	Condition variable
pthread_condattr_	Condition variable attributes
pthread_key_	Thread-specific data
pthread_rwlock_	Read/write locks
pthread_barrier_	Barriers

Dealing with thread safety

In order for any code to be thread-safe one must take specific precautions to prevent multiple threads from accessing a shared resource [7].

1. All access must have no effect on the resource.
2. All accesses are idempotent – the order of operations does not affect the outcome.
3. Only one access is allowed at a time.

Any shared memory location that will be encountered by more than one thread of execution must be protected by a synchronization mechanism for writes where all threads but one are mutually excluded from accessing the resource. When more than one thread accesses a resource (seemingly) simultaneously and there is one writer, a race condition will arise because the outcome depends upon the relative execution order of each thread.

Any portion of code that must be synchronized and protected by mutual exclusion is called a critical section. Furthermore, one must construct the protection mechanism (Figure 17.13) so that all threads must execute the entry and exit routines before entering and exiting the critical section.

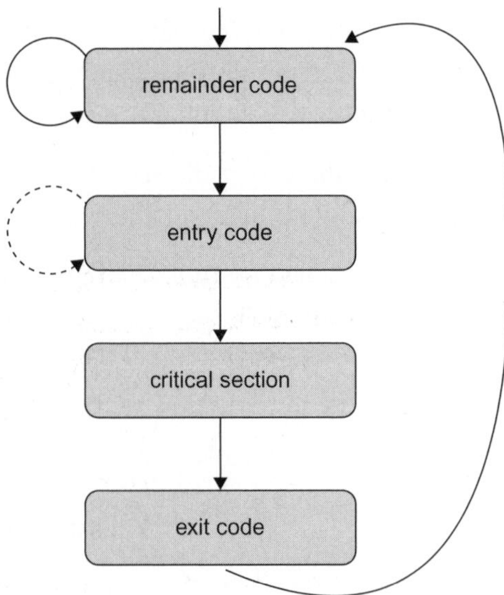

Figure 17.13:
Critical section protection requirements.

For Pthreads specifically, unprotected global or static variables are particularly troublesome and should be avoided. Threads that allocate memory on the stack can take advantage of the thread's stack space offering automatic privacy. Many functions return a pointer to static data, which can be a problem. This can be remedied by allocating memory on the heap and returning a pointer. Using thread-safe variants of library function calls is also recommended. Furthermore, any third-party libraries should also be vetted for thread safety and thread-safe calls should be employed.

Implementing synchronizations and mutual exclusion

Mutual exclusion is enforced when no two threads are in their critical section at the same time. Additionally, this means that deadlock freedom and starvation freedom must be maintained. Table 17.2 describes this problem [7]. Many initial attempts were made to solve this problem (Dijkstra and Dekker Algorithms) [8,9,10] and later efforts are popular [11,12,13], with Petersen's algorithm [9] being most popular. An interesting treatment of mutex algorithm myths is found in Alagarsamy [14].

Table 17.2: Mutual exclusion properties.

Mutual exclusion	No two processes are in their critical sections at the same time
Deadlock-freedom	If a process is trying to enter its critical section, then some process, not necessarily the same one, eventually enters its critical section
Starvation-freedom	If a process is trying to enter its critical section, then this process must eventually enter its critical section

Threads compete for resources, cooperating to share them or cooperating amongst themselves via some type of communication method to guarantee a certain outcome. Depending on the interaction between threads, there are many opportunities for the programmer to fall prey to race conditions, deadlocks, and starvation.

Deadlock [15] is a phenomenon that arises when two threads both hold a resource that the other needs to continue and they are both waiting on the other to release it. However, without external interference there is no possibility of releasing the resource. This is termed circular waiting. This can usually be prevented by verification of the lock ordering – the order in which locks are acquired and released. One rule of thumb is to acquire locks in ascending order and release in descending order. When using C++, concepts such as RAII (Resource Acquisition Is Initialization), leveled locking and lock guards/scope locks can be helpful to avoid missing locks [16]. Algorithm 1 illustrates a common C++ scope locking technique. When an object goes out of scope it is destroyed. The `ScopeLock` class destructor ensures that the mutex is unlocked when the object is destroyed because the mutex unlock is called in the destructor of the object as the stack is wound down.

Algorithm 1 C++ Scope Lock

```
class ScopeLock {
private:
  pthread_mutex_t &lock_;

public:
  ScopeLock(pthread_mutex_t &lock) : lock_(lock) {
    pthread_mutex_lock(&lock_);
  }
  ~ScopeLock() {
    pthread_mutex_unlock(&lock_);
  }
};
```

Starvation can happen when attempting to enforce mutual exclusion in a heavily contended critical section. The kernel may schedule two threads in such a way that a third thread has to wait indefinitely for a shared resource, thereby starving it (Figure 17.13). The third thread makes no progress. Thus one of the goals of certain locks is to be fair, thereby preventing starvation.

Mutexes, locks, nested locks

Using Pthreads, one can implement synchronization and mutual exclusion using specific Pthreads calls. This is called a mutex, which will effectively protect the critical section – even so without proper implementation the mutex is still subject to deadlock and starvation. It's the programmer's responsibility to guarantee that all uses of the shared resource are protected by a mutex. In Pthreads, only one thread may lock the mutex object at the same time. Any thread that tries to lock the mutex object will block until the thread that holds the mutex releases the object. At this point, one of the threads – not necessarily the thread that arrived first – will be allowed to enter the critical section.

Rules of thumb for critical sections:

- Time: make the critical section as small and as short as possible – some instructions will take longer to execute.
- Space: execute the minimal amount of instructions during the lock – execute a minimum number of instructions.
- Do not lock any section of code that executes undeterministically.
- When dealing with containers that hold data, prefer locking data items and structures whenever possible as opposed to the entire container – balance this against granularity concerns.

Mutex

In order to use a mutex, it's necessary to initialize it first and destroy it when finished. This resource initialization/destruction paradigm is common throughout Pthreads.

A partial example of initializing and locking a critical section with a mutex is in Algorithm 2.

Algorithm 2 mutex example

```
#include <pthread.h>
....

pthread_mutex_t mutex;
int global;

main()
{
pthread_mutex_init(&mutex,NULL); // dynamic initialization

// some code to create and join threads

pthread_mutex_destroy(&mutex);
}

void thread_one()
{
// some code for thread one
pthread_mutex_lock(&mutex);
++global;
pthread_mutex_unlock(&mutex);
// some other code for thread one
}

void thread_two()
{
// some code for thread two
pthread_mutex_lock(&mutex);
--global;
pthread_mutex_unlock(&mutex);
// some other code for thread two
}
```

Condition variables

Condition variables are a method of enforcing mutual exclusion based on a change in a variable. For instance, one can create a bounded buffer, shared queue, or software FIFO using two condition variables and a mutex as illustrated in Algorithm 3. In this instance a C++ class is created that wraps a standard library `queue` object and uses the `ScopeLock` class (a standard C class) from above to enforce lock discipline.

Algorithm 3 Simple concurrent queue using two condition variables and a mutex

```
class IntQueue
{
private:
  pthread_mutex_t mutex_;
  pthread_cond_t more_;
  pthread_cond_t less_;
  std::queue<int> queue_;
  size_t bound_;

public:
  IntQueue(size_t bound) : bound_(bound) {
    pthread_mutex_init(&mutex_, NULL);
    pthread_cond_init(&less_, NULL);
    pthread_cond_init(&more_, NULL);
  }
  ~IntQueue() {
    pthread_mutex_destroy(&mutex_);
    pthread_cond_destroy(&more_);
    pthread_cond_destroy(&less_);
  }
  void enqueue(int val) {
        pthread_mutex_lock(&mutex);
    while(queue_.size() >= bound_)
        pthread_cond_wait(&less_,&mutex_);
    queue_.push(val);
    pthread_cond_signal(&more_);
    pthread_mutex_unlock(&mutex);
  }
  int dequeue() {
        pthread_mutex_lock(&mutex);
    while(queue_.size() == 0) {
      pthread_cond_wait(&more_, &mutex_);
    }
    int ret = queue_.front();
    queue_.pop();
    pthread_cond_signal(&less_);
        pthread_mutex_unlock(&mutex);
    return ret;
  }
  int size() {
    ScopeLock lock(mutex_);
    return queue_.size();
  }
};
```

Granularity

Granularity is the ratio of computation to communication in a parallel program. Basically, a program will have sections that compute and sections that communicate. In this case, communication means anything that has to do with controlling, locking, and destroying threads. There are essentially two basic types of granularity in parallel computing; fine-grained and coarse-grained.

Fine-grained

Fine-grained parallelism is small amounts of work done in proportion to the calculation or a low computation to communication ratio. This can facilitate load balancing. However, significant amounts of time will be spent coordinating the events and communicating their outcome to the other threads. It's also possible to produce a situation where there is more communication than computation. For example, the program spends most of its time in the kernel dealing with mutexes or condition variables.

Coarse-grained

Coarse-grained is the opposite of fine-grained: significant amounts of work are being done with little communication or there is a high computation to communication ratio. This would seem to indicate that the performance would increase. However, depending on the algorithm implementation, it may require more effort to achieve a reasonable load balance across a given machine.

Approach

A useful rule of thumb is that there must be enough work to amortize the cost of communication over the computation. It's better to start with a coarse-grained approach and look for opportunities to implement fine-grained parallelism. More parallelism is usually better, but this alone is not the determining factor for performance. This balance is usually dependent on the scheduling strategies, algorithm implementation, and the computation to communication ratio [17]. Maximum performance is only realized after considerable experimentation and applied performance tuning. Additionally, the number of concurrent work items should be close to the number of cores in the machine.

When using most Pthreads primitives the library will ask the kernel to help it perform the task, which in turn causes its own set of problems. It's good to have an idea of the relative overhead for Pthreads calls. This knowledge combined with understanding the potential concurrency in the software (Amdahl's/Gustavson's law [18]) will help with the optimization process.

Implementing task parallelism

Task parallelism is a basic method of implementing parallelism. It implies that each task is executed with a separate thread and the threads are mapped to different processors or nodes on a parallel computer. The threads may or may not communicate with each other to pass data as part of the program structure. It's likely that tasks are different and possibly the algorithm has imposed control and data flow dependencies thereby ordering the tasks and limiting the amount of parallelism. Implementing task parallelism with Pthreads is essentially:

- creating or identifying a group of program functions that will be used as tasks - called thread functions;
- creating the threads that will execute the thread functions and passing the necessary data to the functions;
- joining with and retrieving the results returned from the thread functions if any;
- at the very least all critical sections must be protected – locations where shared resources will be changed by at least one thread and accessed by others.

Creation and join

Threads are created and joined using the `pthread_create` and `pthread_join` calls.

Threads can also send and receive information to each other. This mechanism allows threads to communicate. Algorithm 4 illustrates creating and joining of threads. Notice that we pass a thread number to the thread. In this example, with a small modification, we could retrieve the value returned using the `pthread_exit` call in the thread function using the second parameter of `pthread_join`.

Algorithm 4 pthreads creation and join

```
#include <pthread.h>
#include <stdio.h>
#include <stdlib.h>
#include <string.h>
#define NUM_THREADS 5

void *print_hello( void *threadid )
{
        printf( "\n%d: Hello World!\n", ( int ) threadid );
        pthread_exit( NULL ); // potenitally return some value here
}

int main()
{
        static pthread_t threads[ NUM_THREADS ];
        int rc, t;
        for ( t = 0; t < NUM_THREADS; t++ ) {
                printf( "Creating thread %d\n", t );
                rc = pthread_create( &threads[ t ], NULL, print_hello, ( void * ) t );
                if ( rc ) {
                        printf( "ERROR; pthread_create() returned %d\n", rc );
                        printf( "Error string: \"%s\"\n", strerror( rc ) );
                        exit( -1 );
                }
        }
        for ( t = 0; t < NUM_THREADS; t++ ) {
                printf( "Waiting for thread %d\n", t );
                rc = pthread_join( threads[ t ], NULL); // potentially get a return value here
                if ( rc ) {
                        printf( "ERROR; pthread_join() returned %d\n", rc );
                        printf( "Error string: \"%s\"\n", strerror( rc ) );
                        exit( -1 );
                }
        }
        return 0;
}
```

Parallel-pipeline computation

A pipeline is essentially a collection of tasks that are executed sequentially. The input of the first task is obtained from some data source and the result of one stage is fed to the next. Each block in the pipeline represents one parallel task. The pipeline consists of three separate phases.

Receive – a task is input
Compute – perform some computation on the task
Send – send the task to the next stage.

Figure 17.14 illustrates the temporal and data dependencies that are present in a parallel-pipeline system. A pipeline can be created using the Queue concept introduced earlier, where each stage in the pipeline is separated by a queue object. Each stage has one or more

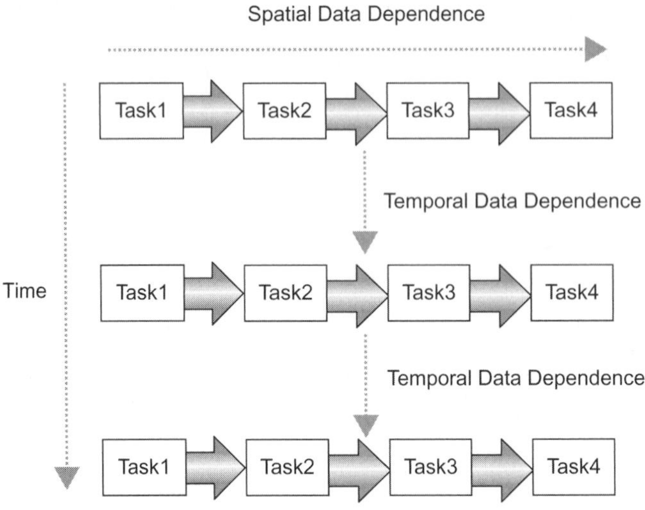

Figure 17.14:
Temporal and data dependencies.

threads that remove a data item from the previous queue, perform some work and place the data object in the queue of the next block.

Master/worker scheme

The master/worker scheme is a technique for a task pool with dynamic task distribution. A master thread hands off work to worker threads and collects the results. In this scheme, the many-to-one communication system enables the master to evenly distribute the work by supplying a worker with a new task each time a result is collected. It's also possible to give many tasks to a worker provided this does not affect load balancing. Figure 17.15 illustrates the basic premise.

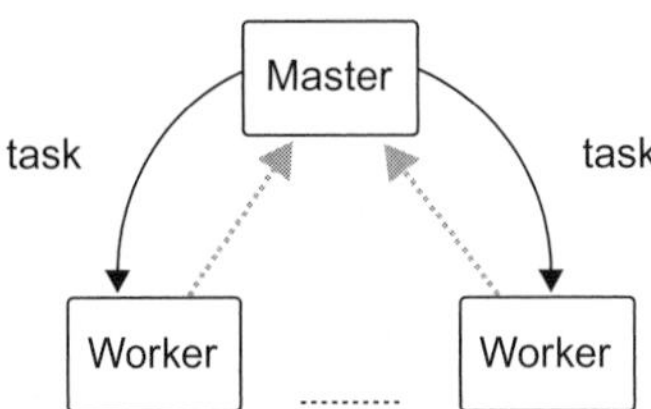

Figure 17.15:
Master/worker scheme.

The master/worker system basically relies on the relatively smooth operation of the master thread. It's responsible for collecting results and emitting tasks. When a large number of workers are used, the master thread may become overloaded for obvious reasons.

Conversely, allowing the worker threads to perform more work (coarse-grained approach) might limit the dynamic nature of the system and affect load balancing.

To combat these problems, it's possible to set up a hierarchy of master/worker thread systems as a tree, with worker processes the leaves and sub-masters as the inner nodes.

Divide-and-conquer scheme

The divide and conquer is an important algorithmic expression used to solve many sorting, computational geometry, graph theory, and numerical problems. The algorithm has three distinct phases:

Divide phase – a problem is split into one or more independent sub-problems of smaller size
Conquer phase – each sub-problem is solved recursively or directly
Combine phase – finally the sub-solutions are combined to a solution of the original problem instance.

In the divide-and-conquer model, one or more threads perform the same task in parallel (SPMD model). There is no master thread and all run independently. Recursive calls can be made concurrently only if the calls write to different parts of the program's memory. Divide and conquer algorithms are subject to load-balancing problems when the sub-problems are not uniform. If possible these sub-problems can be reduced further.

Task scheduling considerations

The determination of task granularity is a partitioning problem. The program must be decomposed into a set of tasks suitable for parallel execution [19]. The grain size can be defined as a series of instructions organized as a task. Depending on the language, this may be a function or a loop body.

An efficient use of the available resources on a parallel system requires enough tasks to spread over the processor cores allowing tasks to execute in parallel.

The programmer must determine the optimal task size that will give the shortest execution time. The larger the task size, the less parallelism there is on a given machine. A smaller task size will result in greater parallel overhead (communication and synchronization).

The general solution to the granularity problem is NP-complete [20]; however, it's possible to find a near-optimal solution to a sub-problem [21].

Techniques such as task packing [22,23] and work stealing [24,25] are also beneficial to arrive at a tuned scheduling algorithm.

Thread pooling

A thread pool is a collection of threads that will perform a given function or task. The dynamics of the pool and its size may be controlled by the programmer and frequently depend on the state of the system such as the number of tasks or processors. The pool is tuned to provide the best performance given the load and machine characteristics. Primarily, this technique allows the programmer to reuse threads and avoid the overhead of creating and destroying threads multiple times.

Affinity scheduling

Depending on the algorithm, resource acquisition and management scheme and the workload, certain threads may benefit from having their affinity set to specific processors. In some instances the operating system kernel will also have support for scheduling threads based on power, cache, CPU or other resources. For example, the kernel may be able to detect that a thread will benefit from continued execution on a given processor based on the cache usage. This cache-aware version is known as cache affinity scheduling.

However, on most processor architectures, migration of threads across cache, memory or processor boundaries is expensive (TLB flush, cache invalidation) and can reduce program performance. The programmer is able to set affinities for certain threads to take advantage of shared caches, interrupt handing and matching computation with data (locality). Additionally, by setting the affinity to a single CPU and excluding other threads from using that CPU, that thread effectively owns the processor.

Pthreads affinity

Affinity is set on different operating systems using different calls. For Linux, it's `sched_setaffinity` and `pthread_setaffinity_np` (`np` refers to non-portable), for Solaris it's `processor_bind`. Both have similar semantics.

Affinity can be set using the `sched_setaffinity` call, which will bind the thread to the processor. The mask is a bitmap of all the cores in the machine as illustrated in Figure 17.16. Algorithm 5 is a code snippet showing the function call for cache affinity scheduling. If `sched_setaffinity` is called again later with a different mask value, the OS will migrate the thread to the requested processor.

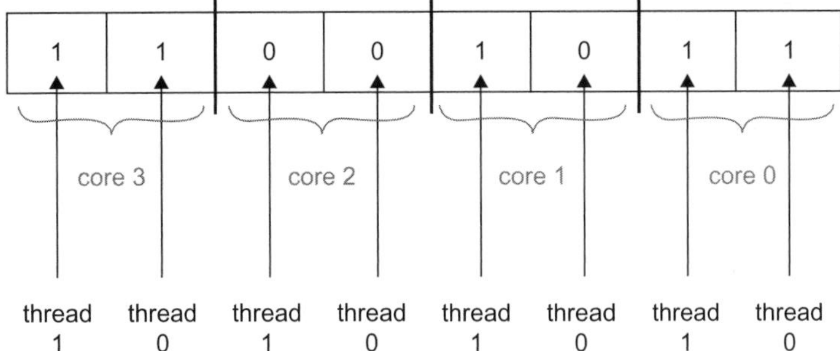

Figure 17.16:
Affinity mask.

Algorithm 5 sched_setaffinity Example

```
unsigned long mask = 1; /* processor 0 */

/* bind the calling process to processor 0 */
if (sched_setaffinity(0, sizeof(mask), &mask) <0)
        {
        perror("sched_setaffinity");
        }
```

Event-based parallel programs

Event-based coordination example:

- Task definition
- Event flow
- Ordering

Implementing loop parallelism

Loop parallelism (data parallelism) is potentially the easiest to implement while achieving the best speed-up and scalability. By dividing the loop iteration space by the number of processors, each thread has an equal share of the work. If the loop iterations have no dependencies and the iteration space is large enough, good scalability can be achieved. Additionally, this implies that each iteration of the loop will take relatively the same amount of time and the program might therefore be free of load-balancing problems. An example of loop parallelism using pthreads is illustrated in Algorithm 6.

Algorithm 6 Loop parallelism - partial example

```
#include <pthread.h>

struct ThreadParam {
        int startIndex_;
        int endIndex_;
        int threadNb_;  // thread number
        pthread_t threadID_; // pthreads thread object
        VectorsStruct *vectors_; // vectors we're going to calculate
};

static void *threadFunction(void *paramPtr) {
   ThreadParam *param = (ThreadParam *)paramPtr; // get our "instructions"
   std::cout<<"Thread: "<<param->threadNb_<<" from "<<param->startIndex_<<" to "
               << param->endIndex_<< std::endl;
   compute(param->vectors,param->startIndex_, param->endIndex_); // compute the vectors
   return NULL;
}

main{}
{
  int nthreads = 8; // Adjusted for the witdth of the machine
  ThreadsParam* paramPtr[nthreads]; // each thread needs it's set of "instructions"
  VectorsStruct vectors(A, B, C); // need something to calculate

  /* Creation of the threads. */
  for(int i = 0; i < nthreads; ++i)
  {
        int startIndex = (size * i) / nthreads; // each thread gets its own start index
        int endIndex = (size * (i + 1)) / nthreads; // each thread gets its own end index
        ThreadParam *paramPtr[i] = new ThreadParam(startIndex, endIndex, i + 1, vectors);
        int status = pthread_create(&paramPtr->threadID_, NULL, threadFunction, paramPtr);
        // check status
  }

  // join on the threads and delete ThreadsParam array.
}
```

Aligning computation and locality

One of the key considerations for performance-oriented codes is locality. As the latency of memory accesses becomes high relative to processor cycle times, application performance is increasingly limited by memory performance. It's important to keep data close to the processor that is performing the computation. Equally, the program must be structured in such a way as to allow the microprocessor caches to make most efficient use of memory. There are two types of locality involved:

temporal locality – where a memory location used is likely to be used again;
spatial locality – if a data item is referenced the neighboring data locations may also be used.

There are many techniques for locality optimization of codes. *Cache blocking* is reorganizing data objects to fit in the microprocessor cache. *Loop tiling* is also a technique to break a loop's iteration space into smaller blocks, thereby ensuring that the data of interest stays in the cache.

Non-uniform memory access (NUMA) considerations

Recent microprocessors where the entire memory space is shared but each processor is connected to a node with a dedicated memory controller are popular (see Figure 17.17). This allows machine designers to build larger machines but the programmer must take greater care with data and memory affinity. Off-node data access times will be greater than access times within a node, thus access time to memory is not always uniform. Specific code optimizations are necessary to guarantee performance. These architectures are called NUMA – *non-uniform memory access.*

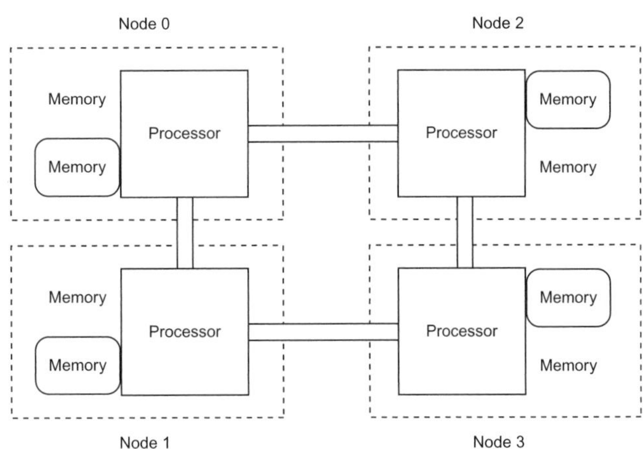

Figure 17.17:
Each processor is connected to a node with dedicated memory.

First-touch placement

First-touch placement allocates memory on the NUMA containing the processor that first touches (writes to) the memory. A first-touch memory placement policy can greatly improve the performance of applications where data accesses are made mostly to the memory local to each processor with first-touch placement. First-touch placement is the default on most Unix-like operating systems and usually there is an API that allows for the manipulation of the placement policies.

Programmers must take care to initialize their data structures using the thread that will also perform the computation. This will ensure that memory is placed closest to the node when the thread is executing. Additionally, threads should be pinned to the processor on the node where the memory of interest is located. This will guarantee the best memory performance.

Message-passing implementations

The Multicore Association (MCA) has created two specifications that address the area of inter-process communications between CPUs in a multicore system. These specifications include the Multicore Communication API (MCAPI) and the Multicore Resource Management API (MRAPI).

In order to understand how MCAPI might fit into your system, we must first look at how to divide up the system and its resources among the operating systems and CPUs. The system itself must be designed both with the hardware and with the software in mind. What are the requirements of the system? What is the minimum latency needed in processing a datagram? Are there any deterministic requirements that need to be adhered to? Can my application be parallelized?

It's important to note the differences between asymmetric multiprocessing (AMP) and symmetric multiprocessing (SMP). In some situations, SMP-capable hardware is best used by running a single operating system across all SMP-capable cores. However, that may not always be the case. Sometimes dividing up a system that is SMP-capable with several operating system instances similar to AMP systems can be an advantage. This would include running an application directly on a CPU without an operating system, otherwise known as a "bare-metal" application.

Once it is determined that using AMP is an advantage, or deemed a requirement in your system design, there must be an inter-processor communication (IPC) mechanism for passing messages between those instances. As previously stated, MCA has two specifications that address the needs of IPC between CPUs: MCAPI and MRAPI. MCAPI specifically deals with the need to pass messages between nodes in the system. MRAPI deals with resources, such as sharing memory and synchronization objects between operating system instances.

MCAPI

Let's first look at MCAPI in detail by exploring the concept of a node, an endpoint, and a channel.

The first concept is the **node**. A node is a CPU, an operating system instance, a thread, or a process. MCAPI deals with passing messages between these nodes. Each node is established and creates a set of endpoints for communication between nodes. It's up to you, the system designer, to decide what is appropriate; nodes don't have to all be the same in your system. For instance, you can have two operating systems running side-by-side on separate CPU combinations. On the first operating system, you may want five processes running on that CPU, so there are five nodes in the first operating system. On the second operating system, you might consider the entire operating system as a single node.

There are two types of communication between nodes: **connection-less** and **connected**. A connection-less endpoint can receive communication from many different nodes at any time. A channel is connected when communication passes between two distinct endpoints. Since the channel is connected, no other nodes can connect to that endpoint.

A channel can be either "socket-like" in its message passing, where all messages appear in the order in which they are transmitted, or they can be "scalar-based", where a simple integer message will be passed between endpoints. For example, a frame of video would be passed in its entirety as a datagram, where a command can be passed as a scalar.

By using MCAPI at a very low layer to pass messages between operating systems, you can abstract away all of the hardware differences and uniqueness from the application.

An MCAPI programming source code example is shown in Figure 17.18. In the example there are several example functions.

```
/****************
* Include Files
****************/
…
/* IPC */
#include          "mcapi/inc/mcapi.h"

/***************
IPC connection
***************/

/* MCAPI definitions */

#define           LOCAL_NODEID          1
#define           REMOTE_NODEID         0

static const struct

[**UNRESOLVED****UNRESOLVED****UNRESOLVED****UNRESOLVED**]ports[2] = {
[**UNRESOLVED**],[**UNRESOLVED**]};

mcapi_pktchan_recv_hndl_t     send_handle;
mcapi_pktchan_recv_hndl_t     recv_handle;
mcapi_endpoint_t              local_rm_endpoint;
mcapi_endpoint_t              remote_rm_endpoint;

/***********************************************************************
*
*   FUNCTION
*
*       Initialization
*
*   DESCRIPTION
*
*       This task initializes the IPC.
*
***********************************************************************/
void  Initialization()

      {mcapi_version_tmcapi_version;mcapi_status_tmcapi_status;mcapi_endpoint
_tlocal_send_endpoint;mcapi_endpoint_tlocal_recv_endpoint;mcapi_endpoint_trem
ote_recv_endpoint;mcapi_request_trequest;size_tsize;/* Initialize MCAPI
*/mcapi_initialize(LOCAL_NODEID, &mcapi_version, &mcapi_status);/* Create a
local send endpoint for print job processing. */if(mcapi_status ==
MCAPI_SUCCESS)[**UNRESOLVED**]

      /* Create a local receive endpoint for print job processing. */
      if(mcapi_status == MCAPI_SUCCESS)

[**UNRESOLVED**]
      /* Create a local send endpoint for resource monitor. */
      if(mcapi_status == MCAPI_SUCCESS)

[**UNRESOLVED**]

      /* Open receive side */
      if(mcapi_status == MCAPI_SUCCESS)

[**UNRESOLVED**]
      /* Wait for the rx side to open. */
      mcapi_wait(&request, &size, &mcapi_status, 0xFFFFFFFF);
      /* Wait till foreign endpoint is created */
      if(mcapi_status == MCAPI_SUCCESS)
```

```
[**UNRESOLVED**]
      /* Connect node 0 transmitter to node 1 receiver */
      if(mcapi_status == MCAPI_SUCCESS)
[**UNRESOLVED**r]

      /* Wait for the connect call to complete. */
      mcapi_wait(&request, &size, &mcapi_status, 0xFFFFFFFF);

      printf("Connected \r\n");

      /* Open transmit side */
      if(mcapi_status == MCAPI_SUCCESS)

[**UNRESOLVED**]

      /* Wait for the tx side to open */
      mcapi_wait(&request, &size, &mcapi_status, 0xFFFFFFFF);

      /* Get the remote resource monitor endpoint */
      remote_rm_endpoint = mcapi_get_endpoint(REMOTE_NODEID,
ports[REMOTE_NODEID].rm_rx, &mcapi_status);

      if(mcapi_status == MCAPI_SUCCESS)

[r**UNRESOLVED**]
}
/************************************************************************
*
*    FUNCTION
*
*        Sample
*
*    DESCRIPTION
*
*        This task receives a job and responds to job over MCAPI.
*
*
************************************************************************/
void  Sample()

      {STATUSstatus;mcapi_status_tmcapi_status;UINT32size;UINT32bytesReceived
,type,cmd;unsigned char *in_buffer;unsigned char
out_buffer[MAX_SIZE];mcapi_uint64_ttmp;/* Receive image from foreign node
*/mcapi_pktchan_recv(recv_handle, (void **)in_buffer,(size_t*)&size,
&mcapi_status);/* Do something with MCAPI buffer */… /* Free MCAPI buffer
*/if(mcapi_status == MCAPI_SUCCESS)[**UNRESOLVED**]
      …
      /* Respond to message with data to send in out_buffer */
      mcapi_pktchan_send(send_handle, out_buffer, MAX_SIZE, &mcapi_status);
      if(mcapi_status != MCAPI_SUCCESS)
[n]
      if ( /* Complete then clean up */ )

            {/* Finalize current nodes MCAPI instantiation
*/mcapi_finalize(&mcapi_status);if(mcapi_status != MCAPI_SUCCESS)[n]
      }
}
```

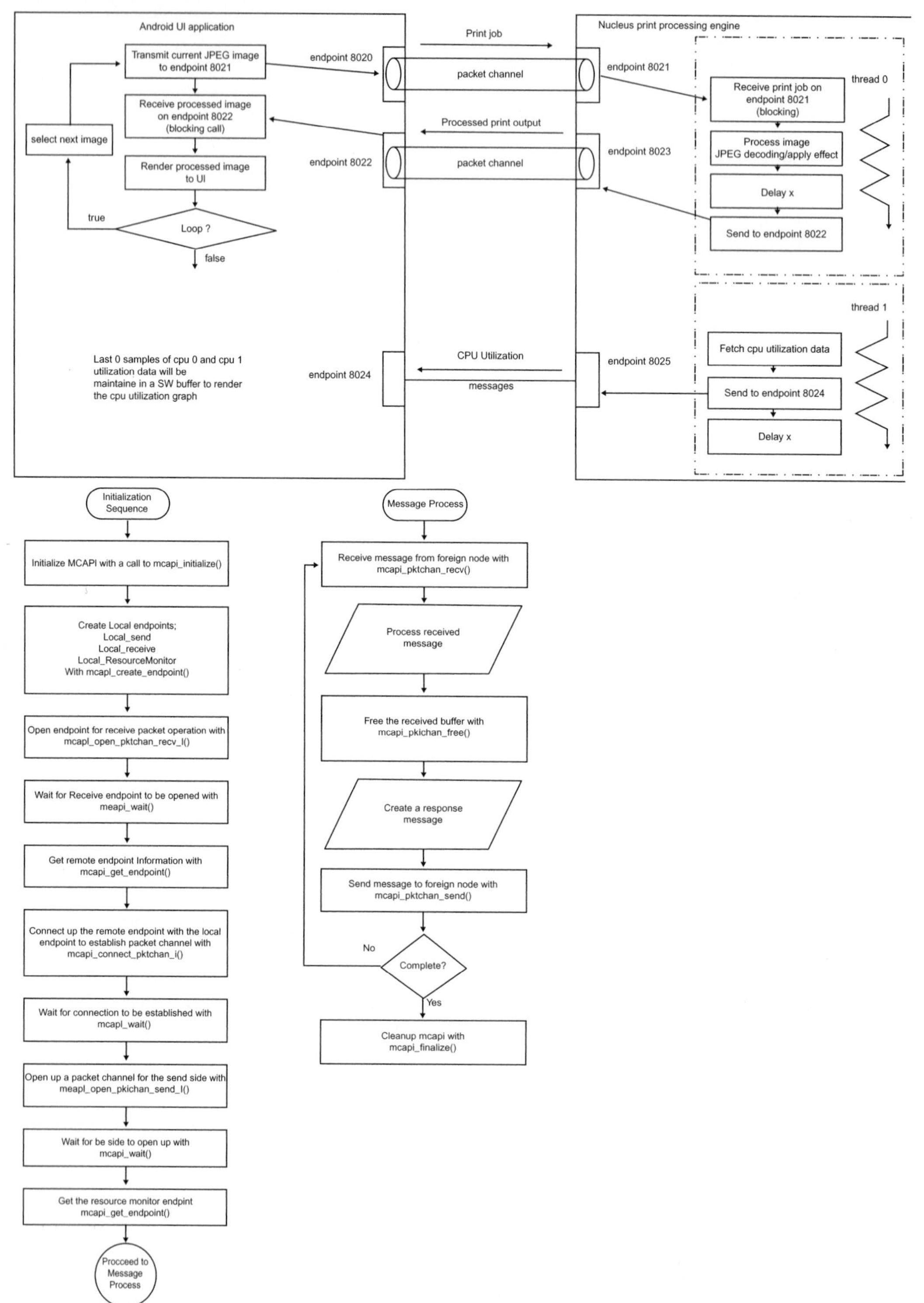

Figure 17.18:
MCAPI programming source code.

Load balancing

One of the strengths of MCAPI is the ability to move an application or thread of execution from one node to another. This may be an advantage when load balancing the system after the system has already been architected. One scenario might be a CPU or operating system that is starving the rest of the system because it cannot process all the threads in time. Another situation might be where the application is divided up in such a way that it has several threads on each operating system executing in parallel or on the set of cores, which are available and yet are being starved because higher-priority threads of execution are running on those cores. With load balancing these types of problems can be migrated at compile/build time to other cores in the system where CPU bandwidth is available.

MRAPI

MRAPI provides memory sharing and synchronization APIs between processing nodes.

Memory-sharing APIs allow a single block of memory, owned by one operating system, to be shared among several nodes in a system. These APIs can enforce only one writer or multiple readers which can access the memory block at any time.

Synchronization APIs provide applications running on different nodes the ability to synchronize their activities. An MRAPI semaphore is a system-wide semaphore that can be accessed by any node in the system, preventing access by multiple nodes to a shared resource.

MCAPI and MRAPI in multicore systems

Let's take a look at some ways in which MCAPI/MRAPI can be used in a multicore system to provide the necessary intercommunication framework between nodes. In this example, we have four cores with each core allocated a set amount of memory from main memory. In addition, there are shared memory regions that are shared by all cores.

First, MRAPI initializes any shared memory region that will be accessible between nodes in the system.

Next, during MCAPI initialization, the MRAPI shared memory is divided up among each of the endpoints or channels that have been established between each of the nodes. Those nodes can be local or remote; but the shared memory piece must be used in order to pass messages between nodes. Interrupts may be used to interrupt current node processing in order to minimize system latency for higher-priority communications.

The combination of using MCAPI and MRAPI together is a compelling approach that allows full-featured APIs to be implemented in an asymmetric multicore processing system across however many nodes you have in a particular system. This even includes nodes that are not local to all other nodes, but need to be passed through intermediate nodes in order to get data through to where it needs to go by setting up a route. It's important to note that the way your system is architected will either enable or impair the ability to pass messages efficiently throughout the system.

Playing-card recognition and sorting example

If we take an example of an application that takes a shuffled deck of cards and sorts them, we can divide that into several tasks. The first task is making a very simple decision: is the card red or black? The second task is also quite simple as it's going to determine the card is red if it's a diamond or heart, or black if it's a club or spade. This can be a determined if the symbol points to the top as is the case for diamonds and spades, but is not the case for hearts or clubs. The third set of tasks are all identical; they take whatever they are assigned and place them in card order 2–10, Jack, Queen, King, and Ace.

Now let's complicate things a bit by adding image processing to decipher what the suit and rank is of each card. We need to process the card as a bitmap for each of the stages, yet each task needs access to the some bits of information on each card.

Using an edge-detection algorithm, illustrated in Figure 17.19, we can process where each of the items are and decipher the difference between where the rank is and where the suit is. Can we run each task in parallel? In this case we can, as we hold on to the original data set and pass copies to each of the nodes for processing or evaluation. Once its disposition,

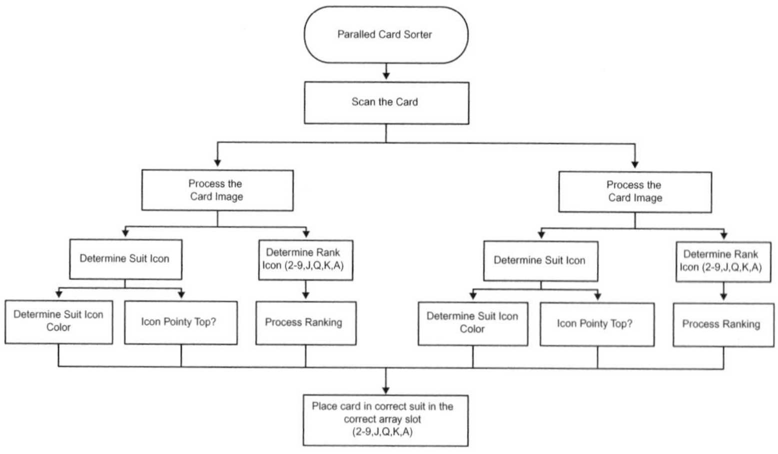

Figure 17.19:
Playing-card recognition and sorting example.

color, suite and rank is fully determined, then the card image is placed appropriately in the correct position.

Now let's complicate this even more by having multiple decks processed, where we now need to synchronize between decks to make sure we've moved on. What if a card is missing or some data takes too long to process? These conditions can occur and must be handled.

Let's look at that last set of tasks where there are four identical threads of execution. They all act on a different data set determined by a previous task. These new tasks must determine the card's rank, and arrange it to be placed in sequence. The rank is the same but the suit is different. The algorithm is identical and highly parallel. Would it make more sense to break it down between four separate nodes, or a single node that supports multiple threads? While this may be a contrived example, it should help us understand how best to decompose the system into what needs to be accomplished.

We may want to have a DSP first process the image of a card into its core components and decipher where the rank is, and where the suit is. Once that data is known, it can be passed to the first thread. Is it red or black? And to a separate node whether it's pointing at the top or not? The rank image can be passed to a third node to process its rank. The third node will take more time to process, so running this on several nodes is advisable. Remember, the goal is to make this algorithm as fast as possible so that when the third task is completed, the card is fully defined and can be placed in a sorted order.

Using a hybrid approach

Using standard POSIX threads inside a node and using MCAPI with MRAPI between nodes, you can develop a system architecture that allows high portability to any system that supports both MCAPI/MRAPI and POSIX. This allows for portability between varied systems. However, load balancing between nodes, where a thread of execution would migrate to a different node, would cause a change in API because what once was local is now remote or vice versa. The solution is to use MCAPI/MRAPI for all messaging between threads as well as nodes. If the communications do not leave the node, the MCAPI/MRAPI layer would translate into native message passing like POSIX on the node. While there is an added layer of abstraction in using MCAPI/MRAPI on a single node the added benefit of being able to load balance across nodes makes using the MCAPI/MRAPI as a common API for all types of inter-/intra-node communications a benefit. That is unless you are trying to squeeze every CPU cycle out of the environment; then using MCAPI/MRAPI as a communication layer to allow for future flexibility in system architecture may be superseded by the need for speed.

We could take the above example and use MCAPI/MRAPI APIs on a single operating system instance with either a single node or multiple nodes and create all the appropriate endpoints and set up all the appropriate tasks and the algorithm will run. This is an easy way to test the application on a single-core operating system node, prior to having the multicore hardware available. While it does not test all the parallel threading, the logical nature of the algorithms can be tested.

References

[1] D. Knuth, Structured programming with go to statements, Comput. Surv. 6 (1974) 268.
[2] Available from: http://folklore.org/StoryView.py?project = Macintosh&story = Creative_Think.txt.
[3] R. Johnson, Open Source POSIX Threads for Win32, Redhat, 2006.
[4] D.B. Bradford Nichols, J.P. Farell, Pthreads Programming, O'Reilly & Associates, 1996.
[5] C.J. Northrup, Programming with UNIX Threads, John Wiley & Sons, 1996.
[6] D.R. Butenhof, Programming with POSIX Threads, Addison-Wesley, 1997.
[7] G. Taubenfeld, Synchronization Algorithms and Concurrent Programming, Prentice Hall, 2006.
[8] E.W. Dijkstra. Cooperating sequential processes (Techniche Hogeschool, Eindhoven, 1965). Reprinted in: F. Genuys (Ed.), Programming Languages (1968) 43.
[9] G.L. Peterson, Myths about the mutual exclusion problem, Inf. Process Lett. 12 (1981) 115–116.
[10] E. Dijkstra, Solution of a problem in concurrent programming control, Commun. ACM (Jan. 1965).
[11] J.H. Anderson, A fine-grained solution to the mutual exclusion problem, Acta Informatica 30 (1993) 249–265.
[12] M. Raynal, Algorithms for Mutual Exclusion, MIT Press, 1986.
[13] J.H. Anderson. Lamport on mutual exclusion: 27 years of planting seeds. PODC: Twentieth ACM SIGACT-SIGOPS Symposium on Principles of Distributed Computing. 12, 2001. pp. 3–12.
[14] K. Alagarsamy, Some myths about famous mutual exclusion algorithms, SIGACT News 34 (2003) 94–103.
[15] T.A. Cargill, A robust distributed solution to the dining philosophers problem, Softw. Pract. Exp. 12 (1982) 965–969.
[16] M. Suess, C. Leopold, Generic locking and deadlock-prevention with C++, Parallel Comput.: Architectures, Algorithms Appl. 15 (2008) 211–218.
[17] D.K. Chen, H.M. Su, P.C. Yew. The impact of synchronization and granularity on parallel systems. Proceedings of the Seventeenth International Symposium on Computer Architecture, June 1990, pp. 239–249.
[18] M.D. Hill, M.R. Marty, Amdahl's law in the multicore era, IEEE Comput. (Jan. 2008) 1–6.
[19] V. Sarkar, Partitioning and Scheduling Parallel Programs for Execution on Multiprocessors, Pitman, 1987.
[20] O. Sinnen, Task Scheduling for Parallel Systems, John Wiley & Sons, 2007.
[21] M. Garey, D.S. Johnson, Computers and Intractability: A Guide to the Theory of NP-Completeness, Freeman, 1979.
[22] J. Beck, D. Siewiorek. Automated processor specification and task allocation for embedded multicomputer systems: the packing-based approaches. Symposium on Parallel and Distributed Processing (SPDP '95), Oct. 1995, pp. 44–51.
[23] J.E. Beck, D.P. Siewiorek, Modeling multicomputer task allocation as a vector packing problem, ISSS (1996) 115–120.
[24] K. Agrawal, C. Leiserson, Y. He, W. Hsu, Adaptive work-stealing with parallelism feedback, Trans. Comput. Syst. (2008) 26.
[25] M. Michael, M. Vechev, V. Saraswat. Idempotent work stealing. PPoPP '09: Proceedings of the Fourteenth ACM SIGPLAN Symposium on Principles and Practice of Parallel Programming, Feb. 2009.

CHAPTER 18

Safety-Critical Software Development

Mark Kraeling

Chapter Outline

Software Engineering for Embedded Systems.
DOI: http://dx.doi.org/10.1016/B978-0-12-415917-4.00018-9
© 2013 Elsevier Inc. All rights reserved.

Introduction

Embedded systems that are sold or upgraded may need to comply with a variety of safety standards based on the market and intended use. These standards can also outline requirements that need to be met based on international standards. Standards such as those based on IEC attempt to develop a common set of standards, so that each individual country and/or market doesn't have completely separate requirements.

This chapter is devoted to looking at various safety-critical software development strategies that could be used with a variety of safety requirements. Some of the strategies may not make sense for your particular product or market segment.

The first part of the chapter goes over some basic strategies that can be used for the up-front project planning for a safety-critical project.

The second part discusses fault, hazard, and risk analyses. For safety-critical projects, the early and continuous focus should be on what fault scenarios exist, the hazard that could occur if failures occur, and what risk it poses to the product and its environment.

The third part of the chapter goes over the basics of safety-critical architectures that are used, and the pros/cons of each.

The last part concentrates on strategies in software development and implementation.

Getting a clear picture of the various standards that your project will need to meet up front, following the appropriate implementation strategies listed, and watching out for the certification "killers" will help to make a safety-critical product launch more successful.

Which safety requirements?

One of the most important aspects of developing safety-critical software is determining which requirements and standards are going to be followed.

Depending on the understanding of the safety requirements of your product or the intended market, you may need to get outside help to determine what needs to be met. Consider following the steps below to aid in your safety certification effort.

1. Customer interaction: if you are entering a new market, the intended customer for that market probably knows the starting point of which safety requirements need to be met. They may be able to provide information on the safety standards that a similar product already meets. If the end customer is just using the product without a lot of technical background, then this step should be skipped.
2. Similar product in same intended market: it may be more straightforward to see what safety requirements and standards a similar product meets. For instance, if your company or a partner already sells a medical device to the same market, and your product is similar, this may be a good place to start.
3. Competitive intelligence: doing basic research on the Internet or from freely available open information from marketing materials may help determine a good starting point as well. Often, paperwork needs to be filed with agencies on which specific standards were met.
4. Professional assistance: each market or market segment normally has agencies or contract facilities that can aid in determining which standards need to be met. Paying a little up front, especially after gathering necessary information from steps 1–3 above, will help make this particular step pay off in the long run.

After gathering this information, you should have a good idea about which standards need to be met. During this investigation, also determine whether or not it is a self-certification activity, a standardized assessment activity, or a fully-fledged independent assessment certification.

For the sets of requirements that need to be met, the team should develop a strategy and initial analysis of how they will comply with the requirements. This could mean compliance could be by design, by analysis, or by testing.

As an example for design, there may be requirements for redundancy. The design could include a dual-processor design or redundant communications paths. As an example for analysis, if a certain bit error rate needs to be detected, then an appropriate-length CRC could be calculated. Through a mathematical equation, the bit error rate could be determined. Using testing as a means of compliance is fairly self-explanatory, as each of the requirements listed would have a corresponding test plan and procedure.

Finally, the team should determine how the evidence should be organized and presented.

Regardless of whether self-certification, an auditor, or full-fledged independent assessment needs to be performed, all standards and dates need to be listed and agreed on. If this specific list can be put into a contract and signed, then it should be done to protect the team. If there is no customer contract that would list this type of documentation, then even an agreement between the project team and management could be written.

If using an independent assessor (which is normally paid for by the product team) then agree to the set of documentation, the means of compliance, and the evidence that needs to be provided up front. Also agree on which party will determine whether a newer standard is released while in the early project stages. Also agree in principle (and in writing) on when the project is far enough along so that the standards list and specification dates can be frozen. If this is all discussed and agreed upon up front, safety certification becomes much easier.

Certification killers

There are also items to watch out for during the safety certification process. Many of these were lost battles on multiple projects historically in the past. Through multiple products and assessor providers, these are the items that will most certainly hinder or even kill your certification effort:

- Failure to recognize safety requirements as real
- Unclear requirements or requirements never agreed upon up front
- Lack of clear evidence of compliance
- Not doing homework up front and finding more safety standards that need to be met throughout the development process
- Lack of dedicated resources, or resources that jump between projects
- Scope and requirements creep
- Trying to safety certify too many things – not developing a boundary diagram and having everyone agree to it
- Not accounting for enough resources to document the safety case and test based on those requirements
- Not using a single contact to interface with the assessor (too many cooks!)
- Not being honest with the weaknesses of the proposed system

- Waiting until the last minute to submit documentation
- Failure to develop a relationship with the local country where the product will be deployed
- Failure to properly sequence certification tasks
- Qualification of software tools and OS to the appropriate safety level.

Project planning strategies

The following rules can be applied to help safety-critical software development projects. The strategies listed are typically looked at very early in the project development life-cycle, before the software is written. These strategies were developed and refined during multiple product certification efforts, and following these helps reduce the amount of money and resources spent on the overall effort.

Strategy 1: determine the project certification scope early

Following some of the guidelines and directives listed in the previous section, "Which safety requirements?", identify which standards your product needs to meet. Determining whether it is a consumer product, whether it has safety implications for the public, and satisfying the customer with the particular certification are guidelines in this step.

Strategy 2: determine feasibility of certification

Answer questions up front whether the product and solution are technically and commercially feasible. By evaluating the top-level safety hazards, and the safety objectives, basic defensive strategies can be developed up front. Involve engineering to determine the type of architecture that is required to meet those defensive strategies; drastic architectural differences from the base product increase risk and cost.

Strategy 3: select an independent assessor (if used)

Find an assessor that has experience with your market segment. Various assessors have specialty industries and areas, so find out if they have experience in certifying products in your industry. Once an assessor becomes comfortable with your overall process and the development procedures, it makes certification of subsequent products much easier.

Strategy 4: understand your assessor's role (if used)

The assessor's job is to assess your product with respect to compliance with standards and norms. Do not rely on the assessor to help design your system; the assessor is neither responsible nor obligated to tell you that you are heading down a wrong path! The assessor's role is to determine whether the requirements have been met, resulting in a report of conformity at the conclusion of the project.

Strategy 5: assessment communication is key

Having a clear line of communication between your team and the group controlling the standards that need to be met is extremely important. Be sure to document all meetings and action items. Document decisions that have been mutually decided during the development process, so that the assessor and team stay on the same page. Ask for a position on any unclear issues or requirements as early as possible. Insist on statements of approval for each document that will be used.

Strategy 6: establish a basis of certification

List all of the standards and directives that your product needs to comply with, including issue dates of the documents. In conjunction with your assessment, agree, disagree, or modify on a paragraph-by-paragraph basis. Consider placing all of the requirements in a compliance matrix, so they can be tracked with the project team. Finally, do not be afraid to propose an "alternate means of compliance" if required.

Strategy 7: establish a "fit and purpose" for your product

Establishing a fit and purpose up front will prevent future headaches! The "fit" for your product is the space that you plan on selling into. If selling a controller for an overhead crane, then state that up front and don't incorporate requirements needed for an overhead lighting system. The "purpose" is what the product is supposed to do or how it is going to be used. Help by clearly defining the system boundary, and what portions of your overall system and product are included in the certification. Consider things like user environment, operating environment, and the integration with other products. Also considerations such as temperature and altitude can impact the circuit design, so those should be defined well in advance for successful product certification.

Strategy 8: establish a certification block diagram

Generate a hardware block diagram of the system with the major components such as modules and processing blocks. Include all of the communication paths, as well as a brief summary of the information flow between the blocks. Identify all of the external interfaces, including the "certification boundary" for the system on the diagram.

Strategy 9: establish communication integrity objectives

Up front before the system design, determine the "residual error" rate objectives for each digital communication path. Defining CRC and Hamming distance requirements for the paths also helps determine the integrity levels required. Also discuss with the assessor up front how the residual error rate will be calculated, as this could drive specific design constraints or necessary features.

Strategy 10: identify all interfaces along the certification boundary

Up front generate a boundary "Interface Control Document". From this document, identify all of the required Safety Integrity Levels for each of the interfaces. At this point, research with the potential parties that own the other side of the interface can begin, to make sure they can comply. Quantify and qualify the interface, including defining acceptable ranges, magnitudes, CRC requirements, and error checking.

Strategy 11: identify the key safety defensive strategies

Identify and have the safety defensive strategies used to achieve the safety objectives for the program. Define key terms such as fault detection, fault accommodation, and the "fail safe" states. During initial architecture and design, keep track of early failure scenarios that could occur. It is difficult to find all of them early in the project, but changes in the architecture and system design are more easily done on the front end of the project.

Strategy 12: define built in test (BIT) capability

Identify the planned BIT coverage, including initialization, periodic, conditional, and user-initiated. Define a manufacturing test strategy to check for key safety hardware components before shipping to the end user. After identifying each of these built-in-test functions, review with the assessor and get agreement.

Strategy 13: define fault annunciation coverage

While keeping the system and user interface in mind, define which faults get annunciated. Determine when they should be announced to the operator or put into the log. Determine the level of information that is given to the end user and what is logged. Define the conditions that spawn a fault, and also what clears that particular fault. Define any fault annunciation color, text, sound, etc. After these are defined make sure the assessor agrees!

Strategy 14: define reliance and expectation of the operator/user

Clearly define any reliance that is placed on the operator or user to keep the system safe. Determine the user's performance and skill level, and the human factors involved with safety and vigilance. When placing safety expectations on the user, make sure the end customer agrees with the assessment. And as stated, make sure your assessor agrees with it as well.

Strategy 15: define plan for developing software to appropriate integrity level

For each of the formal methods, address the compliance with each element of the applicable standard you are certifying to. The software safety strategy should include both control of integrity and application of programming defensive strategies. The plan should include coding standards, planned test coverage, use of commercial off-the-shelf products (COTS), software development rules, OS integrity requirements, and development tools. Finally, define and agree on software performance metrics up front.

Strategy 16: define artifacts to be used as evidence of compliance

List all of the documents and artifacts you plan to produce as part of the system safety case. List how you plan to cross-reference them to requirements in the system. Make sure any document used as evidence of compliance is approved for release via your configuration control process. Test documentation must have a signature and date for each test case. Above all, make sure your assessor agrees with your document and artifact plan up front.

Strategy 17: plan for labor-intensive analyses

Plan on conducting a piece-part FMEA (failure modes and effects analysis), which is very labor-intensive. Also plan on a system-level FMEA, and a software error analysis. It is recommended that probabilistic fault trees are used to justify key defensive strategies and to address systematic failures. More information on FMEAs is in one of the following sections, "Hazard analysis".

Strategy 18: create user-level documentation

Plan on having a users' manual that includes the following information: system narrative, normal operating procedures, abnormal operating procedures, emergency procedures, and safety alerts. Also include a comprehensive maintenance manual that contains the following: safety-related maintenance, required inspections and intervals, life-limited components, dormancy elimination tasks, and instructions on loading software and validating the correct load.

Strategy 19: plan on residual activity

Any change to your certification configuration must be assessed for the impact on your safety certification. There could be features added to the original product, or part changes that need to be made that could affect the safety case. Some safety certifications also require annual independent inspections of manufacturing and/or quality assurance groups. Residual activity (and thus residual cost) will occur after the certification effort is complete.

Strategy 20: publish a well-defined certification plan

Document a certification plan, which includes all previous rules, time-line events, resources, and interdependencies. Include a certification "road map" that can be referred to throughout the development process, to have a snapshot of the documentation that is required for the required certification process.

Faults, failures, hazards, and risk analysis

Once the project planning phase of the project is complete, it is important to do an assessment of where the risks may be for the system being designed. In order to measure the overall risk for the product, a risk analysis needs to be performed.

Before getting to the risk assessment, a list of safety-critical terms will be explored.

Faults, errors, and failures

A **fault** is a characteristic of an embedded system that could lead to a system error. An example of a fault is a software pointer that is not initialized correctly under specific conditions, where use of the pointer could lead to a system error. There are also faults that could exist in software that never manifest themselves as an error, and are not necessarily seen by the end user.

An **error** is an unexpected and erroneous behavior of the system; that is, unexpected by the end user. This is the exhibited behavior of the system whenever a fault or multiple faults occur. An example could be a sub-process that quits running within the system from a software pointer that is not initialized correctly. An error may not necessarily lead to a system failure, especially if the error has been mitigated by having a process check to see if this sub-task is running, and restarting it if necessary.

For an embedded system, a **failure** is best described as a system event not performing its intended function or service as expected by its users at some point in time. Since this is largely based on the user's perception or usage of the system, the issue itself could be in the initial system requirements or customer specification, not necessarily the software itself.

However, a failure could also occur based on an individual error or erroneous system functionality based on multiple errors in the system. Following the example above, the software pointer initialization fault could result in a sub-task running error, which when it fails causes a system failure such as a crash or user interface not performing correctly.

An important aspect is that for the progression of these terms, they may not necessarily ever manifest themselves at the next level. An uninitialized software pointer is a fault, but if it is never used then an error would not occur (and neither would the failure). There may also need to be multiple instances of faults and errors, possibly on completely different fault trees, in order to progress to the next state. Figure 18.1 shows the progression for faults, errors, and failures.

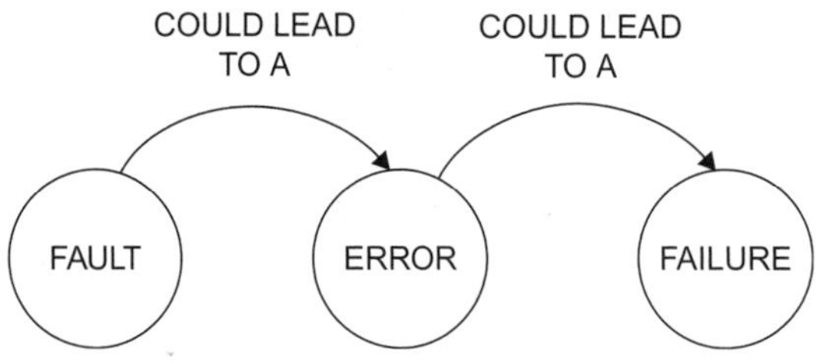

Figure 18.1:
Progression of Faults, Errors, and Failures.

For safety-critical systems, there are techniques that can be used to minimize the progression of faults to errors to failures. All of these impact the reliability of the system, as discussed in the next section.

Availability and reliability

Availability and reliability are related terms, but are not the same. **Availability** is a measure of how much the embedded system will be running and delivering the expected services of the design. Examples of high-availability systems include network switches for voice and data, power distribution, and television delivery systems. **Reliability** is the probability that an embedded system will deliver the requested services at a given point in time. Even though these terms are related, a high-availability system does not necessarily mean the system will also be highly reliable.

An example of a system that could have high availability but low reliability is a home network system that has faults. In this example, if every 100th packet is dropped, causing a retry to occur, to the user it will seem like a very available system. There aren't any periods of a total outage, but just periods in the background where packets need to be resent. The fault could be causing an error to occur, with delays waiting for processes to restart. The system itself stays up, the browser or whatever user interface stays running, so the user doesn't perceive it as a system failure.

Safety-critical systems are examples of high-reliability systems, and, in the case of systems that are monitoring other safety-critical systems, highly available. Systems that are both highly reliable and highly available are said to be dependable. A dependable system provides confidence to the user that the system will perform when they want it to, as it is supposed to. Addressing how to handle faults, which could lead to a system failure, is the source for system dependability.

Fault handling

There are four aspects of faults that should be evaluated as part of a safety-critical system. The four types for faults are avoidance, tolerance, removal, and prediction.

Fault avoidance in a safety-critical system is largely an exercise in developing a system that helps prevent the introduction of software and hardware faults into the system. Formal design and development practices help developers avoid faults. One approach in fault avoidance is designing a software system with a single thread of execution, as opposed to a multi-tasking pre-emptive type of task scheduling. This helps avoid issues of parallelism, or timing issues that could occur if a portion of one section of code is impacted in a negative way by another. For this example, it would be unreasonable to include every timing aspect or order that is a part of normal system testing. There are safety-critical programming practices listed in the section "Software implementation strategies" that target fault avoidance.

Fault tolerance is a layer of software that is able to "intercept" faults that occur in the system and address them so that they do not become system failures. An important aspect of safety-critical systems is the characteristic that fault-tolerant systems have excellent fault detection. Once an individual hardware or software component has been evaluated as "failed", then the system can take appropriate action. Performing fault detection at a high level in the software should only be done when multiple variables need to be evaluated to determine a fault. One example of good fault detection is evaluation of a temperature sensor. If the sensor has an "out-of-range" low or high value coming into an A/D converter, the software should clearly not use this value. Depending on the criticality of this input to the system, there may be a redundant sensor which should be used (higher criticality). If this input is not critical to the system, then another possible solution could be to use another temperature sensor as an approximation to this one. Architecture, hardware, and software designs all have an impact on a system's ability to be fault-tolerant.

Fault removal consists of either modifying the state of the system to account for the fault condition, or removing the fault through debugging and testing. The most difficult aspect of "dynamic" fault removal is to safely determine how to do this. The changing of the fault is typically done with non-critical data that is part of the safety-critical system. Building upon the example that was outlined above, a safety-critical system simply logs a temperature value for environmental evaluation at a later date (it is not used in any control loops or decisions). If the example temperature sensor is an ambient sensor, and it has failed, it switches over to use an ambient sensor that is integrated into the hardware that is less accurate. For the logs, having a less accurate temperature is evaluated as being better than having no ambient temperature at all. Safety-critical systems' primary focus for fault removal is testing and debugging of the system itself. Systems test procedures cover all of the functionality for the safety-critical system, and often require 100% coverage for lines of code in the system as well as different combinations of execution and inputs. Reiterating and addressing faults in this manner is much easier than the complexity of doing it dynamically.

Finally, **fault prediction** is an often missed aspect of safety-critical systems. Being able to predict a fault that may occur in the future and alerting a maintenance person or maintainer is very valuable in increasing the dependability of the system. Examples include sensors that may have spurious out-of-range values, where tossing out those values keeps the system running. However, if the number of out-of-range values increases from a typical one occurrence per day to one occurrence per minute, we are possibly getting nearer to having a failed sensor. Flagging that occurrence and repairing it during a time when the user expects the system to be down is much more dependable than having that sensor fail and cause the system to be unavailable.

Hazard analysis

Designing safety-critical systems should address hazards that cause the system to have a failure that leads to tragic accidents or unwanted damage. A hazard is any potential failure that causes damage. Safety-critical systems must be designed where the system operation itself is always safe. Even if a particular aspect of the system fails, it should still operate in a safe state.

The term "fail safe" is used to describe a result where the system always maintains a safe state, even if something goes terribly wrong. A safe state for a locomotive train would be to stop. Some systems, such as aircraft fly-by-wire, do not have a fail-safe state. When dealing with these types of systems, multiple levels of redundancy and elimination of single points of failure need to occur as part of the system design.

Performing a hazard analysis is key to the design of safety-critical embedded systems. This analysis involves identifying the hazards that exist in your embedded system. It is based on a preliminary design or architecture that has been developed – even if it is just a sketch in its preliminary form.

In this process, an architecture for the safety-critical system is proposed, and iterated until it seems, at this point, that the architecture could support being highly reliable and available with mitigation for the hazards that could be present. Once this is complete, additional hazard analyses will need performed on all aspects of the safety-critical system in more detail.

During sub-system design, hazard analysis will continue to be performed. When more details are known, one effective way to do this is by performing an **FMEA**. This is a systematic approach to numerically evaluating each of the failures in the system, and provides clarity into the classification of each of the failures. Once the failures are understood with their effects, then mitigations can be performed, such as detection, removal, or functional additions into the system to mitigate the condition.

An example work product from an FMEA analysis is shown in Figure 18.2.

Function	Potential failure	Potential effects of failure	Severity rating	Potential cause	Occurence rating	Mitigation plan	Detection rating	RPN
Vehicle speed sensor	Sensor fails high (sensor out-of-range)	Cruise control goes off from on	5	Sensor high side shorts high	2	Add overload to sensor connection	3	30

Figure 18.2:
Example FMEA line item.

For an FMEA, each failure condition is evaluated for how often it occurs, the severity of the consequence when it occurs, and how often it can be detected when it occurs. These are typically ranked from 1 to 10, and then an overall score for each failure (risk priority number) is calculated by multiplying these numbers together. This number helps rank the order in which to evaluate the failures, but by no means should any of the failures be ignored! Rules should be set up and put in place for failures that cannot be detected or have serious consequences when they occur. Another important aspect of an FMEA is that it tends to focus on individual failures, where bigger issues could occur when multiple failures happen at the same time.

A **fault-tree analysis** is a top-down approach to doing a hazard analysis. This helps discern how different combinations of individual faults could cause a system failure to occur. The fault tree isn't focused on just software, but includes hardware and user interaction that could cause the failures to occur. Its top-down approach starts with the faults themselves, and puts a sequence of logical paths together to address how the eventual failure could occur.

Figure 18.3 shows a fault tree.

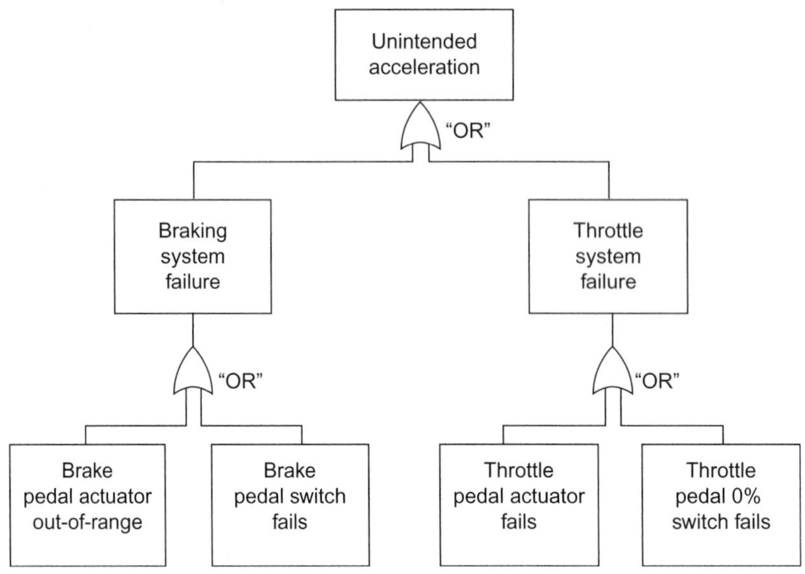

Figure 18.3:
Example fault tree.

An **event-tree analysis** is done in the opposite way to a fault tree analysis, as it is a bottom-up approach to the hazard analysis. The analysis starts with the failure itself and then analyzes how that particular failure could occur from a combination of faults. This type starts with the undesired event itself, such as "engine quits running", and then determines how this could possibly happen with individual faults and errors that occur.

Figure 18.4 shows an example event tree, with the numbers representing the probability that taking that branch could occur.

In safety-critical systems, hazards that can result in accidents, damage, or harm are classified as risks, and should require a risk analysis.

Risk analysis

A risk analysis is a standard method where each of the hazards identified is evaluated more carefully. As part of this process each hazard is evaluated based on the likelihood of the failure occurring, along with the potential for damage or harm when it occurs. A risk analysis helps determine whether the given hazard is acceptable, how much risk we are willing to accept, and whether there needs to be any mitigation or re-design for that failure.

The initial step for risk analysis is evaluation. In this step, the input from the FMEA is used to make certain that the classification is correct. Things like its probability, its estimated

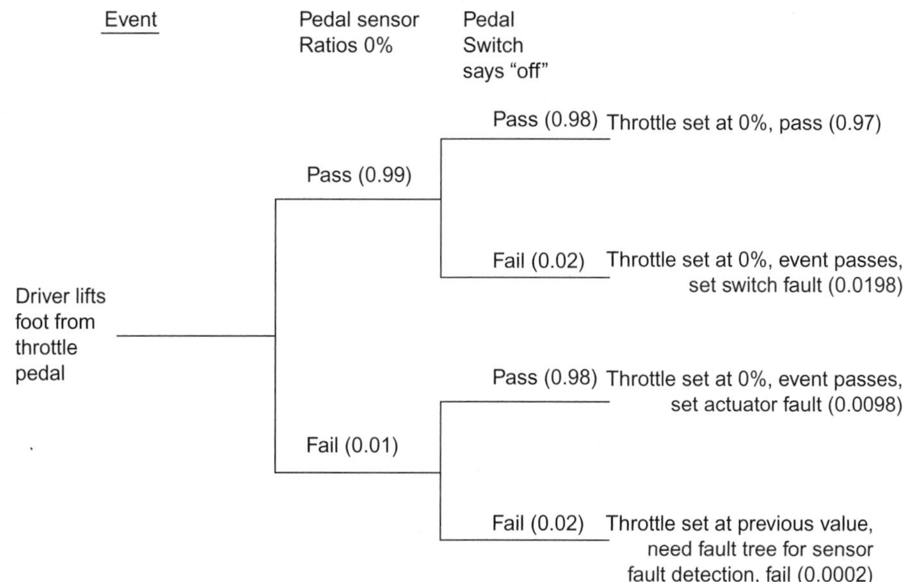

Figure 18.4:
Example event tree.

risk to the overall system, and its severity are evaluated. Discussion for a single failure being evaluated should occur for as long as it needs to – primarily because FMEAs tend to go over many singular failures and risk evaluation may look at multiple elements. Once the evaluation is done, the failure should be given an acceptability rating. The rating can have a value of unacceptable, acceptable, or tolerable. Unacceptable means the failure must be eliminated – requiring redesign or further design efforts. Acceptable means the team accepts the hazard and its mitigation as currently designed (accepting risk). The third tolerable type means a more careful evaluation of the risk should be done to mitigate it or eliminate it.

The other steps for risk analysis use the same tools as the hazard analysis, including performing a fault-tree or event-tree analysis as discussed in the previous section. The risk analysis has the added benefit of looking at the system as a whole – where an FMEA tends to look at individual failures. Changes in the architecture of the entire system or even just a sub-system may be required to eliminate or mitigate the risks that are identified. A key strategy in architectures to help mitigate or eliminate risks is the concept of redundancy.

Redundancy simply means doing the same thing in more than one way. This could include a combination of the same software running on two processors, multiple processors, or even a combination of hardware and software. The next section of this chapter discusses various safety-critical architectures that could be used to mitigate risk.

Safety-critical architectures

A large part of creating a safety-critical system is deciding on the system/software architecture that is going to be used. Consider the processor architecture in Figure 18.5.

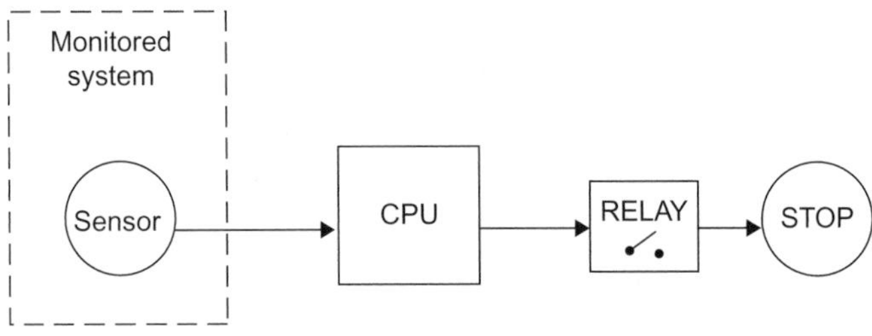

Figure 18.5:
Example stopping system.

In this configuration, if running safety-critical software, what happens if the processor does something that is unexpected? What if the processor runs something out of a bad memory location, or there is a latent failure that only exhibits itself after some period of time?

This processor wouldn't be able to satisfy a truly safety-critical system by itself. Depending on the safety level, there may be external components that can be added around the processor to perform the desired safety function in parallel if the processor cannot do so. As the complexity of the interface goes up, replicating with circuitry may not satisfy the mitigation that is being performed for failures that can happen in your system. This would especially be true if the nature of the critical data is contained within serial messages or Ethernet frames. When the amount of safety-critical data increases, or the number of safety mechanisms increases, it is time for a different architecture.

The following sections outline various architectures that could be used for a safety-critical system. For each architecture, notes are included to outline various aspects, including positives and negatives.

"Do-er" / "check-er"

In the architecture in Figure 18.6, one processor is still performing a majority of the embedded system work. In this case, a second processor is added to look at the safety-related data to make assessments about that data. It then looks at the output of the main processor, and makes a decision as to whether that processor is doing what it is supposed to do.

As an example, say there is a bit of information in the serial stream that means "STOP" and a separate discrete input signal that also means "STOP". Both processors could be designed

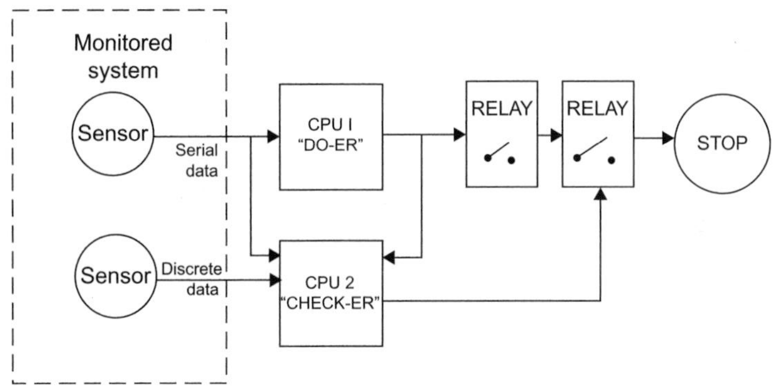

Figure 18.6:
Basic do-er check-er diagram.

to have visibility to both pieces of data. The main processor would process the safety-critical "stop" logic, along with all of the other operations it is performing. The secondary processor would simply look to see whether the main processor ordered a stopping process based on this data, and would take action if the main processor did not. Maybe the main processor stops in a more graceful way, where the secondary processor does something more abrupt (like turning the driveline off).

This architecture lends itself to systems where there is a "safe" state that the system can reside in. It is also good because the complexity on the secondary processor side is limited to just the safety functions of the system. The main processor still runs all of the other non-safety code (the secondary does not).

When the complexity of the safety case goes up, or the safety-critical level goes up, then a different architecture is needed to process data.

Two processors

In the architecture in Figure 18.7, there are two processors, which could be identical, that handle the safety aspects of the system. Each of the processors labeled "A" and "B" performs the same operations and handles the same data. The other processor labeled "C" performs clean-up tasks and executes code that has nothing to do with the safety aspects of the system. The two safety processors operate on the same data.

Various tricks can be done on the two processors to make them a little different. First, the memory maps for the processors can be shifted so that a software error dealing with memory on one processor wouldn't be the same memory on the other processor. They could also be clocked and operated separately – maybe there isn't a requirement to have

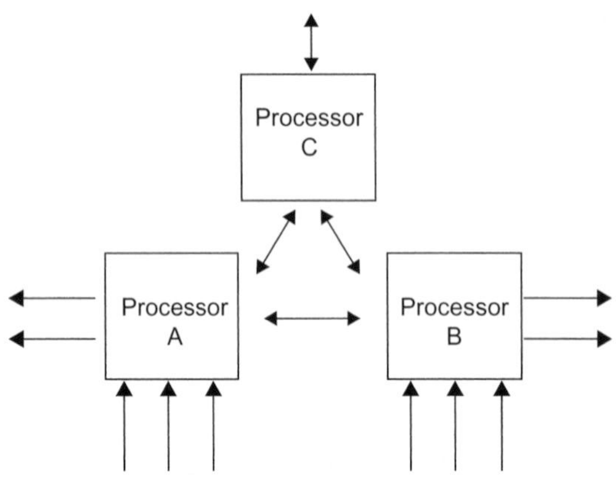

Figure 18.7:
Safety two processor diagram.

the processors execute instructions in lock-step with each other. For this architecture, if the processors disagree then the system would arrive at a "safe state" for the system. For this and the previous architectures listed, it assumes there is a "stop" or "safe" state for the embedded system. If the system must continue to operate, then a more complex system architecture is needed.

"Voter"

The architecture in Figure 18.8 shows a "voter" type of system. For this type of system, the processors actually vote on what should be done next. Information is compared between all of them, and the decision with the greatest number of votes wins. The indecision of the processors is logged and flagged, so that maintenance can be done on the system. There also needs to be a periodic checking of the interpretation of the voting mechanism, so that the voting mechanism itself is known to work and doesn't have a latent failure.

This type of architecture is a large jump in complexity. There are numerous test cases that need to be performed to evaluate this system – and the number of possibilities sharply increases. Embedded engineers spend their entire lives dealing with the intricacies of systems like this, and development is not quick or even regular in terms of time.

Selecting the right architecture up front based on the safety requirements is extremely important. Having to shift from one architecture to another after development has started is expensive and complicated.

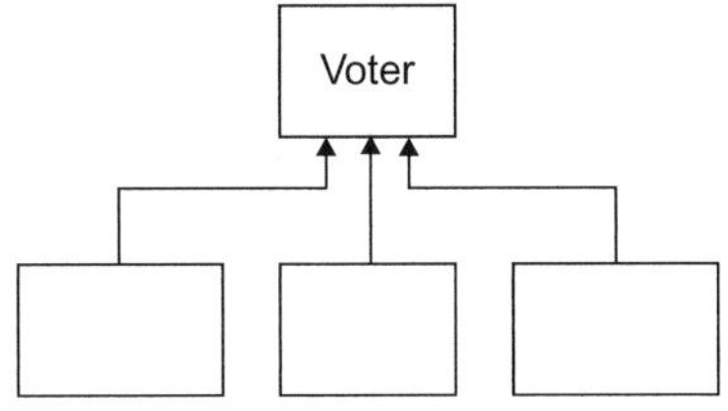

Figure 18.8:
Safety voter processor diagram.

Software implementation strategies

After the project planning, hazard/risk analysis, and architecture are complete, there should be a good understanding of which requirements are safety-critical. For software development, it is important to treat these as special – even following a separate process to make sure they are designed, coded, and unit-tested correctly.

It is difficult to have a single process that fits every type of safety-critical application or project. This section's intent is to point out different strategies that should be considered when doing development. The safety requirements for your project may require many of the items listed here, so this provides a good start for things to consider. If you are using an independent assessor, there may be particular and specific items that need to be included as well.

Strategy 1: have a well-defined, repeatable peer-review process

One of the most critical process items for safety-critical software is having a well-defined peer-review process. There must be a process for peer reviews, and consistency in what information is provided and the amount of time that is available for review prior to the meeting. The reviewers may include systems, systems test, safety, and configuration management.

There also must be recognition by the peer-review leader if the reviewers have not had sufficient time to prepare. In this case, the meeting should be re-scheduled. For safety-critical code development and code sections, it is really important to have independent assessment of the source code so that a single person isn't walking the group through the code where their opinion could come into play. This independent assessment can be a person outside the organization or someone who reports in a different chain of command in the organization.

An example software peer-review process is shown in Figure 18.9.

LIVERPOOL JOHN MOORES UNIVERSITY
LEARNING SERVICES

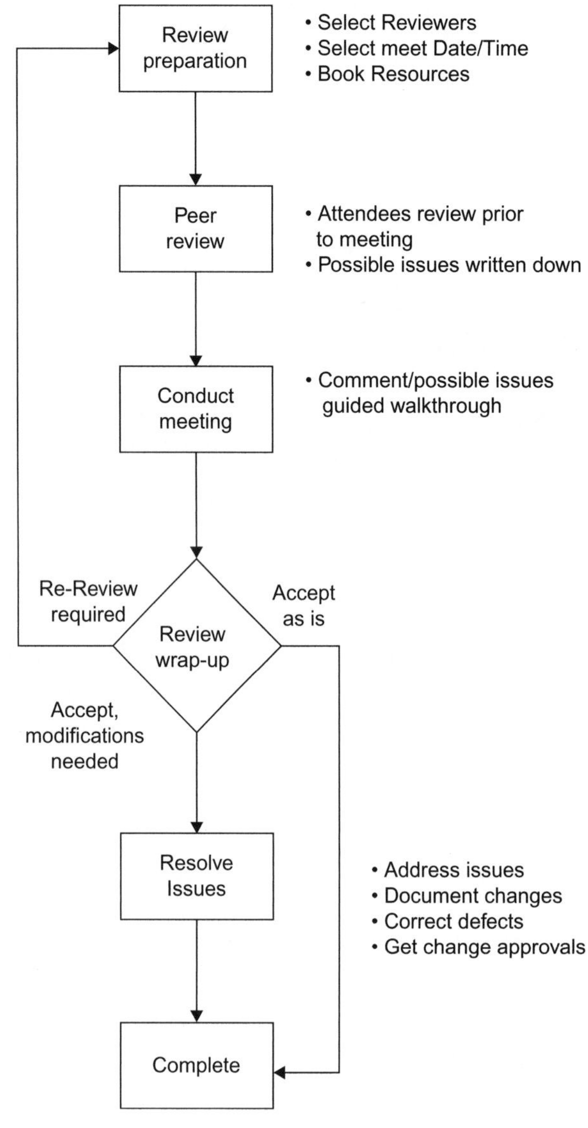

Figure 18.9:
Example peer review process.

Strategy 2: consider using existing safety coding standards

In addition to the strategies listed here, safety standards exist that define rules for programmers to follow when implementing safety-critical code.

One particular standard, called MISRA C, initially established 127 guidelines for using C in safety-critical applications. It checks for mistakes that could be made that are entirely "legal" when using the C programming language, but have unintended consequences when executed. Based in the UK, the Motor Industry Software Reliability Association (MISRA) felt there were areas of automobile design where safety was extremely important. Their first standard was developed in 1998 and included 93 required rules of the 127 total guidelines. The remaining 34 were advisory.

The MISRA standards were updated in 2004 to include additional guidelines. It increased the number to 121 required rules and 20 advisory rules, to bring the total to 141. This newer version of the standard also split the rules into categories, such as "Run-Time Failures". The MISRA C standard document is available at their website: http://www.misra-c.com. There is also a set of guidelines for C++, in a separate MISRA C++ document.

For an example of a rule, one states "All code shall conform to ISO 9899 standard C, with no extensions permitted". In simple terms that means that using extensions or in-line assembly would be considered non-conformity to this rule. However, along with this rule is the following comment: "It is recognized that it may be necessary to raise deviations to permit certain language extensions, for example to support hardware specific features." So with this, it is clear that the standard permits low-level hardware manipulation or handling of interrupt routines – as long as it is in a localized, standard area and also done in a repeatable way. This particular standard was written with embedded systems in mind!

For the 93 required rules, all of them can be checked using a static code analyzer (see Strategy 16: static code analysis, below). Many embedded compiler vendors include support for various sets of rule-checking standards. There are also separate programs that can be run during the build for each of the source files that can check compliance and print reports for software modules. Running any of these tools is checking for compliance only – there is no MISRA certification process that software can go through.

Strategy 3: handle all combinations of input data

For data that is processed by a safety-critical system, it is important to address and account for every combination of input value, including both external data and intermediate data.

Checking the external data that is coming into your system for all possible values certainly makes sense. The interface specification that was written to interface with the other system may state that a particular data item can only have specific values, but it is important to check that a different value has showed up. This could definitely come about later in the life-cycle of the product, where the other system's baseline is updated with new software and yours is missed. Or it could come about because of a misinterpretation of the specification implementing the interface by either party.

For example, if a data element can have value "0" meaning "Stop", and a value of "1" which means "Go", then what happens if the variable is any other value? Maybe someone adds a new value at a later time, “2”, which means “Proceed with caution”. In this case, logic should be put together to specifically check for each case, and also have logic that catches the other case as well. In this situation, notifying someone and/or logging the mismatch is important to help correct the situation in the future. An example of this is shown below:

```
if ( input_data_byte = = 0 )
{
   Movement = STOP;
}
else if ( input_data_byte = = 1 )
{
   Movement = GO;
}
else
{
   Movement = STOP; // Most restrictive case here
   Log_Error( INP_DATA_BYTE_INV, “Unknown Value” );
}
```

For an intermediate variable declared in your system, it is also important to do the same type of checking. Every “if” statement should have an “else”, and every “switch” should have a default case encompassing the values that are unexpected. More complex combinations of conditions for “if” statements should also have the same “else” condition covered. Having these alternate paths that “should” never be executed helps to better understand the system as a whole. It also helps the programmer explore alternative paths and corner cases that may exist.

Strategy 4: specific variable value checking

When writing safety-critical software code, it is important to check for a specific value for the permissive condition you are looking for. Consider the following code:

```
if ( relay_status ! = RELAY_CLOSED )
{
   DO_Allow_Movement(); // Let the vehicle move, everything OK
```

```
}
else
{

   DO_Stop(); //The relay isn't positioned correctly, stop!

}
```

In the example above, the code wishes to look for the relay being open in order to allow movement. The variable "relay_status" has two values, RELAY_OPEN and RELAY_CLOSED. But, depending on the size of variable that was declared, there are actually many more values that it can have! What if the memory actually has a value of something else? With the code above, movement would be allowed. This isn't good practice. For the most permissive state, always check for a single value (or range when appropriate). The following code is the correct way to write this code block:

```
if ( relay_status = = RELAY_OPEN )
{

   DO_Allow_Movement(); // Let the vehicle move, everything OK

}
else if ( relay_status = = RELAY_CLOSED )
{

   DO_Stop(); // It is closed, so we need to stop

}
else // This case shouldn't happen -
{

   DO_Stop(); //The relay isn't positioned correctly, stop!

   Log_Error( REL_DATA_BYTE_INV, "Unknown Value" );

}
```

Another way that the code block could be written, based on how the code is structured, is to set the most restrictive case in the code at the start of execution. Then specific steps are taken and values are checked in order to allow movement. For the simple code block above, DO_Stop() would be moved outside the conditional "if" and then the code would allow movement if certain checks passed.

Strategy 5: mark safety-critical code sections

For code sections that are safety-critical in your code, there should be a special way that the code section is marked. This is more for maintenance of the code later – or if the code is used by another group for their project later on. The real safety-critical sections should be marked with comment blocks that say why it is safety-critical, and also refer back to the specific safety requirements that were written. This would also be an appropriate place to refer to any safety analysis documentation that was done as well.

The following is an example of a header that could be used for a safety-critical code section:

```
/****************************************************
****************************************************
** SAFETY-CRITICAL CODE SECTION
** See SRS for Discrete Inputs for Requirements
** Refer to Document #20001942 for Safety Analysis
**
** This code is the only place that checks to make
** sure the lowest priority task is being allowed
** to run. If it hasn't run, then our system is
** unstable!
*********** START SAFETY-CRITICAL SECTION **********/
  // LOW_PRIO_RUN is defined as 0x5A3C
  if ( LP_Flag_Set = = LOW_PRIO_RUN )
  {
    LP_Flag_Set = 0;
  }
  else
  {
    // The system is unstable, reset now
    Reset_System();
  }
/*********** STOP SAFETY-CRITICAL SECTION ***********/
```

For the example above, you can see that we are just resetting the system. This may not be appropriate, depending on what task your system is performing and where it is installed. Code like this may be appropriate for a message protocol translation device that has safety-critical data passing through it, but is likely not appropriate for a vehicle!

Strategy 6: timing execution checking

For processors that run safety-critical code, it is important to check that all intended software is able to run in a timely manner. For a task-based system, the highest-priority task should check to make sure that all of the other lower-priority tasks are able to run. Time blocks can be created for the other tasks – such that if one lower-priority task runs every 10 ms and another runs every 1 s, the checking is done appropriately. One method is to check to make sure tasks are not running more than 20% slower or faster than their intended execution rate.

The rate at which the task timings are checked would be dependent on the safety aspect of the code in the task that is being checked.

Another system check is to make sure that the entire clock rate of the system hasn't slowed down and fooled the entire software baseline. Checks like this need to look at off-core timing sources so that clock and execution rates can be compared. Depending on how different timers are clocked on the system, it could come from an on-die internal check – but only if what you are checking against is not running from the same master clock input. One example is checking the execution timing of a task in comparison with the real-time clock on the chip – if it is running from an external crystal or other input. When going this route, there may also be requirements that the source code doesn't know how (or is not mapped) to change the clock input for the RTC chip.

Strategy 7: stale data

Another safety-critical aspect of a system is performing operations to make sure that we do not have stale data in the system. Making decisions on data that is older than we expect could have serious consequences while running!

One example of this is an interface between a processor and an external logic device, such as an FPGA. The logic device is accessed through a parallel memory bus, and the processor uses the interface to read input data from a memory buffer. If the data is used as an input to any kind of safety-critical checking, we do not want the data to be stale. In this example, this could occur if the process that collects that data on the FPGA stops or has a hardware fault on its input side. The interface should add some kind of counter for the data blocks, or have a handshaking process where the memory is cleared after it is read. Additional checks may need to be put in place as well, such as the processor having a way to check to make sure the memory block was cleared after the request.

There are many methods to get rid of stale data, largely based on how the data is coming in and where it is coming from. There may be a circular buffer that is filled with DMA or memory accesses. For this case, checking to make sure data is still coming in is important. There may also be serial streams of data that is again placed in a specific memory location. Our safety application comes along and operates on that data. Here are some things to consider:

- First, determine whether there is a way to delete the incoming data once your safety-critical code has run and generated outputs. Clearing out this memory space is a great way to make sure that the data is gone before the functionality is run again.
- Second, when dealing with serial data or sets of data, consider using sequence numbers to order the data. This will allow the software to remember which set was processed last time, so that an expected increase in sequence number would show the data is newer.
- Third, for large blocks of data where it is impractical to clear the entire memory space, and there is also no sequence number, things are a little more difficult. For these large blocks, there should be a CRC or error check of the data itself to make sure it is correct. After processing this data, selectively modifying multiple bytes can help create a CRC mismatch. There is probability to this – there shouldn't be a probable situation where data is changed and the CRC is still good.

Strategy 8: comparison of outputs

Depending on the processor architecture being used, when there is more than one processor the outputs of the safety-critical functions should be cross-checked. This allows each of the processors in the architecture to make sure the other processor is taking appropriate action based on the inputs. There are a variety of ways to check this.

One of the easier ways is for the outputs of one processor to also be run in parallel to be inputs on another processor. Again depending on the architecture, this would be a check to make sure that the other processor(s) is doing what you expect when presented with the same data. For an output that is a serial stream, this could also be run in parallel to the intended target as well as fed back into the other processor as an input. A comparison can be done, again to make sure the other processor is doing the same thing that your processor is, as shown in Figure 18.10.

Another way this can occur is to send serial or memory-mapped data directly between the two processors. This allows more checking to be done at intermediate steps in the software process, as opposed to when it comes out of the other processor. If one of the safety-critical

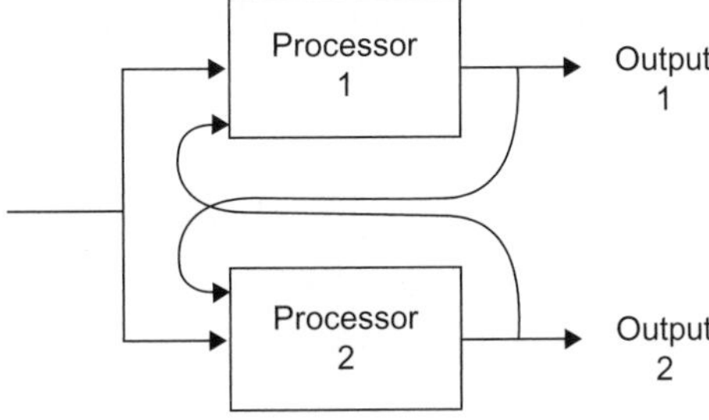

Figure 18.10:
Processors checking actions.

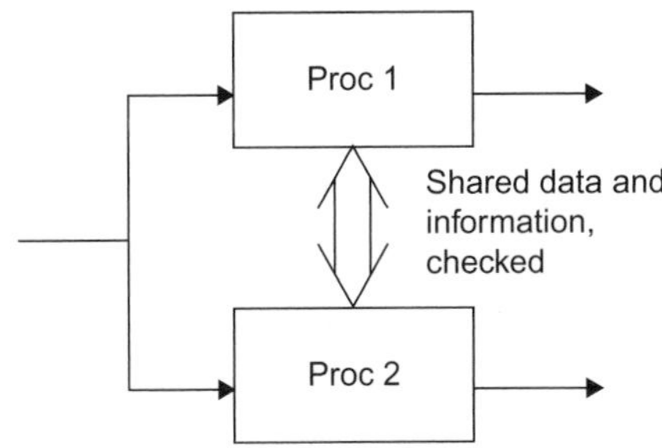

Figure 18.11:
Processors sharing then checking information.

outputs was "ignite" then it is a little late for another processor to be checking for this. In this case, having more checks between the processors would be beneficial before ever getting to the final output case. The latency of the communication channel between them directly corresponds to the regularity and periodocity of the checking. Figure 18.11 shows the basics of this serial or memory-mapped communication.

Strategy 9: initialize data to least permissive state

Initializing data to the least permissive state forces the software and its architecture to continually make decisions on whether to allow any state to be more permissive than the least permissive. In safety-critical systems, least permissive means "the safest condition" for the particular system to be. This starts with the initialization of the code itself – it should be set to start in a safe state without any inputs or incoming data streams. Once the inputs are processed and a decision is made, consider setting the internal variables back to being most restrictive again. When the software runs the next time, it is making the same sort of decision, "can I be more permissive based on inputs" as opposed to having logic that says "we are not restrictive, and should we be?"

Architectures that start from the restrictive state tend to be more understandable when the logic is followed, as opposed to having to look for cases where we should be more restrictive after not being so.

For this case it is permissible to use variables to remember what our last output state was, but they should be used as an input into the logic ("last_output_state") as opposed to the output that the code is generating ("Output_State").

Strategy 10: order of execution

If there are requirements for one code section running before others, safety checks need to be in place to make sure that this has occurred. This certainly comes into play when software is running in different threads of execution, or when tasks and an RTOS may be involved.

For a simple safety-critical application, there is a task that takes raw data and converts it to a filtered, or more meaningful, set of data. There is then a task that takes that data, performs calcuations, and produces an output of the embedded system. For this case, we had better process the input data before attempting to come up with a suitable output.

A check should be in place for this and more complex activities to make sure the order of execution is precisely what is expected. Often failure to execute things in order can result in unexpected behavior if not handled appropriately. This could happen with interrupts that execute (or don't execute) when they are expected. These types of errors tend to be very timing-dependent – so it may be something that happens "every X time" and is hard to catch.

One mitigation for this is to put together a checker to make sure things are done in order, and that the task is allowed to complete (if this is a requirement) before other ordered tasks are run. This can be done using a simple sequence number for the tasks, where it is set to a fixed value to let the next task know that the task ran to the appropriate completion point. Then the next task (where this order is important) checks the value and proceeds only if it matches what it expects.

Another mitigation is to use more of the features in the RTOS to help with ordered execution. Use of semaphores and/or flags may be an alternative. Be careful with this type of solution – because your dependency on the operating system will go up for the safety case with the increase in features that you depend on.

Finally, depending on the safety nature of the code, another idea is to use a simple timer and run the tasks in frames with your own home-spun scheduler. If all the task priorities are the same, and you are comforable writing interupts for the code that needs to "run right now", then ensuring execution order becomes as simple as function calls.

Strategy 11: volatile data checking

Any data that is received from another source offboard of the processor should have its integrity checked. Common ways of doing this involve CRC (cyclic redundancy code) checks of various lengths. Depending on the safety-criticalness of the software, a different CRC other than an established standard may be needed, as described below.

In embedded networks, the parameter that is the most looked at with CRCs is the Hamming distance. This property specifies the minimum number of bit inversions that can be injected into a message without it being detected by the CRC calculation. For a given message bit length, if it had a Hamming distance of 4, that means there exists no combination of 1-, 2-, or 3-bit errors in that message that would be undetectable by the CRC calculation. A paper exploring 16-bit and smaller CRCs, the effect of message length, and Hamming distance that provides a great reference is [1].

Using CRCs and other types of data checking is ideal for streams of data that are coming into your system. When the data arrives, a check can be performed to make sure it is a good message before it is placed into memory. Additional, periodic checks should be made on the data after it is placed in memory, to make sure it isn't altered by errant pointers or memory conditions.

As a strategy, all volatile data that is considered safety-critical, meaning it can alter the safety mechanisms of the system depending on its value, should be checked. For data that is updated by calculation, this data should either be set to the least permissive state before calculation, or have a check performed that makes sure the variable is updated during execution when we expect it to be. This could involve setting it to an invalid state, and then checking at the end of the code to make sure it is not in an invalid state.

For data that is considered safety-critical but may not be updated in a calculation, it and associated variables should be checked with a CRC. For example, let's say there is a test variable that is set to "on" to output data to a maintenance port. A remote tool can set this variable to "on" or "off" as requested. What happens when this volatile memory region becomes corrupted? With no calculation to change it back to the correct value, we could start sending data out of the maintenance port. Again, if this variable is safety-critical in nature, we need to have a check to keep that from happening. Including this variable with others and having a CRC for the set is a good way to see whether this memory has become corrupted from an errant pointer or other situation. Then our program can periodically check the CRCs for these data blocks to know that they are set correctly. Having these CRC calculations on data blocks is, as discussed, especially important for data that is not updated continuously.

Lastly, safety-critical data should be sanity-checked before it is used in calculations throughout the code. This wouldn't include a variable that was just set to one value or another in the previous statements, rather variables that could have influence outside the current function and certainly if it is modified by other threads of execution. For example, we want to execute a section of code every six times a function is called. It is set to a maximum of five or six (depending on decrement logic), and then is decremented when the function is called. If we are executing code that decides whether we should perform our task (value of zero) – what should we also check? Does it make sense to remember the "last" value this variable had to make sure it is different from "current"? It definitely makes sense to make sure the variable is currently set to no higher than six!

A large part of how the volatile data is checked depends on the safety-criticalness of the application. Keep these strategies in mind to lower the chance of dealing with stale, corrupted, or invalid data.

Strategy 12: non-volatile data checking

Non-volatile data is a little easier to check because it isn't supposed to be changing. A useful strategy is to consider having your Makefile calculate a CRC for the program image at build time. If a single CRC for the entire image doesn't provide enough bit error checking for the length of the image, then use multiple CRCs for various sections of the code space. One approach could be to have a CRC cover the first third of the image, another to cover the first two-thirds, and another to cover the whole image. Different variations of this could be used as well.

The primary reason for using multiple CRCs like this is to be able to keep the CRC length the same as the atomic size of the processing unit. This will help speed CRC processing.

The safety case will drive how often the image is checked. Inputs to the safety case include the MTBF data for the hardware involved, how often the system is executing, and the safety-criticality of the code on that single processor itself. If the image checking is assigned to the lowest-priority task (which is typical) then there should be a check at a higher priority to make sure that it is able to run, and that it completes in the time expected.

Another point to the non-volatile data checking is to check the image before running it. Some kind of bootloader or initial program function should check the CRCs upon initialization, and only run the image if the integrity is verified.

Strategy 13: make sure the entire system can run

For a safety-critical system, it may not make sense for a real-time operating system to be running. Depending on the safety requirements for the software that is being written, it may be too cost-prohibitive or complicated to include an RTOS where additional complexities are introduced. Maybe a simple scheduler could also meet the needs, with interrupts to handle time-critical data that is coming in or out. Regardless of what tasking type of system is being used, the system needs to be checked to make sure everything is running correctly.

For a task-based RTOS-type system, this involves making sure that all of the tasks are being allowed to run. It is straightforward to have a high-priority task make sure the lowest-priority task is running. It gets a little more difficult to make sure that all the tasks in the system are running correctly, have enough time to run, and are not hung and doing something unexpectedly. More run-type checking will need to be performed with tasks that have safety-critical code within them. Tasks that contain code that is not safety-critical or part of the safety case probably don't need as much checking,

For a simple scheduler system, where the code runs in a constant loop with some sort of delay at the end of the loop waiting for the frame time to end, checking whether everything was able to run is a little easier. If function pointers (with "const" qualifiers for safety-critical systems) are used, then the checking does become a little more difficult. Since this type of software architecture can get held up at a code location in the main loop forever, it is important to have a periodic interrupt check to make sure that the main code can run.

For both types of systems, it is always good to have an external watchdog circuit that can reset the system (or take other action) if the code appears to quit running altogether.

Another aspect of execution is making sure that the timing you expect is actually real or not. In other words, if you are running an important sequence of code and it needs to run every 10 ms, how do you know it is actually 10 ms, plus/minus some margin? For this type of case it is a good idea to have an external timing circuit that provides a reference that can be checked. A waveform that is an input to your processor could be checked to make sure there is a match. For instance, if you have a simple scheduler that runs every 10 ms, you could have a signal with a period of 10 ms. A mathematical calculation can be done, based on the acceptable margin, of how many "low" or "high" are read in a row at the start of the loop for it to be "accurate enough". When the input is read, it should be either low or high for a number of consecutive samples, and then could shift to the other value for a consecutive number of samples. Any condition where the input changes more often than our consecutive samples could constitute a case where a small time shift is required because the clock input is synchronized with our loop timing.

If timing accuracy has some flexibility, using an output at the start of the main loop to charge an RC circuit could also be used. Based on tolerances and accuracy, if it isn't recharged through the output then an input could be latched showing time expiration, similar to an external watchdog circuit without the reset factor.

Any of these or other methods could be used. But checking to make sure all the code is able to run, and that its execution rate matches what is required, is important.

Strategy 14: remove "dead" code

Another strategy is to remove any code and/or functions that are not currently being called by the system. The reason for this is to ensure that these functions cannot start executing accidentally; they are not covered by testing that is being done so it could certainly lead to unexpected results!

The easiest way to remove "dead code" that is not currently executed is to put conditional compiles around the block of code. It is possible there is special debug or unit test code that you want to include for internal builds, but you never intend this code to be released in the final product. Consider the following block of code:

```
#if defined (LOGDEBUG)

   index = 20;

   LOG_Data_Set( *local_data, sizeof( data_set_t ));

#endif
```

This code block is created whenever a debug version is created, where the conditional definition "LOGDEBUG" is defined at build time. However, a situation could arise where a devloper defines this elsewhere for another purpose, and then this code gets included unexpectedly! In situations where there are multiple conditional compile situations associated with internal releases, consider doing something like the following code block:

```
#if defined (LOGDEBUG)
#if !defined(DEBUG)

   neverCompile

#else

   index = 20;

   LOG_Data_Set( *local_data, sizeof( data_set_t ));

#endif
#endif
```

This block could help when multiple conditional compiles may exist for different features. If "LOGDEBUG" gets defined, and it is not part of an overall "DEBUG" build, then there will be a compiler error when this gets compiled. It is a good way to make sure that code segments are not ending up in the final deliverable – as long as "DEBUG" is never allowed to be defined in external-release software deliverables. This is an excellent way to add extra protection to conditional compiles.

Strategy 15: fill unused memory

For nonvolatile memory that contains the program code, filling unused memory with meaningful data is a good idea. One older processor family decided to have the machine opcode "0xFF" to equate to a "no operation" instruction, where it would use a clock cycle then go on to execute the next instruction! Even for any processor architecture, it is good to protect yourself in case there is an unexpected condition where the program counter gets set to an invalid address.

When the program image is built and linked, it is a good strategy to fill the memory with instructions that cause the processor to reset. There are opcodes that can be used to cause an illegal or undefined interrupt, so that the interrupt routine gets it and does a reset because the unexpected interrupt has code that executes this. Or you could also use instructions that do a software reset, depending on the processor core. Executing in invalid locations isn't a good situation – so for your safety case, determine the best course of action!

Strategy 16: static code analysis

The last strategy to use with safety-critical code development is to run a static code analyzer when the code is compiled. Many different static code analysis packages exist for C and C++, and can also conform to published standards such as MISRA C (discussed in Strategy 2 in this section). With whatever checking that is done as part of static code analysis, there shouldn't be any warnings when the analysis is complete.

Static code checkers typically include a way to "ignore" certain warnings in the code. Since many checks that are done can be considered "optional" or "good practice", there may be instances when the code that is written is really intended to be the way it is, and fixing it to match the checking standard is not optimum. For these situations, it is important to document in the code exactly why you are doing it the way you are doing it, and then include the appropriate "ignore" directive immediately preceding the offending line of code.

Reference

[1] J. Ray, P. Koopman, Efficient high hamming distance CRCs for embedded applications, DSN06 June (2006) <http://www.ece.cmu.edu/~koopman/roses/dsn04/koopman04_crc_poly_embedded.pdf>.

CHAPTER 19

Intellectual Property

Pete Wilson

Chapter Outline

Background

Intellectual property normally means one of two things – the patents or other legal protections you (we use "you" to stand for you personally or your company) have accumulated to protect your inventions, or the inventions and designs themselves. So we may talk about "licensing one's intellectual property", and mean either selling a license to

Software Engineering for Embedded Systems.
DOI: http://dx.doi.org/10.1016/B978-0-12-415917-4.00019-0
© 2013 Elsevier Inc. All rights reserved.

someone to make use of your patented ideas, or selling a license to build, distribute or use a product, as ARM does with its processor and other designs or a tools company like Green Hills does with its compiler and OS products.

In this chapter, we will be concentrating more on the first meaning – dealing with the legal protections around your work – and we will be covering the basics in two major sections, one covering the issues surrounding what you need to do to be sure that you actually do own that software that you wrote or bought, what you need to do when selling it or licensing it to others, including the role of "open software"; and the other covering the various protections you can obtain for your software and any valuable inventions in it.

Before proceeding, a word of caution. The law surrounding intellectual property rights is complex and confusing. As a result, it is simply impossible to provide a comprehensive description of what the issues are, what the law allows or requires, and what you should do. The best we can do in the limited space available is to provide backdrop information which should let you understand the key elements of the key issues; for real guidance you will need to seek legal advice.

In the sections on protection issues, we'll cover the basic protection mechanisms – the use of copyright, obtaining patents, publishing, and maintaining the work as a trade secret (we will not consider trademarks). These various mechanisms have differing costs and provide different protections for different things. We'll cover copyright and patents first, with the same basic organization for each:

Copyright Issues

- What's copyright, and what does it protect?
- How do you obtain copyright for your works?
- How can you detect others' misuse of your software?
- How can you protect yourself from allegations of copyright infringement?

Patent Issues

- What's a patent, and what does it protect?
- How do you decide what to patent?
- How do you obtain a patent?
- How can you detect others' misuse of your software?
- How can you protect yourself from allegations of patent infringement?
- Licensing your patents.

And then we'll discuss why you might choose to publish or keep the work as a trade secret.

Finally we'll end with a word of caution, which we will provide here as well. The law (and patents, and articles, and specifications ...) is not a formal system. Its rules are not provable, and the terms used in the rules do not have unquestionably correct single interpretations. And so interpreting the law is, in fact, a matter of (informed) opinion; if this weren't the case, there'd be no need for a court to decide (for example) whether or not a specific product infringed a specific claim in a patent. Dealing with this uncertainty will generally mean spending money on legal advice; it's a good idea to identify appropriate resources before you have need of them.

Is that software yours?

Obtaining software

As a company whose revenues depend at least partly on your software (maybe, like a development system company, you also sell some hardware; or, like a consultancy, perhaps you sell advice) it could be a most unwelcome shock to discover that the software that you thought you'd developed (or bought/licensed) actually belongs to someone else, and they want it back, along with a substantial sum of money and the opportunity to spend even more in court on lawyers if you don't agree to their terms.

How can this happen?

Pretty simple: currently, the law specifies as a basic, default case that the copyright in a work resides with the author; not, for example, with the person who paid for the work to be done.

Here's one scenario: imagine a lone software genius, slaving late into the night on some hoped-to-be valuable software. After the usual pain and agony, it works. It's so good that he decides to form a company, maybe with some friends. The company somehow monetizes the software – embedded in ROM, sold/licensed as a toolkit, whatever – and does so successfully. However, despite the company having been formed by the author, the company is a separate legal entity from the author. In the absence of an appropriate contract between company and individual, the copyright stays with the author. If, later, there's a boardroom dust-up and the author leaves with bad feelings all round, he might decide to assert his rights and require that the company stop monetizing the software and provide him with a hefty sum for unlicensed prior use.

And he'd likely win, because he owns the copyright in the work.

So when your company uses software written by anyone other than a full-time employee, you must make sure that there's a contract in place which ensures that all necessary rights are transferred. Further, the law requires that the contract be a clear, written contract. Emails, twitters, oral agreements that are recorded etc. don't count as first-class evidence of such a contract. The folk with whom you need such a contract include independent contractors, companies writing custom software for you which employ independent contractors to do the work, and companies selling you software. When you deal with works created by a team of independents, all contributing to the work, you'll need a contract with all of them. And of course when getting software from another company, you will want to know that they have the rights which they wish to license or transfer to you. You should expect to use a "Work for Hire" contract; this specifies that the work done by the employee or contractor is yours, not theirs. Wikipedia provides some helpful insights: http://en.wikipedia.org/wiki/Work_for_hire.

While we cannot offer legal advice, you may find perusing the web for some model contracts helpful; one example is here: http://www.rocketlawyer.com/document/confidential-information-and-invention-assignment-agreement.rl.

As ever, for legal advice, contact a competent lawyer.

Understand that your goals and view of what is good may clash with the vendor's views: for example, when you're dealing with a situation in which an independent contractor has been working for years on a tool (like a compiler), and has refined the internal mechanisms and the ability to retarget source language, assembler syntax and target machine semantics with little work on his part, he will be loath to give you complete rights to the work – because he needs it to continue earning. It's therefore very important that the contract's terms are clear, and provide both sides with what they need.

Copyright protection

Copyright is a specific protection for specific classes of created works:

> *§102 · Subject matter of copyright: In general*
>
> *a. Copyright protection subsists, in accordance with this title, in original works of authorship fixed in any tangible medium of expression, now known or later developed, from which they can be perceived, reproduced, or otherwise communicated, either directly or with the aid of a machine or device. Works of authorship include the following categories:*
>   1. *literary works;*
>   2. *musical works, including any accompanying words;*
>   3. *dramatic works, including any accompanying music;*
>   4. *pantomimes and choreographic works;*
>   5. *pictorial, graphic, and sculptural works;*
>   6. *motion pictures and other audiovisual works;*
>   7. *sound recordings; and*
>   8. *architectural works.*
>
> *b. In no case does copyright protection for an original work of authorship extend to any idea, procedure, process, system, method of operation, concept, principle, or*

discovery, regardless of the form in which it is described, explained, illustrated, or embodied in such work.

And in this context, a "literary work" is defined as:

"Literary works" are works, other than audiovisual works, expressed in words, numbers, or other verbal or numerical symbols or indicia, regardless of the nature of the material objects, such as books, periodicals, manuscripts, phono records, film, tapes, disks, or cards, in which they are embodied.

Thus, software is a literary work.

It is worth understanding the paragraph labeled (b): the protection offered by copyright is for the form of the work, not its meaning. Copyright protection will protect the text of the source of your software, but will not protect any inventions in the software (or the rest of the system – Verilog is a programming language, and thus RTL designs in Verilog can have the same protections as cunning user interfaces or RTOSes written in C). The compiled form of your work is representable in numbers stored on some media, and so it, too, is protectable through copyright.

So if you own the copyright of a literary work, what can you do? You have the right to:

1. reproduce the copyrighted work in copies or phono records;
2. prepare derivative works based upon the copyrighted work;
3. distribute copies or phono records of the copyrighted work to the public by sale or other transfer of ownership, or by rental, lease, or lending.

So as copyright owner you can sell, license, rent, lease, etc., the copyrighted software to anyone you choose; you can make as many copies as you like; and you can prepare derivative works – versions based on but different from the original. And unless you have a signed written contract which gives you specific rights, without owning the copyright you can't do any of these things without infringing.

For light reading, consider going to http://copyright.gov/title17/ for the official posting of all relevant copyright law, including the excerpts above.

Getting copyright

The moment a work is "written down" – stored in tangible form, such as in a file saved from your favorite text editor – you as the author automatically own the copyright in it provided that it is a work containing some "originality". You can't copyright-protect Shakespeare through copy-and-paste into a new file – your work must be differentiable from similar works. The degree to which it must be different and what constitutes originality are likely to become components of discussion when there is any dissent about copyright of a work, and tend to differ between countries.

However, if you discover that someone else appears to be infringing your copyright rights, you may need to sue them. For you to be able to do that (in the USA), you need to have registered your work. If you do this within three months of the original publication of the work, or before any infringement, you can sue for statutory damages and attorney's fees. If you register late, you can only sue for actual damages. Registering your work is fairly straightforward, does not involve the need for legal representation, and isn't very expensive. The process is explained here: http://www.copyright.gov/help/faq/faq-register.html.

Copyright, in the USA, lasts for 70 years after the death of the author.

Patents

Unlike copyright, which protects the outward form or expression of a work, a patent protects an invention. Patents are much more expensive to obtain than copyright in time and money; however, they can be (and are) used to increase the revenues a company can make from its creations.

What is a patent?

The best description is from the US Patent Office, at http://www.uspto.gov/patents/resources/general_info_concerning_patents.jsp:

> *A patent for an invention is the grant of a property right to the inventor, issued by the United States Patent and Trademark Office. Generally, the term of a new patent is 20 years from the date on which the application for the patent was filed in the United States or, in special cases, from the date an earlier related application was filed, subject to the payment of maintenance fees. U.S. patent grants are effective only within the United States, U.S. territories, and U.S. possessions. Under certain circumstances, patent term extensions or adjustments may be available.*
> *The right conferred by the patent grant is, in the language of the statute and of the grant itself, "the right to exclude others from making, using, offering for sale, or selling" the invention in the United States or "importing" the invention into the United States. What is granted is not the right to make, use, offer for sale, sell or import, but the right to exclude others from making, using, offering for sale, selling or importing the invention. Once a patent is issued, the patentee must enforce the patent without aid of the USPTO.*
> *There are three types of patents:*
>
> 1. ***Utility patents*** *may be granted to anyone who invents or discovers any new and useful process, machine, article of manufacture, or composition of matter, or any new and useful improvement thereof;*

2. ***Design patents*** *may be granted to anyone who invents a new, original, and ornamental design for an article of manufacture; and*
3. ***Plant patents*** *may be granted to anyone who invents or discovers and asexually reproduces any distinct and new variety of plant.*

In this discussion, we cover just utility patents. What can be patented? Again, the US PTO has information:

> *In the language of the statute, any person who "invents or discovers any new and useful process, machine, manufacture, or composition of matter, or any new and useful improvement thereof, may obtain a patent," subject to the conditions and requirements of the law. The word "process" is defined by law as a process, act or method, and primarily includes industrial or technical processes. The term "machine" used in the statute needs no explanation. The term "manufacture" refers to articles that are made, and includes all manufactured articles. The term "composition of matter" relates to chemical compositions and may include mixtures of ingredients as well as new chemical compounds. These classes of subject matter taken together include practically everything that is made by man and the processes for making the products.*
>
> . . ..
>
> *Interpretations of the statute by the courts have defined the limits of the field of subject matter that can be patented, thus it has been held that the laws of nature, physical phenomena, and abstract ideas are not patentable subject matter.*

So what can't get patented? An abstract idea cannot; nor can anything already known and described in public; nor can anything obvious to one skilled in the field. In more detail:

> *In order for an invention to be patentable it must be new as defined in the patent law, which provides that an invention cannot be patented if: "(a) the invention was known or used by others in this country, or patented or described in a printed publication in this or a foreign country, before the invention thereof by the applicant for patent," or "(b) the invention was patented or described in a printed publication in this or a foreign country or in public use or on sale in this country more than one year prior to the application for patent in the United States . . ."*
>
> *If the invention has been described in a printed publication anywhere in the world, or if it was known or used by others in this country before the date that the applicant made his/her invention, a patent cannot be obtained. If the invention has been described in a printed publication anywhere, or has been in public use or on sale in this country more than one year before the date on which an application for patent is filed in this country, a patent cannot be obtained. In this connection it is immaterial when the invention was made, or whether the printed publication or public use was by the inventor himself/herself or by someone else. If the inventor describes the invention in a printed publication or uses the invention publicly, or places it on sale, he/she must apply for a patent before one year has gone by, otherwise any right to a patent will be lost. The inventor must file*

on the date of public use or disclosure, however, in order to preserve patent rights in many foreign countries.

Even if the subject matter sought to be patented is not exactly shown by the prior art, and involves one or more differences over the most nearly similar thing already known, a patent may still be refused if the differences would be obvious. The subject matter sought to be patented must be sufficiently different from what has been used or described before that it may be said to be nonobvious to a person having ordinary skill in the area of technology related to the invention. For example, the substitution of one color for another, or changes in size, are ordinarily not patentable.

Once upon a time, you could patent something whose single point of uniqueness was essentially that it hadn't been patented before. For example, you could get a patent for integrating into a single chip functions which had previously been implemented only in separate chips. This sort of "combination" patent (combining two known things to provide an obvious combo) is essentially unpatentable nowadays.

Now, you can combine stuff, but only if doing so requires an inventive step – for example, you might write a disclosure for some cunning method of integrating mechanical stepper motors onto an ordinary CMOS chip to do something which a microcomputer and a stepper could do before. If such a thing were possible, then it would require a definite inventive step – implementing a stepper motor on a CMOS chip sounds rather difficult, and describing how to do that would indeed probably be inventive.

If the issue comes before a court, it may use the seven "Graham Factors" in deciding whether or not an claimed invention is sufficiently non-obvious. From http://en.wikipedia.org/wiki/Inventive_step_and_non-obviousness:

Graham factors

The factors a court will look at when determining obviousness in the United States were outlined by the Supreme Court in Graham et al. v. John Deere Co. of Kansas City et al., *383 U.S. 1 (1966) and are commonly referred to as the "Graham factors". The court held that obviousness should be determined by looking at*

1. *the scope and content of the prior art;*
2. *the level of ordinary skill in the art;*
3. *the differences between the claimed invention and the prior art; and*
4. *objective evidence of nonobviousness.*

In addition, the court outlined examples of factors that show "objective evidence of non-obviousness". They are:

1. *commercial success;*
2. *long-felt but unsolved needs; and*
3. *failure of others.*

> *Other courts have considered additional factors as well. See* Environmental Designs, Ltd. v. Union Oil Co. of Cal., *713 F.2d 693, 697–98, 218 USPQ 865, 869 (Fed. Cir. 1983) (considering skepticism or disbelief before the invention as an indicator of nonobviousness);* Allen Archery, Inc. v. Browning Mfg. Co., *819 F.2d 1087, 1092, 2 USPQ2d 1490, 1493 (Fed. Cir. 1987) (considering copying, praise, unexpected results, and industry acceptance as indicators of nonobviousness);* Diversitech Corp. v. Century Steps, Inc., *850 F.2d 675, 679, 7 USPQ2d 1315, 1319 (Fed. Cir. 1988) (considering copying as an indicator of nonobviousness).*"

Why do patents exist?

Monopolies are generally regarded as A Very Bad Thing. A patent seems to grant a monopoly for an extended period. So why do patents exist?

The simple answer is that society as a whole is improved when things are better. And things can get better through improvements in known stuff, and the creation of entirely new stuff. If a new way of doing something becomes widely known, then the improved way (which reduces costs, improves efficiency, or increases performance) benefits society as a whole. Thus, there's an interest for government to encourage such improvements and inventions.

But if anybody can copy a neat new idea, then the inventor is likely to get zilch for his or her efforts. Thus, there's a tension between publishing for the betterment of the common weal, and the desire to benefit from one's own creativity and hard work.

Government solves this problem with the concept of a patent; a patent allows you to describe your invention in sufficient detail that anyone competent can recreate and reproduce it, but registers with the government an unarguable description of your invention and the date at which the government was informed of your invention.

And then, once you have a patent granted for your invention, the government is saying that it has performed due diligence, and indeed, as far as can be ascertained, you are indeed the inventor of this invention, which is novel, and useful, and not obvious; and that you have a monopoly right to practice that invention. And nobody else has such a right unless they have your permission.

Alongside that is the expectation that you will grant others the right to also practice that invention, in return for some reasonable (generally financial) arrangement.

In this way, you get to invent; society gets to have many people build or practice your invention; and you get rewarded directly (if you choose to build the invention yourself) or indirectly (as others pay you license fees to build or practice what you invented).

Deciding what to patent

Suppose you're in the embedded system business, and you have a neat new control algorithm which is implemented through the use of some cunning software, a synthesizable licensed processor core and some hardware, perhaps implemented in an FPGA. You're an expert in the domain, and to your knowledge nobody has done anything like this before – your system settles to within 0.1% of a required command value ten times quicker than anything done before, and uses fewer transistors and lines of code.

What, if anything, should you patent?

First, you probably cannot patent the algorithm per se. It's an abstract idea. You probably can patent a computer system which executes software which implements the algorithm, and hardware which implements it without a processor, and a combo system which splits the work, provided that there's sufficient novelty and non-obviousness in the hardware.

But should you patent it?

If you do, you will be publishing exactly how to implement your breakthrough approach and implementation. This will cost you money; preparing the invention for patenting with an outside patent attorney isn't free – you should probably budget around $10,000–$100,000 (the lower figure is for a straightforward patent in the USA only; the larger figure for worldwide rights) of direct cost, and an unknown amount of time for the inventor to describe the invention to the attorney and to assist in arguing with the Patent Office when they throw prior art at you. It seems that an average invention for an average patent attorney requires about 20–25 hours of lawyer billable time.

Then – if the patent is granted, which might take several years – you have to keep the patent alive through its nominal 20-year life with scheduled "maintenance fees". Overall, it might cost about $150,000 or so through the life of the patent, done worldwide.

The US PTO publishes a list of its fees at http://www.uspto.gov/web/offices/ac/qs/ope/fee092611.htm. Smaller companies get a price cut, to approximately 50% of the price paid by large entities (such scaling is rarely observed by patent lawyers).

If you do successfully patent the invention, you will generally need to be prepared to act when you discover someone is infringing the patent. How to discover this, and the recourse open to you, is discussed later. However, if you go to court, you need to budget a million or two to cover costs. This can be very burdensome for smaller companies.

You might file patents on your inventions with a completely different aim in mind – to make your company more valuable in the eyes of a (presumably larger) possible purchaser. We'll discuss later how to make money from your inventions through a licensing strategy.

So – what should you patent? It all depends on what you're trying to do. That is, this is a business decision, not a technical one. Factors to consider in making the decision can include the simple one of whether you could afford to defend the patent – to sue someone you found infringing; or would doing so run a high risk of putting you out of business?

Applying for a patent

How do you apply for a patent?

The crudest answer is "follow the instructions at http://www.uspto.gov/patents/resources/types/utility.jsp".

The practical answer is "go to a patent lawyer or patent agent". In the USA, both are recognized as people competent to represent a third party in applying for a patent, the difference being that a patent agent isn't qualified as a lawyer, while the patent attorney is. Wikipedia has a discussion: http://en.wikipedia.org/wiki/Patent_attorney.

What's in a patent?

A granted patent is published in a specific format, well-structured enough that you can parse at least the textual forms of a patent (that is, just the text, no diagrams or formatting; you can obtain text-only versions of published patents by subscribing to services such as Micropatent and Innography, or by obtaining the pdfs from some source (like Google Patents) and running a tool such as Adobe Acrobat or other OCR software to extract the text) to extract the sections, claims etc. without too much trouble.

There are many sections in a US patent. In considering the work needed to prepare an invention for a patent application, there are perhaps three key areas:

- the prior art
- the specification
  - the drawings
  - the explanation
- the claims
  - the claims *are* the invention; the earlier material is just necessary backdrop.

If you're using a patent attorney to prepare your application, you won't need to pay any attention to any other details.

Patent prior art section

You have a duty to bring to the Patent Examiner's attention any relevant prior art that you're aware of. "Prior art" is a technical term – it means "anything related, relevant and similar". The prior art will generally be a list of patents and published papers or books or dissertations which touch on the subject of your invention. You are not required to do an exhaustive search, but it is good practice to ensure that you disclose sources that anyone competent and practicing in the field of your invention should be expected to know.

If you're aware of art which casts a severe shadow across the patentability of your invention, and it's material that folk in the field would be expected to be aware of, and you don't disclose it, and your patent is granted, and someone later finds that publication, you may have to deal with the situation of having been seen to, in essence, defraud the US PTO, which may not be a happy place to be. Plus, your patent will be invalid, and you will have wasted your time and money.

The specification

A patent gives you a monopoly to practice an invention, in exchange for you publishing such a detailed and useful description of how and why your invention works that anyone else competent in the relevant field can replicate the invention. Of course, they are not allowed to do so unless you agree to it, but the requirement that you explain in sufficient detail remains.

Thus, you have to be able to explain what your invention is. Generally, it is helpful to explain what problem or issue your invention solves that was done not at all, or badly, or unacceptably, or inefficiently, beforehand, and to explain how those undesirable prior solutions worked.

Then you get to sketch out at a high level what your invention does.

Then you get into the detail of your invention, comprising drawings and text.

Drawings

You are required to provide diagrams to explain your invention, and they are required to be drawn and labeled in a particular style. Depending on your invention, the drawings might be circuit schematics, silicon process cross-sections, mechanical drawings, tables, flow diagrams ... or any appropriate mix. The drawings must show every feature that is mentioned in a claim. The link above describing the requirements for applying for a patent include the rules for drawing, and your patent attorney will be able to ensure that the submitted drawings meet the formal requirements – your role will be to understand the invention well enough that the drawings can be created, probably informally, and then refined through a process generally using patent-skilled draftsmen.

The resulting figures will give a unique reference number to every element needed for the explanation of how the invention works. In the textual portion of the specification, you will be explaining how the thing works with phrases like "the a/d converter 97 samples the input data, bandwidth limited by the low-pass filter 73 to a maximum of 45 kHz, and provides the digitized results as a serial stream of 17 bit twos-complement values on conductor 56".

Luckily, given a clear description of the invention, the drawings, the numbering, and the explanations will all be written by your patent attorney.

Unluckily, you will need to wade through a (possibly surprising) number of drafts, checking that these laborious descriptions are, in fact, correct.

Specification text

The text of the specification is what explains how your invention works. It (and the drawings) must contain "support" for everything in your claims.

If one of your claims is "In a system including a processor and an A/D converter, a method of reducing 17-bit samples to 5 bits without any loss of accuracy using a down converter comprising x, y and z", you'd better have a description of what a down-converter is and what you have to do to convert 17-bit samples to 5-bit without any loss of accuracy.

Your attorney (and you) are going to want the broadest possible scope for your claims. So when you're describing the invention, think about how you can generalize the thing. It's arguably interesting that you can get a Z80 and a 5-bit A/D to perform magic, but it would be more valuable if what you describe applied to any processor (or none) and any sort of A/D converter. Your attorney will write boilerplate generalizations, but if you can describe a few major variants (especially with an eye to the future unrolling of various versions of Moore's law) then your broader claims will likely have a firmer base. That said, don't try to describe every possible combination and future trend – it'll cost more, and not be any more valuable.

The claims

The specification teaches the world how your invention works in sufficient detail that someone who understands the field can replicate your work. However, the protected invention is what is covered by the claims – nothing more, and nothing less.

It is in the construction of the claims that the value of a good patent attorney will be apparent.

There are two sorts of claims:

- an independent claim
- a dependent claim.

An independent claim is one that stands by itself; generally, it will claim some particular aspect of the invention. It might have language like this (taken from US patent US6754752):

1. *A multi-processing system comprising:*
   - *two or more groups of processing elements, each processing element of each group being coupled by an interconnect and each processing element of each*

group communicating information in accordance with a single communications protocol;

- *a memory contained within each of the processing elements, wherein memory coherency, if established in any one of the two or more groups, is maintained independently within each group, each processing element communicating information within itself using a first transaction format comprising a transaction type field and a target address field;*
- *and system interface circuitry contained within each of the processing elements, the system interface circuitry creating a second transaction format for communication external to a processing element, the second transaction format having more information fields than the first transaction format, the second transaction format comprising a source address field and a target address field.*

An independent claim has a formal structure. The *preamble* is the first section ("1. A multi-processing system comprising:"), setting context (here, the claim is about a multiprocessing system). If anything mentioned in the preamble is mentioned again in the claim, then the fact that the preamble says what it's about is important; if not mentioned again, then the subject area should be looked upon as guidance rather than strict limitation.

The *elements* of the claim are the things mentioned in the rest of the claim. The idea is to make these as general as possible without straying unreasonably from what you actually described in the specification. Anything which infringes the claim must have all the elements described in the claim, operating or connected or whatever as the claim describes.

As always, there are linguistic traps. You'll notice that this claim uses the phrase "coupled" ("*each processing element of each group being* ***coupled*** *by an interconnect*") rather than (e.g.) "connected". A reasonable interpretation of "connected" is "there is a wire or other signal-carrying conduit directly connecting the processing elements". In the real world, you may have bus bridges and the like interposed between the processing elements; or maybe even just drivers and receivers on the edge of a chip to carry the signal from a processing element to the edge of the chip and thence to another chip. So "coupled" would be a better word; a reasonable interpretation is that when A is coupled to B, stuff can get from A to B, but possibly via other agents and not necessarily directly. In general, you want to use terms that are as broad as possible; if you say, "and these two items are glued together" then only glue is covered. You want to say, "glued together or adhered together using any method of adhesion".

A dependent claim is a refinement of an independent claim, thereby 'narrowing' it – that is, making the dependent claim less broad and more limited. An example from the same patent is:

2. *The multi-processing system of claim 1 wherein the interconnect further comprises logic circuitry capable of identifying a group and a selected processing system.*

A dependent claim starts by mentioning a component of a prior claim – dependent or independent – and provides some more detail about what specifically is protected. Here, Claim 2 refines the complete system claimed in Claim 1 by specifying a detail that the interconnect has to have – it has circuitry which can identify a group (etc.).

In practice, you attempt to draft the independent claims as broadly as is reasonable, and then (just in case it turns out that the claim is too broad, and thus invalid due perhaps to prior art being discovered later) you provide the narrower dependent claims as backup.

In addition to there being two sorts of claims, there are two important types of claims:

- an apparatus claim
- a method claim.

An apparatus claim is like Claims 1 and 2 above – it describes an actual piece of equipment. A method claim is, as it suggests, a claim which describes a specific method for achieving something. Often as not, you will want a method claim as well as an apparatus claim – indeed, your patent might well cover similar aspects of the invention from the two angles of an apparatus and a method. However, a method claim and an apparatus claim, even covering the same aspect of the invention, need to be separate. Each claim, to be valid, has to be distinguishable from every other claim. Here's an example, from the same patent, of a method claim:

5. *A method for selectively implementing memory coherency, comprising:*

   – *creating a multi-processing system by providing two or more groups of processing elements, each processing element communicating information within itself using a first transaction format comprising a transaction type field and a target address field and forming a second transaction format for communication external to each processing element, the second transaction format comprising more fields than the first transaction format and designating where the output transaction is to be routed, a type of operation the output transaction implements and whether or not memory coherency is to be maintained by a destination processing element;*
   – *coupling each of the processing elements of each group by an interconnect which communicates information among all processing elements of the two or more groups of processing elements by using a single communications protocol;*
   – *providing a memory within each of the processing elements; and selectively determining which, if any of the two or more groups of processing elements will have coherent memory, wherein memory coherency, if established in any one of the two or more groups, is maintained independently within each group.*

You only need to know this stuff to understand what's going on; your lawyer will know all these things in detail.

Means plus function claims

Once upon a time, you could describe an invention in reasonable detail, and then write claims which, rather than talking about a specific mechanism, invoked a "means for" doing something, without specifying anything further, the support for this being that you'd described a couple of ways of getting something done.

One day, the world woke up to the fact that while you'd *described* just one or two ways of getting something done, your claim covered *every* way of doing it. It's generally considered really bad form to let anyone patent every single way of doing something, because that would stifle all innovation in that field. So nowadays, patents which use language like "means for" are still allowed; but the only means covered by your claims are those explicitly described and explained ("taught") in the specification.

Advice

So what to do to prepare for patenting?

Probably the simplest advice is – assume you're writing an article describing (in complete detail – you're proud of it!) your invention for the technical trade press – perhaps five to ten pages plus helpful diagrams. Think about how future changes in technology and usage patterns might play out, and how you'd take advantage of them in your invention.

Write that article, and use it to brief the attorney. (Later, when so advised by your attorney, you can edit that draft and actually get it published).

If you have a technical manual describing how the invention works (not how to use it), then you can consider using that as the basis for the specification. The upside is that you already had to write it; the downside is that it's probably too long (longer specifications cost more), and may not be written in good patentese.

Licensing patents

If you patent aspects of your inventions, you may have had to spend quite a bit of money. Hopefully, as a real engineer, you'll want to make money by building products incorporating your invention, sell them at a profit, and get rich directly.

But selling stuff involves production, distribution, education, support and more. Other folk may be better at these things than you, and so you might want to have someone else implement and sell the products.

To do this, you'll need to enter a contractual arrangement with a putative vendor, teach them how to build the product, and license them to build and sell the thing. That license should be for both the product design and the patents necessary to build the products.

But even if you choose to build, sell and support your own product yourself, there may be an attraction to making more money from the invention per se, rather than any products.

To do this, you license just the patent(s) to other companies. This, however, is not a process like licensing the design, or the source code. This will generally occur when you discover (just how, see later) that another company is shipping product which infringes (in your opinion) one or more claims of one or more of your patents. Thus, you will be dealing with an unwilling customer – you'll need to convince the lucky "customer" that indeed they do infringe, and that indeed you do have the resources and will to take the dispute as far as necessary. It helps to have a track record of having solid patents, of providing good evidence of real infringement, and of having gone to court. And, ideally, have won. And you can expect that if you accuse company X of infringing your patent, they'll probably accuse you of infringing several of theirs.

The downside is that you have to be prepared to go to litigation, and that can be expensive, and can take a very long time to be resolved. This is not the place to get into details about where to sue whom when – again, legal advice is necessary.

You can sidestep this sort of problem by finding someone else who will act as the attack dog. "Non-practicing entities" – companies whose business is licensing patents which, in general, they have acquired, and who do not make anything nor sell anything else – make money by asserting patents against companies. Since the NPE doesn't actually make anything, they're more or less waterproof – there is (at time of writing) essentially no defense against an NPE. NPEs are generally called "trolls" in the patent industry, the image being that of the evil trolls who live under bridges (which they didn't build) demanding tolls off passing travelers who wish to cross the bridge. Thus, handing over your patents to a troll, for the right financial and legal arrangements, can be an attractive route. Under current law. (You would, of course, be sure to get a license for yourself.)

Problems

With every opportunity comes the possibility of problems. Here we look at a few topics which can turn out to be troublesome if you don't handle them correctly.

Open-source software

Once upon a time, one obtained software from a computer systems vendor, a software vendor, a consultant or one's own employees, all of which cost – one way or another – real money. These days, one can acquire open-source software. This approach can provide you with very large amounts of software, all in source code form, from operating systems (like Linux) through tools (like llvm and gcc compiler toolchains) to applications (like Apache). All free!

However, this approach has repercussions, both business and legal. We will not discuss the technical issues (basically, you get to maintain the software, not a vendor).

The legal side can have major repercussions, because, generally, such software comes with a license which can both require you to perform certain actions and forbid you certain actions.

There are many different "open" or "free" licenses; Wikipedia appears to have a useful summary at http://en.wikipedia.org/wiki/Comparison_of_free_software_licenses. Because of the limitations imposed by some of these licenses, it is vital that you understand the license associated with any such software that you'd like to use, and make sure that any limitations are consistent with your business model.

Licensing and selling software

Just as you had to make sure that the providers of any software that you bought or licensed had the right to license or sell the software to you, so do you need to have clear evidence that you have the right to supply "your" software to others. The rules and issues are the same, but having a clear "paper trail" of where the various components of your products came from will make life easier. Plus, it's just good housekeeping.

When setting terms in the license agreements for your software, you may wish to consider including terms which will smooth the way if bad things appear to happen – going to court is very expensive. An example is the disagreement between Express Logic and Green Hills software. It appears that Green Hills became a reseller of Express Logic's ThreadX RTOS, and eventually developed an equivalent, micro Velosity. Claiming that Velosity's APIs were much too close to ThreadX's APIs, Express Logic accused Green Hills of copyright infringement over at least the APIs. The mechanical issues of the disagreement were taken care of fairly expeditiously, because Express Logic had included a requirement for arbitration in its licensing terms. However, the arbitration did not work out the way Express Logic had hoped; for one side of the story, read: http://rtos.com/news/detail/Express_Logic_Clears_the_Air_Regarding_Ruling_on_Copyright_Infringement_Claim_Against_u-velOSity_RTOS/.

When your software is covered by one or more patents, the license to the software needs to consider what rights should be transferred. Presumably, you don't mind your customer making use of your ideas just so long as what's using the ideas is the software you sold him or licensed to him. But you don't want the fact that he has a license to your software and to use it to give him the rights to practice that patent elsewhere.

Getting acquired

A small company may have as its business strategy the goal of being acquired. Any such acquisition, including investments by venture capitalists and others, is likely to involve due diligence on the acquirers' or investors' part to assure themselves that you have clear title to everything you claim as value. Again, a clear paper trail of where everything came from and the associated rights will be invaluable.

Small companies may find that the writings on these subjects at http://www.iplawforstartups.com/ usefully expand on these issues.

Discovering infringement

One day you may discover that someone else appears to be providing software whose functionality appears to be remarkably similar to one of your own products. The two standard bad ways of this occurring are first, when one of your employees or contractors starts working for some other company, and takes with them the design (or even implementation) of your software; and second, when you license your software to another company and they are inspired by it to create an equivalent.

The questions that come to mind immediately are – how do I stop them and how do I recover the value of lost business?

Discovering copyright infringement

Either eventuality requires that you are able to demonstrate to a court that they have copied your work. You may not be able to do this directly, but if you sue the other entity you can do so during "discovery", a phase prior to the actual trial in which you demand that the other entity provides you with all documents and other materiel which meet certain criteria (chosen by you). In this manner you hope to end up with solid evidence of what their software actually is, and how they developed or acquired it. With that evidence in hand, you can look for evidence of copying and plagiarism. However, lawsuits are very expensive, and plowing through megabytes of source code and documentation can be rather expensive too.

But how could you discover infringement, were you to need to? It depends, of course. In truly blatant cases, you might find header files, or technical documentation, freely available on the web and simply looking at them will give you the evidence you need. But in general, you'll probably need a toolset to look for infringement. However, because the infringement of a copyrighted work is not tightly defined, even if you have an investigative tool you cannot be sure that finding similarities will be sufficient grounds to win an assertion of infringement.

There are tools available. As one example, S.A.F.E ("Software Analysis and Forensic Engineering" – http://www.safe-corp.biz/) offers a number of tools. CodeMatch is said to compare your source files with their source files, and look for close matches – even when their code has had (for example) variable and function names systematically changed and the whole thing translated (for example) into Ruby from C. SAFE also offers BitMatch, which is said to do similar comparisons between executable files; binaries may be more easy to find than source. A further related product is their DocMate, which is said to do a similar analysis on documents rather than software.

If you have a lot of time on your hands, or simply have a firm conviction that they have copied your work, you could try something a little simpler – you could try to use a decompiler to convert their binaries back into a human-readable form. However, this is labor-intensive, and the complexities of a language like C++ (recognizing the use of templates is hard) will likely prevent useful reverse-engineering from happening.

These tools probably all work the same way – in essence, they are probably program transformation tools which can be looked at as building an abstract representation of the code they're given (much as gcc, llvm and other compilers create an internal representation of the meaning of the program they're compiling), and then performing all the optimizations they can on that, and then comparing in some useful way the "shapes" of the resulting "my code" and "their code".

For some general discussion on "software forensics", you can Google. One example is Michael Barr's blog, e.g. http://embeddedgurus.com/barr-code/2011/09/firmware-forensics-best-practices-in-embedded-software-source-code-discovery/.

Discovering patent infringement

Discovering patent infringement isn't as simple as discovering copyright infringement – for copyright, showing that large chunks of their software are the same as large chunks of yours will probably suffice. But for a patent, you need in general to discover what their software is doing, not what the source is. You're looking for algorithms and behaviors, not text or images. Thus the task can be more complicated.

Some patents cover a user interface, rather than the complex mechanisms of the software itself. These can be detected if you get a copy of the possibly infringing software and explore the user interface. If your patent attorney wrote the claims sufficiently broadly, and the examiner was asleep at the wheel, you may well find that an apparently innocuous little invention can turn into a large moneymaker, by reading the claims on many other user interfaces of a nature entirely different from the original invention. Indeed, owners of some of these patents have probably already grossly over-broadened what the claims actually mean, and may already have knocked on your door demanding money with menaces for stuff which would look blindingly obvious to practically anyone vaguely cognizant of the art.

For patents which cover the inner workings of software, which will generally involve patents with method claims, the discovery can be done, as with hardware, via two methods.

The simplest method is one based on a standard. If you have a patent whose claims cover some necessary part of a standard, then you can assert with some confidence that anyone who sells a product meeting that standard infringes your patent; this is one of the reasons companies may invest heavily in upcoming technology areas of interest and manage their relationships with the standards bodies very carefully. Often as not, if you are actually a member of a standards body, you must disclose any relevant IP which is necessary to meet the standard, and to agree to license any such patents to others on a Fair, Reasonable and Non-Discriminatory basis – that is, roughly speaking, you won't charge too much money, and all licensees get essentially the same deal, and nobody's blocked from a license.

The other is reverse engineering of one form or another. This is widely practiced for hardware – there are experts who can take apart a chip, layer by layer, imaging each layer and processing the images to recover a complete schematic. Since the "atoms" of logic circuits – gates, multiplexors, adders, multipliers – and of analog circuits – op amps, phase-locked-loops, A/D converters – are generally very, very similar, it's likely that infringement of circuit patents can be discovered by inspection, possibly aided by some tools. Logic circuit patents (such as a new multiplier) could be found equally straightforwardly. Similarly, infringement of many packaging patents can be detected by inspection. Detecting infringement of silicon process patents can be more burdensome.

However, there is not as yet a widely practiced art of software reverse engineering. The problem is that – unlike hardware – there are very many different ways of doing things. Consider that you have a patent which covers manipulating an ordered list. How many data structures have the effect of keeping things ordered? The standard linked lists have that property. Binary trees do. Simple arrays do. You can probably find a sorting algorithm for the elements of a hash table. Now consider what the chunks of code that perform the maintenance of these structures might look like – there again, there are many choices.

Thus, unlike low-level hardware/circuit patents, most software patents have the deep problem of discoverability. Yes, you can get a ROM image or a hard disk, but then, what do you look for? Decompiling and then reading a few million lines of ugly code may not be an effective use of time.

Avoiding copyright infringement

How can you avoid infringing other folks' copyright or their patents? First, let's look at copyright.

It's more complicated than just "being honest"; for example, how many good ways are there to write a C strcmp() function? If the code you're developing does things that have been done many times before, then it's very likely that there will be substantial similarities between your work and others attempting the same task.

Thus there's no silver bullet against the risk of being accused of infringement. However, your key goal should be avoiding infringement itself. This is fairly straightforward in principle – just require, and enforce (perhaps through code reviews) that everybody be honest and not steal; it may well be worth looking at various workflow tools to make following the rules simple; these will provide evidence (if ever needed) that you are creating all the work you claim as your own. If you do not steal, or inappropriately reuse, other people's work, you will be very unlikely to commit "real infringement". (This doesn't mean you'll win in court, of course.)

The situation is complicated by the legal doctrine that while an employee who moves from one employer to another may not take any of his prior employer's property with him to the new job, he is entitled to the lessons and general domain-specific knowledge he has acquired performing that job. And so, as people are good at recognizing and remembering patterns, there is a reasonable probability that an employee in company A who knows how to construct (say) a decent RTOS will likely use the same approach in developing an RTOS for his new employer company B, even if both new employer and new employee have no desire whatsoever to plagiarize. And just like with strcmp(), how many ways are there of organizing doubly linked lists, priority bit-vectors and other basics of a high-performance RTOS?

It is further complicated by the possibility of one of your new employees being subject to some form of non-compete agreement with his or her prior employer. While it seems that such non-compete agreements are not generally favored by the courts, as with any other legal issue, a messy situation can become very expensive to solve. So appropriate due diligence when hiring is important. Some discussion is available at http://otslawyers.com/wp-content/uploads/2011/07/Hiring-an-EE-with-a-noncompete-May-2011-Employment-Law-Institute-OBERMAN-4-20-11-FINAL.pdf.

Thus – you're always at risk.

And so you should prepare, without too much paranoia, for the worst. If you can demonstrate where all your software came from, and how you developed it, or modified the open-source or other acquired software, and how you tracked and cured bugs, and the various versions held in the code repository, and that no employee was ever asked to nor put into a position where he or she would breach any known non-compete or equivalent contract, you have the tools to show that you didn't steal. Luckily, such an approach is software management 101 in any case, and so need not be an extra burden.

Avoiding patent infringement

Unfortunately, avoiding patent infringement is a much stickier task than avoiding copyright infringement. As we've seen, you can avoid copyright infringement by the simple strategy of not copying; however, that's not an approach which can work for patents because there are too many patents for you to track and there are not enough software-skilled patent lawyers to understand the claims of patents as they emerge and to ensure that you never create anything which infringes.

In the real world, you run the risk of really infringing even when you do so completely innocently (by independent re-invention, for example). Further, you run the risk of having an accusation of infringement stick, whether or not you infringe. Patents are a legal battlefield, not a mathematical, or science-based, or engineering battleground. Claim language can be, and routinely is, twisted by accusers to make a case that your product infringes their claim. This is driven in large part by the fact that – because litigating is so expensive, and the outcome so uncertain – it is a rational decision to pay some money to an accuser whether or not you feel you infringe, simply to keep costs predictable and reasonable, and to avoid years of litigation which can consume much too much of your company's energies and time.

Why is this the situation?

There are probably two major components. The first is that patents are written in English (or other natural language), which does not have a formal semantics. That is, it is in general flatly impossible to assign a single, unarguable meaning to a specification or a claim. Thus, what it means is a question of judgment, and judgment varies by time, court, accuser and alleged infringer. To decide whether a product infringes a claim, the court (if you go to litigation, or are taken there) will perform *claim construction* – it will decide what the terms in a claim really mean. You and your opponent will have the chance to advance your own theories about what the various elements mean.

The construction process is so non-deterministic that it is possible for two courts, considering different cases involving the same claims in the same patents, to arrive at different constructions.

The second component is that there is no guideline for setting the damages for infringing a patent. Common sense suggests that the amount paid for a license should be commensurate with the value illicitly added to the product by practicing the invention *sans* license, but this is not a view which is widely espoused. However, there are roughly two million active patents in the USA today. Even narrowing those down to those relevant to your field will leave you with a very large number of patents. The likelihood is that your product (if a relatively complex system) infringes hundreds, if not thousands, of these. Assume that you actually contributed to the design, adding value, then perhaps only 10% or less of the price of the product is "available" to share amongst the hundreds of infringed patents. Thus, the infringement tax for a given patent should be, at most, way down in the noise. In reality, since there are so many patents, the strong likelihood is that each provides only a minor, incremental advantage over not practicing the invention, and so the actual advantage accruing to an alleged infringer per patent is probably a hundred-fold or thousandfold further reduced.

Naturally, this would sharply reduce the amount of money that a troll could make, and thus this approach has not, to date, been pushed front and center.

Bottom line – it's not possible to know whether you infringe or not, and to discover it is a long-drawn-out, expensive process which can put you out of business.

However, in the real world, despite the possible nightmare scenarios, most companies, most of the time, continue to trade without much interference from intellectual property issues.

CHAPTER 20

Managing Embedded Software Development

Whitson G Waldo III

Chapter Outline

Successful semiconductor suppliers increasingly are providing system solutions to their customers and not just hardware components. The provision of software with hardware for a system solution can differentiate one company among other competitors. It can mean faster time to market with lower development costs for your customer. Their success translates into your success.

The importance of software for fully exploiting hardware capabilities and delivering optimized system performance continues to climb over time. In lockstep, quality is an increasing concern. Quality may be defined either as conformance to the product

Software Engineering for Embedded Systems.
DOI: http://dx.doi.org/10.1016/B978-0-12-415917-4.00020-7
© 2013 Elsevier Inc. All rights reserved.

specifications or as meeting customer needs and expectations. Quality factors include features, performance, and defect levels. Acceptable defect levels typically are considered by customers to be a necessary but insufficient criterion for quality. Under this assumption, the quality emphasis may be correlated more with customer use cases, what the product can and can't do, and how the system performs rather than with defect counts or defect rates per se.

Companies developing software implement quality systems to improve their processes and their products. Examples of these systems include Six Sigma®, ISO9000/ISO9001, and CMMI®. Six Sigma uses statistical methods to solve problems and optimize solutions. At its simplest, ISO9000 may be understood to be a quality system requiring documentation of business practices and then conformance in practice to what was documented. CMMI is a different type of quality system and lends itself well to continuous improvement activities. The CMMI quality system will be studied further in this chapter.

Software is written for many different purposes. The OSI model is one way of explaining the complex composition of software by defining layers, the responsibility of these different layers, and their interactions. The model describes software layers ranging from the physical layer up to applications. Protocols are defined for passing control from one layer to the next.

Three different software development flows are described. These flows provide insight into software development ranging from requirements, through coding, to testing, and finally, product release. General concepts in software development activities are presented. The application of software project management over the software development life-cycle is defined.

Companies typically are organized across functional lines. But most products are created with value added from more than one function. Complexities increase with cross-functional interactions and dependencies. The complications intrinsic to product development flows and urgency from market pressures for on-time deliveries drive the need for continuous management of all details throughout the product development life-cycle. Project management provides the skills and practices for broad ownership of all aspects bringing an idea to reality. The discipline of project management provides capabilities for managing the complexities and myriad details of software and systems development to successfully compete in the market [1].

A program charter is an explicit recognition of the existence of and financial investment in a program. The high-level goals of the program are stated. The power and authority of the office of the program sponsor are conveyed to some degree to the selected program manager. The program charter enables the program manager to get started.

The program manager leads a team of project managers, functional managers, and key individual contributors that is responsible for doing the work. The composition of the core team may change over time as the program advances through its life-cycle. Stakeholders are involved since they have an interest in the team and the outcome of its work.

In order to be profitable, companies must decide how to deploy their scarce resources to create products and services that best meet customers' needs. This requires that decisions be made about what products constitute the portfolio. Portfolio management provides the analysis and methodology to make informed decisions about which products are introduced into the product pipeline and which continue development until they are ramped into production.

The impact of project management can be seen with a view of a product pipeline partitioned by project life-cycle phase. Implementation of project management discipline creates a consistent view over time of the orderly progression of products from concept through production ramp. More products will exist at the mouth of the funnel of the product pipeline than will exist at the pipeline output. Phase reviews will cull out products over the time spanning the development life-cycle that don't meet financial criteria or don't match evolving market requirements in favor of better candidate products. Not every product that is conceived should be brought to market. The discipline of successive reviews provides an evaluation continuum of the likelihood of market success for the product when it is introduced.

For new product introductions, a project manager typically is made responsible for the project execution from the life-cycle phase of project conception until ramp into production. Project management makes an important contribution to new product introduction by bringing relevant management and leadership skills as well as introducing particular management disciplines to a company. It plays a critical role in product life-cycle management.

A project is a related set of work activities with a definite start and end. Any project is defined by the schedule, scope of work, cost and resourcing, quality, and customer satisfaction. The first three of these were originally known as the triple constraint. Now, the term implicitly includes the last two factors as well. The project manager works across functional areas to accomplish the work of the project, making sure everything necessary is addressed and nothing is dropped when handoffs occur between functional areas. Project managers are very much involved in the details of plans and work execution.

Some work is more complex and is composed of multiple projects. Related projects may constitute a program. The program has definite starting and ending dates. Program managers manage project managers, functional managers, and key individual contributors to accomplish the goals of the program. The program manager is responsible for the program schedule, scope of work, cost and resourcing, quality, and customer satisfaction. Program managers typically manage by exception and only get involved in detailed execution when deviations from plan require it.

The project management life-cycle is composed of specific processes. These are initiating, planning, executing, monitoring and controlling, and closing. Each of these specific processes utilize particular knowledge from areas such as integration, scope, time, cost, quality, human resource, communications, risk, and procurement. The knowledge that is applied consists of particular activities depending on which process is being worked through in the life-cycle.

Companies order the work of the project management life-cycle by defining phases of the project life-cycle. These phases typically consist of Concept, Definition, Planning, Execution, Validation, Ramp, and Closure. Processes are developed for each of these phases. The processes define requirements that must be met so a project may graduate from one phase to the next. The processes provide a consistent context under which similar products are developed. This enables best practices to be identified, provides a uniform platform for continuous improvement to be applied, and can gain productivity with appropriate focus on value-added work activities.

A principal responsibility of project and program management is communications and reporting. Communication involves message content, the mode of delivering the message, and distinct activities of transmission, receipt, and verification. Depending upon the forum, communications may be formal or informal. Reports and reviews are a means by which the team is held accountable for progress using the resources provided.

Capability maturity model integration

It is not uncommon for software development companies or organizations to operate with processes guided by the CMMI framework of the Software Engineering Institute (SEI) [2]. Capability maturity model integration is a model enabling process improvement of development, acquisition, and service activities. There are two representations in CMMI models. These are the staged and continuous representations. Tables 20.1 and 20.2 show the staged and continuous representations, respectively.

Table 20.1 for the staged representation shows the Process Areas that must be satisfied to be associated with a particular maturity level. Maturity levels are cumulative, meaning

Table 20.1: Staged representation of CMMI model [2].

Level	Focus	Process Area	
5 Optimizing	Continuous Process Improvement	Organizational Innovation and Deployment	Quality Productivity
		Causal Analysis and Resolution	
4 Quantitatively Managed	Quantitative Management	Organizational Process Performance	
		Quantitative Project Management	
3 Defined	Process Standardization	Requirements Development	
		Technical Solution	
		Product Integration	
		Verification	
		Validation	
		Organizational Process Focus	
		Organizational Process Definition + Integrated Product and Process Development	
		Organizational Training	
		Integrated Project Management + Integrated Product and Process Development	
		Risk Management	
		Decision Analysis and Resolution	
2 Managed	Basic Project Management	Requirements Management	
		Project Planning	
		Project Monitoring and Control	
		Supplier Agreement Management	
		Measurement and Analysis	
		Process and Product Quality Assurance	
		Configuration Management	
1 Initial			Risk Rework

Used by permission; ©2007 by Carnegie Mellon University.

that maturity Level 3 (aka Defined) not only satisfies the Process Areas of its level but also that of Level 2. The staged representation has five levels, with Level 5 being the most mature.

The continuous representation shown in Table 20.2 uses capability levels instead of maturity levels. In this representation, the same Process Areas are categorized. Many of the Process Areas have intuitive meaning or else might be familiar from work usage. The continuous representation has six levels, from 0 to 5, with Level 5 being the most capable.

Each Process Area has specific and generic goals which are required to be done. Associated with these are practices which may either conform to the description provided by SEI or else be substituted appropriately. Table 20.3 shows the Generic Goals and Practices.

Table 20.2: Continuous representation of CMMI model [2].

Category	Process Areas
Process Management	Organizational Process Focus
	Organizational Process Definition + Integrated Product and Process Development
	Organizational Training
	Organizational Process Performance
	Organizational Innovation and Deployment
Project Management	Project Planning
	Project Monitoring and Control
	Supplier Agreement Management
	Integrated Project Management + Integrated Product and Process Development
	Risk Management
	Quantitative Project Management
Engineering	Requirements Management
	Requirements Development
	Technical Solution
	Product Integration
	Verification
	Validation
Support	Configuration Management
	Process and Product Quality Assurance
	Measurement and Analysis
	Decision Analysis and Resolution
	Causal Analysis and Resolution

Used by permission; ©2007 by Carnegie Mellon University.

The generic goal of Level 1 is to Achieve Specific Goals. The single generic practice is to Perform Specific Practices. The generic goal of Level 2 is to Institutionalize a Managed Process. There are ten generic practices associated with this goal. These include Establish an Organizational Policy, Plan the Process, Provide Resources, Assign Responsibility, Train People, Manage Configurations, Identify and Involve Relevant Stakeholders, Monitor and Control the Process, Objectively Evaluate Adherence, and Review the Status with Higher-Level Management.

The generic goal of Level 3 is to Institutionalize a Defined Process. There are two generic practices. The first is to Establish a Defined Process and the second is to Collect Improvement Information. Generic Goal Level 4 also has two generic practices. These are to Establish Quantitative Objectives for the Process and to Stabilize Subprocess Performance. The two generic practices of Generic Goal Level 5, to Institutionalize an Optimizing Process, are to Ensure Continuous Process Improvement and Correct Root Causes of Problems.

Table 20.3: Generic goals and practices [2].

Staged Representation	Generic Goals	Generic Practices	Continuous Representation
	GG1: Achieve Specific Goals	GP1.1: Perform Specific Practices	CL1
ML2; ML3, ML4, ML5	GG2: Institutionalize a Managed Process	CP2.1 Establish an Organizational Policy GP2.2 Plan the Process GP2.3: Provide Resources GP2.4: Assign Responsibility GP2.5: Train People GP2.6: Manage Configurations GP2.7: Identify and Involve Relevant Stakeholders GP2.8: Monitor and Control the Process GP2.9: Objectively Evaluate Adherence GP2.10: Review Status with Higher Level Management	CL2
ML3, ML4, ML5	GG3: Institutionalize a Defined Process	GP3.1: Establish a Defined Process GP3.2: Collect Improvement Information	CL3
	GG4: Institutionalize a Quantitatively Managed Process	GP4.1: Establish Quantitative Objectives for the Process GP4.2: Stabilize Subprocess Performance	CL4
	GG5: Institutionalize an Optimizing Process	GP5.1: Ensure Continuous Process Improvement GP5.2: Correct Root Causes of Problems	CL5

ML=Maturity Level (Staged) CL=Capability Level (Continuous)

Used by permission; © 2007 by Carnegie Mellon University

The highest level, Level 5, signifies the organization has multiple initiatives to improve Process Areas by acting on statistical information to either improve the mean value or tighten the variation of processes under statistical control. Level 4 indicates the organization has many, if not all, processes under statistical process control (SPC). Conventional rules for SPC provide an indication when a response is needed to adjust a process so it stays under statistical control. SPC is one set of tools in the Six Sigma repertoire.

Level 1 denotes that processes are performed to achieve specific work goals. The process could be as elementary as gathering requirements, coding, and delivering the software product. When processes are in place for planning and executing work according to policy with more discipline, the organization is working at Level 2. Level 3 applies yet higher standards of discipline across more Process Areas than Level 2. There is less discrepancy in how processes are applied for successive projects with Level 3 compared to Level 2. The continuous representation has a Level 0, which indicates an incomplete process that either isn't performed or is partially performed.

The OSI model

To provide a system solution for customers means marrying software with hardware to meet particular use cases. The hardware could consist of a system on a chip (SoC) and discrete device components on a board with appropriate input/output (I/O) devices. Substantial software often is architected into layers because of distinct functional purposes.

As an example of the way software may be architected, the seven layers of the Open System Integration (OSI) model form a networking framework defining the types of software that are required. In the OSI model, protocols are defined for passing control from one layer to the next. A commercial system will provide some or all of these types of software. The layers and their names are listed in Table 20.4.

Table 20.4: Seven layers of the OSI model.

Layer #	Layer Name
7	Application layer
6	Presentation layer
5	Session layer
4	Transport layer
3	Network layer
2	Data link layer
1	Physical layer

The bottom layer of the OSI model, layer 1, defines physical-layer protocols for direct interaction with an SoC platform. This layer controls the bit stream at the physical (i.e., electrical and mechanical) layer for transmission and reception. The next higher layer is the data link layer and is written as control code for physical addressing. It is composed of the Media Access Control (MAC) sublayer and the Logical Link Control (LLC) sublayer. The MAC sublayer controls computer access to data and transmission permission such as uplink processing and downlink bit manipulation. The LLC sublayer controls frame synchronization, flow control, and physical layer error checking. The network layer is layer 3 and is concerned with logical addressing. Switching and routing is controlled in this layer for transmitting data from node to node. The first three layers constitute the media layers.

The fourth layer in the OSI model is the transport layer, which makes sure data transfer is complete. It is concerned with reliability and flow control. Layer 5 is the session layer for interhost communication. Connections between applications are established, maintained, and terminated in the session layer. Above this layer is the presentation layer for encryption and decryption. Data are transformed into a type acceptable to the application layer. The top layer, layer 7, is the application layer for end use. The protocols for applications and end-user processes are controlled in this layer. The top four layers constitute the host layers.

For a baseband SoC used in cell phones, a typical architecture includes a microprocessor unit (MPU; e.g., ARM® processor) and a digital signal processor (DSP; e.g., StarCore™ processor). Handset providers increasingly are looking for system solutions combining hardware and software. This means SoC providers must develop software along with their chips in order to enable their customers' success. For example, customers might expect modem software accompany SoC deliveries. Modem software development includes software for layers 1 to 4. Besides development of features and functionality, there are integration and validation activities. The software architecture could define layers 1 to the lower half of layer 4 software to be handled by the DSP. In this case, the MPU would have the upper half of layer 4 and beyond.

A software or systems architect is responsible for defining what software stack elements must be provided to meet the customer use cases. Figure 20.1 shows the software stack running on a femtocell supporting the Long Term Evolution (LTE) radio technology [3]. In this case, the heterogeneous core SoC is Freescale® Semiconductor's QorIQ Qonverge™ PSC9131 with a single digital signal processing (DSP) core (i.e., SC3850) and a single PowerPC (PPC) core (i.e., e500v2). This view is a good example of how complex the software stack can be for a system.

Running on the DSP, the lowest layer includes the MAPLE abstraction layer (MAL) for the femto version of the multi-accelerator platform engine for baseband (MAPLE-B2F), which

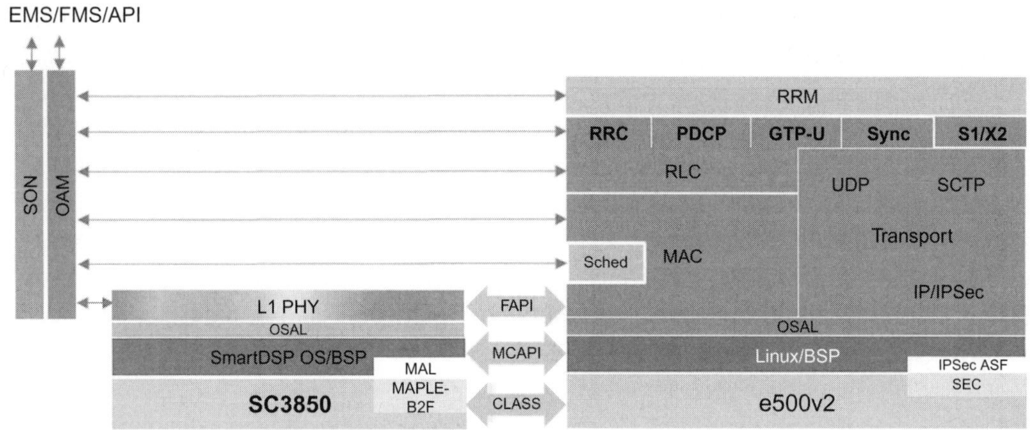

Figure 20.1:
Software stack view of a system on a chip platform.

is a hardware accelerator with firmware. The SmartDSP real-time operating system (RTOS) and its board support package (BSP) including drivers is in this lowest layer and works with the MAL. A driver is software that controls a peripheral or particular piece of hardware. Drivers provide for OS-specific process interrupts, interface to control registers, etc. Above the RTOS is a thin operating system abstraction layer (OSAL) which interfaces with the Layer 1 physical layer (L1 PHY). The FemtoForum application programming interface (FAPI) governs the interface of the PHY layer with upper layers. The chip-level arbitration and switching system (CLASS) is a switch fabric allowing multiple simultaneous accesses between heterogeneous cores.

On the PPC core, the lowest layer includes the Internet protocol security block (IPSec) with application-specific fast path (ASF) processing for packets bypassing the Linux kernel network stack, and a security engine controller (SEC) which is a programmable block handling encryption/decryption, public key, and security protocol. The Linux operating system (OS) and its BSP are in this lowest layer. The multicore application programming interface (MCAPI) exists between the Linux OS and SmartDSP OS. Above the Linux OS is a thin OSAL layer. Interfacing the OSAL from above is the media access control (MAC) layer with a scheduler and a transport layer. The transport layer includes Internet protocol (IP), IPSec, user datagram protocol (UDP), and stream control transmission protocol (SCTP) functionality and support.

Above the MAC and transport layers is the layer supporting the radio link control (RLC) protocol. This layer includes radio resource control (RRC), packet data convergence protocol (PDCP), general packet radio sequence tunneling protocol (GTP-U), synchronization, and S1/X2 interfaces (with functions defined by LTE radio network layer signaling protocol) functionality and support. Above the RLC layer is the radio resource management (RRM) layer.

The PHY layer, MAC layer and scheduler, RLC layer and elements, and RRM layer interface with the operations and maintenance (OAM) layer. The OAM interfaces with the self-organizing network (SON) layer. The OAM and SON interface with the enhanced messaging service (EMS) and fixed mobile substitution (FMS) application programming interfaces (API).

Software development

Three software development models are introduced. The first of these is the V-model. This model is presented first since it is useful for depicting the distinct purposes of basic activities, the expected sequence of those activities (ignoring iterative loops), and dependencies and relationships between activities. The second model is the waterfall model. This traditional model actually predates the V-model. It has a flow of activities proceeding in a linear sequence. The last model is the newest but is now about a decade old. It is known as agile software development. This flow, embracing iterative cycles of incremental software development, has many practices distinct from those associated with the waterfall model.

V-model

Figure 20.2 shows one depiction of what is known as the V-shaped model. The fundamental software development and testing activities and their relationships are depicted in the V-model. This figure shows development activities on one wing and correlated test activities on the other. At the wingtips, the product release must satisfy the use cases in order to be received well by users. Performance testing validates requirements. System testing validates

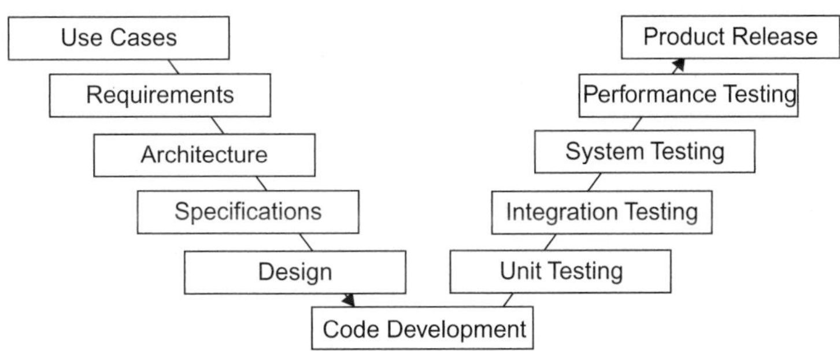

Figure 20.2:
V-model for development and testing.

the software architecture that was specified. The software requirements specifications are tested with integration testing. Unit tests validate the unit or component design.

The first step in this software development process is gathering use cases. Knowing the use cases enables a product manager to generate requirements. To draw a contrast, it is unnecessary to solicit from customers or users a list of what are considered requirements. In fact, such a solicitation might be undesirable since analysis might show lists of requirements containing items unrelated to use cases. Goldplating is the addition of features and functionality in excess of the genuine requirements. Goldplating is economically wasteful since scarce resources have alternative uses.

Product requirements are created against these use cases. Product requirements need to be written so they are actionable by engineering to enable the use cases.

There are various sources of authentic requirements. There could be features in legacy code that need to be carried forward. The engineering team responsible for software development surely has ideas for continuous improvement. Standards compliance may drive feature development. Internal software developers might generate feature requests. Applications engineers might propose features based upon their interaction with customers. After product release, customers might return service requests with feature requests they need. Finally, benchmarking competitive products might highlight missing features that need to be developed.

For example, layer 1 for baseband software is composed of a kernel library, algorithmic code, and application code up to the convergence layer for layer 2. Requirements are composed of critical defects that must be fixed, features, standards adherence, support for use cases (i.e., how customers will use the software: as benchmark code, demonstration code, or integrated into their product), deployment of the code (e.g., in a test harness, lightweight executive environment, or with a scheduler connected to radio link control (RLC)/media access control (MAC) or separated by a queue manager), configuration (e.g., number of users, packet rate, etc.), and convergence to adjacent layers (e.g., layer 2 needs to be concerned with the convergence layers for layers 1 and 3).

Feature analysis is done to understand the product requirements. All this information is used to create a concise set of product requirements. Then a software requirements specification (SRS) is created that provides a high-level description of how the software engineers will satisfy each requirement. A single requirement may spawn multiple SRS responses (e.g., from different components).

A test plan completes the traceability between these operations. A test or set of tests is created for each software specification response. A traceability matrix ties each test to each SRS response. To complete the traceability, each SRS response is linked back to product requirements. Because of the complexity, the work effort is relatively high for engineering to create responses to the requirements, tests against those responses, and traceability linkages.

A test plan should cover static, dynamic, functional tests at the unit, integration, and system levels, plus performance tests. Static analysis tests source code to collect information when it is not actually being executed. Dynamic analysis is done with run-time execution for the purpose of detecting dependencies and collecting temporal information. For example, one type of dynamic analysis tool is the debugger.

Testing is done at several levels and addresses different concerns such as functionality, performance, regressions (i.e., degraded performance or a relatively new defect compared to previous releases), and bug fix validations. Use cases from which tests are developed include new functional applications, existing functional applications, and benchmarking applications.

Manual testing is done for new tests that have been created for code adding new functionality from use cases. Just because these tests have never been run before, they have a high likelihood of catching defects. Unfortunately, creating new tests can be very time-consuming. However, once created, they may be added to an automated testing suite. Over time, the count of automated tests may be substantial. Automated testing helps productivity because of the ease and thoroughness of testing. This approach is key to robust regression testing. However, automated testing is backward-looking in the sense that the suite is a collection of older tests.

Functional tests may be categorized as unit, integration, or system tests. Unit tests are those integral to the component. Integration tests verify interoperability of system components. They may include full high-level tools testing. System tests include all hardware and software interactions including external memory and interfaces. As expected, system tests must confirm that the software is ready for real use cases and applications. These tests are complementary and shouldn't be considered substitutionary. For example, because of limitations in comprehensiveness, passage of system-level tests can't guarantee that components are free from unit-level defects. Field deployment would be the wrong time for any defect to express itself.

Unit tests are developed by the component software developers. They can be the simplest and fastest way to determine whether the change made by a programmer produced the intended result. These tests should be documented so other developers understand what use case is being addressed and how complete it is. The tests should be available for review and for quality audits. In addition to testing per se, all code checked into the mainline needs to be peer reviewed. The costs are least for finding and fixing defects at the unit level.

Integration tests involve multiple components or their interfaces. Often, feature implementation depends on the functionality of another component. Integration tests address this dependency. Due to added complexity, costs are higher for finding and fixing defects at the integration level.

Above this level is system testing with fully integrated software running on a particular target (e.g., emulator, simulator, or hardware populated with the SoC). Ultimately, the system and the scope of system testing are aligned with key customers. In contrast to unit and product testing, system testing might have a lot of manual tests. System-level testing is interested in interactions internally between the different components and externally with interfaces, buses, other software, etc. Peripherals can be exercised as well as data busses. Costs are highest for finding and fixing defects at the system level.

Returning to the traceability matrix, an architect reviews the engineering responses to the requirements and their test plans for correct alignment, completeness, and thoroughness. An architectural definition step could be analogous to or include algorithmic definition. Such an architectural definition is used to design the software. Usability, performance, and features are architectural concerns. Architectural considerations include defining design rules including a common layer approach for different products and consideration of hardware effects so hardware and software partitioning is efficient.

Depending upon the scope and complexity of the software solution required, the architect might decide to publish a detailed software architecture specification. An architectural block diagram will be provided. System dependencies, the programming language(s), and operating system(s) will be specified. Description will be provided of the functionality and performance that must be delivered. How code development is implemented and integrated will be addressed. Subsystems and interfaces will be identified. Communications protocols and security will be defined. Scenarios might be provided to illustrate small use cases.

This information is used to design the software solution. For substantial designs, the software solution needs to determine whether the default is a simple solution which still makes possible addressing a complex need or whether the default is a complex solution for which a simple need is a subset. A peer review is conducted to approve the software design. The functional manager will assign a senior engineer to lead the review. The project manager will record action items and drive them to closure to finish the review.

A peer review is a structured examination of the work product (in this case, the software design) by engineering colleagues for the purpose of determining conformance to standards, the appropriateness of the design for a particular use case and general reuse, and finding faults or errors.

A thorough design review may lead to faster and higher-quality product release by ensuring correctness up front instead of relying on tests or defect reports to find design-related problems more downstream in the process flow. The ideal result from the design review is not only efficient and complete logic but also production of code for which testing discovers no defects. Typically, the finalized design is published in a document.

Code development has its own reviews. Generally, peer reviews are conducted after each operation for algorithm definition, design, coding, and test planning. A code review includes looking at all the code and gaining a detailed understanding of the logic and code development. The purposes of a code review are to ensure the intended task is performed in an efficient manner, no existing functionality is broken, and coding styles are followed.

An abbreviated code review checklist is provided in Table 20.5. In this table, the items being checked off are phrased so that the correct answer is positive. This makes it easy to measure review responses so some quality standard could be applied to this and other code reviews.

Table 20.5: Code review checklist.

No.	Maintainability
1	Does the code completely and correctly implement the design (based on requirements)?
2	Does the code conform to the applicable coding standards?
3	Do libraries have sufficient declarations (external functions, types and other interfaces) in a header file?
4	Are code, comments, revision history, security classification clear, correct, and understandable?
5	Have customer-specific references and general public license contamination been avoided?
	Algorithm/Arithmetic/Logic
6	Are divisors tested for zero and pointers tested for null?
7	Are arithmetic and logical operations correct?
	Data Initialization
8	Are variables and pointers initialized?
	Functional Interface
9	Are imported data and input arguments tested for validity and completeness?
	Conditions/Loops
10	Are all loop entry and exit conditions and branch conditions correct?
11	Are all boundary conditions checked?
	Error Handling
12	Is error handling in place to check for timeouts, transfer failure, access denial, device wrong state (others)?
	Real Time
13	Are multitasking constraints correct?
14	Are thread/process priorities correct?
15	Have appropriate memory locations been used and memory leaks been avoided?

Code review for a bug fix may be easy if only a few lines of code are touched. By comparison, a new feature is more difficult to review since it could require an explanation of what is being accomplished in the logic.

Waterfall model

The waterfall model generally is acknowledged as the traditional software development flow. The V-model was derived from the waterfall model so there is similarity in the activities and their sequence. There is progression through requirements, design, coding, testing, and release. In the example provided, the details are specific to developer tools. But there is general applicability to the development of other software products such as drivers, kernel libraries, board support packages including Linux, or stack layers.

The single lengthiest activity in this software development flow is code development. Code development encompasses fixing previously identified and prioritized defects and adding features. Concurrently, functional test development is done.

In reality, software typically is developed in an iterative cycle. Source code is written and then it gets compiled into what is known as machine code or object code. This is linked with library functions into an executable library image. A debug process can check code as it executes to isolate problems. The source code gets edited for improvements and the cycle begins again.

Compatible with the waterfall model, Table 20.6 shows a linear process flow for creating commercial software like CodeWarrior™. CodeWarrior is a suite of tools to improve the productivity of software developers using SoC products with cores such as StarCore DSP, ARM, or in the Power Architecture® family. As is typical for derivative software products, a couple of iterative development cycles are shown. To simplify the flow, the iterations are linearized.

Table 20.6 shows the operations developing software and their sequence. The flow's emphasis is on component development iterations, although some intermediate CodeWarrior builds are depicted which might have utility for some engineering teams. A process is followed so best practices may be implemented reproducibly and the development is done most efficiently. This process may produce engineering builds or product releases. Product releases may include releases of successive maturity, e.g., Alpha, Beta, and Final product releases.

An Alpha release contains a subset of fully working features. An Alpha product release may go to early users. In the context of SoC platforms, Alpha software could be pre-silicon software available for use on emulator (e.g., such as on the Cadence® Palladium® system or an FPGA system) or simulator targets.

Table 20.6: Software development flow for CodeWarrior Developer tools.

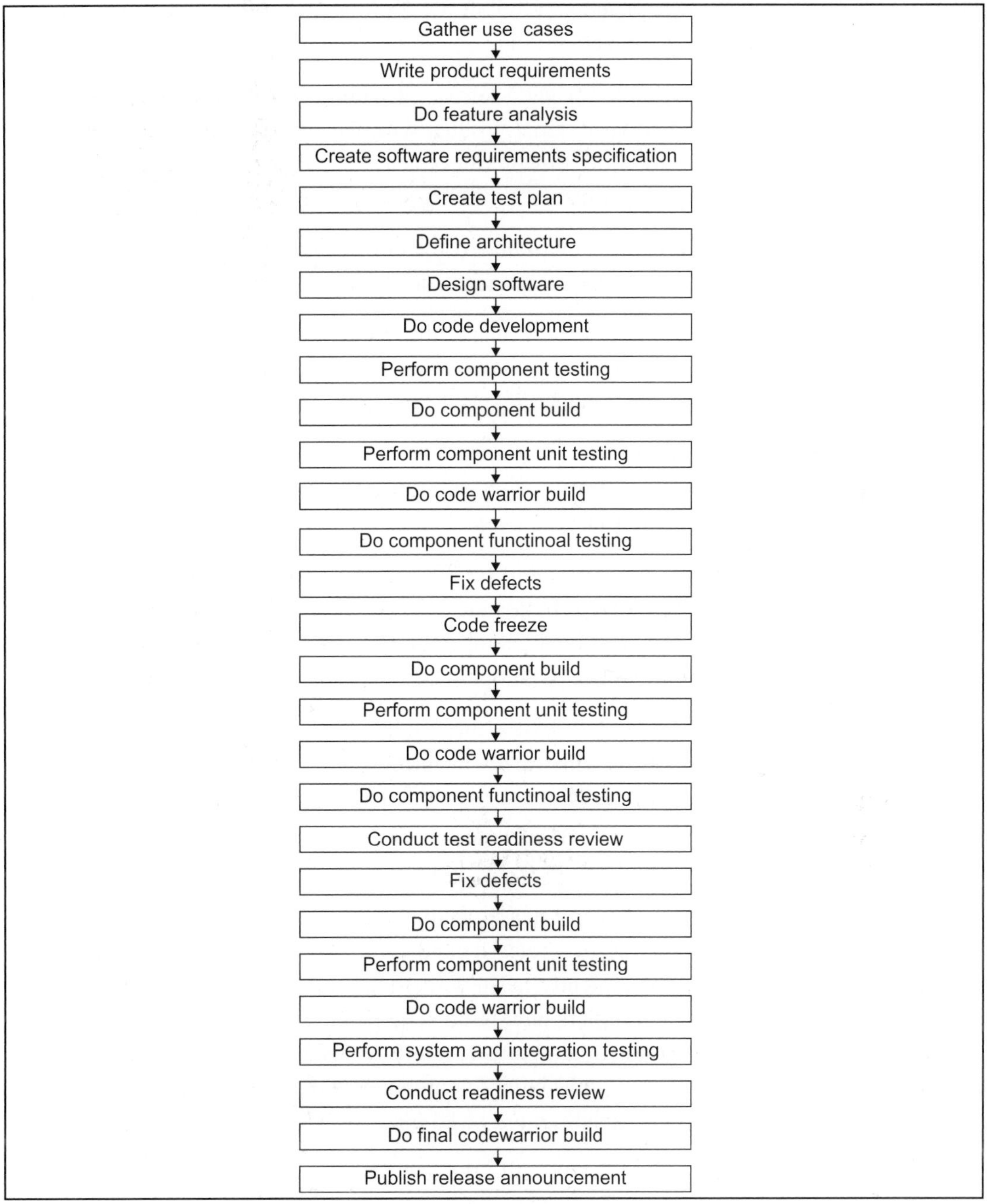

Gather use cases
↓
Write product requirements
↓
Do feature analysis
↓
Create software requirements specification
↓
Create test plan
↓
Define architecture
↓
Design software
↓
Do code development
↓
Perform component testing
↓
Do component build
↓
Perform component unit testing
↓
Do code warrior build
↓
Do component functinoal testing
↓
Fix defects
↓
Code freeze
↓
Do component build
↓
Perform component unit testing
↓
Do code warrior build
↓
Do component functinoal testing
↓
Conduct test readiness review
↓
Fix defects
↓
Do component build
↓
Perform component unit testing
↓
Do code warrior build
↓
Perform system and integration testing
↓
Conduct readiness review
↓
Do final codewarrior build
↓
Publish release announcement

Beta software may be a software release that occurs weeks after silicon populated hardware is available. Beta is feature-complete and eligible for deployment in field trials under specific terms and conditions to selected users.

The Final product release is suitable for wide release providing support for customers. The Final product release should be a very stable product with which users don't observe crashes or data corruption. In addition, this product release has nil defects observed with common use. The usability of this software is the highest among the releases.

Tests are done shortly after software is written. At the conclusion of code development, a component build is done. This enables component unit testing.

Updated builds of all individual components enable their integration into a CodeWarrior build. Then component functional testing may be done. This could be extended unit testing or integration testing between components. Fixes are made for defects that are found.

Software feature development needs to be completed at code freeze. When the software is feature-complete, the focus shifts from working on features to reducing the count of defects. Code freeze occurs from a couple to a few weeks before the release.

New individual component builds are done next. This enables a new round of component unit testing. All the updated component builds are used to create a new integrated CodeWarrior build. Component functional testing follows, which could include extended unit testing or integration testing between components.

A test readiness review is conducted to review the results of code development and testing of all components after code freeze. This review determines what imperative exists to fix remaining defects or bugs for the next integrated build. Then new component builds are made which undergo component unit testing.

A complete toolchain build is composed of the new components. Integration testing and system testing is done on this toolchain release candidate on all release targets (e.g., emulator, simulator, hardware). The first release candidate build is created for functional team testing. If a component subsequently has a defect that must be fixed, a patch build is considered instead of issuing a complete new build. The patch build could pick up even just one new component. Each functional component should be aware of the others and the interactions. By itself or in tandem with multiple components that must be replaced, it could transpire that a new complete integrated build be released.

A general readiness review occurs shortly after the test readiness review and covers all other issues before product release. The release readiness is measured against the test results. A readiness review considers all the defects found, determines the importance of the most critical defects, reviews which defects have workarounds and their respective acceptability, determines whether there are any regressions, and makes a decision about a new fix cycle. If fixes are required, a new build cycle is performed.

A positive review leads to a final toolchain build composed of only trivial changes. Release notes accompany the product release with a list of known defects and available workarounds. A formal release announcement is published to communicate the product release, its intended use, what features it includes, and how it may be picked up.

Agile model

The third software development model discussed is known as agile software development. Agile software development was developed as a simpler and more lightweight, flexible, responsive methodology in contrast to the more complex, substantial, structured, and orchestrated approach associated with the waterfall model. To this end, processes and tools are not valued as much as the way individuals interact to develop code. Developing working software incrementally for customer review and early integration is valued more than presenting design documents or general status reports. Customer collaboration is held to be more important than statements of work or legal contracts. The purpose of each iterative development cycle is to meet requirements which have been updated, reviewed, prioritized, and selected above a cutoff point. The agile flow is intrinsically less susceptible to top-down efforts to over-constrain the project. Flexibility and willingness to change is favored over adherence to a plan.

While the waterfall model typically plans from concept to final delivery, agile software development is done in iterations of short time-frames targeting incremental deliveries. Agile development pointedly deemphasizes production of documentation, but change control needs to be very closely managed. The more intimate customer relationship with the agile flow presents a risk of open-ended engagement, which could have an adverse financial impact. As with waterfall development, the agile approach recognizes the V-model's fundamental activities such as requirements definition, design, coding, and testing and their dependencies and relationships. In this engagement model, customer testing, or joint testing with the customer, may be emphasized for some or all of the functional and performance testing.

Both the waterfall and agile software development models have demonstrated successful deployments over a long period of time. Both models have strengths and weaknesses. The choice of implementation should depend upon market needs. Doubtless, both models will persist among software developers, with hybrid approaches introduced to borrow particular best practices.

Organization

People are organized for work in hierarchies. There are several distinct ways that are common. The most common way to manage people is to organize by work function with individual contributors reporting to a single manager. This is functional management. It provides for specialization, enables learning within the function based on common work assignments, provides a well-defined resource pool that might include sufficient margin to respond flexibly to varying demand, and has a traditional career advancement path.

Program management operating within a functional organization is the weakest possible implementation and will produce the least significant execution improvement over pure functional management. In this organization, program managers must interface and negotiate with functional managers continuously for all aspects of the program, including scope, schedule, and costs (which include resource assignments). The project being worked on within the function may be managed by the functional manager who assumes the project management role or else by a project manager reporting to the functional manager. Since the functional manager controls the resources, software, and hardware tools used, the functional manager effectively controls costs. Because the functional manager may make unilateral decisions about resource levels and work priorities, the schedule is completely dependent upon functional management. The support of any project is completely dependent upon the functional management support. The power and authority at the project level for assigning resources, arranging work priorities, and making decisions reside with the functional manager. Programs usually must work across multiple functions, so the lack of power and authority in program management becomes a primary constraint in what may be done. In this scenario, experience teaches that program management is reduced to a reporting function. The practical effect is diminution of authentic program management into a project coordination role.

Another way people are organized is in a matrix. There are two common matrices. One is a weak matrix where the individual contributors report into functional management for detailed work assignments, status reporting, and performance evaluation while simultaneously being assigned to work on particular projects. In this way, these individual contributors and the project manager report directly to a functional manager but indirectly to a program manager. Figure 20.3 shows a weak matrix reporting structure for a project manager and one functional manager and his engineers.

As a practical matter, there is little difference in execution effectiveness between a weak matrix organization and a functional one. It is clear to individual contributors that their self-interest is served by taking direction from their functional manager whenever there are

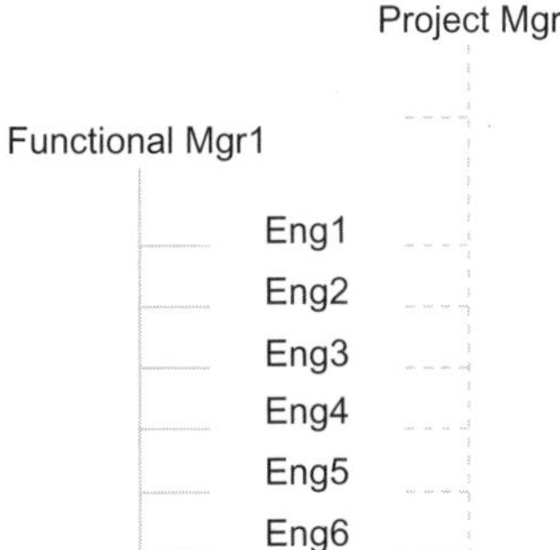

Figure 20.3:
Weak matrix organizational structure.

discrepancies or conflicts since all career rewards and punishment flow from functional management. Whenever differences in direction are communicated between functional management and program management, functional management prevails. The presentation of a core team for program management may be more clearly delineated, but neither power nor authority is invested in the core team to enable its success. As a practical matter, the functional manager retains all the power and authority over the project for resource levels, work priority, and decision-making. As a result, the execution results in a weak matrix are very similar to what is experienced with pure functional management. The execution performance will be on the level of project coordination.

A second matrix is organized as a strong matrix. In this configuration, individual contributors figuratively serve two masters. The functional manager is responsible for hiring and firing of individual contributors, but these workers are assigned to particular projects. Since individual contributors, team leads, and the project manager report to both a functional manager and a program manager, the program manager has the insight to provide weighted input to the functional manager for individual performance assessment. The right to make this weighted input creates capital for the program manager in persuasion and influence where little or none may have existed before. Figure 20.4 shows a strong matrix reporting structure for a project manager and one functional manager and his engineers.

In a strong matrix, removal of resources is a point of negotiation, so the functional manager is unable to make unilateral decisions shifting resources onto other projects for which he has responsibility. Since resourcing decisions are made jointly, the schedule comes under stronger program management control. Initial resources may be negotiated and then changes are made only by negotiation. Work is jointly directed by both the functional manager and program manager. This adds additional scope control to program management. Similarly, since operational expenses driven by census are usually a dominant contributor to total project cost, these are now under more direct program management control. A true strong

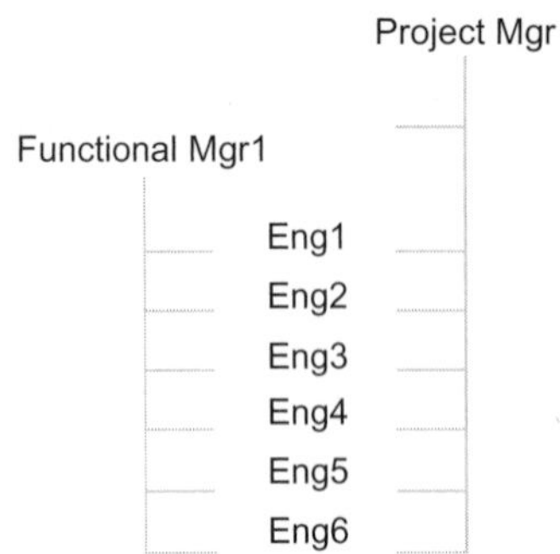

Figure 20.4:
Strong matrix organizational structure.

matrix provides sufficient power and authority to program managers over projects for resources, priorities, and decisions that significant improvement in execution performance relative to functional management is possible.

The last organization is a projectized one. In this configuration, only projects are supported organizationally. Individual contributors work only in projects and report only to project managers who themselves report to a program manager. There are practical problems implementing this if projects aren't all the same scope and scale, and schedules aren't perfectly interlocked. Since functional management doesn't exist, standardization of practices and adaptation of best practices is not as easy. Cross-pollination of learning between projects is impeded. Flexibility for shifting resources to address crisis work is much more difficult. Career paths are more problematic for individual contributors and re-assignment after each project is completed becomes a paramount concern for everyone. The advantages to program management are obvious with the consummate focus on the project and program by everyone associated with the work.

Project management that adds value to the organization should be invested by senior management with sufficient power and authority to manage the project triple constraint. This means the project manager manages, controls, and makes decisions within the project scope, for costs and resources, schedule, quality, and customer satisfaction. This is necessary for authentic project management. In addition, project management adds value by solving problems that arise during the project life-cycle. Finally, project management adds value by providing reports and communications to the team, to stakeholders, and to senior management.

Pitfalls that should be avoided include a heavy application of processes intended to implement particular practices associated with project management but which falls short of implementing authentic project management. At its best, project management exercises power and authority within the project charter and is a light touch that employs processes that help the company do better than it could otherwise do and that helps the company win. The advantages of project management don't stem from the processes themselves but from the superior management approach the discipline offers.

Program charter

The initial responsibility of the program sponsor is to review the program charter that is created by the program manager that defines the program triple constraint at the highest level. At this time, the details of the program scope, cost, schedule, and the means to achieve acceptable quality and customer satisfaction haven't been planned, but these are outlined. Approval of the program charter is the official start of a program and bounds the program so it has limited duration and scope. Key stakeholders and, particularly, core team members should have visibility into the program charter.

The program charter names the program so it has a unique identity. A brief summary of the business case is included. The high-level program objectives are defined. For example, these might include use of a particular generation of technology to create a product filling a need on the product roadmap. Final program deliverables are listed. The core team assignments are made. Budget and resource limitations, as well as any other constraints, are defined. The deadline for final deliverables is defined. The items constituting the triple constraint are prioritized so the relative importance of each is known. The target customer is identified, with customer requirements listed that are necessary for the program to succeed.

"Your customer is relying on you to meet some need by providing a product or service. Product attributes include performance, market timeliness, cost, reliability, and service. Whether the customer is a consumer or an industrial buyer, the product needs to have the performance that is expected, be available at the time of the customer's need, be affordable and recognized as a value by the customer, be reliable and work as advertised or intended, and have assistance or help of some kind available, if needed" [4]. The purpose of the program is to profitably meet the customer's need by provision of a product or service.

Program sponsors want someone to be accountable for results. They have a critical role to play in this. A program sponsor's acceptance of a program charter is an opportunity to be clear about roles and responsibilities. The program manager should be selected carefully and then should be invested directly with the power and authority to manage and lead the program. If this is clearly delegated, then the program manager may be held accountable. The program manager should be the one owner of all program deliverables, issues and their resolution.

Pushing power and authority down to the program manager makes him accountable. The program charter elucidates the original bounds of the program. Program details are clarified over time as the program advances through the life-cycle phases. Within the program boundaries, the program manager should be able to control resource decisions, prioritize work activities, and make decisions. Over the life of the program, problems will arise that require escalation by the program manager. These may be changes in the scope of the program, or in financial expenditures, or in delivery schedules. Through an escalation process, the program manager involves senior management in an evaluation of the resource levels, prioritization of work, or in decision-making to solve the problem. Having solved the particular problem, the program manager resumes normal control of the program.

Stakeholders and the core team

The largest group that is interested in the program is known as stakeholders. This includes people who have direct interest in the program such as the program sponsor, program manager, and core team members. The core team is composed of project managers, functional managers, and key individual contributors. Included among those with a direct interest are the individual contributors doing hands-on program work. In general, these people all have a positive interest in the program. By this it is meant that individual success is aligned with the program and they will be actively working to make the program successful.

Other people may have an indirect interest in the program. This interest may be either positive or negative. These people are stakeholders, too. People like this may include software developers, systems developers, quality system auditors, finance experts, administrative assistants, other managers providing ancillary support, etc. It is important that all stakeholders receive the information they need to do their own jobs well. This information won't be researched by the stakeholders but will be imparted by communication from the program manager.

Some stakeholders may have a negative interest in the program. By this it is meant that their interest is piqued with program difficulties, setbacks, or failures. This description is not meant to comment on the importance of the role they play. Stakeholders like this may include failure analysis engineers ready to assist if needed, safety engineers, environmentalists, managers with a different product competing for the same customer, or managers competing for the resources your program is using.

The program manager routinely interacts with key individual contributors, functional managers, and project managers in a team known as the core team. This core team revolves around clear definition of roles and responsibilities. If these roles and responsibilities haven't been articulated for the organization, then the program manager needs to do it for the core team, so there is clarity and no confusion on who is doing what.

The core team is composed of project managers, functional managers, and key individual contributors representing the major areas in which value is added to the program over its life-cycle. The active membership may evolve over time as the program moves through its life-cycle. For hardware representation, the initial core team might be composed of the product manager, the sales manager, the chip architect, a technical writer, the design project manager or design lead engineer, the lead engineer for design for test (DFT), the project manager for intellectual property (IP) modules (which will be integrated into an SoC), the lead engineer for libraries and input/output pads, the lead packaging engineer, the board project manager, the lead test engineer, and the lead product engineer. Software representation on a core team may include the applications engineering manager, a technical writer, software architects, product manager, build tools manager, project manager for the developer tools, project manager(s) for the operating system(s), and project managers for application software or libraries. Near the end of the program, as the product is getting qualified and ready for ramp into production, the core team may consist of the product manager, the validation lead engineer, the lead product engineer, a supply manager, and the quality engineer.

A core team wheel for DSP software program management is shown in Figure 20.5. This core team is led by the program manager and, going clockwise from the noon position, is composed of the SoC program manager, platform architect, product manager, applications engineering manager, board program manager, developer tools project manager, video applications project manager, voice/audio applications project manager, voice-over-IP frameworks project manager, baseband applications project manager, and real-time OS manager.

Core team members of the program could be core team leaders of projects. For example, the developer tools project manager is a member of the DSP software program manager's core team. But he also is a core team leader in his own right. This core team wheel is shown in Figure 20.6. Note that in this perspective, the DSP software program manager is a member of the developer tools project manager's core team. The other members of the developer tools core team are the component owners and architect.

The program manager will rely upon the core team most for execution success. Most interaction time will be with its members. However, the core team is composed of managers and leaders in their own right. Over the course of the program, these individuals will lead sub-teams to accomplish program goals. The program manager may have an

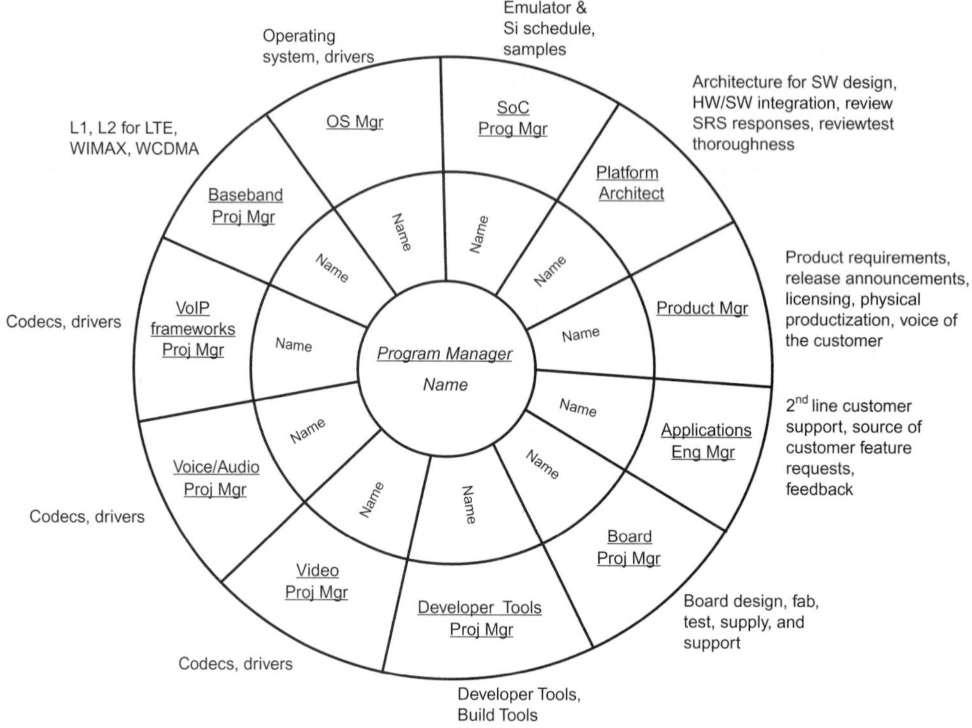

Figure 20.5:
DSP software core team wheel.

active role to play in these sub-team activities although the leadership principle of delegation should be respected.

Product life-cycle management

Project management provides an opportunity to improve business execution whenever projects are done. When project management is employed, executive management has made the decision to employ a sophisticated approach to improving management of people, costs, and work activities.

A project is a coordinated set of activities with a definite beginning and end. There is a prominent role for project management in new product introduction (NPI) since this is an area of recurring complex projects. A simple definition of NPI includes the elements of product definition, development through sample delivery, and then ramp into production. A perspective of how NPI project management fits into the larger business picture is provided in Figure 20.7.

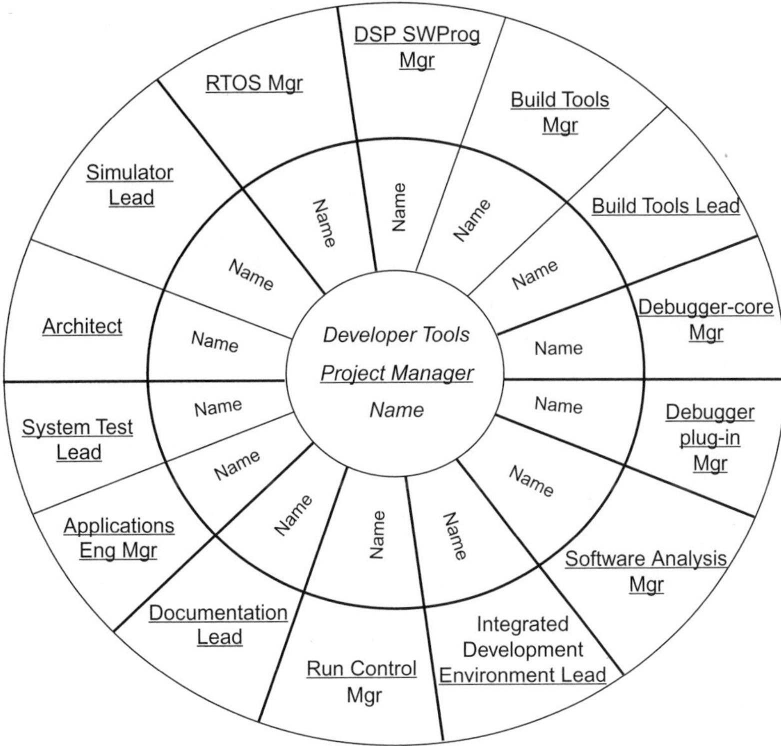

Figure 20.6:
Developer tools core team wheel.

The seminal process in product life-cycle management is developing a market strategy. The strategy considers what markets to compete in and what opportunities exist. The product strategy is created from the market strategy. A new product is considered for its fit on the product roadmap for succeeding an existing product, complementing existing products by filling product holes, or strengthening the product offerings by expanding the market range in which to compete. The financial opportunity is a strategic factor. A decision tree can aid the analysis. Portfolio management clarifies what the product fit would be for strategic alignment. Financial analysis could include first year or lifetime revenues. Pipeline and resource management manages how the product would be developed and introduced in time and its fit relative to other products. This avoids product resource and priority logjams. From this work come customer and vendor collaboration, requirements management, and new product introduction. Work breakdown structures are used to created detailed activities driving schedules for the core team to execute to. A work breakdown structure (WBS) shows the arrangement and relationships of work elements for a product. Product data management completes this collaborative corporate effort through the product life-cycle.

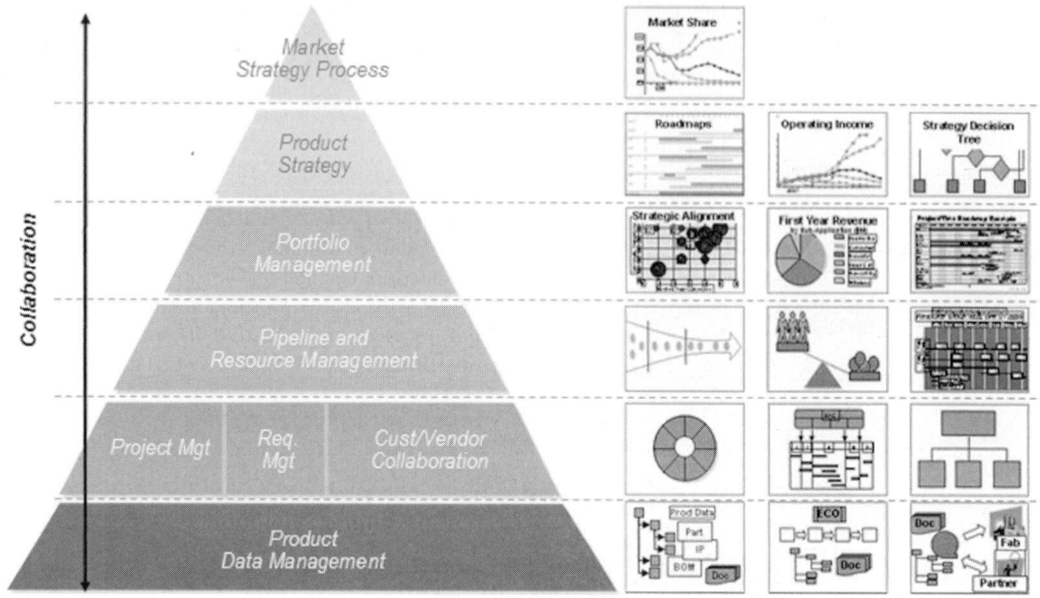

Figure 20.7:
Product life-cycle management [5].

Because of the complexity, program management is most effectively performed by managing by exception to the program plan. A program plan is created that has been reviewed for completeness and is expected to satisfy the triple constraint. During the Execution phase in the program life-cycle, management by exception determines to find significant deviations from the plan to evaluate their importance. This enables focusing time and energy on those important exceptions to the plan that could pose the most risk to execution.

By contrast, project management needs to be much closer to the action. Either the details of the work are tracked by determining the fraction of work completed for each WBS activity (if the project manager owns this responsibility) or else it is managed by exception (if a functional manager is responsible). The project manager consistently should be much more familiar with fine-granularity activity details. The project manager should be managing details closely enough to be aware of slippage of a small fraction of the duration of the lowest-level WBS activity.

Portfolio management

Portfolio management provides guidance on selecting new products being considered for introduction as well as prioritization of existing products. Program management may contribute to portfolio management in selection and authorization of projects. In doing annual planning, prospective projects may be identified by the SoC product management team. This list may be scrubbed for completeness with software product management. Then engineering management may evaluate each project for effort.

When there are multiple projects being executed during one time period, there may be resource constraints. Portfolio management can help with scheduling by evaluating the relative priorities of projects contending for resources. This process can help at the beginning of the year and during it. Conflict management may be handled either through escalation to senior or executive management or else through a change control board populated by key stakeholder decision-makers.

Table 20.7 is a worksheet that suggests a methodology for performing analysis of the portfolio. When all products have undergone evaluation using this process, their respective scores can be used for comparison. This will help management decide how to manage a portfolio of products in the typical environment of scarce resources.

Table 20.7 lists the major categories for evaluation as Strategic Alignment, Product Advantage, Market Attractiveness, Technical Feasibility, Risk, Financials, and Regulatory. Next to each of these major categories is an assignment of which function leads the discussion or provides data for evaluation. For example, the responsibility for Strategic Alignment is shared between Product Management (PDM) and the Program Management Office (PMO) while Technical Feasibility is the responsibility of Research and Development (R&D) (i.e., Engineering).

The use of a panel of evaluators brings collective experience to bear on the different evaluation criteria. If the panel is composed of the same individuals for the evaluation of all products in the portfolio, then there is some normalization of how they perform the evaluations. Otherwise, variation may be observed over time or across products. In Table 20.7, the evaluation panel is composed of a pair each of program managers, product managers, and engineering managers.

Ground rules may be established for scoring each of the criteria. For some (e.g., the item "Performance against budget" under the category "Financials"), the requirement may be to provide objective data for evaluation. Other criteria (e.g., the item "The return on investment is good relative to the risk" under the category "Financials") are subjective but perhaps ranges could be provided against which grades could be defined. Variation can be reduced in the evaluations if the criteria are objective and consistent interpretation is applied. These may include definitions of terms.

Figure 20.8 shows a product pipeline with work progress transitioning from left to right in the figure. Different programs developing new products are captioned as letters. To the left, the pipeline has a wide mouth but narrows to a much smaller exit at the right. This

Table 20.7: Portfolio management worksheet.

Criteria	<Prog Mgr>	<Prog Mgr>	<Prod Mgr>	<Prod Mgr>	<Eng Mgr>	<Eng Mgr>	Avg Score (1-10; 10 is best)	Weight (%)	Weighted Score
Strategic Alignment (PDM/PMO)									
Product fits BU and FSL strategy									
Product leverages core competencies in mkt'ing, technology, mfg'ing									
Product Advantage (PDM)									
Customer needs are understood and effectively addressed by the product									
Product provides unique benefits or value proposition or better meets customer needs									
Meets market window									
Market Attractiveness (PDM)									
Meets market criteria such as minimum market size requirements									
Market provides growth opportunity									
Company can achieve a competitive advantage with this product in this market									
Product meets an existing market need or the need can be readily developed									
Technical Feasibility (R&D)									
Product is technically feasible									
We have or can acquire the needed knowledge and expertise									
The technical gap, complexity, and technical risk can be adequately managed									
Risk (ALL)									
There are no show stoppers									
Risks and uncertainties can be effectively managed and responded to									
Financials (PMO)									
Performance against budget									
The return on investment is good relative to the risk									
Regulatory									
Product meets FCC, environmental, health, safety, and legal policies									
							Totals	0	0

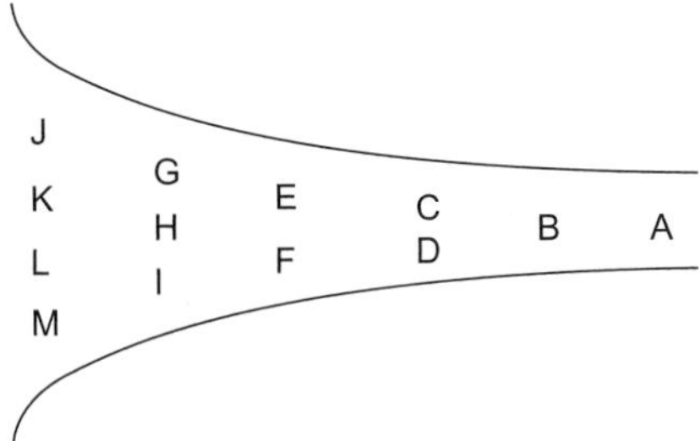

Figure 20.8:
Product pipeline.

indicates more programs are started than are ramped into production. The different life-cycle phases are labeled at the bottom and the new products being developed are aligned with these phases.

This product pipeline is a snapshot in time showing active programs. The Concept phase has the most active programs while Ramp has the least. This indicates that many programs are closed before ramping into production. It is more cost-effective to close programs early in their life-cycle than late, but even programs in the Execution phase are subject to closure. Typically, programs in the Validation and Ramp phases will proceed into volume production.

Project management life-cycle

There are certain generic steps that every project progresses through. Of course, the first step is initiated at the beginning of the project and the last step concludes when the project is closed. The activities within these steps are well defined. These steps are known as project management life-cycle phases.

As Table 20.8 indicates, there are defined knowledge areas that may be applicable to the process groups. These include integration, scope, time, cost, quality, human resources, communications, risk, and procurement.

Integration is applicable to every process group. Planning involves work in every knowledge area. Similarly, monitoring and controlling have activities in every knowledge area.

The Initiating process has two principal activities that are in only the integration knowledge area. These activities include developing a project charter and developing a preliminary project scope statement.

Table 20.8: Project management processes [6].

Process Group Knowledge Area	Initiating	Planning	Executing	Monitoring & Controlling	Closing
Integration	♦ Develop project charter ♦ Develop prelim scope statement	♦ Develop project management plan	♦ Direct and manage project execution	♦ Monitor & Control project work ♦ Integrated change control	♦ Close project
Scope		♦ Scope planning ♦ Scope definition ♦ Create WBS		♦ Scope verification ♦ Scope control	
Time		♦ Activity definition ♦ Activity sequencing ♦ Activity resource est. ♦ Activity duration est. ♦ Schedule dev.		♦ Schedule control	
Cost		♦ Cost estimating ♦ Cost budgeting		♦ Cost control	
Quality		♦ Quality planning	♦ Perform quality assurance	♦ Perform quality control	
Human Resource		♦ Human resource planning	♦ Acquire project team ♦ Develop project team	♦ Manage project team	
Communications		♦ Communications planning	♦ Information distribution	♦ Performance reporting ♦ Manage stakeholders	
Risk		♦ Risk mgmt planning ♦ Risk identification ♦ Qualitative risk anal. ♦ Quantitative risk anal. ♦ Risk response plan		♦ Risk monitoring & control	
Procurement		♦ Plan purchases & acquisitions ♦ Plan contracting	♦ Request seller responses ♦ Select sellers	♦ Contract admin.	♦ Contract closure

The project sponsor is a senior manager or executive under whose budget the program is executed. The project sponsor provides the project manager with authority using a project charter. The project is created formally during the initiating process using this charter, which establishes the project manager as its leader. The project objectives are documented at a high level for the first time. These objectives should be at a sufficiently high level that no revision is required later. The objectives should include fundamental information about schedule, cost, scope, quality, and customer impact. The project charter is approved by the sponsor.

A preliminary scope statement could be a statement of work (SOW) document. The preliminary scope statement includes high-level information about the deliverables and milestones. It lists the stakeholders and the approvals needed for the preliminary scope statement. As its name suggests, the intention is to provide an early definition of what the project scope is and when the project will finish.

The knowledge area of integration is used in the Planning process to develop the project management plan. Planning accounts for the scope knowledge area by scope planning, scope definition, and creating a work breakdown structure. In Planning, time is accounted for by activity definition, activity sequencing, activity resource estimation, activity duration estimation, and schedule development. Cost is handled in the Planning phase by cost estimating and cost budgeting. At this time in the project management life-cycle, quality is planned, human resourcing is planned, and a communications plan is developed. Risk planning involves several elements. These include risk management planning, risk identification, qualitative risk analysis, quantitative risk analysis, and a risk response plan is created. The last knowledge area is procurement. In the Planning phase, purchases and acquisitions as well as contracting are planned.

Integration combines the disparate parts of the project plan. Complicating this, some of the project objectives could require closer management than others. The project management plan comprehensively addresses integration issues and meeting the project goals.

The team's input and review constitute most of the project plan. To ensure acceptability when the project is completed, stakeholder input should be considered. To ensure approvals through the life-cycle of the project, management input should be solicited for inclusion. By the time the project is approved to enter the Execution phase of its life-cycle, most of the planning should have been completed. This doesn't preclude later changes in plans, but these should not be large or disruptive if early work is done well.

The project plan creates the detailed plans within the project charter for the misnomer known as the triple constraint (i.e., scope, schedule, cost, quality, and customer satisfaction). Resources are included in the cost. In addition, the project plan includes risk management, communications management, change management, and any procurement that is required.

Scope planning details how the scope of the project will be managed and how scope changes will be done. The scope needs to be documented so there is alignment among stakeholders concerning what the project will accomplish.

Defining the details of what the project will do is known as scope definition. This work may start with high-level deliverables and proceed by breaking each deliverable into smaller components. This work is not the same as what is done to create a work breakdown structure (WBS).

A WBS is foundational to project management planning. This is an organizational tool that groups work by delivery. It is comprehensive for the activities that are covered so that nothing will be omitted. When it is completed, the WBS defines the total scope of the project.

A WBS is created with the team and should have work broken down into fine-detailed activities. A rule of thumb is that activities should be from one to a few days duration. Smaller durations enable better tracking of progress during execution, which lowers the risk of unrecoverable slippage.

The first level of a WBS comprises the highest-level activities that are oriented to deliverables. The second level provides a breakdown of each of the higher-level activities. This breakdown exercise is repeated. It is likely that some activities will have more levels than others since there is more complexity that may be subdivided. The lowest-level activities are known as work packages. The graphical depiction of the work breakdown of all the activities illustrates the hierarchy of the work in the project.

All the project work should be encompassed in the WBS. Any work outside the WBS is outside the project scope.

A WBS example is provided in Figure 20.9. The WBS construction is hierarchical. The title is the highest level in the hierarchy. The lowest levels are work packages or activities.

The project manager will commonly manage the project execution to the work package level. By contrast, team members could subdivide work packages into even shorter-duration activities. While these are necessary for work completion, they are not usually tracked for progress.

Benefits of the WBS include much improved bottom-up estimation of costs and schedule. Estimation accuracy is improved with small activities instead of large ones. In addition, a WBS provides good visibility for understanding risks. Finally, it is a good communication tool for the team showing the project scope.

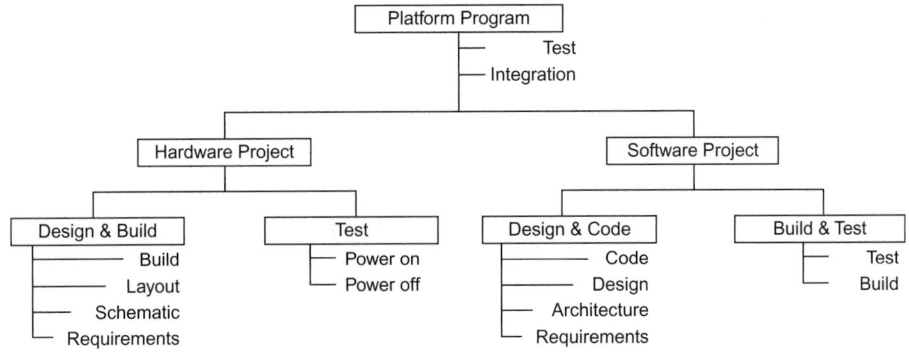

Figure 20.9:
Work breakdown structure.

In Planning, time-based planning depends upon the WBS as a starting point for information. The WBS provides activity definition as a matter of course. Activity sequencing is done with a network diagram where activities are sequenced from the project start to the end. The estimation of each activity's duration enables the network diagram to be used as a tool estimating the project duration.

There are several types of network diagrams showing the relationship of different work activities. Examples include activity-on-node diagrams, activity-on-arrow diagrams, critical-path method (CPM), and program evaluation and review technique (PERT). Figure 20.10 shows the simplest activity-on-node diagram, with the work from Activity A feeding into the work of Activity B. The first two types of diagrams are especially good for showing the flow of work. The latter two are used to estimate project durations.

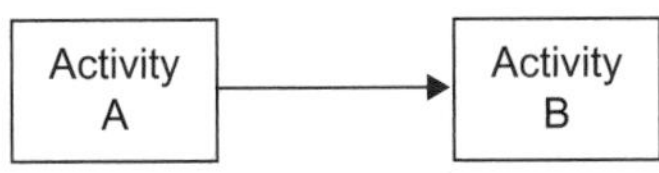

Figure 20.10:
Activity-on-node diagram.

Similar to time estimations, estimation of each activity's resource needs enables a rollup of project resource requirements. This is important for resource management, staffing, and risk management (e.g., diversion, re-assignment, unplanned leave, planned leave, effectiveness, attrition).

Schedule development is done using network diagrams and Gantt charts. The latter are particularly effective for tracking progress. Software programs like Oracle® Primavera or

Microsoft® Project are commonly used to show Gantt charts. These programs allow predecessor and successor relationships to be shown for activity dependencies. An example of a Gantt chart is shown in Figure 20.11.

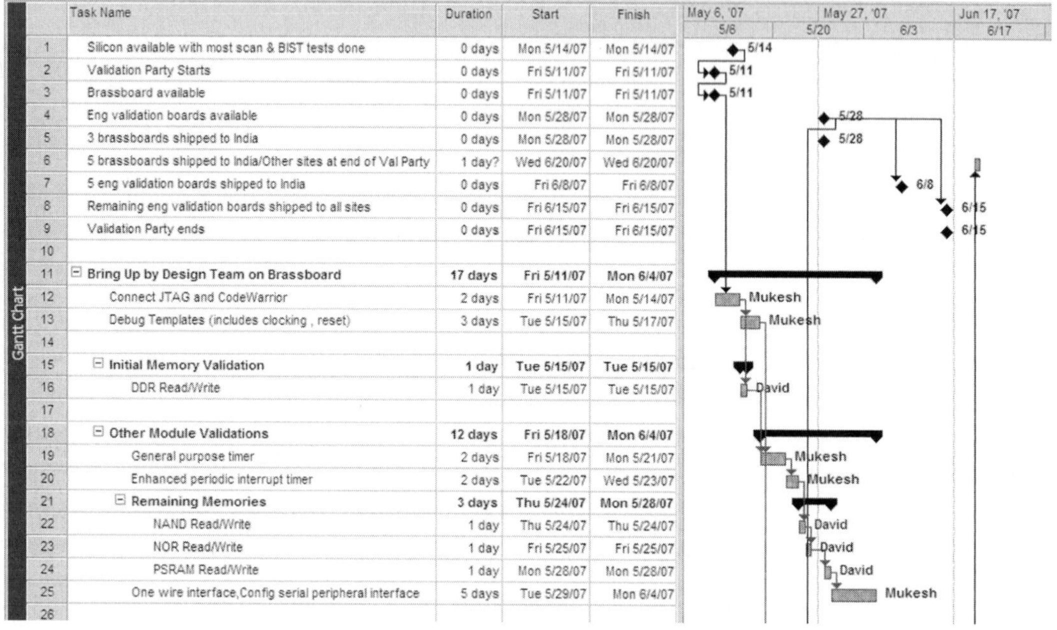

	Task Name	Duration	Start	Finish
1	Silicon available with most scan & BIST tests done	0 days	Mon 5/14/07	Mon 5/14/07
2	Validation Party Starts	0 days	Fri 5/11/07	Fri 5/11/07
3	Brassboard available	0 days	Fri 5/11/07	Fri 5/11/07
4	Eng validation boards available	0 days	Mon 5/28/07	Mon 5/28/07
5	3 brassboards shipped to India	0 days	Mon 5/28/07	Mon 5/28/07
6	5 brassboards shipped to India/Other sites at end of Val Party	1 day?	Wed 6/20/07	Wed 6/20/07
7	5 eng validation boards shipped to India	0 days	Fri 6/8/07	Fri 6/8/07
8	Remaining eng validation boards shipped to all sites	0 days	Fri 6/15/07	Fri 6/15/07
9	Validation Party ends	0 days	Fri 6/15/07	Fri 6/15/07
10				
11	Bring Up by Design Team on Brassboard	17 days	Fri 5/11/07	Mon 6/4/07
12	Connect JTAG and CodeWarrior	2 days	Fri 5/11/07	Mon 5/14/07
13	Debug Templates (includes clocking , reset)	3 days	Tue 5/15/07	Thu 5/17/07
14				
15	Initial Memory Validation	1 day	Tue 5/15/07	Tue 5/15/07
16	DDR Read/Write	1 day	Tue 5/15/07	Tue 5/15/07
17				
18	Other Module Validations	12 days	Fri 5/18/07	Mon 6/4/07
19	General purpose timer	2 days	Fri 5/18/07	Mon 5/21/07
20	Enhanced periodic interrupt timer	2 days	Tue 5/22/07	Wed 5/23/07
21	Remaining Memories	3 days	Thu 5/24/07	Mon 5/28/07
22	NAND Read/Write	1 day	Thu 5/24/07	Thu 5/24/07
23	NOR Read/Write	1 day	Fri 5/25/07	Fri 5/25/07
24	PSRAM Read/Write	1 day	Mon 5/28/07	Mon 5/28/07
25	One wire interface,Config serial peripheral interface	5 days	Tue 5/29/07	Mon 6/4/07
26				

Figure 20.11:
Gantt chart.

Project managers manage costs over the life of the project based on the estimates that are made. Cost estimating may be done in several ways but the two main approaches are top-down and bottom-up. A top-down approach relies on experience from previous projects to scale the costs. It might rely on the expertise of middle managers, senior managers, or experienced project managers to provide some or all of the estimated costs. This approach is best used for a quick estimate where accuracy is not as important.

A bottom-up approach to cost estimation relies on the engineers doing the work to make estimates of the cost and activity durations. These estimates should be based on the WBS. The total costs for the project come from a summation of all activity costs. This approach takes more time to work up but is more accurate.

Cost budgeting includes labor, capital related to the project, royalties and licenses, contractual work, and other project expenses. Of these, labor is usually the largest cost. Since teams may be worldwide, labor costs are usually averaged and applied to the total count. Even though there are variances in salaries due to location, experience, and education, an average typically is applied for the budget.

The budget should consider fixed and variable costs that don't or do change, respectively, with any project activity. Examples of the former include leases and rentals. Salaries, wages, supplies, equipment, and other materials are examples of variable costs. Also, the project will have direct and indirect costs. Direct costs might include travel, wages, and materials. Indirect costs are items like taxes and benefits, and might include some services.

Budget estimates are provided as a range. When the project is closed, the budget estimate should have been within −10% to +25% of actual costs. A budget reserve may be used for risk management. A reserve retains discretionary spending authority within the project for small cost variances from plan.

Quality is conformance to requirements and fitness of use. This definition may be illuminated with an example. Bicycles and sedan cars are both used for transportation. One is faster, safer, and offers more creature comforts. The other offers exercise and a more prolonged and intimate view of the countryside. But they may both be high-quality products if they meet the requirements and do what they are intended to do. If recreational exercise on backwoods trails is a planned activity, then a bike may be a high-quality product. Sedans aren't allowed on these trails and don't provide the requisite exercise, so they wouldn't be a high-quality product for use on bike trails. But getting to the bike trails may make the sedan a quality product. The trails could be difficult or impossible to get to except by motor vehicle, so the bike could be a poor-quality product getting there.

Quality plans for software project management address issues such as the functional and performance match of deliverables against commitments, adequacy and acceptability of the deliverable packaging, out-of-box experience including bring-up and configuration, usability, and reliability over time in the field. Plans for monitoring and controlling should be defined.

Human resourcing planning is fundamental to project management. When the project is approved, financial support is provided as well as the people needed to do the work. One consideration is the count of people in each functional area. Another related consideration is what their experience and qualifications are. Together, these factors may determine whether a particular function is on the critical path or poses undue risks that must be watched more carefully.

How these people report or are accountable to the project manager depends on what type of organization is employed. The four types of organizations are functional, weak matrix, strong matrix, and projectized. Each type of organization provides a different level of visibility to the project manager of the resources that should be doing the work.

A functional management organization has human resources managed exclusively by functional managers. It is possible the project manager might never know the names of the people working on the project even if the count of people is learned. In a functional organization, people are moved from one work activity to another as the functional manager decides. Communication to the project manager of personnel movement from one activity to another might be delayed or never happen.

In a weak matrix, individual contributors and team leaders report to their respective functional managers but there is a dotted-line relationship to the project manager. There is clear communication of core team membership to the pertinent key individual contributors, team leads, and functional managers. The performance review of individuals is still done exclusively by the functional manager. The project manager might know the names of the people as well as the count of people assigned to the project.

In a strong matrix organization, the people assigned to the project report to both their functional manager and the project manager. However, the balance of power lies with the project manager compared to the functional manager. The human resources assigned to the project are known by name. Individuals may not be delayed from their work or moved to other work activities without notification and negotiation with the project manager. The project manager sometimes has input into key individual contributor, team lead, and functional manager performance reviews and might even have a defined weighted contribution.

In a projectized environment, once resources are assigned to the project, all management responsibilities fall to the project manager. For the duration of the project, everyone works on the team and only on the team. Functional managers have no responsibilities for routine work assignments or activity management.

A communications plan is vital for project management since this is such an important function of the job. Communications arguably is the most important skill that a project manager exercises. The scope of communications is across all stakeholders. Understanding who are all the project stakeholders and each of the individual communications needs is paramount to developing a communications plan.

Much communication occurs on a regular basis. These are periodic reports that are required or presentations that must be made to management. These are usually the most formal communications and require adherence to particular formats providing information of particular types and in particular ways. A verbal presentation could be required with written content.

Communications are only effective if the message intended to be sent is identical to what is received and interpreted by the recipient. The sender has principal responsibility for ensuring the communications are acceptable in this sense. To achieve this requires careful editing to ensure phrases and terminology are familiar to the recipient and the presentation is done in an appropriate way.

Communications may be structured to be formal or informal for either verbal or written forms. Formal communications are polished. Formal communications of technical issues, project plans, and reports or presentations made to management rely on written methods and may require particular formats and style. Formal verbal communications are used when making presentations to management and may require a particular presentation style. Informal written communications such as by email or instant messaging are very common. Email communication is appropriate for broadcasting information to the team and routine technical discussions. Informal verbal communications are the most common and occur with team members, peers, and stakeholders across the range of project issues.

The risk management process involves many elements for the purpose of producing a risk management plan. If a methodology doesn't already exist, one needs to be defined. Risks need to be documented so they retain visibility and get managed over time.

Risk identification includes those risks that are common to similar projects plus those that are identified by team members. Risks for the project may be organized according to the triple constraint (i.e., scope, schedule, costs, quality, and customer satisfaction). Understanding the WBS elements provides important insights. Understanding the critical path enables risks to be prioritized. Similarly, activities near the critical path need to be managed for risks so they stay off the critical path. The universe of risks needs to be reduced to a manageable size. The risks that are left should be nontrivial and might include some considered important. For this set of risks, the team needs to understand what could trigger the risk. Understanding the risk triggers may provide options for managing the risk.

Qualitative risk analysis is a method of assessing risks subjectively. This work can prioritize the list of risks. Risk response planning may take advantage of this prioritization. The list of risks with an assessment of their criticality may be used to provide a risk rating for the project itself.

Quantitative risk analysis is a method of assessing risks numerically. For example, one approach would provide a financial analysis. This work can prioritize the list of risks, too.

Analysis of schedules for quantitatively determined confidence levels falls under quantitative risk analysis. Of course, the quality of the analysis depends upon the quality of the input data. The critical-path sequence must be known for the project. For each activity on the critical path, quantitative data are needed for the average time it takes to do the activity and some measure of variation about the average time. Typically, this variation is quantified as the variance or its square root, the standard deviation. The mean time to execute the critical-path sequence is the sum of the average times of each activity on the critical path. The variation about this critical-path mean is the sum of all the respective variances, or the square root of the sum of the variances is found for the standard deviation. For measures of variation other than the variance or for complicated distributions, a technique such as Monte Carlo simulation can be performed to understand the probability distribution.

A risk response plan creates owners for each risk with an action to address the risk. The options for addressing risks include avoidance, mitigation, acceptance, and transference. Avoidance details what actions may be taken to prevent the risk from happening. This addresses the root cause of the risk and eliminates it. Mitigation details actions for reducing either the probability of the risk becoming real or the impact if the risk is actualized. Acceptance takes no specific action for the risk but accepts the impact, if it occurs, as an acceptable cost. Transference takes action to transfer the ownership, or responsibility of managing the risk, to someone else.

The last activities in the Planning process involve procurement decisions. There could be the need to decide whether to build, buy, or partner for some of the work. Particularly for buying and partnering, selection of a supplier, arrangement of work with a contractor, or planning the engagement with a partner will be activities to complete.

The Project Management Process of Execution involves using the integration, quality, human resource, communications, and procurement knowledge areas. Integration activities encompass directing and managing project execution. Quality assurance is performed during Execution. During Execution, the project team is acquired and developed over the course of the project. Communications is summarized simply as information distribution but its importance cannot be overstated. During Execution, use of procurement knowledge is applied by requesting seller responses and selecting sellers.

As mentioned previously, the phase of Monitoring and Controlling uses all knowledge areas. Integration involves monitoring and controlling project work and integrating change control. Monitoring and controlling scope involves verification and control. Monitoring and controlling for time, cost, and quality involve schedule, cost, and quality control, respectively. Human resource monitoring and control involve managing the project team. Communications include project performance reporting and managing stakeholders. Risk monitoring and control are done in this phase. Contract administration involves procurement knowledge.

Project performance reports are of various kinds. These could include status reports and progress reports. There could be reports of a more quantitative nature to show forecasts and analyze trends, variances, or earned value.

Stakeholders are individuals whose interests are positively or negatively impacted by the project. Obvious stakeholders include the sponsor of the project, the project manager, and the members of the project core team. Additional stakeholders include the customer or recipient of the product the project is delivering. Other project managers could be stakeholders if their own project priority or resources are impacted.

Stakeholder management starts with identifying stakeholders and their needs. Their influence and impact on the project has to be assessed. Throughout the project, stakeholders need to be involved. Periodically, reviews should determine whether their needs are being met.

Closing a project involves the integration and procurement knowledge areas. Project closure and contract closure are the respective activities in these knowledge areas. Contract closure occurs before administrative closure.

Contract closure verifies the work was completed in a satisfactory way. Final payments are made and cost accounting is done for the last time. Contract records are updated and become part of the project archived documents. An exercise is done on what lessons were learned during procurement to understand what was done well and what could be done better next time.

Project closure occurs at the end of planned project activities or else when senior management terminates the project. Verification completion ensures the work was completed in a satisfactory way. All documents should be finalized and necessary reports published. Project closure produces archived project documents, presentations, and results. An exercise is done on what lessons were learned during the project to understand what was done well and what could be done better next time. Each project should be formally accepted and closed with senior management approval. After the project is formally closed, resources may be released.

Project life-cycle

The project life-cycle for software has some similarities to the project management life-cycle. The project life-cycle also consists of phases in which particular work is done. Typical project life-cycle phases are Concept, Definition, Planning, Execution, Validation, Ramp, and Closure. Program management's responsibility is to ensure the program is approved by senior management through the life-cycle phases in a timely manner. The work that is actually being done in the program should correspond to the formal phase in which the program is recognized.

The Concept phase evaluates the technical and commercial viability of the product. This includes defining the project at a high level for scope, schedule, and costs. The scope is informed by a market requirements document (MRD) which will include some important use cases. Deliverables for the Concept phase are provided in Table 20.9.

Table 20.9: Concept-phase deliverables.

	Phase Deliverables
Concept	– Market Requirements Doc – Initial requirements – Staffing (count) estimate – Nuclear core team – Prelim risk management plan – Prelim milestones – Prelim scoping of software deliverables – Prelim definition of supported targets

Initial requirements come from different sources. Leading customers could provide use cases from which requirements may be derived. Engineering can supply requirements that result in continuous improvement from a previous related project. And architects may have some requirements based upon an early understanding of use cases and any applicable standards.

Costs will capture full-time engineering equivalents (FTE) required to do the work from start until project closure. In one way to estimate staffing, a similar program that is in or through execution may be scaled or analogized. The closer the programs match and the better the quality of the data from these predecessor programs, the better the scaling estimate will be. In another way, known as Wideband Delphi, an estimate convergence eventually is gotten from experts polled iteratively after sessions that provide information and feedback on the last polling results. Each successive poll for estimates is done secretly by the experts.

In the Concept phase, the core team will involve only a few key individuals such as the product manager, architect, and perhaps some functional management. The preliminary risk management plan might consist of a simple list. The schedule is composed of high-level milestones.

Approval to proceed from the Concept phase into the Definition phase indicates there is authorization in principle to do this project. It is management recognition that there is a good fit in the product pipeline for this NPI project.

In the Definition phase, the principal delivery is the preliminary product requirements document (PRD). The PRD captures business objectives and use cases that drive product requirements. Engineering reviews each of the requirements and accepts or rejects them individually. For those they agree to do, a response from each affected engineering area is linked to each requirement. This information comprises the preliminary software requirements specification (SRS). The engineering work is used to create the preliminary schedule. The PRD, SRS, and use cases get baselined after the Definition phase. Table 20.10 lists deliverables for the Definition phase.

Table 20.10: Definition-phase deliverables.

	Phase Deliverables
Definition	– Use cases – Draft Product Requirements Doc – Draft Software Requirements Spec – Scrubbed milestones – Staffing (teams ID'ed with counts) plan – Full core team – Updated risk management plan – Milestones – Prelim budget

The PRD is developed in phases. Eventually, this document lists all the requirements in the finest granularity created from all the software use cases that the end user or customer provides. The PRD is started in the Definition phase with a subset of requirements consisting of the most critical ones for the project.

An initial software requirements spec (SRS) is created from the PRD. This document provides the engineering responses to the requirements, foremost of which is the agreement or disagreement whether the requirement will be done. It provides the direct linkage to the requirements for the different functional areas that will create the software. Each requirement must have at least one software specification response, but some PRD requirements will have multiple SRS responses. This might be because of coverage and overlapping engineering responsibilities, component interactions, multiple owners, or no clear owner. The software architect has responsibility for determining whether the engineering response in the SRS adequately satisfies the product requirement.

Later in the life-cycle, a traceability report will show the test results (e.g., pass or fail) for each test run against each SRS engineering response which will each be correlated to a specific requirement in the PRD. It should indicate that tests have been run against each SRS entry. The traceability report should clearly state which features have (or have not) been delivered in the release with explicit references to SRS and PRD entries.

Once the initial SRS is ready, high-level milestones may be created. The dates associated with Definition-phase milestones are rough estimates. Also, dependencies are defined to accomplish the work.

The Definition phase is not only concerned with scope, schedule, and cost. For completeness, this phase should begin to address concerns for quality and customer satisfaction, too.

There are many deliverables in the Planning phase. To gain senior management or executive approval for completing the Planning phase requires extensive involvement of the core team. Table 20.11 indicates the deliverables that must be provided in the Planning phase.

Table 20.11: Planning-phase deliverables.

	Phase Deliverables
Planning	– Product Requirements Doc – Software Requirements Doc – Test plan – Traceabilitv matrix – Documentation plan – Staffing (names) plan – Risk management plan – Activity based sched/detailed milestones – Budget – Configuration management plan – Change managment plan – Releases packaging plan – Communications plan

The Planning phase fully develops the PRD with final requirements. This work is a predecessor activity to finishing the SRS. The detailed work activities are captured in this document. The completed SRS enables a detailed schedule to be produced. The static, dynamic, functional, and performance test plans are completed. The traceability matrix exists when there is traceability from the requirements, to engineering responses to those requirements, to test plans against those responses. When an architect reviews the traceability matrix and determines it is correct and complete, then the traceability matrix may be considered finalized.

The PRD, SRS, and use cases get baselined after the Definition and Planning phases. These are the routine baselines that may be expected. However, if a change request is approved, then another baseline is applied. The main causes of change requests are new feature requests and missed dependencies (i.e., internal deliveries from one team to another).

A traceability matrix such as is shown in Table 20.12 couples the software product requirements against the software requirement specification (SRS) and ensures each SRS response is tested. During readiness reviews, the traceability matrix provides a complete view of all the requirements, the response to those requirements, and test results for the product release under consideration.

Documentation is an important deliverable that must be made within the program life-cycle or with the product delivery. Customers will want hardware quick-start guides and a reference manual. A reference manual provides a detailed description of how the hardware

Table 20.12: Traceability matrix.

No.	PRD No.	Requirement	SRS No.	Response	Test ID/Use Case	Result	Comments
1	101	Improve compiler memory usage and compile time	101.1	Implement improvements in compiler linear loop transformation	defect 37422	Pass	build 6
2	101	Improve assembler memory usaqe and compile time	101.2	Implement improvements in assembler	defect 37422	Pass	build 6
3	118	Debugger plug-in will support 4 core processor	118.1	4 core processor will be supported	564	Pass	build 77

works and how to use it. Any software release should include release notes that provide summary information on defects. This helps users and customers avoid unpleasant surprises since defects and workarounds are known up front. Customers may proceed with implementation without wasting time or incurring unplanned delays. Application notes might be provided. These are technical instructions for complex solutions to particular problems.

In the Planning phase, the most accurate estimate of staffing needs to be provided. Some data suggest the highest accuracy of effort estimation comes from bottom-up planning in which the effort estimates are created from a WBS. The WBS captures the scope of work and enables schedule and resources to be determined within practical constraints. Particularly if individual contributors are able to contribute to effort estimates along with functional managers, estimation accuracy improves due to the collective wisdom of the group, which exceeds that of a few experts [7].

Resources for the project should be provided at the project start and maintained until project closure. Over the life of the program, project resource levels will fluctuate as their work demands. In the Planning phase of the life-cycle, the resources should be identified down to the name of the individual doing the work. If the names of the people supposed to be doing the work aren't known, then it is likely no one actually is doing the work. Program management by exception is concerned with knowing that the named resources are still assigned and working on the project as planned and as committed by senior management when the project was approved. Resources that are approved to work on a project should not be removed from the project without negotiation with the project manager.

Each project should have a comprehensive review of risks enumerated during planning, and then the highest-ranking risks need active management. Over the life of the program, risk management will include pursuit of activities to directly address risks. In other words, risk management should be active and not just a passive assessment of risk levels over time. It does little good to just make a list of risks. Instead, activities and owners of those activities should be assigned to respond to each of the most critical risks.

An example of a risk response table is shown in Table 20.13 with several risk examples. This tabulation is a comprehensive format for a large program, rolling up important project risks. The form is patterned after the failure mode and effects analysis used in the automotive industry with some added project management emphases. For smaller programs, this format could be tailored by scaling it down to retain relevance.

Risks and issues may be thought of as related in time. Risks deal with problems that could occur in the future. Issues deal with current problems. It is possible an issue was initially identified as a risk and over the course of time progressed from potential to actual. Active risk management is meant to provide proactive prevention or reduction in impact of problems.

The first column in Table 20.13 just numbers the risks. The next column is the project constraint, which is chosen from the triple constraint. The choices are among schedule, financial, scope, quality and customer satisfaction. Column three is the process function or requirements in which the risk exists. The fourth column is the potential failure mode if the risk is realized. The next or fifth column is the potential effect of the failure.

The sixth column ranks the severity or impact from low (e.g., value equals 1) to high (e.g., value equals 5). The potential cause or mechanism of failure is listed in the seventh column. Column eight ranks the occurrence of the risk or its probability from low to high using the same numerical scale as before. The ninth column lists the way the current design or process control prevents the risk from occurring. The tenth column lists the way a risk would be detected with the current design or process.

Column 11 ranks the detection or exposure of the risk using the previous numerical scale. The product of the three numerical values of the severity, occurrence, and detection is entered as the risk priority number (RPN) value in column 12. The RPN values enable the disparate risks to be prioritized. The 13th column has the recommended action to address the risk. The next column, the 14th column, lists who is responsible for the action to address the risk and what date the completion is targeted. The action taken and the effective date are provided in the 15th column.

The 16th column lists the risk trigger. The next to last column lists one of the risk responses. These choices include mitigation, avoidance, acceptance, or transference. The last column is the contingency plan if the risk response is not effective or acceptable and the risk is realized.

Table 20.13: Risk response table.

No.	Project Constraint	Process Function/ Requirements	Potential Failure Mode	Potential Effect(s) of Failure	Severity (Impact) [1 = low; 5 = high]	Potential Cause(s)/ Mechanism (s) of Failure	Occurrence (Probability) [1 = low; 5 = high]	Current Design/ Process Controls Prevention	Current Design/ Process Controls Detection	Detection (Exposure) [1 = low; 5 = high]	RPN	Recommended Action(s)	Responsibility & Target Completion Date	Actions Taken & Effective Date	Risk Trigger	Risk Response	Contingency Plan
1	Financial	Libraries for new corners	Timing closure (2-3%)	Loss of margin	4	Scaled capacitance models used instead of characterized ones	2	STA	STA	1	8	Consider adding additional margin to critical nets; don't waive violations; use only cz'ed libraries	Design lead, Technology develop lead, 31Jan		Edge of spec Si	Mitigation	Optimize wafer fab process
2	Scope	Validation	Bugs not found	Customers find bugs instead of validation & cz	5	Improve scope of tests by making more exhaustive and random runs	3	validation tests and prioritization	Validation work	3	45	Improve staffing for more thorough validation	IC validation lead, Product eng lead, 9Oct		post-Si Validation	Mitigation	post-TO verif runs with random test pattern; extensive Palladium testing; early OS delivery to MDB
3	Schedule	rev1.0 verification	Bug in module or SoG taped out	HW fix req'd or SW workaround req'd	5	Schedule pressure to tapeout limiting # of verification runs	3	verification runs	RTL & GL verification	3	45	Continue increasing # of verification tests until tapeout is req'd	Module design lead, module verification lead, 31Jan		Tapeout deadline	Mitigation	Continue verification after TO and hope any bug caught can be fixed in metal
4	Customer satisfac	Power consumption	High power consump- tion	Low yield due to lack of margin to specs	5	Models have discrepancy to tester Si cz for available margins	4	Power simulation	Power simulation	3	60	Use high Si utilization, high toggle rate patterns	Design lead, Product eng lead, 9Oct		Si cz	Mitigation	

Projects or small programs may utilize simpler risk management. Table 20.14 is an example of a simpler format while retaining the action oriented focus.

Table 20.14: Simplified risk management table.

No.	Risk Description	Risk Level	Owner	Action to Mitigate Risk	Assigned	Due Date	Closed
2	Start of downlink integration on 8157 platform	High	Matanya	Integrate into scheduler the fix for managing all the writes to the memory mapped registers	29-Aug	4-Sep	4-Sep
1	Schedule risk due to late delivery of boards to Linux team	Med	Sunil	Establish board farm for remote users so boards may be shared and utilization across time zones improved	5-Aug	9-Sep	9-Sep
3	Readiness of antenna interface controller (AIC) driver for RTOS drop	Med	Dov	Eng scheduled for travel for on-site AIC bring up	31-Aug	20-Sep	19-Sep

The program schedule may be high-level and managed by exception. But the underlying project schedules should be more detailed, such as with short-duration activity-based schedules or detailed, shortly spaced milestones. The activities are defined from the work breakdown structure. Activities may be defined for durations of work until it pauses. Pauses may include handoffs, file transfers, software builds, reviews, tests, etc.

Activity durations should be short enough that they are fractions of the time duration between progress reports. For example, if projects are reviewed weekly, then the activities should be of duration less than half a week. This enables insight into progress so issues may be discovered early for response.

It is important to understand what value an activity-based schedule (ABS) provides and what it doesn't. It provides detailed planning for work activities that may include complex interactions and for dependencies that must be met for the work to be successful. Activities are based on work packages. These issues may be worked on in advance. Also, it provides a general methodology for assessing progress between milestones. What it doesn't provide, for complex projects like integrated-circuit design or software development, is an accurate forecast of how the details of reality will unfold. After completion, a comparison of the actual work sequences and durations for these complex projects will likely provide little resemblance to the schedule created in planning. Planned activity durations and sequences won't map exactly onto reality, but the general flows should align. What should be observed is that planned and real major milestone achievements should match. This disconnect between detailed planning and reality, with all its complications and inconveniences, is a factor that could create confusion in the organization if stakeholders are not knowledgeable a priori of the value proposition of activity-based scheduling and the significant differences that may be expected between planning and reality. This is an educational and communications challenge.

Configuration management (CM) involves control of software versions, naming conventions, configuration standardization, and conformance to applicable technical and coding standards. For programs, CM provides a standardized view across projects. A repository of a particular structure is employed for software version control for which there are security and backup procedures. Rules are provided for changes made to the mainline and branches, to shared code, and depending upon the change complexity. There are check-in and check-out criteria so the correct version is always being worked on by teams.

Confusion and wasted work are avoided since teams are known to be working on the expected version. As software complexity grows, CM becomes more vital for maintaining coordinated progress. Code review is a prerequisite to mergers. Components of CM include revision control, change control, and requirements management. Change control manages functional and performance-related change requests as well as non-conforming product. Defect discovery, reporting, tracking, and resolution make management of non-conforming product an important body of work.

Quality expectations should be detailed with supporting plans. Customer engagement and support should be addressed for customer satisfaction.

In the Planning phase, the program manager should start to require project presentations so the whole team becomes familiar with what the work is and how it all relates. These presentations should be shared in the core team meetings. A project website should be the repository for the presentations so they may serve as reference material for the team.

The Execution phase converts the detailed plans into actions. The purpose of this phase is to do the work to bring the product to release. Progress is tracked against plans and problem solving occurs as required. The deliverables expected in the Execution phase are listed in Table 20.15.

It is not unusual that software requirements might change for market reasons based on performance, competitiveness, or to make the product more compelling. So an update to the product requirements and SRS could be required.

In the Execution phase, there should be active management of the risks detailed during planning. Focus is particularly strong on activities that lie on the critical path. Resource assurance, from engineers to the tools they need to do their jobs, needs to be consistently monitored. Important decisions that can't be made at the team level or critical issues that cannot be resolved quickly should be escalated for resolution.

Table 20.15: Execution-phase deliverables.

	Phase Deliverables
Execution	– Test results reviews – Tfaceability matrix reviews – Release reviews – Documentation publications – Resource management – Risk management – Activity and schedule tracking – Budget tracking – Configuration management – Change management – Packaging for releases – Communications

Two general types of program reviews need to be held regularly and frequently with the functional managers or project managers. The first meeting determines progress and issues. In particular, this meeting reviews status, issues, risks, plans, recommendations, escalations, and decisions needed. Decisions may address many things including spending, build or buy choices, prioritization of work, go/no go choices, or re-tooling issues. Program management is responsible for making sure decisions are made in a timely manner so work isn't adversely impacted. Detailed review of project-level risk management activities may be done in this meeting.

The second meeting deals more with program management fundamentals. In particular, the second meeting reviews the project scope to understand if it has changed, the project schedule to understand the rate of progress and the critical path(s), the critical path to learn if it has changed since the last review and the number and description of activities approaching the critical path, resource assignments including changes, the project financials, quality including test results and defect counts, and customer satisfaction. It is possible that there may be multiple critical paths of different activities which require attention.

A basic function of program management is assigning and tracking action items. These action items typically are generated in the different meetings that are held. A simple way for these to be tracked to closure is in a spreadsheet such as is shown in Table 20.16.

Validation phase deliverables are depicted in Table 20.17. In the Validation phase, test results need to be reviewed. These will include static, dynamic, functional, and performance tests. There might be tests run to validate conformance to standards. Similarly, the test results in traceability matrices need to be reviewed so appropriate decisions may be made regarding releases. Pertinent documents are published and product releases are made.

Table 20.16: Action-item tracker.

No.	Category	Description	Owner	Dates: Assigned	Due	Closed	Comment
1	Requirements	Consolidate requirements	Product mgr	2-Jan	9-Jan		including customer requirements, support model, testing riqor
2	Communications	Communicate to the customer the date that the standalone drop can implement the feature request	Program mgr	7-Jan	10-Jan		
3	Support	Finalize workshop agenda	Applications eng mgr	10-Jan	17-Jan		

Table 20.17: Validation-phase deliverables.

	Phase Deliverables
Validation	– Test results reviews – Traceability matrix reviews – Report on conformance to standards – Documentation publications – Product releases

As listed in Table 20.18, the Ramp phase has two important deliverables. The first is to complete the plan transitioning from development into manufacturing or sustaining. The second is to establish support mechanisms for users and customers to make contact for service requests and provide different levels of technical support depending upon the severity of the problem.

The last life-cycle phase is Closure. Program closure actions should be completed before all resources are re-assigned to other projects. There are four typical closure actions, as indicted in Table 20.19. Key documents and collateral needs to be archived. A cost variance analysis is done and a report is published. A lessons-learned exercise is conducted. The last deliverable is release of the resources.

The customer should be notified formally that NPI activities are drawing down and that program management is ending. If routine meetings with the customer have been held, these meetings need to be cancelled in lieu of any meetings that production will want to conduct.

Table 20.18: Ramp-phase deliverables.

	Phase Deliverables
Ramp	– Complete manufacturing transition plan – Establish support mechanisms

Table 20.19: Closure-phase deliverables.

	Phase Deliverables
Closure	– Archive key documents & collateral – Budget variance report – Lessons learned – Release resources

Many pertinent program files find their way to the program manager's computer. All these need to be reviewed with an eye to archiving these in a public repository so they may be retrieved in an orderly fashion later if ever needed. Candidate files for archive include the architecture specification, the design documents, test plans, and validation results, etc.

A summary review should be conducted to compare Planned versus Actual results for the program scope, schedule, costs/resources, quality, and customer satisfaction. Data such as these may be used later for benchmarking purposes to understand opportunities for improvement in program management.

A review should be held with a cross-functional team to document lessons learned during the life of the program. A ground rule should be that only actionable items with an owner may be proffered. These can be followed up to closure and may constitute an important exercise in process improvement. If suggestions aren't actionable, they tend to be in the categories of comments or criticisms. Realistically, it is doubtful that someone later will have the time or interest to do historical research. But actions that have been closed and implemented provide ongoing benefits for the next programs.

Table 20.20 tries to capture important points of five examples of lessons learned. The first column just numbers the different lessons learned. The next column lists the functional area in which the lesson was learned. The third column has a description of the issue. Column four lists the improvement from the learned lesson, which is the action addressing the issue. The correction is located in the fifth column. The sixth column lists the owner of the action associated with the learned lesson. In the column, titles are provided, but, in practice, the owner's name will be listed. The due date for completing the action is in column seven. The next to the last column is the date the action was closed. Comments may be entered in the last column.

Table 20.20: Lessons-learned table.

No.	Functional area	Issue Description	Improvement	Correction Location	Owner	Due Date	Date Closed	Comment
1	Business	Late Products Requirements Document and lack of process to get business filter first before technical assessment and commitment	Make business decisions before adding/changing features when definition is supposed to be frozen	Management Program Review	Product manager	30-Jun	30-Jun	Need business input to Change Review Committee to determine importance
2	Business	Uncompetitively large die area	Incorporate die area optimization in Definition	Management Program Review	IC architect, IC program manager	30-Jun	23-Jun	Now standard practice
3	Technical	Changing Design Collateral (lib.IO's)	Need to freeze library labels at the time of IC architecture spec closure		TechDev	30-Jun	23-Jun	Standard practice for follow-on parts in a technology but wont work for initial part
4	Validation	Late engineering validation board deliveries	Plan for earlier start of engineering validation board requirements and dependent deliveries	Engineering validation board design team	Engineering validation board manager, IC program manager	30-Jun	30-Jun	
5	Technical	IBIS models need re-delivery	Formal internal review after IBIS model generation		IBIS team, product engineering, test engineering	30-Jun	30-Jun	

The program schedule needs to be closed and archived. This could involve updating and closing documents tracking milestones. It could include updating scheduling software using particular required archival procedures such as setting final baselines or printing reports.

Some activities that are common for closure are shown in Table 20.21.

Table 20.21: Closure activities.

No.	Description	Owner	Comment
1	Close all action items		
2	Update all meeting minutes		
3	Document and archive customer project acceptance		
4	Clean up computer workspace files		
5	Archive files		
6	Summary analysis of Planned versus Actuals for triple contraints		Scope, schedule, costs/resources, quality, customer satisfaction
7	Document and archive lessons learned		Track and close actionable items
8	Close project schedule		
9	Formally close project phase		
10	Release resources		

An initial activity could be to follow up and ensure all program action items are closed. At this point in the program, the actions may not be completely dispositioned, but if they're related to NPI, then it could be appropriate to close them at this time.

Formal closure officially ends program activities. The core team members, all the human resources assigned to all the project teams, and the supervisors of all the people assigned to the team need to be notified of this formal ending, so these people may be re-assigned to their next project.

Problem-solving

Solving problems is a principal contribution of a program manager. Before trying to solve any problem, the use case(s) must be understood. This directs the effort correctly and avoids wasting time.

Often, the program manager can solve problems just by listening carefully. Many times, the problem is well recognized by the team and there is consensus on what should be done to fix it. They just need someone to make a decision. In this case, the program manager needs to become familiar with the problem and its impact, understand the proposed fix and why it is considered the best one, and make the decision formally. If the solution isn't so apparent, the best first course of action is to ask those closest to the problem what they think. In any case, when a problem arises, the program manager should go and see the problem. This inevitably leads to better clarity than trying to solve the problem remotely or abstractly.

Complex problems could require more sophisticated problem-solving skills. Problem-solving skills may be sharpened by utilizing some methodologies that have proven their effectiveness. These include Occam's razor, poka-yoke, and the Ford 8D process.

Ockham's razor, attributed to fourteenth-century English philosopher William of Ockham, might provide insight into problems. "Accept the simplest explanation with the fewest assumptions and reject the more fantastic and convoluted explanations." This approach narrows down the list of possible explanations that have to be investigated.

Poka-yoke is a process in which the question "Why?" is asked five times to dig into the root cause of a problem, and then finally the question "How do I fix it?" is asked. This approach drives to the solution that needs to be enacted.

The Ford 8-Discipline (Ford 8D) problem-solving methodology lends itself well to either difficult or subtle problems. The eight steps or disciplines are: form a team, describe the problem, implement containment actions, find the root cause of the problem, choose and verify the permanent corrective actions, implement the permanent corrective actions, prevent recurrence, and congratulate the team.

Finally, any decision that is made should be reasonable and defensible for the circumstances. This is a simple test to apply before communication. If a decision can't pass this test, then it needs to be reconsidered. The circumstances matter since the heat of a crisis may produce different decisions than after calm reflection.

Communications

A principal responsibility of program management is communications and reporting. Internal communications must be made to the program sponsor, senior management, the core team, and stakeholders. Communications occur through many modes including verbal and nonverbal forms, face to face and remotely, in front of large numbers of people and individually, with vice presidents and with individual contributors, with local and international teams.

Communication involves the message and the mode of delivering the message. Written communications may be more formal and are necessary for historical records.
Verbal communication may be more informal but can be important for timeliness, soliciting alignment, or providing advance notice to avoid surprises. Extended discussions are difficult with written messages but are facilitated with higher-baud-rate verbal exchange. Whether written or verbal, communication is successful when the message intended to be imparted

by the presenter is received accurately and understood by the audience. Communication accuracy, clarity, and conciseness aid the achievement of understanding.

Formal communications should be done with a written record. These could be real or they could be soft copies. Formal documents may take different forms. For example, legal documents typically are published in a word-processing document, while presentations to executives may be done in a Microsoft® PowerPoint® slideshow. Email has transitioned over time from being considered an informal mode of communication to the situation now where it may be either a formal or an informal one. Many formal communications that were reserved to hard copy notifications are now done by email. This is true for team communications, company internal news and announcements, or communications to customers or third-party providers.

It is the prerogative of management to require reports. Reports characterize the program. But reports are not program management. Providing these is one of many functions of program management. From the perspective of program management, reports represent overhead to a program and don't in and of themselves add value or improve productivity. From the perspective of senior management, program management needs to carefully consider how to gain the most value from the time having to be spent on communications. This might include tuning the presentation to address escalated issues, solicit management help where it's needed, getting decisions made in a timely manner, and aligning management perception with program reality.

On an ongoing basis, program managers will report the program status, issues, plans, and recommendations to the program sponsor. These reports occur periodically and at phase reviews in the program life-cycle. Program sponsors provide continuing support and perseverance to see the program reach volume manufacturing. Sometimes, it will be necessary to terminate programs before they reach production. This may be due to shifts in corporate strategy, changes in the market, or noncompliance in the program to meeting constraints. Since there is a financial benefit to stopping programs early rather than late, reviews of program assumptions and initial work progress should be especially careful in the early stages of the program life-cycle, in initiation and planning.

Formal reviews usually require public speaking combined with presentation of materials. There are many elements in public speaking. Information needs to be presented in an organized but engaging way. This keeps everyone's attention. An appropriate level of communication needs to be chosen so the expressions and terms are familiar to the audience. This prevents confusion. Speech should be clear and appropriately loud for everyone to hear. But public speaking may involve more than just verbal discourse. If a forum is provided in which a presentation is to be made in person, then personal appearance, dress, and the way in which you physically comport yourself becomes important. Non-verbal communication from body language becomes at least as important as verbal communication, since people are watching and interpreting what they see while they listen.

The format of program status reviews may be required to meet certain requirements. Having uniform format requirements helps the audience understand better and faster the presentation materials from a series of presenters. Once the format is recognized, the information within the presentation is understood. However, the general content of routine updates and reports is similar. This includes status, issues, plans, and recommendations [8]. The issues and recommendations may sometimes be coupled if escalated items are included along with a recommendation for disposition.

Full program reviews should cover the program triple constraint plus status, issues, plans, and recommendations. These comprehensive reviews could occur monthly or quarterly.

Communication to the core team and between core team members is usually informal. There may be some standing weekly meetings to which some or all core team members are invited. One of these might be a technical meeting led by the program manager that is driven by all major issues. The agenda may change slowly over time as issues change with the program maturity. Or the technical meeting might reduce the agenda in any given week to a deep dive into one particular issue. These meetings might have flexibility to devolve from quick updates into working sessions, depending upon the need.

Another weekly communication forum might be for core team member updates. A standard one-page format might be appropriate where the presenter provides the status, issues, plans, and recommendations. This meeting is not a working meeting but is for updates and reports. From this meeting, the program manager will collect escalated issues and action items. He will need to address the escalated issues until they are resolved. The action items need to be assigned to owners and tracked until they are closed.

Also, depending on where the program is in its life-cycle, there will be recurring meetings addressing particular areas of emphasis, e.g., reviews of the architecture specification, readiness to tape out the design database to the mask house, validation and characterization progress of silicon, etc. The program manager is responsible for leading or having conducted the appropriate number of meetings which have durations long enough to be productive but short enough to not waste people's time. In addition, each core area of the program will likely need recurring meetings specialized to their concerns. The program manager may never participate in these narrow-interest meetings but he will want to know they are occurring under the core team member's leadership. Of course, the ultimate informal communication medium is email.

A primary responsibility of program management is customer communications. In these, the program manager represents the company. The relationship is decidedly unequal. Companies are in business to meet customers' needs. Customers provide the financial means to stay in business. The ideal situation builds a relationship so customers consider your company a preferred partner in their success.

Customer communication requirements depend upon the engagement. Even if they are friendly, communications tend to be more formal. Traveling may be required for kickoff meetings and for periodic reviews. As in any type of relationship, meeting in person is always the best way to build a positive relationship with your customer. Teleconferencing is a lower-cost and more common meeting forum. Email exchanges can be prolific but these are informal modes of communication. Formal reports are produced for presentations or to meet specific deliverables. These latter have invariably been scrubbed internally for appropriate content and message.

There may be some documents that are created with joint input. These include legal documents including legal terms, business terms, and statements of work (SOW). Whether it is constituted as a legal document or not, the SOW may be used to define important deliverables and dependencies.

A jointly accessible program website may be maintained so reports can be stored in a central location and archived. This is an advantage over distributions using just email.

An intimate relationship with the customer program manager is preferable. An advantage of this is the opportunity for nemawashi. This Japanese legacy process lays the groundwork for mutual understanding informally before issues come to the fore formally. Nemawashi builds personal relationships and relies upon close, offline discussions. It opens the window more into the customer's perspective in an informal environment. Perhaps most importantly, it prevents unpleasant surprises in a formal environment.

Abbreviations, symbols, acronyms

ABS	activity-based schedule
API	application programming interface
CM	configuration management
CMMI®	Capability Maturity Model Integration
CPM	critical-path method
DFT	design for test
DSP	digital signal processor
FTE	full-time equivalent
HAL	hardware abstraction layer
I/O	input/output
IP	intellectual property
LLC	logical link control
MAC	media access control

MPU microprocessor unit
MRD market requirement document
NPI new product introduction
OS operating system
OSI Open System Integration
PDM product management
PERT program evaluation and review technique
PMO Program Management Office
R&D research and development
RLC radio link control
RPN risk priority number
SoC system on a chip
SOW statement of work
SRS software requirement specification
WBS work breakdown structure

Copyright acknowledgments

Special permission to reproduce the slides "Continuous Representation: PAs by Category" and "Staged Representation: PAs by Maturity Level" from the slide presentation Model-Based Improvement by Scott Reed, copyright 2007 by Carnegie Mellon University, is granted by the Software Engineering Institute.

This Carnegie Mellon University and Software Engineering Institute Material is furnished on an "as-is" basis. Carnegie Mellon University makes no warranties of any kind, either expressed or implied, as to any matter including, but not limited to, warranty of fitness for purpose or merchantability, exclusivity, or results obtained from use of the material. Carnegie Mellon University does not make any warranty of any kind with respect to freedom from patent, trademark, or copyright infringement.

®Capability Maturity Model, CMM, and CMMI are registered in the U.S. Patent and Trademark Office by Carnegie Mellon University.

Special permission to reproduce the slide "Summarizing Generic Goals and Practices" from Introduction to CMMI v.1.2, copyright 2007 by Carnegie Mellon University, is granted by Cepeda Systems & Software Analysis, Inc.

Special permission to reproduce the table "Project Management Processes" from *A Guide to the Project Management Body of Knowledge* (PMBOK® Guide), 3rd edn, Project Management Institute, Inc. 2004. Copyright and all rights reserved. Material from this publication has been reproduced with the permission of PMI.

References

[1] W.G. Waldo, Program Management for System on Chip Platforms, Inkwater Press, 2010.
[2] M.B. Chrissis, M. Konrad, S. Shrum, CMMI® Guidelines for Process Integration and Product Improvement, second ed., Addison-Wesley, 2007.
[3] Unpublished presentation by Paul D'Arcy, 1 Mar, 2011, Freescale® Semiconductor.
[4] W.G. Waldo, Classic Leadership Principles, Inkwater Press, 2004 (p. 72).
[5] Unpublished presentation by Wayne McCleve, 21 Feb, 2009, Freescale® Semiconductor.
[6] *A Guide to the Project Management Body of Knowledge* (PMBOK® Guide), third ed. Project Management Institute, Inc. 2004. Copyright and all rights reserved. Material from this publication has been reproduced with the permission of PMI.
[7] J. Surowiecki, The Wisdom of Crowds, Anchor, 2005.
[8] W.R. Daniels, J.G. Mathers, Change-ABLE Organization, ACT Publishing, 1997.

CHAPTER 21

Agile Development for Embedded Systems

Bruce Douglass

Chapter Outline

Software Engineering for Embedded Systems.
DOI: http://dx.doi.org/10.1016/B978-0-12-415917-4.00021-9
© 2013 Elsevier Inc. All rights reserved.

Introduction

Agile has a bad rap in the embedded systems world. To be fair, some of this is self-inflicted. Very little literature exists for applying agile to embedded systems development and most of what does exist treats embedded systems as a simple variant of IT software. In addition, many self-proclaimed "Agilistas" really don't apply the principles and practices of agile but instead use the term to justify a lack of planning, design, governance, and follow through. Additional concerns that remain largely unaddressed by the agile community are fixed-price bids, hardware-software co-development, and compliance with regulatory agencies and their certification standards.

Still, the notion of agility is compelling – responsiveness to changing requirements, avoiding all the manual paperwork required by many embedded development environments, and addressing the problems incurred with late integration. These are all pain points for virtually every embedded developer. Agile approaches tackle these recurring problems with a combination of reordering work tasks, changing how work tasks are done, and in some cases, avoiding the tasks altogether.

The term "process", used in software development, merely refers to the tasks we perform to create software, their inputs and outputs, their sequencing, and the definition of the steps and work involved in their execution. (We will use the term "task" in this chapter to denote a software developer work task and not a unit of software concurrency, unless otherwise stated.) Process provides guidance to workers in many different roles and allows them to communicate and collaborate during the creation of this complex entity we call "software".

The most common process style, known as waterfall, is based on the idea that we can prescribe a specific linear work organization of tasks. Subsumed in that idea is the notion that we can do so without any significant errors. We know this to be incorrect from man-millennia of global software development experience. Interestingly, the waterfall process got its start in 1970 from a paper by Dr. Winston Royce entitled "Managing the Development of Large Software Systems" [1]. Although Dr. Royce is the first one to discuss the waterfall life-cycle he is clearly not in favor of it. In fact, he states that "An implementation plan . . . keyed only to these steps, however, is doomed". (We software engineers have got to teacher managers to read the text and not just look at the pretty pictures!)

There is ample theoretical and practical evidence that the waterfall life-cycle is deeply and fundamentally flawed and has led to numerous software project failures. These failures can be classified into two types: schedule and quality. A schedule failure means that the effort and calendar time for a project cannot be adequately predicted by a waterfall plan. A quality failure means that the delivered system has too many flaws and these flaws are too severe for the system to be successful for its intended use. The waterfall approach fails because at its core it assumes that one can schedule invention with high predictability and one can implement without defects. We have lots of evidence that simply isn't true.

This is, of course, old news.

Most people move to agile approaches for empirical reasons rather than theoretical purity. Specifically, most people take up agile methods to improve product quality and secondarily to improve performance against schedule. Agile methods achieve these goals because they assume you can't completely plan a project (and therefore have to pay attention to project progress and adjust plans accordingly) and that you can't implement without defects (and therefore you have to test continuously and adjust the implementation accordingly). These realizations led to the creation of the Agile Manifesto [2]:

- Individuals and interactions over processes and tools
- Working software over comprehensive documentation
- Customer collaboration over contract negotiation
- Responding to change over following a plan.

The Manifesto is based on 12 principles for agile software development [2]:

- Our highest priority is to satisfy the customer through early and continuous delivery of valuable software.
- Welcome changing requirements, even late in development. Agile processes harness change for the customer's competitive advantage.
- Deliver working software frequently, from a couple of weeks to a couple of months, with a preference to the shorter timescale.
- Business people and developers must work together daily throughout the project.
- Build projects around motivated individuals. Give them the environment and support they need, and trust them to get the job done.
- The most efficient and effective method of conveying information to and within a development team is face-to-face conversation.
- Working software is the primary measure of progress.
- Agile processes promote sustainable development. The sponsors, developers, and users should be able to maintain a constant pace indefinitely.
- Continuous attention to technical excellence and good design enhances agility.
- Simplicity – the art of maximizing the amount of work not done – is essential.

- The best architectures, requirements, and designs emerge from self-organizing teams.
- At regular intervals, the team reflects on how to become more effective, then tunes and adjusts its behavior accordingly.

There are a number of processes that implement these principles, including Extreme Programming (XP), Lean Software Development, Crystal Clear, and Scrum. Almost all of these well-published processes focus primarily on IT software development for small co-located teams and ignore scalability concerns to big teams and big projects as well as extensions to non-IT domains such as the development of embedded software. Disciplined Agile Delivery [3] is an IBM initiative spearheaded by well-known Agilista Scott Ambler to address the concerns of scaling agile to large, distributed teams. The Harmony process [4] is an agile approach (developed by the author of this chapter) specifically targeting real-time and embedded systems that integrates model-based engineering (MBE) with agile practices.

Embedded developers thinking about applying agile methods typically have two fundamental questions:

1. Is embedded software development just like the development of IT software?
2. Can the methods and practices successful in the latter arena be applied to the former?

The next section will discuss the important differences that affect the application of agile methods to embedded software development.

Agile approaches are characterized by lightweight processes with short iteration cycles (1 to 4 weeks is common), active stakeholder involvement to prioritize and verify requirements, active measurement of progress, dynamic planning, and an emphasis on continual testing and verification.

Fundamental to the agile perspective is the notion of relative measures; there are no absolutes in agile; no "you shalls" or "you shall nots". Applying agile effectively is about balancing the forces that buffet your project, rather than assuming we can absolutely predict them (which is the basis of waterfall planning) or the more common approach of ignoring them altogether. You must select the practices and procedures that make the most sense in the context of the system you're developing, the team that you have, and the industry and business in which you work [5].

What's special about embedded systems?

This entire book is about embedded systems so by now you've probably got a good sense of the differences even if you didn't before picking it up. However, there are some important differences with respect to IT systems that affect how agile practices can be best applied. The most important of these are that embedded software:

- fits into a system whose requirements are allocated to different engineering disciplines, of which software is only one
- uses specialized hardware
- is often co-developed with the hardware
- constrains the selection of programming languages and tools
- has a more challenging testing environment
- must often be highly predictable
- is often subject to tight timeliness constraints
- often has severe resource constraints (such as memory)
- must often be very highly reliable and safety-critical
- is often subject to rigorous external regulation
- is delivered in a shipped, stand-alone product
- is often subject to fixed-price bids.

Let's consider each of these in turn.

Fits into a system whose requirements are allocated to different engineering disciplines of which software is only one

Systems engineering is a separate engineering discipline that concerns itself with overall system properties including system requirements, architecture, and constraints. It does not focus on software or electronic or mechanical aspects but allocates requirements to those disciplines and ensures that if the elements of the different disciplines are properly designed, they will integrate together to give the desired system properties.

System engineering usually starts with black-box functional analysis without regard to implementation technology or discipline. Once the functional and quality of service (including such concerns as cost, heat, weight, power, performance, reliability, safety, and security) are specified, architectural models are developed. A systems architecture identifies subsystems that deliver coherent sets of functionality but will still be (usually) implemented via multiple disciplines. Once the requirements are handed off to the subsystems detailed allocation among the relevant engineering disciplines can take place. Combinations of different engineering solutions are examined in a process known as "trade studies" to find an optimal solution. The outcome of the trade studies is a specific engineering solution using specific technologies – different hydraulic pumps, electronic motors and sensors, and software. This outcome is then used to specify the requirements for the embedded software, including its interfaces to other subsystems and the interfaces of the software to the electronics.

IT systems rarely have this kind of analysis performed and even when it is done, the outcome relies on commercial off-the-shelf (COTS) electronics. Little, if any, consideration is given to many of the qualities of services and design constraints that make the development of embedded systems so challenging.

Uses specialized hardware

By definition, embedded software is a part of a system composed of components from different engineering disciplines. To achieve the system goals, most such systems include specialized sensors and actuators that interact with the software. These are usually not widely supported with standard libraries and open-source tools. Thus, a not-insignificant amount of the embedded developer's time is spent writing "low-level" software such as operating systems (although less now that commercial real-time operating systems are in widespread use), device drivers, and control loops. This kind of software is rarely seen in IT systems.

In addition, because the hardware is so specialized, tooling to support embedded software development may be primitive or missing altogether. There may not even be a run-time debugger for the target environment. It may be difficult to download the software to the target for execution, resulting in time-consuming delays between coding and testing.

Is often co-developed with the hardware

For many systems, appropriate mechanical and electronic parts simply don't exist at the start of the project but must be developed in parallel with the software. This results in three different but related difficulties. First, the hardware is not available when the software is, so development, debugging, and developer testing must often be done with simulators, which must often be written by the developer. Secondly, the embedded developer is designing against hardware specifications and usually such specifications are either inadequate to really understand the hardware/software interaction, or are incorrect in some number of details, or both. That means that the software will have to be modified when the hardware does actually appear. Lastly, because the hardware is being co-developed, even when early hardware is available, it is a scant resource and unavailable much of the time.

Constrains the selection of programming languages and tools

Another of the challenges of the embedded is the limited choice of languages and tools. Few embedded systems are written in Java (with the exception of mobile applications and in automotive infotainment) and none, to our understanding, are written in Perl, Ruby, Python or any of a number of popular languages. At the time of this writing, 80% of embedded systems are developed in C, with the rest being mostly implemented in C++ with a smattering of other languages such as Ada, Java and C#.

Has a more challenging testing environment

Beyond the language itself, the tools for embedded development are often missing or primitive. They often cannot run in the target environment so, while most debugging must be done in the richer host development environment, target testing must repeat much of this work using tools such as logic analyzer, in-circuit emulators, and oscilloscopes. This slows down the testing and makes finding and removing defects more challenging.

The widespread adoption of commercial real-time operating systems has mitigated this problem somewhat but testing in the embedded environment remains an ongoing challenge.

Must often be highly predictable

Predictability of execution comes with a high design-time price tag. It requires additional analysis (such as rate monotonic analysis or queuing theoretic analysis), which takes time and specialized expertise. It may mean that you cannot use standard concurrency architectures used in IT systems but must rely on concurrency design patterns specific to predictable embedded systems (See, for example, ref. [6]). These patterns require additional analysis and tuning to meet the needs of highly predictable systems.

Is often subject to tight timeliness constraints

Most embedded systems are "real-time" systems. A real-time system is one in which timeliness is an aspect of correctness. Timeliness may be expressed in many ways, but the most common is the notion of a deadline. A deadline is a point in time after which a computation isn't just late, it is wrong. IT systems may want to improve bandwidth or throughput to improve customer experience but that is not the same thing as having a plane crash because updates to the control surfaces come too slowly.

Having to deal with timeliness as a first-order design constraint makes embedded systems more difficult to develop. This increases the need for inventiveness and ingenuity on the part of the developer in addition to requiring more complete and thorough specifications, analysis, and testing.

Often has severe resource constraints (such as memory)

One key difference between IT and embedded software is that the former is, to a large degree, divorced from the hardware. The hardware and software may be separately upgraded as necessary for most IT systems. Embedded software, on the other hand, ships as an integrated component of the embedded system. It is true that field-updated embedded software is becoming more common but it is still relatively new. And there are no such over-the-web updates of hardware. Because recurring cost (cost per shipped item) is a key design constraint, there is always a business need to drive down the cost of the hardware by limiting clock speed, decreasing the amount of memory, and using cheaper and less capable parts. Embedded systems must always function within limited resource constraints.

Must often be very highly reliable and safety-critical

Many IT systems are mission-critical – that is, the company depends on the system for fundamental business operation. However, many embedded systems are safety-critical, meaning that their malfunction or misuse can lead to injury or death of one, many, or in some cases, thousands of people. Such systems cannot tolerate requirements or design flaws. The standard lightweight agile requirements mechanisms are inadequate to address the higher standard necessary to ensure safety.

Even if the system is not safety-critical, it may have customer needs for very high reliability. Reliability is a stochastic measure of the availability of system services. Many embedded systems must function without error with a very high mean time between failures (MTBFs) for such services. These include the delivery of electrical power, telecommunications, and space craft. The cost of failure of highly reliable systems is typically very high even when the system is not safety-critical. This requires an addition diligence and rigor not usually associated with agile methods.

Is often subject to rigorous external regulation

Different industries require embedded systems (and software) to adhere to different safety or reliability standards. IEC 61508 is a common European safety standard used directly in a variety of industries, including nuclear power generation. ISO 26262 is a 61508 derivative standard used to specify the development of automotive safety systems. DO-178B, a 1991 standard published by the RTCA, is used to certify aircraft. This standard was updated to DO-178C in February 2012 with supplements to provide guidance for tool qualification, use of modeling, application of object-oriented methods, and formal methods.

Each of these standards has objectives and goals to which the software and/or the software development standard must adhere. In the case of DO-178B, it has been estimated that the cost of adhering to the standard is at minimum an additional 25%–40% of the normal development cost, but is typically more like 75%–150%. This is largely due to additional practices that must be executed (such as quality assurance audits), the development of more thoroughly detailed plans, and the gathering and management of evidence of standard adherence.

Is delivered in a shipped, stand-alone product

As previously mentioned, the core difference between IT and embedded software is that the latter is embedded in a device. This means that the software isn't handed off to the customer, but to manufacturing. In a manufacturing process, the system, including the software, is constructed and then shipped out. It is far more difficult to field-upgrade the system should a problem be discovered, so the software must generally be of higher quality than for IT. Incremental updates to the shipped system are far more costly and take far longer than incremental updates to an IT system.

Is often subject to fixed-price bids

While it is true that some agile papers on dealing with fixed-price bidding are available, for the most part the agile approach requires continual discovery of requirements throughout the project with "just-enough" planning to address the immediate concerns. This naive approach is fundamentally flawed for embedded systems because of the need to "size" the co-developed hardware and the need to hit a market niche. In addition, one of the largest domains for embedded systems is aerospace and defense. In this industry, most contracts are not "time and materials" but fixed price. For this reason, the agile planning approach taken must address this fundamental aspect of embedded projects.

Agile project planning for embedded software

We need project plans. They tell us

- how many developers we need,
- how much and what kind of resources we need and when we need them,
- how much time a project will take and when we can deliver it,
- the project cost,
- the work items that must be performed and who will perform them.

The problem is, though, that all such plans are lies.

They may be mostly true but they are based on hundreds of unproven assumptions, at least some of which are wrong. They are based on the notion that we know everything about the project and with infinite precision. They assume that nothing we believe will change. They often assume nothing else is going on in the company or the world; that technology will be stable throughout the project; that we can accurately predict the ingenuity and inventiveness of our staff; that there will be no earthquakes or tsunamis in the areas in which our suppliers operate; etc. And even then, managers often insist on creating "aggressive" or "optimistic" schedules – these adjectives are synonyms for "inaccurate" and "incorrect". The fact is, we need plans that are as accurate as possible (and that don't pretend to be more accurate than that), adaptable to changing conditions, and adjustable based on evidentiary data about project performance.

As in IT projects, planning for embedded systems have a poor track record industry-wide. We all know that most projects are late, over-budget, and don't meet all of the stakeholder needs. One key reason for this is the widespread notion that it is possible to completely plan a software-intensive project without making mistakes. This is, of course, despite the not-inconsiderable evidence to the contrary.

Agile methods take a different point of view. According to Agilistas, planning is important but it is impossible to do with complete accuracy at the outset. So the agile approach is to create a plan that is cognizant of its own limitations (error) and adjust that plan based on evidence gathered as the project progresses.

Planning needs to take into account the available time, effort, necessary people and other resources, system functionality, required innovation, and key risks to successful project completion. Of course, early on we only have estimates of these aspects but we still need planning to evaluate whether it makes business sense to even begin the project. Is it likely to make more money than it costs to produce? Can we reasonably expect to hit our market window? What is the value to our customers? Do we have the resources, skills and tools necessary to specify, design, and construct the system? We can't answer these questions with absolute certainty but we'd like to believe it is likely and understand what are the likely conditions and events that could inhibit success.

Project vision

In order to be able to do even the most rudimentary planning, the product vision must provide the context, scope and expected functionality for the envisioned system. This vision may be thought of as "very high-level requirements" for the system development. For simple systems, user stories (scenarios) describing the actor-system interaction and the necessary data and control transformations are enough. In more complex systems, a more rigorous set of use cases should be developed, with each use case having a business case description that will be elaborated in more detail after the project is begun.

A user story is a set of natural-language sentences in the stakeholder (business) language that captures how a set of actors (including human users) interact with the system. A user story is a scenario with a small number of minor variants. For an embedded example, consider the cardiac pacemaker set of user stories in Table 21.1.

For simple enough systems, these user stories allow the developers to interact with the stakeholders to understand the underlying stakeholder needs.

Table 21.1: User story examples.

As a heart	I want to receive pacing pulses to my right atrium if I'm beating too slowly and in AAI[1] mode.
As a heart	I want to receive pacing pulse to my right ventricle if I'm beating too slowly or when an intrinsic beat is detected and in VVT mode.
As a heart	I do not want to receive pacing pulses if the intrinsic heart rate is fast enough.
As a physician	I want to be able to set pacing rate.
As a physician	I want to be able to set pulse amplitude and pulse width to "capture" the heart.
As a physician	I want to be able to set the sensor sensitivity to detect intrinsic cardiac activity while rejecting external electromagnetic noise.
As a Holter monitor	I want to be able to receive a record of cardiac activity across a pacing lead terminal pair for storage.
As a Holter monitor	I want to be able to store 48 hours of data sampled at 15 and 10 ms intervals.

[1]Pacemaker modes are characterized with three-letter codes. The first letter refers to the heart chamber being paced (A for atrium, V for ventricle, or D for dual). The second letter refers to the chamber being sensed. The third letter is a qualifier such as whether the pacemaker operates in inhibit (I) mode, triggered (T) mode or another mode of operation.

As an alternative, use cases (A use case contains a set of user stories) combine graphical representation with links to textual statements. These tend to be more work to create and manage but provide higher fidelity. Figure 21.1 shows the same system but organized into use cases. Note that the actors may be people (as in the physician) or devices (as in the case of the Holter monitor) or even organs (as in the case of the heart).

Figure 21.2 shows one of the use cases in more detail. The dashed dependencies represent traceability links that can be viewed in tabular form and traced in a requirements management tool.

In addition to linkages to requirements, it is common to have a semi-formalized statement about the use case. For example, for the use case in the last figure, such a statement might read like Table 21.2.

Both approaches have value and mixed approaches are possible.

At the end of this activity, the overall functionality and system execution context should be understood, as well as the initial time, resource, and cost expectations.

Initial safety/reliability risk assessment

For safety-critical or high-reliability systems, the initial or intrinsic safety assessment must be performed. This assessment identifies the safety and reliability concerns for the envisioned system. Of course, this is done prior to any design, so technological considerations are largely out of scope (they will be considered later in design). The items that should be considered

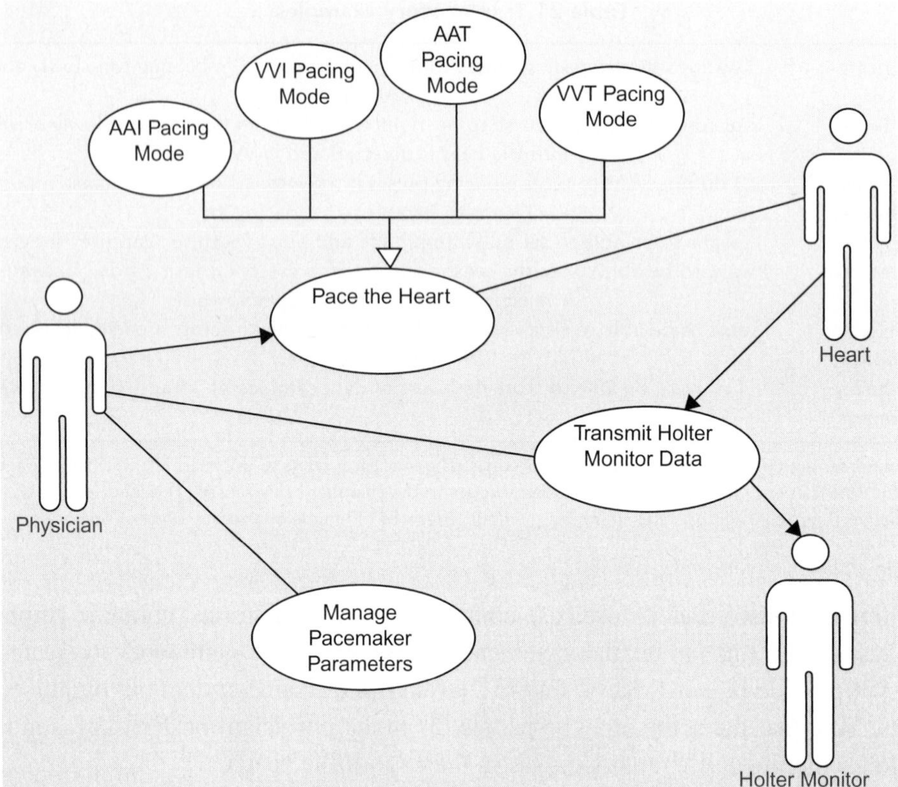

Figure 21.1:
Example use case diagram.

include not only requirements to ensure the intrinsic hazards are addressed, but also the project needs for regulatory compliance and certification. This will strongly influence what evidence is gathered as well as quality assurance and assessments may be necessary during the project.

In safety analysis, the term *risk* is the product of two more primitive values. The first is the *severity* of an undesirable event or condition. How bad is it, for example, if the brake pedal on your automobile no longer influences braking behavior on your car? Severity is specified by applicable standards. In passenger automobiles, the relevant standard is ISO 26262. Severity is addressed in terms of Automotive Safety Integrity Level (ASIL), with level A as the lowest level of concern and level D as the highest [7]. The criticality levels require increasing levels of rigor and evidence of the application of that rigor, as well as increasingly constraining safety requirements.

The second factor that determines risk is *likelihood*. It is fairly likely that a message will be corrupted during transmission or that memory will be corrupted during operation in an electrically noisy environment. It is less likely that high-grade steel will exhibit structural flaws

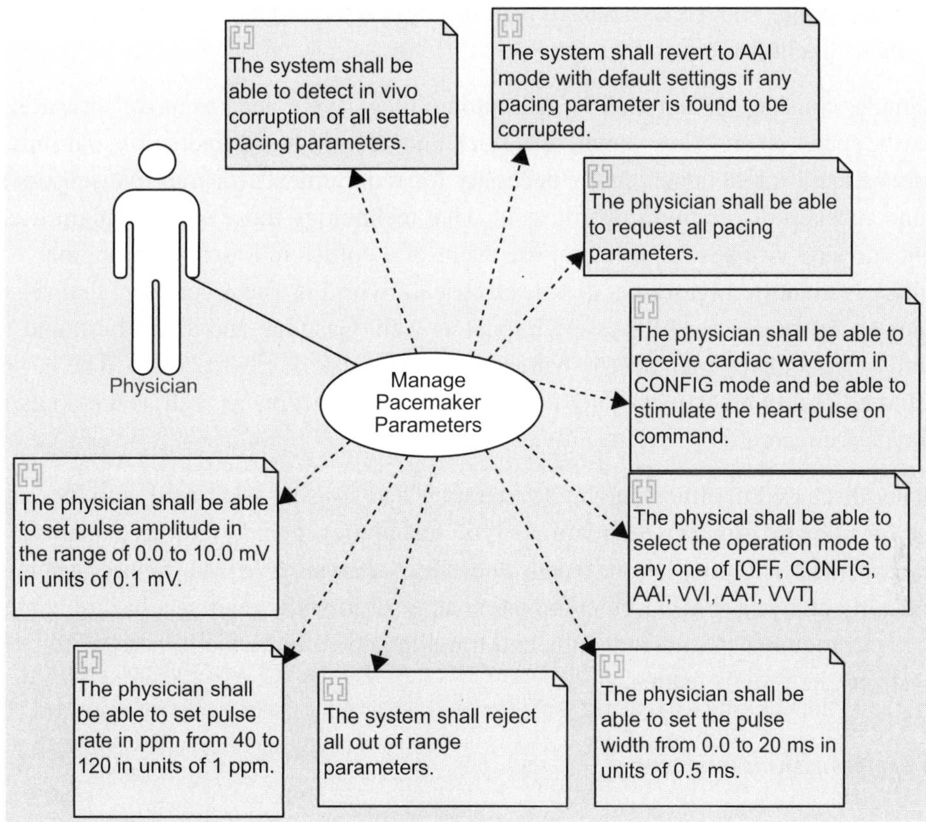

Figure 21.2:
Example use case diagram with traceability links.

Table 21.2: Use case description.

Name	Manage Pacing Parameters
Purpose	Allow the setting and recovery of the pacing parameters as well as the identification of errors in the data, either due to corruption or an attempt to set a value out of range.
Description	This use case allows the physician to set the important pacing parameters (pulse rate, pulse amplitude, pulse width, sensor sensitivity, and pacing mode) in the context of implanting the device. This means that the programming device used by the physician must display the cardiac waveform in real-time as he or she attempts to position the cardiac lead and to stimulate the heart in order to ensure the pacing parameters properly capture the heart when pacing is necessary. Note that to support the heart capture process, the pacemaker must be in the CONFIG mode of operation.
Pre-conditions	The pacemaker is in any operational model. It will continue in that operational mode until commanded otherwise.
Post-conditions	The pacing parameters are stored and used appropriately with the pacing execution use case(s).
Invariants	The pacemaker shall reject all attempts to set invalid pacing parameter values. If a pacemaker parameter value is invalid or out of range, then it will be reset to the default value.

after manufacturing. The risk of a hazard manifestation is the product of the severity of the hazard and its likelihood.

For example, consider an automobile. All automobiles have a need to move forwards and backwards, speed up and slow down, turn, lock and unlock doors, and so on. An initial safety assessment might conclude the necessity for requirements for multiple sensors for brake and accelerator position, regardless of what technology those sensors might use, and for front and side air bags to protect in the event of a collision. Later when engine technology is identified (gasoline, diesel, electrical, hybrid or flux capacitor) that selected technology must be assessed for safety impact as well. Gasoline and diesel burn and potentially explode while an electric battery presents a risk of electrocution. The initial safety and reliability assessment only includes intrinsic concerns as well as any known technological concerns.

This is not discussed in almost any agile literature and so is an additional activity that must be done for relevant projects. Standard analytic techniques include fault tree analysis (FTA), robustness analysis, failure means and effect analysis (FMEA), failure means, effect, and criticality analysis (FMECA), culminating in a summary known as a hazard analysis. This analysis requires specialized skills and training and so is normally performed by specialists on the project team.

Initial project risk assessment

Project risk refers to conditions and events that lead to an unsuccessful project and is quite distinct from system risk, discussed above. Common project risks may include:

- optimistic (unrealistic) schedules
- lack of personnel and other resources
- lack of funding
- inadequate skills of the personnel
- inadequate development platform infrastructure
- lack of tools and automation where needed
- the use of new tools and technologies
- lack of management support
- dysfunctional teams
- staff turnover
- low team motivation
- volatile customer requirements.

The agile way of dealing with such risk factors is to understand them, prioritize them, and then manage them. To understand them, it is important to quantify the degree of risk; how severe is the potentially bad outcome? How likely is it? The product of these values determines the risk. Then rank the project hazards in order of risk and address all those above some critical threshold, preferably in a decreasing fashion. The activities to address the risk are commonly known as *risk mitigation activities* or *spikes*. These are work items – such as taking training or analyzing the impact of using a technology – that are put into the schedule. The outcomes of the spikes are then used to update the plans. Does DDS have too large a memory footprint? Ok, let's perform a spike to figure that out. If so, then what's the back-up plan: write our own middleware layer? Use a different middleware? Use shared memory with no middleware?

The project risks are managed in what is known as a risk management plan or risk list. This plan summarizes the known risks, their analysis, when the spike is to be executed and to whom, and its outcome. This feeds into the initial schedule as well as the schedule updates. Additionally, it is important that during the project the team looks out for encroaching risks and adds them to the risk plan on a frequent basis.

Estimating

The vision, safety/risk assessment, and project risk assessment all aid in the identification of the work to be done. Once this work is complete, work items (work tasks) must be identified and assigned to people to do the work. To predict project performance, these work items must be estimated as to effort. Common agile methods use relativistic and subjective measures, such as story points. For larger and more complex systems, absolute measures can be used.

The idea behind story points is pretty simple. Assign a unitless value to the amount of work required to complete a work item. The next work item gets a value that is a measure of how much more (or less) it is to perform than the previous. This is rough estimation, to be sure, but often that is the only possible degree of precision. For example, you might have five work tasks and assign story points as in Table 21.3.

Table 21.3: User story points example.

User Story	Story Points
Capture cardiac voltage between lead points	5
Transmit cardiac voltage in real-time to device programmer	3
Set/get pacemaker pacing rate	1
Set/get pacemaker pulse amplitude	1
Set/get pacemaker pulse width	1
Auto-capture heart with ramping amplitude and width	8

We're not exactly sure how many hours a story point value of "1" is but three stories take about that much time each. On the other hand, transmission of data takes about 3 times that much, capturing the data to transmit about 5 times that much, and auto-capture about 8 times that much. Then, based on the expected time to achieve a story point (known as the project velocity), we can estimate the number of hours required for any activity. That is, we estimate the relative size of the work effort but the duration of that effort is computed from this value and the expected project velocity.

This approach has much to recommend it. It doesn't require a detailed understanding of the implementation but relies instead on relative difficulty. It can be rescaled as the project runs based on measured project velocity. It works when we are asked to perform tasks that we've not done before. And it doesn't give the impression that we know the exact answer.

Downsides include its reliance on the velocity to come up with a schedule – this value might not be known. It also is more difficult to reuse previously captured metric data about performance on similar tasks. It doesn't allow us to customize the schedule based on different skill levels.

There are many alternatives, such as planning poker, a consensus mechanism for estimating effort. DeMaro and Lister have another approach in which they add risk. The author has published his own BERT (Bruce's Evaluation and Review Technique) and ERNIE (Effect Review for Nanocycle Iteration Estimation) approach that relies on linearized Gaussian estimators.

However you do it, the work (and ultimately duration) of each work item must be estimated so that a schedule can be constructed.

Scheduling

A schedule is a sequenced set of work items. Some work items may be performed in a predecessor-successor relationship while others may be performed in parallel. Each work item must be "resource loaded" – that is, assigned to personnel responsible to perform it. The overall time of the schedule is the sum of the durations, plus delays, of the longest sequence, known as the *critical path*.

A schedule is like a house of cards in that all too often they are built on a poor foundation of inaccurate estimates and bad assumptions. A good schedule is only as good as its aggregate parts; usually this means it isn't very good at all.

To address the problems of scheduling it is necessary to group work items somehow and then deliver the outcome of those related work items together. This is done in a couple of different ways in agile methods.

First, an iteration is a body of work that produces a working system that may (optionally) be delivered to the customer but may be incomplete in its coverage of the stakeholders' full needs. Each iteration is usually in the range of 1 to 4 weeks in length. Most Agilistas recommend that all iterations should be of the same duration (providing a project "heartbeat"), but this is not strictly necessary. Other agile approaches, such as the Harmony process, suggest that relatively equal iterations but minor variations in iteration completion times are unimportant. What is important is that each iteration

- delivers previous functionality plus some new functionality
- delivers a verified and validated solution for the implemented functionality
- continues to make progress towards project completion
- captures performance metrics that enable schedule and plan refinement.

Early iterations are less complete than later iterations and each iteration adds its own functionality and test cases to the system. This leads to a two-level planning approach.

First identify the work items and allocate the work items to iterations. The sequence of the overall set of iterations is the overall schedule. Each iteration implements some coherent set of user requirements, which may be organized by user story or use cases.

Secondly, within each iteration, the order of execution of the work items should be planned. It is not enough to have a big bucket of work items to be worked on in any order. To best implement some of the development practices, work items should be implemented in a coordinated fashion during the iteration.

Any software schedule is an estimate of something not actually known and should be treated as such. Software development remains a craft, not an industrial process. It is inherently chaotic but it is possible to create schedules that are approximately correct. However, most schedules are systematically underestimated, so it is important to track true progress and adjust the plan based on project evidence. This is the topic of the next section.

Project governance for embedded software

Project governance refers to the procedures and practices used to monitor and control projects. Agile governance varies widely from Scrum's "stand-up meetings" to gathering detailed metrics with instrumented tooling such as Rational Team Concert™ on the Jazz™ Platform.

Governance is crucial to project success because, as we discussed in the section before, all software plans are lies. The three steps of governance are:

- gather project performance data
- perform gap analysis
- replan when appropriately.

The biggest mistake in software projects today is that to a very large degree, software projects are ungoverned. There may be a development plan at the outset, but the progress of the project isn't tracked, plans are not adjusted, and everyone at the end, from the manager to the developer to the customer, is surprised by the resulting deviation from the plan. Far too often, software isn't so much "released" as it "escapes". Even when software plans are more or less accurate, project data provides the opportunity to fine-tune your processes, improve product quality, save time and cost, and improve customer satisfaction.

Stand up! (meetings)

Also known as a "stand up", this practice is often exercised daily in agile projects. The idea is to have a short meeting in which two crucial pieces of information are provided. First, the developer presents the current status of their assigned work items. Secondly, they identify existing, pending, or potential roadblocks. These meetings are kept very short, with any necessary following-up taking place outside the meeting per se. Stand ups are very good for sharing information within the team about progress and status, although they don't replace managerial status updates or communication with stakeholders.

Martin Fowler [9] identifies the goals for the stand up as:

- to help start the day well
- to support improvement
- to reinforce focus on the right things
- to reinforce the sense of team
- to communicate what's going on.

While beneficial (and recommended), stand ups don't provide enough information to truly govern the project, nor do they provide the information to the right people. Other methods must be employed to gather project performance data.

Performance metrics

Performance metrics are values that represent some measured quantity of interest. With embedded software projects, metrics can be categorized into metrics about conformance to plan, progress, and quality. One reason why metrics are so crucial is that software projects are like steering a ship in turbulent, chaotic currents. It requires constant attention or you will quickly go off course. Performance metrics may be either leading or lagging indicators. A leading indicator provides data that suggests you are on the right course, while a lagging indicator indicates what you've achieved.

One of the biggest problems seen in the identification and capture of project metrics is that the easiest metrics to measure are against tasks – that is, lagging indicators are easiest to measure and most commonly captured. That may not sound like a bad idea (because it's not) but while they indicate that the work being done correlates to the plan, they do not indicate that the right things are being achieved. The work tasks might be accomplished but are they moving the project towards successful completion?

Metrics are most useful when they track progress against goals and not work tasks. That means that the best metrics are metrics against goals and not assigned work items. This is more than a minor philosophical difference. It often happens, even in good organizations, that metrics are captured because they are easy to measure, but they provide little actual value for project governance. The most common metric in use in aerospace and defense, for example, is code productivity as measured in source lines of code (SLOCs) per unit time. This metric would be extremely useful if the goal was to write a known number of lines of code and we didn't care if that code was correct or needed to be optimized. In actual fact, we don't know how many lines of code we need at the start of a project. We can, at best, hazard a guess. So if I've written 100,000 lines of a project that is expected to yield 200,000 lines am I half-way done? What if the code has a very high number of defects in it? The metric doesn't account for debugging, developer test, or integration test time and rework. What if I'm spending time optimizing code and reducing the number of lines of code to meet performance and memory constraints. Am I doing "negative work" if I optimize 100,000 lines of code to 80,000 while maintaining the same functionality? No, I'm clearly doing real work and making real progress that the metric completely gets wrong.

Further, slavishly following a plan ("turn left!") may not be the right thing when conditions are changing. What's more important, following the sea lane chart or avoiding the big rock in the middle of your path that someone forgot to put on the chart and moving closer to your destination? Goal-based metrics, which are leading indicators, provide better guidance and can lead not only to improved project success but also to better planning in the future.

A common term in this area is key performance indicator (KPI). These are often business or industry-specific metrics. They are gathered during the process activities and analyzed to determine progress and status and to enable corrective action.

Let's look at some potentially useful metrics:

- Conformance metrics
  - Schedule progress – scheduled work items accomplished
  - Standard objectives met – objectives from a regulatory standard achieved
- Progress metrics
  - Velocity (of code, test, or requirements, or of any other work data output or a measure of accomplishment such as story points or use cases) – the rate (normally measured per iteration) at which work is being accomplished
  - Acceleration – the rate of change of velocity over the time of the project
  - Technical debt – the measure of things that are not yet done; also known as "on the plate" metric

    - Iteration cycle time – the steadiness of the project cycle
    - Story point/use case burndown chart – a graphic representation of the achievement of story points or use case over time
    - Test coverage – structural coverage (usually lines of code covered in tests), decision coverage (structural coverage plus branches) or modified condition decision coverage (decision coverage plus independent variation of Boolean conditions in decision points)
- Quality metrics
    - Defect density – the number of defects found per unit of software, often per line of code or 1000 lines of code
- Other goal-oriented metrics
    - Customer satisfaction – usually measured with a customer survey to assess the customer's view of the value of the work products being delivered
    - Requirement volatility – average rate of change of requirements.

Iteration retrospective (party phase)

Agile methods are, to some degree, about applying a closed-loop approach to software development. Most projects are run open-loop; that is, there is some initial plan but metrics about success against the plan are not applied to tune the project for optimal completion. By closed-loop, we mean that we acquire project performance data and use it to modify both what the plan is and how we execute the plan. One of the ways to get the project performance data is via a periodic retrospective, typically performed at the end of each iteration.

A retrospective is sometimes known as a "post-mortem". However, since a post-mortem is something a forensic physician does to determine cause of death, most processes refer to it as either a retrospective or an iteration review. The Harmony process [8, pp. 420–425] goes so far as to (informally) refer to it as the "party phase" with the perspective that it is, in some sense, a celebration of ongoing success.

The key concept of the retrospective is to gather "lessons learned" from the current iteration and apply them to the project to improve project execution performance. The Harmony process identifies five different steps in the retrospective:

- Review the team questionnaire – this questionnaire asks developers, testers and other workers about what is working well in the project and what isn't and solicits suggestions as to corrective measures.
- Review schedule – this step compares the planned iteration post-conditions (work accomplished, project velocity, product quality and other metrics) against actual values. If necessary, replanning is performed to adjust for "truth on the ground".

- Review architecture – the architecture should be scaling; that is, the changes to the architecture should be monotonically decreasing as the project progresses. If this is not true, architectural issues must be examined and the architecture may require rework.
- Review risks – this step examines the outcome of risk mitigation activities (spikes) performed during this iteration and decides what should be done about them. Thought is given to identifying new emerging risks. Finally, the risk management plan is reviewed to ensure that the risk-mitigation activities in upcoming iterations are still relevant, appropriate, and properly prioritized.
- Review process workflows – the effectiveness of the processes is examined to see whether they can be improved. If appropriate, new processes or tooling are put into place to improve project execution.

Agile development practices for embedded

Practices are customary ways of acting in accordance with a set of guiding principles, such as those set out in the Agile Manifesto or those discussed earlier in this chapter. There are several key practices for the successful application of agile methods to the development of embedded systems, discussed below.

Incremental development

Although not specific to agile methods (the notion of incremental or iterative development is more than 20 years old at this point), incremental development remains a key practice for implementation of agile. The basic idea it to take a big problem and divide it into a series of smaller problems. The solution (product) evolves as you add more and more capability to the system. At the end of the iteration, the as-yet-incomplete system is verified and validated against its requirements. The typical time-scale for an iteration is 4–6 weeks but many agile projects are run with iterations as short as 1 week. There is some overhead associated with the V&V activities and releasing the build so most projects find 4 weeks to be a more optimal timeframe.

Iterations produce a primary work product – a verified and validated version of the system – as well as a number of secondary work products, such as defects, change requests, test results, and regulatory compliance data. They are organized around a *mission*, which includes:

- a coherent set of stakeholder or system requirements, usually organized by either user stories or use cases resulting in work items
- defects, identified in previous iterations, to be repaired in the current iteration
- risks to be address with risk mitigation activities (spikes)

- target platforms to be supported (this changes over time, such as moving gradually from host to simulated target to actual target)
- architectural intent – the architectural viewpoints or needs to be addressed
- required external elements, such as testing fixtures, or external systems for integration.

Figure 21.3 shows the overall workflow for iteration in the Harmony process and is not hugely dissimilar from other agile processes. Each iteration, as mentioned, is typically 4–6 weeks in length. Early activities focus on the iteration planning (iteration schedule and finalizing and detailing the requirements to be realized), middle activities focus on the design and implementation, and later activities focus on verification, validation, and process improvement. It is important to note that the process also defines other parallel activities not shown in the figure, such as on-going safety assessment, configuration management, and project governance. Note also the "Continuous Integration" activity in Figure 21.3, a practice that will be discussed shortly.

High-fidelity modeling

Most agile methods do not employ modeling or, if they do, they emphasize lightweight modeling, sometimes known as *model storming*. As such, the practice of *high-fidelity modeling* is perhaps a controversial practice to include in this book. The author of this chapter is a well-known proponent of precise, detailed modeling but both lightweight and high-fidelity approaches will be briefly mentioned so the reader can draw their own conclusions.

Model storming refers to a practice of sketching out a rough concept before writing source code to implement a design idea. Such sketches are done with little or no tooling and are not maintained over the long term. Little investment in time or effort goes into creating such models and correspondingly little value is derived from it.

High-fidelity modeling, on the other hand, formalizes the design concepts to the point where the model executes, may be tested, and source code may be generated automatically from it. A bigger investment is required in tooling as well as in the training of the developer so that they can harness the power of the models and tools. This approach shifts the workload more to modeling and away from the actual writing of source code. Models are maintained in configuration management and are automatically updated as changes are made – either to the model or to the source code. The advantage of this approach is that the level of abstraction is raised to a much higher level than source code, increasing the productivity of the developer about the same amount as moving from source language did for assembly-language programmers. The disadvantages are the reliance on more capable (and expensive) tooling and a need for a higher skill level on the part of the developer.

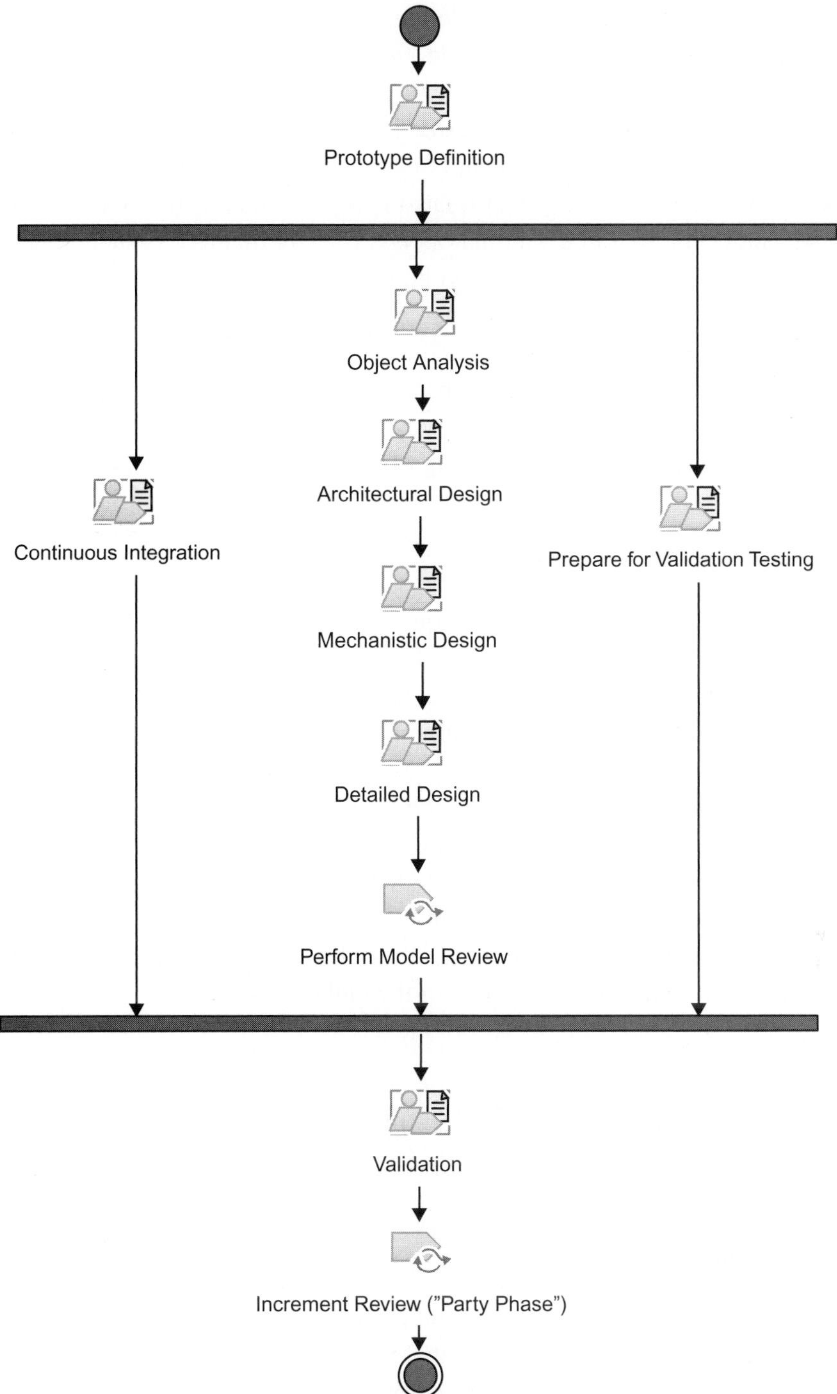

Figure 21.3:
Harmony microcycle iteration workflow.

A potential problem with high-fidelity modeling is that if the source code is created by hand with the high-fidelity models as a guide, then any updates require changes to both the models and the code. This is a classic problem known as "dual maintenance". With model storming, the sketched-out models are discarded anyway, so this is not a problem, but with high-fidelity modeling a bigger investment is made in the design. However, there is a technical solution – there is tooling that treats the source code as just another viewpoint on the system semantics, in the same way that a class or state diagram is such a viewpoint. With appropriate tooling, any viewpoint can be used to update the system semantics in the model and all the other relevant views change because they are all dynamically linked to the model repository. Thus, you can change the class or state diagram and the source code changes to reflect that, or you can change the source code and the diagrams change accordingly. Appropriate tooling can virtually eliminate the dual maintenance problem. (Readers interested in reading more about high-fidelity modeling are referred to ref. [10].)

Executable requirements

Most agile methods characterize software requirements in terms of user stories and, to a lesser degree, use cases. In contrast, more traditional systems approaches emphasize large, monolithic documents contains hundreds or thousands of requirements in the form of "shall" statements. We find value in both approaches for the development of embedded systems. At one extreme, user stories or use cases alone might provide enough information to engineer the system provided that the system is simple enough and sufficiently non-critical. At the other extreme, ensuring that every requirement is properly designed, implemented, verified, and validated with detailed traceability tables is required for safe avionics systems. To ensure such complex and detailed requirements are correct, creating state-driven executable requirements models allows for the execution (and therefore testing) of requirements prior to their inclusion within the embedded design.

In general, if the cost of requirements defects is high, more rigor in the requirements process is justified. For this reason, the use of executable models is far more common in the development of safety-critical and high-reliability cyber-physical systems such as avionics, military, automotive, and medical systems than in the development of consumer devices.

Test-driven development (TDD)

The idea behind TDD is that it is better to avoid defects than to fix them later in the development cycle. Practically, this means rather than the more traditional Code-A-Bunch → Test-A-Bunch cycle → Done, TDD is Code-A-Little → Test-A-Little → Repeat until done. In the Harmony process, this is known as the *nanocycle* and typically lasts 20–60 minutes. The workflow for the nanocycle is shown in Figure 21.4.

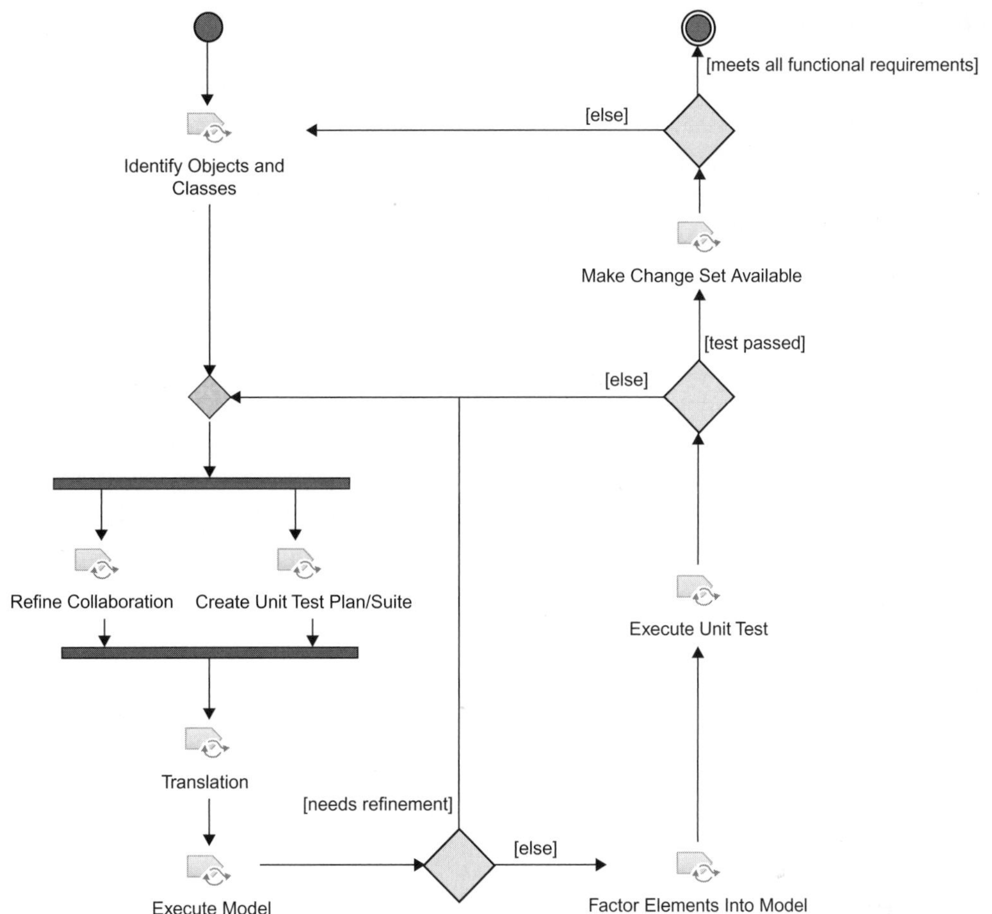

Figure 21.4:
Harmony nanocycle implements test-driven development.

In this rapidly executing loop, the developer identifies some small but relevant portion of the design – perhaps two or three class attributes, a function or two or perhaps a couple of states with even receptors – then creates test cases that verify that portion of the design, applies the test cases and, if correct, moves on to add more design features.

The unit (also known as "developer") tests grow in completeness in parallel with the design and source code. These tests may be created through test tooling or manually. CppUnit, a port of JUnit from Java, is commonly used in source code-centric environments. Alternatively, "test-buddy" classes can be created for the purpose of encapsulating and applying test cases. There is even a standard, The UML Testing Profile [11], that specifies a standard way of specifying test cases using UML representations (e.g., sequence, activity, or state diagrams) so that the power of modeling can be brought to test as well as design.

Continuous integration

In most projects, big integration brings big integration problems. In many large systems, this can mean months to years to get a set of pieces of presumably high-quality software to work together properly. This is usually because more attention is paid to the internals of the subsystems than to the "seams" of the system where subsystems interact. Misunderstandings about interfaces, pre- and post-conditions for services, data formats, and requirements allocation all work to complicate system integration.

Much of the pain can be alleviated directly by integrating both early and frequently throughout the system development, a practice known as *continuous integration.* In this practice, the partially complete work from engineers is brought together to ensure that the functionality implemented from different pieces works properly as a whole. The time basis for integration is typically daily, but it can stretch from truly continuous (engineers can check in new software at anytime and the integration is performed immediately) to weekly. The basic rule is that no engineers are allowed to "break the build" so that integration proceeds smoothly.

A successful build in this context means a number of things:

- The new baseline successfully compiles, links, and loads onto the target (which may not necessarily be the ultimate target).
- The new baseline successfully passes previously passed integration tests (known as regression tests) so that previously working functionality is not broken.
- The new baseline successfully passes new integrated functionality for the features and functionality just added.

A less-than-successful build results in the rejection of the updated (broken) software, a cessation of work on new functionality, and necessitates immediate repair.

The practice of continuous integration can greatly reduce the time for integration at the end but does require more discipline on the part of the developers. First, they must release new software at a rate compatible with the integration timeframe. Secondly, they must perform the TDD cycle so that the software they are delivering to integration is of high quality. (This is in contrast with a more common emphasis on feature completion followed by a period characterized by feature stabilization.) Third, the developers must all work on the related parts of the software so that integratable pieces are created and can be tested with scenarios that go through the important interactions of the involved components.

Change management

Change management provides a workflow for turning requests into updated software. These requests might be from defects identified during testing or system usage or changing requirements. The change management process takes a request through a series of steps that initiate, evaluate, and approve the change request all the way though approval of the changes made to the software. A typical workflow for change management is shown in Figure 21.5. A typical outcome for a change request is a work task assigned to a developer.

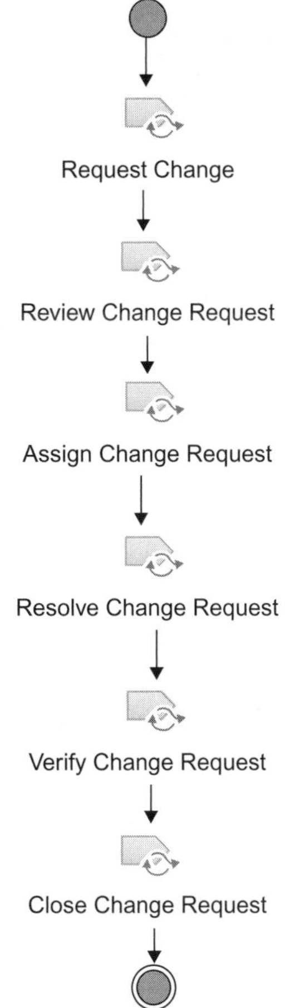

Figure 21.5:
Change management workflow.

Dynamic planning

A common mistake by those not familiar with agile methods is that there is no planning in agile methods. As we have seen, this is clearly not true. Agile is a rigorous approach to development and that includes creating plans for the work to be done. However, while agile methods require planning, they also try not to over-plan, that is, create plans whose details exceed existing knowledge. Certainly, all care should be taken to avoid so-called "optimistic" schedules that are systematically biased towards underestimation.

Agile methods generally propose a two-tier planning scheme. Since agile methods emphasize iterations (sprints), they recommend an overall plan that links together the planned set of iterations with the user stories or use cases allocated to them. Each iteration then has a plan as well, which is finalized at the start of the iteration. The plan is organized around the mission of the iteration, discussed above in the section on incremental development.

The other side of dynamic planning is the frequent updates to the plan. This requires information about project progress so that the difference between the plan and the actual project execution can be quantified. Different metrics capture different information that can be relevant to support project governance. Project velocity, work items completed, and defect density are probably the most commonly used metrics. As previously mentioned, the most useful metrics focus on progress against goals, not against activities.

Risk management

Most projects fail because of a lack of project governance and good risk management is a key to properly governing project uncertainty. Risk is a product of two values; severity (the impact of the manifestation of the undesirable outcome) and likelihood. A risk management plan (aka *risk list*) identifies potential obstacles to project success, along with relevant risk metadata such as a description of the condition or event, risk status, severity, likelihood, risk assessment metrics, risk mitigation activity (or spike), and spike outcome. Risks are really all about stuff you don't know and risk mitigation activities reduce that uncertainty. Typical project risks include:

- optimistic (i.e., unreasonable) schedules
- new middleware, OS, or hardware platform
- new technologies (e.g., languages, such as UML or C++)
- new tools
- lack of team motivation
- lack of team availability
- lack of platform availability when needed
- poor requirements
- lack of managerial commitment
- vendor support
- use of partners or subcontractors.

Spikes are a part of each iteration mission (see the above section on the incremental development practice) and the risks are evaluated and considered within the project life-cycle.

Initially, the risk management plan is done at the project outset, with risks above some threshold value being addressed by an identified spike that is allocated to a planned iteration. Clearly, higher-risk conditions or events should be addressed sooner than lower-risks situations.

In addition to the initial planning, risks are addressed at least twice in each iteration. First, as the iteration itself is planned, the spike is assigned as one or more work items to appropriate team members. Secondly, the outcome of the spike is evaluated during the Increment Review, shown at the bottom of Figure 21.3. Also during this Increment Review, care is taken to look for emerging risks to be added to the Risk Management Plan.

Scaling factors for agile

There are many embedded software projects that are within the agile norm in term of small co-located teams. However, there are others that are clearly not. After all, an aircraft is a big embedded system. A modern automobile has up to 80 processors and 10 million lines of code. Satellites, spacecraft, submarines, UAVs are all large-scale systems often with many millions of lines of code. True, these can be decomposed as "systems of systems" into smaller and simpler component parts but these parts remain complex and they must all work closely together with their counterparts to achieve the mission goals within the embedded, real-time, and mission constraints.

Some key factors that affect how agile scales include:

- team size
- team distribution (co-located or global)
- enterprise discipline (project focus or enterprise focus)
- domain complexity
- regulatory compliance requirement
- organizational complexity (outsourcing, subcontracting, and partnering)
- technical complexity.

Most agile literature assumes small (fewer than 15 person) teams, all co-located, working on domains and using technologies with which the team are all familiar and without any regulatory compliance issues. As those assumptions are violated, the practices must be extended or, at the very least, tailored to meet the project team's needs.

The good news is that agile can be and has been successfully applied to large, distributed, teams building technically complex systems. The bad news is that there isn't much published literature on how to extend the core agile practices to meet those needs.

In general, as the projects lean towards the more difficult (larger and more complex) scale and the project teams face more organizational complexity (e.g., become more distributed and involve more organizations), increasing rigor and ritual are needed. A more comprehensive use of high-fidelity modeling and use of distributed collaboration tools can unburden the teams to a large degree. Although core agile approaches de-emphasize specialization of team member skills, larger teams reintroduce specialized roles, such as architect, quality assurance, safety engineer, and (independent) tester.

Can agile methods help you adhere to standards?

One of the concerns that regulation brings is the volume of documentation required to meet certification needs. Documentation for standards compliance generally comes in four forms:

- plans
- standards
- test results
- quality assurance evidence.

Plans encompass what and how the project is to be run. Plans include everything from schedules and work-breakdown structures to requirements documents and test plans and procedures. Standards refer to industry, company, or projects guidelines such as requirements, modeling, design, or coding standards. Standards are often codified as checklists delineating objective measures to demonstrate adherence and are required by a number of industry standards. Test results show the compliance of the delivered system to system requirements (verification) or to stakeholder needs (validation). Finally, QA evidence demonstrates the adherence of the project team to the plans and standards. This evidence is generally the outcome of audits, reviews, and other verification activities that demonstrate the project was done in accordance with its selected standards.

We can look at one such standard – RTCA's DO-178C – and the evidence it requires. This standard is used for the certification of civil avionics systems and is used increasingly in military systems and other industries as well. The specified life-cycle data from the standard is shown in Table 21.4.

The amount of data looks daunting – as well it should, especially when you consider the depth of information required in traceability records and test coverage. The interesting question is – how can agile help with the development and management of all this life-cycle data?

Being agile doesn't mean that teams don't create documentation or provide evidence of compliance. Being agile means that the team does so in an efficient way so as to minimize additional costs for the documentation for both its initial creation and its management. Some agile practices that can help here include:

- Develop the life-cycle data as a normal outcome of the engineering work.
- Create the documentation as you create the software, not *ex post facto*.
- Use tooling to create and manage the data whenever possible.

Table 21.4: DO-178C life-cycle data.

Abbreviation	Document Title	Description	Section
PSAC	Plan for Software Aspects of Certification	Provides an overview of the project and system for the certification authority including the data that will be developed, the plans by which the project will execute, supplier oversight and additional considerations as necessary.	11.1
SDP	Software Development Plan	Provides a description of the software development procedures and life-cycles, including standards and the development environment.	11.2
SVP	Software Verification Plan	Describes the verification procedures to be used to satisfy the software verification objectives.	11.3
SCMP	Software Configuration Management Plan	Establishes the procedures to be used to achieve the objectives for configuration management of the software and related life-cycle data including configuration management, baselines, traceability, change control and review and problem reporting.	11.4
SQAP	Software Quality Assurance Plan	Describes the methods to be used to achieve quality assurance including standards, procedures, tools, and methods.	11.5
SRS	Software Requirements Standards	This standard defines the criteria to be used to develop and evaluate high-level requirements.	11.6
SDS	Software Design Standards	This standard defines the criteria to be used to develop and evaluate software architecture, and low-level requirements (design).	11.7
SCS	Software Coding Standards	This standard defines the programming languages, methods, rules, and tools to develop and evaluate the software source code.	11.8
SRD	Software Requirements Data	Specifies the high-level requirements allocated to software and derived high-level requirements, both functional and quality of service, including safety requirements.	11.9
SDD	Software Design Description	Defines the software architecture and the low-level requirements that will realize the high-level requirements.	11.10
SC	Source Code	Provides the source code to be used in compiling, linking, and loading the software.	11.11
EOC	Executable Object Code	This is the output of the compiling and linking process – the executable computer instructions that will be loaded onto the target computing platform.	11.12
SVCP	Software Verification Cases and Procedures	Details how the software verification activities are implemented, including review and analysis procedures, test cases and data, and procedures for test execution.	11.13
SVR	Software Verification Results	The output of the software verification activities, including the results of tests, reviews, and analyses.	11.14
SECI	Software Life-cycle Environment Configuration Index	Identifies the configurations for the software development environment including tools, equipment, OS tools and any qualified tools.	11.15

(Continued)

Table 21.4: (Continued)

Abbreviation	Document Title	Description	Section
SCI	Software Configuration Index	Identifies the configuration of the software product and all relevant files including all software life-cycle data.	11.16
PR	Problem Reports	Provide a means to identify and record defects and their resolution.	11.17
SCMR	Software Configuration Management Records	Contains the results of configuration management activities, including baselines, change reports, archive records, and release records.	11.18
SQAR	Software Quality Assurance Records	Contains the results of all software quality assurance activities including review and audit reports, meeting minutes, and software conformity review records.	11.19
SAS	Software Accomplishment Summary	This summary is the primary datum for showing compliance with the PSAC, including any deviations from it.	11.20

Developing systems under the DO-178B/C standards is estimated to cost *at minimum* 25%–40% more than creating systems that don't need to be certified [12]. This cost is largely due to additional processes related to certification and to the creation and management of the required evidence. However, *typical* costs are closer to an additional 75%–150%.

Much of this cost can be reduced by engaging your Designated Engineering Representative (DER) early (and continuously) in the process to ensure that your work and evidence will be accepted. Avoiding rework is a big part of cost reduction for certification of systems. (A DER, commonly used in the USA, represents the FAA for certification and provides regulation and certification guidance to project teams developing avionics systems.)

Another source of cost is *additional* work. Ideally, a team does what is necessary to create the work products (high-level requirements, source code, test cases, or what have you) and *as a natural part of that work* the necessary documentation is created. What is far too common is that a separate task is performed, sometimes long after the original work has been completed, to document what was done. This can add a huge cost because of the recreation of the rationale and data necessary for the documentation. For example, a team using high-fidelity modeling can produce design documentation as a report on the model rather than a separate paper exercise to capture the design hidden within the source code. As you develop relevant model diagrams, add comments and other documentation as you create the views and semantic elements. Here, being agile means creating the documentation or evidence you need as you do the work, not some time in the far-off future.

The DO-178B/C standards do require some evidence which is painful – if not impossible – to manage manually. For example, the standard requires managed traceability between related life-cycle data elements, such as which system requirements result in which software high-level requirements, and how these software high-level requirements map to software architecture and low-level requirements (design), and test cases. In fact, Figure 21.6 provides a pretty good idea of the required traceability for each data element in the required life-cycle data.

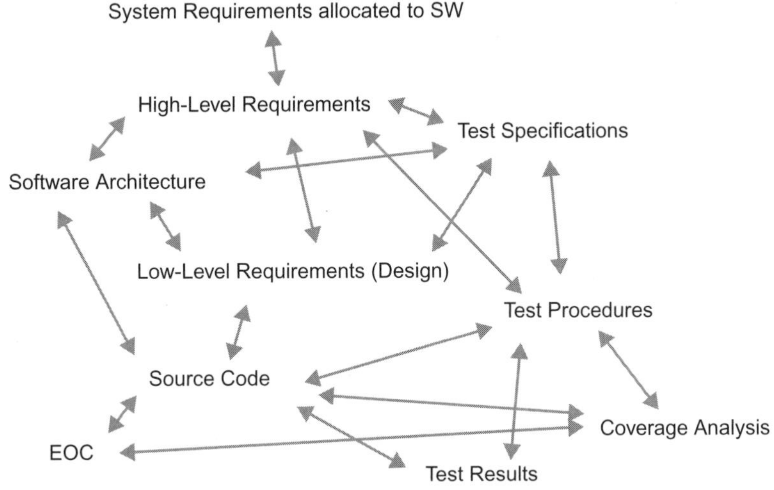

Figure 21.6:
DO-178B/C traceability.

It is infeasible to even initially create all these links manually among the various pieces of the required work products, let alone to manage changes and updates. Tools to manage traceability are a huge asset. While the agile view of "traveling light" has merit, when faced with tasks that are error-prone and hugely effort-intensive, investing in good tooling can be a great asset.

Other areas where tools are a powerful adjunct to the developer are configuration management and testing tools. Testing tools are particularly interesting in a certified environment because of the coverage objectives of the standard. The DO-178C standard requires different levels of coverage depending on the safety level of the system under certification. For Level C, structural testing is required. This means that each line of source code must be executed at least once by some verification test. For level B, decision coverage is required; that is, each branching decision must be tested twice, once where the decision is true and one where it is false. For level A certification, modified condition decision coverage (MC/DC) coverage is required. For this highest level of test coverage, each Boolean fragment must be independently varied to ensure it results in the proper outcome.

For example, consider the code fragment

```
if (x<0 && y>10 && z = = 2)

  func1();
```

For level C, a single test case (true) suffices. For level B, two test cases (one true, one false) is good enough. For level A, a minimum of four cases are needed. Analyzing test coverage by hand and justifying your conclusions is a Herculean undertaking and not recommended. In fact, in this case a *qualified* testing tool that performs coverage analysis is the only reasonable way to achieve level A certification.

(The standard DO-178C provides a supplement, DO-330 "Tool Qualification Considerations", that gives guidance for tool qualification. A qualified tool is one in which you can trust the output without independent verification. A tool must undergo a rigorous qualification verification process to be used in this way. Not all tools in the software development environment must be qualified but tools whose defects could leave a defect undiscovered (such as a testing tool) must be qualified for the team to receive certification credit for its use.)

Summary

Agile methods offer significant project advantages over more traditional software development approaches, notably:

- improved quality
- improved time-to-market
- improved stakeholder and customer satisfaction.

Agile methods achieve these benefits with a combination of changing the order in which tasks are performed, reduction or elimination of tasks that don't add to the development goals of the project, and putting into place metrics and practices for improved project planning and governance.

Adoption of agile methods for the development of embedded software has been impeded by a number of factors, including inherent conservatism on the part of embedded development organizations, the lack of literature on its application in systems domains, and the need to modify the agile practices to take into account the unique aspects of embedded systems. Nevertheless, real benefits are possible through the application of agile methods, even in highly regulated safety-critical systems development.

The most important of the agile practices for embedded systems development include:

- dynamic planning – not planning beyond the knowledge we have with the expectation and practice of updating plans as deeper information becomes available

- governance with goal-based metrics – continuously gathering evidence of progress and success to effectively steer the project and update project plans
- stand-up meetings – tracking progress and roadblocks on a daily schedule with short informal meetings
- retrospectives – paying attention to what is working and what is not and adapting to improve success
- incremental development – developing the system in a series of iterations, each of which is verified and validated against an independent set of requirements
- high-fidelity modeling – use of precise, verifiable models for requirements analysis, architecture, and design to ensure correctness and consistency
- executable requirements – building verifiable requirements models to facilitate understanding of stakeholder needs and system functionality, resulting in early and low-cost identification of missing, incorrect, incomplete, and inconsistent requirements
- test-driven development – the creation and application of unit (developer) tests as the design and code are developed, thereby avoiding defects in the first place
- continuous integration – continuously integrating the work from different engineers to ensure its consistency
- change management – tracking requests for change from their creation through their resolution to improve software quality
- risk management – identification, tracking, and resolution of key project risks to improve project success.

These practices can, individually or collectively, improve the quality and efficiency of most embedded software development environments. That being true, it isn't necessary to apply all of these pactices simultaneously. The best way to adopt agile methods is via an agile approach: first, identify the key pain points of your development organization or project and apply the practices that specifically address your greatest pain. Later, as your team becomes adept in the new methods, you can incrementally add other practices to address secondary issues. Agile methods are not static and agile teams are not stagnant. In their core, agile methods require continuously paying attention, adapting, and verifying improvement to guide increasing development capabilities.

References

[1] Proceedings of IEEE WESCON 26 1970 (August): 1–9, Available from: http://www.cs.umd.edu/class/spring2003/cmsc838p/Process/waterfall.pdf.

[2] Available from: http://agilemanifesto.org/.

[3] Available from: http://disciplinedagiledelivery.com.

[4] Available from: http://www.amazon.com/Real-Time-Agility-Embedded-Development-ebook/dp/B002RQVPA4/ref=sr_1_2?ie=UTF8&qid=1329495806&sr=8–2.

[5] B. Douglass. Rigorous agile is an oxymoron (November, 2010). Available from: <https://www.ibm.com/developerworks/mydeveloperworks/blogs/BruceDouglass/entry/rigorous_agile_is_an_oxymoron?lang=en>.

[6] B.P. Douglass, Real-Time Design Patterns, Addison-Wesley, 2002.
[7] ISO/CD 26262−9: Road vehicles – Functional Safety – Part 9: ASIL-oriented and safety-oriented analyses. ISO, 2008.
[8] B.P. Douglass, Real-Time Agility, Addison-Wesley, 2009.
[9] Available from: http://www.martinfowler.com/articles/itsNotJustStandingUp.html.
[10] B.P. Douglass, Real-Time UML, 3rd Edition: Advances in the UML for Real-Time Systems, Addison-Wesley, 2004.
[11] P. Baker, Z. Ru Dai, J. Grabowski, I. Schieferdecker, C. Williams, Model-Driven Testing: Using the UML Testing Profile, Springer, 2007 (or the originating specification ptc/03-08-03 from the OMG website <www.omg.org>).
[12] V. Hilderman, T. Baghai, Avionics Certification: A Complete Guide to DO-178 (Software), DO-254 (Hardware), Avionics Communications, 2007.

Bibliography

Available from: http://www-01.ibm.com/software/rational/products/rtc/.
T. de Marco, T. Lister, Waltzing with Bears, Dorset Publishing, 2003.

CHAPTER 22

Embedded Software for Automotive Applications

Inga Harris

Chapter Outline

Software Engineering for Embedded Systems.
DOI: http://dx.doi.org/10.1016/B978-0-12-415917-4.00022-0
© 2013 Elsevier Inc. All rights reserved.

The purpose of this chapter is to introduce the embedded environment of the automotive electronic system. This automotive embedded software environment is more intense than any other embedded system: with rigorous planning, architecting, development, testing, validation and verification taking up to 5 years from concept to production. In an automotive system, millions of people's lives are dependent on the components, hardware and software working perfectly from mile 1 to mile 200,000 and beyond without one single failure, over 20 years, and from temperatures below freezing to above 100°C. This chapter will describe the key steps, processes, and quality aspects which must be considered by the automotive embedded software engineer, but does not prescribe any specifics about how this must be done, as no such rules exist.

To write good automotive software an engineer should have knowledge of how and why the automotive vehicle evolved into the complex system that it is today. The differences between the different automotive submarkets, which are developed independently but have to work in unison, must also be understood by the software engineer. What the quality levels are and why such strict quality levels exist, along with how quality is tested and measured must be understood. An automotive software engineer must know the automotive industry standards and in which direction the market is moving over the next decade. This chapter touches on all of these topics and provides examples and links to the industry bodies and regulations. Most if not all of the other chapters in this book apply to automotive applications. This chapter highlights the key areas.

A bit of history to set the scene

The automotive industry was born in the eighteenth century when the first self-propelled steam vehicles were invented for military use. Within months of these vehicles being used the very first recorded motor accident happened when a large three-wheeled artillery carriage knocked down part of a wall.

Auto electronics: 1911–2000

In 1911 the Cadillac 20/30 hp model was on sale with ignition, electric lighting and electric self starting developed by Charles F. Kettering's Dayton Engineering Laboratories Company (Delco). This marked the start of electronic content in vehicles. As history shows in many other industries, war is often a key driver in technology innovation. The First World War switched the focus from automotive road vehicles to war machines, but shortly after the war ended and the post-war sales slump showed signs of recovering, focus and development of road vehicles resumed.

- Marconi began experimenting with wireless receivers (radios) in Daimler road vehicles.
- Trico introduced electric windscreen wipers as a speed-consistent alternative to previous vacuum driven wipers.

The 30 s: the great depression of the 1930s again pushed many companies into financial difficulties and while advances in mechanical components continued, e.g., gear boxes and suspension, electronic content remained minimal, by today's standards.

The 40 s: the Second World War again swung focus from road vehicles to the military needs but this war, with its heavier bombing, had a longer-lasting effect on the industry. This war destroyed factories and also forced the introduction of petrol rationing. That didn't stop Packard introducing electrically powered seats and windows in 1947 and Buick introducing a fully automatic gearbox the following year.

The 50 s: the 1950s brought the Suez crisis in Europe and tail fins and rocket-shaped tail lamps in the USA but the automobile industry was focusing on performance. Packard continued to lead innovation on the electronic side with push-button transmissions, power door locks and in-vehicle record players in 1957 but sadly these innovations ceased production the following year.

The 60 s: the 1960s really saw the industry take off and road infrastructures were developed to support the faster vehicles. With speed came safety, and seatbelts started to become installed as standard.

The 70 s: in the 1970s airbags were developed in reaction to the increase in fatal road vehicle accidents. The Arab Israeli War caused fuel supply problems and a steep rise in fuel prices for motorists throughout the world. This war caused the realization that oil is a finite resource and manufacturers started to look at ways of improving fuel economy. Later in that decade American road vehicles started to come with catalytic converters in the exhaust system in an effort to cut air-polluting emissions.

The 80 s: the industry was naturally maturing by the 1980s and all the key drivers of automotive electronics were in place; pleasure, safety, economy and emissions. Many companies merged and start working together to form industry standards which made development and integration between system components easier to do.

The 90 s: governmental regulatory bodies such as the Environmental Protection Agency (EPA) and the European Commission introduced exhaust emissions controls in the 1990s. Bosch developed the Controller Area Network (CAN) bus standard in the 1980s with the CAN2.0 specification released in 1991, which allows microcontrollers and devices to communicate directly with each other in a vehicle without the need for a host computer. This communications standard was readily adopted by the automotive industry but also found its way into the industrial and medical industries. Alternative networks, such as Local Interconnect Network (LIN), Media Oriented Systems Transport (MOST®) and FlexRay™, were also under development. Table 22.1 shows five automotive communication protocols which are present in recent vehicle models. Each protocol has its place as the vehicle subsystems differ so greatly. There is a network for slow, cost-conscious nodes, traditional vehicle network nodes with some cost constraints but high data rates in the noisy environment, and networks for state-of-the-art communications including auto video and real-time diagnostics.

Electronic content growth drivers

It became increasingly difficult to manage all the vehicle components as the developers added more functionality and performance at the same time as being constrained by vehicle specification targets and regulations. Electronic content was once a simple circuit of switches, relays and fuses that could be drawn on a large piece of paper. Figure 22.1 shows the entire electronic content of a 1970s Mini Clubman. The electronic system contains little more than lamps, indicators, battery, a horn, a starter motor, switches and relays. Compare that with the instrument cluster wiring diagram of the 1997 Volvo 960 shown in Figure 22.2.

Table 22.1: Comms comparison table.

Protocol	Applications	Physical	Cost	Bandwidth	Advantages	Disadvantages
LIN	Door Locks, Climate Control, Seat Belts, Sunroof, Lighting, Window Lift, Mirror Control	1 wire	Low	20 kbits/sec	Low cost and easy to use	Speed/Bandwidth
CAN	Body Systems, Engine Management, Transmission	2 wire	Medium	1 Mbits/sec	Global Mature, Proven, Standard	Speed/Bandwidth limitations
FlexRay	Drive-by-Wire, Brake-by-Wire, Advanced Safety and Collision Avoidance Systems, Steer-by-Wire, Stability Control, Camera-Based Monitoring Systems	2 Channel, 2 Wire, normally Fibre Optic	High	10 Mbits/sec	High data rate and Redundancy	Limited adoption, Clock accuracy and voltage levels
MOST	Multimedia, Infotainment	2 Wire, Fibre Optic	High	25 Mbits/sec	Specifically design for automotive multimedia	Limited adoption (niche), High Cost
Ethernet	Programming ECUs, Multimedia	2 wire	Medium	100 Mbits/sec	Global Standard, large bandwidth	Noise Immunity, Cable Cost, new in automotive space

You can see that over 20 years a lot of electronic content had evolved, including significantly more dashboard indicators and the inclusion of electronic climate control, cruise control, radio, oil pressure, fuel level, engine control, transmission control, ABS control and speed control system connections on the right-hand side of the figure as well as other connections listed in the middle, e.g., supplemental restraints. The communication protocols which enable the data and commands to be transferred all around the vehicle cannot be controlled without drivers. Even the sensors which transform the vehicle's activities into the electronic domain need software to make meaningful sense of the reading and react to it. This wiring diagram is 15 years old; imagine how that would look today. Figure 22.3 shows a 3D instrument cluster with no analog gauges at all; the dashboard has become a computer screen.

The automotive market is experiencing unprecedented electronic control evolution. It is providing consumers with vehicles that are safer, more fuel efficient and more pleasant to drive than any previous generation, vehicles that are an extension of the owner's personal life. A lot of this can be attributed to the successful expansion of the global markets,

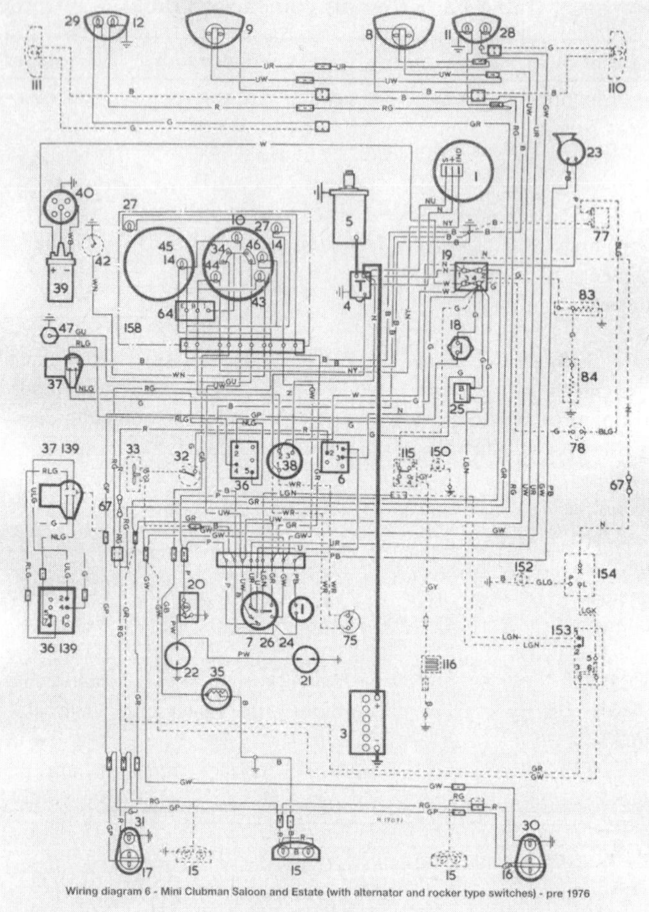

Figure 22.1:
Wiring diagram of 1976 Mini Clubman saloon and estate.

encompassing all aspects of the industry, from government environmental mandates, to vehicle design and manufacturing, to semiconductor solutions design.

The resultant embedded SW growth

Embedded automotive system software in today's road vehicles is millions of lines long and distributed across hundreds of components of various types and architectures. It has evolved this way over many decades. When software was first used in the mainstream, high-volume vehicle systems it would have been written on a 4- or 8-bit microcontroller architecture. There were just a few software-driven components in the vehicle which did

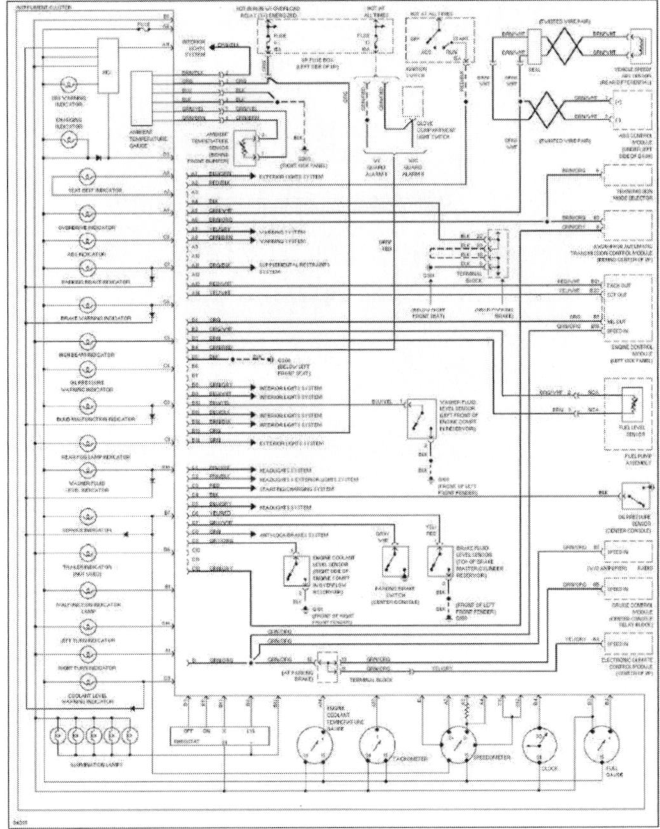

Figure 22.2:
Instrument cluster wiring diagram of 1997 Volvo 960.

some timing control and some basic communication and computation, possibly some analog-to-digital conversion. As more advanced, higher-speed communication protocols were introduced the software was typically ported onto an 8- or 16-bit device but powertrain and airbag applications demanded 32-bit performance at a much earlier time than other systems due to the complex timing requirements. Motor control systems were the initial candidate for electronic control as windscreen wipers, electric windows and mirrors, power steering and seat belt pre tensioner systems were introduced across many global platforms early on in the industry's electronics evolution. In the 1990s the introduction of the self-diagnostic and reporting requirement of the vehicle system known as On Board Diagnostics Two (OBDII) forced the move to embedded software in vehicles for any system that was affected but had not yet moved. After the introduction of OBDII almost every component of the vehicle which moved was controlled by software.

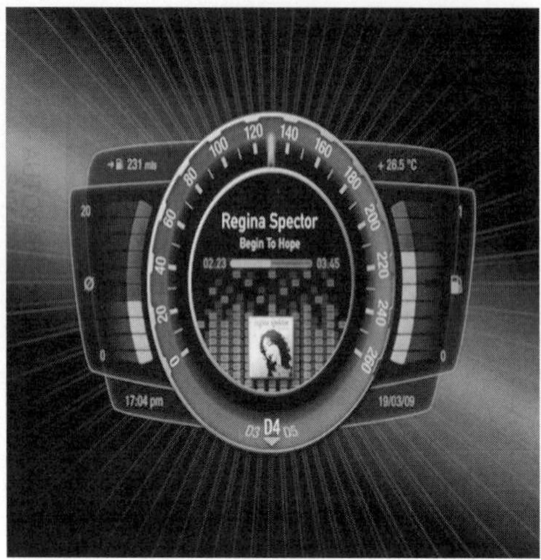

Figure 22.3:
Icon instruments 610 × 457.

Automotive programming languages

In general the automotive industry lags behind other industries such as the computer and networking industries mainly due to the extreme levels of safety and reliability required.

During the first few decades of electronic expansion in vehicles, when software content was growing, assembly code was the language of choice. The functionality of the software was manageable. Development tools were not advanced and memory availability for the storage of the software routines was not an infinite resource, a few kilobytes rather than tens of megabytes. A big disadvantage of writing in assembly was and still is its lack of portability across devices and across platforms. In an environment which is evolving at such a fast pace the adoption of C was quick. This enabled functions to be written at a higher level and made to be more portable with low-level drivers handling the differences and the C compilers managing the core resource allocation. The adoption of C did mean that code size grew quickly but the advantage of a shorter development time and significantly increased reusability was too great to discount.

Memory technology switched from EPROM and ROM solutions to flash NVM technology and the costs came down so that large memory devices were affordable. The automotive industry is addicted to C and is not showing any indication of a move away. Some submarkets such as the previously mentioned instrumentation cluster are advancing but this is more due to the evolution of the dashboard into a computer system rather than an automotive safety and control environment. C++ is used in some cases, but not to its full capability.

Summary of implications

With so much history and with a high level of complexity, reliability and quality (mandated by governments, worldwide treaties and industry consortium bodies for safety and emissions), automotive embedded software is diverse, complex and requires understanding of the system it runs in, and the devices it runs on and in partnership with. These systems are developed based on existing platforms and are worked on by teams of engineers over many continents and many separate companies. This means that the required functionality, where (on which hardware) it must be achieved and how it must be achieved (which standards it must conform to) so that it operates with other components without conflict must be known, risk-assessed and quality-checked before any of it is put on a device in a system for testing. In many cases this phase of the development cycle is the hardest, longest part, and will involve the vehicle manufacturers, submodule architects/designers and component suppliers. Once you have all that information in place the software is relatively easy to output, test and integrate.

Automotive segments and how they differ

The automotive electronics industry can be broken down into various market subsegments. Each subsegment has its own nuances and priorities based on the standard automotive framework, with the exception being the modern infotainment market, which is more like a consumer application with some automotive characteristics. Figure 22.4 shows the five automotive subsegments which are present inside a typical modern vehicle and the following five sections describe these major automotive subsegments.

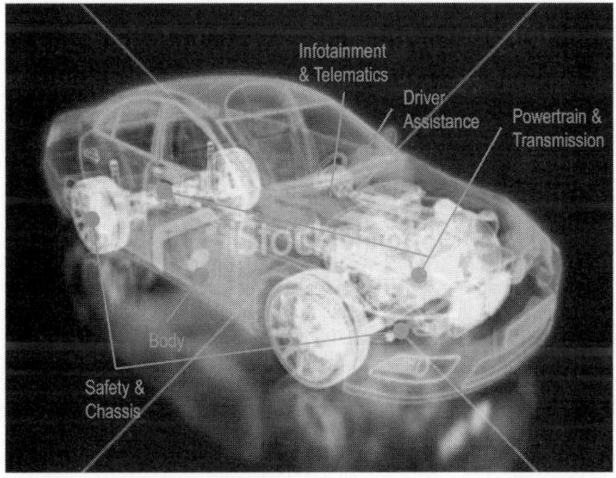

Figure 22.4:
Vehicle subsystems.

Body

Body electronics systems encompass a broad variety of applications inside the vehicle cabin, consisting of comfort, safety and networking functions (such as the body controller and central gateway), windows, doors, seats, lighting and heating, ventilation and air conditioning, known as HVAC. Reducing power consumption and improving comfort are the key trends that are driving body electronics systems.

The central body control module (BCM) is the primary hub that maintains body functions, such as internal and external lighting, security and access control, comfort features for doors and seats and other convenience controls.

The gateway serves as the information bridge between various in-vehicle communication networks, including Ethernet, FlexRay™, CAN, LIN and MOST® protocols. It also serves as the vehicle's central diagnostic interface. Figure 22.5 shows a simple block diagram on a BCM and Gateway system.

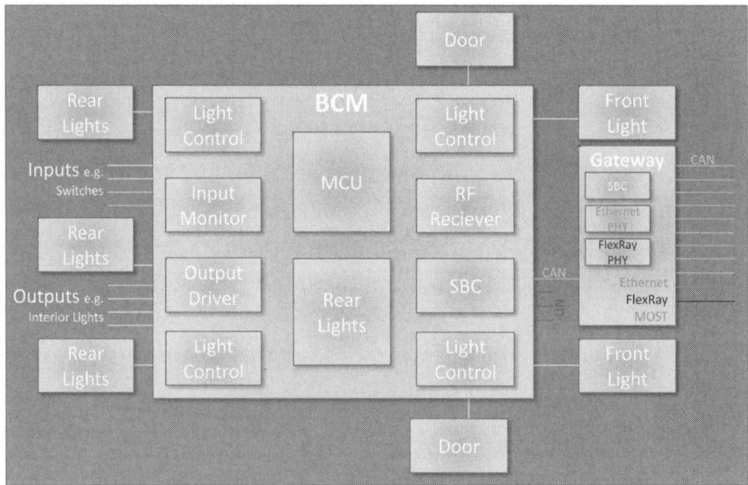

Figure 22.5:
BCM and gateway block diagram.

Centralized door modules typically control several motors (e.g., window lift, door locks and mirrors) and are quite similar to seat control modules. Distributed systems incorporate smart actuators where networked mixed-mode control devices are directly mounted on the actuator to help reduce the electronic control unit (ECU) developer's design effort.

Exterior lighting plays an important role in the safety of vehicle passengers and other road users. Different types of lamps (e.g., halogen, xenon or LED) are used in a variety of lighting functions, such as brake lights, turn indicators, low- and high-beam headlights and others. More advanced functions include light bending, leveling and shaping to adapt to changing driving conditions.

HVAC systems require several electric motors for blowers and flaps. The motor control is based on a variety of sensor inputs. Newer systems use fewer sensors and model the vehicle interior, requiring the higher computing performance of 32-bit microcontrollers. Hbridge drivers with PWM, low unloaded current use, over-current and over-temperature protection, and load current feedback control motors more efficiently. Distributed systems incorporate smart actuators where networked mixed-mode control devices are directly mounted on the actuator to help reduce the ECU developer's design effort.

Chassis and safety

The chassis electronic system includes the braking systems, steering control and suspension. These systems are pertinent to the vehicle's safety. Improving driving comfort and increasing vehicle safety are the key trends that are driving today's chassis electronics systems.

Electronic stability control (ESC) helps drivers maintain control of their vehicles. The microcontroller and a set of sensors measure the vehicle's lateral and longitudinal acceleration, angular velocity, wheel speed, and steering angle. By controlling the actuators in the antilock braking system the ESC system can achieve a reduction of 30% of single-vehicle car crashes and around 60% of single-vehicle sport utility vehicle (SUV) crashes.

Dual-core microcontrollers enable individual control of brake forces at each wheel. If loss of steering control is detected, the ESC can take control of braking from the driver and use active suspension functions to stabilize the vehicle. By increasing the computing power of the ESC system, active and passive safety systems can be networked together to improve the overall safety.

The central electronic elements of today's power steering systems are 16- and 32-bit single or dual-core microcontrollers designed for safety-critical applications. These controllers can provide enhanced computing power and specialized peripherals for complex electric motor control functions. For MOSFET power stage control, integrated predrivers are typically used to interface with the microcontroller directly or via an SPI link. These connections between the microcontroller and the power stage are designed with some level of fault tolerance, e.g., fault detection, replication and redundancy to ensure a robust solution in this noisy environment.

Tire-pressure monitoring systems (TPMS) are incorporated for improved vehicle safety. A TPMS solution provides real-time tire pressure monitoring and alerts the driver to

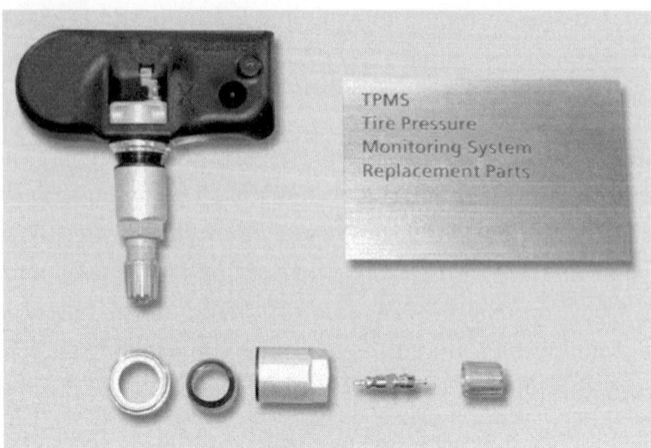

Figure 22.6:
TPMS.

improperly inflated tires. The tire-pressure monitor system integrates a pressure sensor, an 8-bit microcontroller, a radio frequency (RF) transmitter and a two-axis accelerometer sensor with *X* and *Z* axis as shown in Figure 22.6. This is normally installed in a module on the wheel rims to provide independent, real-time air pressure measurements for each tire that can be transmitted to the vehicle instrument cluster to instantly inform the driver.

Another key system concerning vehicle safety is the airbag system. The central component of an airbag system is a control unit that combines a 16- or 32-bit microcontroller with a set of local acceleration sensors. Depending on the complexity of the system, additional satellite sensors provide supplementary crash information via standardized sensor buses. Processed sensor inputs are used to fire front, side and curtain airbags with specialized multi-channel squib driver circuits. Advanced sensing solutions have intuitive signal processing including fault and overload diagnostic system alerts to help make decisions about airbag deployment. As an additional safety factor, highly efficient switched-mode power supply components allow the system to keep operating for several hundred milliseconds if the battery connection is lost during an accident.

Driver assistance

Advanced driver-assistance systems (ADAS) are one of the fastest-growing safety application areas due to the desire to reduce vehicular accidents and fatalities.

Beyond passive safety systems, active safety systems play a major role in reducing traffic fatalities and the monetary impact of vehicular accidents. ADAS systems include long- and medium-range radar and vision systems. Developing an ADAS system requires state-of-the-art yet cost-effective RF technology that can be embedded in the vehicle for exterior object detection and classification. A state-of-the-art radar system can tell a vehicle from a pedestrian, from a wall, and know the location and potential corrective path. Extraordinary computation power is needed to make the system efficient, but to become more prevalent in the marketplace the cost must be very low.

Active safety systems include adaptive cruise control (ACC) and collision-warning systems with automatic steering and braking intervention. In a collision-warning system, a microcontroller-controlled 77 GHz transmitter emits signals reflected from objects ahead, to the side and to the rear of the vehicle, which are captured by multiple receivers integrated throughout the vehicle. Using a high-performance 32-bit single- or dual-core microcontroller with embedded flash and RAM, the radar system can detect and track objects in the frequency domain, triggering a driver warning of an imminent collision and initiating ESC emergency intervention.

Camera systems in ADAS can display what is behind or beside the vehicle, even at night on screen. They can also analyze the video content for automatic lane-departure warning systems and high/low-beam headlight control. An image sensor interface provides incoming video frames to a single- or dual-core architecture optimized with DSP extensions for image improvement filtering and edge or spot detection. Additional system requirements include an appropriate communication interface, an integrated DRAM interface for fast access to external memory and embedded flash for low system cost.

Powertrain and transmission

Powertrain systems solidified electronic control technology in vehicles, from motorcycle engines to the latest high-end powertrain technology in diesel, spark ignition, hybrid and electric vehicles.

The transmission system ensures that engine torque output is efficiently transferred to the road, providing the traction and control the driver requires. Today, most vehicle manufacturers are turning to electronically controlled transmission systems to provide the precise control necessary for new-generation automated manual dual-clutch transmissions and fully automatic transmissions with up to eight different speeds. Electronically controlled transmissions help improve fuel efficiency and reduce driver workload. Designing powertrain and transmission applications that meet government regulations and consumers' requirements for cleaner, more fuel-efficient vehicles while delivering best-in-class engine control performance for an uncompromised driving experience are the key trends that are driving today's powertrain and transmission systems.

The gasoline engine is the most common drive technology in the world. Modern gasoline engines are able to meet very stringent CO_2 regulations, are cost-effective to manufacture and remain the primary choice for urban driving. Common-rail fuel-injection technology has dramatically improved the performance and efficiency of diesel engines. Consequently, public perception of diesel engines has changed, due to improved performance and fuel efficiency, reduced noise and lower smoke emissions. High-pressure injection systems and efficient exhaust-gas treatment modules will guarantee even more eco-friendly and fuel-efficient driving in the future. The gasoline direct injection (GDI) technology, with its potential 20% improvement in fuel savings, is expected to grow significantly in the coming years.

Consumer demand for mobility in emerging markets is leading the motorcycle manufacturers to move from mechanically to electronically controlled systems to meet stricter emissions regulations. In the west, the vehicle makers see engine downsizing as an opportunity to reduce CO_2 levels significantly and to boost the fuel economy.

Hybrid vehicles combine an internal combustion engine and a battery-powered electric motor to power the drivetrain, improving fuel economy and reducing harmful emissions. In addition to the internal combustion engine control unit, other modules are required to control the electric traction motor, recharge the battery and manage the energy used to run the start/stop system, fuel and water pumps. The start/stop system is the first step in the vehicle electrification. Also referred to as micro-hybrid technology, this system turns the engine off when it would normally idle in neutral and restarts it instantly when the accelerator is pressed. This is a particularly effective system in urban "stop and go" driving conditions where fuel consumption and CO_2 emissions can be improved by up to 15%. Electronically controlled fuel and water pumps can more precisely deliver accurate fuel and coolant flow and pressure within the engine environment and operate only when required. This helps ensure not only economical fuel management but also that the engine runs at optimum temperatures for the most efficient operation. Electronic control is essential for vehicle makers to develop a beltless engine and to remove all-engine driven loads, such as electric power steering and the A/C compressor, which need to operate even when a hybrid vehicle has its engine off. Distributed systems incorporate smart actuators where networked mixed-mode control devices are directly mounted on the actuator to help reduce the ECU developer's design effort. Figure 22.7 is a map of all the powertrain and transmission systems in a standard vehicle.

Infotainment and telematics

The automotive infotainment market is increasingly influenced by portable and mobile consumer electronics technology. Driver information system complexity is increasing at an exponential rate. In recent years we have seen the addition of navigation systems, 3 G wireless access, high-resolution color displays, speech recognition, USB and Bluetooth® connectivity and so on. Most of the increased complexity is in the amount of software the

Figure 22.7:
Powertrain.

system has to run. Consumers expecting more and more multimedia features in their vehicles have driven the increased growth rate and forced a reduction of design cycle time for products. The evolving world of instrument clusters is moving from purely mechanical gauges towards systems that incorporate displays of various types across the entire range of applications. The systems range from displays with a single gauge to fully reconfigurable graphical instrument clusters shown on large displays in the dashboard (see Figure 22.3). The mid-end dashboard instrumentation clusters have moved to TFT LCD display-based systems with the simultaneous drive capability of gauges, LEDs buzzers and LCD displays, as shown in Figure 22.8. The microcontrollers which support this market space provide basic image manipulation all the way to Open GL ES and Open VG graphics support enabling graphics reuse across various products.

Telematics is the integrated use of telecommunications and informatics within road vehicles. This technology sends, receives and stores information via telecommunication components. A telematic system includes global positioning system (GPS) technology which is integrated with ECUs and mobile communications technology in an automotive navigation system.

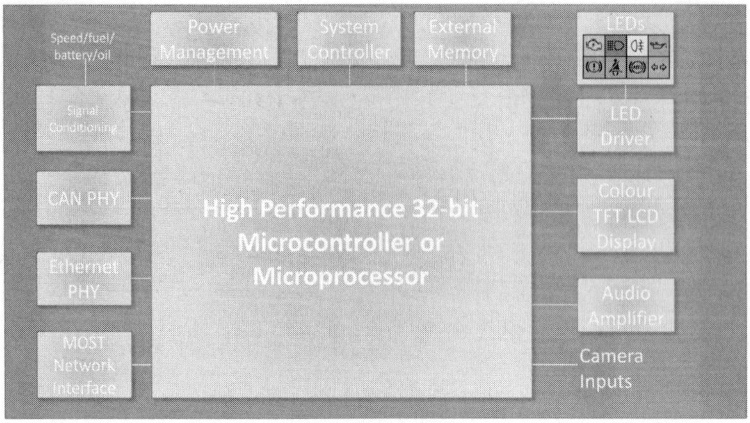

Figure 22.8:
Instrument cluster block diagram.

Automotive subsegment summary

Table 22.2 lists each of the described automotive market and their characteristics for comparison purposes.

Automotive quality

In the previous section various automotive subsegments were introduced from a functionality point of view. The fundamental purpose of the embedded software is to fulfill the requirements of the application and the associated quality needs by addressing them all by effectively utilizing the capabilities of the available hardware with quality software routines in a supporting role. This means that the software engineer must be aware of the hardware functionality and risks, and write functions and routines in a way that ensures quality of the entire automotive system. As you saw in Figure 22.2, showing the Volvo instrument cluster, the separate application modules are highly interconnected and software in one application area can have an effect on another.

Planning for Murphy's law

The automotive market segment requires real-time reactions to high-speed data as engines rotate at thousand of revolutions per minute. Imagine the case where a heavy-use interrupt service routine is being executed by the core when a rare random but high-impact event occurs. The reaction to this event could be delayed if the core does not react appropriately and quickly, possibly causing an incident and in the worst case causing a fatality. Such a situation could occur if the interrupt priorities where incorrectly set up for this rare random

Table 22.2: Auto subsegment summary.

Subsegment	Application	Maturity	Market Driver	Major Function/ Feature
Body	BCM	High	Driving Comfort	Control
	Gateway	High	Power Consumption	Communications
	Exterior Lighting	High	Power Consumption	Control
	HVAC	High	Driving Comfort	Motor Control
Chassis and Safety	ESC	Medium	Safety	Breaking Control
	Power Steering	High	Driving Comfort	Motor Control
	TPMS	Medium	Safety	Sensors
	Airbag	High	Safety	Sensors
Driver Assistance	ACC	Low	Safety	DSP
	Visual System	Low	Safety	DSP
Powertrain and Transmission	Gasoline	High	Fuel Efficiency and Emmissions	Efficiency Control
	Diesel Common Rail Fuel Injection	High	Fuel Efficiency and Emmissions	Efficiency Control
	Hybrid	Low	Fuel Efficiency and Emmissions	Efficiency Control
	Start Stop	Medium	Fuel Efficiency and Emmissions	Efficiency Control
	Fuel/Water Pumps	High	Fuel Efficiency and Emmissions	Efficiency Control
Infotainment and Telematics	Instrumentation Cluster	Medium	Driving Comfort	Data Displays
	GPS	Medium	Driving Comfort	Graphics

event that was not fully considered when the software was being developed or if the core disabled interrupts while this heavy load interrupt was being run with the intention of having that interrupt complete as soon as possible. This would be unlikely to be highlighted as an issue during the system verification as rare random events are hard to simulate in a test environment and even harder to create in real-world tests as test time is limited to weeks and months rather than years. This quality incident could remain dormant in millions of vehicles over various platforms for years until that exact condition was stumbled upon. Having a total focus on software and system quality from the outset of the project based on a solid risk assessment profile and sound software practices documented along with a robust configuration management tool goes a long way to ensuring that quality is maintained in the final system. Automotive systems should be reviewed with Murphy's Law in mind: anything that can go wrong, will go wrong.

Fault-tolerant communications

In all communications, errors are recognized as a fact of life, and hence provisions for error control have been included in most protocol standards. The most challenging aspect of ensuring a fault-tolerant communication path is balancing the traditional redundancy approach with error detection and recovery mechanisms that are built into most of the communication protocols against risk, impact, probability and cost. It is essential to understand what capability the communication hardware of the microcontroller has in-built and to ensure that it is enabled and used wherever possible.

Ignoring an error interrupt source is one of the cardinal sins of automotive embedded software as Murphy 's Law definitely applies. If it can go wrong, it will go wrong, especially if you think it is impossible. Once the hardware capability is understood and enabled with associated software routines and interrupt routines in place, normally through software drivers, any identified gaps in fault tolerance communications can be closed by robustly written software functions. Normally communication modules on the microcontroller will provide some form of parity, handshaking, ACK/NACK signaling or ECC generation to support fault identification and correction. If the system uses custom communication protocols one or more of the listed fault-finding methods should be designed into the protocol to ensure that the information sent is received correctly, on time and potentially received in the correct order or the order identifiable. In the automotive environment the timeliness of the message reception must not be adversely hampered by fault checking.

Fault-tolerant software

Within just 30 years, software in road vehicles went from 0 over 10 million lines of code. The size and structure of the embedded software and hardware systems in vehicles are enormous. The automotive application functions are built on top of real-time operating systems and devices and peripheral drivers. Most of the software is real-time critical. Thousands of individual functions are realized and controlled by software in high-end vehicles with no less than 70 individual, yet connected, control units. Approximately 40% of the production costs of a vehicle can be due to the electronic content infrastructure and software costs alone. The speed of the development, the complex requirements and the cost pressure bring enormous challenges and risks but also opportunities and high potential for improvements. Historically control theory played a prominent role in vehicle development. Today, a lot of the software in vehicles is not actually control-based, but event-based. The challenge here is to find the right theory and methodology to combine control theory and the engineering of discrete event systems. Data management is very distributed and uncoordinated. Each of the ECUs contains and manages their own data. This could lead to a conflicting situation in vehicles where a submodule's local data tells the module that the vehicle is moving, while another submodule believes that the vehicle has stopped based on its data. If this case were not planned for in advance it could not be resolved. Conflicts such as these must be resolvable. Replication, redundancy and output comparison are frequently used in the automotive environment.

Zero-defect software

Unlike other markets where consumers are used to updating firmware regularly, the automotive market frowns upon such updates as these are effectively recalls. Zero-defect (ZD) software development is not the same as bug-free software. It is a practice of developing software that is maintained in the highest-quality state throughout the entire development process. Defects are characteristics of the developing software that would not be suitable for the final product as is. This generic definition encompasses bugs as well as unwanted deviations from the expected and desired final outcome. Defects in the development of an automotive application could include a delay or jitter in an output signal, a lower system frequency than the final product, or any unfinished features.

The most common development approach in software engineering is to postpone major testing until the final quality assurance (QA) phase of development, where defects are often discovered for the first time. Experience shows that the majority of bugs are not detected and consequently not resolved until long after their introduction but the longer a defect exists, the harder it is to fix. On large software products such as any automotive application, each individual stage of development in which a defect proliferates will increase the cost of fixing the defect by up to 50 times. A defect which is introduced in the early design phases can cost hundreds of times more to fix if it is only caught in the testing phase than it would if it were fixed soon after its introduction. Maintaining the software product in what is believed to be a defect-free state throughout the development process is paramount.
The typical software engineer writes an average of ten lines of code a day while the rest of the day is spent on debugging. ZD shortens schedules by eliminating most debugging time and decreases the likelihood of in-field issues and ensures problems do not proliferate. Figure 22.9 describes some key points to bear in mind when developing ZD automotive software.

Risk management and failure modes

Risk management can be defined as the identification, analysis, and prioritization of risks (defined in ISO 31000 as the effect of uncertainty on objectives, whether positive or negative) followed up with a coordinated use of available resources to reduce, observe, and control the likelihood and impact of deviations from expected behavior. The first step is the identification, characterization and assessment of potential threats. Then the system's vulnerabilities can be assessed and the consequences identified. The next step is to find ways to reduce those risks. There are four kinds of reaction to identified risks; avoid, prevent, share or accept. Once that data is collected a mitigation plan can be drawn up and prioritized based on an appropriate strategy. A process must exist to make sure that the identified risks are monitored and managed during the project to reduce the likelihood that

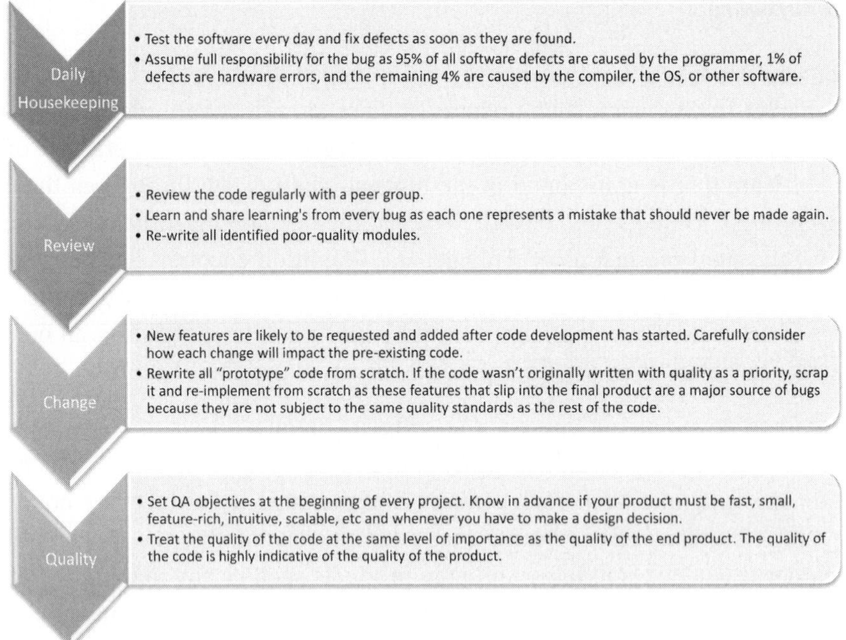

Figure 22.9:
ZDSW chart.

they will occur and to reduce the impact if they do. It is good practice to create a risk register which lists risks in a prioritized order. For each identified risk, the risk register should include fields such as:

- risk identification number
- description
- consequence
- probability (high, medium or low)
- planned actions to mitigate the risk
- contingency plan (what you'll do if the risk happens)
- risk owner (a member of the project team)
- status (e.g., closed: no longer a risk).

Be aware that new risks can be identified at any stage of development. If they are significant they should be added to the risk register document.

Failure modes and effects analysis

Failure modes are any errors or defects in a process or design that affect the customer. The failure mode can be potential or actual. This term was first used in manufacturing industries during various phases of the product life-cycle and has now found its way into all other industries. Effects analysis is the investigation of the consequences of those failures. Failure modes and effects analysis (FMEA) is a common process used in the automotive industry. FMEA analyzes potential failure modes within a system for classification by the severity and likelihood of the failures. A successful FMEA activity enables a team to identify potential failure modes based on past experiences with similar products or processes, allowing the team to design those failures out of the system with minimum effort and resource expenditure, reducing development time and reducing development costs. The process for conducting an FMEA is typically three main stages. The first stage looks at the cause of a failure mode and the number of times it occurs. A failure mode is given an occurrence ranking as shown in Table 22.3.

The next stage determines the severity of the failure mode. As a failure mode in a single component can lead to a failure mode in another component, each failure mode should be listed in technical terms and for each function. This means that the ultimate effect of each failure mode needs to be considered. A failure mode is given a severity ranking, as shown in Table 22.4. The final stage is to test the action's efficiency and verify it. A number is given to rank the ability of planned tests to remove defects or to detect failure modes in time. This number measures the risk that the failure will escape detection. A failure mode is given a detection ranking as shown in Table 22.5.

After ranking the severity, occurrence and detectability, the risk priority number can be calculated by multiplying these three numbers. This has to be done for the entire design.

Table 22.3: FMEA occurrence.

Rating	Meaning
1	No known occurrences on similar products or processes
2/3	Low (relatively few failures)
4/5/6	Moderate (occasional failures)
7/8	High (repeated failures)
9/10	Very high (failure is almost inevitable)

Table 22.4: FMEA severity.

Rating	Meaning
1	No effect
2	Very minor (only noticed by discriminating customers)
3	Minor (affects very little of the system, noticed by average customer)
4/5/6	Moderate (most customers are annoyed)
7/8	High (causes a loss of primary function; customers are dissatisfied)
9/10	Very high and hazardous (product becomes inoperative; customers angered; the failure may result unsafe operation and possible injury)

Table 22.5: FMEA detection.

Rating	Meaning
1	Certain - fault will be caught on test
2	Almost certain
3	High
4/5/6	Moderate
7/8	Low
9/10	Fault will be passed to customer undetected

When this has been completed it is easy to determine the areas of greatest concern. The failure modes which have the highest risk priority number (RPN) are the failure modes which should be given the highest priority for corrective action execution.

An automotive software FMEA example is shown in Table 22.6.

Development and test

Subsystem interoperability

The vehicle industry is vertically organized. In software engineering terms it would be described as modular. Automotive mechanical engineers developed, over 100 years, the various subsystems in vehicles to work independently and be manufactured independently. This enables a significant division of labor and as a result third-party suppliers can take over a considerable part of the engineering, the development, and also the production. The vehicle parts are produced by a complex supply chain and in some cases only assembled by the vehicle manufacturer. A vehicle can be considered to be a kit of subparts that are assembled by the vehicle manufacturer (OEM) but in some cases this too is subcontracted. However, now quite unrelated and independent functions such as braking, steering, or controlling the engine, which were freely controlled by the driver, are starting to interact. The vehicle is evolving from an assembled device of mostly discrete systems, which affected each other only by the odd vibration and a bit of heat, into a fully integrated system with communication busses, centralized control and real system dependencies, such as real-time video and radar system directly affecting the vehicle's braking control units. As a result unintentional feature interactions have become an issue. This means that the need for a full system specification and a solid understanding of the various interlinked systems is more important than ever to enable thorough testing and a highly reliable end product, a reliable and safe vehicle. The following development and test section of this chapter suggests steps that can be taken to achieve the required standards in automotive safety in an integrated automotive system.

Table 22.6: Example FMEA entry.

Functionality	Fault mode	Fault cause	Fault/Failure effects						Failure detection method / observable symptoms	Mitigation Plan	Design Recommendation	Remarks
			Description	Failure root cause	Occurence	Severity	Detection	Risk Index				
"Flash based variable" which provides information needed for the determination of the active memory area	Permanent ECC error or invalid value in the active memory area	– HW error in the flash memory – Insufficent margin (low voltage condition during flash programming) – ECC caused by exceeded number of allowed erase cycles	All blocks from memory area are lost.	Memory with corrupted header is not recoverable.	1	8	1	8				
	Transient ECC error or invalid value in the active memory area – the parameter is read corectly during initialization, but gets corrupted in runtime	– Insufficent margin (low voltage condition during flash programming), temperature, radiation, ...	None - the memory is accessible normally till the next reset; then another fault mode may apply based on whether swap operation happened before reset or not	N/A	4	6	4	96				
	Transient ECC error or invalid value in the active memory area – the parameter is read corectly during one initialization and incorrectly during another initialization		Newly written blocks are lost after the next reset.	Parameter is read correctly during initialization, the memory area is recognized as an active one and new blocks are written to the memory. Then, during the next initialization, the	2	6	4	48				

(Continued)

Table 22.6: (Continued)

Functionality	Fault mode	Fault cause	Fault/Failure effects						Failure detection method / observable symptoms	Mitigation Plan	Design Recommendation	Remarks
			Description	Failure root cause	Occurence	Severity	Detection	Risk Index				
				parameter is read incorrectly because of low margin. Therefore the previous memory area with the obsolete data is recognized as an active one and all blocks writen in a previous step are lost.								
	ECC error or invalid value in the alternate memory area	– Interruption of the data write operation (MCU reset, MCU power drop, flash HV abort (e.g. cancel operation)) – Interruption of the erase operation	No failure effect.	N/A	3	3	5	45				

Software specifications

An automotive software requirement specification (SRS) will look like any other safety- and quality-conscious SRS. It will describe the behaviors of the system which is to be developed, include use cases that describe the software and its interactions with the hardware and other platforms and contain non-functional requirements such as performance, quality and constraints. The IEEE Standard 830 1998 Recommended Practice for Software Requirements Specifications (http://ieeexplore.ieee.org/stamp/stamp.jsp?tp = &arnumber = 720574&userType = inst&tag = 1) is a commonly used reference for the best-in-class practice for SRSs. The only difference you may observe for automotive software is a stronger focus on the QA, validation and verification aspects of SRS and the references to compliance with other standards, some of which are described in the later sections of the chapter.

Software architecture

The thousands of functions running inside a vehicle address many different high-level functions including fundamental driving tasks and other features such as comfort and infotainment. These functions do not stand alone as they exhibit a high dependency on each other and many functions are very sensitive to other functions operating at the same time.

Models are developed to enable a better understanding of how to portray a structured view of a multifunctional system like those found in vehicles. Due to the complex functionality and all the associated issues there needs to be a sophisticated structural view of the architecture of the vehicle that addresses all the views that are relevant so that hardware and software engineers are able to develop a robust end-product, therefore the modeling approach has to be flexible enough to deal with all the aspects of the product architecture.

- The functional high-level user view captures all the software-based functionality offered by the vehicle to all the users, including the obvious drivers and passengers but also garage and maintenance engineers and even the production line staff, as shown in Figure 22.10. The functionality-level model captures families of services and its aim is to enable an understanding of how the services are offered and how they depend on and interface with each other. This can be modeled by feature (or function) hierarchies. If data or message flow among services is already identified, techniques such as message sequence charts can be used.
- The logical architecture level addresses the logical component architecture. In a logical architecture, the functional hierarchy model is split up into a distributed system of interacting components as shown in Figure 22.11. At this level the distributed system is shown regardless of whether the components are implemented by hardware or software and regardless of how many different components implement those functions. The

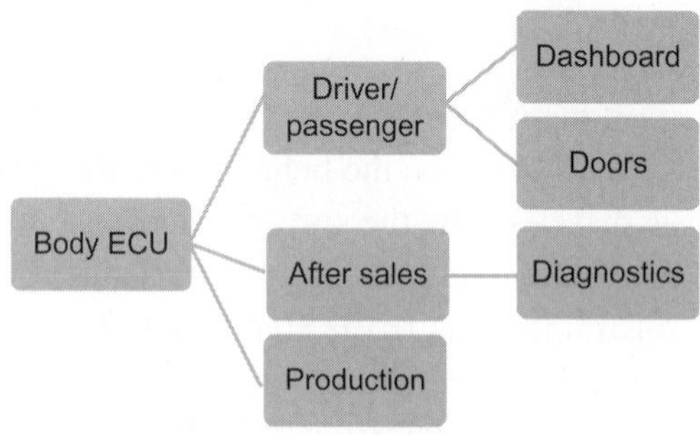

Figure 22.10:
SW architecture: feature hierarchy.

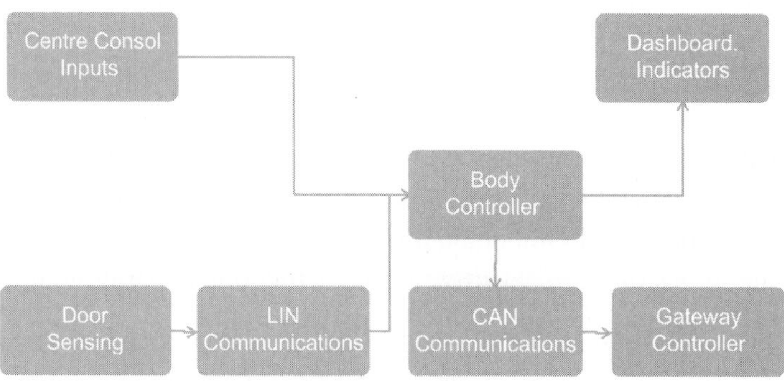

Figure 22.11:
SW architecture: logical architecture, doors and dashboard.

logical architecture can be described as interfaces with inputs and outputs that realize the functions in the system. Through their interaction, the model illustrates their observable behavior as described at the functionality level and these interactions can be used to define the automotive system's decomposition. The logical architecture describes abstract solutions and the protocols and abstract algorithms used in these solutions. This enables conceptual reuse of services that differ only in the way they are deployed from one vehicle design to another and it also identifies common services needed across the vehicles infrastructure.

- At the model clustering level, the logical architecture is rearranged in a way that makes it obvious what the software will do, as shown in Figure 22.12. This means that further decomposition of software components from the logical architecture is done until a sufficient granularity is reached and then they are rearranged into clusters.

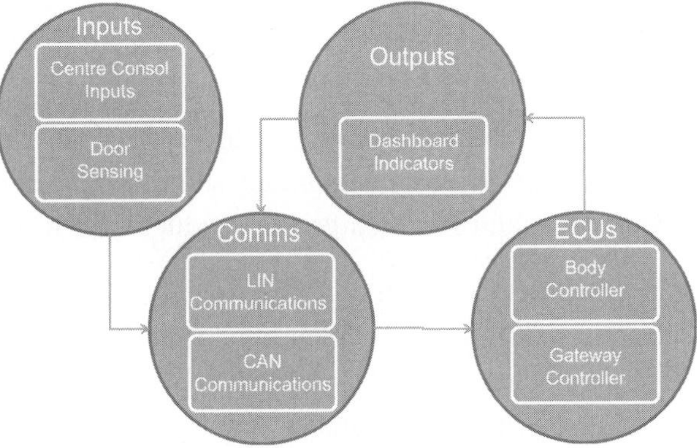

Figure 22.12:
SW architecture: clustering.

- The software architecture is the classic division of software in platforms; operating systems and drivers on one side and the application software represented as tasks on the other side. The high-level software architecture is derived from the logical architecture. If appropriate tools are available, a significant portion of the code can be generated from the logical architecture (a process known as autocoding). The target code, in terms of the tasks and processes, as well as the scheduling is derived from the high-level software architecture and is closely related to the software infrastructure such as the operating system and the scheduler.
- The hardware architecture level consists of all the physical components including sensors, actuators, bus systems, communication lines, ECUs, MMI, and many more. Within one ECU the model can define the hardware architecture that exists in the processor, the hardware I/O and the memory. Specific automotive requirements for the hardware must be specified and satisfied in the hardware architecture, such as electromagnetic compatibility, temperature tolerance and the packaging (physical construction space) of the device.
- Finally there is the software/hardware co-design model, a deployment function that relates hardware to software. The hardware/software and the deployment function represent a concrete realization of the logical architecture that describes the interaction between the logical components. The design of automotive systems has become a driver for electronic design automation (EDA) and co-design as the line between hardware and software becomes faint due to the distributed nature of computing in the vehicle. Any deployment architecture has to take into account the vehicle network topologies and technologies as different functionalities have different communication requirements.

Modeling

Modeling has the potential to help to improve the quality of an automotive software system. Starting with the product documentation, making any loose descriptions precise, the development team can analyze the requirements better and then reuse, redevelop and generate new code appropriately, and finally sign the product over to the production line.

Today models and model-based development are used to some extent in the automotive industry but their use is sparse. Modeling is applied only at particular stages in the development process, so a lot of their benefits are diluted. Because the models are rough and the modeling languages are not formalized, a higher benefit is not achieved. Typical model use case examples are consistency checking or the generation of tests from the models.

Another issue in which models could help is in the communication between the different companies, e.g., OEMs and first- and second-tier suppliers. Using models in an integrated seamless way, developments teams can have a strong vision of the model-based process in the automotive industry. After a business requirement is captured and the key requirements are brought together, a model can split the requirements into functional and nonfunctional requirements.

- Functional requirements are formalized by a function hierarchy where all the individual features are described by state machines or by interaction diagrams. In the function hierarchy, dependencies are introduced.
- The nonfunctional requirements are process quality requirements for the product.

The model helps developers to understand how the product quality requirements determine properties of the software product.

A quality-driven architecture is created onto which the functional requirements are drawn. In the decomposition the model specifies a logical architecture and the interfaces of the model's logical components. At this level of model a proof of concept of the logical architecture is possible as long as there are formal models for the logical components and their composition. This provides proof that at the application level the architecture is correct.

From here the decomposition of the components into software parts and the hardware architecture is started.

Autocoding and drivers

Automatic (non-manual) code-generation tools can be used to convert software state diagrams into executable code, enabling a model-based approach to software design and development. The primary advantages of this are reduced development time and consistency between the system design and its implementation, but to the detriment of code size and execution time as the autocode generator tool cannot take advantage of the hardware accelerator systems which the semiconductor device has on board and it has no knowledge of existing routines and resources. Using established robust coding templates, state chart models can be automatically mapped into the automotive application code by means of a state chart autocoding tool. Rather than using state charts as just part of the design documentation definition files, they can be continuously used and maintained with the source code, and then they would be subjected to the same level of quality and review. Joint reviews of the state charts by system engineers and software engineers can quickly identify poorly worded and misunderstood requirements, and provide an opportunity to improve and correct them before a mistake is made.

In non-embedded software environments a driver is a computer program which allows a high-level computer program to interact with a hardware component. In embedded software engineering a driver is code which allows application code to be written without caring how it is executed on the hardware, allowing for the code to be transferrable across platforms which have different hardware implementations and low-level drivers. Drivers are often provided by the device manufacturer or a third-party provider. In the automotive market low-level drivers are required due to the extremely high level of code evolution, reuse and the complex design and because of the build hierarchy of the vehicle. When using a low-level driver it is important to have a strong relationship with the developer as often changes in the way drivers are exercised from one generation of ECU to the next can highlight areas for improvement and in the worst case driver defects. Even with low-level drivers available the automotive industry still struggles with interoperability so a driver standard called AUTOSAR was defined. AUTOSAR is described later in the chapter.

Bench testing

Once the software is functionality-completed it must be tested. A minimum level of recommended bench test activities includes unit level tests, system level testing such as functional tests (requirement-based tests and partition tests) and structural coverage tests. Part 6 of the ISO 26262 standard, which is covered later in this chapter, addresses the recommendations for software testing and verification. Bench validation and verification test cases must support all levels of code coverage:

- generation and compilation of complete test functions and driver programs for both device and system testing
- regression testing
- test case mapping
- robustness testing
- out-of-bounds values and boundary condition testing on a host, simulator and on embedded target systems.

In the cases where an automotive standard plan is in place and has been fully reviewed, simply executing to that plan and recording as much data as possible are all that is needed during the bench testing phase. A good software engineer will be able to notice any deviations, glitches and odd effects observed during bench testing which might not necessarily cause a test to fail and investigate them further in case this is a warning of issues to come.

Trace and debug

Automotive quality software testing requires very high levels of test coverage of the software working together with the hardware. As the microcontroller's internal data and the software flow is not visible to the outside, work trace and debug tools exist to enable software test engineers to access the internal functionality and gather information to monitor correct operation information on the application. The device will have a debug port, frequently JTAG/Nexus, to enable the tool access. The debug functionality involves either request/response interactions, or packets transferred through the debug port, and includes:

- Run-time control: debug tools can start and stop the processor modify registers, and single step machine instructions;
- Memory access: debug tools can support memory access while the processor is running. Such access is required in debugging systems where it is not possible to halt the system under test. An example would be engine control, where stopping digital feedback loops can create physically dangerous situations.
- Breakpoints: programs stop when a defined event (often referred to as a watchpoint) or a breakpoint has occurred. The event can be specified as a code execution address, or as a data access (read or write) to an address with a specified value. Breakpoints can be set at any memory mapped address, including flash, RAM and ROM memory. Cores may also provide special breakpoint instructions.
- Trace: most tools depend on a high-speed auxiliary port to offload the large quantities of data without negatively impacting program execution. Three types of event tracing are defined:
  - Program trace: branch tracing compresses program execution data, by emitting messages at branch or exception instructions only. Trace data analysis can be used to reconstruct the programs flow. Figure 22.13 shows a typical screenshot of a program trace tool.
  - Data trace: accesses (reads and or writes) to memory locations may be tracked, limited by range (start and stop address) and access type.
  - Ownership trace: an operating system may write a task identifier to a debug register when switching tasks, forcing an ownership trace message to be emitted.

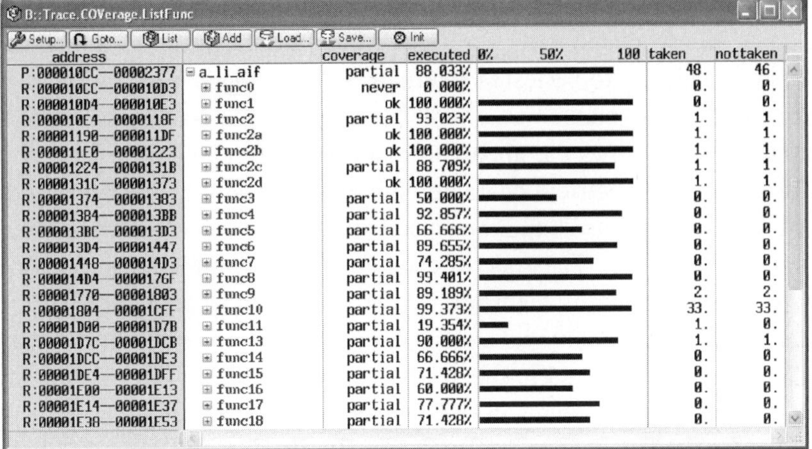
B::Trace.COVerage.ListFunc

Setup... Goto... List Add Load... Save... Init

address		coverage	executed	0% 50% 100	taken	nottaken
P:000010CC—00002377	a_li_aif	partial	88.033%		48.	46.
R:000010CC—000010D3	func0	never	0.000%		0.	0.
R:000010D4—000010E3	func1	ok	100.000%		0.	0.
R:000010E4—0000118F	func2	partial	93.023%		1.	1.
R:00001190—000011DF	func2a	ok	100.000%		1.	1.
R:000011E0—00001223	func2b	ok	100.000%		1.	1.
R:00001224—0000131B	func2c	partial	88.709%		1.	1.
R:0000131C—00001373	func2d	ok	100.000%		1.	1.
R:00001374—00001383	func3	partial	50.000%		0.	0.
R:00001384—000013BB	func4	partial	92.857%		0.	0.
R:000013BC—000013D3	func5	partial	66.666%		0.	0.
R:000013D4—00001447	func6	partial	89.655%		0.	0.
R:00001448—000014D3	func7	partial	74.285%		0.	0.
R:000014D4—0000176F	func8	partial	99.401%		0.	0.
R:00001770—00001803	func9	partial	89.189%		2.	2.
R:00001804—00001CFF	func10	partial	99.373%		33.	33.
R:00001D00—00001D7B	func11	partial	19.354%		1.	0.
R:00001D7C—00001DCB	func13	partial	90.000%		1.	1.
R:00001DCC—00001DE3	func14	partial	66.666%		0.	0.
R:00001DE4—00001DFF	func15	partial	71.428%		0.	0.
R:00001E00—00001E13	func16	partial	60.000%		0.	0.
R:00001E14—00001E37	func17	partial	77.777%		0.	0.
R:00001E38—00001E53	func18	partial	71.428%		0.	0.

Figure 22.13:
Program trace.

- Memory substitution and port replacement: allows physical memory or device port accesses to be emulated over the auxiliary debug port.
- Data acquisition: high-bandwidth prototyping could demand high-speed transfer of significant amounts of data via a port to the debug tools. The data-acquisition process uses a lower-bandwidth protocol than that used in data trace to increase efficiency, which is essential to support calibration in automotive applications.

The collected data can be analyzed for expected and correct operation of the system software and hardware.

Final-phase testing

On the road tests are done when the system is thought to be in a completed state, i.e., all the software specification items are in place and completely tested in the bench environment. In many cases, the most effective way to test an embedded system is to physically connect it to the real vehicle. In other cases, hardware in the loop (HIL) simulation is more effective. While the usage of HIL enhances the quality of the testing by increasing the scope of the testing, the ideal condition to test the embedded system is the real-world vehicle environment. Most of the time the vehicle imposes various limitations on the testing's scope, e.g., in an engine control unit, testing at or beyond the range of the defined ECU parameters, at the expected failure condition, would lead to a dangerous test condition for the test engineer.

HIL is often used in the development and test of complex real-time embedded systems. HIL simulations recreate the complexity of the vehicle on the test platform. The complexity of the vehicle is included in HIL tests by adding a mathematical representation of all associated active systems which are the vehicle simulation. The embedded system which is to be tested interacts with this vehicle simulation. Engine dynamics are emulated by mathematic models and are executed by a dedicated processor. In addition, an I/O unit allows the apparent connection of vehicle sensors and actuators. HIL simulations include electrical characteristic emulations of any sensors and actuators as this electrical mimicry acts as the interface between the vehicle simulation and the embedded system under test. The state of each electrically emulated sensor is controlled by the vehicle simulation and is feedback by the embedded system under test. Similarly, the embedded system implements its control tasks by outputting actuator control signals. The ECU under test is connected to the system and exposed to a set of vehicle maneuvers executed by the simulator. Changes in the control signals result in changes to variables in the vehicle simulation.

As an example, a HIL simulation platform for the development of an automotive anti-lock braking (ABS) system may have a mathematical model for each of the subsystems in the simulation environment:

- sensors: suspension, wheels, tires, roll, pitch and yaw
- actuators: the brake system's hydraulic components
- external influences: road characteristics.

HIL simulation is a key part of the process of safely integrating the testing of human factors and is a method of ensuring usability and system consistency. For real-time systems such as vehicles, human-factor test development is the collection of data from a person in the loop testing for components that will have a human interface. Because in-vehicle driving tests which record the performance and diagnostic functionality of Engine management systems are time-consuming, expensive and not reproducible, HIL simulators allow developers to validate their automotive hardware and software solutions, while still managing to respect quality requirements and time-to-market restrictions.

When testing a new ECU software release, experiments can be performed open loop and therefore several engine dynamic models are no longer required. In this case, a micro-HIL system (MHIL) offers a simpler and more economic solution than the full-size HIL system as it is simplified into a portable device consisting of a signal generator, an I/O processing board, and a board containing the actuators which are to be connected to the ECU.

When all the systems are in place for the final road testing, testing begins. At this time the system is assumed to be safe! All environments are used for testing: day, night, highways, towns, countryside, airstrips, race tracks, extreme temperatures, hot deserts, soaking wet terrain and ice fields, mountains, bump tracks, etc., to ensure that the vehicle is road-safe and there are no areas of concern.

Calibration

Vehicle calibration is used throughout the engine development process, from early engine mapping through to final end of manufacturing line calibration and vehicle sign-off. Calibration is done to maximize the vehicle's performance, fuel economy and drivability objectives in conjunction with satisfying the requirements for the control of exhaust emissions as demanded by legislation. As well as powertrain electronics calibration it is also possible to calibrate associated subfunctions such as cooling, fan control, air conditioning systems, alternator control and transmission control. The controlled calibration set-up includes environment control and a rolling road which is tightly controlled so that the entire vehicle performance can be mapped, analyzed and tweaked to improve the overall performance of the vehicle systems and collect the performance specification data. as illustrated in Figure 22.14.

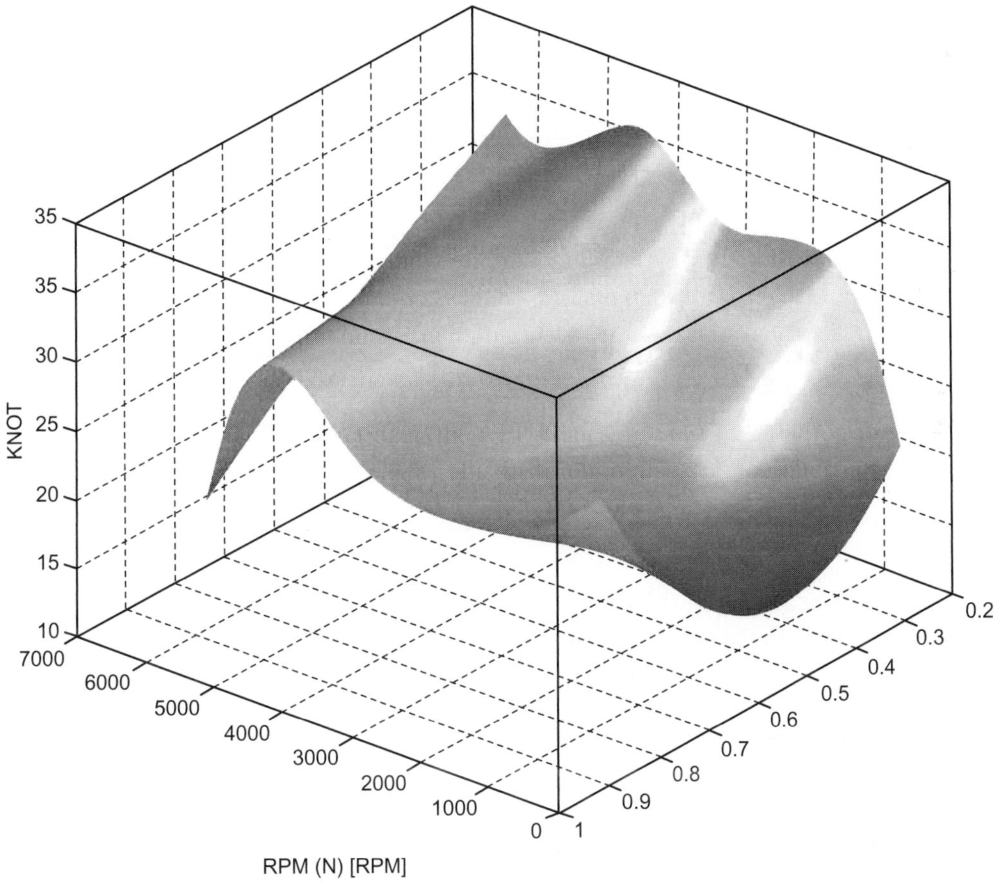

Figure 22.14:
MathWorks powertrain calibration.

Maintenance/product lifetime support

Unlike most other industries, excluding military and aerospace, an automotive product is expected to be supported and maintained for over 15 years from its introduction. Semiconductor and other component suppliers guarantee this availability and support but inevitably at some point over those 15 years somebody is going to need to access the software again . . . and understand it. Whether it be due to a product field return or factory transfer the software must be locatable, identifiable, configuration-managed, well-commented and written in a reusable manner. Fortunately the days of ROM codes stored as binary files of meaningless 1 s and 0 s are mainly gone. ASCII hexadecimal file formats (often referred to an S record) are still commonly used in the archiving of software. In the right hands the software is somewhat recoverable and modifiable although the original format is lost. Some minor modifications can be made. The art of reading S records (hexadecimal machine code with checksums) is a dying one. All automotive companies will have a strict and robust configuration management system (CMS). Vesta, Subversion and Concurrent Version System (CVS) are open-source clients which do the CMS role well if used correctly by all involved parties.

Automotive diagnostics

On-board diagnostics (OBD) is a generic term which refers to a vehicle's self-diagnosis and reporting capability. The amount of diagnostic information available has varied widely since the introduction of the on-board vehicle computers which made OBD possible. Early incarnations of OBD would simply illuminate a light if a problem was detected but would not provide any information as to the nature of the problem. Modern diagnostic implementations use a digital communication port to provide real-time data and a series of diagnostic trouble codes (DTCs) which enable identification of malfunctions within the vehicle.

MIL

A malfunction indicator lamp (MIL) indicates a malfunction of the computerized engine management system to the driver via the dashboard. An example of a MIL is shown in Figure 22.15. The following malfunctions are some that could be indicated by the MIL:

- catalyst efficiency
- fuel system
- mass air flow sensor
- intake air temperature sensor
- engine coolant temperature sensor
- throttle position sensor
- O_2 sensors

Figure 22.15:
Malfunction indicator light.

- injector
- cylinder misfire
- crankshaft position sensor
- camshaft position sensor
- evaporative emission control system
- vehicle speed sensor
- idle control valve
- power supply
- ECM
- power stage
- canister close valve
- fuel tank pressure sensor
- watchdog.

Data logger

With the need for more diagnostic information than the MIL could provide data loggers were introduced. The most widely known use of a data logger is an airplane's black box. Data loggers store a wide range of vehicle parameters for analysis on a computer at a later date, but the system does not include an in-vehicle display. These systems, where available, are only accessed when needed, by the automotive technicians in a garage with specialist equipment and software, when something is not working as expected, indicated to the driver by the MIL. The technology could be used more widely and advance further, but the consumer distrust of the data storage aspect has limited this tool's adoption. The data logger is used heavily in the motor racing industry as it sends real-time data on the race vehicle's performance and environment to the control van at the circuit side and the main data analysis unit at the race team headquarters using wireless telecommunications technology. The data logger interfaces with the engine control module, which monitors the input and output signals. When the ECU detects an irregularity, the data logger records the diagnostic trouble code and then outputs that information to the self-diagnosis output terminal. The diagnosis results can be read out by a specialist tool. The diagnostic trouble code will be held in the engine control module memory if stored in non-volatile memory (NVM), or as long as battery power is maintained if stored in RAM, or until it is erased by the specialist tool.

OBD II

The OBD II standard specifies the diagnostic connector form factor and its pin out, the electrical signaling protocols and the messaging format. The standard also outlines a list of vehicle parameters which must be monitored along with how to encode the data for each. The OBD II standard defines an extensive list of diagnostic trouble codes (DTCs). The OBD II standard means that a single tool can query the on-board computer(s) in any vehicle. The need for the OBD II standard was prompted by emissions requirements, and although only emission-related codes and data are required to be transmitted through it by the OBD II definition most manufacturers have made the OBD II data link connector the only port in the vehicle which all systems are diagnosed and programmed.

OBD II DTCs are four digits preceded by a letter:

B stands for body
C stands for chassis
P stands for powertrain
U stands for network.

The OBD II standardized hardware interface is a female 16-pin (2×8) J1962 connector which is required to be located within 2 feet of the steering wheel. The European (EOBD) and Japanese (JOBD) regulations are those regions' equivalent of OBD II. The technical implementations of these regional equivalents are essentially the same as OBD II. There are five allowable signaling protocols in OBD II:

1. SAE J1850 pulse width modulation running at 41.6 kbit/s.
2. SAE J1850 variable pulse width running at 10.4/41.6 kbit/s.
3. ISO 9141 2, which is an asynchronous serial data protocol running at 10.4 kbaud, somewhat similar to RS 232 with different signal levels and communications on a single, bidirectional line without an additional handshake signal.
4. ISO 15765 CAN running at 250 kbit/s or 500 kbit/s.
5. ISO 14230 Keyword Protocol 2000.

Automotive standards

MISRA

The Motor Industry Software Reliability Association (MISRA) is the industry body that produces guidelines for software development for electronic components used in the automotive industry. The goal of this organization is to advise the automotive industry in the creation and application of safe, reliable software within vehicles. MISRA guidelines exist which define a common standard of development guidelines for vehicle-based software. The guidelines are given to achieve the following goals:

- ensure safety
- bring in robustness and reliability to the software
- ensure that human safety takes precedence when in conflict with security of property
- ensure that random and systematic faults are considered in system design
- demonstrate robustness and not just rely on the absence of failures
- consider safety across the design, manufacture, operation, servicing and disposal of products.

MISRA C is a software development standard for the C programming language and the MISRA C: 2004 document contains over 140 rules, most of which are required and some are advised. They are divided into categories which range from "Environment" to "run-time" failures. Many software tools claim to check code for MISRA conformance but there is no MISRA certification process. The Exemplar Suite for MISRA C: 2004 is available from the MISRA forum (http://www.misra.org.uk/). This allows tool users to evaluate and compare the support provided by the various MISRA tools and it also gives the tool implementers some guidance as to the intent of the rules within MISRA C: 2004. Most of the guidelines can be checked by using tools that perform static code analysis. The remaining guidelines do require the use of dynamic code analysis, i.e., can only be tested for when the software is executing.

AUTOSAR

AUTOSAR, which stands for AUTomotive Open System ARchitecture, is an open and standardized automotive software architecture developed by automobile manufacturers, suppliers and tool developers. AUTOSAR's objective is to establish a de facto open standard for automotive electronics architectures, in a space where only proprietary software standards exist, that provides a basic infrastructure to assist with developing vehicle software, user interfaces and management. As stated on the official website, the goals of AUTOSAR are:

- implementation and standardization of basic system functions as an OEM-wide "standard core" solution

- scalability to different vehicle and platform variants
- transferability of functions throughout the network
- integration of functional modules from multiple suppliers
- consideration of availability and safety requirements
- redundancy activation
- maintainability throughout the whole "product life-cycle"
- increased use of "commercial off-the-shelf hardware"
- software updates and upgrades over the vehicle lifetime.

These goals are achieved by using a software architecture that supports a design model based on components as shown in Figure 22.16. The design model is enabled by AUTOSARs automated methodology of creating the software for the ECUs, starting from the design model and the properties and physical topology of the hardware. The AUTOSAR project has forced a paradigm shift in automotive software development, from a module-based approach to a function-based approach. The AUTOSAR standard enables use of the component-based software design model for the design of the entire vehicle system.

To make a component-based design possible, AUTOSAR is a layered architecture that ensures that the functionality is decoupled from the supporting hardware and software as shown in Figure 22.16 and described below.

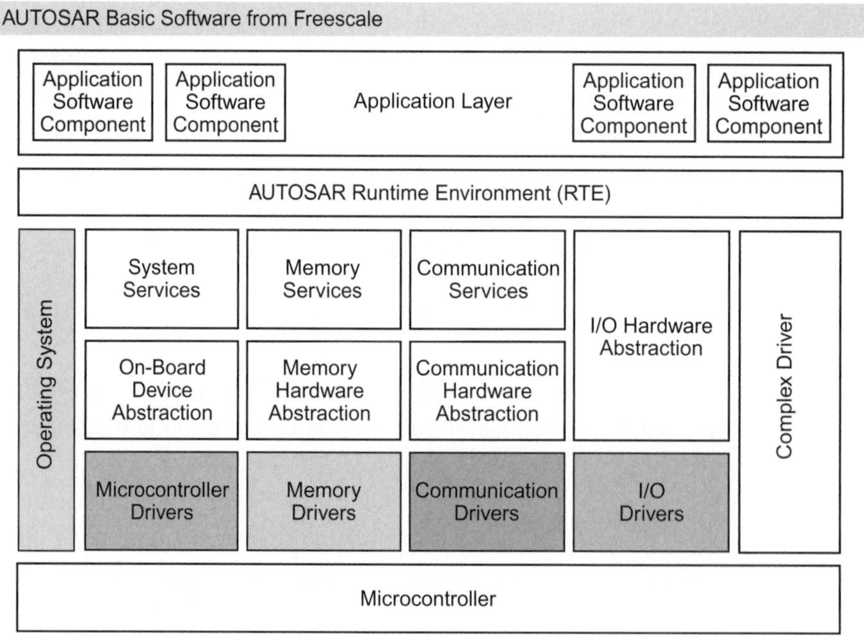

Figure 22.16:
AUTOSAR.

- Basic software layer: the basic software components are standardized software drivers that do not have any functionality but offer hardware-dependent and hardware-independent services to the run-time environment, achieved through an application programming interface. The layer is not entirely hardware-independent but does make the upper layers hardware-independent.
- Run-time environment: the run-time environment handles the information exchange between the application software components above and connects the application software components to the right hardware.
- Application layer: the application layer is not composed of standardized software. It is the layer where the actual functionality is situated. The layer is composed of application software components which interact with the run-time environment.

Standardized interfaces for all the application software components required to build the automotive applications are specified in the AUTOSAR standards. Because AUTOSAR only defines the interfaces and data format, there is flexibility to choose how functionality is achieved. The basic software and runtime environment are the virtual function bus in the design model as shown in Figure 22.17. This abstract component interconnects the different application software components and transfers the information exchanged between them. This virtual bus makes it possible for designers to focus on the application instead of the infrastructure software because by using the bus the software components do not need to know which of the other application software components they communicate with. This makes it possible to validate the interaction of all components and interfaces before starting the software implementation.

When the layered architecture is used on every ECU it is possible to design a vehicle system without thinking in terms of ECUs at all, i.e., the designers have a number of software components but they do not know on which ECU a specific software component is run or what hardware is connected together.

AUTOSAR created a four-step methodology that can be used to create the system architecture from the design model.

Step 1: input descriptions

This step is the creation of descriptions of the software, system and hardware.

- The software component description is independent of the final implementation of the software components. The interfaces and the hardware requirements are to be defined.
- The connections between ECUs are specified along with the available data buses, protocols, function clusters and the communication matrix and attributes, e.g., data rates, timing and latency.
- The required hardware, such as processors, sensors and actuators, needs to be specified along with the signal-processing methods and programming capabilities.

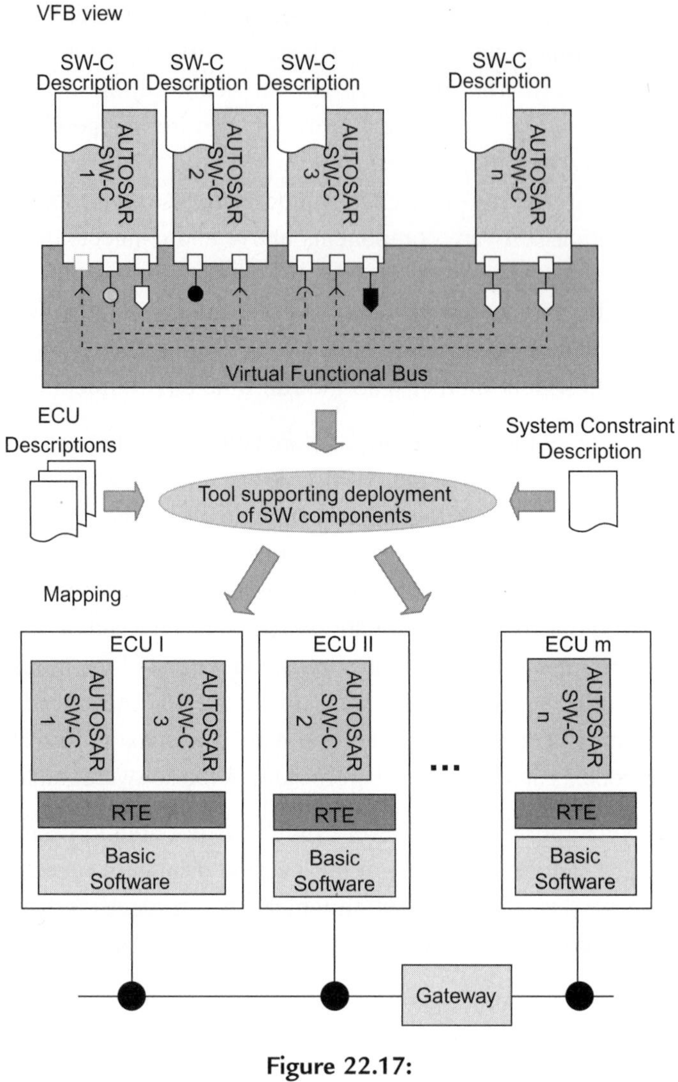

Figure 22.17:
Virtual bus.

Step 2: system configuration

This step distributes the software components that were described in the previous step, to the different system ECUs. ECU resources and system constraints must be taken into account and it may take a few attempts to get the balance correct.

Step 3: ECU configuration

The basic software and run time environment for each ECU is configured.

Step 4: generation of software executables

Based on the configuration of the ECU from the previous step, the software executables are now generated. It's necessary to specify the implementation of each software component.

This methodology is automated by AUTOSAR tool chains. All subsequent steps which are taken to reach the final generation of executable code are supported by defining exchange formats, frequently using XML, and work methods for each step.

To support this AUTOSAR methodology a formal description of all methodology related information is modeled in UML, which has the following benefits:

- the structure of the information can be clearly visualized
- the consistency of the information is guaranteed
- by using XML, a data exchange format can be generated automatically from the meta-model and be used as input
- easy maintenance of the entire vehicular system.

AUTOSARs implementation comes with some challenges. It lacks information about timing requirements in the meta-model but there are high-level timing requirements such as end-to-end latencies that specify time domain behavior of the system at the logical level of system functions. There are also timing-relevant implementation details at the system level. Even though a meta-model which captures high-level requirements will support the development of automotive systems, it can still be difficult to find timing issues like buffer overflow. This is due to nonfunctional delays such as buffering of signals and allocation of memory.

Manually developed systems can be designed to be more efficient than software built from plug-in software components, therefore smaller systems designed to the AUTOSAR standard need more memory space and more computing power than they did previously. The extra cost of these ECU resources is a real issue in the cost-driven automotive business. For complex ECUs the situation is different as here the availability of a common platform enables high reuse of the basic functions by the application software.

AEC

The Automotive Electronics Council (AEC) is an organization that sets qualification standards for the supply of components in the automotive electronics industry. The AEC Component Technical Committee is the standardization body for establishing standards for reliable, high-quality electronic components. Components meeting these specifications are suitable for use in the harsh automotive environment without additional component-level qualification testing. During the AEC's development of Q100 (Stress Test Qualification for Integrated Circuits), IC suppliers had an opportunity to comment on the document, which represented the preferred qualification document for Chrysler, Delco Electronics, and Ford. The Q100 standard encouraged the open exchange of standardized qualification data and stated that if a part was qualified to the specification levels in this document, it was qualified for all three companies.

Following this successful standard introduction, qualification specifications for other component categories were developed: AEC Q101 for discrete parts and AEC Q200 for passive parts.

These standards establish a minimum set of qualification requirements which must be achieved for a device to be deemed suitable for use in an automotive environment. The most common AEC references seen mentioned are operating temperature grades which the product has achieved:

- Grade 0: 40°C to +150°C ambient operating temperature range
- Grade 1: 40°C to +125°C ambient operating temperature range
- Grade 2: 40°C to +105°C ambient operating temperature range
- Grade 3: 40°C to +85°C ambient operating temperature range
- Grade 4: 0°C to +70°C ambient operating temperature range.

The selection of a device for automotive application must meet the AEC grade for that application's temperature profile.

Automotive safety

ISO 26262

All corners of the automotive industry are under pressure to provide new and improved vehicle safety systems, ranging from airbag deployment systems to complex advanced driver assistance systems (ADAS) with accident prediction and avoidance capability. Such safety functions are performed by electronics, and ISO 26262 has been introduced to enable the design of electronic systems that can prevent dangerous failures or control them if they occur.

ISO 26262 is a recently introduced functional safety standard, titled Road Vehicles – Functional Safety. It describes an automotive safety life-cycle (management, development, production, operation, service followed by decommissioning) and outlines the necessary activities during these life-cycle phases. It covers functional safety aspects of the entire development process including requirements specification, design, implementation, integration, verification, validation, and configuration. It also provides an automotive-specific risk-based approach for determining risk classes known as Automotive Safety Integrity Levels (ASILs) and uses ASILs to specifying the necessary safety requirements to achieve an acceptable residual risk. It also describes safety requirements for validation and measures to ensure a sufficient and acceptable level of safety has been achieved.

From the very start of the design process, evidence must be collected to show that the product has been developed according to the ISO 26262 standard. Any potential deviations that are identified must be documented to ensure that adequate mitigation is in place. Tools are available to support this additional element to automotive quality assurance.

Designing safety systems while achieving the functional safety requirements is a challenge for system designers, especially when they are also tasked with managing increased application complexity and shortened time-to-market deadlines. The challenge is to architect their system in a way that prevents dangerous failures or control them when they do occur. These dangerous failures could arise from events such as:

- random hardware defects
- systematic hardware defects
- systematic software defects.

ISO 26262 is applied to ensure that electronic systems in automotive applications are completely safe.

ASIL

The ISO 26262 standard defines four ASILs, with ASIL D being the most stringent safety level. Table 22.7 shows the three higher ASIL levels which are most commonly stated as targets for automotive applications in development now.

Functional safety systems rely not only on microcontrollers, but also depend upon companion power management devices and sensors. Hardware safety concepts focus on detecting and mitigating single-point, latent and dependent faults. This can be achieved through the use of built-in safety features, including self-testing, monitoring and hardware-based redundancy in microcontrollers, power management ICs and sensors.

Table 22.7: ASIL.

	ASIL B	ASIL C	ASIL D
Probability of violation of safety goal *e.g., Random hardware failure*	$<10^{-7}$	$<10^{-7}$	$<10^{-8}$
Single point fault metric *i.e., immediate potential to cause a hazard*	>90%	>97%	>99%
Latent fault metric *i.e., can become dangerous in conjunction with a second fault*	>60%	>80%	>90%

Safety Microcontrollers may have some, if not all, of the following built-in safety features:

- lock-step cores
- ECC on memories
- redundant functions
- monitor modules
- built in self-test
- fault collection and control.

Analog and power management devices may have the following built-in safety features:

- voltage monitors
- external error monitor
- advanced watchdog
- built in self-test.

Sensors may have the following built-in safety features:

- timing checker
- digital scan of signal chains
- DSI3 and PSI5 safety data links
- ECC on memories
- triggered self-test.

Each of the built-in features must be utilized to reach the required ASIL level and in some cases additional software routines will be required to reach the target ASIL.

Automotive security

As with any desirable, high-value item the problem of theft must be addressed. In vehicles, that started with the introduction of key access and then keyed start. Then use of the crowbar and jump starting was invented.

What it used to mean: car alarms etc.

When advanced vehicle security first became mainstream the solution was an electronic device installed in a vehicle in an attempt to discourage theft of the vehicle itself, its contents, or both, known as the car alarm. This was taken one step further with the introduction of immobilizers, which prevented the engine from running unless the correct key was present. This prevented the vehicle from being hotwired if entry had been achieved.

What it means today: hacking

With the advances made in vehicle entry, vehicle immobilizers and vehicle theft reports falling in numbers worldwide, protection of the vehicle's electronic systems from "chipping" was tackled by vehicle manufacturers. Chipping is the term used for reprogramming the computer that controls a vehicle's engine. A manufacturer's warranty is invalidated by a chipped engine as the extra power taken from the engine can cause severe damage.

From a legislative standpoint modifying the vehicle's program will have a detrimental effect on the fuel economy and emissions as the vehicle was calibrated to maximize those parameters. Most semiconductor manufacturers support prevention of post-factory access to the device's software for modification or complete reloading by offering some level of device security. That could be a low-level hardware interface whereby access would only be possible through specialized hardware, but which only stops access if you can't get the hardware, to more advanced censorship solutions which lock the device at the end of the production line so that only those with knowledge of the 64-bit key can open the device for debug or reprogramming. Some censorship methods lock the device so that no one can ever access it again; however, this does make in-field updates infinitely harder to do.

What it will mean tomorrow: counterfeiting

The next level of security for vehicles is the prevention of counterfeiting modules. With so much development time, effort and cost going in to each of the 100 + ECUs in a vehicle, coupled with the fact that these systems are tested to the highest quality level and are known to work together in a safe state, the manufacturers are focusing on ensuring that no one can go out and develop a compatible module to replace the original. Automotive embedded system cryptographic modules for secure communication in the presence of third-party modules are being developed in partnership with vehicle manufacturers, software houses and semiconductor suppliers. In-vehicle cryptography algorithms are built around computational hardness assumptions, making the algorithms hard to break by anyone without prior knowledge. It is theoretically possible to crack these algorithms but it is infeasible to do so by any practical method. An automotive cryptographic system would not prevent an ECU being removed and replaced. Instead if the module was not original and therefore not authorized on the vehicle network, the vehicle can make life interesting. Depending upon which functional ECU is counterfeited, the network may allow the module to function as intended but could blink a light on the dashboard, causing some annoyance to the driver, or could limit the infotainment system audio level to force the driver to seek out a dealership to address the issue in the future. If a counterfeit module is detected in a safety-critical system the vehicle could disable the vehicle engine completely.

The near future of the automotive market

Performance

With the absolute drive for reduced emissions and higher fuel economy it is easy to achieve these to the determent of driving experience; for example, if acceleration was limited the fuel economy would increase but drivers would become very frustrated with the lack of power. Electric vehicles are a great example of this as they have relatively slow 0 to 60 mph figures when compared with combustion vehicle performance figures, which drivers are now accustomed to. However, the systems are evolving and electric racing and rally vehicles are emerging, enabling the technology developed in them to move into the mainstream market. Major redesigns of the propulsion of electrified vehicles mean that precise motor control is at the forefront of the environment/performance battle.

The emergence of multicore

The demand for rapid performance scaling of the automotive semiconductor product is immense and Moore's Law is struggling to enable the performance ramp-up. Microcontrollers must provide more processing MIPS at the same power consumption. To help meet these performance targets significant changes in the microcontroller architecture are taking place. The microcontroller must be re-architected in order to manage the synchronization issues, energy dissipation limitations, and fault handling requirements of the emerging billion-transistor automotive devices. The single-processor architecture is being replaced by multicore devices that communicate via networks on chip. These emerging multicore devices provide an ideal execution environment for the integration of multiple automotive ECUs into a single device. However, there are major obstacles for software engineers to overcome with the emergence of multicore for automotive applications. All existing software functions are serially coded, i.e., the core does one thing at a time. In multicore-enabled software the software function can be doing two or more things at once, as shown in Figure 22.18.

In networking and computing environments where multicore is the norm this issue is not as concerning, as these applications tend to run orthogonal software or completely independent functions. For example, a networking multicore processor moves data in and out across over 10 s of cores; a computer runs user application SW on one core and another application or the fan control, etc., on the other and uses TDM to give each function its own processing slot. If you are slamming on the breaks at 70 mph in a vehicle you don't really want the CPU to stop doing that and starting scanning the vehicle network for another command. In a multicore device with a shared memory what could result if one core reads data from RAM while the other is updating that same data which it has stored

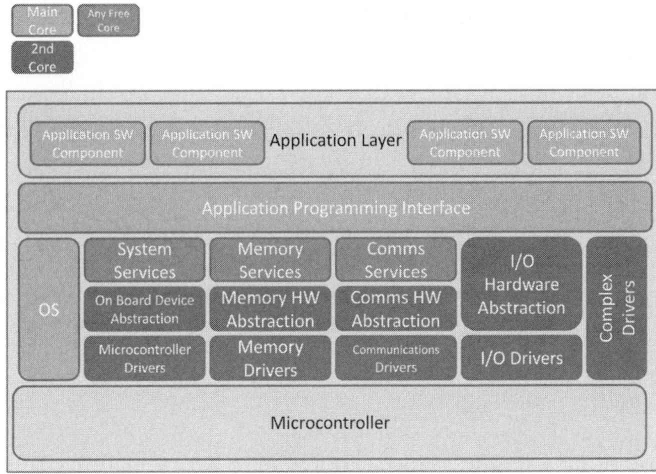

Figure 22.18:
Multicore.

locally in its cache and writes back at a later time? An engine misfire or complete stall at high speed isn't beyond the realms of the possible.

The connected vehicle

Market demand for mobile connectivity embedded in the vehicle is growing rapidly and as a result vehicle manufacturers are in a race to out-specify each other's vehicles. Mid- to high-range vehicles need mobile phone connectivity with information displays on the center console, controls on the steering wheel and center console knobs and buttons to control phone functions, essentially an advanced hands-free kit, as standard. Speech recognition and mobile internet connection via WiFi and 3 G will become the norm as infotainment in vehicles becomes as important as vehicle safety in the consumer's eye. Online data will be used to augment vehicle technology when the vehicle is online to access this data; therefore the vehicle will have its own IP address. It will know where it is via its GPS and be able to access personalized data about the world around it, e.g., the cheapest fuel in a 5-mile radius or a traffic incident on or near the planned route, an estimated time of arrival at destination and the best available parking space when the vehicle arrives.

The issue with the automotive industry is the time it takes to get a product from concept to production. An infotainment system development cycle starts 3 years before the product is launched and it takes a few more years to roll that product out across the entire vehicle range. If the automotive industry decided to reinvent the music player we would only just be getting a flash-based MP3 player. Because the consumer market moves much faster, by the time the product is available the consumer wants more functionality, or the latest phone is not compatible with the latest infotainment system. In order to stand a chance of keeping up with consumer technology, vehicle manufacturers must future-proof their infotainment system. In many cases, new features can be added with a software change but in the automotive industry software is frozen between 6 and 12 months before launch. Systems must be designed from the outset to accommodate the real world where APIs and drivers can change daily. It is impossible for anyone to predict what the hot new consumer application will be in 3 years time when the product is launched so the product must be designed to be expandable.

All this mobile connected content is helping to drive another future trend: automation.

The automated vehicle

By adding a plethora of new features inside the vehicle the probability of driver distraction causing a safety concern is extremely high. While systems are designed to minimize safety fears the automated vehicle is also evolving to bolster road safety. Lane keeping, adaptive cruise control, road sign recognition and collision-avoidance systems assist the driver in this information-overloaded situation.

It is too easy to miss a speed-limit sign, a stop sign or a lane closure sign, to drift out of your lane for a short time, not observe a brake light 20 meters ahead or (if you really are distracted) a wall in front of you. Sensor information systems warn or inform the driver about events that may have been unnoticed by them, such as the lane departure warning system (LDWS), the rear view alarm, which is common in its most basic form of beeps when reversing close to an object in most vehicles, visibility aids for the driver to eradicate blind spots and enhanced vision systems such as night vision, radar and wireless vehicle safety communications. Corrective-action systems modify the driver's instructions so enable them to drive in a more effective way; for example, the most widely deployed system of this type is ABS.

The anti-lock braking system (ABS), often coupled with electronic brake force distribution, prevents the brakes from locking and losing traction while braking. Traction-control systems actuate brakes or reduce throttle to restore traction if driven wheels begin to spin. Four-wheel drive, with a center differential, distributes power to all four wheels, lessening the chances of wheelspin. It also suffers less from oversteer and understeer. Electronic stability, acceleration slip regulation and the electronic differential lock use lots of sensors to take over when the vehicle senses a possible loss of control. The vehicle's control unit can reduce power from the engine and apply the brakes on a per-wheel basis to prevent the vehicle from understeering or oversteering. Dynamic steering response corrects the rate of the power steering system to adapt it to the vehicle's speed and road conditions. In Japan the system is evolving ahead of the rest of the world where an infrastructure-based driver warning/informing system is under development with full governmental support.

Systemic systems are those such as automatic parking where the vehicle "reads" the parking space, calculates the maneuver and then executes that maneuver. Other systems are those such as adaptive cruise control, as used by Ford and Vauxhall, or distance control assist, as developed by Nissan. There is a move to introduce dead-man's braking into automotive applications, which is a switch that is automatically operated if the human operator becomes incapacitated, such as through death or loss of consciousness, primarily for heavy vehicles. The inclusion of ADAS, while increasing the amount of data presented to the driver, can also be used by the vehicle to take over control from the driver in a critical situation.

The Hollywood-predicted day of the autonomous, autopiloted vehicle is still some way off forecourt availability, but development and road testing of such systems has started. Automated vehicle systems have the following potential benefits:

- reducing the number of, and severity of, crashes due to the autonomous system's increased reliability compared with human driver reactions
- increasing road network capacities due to a reduction in inter-vehicle safety gap length and the ability to better manage traffic flow
- relieving vehicle occupants of driving and navigation chores
- alleviation of parking scarcity, as vehicles could drop off their passengers at the destination and then park themselves where space is not as scarce and then return as needed to pick up passengers
- removal of constraints on the occupants' state; it would not matter if the driver knew how to drive a vehicle or if their state of mind was not suitable for driving a traditional vehicle and many disabilities would no longer prevent a person from using a road vehicle and being the "driver"
- elimination of redundant passengers as the human is no longer required to take the vehicle anywhere; the robotic vehicle can drive unaccompanied to wherever it is required.

Some of these potential benefits apply to a very futuristic world and have been envisaged by Hollywood sci-fi writers for decades but are slowly becoming possible. Most automated vehicle development projects do not aim explicitly to create a fully autonomous vehicle but they are seen as an incremental step towards a proof of concept. The systems which are under development are concentrating on sensor information translation, corrective actions and general systems.

Conclusion

The physical task of writing embedded software for automotive applications versus other application areas is not significantly different. Modules, registers, processors and buses are all similarly architected. The key differences are the quality standards, which must absolutely be followed for any automotive application development and test project, as faults can be deadly. All aspects of the automotive software are affected by quality levels and measures, from fault-tolerant communication and zero-defect processes such as FMEA, though to the functional safety standard ISO 26262. Various processes exist to help software engineers write high-quality, fault-tolerant, interoperable code such as modeling, autocoding and advanced trace and debug assisted by the emergence of the AUTOSAR and ISO 26262 standards, as well as more traditional standards such as AEC, OBD-II and MISRA. The paradigm shift from the traditional single-core microcontrollers to the multicore microcontrollers, which will dominate this decade, places the embedded software engineer in a tight corner, as the software which has been developed and has evolved over decades needs to be completely re-architected for the next-generation vehicle platform while maintaining the defect-free quality status. At the same time as multicore is becoming a reality the connected vehicle concept brings in new factors which have the potential to cause system disturbance. When software engineers use all the tools, techniques and processes which have been developed, the next-generation software challenge is achievable.

CHAPTER 23

Programming for I/O and Storage

Xin-Xin Yang

Chapter Outline

Software Engineering for Embedded Systems.
DOI: http://dx.doi.org/10.1016/B978-0-12-415917-4.00023-2
© 2013 Elsevier Inc. All rights reserved.

Input and output (I/O) devices are very important components in the embedded system. In this book, I/O devices refer to all the components in the embedded system except the CPU and memory, e.g., device controllers and I/O channels. This I/O diversity makes the I/O management in the embedded system a very complicated subsystem. One of the basic functions of the embedded OS is to control and manage all of the I/O devices, and to coordinate multiple processes accessing I/O devices simultaneously.

The storage in this book refers to external storage devices such as NOR/NAND flash, eSDHC, U-Disk, HDD and SSD, which are commonly used in embedded systems. With the recent development of cloud computing, storage technology plays a more and more important role in the whole system and is moving faster and faster.

The key task for device management is to control the I/O implementation between the CPU and the devices, in a way which meets the user's I/O application requirement. The operating system must send commands to the devices, respond to interrupts and handle exceptions from the devices. It should also provide a simple and easily used interface between the devices and other parts of the system. Therefore, the I/O management module needs to improve the parallel process capability between the CPU and I/O devices, I/O devices and I/O devices, to get the best utilization efficiency of the system resources.

The I/O management module should provide a unified, transparent, independent and scalable I/O interface.

This chapter introduces the data transfer mode between the CPU and I/O devices, interrupt technology, the I/O control process and the device driver implementation process. In the second part of this chapter, a programming model for storage devices is introduced, including feature support and performance optimization.

I/O device and I/O controller

Category of I/O devices

There are many types of I/O devices in embedded systems with complicated structures and different working models. In order to manage them efficiently, the OS usually classifies these devices from different perspectives.

Subordination category

System device: standard devices which are already registered in the system when the OS boots up. Examples include NOR/NAND flash, touch panel, etc. There are device drivers and management programs in the OS for these devices. The user applications only need to call the standard commands or functions provided by the OS in order to use these devices.

User device: non-standard devices which are not registered in the system when the OS boots up. Usually the device drivers are provided by the user. The user must transfer the control of these devices in some way to the OS for management. Typical devices include SD card, USB disk, etc.

Usage category

Exclusive device: a device which can only be used by one process at a time. For multiple concurrent processes, each process uses the device mutually exclusively. Once the OS assigns the device to a specific process, it will be owned by this process exclusively till the process releases it after usage.

Shared device: a device which can be addressed by multiple processes at a time. The shared device must be addressable and addressed randomly. The shared device mechanism can improve the utilization of each device.

Virtual device: a device which is transferred from a physical device to multiple logical devices by utilizing virtualization technology. The transferred devices are called virtual devices.

Characteristic category

Storage device: this type of device is used for storing information. Typical examples in the embedded system include hard disk, solid-state disk, NOR/NAND flash.

I/O device: this type of device includes two groups – input devices and output devices. The input device is responsible for inputting information from an external source to the internal system, such as a touch panel, barcode scanner, etc. In contrast, the output device is responsible for outputting the information processed by the embedded system to the external world, such as an LCD display, speaker, etc.

Information transferring unit category

Block device: this type of device organizes and exchanges data in units of data block, so it is called a block device. It is a kind of structural device. The typical device is a hard disk. In the I/O operation, the whole block of data should be read or written even if it is only a single-byte read/write.

Character device: this type of device organizes and exchanges data in units of character, so it is called a character device. It is a kind of non-structural device. There are a lot of types of character device, e.g., serial port, touch panel, printer. The basic feature of the character device is that the transfer rate is low and it's not addressable. An interrupt is often used when a character device executes an I/O operation.

Therefore, we can see that there are many types of I/O devices. The features and performance of different devices vary significantly. The most obvious difference is the data transfer rate. Table 23.1 shows the theoretical transfer rate of some common devices in embedded systems.

Table 23.1: Theoretical maximum data transfer rate of typical I/O devices.

I/O Device	Theoretical Date Rate
Keyboard	10 B/s
RS232	1.2 KB/s
802.11g WLAN	6.75 MB/s
Fast Ethernet	12.5 MB/s
eSDHC	25 MB/s
USB2.0	60 MB/s
10G Ethernet	125 MB/s
SATAII	370 MB/s
PCI Express2.0	625 MB/s
Serial Rapid IO	781 MB/s

I/O controller

Usually the I/O device is composed of two parts – a mechanical part and an electronic part. The electronic part is called the device controller or adapter. In the embedded system, it usually exists as a peripheral chip or on the PCB in an expansion slot. The mechanical part is the device itself such as a disk or a memory stick, etc.

In the embedded system, I/O controllers (the electronic part) are usually connected to the system bus. Figure 23.1 illustrates the I/O structure and how I/O controllers are connected in the system.

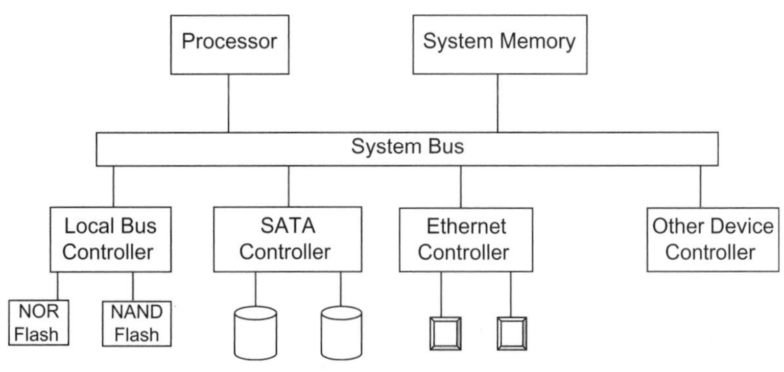

Figure 23.1:
I/O structure in a typical embedded system.

The device controller is an interface between the CPU and the device. It accepts commands from the CPU, controls the operation of the I/O device and achieves data transfer between the system memory and device. In this way, it can free up the high-frequency CPU from the control of the low-speed peripherals.

Figure 23.2 shows the basic structure of the device controller.

It contains the following parts:

- Data registers: they contain the data needing to be input or output.
- Control/status registers: the control registers are used to select a specific function of the external devices, i.e., select the function of a multiplexed pin or determine whether the CRC is enabled. The status registers are used to reflect the status of the current device, i.e., whether the command is finished or whether an error has occurred.
- I/O control logic: this is used to control the operation of the devices.
- Interface to CPU: this is used to transfer commands and data between the controller and the CPU.

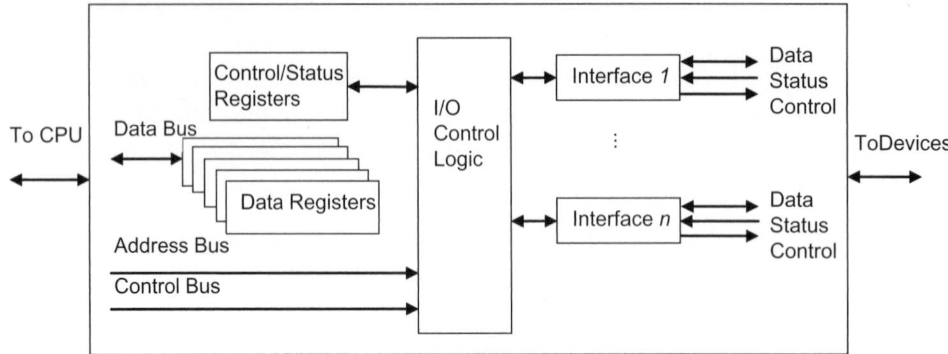

Figure 23.2:
Basic structure of a device controller.

- Interface to devices: this is used to control the peripheral devices and return the devices' status.

From the above structure, we can easily summarize the main function of the device controller:

- Receive and identify the control command from the CPU and execute it independently. After the device controller receives an instruction, the CPU will turn to execute other processes. The controller will execute the instruction independently. When the instruction is finished or an exception occurs, the device controller will generate an interrupt; then the CPU will execute the related ISR (interrupt service routine).
- Exchange data. This includes data transfer between the devices and the device controller, as well as data transfer between the controller and the system memory. In order to improve the efficiency of the data transfer, one or more data buffers are usually used inside the device controller. The data will be transferred to the data buffers first, then transferred to the devices or CPU.
- Provide the current status of the controller or the device to the CPU.
- Achieve communication and control between the CPU and the devices.

Memory-mapped I/O and DMA

As shown in Figure 23.2, there are several registers in every device controller which are responsible for communicating with the CPU. By writing to these registers, the operating system can control the device to send data, receive data or execute specific instruction/commands. By reading these registers, the operating system can get the status of the devices and see if it is ready to receive a new instruction.

Besides the status/control registers, many devices contain a data buffer for the operating system to read/write data there. For example, the Ethernet controller uses a specific area of RAM as a data buffer.

How does the CPU select the control registers or data buffer during the communication? There are three methods.

1. Independent I/O port. In this method, the memory and I/O space are independent of each other, as shown in Figure 23.3(a). Every control register is assigned an I/O port number, which is an 8-bit or 16-bit integer. All of these I/O ports form an I/O port space. This space can only be visited by dedicated I/O commands from the operating system. For example,

   ```
   IN REGA, PORT1
   OUT REGB, PORT2
   ```

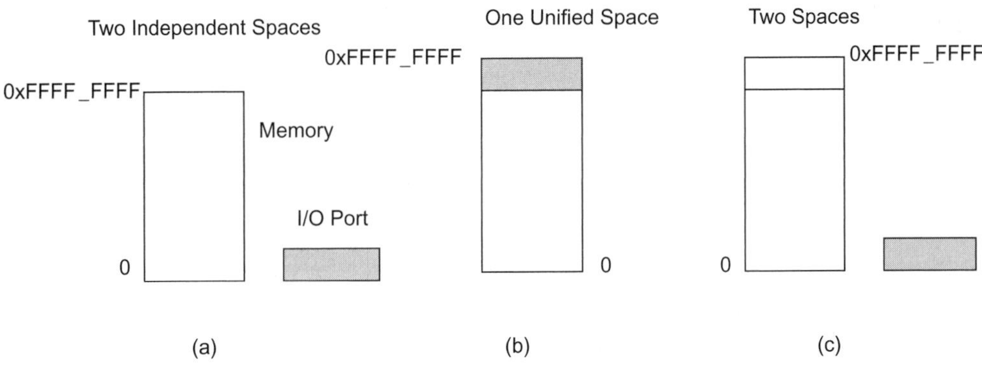

Figure 23.3:
(a) Independent I/O and memory space. (b) Memory-mapped I/O. (c) Hybrid Solution.

   The first command is to read the content of PORT1 and store it in the CPU register REGA. Similarly, the second command is to write the content of REGB to the control register PORT2.

2. Memory-mapped I/O. In this method, all the registers are mapped to the memory space and no memory will be assigned to the same address, as shown in Figure 23.3(b). In most of the cases, the assigned addresses are located at the top of the address space. Such a system is called memory-mapped I/O. This is the most common method in embedded systems, such as in ARM® and Power® architectures.
3. Hybrid solution. Figure 23.3(c) illustrates the hybrid model with memory-mapped I/O data buffers and separate I/O ports for the control registers.

The strength of the memory-mapped I/O can be summarized as:

- In a memory-mapped I/O mode, device control registers are just variables in memory and can be addressed in C the same way as any other variables. Therefore, an I/O device driver can be completely written in the C language.
- In this mode, there is no special protection mechanism needed to keep user processes from performing I/O operations.

The disadvantages of memory-mapped I/O mode can be summarized as:

- Most current embedded processors support caching of memory. Caching a device control register would cause a disaster. In order to prevent this, the hardware has to be given the capability of selectively disabling caching. This would increase the complexity of both the hardware and software in the embedded system.
- If there is only one address space, all memory references must be examined by all memory modules and all I/O devices in order to decide which ones to respond to. This significantly impacts the system performance.

Even if a CPU has memory-mapped I/O, it still needs to visit the device controllers to transfer data to them. The CPU can transfer data to an I/O controller one byte by one byte, but this method is not efficient enough and wastes the CPU bandwidth. In order to improve the efficiency, a different scheme, called DMA (direct memory access) is used in embedded systems. DMA can only be used if the hardware contains a DMA controller, which most embedded systems do. Usually most of the controllers contain an integrated DMA controller such as a network card or a disk controller.

The DMA controller transfers blocks of data between the many interface and functional blocks of this device, independent of the core or external hosts. The details of how the DMA controller works and is programmed have already been discussed in this chapter.

Figure 23.4 shows a block diagram of the DMA controller in the Freescale QorIQ P1022 embedded processor. The DMA controller has four high-speed DMA channels. Both the core and external devices can initiate DMA transfers. The channels are capable of complex data movement and advanced transaction chaining. Operations such as descriptor fetches and block transfers are initiated by each channel. A channel is selected by arbitration logic and information is passed to the source and destination control blocks for processing. The source and destination blocks generate read and write requests to the address tenure engine, which manages the DMA master port address interface. After a transaction is accepted by the master port, control is transferred to the data tenure engine, which manages the read and write data transfers. A channel remains active in the shared resources for the duration of the data transfer unless the allotted bandwidth per channel is reached.

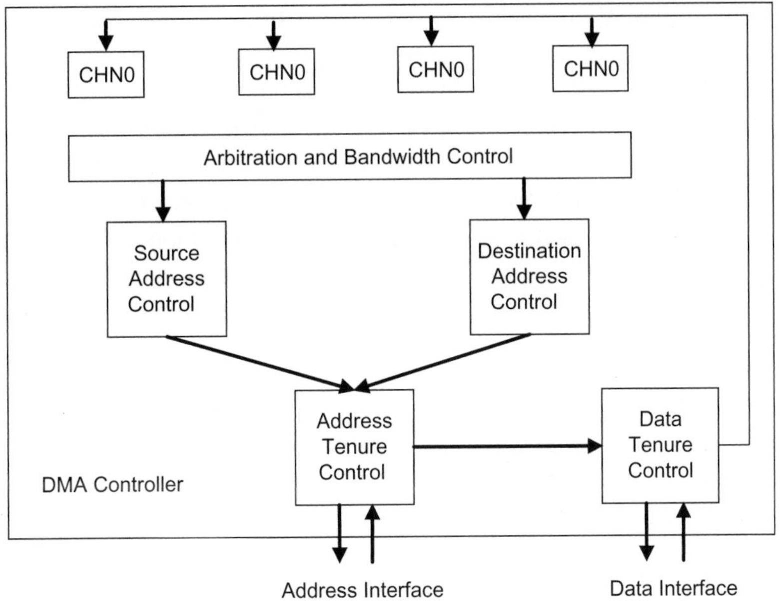

Figure 23.4:
DMA controller on P1022 processor.

The DMA block has two modes of operation: basic and extended. Basic mode is the DMA legacy mode, which does not support advanced features. Extended mode supports advanced features such as striding and flexible descriptor structures.

Flash, SD/SDHC and disk drive

Storage technology in embedded systems has developed very fast in recent years. Flash memory, eSDHC and disk drive are the typical representatives.

Flash memory

Flash memory is a long-life and non-volatile storage chip that is widely used in embedded systems. It can keep stored data and information even when the power is off. It can be electrically erased and reprogrammed. Flash memory was developed from EEPROM (electronically erasable programmable read-only memory). It must be erased before it can be rewritten with new data. The erase is based on a unit of a block, which varies from 256 KB to 20 MB.

There are two types of flash memory which dominate the technology and market: NOR flash and NAND flash. NOR flash allows quick random access to any location in the memory array, 100% known good bits for the life of the part and code execution directly from NOR flash. It is typically used for boot code storage and execution as a replacement for the older EPROM and as an alternative to certain kinds of ROM applications in embedded systems. NAND flash requires a relatively long initial read access to the memory array compared to that of NOR flash. It has 98% good bits when shipped with additional bit failure over the life of the part (ECC is highly recommended). NAND costs less per bit than NOR. It is usually used for data storage such as memory cards, USB flash drives, solid-state drives, and similar products, for general storage and transfer of data. Example applications of both types of flash memory include personal computers and all kinds of embedded systems such as digital audio players, digital cameras, mobile phones, video games, scientific instrumentation, industrial robotics, medical electronics and so on.

The connections of the individual memory cells in NOR and NAND flash are different. What's more, the interface provided for reading and writing the memory is different. NOR allows random access for reading while NAND allows only page access. As an analogy, NOR flash is like RAM, which has an independent address bus and data bus, while NAND flash is more like a hard disk where the address bus and data bus share the I/O bus.

SD/SDHC

Secure Digital (SD), with the full name of Secure Digital Memory Card, is an evolution of old MMC (MultiMedia) technology. It is specifically designed to meet the security, capacity, performance, and environment requirements inherent in the emerging audio and video consumer electronic devices. The physical form factor, pin assignments, and data transfer protocol are forward-compatible with the old MMC. It is a non-volatile memory card format developed by the SD Card Association (SDA) for use in embedded portable devices. SD comprises several families of cards. The most commonly used ones include the original, Standard-Capacity (SDSC) card, a High-Capacity (SDHC) card family, an eXtended-Capacity (SDXC) card family and the SDIO family with input/output functions rather than just data storage.

The Secure Digital High Capacity (SDHC) format is defined in Version 2.0 of the SD specification. It supports cards with capacities up to 32 GB. SDHC cards are physically and electrically identical to standard-capacity SD cards (SDSC). Figure 23.5 shows the two common cards: one SD, the other SDHC.

The SDHC controller is commonly integrated into the embedded processor. Figure 23.6 shows the basic structure of an MMC/SD host controller.

Hard disk drive

A hard disk drive (HDD) is a non-volatile device for storing and retrieving digital information in both desktop and embedded systems. It consists of one or more rigid (hence "hard") rapidly rotating discs (often referred to as platters), coated with magnetic material and with magnetic heads arranged to write data to the surfaces and read it from them.

Figure 23.5:
SanDisk 2 GB SD card and Kingston 4 GB SDHC card.

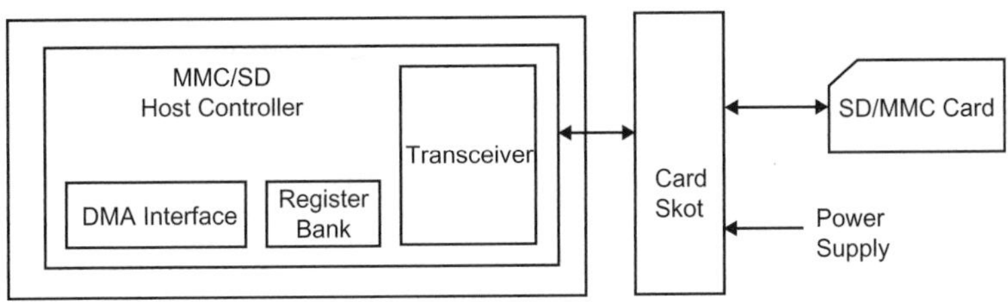

Figure 23.6:
Basic structure of an SD controller.

Hard drives are classified as random access and magnetic data storage devices. Introduced by IBM in 1956, the cost and physical size of hard disk drives have decreased significantly, while capacity and speed have been dramatically increasing. In embedded systems, hard drives are commonly used as well, such as data center and NVR systems. The advantages of the HDD are the recording capacity, cost, reliability, and speed.

The data bus interface between the hard disk drive and the processor can be classified into four types: ATA (IDE), SATA, SCSI, and SAS.

ATA (IDE): Advanced Technology Attachment. It uses the traditional 40-pin parallel data bus to connect the hard disk. The maximum transfer rate is 133 MB/s. However, it has been replaced by SATA due to its low performance and poor robustness.

SATA: Serial ATA. It has good robustness and supports hot-plugging. The throughput of SATA II is 300 MB/s. The new SATA III even reaches 600 MB/s. It is currently widely used in embedded systems.

SCSI: Small Computer System Interface. It has been developed for several generations, from SCSI-II to the current Ultra320 SCSI and Fiber-Channel. SCSI hard drives are widely used in workstations and servers. They have a lower CPU usage but a relatively higher price than SATA.

SAS: Serial Attached SCSI. This is a new generation of SCSI technology. Its maximum throughput can reach 6 Gb/s.

Solid-state drive

The solid-state drive (SSD) is also called a solid-state disk or electronic disk. It is a data storage device that uses solid-state memory (such as flash memory) to store persistent data with the intention of providing access in the same manner as a traditional block I/O hard disk drive. However, SSDs use microchips that retain data in non-volatile memory chips. There are no moving parts such as spinning disks or movable read/write heads in SSDs. SSDs use the same interface as hard disk drives, such as SATA, thus easily replacing them in most applications. Currently, most SSDs use NAND flash memory chips inside, which retain information even without power.

Although there is no spinning disk inside an SSD, people still use the conventional term "Disk". It can replace the hard disk in an embedded system.

Network-attached storage

Network-attached storage (NAS) is a computer in a network environment which only provides file-based data storage services to other clients in the network. The operating system and software running on the NAS device only provide the functions of file storage, reading/writing and management. NAS devices also provide more than one file transfer protocol. The NAS system usually contains more than one hard disk. The hard disks usually form a RAID for providing service. When there is NAS, other servers in the network do not need to provide the file-server function. NAS can be either an embedded device or a software running on a general computer.

NAS uses a communication protocol with file as the unit, such as NFS commonly used in Linux or SMB used in Windows. Among popular NAS systems is FreeNAS, which is based on FreeBSD and Openfiler based on Linux.

With the development of cloud computing, NAS devices are gaining popularity. Figure 23.7 shows a typical application example of NAS. Embedded processors are widely used in NAS storage servers.

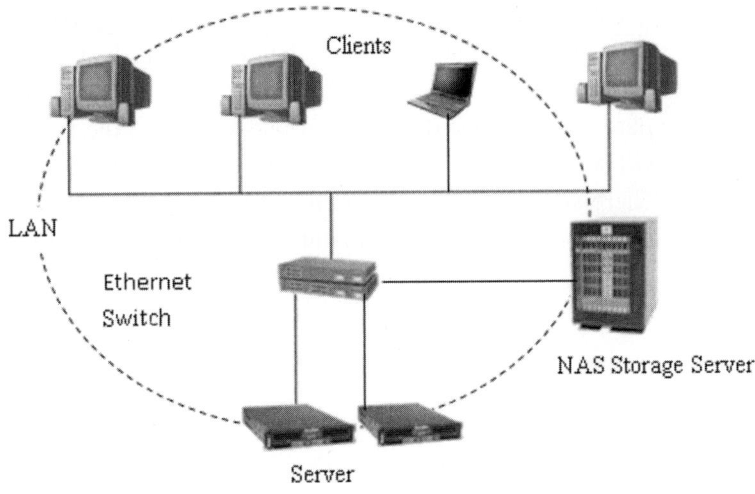

Figure 23.7:
An example of NAS.

I/O programming

After the introduction and discussion of I/O hardware, let's focus on the I/O software – how to program the I/O.

I/O control mode

The I/O control mode refers to when and how the CPU drives the I/O devices and controls the data transfer between the CPU and devices. According to the different contact modes between CPU and I/O controller, the I/O control mode can be classified into four sub-modes.

Polling mode

Polling mode refers to the CPU proactively and periodically visiting the related registers in the I/O controller in order to issue commands or read data and then control the I/O device.

In polling mode, the I/O controller is an essential device, but it doesn't have to support the DMA function. When executing the user's program, whenever the CPU needs to exchange data with external devices, it issues a command to start the device. Then it enters wait status and inquires about the device status repeatedly. The CPU will not implement the data transfer between the system memory and the I/O controller until the device status is ready.

In this mode, the CPU will keep inquiring about the related status of the controller to decide whether the I/O operation is finished. Taking the input device as an example, the device stores the data in the data registers of the device controller. During the operation, the application program detects the Busy/Idle bit of the Control/Status register in the device controller. If the bit is 1, it indicates that there is no data input yet; the CPU will then query the bit at next time in the loop. However, if the bit is 0, it means that the data is ready, and the CPU will read the data in the device data register and store it in the system memory. Meanwhile, the CPU will set another status register to 1, informing the device it is ready to receive the next data. There is a similar process in the output operation. Figure 23.8 shows a flow chart of the polling mode. Figure 23.8(a) is the CPU side, while (b) focuses on the device side.

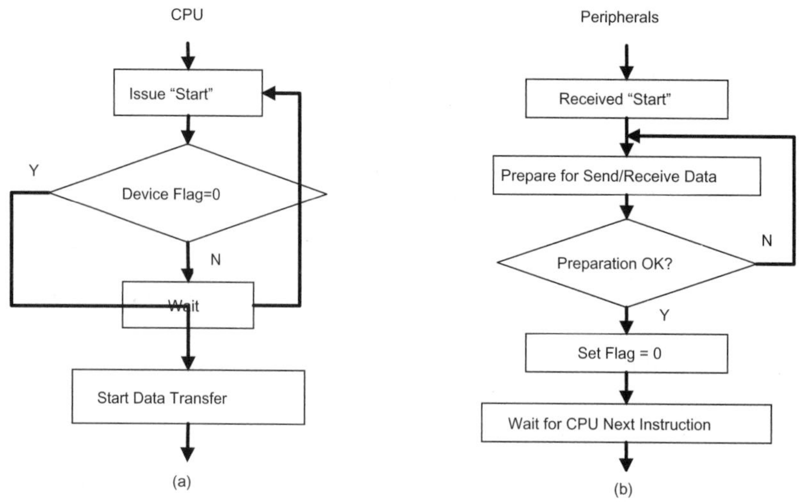

Figure 23.8:
Flowchart of polling mode.

Although the polling mode is simple and doesn't require much hardware to support it, its shortcomings are also obvious:

1. The CPU and peripheral devices can only work serially. The processing speed of the CPU is much higher than that of the peripheral devices, therefore most of the CPU time is used for waiting and idling. This significantly reduces the CPU's efficiency.
2. In a specific period, the CPU can only exchange data with one of the peripheral devices instead of working with multiple devices in parallel.
3. The polling mode depends on detecting the status of the register in the devices; it can't find or process exceptions from the devices or other hardware.

Interrupt control mode

In order to improve the efficiency of CPU utilization, interrupt control mode is introduced to control the data transfer between the CPU and peripheral devices. It requires interrupt pins to connect the CPU and devices and an interrupt-enable bit in the control/status register of the devices. The transfer structure of the interrupt mode is illustrated in Figure 23.9.

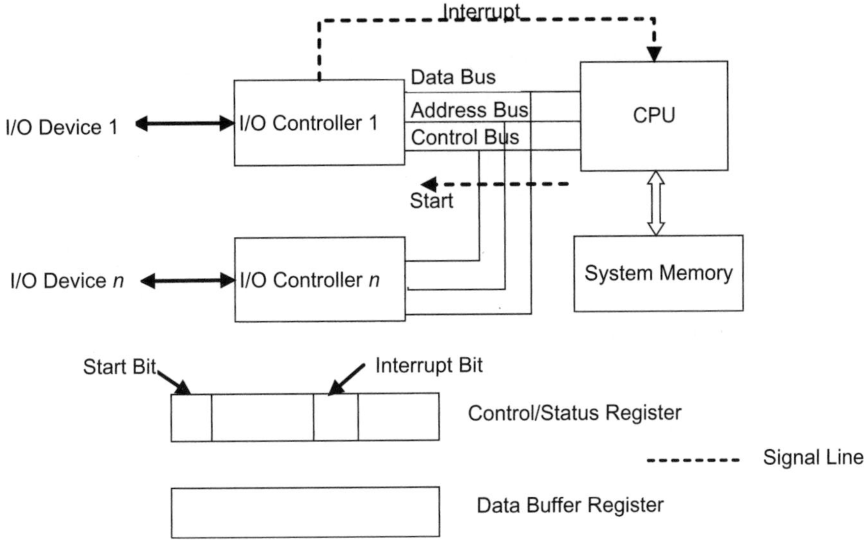

Figure 23.9:
Structure of interrupt control mode.

The data transfer process is described as follows.

1. When the process needs to get data, the CPU issues a “Start” instruction to start the peripheral device preparing the data. This instruction also sets the interrupt-enable bit in the control/status register.
2. After the process starts the peripheral device, the process is released. The CPU goes on to execute other processes/tasks.
3. After the data is prepared, the I/O controller generates an interrupt signal to the CPU via the interrupt request pin. When the CPU receives the interrupt signal, it will turn to the predesigned ISR (interrupt service routine) to process the data.

A flowchart of the interrupt control mode is shown in Figure 23.10. Figure 23.10(a) shows the CPU side while (b) focuses on the device side.

While the I/O device inputs the data, it doesn’t need the CPU to be involved. Therefore, it can make the CPU and the peripheral device work in parallel. In this way, it improves the system efficiency and throughput significantly. However, there are also problems in the interrupt control mode. First, the size of the data buffer register in the embedded system is

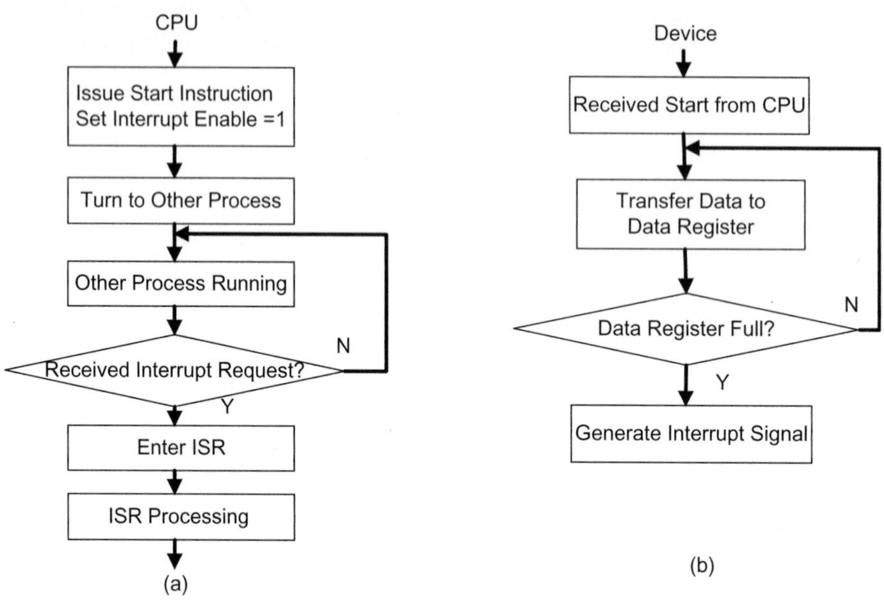

Figure 23.10:
Flowchart of interrupt control mode.

not very big. When it is full, it will generate an interrupt to the CPU. In one transfer cycle, there will be too many interrupts. This will occupy too much of CPU bandwidth in processing the interrupts. Second, there are different kinds of peripheral devices in embedded systems. If all of these devices generate interrupts to the CPU, the number of interrupts will increase significantly. In this case, the CPU may not have enough bandwidth to process all the interrupts, which may cause data loss, which is a disaster in an embedded system.

DMA control mode

DMA, as introduced in section 1, refers to the transfer of data directly between I/O devices and system memory. The basic unit of data transfer in DMA mode is the data block. It is more efficient than the interrupt mode. In DMA mode, there is a data channel set up between the system memory and I/O devices. The data is transferred as blocks between memory and the I/O device, which doesn't need the CPU to be involved. Instead, the operation is implemented by the DMA controller. The DMA structure is shown in Figure 23.11. The data input process in DMA mode can be summarized as:

1. When the software process needs the device to input data, the CPU will transfer the start address of the memory allocated for storing the input data and the number of bytes of the data to the address register and counter register, respectively, in the DMA

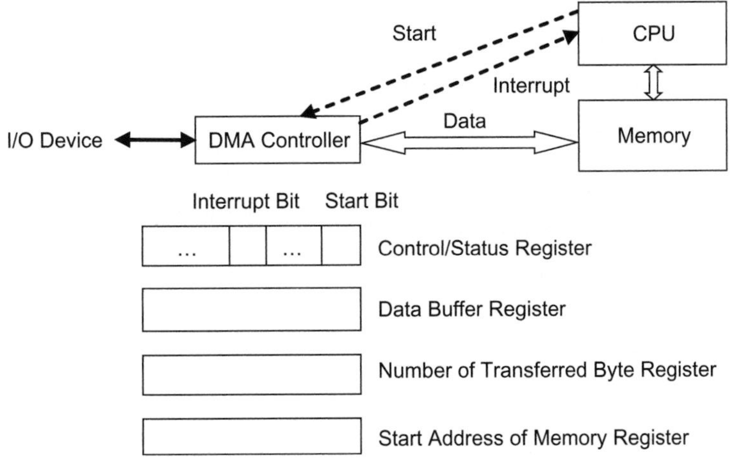

Figure 23.11:
DMA control mode.

controller. Meanwhile, it will also set the interrupt-enable bit and start bit. Then the peripheral device starts the data transfer.

2. The CPU executes other processes.
3. The device controller writes the data from the data buffer register to the system memory.
4. When the DMA controller finishes transferring data of the predefined size, it generates an interrupt request to the CPU. When receiving this request, the CPU will jump to execute the ISR to process the data further.

A flowchart of the DMA controller is shown in Figure 23.12. Figure 23.12(a) shows the CPU side while (b) focuses on the device side.

Channel control mode

Channel control mode is similar to the DMA mode but has a more powerful function. It reduces CPU involvement in the I/O operation. DMA processes the data in unit of data block, while the channel mode processes the data in units of data group. The channel mode can make the CPU, I/O device and the channel work in parallel, which improves the system efficiency significantly. Actually, the channel is a dedicated I/O processor. Not only can it effect direct data transfer between the device and system memory, it can also control I/O devices by executing channel instructions.

The coprocessor in the SoC architecture is a typical channel mode. For example, the QUICC Engine and DPAA in Freescale QorIQ communication processors use the channel mode to exchange data with the CPU.

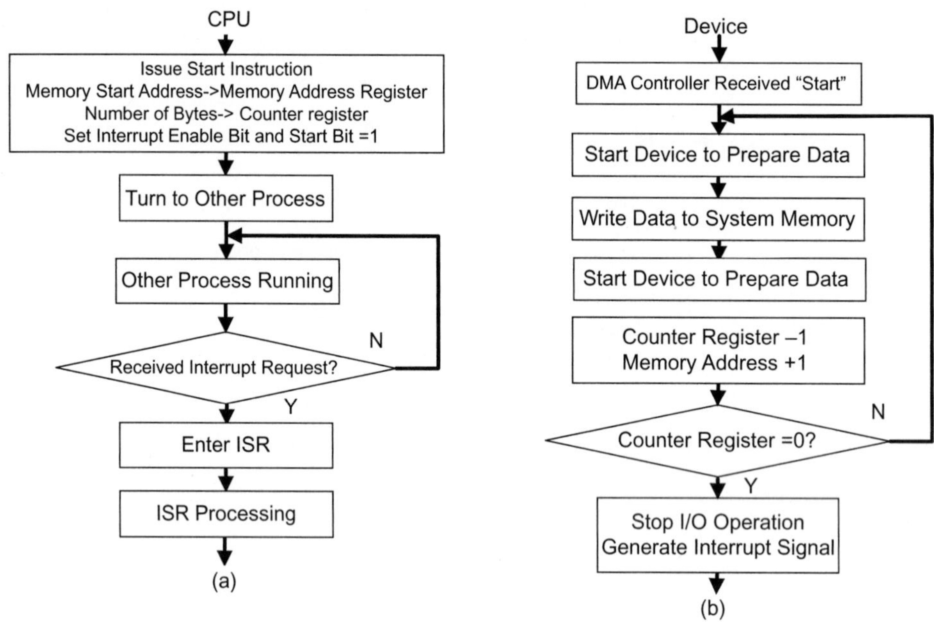

Figure 23.12:
Flowchart of DMA control mode.

I/O software goals

The general goal of I/O software design is high efficiency and universality. The following items should be considered.

Device independence

The most critical goal of I/O software is device independence. Except for the low-level software which directly controls the hardware device, all the other parts of the I/O software should not depend on any hardware. The independence of I/O software from the device can improve the design efficiency, including software portability and reusability of the device management software. When the I/O device is updated, there is no need to re-write the whole device management software, only the low-level device driver.

Uniform naming

This is closely related to the device-independence goal. One of the tasks of I/O device management is to name the I/O devices. Uniform naming refers to the use of a predesigned and uniform logic names for different kinds of devices. In Linux, all disks can be integrated into the file system hierarchy in arbitrary ways so that the user doesn't need to be aware of which name is related to which device. For example, an SD card can be mounted on top of the directory /usr/ast/backup so that copying a file to /usr/ast/backup/test copies the file to the SD card. In this way, all files and devices are addressed in the same way – by a path name

Exception handling

It is inevitable that exceptions/errors occur during I/O device operation. In general, I/O software should process the error as close as possible to the hardware. In this way, device errors which can be handled by the low-level software will not be apparent to the higher-level software. Higher-level software will handle the error only if the low-level software can't.

Synchronous blocking and asynchronous transfer

When the devices are transferring data, some of them require a synchronous transfer while some of them require an asynchronous transfer. This problem should be considered during the design of the I/O software.

I/O software layer

In general, the I/O software is organized in four layers. From bottom to top, they are interrupt service routine, device drivers, device-independent OS software and user-level I/O software, as shown in Figure 23.13.

After the CPU accepts the I/O interrupt request, it will call the ISR (interrupt service routine) and process the data. The device driver is directly related to the hardware and carries out the instructions to operate the devices. The device-independent I/O software implements most functions of the I/O management, such as the interface with the device driver, device naming, device protection and device allocation and release. It also provides storage space for the device management and data transfer. The user-level I/O software provides the users with a friendly, clear and unified I/O interface. Each level of the I/O software is introduced below.

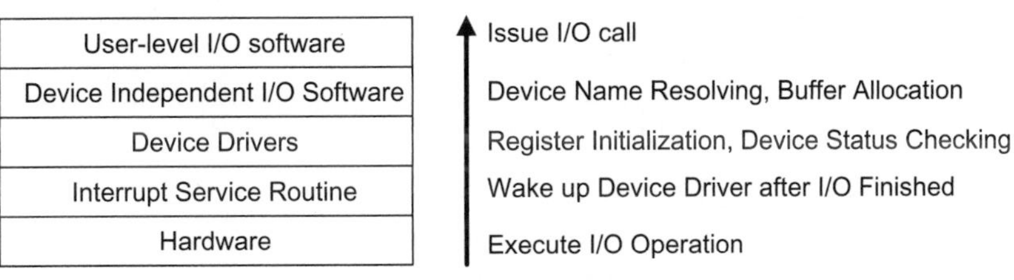

Figure 23.13:
I/O software layer.

Interrupt service routine

In the interrupt layer, data transfer between the CPU and I/O devices takes the following steps.

1. When a process needs data, it issues an instruction to start the I/O device. At the same time, the instruction also sets the interrupt-enable bit in the I/O device controller.
2. After the process issues the start instruction, the process will give up the CPU and wait for the I/O completion. Meanwhile, the scheduler will schedule other processes to utilize the CPU. Another scenario is that the process will continue to run till the I/O interrupt request comes.
3. When the I/O operation is finished, the I/O device will generate an interrupt request signal to the CPU via the IRQ pin. After the CPU receives this signal, it starts to execute the predesigned interrupt service routine and handling the data. If the process involves a large amount of data, then the above steps need to be repeated.
4. After the process gets the data, it will turn to Ready status. The schedule will schedule it to continue to run in a subsequent time.

As mentioned in section 2.1 the interrupt mode can improve the utilization of the CPU and I/O devices but it has shortcomings as well.

Device driver

A device driver is also called a device processing program. The main task is to transform the logical I/O request into physical I/O execution. For example, it can transform the device name into the port address, transform the logical record into a physical record and transform logical operation into physical operation. The device driver is a communication program between the I/O process and the device controller. It includes all the codes related to devices. Because it often exists in the format of a process, it is also called a device-driving process.

The kernel of the OS interacts with the I/O device through the device driver. Actually, the device driver is the only interface which connects the I/O device and the kernel. Only the device driver knows the details of the I/O devices. The main function of the device driver can be summarized as follows.

1. Transfer the received abstract operation to a physical operation. In general, there are several registers which are used for storing instructions, data and parameters in each device controller. The user space or the upper layer of software is not aware of the details. In fact, they can only issue abstract instructions. Therefore, the OS needs to transfer the abstract instruction to a physical operation; for example, to transfer the disk number in the abstract instruction to the cylinder number, track number and sector number. This transfer work can only be done by the device driver.

2. Check the validity of the I/O request, read the status of the I/O device and transfer the parameters of the I/O operation.
3. Issue the I/O instruction, start the I/O device and achieve the I/O operation.
4. Respond in a timely manner to interrupt requests coming from device controller of the channel and call the related ISR to process them.
5. Implement error handling for the I/O operation.

Device-independent I/O software

The basic goal of device-independent I/O software is to provide the general functions needed by all devices and provide a unified interface to the user-space I/O software. Most of the I/O software is not related to any specific device. The border between the device driver and device-independent I/O software depends on the real system needs. Figure 23.14 shows the general functions of device-independent I/O software.

Device Naming
Device Protection
Provide Device Independent Block
Buffer Technology
Block Device Store and Allocate
Exclusive Device Allocate & Resign
Report Error Information
Unified Interface with Device Driver

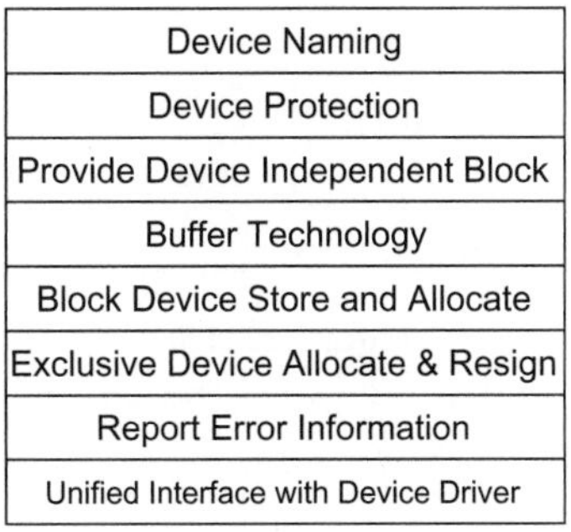

Figure 23.14:
Basic function of device-independent I/O software.

User-level I/O software

Most of the I/O software exists in the OS, but there are also some I/O operation-related I/O system calls in the user space. These I/O system calls are realized by utilizing the library procedure, which is a part of the device management I/O system. For example, a user space application contains the system call:

```
count = read(fd,buffer,nbytes);
```

When the application is running, it links the library process `read` to build a unified binary code.

The main tasks of these library procedures are to set the parameters to a suitable position, then let other I/O processes implement the I/O operation. The standard I/O library includes a lot of I/O-related processes which can be run as part of the user application.

Case study: device driver in Linux

As discussed in section 2.3, device drivers play an important role in connecting the OS kernel and the peripheral devices. It is the most important layer in the I/O software. This section will analyze details of the device driver by taking Linux as an example (Figure 23.15).

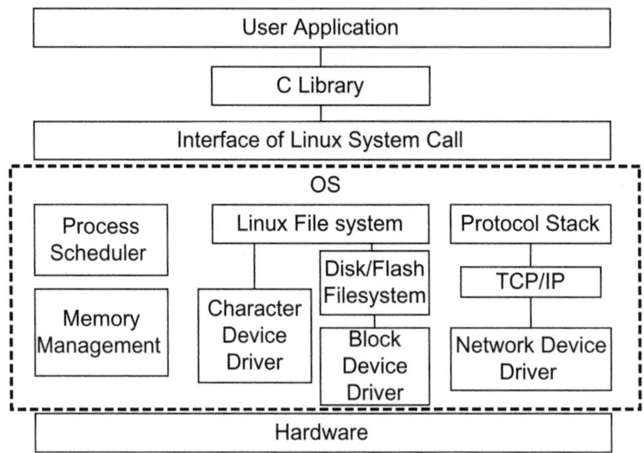

Figure 23.15:
Linux device driver in the whole OS.

In Linux, the I/O devices are divided into three categories:

- character device
- block device
- network device.

There is much difference between the design of a character device driver and a block device driver. However, from a user's point of view, they all use the file system interface functions for operation such as `open()`, `close()`, `read()` and `write()`. In Linux, the network device driver is designed for data-package transmitting and receiving. The communication between the kernel and the network device and that between the kernel and a character device or a block device are totally different. The TTY driver, I2C driver, USB driver, PCIe driver and LCD driver can be generally classified into these three basic categories; however, Linux also defines specific driver architectures for these complicated devices.

In the following part of this section, we will take the character device driver as an example to explain the structure of a Linux device driver and the programming of its main components.

cdev structure

The Linux2.6 kernel uses the cdev structure to describe the character device. The structure of the cdev is defined as

```
struct cdev
{
   struct kobject kobj; /* Inside object of kobject */
   struct module *owner; /* Module that blongs to */
   struct file_operations *ops; /* Structure of file operation */
   struct list_head list;
   dev_t dev;          /* Device number */
   unsigned int count;
};
```

The member of `dev_t` in the `cdev` structure defines the device number. It is 32 bit. The upper 12 bits are for the main device number while the lower 20 bits are for the subdevice number.

Another important member in the `cdev` structure, `file_operations`, defines the virtual file system interface function provided by the character device driver.

Linux kernel 2.6 provides a group of functions to operate the cdev:

```
void cdev_init(struct cdev*, struct file_operations *);
struct cdev *cdev_alloc(void);
void cdev_put(struct cdev *p);
int cdev_add(struct cdev *, dev_t, unsigned);
void cdev_del(struct cdev *);
```

The `cdev_init()` function is used to initialize the members of `cdev` and set up the connection between the `cdev` and `file_operations`. The source codes are shown below:

```
void cdev_init (struct cdev *cdev, struct file_operation *fops)
{
   memset(cdev, 0, sizeof *cdev);
   INIT_LIST_HEAD(&cdev->list);
   cdev->kobj.ktype = &ktype_cdev_default;
   kobject_init(&cdev->kobj);
   cdev->ops = fops;
}
```

The `cdev_alloc()` function is used to dynamically apply `cdev` memory:

```
struct cdev *cdev_alloc(void)
{
```

```
    struct cdev *p = kzalloc(sizeof(struct cdev), GFP_KERNEL);

    if (p) {

        memset(p, 0, sizeof(struct cdev));

        p->kobj.ktype = &ktype_cdev_dynamic;

        INIT_LIST_HEAD(&p->list);

        kobject_init(&p->kobj);

    }

    return p;

}
```

The `cdev_add()` function and `cdev_del()` function can add or delete a `cdev` to or from the system, respectively, which achieves the function of character device register and un-register.

Register and un-register device number

Before calling the `cdev_add()` function to register the character device in the system, the `register_chrdev_region()` or `alloc_chrdev_region()` function should be called in order to register the device number. The two functions are defined as:

```
int register_chrdev_region(dev_t from, unsigned count, const char *name);
int alloc_chrdev_region(dev_t *dev,unsigned baseminor,
    unsigned count, const char *name)
```

The `register_chrdev_region()` function is used when the starting device number is known, while `alloc_chrdev_region()` is used when that number is unknown but it needs to dynamically register an unoccupied device number. When the function call occurs, it will put the device number into the first parameter dev.

After the character device is deleted from the system by calling the `cdev_dev()` function, the `unregister_chrdev_region( )` function should be called to un-register the registered device number. The function is defined as:

```
void unregister_chrdev_region(dev_t from,unsigned count)
```

In general, the sequence of registering and un-registering the device can be summarized as:

```
register_chrdev_region()–> cdev_add()   /* Existing in loading */
cdev_del()–>unregister_chrdev_region()   /* Existing in Unloading */
```

The `file_operations` structure

The member functions in the `file_operations` structure are the key components in the character device driver. These functions will be called when the applications implement the system calls such as `open()`, `write()`, `read()` and `close()`. The `file_operations` structure is defined as;

```
struct file_operations
{

 struct module *owner; /*The pointer of the module of this structure. The value usually is
THIS_MODULES */

 loff_t (*llseek) (struct file *, loff_t, int); /* Used for modifying the current read/write
position of the file*/

 ssize_t (*read) (struct file *, char __user *, size_t, loff_t *); /* Read data from the
device */

 ssize_t (*write) (struct file *, const char __user *, size_t, loff_t *); /* Write data to the
device */

 ssize_t (*aio_read) (struct kiocb *, const struct iovec *, unsigned long, loff_t); /*
Initialize an asynchronous read operation */

 ssize_t (*aio_write) (struct kiocb *, const struct iovec *, unsigned long, loff_t); /*
Initialize an asynchronous write operation */

 int (*readdir) (struct file *, void *, filldir_t); /* Used for reading directory */

 unsigned int (*poll) (struct file *, struct poll_table_struct *); /* Polling function*/

 int (*ioctl) (struct inode *, struct file *, unsigned int, unsigned long); /* Execute the
device I/O control instruction */

 long (*unlocked_ioctl) (struct file *, unsigned int, unsigned long); /* Use this function
pointer to replace the ioctrl when not using BLK file system */

 long (*compat_ioctl) (struct file *, unsigned int, unsigned long); /* The 32 bit ioctl is
replaced by this function pointer in 64-bit system */

 int (*mmap) (struct file *, struct vm_area_struct *); /* Used to map the device memory to the
process address space */

 int (*open) (struct inode *, struct file *);

 int (*flush) (struct file *, fl_owner_t id);
```

```
int (*release) (struct inode *, struct file *);

int (*fsync) (struct file *, struct dentry *, int datasync); /* synchronize the data for
processing */

int (*aio_fsync) (struct kiocb *, int datasync); /Asynchronous fsync */

int (*fasync) (int, struct file *, int); /* Inform device that the fasync bit is changing */

int (*lock) (struct file *, int, struct file_lock *);

ssize_t (*sendpage) (struct file *, struct page *, int, size_t, loff_t *, int); /* Achieve
another part of send file call. Kernel call sends the data to related file with one data page
each time. The device driver usually sets it as NULL */

unsigned long (*get_unmapped_area)(struct file *, unsigned long, unsigned long, unsigned
long, unsigned long); /* Find a position in the process address to map memory in the low level
device */

int (*check_flags)(int); /* Enable the module to check the flag being transferred to fcntl
(F_SETEL...) call */

int (*flock) (struct file *, int, struct file_lock *);

ssize_t (*splice_write)(struct pipe_inode_info *, struct file *, loff_t *, size_t, unsigned
int);

ssize_t (*splice_read)(struct file *, loff_t *, struct pipe_inode_info *, size_t, unsigned
int);

int (*setlease)(struct file *, long, struct file_lock **);

};
```

Linux character device driver composition

In Linux, the character device driver is composed of the following parts:

- Character device module registration and un-registration.

The functions for character device module load should perform device number application and device registration. The functions for character device module unload should perform device number un-register and cdev deletion. Below is a template of these modules:

```
/* ——— Device Structure ——— */
struct xxx_dev_t
{

  struct cdev cdev;
```

```
    ...
} xxx_dev;
/* ——— Device Driver Initialization Function ——— */
static int __init xxx_init(void)
{
    ...
    cdev_init(&xxx_dev.cdev, &xxx_fops); /* Initialize cdev */
    xxx_dev.cdev.owner = THIS_MODULE;
    if (xxx_major) /* Register device number */
        register_chrdev_region(xxx_dev_no, 1, DEV_NAME);
    else
        alloc_chrdev_region(&xxx_dev_no, 0, 1, DEV_NAME);
    ret = cdev_add(&xxx_dev.cdev, xxx_dev_no, 1); /* Add the device */
    ...
}
/* ——— Device Driver Exit Function ——— */
static void __exit xxx_exit(void)
{
    unregister_chrdev_region(xxx_dev_no, 1); /* Unregister the occupied device number */
    cdev_del(&xxx_dev.cdev);
    ...
}
```

- Functions in the `file_operations` structure.

The member functions in the `file_operations` structure are the interface between the Linux kernel and the device drivers. They are also the eventual implementers of the Linux system calls. Most of the device drivers will execute the `read()`, `write()` and `ioctl()` functions. Below is the template of read, write and I/O control functions in the character device driver.

```
/* ——— Read the Device ——— */
ssize_t xxx_read(sturct file *filip, char __user *buf, size_t count, loff_t *f_pos)
{
    ...
    copy_to_user(buf, ..., ...);
    ...
}
/* ——— Write the Device ——— */
ssize_t xxx_write(struct file *filp, const char __user *buf, size_t count, loff_t *f_pos)
{
    ...
    copy_from_user(..., buf, ...);
    ...
}
/* ——— ioctl function ——— */
```

```
int xxx_ioctl(struct inode *inode, struct file *filp, unsigned int cmd, unsigned long arg)
{
  ...
  switch (cmd)
  {
    case XXX_CMD1;
     ...
     break;
       case XXX_CMD2;
       ...
       break;
     default;
     return - ENOTTY;
  }
  return 0;
}
```

In the read function of the device driver, `filp` is the file structure pointer while `buf` is the memory address in user space which cannot be directly read or written; `count` is the number of bytes that need to be read; `f_pos` is the read offset relative to the beginning of the file.

In the write function of the device driver, `filp` is the file structure pointer while `buf` is the memory address in user space which cannot be directly read or written; `count` is the number of bytes that need to be written; `f_pos` is the write offset relative to the beginning of the file.

Because the kernel space and the user space cannot address each other's memory, the function `copy_from_user()` is needed to copy the user space to the kernel space, and the function `copy_to_user()` is needed to copy the kernel space to user space.

The `cmd` parameter in the I/O control function is a pre-defined I/O control instruction, while `arg` is the corresponding parameters.

Figure 23.16 shows the structure of the character device driver, the relationship between the character device driver and the character device and the relationship between the character device driver and the applications in user space which addresses the device.

Storage programming

As discussed in section 1.4 the storage subsystem plays an important role in embedded systems. Most storage devices are block devices. How to program the storage system is one of the key topics in embedded system software design. This section will focus on how to program the popular storage devices such as NOR flash, NAND flash, SATA hard disk and so on. The Linux OS will be used as well as an example.

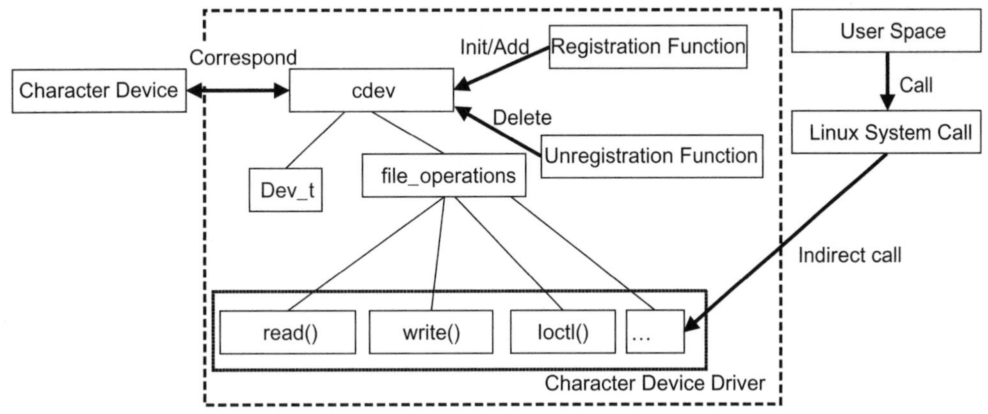

Figure 23.16:
The structure of the character device driver.

I/O for block devices

The operation of a block device is different from that of a character device.

A block device must be operated with block as the unit, while character device is operated with byte as the unit. Most of the common devices are character devices since they don't need to be operated with a fixed size of block.

There is corresponding buffer in a block device for an I/O request. Therefore, it can select the sequence to respond to the request. However, there is no buffer in a character device which can be directly read/written. It is very important for the storage device to adjust the read/write sequence because to read/write continuous sectors is much faster than to read/write distributed sectors.

A character device can only be sequentially read/written, while block device can be randomly read/written. Although a block device can be randomly addressed, it will improve the performance if sequential read/writes can be well organized for mechanical devices such as hard disks.

The block_device_operations structure

In the block device driver, there is a structure `block_device_operations`. It is similar to the `file_operations` structure in the character device driver. It is an operation set of the block device. The code is:

```
struct block_device_operations
{

   int (*open) (struct inode *, struct file *);
```

```
    int (*release) (struct inode *, struct file *);
    int (*ioctl) (struct inode *, struct file *, unsigned, unsigned long);
    long (*unlocked_ioctl) (struct file *, unsigned, unsigned long);
    long (*compat_ioctl) (struct file *, unsigned, unsigned long);
    int (*direct_access) (struct block_device *, sector_t, unsigned long *);
    int (*media_changed) (struct gendisk *);
    int (*revalidate_disk) (struct gendisk *);
    int (*getgeo)(struct block_device *, struct hd_geometry *);
    struct module *owner;
};
```

The main functions in this structure are:

- Open and release

```
int (*open) (struct inode *inode, struct file *flip);

int (*release) (struct inode *inode, struct file *flip);
```

When the block device is opened or released, these two functions will be called.

- I/O control

```
int (*ioctl) (struct inode *inode, struct file *filp, unsigned int cmd, unsigned long
arg);
```

This function is the realization of the `ioctl()` system call. There are many I/O requests in the block device which are handled by the Linux block device layer.

- Media change

```
int (*media_changed) (struct gendisk *gd);
```

The kernel calls this function to check whether the media in the drive has changed. If changed, it returns non-zero, otherwise it returns zero. This function is only used for portable media such as SD/MMC cards or USB disks.

- Get drive information

```
int (*getgeo)(struct block_device *, struct hd_geometry *);
```

The function fills in the `hd_geometry` structure based on the drive's information. For the hard disk, it contains the head, sector, cylinder information.

```
struct module *owner;
```

A pointer points to this structure, which is usually initialized as `THIS_MODULE`.

Gendisk structure

In the Linux kernel, the gendisk (general disk) structure is used to represent an independent disk device or partition. Its definition in the 2.6.31 kernel is shown below:

```
struct gendisk {

 /* major, first_minor and minors are input parameters only,

   *don't use directly.  Use disk_devt() and disk_max_parts().

  */

 int major;   /* major number of driver */

 int first_minor;

 int minors;           /* maximum number of minors, =1 for

                              * disks that can't be partitioned. */

 char disk_name[DISK_NAME_LEN];/* name of major driver */

 char *(*nodename)(struct gendisk *gd);

 /* Array of pointers to partitions indexed by partno.

  * Protected with matching bdev lock but stat and other

  * non-critical accesses use RCU.  Always access through

  * helpers.

  */

  struct disk_part_tbl *part_tbl;

  struct hd_struct part0;
  struct block_device_operations *fops;

  struct request_queue *queue;

  void *private_data;
  int flags;

  struct device *driverfs_dev;

  struct kobject *slave_dir;
  struct timer_rand_state *random;

  atomic_t sync_io;  /* RAID */

  struct work_struct async_notify;
```

```
#ifdef CONFIG_BLK_DEV_INTEGRITY
 struct blk_integrity *integrity;
#endif
 int node_id;
};
```

The `major`, `first_minor` and `minors` represent the disk's major and minor number. The `fops` is the `block_device_operations` structure as introduced above. The `queue` is a pointer that the kernel uses to manage the device I/O request queue. The `private_data` is used to point to any private data on the disk.

The Linux kernel provides a set of functions to operate the gendisk, including allocate the gendisk, register the gendisk, release the gendisk, and set the gendisk capacity.

Block I/O

The `bio` is a key data structure in the Linux kernel which describes the I/O operation of the block device.

```
struct bio {
 sector_t  bi_sector; /* device address in 512 byte       sectors */
 struct bio  *bi_next; /* request queue link */
 struct block_device *bi_bdev;
 unsigned long  bi_flags; /* status, command, etc */
 unsigned long  bi_rw;  /* bottom bits READ/WRITE,
                          * top bits priority
                         */
 unsigned short  bi_vcnt; /* how many bio_vec's */
 unsigned short  bi_idx; /* current index into bvl_vec */
 /* Number of segments in this BIO after
  * physical address coalescing is performed.
  */
 unsigned int  bi_phys_segments;
 unsigned int  bi_size; /* residual I/O count */
```

```
    /*
     * To keep track of the max segment size, we account for the
     * sizes of the first and last mergeable segments in this bio.
     */
    unsigned int bi_seg_front_size;
    unsigned int bi_seg_back_size;
    unsigned int bi_max_vecs; /* max bvl_vecs we can hold */
    unsigned int bi_comp_cpu; /* completion CPU */
    atomic_t bi_cnt; /* pin count */
    struct bio_vec *bi_io_vec; /* the actual vec list */
    bio_end_io_t *bi_end_io;
    void *bi_private;
#if defined(CONFIG_BLK_DEV_INTEGRITY)
    struct bio_integrity_payload *bi_integrity; /* data integrity */
#endif
    bio_destructor_t *bi_destructor; /* destructor */
    /*
     * We can inline a number of vecs at the end of the bio, to avoid
     * double allocations for a small number of bio_vecs. This member
     * MUST obviously be kept at the very end of the bio.
     */
    struct bio_vec bi_inline_vecs[0];
};
```

Block device registration and un-registration

The first step of the block device driver is to register itself to the Linux kernel. This is achieved by the function `register_blokdev()`:

```
int register_blkdev(unsigned int major, const char *name);
```

The `major` is the main device number that used by the block device. The `name` is the device name which will be displayed in the /proc/devices. If the `major` is 0, the kernel will allocate a new main device number automatically. The return value of `register_blkdev()` is the number.

To un-register the block device `unregister_blkdev()` is used:

```
int unregister_blkdev(unsigned int major, const char *name);
```

The parameter which is transferred to `unregister_blkdev()` must match the one transferred to `register_blkdev()`. Otherwise it will retun −EINVAL.

Flash device programming

MTD system in Linux

In Linux, the MTD (Memory Technology Device) is used to provide the uniform and abstract interface between the flash and the Linux kernel. MTD isolates the file system from the low-level flash. As shown in Figure 23.17, the flash device driver and interface can be divided into four layers with the MTD concept.

- Hardware driver layer: the flash hardware driver is responsible for flash hardware device read, write and erase. The NOR flash chip driver for the Linux MTD device is located in /drivers/mtd/chips directory. The NAND flash chip driver is located at /drivers/mtd/nand directory. Whether for NOR or NAND, the erase command must be implemented before any write operation. NOR flash can be read directly with byte units. It must be erased with block units or as a whole chip. The NOR flash write operation is composed with a specific series of commands. For NAND flash, both read and write operations must follow a specific series of commands. The read and write

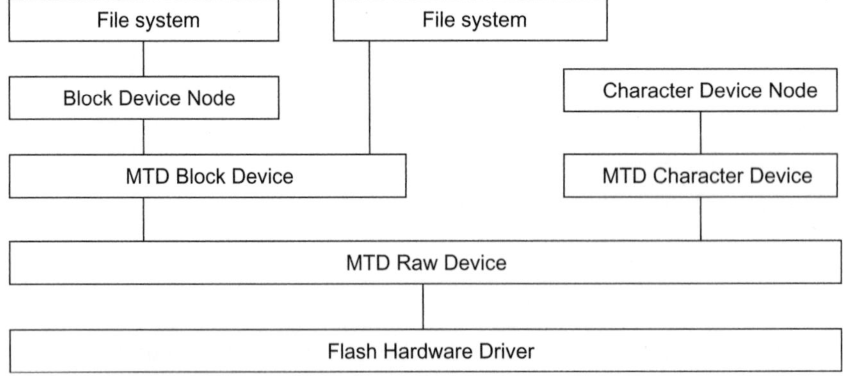

Figure 23.17:
MTD system in Linux.

operations on NAND flash are both based on page (256 byte or 512 byte), while the erase is based on block (4 KB, 8 KB or 16 KB).

- MTD raw device layer: the MTD raw device is composed of two parts: one is the general code of the MTD raw device, the other is the data for each specific flash such as partition.
- MTD device layer: based on the MTD raw device, Linux defines the MTD block device (Device number 31) and character device (Device number 90), which forms the MTD device layer. MTD character device definition is realized in mtdchar.c. It can achieve the read/write and control to MTD device based on file_operations functions (lseek, open, close, read, write and ioctl). The MTD block device defines a mtdbli_dev structure to describe the MTD block device.
- Device node: the user can use the mknod function to set up MTD character device node (with main device number 90) and MTD device node (with main device number 31) in the /dev directory.

After the MTD concept is introduced, the low-level flash device driver talks directly to the MTD raw device layer, as shown in Figure 23.18. The data structure to describe the MTD raw device is mtd_info, which defines several MTD data and functions.

The mtd_info is a structure to represent the MTD raw device. It's defined as below:

```
struct mtd_info {

 u_char type;
```

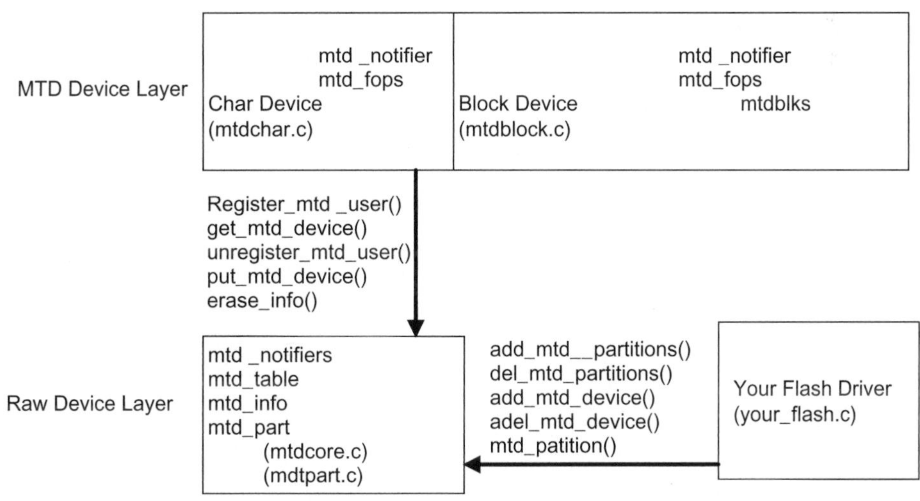

Figure 23.18:
Low-level device driver and raw device layer.

```
uint32_t flags;

uint64_t size; // Total size of the MTD

/* “Major” erase size for the device. Naïve users may take this

 * to be the only erase size available, or may use the more detailed

 * information below if they desire

 */

uint32_t erasesize;

/* Minimal writable flash unit size. In case of NOR flash it is 1 (even

 * though individual bits can be cleared), in case of NAND flash it is

 * one NAND page (or half, or one-fourths of it), in case of ECC-ed NOR

 * it is of ECC block size, etc. It is illegal to have writesize = 0.

 * Any driver registering a struct mtd_info must ensure a writesize of

 * 1 or larger.

 */

uint32_t writesize;
uint32_t oobsize;   // Amount of OOB data per block (e.g. 16)

uint32_t oobavail;  // Available OOB bytes per block
/*

 * If erasesize is a power of 2 then the shift is stored in

 * erasesize_shift otherwise erasesize_shift is zero. Ditto writesize.

 */

unsigned int erasesize_shift;

unsigned int writesize_shift;

/* Masks based on erasesize_shift and writesize_shift */

unsigned int erasesize_mask;

unsigned int writesize_mask;
// Kernel-only stuff starts here.

const char *name;
```

```
int index;

/* ecc layout structure pointer - read only ! */

struct nand_ecclayout *ecclayout;

/* Data for variable erase regions. If numeraseregions is zero,

 * it means that the whole device has erasesize as given above.

 */

int numeraseregions;

struct mtd_erase_region_info *eraseregions;

/*

 * Erase is an asynchronous operation.  Device drivers are supposed

 * to call instr->callback() whenever the operation completes, even

 * if it completes with a failure.

 * Callers are supposed to pass a callback function and wait for it

 * to be called before writing to the block.

 */

int (*erase) (struct mtd_info *mtd, struct erase_info *instr);

/* This stuff for eXecute-In-Place */

/* phys is optional and may be set to NULL */

int (*point) (struct mtd_info *mtd, loff_t from, size_t len,

            size_t *retlen, void **virt, resource_size_t *phys);

/* We probably shouldn't allow XIP if the unpoint isn't a NULL */

void (*unpoint) (struct mtd_info *mtd, loff_t from, size_t len);

/* Allow NOMMU mmap() to directly map the device (if not NULL)

 * - return the address to which the offset maps

 * - return -ENOSYS to indicate refusal to do the mapping

 */
```

```
unsigned long (*get_unmapped_area) (struct mtd_info *mtd,

      unsigned long len,

      unsigned long offset,

      unsigned long flags);

/* Backing device capabilities for this device

 * - provides mmap capabilities

 */

struct backing_dev_info *backing_dev_info;

int (*read) (struct mtd_info *mtd, loff_t from, size_t len, size_t *retlen, u_char *buf);

int (*write) (struct mtd_info *mtd, loff_t to, size_t len, size_t *retlen, const u_char
*buf);

/* In blackbox flight recorder like scenarios we want to make successful

  writes in interrupt context. panic_write() is only intended to be

  called when its known the kernel is about to panic and we need the

  write to succeed. Since the kernel is not going to be running for much

  longer, this function can break locks and delay to ensure the write

  succeeds (but not sleep). */

int (*panic_write) (struct mtd_info *mtd, loff_t to, size_t len, size_t *retlen, const
u_char *buf);

int (*read_oob) (struct mtd_info *mtd, loff_t from,

  struct mtd_oob_ops *ops);

int (*write_oob) (struct mtd_info *mtd, loff_t to,

  struct mtd_oob_ops *ops);

/*

 * Methods to access the protection register area, present in some

 * flash devices. The user data is one time programmable but the

 * factory data is read only.

 */
```

```
int (*get_fact_prot_info) (struct mtd_info *mtd, struct otp_info *buf, size_t len);

int (*read_fact_prot_reg) (struct mtd_info *mtd, loff_t from, size_t len, size_t *retlen,
u_char *buf);

int (*get_user_prot_info) (struct mtd_info *mtd, struct otp_info *buf, size_t len);

int (*read_user_prot_reg) (struct mtd_info *mtd, loff_t from, size_t len, size_t *retlen,
u_char *buf);

int (*write_user_prot_reg) (struct mtd_info *mtd, loff_t from, size_t len, size_t *retlen,
u_char *buf);

int (*lock_user_prot_reg) (struct mtd_info *mtd, loff_t from, size_t len);

/* kvec-based read/write methods.

  NB: The 'count' parameter is the number of _vectors_, each of

  which contains an (ofs, len) tuple.

*/

int (*writev) (struct mtd_info *mtd, const struct kvec *vecs, unsigned long count, loff_t to,
size_t *retlen);

/* Sync */

void (*sync) (struct mtd_info *mtd);

/* Chip-supported device locking */

int (*lock) (struct mtd_info *mtd, loff_t ofs, uint64_t len);

int (*unlock) (struct mtd_info *mtd, loff_t ofs, uint64_t len);

/* Power Management functions */

int (*suspend) (struct mtd_info *mtd);

void (*resume) (struct mtd_info *mtd);

/* Bad block management functions */

int (*block_isbad) (struct mtd_info *mtd, loff_t ofs);

int (*block_markbad) (struct mtd_info *mtd, loff_t ofs);

struct notifier_block reboot_notifier;  /* default mode before reboot */

/* ECC status information */
```

```
struct mtd_ecc_stats ecc_stats;

/* Subpage shift (NAND) */

int subpage_sft;

void *priv;

struct module *owner;

struct device dev;

int usecount;

/* If the driver is something smart, like UBI, it may need to maintain

 * its own reference counting. The below functions are only for driver.

 * The driver may register its callbacks. These callbacks are not

 * supposed to be called by MTD users */

int (*get_device) (struct mtd_info *mtd);

void (*put_device) (struct mtd_info *mtd);

};
```

The functions read(), write(), erase(), read_oob() and write_oob() in the mtd_info are the key functions that the MTD device driver needs to perform.

In the Flash driver, the two functions below are used to register and un-register the MTD device.

```
int add_mtd_device(struct mtd_info *mtd);
int del_mtd_device(struct mtd_info *mtd);
```

For MTD programming in the user space, mtdchar.c is the interface of the character device, which can be utilized by the user to operate flash devices. The read() and write() system call can be used to read/write to/from flash. The IOCTL commands can be used to acquire flash device information, erase flash, read/write OOB of NAND, acquire the OOB layout and check the damaged blocks in NAND.

NOR flash driver

Linux uses a common driver for NOR flash which has a CFI or JEDEC interface. This driver is based on the functions in mtd_info(). It makes the NOR flash chip-level device driver simple. In fact, it only needs to define the memory map structure map_info and call the do_map_probe.

The relationship between the MTD, common NOR flash driver and map_info is shown in Figure 23.19.

The key of the NOR Flash driver is to define the map_info structure. It defines the NOR flash information such as base address, data width and size as well as read/write functions. It is the most important structure in the NOR flash driver. The NOR flash device driver can be seen as a process to probe the chip based on the definition of map_info. The source code in Linux kernel 2.6.31 is shown as below:

```
struct map_info {
      const char *name;
      unsigned long size;
      resource_size_t phys;
#define NO_XIP (-1UL)

 void __iomem *virt;
 void *cached;

 int bankwidth; /* in octets. This isn't necessarily the width
      of actual bus cycles - it's the repeat interval
      in bytes, before you are talking to the first chip again.
      */
#ifdef CONFIG_MTD_COMPLEX_MAPPINGS
 map_word (*read)(struct map_info *, unsigned long);
```

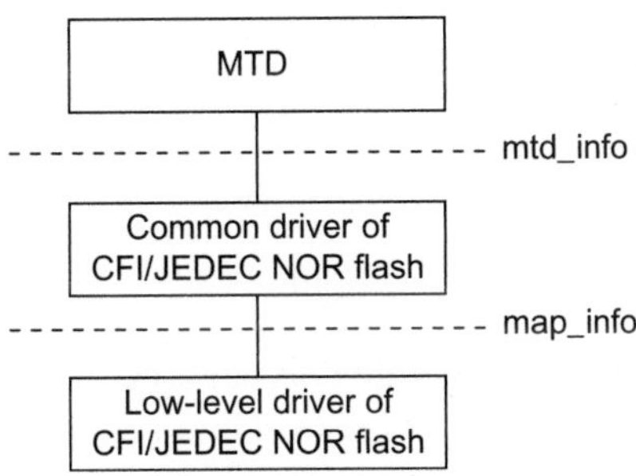

Figure 23.19:
Relationship between MTD, common NOR driver and map_info.

```
 void (*copy_from)(struct map_info *, void *, unsigned long, ssize_t);

    void (*write)(struct map_info *, const map_word, unsigned long);

    void (*copy_to)(struct map_info *, unsigned long, const void *, ssize_t);

    /* We can perhaps put in 'point' and 'unpoint' methods, if we really

    want to enable XIP for non-linear mappings. Not yet though. */

#endif

 /* It's possible for the map driver to use cached memory in its

   copy_from implementation (and _only_ with copy_from). However,

   when the chip driver knows some flash area has changed contents,

   it will signal it to the map driver through this routine to let

   the map driver invalidate the corresponding cache as needed.

   If there is no cache to care about this can be set to NULL. */

 void (*inval_cache)(struct map_info *, unsigned long, ssize_t);

 /* set_vpp() must handle being reentered - enable, enable, disable

   must leave it enabled. */

   void (*set_vpp)(struct map_info *, int);

   unsigned long pfow_base;

   unsigned long map_priv_1;

   unsigned long map_priv_2;

   void *fldrv_priv;

   struct mtd_chip_driver *fldrv;

};
```

The NOR flash driver in Linux is shown in Figure 23.20. The key steps are:

1. Define map_info and initialize its member. Assign name, size, bankwidth and phys based on the target board.
2. If flash needs partitions, then define the mtd_partition to store the flash partition information of the target board.

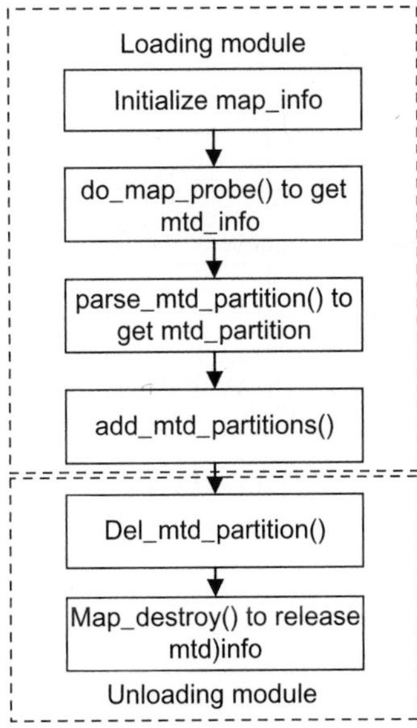

Figure 23.20:
NOR flash device driver.

3. Call the do_map_probe() based on the map_info and the checked interface type (CFI or JEDEC etc.) as parameters.
4. During the module initialization, register the device by calling add_mtd_device() with mtd_info as a parameter, or calling add_mtd-partitions() with mtd_info, mtd_partitions and partition number as parameters.
5. When unloading the flash module, call del_mtd_partitions() and map_destroy to delete the device or partition.

NAND flash device driver

Similar to that of NOR flash, Linux realizes the common NAND flash device driver in the MTD layer through the file drivers/mtd/nand/nand_base.c, as shown in Figure 23.21. Therefore, the NAND driver at chip level doesn't need to perform the read(), write(), read_oob () and write_oob() functions in mtd_info. The main task focuses on the nand_chip structure.

MTD uses the nand_chip structure to represent a NAND flash chip. The structure includes the low-level control mechanism such as address information, read/write method, ECC mode and hardware control of the NAND flash. The source code in Linux kernel 2.6.31 is shown below:

```
struct nand_chip {

    void __iomem *IO_ADDR_R;
```

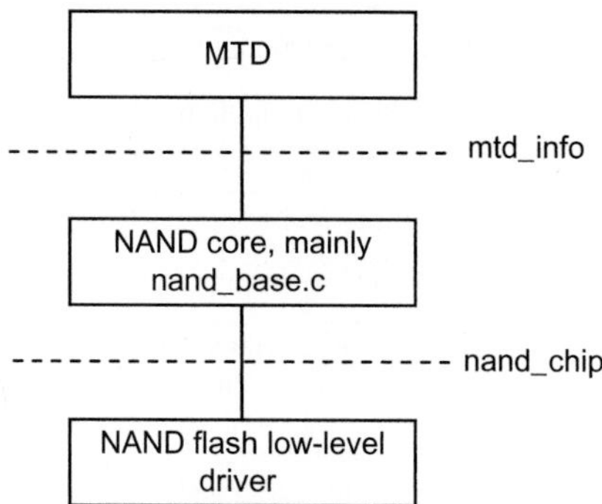

Figure 23.21:
NAND flash driver in Linux.

```
void __iomem *IO_ADDR_W;

uint8_t (*read_byte)(struct mtd_info *mtd);

u16 (*read_word)(struct mtd_info *mtd);

void (*write_buf)(struct mtd_info *mtd, const uint8_t *buf, int len);

void (*read_buf)(struct mtd_info *mtd, uint8_t *buf, int len);

int (*verify_buf)(struct mtd_info *mtd, const uint8_t *buf, int len);

void (*select_chip)(struct mtd_info *mtd, int chip);

int (*block_bad)(struct mtd_info *mtd, loff_t ofs, int getchip);

int (*block_markbad)(struct mtd_info *mtd, loff_t ofs);

void (*cmd_ctrl)(struct mtd_info *mtd, int dat,

    unsigned int ctrl);

int (*dev_ready)(struct mtd_info *mtd);

void (*cmdfunc)(struct mtd_info *mtd, unsigned command, int column, int page_addr);

int (*waitfunc)(struct mtd_info *mtd, struct nand_chip *this);

void (*erase_cmd)(struct mtd_info *mtd, int page);

int (*scan_bbt)(struct mtd_info *mtd);

int (*errstat)(struct mtd_info *mtd, struct nand_chip *this, int state, int status, int
page);
```

```
int (*write_page)(struct mtd_info *mtd, struct nand_chip *chip,
    const uint8_t *buf, int page, int cached, int raw);
int chip_delay;
unsigned int options;
int page_shift;
int phys_erase_shift;
int bbt_erase_shift;
int chip_shift;
int numchips;
uint64_t chipsize;
int pagemask;
int pagebuf;
int subpagesize;
uint8_t cellinfo;
int badblockpos;
nand_state_t state;
uint8_t *oob_poi;
struct nand_hw_control *controller;
struct nand_ecclayout *ecclayout;
struct nand_ecc_ctrl ecc;
struct nand_buffers *buffers;
struct nand_hw_control hwcontrol;
struct mtd_oob_ops ops;
uint8_t *bbt;
struct nand_bbt_descr *bbt_td;
```

```
    struct nand_bbt_descr *bbt_md;

    struct nand_bbt_descr *badblock_pattern;

    void *priv;
};
```

Because of the existence of MTD, the workload to develop a NAND flash driver is small. The process of a NAND flash driver in Linux is shown in Figure 23.22. The key steps are:

1. If flash needs partition, then define the mtd_partition array to store the flash partition information in the target board.
2. When loading the module, allocate the memory which is related to nand_chip. Intialize the hwcontro(), dev_ready(), calculate_ecc(), correct_data(), read_byte() and write_byte functions in nand_chip according to the specific NAND controller in the target board.

If using software ECC, then it is not necessary to allocate the calculate_ecc() and correct_data() because the NAND core layer includes the software algorithm for ECC. If using the hardware ECC of the NAND controller, then it is necessary to define the calculate_ecc() function and return the ECC byte from the hardware to the ecc_code parameter.

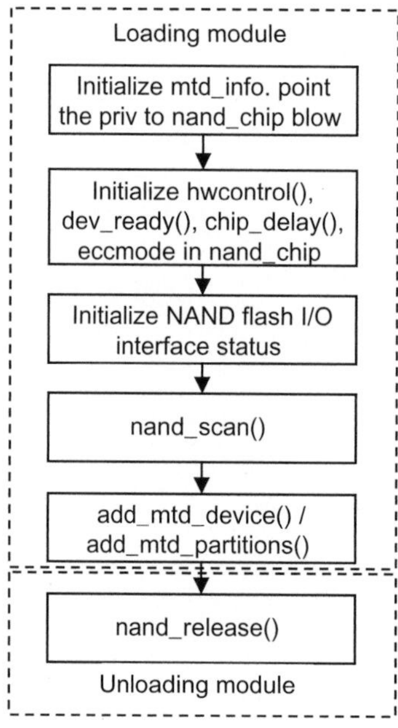

Figure 23.22:
NAND flash device driver.

3. Call nand_scan() with mtd_info as parameter to probe the existing of NAND flash. The nand-scan() is defined as:

```
int nand_scan(struct mtd_info *mtd, int maxchips);
```

4. The nand_scan() function will read the ID of the NAND chip and initialize mtd_info based on mtd→priv in the nand_chip.
5. If a partition is needed, then call add_mtd_partitions() with mtd_info and mtd_partition as parameters to add the partition information.
6. When unloading the NAND flash module, call the nand_release() function to release the device.

Flash translation layer and flash file system

Because it is impossible to write directly to the same address in the flash repeatedly (instead, it must erase the block before re-writing), the traditional file systems such as FAT16, FAT32, and Ext2 cannot be used directly in flash. In order to use these file systems, a translation layer must be applied to translate the logical block address to the physical address in the flash memory. In this way, the OS can use the flash as a common disk. This layer is called FTL (flash translation layer). FTL is used for NOR flash. For NAND flash, it's called NFTL (NAND FTL). The structure is shown in Figure 23.23.

The FTL/NFTL needs not only to achieve the mapping between the block device and the flash device, but also to store the sectors which simulate the block device to the different addresses in the flash and maintain the mapping between the sector and system memory. This will cause system inefficiency. Therefore, file systems which are specifically based on

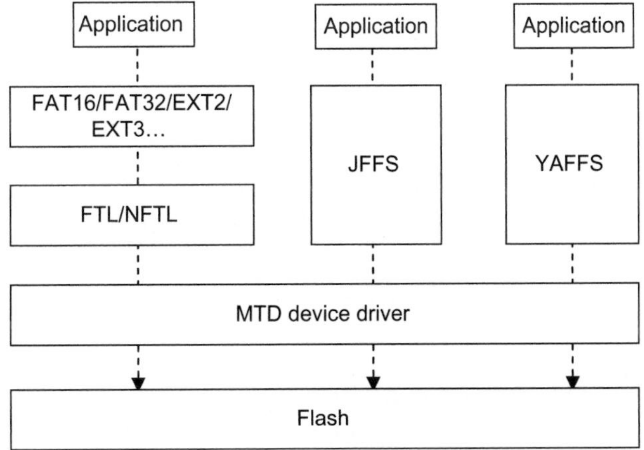

Figure 23.23:
FTL, NFTL, JFFS and YAFFS structure.

Flash device will be needed in order to improve the whole system performance. There are three popular file systems:

- JFFS/JFFS2: JFFS was originally developed by Axis Communication AB Inc. In 2001, Red Hat developed an updated version, JFFS2. JFFS2 is a log-structured file system. It sequentially stores the nodes which include data and meta-data. The log structure can enable the JFFS2 to update the flash in out-of-place mode, rather than the disk's in-place mode. It also provides a garbage collection mechanism. Meanwhile, because of the log structure, JFFS2 can still keep data integrity instead of data loss when encountering power failure. All these features make JFFS2 the most popular file system for flash. More information on JFFS2 is located at: http://www.linux-mtd.infradead.org/.
- CramFS: CramFS is a file system developed with the participation of Linus Torvalds. Its source code can be found at linux/fs/cramfs. CramFS is a kind of compressed read-only file system. When browsing the directory or reading files, CramFS will dynamically calculate the address of the uncompressed data and uncompress them to the system memory. The end user will not be aware of the difference between the CramFS and RamDisk. More information on CramFS is located at: http://sourceforge.net/projects/cramfs/.
- YAFFS/YAFFS2: YAFFS is an embedded file system specifically designed for NAND flash. Currently there are YAFFS and YAFFS2 versions. The main difference is that the YAFFS2 can support large NAND flash chips while the YAFFS can only support 512 KB page-size flash chips. YAFFS is somewhat similar to the JFFS/JFFS2 file system. However, JFFS/JFFS2 was originally designed for NOR flash so that applying JFFS/JFFS2 to NAND flash is not an optimal solution. Therefore, YAFFS/YAFFS2 was created for NAND flash. More information of YAFFS/YAFFS2 is located at: http://www.yaffs.net/.

SATA device driver

As introduced in section 1.4, SATA hard disks and SATA controllers are widely used in embedded systems. The SATA device driver structure for Linux is shown in Figure 23.24.

The Linux device driver directly controls the SATA controller. The driver directly registers the ATA host to SCSI middle level. Due to the difference between ATA protocol and SCSI protocol, LibATA is used to act as a translation layer between the SCSI middle layer and the ATA host. In this way, the SATA control model is merged into the SCSI device driver architecture seamlessly.

In the Linux kernel, the SATA driver-related files are located at /driver/ata. Taking the SATA controller in the Freescale P1022 silicon driver in Linux kernel 2.6.35 as an example, the SATA middle layer/LibATA includes the following files:

SATA –lib:
- libata-core.c
- libata-eh.c
- libata-scsi.c
- libata-transport.c

SATA-PMP:
- libata-pmp.c

AHCI:
- ahci.c
- libahci.c

The SATA device driver is:

FSL-SATA:
- sata_fsl.c (sata_fsl.o)

Performance improvement of storage systems

In the current embedded system, I/O performance plays a more and more important role in the whole system performance. In this section, storage performance optimization of SDHC and NAS is discussed as a case study.

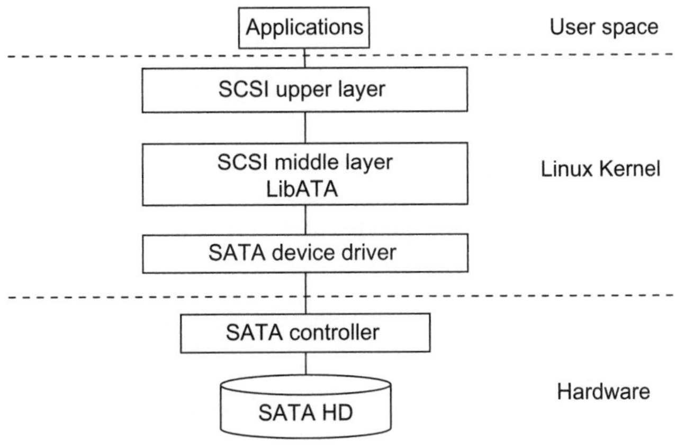

Figure 23.24:
SATA device driver in Linux.

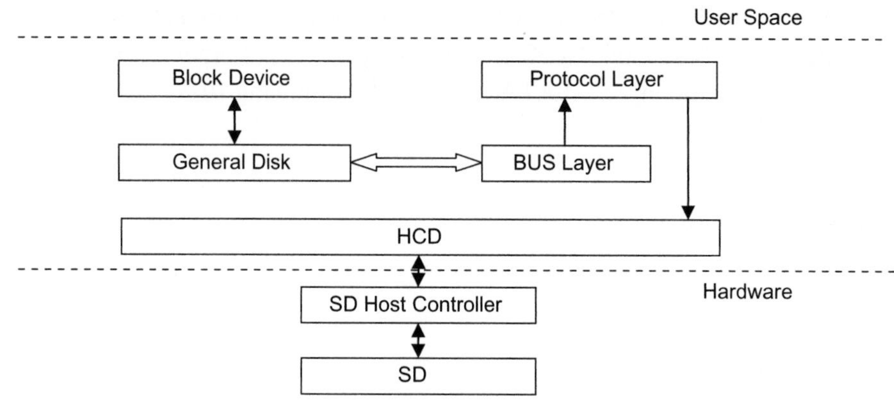

Figure 23.25:
SDHC driver in Linux.

Case study 1: performance optimization on SDHC

SD/SDHC Linux driver

As introduced in section 1.4, SD/SDHC is becoming a more and more popular storage device in embedded systems. The SDHC driver architecture for Linux is shown in Figure 23.25. It includes the modules:

- Protocol layer: implement command initializing, response parsing, state machine maintenance
- Bus layer: an abstract bridge between HCD and SD card
- Host controller driver: driver of host controller, provides an operation set to host controller, and abstract hardware
- Card driver: register to drive subsystem and export to user space.

Read/write performance optimization

Based on the analysis of the SDHC driver, the methods below can be applied to improve performance:

- Disk attribute: from the perspective of a disk device, write sequential data will get better performance.
- I/O scheduler: different strategies with the I/O scheduler will produce different performance.
- SDHC driver throughput: enlarged bounce buffer size will improve SDHC throughput. The faster that block requests return, the better performance will be.

- Memory management: the fewer dirty pages there are waiting to write back to the device directly, the better performance will be.
- SDHC clock: for hardware, the closer it is to maximum frequency, the better performance will be.

Freescale released patches based on each of the above methods and included them in its QorIQ SDK/BSP. For example, the maximum block number in a read/write operation depends on the bounce buffer size. A patch to increase the bounce buffer size is provided below:

```
From 32ec596713fc61640472b80c22e7ac85182beb92 Mon Sep 17 00:00:00 2001
From: Qiang Liu<b32616@freescale.com>
Date: Fri, 10 Dec 2010 15:59:52 +0800

Subject: [PATCH 029/281] SD/MMC: increase bounce buffer size to improve system
throughput

The maxmium block number in a process of read/write operation dependson bounce buffer size.
Signed-off-by: Qiang Liu<b32616@freescale.com>
–

 drivers/mmc/card/queue.c |   4 ++++
 1 files changed, 4 insertions(+), 0 deletions(-)

diff -git a/drivers/mmc/card/queue.c b/drivers/mmc/card/queue.c
index d6ded24..7d39fe5 100644
– a/drivers/mmc/card/queue.c
+++ b/drivers/mmc/card/queue.c
@@ -20,7 +20,11 @@

 #include<linux/mmc/host.h>
 #include "queue.h"

 + #ifdef CONFIG_OPTIMIZE_SD_PERFORMANCE
 + #define MMC_QUEUE_BOUNCESZ 262144
 + #else
 #define MMC_QUEUE_BOUNCESZ 65536
 + #endif

#define MMC_QUEUE_SUSPENDED (1 << 0)
-
1.7.5.1
```

All the other patches are included in the Linux SDK/BSP, which can be found at http://www.freescale.com/webapp/sps/site/prod_summary.jsp?code = SDKLINUX& parentCode = null&nodeId = 0152100332BF69 (Linux SDK v.1.0.1),

Test result

The Freescale P1022, which has an on-chip eSDHC controller, is selected as the test silicon and the P1022DS board is selected as a test platform. The P1022 is a dual-core SoC processor with two Power e500v2 cores. Its main frequency is 1066 MHz/533 MHz/800 MHz (Core/CCB/DDR). The SanDisk, SDHC 32G Class 10 card is used for performance testing. The application IOZone is used for benchmarking. The test result is shown in Figure 23.26. The original read and write speeds are 19.96 MB/s and 12.54 MB/s, respectively. Four methods are applied to improve the performance: delay timepoint of metadata writing, enlarge bounce buffer to 256 KB, implement dual-buffer request and adjust CCB frequency clock to 400 MB. Each method has an impact slightly, but as a whole the performance gets a significant improvement of 15% on read and 55% on write, to 22.98 MB/s read and 19.47 write.

Case study 2: performance optimization on NAS

With the development of cloud computing, NAS devices are gaining popularity. Freescale QorIQ processors are widely used in the NAS server industry. NAS performance is one important aspect that software needs to address. In this section, the software optimization of NAS is discussed with theoretical analysis and a test result.

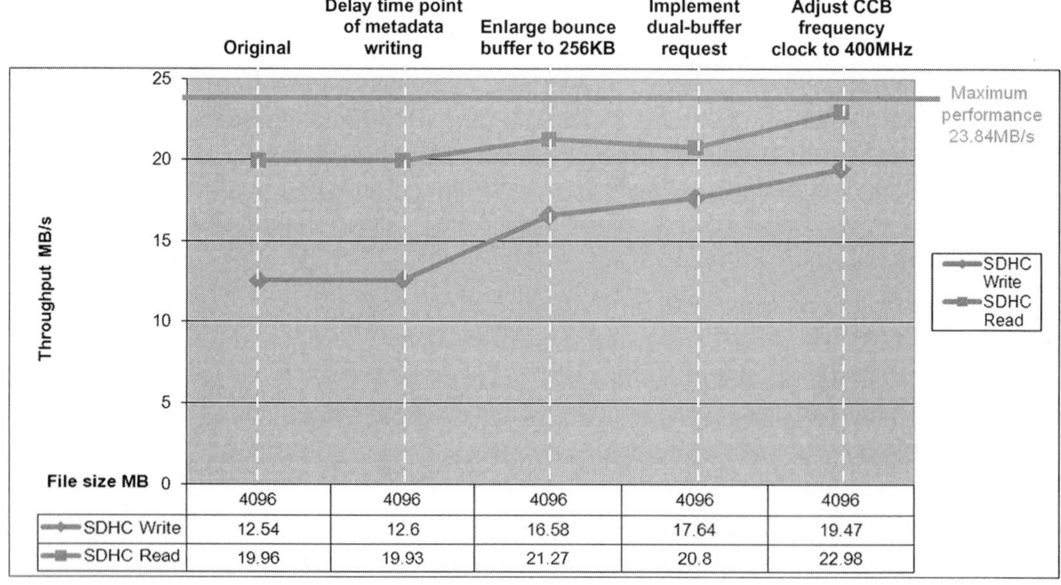

File size MB	4096	4096	4096	4096	4096
SDHC Write	12.54	12.6	16.58	17.64	19.47
SDHC Read	19.96	19.93	21.27	20.8	22.98

Figure 23.26:
SDHC performance optimization on P1022DS board.

Performance optimization method analysis

1. SMB protocol. SMB1.0 is a "chattiness" protocol rather than a streaming protocol. It has a block size that is limited to 64 KB. Latency has a significant impact on the performance of the SMB1.0 protocol. In SMB1.0, enable Oplock and Level2 oplocks will improve the performance. Oplock supports local caching of oplocked files on the client and and Level 2 oplocks allow files to be cached read-only on the client when multiple clients have opened the file. Pre-reply write is another way to optimize the SMB. It is helpful to parallelize NAS write on the server.
2. Sendpages. The Linux kernel's sendfile is based on a pipe. The pipe supports 16 pages. The kernel sends one page at a time. This impacts the overall performance of the sendfile. In the new sendfile mechanism, the kernel supports the sending of 16 pages at a time. This is shown in Figure 23.27. The patch for the standard Linux kernel 2.6.35 is described below:

```
From 59745d39c9ed864401b349af472655ce202e4c42 Mon Sep 17 00:00:00 2001
From: Jiajun Wu <b06378@freescale.com>
Date: Thu, 30 Sep 2010 22:34:38 +0800
Subject: [PATCH] kernel 2.6.35 Sendpages

Usually sendfile works in send single page mode. This patch removed the
page limitation of sendpage. Now we can send 16 pages each time at most.

Signed-off-by: Jiajun Wu <b06378@freescale.com>
```

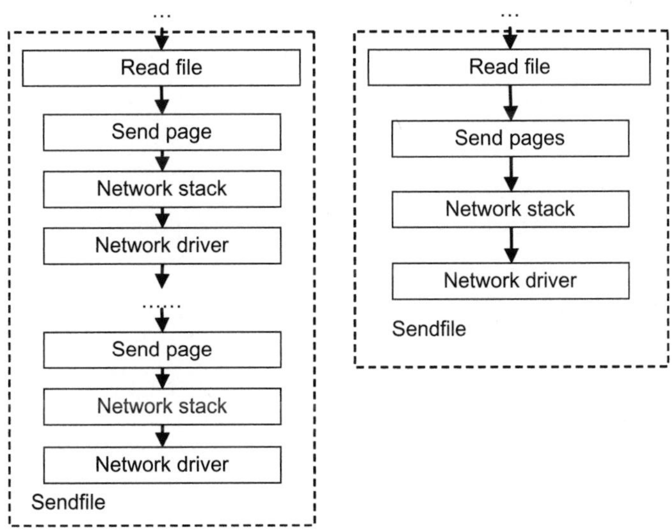

Figure 23.27:
Optimization of sendfile/sendpage.

```
-
 fs/Kconfig      | 6+++
 fs/splice.c     | 96++++++++++++++++++++++++++++++++++++++++
+++++++++-
 include/net/tcp.h| 1+
 net/ipv4/tcp.c   | 15++++++++
 net/socket.c    | 6+++
 5 files changed, 123 insertions(+), 1 deletions(-)

diff -git a/fs/Kconfig b/fs/Kconfig
index ad72122..904a06a 100644
— a/fs/Kconfig
+++ b/fs/Kconfig
@@ -62,6 +62,12 @@ config DELAY_ASYNC_READAHEAD
   This option enables delay async readahead in sendfile that impoves
   sendfile performance for large file.
+ config SEND_PAGES
+ bool "Enable sendpages"
+ default n
+ help
+   This option enables sendpages mode for sendfile.
+
 source "fs/notify/Kconfig"

 source "fs/quota/Kconfig"
diff -git a/fs/splice.c b/fs/splice.c
index cedeba3..b5c80a9 100644
— a/fs/splice.c
+++ b/fs/splice.c
@@ -33,6 +33,12 @@
 #include<linux/security.h>
 #include<linux/gfp.h>

+#ifdef CONFIG_SEND_PAGES
+#include<net/tcp.h>
+#include<linux/netdevice.h>
+#include<linux/socket.h>
+extern int is_sock_file(struct file *f);
+#endif /*CONFIG_SEND_PAGES*/
 /*
  * Attempt to steal a page from a pipe buffer. This should perhaps go into
  * a vm helper function, it's already simplified quite a bit by the
```

```
@@ -690,6 +696,78 @@ err:
 }
 EXPORT_SYMBOL(default_file_splice_read);
+#ifdef CONFIG_SEND_PAGES
+static int pipe_to_sendpages(struct pipe_inode_info *pipe,
+      struct pipe_buffer *buf, struct splice_desc *sd)
+{
+ struct file *file = sd->u.file;
+ int ret, more;
+ int page_index = 0;
+ unsigned int tlen, len, offset;
+ unsigned int curbuf = pipe->curbuf;
+ struct page *pages[PIPE_DEF_BUFFERS];
+ int nrbuf = pipe->nrbufs;
+ int flags;
+ struct socket *sock = file->private_data;
+
+ sd->len = sd->total_len;
+ tlen = 0;
+ offset = buf->offset;
+
+ while (nrbuf) {
+       buf = pipe->bufs + curbuf;
+
+       ret = buf->ops->confirm(pipe, buf);
+       if (ret)
+       break;
+
+       pages[page_index] = buf->page;
+       page_index++;
+       len = (buf->len < sd->len) ? buf->len : sd->len;
+       buf->offset += len;
+       buf->len -= len;
+
+       sd->num_spliced += len;
+       sd->len -= len;
+       sd->pos += len;
+       sd->total_len -= len;
+       tlen += len;
+
```

```
+       if (!buf->len) {
+       curbuf = (curbuf + 1) & (PIPE_DEF_BUFFERS - 1);
+       nrbuf-;
+   }
+   if (!sd->total_len)
+    break;
+ }
+
+ more = (sd->flags & SPLICE_F_MORE) || sd->len < sd->total_len;
+ flags = !(file->f_flags & O_NONBLOCK) ? 0 : MSG_DONTWAIT;
+ if (more)
+       flags |= MSG_MORE;
+
+ len = tcp_sendpages(sock, pages, offset, tlen, flags);
+

+ if (!ret)
+  ret = len;
+
+ while (page_index) {
+       page_index-;
+       buf = pipe->bufs + pipe->curbuf;
+       if (!buf->len) {
+           buf->ops->release(pipe, buf);
+           buf->ops = NULL;
+           pipe->curbuf = (pipe->curbuf + 1) & (PIPE_DEF_BUFFERS - 1);
+           pipe->nrbufs-;
+           if (pipe->inode)
+               sd->need_wakeup = true;
+       }
+ }
+
+ return ret;
+ }
+ #endif/*CONFIG_SEND_PAGES*/
+
 /*
  * Send 'sd->len' bytes to socket from 'sd->file' at position 'sd->pos'
  * using sendpage(). Return the number of bytes sent.
@@ -700,7 +778,17 @@ static int pipe_to_sendpage(struct pipe_inode_info *pipe,
```

```
 struct file *file = sd->u.file;
 loff_t pos = sd->pos;
 int ret, more;
-
+#ifdef CONFIG_SEND_PAGES
+ struct socket *sock = file->private_data;
+
+ if (is_sock_file(file) &&
+  sock->ops->sendpage == tcp_sendpage){
+  struct sock *sk = sock->sk;
+  if ((sk->sk_route_caps & NETIF_F_SG) &&
+   (sk->sk_route_caps & NETIF_F_ALL_CSUM))
+   return pipe_to_sendpages(pipe, buf, sd);
+ }
+#endif
 ret = buf->ops->confirm(pipe, buf);
 if (!ret) {
  more = (sd->flags & SPLICE_F_MORE) || sd->len < sd->total_len;
@@ -823,6 +911,12 @@ int splice_from_pipe_feed(struct pipe_inode_info *pipe, struct
splice_desc *sd,
   sd->len = sd->total_len;
  ret = actor(pipe, buf, sd);
+#ifdef CONFIG_SEND_PAGES
+ if (!sd->total_len)
+  return 0;
+ if (!pipe->nrbufs)
+  break;
+#endif /*CONFIG_SEND_PAGES*/
  if (ret <= 0) {
   if (ret == -ENODATA)
    ret = 0;
diff -git a/include/net/tcp.h b/include/net/tcp.h
index a144914..c004e0c 100644
- a/include/net/tcp.h
+++ b/include/net/tcp.h
@@ -309,6 +309,7 @@ extern int     tcp_v4_tw_remember_stamp(struct
inet_timewait_sock *tw);
 extern int  tcp_sendmsg(struct kiocb *iocb, struct socket *sock,
     struct msghdr *msg, size_t size);
```

```
    extern ssize_t   tcp_sendpage(struct socket *sock, struct page *page, int offset,
size_t size, int flags);
   +extern ssize_t   tcp_sendpages(struct socket *sock, struct page **pages, int offset,
size_t size, int flags);
    extern int   tcp_ioctl(struct sock *sk,
         int cmd,
   diff -git a/net/ipv4/tcp.c b/net/ipv4/tcp.c
   index 65afeae..cd23eab 100644
   – a/net/ipv4/tcp.c
   +++ b/net/ipv4/tcp.c
   @@ -875,6 +875,20 @@ ssize_t tcp_sendpage(struct socket *sock, struct page *page, int
offset,
     return res;
    }
   +ssize_t tcp_sendpages(struct socket *sock, struct page **pages, int offset,
   +      size_t size, int flags)
   +{
   + ssize_t res;
   + struct sock *sk = sock->sk;
   +
   + lock_sock(sk);
   + TCP_CHECK_TIMER(sk);
   + res = do_tcp_sendpages(sk, pages, offset, size, flags);
   + TCP_CHECK_TIMER(sk);
   + release_sock(sk);
   + return res;
   +}
   +
    #define TCP_PAGE(sk) (sk->sk_sndmsg_page)
    #define TCP_OFF(sk) (sk->sk_sndmsg_off)
   @@ -3309,5 +3323,6 @@ EXPORT_SYMBOL(tcp_recvmsg);
    EXPORT_SYMBOL(tcp_sendmsg);
    EXPORT_SYMBOL(tcp_splice_read);
    EXPORT_SYMBOL(tcp_sendpage);
   +EXPORT_SYMBOL(tcp_sendpages);
    EXPORT_SYMBOL(tcp_setsockopt);
    EXPORT_SYMBOL(tcp_shutdown);
   diff -git a/net/socket.c b/net/socket.c
   index 367d547..3c2cfad 100644
   – a/net/socket.c
```

```
+++ b/net/socket.c
@@ -3101,6 +3101,12 @@ int kernel_sock_shutdown(struct socket *sock, enum
sock_shutdown_cmd how)
  return sock->ops->shutdown(sock, how);
 }
+int is_sock_file(struct file *f)
+{
+ return (f->f_op == &socket_file_ops) ? 1 : 0;
+}
+EXPORT_SYMBOL(is_sock_file);
+
 EXPORT_SYMBOL(sock_create);
 EXPORT_SYMBOL(sock_create_kern);
 EXPORT_SYMBOL(sock_create_lite);
-
1.5.6.5
```

This patch is also included in Freescale QorIQ Linux SDK v.1.0.1.

3. Other methods include: software TSO (TCP segmentation offload), enhanced SKB recycling, jumbo frame and client tuning, etc. All the patches are included in Freescale QorIQ Linux SDK v.1.0.1 which can be found at: http://www.freescale.com/webapp/sps/site/prod_summary.jsp?code = SDKLINUX&parentCode = null&nodeId = 0152100332BF69.

Test result

Freescale P2020 is selected as the test silicon and the P2020DS board is selected as the NAS server. The P2020 is a dual-core SoC processor with two Power e500v2 cores. Its running frequency is 1200 MHz/600 MHz/800 MHz (Core/CCB/DDR). The Dell T3500 is selected as a NAS client. The system test architecture is shown in Figure 23.28.

For a single SATA drive and RAID5, the NAS performance is shown in Figure 23.29 and Figure 23.30.

From the two figures in the result, we can see that NAS optimization makes the P2020DS achieve a good NAS performance.

Summary

This chapter first introduces the concept of I/O devices and I/O controllers. Then it focuses on I/O programming. It introduces the basic I/O control modes, including polling mode, interrupt control mode, DMA control mode and channel control mode. The I/O software goals include device independence, uniform naming, exception handling and synchronous

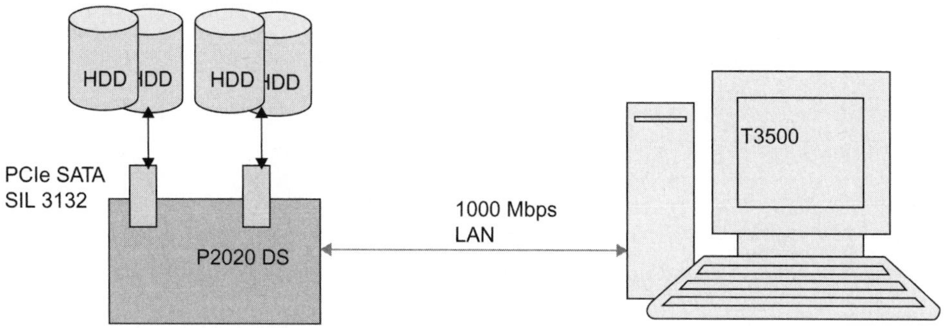

Figure 23.28:
NAS performance test architecture.

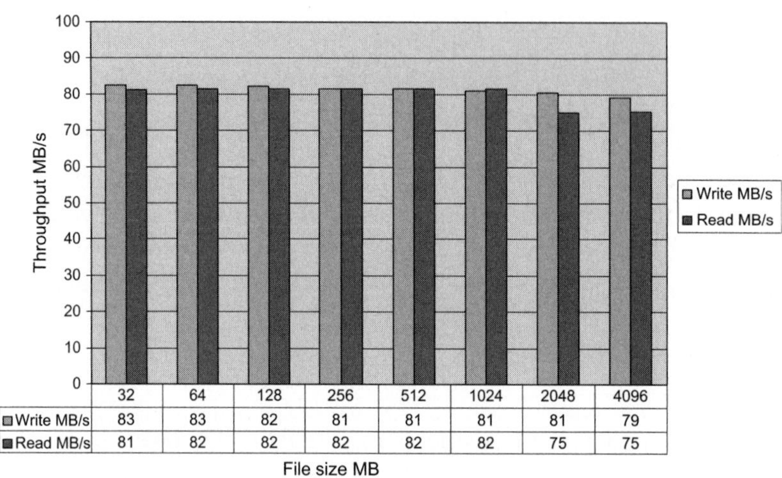

	32	64	128	256	512	1024	2048	4096
Write MB/s	83	83	82	81	81	81	81	79
Read MB/s	81	82	82	82	82	82	75	75

Figure 23.29:
P2020DS single-drive NAS result.

blocking and asynchronous transfer. The I/O software layer is the focus of I/O programming, which includes interrupt service routines, device drivers, device-independent I/O software and user-level I/O software. As a case study, the Linux driver is described in detail in the chapter.

Then the chapter introduces storage programming, including I/O for block devices, the gendisk structure, block I/O and block device registration and un-registration. Flash devices (NOR and NAND) and SATA are used as examples on how to develop Linux device drivers for storage devices. At the end, two cases with the Freescale Linux SDK/BSP are studied to illustrate how to optimize performance on SDHC devices and NAS.

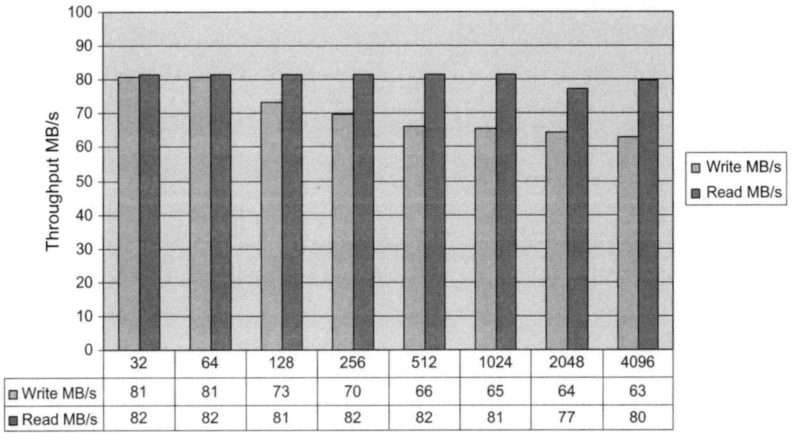

	32	64	128	256	512	1024	2048	4096
Write MB/s	81	81	73	70	66	65	64	63
Read MB/s	82	82	81	82	82	81	77	80

Figure 23.30:
P2020DS RAID5 NAS result.

Bibliography

[1] Available from: http://www.kernel.org/.
[2] Available from: http://en.wikipedia.org/wiki/Flash_memory.
[3] Available from: http://en.wikipedia.org/wiki/Secure_Digital.
[4] Available from: http://en.wikipedia.org/wiki/Hard_disk_drive.
[5] Available from: http://en.wikipedia.org/wiki/SSD.
[6] Available from: http://zh.wikipedia.org/wiki/%E7%A1%AC%E7%9B%98.
[7] Available from: http://en.wikipedia.org/wiki/Network-attached_storage.
[8] Available from: http://www.linux-mtd.infradead.org/.
[9] Available from: http://sourceforge.net/projects/cramfs/.
[10] Available from: http://www.yaffs.net/.
[11] Available from: http://www.freescale.com/webapp/sps/site/prod_summary.jsp?code = SDKLINUXDPAA.
[12] Available from: http://www.freescale.com/webapp/sps/site/prod_summary.jsp?code = SDKLINUX&parentCode = null&nodeId = 0152100332BF69.
[13] QorIQ™ P1022 Communications Processor Reference Manual. http://www.freescale.com/webapp/sps/site/prod_summary.jsp?code = P1022&nodeId = 018rH325E4DE8AA83D&fpsp = 1&tab = Documentation_Tab.
[14] Jianwei Li, et al., Practical Operating System Tutorial, Tsinghua University Press, 2011.
[15] Yaoxue Zhang, et al., Computer Operating System Tutorial, third ed., Tsinghua University Press, 2006.
[16] A.S. Tanenbaum, Modern Operating Systems, third ed., China Machine Press, 2009.
[17] Baohua Song, Linux Device Driver Development Details, Posts & Telecom Press, 2008.

CHAPTER 24

Embedded Software for Networking Applications

Srinivasa Addepalli

Chapter Outline

Software Engineering for Embedded Systems.
DOI: http://dx.doi.org/10.1016/B978-0-12-415917-4.00024-4
© 2013 Elsevier Inc. All rights reserved.

Introduction

Many network appliances are embedded and purpose-built devices. Appliance vendors are constantly adding multiple functions in devices. These devices support a large number of protocols to enable LANs (local area networks), WANs (wide area networks) and diverse networks. Interconnectivity of networks among multiple organizations and enablement of access to internal resources from external networks such as the Internet are forcing network devices to be resilient to attacks targeted at them as well as at resources in internal networks. Due to these factors, embedded software in network devices is no longer simple and its complexity is reaching the levels of enterprise server application programs.

To mitigate the complexity of device implementations, embedded software developers are increasingly dependent on general-purpose operating systems such as Linux and NetBSD. Operating systems provide multiple processing contexts, concurrent programming facilities, and various abstractions that hide hardware IO devices and accelerators from applications. These facilities are being used by programmers to develop embedded software faster and to maintain software easily.

Networks in organizations have migrated from 10 Mbps Ethernet hubs to 100 Mbps.Now even 1 Gbps Ethernet networks are common. Lately, 10 Gbps Ethernet networks have been introduced in organizations. In the next few years, one will probably see 40 Gbps and 100 Gbps networks in use. Embedded network devices are expected to handle these rates in the future. Network device vendors can no longer meet high data traffic rates with single-core or few-core processors. Instead, they require multicore with many core processors. However, multicore programming is not simple and getting scalable performance is a very big challenge that developers face.

This chapter will discuss design and programming considerations in the development of network applications, with a focus on multicore programming. First, it provides details on the system architecture of devices. Second, it gives an overview of multicore SoCs. Third, it introduces some popular network programming models and the structure of packet-processing applications. Finally, it discusses Linux operating system features that help in network programming.

Even though this chapter keeps network infrastructure devices in mind while explaining network programming concepts, these concepts are equally valid for any devices that need to interact with the external world.

System architecture of network devices

There are many types of network devices one can find in homes, offices and data center networks. Layer 2 switch devices and to some extent layer 3 switch devices are frequently seen in many networks. These devices provide high-speed connectivity among end stations in enterprises, schools, campuses and data centers. Data center networks have many other devices such as load-balancer devices to balance the traffic across multiple servers in server farms. There are also network security devices such as firewalls, IP security devices, and intrusion prevention and detection devices to protect servers from attacks originating from external networks. All of these devices are called network infrastructure devices and most of them are embedded and purpose-built.

Before going into the details of the system architecture of network devices, it is important to refresh some networking concepts. Networking and data communication courses in colleges and universities teach the open systems interconnection (OSI) model in great detail. The Internet Protocol Suite, commonly known as TCP/IP, is a set of protocols that run the Internet. TCP/IP stack protocols implement the first four layers of the OSI model – the physical layer, the data link layer, network layers and the transport layer. The Transmission Control Protocol of the TCP/IP suite also implements a partial session layer, the fifth layer of the OSI model, in terms of connection (session) management between local and remote machines. The Internet Protocol Suite does not implement the session checkpoint and recovery features of the session layer of the OSI model. The presentation and application layers of the OSI model are not exactly mapped into any protocol in the Internet Protocol Suite and are left to applications running on the TCP/IP stack.

The Ethernet protocol is the most prominent physical and data link layer protocol in the Internet Protocol Suite. Internet Protocol v4 (IPv4) and Internet Protocol v6 (IPv6) are network layer protocols. The Transmission Control Protocol (TCP), User Datagram Protocol (UDP), and Stream Control Transmission Protocol (SCTP) are some of the common transport layer protocols.

All network devices work at different layers of the Internet Protocol suite. L2 switch devices work at the data link layer, L3 switch devices work at the network layer, load balancer and security devices typically tend to work at the transport and session layers.

Though the functionality in these devices is different as they serve different purposes, the basic system-level architecture of network devices tends to be same. Hence, programming methods and techniques used to develop network devices tend to be similar in nature. We believe that understanding the system-level architecture helps developers debug and maintain software efficiently. Hence the rest of this section provides some details of high-level software blocks in network devices.

Data, control, service and management planes

Figure 24.1 shows an abstract functional view that many network devices conform to, which includes data, control, service and management planes.

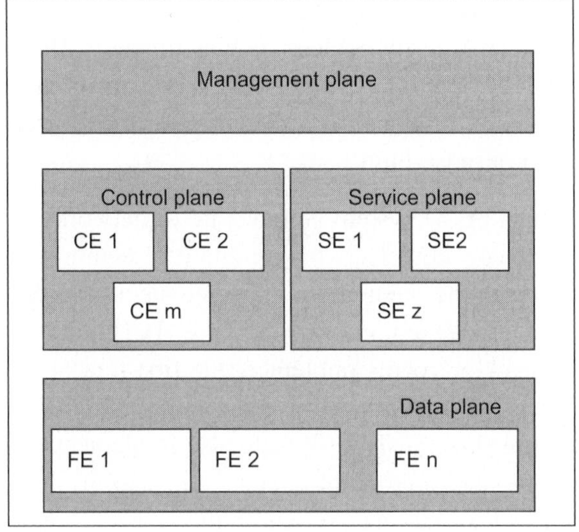

Figure 24.1:
System architecture of network devices.

The data plane, also called the "data path", is a set of forwarding engines (FE) with each forwarding engine implementing a function such as L3 routing, IPsec, firewall, etc. The data plane is the first software component that receives packets from networks using an IO device such as Ethernet. Each FE is programmed with a set of flow contexts by control and service planes. Flow context is a memory block which contains information on actions that are to be taken on the packets, corresponding to a flow.

Any FE, upon receiving a packet, first extracts the packet fields, searches for the matching flow context and then works on the packet as per the actions in the flow context. Actions include modification of the packet, information about the next destination of the packet, updating statistics counters in the flow context, etc. Data paths are normally updated with flow contexts by control and service planes. Two different ways in which flow contexts are updated by control and service planes:

- Reactive updates: control and service plane software engines update flow contexts on an on-demand basis as part of exception packet processing. When an FE does not find a matching flow context as part of the packet processing, it sends the packet to the service plane for further processing. These packets are called exception packets. An appropriate service plane engine (SE), with the help of configuration information or information that is negotiated among devices using control plane protocols, determines the type of actions required and creates a flow context in the right FE.
- Proactive updates: unlike reactive updates, proactive updates are created in data-plane forwarding engines by service and control planes even before packets hit the device.

Reactive updates are normally associated with inactivity timers. A flow context is considered inactive if there are no incoming packets matching the flow for a configured amount of time. The data plane normally removes inactive flows to make room for new flow contexts. Flow contexts of some forwarding engines are associated with a specific lifetime too. Flow contexts having a specific lifetime get deleted by the data plane after living for the time programmed in the context irrespective of packet activity.

Table 24.1 gives the flow context information of some popular forwarding engines.

Table 24.1: Flow contexts of some popular forwarding engines.

Forwarding Engine	Key Fields to Find the Matching Flow Context	Important Action Information
L2 bridge/switch	Destination MAC address	Outbound port
L3 router	Destination IP address and optionally source IP address and type of service (ToS)	Outbound interface, gateway IP address, path MTU
L4 forwarding (load balancer, firewall, NAT etc.)	Source IP address, destination IP address, IP protocol. In the case of TCP and UDP protocols source port and destination port are also used as key fields	NAT information on source IP, destination IP, source port, destination port, TCP sequence number, IP ID etc.
IPsec	Inbound tunnel (flow context) is identified by destination IP address and SPI (Security Protocol Index)	Key information to decrypt and check the integrity of the packet

The service plane contains multiple service engines (SE). Service engines typically process exception packets coming from forwarding engines, enforce configured policies and update flow contexts in forwarding engines. For example, the firewall service engine enforces ACLs (access control lists) created via management engines upon receiving exception packets. Based on the actions defined in the ACL matching rule, either a flow context is added in the data plane or the packet is dropped.

The control plane also contains multiple engines called control engines (CEs). CEs typically implement protocols which interact with peer network devices. The result of control plane protocols is either directly or indirectly used to create flow contexts in forwarding engines. In the case of routers, results of OSPF, BGP, RIP, and other routing control plane protocols are used to create routing flow contexts in the routing forwarding engine. In the case of IPsec devices, the result of the Internet Key Exchange (IKE) control plane protocol is used to create the IPsec tunnel contexts in the Ipsec forwarding engine.

The management plane provides human interaction to the network device functionality. Typical network devices provide multiple management engines, including the command line interface (CLI), web-based GUIs, SNMP and Netconf.

The performance of network devices is rated in two aspects – throughput of devices and creation rate of flow contexts. Forwarding engine implementation determines the throughput and service plane implementation determines the context creation rate. With increasing traffic in networks and complexity of forwarding engines, throughput and flow creation rate requirements are going up. Single-core processors are no longer able to provide the scale that is required. Network equipment vendors are increasingly looking at multicore processors and SoCs (system-on-chips) to increase the performance of devices. Thus, embedded system development increasingly requires multicore programming. Before going into the details of programming models and programming techniques on multicore processors to implement data and service planes, it is important to have the background on multicore SoCs. The next section introduces multicore SoCs and the capabilities of these SoCs that help efficient programming.

Multicore SoCs for networking

The multicore system-on-chip (SoC), as shown in Figure 24.2, consists of multiple general-purpose cores with multiple peripheral controllers. Multicore SoCs reduce the cost of network devices as they integrate cores, IO devices (such as Ethernet controllers) and hardware accelerators (such as crypto, pattern matching and compression accelerators) in a single die. With multicore SoCs, very few external chips, such as Ethernet phys, DDR, and flash memory, are required in order to build device hardware boards.

Cores

Multicore SoCs have more than one general-purpose core. MIPS, Power and ARM based multicore SoCs are common in the market. Many general-purpose operating systems such

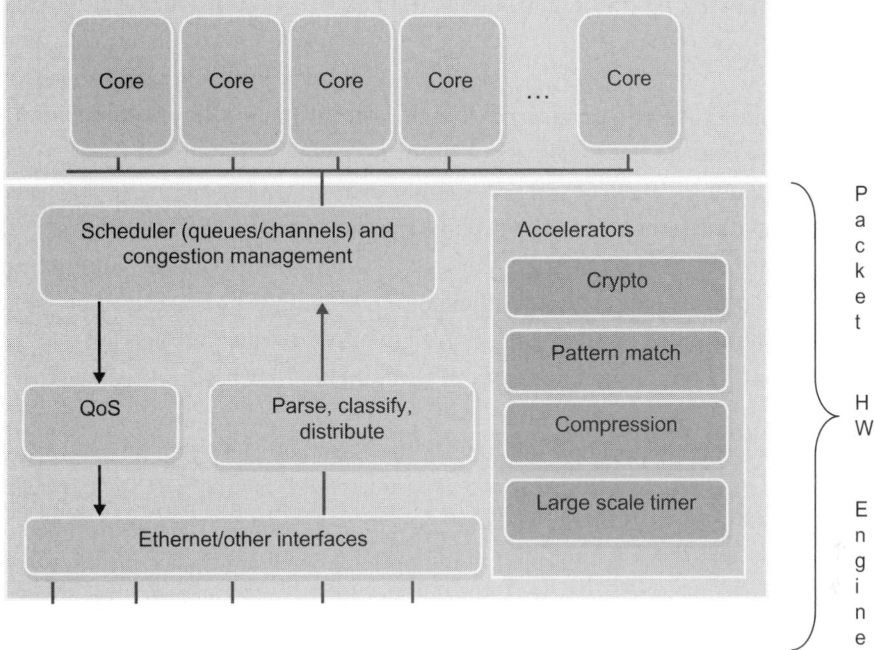

Figure 24.2:
Multicore SoC architecture.

as Linux and NetBSD are available on multicore SoCs. Hence, network software developers can develop networking applications on these cores using general-purpose operating system programming concepts.

Packet engine hardware (PEH) block

The packet engine is an essential part of multicore SoCs. The PEH works on top of the Ethernet and interface ports. Its main purpose is to distribute packets across multiple cores, ensuring that the multiple cores can be utilized for packet processing. Since it is a critical part in utilizing multiple cores, this section details the capabilities of this block and the facilities it provides to software.

The PEH provides different schemes to distribute packets across cores. To address the different requirements of networking applications, PEHs in Multicore SoCs provide various options for software to control packet distribution. To handle the various types of flow contexts of different network devices, PEHs provide programmability to distribute the packets based on a set of header fields. For example, a PEH can be programmed to do 5-tuple (source IP address, destination IP address, IP protocol, source port and destination port) based packet distribution.

PEHs have the following hardware sub-blocks to enable packet distribution.

Parser

The parser hardware block parses incoming packets from the Ethernet block and extracts header field values. Parsers have the capability of checking the integrity of the packets – Ethernet CRC validation, IP checksum validation, even transport layer checksum validation and packet length validations. If a validation of the packet fails, the parser drops the packet. If all validations are successful, then the parser block proceeds to extract fields from the packet. Parser sub-blocks also have intelligence to reassemble IP fragments to the full IP packet. Note that non-initial IP fragments don't contain the transport header. The parser, to get hold of transport header fields, reassembles fragments first before it parses the transport header.

Distribution

The distribution hardware sub-block uses the extracted values of fields to decide on a queue to place the packet. The distribution hardware applies a hash algorithm on the extracted fields' values and uses the hash result to choose one of the queues. CRC-32 and CRC-64 are popular algorithms used by the PEH for calculating hash values. Since all packets belonging to a flow would result in the same hash value, all packets in the flow would get placed in the same queue. To facilitate the above, the distribution hardware block provides facilities for software to program a set of queues and the number of bits from the hash result.

Classification

The classification hardware block is also used to place incoming packets in queues. This block provides flexibility for software to assign specific queues to specific flows. As noted before, the distribution hardware block selects the queues based on the hash result on the header fields' values, but does not select queues on specific values of header fields. The classification hardware block selects the queues based on specific values of fields. As an example, software can program the classification block to place web GUI (TCP destination port 80) traffic in a specific queue with different (higher) priority than the queues used by hash-based distribution. This example configuration would ensure that traffic to port 80 is given higher priority than other traffic by the PEH scheduler.

Scheduler, queues and channels

Queues and channels are mechanisms used to transfer packets between the PEH and cores. As discussed above, queues are used by distribution and classification hardware blocks to place incoming packets. Cores place packets in queues for sending them out or to access hardware acceleration engines. Queues can also be associated with priority. The distribution hardware can be programmed to use priority fields in the packet to use different queues in addition to the hash result. The scheduler block schedules the packets from the queues as per priority. When a core asks for new work (packet) from the PEH, the scheduler in the PEH considers the priority of queues first and then uses a round-robin or weighted round-robin selection mechanism to select a queue from equal-priority queues. Once the queue is selected, then the packet/work from that queue is given to the requesting core.

Channels in the PEHs provide a mechanism to bundle a set of queues. They are typically used if multiple networking software applications require different types of packets. Consider the case in which an L2 switch application processes packets belonging to L2 flows coming from some Ethernet ports and an L4 load balancer processes packets belonging to L4 flows coming from different Ethernet ports. L2 flows are typically identified based on the "destination MAC address" field of the Ethernet header, whereas L4 flows are identified based on header fields (5-tuple) from IP and transport headers. Software, in this case, programs the parser to identify the flows using the destination MAC address field of packets received on Ethernet ports dedicated to the L2 switch application. Software also programs the parser to identify the flows using 5-tuples of the packets coming from Ethernet ports associated with the L4 load balancer. Software also programs distribution hardware with two sets of queues – one set of queues is used to place the packets corresponding to L2 flows and another set of queues is used to place the packets of L4 flows. Then software connects each parser configuration with a set of queues.

The PEH, upon receiving an incoming packet, selects the parser configuration based on the incoming Ethernet port, extracts relevant fields, calculates a hash on the fields' values, identifies the associated queue-set, selects the queue based on the hash result and places the packet in the queue.

In the above example, two channels are associated with two sets of queues. Cores when they need a new packet (work) can request the packet from one or more channels. For example, if some cores are dedicated to the L2 switch application, then these cores would request work on a channel associated with L2 flows. If some cores are programmed to handle both L2 and L4 work, then these cores request packets from both channels.

PEHs support many channels to enable development of multiple networking applications on a device. Schedulers in the PEHs are capable of not only selecting a queue from the set of queues as part of the de-queue operation by cores, but are also capable of applying a scheduling algorithm to select a channel.

Essentially, PEHs provide flexibility for software to bundle the packets in flows as required by applications and distribute the packets of these flows across multiple cores via queues and channels.

Accelerators

PEHs also include several acceleration blocks to take the load away from the cores on routine and computationally intensive algorithmic tasks. There are three types of acceleration engines in PEHs – look-aside accelerators, ingress accelerators, and egress accelerators.

Look-aside accelerators are the ones used by the software running in cores while processing the packets. Cryptography, pattern matching, compression/decompression, de-duplication and timer management are some examples of acceleration units that are normally included in multicore SoCs.

Ingress acceleration is done by PEHs on the incoming packets before they are handed over to software running on the cores, in order to save core cycles in certain tasks. Parsing of headers and making extracted values of header fields available along with the packets to software is one type of ingress acceleration. Similar to this, some other popular ingress accelerations in PEHs include packet header integrity checks, reassembly of IP fragments into full IP packets, aggregation of consecutive TCP segments and de-tunneling.

Egress acceleration is done by PEMs before transmitting packets to the interfaces. Cores, after processing the packets, send the packets to the PEH. The PEH then applies actions before sending them out. Quality of service shaping, link aggregation and tunneling are some of the acceleration functions that are part of PEHs.

Buffer manager

This is also called the "free pool manager" in the networking industry. Its main purpose is to maintain free buffer pools. It provides services such as "allocate" and "release". The "allocate" operation gets a free buffer from the given buffer pool and the "release" operation releases the buffer to the pool. Buffer pools are used by the PEH as well as cores. The PEH uses these pools to allocate buffers to store incoming packets. It frees the buffers to the pools after transmitting the packets out. Multicore SoCs provide a large number of buffer pools for software usage too. Software can avoid expensive memory management in software and can take advantage of these pools.

Network programming models

Network packet-processing applications are normally implemented in two programming models – the pipeline programming model and the run-to-completion programming model.

Pipeline programming model

In the pipeline programming model, each function is executed on a core with functions arranged in pipeline fashion. If it is a single-function device, then the function is divided into sub-functions. Whatever the case may be, a core does the assigned job on packets before handing them over to next function/sub-function.

As an example, consider an embedded network device implementing three functions (A, B and C). Each function is assigned to one core each. As shown in Figure 24.3, Function A receives the packet first, processes the packet, and then the queues the packet to Function B. Function B does its processing and queues the packet to Function C. Function C, after processing the packet, sends it out by queuing the packet to the PEH.

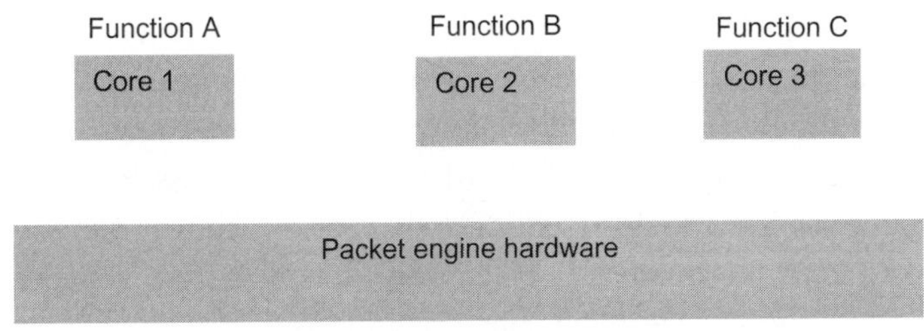

Figure 24.3:
Pipeline programming model.

At times, there may be more cores than the functions. Functions would need to get divided into multiple sub-functions to take advantage of all cores.

The pipeline model is commonly used by developers while migrating single-core programs to multicore SoCs in order to avoid concurrency issues associated with multicore programming.

Though on the surface it looks simpler, pipeline programming has several complexities:

- All functions may not take the same number of core cycles to process the packet. Due to this, the performance of the device is limited to throughput of the most demanding function and thus resulting in underutilization of cores that run other functions. In the above example, if A consumes 2000 core cycles, B consumes 1000 core cycles and C consumes 500 core cycles per packet, then the cores assigned to B and C are underutilized. The core running Function B is utilized only 50% and the core running Function C is utilized only 25%.
- Pipelining leads to higher latency of packets. In the above example, cores implementing Function A and Function B queue the packets to Function B and Function C respectively after doing their jobs. Enque and Deque operations associated with the

queue management itself use up precious core cycles and also contribute to the latency of the packets.

- If there are fewer functions than the cores, some functions are to be broken into multiple sub-functions. This task may not be simple.

Run-to-completion programming

In this programming model, every core processes all functions needed on the packets. Essentially, the cores run all the functions. All cores receive the packets, process the packets and send them out as shown in Figure 24.4. In this model, multiple cores receive the packets from the PEH. This programming model requires PEHs to provide packets from different flows to different cores. As discussed in the previous section, PEHs can be programmed to identify flows and queue packets to different queues using hash results on packet fields. It is very important that only one core processes the packet of any queue at any time in order to ensure packet ordering within a flow. Networking applications require maintenance of packet ordering from ingress to egress within a flow. PEHs can be programmed to block de-queuing of packets from a queue by other cores if a previous packet from the queue is being processed. The core processing the packet can signal the PEH to remove the block once it processes the packet. This kind of handshaking between cores and PEH hardware ensures that the packet ordering is maintained within a flow.

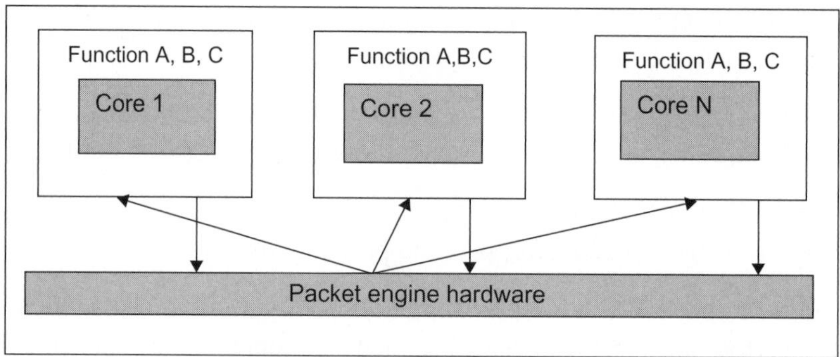

Figure 24.4:
Run-to-completion programming model.

Since packets belonging to a flow are processed by one core at a time to preserve the packet ordering, a given flow's performance is limited to what one core can process. In typical deployments, there would be a large number of flows and hence multiple cores are utilized with PEH distributing the flows. If a deployment has fewer flows than cores, then some of the cores are underutilized. Though this may seem like a limitation, the run-to-completion model is accepted in industry since many network deployments have a large number of simultaneous flows.

Having said that, there could be some instances where a very high throughput is required on few flows. To utilize the cores effectively, the flows need to be processed by multiple cores in the pipeline model. To improve performance further, multiple cores can be used at each pipeline stage. That is, a hybrid model combining run-to-completion and the pipeline model is required. As shown in Figure 24.5, cores are divided into three pipeline stages where each stage itself gets implemented in run-to-completion fashion.

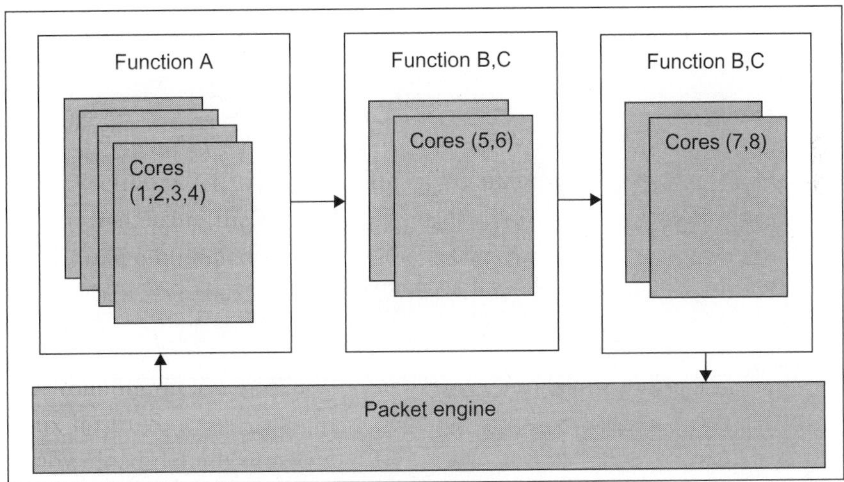

Figure 24.5:
Hybrid programming model.

The run-to-completion model utilizes multiple cores for a function or set of functions. This being a popular programming model to implement packet-processing applications, the rest of the chapter focuses on related programming techniques that programmers need to be aware of. Multicore programming techniques suitable for network programming are similar to any multicore programming, with subtle differences. The rest of the chapter focuses on the structure of packet-processing engines and then describes some important multicore programming techniques that are useful for packet-processing applications.

Structure of packet-processing software

Data-plane (DP) and service-plane (SP) engines are the main packet-processing engines in network devices. The structure of packet-processing software whether it is DP or SP software is similar in nature. Though the rest of the chapter mainly uses the term DP and forwarding engines while describing structure and programming techniques, it is equally applicable for SP engines too.

Figure 24.6 shows a data plane with multiple forwarding engines (FE1, FE2 to FE N), with each engine implementing a device function. In the run-to-completion model, FEs call the next FE by function calls. In the above example, FE1 processes the packet and hands it over to FE2 by calling a function of FE2. FE2 does its processing and hands over the packet to the next FE module until the packet is sent out by the last FE (FE N).

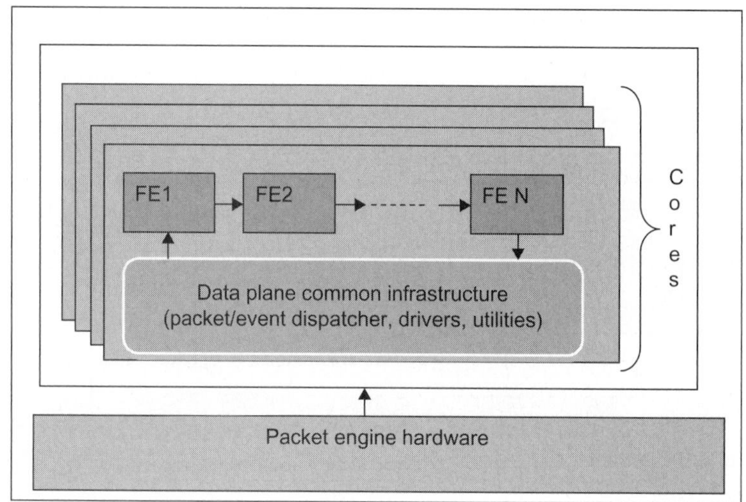

Figure 24.6:
Data-plane architecture.

- Note: alternative mechanism of calling the next FE: to maintain modularity, many data path implementations use the approach of functions pointers. Consider an example where FE1, after processing a packet, needs to select one of the next FEs. Let us also assume that FE1 uses a packet header field to decide on the next FE to send the packet to. One approach is to call functions by the name of next FEs based on the value of field in the packet. Another approach is where neighboring FEs register with function pointers along with packet field values to the current FE (FE1) at initialization. While packet processing, FE1 finds the function pointer based on the field value of the current packet, gets the corresponding function pointer from the registered list and calls the next FE using the function pointer. This modularity allows new FEs to be added in the future on top of FE1 without any changes to FE1.

Data-plane infrastructure (DP-Infra)

Software architects and programmers strive for modularity by dividing the problem into manageable modules. With increasing complexity of DP implementations due to the large number of FEs and the complexity of FEs, modularity is required in DP implementations too. DP-Infra is a set of common modules which are required by DP FEs. By separating out the common functionality of FEs, it provides several advantages – reusability (hence faster to add more FEs in future), maintainability, and easy portability of FEs across multiple different SoCs due to abstraction of the hardware. It is important to understand at this time that the initial FE (FE1 in above diagram) gets packets from the DP-Infra sub-module. Similarly, the last FE sends out the packets to the PEH (packet engine hardware) using DP-Infra. Forwarding engines also interact with the DP-Infra to interact with AEs (acceleration engines) in PEH.

- Note: this chapter does not get into the details of DP-Infra. At a very high level, modules in DP-Infra typically include dispatcher, drivers, packet buffer manager, timer manager, etc. The dispatcher module dispatches packets to requestors – drivers and FEs. Drivers are software modules that hide details of hardware by providing easy-to-use API functions for FEs to access hardware accelerators and devices. Packet buffer, timer and other utilities are mainly easy-to-use library facilities providing consistent programming methods across FEs. By the way, DP-Infra is typically provided by multicore SoC vendors as part of their software development kits to jumpstart DP and SP development on SoCs.

Structure of the forwarding engine

Forwarding engines follow a structure similar to that shown in Figure 24.7. Forwarding engines receive packets from previous FEs or from the DP-Infra.

First, FEs parse packet headers and extract fields of interest. If it is the first FE receiving the packets from the PEH, it can use parse results that were extracted by the PEH. As described earlier, PEHs of multicore SoCs can be programmed to understand the flows and distribute the flows across cores. PEHs extract fields and values of packet headers to do this job. The FE receiving packets from PEH can take advantage of PEH parser results.

Second, the flow lookup step, using fields extracted in the previous step, determines the matching flow context in the flow context database (flow DB). If there is no matching flow, the packet is sent to the service plane. These packets are called exception packets. As part of exception packet processing, a flow may be created by the SP in the flow context database through the flow management module. If there is a matching flow in the database, then the actual packet processing gets done.

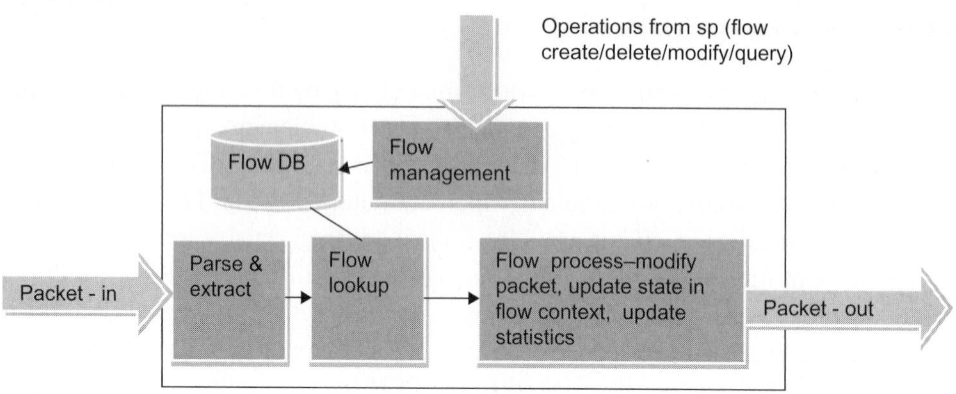

Figure 24.7:
Structure of forwarding engine.

Third, the flow process step processes the packet based on state information in the flow context. It could result in a new packet, modification of some fields in the packet header or even dropping the packet. In this step, new state values might be updated in the flow context. This step also updates statistics. Maintenance of statistics is quite common in networking applications. Statistics counters such as byte count and packet count are normally kept on a per flow context basis. There are some counters which can be updated across the flow contexts and those are called global counters.

Finally, the updated packet is sent out to the next FE. If the current FE is the last module, it typically sends the packet out using DP-Infra.

Packet-processing application requirements

There are some requirements which developers need to keep in mind while developing an FE in the run-to-completion model.

- Packet ordering must be preserved in a flow.
- Performance scaling is expected to be almost linear with number of cores assigned to the data plane.
- Latency of the packet from ingress to egress needs to be kept as small as possible.

Performance scaling is one of the activities developers spend most of their time on, much more than the time they spend on implementation of data-plane modules. There are two kinds of performance considerations developers need to keep in mind: multicore-related performance items and typical programming items.

Network application programming techniques

Multicore performance techniques for network application programmers

Network programmers use a variety of techniques to achieve better performance while developing packet-processing applications in the DP and the SP.

Locks are used in multicore programming to keep the data integrity in data structures such as hash tables. Locks ensure that only one core accesses and changes the data structures at any point in time. This is typically achieved by placing the pieces of code which are modifying and accessing the data structures under locks. While a core is accessing a data structure with a lock on it, any other core trying to do any operation on the data structure is made to spin until the lock is released. Since cores don't do any useful job during spin, the performance of packet processing does not scale with multiple cores if there are many locks in the packet-processing path. Hence networking programmers need to ensure that their packet-processing code is lock-free as much as possible.

Avoid locks while looking for flow context

Hash table

Packet-processing modules in the DP or SP use various data structures to store flow contexts. The hash table is one of the most popular data structures used in network programming. Hence the hash table data structure is used to describe some of the programming techniques here.

The hash table organization is as shown in Figure 24.8. It is an array of buckets with each bucket having flow context nodes arranged, typically, in a linked-list fashion. Nodes in the buckets are also called collision nodes. The hash table, like any other data structure,

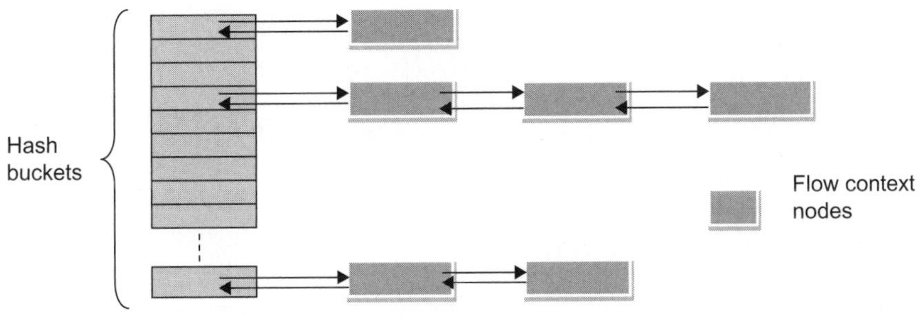

Figure 24.8:
Hash table organization.

provides add, delete and search operations on the nodes. Every hash table is associated with key parameters. Nodes are added, deleted and searched based on the values of the key parameters identified for the hash table. For any operation, the hash is calculated first on the key values. The Bob Jenkins hash algorithm is one of the most popular hash algorithms used to calculate a hash. Some bits from the hash result are used as the index to the hash bucket array. Once the bucket is determined, an add operation adds the node to the bucket linked list either at the head or the tail. A search operation finds the matching node by doing an exact match on collision nodes. A delete operation deletes the node from the bucket linked list.

The following set of structures and code pieces provides an implementation of a hash table in the C language. Though the C structures have many more variables, only relevant fields are described here. Other variables will be described in other sections of the document.

Flow_t: This C structure represents the nodes in a hash table.

- *next* and *prev* pointers are used to link the nodes in the bucket double linked list.
- *key1* and *key2* variables in the structure store the key values of the node. These values uniquely identify the flow context (node) in the hash table.

Flow_Hash_Bucket_t: C structure used to represent a bucket. It contains the dummy Flow_t node as head of the linked list.

```
typedef struct Flow_s {
   struct rcu_head rcuh;
   struct Flow_s *next;
   struct Flow_s *prev;
   struct futex in_use_lock;
   char in_use;
   struct backlogQ_s backlogQ;
   unsigned int sr_array_index;
   struct Flow_Hash_table_s *table;
   int key1;
   int key2;
   int sv1, sv2;
   int s1, s2, s3, s4;
}Flow_t;

typedef struct pkt_s {
   struct pkt_s *next;
   int buff_size;
   unsigned char *buff;
}pkt_t;

struct backlogQ_s {
   pkt_t *head;
   pkt_t *tail;
};
```

```
typedef struct Flow_Hash_Bucket_s {
    Flow_t  head;
}Flow_Hash_Bucket_t;

typedef struct Flow_Hash_Table_s {
    int number_of_buckets;
    Flow_Hash_Bucket_t *buckets;
    struct futex list_lock;
    unsigned int  cookie_val;
    struct Flow_Safe_Reference_Node_s *sr_array;
    struct Flow_Safe_Reference_Node_s
*free_index_list;
}Flow_Hash_Table_t;

typedef struct Flow_Safe_Reference_Node_s {
    unsigned int cookie_val;
    Flow_t *flow_node;
    int array_index;
    struct Flow_Safe_Reference_Node_s *next;
}Flow_Safe_Reference_Node_t;
```

Listing 24.1:
Safe reference array.

Flow_Hash_Table_t: this C structure represents the hash table.

- *number_of_buckets*: indicates the number of buckets in the hash table.
- *buckets*: array of buckets.
- *list_lock*: lock used to protect the hash table integrity.

A search operation is issued on the hash table on a per-packet basis in any typical forwarding engine. Since it is a per-packet operation, the search operation needs to be very fast in order to achieve good performance. An add operation is executed on the hash table for every new flow, typically, as part of exception packet processing. A delete operation is executed to remove a flow upon inactivity or after the life of a flow has expired. In the run-to-completion programming model, many cores process the packets and add/delete flows. These operations may happen concurrently. To protect hash table integrity, locks are required to provide mutually exclusive access to the hash table.

The search function, as shown in Listing 24.2, takes the table pointer representing the hash table, *hash_key*, which is result of a hash function such as the Jenkins hash algorithm on key values. This function, first, gets the linked list head of the bucket and then does collision resolution using *key1* and *key2* fields. Note the statements *LOCK_TAKE()* and *LOCK_RELEASE()*. The *LOCK_TAKE* function takes the lock. If the lock is already taken by some other core, then the current core spins until the lock is released by the core that took the lock. The *LOCK_RELEASE* function releases the lock. Since cores spin waiting for the lock, performance does not scale with number of cores if there are more locks and/or if there is significant code that gets executed under locks.

Avoiding locks

Modern operating systems including Linux support many different types of mutex functions. Pthreads in Linux supports at least three kinds of mutex primitives – spinlocks (*pthread_spin_lock* and *pthread_spin_unlock*), mutexes (*pthread_mutex_lock* and *pthread_mutex_unlock*) and futexes (fast mutex operations using *futex_down* and *futex_up*). These sets differ in the performance of the mutex operation itself, but the cores stall during contention in all cases. So, lock-less implementation is the best way to scale the performance with numbers of cores. Enter the world of Read-Copy-Update (RCU) primitives.

Read-Copy-Update is a synchronization mechanism supported by many modern operating systems. It improves the performance of the read-side of a critical section. In the above example, the search function is a read-side critical section as it does not update the hash table data structure. Add/Delete functions are write-side critical sections as they update the data structure. RCU provides wait-free read-side locking and hence many cores can do the search operation at the same time. Due to this, the packet-processing application

```
Flow_t *Flow_Search_Node(Flow_Hash_Table_t *table, unsigned int hash_key,
             unsigned int key1,  unsigned int key2,
             unsigned int *sf_index, unsigned int *cookie_val  )
{

   Flow_t *temp, *head;
   unsigned int   array_index;
   unsigned int   cookie;
   Flow_t        *flow;

   LOCK_TAKE(&table->lock);

   {
       /** Start from head  **/
       head = &table->buckets[hash_key % table->number_of_buckets].head;
       temp = head->next;

       while(temp != head)
       {
           if ((key1 == temp->key1) && (key2 == temp->key2))
           {

                 break;
           }

           temp = temp->next;
       }

       if (temp == head )
       {
          /** No Match found **/
          temp = NULL;
       }
       else
       {
        *sf_index = temp->sr_array_index;
        *cookie_val = table->sr_array[temp->sr_array_index].cookie_val;

       }

   }

   LOCK_RELEASE(&table->lock);

   return(temp);

}
```

Listing 24.2:
Search function.

performance can be scaled with the cores. rcu_read_lock() and rcu_read_unlock() are RCU primitives. These are similar to reader locks, but very fast. In many CPU architectures supporting in-order instruction execution, RCU read lock/unlock primitives don't do anything really much and are practically stub functions. Even in OOO (out-of-order) execution-based CPU architectures, these primitives mainly do the "memory bar" (memory fence) operations and hence are very fast. In some operating systems, lock primitive disables preemption.

Though the RCU mechanism improves the performance of read operations (search), normal locks are still required for add/delete operations. Delete operations need additional work when RCUs are used for read-side protection. A delete operation is expected to postpone the freeing of a node that is removed from the data structure until all cores have finished accessing the node. This is achieved by calling synchronize_rcu() or call_rcu() functions after removing the node from the data structure in the delete operation. synchronize_rcu is a synchronous operation. Once this function returns, the caller can assume that it is safe to free the node. call_rcu is an asynchronous operation. This function takes a function pointer as an argument. This function pointer is called by the RCU infrastructure of the operating system once the operating system determines that all other cores have finished accessing the node. The RCU infrastructure calls the callback function pointer once it determines that all the cores have finished their current execution cycle.

There are two primitives that programmers need to be aware of while using RCUs. They are rcu_assign_pointer() and rcu_dereference(). rcu_assign_pointer is used to assign new values to the RCU protected pointer and is needed for readers to see the new value assigned by the writers. The rcu_deference() primitive is used to get the pointer value from the RCU protected pointer.

Please see the hash table search, add and delete functions following listings to understand the usage of RCUs.

A modified search function with RCUs is given in Listing 24.3.

Look at the bold red statement in Listing 24.3. Since the *next* pointer may be updated by the add and delete functions, it is necessary to de-reference it using the *rcu_dereference*() function. *rcu_read_lock* and *rcu_read_unlock* functions are used to showcase the read side of a critical section of the search operation.

Now let us look at the add and delete functions in Listing 24.4 and Listing 24.5.

Note that the add function still goes with mutex locks. Check the linked-list addition using *rcu_assign_pointer*() primitives. *rcu_assign_pointer(new_flow->next, head->next)* is the same as *new_flow->next* = *head->next* except that *head->next* always sees a new value.

Look at the bold red items in the above listing. A mutex lock is used to protect the critical section. Since RCU protection is used in the search operation, a flow that is removed from the hash table should not be freed immediately. The *call_rcu* function takes the function

```
Flow_t *Flow_Search_Node(Flow_Hash_Table_t *table, unsigned int hash_key,
               unsigned int key1,   unsigned int key2,
               unsigned int *sf_index, unsigned int *cookie_val  )
{

   Flow_t *temp, *head;
   Flow_t         *flow;

   rcu_read_lock();

   {
       /** Start from head  **/
       head = &table->buckets[hash_key % table->number_of_buckets].head;
       temp = (Flow_t*)rcu_dereference(head->next);

       while(temp != head)
       {
           if ((key1 == temp->key1) && (key2 == temp->key2))
           {
               Break;
           }

           temp = (Flow_t*)rcu_dereference(temp->next);
       }

       if (temp == head )
       {
          /** No Match found **/
          temp = NULL;
       }
       else
       {
        *sf_index = temp->sr_array_index;
        *cookie_val = table->sr_array[temp->sr_array_index].cookie_val;

       }

   }

   rcu_read_unlock();

   return(temp);

}
```

Listing 24.3:
Modified search function.

pointer and pointer to *rcu_head*. In the above case, *Flow_RCU_free_fn* is passed along with the *rcu_head* pointer to the *call_rcu* API function. By defining *rcu_head* in the flow context record, it is possible to get the flow context in the *Flow_RCU_free_fn*(). When *Flow_RCU_free_fn* is called by the RCU infrastructure of operating system, the flow is freed as shown above.

```
unsigned int Flow_Add_Node( Flow_Hash_Table_t *table, unsigned int hash_key,
  Flow_t *new_flow,unsigned int *sf_index, unsigned int *cookie_val)

{
   unsigned int free_index;

   LOCK_TAKE(&table->list_lock);


   /** Get free array index **/

   if ((free_index = Flow_get_free_sr_index(table)) == 0 )
      return 0;


   if (table->cookie_val == 0 )  table->cookie_val++;
   table->sr_array[free_index].cookie_val = table->cookie_val++;
   table->sr_array[free_index].flow_node = new_flow;
   table->sr_array[free_index].next = NULL;

   /** Adding the flow should be the last step **/
   /** Add flow to circular double linked list in the beginning,
       right after head
   **/

   {
      Flow_t *head;
      head =  &table->buckets[hash_key % table->number_of_buckets].head;

      new_flow->sr_array_index = free_index;
     /* DLL Manipulations, but RCU purposes, we need to use
         rcu_assign_pointer to take care of CPUs with weak ordering*/
      rcu_assign_pointer(new_flow->next, head->next);
      rcu_assign_pointer(head->next->prev,new_flow);
      rcu_assign_pointer(head->next, new_flow);
      rcu_assign_pointer(new_flow->prev,  head);

   }
   new_flow->table = (struct Flow_Hash_table_s*)table;

   LOCK_RELEASE(&table->list_lock);

  *sf_index = free_index;
  *cookie_val = table->sr_array[free_index].cookie_val;
   return(1);
}
```

Listing 24.4:
Add operation.

Avoid reference counting

Network packet-processing applications, as discussed, find the matching flow context entry upon receiving a packet. The flow process step in packet-processing applications refers to the flow context node multiple times, including accessing and updating state variables and

```
unsigned int Flow_Remove_Node(Flow_Hash_Table_t *table,
    Flow_t *flow)
{
    struct Flow_Safe_Reference_Node_s *TmpFreeList;
    unsigned int array_index;

   LOCK_TAKE(&table->list_lock);


    /** Invalidate the sr_array node, but don't put in the
        free list yet. Freeing to the linked list would be done as part
        of RCU callback.
        Do this before removing the flows.
    **/

    array_index = flow->sr_array_index;
    table->sr_array[array_index].cookie_val = 0;
    table->sr_array[array_index].flow_node = NULL;

    /** Remove flow from hash list, but don't initialize the pointers to NULL as
     ** other thread will continue to traverse the linked list
    **/

       /** Make this DLL steps RCU friendly*/
       rcu_assign_pointer(flow->next->prev, flow->prev);
       rcu_assign_pointer(flow->prev->next, flow->next);
       LOCK_RELEASE(&table->list_lock);

    /** Set up the callback for RCU infrastructure to indicate us when
     ** all threads complete their current scheduled cycle
     **/
    call_rcu(&flow->rcu_head, Flow_RCU_free_fn );
}

void Flow_RCU_free_fn(struct rcu_head *ptr)
{
     Flow_t *flow;
     Flow_Hash_Table_t *table;

     flow = container_of(ptr,  Flow_t, rcuh);

     table = flow->table;

     LOCK_TAKE(&(table->list_lock));

     /** Free the array index into free sr list **/
     Flow_free_sr_node(flow->table, flow->sr_array_index);

     LOCK_RELEASE(&table->list_lock);

     free(flow);

}
```

Listing 24.5:
Delete operation.

updating statistics. While the flow context record is being accessed, the flow should not be deleted and freed by any other core. Traditionally this is achieved by applying "reference counting".

The reference counting mechanism is typically implemented by two variables in the flow context records: *ref_count* and *delete_flag*. Packet-processing applications normally increment the reference count of matched flows as part of the search operation. Once the packet processing is done, the reference count is decremented. A non-zero positive value in *ref_count* indicates that the flow is being used by some threads/cores. When a core or a thread is trying to delete a flow, *ref_count* is checked first. If it is 0, then the core removes it from the data structure and frees the flow. If it has a non-zero value, the core/thread marks the flow for deletion by setting the *delete_flag*. As cores stop using the flow, they decrement the *ref_count*. The last core/thread that de-references the flow (*ref_count* == 0) frees the entry if the flow is marked for deletion. Since there are two variables to implement the reference count mechanism, locks are used to update or access these two variables atomically.

There are mainly two issues associated with the reference counting mechanism.

- Locks are required in implementing the reference counting mechanism. Hence, there would be performance scaling issues with increasing number of cores.
- Error prone: programmers should ensure that the reference count is decremented in all possible packet paths when the flow is no longer required. While developing forwarding engines for the first time, programmers might handle this carefully. But developers may not be as careful or knowledgeable in the code maintenance phase.

Due to the above issues, programmers are advised to avoid reference counting mechanisms. The RCU mechanism described above avoids the need for reference counting. As discussed above, the RCU-based delete operation postpones the freeing-up of the node until all other threads/cores complete their current run-to-completion cycle. Therefore any core that is doing the flow process step can be sure of the flow's existence until the current run-to-completion cycle is completed. In essence, RCU-based data structures such as the RCU-based hash table provide two great benefits – avoiding locks during the flow lookup step and avoiding error-prone reference counting mechanisms.

There is another reason why the reference counting mechanism is used by programmers. At times, the neighboring modules need to store the reference to the flow contexts of a module. Once the reference is stored, the neighbor modules might use the information in the flows at any time during its processing. If no care is taken, neighbor module might de-reference the stale pointers of the deleted flows. In the best case, this may lead to accessing wrong information and in the worst case it may lead to system stability issues. A reference counting mechanism is used to protect software from these issues. Coding needs to be done carefully to ensure that *ref_count* is incremented and decremented at the right places in neighbor modules. Since the reference counting mechanism is not just limited to the local module, but extends to neighbor modules, this method is prone to even more implementation errors. A safe reference method, in addition to RCU, is an additional technique programmers can use to eliminate the reference counting mechanism entirely.

Safe reference mechanism

In the reference counting mechanism, neighbor modules store the reference by pointer. In the safe reference mechanism, neighbor modules store an indirection to the pointer to a flow context. Indirection happens through an array and includes two important variables – index and cookie. A module that expects a neighbor module to store a reference to its flow contexts defines a safe reference array data structure in addition to data structures such as the hash table. As part of the flow context addition operation, the flow context is not only kept in the hash table, it is also referred from one of the elements in the safe reference array. Also, a unique cookie is generated upon each addition operation. This cookie value is also added to the safe reference array element. Please see Figure 24.9.

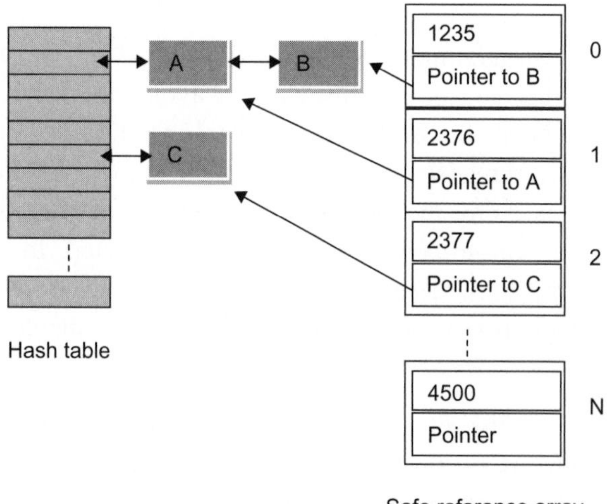

Figure 24.9:
Hash table with safe reference array.

The neighbor module is expected to store Index 1 and Cookie 2376 to refer to flow context A. Since it is no longer a pointer, neighbor modules can't access the flow context information directly. The module owning the flow context A provides macros/ API functions for neighbor modules to access any information from flow A. Neighbor modules are expected to pass safe reference (index and cookie values) to get the needed information. The module providing the API/macro is expected to check for the validity of the reference by matching the cookie value given with the cookie value in the safe reference array. If the cookie values don't match, it means that the node was deleted and the module returns an error to the caller. In essence, using safe references instead of pointers, modules can delete their nodes safely without worrying about neighbor modules. It not only eliminates the need for reference counting and associated performance degradation, but it also makes software more modular as it forces neighbor modules to access information via API/macros.

Listing 24.1 has *sr_array* in the *Flow_Hash_Table_t* structure that defines the safe reference array. The array size is maximum number of nodes supported by that module. Normally, this array is allocated along with the hash table initialization. *free_index_list* maintains the free indices in a linked-list fashion. This helps in finding the free index fast during flow creation.

Listing 24.1 also has the C structure *Flow_Safe_Reference_Node_t*, which defines the array element in the safe reference array. It contains cookie_val and a pointer to the flow context *flow_node*. It also has two housekeeping variables – the *next* pointer is used to maintain the *free_index_list* linked list and *array_index* is to denote the index on the array which this element represents.

The add operation function listed in Listing 24.4 has logic to populate the safe reference array element after getting hold of the free array index and the unique cookie value. It gets the unique cookie value from *cookie_val* in the hash table, which gets incremented every time it is used, thereby maintaining uniqueness. Value 0 is reserved to indicate the free element and hence it avoids using 0 as cookie. Essentially, there is one array element used for every new flow context. The index to this array element is also stored in the flow to help in finding the array element from the flow context. Usage of this can be seen from the delete operation.

```
if ((free_index = Flow_get_free_sr_index(table)) = = 0 )

   return 0;

  if (table->cookie_val = = 0 ) table->cookie_val++;

  table->sr_array[free_index].cookie_val = table->cookie_val++;

  table->sr_array[free_index].flow_node = new_flow;
```

```
table->sr_array[free_index].next = NULL;

new_flow->sr_array_index = free_index;
```

The delete operation function in Listing 24.5 has logic to invalidate the safe reference array element. The RCU callback function frees the safe reference element to the free linked list. The following code piece in the *Flow_Remove_Node*() invalidates the safe reference element.

```
array_index = flow->sr_array_index;

table->sr_array[array_index].cookie_val = 0;

table->sr_array[array_index].flow_node = NULL;
```

The following code piece in the *Flow_RCU_free_fn*() puts the safe reference array in the free linked list.

```
Flow_free_sr_node(flow->table, flow->sr_array_index);
```

Flow parallelization

The flow parallelization technique allows a flow to be processed by only one core at any given time. Independent flows are parallelized across cores instead of packet parallelization, where packets within a flow may get processed by multiple cores simultaneously. Note that the flow parallelization technique does not bind a flow to a core permanently. It only ensures that only one core processes any given flow at any point in time.

Let us see some of the issues with packet parallelization. In packet parallelization mode, packets are distributed across cores with no consideration to flows. Many forwarding applications tend to maintain state variables which get updated and accessed during packet processing. If multiple packets of a flow get processed by more than one core at a time, then there would be a need to ensure the integrity of state variables in the flow. Mutual exclusion (a lock) is required to ensure the integrity of state variables. If state variables are updated or accessed at multiple places during the flow processing step, then more instances of locking are required to protect these variables. This will reduce the overall performance of the system.

Many networking applications require packet ordering to be maintained with a flow. If multiple cores process packets of a flow at the same time, then there is a good possibility of packet misordering. Note that packet-processing cycles may not be exactly the same across packets due to various conditions that happen in the system such as core preemption, interrupt processing, etc. Hence, a newer packet may get processed fast and sent out before the packet that was received earlier on by some other core. Some applications are very sensitive to packet order and hence packet ordering is expected to be maintained by packet-processing applications.

The flow parallelization programming technique is used to overcome the above issues – eliminate locks during the packet-processing path and keep packet order.

As discussed in the section on multicore SoCs in networking, the PEH tries to help in flow parallelization by bundling packets of a flow into one queue. As long as only one core processes the queue at a time, flow parallelization is achieved without any special software programming techniques. The first forwarding engine in the data plane might benefit from the PEH way of bundling the packets. But software-based flow parallelization is required in other forwarding engine modules in cases where the granularity or flow definition is different in these engines. Consider an example of multiple forwarding engines in the data plane as shown in Figure 24.6. Assume that FE1 flow granularity is based on 5-tuples (source IP, destination IP, protocol, source port and destination port) and FE2 flow granularity is based on 2-tuples (source IP and destination IP). Packets belonging to more than one flow of FE1, where flows are processed by different cores, might fall into a single flow of FE2. In the run-to-completion model, the FE2 entry point is called by FE1 by a function call. Hence, in this example, FE2 would see packets to one FE2 flow coming into it from multiple cores. Here the flow parallelization technique is required in FE2 to avoid issues associated with packet parallelization as describe above.

There are cases where an FE receiving packets from the PEH directly may also need to implement software flow parallelization techniques. One case is where packets belonging to a flow come from two sources from the PEH. Many stateful packet-processing applications have two sub-flows. The two sub-flows normally are the forwarding sub-flow (client to server flow) and the reverse sub-flow (server to client flow). Consider an example of a NAT device. The NAT flow contains two sub-flows with different 5-tuple parameters. Since PEHs don't have knowledge of these two sub-flows belonging to a flow, the PEH might place packets of these two sub-flows into two different queues. Hence packets belonging to a flow may get processed by different cores at the same time. Therefore, flow parallelization may even be required in FEs that receive packets directly from PEHs.

The software technique to parallelize flows is simple. The rest of this section describes one implementation of flow parallelization. Figure 24.7 shows the step Flow lookup. Once the flow is found, flow is checked if it is being processed by any other core/thread. This can be done by maintaining a field *in_use* in the flow context. If this variable value is 1, this flow is being used by some other core/thread and the current core/thread queues the packet to a flow-specific *backlog* queue. If the flow is not in use (*in_use* is 0), then the flow is marked by setting *in_use* to 1 and the packet gets processed further. Once the packet is processed and sent to the next FE, it goes and checks whether any packets are in the backlog queue. If so, it processes all packets in the backlog queue and unmarks the flow by setting *in_use* to 0. Essentially, this technique ensures that only one packet in the flow gets processed by any core at any point in time.

Since *in_use* and the backlog queue are to be used together, this technique requires access to these two variables atomically and hence a lock is used. That is, one lock is required to implement the flow parallelization technique, but it avoids any further locks during packet processing and also helps in maintaining the packet order. Since the rest of processing does not require locks, it also provides a very good maintenance benefit in the sense that programmers need not be concerned about multicore programming issues if new code is added or existing code is modified in the flow processing step of Figure 24.7.

As shown in Listing 24.1, there are three variables in *Flow_t* that help in implementing flow parallelization. *in_use_lock* is a lock variable to protect *in_use* and *backlogQ*. *in_use* flag indicates whether or not the flow is being used. *backlogQ* is used to store the packets if the flow is being used by some other thread/core.

As shown in Figure 24.7 (the structure of forwarding engine), the code path of the flow engine looks like this:

```
FE_entry_point(pkt)
{

    extract_fields(pkt, &key_value1, &key_value2,....);

    flow = Flow_Search_Node(...., key_value1, key_value2,....);

    Flow_Process(flow, pkt, ...);

}
```

With flow parallelization, code path looks like this:

```
FE_entry_point(pkt)
{
       .......
       ........
  extract_fields(pkt,  &key_value1, &key_value2, ....);
 flow = Flow_Search_Node(...., key_value1,  key_value2, ....);
  LOCK_TAKE(&flow->in_use_lock);

   if (flow->in_use == 0)
   {
      flow->in_use = 1;
      LOCK_RELEASE(&flow->in_use_lock);

      Flow_Process(flow, pkt);

      /** If there are any packets added to backlog queue, process them
          here **/

      process_backlog_packets(flow);

   }
   else
   {
     /** Add pkt to end of the list **/

     pkt->next = NULL;
     if (flow->backlogQ.head == NULL )
     {
        flow->backlogQ.head = flow->backlogQ.tail = pkt;
     }
     else
     {
       flow->backlogQ.tail->next = pkt;
       flow->backlogQ.tail = pkt;

     }
     LOCK_RELEASE(&flow->in_use_lock);
   }

}
process_backlog_packets(Flow_t *flow)
{
   pkt_t *pkt;

   LOCK_TAKE(&flow->in_use_lock);

   do
   {
     if ( flow->backlogQ.head == NULL )
     {
       flow->in_use = 0;
       LOCK_RELEASE(&flow->in_use_lock);
       break;
     }
     pkt = flow->backlogQ.head;
     flow->backlogQ.head = pkt->next;
     if (flow->backlogQ.head == NULL ) flow->backlogQ.tail = NULL;

     LOCK_RELEASE(&flow->in_use_lock);
     Flow_Process(flow,pkt);
     LOCK_TAKE(&flow->in_use_lock);

   } while(1);
}
```

Listing 24.6:

FE1.

```
FE_entry_point(pkt)
{
        .....
        ......
        extract_fields(pkt,  &key_value1, &key_value2, ....);
        flow = Flow_Search_Node(....,  key_value1,  key_value2, ....);
        Flow_Process(flow, pkt, ...);
}
```

Listing 24.7:

Forwarding engines.

Once the above changes are made, any changes to *Flow_Process*() function in the future work without having to worry about complexities associated with multicore programming. Please see *FE_Entry_Point*() and *process_backlog_packes*(). The *FE_Entry_Point*() function queues the packet to the backlog queue if the flow is in use. Otherwise, the *Flow_Process*() function is invoked after setting the *in_use* flag. Once the *Flow_Process*() is done on the packet, *process_backlog_packets*() is called, which processes any packets queued while the previous packet was being processed.

Reducing cache thrashing associated with updating statistics

Many networking applications update two types of statistics – flow-specific statistics and global statistics. When multiple cores are used, statistics variables are updated using atomic operations such as *atomic_inc*() and *atomic_add*().

Any increment operation on a variable internally involves the following steps by cores. For example *atomic_inc*(*stats_var1*) involves:

- Reading *stats_var1* from memory.
  - If this variable is not in the cache, *stats_var1* is read into the cache from DDR.
- Note: cores read one cache line of data into the caches. Cache line size is typically in the range 32 to 128 bytes in many CPU architectures.
- Increment operation.
- Writing back *stats_var1* to memory: this operation not only updates the local cache, but it results in cache invalidations in other cores. The cache invalidation operation invalidates the entire cache line corresponding to *stats_var1* memory location.

Cores normally have two kinds of caches – the L1 cache, which is very near the core, and the L2 cache, which is little farther away from the core. Finally, there is DDR memory, which is farthest from the cores. L1 cache latency is typically of the order of 2 to 3 cycles. L2 cache latency is around 10 to 15 cycles and DDR latency is around 100 + cycles. Cores access memory for both instructions and data. Cores typically stall until the data is available to operate. If the data is available in the caches, CPU stall cycles are fewer. Hence, programmers like to ensure that the data is in the cache as much as possible.

As discussed above, *atomic_inc*() and *atomic_add*() operations update the memory with new values. This results in invalidation of this memory location in other core caches. When another core tries to do an *atomic_inc*() operation on the same statistics variable, it goes to DDR memory as the cache for this memory location is no longer valid in its cache. The core needs to wait for 100+ cycles for DDR access.

Consider a case where cores are processing packets in round-robin fashion and let us also assume that the processing of each packet results in *stats_var1* getting incremented. Also consider that there are two cores working on this packet-processing application. Core 1 getting packet 1 increments *stats_var1* and this invalidates the core2 cache line having *stats_var1*. When packet 2 is processed by core 2, it needs to get the *stats_var1* from DDR as the *stats_var1*-related cache line was invalidated. When core 2 updates *stats_var1* with a new value, this results in invalidation of the core 1 cache line having *stats_var1*. When packet 3 is processed by core 1, core 1 needs to go to DDR to fill its cache and the update of statistics variable invalidates the core 2 cache, and this can go on if packets are being processed alternately by cores. This effectively masks the cache advantage and hence leads to performance issues.

Programmers can avoid these repeated cache invalidations by ensuring that the flow is processed by the same core all the time. Though this is possible in some applications, it is not typically advised to bind flows to cores as it may result in under-utilization of cores. Moreover this technique only works for flow-based statistics variables at most and can't be applied to global statistics.

Per-core statistics is one of the techniques programmers are increasingly using to reduce cache thrashing issues associated with statistics updates by multiple cores. This technique defines as many statistics copies as there are cores. Each core updates its copy of statistics only. Due to this, there is no need for atomic operations on the statistics variables.

Example: consider a module having two global counters that get updated for each packet. Per CPU statistics are defined as shown below.

```
structmodStatistics{
intCounter1;
intCounter2;
};
structmodStatisticsstatsArray[NR_CPUS];
```

NR_CPUS: number of cores dedicated to the module. This could be number of threads if the module is implemented in Linux user space using pthreads.

The core that is processing the packet is used as the index on the *statsArray* to increment the appropriate statistics counter. The code to increment Counter1 is:

```
statsArray[core_id].Counter1++;
```

When a management plane module requires to look at the consolidated statistics variables, all counters in the array are added and returned. For example, the following code gives information on the *Counter1* counter.

```
for ( ii=0, sum_counter1 = 0; ii<NR_CPUS; ii++ )
sum_counter1+ =statsArray[ii].Counter1;
```

Even though the above logic eliminates the need for atomic operations, cache thrashing issues don't go away entirely as counters defined in an array belonging to different cores might fall on the same cache line. For example, core 0's *Counter2* and core 1's *Counter1* might fall on the same cache line. When CPUs update any memory location in a cache line, the entire cache line of data is considered dirty. That is, if core 0 updates *Counter2*, it results in invalidation of *Counter1* of core 1 as they share the same cache line. Due to this, updating of *Counter1* by core 1 at a later time results in DDR access. To avoid the cache thrashing scenarios, the statistics block itself can be made cache aligned. This is typically done by defining the structure aligned to the cache line as shown below. Here, the code assumes that the cache line size is 32 bytes.

```
structmodStatistics {
intCounter1;
intCounter2;
}__attribute__(aligned(32));
```

The above definition solves the cache thrashing issue associated with the sharing of a cache line across multiple statistics counters belonging to different cores. But it increases the size of the statistics structure. Assuming that *int* is 4 bytes long, without any aligned attribute, the size of the *modStatistics* structure is 8 bytes. With cache aligned, the size could be one cache line size (32 bytes), 24 bytes of wastage. This memory inefficiency could be a problem if the *aligned* attribute is used for statistics in flow contexts where there are large numbers of flows. As indicated above, per-core statistics are not required in flow contexts if the specific application can live with binding flows to specific cores. In cases where this is not possible, a programming technique is used which lumps all statistics counters corresponding to all flow contexts in core-specific contiguous memory blocks. Let us assume that there are four statistics counters on a per-flow context basis as shown below.

```
struct FelFlowStats_s {

  Int counter1, counter2, counter3, counter4;
```

```
};
Struct Felflow_s {
struct FelFlowStats_s stats;
} FelFlow_t;
```

Statistics blocks are referred from the flow context using an array of pointers as shown below.

```
struct Felflow_s {
```

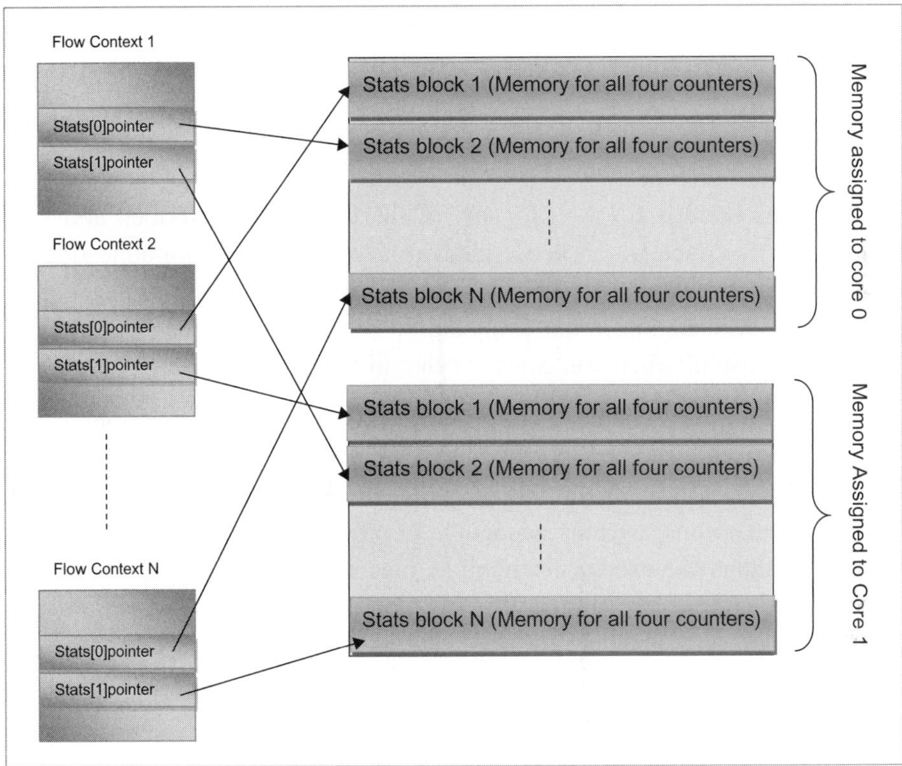

Figure 24.10:
Software-based statistics management.

```
struct FelFlowStats_s *stats[NR_CPUS];
} FelFlow_t;
```

The organization of statistics looks like Figure 24.10 where there are two cores (NR_CPUS = 2).

This programming method ensures that core-0-specific counters across flow contexts are within a contiguous memory block. Similarly core 1 statistics counters across all flow contexts are in another memory block. These bigger memory blocks are cache aligned. No cache alignment is required across stats blocks. Any update by counters by core 0 does not thrash core 1 cache as core 0 and core 1 statistics for any flow are not on the same cache line and vice versa. But it adds one additional complexity where stats blocks are allocated as part of flow context creation. This may add to a few more core cycles during flow context set-up, but cache thrashing on a per-packet basis is avoided. Since there will be a good number of packets within a flow, this trade-off in flow creation is accepted in many implementations.

Statistics acceleration

Some multicore SoCs provide a special feature called statistics acceleration. If these SoCs are used, then there is no need for any of the techniques described above. Only one copy of statistics counters can be defined in flow contexts. No atomic operation is required and there are no cache thrashing issues. It simplifies programming quite a bit. Note that statistics acceleration is not available on many SoCs and hence the above techniques are still useful where statistics acceleration is not available.

Multicore SoCs supporting statistics acceleration provide special instructions to update statistics. These instructions increment, add and perform other operations on counters without involving the cache. Also, multiple cores can fire these instructions at the same time. Statistics accelerators have the capability to pipeline fired operations and ensure that all fired operations are executed reliably. Cores do not wait for operation completion and move on to execute further instructions. This is considered acceptable as statistics counters are only updated but not checked during the packet-processing path. In summary, having the statistics acceleration feature in SoCs does not increase memory requirements, avoids atomic operations, and simplifies coding.

General performance techniques for network application programmers

Use cache effectively

Packet processing performance can benefit significantly if programming is done to take advantage of core caches effectively. As discussed earlier in this chapter, if cores do not find data in the caches they go to DDR. The core stalls until the data is available in its registers, which can be of the order of 100 core cycles. Performance can be improved if programmers ensure that data is in the caches. Programmers can ensure this by following some good coding practices. Some of the methods that can be used to take advantage of caches are described below.

Software-directed prefetching

Many CPU architectures provide a set of instructions to warm its L1 or L2 cache with cache line worth of data from a given memory location. The Linux operating system, for example, defines an API function which can be used to prefetch data from DDR into the L1 cache.

```
char*ptr;
ptr = <Pointer to memory location to fetch data from>
prefetch(ptr);
```

Linux and CPU architectures don't generate an exception even if an invalid pointer is sent to the *prefetch*() API built-in function and hence it can be used safely. *prefetch*() does actual prefetching in the background, that is, the core does not stall waiting for data to be placed in the cache and goes on executing further instructions. Hence it can be used to fetch data that is required at a later time.

In data-plane processing, this technique can be used to fetch the next module flow context while the packet is being processed in the current module. For example, FE1 in Figure 24.6 can prefetch the FE2 flow context while FE1 is processing the packet. By the time FE2 gets hold of the packet, the FE2 context would have already been fetched into the L1 cache by the core subsystem, thereby saving on-demand DDR accesses. Though this may not be possible in some cases, it is possible in many cases. For example, it is possible to do prefetching of the FE2 flow context in FE1 if the FE1 flow context is a subset of the FE2 flow context.

The prefetch operation can also be issued in any memory/string library operations. Memory copy, *strcpy*, *strstr* or any operations of this sort can use prefetch of the next cache line of data while working on current data.

Use likely/unlikely compiler built-ins

Cores having intelligent prediction logic proactively fetch instructions in the memory next to the instruction that is being executed into the caches. Core usage is more optimal if instructions that are going to be executed are available in the caches. Conditional logic (if condition) in the programs is one of the main reasons why the next instruction that gets executed is not in the caches. Thus, the next instruction fetch results in DDR stalls. By using likely/unlikely built-in primitives programmers can ensure that most commonly executed code is together.

Locking critical piece of code in caches

Cache size is often less than the data path code size. Hence cores make space for new code by removing old code from the cache. CPU architectures provide a facility to lock some code (memory location and size) permanently in the cache. Programmers can take advantage of this feature to lock small, commonly executed code in caches. It improves the performance of data-plane engines. However, this feature in CPU architectures should be used carefully as the locked portion of the cache is dedicated and hence the overall cache available for the rest of the code is reduced.

General coding guidelines

Some additional guidelines that help in embedded programming:

- Do not initialize function local variables when they are declared. Initialize them only when required. Based on the code path that is being taken at that time, some local variables may not be used at all. In those cases, core cycles need not be expended to do the initializations.
- Define inline and macros for most commonly used operations.
- Avoid buffer copies, string compares, and allocations in the packet-processing path as much as possible.
- Utilize hardware acceleration features. Some examples are:
  - Packet parsing and fields extracted by hardware
  - TCP, IPv4 checksum verification on incoming packets and generation on outgoing packets
  - IP reassembly, IP fragmentation, TCP large receive offload, TCP segmentation offload, etc.
  - Quality of service
  - Cryptography, compression/decompression, timer, XML, and pattern-matching offloads.

Linux operating system for embedded network devices

General-purpose operating systems such as Linux are used to implement control and management planes. A bare-metal executive in a separate partition with dedicated cores is one popular approach to implementing data-plane engines. As the complexity of data-plane engines goes up, general-purpose operating systems are preferred by system designers. By using general operating systems to implement software for all planes, designers have a choice of dedicating cores as well as sharing cores across multiple software entities.

Since Linux is one of the popular operating systems used in network devices, this section concentrates on Linux. Linux, like other general-purpose operating systems, has two execution spaces – kernel and user space. Control and management-plane software are typically implemented as Linux user-space executables in order to take advantage of the vast repository of libraries and also the availability of debugging utilities. Since the data plane and service plane deal with hardware devices, kernel-space programming is used initially by developers. With the increasing complexity of data-plane engines, Linux user-space programming is being looked at to implement DP engines too.

There are some concerns in developing DP engines in Linux user space. This section discusses some of the concerns and how the Linux operating system mitigates those concerns.

Translation lookaside buffer (TLB) misses associated with user-space programming

Concerns: unlike the Linux kernel, user-space programs use virtual addresses. Virtual addresses do not have one-to-one correspondence with physical addresses. Cores need to get hold of physical address from virtual address to read instructions or access data. Cores use the TLB cache to get hold of physical address from virtual addresses. The TLB is a cache that the MMU (memory management unit) uses to maintain virtual address to physical address mappings. Operating systems such as Linux use one TLB entry to map one page (4 Kbytes worth). The number of TLB entries is limited in multicore SoCs, typically in the range of a few thousands. Even though program sizes may not be large, the memory required for millions of flow contexts could be huge. That could result in many TLB misses while accessing flow context nodes. When the core finds that there is no mapping available in the TLB for virtual memory while accessing the memory, it generates a fault. The Linux kernel services this fault and at the end fills up a TLB entry by referring to the page table associated with user-space processes. Due to this additional processing overhead, performance can drop if there are many TLB misses.

Solution: the Linux operating system has a facility called huge pages (also called hugetlbfs). Rather than using 4-K pages, it allows user-space programs to use huge pages of different sizes. Many CPU architectures including Power cores support huge pages up to 256 Mbytes. Only one TLB entry is required for each huge page. Data-plane engines supporting millions of flows can be addressed by very few TLB entries. It reduces TLB misses and in many cases TLB misses reach zero when huge pages are used. The Linux loader also supports loading of text and data segments on huge pages, thereby reducing the TLB misses associated with instructions too.

Luckily, multicore SoCs are increasingly providing a feature called hardware page table walk. This hardware feature walks through the user-space page tables when there is a

TLB miss. Since cores are not involved in servicing TLB misses, performance does not suffer. If a multicore SoC has this feature, programmers don't need to do anything to avoid TLB misses. That is, huge pages are not required when using multicore SoCs with hardware page table walk support. Multicore SoC vendors provide this support in Linux. Hence DP developers don't even need to be aware of this feature.

TLB misses are avoided either by using multicore SoC with hardware page table walk support or by using huge pages support provided by Linux.

Access to hardware peripherals and hardware accelerators

Concerns: traditional hardware peripherals and accelerators understand only physical memory addresses. Drivers in the Linux kernel space are used to work with hardware devices. Accessing hardware devices such as the Ethernet controller and accelerators through the kernel from user space involves multiple context switches and buffer copies.

Solution: Linux provides memory mapping functionality, whereby hardware device registers can be mapped directly to user space. Data-plane engines in user-space processes can access hardware devices without any kernel intervention. Using memory map functionality (*mmap*), even physical memory space can be mapped into user space. User-space processes can program physical addresses for packet buffers in the hardware devices and access the mapped addresses in user space, thereby avoiding any copies from virtual address buffers to physical addresses.

Multicore SoCs provide a feature called IOMMU (IO memory management unit) whereby hardware devices have intelligence to convert virtual memory addresses to physical addresses before accessing any data from memory. The IOMMU hardware block has intelligence to look at the page tables to determine the physical addresses from the programmed virtual addresses. User-space programs using these multicore SoCs don't even need to worry about memory mapping of registers or physical memory and yet access hardware devices and accelerators directly using virtual addresses.

Linux UIO (user-space IO) functionality allows interrupt delivery to user-space programs via the Linux file IO framework. User-space programs waiting on *epoll*() or *select*() function calls on UIO file descriptors are woken up when the interrupt is generated.

The interrupt delivery mechanism and the ability to access hardware directly from user space are also helping user-space-based DP implementations.

Deterministic performance

Concerns: bare-metal-based data-plane implementations are run in a separate partition with dedicated cores. Since the cores are dedicated, there is determinism in performance. Since

Linux is a general-purpose operating system, cores are shared across multiple tasks and hence the performance determinism can't be guaranteed.

Solution: pthreads in Linux can be used to create multiple threads in a Linux user-space process. Each thread can be associated with a core (Linux calls it core affinity). Since it is one Linux user-space process, the entire virtual address space is shared by all threads, allowing the run-to-completion programming model even in Linux as in bare-metal executives. Linux also provides mechanisms to dedicate cores to threads. Once dedicated, the Linux OS does not schedule these cores to any other user processes or threads. It does not even execute interrupts on dedicated cores, thereby providing deterministic performance as achieved in bare-metal executives.

In essence, the Linux operating system advances in using multicore SoCs are paving the way for developing data-plane engines too in the Linux user space without sacrificing performance.

Summary

The move to multicore is occurring not only in high-end applications, but even in mid- and low-end networking applications. Achieving multicore performance is only possible if software takes advantage of the multiple cores. Multicore programming is not as simple as single-core programming. A new mindset is required from architecting, designing to coding. Networking application development in multicore SoCs should not only concentrate on achieving scalable performance, but also ease development and be maintainable for a long time. Some of the programming techniques listed in this chapter should help in achieving this goal. Happy multicore network programming.

CHAPTER 25

Linux for Embedded Systems

Mark Kraeling and Andrew McKay

Chapter Outline

Introduction

The purpose of this chapter is to introduce the use of Linux for embedded applications. Linux was originally written as a kernel for PC clone computers, running an Intel 386-

Software Engineering for Embedded Systems.
DOI: http://dx.doi.org/10.1016/B978-0-12-415917-4.00025-6
© 2013 Elsevier Inc. All rights reserved.

based processor. Without going through a full history of the operating system, it was originally based on an operating system called Minix which was being used as a teaching aid for university students. It was released as a GNU GPL (General Public License) with the source code. This helped it be free for all to copy, use, and change.

Now many distributions exist to help get people started in using Linux. Many of these are commercial ventures, where the company may charge for support or enhanced packages that are not part of the GPL license. One operating system based on the Linux kernel is available called "Debian". This organization of developers (http://www.debian.org) still maintains the concept of providing a "free" operating system. Debian also provides numerous packages for the operating system – again all free. For embedded development, it is more typical to get source code and a kernel specific for your processor environment as opposed to a general distribution.

Why Linux for embedded?

In order to make a decision on which operating system to use, a careful analysis of the timing and feature requirements should be made. Any application that has very stringent timing requirements, such as something that must happen every millisecond (with a very tight deviation requirement) should probably shy away from Linux. These types of applications with stringent deadlines for execution are sometimes classified as "hard" real-time systems. For this classification, the mission of the embedded software cannot be carried out successfully if the timing is not met appropriately. For these types of timing-based applications, Linux isn't a good fit. Also, if your processor environment doesn't have sufficient RAM or a protected mode for the memory, Linux should not be used. Processors like the ARM® Cortex M series fall into this category. The other major consideration is that Linux device drivers can often be complex, so if you are using a board that has no support for Linux already, it can be very time-consuming to get the driver structure working correctly.

If your application is performing networking, requires graphics capability, or requires many user-generated applications to run concurrently, Linux should definitely be considered. Many hardware reference boards and designs for embedded that perform these types of functions include support for Linux already (so time isn't spent driver-writing). Operating systems like Android run with a modified Linux kernel that specializes in the user experience along with varied methods of communication including Bluetooth and Cellular. Processors like the ARM® Cortex A series are excellent candidates for running Linux. Existing processor and hardware reference designs that use this processor core typically have excellent support from various Linux-based kernel distributions.

Linux distributions

There are many different distributions of the Linux-based kernel and packages. For the GNU/Linux distributions, most had their origin in Debian, which was started in 1993. Distributions such as Knoppix, Ubuntu, and Progeny are all descendants of the Debian distribution. Other distributions were started from the GNU/Linux predecessor to Debian, such as Slackware, Gentoo, and Red Hat. There are many active distributions available, and each of them has strengths and weaknesses for the hardware platform being used, and the application that is desired.

Figure 25.1 shows the ancestry tree for the various distributions.

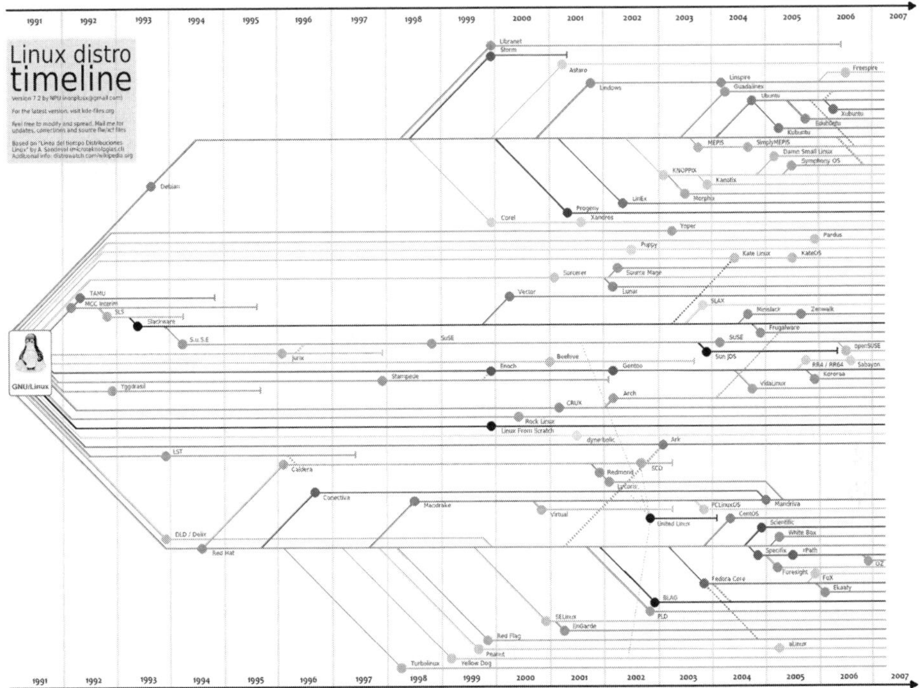

Figure 25.1:
Ancestry tree for the various distributions of Linux. Graphic from: http://www.kde-files.org/CONTENT/content-pre1/57722-1.png.

There are highly specialized distributions like AsteriskNOW, which is a package that allows the user to create their own voicemail, FAX server, and VOIP system. It is based on the CentOS version of Linux. There are many other specialized distributions that focus on specific applications, including home automation, network management, graphic design, and software development.

Distributions are a great way to get started with embedded development. Using a distribution on a development PC makes integration with the embedded target easier. There are also numerous virtual machine applications that allow running multiple different operating systems on the native host system for development. For instance, if the host PC provided by the company runs Windows 7, a virtual machine package can be installed that allows other operating systems to run inside a window on Win7. It is also a great way to try different distributions that run on PC platforms without installing it natively on the machine. Within this virtual machine it allows the user to select which operating system to run in the window.

Embedded platforms suitable for Linux

The most popular Linux distributions are for x86 PC-compatible computers. However, most embedded systems do not use x86 architecture, so Linux has been ported to many other embedded processor families. This includes ARM®, PowerPC, MIPS, and StrongArm®. Processors that are built using these families have differing implementations, with differences in processing power, on-chip memory, I/O, cost, and power consumption.

For embedded applications, they typically need to operate in a "headless" fashion. This means that there is no operator interaction in order to start the operating system and run the embedded applications. Linux was originally developed to use a console to interact, log in, and start the operating system with a PC. Linux has the capability of automating this process, and making the console device a "NULL" device at startup. If operator interaction is required after the system is started, this can be done through a TTY interface or remote login.

Another requirement for Linux is to have a bootable device for the platform. This is typically a flash-based device, as opposed to a hard drive that would be used on a PC x86 system. Depending on the hardware, this device could be some type of flash device that emulates an IDE hard drive, or a more standard SD or microSD flash card that contains the bootloader and program image for the system. Another option is using a RAM disk, which will use a portion of the available RAM memory to emulate a disk drive. For this option, there still needs to be some kind of booting support in order to start the system.

The last requirement for selectioning a platform for Linux is having sufficient memory. The default Linux system has a fairly large memory footprint in comparison with other embedded operating systems. The size of the distribution itself is in the hundreds of megabytes. The kernel within this distribution has a typical size of around 2 megabytes. For smaller embedded systems, it is better to not start with a standard distribution, and instead start with a more specialized distribution for your platform, or build your own. The kernel also uses approximately 4 megabytes of volatile RAM memory. As mentioned above, this amount of RAM required will increase if a RAM drive is also used to simulate a disk drive while operating.

The following are some development boards that are available that are suitable for Linux embedded system development. These reference boards could be used as is if the application is more hobbyist in nature, or most come with schematics and layout assistance to use the same processor and even memory interfaces on your own board:

Arndale Board (http://www.arndaleboard.org)
 Processor: Samsung Exynos 5 (core: ARM Cortex A15) – 1.7 GHz
 RAM: 2 GB DDR3L
 Flash: [microSD slot]
 Other HW: SATA 3, JTAG, USB 3.0 host, USB 2.0 OTG, HDMI, Ethernet, serial

BeagleBoard-xM (http://www.beagleboard.org)
 Processor: TI DM3730 (core: ARM Cortex A8) – 1 GHz
 RAM: 512 MB LPDDR
 Flash: [microSD slot]
 Other HW: DVI-D, JTAG, USB-OTG, 10/100 Ethernet, audio in/out, RS-232, DSP core

BeagleBone (http://www.beagleboard.org)
 Processor: TI Sitara AM335x (core: ARM Cortex A8) – 720 MHz
 RAM: 256MB DDR2
 Flash: [microSD slot]
 Other HW: FTDI-Serial/JTAG, 10/100 Ethernet, USB host, USB client

Micro2440 Stamp Module (http://www.friendlyarm.net)
 Processor: Samsung S3C2440A (core: ARM920T) – 400 MHz
 RAM: 64 MB SDRAM
 Flash: 2 MB NOR
 Other HW: Serial, Analog I/O, user LEDs

ODROID-X Development Board (http://www.hardkernel.com)
 Processor: Sansung Exynos 4412 (core: ARM Cortex A9) – 1.6 GHz
 RAM: 1 GB LPDDR2
 Flash: [SD slot]
 Other HW: USB host * 6, 10/100 Ethernet, audio in/out, MicroHDMI, module header

There are many other development and reference boards available. Choose one based on the hardware interfaces that are needed, and the processor core that is desired. For instance, for the BeagleBoard-xM and the BeagleBone boards above, the xM board has a DVI-D interface and a DSP onboard. If there are video or signal-processing requirements this would be a better choice over the BeagleBone. Various add-on boards exist for both development boards that add various interfaces to the existing board, like VGA to the BeagleBone. Price and availability are important as well after narrowing down the choices based on hardware needs. Using the example above, the xM board has a 40% price adder at the time of publication over the BeagleBone.

Licensing

An open-source software (OSS) license is essentially a copyright license applied to computer software that makes the source code available for the community to use. This license allows end users to review and modify/customize the source code. Most open-source licenses are free, which enables modification, redistribution, and commercial use without having to compensate the original author. Other open-source licenses permit modification of the source code for personal use only or only permit non-commercial redistribution. Many open-source licenses have additional restrictions such as a requirement to maintain the name of the authors along with a copyright statement within the source code. The most popular set of free open-source software licenses are approved by the Open Source Initiative (OSI) based on the Open Source Definition (OSD). The OSD has ten basic concepts:

1. Free redistribution.
2. Source code.
3. Derived works.
4. Integrity of the author's source code.
5. No discrimination against persons or groups.
6. No discrimination against fields of endeavor.
7. Distribution of license.
8. License must not be specific to a product.
9. License must not restrict other software.
10. License must be technology-neutral.

OSS is based on the concept of content licensing. There are a number of rules which open-source licenses must adhere to. The fundamental rule is the following: "Any person who receives the software is allowed to modify it, and to redistribute the modified version to whomever they please." Open-source software is essentially the opposite of proprietary software. When software is released under an open-source license, you no longer have any control over who uses the software or how the software is used. This is why it's difficult to make money by directly selling copies of OSS. Since recipients are permitted to change the software, it is impossible to impose any controls over how the software is used.

Many embedded software programs have software components from various other organizations. When considering what license to use for a given software program, don't forget to consider the licenses already being used by the software components. These existing licenses may well constrain the licensing choices. If the embedded software is going to be built or linked with other embedded software, and the resulting software build will then be distributed, then a license must be chosen which is compatible with the existing software.

It is common to provide a license that is readily understood by the industry. Potential contributors who are confronted with an unfamiliar license will move on to another project with more familiar licensing. If the goal is to encourage contributors, a well-known license must be used. Some examples are:

- GNU General Public License (GPL)
- BSD License
- Mozilla Public License (MPL)
- Academic Free License (AFL)
- Open Software License (OSL).

Embedded software organizations should keep track of all of the "approved" licenses for their organization. An example list of open-source licenses is shown in Figure 25.2.

Getting started with Embedded Linux

Memory management unit

A main requirement for Linux is that the processor supports a memory management unit (MMU). This allows the Linux kernel to provide consistent address space across different processor platforms, memory mapping, memory protection, and memory sharing. That said, a variant of Linux called uClinux exists and it is specifically designed for use on processors without an MMU. This section will focus on Linux running on an ARM processor with an MMU.

Bootstrapper

A first-stage bootloader or bootstrapper is a small piece of code that runs right after boot. It initializes the processor and then loads a larger application into executable memory before starting the application's execution. A bootstrapper may be required when code is stored in memory that the processor is unable to execute out of, such as SPI data/serial flash. Some ARM class processors may require a bootstrapper depending on the external memory devices that are used to store code.

Column1	License Name	Publisher	Attribution/Disclaimer Requirements (giving credit to author)	Linking from Code with a different license	Grant license to contributors patents	Name	Abbreviation	Link to official version	Intended Uses
APACHE1.1	Apache 1.1	The Apache Software Foundation	Yes	Yes	no	Apache Software License	APACHE1.1	http://www.apache.org/licenses/LICENSE-1.1	
APACHE2.0	Apache 2.0	The Apache Software Foundation	Yes	Yes	Yes	Apache License 2.0	APACHE2.0	http://www.apache.org/licenses/LICENSE-2.0	Release Only Object Code Externally; Release Source Code Externally; Recipient Needs Redistribution Rights; Enable Recipient to Reuse in Open Source Code (check license compatibility); Enable Recipient to Reuse in Proprietary Code; Linking from Code with a Different License; Encourage Community Contributions; Release under Proprietary License; Protect Sensitive IP (if no source distributed); Sell the Software; Grant License to Patents; Internal Use
ART2.0	Artistic License	Unknown		Yes		Artistic License	ART2.0	http://www.opensource.org/licenses/artistic-license-2.0.php	
BSD	BSD License	University of California	Yes	Yes	No	New BSD License (2-clause)	BSD	http://www.opensource.org/licenses/bsd-license.php	Internal Use; Release Only Object Code Externally; Release Source Code Externally (optional); Recipient Needs Redistribution Rights; Enable Recipient to Reuse in Open Source Code (check license compatibility); Enable Recipient to Reuse in Proprietary Code; Linking from Code with a Different License; Encourage Community Contributions; Release under Proprietary License; Protect Sensitive IP; Sell the Software; Use in GPLv2 projects like the Linux kernel or U-Boot; Use in BSD projects like FreeBSD
ECLIPLSE1.0	Eclipse Public License 1.0 (EPL)	Eclipse Foundation	NO?	Yes	Yes	Eclipse Public License	ECLIPLSE1.0	http://www.opensource.org/licenses/eclipse-1.0.php	Release Source Code Externally; Recipient Needs Redistribution Rights; Enable Recipient to Reuse in Open Source Code (check license compatibility); Enable Recipient to Reuse in Proprietary Code Linking from Code with a Different License; Encourage Community Contributions Release under Proprietary License; Sell the Software; Grant License to Patents; Force recipient to Release Under the Same License (not as restrictive as GPL); Limit use to FSL products (or other similar restrictions); Internal Use
GPL1.0	GPL (1.0)	Free Software Foundation		no	silent	GNU General Public License (GPL) Ver. 1 1989	GPL1.0	http://www.gnu.org/licenses/gpl-1.0.html	Release Source Code Externally; Recipient Needs Redistribution Rights; Enable Recipient to Reuse in Open Source Code; Encourage Community Contributions; Force recipient to Release Under the Same License; Internal Use
GPL2.0	GPL (2.0)	Free Software Foundation		No	debatable (v3 seems to indicate yes)	GNU General Public License (GPL) Ver. 2, June 1991	GPL2.0	http://www.gnu.org/copyleft/gpl.html	Release Source Code Externally; Recipient Needs Redistribution Rights; Enable Recipient to Reuse in Open Source Code; Encourage Community Contributions; Force recipient to Release Under the Same License; Reuse in GPLv2 projects like the Linux kernel or U-Boot; Internal Use
GPLv3	GPL(3.0)	Free Software Foundation		No (except for linking GNU AGPLv3 with GNU GPLv3	Yes	GNU General Public License (GPL) Ver. 3, 2005	GPL3.0	http://www.gnu.org/copyleft/gpl.html	Release Source Code Externally; Recipient Needs Redistribution Rights; Enable Recipient to Reuse in Open Source Code; Encourage Community Contributions; Grant License to Patents; Force recipient to Release Under the Same License; Internal Use
LGPL2.1	LGPL (2.1)	Free Software Foundation		Yes	No?	GNU Library or "Lesser" General Public License (LGPL), V2.1	LGPL2.1	http://www.gnu.org/licenses/lgpl-2.1.html	Release Source Code Externally; Recipient Needs Redistribution Rights; Enable Recipient to Reuse in Open Source Code; Linking from Code with a Different License; Encourage Community Contributions; Force recipient to Release Under the Same License; Reuse in GPLv2 projects like the Linux kernel or U-Boot; Internal Use
LGPLv3									
MIT	MIT License	Unknown	Yes	Yes	No	MIT License	MIT	http://www.opensource.org/licenses/mit-license.php	
MPL1.0	Mozilla Public License (1.0)	Unknown	no?	Yes	no?	Mozilla Public License, (MPL), 1.0	MPL1.0	http://www.opensource.org/licenses/mozilla1.0.php	
MPL1.1	Mozilla Public License (1.1)	Unknown	no?	Yes	no?	Mozilla Public License (MPL), 1.1	MPL1.1	http://www.opensource.org/licenses/mozilla1.1.php	
PHP	PHP License (3)	PHP Group	Yes	Yes?	No?	PHP License	PHP	http://www.opensource.org/licenses/php.php	
PHP	PHP License (4)	PHP Group	Yes	Yes?	No?	PHP License	PHP	http://www.opensource.org/licenses/php.php	
PYTHON	Python License (CNRI Python License)	Corporation for National Research Initiatives	no?	yes?	no?	Python License (CNRI Python License)	PYTHON	http://www.opensource.org/licenses/pythonpl.php	
PYTHONSF	Python Software Foundation (PSF) License (2.1.1)	Python Software Foundation	"Copyright © 2001, 2002, 2003, 2004, 2005, 2006 Python Software Foundation; All Rights Reserved" must be retained in Python alone or in any derivative version prepared by Licensee	yes (silent)	no (silent)	Python Software Foundation License	PYTHONSF	http://www.opensource.org/licenses/PythonSoftFoundation.php	Release Only Object Code Externally; Release Source Code Externally; Recipient Needs Redistribution Rights; Enable Recipient to Reuse in Open Source Code (check license compatibility); Enable Recipient to Reuse in Proprietary Code; Linking from Code with a Different License; Encourage Community Contributions; Release under Proprietary License; Protect Sensitive IP (if no source distributed); Sell the Software; Grant License to Patents; Internal Use
SLEEPYCAT	Sleepycat License	University of California & Harvard University	No	yes	Yes	Sleepycat License:	SLEEPYCAT	http://www.opensource.org/licenses/sleepycat.php	
Sun Industry Standards Source License (SISSL)	SISSL					Sun Industry Standards Source License (SISSL)	SISSL	http://www.opensource.org/licenses/sisslpl.php	
Echelon									
SUNPL						Sun Public License	SUNPL	http://www.opensource.org/licenses/sunpublic.php	
Common	CDDL			Yes					
SYBASE1.0						Sybase Open Watcom Public License, 1.0	SYBASE1.0	http://www.opensource.org/licenses/sybase.php	
UoI-NCSA						University of Illinois/NCSA Open Source License	UoI-NCSA	http://www.opensource.org/licenses/UoI-NCSA.php	
VOVIDA1.0						Vovida Software License, Version 1.0	VOVIDA1.0	http://www.opensource.org/licenses/vovidapl.php	
W3C						W3C License	W3C	http://www.opensource.org/licenses/W3C.php	
Dual BSD/GPL2									Release Only Object Code Externally; Release Source Code Externally (optional); Recipient Needs Redistribution Rights; Enable Recipient to Reuse in Open Source Code (check license compatibility); Enable Recipient to Reuse in Proprietary Code; Linking from Code with a Different License; Encourage Community Contributions; Release under Proprietary License; Protect Sensitive IP; Sell the Software; Reuse in GPLv2 projects like the Linux kernel or U-Boot; Use in BSD projects like FreeBSD; Internal Use

Figure 25.2:
An example list of open source licenses.

It is possible to boot a Linux kernel with a bootstrapper or first-stage bootloader. However, because of the limited functionality that it would typically provide, it is recommended to use it to load a fully functional bootloader such as DAS U-Boot or Redboot.

In the case of Atmel's AT91 processor, the boot ROM code stored inside the processor is designed to search for an image in a particular memory location in SPI data flash, NAND flash or SDCARD. Once it has found a boot image, the code is loaded into internal SRAM and executed. Since internal SRAM is quite limited, a typical application would not be able to run within the memory constraints. Therefore it is the job of the boostrapper to:

1. configure GPIOs;
2. configure internal clocks;
3. initialize external SDRAM;
4. load an application from external memory into SDRAM;
5. start execution of the main application.

Often bootstrapper code is provided by the processor vendor. Atmel provides an application called AT91Boostrap for booting their AT91 series processors.

Bootloader

Fully functional bootloaders tend to be larger pieces of code than bootstrappers so they are often loaded with a bootstrapper application once SDRAM has been initialized. In some processor architectures a bootloader may be stored in flash that the processor is capable of executing from. In this case the bootloader may self-bootstrap. That is, it contains a small piece of code that initializes SDRAM and copies the rest of its own image into SDRAM for execution.

Requirements to boot Linux on ARM

According to the ARM Booting document found in the documentation that ships with the Linux kernel source (Documents/arm/Booting) a bootloader should:

1. set up and initialize the RAM;
2. initialize one serial port (optional);
3. detect the machine type;
4. set up the kernel tagged list;
5. call the kernel image.

The first job of the bootloader is to ensure that the RAM on the system is initialized for the kernel. The kernel does not contain any code to detect and initialize RAM so the bootloader must perform this task. It is also good practice for the bootloader to run a quick memory test prior to booting the kernel to ensure that the hardware is functioning correctly.

To aid in debugging the kernel while it boots, the bootloader should initialize one serial port for the kernel to use. This is often called the console port. It is possible for the kernel to initialize a console port on its own based on arguments passed to the kernel. However, until such time that the console port is initialized any messages printed during the boot will not be output. This means that if the kernel crashed during boot prior to a console port being initialized, the reason for the crash would be unknown.

The kernel expects to be told what type of machine it is running on so that it can perform the proper initialization for that machine. The bootloader has a responsibility to provide that information to the kernel. It is possible that the bootloader either provides a hardcoded machine type or detects the type of hardware that it is running on and provides the appropriate machine type to the kernel.

The kernel tagged list is a structure set up in memory to pass information about the system to the kernel. The kernel tagged list may contain information such as system memory, root file system location, machine type.

After performing all of the above tasks the bootloader must then call the kernel image.

For a full description of requirements to boot the Linux kernel on an ARM platform see the documentation provided in Documents/arm/Booting or the Linux kernel source.

Advanced bootloader functionality

The previous section covered the functionality that a bootloader has to support to boot a Linux kernel. However, modern bootloaders are capable of much more functionality. This functionality may include:

1. serial console to interact with the bootloader;
2. managing images stored in flash;
3. loading images via serial port;
4. loading images via Ethernet;
5. loading images via TFTP;
6. modifying parameters passed to the kernel;
7. system test.

DAS U-Boot

DAS U-Boot, the Universal Bootloader, is an open-source application that builds for several different platforms (PowerPC, ARM, MIPS, and X86) and provides many of the previously mentioned advanced features. It is normally configured to load and boot the kernel automatically. However, it is possible to interrupt the normal boot sequence and get on to the command line of U-Boot via a console serial port. DAS U-Boot is available at http://www.denx.de/wiki/U-Boot/WebHome.

Kernel

Choosing a kernel version can be tricky; therefore it is recommended to check with the processor vendor to see what versions of the kernel are supported. When choosing a processor it is also a good idea to determine whether the processor is supported in the mainline kernel. Choosing a processor with mainline kernel support makes staying up to date with the latest kernel much easier.

In July of 2011 the Linux kernel moved to version 3.0, leaving behind the 2.6 series of the kernel, which is now EOL. However, Linux 2.6 is still a good choice for embedded applications. Embedded applications often do not require the bleeding-edge functionality of the latest kernel and benefit greatly from the stability that older kernel versions may provide. Conversely if any issues arise while running an older version of the kernel it may be harder to get support from the Linux community.

A general rule of thumb for choosing a kernel version to use within a project is to use the newest stable release that can be run on the processor. There are other external factors that may come into effect that may not allow the use of the absolute latest kernel such as drivers that have not yet been ported to that particular kernel version. Typically speaking, once a kernel has been chosen for a particular project, there is no need to change versions of the kernel unless a newer kernel version provides new functionality that would be a benefit to the project.

Boot parameters

The Linux kernel can be passed parameters during boot that affect what the kernel does during boot and execution. These parameters may include what block device should be used for the root file system, how much memory the system has, devices to use as console, or whether the kernel should provide debug information during boot. A list of the parameters that can be passed to the kernel is maintained at http://www.kernel.org/doc/Documentation/kernel-parameters.txt.

Kernel drivers

There are three classes of device drivers within the Linux kernel. They are character devices, block devices, and finally network devices. This section will describe the similarities and differences of these types of drivers. It is beyond the scope of this book to provide sample drivers for each class of device driver. A good reference for device drivers is *Linux Device Drivers* by Jonathan Corbet, Alessandro Rubini, and Greg Kroah-Hartman (http://lwn.net/Kernel/LDD3/). It is current as of Linux 2.6.10 and is still applicable to newer versions of the Linux kernel.

Device nodes

Device nodes (devnode) are located in the /dev directory. They are used by applications running on Linux to communicate with drivers that handle character and block devices. To interact with a driver an application will use the open, close, read, write, and ioctl (IO Control) system calls.

A devnode is defined with a major and minor number. Typically the major number is used to define the type of device and the minor number is used to define an instance of that device. Devnodes are created using the command-line tool mknod and are located in the /dev directory. The mknod command takes arguments that include the node type: block, character or pipe, the major number and the minor number.

When a driver registers itself with the kernel, it registers itself as a character or block driver along with its major and minor number. This allows the Linux kernel to associate the driver with a devnode and then when a Linux application opens the devnode the correct driver will handle the system calls made by the application.

Character devices

As mentioned in the Device Nodes section, character devices are accessed through device nodes in the /dev directory. Character drivers are used for devices that require streams of data such as serial ports, parallel ports and consoles. A Linux application connects to a character device using the open system call and disconnects from the device using the close system call. It uses the read system call to read available bytes from the character device, and the write system call to write bytes to the character device. The ioctl system call is used to control the settings of the character device. In the case of a serial port, the ioctl system call would be used to set the BAUD rate, number of data bits, parity bits, and number of stop bits.

Block devices

As mentioned in section 2.4.2.1, block devices are accessed through device nodes in the /dev directory. Block device drivers are used for devices that require blocks of data such as hard drives and flash chips. A Linux application connects to a block device using the open system call and disconnects from the device using the close system call. Unlike UNIX drivers Linux does allow block devices to be accessed in a stream through the read and write system calls. However, the driver will buffer the data until one block is received and then flush it to the hardware. Block devices also support the ioctl function. The ioctl function may be used to access information about the block device, access out of band (OOB) information or perform block-level erases.

Network devices

The third type of device, the network device, is quite different from the previous two types of devices. Network device drivers are not accessed through devnodes and are not mapped to the file system in any manner. Network device drivers, whether they are hardware drivers or protocol drivers, handle data at a packet level and they are accessed through system calls relating to the handling of packets.

Basic kernel driver example

Kernel drivers are written in C and can be written outside the kernel source tree. During development it is typical to build a driver as a module. After the driver has been completed it is up to the system designer to decide whether the driver should be built statically in the kernel or as a separate loadable module. The following piece of code is a sample Hello World driver that can be compiled as either a kernel module or built-in driver.

```
/* Basic Kernel Module */
/* Adapted from "The Linux Kernel Module Programming Guide" */
/* http://tldp.org/LDP/lkmpg/2.6/html/lkmpg.html */

#include<linux/module.h> /* Required for Module Support */
#include<linux/kernel.h> /* Required for printk log levels */
#include<linux/init.h> /* Required for module_init and module_exit macros */

static int __init hello_start(void)
{

    printk(KERN_INFO "Hello from the Kernel\n");

    /* Return Success */

    return (0);

}
static void __exit hello_exit(void)
{

    printk(KERN_INFO "Goodbye from the Kernel\n");

}
module_init(hello_start);
module_exit(hello_exit);
```

There are a few things to note about the source code:

- The three include files at the top are the minimum required header files for a driver file. Note that linux/module.h is not required if the driver is only ever built into the kernel directly.

- At the bottom of the file are two macros, the module_init macro and the module_exit macro. These macros tell the kernel which functions to call when the driver is loaded and unloaded from the system.
- The prototypes for the two functions use an _init and _exit macro. This is used by the linker when building a built-in driver. The _init macro is used to denote a function that is used for initialization of the driver. After execution it is possible for the kernel to clean this memory up for later use. The _exit macro is used to denote a function that does not need to be included when built as a built-in driver. Since a built-in driver by definition will never exit, this function can be excluded by the linker.

To compile this driver on a standard Linux machine the following makefile is written:

```
obj-m += hello_driver.o

all:
    make -C /lib/modules/$(shell uname -r)/build M=$(PWD) modules

clean:
    make -C /lib/modules/$(shell uname -r)/build M=$(PWD) clean
```

To compile this Hello World driver *make all* is called from the command line. Once the driver is built the directory will contain the following files:

```
hello_driver.c  hello_driver.mod.c hello_driver.o modules.order
hello_driver.ko hello_driver.mod.o Makefile   Module.symvers
```

The actual driver is called hello_driver.ko. To load this driver the insmod command is used. Note that an insmod must be run by the root user. Running dmesg after installing the module reveals the message printed by the driver during load.

```
amckay@Zen:~/WIP/hello_driver$ insmod hello_driver.ko
amckay@Zen:~/WIP/hello_driver$ dmesg | tail -n 3
[ 6039.800909] Disabling lock debugging due to kernel taint
[ 6039.800914] hello_driver: module license 'unspecified' taints kernel.
[ 6039.801206] Hello from the Kernel
```

To unload the driver the rmmod command is used. Instead of specifying the filename of the driver, only the name of the driver needs to be used.

```
amckay@Zen:~/WIP/hello_driver$ rmmod hello_driver
amckay@Zen:~/WIP/hello_driver$ dmesg | tail -n 4
[ 6039.800909] Disabling lock debugging due to kernel taint
[ 6039.800914] hello_driver: module license 'unspecified' taints kernel.
[ 6039.801206] Hello from the Kernel
[ 6054.434776] Goodbye from the Kernel
```

In the messages output by the kernel when the module was loaded there was a message printed that said *module license 'unspecified' taints kernel.* This is output because the driver did not specify its license type. A kernel is tainted when a proprietary driver is loaded to the kernel. The Tainted Kernels section will outline the pitfalls of running a tainted kernel.

To ensure that the kernel is not tainted the MODULE_LICENSE macro is used to specify what license the driver is distributed under. A couple of other important macros are the MODULE_AUTHOR and MODULE_DESCRIPTION macros. These are used to document who wrote the driver and what the driver does. Modifications to the driver as shown below will now allow the driver to be loaded without tainting the kernel and document the driver author and description.

```
/* Basic Kernel Module */
/* Adapted from "The Linux Kernel Module Programming Guide" */
/* http://tldp.org/LDP/lkmpg/2.6/html/lkmpg.html */

#include<linux/module.h> /* Required for Module Support */
#include<linux/kernel.h> /* Required for printk log levels */
#include<linux/init.h> /* Required for module_init and module_exit macros */

static int __init hello_start(void)
{

   printk(KERN_INFO "Hello from the Kernel\n");

   return (0);

}
static void __exit hello_exit(void)
{

   printk(KERN_INFO "Goodbye from the Kernel\n");

}
module_init(hello_start);
module_exit(hello_exit);
MODULE_LICENSE("GPL");
MODULE_AUTHOR("Andrew McKay");
MODULE_DESCRIPTION("A simple Hello World driver");
```

Debugging

Tainted kernels

Running a tainted kernel can be an issue when trying to get support from the community. Two common reasons for the kernel to become tainted are that an out-of-tree module has been loaded, or that a module with a proprietary license was loaded into the system. When asking for help from the Linux community it is best to recreate the issue with a non-tainted kernel if it is possible. It is still possible to ask for some help with a tainted kernel. However, members of the community will likely call into question the quality of the proprietary or custom code.

To determine whether the kernel that is currently running is tainted the */proc/sys/kernel/tainted* file should be read. If the file returns 0 then the kernel is currently not tainted. If the file returns a non-zero number then the kernel is tainted. The following bits define the reason that the kernel has become tainted:

```
#define TAINT_PROPRIETARY_MODULE     0
#define TAINT_FORCED_MODULE          1
#define TAINT_UNSAFE_SMP             2
#define TAINT_FORCED_RMMOD           3
#define TAINT_MACHINE_CHECK          4
#define TAINT_BAD_PAGE               5
#define TAINT_USER                   6
#define TAINT_DIE                    7
#define TAINT_OVERRIDDEN_ACPI_TABLE  8
#define TAINT_WARN                   9
#define TAINT_CRAP                  10
#define TAINT_FIRMWARE_WORKAROUND   11
#define TAINT_OOT_MODULE            12
```

Printk

Printk is the recommended approach to debugging issues within the kernel. Printk, similarly to printf, is a function that takes a formatted string and a list of data type parameters to place within the string. Printk messages are printed to console and command-line interfaces depending on what level of printk messages they are currently configured to output. Messages printed with printk are also available to be viewed using the *dmesg* command on the command line, and may be logged to /var/log/messages as well.

Printk supports multiple levels of message based on their priority. The kernel supports the following message levels where lower numbers define a higher message priority:

```
#define KERN_EMERG "<0>" /* system is unusable  */
#define KERN_ALERT "<1>" /* action must be taken immediately */
#define KERN_CRIT "<2>" /* critical conditions  */
#define KERN_ERR "<3>" /* error conditions  */
#define KERN_WARNING "<4>" /* warning conditions  */
#define KERN_NOTICE "<5>" /* normal but significant condition */
#define KERN_INFO "<6>" /* informational  */
#define KERN_DEBUG "<7>" /* debug-level messages  */
```

To output a message with printk at a certain message level, printk is called as follows:

```
printk(KERN_WARNING "This is my warning message\n");
```

Printk is useful for debugging simple problems within the kernel. However, debugging timing-critical or race-condition type bugs can prove to be difficult with printk. Generally speaking debugging with printk is sufficient for most bugs within the kernel.

A file in the proc filesystem controls the levels of printk that are output to the console. Using *cat* to output this file will output four numbers to the terminal

```
amckay@Zen:/proc/sys/kernel$ cat printk
4	4	1	7
```

In order, the numbers represent the current console log level, the default message log level, the minimum console log level, and finally the default console log level. These items are defined as follows:

Current console log level	The priority of messages that are output to the console. Any message of this log level or lower will be output to the console.
Default message log level	Any message without a specified priority will output with this priority.
Minimum console log level	The highest priority level of message that the console can be set to. Any message with a higher priority than this value will be output to the console no matter what the current console log level is set to.
Default console log level	The message priority that a console will default to.

By writing to the /proc/sys/kernel/printk, the current console log level can be modified. To set the console so that all printk messages are output it should be written to 7 using *echo*. Note that it is necessary to be root on the system to write to this file.

```
root@Zen:/proc/sys/kernel# echo 7>printk
root@Zen:/proc/sys/kernel# cat printk
7	4	1	7
```

Kernel Panic/Oops

When the Linux kernel has determined that something has gone wrong internally, it will output either a kernel Oops or a kernel Panic message. The difference between an Oops and a Panic is the severity of the issue. When a kernel Oops happens, the kernel is usually capable of continuing execution. Because there is no guarantee as to the state of the operating system after a kernel Oops, it is best to save as much information about the state of the system and then reboot. When a kernel Panic happens, Linux halts and the system will require a reboot.

The location of a driver can impact whether the kernel fails with an Oops or a full-on Panic. Often if a driver that is loaded as a module crashes, the kernel is able to unload the driver and continue execution. Conversely if a driver built statically into the kernel crashes, the kernel will likely not be able to continue execution. During driver development it is best to develop the driver as a module as it will still be possible to interact with the system after a crash. This can be important in helping to gather as much information about the state of the system and what went wrong with the code.

Depending on what kernel options are enabled it may be possible to debug where in execution the kernel was when it crashed. The important item to make sure is enabled in the kernel is KALLSYMS. This option ensures that all symbol information is retained in the kernel image and output in the kernel Oops message. Without this information only memory addresses will be output in the message. If the System.map file or vmlinux file is still available it is still possible to debug a kernel Oops without KALLSYMS enabled; however, it is much more difficult. In later versions of the kernel KALLSYMS is automatically enabled when the kernel is configured with EXPERT enabled. The kernel Oops message will also note if the kernel has been tainted. This is one of the first places that members of the Linux community will look while reviewing a kernel Oops message when offering support.

The following output is a sample kernel Oops with KALLSYMS enabled. From this output it is possible to determine that the kernel crashed in a function called vlan_proc_init which was called from vlan_init_net. The output includes output of the stack. The stack is also interpreted, which gives a longer history of the function calls that led up to the crash. Combining this message along with printk messages outlined in the previous section will prove to be a powerful tool in hunting most bugs within the Linux kernel.

```
Unable to handle kernel NULL pointer dereference at virtual address 00000000
pgd = c3bec000
[00000000] *pgd = 23bdb031, *pte = 00000000, *ppte = 00000000
Internal error: Oops: 17 [#1] PREEMPT
Modules linked in: 8021q(+)
CPU: 0  Not tainted (2.6.30.9 #1)
PC is at vlan_proc_init + 0 × 34/0xec [8021q]
LR is at vlan_init_net + 0 × 4c/0 × 74 [8021q]
pc : [<bf002840>]  lr : [<bf0001a0>]  psr: 20000013
sp : c3b9ff10 ip : 00000000 fp : 4001f740
r10: 00000000 r9 : c3b9e000 r8 : c025b32c
```

```
r7 : c025b31c r6 : 00000000 r5 : c028056c r4 : c028056c
r3 : c3b9e000 r2 : 00000002 r1 : 00000000 r0 : c028056c
Flags: nzCv IRQs on FIQs on Mode SVC_32 ISA ARM Segment user
Control: 0005317 f Table: 23bec000 DAC: 00000015
Process modprobe (pid: 532, stack limit = 0xc3b9e268)
Stack: (0xc3b9ff10 to 0xc3ba0000)
ff00:          c028056c 00000002 c3aacc80 c028056c
ff20: 00000000 bf0001a0 bf004f20 bf00511c 00000000 c0155984 c3811850 c0155c2c
ff40: bf008000 000c10b0 00000000 00006710 c001cf88 bf008030 bf008000 c001c2f4
ff60: bf004f6c 000c10b0 00000000 00006710 c001cf88 bf004f6c 000c10b0 00000000
ff80: 00006710 c005a058 000c10c0 00006710 000c10b0 00006710 00000001 00000000
ffa0: 00000080 c001cde0 00006710 00000001 000c10c0 00006710 000c10b0 000c1090
ffc0: 00006710 00000001 00000000 00000080 000c10b0 000c101c 000c1090 4001f740
ffe0: bedb8aa8 bedb8a98 0001bccc 401d9840 60000010 000c10c0 00000000 00000000
[<bf002840>] (vlan_proc_init + 0 × 34/0xec [8021q]) from [<bf0001a0>] (vlan_init_net
+ 0 × 4c/0 × 74 [8021q])
[<bf0001a0>] (vlan_init_net + 0 × 4c/0 × 74 [8021q]) from [<c0155984>] (register_perne
t_operations + 0 × 1c/0 × 24)
[<c0155984>] (register_pernet_operations + 0 × 1c/0 × 24) from [<c0155c2c>] (register_
pernet_gen_device + 0 × 58/0 × 94)
[<c0155c2c>] (register_pernet_gen_device + 0 × 58/0 × 94) from [<bf008030>] (vlan_prot
o_init + 0 × 30/0xb4 [8021q])
[<bf008030>] (vlan_proto_init + 0 × 30/0xb4 [8021q]) from [<c001c2f4>] (do_one_initc
all + 0 × 5c/0 × 1bc)
[<c001c2f4>] (do_one_initcall + 0 × 5c/0 × 1bc) from [<c005a058>] (sys_init_module + 0 × 8
c/0 × 188)
[<c005a058>] (sys_init_module + 0 × 8c/0 × 188) from [<c001cde0>] (ret_fast_syscall + 0x
0/0 × 2c)
Code: e5922000 e3520000 e5901308 0a000002 (e5910000)
–[ end trace bad8d707ee821b7b ]–
note: modprobe[532] exited with preempt_count 1
BUG: scheduling while atomic: modprobe/532/0 × 40000002
Modules linked in: 8021q(+)
[<c0022600>] (unwind_backtrace + 0 × 0/0xd4) from [<c01c5080>] (__schedule + 0 × 68/0 × 34
c)
[<c01c5080>] (__schedule + 0 × 68/0 × 34c) from [<c01c5388>] (schedule + 0 × 24/0 × 40)
[<c01c5388>] (schedule + 0 × 24/0 × 40) from [<c002d9b4>] (__cond_resched + 0 × 24/0 × 40)
[<c002d9b4>] (__cond_resched + 0 × 24/0 × 40) from [<c01c549c>] (_cond_resched + 0 × 40/0x
54)
[<c01c549c>] (_cond_resched + 0 × 40/0 × 54) from [<c0074fbc>] (unmap_vmas + 0 × 528/0 × 5d8
)
[<c0074fbc>] (unmap_vmas + 0 × 528/0 × 5d8) from [<c0077bb4>] (exit_mmap + 0xbc/0 × 1a8)
[<c0077bb4>] (exit_mmap + 0xbc/0 × 1a8) from [<c003088c>] (mmput + 0 × 38/0xe0)
[<c003088c>] (mmput + 0 × 38/0xe0) from [<c00343e4>] (exit_mm + 0 × 144/0 × 148)
[<c00343e4>] (exit_mm + 0 × 144/0 × 148) from [<c0035b54>] (do_exit + 0 × 158/0 × 660)
[<c0035b54>] (do_exit + 0 × 158/0 × 660) from [<c0020b44>] (die + 0 × 17c/0 × 19c)
[<c0020b44>] (die + 0 × 17c/0 × 19c) from [<c0023550>] (__do_kernel_fault + 0 × 64/0 × 74)
[<c0023550>] (__do_kernel_fault + 0 × 64/0 × 74) from [<c0023764>] (do_page_fault + 0 × 20
4/0 × 21c)
[<c0023764>] (do_page_fault + 0 × 204/0 × 21c) from [<c001c234>] (do_DataAbort + 0 × 30/0x
```

```
90)
[<c001c234>] (do_DataAbort+0x30/0x90) from [<c001c9ac>] (__dabt_svc+0x4c/0x60)
Exception stack(0xc3b9fec8 to 0xc3b9ff10)
fec0:      c028056c 00000000 00000002 c3b9e000 c028056c c028056c
fee0: 00000000 c025b31c c025b32c c3b9e000 00000000 4001f740 00000000 c3b9ff10
ff00: bf0001a0 bf002840 20000013 ffffffff
[<c001c9ac>] (__dabt_svc+0x4c/0x60) from [<bf0001a0>] (vlan_init_net+0x4c/0x74 [
8021q])
[<bf0001a0>] (vlan_init_net+0x4c/0x74 [8021q]) from [<c028056c>] (0xc028056c)
Segmentation fault
```

Proc file system

The proc file system or procfs is a special file system in the Linux kernel that allows communication between application and kernel code. Originally it was used to present information about processes that were currently running on the system. Later on it was extended to allow communication with the internals of the kernel.

Procfs is typically mounted to the file system at /proc. The contents of procfs look like:

```
1    1477 1751 1859 23   6451 886        driver        net
10   1480 1755 1864 237  6507 9          execdomains   pagetypeinfo
1006 1481 1758 1872 242  6515 919        fb            partitions
1019 15   1760 1881 25   6531 930        filesystems   sched_debug
1022 1509 1776 1883 26   6532 951        fs            schedstat
1050 1510 1783 19   27   654  965        interrupts    scsi
1055 1541 1789 1913 28   659  973        iomem         self
1070 1542 1798 1914 29   6685 986        ioports       slabinfo
1071 1543 1799 1915 295  6686 988        irq           softirqs
1072 1545 18   1916 296  6785 994        kallsyms      stat
1074 1550 1802 1917 3    680  998        kcore         swaps
1079 1552 1806 1918 30   6836 999        key-users     sys
1082 1555 1810 1919 31   685  acpi       kmsg          sysrq-trigger
1083 16   1813 1972 382  698  asound     kpagecount    sysvipc
1089 1668 1815 1988 39   7    buddyinfo  kpageflags    timer_list
1096 17   1819 1989 390  717  bus        latency_stats timer_stats
1125 1714 1827 1990 48   723  cgroups    loadavg       tty
12   1716 1830 2    49   725  cmdline    locks         uptime
13   1720 1832 20   50   727  consoles   mdstat        version
132  17221837 2022 53    731  cpuinfo    meminfo       vmallocinfo
1328 1723 1843 2030 54   747  crypto     misc          vmstat
1333 1726 1850 2033 5971 76   devices    modules       zoneinfo
1351 1740 1852 2090 6    790  diskstats  mounts
14   1743 1854 21   6403 8    dma        mtd
1424 1745 1856 22   6419 885  dri        mtrr
```

The directories named with numbers are associated with the process ID (PID) of currently executing tasks. Other various files and directories report information about the system. Typically drivers will create proc files within the driver folder.

The following are some important files in procfs to note:

/proc/cmdline	Reports the parameters passed to the kernel at boot. `BOOT_IMAGE=/boot/vmlinuz-3.2.0-aacm-custom2-core2duo root=UUID=eefc2430-592b-4262-bd96-62bbee662af5 ro crashkernel=384M-2G:64M,2G-:128M`
/proc/cpuinfo	Reports information about the CPU that the kernel is running on.

```
processor       : 0
vendor_id       : GenuineIntel
cpu family      : 6
model           : 23
model name      : Intel(R) Core(TM)2 Duo CPU    T9300 @
2.50 GHz
stepping        : 6
microcode       : 0x60c
cpu MHz         : 800.000
cache size      : 6144 KB
physical id     : 0
siblings        : 2
core id         : 0
cpu cores       : 2
apicid          : 0
initial apicid  : 0
fdiv_bug        : no
hlt_bug         : no
f00f_bug        : no
coma_bug        : no
fpu             : yes
fpu_exception   : yes
cpuid level     : 10
wp              : yes
flags           : fpu vme de pse tsc msr pae mce cx8 apic sep
mtrr pge mca cmov pat pse36 clflush dts acpi mmx fxsr sse sse2
ss ht tm pbe nx lm constant_tsc arch_perfmon pebs bts
```

```
aperfmperf pni dtes64 monitor ds_cpl vmx est tm2 ssse3 cx16
xtpr pdcm sse4_1 lahf_lm ida dts tpr_shadow vnmi flexpriority
bogomips        : 4987.85
clflush size    : 64
cache_alignment : 64
address sizes   : 36 bits physical, 48 bits virtual
power management:
processor       : 1
vendor_id       : GenuineIntel
cpu family      : 6
model           : 23
model name      : Intel(R) Core(TM)2 Duo CPU    T9300 @
2.50 GHz
stepping        : 6
microcode       : 0×60c
cpu MHz         : 800.000
cache size      : 6144 KB
physical id     : 0
siblings        : 2
core id         : 1
cpu cores       : 2
apicid          : 1
initial apicid  : 1
fdiv_bug        : no
hlt_bug         : no
f00f_bug        : no
coma_bug        : no
fpu             : yes
fpu_exception   : yes
cpuid level     : 10
wp              : yes
flags           : fpu vme de pse tsc msr pae mce cx8 apic sep
mtrr pge mca cmov pat pse36 clflush dts acpi mmx fxsr sse sse2
ss ht tm pbe nx lm constant_tsc arch_perfmon pebs bts
aperfmperf pni dtes64 monitor ds_cpl vmx est tm2 ssse3 cx16
xtpr pdcm sse4_1 lahf_lm ida dts tpr_shadow vnmi flexpriority
bogomips        : 4987.50
clflush size    : 64
cache_alignment : 64
```

```
address sizes    : 36 bits physical, 48 bits virtual
power management:
```

/proc/meminfo Reports the current memory usage of the system.

```
MemTotal:         3924760 kB
MemFree:          2267780 kB
Buffers:          78888 kB
Cached:           1077832 kB
SwapCached:       0 kB
Active:           675904 kB
Inactive:         874936 kB
Active(anon):     394880 kB
Inactive(anon):   14636 kB
Active(file):     281024 kB
Inactive(file):   860300 kB
Unevictable:      0 kB
Mlocked:          0 kB
HighTotal:        3214024 kB
HighFree:         1706680 kB
LowTotal:         710736 kB
LowFree:          561100 kB
SwapTotal:        2104316 kB
SwapFree:         2104316 kB
Dirty:            132 kB
Writeback:        0 kB
AnonPages:        394116 kB
Mapped:           152124 kB
Shmem:            15404 kB
Slab:             58168 kB
SReclaimable:     40992 kB
SUnreclaim:       17176 kB
KernelStack:      3016 kB
PageTables:       9492 kB
NFS_Unstable:     0 kB
Bounce:           0kB
WritebackTmp:     0 kB
CommitLimit:      4066696 kB
Committed_AS:     1892516 kB
VmallocTotal:     122880 kB
VmallocUsed:      54240 kB
```

	`VmallocChunk: 64220 kB`
	`HardwareCorrupted: 0 kB`
	`AnonHugePages: 0 kB`
	`HugePages_Total: 0`
	`HugePages_Free: 0`
	`HugePages_Rsvd: 0`
	`HugePages_Surp: 0`
	`Hugepagesize: 2048 kB`
	`DirectMap4k: 12280 kB`
	`DirectMap2M: 901120 kB`

/proc/partitions	Reports partitions detected by the kernel within block devices:
	`major minor #blocks name`
	`8 0 732574584 sda`
	`8 1 341795840 sda1`
	`8 2 1 sda2`
	`8 5 388670464 sda5`
	`8 6 2104320 sda6`
	`11 0 1048575 sr0`

/proc/sys/ kernel/printk	Controls the priority of printk messages that are output to the console. `4 4 1 7` See the Printk section for a more complete description
/proc/sys/kernel/ tainted	Reports whether the kernel that is currently running is tainted. `0`

For further information about what is available through procfs read the manpage (man proc).

Procfs is useful in driver development for passing information between applications and the kernel. The standard API for application/driver interaction is to use the open, close, read, write, and ioctl functions. However, this requires that an application be written to perform these functions. Sometimes it is useful to be able to control a driver directly from the command line using procfs.

As an example of how a driver interacts with procfs the Hello World driver in the Basic Kernel driver example is extended as follows. Two functions are added to the driver: one to handle reads of the registered procfs file and one to handle writes to the registered procfs file. The hello_start function now includes code to register a directory called /proc/driver/hello_driver in procfs and a file called info within that directory. It then associates the read and write handlers with the info file in procfs. Modifications to the driver are shown below.

```
/* Basic Kernel Module */
/* Adapted from "The Linux Kernel Module Programming Guide" */
/* http://tldp.org/LDP/lkmpg/2.6/html/lkmpg.html */

#include<linux/module.h> /* Required for Module Support */
#include<linux/kernel.h> /* Required for printk log levels */
#include<linux/init.h>   /* Required for module_init and module_exit macros */
#include<linux/proc_fs.h> /* Required for procfs support */

#define HELLO_PROC_DIR "driver/hello_driver"
#define HELLO_PROC_INFO "info"
#define PROC_WRITE_LEN 256

static struct proc_dir_entry *hello_proc_dir;
static struct proc_dir_entry *hello_proc_info;
static char proc_write_value[PROC_WRITE_LEN];

static int hello_proc_read(char *buffer, char **start, off_t offset,
                   int count, int *eof, void *data)
{
     int len = 0;
     if (len<count){
          len += sprintf(buffer+ len, "Hello from the Kernel through ProcFS\n");
          len += sprintf(buffer+ len, "Last Write to Info: %s\n", proc_write_value);
          *eof = 1;
          return(len);
     }
     return(0);
}

static int hello_proc_write(struct file* file, const char* buffer,
                            unsigned long count, void* data)
{
     int len = 0;
     if (count<PROC_WRITE_LEN){
          len = count;
     }else{
          len = PROC_WRITE_LEN;
     }
```

```
    strlcpy(proc_write_value, buffer, len);
    return (count);
}

static int __init hello_start(void)
{
    int retval = 0;
    printk(KERN_INFO "Hello from the Kernel\n");
    printk(KERN_INFO "Adding /proc/%s\n", HELLO_PROC_DIR);
    hello_proc_dir = proc_mkdir(HELLO_PROC_DIR, NULL);
    if (!hello_proc_dir){
        printk(KERN_ERR "Failed to add /proc/%s\n", HELLO_PROC_DIR);
        retval = -ENOSPC;
        goto hello_start_out1;
    }
    printk(KERN_INFO "Adding /proc/%s/%s\n", HELLO_PROC_INFO, HELLO_PROC_INFO);
    hello_proc_info = create_proc_entry(HELLO_PROC_INFO, 0644, hello_proc_dir);
    if (!hello_proc_info){
        printk(KERN_ERR "Failed to add /proc/%s/%s\n", HELLO_PROC_INFO, HELLO_PROC_INFO);
        retval = -ENOSPC;
        goto hello_start_out2;
    }
    hello_proc_info->read_proc = hello_proc_read;
    hello_proc_info->write_proc = hello_proc_write;
    return (retval);
hello_start_out2:
    printk(KERN_INFO "Remove /proc/%s\n", HELLO_PROC_DIR);
    remove_proc_entry(HELLO_PROC_DIR, NULL);
hello_start_out1:
    return (retval);
}

static void __exit hello_exit(void)
{
    printk(KERN_INFO "Removing /proc/%s/%s\n", HELLO_PROC_DIR, HELLO_PROC_INFO);
    remove_proc_entry(HELLO_PROC_INFO, hello_proc_dir);

    printk(KERN_INFO "Removing /proc/%s\n", HELLO_PROC_DIR);
    remove_proc_entry(HELLO_PROC_DIR, NULL);
```

```
    printk(KERN_INFO "Goodbye from the Kernel\n");
}
module_init(hello_start);
module_exit(hello_exit);
MODULE_LICENSE("GPL");
MODULE_AUTHOR("Andrew McKay");
MODULE_DESCRIPTION("A simple Hello World driver using ProcFS");
```

The function of this driver is to report information about the driver when /proc/driver/hello_world/info is read. It also will save up to 256 characters written to /proc/driver/hello_world/info and report back these characters on subsequent reads.

The driver is loaded to the system in the same manner as previously and reports that it has registered a directory and file within procfs:

```
[18441.945329] Hello from the Kernel
[18441.945333] Adding /proc/driver/hello_driver
[18441.945347] Adding /proc/driver/hello_driver/info
```

When the info file is output to the terminal the following message is reported:

```
amckay@Zen:~/WIP/hello_driver$ cat /proc/driver/hello_driver/info
Hello from the Kernel through ProcFS
Last Write to Info:
```

Information can be written back to the /proc/driver/hello_driver/info file and it will be saved and reported on subsequent reads:

```
amckay@Zen:~/WIP/hello_driver$ echo "Hello from the command line" > /proc/driver/
hello_driver/info
```

Following the previous write, the file will now report the following message:

```
amckay@Zen:~/WIP/hello_driver$ cat /proc/driver/hello_driver/info
Hello from the Kernel through ProcFS
Last Write to Info: Hello from the command line
```

Strace

Often crashes within the kernel will be caused by an application interacting with the kernel in a certain way that a developer may not have considered. To understand what might be going on between the application and kernel a tool called strace is very useful.

Strace is a command-line application available on Linux that will output the system calls that an application makes as it is running. Using strace is as simple as typing strace on the terminal, followed by the application that is to be monitored for system calls. The following is output from strace when *ls* is executed:

```
amckay@Zen:~/WIP/linux-3.2$ strace ls
execve("/bin/ls", ["ls"], [/* 45 vars */]) = 0
brk(0)                                  = 0x8af9000
access("/etc/ld.so.nohwcap", F_OK)      = -1 ENOENT (No such file or directory)
mmap2(NULL, 8192, PROT_READ|PROT_WRITE, MAP_PRIVATE|MAP_ANONYMOUS, -1, 0) = 0xb7891000
access("/etc/ld.so.preload", R_OK)      = -1 ENOENT (No such file or directory)
open("/etc/ld.so.cache", O_RDONLY|O_CLOEXEC) = 3
fstat64(3, {st_mode=S_IFREG|0644, st_size=89319, ...}) = 0
mmap2(NULL, 89319, PROT_READ, MAP_PRIVATE, 3, 0) = 0xb787b000
close(3)                                = 0
access("/etc/ld.so.nohwcap", F_OK)      = -1 ENOENT (No such file or directory)
open("/lib/i386-linux-gnu/libselinux.so.1", O_RDONLY|O_CLOEXEC) = 3
read(3, "\177ELF\1\1\1\0\0\0\0\0\0\0\0\0\3\0\3\0\1\0\0\0@A\0\0004\0\0\0"..., 512) = 512
fstat64(3, {st_mode=S_IFREG|0644, st_size=120748, ...}) = 0
mmap2(NULL, 125852, PROT_READ|PROT_EXEC, MAP_PRIVATE|MAP_DENYWRITE, 3, 0) = 0xb785c000
mmap2(0xb7879000, 8192, PROT_READ|PROT_WRITE, MAP_PRIVATE|MAP_FIXED|MAP_DENYWRITE, 3, 0x1c)
= 0xb7879000
close(3)                                = 0
access("/etc/ld.so.nohwcap", F_OK)      = -1 ENOENT (No such file or directory)
open("/lib/i386-linux-gnu/librt.so.1", O_RDONLY|O_CLOEXEC) = 3
read(3, "\177ELF\1\1\1\0\0\0\0\0\0\0\0\0\3\0\3\0\1\0\0\0\320\30\0\0004\0\0\0"..., 512) = 512
fstat64(3, {st_mode=S_IFREG|0644, st_size=30684, ...}) = 0
mmap2(NULL, 33360, PROT_READ|PROT_EXEC, MAP_PRIVATE|MAP_DENYWRITE, 3, 0) = 0xb7853000
mmap2(0xb785a000, 8192, PROT_READ|PROT_WRITE, MAP_PRIVATE|MAP_FIXED|MAP_DENYWRITE, 3, 0x6) =
0xb785a000
close(3)                                = 0
access("/etc/ld.so.nohwcap", F_OK)      = -1 ENOENT (No such file or directory)
open("/lib/i386-linux-gnu/libacl.so.1", O_RDONLY|O_CLOEXEC) = 3
read(3, "\177ELF\1\1\1\0\0\0\0\0\0\0\0\0\3\0\3\0\1\0\0\0\200\24\0\0004\0\0\0"..., 512) = 512
fstat64(3, {st_mode=S_IFREG|0644, st_size=30300, ...}) = 0
mmap2(NULL, 4096, PROT_READ|PROT_WRITE, MAP_PRIVATE|MAP_ANONYMOUS, -1, 0) = 0xb7852000
mmap2(NULL, 33088, PROT_READ|PROT_EXEC, MAP_PRIVATE|MAP_DENYWRITE, 3, 0) = 0xb7849000
mmap2(0xb7850000, 8192, PROT_READ|PROT_WRITE, MAP_PRIVATE|MAP_FIXED|MAP_DENYWRITE, 3, 0x6)
= 0xb7850000
close(3)                                = 0
access("/etc/ld.so.nohwcap", F_OK)      = -1 ENOENT (No such file or directory)
open("/lib/i386-linux-gnu/libc.so.6", O_RDONLY|O_CLOEXEC) = 3
read(3, "\177ELF\1\1\1\0\0\0\0\0\0\0\0\0\3\0\3\0\1\0\0\0000\226\1\0004\0\0\0"..., 512) = 512
fstat64(3, {st_mode=S_IFREG|0755, st_size=1713640, ...}) = 0
mmap2(NULL, 1723100, PROT_READ|PROT_EXEC, MAP_PRIVATE|MAP_DENYWRITE, 3, 0) = 0xb76a4000
mmap2(0xb7843000, 12288, PROT_READ|PROT_WRITE, MAP_PRIVATE|MAP_FIXED|MAP_DENYWRITE, 3,
0x19f) = 0xb7843000
mmap2(0xb7846000, 10972, PROT_READ|PROT_WRITE, MAP_PRIVATE|MAP_FIXED|MAP_ANONYMOUS, -1, 0)
= 0xb7846000
close(3)                                = 0
access("/etc/ld.so.nohwcap", F_OK)      = -1 ENOENT (No such file or directory)
open("/lib/i386-linux-gnu/libdl.so.2", O_RDONLY|O_CLOEXEC) = 3
read(3, "\177ELF\1\1\1\0\0\0\0\0\0\0\0\0\3\0\3\0\1\0\0\0`\n\0\0004\0\0\0"..., 512) = 512
fstat64(3, {st_mode=S_IFREG|0644, st_size=13940, ...}) = 0
mmap2(NULL, 16504, PROT_READ|PROT_EXEC, MAP_PRIVATE|MAP_DENYWRITE, 3, 0) = 0xb769f000
mmap2(0xb76a2000, 8192, PROT_READ|PROT_WRITE, MAP_PRIVATE|MAP_FIXED|MAP_DENYWRITE, 3, 0x2) =
0xb76a2000
close(3)                                = 0
access("/etc/ld.so.nohwcap", F_OK)      = -1 ENOENT (No such file or directory)
open("/lib/i386-linux-gnu/libpthread.so.0", O_RDONLY|O_CLOEXEC) = 3
read(3, "\177ELF\1\1\1\0\0\0\0\0\0\0\0\0\3\0\3\0\1\0\0\0p[\0\0004\0\0\0"..., 512) = 512
fstat64(3, {st_mode=S_IFREG|0755, st_size=124663, ...}) = 0
mmap2(NULL, 107008, PROT_READ|PROT_EXEC, MAP_PRIVATE|MAP_DENYWRITE, 3, 0) = 0xb7684000
mmap2(0xb769b000, 8192, PROT_READ|PROT_WRITE, MAP_PRIVATE|MAP_FIXED|MAP_DENYWRITE, 3, 0x16)
= 0xb769b000
mmap2(0xb769d000, 4608, PROT_READ|PROT_WRITE, MAP_PRIVATE|MAP_FIXED|MAP_ANONYMOUS, -1, 0) =
0xb769d000
close(3)                                = 0
access("/etc/ld.so.nohwcap", F_OK)      = -1 ENOENT (No such file or directory)
open("/lib/i386-linux-gnu/libattr.so.1", O_RDONLY|O_CLOEXEC) = 3
read(3, "\177ELF\1\1\1\0\0\0\0\0\0\0\0\0\3\0\3\0\1\0\0\0@\f\0\0004\0\0\0"..., 512) = 512
fstat64(3, {st_mode=S_IFREG|0644, st_size=17816, ...}) = 0
```

```
mmap2(NULL, 20584, PROT_READ|PROT_EXEC, MAP_PRIVATE|MAP_DENYWRITE, 3, 0) = 0xb767e000
mmap2(0xb7682000, 8192, PROT_READ|PROT_WRITE, MAP_PRIVATE|MAP_FIXED|MAP_DENYWRITE, 3, 0x3)
= 0xb7682000
close(3)                    = 0
mmap2(NULL, 4096, PROT_READ|PROT_WRITE, MAP_PRIVATE|MAP_ANONYMOUS, -1, 0) = 0xb767d000
mmap2(NULL, 4096, PROT_READ|PROT_WRITE, MAP_PRIVATE|MAP_ANONYMOUS, -1, 0) = 0xb767c000
set_thread_area({entry_number:-1 -> 6, base_addr:0xb767c740, limit:1048575, seg_32bit:1, contents:0, read_exec_only:0,
limit_in_pages:1, seg_not_present:0, useable:1}) = 0
mprotect(0xb7843000, 8192, PROT_READ)  = 0
mprotect(0xb7682000, 4096, PROT_READ)  = 0
mprotect(0xb769b000, 4096, PROT_READ)  = 0
mprotect(0xb76a2000, 4096, PROT_READ)  = 0
mprotect(0xb7850000, 4096, PROT_READ)  = 0
mprotect(0xb785a000, 4096, PROT_READ)  = 0
mprotect(0xb7879000, 4096, PROT_READ)  = 0
mprotect(0x8061000, 4096, PROT_READ)   = 0
mprotect(0xb78b4000, 4096, PROT_READ)  = 0
munmap(0xb787b000, 89319)           = 0
set_tid_address(0xb767c7a8)         = 6394
set_robust_list(0xb767c7b0, 0xc)    = 0
futex(0xbfca85a4, FUTEX_WAIT_BITSET_PRIVATE|FUTEX_CLOCK_REALTIME, 1, NULL, b767c740) = -1
EAGAIN (Resource temporarily unavailable)
rt_sigaction(SIGRTMIN, {0xb7689570, [], SA_SIGINFO}, NULL, 8) = 0
rt_sigaction(SIGRT_1, {0xb76895f0, [], SA_RESTART|SA_SIGINFO}, NULL, 8) = 0
rt_sigprocmask(SIG_UNBLOCK, [RTMIN RT_1], NULL, 8) = 0
getrlimit(RLIMIT_STACK, {rlim_cur=8192*1024, rlim_max=RLIM_INFINITY}) = 0
uname({sys="Linux", node="Zen", ...})  = 0
statfs64("/selinux", 84, {f_type="EXT2_SUPER_MAGIC", f_bsize=4096, f_blocks=85353101, f_bfree=75066663,
f_bavail=70794215, f_files=21364736, f_ffree=21047172, f_fsid={-1958319533, -1754772041}, f_namelen=255,
f_frsize=4096}) = 0
brk(0)                      = 0x8af9000
brk(0x8b1a000)                    = 0x8b1a000
open("/proc/filesystems", O_RDONLY|O_LARGEFILE) = 3
fstat64(3, {st_mode=S_IFREG|0444, st_size=0, ...}) = 0
mmap2(NULL, 4096, PROT_READ|PROT_WRITE, MAP_PRIVATE|MAP_ANONYMOUS, -1, 0) = 0xb7890000
read(3, "nodev\tsysfs\nnodev\trootfs\nnodev\tb"..., 1024) = 304
read(3, "", 1024)               = 0
close(3)                    = 0
munmap(0xb7890000, 4096)          = 0
open("/usr/lib/locale/locale-archive", O_RDONLY|O_LARGEFILE|O_CLOEXEC) = 3
fstat64(3, {st_mode=S_IFREG|0644, st_size=8748544, ...}) = 0
mmap2(NULL, 2097152, PROT_READ, MAP_PRIVATE, 3, 0) = 0xb747c000
mmap2(NULL, 1253376, PROT_READ, MAP_PRIVATE, 3, 0x4a5) = 0xb734a000
close(3)                    = 0
ioctl(1, SNDCTL_TMR_TIMEBASE or TCGETS, {B38400 opost isig icanon echo ...}) = 0
ioctl(1, TIOCGWINSZ, {ws_row=61, ws_col=231, ws_xpixel=0, ws_ypixel=0}) = 0
openat(AT_FDCWD, ".", O_RDONLY|O_NONBLOCK|O_LARGEFILE|O_DIRECTORY|O_CLOEXEC) = 3
getdents64(3, /* 57 entries */, 32768)  = 1904
getdents64(3, /* 0 entries */, 32768)  = 0
close(3)                    = 0
fstat64(1, {st_mode=S_IFCHR|0600, st_rdev=makedev(136, 2), ...}) = 0
mmap2(NULL, 4096, PROT_READ|PROT_WRITE, MAP_PRIVATE|MAP_ANONYMOUS, -1, 0) = 0xb7349000
write(1, "arch  COPYING\tcrypto\t   dri"..., 173arch  COPYING   crypto     drivers  fs    init  Kbuild  kernel
MAINTAINERS  mm          modules.order  net    REPORTING-BUGS  scripts  sound     tools  virt    vmlinux.o
) = 173
write(1, "block  CREDITS\tDocumentation  fi"..., 173block  CREDITS    Documentation  firmware  include  ipc  Kconfig
lib    Makefile    modules.builtin  Module.symvers  README  samples      security  System.map  usr   vmlinux
) = 173
close(1)                    = 0
munmap(0xb7349000, 4096)          = 0
close(2)                    = 0
exit_group(0)                 = ?
```

Applications

Cross compiling

A cross-compiler is a compiler that runs on one architecture that is capable of running code on another architecture. Typically bootloaders and the Linux kernel are built with cross-compilers. Linux applications can be built with cross-compilers as well. Since most development machines are x86 based, it is common to have a compiler that runs on that architecture that can build applications for ARM-, PowerPC-, or MIPs-based platforms. Though these platforms are capable of compiling code for themselves it is often beneficial to build code on an x86-based platform for the performance enhancement that modern desktop/laptop machines have over most embedded systems.

Busybox

Busybox is an application suite that provides core UNIX/Linux application support. Busybox is designed to be small and lightweight. While it does not provide the full functionality for all the commands that would typically be supported on a non-embedded platform it is still very powerful. Busybox is available at http://www.busybox.net/.

Busybox compiles to one binary application that is typically located in /bin. Symbolic links are created with various names to the Busybox binary. When a symbolic link is called from the command line, Busybox checks the value passed within argv[0] and executes the proper application.

Busybox provides a simple init application. Init is the first task that is started on Linux. Using an inittab script, init will start various daemons and applications on the system. The init application in Busybox init is very lightweight and only supports starting applications at boot and does not support run-levels that full-blown Linux distributions have.

SysVinit

System V Initialization or sysVinit is an initialization application typically found on fully functional Linux systems. It is also very useful on embedded systems and allows the Linux system to run at different runlevels. While sysVinit supports eight different runlevels only seven are used in Linux. They are defined as:

ID	Name
0	Halt
1	Single User Mode
2	Multi User Mode
3	Multi User Mode with Networking
4	User Definable
5	Multi User Mode with GUI
6	Reboot
S	Run Once at Boot

SysVinit uses scripts that are located in /etc/init.d to start processes based on the runlevel. Each of these shell scripts at a minimum must take a start and stop argument. SysVinit will pass this argument depending on the action that needs to be taken.
For each runlevel there is a directory name /etc/rcN.d where N is the run level ID. Within each of these directories symbolic links are created pointing to the scripts in /etc/init.d. The symbolic links have the following naming convention [S/K][Order]name. The S and K denote whether sysVinit should start or kill the task. Order is a number that sysVinit will use to determine the order that the scripts should be run. It starts at the lowest-numbered script and works its way through the scripts in increasing order. Finally the name is used so that the user can identify the script's function.

On a typical Linux system the rc3.d or Multi User with Networking runlevel directory will look as follows:

```
root@Loco-3456:/etc/rc3.d# ls -al
total 20
drwxr-xr-x  2 root root 4096 2012-10-01 09:11
drwxr-xr-x 135 root root 12288 2012-10-06 14:13
-rw-r-r-  1 root root  677 2012-01-20 04:03 README
lrwxrwxrwx  1 root root  22 2011-11-22 23:23 S20boinc-client -> /init.d/boinc-client
lrwxrwxrwx  1 root root  20 2011-11-14 22:05 S20fancontrol -> /init.d/fancontrol
lrwxrwxrwx  1 root root  20 2011-11-14 22:05 S20kerneloops -> /init.d/kerneloops
lrwxrwxrwx  1 root root  27 2011-11-14 22:05 S20speech-disp -> /init.d/speech-disp
lrwxrwxrwx  1 root root  23 2012-07-09 13:11 S20uml-util -> /init.d/uml-util
lrwxrwxrwx  1 root root  19 2011-11-14 22:05 S25bluetooth -> /init.d/bluetooth
lrwxrwxrwx  1 root root  14 2011-11-14 22:05 S50cups -> /init.d/cups
lrwxrwxrwx  1 root root  20 2011-11-14 22:05 S50pulseaudio -> /init.d/pulseaudio
lrwxrwxrwx  1 root root  15 2011-11-14 22:05 S50rsync -> /init.d/rsync
lrwxrwxrwx  1 root root  15 2011-11-14 22:05 S50saned -> /init.d/saned
lrwxrwxrwx  1 root root  19 2011-11-14 22:05 S70dns-clean -> /init.d/dns-clean
lrwxrwxrwx  1 root root  18 2011-11-14 22:05 S70pppd-dns -> /init.d/pppd-dns
lrwxrwxrwx  1 root root  24 2011-11-14 22:05 S90binfmt-sup -> /init.d/binfmt-sup
lrwxrwxrwx  1 root root  17 2011-11-23 19:57 S91apache2 -> /init.d/apache2
lrwxrwxrwx  1 root root  22 2011-11-14 22:05 S99acpi-support -> /init.d/acpi-support
lrwxrwxrwx  1 root root  21 2011-11-14 22:05 S99grub-common -> /init.d/grub-common
lrwxrwxrwx  1 root root  18 2011-11-14 22:05 S99ondemand -> /init.d/ondemand
lrwxrwxrwx  1 root root  18 2011-11-14 22:05 S99rc.local -> /init.d/rc.local
```

Note for the rc3.d runlevel all the scripts being called start with an S and therefore will be starting tasks on the system.

SysVinit uses a configuration file called inittab to start the first tasks on the Linux system and to set the runlevel of the system after a successful boot. The inittab configuration file is also capable of starting tasks at boot, starting respawnable tasks, taking action for keyboard sequences such as ctrl-alt-del, taking action for custom system request events, or taking action during power-sensing events sent by a UPS or power-management system.

Example application

Using devices in a Linux application is as simple as opening a devnode and interacting with it using read and write commands. The ioctl system call is used to control the settings of the driver. Commonly used devices such as serial ports have libraries that have been written that already interact with the ioctl system call. The following application shows how a user application would interact with a serial port. First it opens the serial port and then it uses functionality exported by termios.h to configure the serial port with a baud rate of 115200 KBps and 8 data bits. After configuring the port the application writes "Hello Serial Port!" out of the serial port.

```
#include<fcntl.h>
#include<stdio.h>
#include<stdlib.h>
#include<string.h>
#include<termios.h>

#define SERDEV "/dev/ttyS4"
#define MESSAGE "Hello Serial Port!\n"


 int main(int argc, char *argv[]){
 int serport;
 struct termios serport_termios;

 printf("Opening Serial Device: %s\n", SERDEV);        //Open Serial Port
 serport = open(SERDEV, O_RDWR);
 if(serport <= 0){
  printf("Error opening Serial Device: %s\n", SERDEV);
  return -1;
 }

 tcgetattr(serport, &serport_termios);           //Read Serial Settings
 cfmakeraw(&serport_termios);           //Set Serial Port RAW
 serport_termios.c_cflag = B115200 | CS8 | CLOCAL | CREAD; //Set BAUD Rate and Data Bits
 tcsetattr(serport, TCSANOW, &serport_termios);         //Write Serial Settings
 write(serport, MESSAGE, strlen(MESSAGE));          //Write Message
 close(serport);            //Close Serial Port
 return 0;

}
```

Running Linux on a reference board

Reference platforms

Reference boards are a great way to get started running Linux on an embedded platform. Many reference designs provide the schematics, bill of materials, and layout files so that the reference design can be moved over to your own production board with a bit more ease.

There are many different reference boards available. For this section, the sub-$100 BeagleBone board will be used to show a start-to-finish set-up of the board itself to prepare it for embedded development. There are multiple vendors that sell the BeagleBone board, and it comes with an initial start-up USB cable and microSD card already capable of booting the system. In this section we will get our own distribution and start from the beginning.

Starting with BeagleBone

The following hardware interfaces are available on the base BeagleBone:

- USB host
- USB client
- 10/100 Ethernet
- Interface headers (for access to additional processor I/O, and plug-in modules)
- FTDI-based serial/JTAG (for simultaneous connection to JTAG/USB/serial port).

Figure 25.3 is a picture of the BeagleBone, measuring 3.4" x 2.1" in size:

Getting started

The BeagleBone hardware is available from a variety of distributors. Visiting the website for BeagleBoard will provide a list of the vendors where it can be ordered.

When the board arrives, it contains the board itself, a USB cable for connecting it to your computer, and a microSD card with a date code on it that matches the provided default images. An excellent resource to better understand this provided microSD disk is located at http://circuitco.com/support. After selecting the BeagleBone from this webpage, a list of the various hardware revisions and image files are provided in a wiki format. Before attempting to create an image, it is recommended to download the latest version that is supported by your hardware revision (stamped on the box and on the top of the board).

Another recommendation is setting up a host Linux environment for development. If the primary computer for development is running Windows, there are a few options. First, many Linux distributions provide a dual-boot option for your computer during installation. Ubuntu, for instance, will install a "grub" boot menu when the computer is

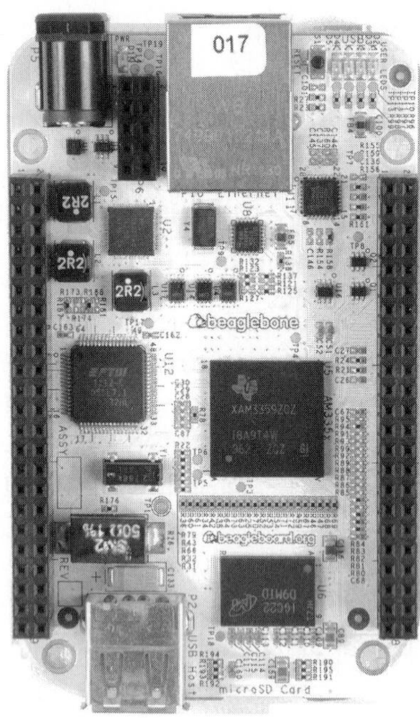

Figure 25.3:
A picture of the BeagleBone from http://beagleboard.org.

started, so either Linux or Windows can be selected for startup. The second option is to install a virtualization package that will allow Linux to run inside Windows. VirtualBox and VMWare are candidate packages that have an option to install a "freeware" version. The third option is finding an older PC machine that may not be in use any longer – it may be too slow to run the latest Windows version but may run a Linux distribution just fine!

The rest of this section for running BeagleBone will use instructions based on running in a Linux host environment. If there isn't an opportunity to dual-boot, run a virtualization package, or use an older machine, equivalent Windows-based instructions can be found on the Internet to get up and running.

Linux SDK

In order to get the correct drivers installed for the BeagleBone, it is necessary to download the Linux Sitara SDK. This image has the FTDI drivers that are needed in order to get the host Linux operating system to talk with the BeagleBone. The following steps should be performed to get the drivers:

Step 1: Download the Sitara SDK
Go to http://beagleboard.org/project/amsdk/, which has a link to the TI website.

Step 2: Burn the image

Follow step 3 in section 3.2.3 below to determine the device drive, and how to burn the image based on the file format.

Step 3: Start BeagleBone

Plug the BeagleBone board into the host PC using the supplied USB cable. Depending on whether you are running Linux on the host PC natively or using a virtualization program, the BeagleBone should be recognized and a folder "START_HERE" should appear. When the directory is opened, a script file START_HERE.sh should be executed to load the correct drivers.

Step 4: Copy support files

There are support applications and guides in this START_HERE directory. Copy them over to your host system so they can be accessed once you start changing the BeagleBone image.

Getting default image

As described in section 3.2.1, the default image available from http://circuitco.com/support is a great way to make sure the board and your development environment are running correctly. If the image obtained runs, then the setup can be verified – this will make it easier to debug when you start creating your own images!

Step 1: Enter Linux host OS

Whether running on a native host system or in a virtualization environment, log into the Linux host OS.

Step 2: Download default image

Go to http://circuitco.com/support and click on "BeagleBone". Find the distribution that matches the revision of the hardware that you have. Download it!

Step 3: Burn the image

Use a blank 4 GB microUSB card – the distribution size is now larger than 2 GB so those size cards will no longer work. Determine the device ID for the microSD card on your host computer by issuing the following command:

```
-$ df
```

Find a drive in the format of /dev/sdX or /dev/diskX that matches the expected size for the microSD card. Then unmount that drive using the following command:

```
-$ umount /dev/sdX
```

Substitute the letter "X" in the following to match the drive and type the following (for "xz" files):

```
-$ xzcat IMAGENAME.img.xz | sudo dd of = /dev/sdX bs = 8 M
```

Or type the following (for "gz" files):

```
-$ zcat IMAGENAME.img.gz | sudo dd of = /dev/sdX bs = 8 M
```

Step 4: Plug in the BeagleBone board to the host computer

Device driver software should install correctly – if there is an error message then search for the specific error code and "BeagleBone" on the Internet. As long as the Sitara SDK is installed as discussed in 3.2.2, the drivers should be available and ready.

Getting Linux distribution

There are many Linux distributions that are already setup to run on BeagleBone. Here is a partial list of the distributions that are available along with instructions on how to get the image.

- Angstrom Demo Image [http://beagleboard.org/project/angstrom/]
  ```
  -$ wget http://www.angstrom-distribution.org/demo/beaglebone/Cloud9-IDE-eglibc-ipk-v2012.01-core-beaglebone-2012.01.11.img.gz
  -$ zcat Cloud9-IDE-eglibc-ipk-v2011.12-core-beaglebone-2012.01.11.img.gz | sudo dd of = /dev/sdX bs = 8 M
  ```
- Ubuntu 11.04 for BeagleBone [https://wiki.ubuntu.com/ARM/OmapNetbook]
  ```
  -$ wget from http://cdimage.ubuntu.com/releases/11.04/ubuntu-12.04-preinstalled-desktop-armhf + omap.img.gz
  -$ zcat ubuntu-12.04-preinstalled-desktop-armhf + omap.img.gz | sudo dd of = /dev/sdX bs = 8 M
  ```
- Android [http://arowboat.org]
  A TI wiki page is an excellent resource for setting up and getting an Android image with appropriate drivers running on the BeagleBone. It also includes instructions on enabling video if you have the appropriate add-on "hood" module for the BeagleBone like the LCD Touch Screen option or a DVI-D interface. Instead of typing the instructions here, please go to the following link for instructions: http://processors.wiki.ti.com/index.php/AM335X_EVM-SK_Android_Devkit_Guide.
- Gentoo
  Gentoo is another distribution of Linux that works well for BeagleBone, especially where a certain degree of configurability freedom is required. It allows the user to only grab the packages and features that are needed, and is supported by a fairly large user community. A page for installing Gentoo on BeagleBone is provided on this link: http://dev.gentoo.org/~armin76/arm/beaglebone/install.xml.

For the development board or reference design that is being used, careful Internet searches can be performed to determine a good starting point for the distribution. For boards like the BeagleBone, with a large number of users, there is plenty of information and help on the Internet when it is needed!

Embedded Linux

It is unlikely that a user would want to run Ubuntu on the BeagleBone. This is because the amount of extra software that exists causes the embedded processor to slow down to an almost painful pace. It also requires quite a bit of memory resources, which may be needed for the programs that are being written. The following items are typically needed for an embedded Linux platform:

- Cross-compiler toolchain: depending on the host computer system and the target, cross-compiling allows the user to specify that the binaries should be created using a different target from the host. For the BeagleBone, a program like gcc should be present so programs can be developed on the host system, but debugged or have small changes take place on the target.
- File system: the standard Linux directory structure with /bin and /etc, with appropriate files so the system can initialize and run.
- Board support package: for the Linux distribution that is used on the target board, it is important to have a board support package so the kernel knows how to run on the target system.
- Application source: for the distribution, it is important to be able to quickly get applications like python or cron, so that the application you are writing can take full advantage of Linux functionality that is already built-in.

Building Angstrom

Angstrom is a fairly typical embedded operating system that runs on the BeagleBone. The website has a distribution builder, so that only the components that are desired are built in. It also has the necessary boot files for the BeagleBone embedded target.

When using a default image, as described in section 3.2.3, the image already has the necessary partitions in the image file for running Linux. When grabbing files and creating your own Linux file system, it is necessary to format the SD card with the correct partitions. The following instructions go through the steps to create a bootable SD card for the BeagleBone:

Step 1: Format the SD card

The following file can be downloaded directly from the Angstrom Distribution website, called mkcard.txt.

```
-$ wget http://downloads.angstrom-distribution.org/demo/beaglebone/mkcard.txt
```

Rename the file to be a shell script, which it is, and make it executable:

```
-$ mv mkcard.txt mkcard.sh
-$ sudo chmod +x mkcard.sh
```

Execute the script to format the SD card – substituting the letter X with the appropriate drive letter for the SD card

```
-$ sudo./mkcard.sh /dev/sdX
```

After this executes, then mount both partitions with one named "boot" and one named "Angstrom". Having both mounted will be necessary to start copying files.

Step 2: Build the distribution

Angstrom has an online builder to put together the package that is needed for the target. Go to the website http://narcissus.angstrom-distribution.org. From here there are drop down selections for the build configurability for the image that is desired. For the option "Select the machine to build rootfs for" see if BeagleBone is listed. It has appeared on the list and also been taken away. If BeagleBone is not listed, go to the alternative site, http://dominion.thruhere.net/koen/narcissus. It operates the same way, except that BeagleBone should be listed!

Depending on whether you are using graphics, there is an option to do "console only" as opposed to a graphical system. If you do not have any optional graphics modules for the BeagleBone, this is the best option for sure. It will limit the amount of resources that are used by the board.

There are additional options below, including building in development packages and platform-specific packages. Definitely choose to include the bootloader files, because those will be needed to setup the boot partition on the SD card that has been created. Your selections may vary, but as an example the following can be chosen for the BeagleBoard on this builder page:

Machine: beaglebone

Image name: (random default)

Complexity: simple

User environment: console only

Additional packages: python, perl, busybox replacements, native (on-target) SDK

Network-related packages: Dropbear SSH server, NTP, NTP client

Platform-specific packages: bootloader files

Once the options are chosen, select "Build Me" to create the image. At the time the image above was created, it was approximately 50 MB is size for the tar and gzip file.

Step 3: Copy onto SD card

We need to extract the bootloader files for the boot partition. This can be done by extracting the boot files out of the .tar.gz file. As long as the two partitions were mounted in step 1 above, the following commands should work:

```
-$ tar -wildcards -xzvf random-xxxxxx-image-beaglebone.tar.gz./boot/*
-$ cp u-boot.img /mnt/boot/u-boot.img
-$ cp MLO /mnt/boot/MLO
-$ cp uImage-*.bin /mnt/boot/uImage
```

Once the boot files above are copied, the main partition can be populated. The following command copies over the Angstrom distribution that was created to the main partition:

```
-$ sudo tar -xvz -C /mnt/Angstrom -f random-xxxxxx-image-beaglebone.tar.gz
-$ sync
```

Step 4: Unmount and boot

Unmount the two SD card partitions, and move the card over to the BeagleBone. Open the console port on the host system, and boot your BeagleBone. It should boot correctly! From here, when you are connected through the console port to your BeagleBone, you can download additional packages using the command "opkg" and further configure your target.

APPENDIX 1

'C' Syntax Coding Standard: Source Code Development

Robert Oshana

This document was edited and reformatted from the original work of Daniel Moone, who wrote a document originally called the C Coding Standard *in 1992. It has undergone multiple revisions, with the latest version in 2009 renamed to the* C Syntax Coding Standard. *Dan's experience includes embedded development in automotive, medical, and industrial fields, where many of the terms and definitions in this standard are founded. Special thanks to him for allowing the book* Software Engineering for Embedded Systems *to provide this information to the readers.*

– Editors Mark Kraeling and Rob Oshana

Abstract

This appendix includes a syntax standard which could be considered for an embedded project. It includes a style guide and naming conventions for variables and declarations. It can be used as is, or modified to fit the particular application being developed. Using a standard for coding can help with providing uniformity in the code baseline, which helps with readability and maintainability among all of the developers. It also suggests practices that help reduce bugs in the code, such as initialization order and conventions that should be avoided.

Scope

Purpose

The purpose of this document is to specify language independent and dependent requirements for software coding standards. The requirements specified in this document are a mandatory part of this standard.

Objective

The foundations of this standard is to produce code that is easy to read and understand while promoting portability. The objective is to limit code constructs and flag some suspicious and possibly non-portable constructs (likely to be bugs) in C language source code, the hope being that applications produced using this standard will be not only readable and understandable but will also be maintainable and testable.

Applicability

This document applies to any embedded development project using the 'C' programming language.

References

[1] ANSI/IEEE Std 620.12-1990, IEEE Standard Glossary of Software Engineering Terminology.

[2] ANSI/IEEE Std 983-1986, IEEE Guide for Software Quality Assurance Planning.

[3] ANSI/IEEE Std 1008-1987, IEEE Standard for Software Unit Testing.

[4] DOD-STD-2167 A, Defense System Software Development, DOD, Washington DC, 1988.

[5] B. Kernighan, D. Ritchie, The C Programming Language, Prentice-Hall, Englewood Cliffs, NJ, 1988.

[6] M. Bolsky, The C Programmer's Handbook, Prentice-Hall, Englewood Cliffs, NJ, 1985.

[7] N. Gehani, Advanced C, Computer Science Press, Rockville, MD, 1985.

[8] IBM SC26-4353-0, Systems Application Architecture, Common Programming Interface C Reference, IBM, Armonk, NY, 1987.

[9] E. Yourdon, L. Constantine, Structured Design, Englewood Cliffs, NJ: Prentice-Hall, 1979.

[10] S.H. Caine, E.K. Gordon, PDL-A tool for software design. National Computer Conference, 1975, pp. 271–276.

[11] M. Daniel. C Coding Standard, multiple versions and iterations starting in 1992.

Definitions

The definitions listed below establish meaning in the context of this standard. Other definitions can be found in ANSI/IEEE Std 620.12-1900 [1].

conventions: requirements employed to prescribe a disciplined, uniform approach to providing consistency in a software product, that is, uniform patterns or forms for arranging data.

definition: an **object*definition*** is used to specify the properties of and to allocate storage for the **object** [7]. ***Definitions*** are **declarations** that allocate storage [8].

declaration: an **object*declaration*** is used only to specify the properties of an **object**; no storage is allocated for the **object** [7]. ***Declarations*** establish names and define characteristics such as size, scope, and data type [8].
extendibility: the ease with which a system or component can be modified to increase its storage or functional capabilities.
flexibility: the ease with which a system or component can be modified for use in applications or environments other than those for which it was specifically designed.
maintainability: the ease with which a software system or component can be modified to correct faults, improve performance or other attributes, or adapt to a changed environment.
object:

(1) A region of storage [7].
(2) An **object**, sometimes called a variable, is a location in storage [5].
(3) An **object**, an encapsulation of data and services that manipulate that data [1].

practices: requirements employed to prescribe a disciplined, uniform approach to the software development process.
readability: a program listing that conforms to the form and format specified in this standard.
reliability: the ability of a system or component to perform its required functions under stated conditions for a specified period of time.
standards: mandatory requirements employed and enforced to prescribe a disciplined, uniform approach to software development, that is, mandatory conventions and practices are in fact standards.
testability: the ability to detect software anomalies with the tools provided (e.g., symbolic debuggers, emulators). The available tools will dictate certain programming constructs/constraints needed to achieve module **testability** objectives.
understandability: the ease with which the essence (i.e., the basic functionality) of a software system or component can be understood/comprehended.

Rules and Conventions

The following subparagraphs define the requirements for rules and conventions applicable to software coding standards.

Presentation Style

This section describes the rules and conventions for the format of the source code which may include paper listings, listing stored on electronic media, or both.

Indentation and spacing

Indentation

Four (4) spaces per indent are recommended. Tabs should be allowed because there is not a uniform definition as to what constitutes a tab. This indentation rule would apply to all language constructs.

When the object of a conditional expression requires a block of code causing an opening brace ({) to be used, the brace is put on its own line. The closing brace (}) is also put on a line by itself. The exception is the `do{}while` statement where the `while` condition is put on the same line as the closing brace. The braces are indented at the same level as the conditional statement.

```
Column: * * * * * * *
  12345678901234567890123456789
    do
    {
      for ( ...; ...; ... )
      {
       if ( ... )
        {
         switch ( ... )
          {
           case ...:
             ...;
             case ...:
             {
              ...;
               ...;
                }
                default:
                ...;
```

```
            break;
          }
        }
        else if ( ... )
        {
          while ( ... )
          {
            ...;
          }
        }
        else
        {
          for ( ...; ...; ... )
            ;
        }
      }
    } while ( ... );
  123456789012345678901234567890123456789
  *   *   *   *   *   *   *   *
```

Spacing

In addition to the previously mentioned indentation rules, spaces should be used to enhance readability. The following are examples of approved spacing conventions (please note that there is **no** whitespace between for function name and the following "("):

Function declaration/definition:

```
f( void )                // Space between function name and '(' is not
f( type arg )            // recommended [i.e., "f ("]. A ',' should
f( type arg, type arg )  // immediately follow all arguments.
```

Function invocation and passing values:

```
f()                    // Space between function name and '(' is not
f( arg )               // recommended [i.e., "f ("].
f( arg, arg )          // ',' shall immediately follow all arguments.
f( arg,                // If the argument list is too long to fit on

   arg,                // one line, then the argument list should be

   arg,                // split at the ',' character(s) and continued

  arg )                // on the next line. Alignment should be

f( arg, arg,           // maintained.

  arg, arg )           // Ref §3.2.1.1.1 Function Argument List Names, p.13
```

Expressions and operations:

```
lvalue = ( a + ( b * c )); // operator preceded and followed by one
lvalue = ((( d * e ) / f ) / g ); // space; multiple parentheses are to be
lvalue = ( h + ( j / k )); // grouped with no spaces.
lvalue = l + m + n;
lvalue = o() + p() + q();
lvalue = r( s ) + t( u, v ) - w( x, y, z );
```

Array subscripts:

```
code[u][d][t] = 0;       // NO space between identifier and '['
```

or

```
code[ u ][ d ][ t ] = 0; // spaces around subscripts are optional
code[ u ][d][ t ] = 0;  // inconsistent spacing should be avoided
```

Structure and union member specification:

```
roster->name // NO space around "->"
```

Unary expressions (++, -, +, -, !, ~, &, *, cast, sizeof an object):

```
i++;   // NO spaces between identifier and operator
-j;
k = -1;
while ( !right )
~mask
p_to_y = &y;
*p_to_y = 3;
(double)dtrdsp
(uint32)tvol
(char *)buff
(uint16*)val
```

```
sizeof( uint16 )
```

Binary expressions (*, /, %, +, -, <<, >>, <, >, <=, >=, ==, !=, &, ^, |, &&, ||):

```
sites * num * cost // operator preceded and follow by one space
unscaled_value / 256
( a / b ) * b + a % b
bmap = mask << ptbl[i].bit_num
for ( i = 0; i <= MAX_PARM; i++ )
while (( ptbl[ i ].bmap & CLASS_MASK ) != class )
if ( strcmp( string1, string ) == 0 )
mask = feat_enabl & feat_avail
(( MIN_LIMIT <= value ) && ( value <= MAX_LIMIT ))
if (( key == YES ) || ( key == NO ))
```

Assignment expressions:

```
a = a * ( b + c ); // operator preceded and follow by one space
a *= b + c;
*pointer = *(pointer++) - 1;
*(pointer++) -= 1;
test = test ^ pre_test;
test ^= pre_test;
```

Alignment of assignment operators is expected. For example:

```
local_a   = foo_one();
local_two = foo_two();
```

is preferred over:

```
local_a = foo_one();
local_two = foo_two();
```

Conditional expressions (?:):

```
x = ( y>z ) ? y : z; // Spaces around conditional operators. All

                      // other appropriate spacing requirements

                     // (e.g., assignment expressions) also apply.

                    // Reference §3.4.3.3 Conditional Expression, p.25
```

Statements:

```
for ( expression1; expression2; expression )
if ( expression )
switch ( expression )
while ( expression )
```

Declarators:

```
*node
name[NAME_LEN + 1]
buffer[ MAX_COLUMNS + 1 ]
record_t *get_record( storage )
char* get_field( record )
uint16 * get_feat_mask( void ) // " * " not recommended
( *volatile points[3][2] )()
```

Whichever style is adopted by the developer, it should be maintained throughout the file. A mixing of styles is **not** recommended. Maintenance programmers should be required to maintain a style consistent with the original documents style as long as the original document meets standards.

Nesting

The maximum number of nesting levels shall be eight (8). The following is an example of the maximum number of nested levels allowed and how to determine the actual nesting level.

```
pf_t nesting( void )
{

  pf_t retval;

  do                                    // level 1

  {

    for ( ..., ..., ... )              // level 2

    {

    if ( ... )                        // level 3

    {

      switch ( ... )                 // level 4

    {

      case ...:                     // level 5

    {

    while ( ... )                  // level 6

         {

         retval = funcs(); // level 7
```

```
            if ( retval = = FAILED )

            {

1234567890123456789012345678901 23

      ...;                   // level 8

* * * * * * * * *

            }

          }

        }

       }

      }

    }

  } while ( ... );

  return retval;

} // END: nesting()
```

Each `break` or `continue` statement used within a `for` or `while` loop shall count as one nesting level.

```
while ( ... )     // level n
{

  if ( !something_to_do )

  continue;   // level n + 1

  do_something();

}
```

produces the same number of nesting levels as:

```
while ( ... )    // level n
{

  if ( something_to_do )

  do_something(); // level n + 1

}
```

A nesting shall never exceed the average specified code aggregate size of 100 non-expandable statements. Reference §3.1.5 Code aggregate size.

If the size of a nest is extensive and there is difficulty in determining which ending brace goes with which beginning brace then the ending brace should be labeled. Examples of appropriate labeling techniques follow:

```
main()
{
  do                              // level 1
  {
    for ( ..., ..., ... )         // level 2
    {
      if ( ... )                  // level 3
      {
      switch ( ... )              // level 4
    {
      case ...:                   // level 5
      {
        while ( ... )   // level 6
        {
         } // END while ...
          } // END case ...
          } // END switch ...
     } // END if ...
    } // END for ...
  } while ( ... );
} // END: main()
```

Capitalization

Restrictions on the use of capitalized text are identified.

All objects shall be constructed from alphanumeric characters plus the underscore. Objects whose scope is file shall use only lower-case letters. Objects whose scope is global (i.e., external linkage) shall be "Title Cased". Reference §3.2.1.1 Variable names.

Integer, character, and floating constant names regardless of scope (i.e., file or global) can be constructed with upper-case alphabetic, numeric, and underscore characters. Enumerated constants shall be constructed from upper case alphabetic and underscore characters. Reference §3.2.1.3 Constant names.

Information presentation

Uniform presentation of information throughout the source code.

Definitions shall be listed at the beginning of a program. All definitions and `const` qualifiers shall be declared prior to the body of the program.

All local variables shall be located immediately after the program's definition and before the first executable statement and they shall be listed in alphabetical order.

The following construct is **NOT** acceptable:

```
uint8 i = 1;     // i defined at external level
main()

  {

printf( "%d\n", i );                // prints 1

   {

uint8 i = 2;                       // i and j defined at
uint8 j = 3;     // internal level
printf( "%d\n%d\n", i, j );       // prints 2, 3

     {

uint8 i = 0;     // i redefined again
printf( "%d\n%d\n", i, j );     // prints 0, 3

     }

printf( "%d\n", i );          // prints 2

  }

printf( "%d\n", i );        // prints 1
}  // END: main()
```

Multiple variables using the same names are **NOT** allowed in a function's scope (i.e., the same identifiers shall **NOT** be used more than once in any one function).

Comments

Conditions under which comments are provided and the format to be used.

Comments should not appear inline. If required, comments are to appear to the right of the source, one comment per line, aligned "blocked to the block". This "blocked to the block" requirement shall apply to all consecutive lines containing comments.

```
#define FOREVER for(;;)                                 // for(;;) is an infinite loop

                                                       // equivalent to while(1).

FOREVER
{
   if ( a )                                          // Here is some cryptic code that

   {                                                // satisfies some particular requirement

   perform_a();                                    // such that drawing attention to this

   }                                              // block code is desired.

   else

   {

     if ( b )

      {                                        // Here is another equally cryptic block

      perform_b();                            // of code needing clarification.  Notice

     clarify();                              // the different blocking used. While only

     notice();                              // consecutive lines containing comments

      consecutive();                       // are required to have the same comment

      bck_n_frth();                       // blocking, the back-and-forth blocking

      }                                  // style shown below is discouraged.

   else if ( c )

      {                                 // Back-and-forth blocking style.

      perform_c();                     // Cryptic call requiring comment.

      obvious_function_call();

         something_strange();   // Function needing explanation.
```

```
      self_explanatory_call();

      more_strange_stuff();          // A comment needed.

   }

     else

    {                                // Preferred comment blocking.

      perform_c();                  // Cryptic call requiring comment.

      obvious_func_call();

      something_strange();         // Function needing explanation.

      self_explanatory_call();

       more_strange_stuff();     // A comment needed.

         you_get_my_meaning();  // Explanation required?

     }

   }

}  // END FOREVER
```

There are times when a block that crosses the source from column 1 to column 70 is more desirable. Certainly if the amount of nesting in the code would force the comments to start too far to the right, a set of block comments is preferred.

```
// ——————————————————————————————————————————————————————————
// Function find_name. This function searches an array of names to
// see if a given name already exists in the array. It returns a
// pointer to the name or NULL if the name if not found.
// Reference Appendix F – Function Template, p.53
// ——————————————————————————————————————————————————————————
// char **array is a pointer to arrays of pointers (existing names)
// char *string is a pointer to character array entered (new name)
char *find_name( char **array, char *string )
{

  for ( ; *array != (char *)NULL; array++ ) // for each name

   {

    if ( strcmp( *array, string ) == 0 )   // if strings match

     break;                               // found it!
```

```
    }

    return *array;        // return the pointer

}  // END: find_name()
```

Reference §3.4.1.8.1 Arrays, for an example on how to comment multidimensional arrays.

Code aggregate size

Size of code aggregates shall on average be limited to 100 or at most 200 executable, non-expandable statements.

Naming

This section describes the rules and conventions governing the selection of identifiers used in the source code listing.

Naming conventions

No name shall exceed 31 characters in length. Use standard abbreviations to shorten name length while maintaining understandability. Reference §3.2.2 Standard abbreviations.

Filenames shall not be longer than 32 characters including the file's extension.

Variable names

An object, sometimes called a variable, is a location in storage.

Public objects and public functions (i.e., globals) should be prefixed by some indicator as to their origin (e.g., source code file). As an example, given files of name:

Source code file `timing_matrix.c`
Include file `timing_matrx.h`

with abbreviation TM (i.e., a unique two-to-five-character acronym) then all global variables and public functions as listed in `timing_matrx.h` should be prefixed with "TM_"

Acronym TM
Prefix "`TM_`"
Variable declaration `float TM_Timing_Matrix[7][24][365];`
Function declaration `*float[][][] TM_Return_Timing_Matrix_Pointer( void );`

Reference §3.2.1.2 Function names, for additional function naming conventions.

All objects shall be constructed from alphanumeric characters plus the underscore. Objects whose scope is file shall use only lower-case letters. Objects whose scope is global (i.e., external linkage) shall be "title cased" and prefixed.

Given:

Source code file `rugged_rock.c`
Include file `rugged_rock.h`

Variable Names:

File scope as declared in `rugged_rock.c`:

```
static boolean_t around_the_rugged_rock; // prefix "RR_" optional
```

Global scope as declared in `rugged_rock.h`:

```
boolean_t RR_The_Ragged_Rascal_Ran = B_FALSE;
```

All objects of file scope shall be declared in the source code file. All objects of global scope shall be declared in the include file. Types and variables shall be defined to give them the smallest scope possible.

Names for hardware objects like on-chip timers or A/D units or any hardware port should provide some indication as to the type of hardware involved. This indicator should be capitalized, the rest of the variable should be lower case. For instance, references to registers in a System Integration Module would start with "`SIM_`".

Pairs of diverse or redundant files will use suffixes consisting of an underscore and a single character (e.g., `ds_get_speed_A.c`, `ds_get_speed_B.c`).

Function argument list names The variable names used within one function shall be maintained across function boundaries where their meaning is not lost or misunderstood. For instance, the following are **not** acceptable:

```
uint16 convert_file_to_view( ... )
{

   char    data_buffer[NUM_LEN + 1];    // converted text data

   char    fline_buffer[MAX_LEN + 1]; // text from file

   uint16    item_genre;             // item type (feat or parm)

   char    *line_position;         // index into fline_buffer

   PARM_REC *ptbl;                // address of parm table

   uint16    table_index;       // parm/feat table index

     cnvt_parm_val( item_genre, ptbl, table_index,

        line_position, data_buffer );

}
```

```
void cnvt_parm_val(uint16 genre, PARM_REC *ptbl, uint16 index,

     char *line, char *buffer )

{

  ...

}
```

and shall be renamed to be consistent across the function boundary (the original comments have been replaced to provide an explanation for each change):

```
void convert_file_to_view( ... )
{

  char   data_buffer[NUM_LEN + 1];

  char   fline_buffer[MAX_LEN + 1];

  char   *fline_position; // Renamed to provide a better

                          // "link" between itself and the

                          // buffer with which it is used.

  uint16 item_genre;

  PARM_REC *ptbl;

  uint16   table_index;

  cnvt_parm_val( item_genre, ptbl, table_index,

     fline_position,      // dito

     data_buffer );

}
void cnvt_parm_val( uint16   item_genre,     // Names changed

     PARM_REC *ptbl,                         // to maintain

     uint16 table_index,                     // consistency

     char   *fline_position,                 // with convert_

     char   *data_buffer )                   // file_to_view()

{    // names.

  ...

}
```

Remember that this requirement shall be invoked whenever an argument's name does not lose its meaning when viewed from the perspective of either the calling or called routine. For instance,

```
char  old_fname[];
char  new_fname[] = { "12345678.123" );
strcpy( old_fname, new_fname );
```

would **not** be renamed:

```
char  *dest;
char  source[] = { "12345678.123" );
strcpy( dest, source );
```

just because the `strcpy()` is coded:

```
int strcpy( char *dest, char *source )
```

nor would you change the `strcpy()` code to:

```
int strcpy( char *old_fname, char *new_fname )
```

The first example above is tied to a specific function within the system and because of this, consistency in names within this entire function is not only desired but is required. No meaning is lost between the various routines while both understandability and maintainability are enhanced.

Function names

Functions names are constructed from alphanumeric characters plus the underscore (`a-z`, `0-9`, `_`). Numeric characters are discouraged but may be allowed on a case-by-case basis. The name shall follow the verb-noun convention [e.g., `generate_alarm()`] [9]. It is further recommended that the name be composed of a single verb followed by a single noun. Be precise, not verbose. A name of `fetch_bucket()` is preferred over `fetch_bucket_from_bottom_of_hill_after_jill_tossed_it_there()`. Reference Appendix B – Suggested module names.

Object-oriented related functions [Reference §2 Definitions, object (3)] shall contain a verb followed by an underscore character and the `object_name` [e.g., `check_object_name()`, `get_object_name()`, `set_object_name()`]. Function names for accessing an object's attribute(s) shall be of the form verb_noun_attribute [e.g., `get_object_name_id()`].

The prefix "`is`" or "`is_`" for function names shall be reserved for Boolean functions returning `boolean_t`, Boolean, etc. exclusively [e.g., `isxdigit()`].

Reference §3.2.1.1 Variable names, for additional function naming conventions.

Constant names

Declarations (i.e., single line #define's containing no arguments), objects utilizing the type-qualifier const, and enumerations shall be referred to as constants.

Integer, character, and floating constant names regardless of scope (i.e., file or global) can be constructed with the underscore character plus either:

- upper case alphanumeric characters or
- lower-case alphanumeric characters suffixed with a "_k".

The "_k" suffix is reserved for integer, character, and floating constant names.

```
#define LITERS_PER_BIT 0.1736407 // Acceptable but not preferred
#define MAX_PARM    31
#define PROMPT      ':'
const float  liters_per_bit_k = 0.1736407; // Preferred
const double pi_k      = 3.1415926;
const char  *warning_msg_k   = "Warning!";
```

Use symbolic values instead of literals whenever it improves code readability or maintainability. The following construct:

```
if ( velocity = = 512 )
```

should be rewritten:

```
static const uint16 max_velocity_k = 512;
if ( velocity = = max_velocity_k )
```

Enumerated constants shall be constructed from upper-case alphabetic characters plus the underscore character.

```
typedef enum { CIRCLE, RECT, TRIANGLE, POINT } figure_class_t;
```

Macro names

Macros (i.e., single or multiple line #define's having arguments) regardless of scope shall conform to the same naming convention prescribed for function names except for the requirement that they follow a verb-noun naming convention [9]. Reference Appendix B – Suggested module names.

```
#define CLRBIT(m,b) (( m ) &= ~( 1 L << ( b )))  // clear bit b in mask m
#define SETBIT(m,b) (( m ) |= 1 L << ( b ))       // set  bit b in mask m
#define TSTBIT(m,b) (( m ) & 1 L << ( b ))        // test bit b in mask m
```

typedef names

`typedef` declaration names shall be constructed from lower-case alphabetic characters plus the underscore. All `typedefs` shall have the suffix "`_t`" (for non-`union` types) and "`_u`" (for `union` types). The "`_t`" and "`_u`" suffix is reserved for `typedefs`.

```
typedef enum { CIRCLE, RECT, TRIANGLE, POINT } figure_class_t;
// pfi_t = = pointer to a function returning an integer
typedef int16 ( *pfi_t )();
typedef union
{

   FLOAT v[MAXNEL];

   FLOAT m[NPR][NER];

} mea_u;
```

Each `struct`, `union`, and `enum` type shall be named, and shall be defined as a `typedef`. Given the following `struct` construct:

```
struct car_status
{

   ...

};
```

the code shall be rewritten using a `typedef`:

```
typedef struct
{

   ...

} car_status_struct_t;
car_status_struct_t car_status;
```

Tag names

Structure and `union` tags shall conform to the same naming convention prescribed for `typedef` names.

```
struct tag
{

  ...;  // list of declarations

};
```

Enumeration tags shall conform to the same naming convention prescribed for `typedef` names.

```
enum figure_class_t { CIRCLE, RECT, TRIANGLE, POINT };
```

The tag mechanism is redundant in the presence of the more general `typedef` declaration, with `typedef` being the preferred form. If both tags and `typedef`s are used, they shall be identical.

Member names

Structure and `union` member names shall conform to the same naming convention prescribed for variable names.

Label names

Statement labels are **not** allowed.

Standard abbreviations

When abbreviations are used in conjunction with additional text, they shall be either prefixed or suffixed of a '_' (underscore) or both prefixed and suffixed with an underscore to accent their use. Reference Appendix A – Approved Standard Abbreviations, for a list of approved abbreviations.

Reserved words

Restrictions on the use of reserved words and keywords are identified.

The "_g" suffix is reserved for variables of global scope; optional.
The "_k" suffix is reserved for integer, character, and floating constant names; required.
The "_t" suffix is reserved for `typedef` declaration names excluding `union`'s; required.
The "_u" suffix is reserved for `typedef` declaration names for `union`'s; required.
The prefixes "is" and "is_" are reserved for Boolean functions.
The following is the standard true/false enumeration found in `portable.h`:

```
typedef enum { B_FALSE = 0, B_TRUE = 1 } boolean_t;
```

The following are the standard success/failure definitions found in `portable.h`:

```
typedef enum { PASSED = 0, FAILED = 1 } pf_t;
```

Restrictions on the implementation language

This section includes a description of any restrictions imposed on the use of constructs and features of the implementation language due to project, machine-dependent characteristics, or tools.

Language constructs and features

This section addresses the allowed use of constructs and features of the C language.

Data and declarations

The use of system-wide global variables is to be avoided. The obvious exception is description of hardware. Another exception is system-wide status indicators to allow communication between, for instance, the diagnostic and administrative/control systems.

Type specifiers

All integer storage is defined as unsigned unless there is a reason for the storage to be signed. For instance, revolutions-per-minute are always positive (negative RPMs do not exist). However, an analog voltage may be from −5 V to 5 V, and a negative voltage is meaningful.

`unsigned` shall always be used if the most significant bit is expected to contain a specific piece of information. This is true in the case of bit masks, which shall always be declared as `unsigned`. Unsigned quantities are guaranteed by the C language definition to be shifted logically (i.e., vacated bits are replaced by 0 bits). Shifting of signed quantities is done either logically or arithmetically (i.e., vacated bits are replaced by a copy of the sign bit); not something you want to have done on your bit mask [6].

Character strings shall be declared as type `char` without regard to the data stored in them. The integer type would not be used for objects such as zip code and social security number because computations are not performed on these objects. The integers, longs, floats, doubles, and like types shall be restricted to variables upon which some computation is possible (regardless of the probability) and unsigned integers and longs (e.g., `uint16`, `uint32`) for masks containing bitwise information.

typedef

`typedef` declarations shall be required whenever there shall be multiple instantiations of the same type.

```
typedef uint16 feat_tbl_mask_t;
typedef uint32 parm_tbl_mask_t;
typedef struct
{

   char street_nbr[];    // [] highlights that street_nbr[] is an array

   char street_name[]; // Ref §3.4.1.8.1.1 Character Strings, p.21

   char city[];        // ...

   char state[];    // ...
```

```
  char zip_code[];   // ...

} address_t;
```

Structure and union declarations

Bit fields

With these declarations:

```
#define UNAVAILABLE 0
#define AVAILABLE   1
#define DISABLED    UNAVAILABLE
#define ENABLED     AVAILABLE
typedef struct
{

  unsigned automotive_governor             : 1;

  unsigned cruise_control                  : 1;

  unsigned engine_protection               : 1;

  unsigned engine_protection_shutdown      : 1;

  unsigned                                 : 4;

  unsigned fuel_log                        : 1;

  unsigned gear_down_protection            : 1;

  unsigned idle_shutdown                   : 1;

  unsigned idle_shutdown_in_pto            : 1;

  unsigned idle_shutdown_override          : 1;

  unsigned                                 : 3;

  unsigned j1922_control_monitor           : 1;

  unsigned low_idle_adjust_switch          : 1;

  unsigned mpg_monitor                     : 1;

  unsigned progressive_shift               : 1;

  unsigned                                 : 4;

  unsigned pto                             : 1;

  unsigned remote_pto                      : 1;
```

```
  unsigned vss                                   : 1;

  unsigned      : 5;

} ecm_flags_u;
```

and these definitions:

```
ecm_flags_u avail_flags;
ecm_flags_u enabl_flags;
```

provides for the following assignment statements:

```
avail_flags.automotive_governor = AVAILABLE;
avail_flags.vss                 = AVAILABLE;
enabl_flags.pto                 = ENABLED;
enabl_flags.remote_pto          = DISABLED;
```

Unions

Given the `UNAVAILABLE`, `AVAILABLE`, `DISABLED`, `ENABLED`, and `ecm_flags_u` declarations above (Reference 3.4.1.3.1 Bit fields) plus declaration:

```
union flags
{
ecm_flags_u flags;
uint32 store;
};
```

and these definitions:

```
union flags avail;
union flags enabl;
```

provides for the following assignment statements:

```
avail.store = (uint32)UNAVAILABLE;
enabl.store = (uint32)UNAVAILABLE;
avail.flags.vss = AVAILABLE;
avail.flags.pto = AVAILABLE;
enabl.flags.vss = ENABLED;
```

Enumerations

Reference §3.2.1.3 Constant names.

Reference §3.2.1.5 typedef names.

```
Reference §0 typedef struct
{

  ...
```

```
} car_status_struct_t;
car_status_struct_t car_status;
Tag names
```

Reference §3.2.3 Reserved words.

Pointer declarations

Reference §5.3 Mismatches of types.

Array declarators

Reference §3.4.1.8.1 Arrays.

Character strings

"By convention, strings in C are terminated with the null character \0. String processing in C is based on this convention" [7].

Null terminating facilitates the use of the intrinsic C functions and, when standardized, eliminates any ambiguity about whether or not a string should be treated as a string or just a set of characters occupying a given memory location.

To preserve and in turn utilize this convention to its fullest, all character strings shall be null (i.e., '\0') terminated. This requirement shall be reflected in the sizing and the initialization (Reference §3.4.1.8.1.1 Character strings) of all character strings.

If the length of a particular character string is a fixed length (e.g., `STR_LEN`), then all declarators used to store that entity shall be sized using the "`+ 1`" notation (e.g., `STR_LEN + 1`). This notation highlights the fact that while the entity being stored is of length `STR_LEN`, the string to hold that entity has been sized for a null terminator.

With these declarations:

```
#define FILE_NAME_LEN 12
#define FILE_ROOT_LEN 8
#define EXTENSION_LEN 3
```

and these definitions:

```
char fname[FILE_NAME_LEN + 1];
char s[];
```

allow for null terminated strings thus facilitating the use of intrinsic C string manipulation functions:

```
sprintf( fname, "%s.%s, "config", "sys" );
strcpy( fname, "12345678.123" );
strncpy( fname, "87654321", FILE_ROOT_LEN );
strlen( fname );
```

```
fname[0] = '\0';
strcat( fname, "config.sys" );
strcmp( fname, "config.sys" );
s = strchr( fname, '.' );
*(++s) = '\0';
strncat( fname, "sys", EXTENSION_LEN );
strncmp( s, "sys", EXTENSION_LEN );
fname[FILE_NAME_LEN] = '\0';
printf( fname );
```

Function declarators

All functions shall be prototyped (i.e., declared). Reference §3.4.2 Functions.

All function definitions shall conform to the "new-style" format [5]. The following style is acceptable:

```
int strcpy( char *dest, char *source )
{

  ...;

} // END: strcpy()
```

while the next example is **not** acceptable:

```
int strcpy( dest, source )
char *dest;
char *source;
{

  ...;

}
```

Some existing C compilers do not check for type mismatches between the caller and called or even between a function's prototype and the actual implementation, if the "old-style" is used.

Initialization

Arrays

Single-dimensional arrays can use either one of the two (2) initialization styles (i.e., single line, everything one line including the braces, or multiple line with braces on separate lines).

```
static uint8 digits[10] =
{
1, 2, 3, 4, 5, 6, 7, 8, 9, 0
};
```

```
static uint8 digits[10] = { 1, 2, 3, 4, 5, 6, 7, 8, 9, 0 };
```

while the next example is **not** acceptable:

```
static uint8 digits[20] = { 0, 1, 2, 3, 4, 5, 6, 7, 8, 9, 10,

      11, 12, 13, 14, 15, 16, 17, 18, 19 };
```

The preceding example shall be rewritten as:

```
static unit8 digits[20] =
{

   0, 1, 2, 3, 4, 5, 6, 7, 8, 9,

   10, 11, 12, 13, 14, 15, 16, 17, 18, 19

};
```

Multidimensional arrays shall accent their row and column initializations by explicitly enclosing each column's values within its own set of braces. The following construct is required:

```
static uint32 salary_tbl[3][5] =
{

   { 500, 550, 600, 650, 700 },   // ...

   { 600, 670, 740, 810, 880 },   // ...

   { 740, 840, 940, 1040, 1140 }   // ...

};
```

while both of the following examples are **not** allowed:

```
static uint32 salary_tbl[3][5] =
{

   500, 550, 600, 650, 700,

   600, 670, 740, 810, 880,

   740, 840, 940, 1040, 1140

};
static uint32 salary_tbl[3][5] =
{

   500, 550, 600, 650, 700, 600, 670, 740, 810, 880, 740, ...

};
```

Commenting of multidimensional arrays is accomplished using the following style:

```
static uint32 salary_tbl[3][5] =
{
  {
    500,  // ...
    550,  // ...
    600,  // ...
    650,  // ...
    700   // ...
  },
  {
    ...
  }
};
```

Character strings

The following three array sizing/initialization styles are **not** acceptable:

```
char name1[] = { 'J', 'a', 'n' };
char name2[3] = { "Feb" };
char *name3   = { 'M', 'a', 'r' };
```

These three declarations create the following elements:

```
Element Value Element Value Element Value
name1[0] 'J' name2[0] 'F' name3[0] 'M'
name1[1] 'a' name2[1] 'e' name3[1] 'a'
name1[2] 'n' name2[2] 'b' name3[2] 'r'
```

while the next examples are acceptable. They are ordered from the most to the least preferred style:

```
char name4[] = { "April" };       // [] highlights that it is an array
                                  // and is the preferred style
                                  // array size established by compiler
char *name5   = { "May" };        // array size established by compiler
char name6[5] = { "June" };       // array size hard coded
```

These three declarations create the following elements:

```
Element  Value Element  Value Element  Value
name4[0] 'A'   name5[0] 'M'   name6[0] 'J'
name4[1] 'p'   name5[1] 'a'   name6[1] 'u'
name4[2] 'r'   name5[2] 'y'   name6[2] 'n'
name4[3] 'i'   name5[3] '\0'  name6[3] 'e'
name4[4] 'l'   name6[4] '\0'
name4[5] '\0'
```

All character strings shall be null (i.e., '\0') terminated. Reference §3.4.1.6.1 Character strings.

Enumerations

The single-dimensional array initialization rules (Reference §3.4.1.8.1 Arrays) shall apply to enumeration type declarations.

Structures

Single-dimensional structures can use either one of the two (2) initialization styles (i.e., single line, everything one line including the braces, or multiple line with braces on separate lines).

Given declaration:

```
typedef struct
{

   char street_nbr[];   // [] highlights that street_nbr is an array

   char street_name[]; // Ref §3.4.1.8.1.1 Character Strings, p.21

   char city[];         // ...

   char state[];       // ...

   char zip_code[]; // ...

} address_t;
```

the following definition styles are acceptable:

```
static address_t tmp_adrs =
{

   "654", "Holly", "St. Paul", "MN", "55104"

};
static address_t tmp_adrs = { "654", "Holly", "St. Paul", "MN", "55104" };
```

while the next definition is **not** acceptable:

```
static address_t tmp_adrs = { "654", "Holly", "St. Paul",      "MN", "55104" };
```

Multidimensional structures shall accent each dimension's initialization by explicitly enclosing each dimension's values within a set of braces. The following two construction/comment styles are acceptable:

```
static address_t perm_adrs[2] =
{

  { "12345", "Bee Cave Rd", "Austin",   "TX", "78746-0000" }, // ...

  { "4261", "Home Ave",   "Columbus", "IN", "10274"   }  // ...

};
static address_t perm_adrs[] =
{

  {

    "12345",           // ...

    "Bee Cave Rd",     // twisty + speed traps = trouble

    "Austin",          // In the heart of Texas.

    "Texas",           // In heaven as it is in Texas!!!

    "78746-0000"     // ...

  },

  {

   ...

  }

};
```

Functions

Functions shall be limited to the performance of a *single purpose*. Control flows telling a function what to do and how to do it (i.e., "nag flags") shall be strictly limited. If a nag flag/control flow changes a function's *single purpose*, then that function should be reconstructed to conform to the *single purpose* criteria.

All functions shall be prototyped. Functions whose scope is global shall be prototyped in an include file which shall be referenced in the file containing the function. Functions whose scope is file (i.e., locally defined static functions) shall be prototyped under the banner "LOCAL PROTOTYPES" in the source file.

A function's error handling requirements shall be defined in the "RESTRICTIONS, SIDE EFFECTS, ERROR HANDLING, AND NOTES" section of the function header.

Function invocation

All invocations to functions returning the PASSED/FAILED success/failure indications shall be explicitly checked and processed immediately upon their return to the calling function.

All file input/output operations [e.g., fclose(), ferror(), feof(), fopen(), fgets(), fputs(), fseek(), ftell(), rename(), unlink()] shall be explicitly checked for a success/failure condition immediately upon their return to the calling function and the appropriate action taken.

A function's error processing could even be to ignore the returned success/failure indicator. Whatever the case may be, an explanation is required in the ERROR HANDLING section of the function's header.

Testability requirements mandate that the code be constructed to allow for the setting of breakpoints both before and after a function is called during emulator debugging. For instance:

```
if ( lock_out() = = FAILED )
perror();
else

...
```

is **not** an acceptable construction. It shall be rewritten as:

```
pf_t status;

...

status = lock_out();
if ( status = = FAILED )
perror();
else

   ...
```

Given:

```
FILE *fptr;
```

the following construct:

```
if (( fptr = fopen( ... )) != (FILE *)NULL )

   ...
```

shall be rewritten:

```
fptr = fopen( ... );
if ( fptr != (FILE *)NULL )

   ...
```

The C language does not specify the order of evaluation for function call arguments or for the operands of binary operators. Thus avoid writing such ambiguous expressions as:

```
z = ( x * ++y ) / f( y );
f( ++i, x[ i ] );
```

In the example above, `++y` and `f( y )` may not be evaluated in the same order by all C compilers [8].

Expressions and operators

Constant expression

It is poor programming practice to use numeric constants, especially when their meaning is not immediately obvious. Numeric constants are better represented by symbolic constants associated with them by `#define` [6].

Use constants instead of variables for constant values; use `const uint16 max_altitude_t = 50000` instead `uint16 max_altitude = 50000`).

Constants are to be replaced by `#define`s or declared using the type-qualifier `const`. It is permissible for multiple `#define`s to resolve to the same string when the group can identify an advantage; for instance:

```
#define HALT_FLAG 0×01
#define FIRST  HALT_FLAG
```

is permissible. The intent here is to improve the ability to scan a library of source for occurrences of a token like `HALT_FLAG`.

Additionally, multiple `#define`s are only allowed where there is a meaningful connection between the values being defined. If they are not related, then separate `#define`s are required. Also reference §3.4.3.5 Assignment expression.

Unary expression

The use of the unary expression ! (logical negation) operator shall be restricted to tests involving boolean expressions.

Given:

```
FILE *fptr;
fptr = fopen( ... );
```

the following construct:

```
if ( !fptr )

   ...
```

shall be rewritten:

```
if ( fptr = = (FILE *)NULL )

   ...
```

Conditional expression

The use of the conditional expression `?:` shall be discouraged. Testability requirements mandate that only one executable statement exists per line to allow for the setting of breakpoints on every executable statement during emulator debugging. The conditional expression `?:` prevents the setting of breakpoints in this manner.

The following construct:

```
boolean_t check_range( uint16 value )
{

   return (( MINVAL<= value ) && ( value<= MAXVAL )) ? B_TRUE : B_FALSE;

}
```

shall be rewritten:

```
boolean_t check_range( uint16 value )
{

   boolean_t in_range;

   if (( MINVAL<= value ) && ( value<= MAXVAL ))

      in_range = B_TRUE;

   else

      in_range = B_FALSE;

   return in_range;

   } // END: check_range()
```

The construct:

```
memset( ccr->line[FIRST_DOT_LOC], '.', num_dots ? num_dots : MAX_DOTS );
num_dots = ( num_dots<MAX_DOTS ) ? num_dots + 1 : 0;
```

shall be rewritten similar to the following:

```
if ( num_dots>= MAX_DOTS )

  num_dots = 0;

else

  num_dots++;

memset( ccr->line[FIRST_DOT_LOC], '.', num_dots );
```

Conditional expressions are acceptable in instances similar to the following:

```
#define NEGATIVE(x)  ((x)<0 ? B_TRUE : B_FALSE )
#define NATURAL(x)   ((x)>= 0 ? B_TRUE : B_FALSE )
#define POSITIVE(x)  ((x)>0 ? B_TRUE : B_FALSE )
```

Comma expression

The comma expression is **not** allowed. The following construct:

```
wave = ( intensity + = incr, intensity *= mult, splash( intensity ));
```

shall be rewritten:

```
intensity + = incr;
intensity *= mult;
wave = splash( intensity );
```

Assignment expression

Multiple assignment expressions (e.g., `i = j = 0`) are only allowed where there is a meaningful connection between the values being equated. If they are not related, then separate equates are required. In the example `i = j = 0`, assigns in order the value `0` (zero) to `j` and the value `j` to `i`.

Also, be wary of the construct "`lvalue = j = = 0`", "`lvalue = j ! = 0`", or like statements. In this case, the right-hand expression is evaluated as a Boolean expression and the results are stored in `lvalue`. These statements should be rewritten in the following format:

```
boolean_t lvalue;
unit16 j;
if ( j = = 0 )

  lvalue = B_TRUE;
```

```
else
   lvalue = B_FALSE;
```

Grouping and evaluating exceptions

The C language does not specify the order of grouping operands with operators in an expression that contains more than one instance of an operator that has both associative and commutative properties. The compiler can rearrange operands in such an expression and not even parentheses can guarantee an order of grouping within the expression. The operators that have the same associative and commutative properties are: `*`, `+`, `&`, `|`, and `^`. The grouping of operands can be forced by grouping the expression in parenthesis and preceding it with a unary plus (+) operator [8].

The parentheses in the following expression do not guarantee the order of grouping operands with the operators:

```
x = f() + ( g() + h() );
```

The order may be guaranteed by placing a unary plus (+) in front of the parenthesis:

```
x = f() + +( g() + h() );
```

Statements

No more than one statement on a single line. For instance:

```
while ( i = = test_value ) test_time = Timer1;
```

is **not** an acceptable construction. The object of the `while` statement should be on a separate line:

```
while ( i = = test_value )
   test_time = Timer1;
```

is acceptable.

`break`

The use of the `break` statement in loop constructs (e.g., `do{}while`, `for`, `while`) shall be discouraged because `break` and `continue` are little more than `goto` statements and `goto`s are **not** allowed. If used, they shall be restricted to at most only one occurrence per loop and shall never be used in conjunction with a `continue` statement in the same loop. The use of multiple `break` statements or the combination of `break` and `continue` statements within the same loop falls under the category of fractured control flow and shall not be used. Reference 3.4.4.9 `switch`, for additional usage requirements.

```
//
// This program counts the characters in strings that are part of an
// array of pointers to characters. The count stops when one of the
// digits 0 through 9 is encountered and resumes at the beginning of
// the next string. Reference Appendix F – Function template
//
#define NUM_OF_STRINGS 3
static char *strings[NUM_OF_STRINGS] = { "ab", "c5d", "e5" };
main()
{

  uint16      letter_count = 0;

  char       *pointer;

    register uint16 ui;      // ui defined for block use.

                             // The register storage class is an

                             // attempt to improve the loop's efficiency.

  for ( ui = 0; ui < NUM_OF_STRINGS; ui++ ) // for each string

  {

  // for each character in the string

    for ( pointer = strings[ui]; *pointer != '\0'; pointer++ )

    {

         // if the character was a number

    if (( '0' <= *pointer ) && ( *pointer <= '9' ))

         break;

      letter_count++;

    }

   }

  printf( "letter count = %d\n", letter_count );

}  // END: main()
```

Be aware, compilers typically ignore the `register` type qualifier. The use of `register` is **not** recommended and should be avoided. Choose the correct type for the variable and let the compiler handle register allocation.

continue

The use of the `continue` statement shall be discouraged. If used, they shall be restricted to at most only one occurrence per loop and shall never be used in conjunction with a `break` statement in the same loop. The use of multiple `continue` statements or the combination of `continue` and `break` statements within the same loop falls under fractured control flow. The following example shows a `continue` statement in a nested loop.

```
//———————————————————————————————————————————————————
// This program counts the characters in strings that are part of an
// array of pointers to characters. The count excludes the digits
// 0 (zero) through 9. When the inner loop encounters a number in
// the array strings, that iteration of the loop is terminated.
// Execution continues with the next expression of the inner loop.
// The inner loop is terminated when the '\0' null terminator is
// encountered. Reference Appendix F – Function template
//———————————————————————————————————————————————————
#define NUM_OF_STRINGS 3
static char *strings[NUM_OF_STRINGS] = { "ab", "c5d", "e5" };
main()
{

    uint16 ui;

    unit16 letter_count = 0;

    char *pointer;

    for ( ui = 0; ui < NUM_OF_STRINGS; ui++ ) // for each string

{

     // for each character in the string

     for ( pointer = strings[ui]; *pointer != '\0'; pointer++ )

     {

         // if the character was a number

          if (( '0' <= *pointer ) && ( *pointer <= '9' ))

         continue;

      letter_count++;

     }

    }

    printf( "letter count = %d\n", letter_count );
```

```
}  // END: main()
```

do{}while

Loops requiring at least one execution should use the `do{}while` construct and not the `for` or `while` constructs. When the `while` statement is used in loop requiring at least one execution, the loop control expression has to be preconditioned to a true state to gain entry into the loop and every time thereafter to check when looping is completed. If preconditioning is needed to enter a loop then the `do{}while` construct should be considered.

for

The following `for` statement prints the value of count 20 times. The `for` statement initially sets the value of `count` to one. After each execution of the statement, `count` is incremented.

```
for ( count = 1; count<= 20; count++ )

  printf( "count = %d\n", count );
```

For comparison purposes, the preceding example can be written using the following sequence of statements to accomplish the same task. Note the use of the `while` statement instead of the `for` statement.

```
count = 1;
while ( count<= 20 )
{

   printf( "count = %d\n", count );

   count++;

}
```

The following `for` statement does not contain an initialization expression.

```
for ( ; index>10; index- )
{
  list[index] = var1 + var2;
  printf( "list[%d] = %d\n", index, list[index] );
}
```

The `for` statement shall contain only loop control parameters. The following construct:

```
const uint16 increment = 50;

...

for ( i = 0, j = increment; i<10; i++, j + = increment )
{
```

```
    printf( "i = %d and j = %3d\n", i, j );

}
```

shall be rewritten as:

```
const uint16 increment = 50;

...

j = increment;
for ( i = 0; i<10; i++ )
{

    printf( "i = %d and j = %3d\n", i, j );

    j + = increment;

}
```

A single `for` statement shall control only one loop:

```
uint16 code[4][3][6];
for ( first = 0; first<= 3; first++ )

        for ( second = 0; second<= 2; second++ )

          for ( third = 0; third<= 5; third++ )

              code[first][second][third] = 100;
```

The following construct initializing the elements of the array `price`:

```
for ( i = 0; i<3; price[i++] = 0 );
```

shall be rewritten as:

```
for ( i = 0; i<3; i++ )

    price[i] = 0;
```

`goto`

The use of the `goto` statement is **not** allowed. The use of the `goto` statement is considered harmful because it hampers program understandability.

`if`

Ambiguity exists when the `else` is omitted from a nested `if` sequence. In such cases, the `else` is associated with the closest previous un-`else`'ed `if` at the same block level [6]. Use braces to prevent ambiguity.

```
if ( n>= 0 )

  for ( i = 0; i<n; i++ )

    if ( s[i]>0 )

    {

     printf( "..." );

    }

else

   printf( "error - n is negative\n" );
```

The indentation shows unequivocally what was intended but the inner `if` is associated with the `else` statement. Use braces when there are nested `if`s [5].

```
if ( n>= 0 )
{

   for ( i = 0; i<n; i++ )

      if ( s[i]>0 )

         printf( "..." );

}
else

   printf( "error - n is negative\n" );
```

Repeated `if`/`else if` statements containing the same test (e.g., "`box_type = = ...`") shall be avoided.

Given:

```
typedef enum
{

  COLOR_LIGHT_BOX, END_BOX, REPEATER_BOX, IWP_BOX, UNKNOWN_BOX

} box_t;
```

the following construct:

```
if ( box_type = = END_BOX )

  format_end_box_entry( entry, str );

else if ( box_type = = COLOR_LIGHT_BOX )
```

```
  format_color_light_box_entry( entry, str );

else if ( box_type = = REPEATER_BOX )

  format_repeater_box_entry( entry, str );

else if ( box_type ! = IWP_BOX )

  log_error( Verr_RecInit, S_File, __LINE__,

      "Unknown Box Type", 16, B_FALSE );
```

should be rewritten as:

```
switch ( box_type )
{

  case END_BOX :

    format_end_box_entry( entry, str );

    break;

  case COLOR_LIGHT_BOX :

    format_color_light_box_entry( entry, str );

    break;

  case REPEATER_BOX :

    format_repeater_box_entry( entry, str );

    break;

  case IWP_BOX :

    break;

  default :

    log_error( Verr_RecInit, S_File, __LINE__,

        "Unknown Box Type", 16, B_FALSE );

    break;           // break statement mandatory

}
```

Null (;) statement

A null statement shall appear on a line by itself:

Acceptable:

```
main()
{

   uint16 ones;

   uint16 thousands;

   for ( thousands = 0; thousands<1000; thousands++ )

   {

     for ( ones = 0; ones<1000; ones++ )

   {

        ; // A null statement shall appear on a line by itself

   }

   }

} // END: main()
```

Preferred:

```
main()
{

   uint16 ones;

   uint16 thousands;

    for ( thousands = 0; thousands<1000; thousands++ )

      for ( ones = 0; ones<1000; ones++ );

         // A null statement shall appear on a line by itself

} // END: main()
```

not acceptable (null statement **not** on a line by itself):

```
main()
{

   uint16 ones;
```

```
    uint16 thousands;

    for ( thousands = 0; thousands<1000; thousands++ )

      for ( ones = 0; ones<1000; ones++ );     // NOT allowed

}
```

return

A function shall contain only one `return` statement except for functions of type `void`. The `return` statement for `void` functions is optional. Void functions shall be restricted to functions that always exit normally (i.e., without error). All functions shall be constructed in such a manner that there exists only one exit point regardless of whether or not a `return` statement is used. This exit point shall be at the *bottom* of the function body (e.g., the last instruction).

All functions shall return a success/failure indication if there exists any possibility of it exiting in an abnormal state regardless of whether it is the perception at the function's level that the success/failure indicator is needed or not. The following are the standard success/failure `PASSED/FAILED` declarations of type pf_t found in `portable.h`.

switch

The following example is a `switch` statement that contains several `break` statements. Each `break` statement signals the end of a specific clause and ends the execution of the `switch` statement. The "mandatory" `break` statements in the following examples (although optional from a pure C language perspective) are required for the setting of a breakpoint following the execution of the `switch`'s statement(s). This is a testability requirement to facilitate emulator debugging.

```
char key;
printf( "Enter an arithmetic operator: " );
scanf( "%c", &key );
switch ( key )
{

    case '+' :

        add();

        break;

    case '-' :

        subtract();

        break;
```

```
    case '*' :

      multiply();

      break;

    case '/' :

      divide();

      break;

    default :

      printf( "invalid key\n" );

      break; // break statement mandatory

}
```

The following `switch` statement contains several `case` labels that are not immediately followed by statements:

```
typedef enum
{

    JAN = 1; FEB, MAR, APR, MAY, JUN, JUL, AUG, SEP, OCT, NOV, DEC

} months_t;
months_t month;

...;

switch ( month )
{

    case DEC:

    case JAN:

    case FEB:

      printf( "month %d is a winter month\n", month );

      break;

    case MAR:

    case APR:

    case MAY:
```

```
    printf( "month %d is a spring month\n", month );
    break;
  case JUN:
  case JUL:
  case AUG:
    printf( "month %d is a summer month\n", month );
    break;
  case SEP:
  case OCT:
  case NOV:
    printf( "month %d is a fall month\n", month );
    break;
  default:
    printf( "%d not a valid month\n", (int)month );
    break;          // break statement mandatory
}
```

If the expression `month` had the value `MAR`, the system would pass control to the statement:

```
printf( "month %d is a spring month\n", month );
```

The `break` statement would pass control to the statement following the switch body.

If the `switch` expression matches a `case` expression, the statements following the `case` expression are executed until a `break` statement is encountered or the end of the switch body is reached. In the following example, `break` statements are not present.

This type of construction is acceptable if it is explicitly stated in the comments that a "`fall through`" or "`fall thru`" is intended. This is to remove any doubt from someone other than the author that the following statement(s) is to be executed.

```
uint8 strl;       // length of text to be searched
char *text;       // source string containing text to be searched
uint8 capa;       // total number of capital 'A'
uint8 lettera;    // total number of 'A' and 'a'
uint8 total;      // total number of character in source string
```

```
strl = strlen( text );
for ( i = 0; i<strl; i++ )
{

    switch ( text[i] )

    {

     case 'A':                 // If the value of c is equal to 'A',

       capa++;                // all 3 counters are incremented.

                            // Fall thru to case 'a' intended.

    case 'a':              // If the value of c is equal to 'a',

    lettera++;           // letter a and total are increased.

                       // Fall thru to default case intended.

     default:          // Only total is increased if c is not

     total++;        // equal to 'A' or 'a'.

    break;          // break statement mandatory

    }

}
```

The use of multiple `break` statements in case constructs is **not** allowed. This continues the proscription against fractured control flow since the `break` statement is nothing but a glorified `goto` statement and `goto`s are **not** allowed.

while

`while` statement expressions shall be restricted to loop control. The following construct:

```
while (( key = getchar()) = = ' ' || key = = '\n' || key = = '\t' )

    ;
```

shall be rewritten:

```
do
{

    key = getchar();

} while ( key = = ' ' || key = = '\n' || key = = '\t' );
```

Complexity

This section describes controls and restrictions on the complexity of code aggregates.

When a single statement is too complex to fit well on one line, align like parts together if possible. For instance, if you are starting with something like:

```
if ((( a = = b ) && ( c>d )) || (( e != f ) && ( g<h )) || ( i<j ))
```

the statement should be rewritten:

```
if ((( a = = b ) && ( c>d )) ||   \
    (( e != f ) && ( g<h )) ||    \
    ( i<j     ))
```

Statements should be constructed to enhance their understandability, maintainability, and testability.

Problematic constructs

Constants versus `sizeof` operator

The use of the `sizeof` operator to refer to the size of the object shall be encouraged. A constant is often used to represent the size of some object but such usage in not portable. The following macro yields the number of elements in an array in a portable manner:

```
#define NUM_ELEM(array) ( sizeof( array ) / sizeof( *( array )))
```

Multicharacter character constants

The use of multicharacter character constants is **not** allowed. Because character constants are really objects of type `int`, the C language definition allows multicharacter character constants. However, the order in which the characters are assigned in a word varies on different machines [6].

Mismatches of types

Do not mismatch data type/values (e.g., a pointer is not an integer is not a character and in turn NULL is not the same thing as `0` (zero) is not the same thing as `'\0'`). The only *safe* constant that can be assigned to a pointer is NULL, when NULL is cast to the pointer type. Do not equate pointers to `uint32` and vice versa. This will only work until the size of the pointers change.

Machine's word size

The size of an `int` type depends on the machine's word size, which varies on different machines. For this reason, a machine's word size can affect constants such as bit masks.

```
#define MASK 0xfff8  // WRONG
int x;
x &= MASK;
```

The above will clear the three least significant bits of `x` correctly, only when an `int` is 16 bits in size and where `x` is declared as likewise. On the other hand, the most significant bits of `x` will be cleared when an `int` has more than 16 bits or when `x` is declared as a inappropriate (for this mask) data type such as an `uint16`. To avoid these problems, use this `#define` declaration instead [6]:

```
#define MASK (~0x07) // RIGHT
uint16 x;
x &= MASK;
```

Source and include file layouts

Source code

All source files (with extension `.c`) will follow one of these standard formats with the header structure as specified. Each source file will have a corresponding header file (same name with `.h` extension) whenever there are global coding elements that need to be read from other modules.

Regardless of whether the software development methodology is structured or object-oriented, a requirement for organizing the code is that the source code file should not be a haphazard collection of elements. Everything in a single source code file should be logical and by design. For structured design, everything in the file should be oriented towards function(s)s as represented in a design element such as function block on the structure chart. For those implementing an object-oriented design, everything in the file should be solely for that object.

Reference Appendix C – Source code template.

Multiple function rules

Multiple functions may reside in a single file as long they conform to the following rules:

- Structure-oriented source files shall contain only one (1) non-static function and that function name (e.g., "`verb_noun`") shall be identical to the filename (i.e., `verb_noun.c`). This non-static function shall be the first function body found in the file.

- Object-oriented [Reference §2 Definitions, object (3)] source files may contain multiple non-static (i.e., public) functions and the object's name (e.g., "`object_name`") shall be identical to the filename (i.e., `object_name.c`).
- For each source code file, there shall be at most a single include file (e.g., `verb_noun.h`, `object_name.h`).
- All locally defined static functions shall be prototyped. These prototypes shall be alphabetically ordered in the `LOCAL PROTOTYPES` section.
- All functions shall be preceded with the appropriate header. Reference Appendix F – Function template.
- For a structure-oriented source file, the locally defined static function(s) shall support the one non-static function for which the file is named. Locally defined static function(s) shall not become the hiding places for little chunks of code just because the author "wanted to do it their own way" or simply did not want to investigate whether or not a static function's functionality was already being performed by another function.
- For an object-oriented source code file, the locally defined function(s) (both public and static) shall support the object for which the file is named.
- Structure-oriented source code files shall be no larger than three (3) times the maximum code aggregate size. Reference §3.1.5 Code aggregate size.
- The maximum code aggregate size for object source file shall be determined by the size of the functions (public, protected, and private) that constitute the object's definition. The maximum code aggregate size restriction as specified in §3.1.5 does not apply. It shall be the responsibility of the designer and reviewer(s) to determine what is acceptable but file lengths in the four figures (i.e., > 999 executable, non-expandable statements) are not allowed.

Reference §3.2.1.2 Function names, for function-naming conventions.

Include files

Place declarations of data types, symbolic constants, and macros shared by more than one program in a single header (i.e., `include`) file so that changes can be made in one place. ***Don't*** place external variable definitions that allocate storage in header files. Use header files ***solely*** for preprocessor statements and `typedef`s [6].

All header files (with extension `.h`) should follow a standard format for the file. The header file should be wrapped with `#ifndef`/`#define`/`#endif` in case it is included multiple times by a source file. For example, if `api_serial.h` is the filename, then after the header the rest of the file should be wrapped with `#ifndef API_SERIAL_H`, `#define API_SERIAL_H`, and then followed with the `#endif` at the end of the file. Reference Appendix D – Standard include file template.

All include files should be compilable as standalone entities.

portable.h

To minimize concerns with porting code from one platform to another, all constructs associated with a machine unique characteristics (e.g., word size, processor speed) shall be captured as more as practicable in one file `portable.h`. This makes `portable.h` one of the most important files in the system with "portability" extending far beyond just the calling conventions. Reference §7.2.1 `portable.h`, for the machine-dependent characteristics associated with `portable.h`.

`portable.h` shall not include any other header files and should be written so it is not dependent on other files. `portable.h` shall not contain any function prototypes. Reference Appendix E – `portable.h` include file template.

Characteristics

Project characteristics

Project characteristics may include, but are not limited to, safety or security considerations in the operational environment.

Machine-dependent characteristics

Machine-dependent characteristics may include input/output features, word-length-dependent features, use of floating-point arithmetic, etc.

Use header (i.e., include) files to contain environment-specific and hardware-dependent information. Use header files to isolate data and environment-dependent data such as filenames or options. Place anything that can vary across systems, or even within the same system, in header files where it (they) can be easily located and modified [6].

portable.h

Application definitions

Any definitions that are present in the `portable.h` file should never be defined anywhere else in the system. This includes `B_TRUE`, `B_FALSE`, `PASSED`, and `FAILED`. An alternative to `PASSED`/`FAILED` is the usage of `PASS`/`FAIL`. Choose one convention or the other – mixing them could have bad results! This will force the project to never have multiple definitions and meeting for the same variable.

Storage sizes and base classes

Source code in the application should never use compiler- or architecture-dependent storage sizes and classes. As an example, code should not declare an `unsigned int` variable in the code. Instead, this file will declare new type definitions (e.g., `UINT8`, `INT16`) so that consistent storage definitions are used throughout. Standard C library calls can continue to use both `unsigned char` and `char` as necessary to maintain compatibility. Also, the normal `char` can be used to represent characters (e.g., 'x') or character strings (e.g., "xfer").

Here is an example of the new type definitions:

```
typedef unsigned char  uint8; // Alternative: uint8_t to show typedef
typedef unsigned int   uint16;
typedef unsigned long int uint32;
typedef signed char   int8;
typedef signed int    int16;
typedef signed long int  int32;
```

Processor speed and timeframes

Another piece of information will be the base periodic frame time. This `#define` will use a somewhat non-descriptive name, called `FRAME_TIME_MS`. This is because it is expected that this will be used whenever another timer or base time needs to be created. For instance, if the base frame timing for the `main()` is 10 ms, this `#define` will have the value "10". If a routine is called with every major frame, and needs to use a 1.1 second timer, its definitions might look something like this:

```
#define IO_TIMEOUT_TIMER (UINT16)( 1.1 * 1000.0 / FRAME_TIME_MS ) // 1.1 secs
```

If a routine is executed in a sub-frame, then the application should consider declaring a separate frame time constant, but it should also be based on `FRAME_TIME_MS`. The goal is to be able to change this frame time definition in `portable.h` without having to change any other code.

Tool characteristics

Tool characteristics may include optimization options, etc.

Some compilers provide a switch(es) for various *optimization* options. These options should be scrutinized and the ramifications of their use should be ***clearly*** understood before being invoked.

As an example, it is common for compilers (especially those targeted towards embedded real-time applications) to provide a switch(es) for memory optimization. When invoked, these options would attempt to *pack* objects into a minimal storage space. This sounds great but be forewarned that this may also get you into trouble. If an object requires an odd number bytes for storage and you have invoked the *optimize memory* option, the object declared immediately afterwards could be storage at an *odd* address. This *packing/odd addressing* has two *you-had-better-watch-out-for-these* aspects depending on the target computer's architecture and addressing modes. The first *you-had-better-watch-out-for* deals with the overlaying of objects-on-objects as in the case of `unions` and memory-mapped software (e.g., software mapped on a specific hardware implementation) and the other *watch-out* involves *odd byte* addressing.

While the potential negative associated with *odd byte* addressing can usually be avoided by **not** invoking the *optimize memory* option the objects-on-objects problem takes more thought. `unions` will require the developer to possess a detailed knowledge regarding the size (to the bit, byte and word levels) for each object contained in a `union`. Lest anyone suggest that we *just say no* to `unions`, there are legitimate uses for `unions` especially in the manipulation of structures containing bit fields. Reference §3.4.1.3.1 Bit fields and §3.4.1.3.2 Unions. Bit fields are especially useful in the manipulation of individual bits when `unions` overlay `structs` which overlay hardware. For memory-mapped software, the *fix* can be as simple as ensuring that there are *no blank spots* (i.e., no *odd byte* length objects) in the software declarations.

Appendix A – Approved standard abbreviations

```
addr/adrs address
anal analyze/analysis
auto  automated/automatic
cal   calibrate/calibration
calc  calculate/compute
cfg   config/configuration
chk   check
cksum checksum
clr   clear
cls   class
comp  compare
conv  convert/conversion
del   delete/remove
dev   develop/development
dspl  display
feat  feature(s)
fname filename
fptr  file pointer
flt   fault
func  function
gen   generate
gui   graphical user interface
hdr   header
init  initial / initialize / initialization
len   length
loc   locate/location
mgr   manager
mon   monitor
```

```
msk  mask
nbr/num number
parm parameter(s)
perc percent
perf perform/performance
pres pressure
proc process
pswd password
ptr  pointer
ptrn pattern
rd   read
rec  record
scrn screen
std  standard
stat status
str  string
sys  system
tbl  table(s)
temp temperature
tmp  temporary
tst  test
val  value
ver  version
vld  validate/validation
vfy  verify/verification
wr   write
x... trans...
xfer transfer
xform transform
```

Appendix B – Suggested module names

Afferent processes with external sources of data:

- `accept` (usually asynchronous)
- `find`
- `get`
- `input`
- `load`
- `obtain`

Afferent process with internal sources of data:

- `create` (`cre`, Reference Appendix A – Approved standard abbreviations)
- `develop` (`dev`)
- `form`
- `generate` (`gen`)
- `setup`

Transform processes:

`analyze (anal)`
`calculate (calc)`
`compute (calc)`
`convert (conv)`
`do`
`perform (perf)`
`process (proc)`
`transform (xform)`
Specific verbs like `sort`, `validate`, etc.
Function-oriented nouns like `inversion`, `squareroot`, etc.

Efferent process with external targets:

`deliver`
`output`
`produce (prod)`
`put`
`save`
`store`
`write (wr)`

Specific verbs like `list`, `print`, `punch`, etc.

Some of these verbs are somewhat ambiguous:

`create` (could be afferent or efferent)
`deliver` (could be afferent or efferent)
`do` (could be anything)
`generate` (could be afferent or efferent) (`gen`)
`perform` (could be anything) (`perf`)
`process` (could be afferent or transform) (`proc`)

[9] Table 10.1 Suggested Module Names, p. 203.

Appendix C – Source code template

```
//= ________________________________________________________________
//=
//= NAME: $Workfile: filename.c$
//=
//= REVISION: $Revision: $
//=
//= MNEMONIC: "unique two-to-five character acronym"
//=
//= PURPOSE:
//=
```

```
//= DESCRIPTION:
//
//= RESTRICTIONS, SIDE EFFECTS, ERROR HANDLING, AND NOTES:
//
//= AUTHOR: $Author: $
//=
//= CONTROL: $Date: $
//=
//= COPYRIGHT:
//=  Copyright (c) 2012<Legal Company Name>
//=  Unpublished Work
//=  All Rights Reserved
//=
//= ----------------------------------------------------------------------
// $NoKeywords$
#define _FILENAME_C_
// ----------------------------------------------------------------------
// Comment block containing free-flowing text.
// Reference §3.1.4Comments.
// This section can be replicated as many times as required.
// ----------------------------------------------------------------------
// ----------------------------------------------------------------------
// SYSTEM INCLUDE FILES
// ----------------------------------------------------------------------
// ----------------------------------------------------------------------
// APPLICATION INCLUDE FILES
// ----------------------------------------------------------------------
#include<portable.h>
#include<filename.h>
// ----------------------------------------------------------------------
// LOCAL DECLARATIONS
// ----------------------------------------------------------------------
// ----------------------------------------------------------------------
// GLOBAL VARIABLES (extern)
// ----------------------------------------------------------------------
// ----------------------------------------------------------------------
// FILE SCOPE VARIABLES (static)
// ----------------------------------------------------------------------
// ----------------------------------------------------------------------
// LOCAL PROTOTYPES
// ----------------------------------------------------------------------
// ----------------------------------------------------------------------
// PUBLIC FUNCTIONS
// ----------------------------------------------------------------------
// ----------------------------------------------------------------------
// All public function(s) in this file should reside here.
// These function(s) should be placed in either alphabetic or logic order.
// Consistency of ordering should be maintained regardless of which ordering is
// chosen.
// ----------------------------------------------------------------------
```

```
//—————————————————————————————————
// Reference Appendix F – Function template
//—————————————————————————————————
type public_function_name()
{
#ifdef PARM_CHK
#endif // PARM_CHK

 ...;

} // END: public_function_name()
//—————————————————————————————————
// LOCAL FUNCTIONS
//—————————————————————————————————
//—————————————————————————————————
// All static function(s) in this file should reside here.
// These function(s) should be placed in either alphabetic or logic order.
// Consistency of ordering should be maintained regardless of which ordering is
// chosen.
//—————————————————————————————————
//—————————————————————————————————
// Reference Appendix F – Function template
//—————————————————————————————————
static type local_function_name()
{
#ifdef PARM_CHK
#endif // PARM_CHK

  ...;

} // END: local_function_name()
// EOF: filename.c
#undef _FILENAME_C_
```

Appendix D – Standard include file template

```
//=—————————————————————————————————
//=
//= FUNCTION: $Workfile: filename.h$
//=
//= REVISION: $Revision: $
//=
//= PURPOSE:
//=
//= USAGE DESCRIPTION:
//
//= AUTHOR: $Author: $
//=
//= CONTROL: $Date: $
```

```
//=
//= COPYRIGHT:
//=  Copyright (c) 2012<Legal Company Name>
//=  Unpublished Work
//=  All Rights Reserved
//=
//= ————————————————————————————————————————
#ifndef _FILENAME_H_
#define _FILENAME_H_
// ————————————————————————————————————————
// Comment block containing free-flowing text.
// Reference§3.1.4Comments.
// This section can be replicated as many times as required.
// ————————————————————————————————————————
// ————————————————————————————————————————
// SYSTEM INCLUDE FILES
// ————————————————————————————————————————
// ————————————————————————————————————————
// The list of included files should be restricted to the minimum set of files
// needed to resolve all symbols contained in this file (i.e., include files
// should be "free standing" and if compiled by themselves should be errorless
// and warning free).
// ————————————————————————————————————————
// ————————————————————————————————————————
// APPLICATION INCLUDE FILES
// ————————————————————————————————————————
// ————————————————————————————————————————
// DECLARATIONS
// ————————————————————————————————————————
#ifdef _FILENAME_C_
// Definition of global variables (storage allocation).
#else
// Declarations of global variable (extern).
#endif // _FILENAME_C_
// ————————————————————————————————————————
// PROTOTYPES
// ————————————————————————————————————————
#endif // _FILENAME_H_
// EOF: filename.h
```

Appendix E — `portable.h` include file template

```
//= ————————————————————————————————————————
//=
//= NAME: $Workfile: portable.h$
//=
//= REVISION: $Revision: $
//=
//= PURPOSE:
```

```
//=
//= USAGE DESCRIPTION:
//
//= AUTHOR: $Author: $
//=
//= CONTROL: $Date: $
//=
//= COPYRIGHT:
//=  Copyright (c) 2012 <Legal Company Name>
//=  Unpublished Work
//=  All Rights Reserved
//=
//= ________________________________________________________________
#ifndef _PORTABLE_H_
#define _PORTABLE_H_
// ________________________________________________________________
// Comment block containing free-flowing text.
// Reference §3.1.4Comments.
// This section can be replicated as many times as required.
// ________________________________________________________________
// ________________________________________________________________
// DECLARATIONS
// ________________________________________________________________
typedef enum { B_FALSE = 0, B_TRUE = 1 } boolean_t;
typedef enum { PASSED = 0, FAILED = 1 } pf_t;
// Alternate of line above, chose one or the other
// typedef enum { PASS = 0, FAIL = 1 } pf_t;
typedef unsigned char   uint8;  // Alternative use uint8_t
typedef unsigned int    uint16;
typedef unsigned long int uint32;
typedef signed char   int8;
typedef signed int    int16;
typedef signed long int  int32;
#endif // _PORTABLE_H_
// EOF: portable.h
```

Appendix F – Function template

```
//= ________________________________________________________________
//=
//= FUNCTION: function_name  (Extended function name, if any)
//=
//= PURPOSE:
//=
//= DESIGN DESCRIPTION:
//=
//= SAFETY, RESTRICTIONS, SIDE EFFECTS, ERROR HANDLING, AND NOTES:
//=
//= ________________________________________________________________
```

```
// ------------------------------------------------------------------
// Comment block containing free-flowing text.
// Reference §3.1.4Comments.
// This section can be replicated as many times as required.
// ------------------------------------------------------------------
type function_name()
{
#ifdef PARM_CHK
#endif // PARM_CHK

   ...;

} // END: function_name()
```

APPENDIX 2

On the C++ Programming Language for Embedded Software, Systems, and Platforms

Introduction

The are a number of reasons developers may want to consider using C++ as the programming language of choice when developing for an embedded device. C++ does compare with C in terms of syntactical similarities, in addition to memory allocation, code reuse and other features. There are also reasons to take caution when considering C++ and its related toolsets. One reason is that functionality and performance vary across compilers due to differing implementations of the standard by individual vendors and open-source offerings. In addition, C++ and its libraries tend to be much larger and more complex than their C language counterparts. As such, there tends to be a bit of ambiguity in the community around C++ as a viable option for embedded computing, and more specifically what features of the language are conducive to embedded computing and what features should generally be avoided.

When characterizing the cost of various aspects of using C++ for embedded software development, we characterize cost as something that requires runtime resources. Such resources may be additional stack or heap space, additional computational overhead, additional code size or library size, etc. When something can be done offline a priori by the compiler, assembler, linker or loader, we consider those features to be inexpensive and in some cases absolutely free. As behaviors differ across compilers and vendors, the burden is ultimately placed on the developer and designer to ensure that said benefits are actually achieved with a given development environment for the target architecture. Lastly, development tools change over time as new functionality is added, features are deprecated, performance is tuned and so forth. Development tools are highly complex interdependent software systems, and as such there may periodically be regressions in performance of legacy software as tools evolve. A periodic re-evaluation of features and performance is encouraged. The topics discussed in this section are furthermore presented as general trends, and not meant to be an absolute for any specific target or toolset implementation.

Relatively inexpensive features of C++ for embedded

The following section details C++ language features that are typically handled automatically by the compiler, assembler, linker and/or loader effectively free. That is to say they typically will not incur additional computational or storage overhead at run-time, or increase code size.

Static constants

C++ allows users to specify static constants in their code rather than use C-style macros. Consider the example below:

C language:

```
#define DRIVE_SHAFT_RPM_LIMITER 1000
```

C++ language:

```
const int DRIVE_SHAFT_RPM_LIMITER = 1000
```

Developers may take pause in that the C++ language implementation will require additional storage space for the variable DRIVE_SHAFT_RPM_LIMITER. It is the case, however, that if the address of said variable is not used within the code and rather the literal value 1000 is used in computation, the compiler will fold in the value as a constant at compilation time, thus eliminating the storage overhead.

Ordering of declarations and statements

In the C programming language, programmers are required to use a specific sequence whereby blocks start with declarations followed by statements. C++ lifts this restriction, allowing declarations to be mixed in with statements in the code. While this is mostly a syntactical convenience, developers should also use caution regarding the effect on the readability and maintainability of their code.

Function overloading

Function overloading pertains to the naming conventions used for functions, and the compiler's ability to resolve at compile time which version of a function to use at the call site. By differentiating between various function signatures, the compiler is able to disambiguate and insert the proper call to the correct version of the function at the call site. From a run-time perspective, there is no difference.

Usage of namespaces

Leveraging code reuse has the obvious benefits of improving reliability and reducing engineering overhead, and is certainly one promise of C++. Reuse of code, especially in the context of large software productions, often comes with the challenge of namespace collisions between C language functions depending on how diligent past developers have been with naming convention best practices. C++'s classes help to avoid some of these collisions, but not everything can be constructed as a class (see previously); furthermore existing C language libraries must still be accommodated in many production systems.

C++'s namespaces resolve much of this problem. Any variables within the code are resolved to a given namespace, if nothing else the global namespace. There should be no penalty in using these name spaces for organizational advantage.

Usage constructors and destructors

C++ adds the functional of "new" and "delete" operators for provisioning and initializing heap-based objects. It is functionally equivalent to using malloc and initialization in C, but has the added benefit of being easier to use and less prone to errors in a multi-step allocation and initialization process. C++'s "delete" functionality is also similar to "free" in C; however, there may be run-time overhead associated with it. In the case of C, structs are not typically destructed like objects in C++. Default destructors in C++ should be empty, however. One caveat with new/delete is that certain destructors may throw run-time exceptions which would in turn incur overhead. Run-time exceptions are described in more detail in the following subsections.

Modestly expensive features of C++ for embedded

The following groups of features do not necessarily need to impact the program run-time versus their C programming counterparts, but in practice they may have an effect depending on maturity and robustness of the compiler and related tools.

Inlining of functions

The subject of inlining functions for C++ is a very broad one, with far-reaching performance impacts ranging from run-time performance to code size and beyond. When designating a function to be inlined, typically the "inline" keyword is used. Some compilers will take this as a hint, while others will enforce the behavior. There may be other pragmas available within a given toolset for performing this action in a forceable manner, and documentation should be revisited accordingly. One of the costs associated with function inlining is naturally growth in code size, as, rather than invoke the function via a call site at run-time, the compiler inserts a copy of the function body directly where the call site originally was. Additionally, there may be performance impacts due to challenges in register allocation across procedure boundaries or increase in register pressure within the calling function. It is advised to closely consider the impact of inlining for your target when using C++.

Constructors, destructors and data type conversions

If a developer does not provide constructors and destructors for a given C++ class, the compiler will automatically provision for them. It is true that these default constructors and destructors may not ever be required; moreover the developer may have explicitly omitted them, as they were not required. Dead-code elimination optimizations will likely remove these unused constructors and destructors, but care should be taken to ensure this is in fact the case. One should also take caution when doing various copy operations and conversion operations: for example, passing a parameter to a member function by value, in which a copy of the value must be created and passed using the stack. Such scenarios may inadvertently lead to invocation of constructors for the value being copied, which subsequently cannot be removed by dead-code elimination further on in the compilation process.

Use of C++ templates

The use of templates within C++ code for embedded systems should come with no overhead, as in principle all of the work is done ahead of time by the build tools in instantiating the right templates based on source code requirements. The parameterized templates themselves are converted into non-parameterized code by the time it is consumed by the assembler. In practice, however, there have been cases of compilers that behave in an overly conservative (or aggressive, depending on your view point) manner, and instantiate more template permutations than were required by the program. Ideally dead-code elimination would prune these out, but that has been shown to not always be the case on some earlier C++ compilers.

Multiple inheritance

With C++'s class inheritance, users can add and expand functionality of classes for a specific use case. For example, perhaps there is a packetized channel communications manager that a user has an implementation of, which can be expanded to UDP management versus TCP/IP management, both of which are derived by inheriting from multiple base classes. In order to accommodate this, compilers use what is called a virtual table to basically perform the book-keeping of functions in the inheritance table. Multiple inheritance expands single inheritance to allow a given class to inherit from multiple other classes. While this seems good on paper, as the inheritance hierarchy grows in complexity so does the size of the virtual tables required to manage these resources. Use caution when considering multiple inheritance, or consider using composition design methods instead. The code snippets below detail how to achieve the functional benefits of multiple inheritance, while instead using composition design to avoid expansive growth in virtual tables.

Multiple inheritance with virtual tables example:

```
#include<stdio.h>
class base_class_00
{
public:
 base_class_00(){};
 ~base_class_00(){};
private:
};
class base_class_01
{
public:
 base_class_01(){};
 ~base_class_01(){};
private:
};
class final_class_minheret : public base_class_00,
                              public base_class_01
{
 // Compiler will need virtual tables to manage inherited classes
 // and book keeping, this will increase size!!!
public:
 final_class_minheret(){};
 ~final_class_minheret(){};
private:
};
```

The example above illustrates the typical C++ use case of building a class using multiple inheritance, which will also incur overhead due to the code size requirements for maintaining the virtual tables. Rather than incur this penalty, the developer may want to build similar functionality via the composition design model whereby, rather than inheriting multiple classes, a class simply contains pointers to instances of the formerly inherited class.

Composition without virtual tables example:

```
#include<stdio.h>
class base_class_00
{
```

```
public:
 base_class_00(){};
 ~base_class_00(){};
private:
};
class base_class_01
{
public:
 base_class_01(){};
 ~base_class_01(){};
private:
};
class final_class_composition
{
 //
public:
 final_class_composition()
 {
  _a = new base_class_00();
  _b = new base_class_01();
 };
 ~final_class_composition()
 {
  delete _a;
  delete _b;
 }
private:
 base_class_00 *_a;
 base_class_01 *_b;
};
```

Encapsulation of architecture-specific data types

For certain embedded platforms, there may be non-standard data types supported by the architecture. Consider a signal-processing architecture that has a 24-bit data type with native support for 24-bit arithmetic in the processor. These types of arithmetic are often supported in C via native intrinsics in the source code, as can be seen below:

```
void compute( fract24 sample_a, fract24 sample_b )
{
      /* some computation     */
      /* fract24_mpy is native instruction on processor target */
      product = fract24_mpy ( sample_a , sample_b );
}
```

The reason for supporting such computation in C is that the data types for such instructions typically do not map well to the standard "char, short, long" data types that are native within the language. In addition, the instructions themselves may be highly application domain specific, such as multiply and accumulate with saturating arithmetic. As such, typical C compiler implementations will rarely identify such patterns at compile time and need assistance in ensuring that the most computationally efficient instruction is selected at computation time. The developer effectively aids in this process by using the intrinsic, in this case fract24_mpy(), that matches the instruction of choice on the target processor.

C++ developers may be tempted to create custom C++ classes for handling of such non-standard data types associated with these systems. For example, the fract24 data type could be abstracted into its own C++ class, with related public member functions that support the arithmetic operations such as addition, multiplication, etc. While this would allow for more portable code, in that the functions can be ported to different architectures, it often comes with additional overhead. This is evident in the fact that while the C implementation will keep the fract24 data type as a number presumably in a register, the C++ implementation will require an object to be created and stored in memory for each fract24 instance. This will require additional memory usage, constructor/destructors, as well as having an impact on performance depending on how objects are handled by lower-level ABI functionality.

Typically costly features of C++ for embedded

This last section details portions of the C++ language that unfortunately have significant impact on program run-time behavior. Designers should seriously consider whether these features are allowed within their embedded project or coding style documents, perhaps allowing their usage on an as-needed case-by-case basis.

Run-time type identification (RTTI)

This language feature is of value with relation to pointers to objects in memory, and determining dynamically at run-time what those object types are. As such, it requires maintaining a book-keeping hierarchy in place at run-time to differentiate type information, somewhat analogous to the virtual table use case mentioned earlier. Thus, the disadvantages become two-fold: (1) the overhead required in order to maintain the RTTI information dynamically at run-time in memory, and (2) the run-time computational overhead incurred in determining said information and updating the table.

Exception handling

Exception handling provides a rather elegant means of handling abnormal run-time behavior in a C++ application, but comes with significant overhead typically not conducive to embedded systems. For starters, exception handling requires the maintenance of the RTTI tables described previously. In addition, the ability to throw/catch exceptions requires significant run-time resources to perform the requisite book-keeping pertaining to call stacks, etc. Objects need to be destructed, and open scopes must be analyzed to determine whether or not they can handle the type of exception currently being processed. There is also additional code size required for tracking this information. As such, while an elegant design feature within the language, it is recommended that designers avoid using this feature in their systems.

Summary

C++ affords a number of features that lend themselves to the development of embedded systems, more specifically application and systems-level software for a given product or platform. Managers and developers alike should take pause when introducing C++ to their development environment, taking care to observe both performance of code across tool releases, quality of code generated by software developers and engineers, as well as maintainability and scalability of code bases within and across platforms. With proper planning and diligence, C++ provides an attractive offering for portability and performance in the embedded environment beyond that of the C language, while not necessarily suffering the overhead of various alternatives in the emulated or interpreted spaces.

CASE STUDY 1

Software Performance Engineering

Robert Oshana

Introduction and project description

Expensive disasters can be avoided when system performance evaluation takes place relatively early in the software development life-cycle. Applications will generally have better performance when alternative designs are evaluated prior to implementation. Software performance engineering (SPE) is a set of techniques for gathering data, constructing a system performance model, evaluating the performance model, managing risk of uncertainty, evaluating alternatives, and verifying the models and results. SPE also includes strategies for the effective use of these techniques. Software performance engineering concepts have been incorporated into a Raytheon Systems Company program developing a digital signal-processing application concurrently with a next-generation DSP-based array processor. Algorithmic performance and an efficient implementation were the driving criteria for the program. As the processor was being developed concurrently with the software application a significant amount of the system and software development would be completed prior to the availability of physical hardware. This led to incorporation of SPE techniques into the development life-cycle. The techniques were incorporated cross-functionally into both the systems engineering organization responsible for developing the signal-processing algorithms and the software and hardware engineering organizations responsible for implementing the algorithms in an embedded real-time system.

Consider the DSP-based system shown in Figure CS1.1. The application is a large, distributed, multi-processing embedded system. One of the sub-systems consists of two large arrays of digital signal processors (DSP). These DSPs execute a host of signal-processing algorithms (various-size FFTs and digital filters, and other noise-removing and signal-enhancing algorithms). The algorithm stream being implemented includes both temporal decomposition of the processing steps as well as spatial decomposition of the data set. The array of mesh-connected DSPs is used because the spatial decomposition required maps well to the 2D mesh hardware architecture. The required throughput of the system drives the size of the array. The system is a data-driven application, using interrupts to signal the arrival of the next sample of data. This system is a "hard" real-time system in the sense that missing one of the data-processing deadlines results in a catastrophic loss of system performance.

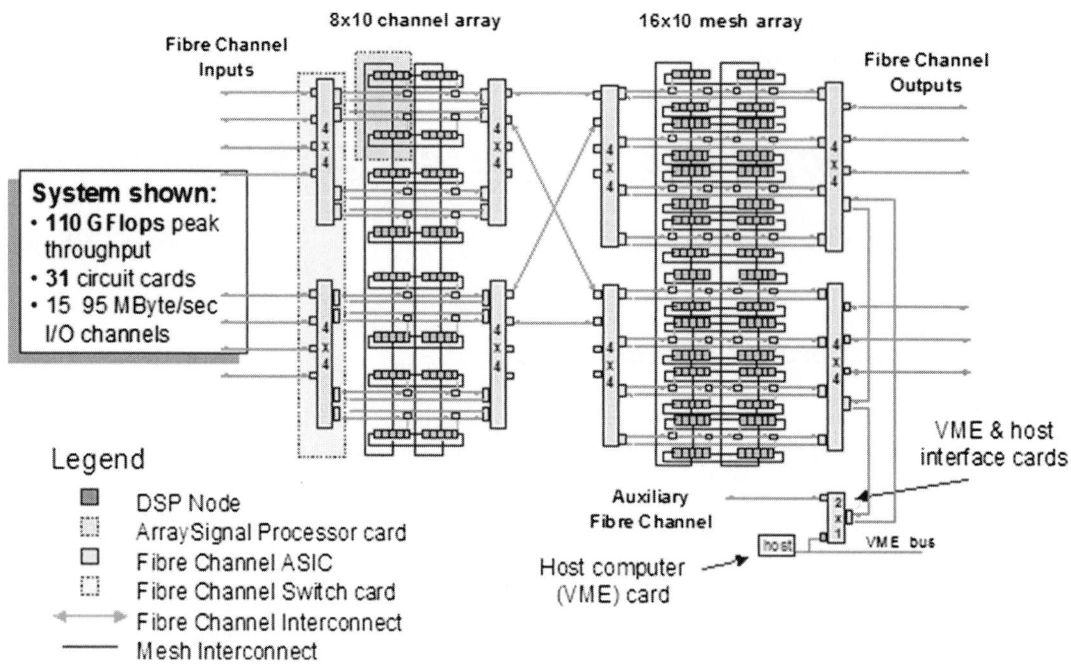

Figure CS1.1:
DSP array architecture in mesh configuration.

This system was a hardware-software co-design effort. This involved the concurrent development of a new DSP-based array processor using high-performance DSP devices. In this project, the risk of the delivered system not meeting performance requirements was a serious concern. To further complicate matters the algorithm stream was being enhanced and revised as part of the development effort. The incorporation of SPE techniques into the development processes of the various functional organizations was deemed critical to mitigating these risks.

The issue of performance was addressed from the inception of the program throughout its development phases. The main measures of performance are captured in three metrics:

- processor throughput
- memory utilization
- I/O bandwidth utilization.

These are the metrics of choice because monthly reporting of these metrics was a customer requirement for the program. Initial estimates of these metrics were made prior to the start of the program and updated monthly during the development effort. Uncertainties associated with key factors driving these estimates were identified. Plans for resolving these uncertainties during the development effort were developed and key dates identified.

Updating the metrics and maintaining the associated risk-mitigation plans was a cross-functional collaborative effort involving systems engineering, hardware engineering and software engineering.

Initial performance estimates and information requirements

The information generally required for a SPE assessment is [1]:

- Workload: the expected use of the system and applicable performance scenarios. We chose performance scenarios that provided the array processors with the worst-case data rates. These worst-case scenarios were developed by interfacing with the users and our system engineers.
- Performance objectives: this represents the quantitative criteria for evaluating performance. We used CPU utilization, memory utilization, and I/O bandwidth because of the customer requirement that we report on these monthly.
- Software characteristics: this describes the processing steps for each of the performance scenarios and the order of the processing steps. We had accurate software characteristics due to an earlier prototype system using a similar algorithm stream. We also had an Algorithms Description document detailing the algorithmic requirements for each of the functions in the system. From this a discrete event simulation was developed to model the execution of the algorithms.
- Execution environment: this describes the platform on which the proposed system will execute. We had an accurate representation of the hardware platform due to involvement in the design of the I/O peripherals of the DSP as well as some of the DSP core features. The other hardware components were simulated by the hardware group.
- Resource requirements: this provides an estimate of the amount of service required for the key components of the system. Our key components were CPU, memory and I/O bandwidth for each of the DSP software functions.
- Processing overhead: this allows us to map software resources onto hardware or other device resources. The processing overhead is usually obtained by benchmarking typical functions (FFTs, filters) for each of the main performance scenarios.

CPU throughput utilization was the most difficult metric to estimate and achieve. Therefore, the rest of this paper will focus primarily on the methods we used to develop an accurate estimate for the CPU throughput utilization metric.

Developing the initial estimate

The process used to generate the initial performance metric estimates is shown in Figure CS1.2. This flow was used throughout the development effort to update the metrics. The algorithm stream is documented in an algorithm document. From this document the

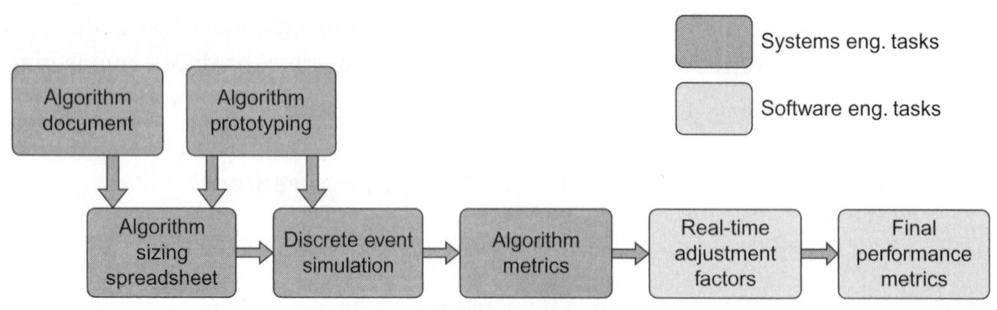

Figure CS1.2:
Performance metric calculation flow.

systems engineering organization developed a static spreadsheet model of the algorithm stream which provided estimates of throughput and memory utilization for each of the algorithms in the algorithm requirements document. The spreadsheet includes allowances for operating system calls and inter-processor communication. The systems engineering organization used a current-generation DSP processor to perform algorithm prototyping and investigation activities. The results of this work influenced algorithm implementation decisions and were used to develop the discrete event simulations used to estimate the performance metrics. A discrete event simulation was used to model the dynamic performance of the algorithm stream. The simulation model included allowances for operating-system task switches and associated calls. The initial algorithm spreadsheet of resource allocations for each algorithm and discrete event simulation processes provide the system engineering "algorithm" performance metrics. At this point the metrics reflect the throughput, memory, and I/O bandwidth required to perform the algorithms defined in the algorithm document and implemented using the prototype implementations. The software engineering organization then updates the performance metrics to reflect the costs of embedding the algorithm stream in a robust, real-time system. These metric adjustments include the effects of system-level real-time control, built-in test, formatting of input and output data, and other "overhead" functions (processing overhead) required for the system to work. The results of this process are the reported processor throughput, memory utilization and I/O utilization performance metrics.

Key factors in the spreadsheet that influence the processor throughput metric are:

- the quantity of algorithms to implement
- elemental operation costs (measured in processor cycles)
- sustained throughput to peak throughput efficiency
- processor family speed-up.

The quantity of algorithms to perform is derived from a straightforward measurement of the number of mathematical operations required by the functions in the algorithm stream. The number of data points to be processed is also included in this measurement. The elemental operation costs measure the number of processor cycles required to perform multiply accumulate operations, complex multiplies, transcendental functions, FFTs, etc. The sustained throughput to peak throughput efficiency factor de-rates the "marketing" processor throughput number to something achievable over the sustained period of time a real-world code stream requires. This factor allows for processor stalls and resource conflicts encountered in operation. The processor family speed-up factor was used to adjust data gained from benchmarking on a current-generation processor. This factor accounted for the increase in clock rate and number of processing pipelines in the next-generation device compared to its current-generation predecessor.

Key factors in the spreadsheet that influence the memory utilization metric are:

- size and quantity of intermediate data products to be stored
- dynamic nature of memory usage
- bytes/data product
- bytes/instruction
- size and quantity of input and output buffers based on worst-case system scenarios (workloads).

The size and quantity of intermediate data products are derived from a straightforward analysis of the algorithm stream. A discrete event simulation was used to analyze memory usage patterns and establish high-water marks. The bytes/data product and bytes/instruction were measures used to account for the number of data points being processed and storage requirement for the program load image.

All of these areas of uncertainty are the result of the target processor hardware being developed concurrently with the software and algorithm stream. While prototyping results were available from the current-generation DSP array computer, translating these results to a new DSP architecture (superscalar architecture of the C40 versus the very long instruction word (VLIW) of the C67 DSP), different clock rate, and new memory device technology (synchronous DRAM versus DRAM) required the use of engineering judgment.

Tracking the reporting metrics

The software development team is responsible for estimating and reporting metrics related to processor throughput and memory. These metrics are reported periodically to the customer, and are used for risk mitigation. Reserve requirements are also required to allow for future growth of functionality (our reserve requirement was 75% for CPU and memory). Throughout the development life-cycle, these estimates varied widely based on the different modeling techniques used in the estimation and hardware design decisions which influenced the amount of hardware available to execute the suite of algorithms as well as

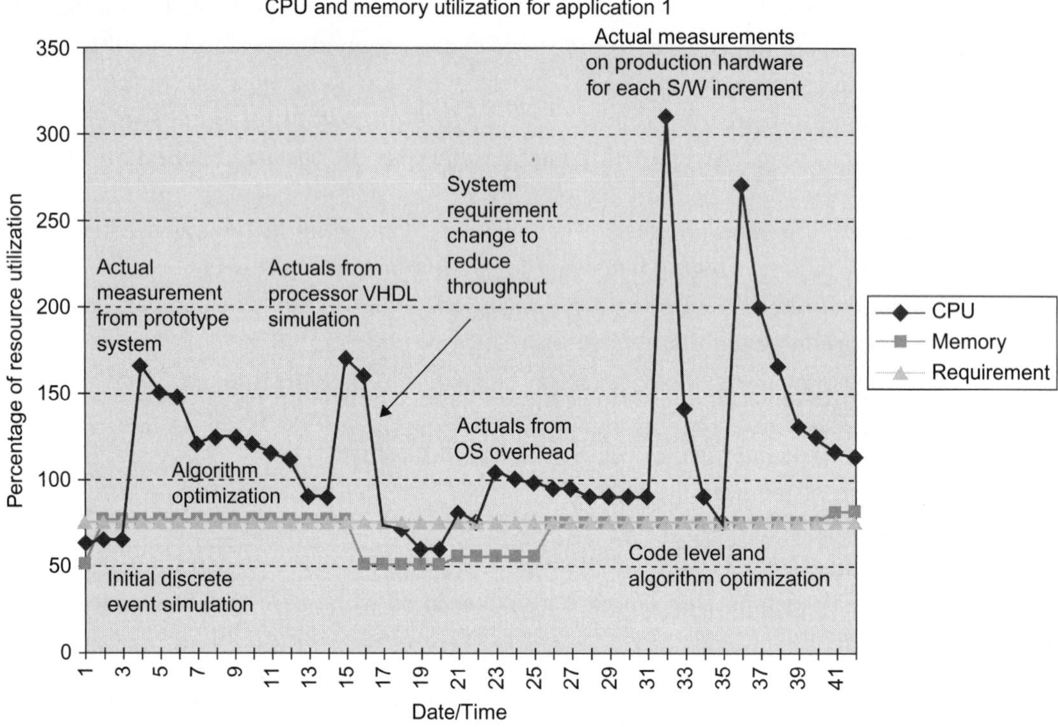

Figure CS1.3:
Resource utilization metric for application 1.

measurement error. Figure CS1.3 shows the metric history for throughput and memory for the first array processor application. There is a wide variability in the throughput throughout the life-cycle, reflecting a series of attempts to lower the throughput estimate followed by large increases in the estimate due to newer information. In Figure CS1.3, the annotations describe the increases and decreases in the estimate for the CPU throughput measurement. Table CS1.1 describes the chronology of this estimate over the course of the project (not completed as of this writing).

The first large increase in the estimate came as a result of implementing the algorithm stream on a prototype current-generation processor. These measurements were then scaled based on the anticipated performance of the next-generation processor. An effort was then undertaken to optimize the implementation of the algorithm stream to lower the throughput estimate.

The next unexpected increase came from running representative benchmarks on the next-generation cycle-accurate simulator. This simulation allowed us to estimate the true cost of external memory accesses, pipeline stalls, and other processor characteristics that increased the cost of executing the algorithms. These results led the development teams to undertake

Table CS1.1: Chronology of CPU throughput reduction for application 1.

Increase or Decrease in Metric	Explanation
Initial discrete event simulation was used as the starting point for the metric estimation	Discrete event simulation was built using algorithm cycle estimations and first-order modeling for task iterations due to context switching, etc.
Measurement on prototype C40-based array	Prototype code was ported to a C40-based DSP small-scale array and measured. The measurement was then scaled based on the speedup of the C67-based DSP full-scale array
Algorithm-level optimization	Algorithms were made more efficient using algorithm re-structuring methods and reducing complexity in other areas of the algorithm stream
Processor VHDL'measurement	Big increase in throughput measurement was due to unexpected high cost of accessing data from external (off-chip) memory. Several benchmarks were performed and scaled to the entire application
System-level requirement change	Project decision was made to change a system-level parameter. This caused significant algorithm restructuring and was an unpopular decision with the customer
OS-level overhead measured	Because the processor was new, the COTS OS was not immediately available. This point indicated the first time to run the application in a multi-tasking environment with the OS
Actuals on production hardware array of DSPs for each software increment	The production code was initially developed without code optimization techniques in place (Make it work right and then make it work fast). Initial measurement for the full algorithm stream was not entirely optimized when we first took the measurement
Continued code and algorithm-level optimization	Dedicated team in place to work code optimization and other algorithm transformation techniques to reduce CPU throughput (i.e., taking advantage of symmetry in the algorithms and innovative techniques to reduce communications between DSPs which were expensive)

another significant effort to optimize the algorithm stream for real-time operation. The main techniques undertaken during this phase included instrumentation of the direct memory access (DMA) to stage data on and off chip, re-structuring of code to allow critical loops to pipeline, assembly-language implementation of critical algorithm sections, and efficient use and management of on-chip memory, where memory access time is much shorter.

The representative benchmarks showed us that we could reduce the throughput using code-level optimization techniques (use of on-chip memory, pipelining of important loops, etc.) but we were still in danger of not meeting our overall throughput requirement. It was at this time that a system requirement was modified to reduce throughput. Although a very unpopular decision with the customer (the change reduced data rate and performance of the algorithms), it allowed us to save money by not having to add additional hardware to the system (which is more cost per unit delivered). Algorithm studies also showed that we could still meet system performance by improvements in other areas of the system.

The third major increase came when we measured the full application on the target array of DSPs. The main reason for the increase was the fact that many of the algorithms were not optimized. Only a small percentage of algorithms were benchmarked on the processor VHDL simulator (representative samples of the most commonly used algorithms such as the FFTs and other algorithms called inside major loops in the code). The software group still needed to employ the same optimization techniques for the remaining code for each of the software increments being developed. By this time the optimization techniques were familiar to the group and the process went fairly fast.

The memory estimate, although not as severe as the throughput estimate, continued to grow throughout the development cycle. The main reasons for the increase in memory were:

- additional input and output buffers required for a real-time system to operate;
- additional memory was required for each section of code that is instrumented to use the DMA (although this does save on throughput cycles);
- additional memory is needed for code-optimization techniques such as loop unrolling and software pipelining which cause the number of instructions to increase.

The life-cycle throughput estimates for the second array processor application is shown in Figure CS1.4. A similar pattern in the reported numbers is seen here due to the same basic issues. Table CS1.2 shows the chronology of this CPU utilization estimation.

Once again the initial discrete event simulation proved to be inaccurate and the prototype system measurements were much higher than anticipated due to overly aggressive estimates of the CPU throughput, failure to account for realistic overhead constraints, etc. A long process of code and algorithm optimization was able to bring the estimate back down close to the goal before the VHDL simulation measurements uncovered some other areas that made us increase the estimate. The increase in the estimate in this application resulted in several risk-management activities being triggered.

The estimate in month 5 was high enough and was made early enough in the program schedule that the program was able to add more hardware resources to reduce the algorithm distribution and lower the throughput estimate. This was made at the expense of more power and cooling requirements as well as more money for the hardware (no new designs were required, just more boards). These increases in power and cooling had to be offset by sacrifices elsewhere to maintain overall system requirements on these parameters.

The measurement in month 19 caused consternation among the managers as well as the technical staff. Although we felt continued optimization at the code level would drop the

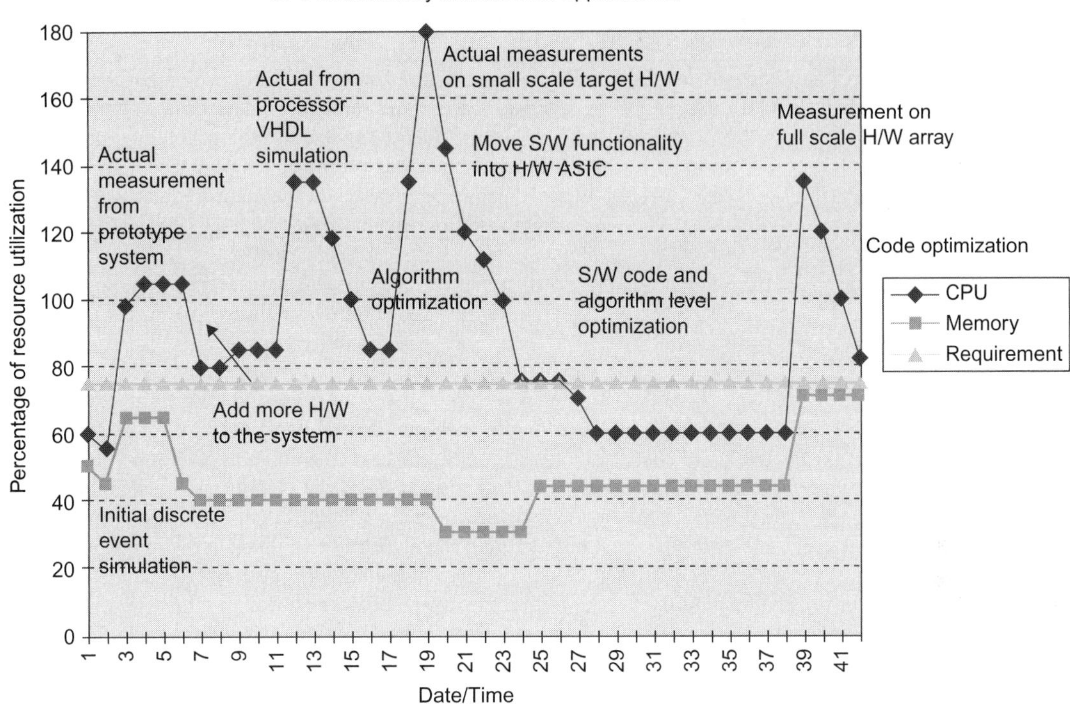

Figure CS1.4:
Resource utilization metric for application 2.

number significantly, meeting the application requirement of 75% CPU throughput (25% reserved for growth) would be hard to accomplish.

One contributor to the CPU throughput estimate increase was a result of an under-estimation of a worst-case system scenario which led to an increase in data rate for the processing stream. This resulted in several algorithm loops being executed more frequently, which increased the overall CPU utilization.

The decision was made to move some of the software functionality being done in the DSPs into a hardware ASIC to reduce the throughput significantly (there were a sufficient number of unused gates in the ASIC to handle the increased functionality). With this decision coming so late in the development cycle, however, significant re-design and re-work of the ASIC and the interfaces were required, which was extremely expensive for the hardware effort, as well as causing delays in the system integration and test phase.

The last increase in CPU utilization was a result of scaling the algorithms from the small (single node) DSP benchmark to the full array of DSPs. The increase was mainly due to a mis-estimation in the overhead associated with inter-processor communication. Once again,

Table CS1.2: Chronology of CPU throughput reduction for application 2.

Increase or Decrease in Metric	Explanation
Initial discrete event simulation was used as the starting point for the metric estimation	Discrete event simulation was built using algorithm cycle estimations and first-order modeling for task iterations due to context switching, etc.
Measurement on prototype C40-based array	Prototype code was ported to a C40-based DSP small scale array and measured. The measurement was then scaled based on the speedup of the C67-based DSP full-scale array
Add more hardware to the system	Number of DSP nodes was increased by adding more DSP boards. Good hardware design made scalability relatively easy
Processor VHDL measurement	Big increase in throughput measurement was due to unexpected high cost of accessing data from external (off-chip) memory. Several benchmarks were performed and scaled to the entire application
Algorithm optimization	Because of the nature of the algorithms, we were able to significantly cut CPU throughput utilization by restructuring the algorithms to pipeline the major loops of the algorithm stream
Actual measurement on small-scale target Hardware	In our hardware/software co-design effort, we did not have full-scale hardware until late in the cycle. Initial benchmarking for this application was performed on a single node prototype DSP card
Move software functionality into hardware ASIC	Decision was made for risk mitigation purposes to move part of the algorithm stream into a hardware ASIC in another sub-system, saving significant CPU cycles in the application software
Software code and algorithm-level optimization	Dedicated team in place to work code optimization and other algorithm transformation techniques to reduce CPU throughput
Measurement on full-scale hardware	Measuring the application CPU throughput on the full-scale hardware showed that we had under-estimated the overhead for communication among all the array nodes. We developed a tailored comm API to perform intra-node communications more quickly

the development teams were faced with the difficult challenge of demonstrating real-time operation given these new parameters. At this late date in the development cycle, there are not many options left for the system designers. The main techniques used at this point to reduce the throughput estimate were additional code optimization, assembly-language implementation of additional core algorithms, additional limited hardware support, and a significant restructuring of the algorithm control flow to circumvent the use of slow operating system functions. For example, we eliminated some of the robustness in the node-to-node communication API in order to save valuable CPU cycles.

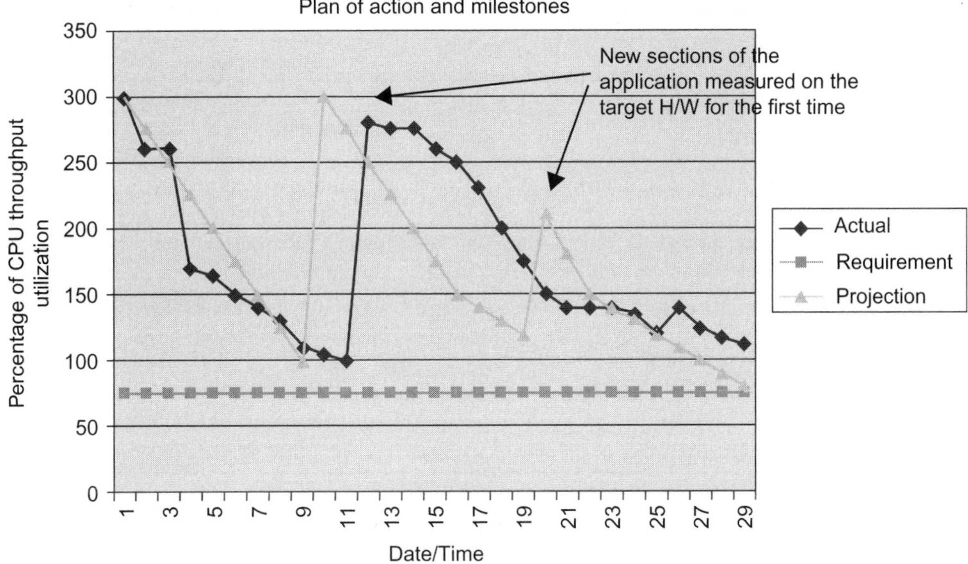

Figure CS1.5:
Plan of action and milestones for application 1.

It did not take long for management to realize that these "spikes" in the CPU throughput utilization would continue until all of the application had been measured on the target system under worst-case system loads. Rather than periodically being surprised by a new number (we were optimizing the code in sections so every few months or so we would have actuals for a new part of the algorithm stream) we were asked to develop a Plan of Action and Milestones (POA&M) chart which predicted when we would have new numbers and the plan for reducing the throughput after each new measurement that would support completion by the program milestone. In the plan we predicted the remaining spikes in the estimate and the plan for working these numbers down (Figure CS1.5). This new way of reporting showed management that we knew increases were coming and had a plan for completing.

Reducing the measurement error

The performance engineering plan detailed when hardware and software tools would become available which could be used to reduce the errors in the performance metrics. These availability dates when combined with the system development schedule provided decision points at which design trade-offs would be performed balancing algorithm, hardware, and software design points to yield a system that met cost and performance goals. Table CS1.3 lists the tools identified and the error factors reduced by them.

Table CS1.3: Tools identified in performance plan and errors resolved by them.

Tool	Error Factors Resolved
Code-generation tools (compiler, assembler, linker)	Compiler efficiency Quality of generated assembly code Size of load image
Instruction-level processor simulator	Utilization of dual processor pipelines Cycle counts for elemental operations
Cycle-accurate device-level VHDL model	Effect of external memory access times Instruction caching effects Device resource contention between processor and DMA channels
Single DSP test card	Validate VHDL results Run-time interrupt effects
Multi-DSP test card	Inter-processor communication resource contention effects

As these tools became available, benchmark code was executed using them and the performance metrics updated accordingly. This data was used to support program-level decision points to review the proposed computer design. This review included hardware resources in the computer, algorithmic functionality assigned to the computer, and the proposed software architecture. At various decision points all of these areas were modified. The computer hardware resources were increased through the addition of more DSP processor nodes. The clock rate of the DSP was increased by 10%. Some algorithms were moved to other portions of the system. The software architecture was reworked to reduce overhead by eliminating extraneous interrupts and task switches. All aspects of the design were considered and adjusted as appropriate to meet the performance and cost objectives.

The performance plan also included the use of analytical tools to address the overall schedulability and large-scale performance of the array processor. We attempted to use rate monotonic analysis (RMA) to validate the schedulability of the software architecture [3,4,5]. RMA is a mathematical approach to determining schedulability under wors- case task phasings and allows the designer to determine ahead of time whether the system will meet its timing requirements. RMA has the advantage over discrete event simulation in that the model is easier to develop and change and the model provides a conservative answer that guarantees schedulability (using a simulation, it becomes hard to predict how long to execute the model before a certain set of task phasings causes the system to break). One powerful feature of RMA tools is the ability to identify blocking conditions. Blocking and preemption are the most common reasons for missing deadlines and are one of the main focuses of most RMA tools. We were interested in using RMA because the model could identify potential timing problems even before the system is built. Alternative designs could be analyzed quickly before actually having to implement design. Our attempt at using RMA provided only a high-level look at schedulability but not the details. The tools used did not scale well to large systems with thousands of task-switch possibilities and non-preemptible sections (one of the compiler optimization techniques produced software pipelined loops which, because of the nature of the processor pipeline, turn off interrupts during the pipelined loop, thereby creating a small non-preemptible section; attempting to input and model thousands of these conditions proved to be too cumbersome for our application without becoming too abstract for our purposes).

As the array computer hardware was being developed concurrently with the software, the software team did not have target hardware available to them until late in the development life-cycle. To enable the team to functionally verify their software prior to the availability of hardware an environment was developed using networked Sun workstations running Solaris. Using features of the Solaris operating system, the environment enabled small portions of the array computer to be created with inter-processor communication channels logically modeled. The application code was linked to a special library that implemented the DSP operating system's API using Solaris features. This enabled the team to functionally verify the algorithms, including inter-task and inter-processor communications, prior to execution on the target hardware.

The fundamental approach was to make the application work correctly and then attempt to add efficiency to the code ("make it work right – then make it work fast!"). We felt this was required for this application for the following reasons:

- Given the hardware/software co-design effort, the processor (and user documentation) was not available so the development team did not thoroughly understand the techniques required to optimize the algorithm stream.
- The algorithms themselves were complicated and hard to understand and this was seen as a risk by the development team. Making the algorithm stream run functionally correct was a big first step for a development team tackling a new area.
- Optimization of an algorithm stream should be performed based on the results of profiling the application. Only after the development team knows where the cycles are being spent can they effectively optimize the code. It does not make sense to optimize code that is executed infrequently. Removing a few cycles from a loop that executes thousands of times, however, can result in a bigger savings in the bottom line.

Conclusions and lessons learned

Estimating throughput may not be exact science but active attention to it during life-cycle phases can mitigate performance risks and enable time to work alternatives while meeting overall program schedules and performance objectives. This needs to be a collaborative effort across multiple disciplines. System performance is the responsibility of all parties involved. There are no winners on a losing team.

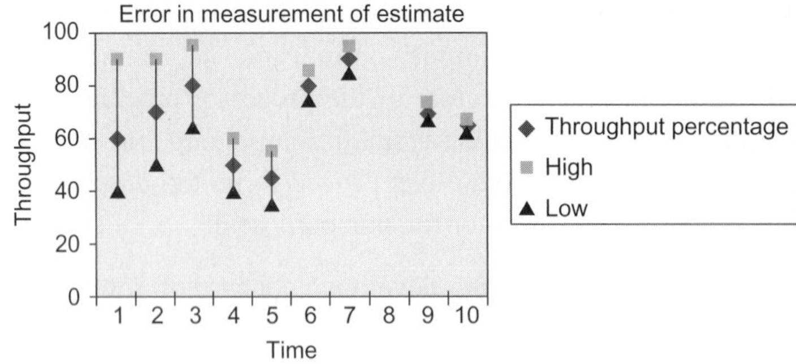

Figure CS1.6:
Improvement in accuracy in estimate over time.

Processor CPU, memory, and I/O utilization are important metrics for a development effort. They give early indications as to problems and provide ample opportunity for the development teams to take mitigation actions early enough in the life-cycle. These metrics also give management the information necessary to manage system risks and allocate reserve resources (i.e., money and schedule) where needed. Often, one or more of these metrics will become an issue at some point during the development cycle. To obtain a system solution to the problem, sensitivity analysis is usually performed, examining various alternatives that trade off throughput, memory, I/O bandwidth, as well as cost, schedule, and risk. When performing this analysis, it is essential to understand the current accuracy in the metric estimates. Early in the life-cycle the accuracy will be less than in later stages, where the measurements are much more aligned to the actual system due to the simple fact that more information is available (Figure CS1.6).

There were several lessons learned in this experience;

- Prototype early in the development life-cycle; several of the surprises we encountered could have been uncovered earlier if the proper level and type of prototyping was performed. Although prototyping was scheduled early in the life-cycle, schedule pressures forced the development team to dedicate a limited amount of resources to this early in the development cycle.
- Benchmark – don't rely totally on the processor marketing information; most processors will never achieve the throughput proposed in the literature. The numbers are often theoretical. In many cases, the actual is much lower and very dependent on how the application maps to the processor architecture (DSPs run DSP-like algorithms very well but they are not very good at finite-state machines and other "control" software). Marketing information for processors will show how well they perform on the best-mapped algorithms the processors support.
- Analyze the functions executing most often; these areas are where the hidden cycles can come back to haunt a development team. Eliminating just a few cycles from a

function that executes many times will have significant impact on the overall throughput.

- Don't ignore the interfaces; real-time systems carry an inherent "overhead" that never seems to be accounted for in throughput estimates. Although the signal-processing algorithms may be where the main focus is from a system requirements and functionality point of view, real-time systems also need throughput for interrupt handling, data packing and unpacking, data extraction, error handling, and other management functions that are easily overlooked in throughput estimates. Many battles were fought over how much of the timeline should be devoted to overhead tasks.
- Benchmarks of discrete algorithms don't scale well to real-time systems; benchmarking an individual algorithm inherently implies that algorithm has complete control and use of all the processor resources including internal and external memory, the DMA controller, and other system resources. In reality, there may be other tasks competing for these same resources. Assumptions made when benchmarking individual algorithms may not apply when the system is put together and running under full system loads. Resource conflicts result in additional overhead that can easily be overlooked when forming throughput estimates.
- Keep management informed; as we approach the completion of the code-level optimization effort, it appears the model we established early in the project was a relatively accurate estimate. However, it took a substantial amount of resources (schedule and budget) to accomplish this goal. Along the way, the estimate periodically rose and fell as we optimized and measured our algorithm stream. The reporting period for these metrics was short enough to catch these spikes, which caused premature concern from management. A longer reporting interval may have "smoothed" some of these spikes.
- Budget accordingly; the two-pass approach of functional correctness followed by code optimization will take more time and more resources to accomplish. This needs to be planned. A one-pass approach to code-level optimization at the same time the functionality is being developed should be attempted only by staff experienced in the processor architecture and the algorithms.

References

[1] C.U. Smith, Performance engineering for software architectures. Twenty First Annual Computer Software and Applications Conference, 1997, pp. 166–167.

[2] M. Baker, W. Smith, Performance prototyping: a simulation methodology for software performance engineering, Proceeding of the Computer Systems and Software Engineering (1992) 624–629.

[3] R. Oshana, Rate monotonic analysis keeps real time systems on track, EDN (September 1, 1997).

[4] C. Liu, J. Layland, Scheduling algorithms for multiprogramming in a hard real time environment, Journal of the Association for Computing Machinery 20 (1973) 46–61.

[5] R. Obenza, Rate monotonic analysis for real-time systems, Computer 26 (1993) 73–74.

References

CASE STUDY 2

A User Interface: Police Command and Control System

Robert Oshana

Introduction

This user interface design case study will walk through a process used to develop an embedded system user interface using a process and series of steps similar to those techniques discussed in Chapter 14 on user interface design. These steps are summarized below.

Key steps in the analysis phase

Describe the vision
Describe the metaphors and mental models to be used.
Elicitation and task analysis

- Develop a data model of the system
- Develop a task list
- Develop the appropriate user profiles
- Develop a vivid scenario
- Develop the appropriate use cases and scenarios
- Develop a hierarchical task analysis (HTA)
- Develop a concur task tree

First design

- Create a first design using virtual windows
- Develop a CREDO matrix to verify the virtual windows
- Develop a first prototype using hand sketches (low-fidelity hand-drawn mockup)
- Identify the gestalts that you are using in your design
- Describe how the gestalts are suitable for the user tasks
- Describe the data presentation steps you have taken
- Describe the mental models used for data, functions, and domain
- Perform usability testing on first prototype with one of the other students in the class
    - Perform a "thinking out loud test" with at least one user
    - Perform a heuristic evaluation on the prototype

- Perform a "problem counts" analysis
- Create a defect list.

Develop a second prototype using available tools (high-fidelity tool drawn mockup)

- Develop a functional prototype (screen prototype)
- Develop the functional design
- Attach semantic and search functions to the virtual windows
- Define undo mechanisms
- Transform virtual windows to real screens
- Add navigation functions to the screens
- Describe the color you will use in the prototype
- Choose presentation formats for functions
- Support transition from novice to expert
- Put pieces together into a prototype
- Usability test and defect correction
- Create a test log and test report
- Develop a support plan for the product, including user documentation.

Police command and control system

It is a requirement of a police service that it responds as quickly as possible to reported incidents and the objective of a command and control system is to ensure that incidents are logged and routed to the most appropriate police vehicle. Factors that must be taken into account in deciding which vehicle to send to which incident include:

- The type of incident: some incidents are more serious than others and require a more urgent response. It is recommended that classes of response be identified and incidents allocated to these classes.
- The position of available vehicles: in general, the best strategy is to send the closest vehicle to respond to an incident. Take into account that the position of vehicles may not be known exactly and it may be necessary to send a message to vehicles to determine their current position.
- The type of vehicles available: some incidents require a number of vehicles, others such as traffic accidents, may require specialized vehicles and so on.
- The location of the incident: in some areas, it may be unwise simply to respond to an incident by sending a single vehicle. In other areas, a single vehicle or policeman may be all that is needed to respond to the same type of incident.
- The need to alert other emergency services such as fire and ambulance services: the system should automatically alert these services if necessary.
- The system should allow details of the reporter of incidents to be logged.

A system such as this one is open to almost indefinite expansion. For example, police vehicles may include fax terminals so that written information may be faxed when a vehicle is routed to an incident. A user interface for a system control room should be prototyped.

Description and conceptual model for the police command and control system

- Concepts
  1. FIR
  2. Search information
  3. Incident monitoring and classification
  4. Command and control police vehicles
  5. Alert other emergency services
  6. Extension of the existing system
  7. Archive incident history
- Key metaphors:

1. **FIR:** this is an acronym for first information report; this term refers to the first information report, which is provided by the victim of an incident or the person reporting it, to the police service dispatcher.
2. **Threat level:** this term refers to the degree of threat posed by the incident in question; this would help assess the number of people and kind of equipment to be dispatched along with the rescue/police teams, so that the situation can be combated in an appropriate way.
3. **Satellite view:** this term refers to the view of the area/county that is made available to the 911 dispatcher as well as all the rescue/police teams of the county. This doesn't provide them with real-time pictures; however, a map view provides the dispatcher/field officer with a diagrammatic representation of the county/city. Thus the people can zoom-in, zoom-out, and pan the map to get a better estimate of the region as well as the positions of rescue teams/field officers.
4. **Driving Directions:** the idea for driving directions is that the map would be overlaid with a thick line or arrows from a source point to a destination point on the map, so that the field officers can be guided and their routes calculated dynamically so as to reduce the response time for rescue operations.
5. **GPS:** acronym for global positioning system, it is a small device attached to each of the computers in the entire system architecture. These devices can pin-point the latitude, longitude and altitude where they currently are and hence would help maintain/ update positions of the devices on the map.
6. **Teams:** this term is generic for a group of people and equipment since different emergencies require different kinds of skills and equipment; e.g., a fire would require fire engines, firemen, paramedics and at times even the police to help with the

crowd, whereas people being held hostage by armed people would require specially trained men such as SWAT.

7. **Classes of vehicles:** this term corresponds to the type of vehicle required depending upon the nature of emergency; e.g., fire would require a fire engine, whereas a pursuit would require some high-speed police vehicles and even a chopper.
8. **Dispatch vehicles:** stands for the action of ordering vehicles to reach a specified location for a rescue and/or emergency.
9. **TTA (time to arrive)**: refers to the window of time between the arrival of the rescue team at the location and the time when it was dispatched by the 911 dispatcher. This would give the people concerned a better idea of time and hence they can plan out things accordingly. For example, when someone requests backup the team can see how much time it would take, thus they can either go ahead and start the operation or stand by for the backup to arrive.
10. **Search for vehicles:** this corresponds to the fact that a dispatcher will have to search for a vehicle before he or she can go ahead and dispatch it to the incident location. The search would be partly the responsibility of the system in the sense that it will display all the vehicles in the neighborhood of the incident and display them on the map for the dispatcher to choose; the user part of the search would be then to pick and choose the vehicles which are displayed onto the map by the user.
11. **Send intimation:** the concept here is that the vehicle which has to be dispatched at the scene of crime/incident needs to be intimated of the same by the dispatcher. There are two ways to do this: one where the intimation is sent through the police wireless and the other where the central system alerts the police vehicle's computer through a software notification. Though both of them will be triggered simultaneously, only the intimation through the automated system will be sent by the system. The dispatcher will do verbal communication through the wireless.
12. **Occurrence location:** this term refers to the venue of incidence occurrence as reported by the reporter. This would be required by the dispatcher and all the teams and vehicles reaching the emergency venue.
13. **Reporter:** This refers to a person who is reporting the incident to the dispatcher. In certain cases the victim can be the reporter.
14. **Reporter Information:** this term refers to the information furnished about the person reporting the incident to the reporter. This is recorded for official purposes and for the track record, and can be left blank if the reporter wants to stay anonymous.
15. **Archives:** this refers to the archiving the incidents that have been closed, i.e., which are no longer active; hence they can be stored in a persistent storage so that they can be later reviewed or retrieved if need arises, such as for pressing the charges or for presentation to the jury, etc.

16. **Search:** this refers to the facility to search the archives for a given incident based on criteria like the date, location, FIR number, etc., to make document retrieval easier and faster.

Data-gathering approaches for the system

The primary approaches for data gathering that have been employed for gaining an insight into the system and user requirements are as follows.

- Interviews: a very good method for data gathering would be interviewing a police officer as well as a dispatcher. In this case study conversations were held with one of the officers from the university police department; this officer was quite helpful and understanding and was actually patient enough to answer some of the queries. Good insight was received into the way a police department works. Though the university police department doesn't employ many of the methods that other police departments employ, enough information was gathered to make the time investment worthwhile. For example the police department does not use mobile computers to stay connected with their control center; however, a larger police department is equipped with mobile computers that are connected to the internet and stay online on their virtual private networks so they are capable of receiving real-time alerts and warnings and any other information sent their way.
- Direct observation: this is another effective method for gaining insight into the user's needs and activities and also to establish the dos and don'ts for your system. This was the major basis used to determine a set of requirements although there was familiarity with the existing systems that are in place and an understanding of the flow of events and what needs to go into such situations.
- Studying documentation: since the system has to operate sticking to a set of rules and regulations, which are well documented, a good data gathering approach would be to study and analyze the rules and regulations that govern the operation of the police sub-system of the law: for example, whether a person can tip off the p[olice about an incident anonymously or is it compulsory for the person tipping off to reveal his or her identity to the dispatcher. Detailed documentation was not studied but general knowledge relating to law and order and also the way they function from the perspective of the common man was used in this case study.

Other approaches that can be used to gather data for this system are described below

- Focus groups: this method involves a group interview with one or more of the people listed below to gain an insight into things and to get a better understanding of who needs what, and whose needs conflict with whose.
  - Dispatcher
  - Field Police Officer

- A fire fighter
- A paramedic
- A senior level-officer who supervises the investigations that follow any incident

- Researching similar products: another effective way to understand the user requirements is to research a similar product and observe it for its pros and cons.

Use case diagram and use case scenarios for the system

A use case is a list of steps, typically defining interactions between a role (referred to as an actor) and a system, to achieve a goal. The actor can be a human or an external system.

Figure CS2.1 shows a use case diagram for the police command and control system.

An example use case scenario is described below:

1. The dispatcher chooses to file an FIR (first information report) after receiving a call regarding an incident.
2. The dispatcher enters the relevant information in the FIR, including the name of the reporter.

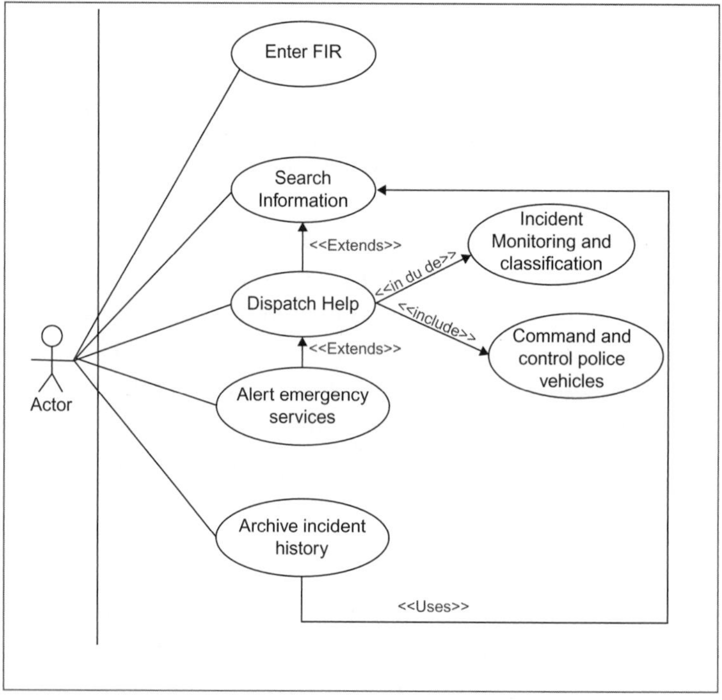

Figure CS2.1:
Use case diagram for PC&CS (police command & control system).

3. The system automatically fills out the phone number from which the call was made using incoming-caller identification
4. The dispatcher enters the location and street address of the incident being reported.
5. The dispatcher enters the type of incident, e.g., riot, rampage, etc.
6. The system suggests types of incidents based on the input it has seen thus far.
7. The system also checks the checkboxes for the other emergency services that need to be alerted based on a mapping from incident types to emergency services built into the system.
8. The dispatcher enters a description for the incident as described by the reporter who has made the call.
9. The dispatcher selects the type of units that should be sent out for that incident type and also specifying how many of each to be sent out.
10. The system searches for the vehicles that match the types specified by the user and are closest to the location of the incident.
11. The system sends a summary of the incident and a command to respond to the incident to the vehicle's system and waits for a confirmation.
12. After confirmation, the dispatcher tracks the incident based on its ID and tuning into the police service scanner.
13. The user marks the incident as "Closed" when the police service team resolves the incident.
14. The system automatically goes ahead and archives it, in case it should be required later, and closes the FIR.

An alternative course of action for this use case:

4. Another dispatcher tries to enter an FIR for the same incident at the same location.
    - 4.1. The system displays a warning message stating that a similar incident has already been added to the system: should the system augment it or should it create another FIR?
    - 4.2. The user chooses to augment the existing FIR with the information specified by the caller.
    - 4.3. The system appends the information to the existing FIR
10. The system does not find an unassigned vehicle anywhere near the incident location
    - 10.1. The system informs the dispatcher about the status through an error message.
    - 10.2. The dispatcher is shown the map centered at the incident in question.
    - 10.3. The dispatcher picks a vehicle already busy with a previous assignment and assigns it to the incident in question by dragging it and dropping it to the incident.
    - 10.4. The system warns the dispatcher about the vehicle already being busy.
    - 10.5. The dispatcher chooses to go ahead with the assignment.
12. The system waits for confirmation but doesn't receive it.
    - 12.1. The system waits for a specific amount of time, after which it times out.
    - 12.2. The system alerts the user about the failed status of the confirmation.

12.3. The dispatcher can re-send the command to the vehicle and the system returns to step 11 or the dispatcher can contact the vehicle through the police scanner.

Essential use case

An essential use case is a simplified, abstract, generalized use case that captures the intentions of a user in a technology- and implementation-independent manner. An essential use case is a structured narrative, expressed in the language of the application domain and users, and an abstract, technology-free and implementation-independent description of one task or interaction. An essential use case for the police command and control system is shown below.

User Intention	System Responsibility
The user hits F1	
	The system opens up a new FIR form for the user to fill out
The dispatcher enters the relevant information for the person calling	
	The system fills out the number from which the call was made using the caller identification
The dispatcher enters the location and street address for the incident	
	The system suggests the user street addresses, should it find that the user has entered a wrong one
The dispatcher enters the description for the incident The dispatcher enters the type of incident	
	The system suggests to the dispatcher the types of incidence which match the words the dispatcher has entered until that point The system selects the other emergency services that need to be informed based on the type of incident
Dispatcher selects the type and quantity of units to respond to that incident	
	System searches for the vehicles closest to the incident and matching the type specified by the users System selects the vehicles as per the quantity specified and sends them the incident info and command to respond to them System waits for a confirmation from the vehicles contacted
The dispatcher tunes into the police wireless to stay updated on developments	
The dispatcher marks the FIR closed when the FIR has been responded to by the officers and things are back to normalcy	
	The system archives the FIR for future retrievals

Scenarios

Scenarios are built on the information gathered in initial system workflow analysis. Scenarios can focus on the functional level or the task-level detail. High-level scenarios, similar to what are discussed below, are used in the analysis phase for new products. More detailed scenarios are used later in the design phase of new products or when redesigning existing products.

Scenarios are generally individual, fictional accounts of workflow data. They are descriptions of a person using a product to achieve a particular goal. Scenarios are narratives that tell a story describing one or more tasks in a specific environmental situation.

Scenario development identifies important aspects of using a product in the real world. Scenarios are useful throughout the user interface design process, and can also be useful in developing task descriptions for usability testing.

User interface scenario for police command and control (perfect-world scenario)

Kristi is working her late night shift as a dispatcher for the police service center from mid-night until six o'clock in the morning. She's had a couple of coffees to keep her awake and alert. She's generally browsing the dispatcher software and exploring it. Around four o'clock, she gets a distress call from a lady named Elisha, located in Garland, TX; her apartment was broken into and most of her valuables were stolen, Kristi hits F1 key on the panel and asks Elisha for the street address where her apartment is located. Elisha tells her 4839 Buckingham Road, Garland, Texas. Kristi then asks Elisha for her apartment number and Elisha responds with 1505, which Kristi promptly goes ahead and enters; the system automatically logs and shows the incoming caller's phone number on the respective field of the FIR form along with the date and time. Kristi finally asks for the caller's first name and last name, upon which Elisha replies back with Elisha Cuthbert, which is then entered into the respective fields by Kristi.

Kristi puts the caller on hold and proceeds to dispatch the police team to the spot. She selects the "Local police team" from the menu and sets the Threat Level to "Moderate". The system shows the current local police in the vicinity of the incident location. The system identifies the nearest police vehicles and highlights those vehicles for Kristi. Kristi selects a particular vehicle and hits the "Save and dispatch" button on the interface. The incident details are sent to the police officer on his or her system. The officer confirms the reception of the details and heads towards the scene location. The form window disappears and on the main window a new event shows up flashing red and blue with the heading "Garland Robbery Incident"; also the location is marked on the map with the same tag. The tag system shows the TTA to be

1 min 30 seconds and encircles the assigned vehicle rushing to the scene with a marker the same color as the marker highlighting the incident location.

Kristi finally tells the caller that help is on its way even as they speak and that it would take roughly 1.5 minutes for the team to reach the spot. The caller thanks Kristi and hangs up. The system continues to track the active incident by assigning the same highlighting color to the incident location as the "Garland robbery incident". Kristi continues to keep a watch on the scene through her interface and hits the tune-in button on the front end, which switches her headset to the rescue team scanner so that she can be alerted of any subsequent updates on the scene.

Imperfect-world scenario

Gerald is a police service dispatcher; he is working his normal routine shift from eight o'clock in the morning till two o'clock in the afternoon. He has recently joined the work, and though he is acquainted with the systems and interfaces thanks to the police training imparted to him, he lacks the intuitiveness and the insight that comes from experience and age. Around 12 noon he gets a tip-off call from a person stating that there is a clash between two groups on Greenville, TX. Gerald hits F1 and asks the person to say the street address, hearing which the person responds with Greenville and University Boulevard intersection. The system automatically logs the caller's phone number along with the date and time. Gerald briefly enters a description for the incident as "clash between two groups". Gerald asks the person for his name, upon which the person requests anonymity, hence Gerald goes ahead and puts "anonymous tip" in the name field. Gerald puts the person on hold and clicks on the "choose teams for dispatch checkbox"; a sub-panel pops up with all the units available to him, with a textbox next to each. Gerald assumes that a clash can turn into a riotous situation and hence decides to alert police units, paramedics and riot control units. He sets the threat level to "High". The system shows the vehicles of the police units, paramedics and control units that are nearest to the location of the incident. Gerald chooses the appropriate number of vehicles of each type – three police units, two paramedics and two riot control units – and clicks on "save and dispatch".

The form window disappears and on the main window a new event shows up flashing red and blue with the heading "Greenville Clash/Riot"; also the location is marked on the map with the same tag. The tag system shows the TTA to be 1 min and encircles the vehicles rushing to the scene with a marker the same color marker as the marker highlighting the incident location.

Gerald finally tells the caller that help is on its way even as they speak and that it would take roughly 1 minute for the teams to reach the spot. The caller thanks Gerald and hangs up. Gerald continues to keep a watch on the scene through his interface and hits the tune-in button on the front end, which switches his headset to the rescue team scanner so that he can be alerted of any subsequent updates on the scene.

The first vehicle arriving at the spot is a police car driven by Officer Jim; he notifies the dispatcher of the same. Jim also tells the dispatcher that the groups are clashing fiercely and some of them seem to possess weapons, thus he needs armed police back-up. Also, some people have set a vehicle on fire and hence Jim asks Gerald for help from the Fire Services. Gerald immediately clicks on the incident icon on the map, and chooses the option of dispatching more units, upon which he gets the previous form with current units on the case. He chooses SWAT teams in addition to the current set and the system shows the SWAT teams that are nearest to the location of the incident. Gerald chooses four SWAT teams. Gerald also clicks on the "Contact emergency fire services" check box and clicks on save and dispatch. The system sends the details about the incident to the emergency services and waits for a confirmation from their end. After, Fire Services confirm the reception of the alert, the TTA on the system is updated to 1 min 30 seconds, upon which Gerald notifies Jim to hold on for another one and a half minutes as the SWAT team and Fire Services backup is on its way.

Scenario for a typical user of the PC&CS

Andres is a dispatcher with the Dallas police department; he has just walked into his room and begun his shift at work; he puts on his headset and opens a can of diet coke, a drink he's very fond of. Just then he receives a transmission from Officer Mike Hannigan bearing call number DPO213. Andres picks up the incoming call by clicking on the incoming call, which is being circulated to all the terminals with dispatchers so as to be responded by any free dispatcher. The officer notifies Andres that he is in pursuit of a car which was detected to be speeding and has just now run over a pedestrian on the Spring Valley entrance to I-75, northbound on I-75 and doing over 90 miles per hour on the expressway. The officer requests paramedics to be rushed to the scene of the accident pronto and thereafter calls for two or three backup vehicles to assist him in chasing down the speeding car. Andres quickly hits F4 on his keypad and his headset switches over to the paramedic wireless frequency. Andres duly notifies them of the situation with the location of incident, which he had taken down during the officer's message broadcast. The paramedics acknowledge him and Andres hits the Esc key to revert to the original police frequency channel; he then hits F1 and fills out the rest of the details such as the description of the situation, the accident location for FIR purposes, and the details of the reporter as officer Mike Hannigan with his call number being recorded in the identification phone number field. Andres selects three police vehicles and one helicopter to be dispatched and clicks submit. The system registers the event and shows the icon flashing red and blue and shows the TTA to be 2 min. Andres stays tuned to the frequency should the officer contact him again. Officer Mike Hannigan is heard broadcasting on the police wireless his call number and stating that he is moving out of the Dallas city limits and needs the Richardson police to assist him in the pursuit of the vehicle. Andres, who's been listening to the dispatch, selects all the police vehicles on the map who are racing to assist Officer Mike Hannigan, right clicks on the selected vehicle's icon and selects "Cancel last order"; however, he leaves out the helicopter so that the officer is assisted from the air until the Richardson police join him in the pursuit. Andres knows that there is nothing much he can do to help his officer out there, but beyond the call of his duty he stays tuned in and continues to listen to the updates from the helicopter above the officer and the officer himself. After around 5 minutes the helicopter updates the police units in pursuit that the vehicle has been given a pit maneuver by officer Mike Hannigan and has crashed to the side lane. There has been no accident with other cars passing by; however, he requests paramedics for the officer as well as the suspect should they need one. After another 5 minutes Officer Mike Hannigan confirms on the scanner that the suspect has been apprehended and is being taken over to Richardson police department for further questioning and that the pursuit has ended. Hearing this Andre clicks onto the incident icon and logs in the details of the ending of the pursuit and then clicks "Save" and "Close the incident", after which the icon is removed from the map and also from the active incidents listing onto the screen.

Hierarchical task analysis

In user interface design, a hierarchy can be thought of as an organization of elements. Based on Seels and Glasgow, these elements are based on prerequisite relationships and describe the path of experiences a learner must take to achieve any single behavior that appears higher in the hierarchy. The user interface designer breaks down a task from top to bottom. This in turn shows a hierarchical relationship amongst the tasks. Instruction is then sequenced bottom up. This is shown below for the police command and control system in Figure CS2.2.

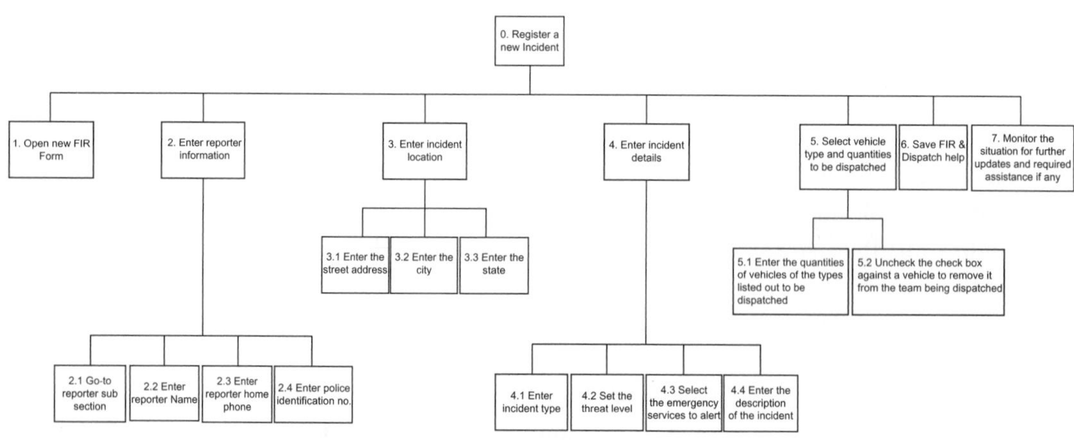

Figure CS2.2:
Hierarchical task analysis for PC&CS.

Task: Assigning vehicle(s) to the location of incident.

0. Register a new incident
1. Open new FIR form
2. Enter reporter information
   - 2.1. Go to reporter info sub-section
   - 2.2. Enter reporter name
   - 2.3. Enter reporter home phone
   - 2.4. Enter police identification number
3. Enter incident location
   - 3.1. Enter the street address
   - 3.2. Enter the city
   - 3.3. Enter the state
4. Enter incident details
   - 4.1. Enter the incident type
   - 4.2. Set the threat level
   - 4.3. Select which other emergency services to alert
   - 4.4. Enter the description for the incident
5. Select vehicle type and quantities to be dispatched
   - 5.1 Enter the quantities of vehicles of the types listed out to be dispatched
   - 5.2 Uncheck the checkbox against a vehicle to remove it from the team being dispatched
6. Save FIR & dispatch help
7. Monitor the situation for further updates and required assistance if any.

Plan 0: Do 1, 2, 3, 4, 5, 6 and 7

Plan 2: Do 2.1, 2.2, 2.3

If the reporter requests anonymity do 2.1

If the reporter is a police officer himself do 2.1, 2.4

Plan 3: Do 3.1, 3.2, 3.3

Plan 4: Do 4.1, 4.2, 4.3, 4.4

Plan 5: Do 5.1

If a vehicle is to be removed from the team being dispatched go to 5.2.

Primary interaction styles for the PC&C system

Interaction styles refer to all the ways the user can communicate or interact with the computer system. Types of interaction styles are usually command language, instructing, form fill in, menu selection, and direct manipulation.

Direct manipulation refers to the idea of "direct manipulation of the object of interest". This means that objects of interest are represented as distinguishable objects in the user interface and can be manipulated in a direct fashion.

Direct manipulation user interfaces can be defined by the following characteristics:

- visibility of the object of interest;
- rapid, reversible, incremental actions;
- replacement of complex command-language syntax by direct manipulation of the object of interest.

Below are some primary interaction styles for the PC&C system.

- Direct manipulation: the system will employ a map widget to guide the user to the location of the incident and to view all the vehicles in the vicinity of the incident. The user can also see and determine the type of the vehicles, and the status (busy or not engaged) is made available to the user. The user can drag and drop vehicles on the incident located on the map to dispatch the vehicle for that incident.
- Instructing: the system takes command or instructions from the user to implement tasks and provides the user with feedback; hence its primary interaction type would be instructing since the user only tells the system what to do and the system doesn't really reciprocate the commands, it only provides feedback.

The reasons for choosing direct manipulation or instructing are as follows

- Direct manipulation is faster in certain cases as opposed to the user having to type in commands for the same task. Let's consider a scenario where the user wants to relocate a vehicle on the map from one location to other: through command or instruction the user will have to type in the address of the new location along with the command to relocate or click on the vehicle and then click on "send to address" and then enter the new address; however, the power of direct manipulation can be used here, which is more intuitive and fits better in the mental model of the user. The user can straight away drag the vehicle to the new desired location on the map; this would take far less time on the part of the user than to issue commands. Also humans perceive the relocation of things as the ability to pick up a thing and place it at the new location, hence it doesn't break any conventions either.
- Instructing was chosen as another method of interaction as the system needs to only perform the tasks as demanded by the user of the system; conversing would not fit very well here as time is critical in this application and instructing would achieve the goals of the user much faster and possibly with far fewer errors than conversing. The system only needs to provide feedback in terms of status and process completion and does not actually need to talk back to the user.
- Conversing can also not be used for another reason given the environment for such scenarios as at any given time there would be more than one dispatcher working for the police services, probably in the same room within cubicles; also since the person reporting the incident would be on the telephone line, commands used for conversing

can be confusing to the person reporting the incident as well as interfering with the work of other co-workers, who would be dispatchers too. This is a major criterion since recording of information needs to be very precise as well as fast in a case like that of this system.

- Exploring is not an option here as the requirements of the system do not allow three-dimensional exploring of the location or anything else on the system by the user.

Design approaches to overcome user limitations of cognition, perception and learning

The cognitive approach to user interface design takes into consideration the abilities of the human brain and sensory perception and uses this to develop a user interface that will support the end user.

One approach is the use of metaphors. When used accurately, metaphors are an effective way to communicate an abstract concept or procedure to users. Desktop computers use a "desktop" metaphor to represent data as folders, document files, and other applications. Metaphors rely on a user's familiarity with other concepts such as human affordances, to aid users in understanding the actions they can perform with their data based on the form it takes. As an example, a user can move a file into the "trash can" to delete it. One of the benefits of using metaphors in user interface design is learnability. Users who can understand and relate to the metaphor are generally able to learn to use a new system quickly.

Another cognitive issue to consider is the user's attention span. Attention span varies based on environment of use, and the perceived mental workload involved in completing a specific task. Users generally can focus well on only one task at a time.

Workload is measured by the amount of information communicated to each sensory system (visual, auditory, etc.) at a given moment. A good example is Adobe Flash. Some user interfaces incorporate Adobe Flash in the system to impress the user. However, if the Flash presentation does not directly support the user's task, the user's attention may become distracted, or overloaded, by too much auditory and visual information.

Overloading the user's memory is a common problem in user interfaces.

The user of the system would be a dispatcher; apart from the inherent limitations which are attached to a user, the system user would be fatigued and stressed out as well, which I need to take care of. Also since the user would typically spend most of his/her time in front of the computer screen, care has to be taken so that the color combinations and use of other effects are minimal so that the interface is serene and simple rather than jazzy and startling, which can be stressful to work with after a couple of hours in front of it.

Below are the design approaches used in the design of the user interface, which would help users to carry out their task much more efficiently and fruitfully.

- Suggestive/predictive search: first of all as the dispatcher would be in a hurry and most of the tasks that he/she needs to carry out like typing down the details of the incidents, etc., have critical time requirements, where every second matters, and for a stressed person and especially when the person reporting the incident is in a state of panic, it is very easy for the person to commit typographic errors while taking down the information. The PC&C system will provide a suggestive/predictive text input to fields like location, type of incident, etc., so that the user can quickly select the option that he/she set out to type and move ahead to the next field. For example, if an incident is to be logged about a robbery at Matilda and Milton, when the user sets out to enter the type of incident he she hits "r" then the system goes ahead and suggests "Ransom" and "Robbery"; after the user enters the second character, which would be "o", the system would only suggest "Robbery" which, if the user hits the Enter button or clicks on the suggestion the field, would be automatically filled out by the system. This avoids a lot of errors on the part of the user and also saves time inputting the information.
- Auto selection and dispatching of rescue vehicles: for dispatching the vehicles where there is a possibility that the user can go wrong, a task will choose the closest requested units and assign them to the task at hand; this way all the user has to do is select the type and number of vehicles and the system would do the rest.
- Delineating system and user responsibilities: since time is a constraint for the user and again to avoid errors on the part of the user, the task of registering the caller ID of an incoming call to the system in the FIR form is used, so that the user saves time as well as any errors that might occur if the caller has to dictate it, since the caller might be calling from an environment which may be noisy due to various reasons like wind, traffic, voices, etc.; not only that, the caller may be of different origin so there might be pronunciation and accent issues which can be overcome by this method. Since nowadays nearly everyone carries a cellular phone and almost 90% of the time the identification number (a home or cellular phone number so that the reporter can be tracked down should a legal need arise) would be the same as the number he/she is calling form, although the interface has provision for an alternative identification number so that the caller can be tracked down, by default the system puts the same number as the one on the incoming caller ID into this field, but the operator/dispatcher can overwrite it (suppose the person is calling from a public phone).
- Auto-alert to emergency services: this interface has incorporated another feature into the interface/design, for when the dispatcher selects the type of the incident such as robbery or riot, etc., since each of these incidents can require fire services or the paramedics or both; e.g., a riot would require the assistance of the paramedics to complete the rescue operation, maybe even the fire services. The system selects the

emergency services to be notified depending upon the type of incident (which can be mapped at the back-end, so that each incident has an associated set of services to be notified); though all the services show up on the form, only the ones that are mapped are check-boxed by the system. This allows the dispatcher the flexibility to edit the services to be alerted, should he/she require it in certain special circumstances, while by default making sure that relevant emergency services are notified if the dispatcher is in a hurry and overlooks the notify sub-panel.

- The active incidents and busy vehicles are highlighted: since the user will have a plethora of information on the screen and using a map brings its own benefits and drawbacks to the table, to help the user (the dispatcher) the system shows all the incidents that are active at a given time, flashing in red. This ensures that the user would be easily able to locate incidents on the map. Also the vehicles shown on the map that are busy carry a red visible bubble on their icons, indicating that they are already assigned to some other task and should not be used unless unavoidable; the ones that are currently not assigned any task have no bubble associated with them; hence this shows which vehicles and incidents are currently active, without overuse of colors.
- Map interface: the above limitations can be overcome, though partially, using the map interface for locating the vehicles. One of the advantages of map-based interfaces is that they enable users to browse information while maintaining a relative position with the location of the incident. The users will also be able to use the basic functions of the map interface such as browsing through the maps to different locations. The users can also view the vehicles with their types and the status (busy or not engaged). The basic map functions like filtering out the unnecessary information or icons have been added to this interface. Thus all the relevant data can be presented without the user interface being cluttered. It is possible to view a list of the vehicles being viewed currently on the map, enabling the user to browse through the list. The map interface does have disadvantages, such as a lot of location information is superimposed on the map images. However, this can be solved by employing map scale flexibility in displaying data at different zoom levels on the map.

External cognition approaches to overcome user limitations

- Cognitive benefits of using a map: the usage of the map as an interface for this system is an external cognitive approach. The user is more adept at tracking locations on a map rather than from a list of written text. Also, identification and the direction to the spot of incident can be identified easily on a map.
- Externalizing to reduce memory load: the system reminds users of various events in the form of warnings, balloon notifications and error messages; e.g., upon automatic notification to the emergency services, if the system does not receive an

acknowledgment from them within a fixed timeout period, the system notifies the user of the same so as to enable him to perceive the state of the system and take necessary corrective actions.

- Computational offloading: the system automatically calculates the rescue vehicles closest to the scene of incident and dispatches them if the dispatcher has selected the types and quantities of the vehicles to be dispatched. Also the system ensures that only vehicles that are free at that moment and in the vicinity are assigned to respond to the incident instead of a vehicle that is already assigned to an incident. This saves a lot of time and trouble and also reduces the error space on the part of the user as the user can accidentally assign vehicles that are further away or might be busy responding to another call.
- Use of icons and colors: the vehicles on the map can be assigned common icons. For example: a red truck with a light can be used to represent a fire truck. Assigning familiar icons to the vehicles reduces the user limitation of remembering the vehicle type.
- Annotation and cognitive tracing: an active incident can be viewed on the map with the status of the incident, a brief description of the incident and flashing in red. The user can browse through the map to view the current active incidents, and thus the need to always perform search operations for active incidents is reduced.
- Consistency with mental models: the model of a paper register where the incidents are logged is modeled into the system where homogeneity of this concept is maintained. The procedure of logging the information will be similar to that in the paper system; however, due to automation of most of the logging techniques, the system can perform the operation faster as compared to the earlier system.

Error messages and warnings for PC&CS

Errors messages are important in user interface design. The characteristics of good error messages:

- A problem: states that a problem occurred.
- A cause: explains why the problem occurred.
- A solution: provides a solution so that users can fix the problem.

Additionally, good error messages are presented in a way that is:

- Relevant: the message presents a problem that users care about.
- Actionable: users should either perform an action or change their behavior as the result of the message.
- User-centered: the message describes the problem in terms of target user actions or goals, not in terms of what the code is unhappy with.

- Brief: the message is as short as possible, but no shorter.
- Clear: the message uses plain language so that the target users can easily understand problem and solution.
- Specific: the message describes the problem using specific language, giving specific names, locations, and values of the objects involved.
- Courteous: users shouldn't be blamed or made to feel stupid.
- Rare: displayed infrequently. Frequently displayed error messages are a sign of bad design.

Figure CS2.3 shows some example error messages for the PC&C system.

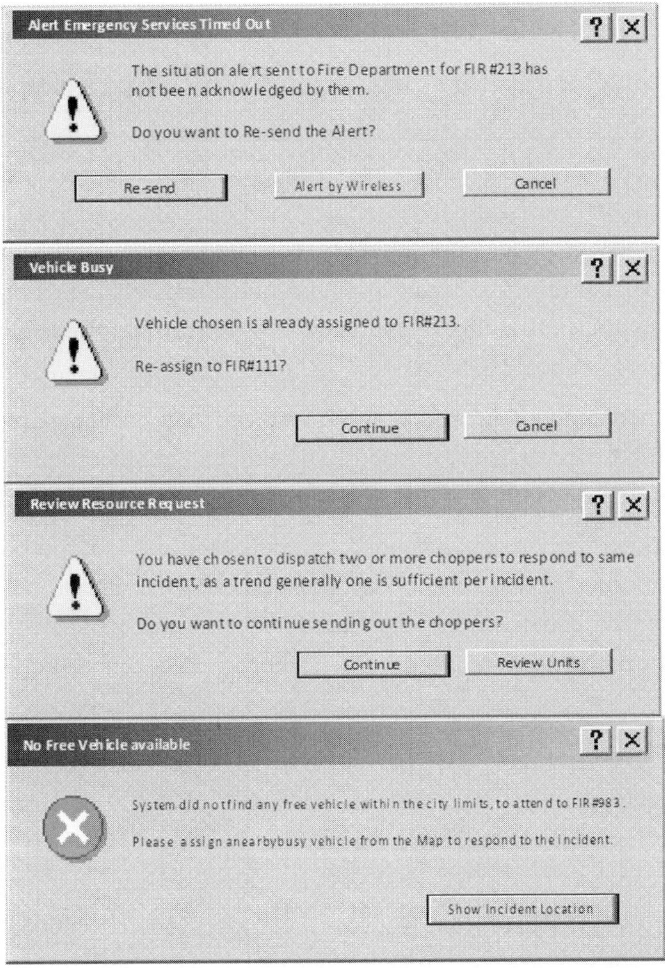

Figure CS2.3:
Error messages for the police command and control system.

Data model (entity relationship diagram) and virtual windows for PC&CS

Soren Lauesen (*Virtual Windows: Linking User Tasks, Data Models, and Interface Design*, by Soren Lauesen and Morten Borup Harning) describes user interface design as comprising three major activities:

1. organizing data into a set of windows or frames
2. defining functions that let the user control the system
3. designing the graphical appearance of windows and functions.

These three design activities build on previous analysis results such as hierarchical task analysis and data modeling. These activities also include checking activities such as reviews and usability tests. The goal of this process is to create a user interface that is easy to learn, easy to understand, and also supports user tasks efficiently.

The approach we will take uses two systematic approaches that have been used quite extensively.

1. Data-oriented approach: this starts with a description of the data the system must maintain; a data model (entity relationship diagram, ERD) will be used to create this. Using the ERD, user interface designers define a set of windows such that all data is visible. The functions generally are standard functions for creating, updating, and deleting data.
2. Task-oriented approach: traditional approach used for user interface design discussed in previous sections.

A virtual-windows technique is used to pull these two together. This approach uses data and tasks at the same time. The approach is used to design and test the graphical appearance of the interface before the functions are fully defined.

Lauesen describes a virtual window as a picture on an idealized screen. These idealized screens or window show data but have no widgets (buttons, menus, etc.). Gestalts are used to format and organize the data in these virtual windows. Complex applications need several virtual windows.

The process of creating the data model (ERD) and the virtual windows are shown in Figures CS2.4 and CS2.5.

Analysis of virtual windows using a CREDO matrix

CREDO stands for Create, Read, Edit, Delete, Overview and represents the different operations on data in a system. We can check whether we have all proper operations on the data in a system by comparing the user interface windows (virtual windows at this point) against the different data types. This is shown in Tables CS2.1 and CS2.2.

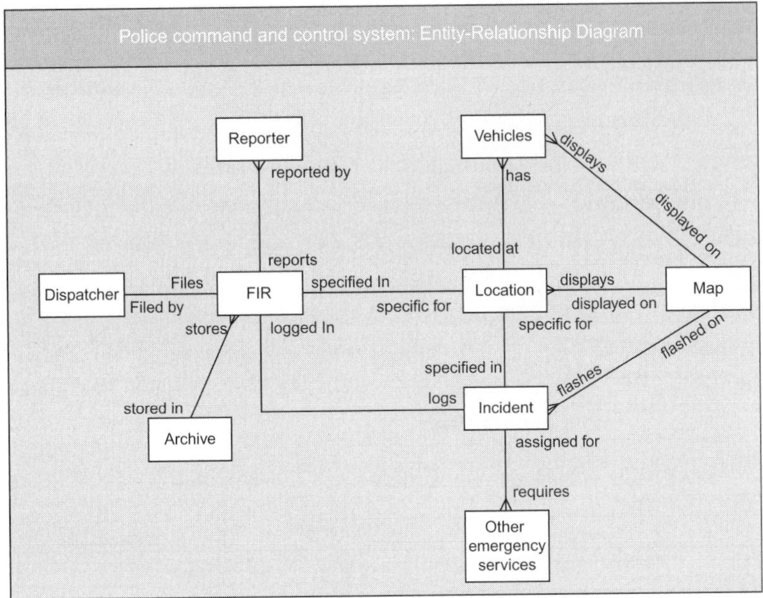

Figure CS2.4:
ERD for PC&CS.

First iteration: a low-fidelity prototype for the PC&C is shown in Figure CS2.6, CS2.7, and CS2.8.

Identifying gestalts in PC&CS user interface design

The operational principle of gestalt psychology describes the brain as holistic, parallel, and analog, with self-organizing tendencies. The gestalt principle maintains that the human eye sees objects in their entirety before perceiving their individual parts. The gestalt psychologists believe that perception is the product of complex interactions among various stimuli. This is different from the behaviorist approach, which is based on understanding the elements of cognitive processes. The gestalts, on the other hand, look to understand their organization. This gestalt effect is essentially the form-generating capability of our senses with respect to the visual recognition of figures and whole forms rather than a collection of simple lines and curves.

Some of the gestalt laws include;

- Law of proximity
- Law of similarity
- Law of Prägnanz (figure-ground)
- Law of symmetry
- Law of closure.

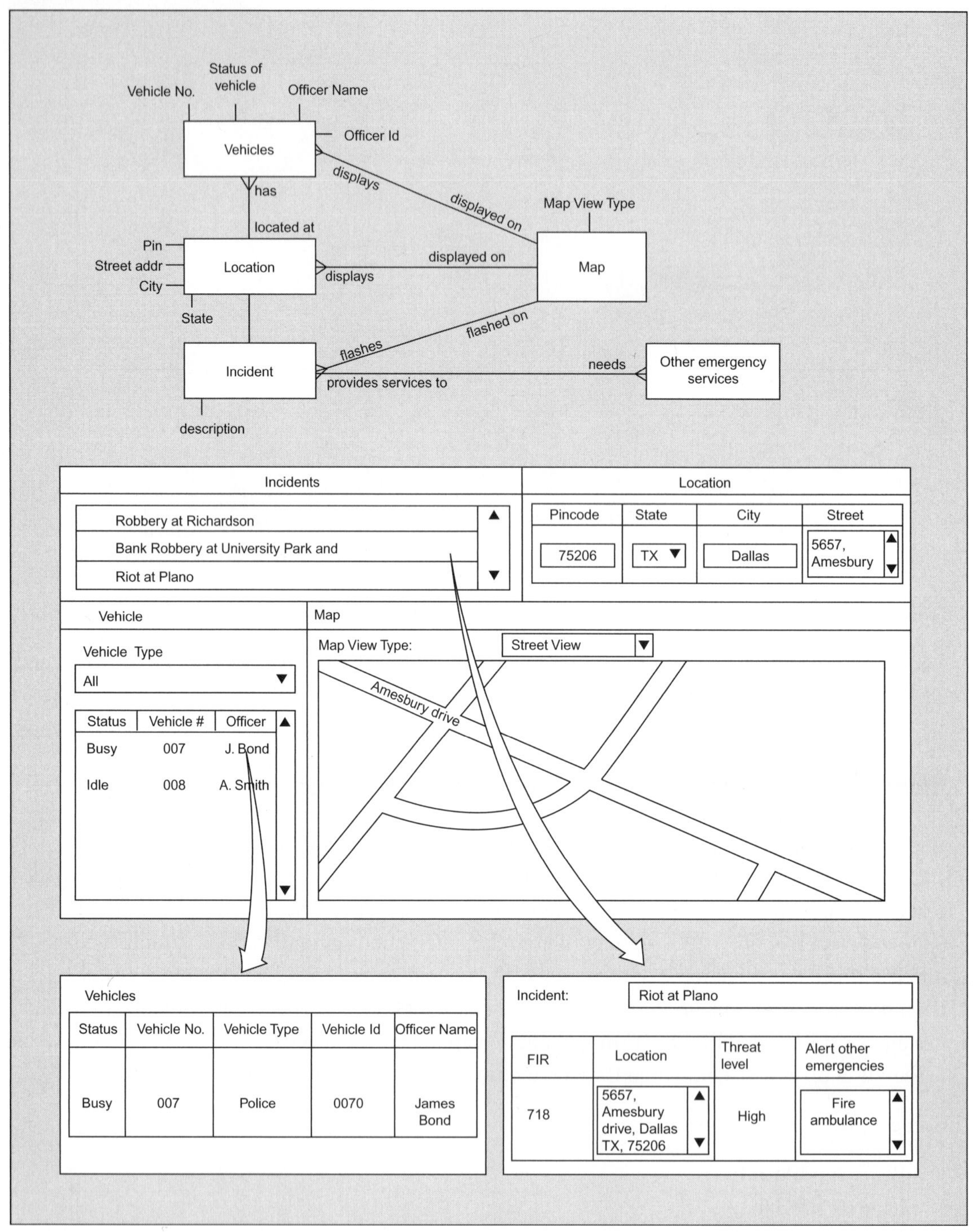

Figure CS2.5:
Virtual window for PC&CS.

Table CS2.1: CREDO matrix for the PC&C system (data model versus virtual windows).

Entity Virt. Window	Dispatcher	FIR	Reporter	Location	Incident	Vehicles	Map	Archive	Other Emergency Services
Login Screen	CRE								
FIR		CREO	CREdO	CREdO	CREdO	RO		CREO	CREO
Tracker Screen	RO	RO		RO	ReO	RO	REO		RO
Missing fncts	D	D	(D)	(D)	(D)	CED	CD	D	D

Table CS2.2: CREDO matrix for the PC&C system (data model versus tasks).

Entity Task	Dispatcher	FIR	Reporter	Location	Incident	Vehicles	Map	Archive	Other Emergerncy Services
Login	CRE								
Search info	RO	RO	REO	RO	RO	RO	RO	REO	RO
Dispatch help		RO	RO	ReO	ReO	RO	ReO		RO
File FIR	RO	CREO	CREO	CREO	CREO	RO		CREO	RO
Archive		REO						CREO	
Missing tasks	D	D	D	D	D	CED	C(E)D	D	CED

The gestalts used in the above low-level prototyping are:

Screen 1: FIR screen (Figure CS2.6)

1. Laws of proximity
   The widgets for FIR inputs are arranged in a tabular format in close proximity to each other. The reporter input data widget and the location input data widget are placed side by side. The incident details are also arranged in a column format where the Incident information and the description of the incident are placed using the laws of proximity. The dispatch vehicles details also use a law of proximity where the overview of the vehicles dispatch is shown alongside the input widget for dispatching vehicles.
2. Laws of closure
   The Fir details, incident details and dispatch vehicles tables are separated using the laws of closure.
3. Law of parallel movement
   The screen uses the law of parallel movement in the case of the input screens. For instance, the dispatcher inputs the information in one widget in a vertical fashion and moves from one widget to another in a section in horizontal fashion.

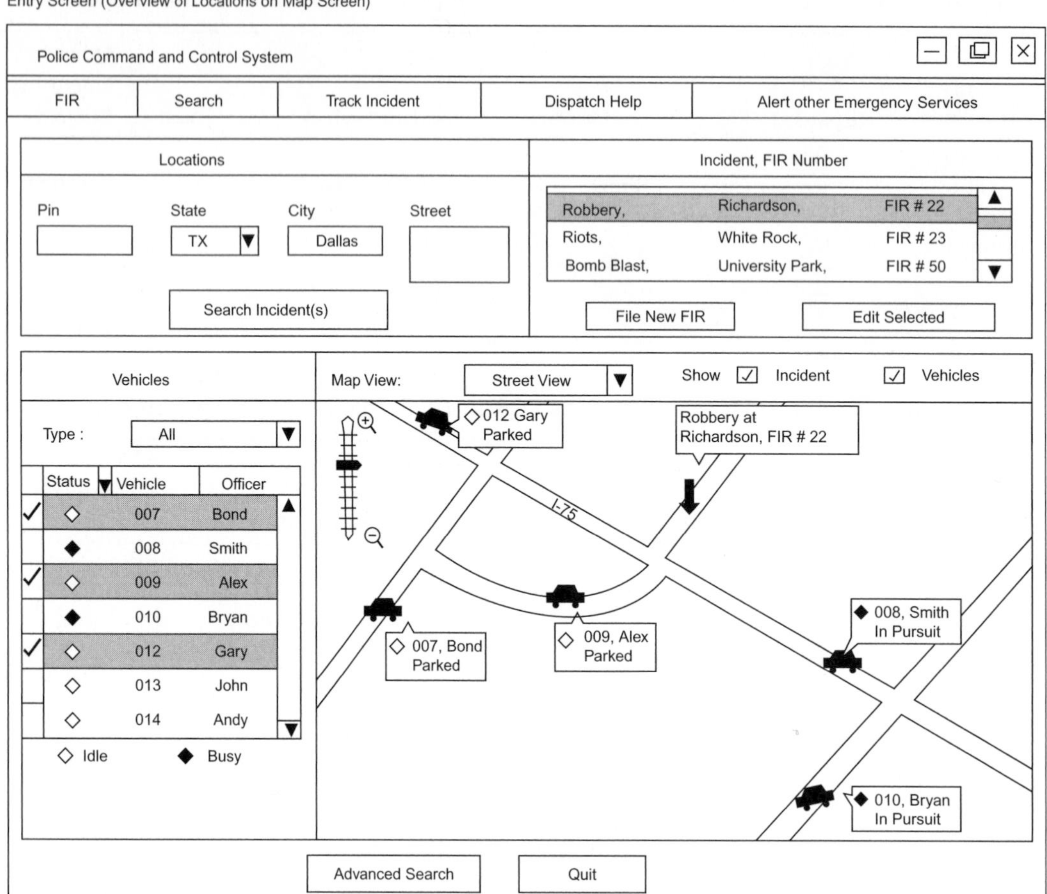

Figure CS2.6:
Low-fidelity prototype – first iteration for PC&CS – entry screen.

4. Law of lines
   The reporter input widget uses the law of lines to separate the reporter information from the police identification information input.
5. Column gestalts
   The screen uses clear column gestalts by separating different widgets into different columns. These widgets altogether serve different purposes yet they are related to each other and hence represented in different columns. For instance, the reported information input and location information input are placed as two columns in the FIR details table.

Screen 2: Overview of locations and incidents on map (Figure CS2.7)

1. Laws of proximity

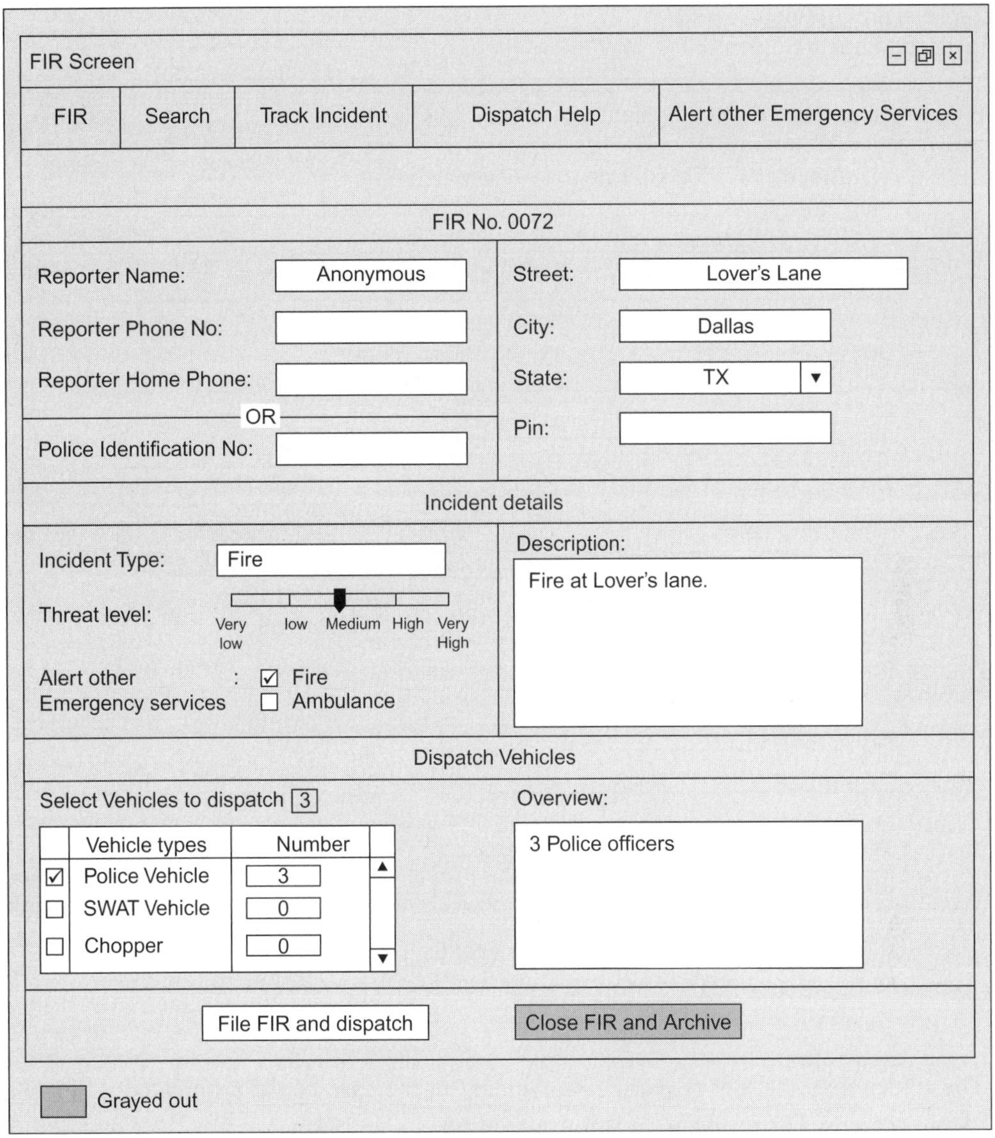

Figure CS2.7:
Low-fidelity prototype – first iteration for PC&CS – FIR screen.

The widgets for location information search and the results of the search are arranged in a tabular format in close proximity to each other. The vehicles overview data widget and the map showing the incident details also show the law of proximity in gestalts.

2. Laws of closure
   The incident details, map and vehicles details are separated using the laws of closure.
3. Law of parallel movement

Low level prototyping:-
Advanced Search Screen:

Police Command and Control System
FIR | Search | Track Incident | Dispatch Help | Alert other Emergency Services Menu
Advanced Search
FIR
FIR ID :
FIR Description :
Search FIR
Location
Pin Code :
State : Texas, (TX)
City : Dallas
Street : 5657, Amesbury Dr
Search Location
Incident
Incident Id :
Status : Active Closed
Incident description :
Threat level : Very low low Medium High Very High
Search Incident
Search All

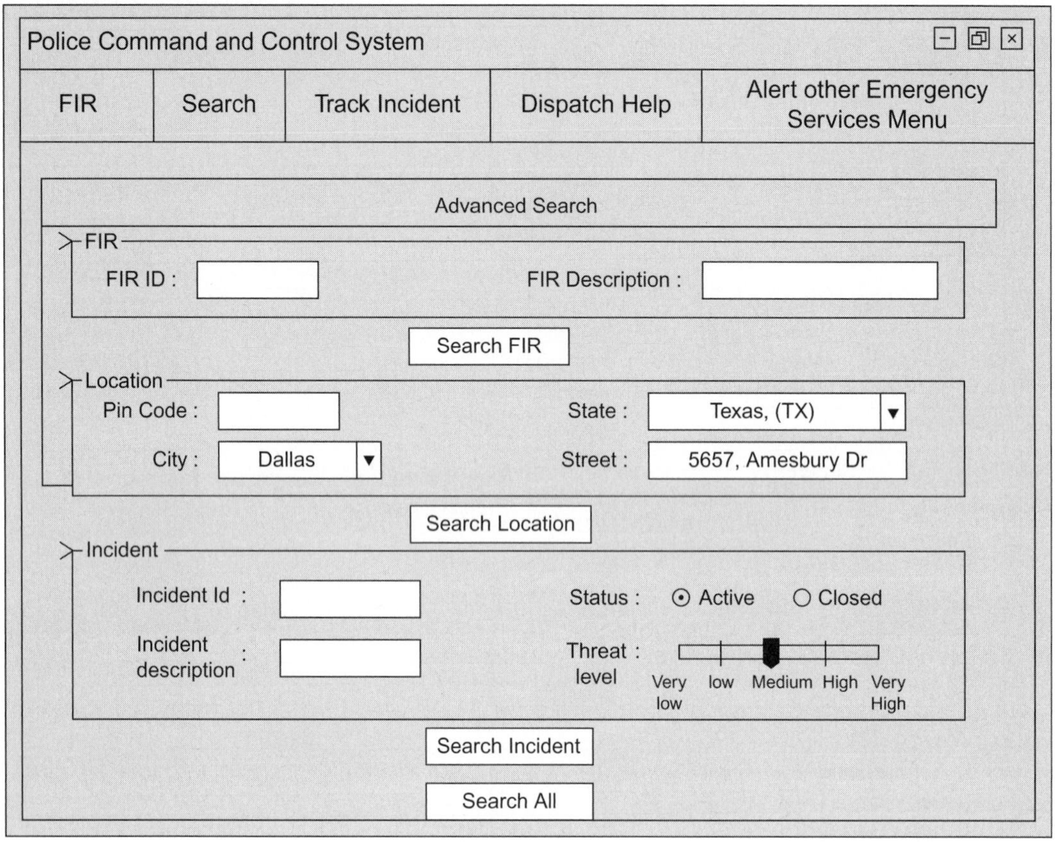

Figure CS2.8:
Low-fidelity prototype – first iteration for PC&CS – advanced search screen.

The screen uses the law of parallel movement in the case of the arrangement of the output screens. For instance, location search results are shown in a widget parallel to the location search widget.

4. Law of lines
   The reporter input widget uses the law of lines to separate the location search input and results from that of map and vehicles overview.
5. Column gestalts
   The screen uses clear column gestalts by separating different widgets into different columns. These widgets altogether serve different purposes yet they are related to each other and hence represented in different columns.

Screen 3: Advanced search screen (Figure CS2.8)

1. Laws of proximity
   The widgets for information search are divided but placed using the laws of proximity in gestalts.
2. Laws of closure
   The incident details, map and vehicles details are separated using the laws of closure.
3. Law of lines
   The different search widgets like FIR, location and incident are input widgets that are placed on the screen using the law of lines. They are separated from each other using simple line demarcation.
4. Column gestalts
   The screen uses clear column gestalts by separating different widgets into different columns. These widgets altogether serve different purposes yet they are related to each other and hence represented in different columns.

Data presentation techniques

There are many possible data presentation techniques for user interface design. This section describes those techniques used for the PC&C system.

Screen 1: FIR screen (Figure CS2.6)

The FIR Screen is mainly an input screen that can be configured to show the data also in the case of search results. The data is represented here mainly using the standard input fields.

- Reported information input widget: this information is taken from text boxes since this data will most frequently be new information.
- Location information input widget: the street address is represented using a scrollable text area instead of a text box to accommodate more characters. This approach will help in restricting the size of the input area. The City field is taken from a text box that can implement predictive search for faster input. The State field is a drop-down box, because the number of states is restricted and is not vulnerable to change. Pin code is a text field input.
- Incident details input widget: the Incident type field is a text input field coupled with predictive/suggestive search which shows the values of the most frequently used Incident types in alphabetical order. Threat level uses a slider to indicate the level of threat, which is set as average by default. The idea behind using a slider for threat level was to enable faster input for the user, since an options menu or drop-down box could be time-consuming. Also, a slider is another cognitive approach towards showing the

increasing threat levels. The description for an incident can be multiple lines and hence I use a text area for the same.

- Dispatch vehicle details widget: the predefined vehicle types and the numbers of vehicle types are arranged in a table structure with check boxes. The user can select the type of vehicle and input the number for that type. The number of vehicles text box is zero by default. The overview window is a list box, which summarizes the selected vehicles with their respective numbers.

Screen 2: Overview of locations and incidents on the map interface (Figure CS2.7)

The Overview screen is mainly used to perform quick searches and find the incident locations and status on the map of the city.

- The search location widget: the placement of the input fields for the search is done in the order of most specific to the least specific search. The type of input fields used to represent Pin, State, City and Street are same as the previously mentioned FIR screen for similar reasons.
- The result of the search: Incident and FIR details: the details of the FIR are shown in a scrollable list box separated by commas with an example entry shown below the list box for help purpose.
- Vehicles widget: the vehicles are represented in a scrollable table that can be sorted based on any of the columns. This will help in identifying entire details of the vehicles, which are present at the site. The vehicles can also be filtered using the Vehicle Type, which is represented as a drop-down menu.
- Map widget: the map widget is shown alongside the list of vehicles and the data is represented on the map in the form of icons. The map view type can vary from street view to satellite view depending on the user preferences. The map shown is a standard map widget with the replica of a top view of the locality. The vehicles on the map can be shown as icons with varying shapes depending on the type of vehicle. The details for a vehicle can be shown in the form of a pop-up on the icon. The incident location is represented distinctly with the use of a different icon and the details of that can also be viewed in the form of a pop-up. The map can be panned and zoomed to enable moving around the selected locality.

Screen 3: Advanced search (Figure CS2.8)

- The data is represented in a similar way to the data in earlier form fields since most of the inputs are the same.

Usability testing on the first prototype

This section describes the testing techniques used for the PC&C system.

Heuristic evaluation is a usability inspection approach for user interface software that can help to identify usability problems in the user interface design. The approach involves evaluators examining the interface and judging its compliance with recognized usability principles (the "heuristics"). The heuristics are defined by Jacob Nielsen;

- **Visibility of system status:** the system should always keep users informed about what is going on, through appropriate feedback within reasonable time.
- **Match between system and the real world:** the system should speak the user's language, with words, phrases and concepts familiar to the user, rather than system-oriented terms. Follow real-world conventions, making information appear in a natural and logical order.
- **User control and freedom:** users often choose system functions by mistake and will need a clearly marked "emergency exit" to leave the unwanted state without having to go through an extended dialogue. Support undo and redo.
- **Consistency and standards:** users should not have to wonder whether different words, situations, or actions mean the same thing. Follow platform conventions.
- **Error prevention**: even better than good error messages is a careful design which prevents a problem from occurring in the first place. Either eliminate error-prone conditions or check for them and present users with a confirmation option before they commit to the action.
- **Recognition rather than recall:** minimize the user's memory load by making objects, actions, and options visible. The user should not have to remember information from one part of the dialogue to another. Instructions for use of the system should be visible or easily retrievable whenever appropriate.
- **Flexibility and efficiency of use:** accelerators – unseen by the novice user – may often speed up the interaction for the expert user such that the system can cater to both inexperienced and experienced users. Allow users to tailor frequent actions.
- **Aesthetic and minimalist design:** dialogues should not contain information which is irrelevant or rarely needed. Every extra unit of information in a dialogue competes with the relevant units of information and diminishes their relative visibility.
- **Help users recognize, diagnose, and recover from errors:** error messages should be expressed in plain language (no codes), precisely indicate the problem, and constructively suggest a solution.

- **Help and documentation:** even though it is better if the system can be used without documentation, it may be necessary to provide help and documentation. Any such information should be easy to search, focused on the user's task, list concrete steps to be carried out, and not be too large.

The heuristic evaluation summary for the PC&C is shown in Table CS2.3.

According to the heuristic evaluation and the usability testing, many suggestions for modifying the first prototype were suggested by the user. Summarizing the possible changes in the first prototype:

- Rearranging the widgets to avoid clutter and visual noise.
- Merging common functionalities into a single widget to make the design compact.
- Restructuring the menu bar to that of standard desktop applications.
- Adding a toolbar for quick access to most frequently used actions.
- Redesigning some parts of the widgets according to the suggestions after usability testing by the user. For instance, adding affordance to the threat-level slide bar.
- Adding more icons to indicate vehicle types and status of the application.
- Using tabs wherever applicable to use the same window space for different functionalities and thus avoiding confusion due to various instances of the application. Tabs also provide easier navigation than using column gestalts between widgets.
- Modularization of different actions to enable a classified approach towards navigation.

Second iteration – low-fidelity prototype

The motivation to create a second low-fidelity prototype is to overcome all the problems that were found out in the first low-fidelity prototype after usability testing. The approach devised to redesign this low-level fidelity prototype is to classify the data and represent it on the screen using a well-defined taxonomy. The data remains the same and in some cases is duplicated across the different tasks but the visual coherence is maintained. The data classifications or taxonomies are arranged in a dynamic side taskbar. This taskbar will act as a container for frequently used functions for that specific classification of data. For instance, the location tab will contain the current locations of the active incidents that can be viewed on the current scope of the map. Thus, this acts as a quick overview to the locations where there are active incidents taking place and hence can be used a visual aid to view the map in an organized manner. This approach will improve upon the earlier low-fidelity prototype by maintaining an aesthetic and minimalist design. The gestalts from the earlier prototypes are maintained and the new design approach uses the taskbar to toggle between different forms.

Table CS2.3: Results of heuristic evaluation.

Heuristic	Conformance Question	Evidence of Conformance
Visibility of system status	Are users kept informed about system progress with appropriate feedback within reasonable time?	Yes. The system uses a suggestive and predictive approach towards input fields like City where the text box pops up the data matching to the typed in characters relevant to that field in a sorted order. When the incident is filed, the system indicates a time to arrive to the location of incident.
Match between system and the real world	Does the system use concepts and language familiar to the user rather than system-oriented terms. Does the system use real-world conventions and display information in a natural and logical order?	Yes, the system uses language familiar to the user. Commonly used terms like FIR, incident, alert emergency, dispatch etc. by the dispatchers are used to maintain real-world convention. The information is displayed mainly on the map that is logical in this case, because the requirements involved showing an overview of the location of the incident to the dispatcher.
User control and freedom	Can users do what they want when they want?	Usage of maps enables the user to move around the location of the incident, to look out for vehicles and monitor the incidents. The user can also search for incidents, FIRs, and vehicles. Emergency services are not dispatched until the entire FIR information is saved, which can be a constraint.
Consistency and standards	Do design elements such as objects and actions have the same meaning or effect in different situations?	Menu list is inconsistent across the screens and standard menu items are missing. The slide bar for threat level doesn't have the affordance to show the increasing level. Gestalts are noisy and the subdivisions within a window are too glaring and overdone. There is no need for three search buttons in the advanced search screen.
Error prevention	Can users make errors that good designs would prevent?	The user can make an error by selecting some menu items that are not relevant to that screen. In the rest of the cases, errors are largely prevented by use of good design techniques. For instance, the system uses pop-up warnings wherever applicable to help deal with the data that is entered in some fields.
Recognition rather than recall	Are design elements such as objects, actions and options visible? Is the user forced to remember information from one part of a system to another?	No. The use of too many widgets on the overview of locality and incident screen causes inconvenience. The overview page has a lot of information, which may

(Continued)

Table CS2.3: (Continued)

Heuristic	Conformance Question	Evidence of Conformance
		never be used. Also, the FIR registration screen doesn't follow good gestalts. The icons designed for the vehicles are not enough to distinguish the type of the vehicle.
Flexibility and efficiency of use	Are task methods efficient and can users customize frequent actions or use short cuts?	The user needs to press F1 key to file a new FIR, which violates the standard use of F1 for showing the help file. The user cannot use shortcuts to submit the FIR form and hence this can affect the speed of filling up the form. The form is submitted only on clicking the File FIR and dispatch button. The user cannot customize frequent action using this prototype.
Aesthetic and minimalist design	Do the screens contain irrelevant or rarely needed information?	The screens do contain irrelevant or rarely needed information, infact the screens are designed to hold as much information as possible.
Help users recognize, diagnose and recover from errors	Are error messages expressed in plain language (no codes), do they accurately describe the problem and suggest a solution?	The error and warning messages are designed in a manner that describe the problem, the cause of the problem and suggests a solution. Thus, the error messages are very well designed and prompt the user to perform the actions to avoid or rectify them.
Help and documentation	Is appropriate help information supplied, and is this information easy to search and focused on the user's tasks?	No. The system tries to show all the functionalities on the screen and thus expects the user to navigate and learn about them. The help documents for the system are not present, however some help functionalities are provided for critical functionalities like searching location.

The menu structure for the earlier prototype was poorly designed and didn't match the standard menu bars for desktop applications. The menu structure is also redesigned to match the standard menu structure and the menu items are grouped into four main menu items, namely File, View, Tools and Help.

Figures CS2.9, CS2.10, and CS2.11 show the dynamic taskbar, which is placed on the left-hand side of the primary window. Upon clicking any of the buttons on the taskbar, the button expands to show the details as shown; this helps reduce clutter as well as providing the user with a view that is oriented towards a specific perspective.

Figure CS2.12, CS2.13, and CS2.14 show the Hierarchical menu bar, the Entry Screen, and the FIR Screen, respectively.

Usability test and defect correction for the second iteration of the low-fidelity prototype

The first hand-drawn low-fidelity prototype was evaluated by performing a thinking-out-loud test and analysis; after studying the needs and feasibility several changes were incorporated. This was presented to a naive user; after a briefing session of 5 minutes, his feedback on things, the issues with current design and his suggestions as to how he would expect the interface to be were documented. The prime issues are summarized below.

- Problem 1: context of many buttons on the left task panel not obvious to user at first.
- Problem 2: data on the left task panel redundant and hence confusing to the user.

Locations
City State Pin
Dallas Tx 75206
Plano Tx 75216
Garland Tx 12345
Incidents
FIRs
Vehicles
Officers
Search

Locations
Incidents
Incident | Time & Date | Threat Level
Robbery | 23:30 5/12/12 | Medium
Riot | 23:45 5/12/12 | High
Shootout | 23:45 5/12/12 | Very High
FIRs
Vehicles
Officers
Search

Figure CS2.9:
Low-fidelity prototype – second iteration for PC&CS – dynamic side taskbar.

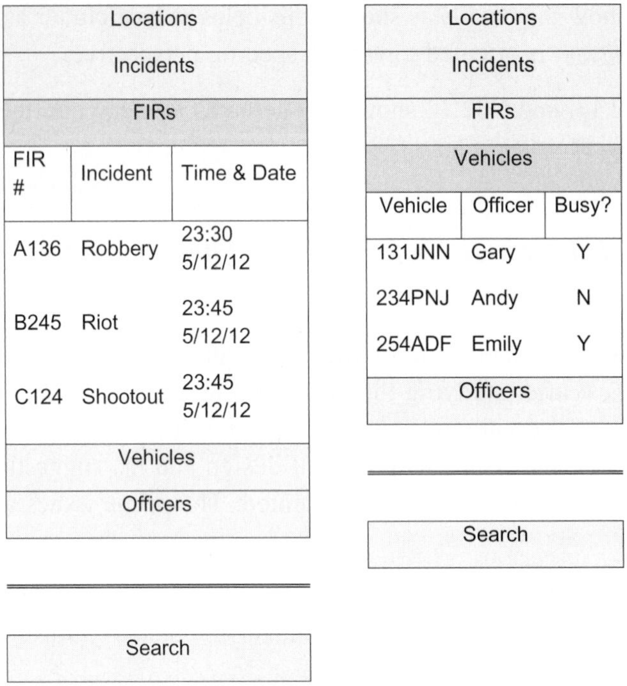

Locations

Incidents

FIRs

FIR #	Incident	Time & Date
A136	Robbery	23:30 5/12/12
B245	Riot	23:45 5/12/12
C124	Shootout	23:45 5/12/12

Vehicles

Officers

Search

Locations

Incidents

FIRs

Vehicles

Vehicle	Officer	Busy?
131JNN	Gary	Y
234PNJ	Andy	N
254ADF	Emily	Y

Officers

Search

Figure CS2.10:
Low-fidelity prototype – second iteration for PC&CS – dynamic side taskbar.

Locations

Incidents

FIRs

Vehicles

Officers

Badge #	Officer	Vehicle
PD1234	Andy	131JNN
PD8732	Emily	234PNJ
PD9854	Emily	254ADF

Search

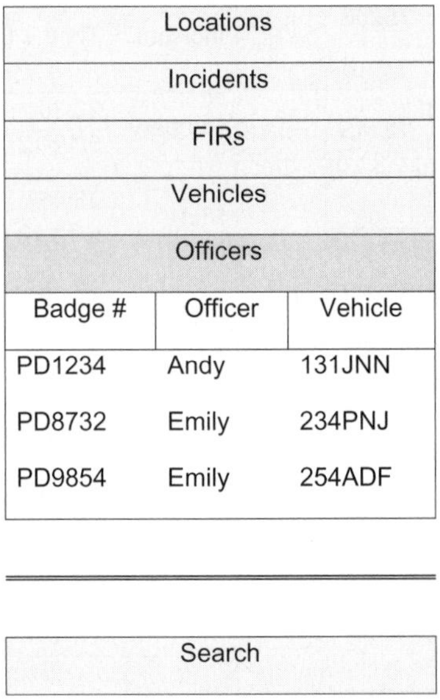

Figure CS2.11:
Low-fidelity prototype – second iteration for PC&CS – dynamic side taskbar. The menu structure for the second iteration of the low-fidelity prototype is as shown in Figure CS2.12.

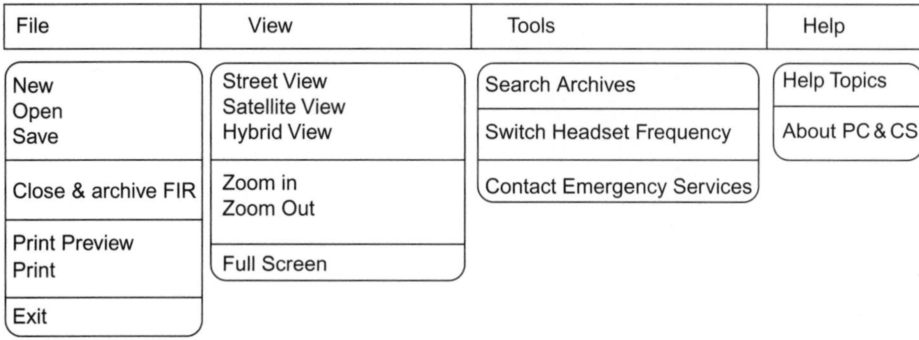

Figure CS2.12:
Low-fidelity prototype – second iteration for PC&CS – hierarchical menu bar. The screen prototypes for the second iteration of the low-fidelity prototype are shown in Figures CS2.13 and CS2.14.

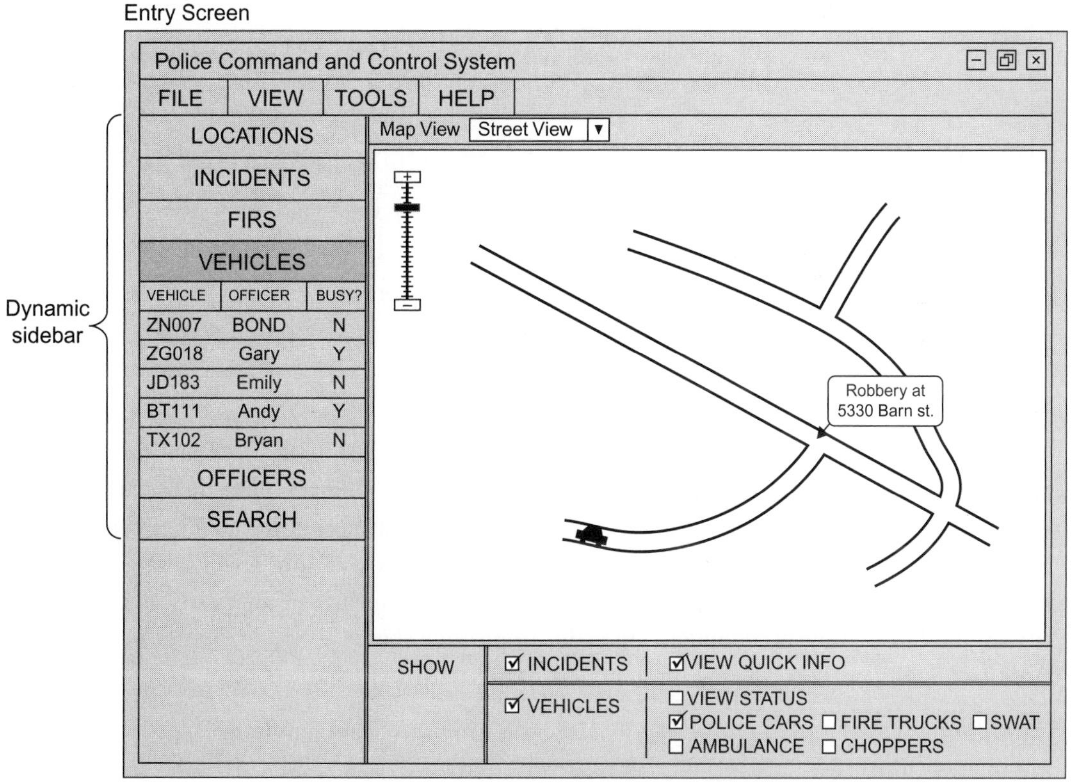

Entry Screen

Police Command and Control System

FILE | VIEW | TOOLS | HELP

Dynamic sidebar

LOCATIONS

INCIDENTS

FIRS

VEHICLES

VEHICLE	OFFICER	BUSY?
ZN007	BOND	N
ZG018	Gary	Y
JD183	Emily	N
BT111	Andy	Y
TX102	Bryan	N

OFFICERS

SEARCH

Map View Street View

Robbery at 5330 Barn st.

SHOW ☑ INCIDENTS | ☑ VIEW QUICK INFO

☑ VEHICLES | ☐ VIEW STATUS ☑ POLICE CARS ☐ FIRE TRUCKS ☐ SWAT ☐ AMBULANCE ☐ CHOPPERS

Figure CS2.13:
Low-fidelity prototype – second iteration for PC&CS – entry screen.

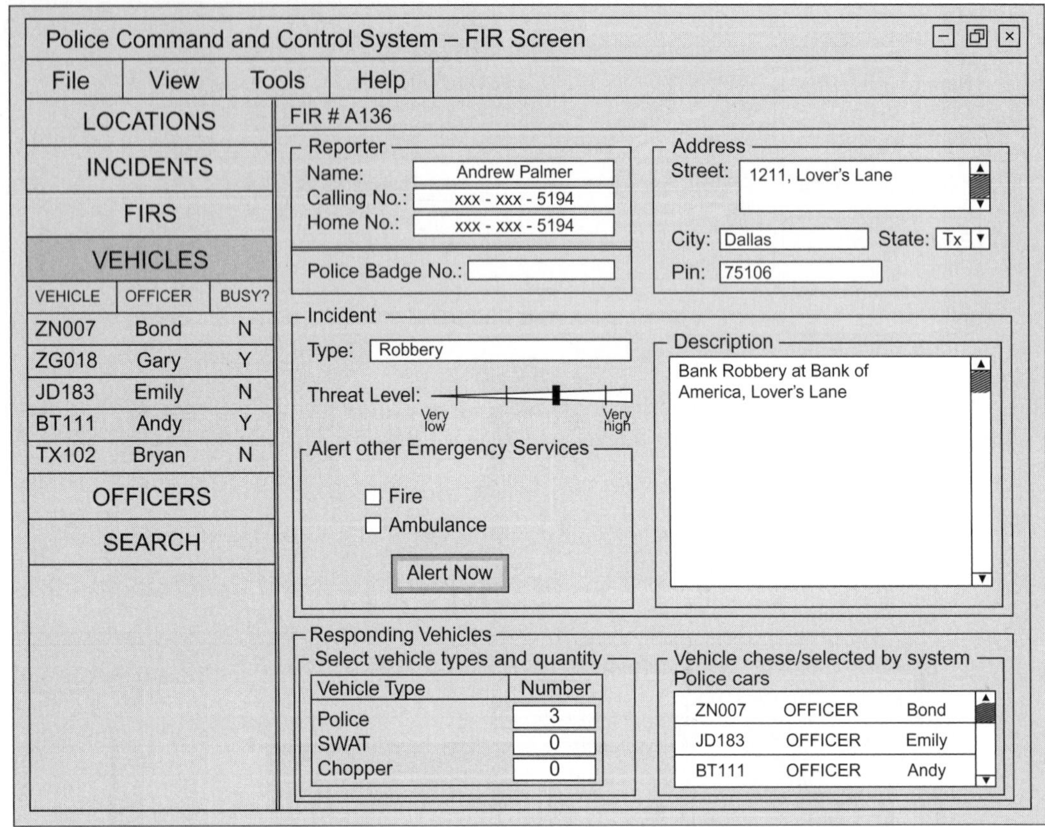

Figure CS2.14:
Low-fidelity prototype – second iteration for PC&CS – FIR screen.

Solution for 1 and 2: side task bar re-modeled.

The first feedback received from the user was that the task bar on the left has too many buttons and the user didn't quite understand the need at the first pass for each of them until he was briefed about the various situations and then the buttons started making sense to him. Once the user started getting the hang of things like how to file an FIR, how to edit one and how to dispatch help to the site of an incident, it unearthed an overlooked bug; the data on the left pane was redundant. In order to provide the user with different views in terms of a resource, redundancy was created in presenting the data.

The solution was removing all redundancy and letting the user change the way data is presented to him.

Earlier the system provided the user with a "viewing data through a straw" for several views; tabs for Officer and Vehicle, so that the user can search either one of them or look at them in a particular order; however, they are connected, and hence one table for details of vehicle and assigned officer can do the same task, so these were merged and the user provided with sorting functionalities for each column so that the user can sort them and hence have a taxonomy. This was the case with Location, FIR, and Incident tabs on the pane; hence these were deleted as well.

Now when the user clicks on one of the FIRs the map is centered at the location of the incident with only the units involved in the incident being displayed. Similarly when the user clicks on a vehicle the map is centered at that vehicle, providing the user the view he or she needs to assess the situation in real time and alter the tasks assigned to these vehicles on the fly.

Figures CS2.15 and CS2.16 show the redesigned left pane with the changes.

- Problem 3: difficult to search for data within these pane tabs if too many data lines are presented.

Solution: quick search added for each expanded tab.

When the tab is expanded and there are too many lines of data present, although these tabs are scrollable, in situations where the user might want to search for say officer "Mike

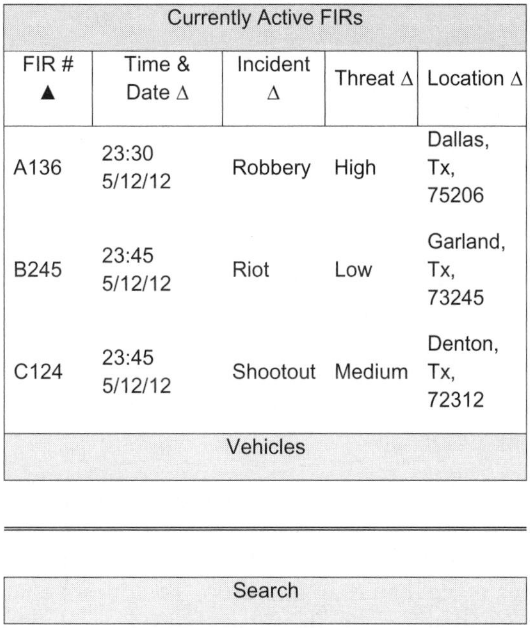

Currently Active FIRs				
FIR # ▲	Time & Date Δ	Incident Δ	Threat Δ	Location Δ
A136	23:30 5/12/12	Robbery	High	Dallas, Tx, 75206
B245	23:45 5/12/12	Riot	Low	Garland, Tx, 73245
C124	23:45 5/12/12	Shootout	Medium	Denton, Tx, 72312
Vehicles				

Search

Figure CS2.15:
Low-fidelity prototype — second iteration for PC&CS — dynamic side taskbar.

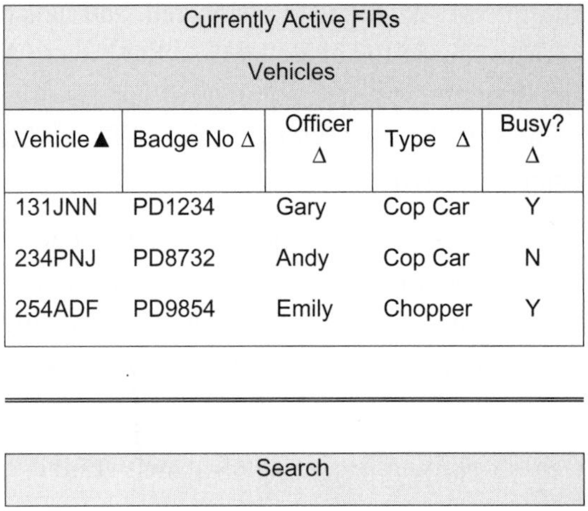

Currently Active FIRs				
Vehicles				
Vehicle ▲	Badge No Δ	Officer Δ	Type Δ	Busy? Δ
131JNN	PD1234	Gary	Cop Car	Y
234PNJ	PD8732	Andy	Cop Car	N
254ADF	PD9854	Emily	Chopper	Y

Search

Figure CS2.16:
Low-fidelity prototype – second iteration for PC&CS – dynamic side taskbar.

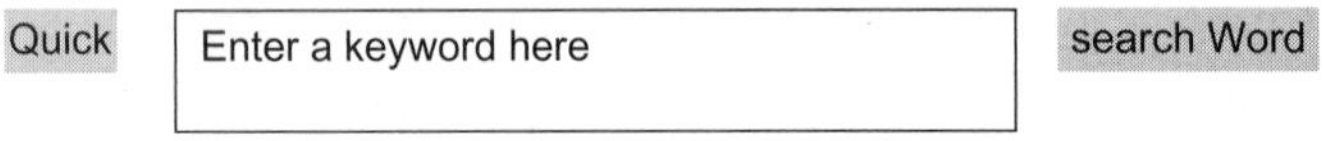

Quick	Enter a keyword here	search Word

Figure CS2.17:
Low-fidelity prototype – second iteration for PC&CS – quick-search bar.

Hanigan", he or she will have to go through the entire list. A small quick-search box was added at the beginning of the table underneath the tab to address this issue. The search box would work like a keyword search from the data being presented underneath it, thus a user searching for "Mike" would get all the lines that have that word in them.

For quick access a quick search was added to the "Currently Active FIRs" as well to speed up user access should he or she need to search for a needle in a haystack (Figure CS2.17).

- Problem 4: User wants to assign a vehicle he or she has found in the table under the vehicle pane to an active incident: there is no way to do it other than drag and drop the vehicle to the incident.

Solution: add right-click context menu to items on the task pane as well as the map.

If the user wants to assign a vehicle to an incident from the data on the task pane, he or she cannot do it by any means other than drag and drop. To address context menus for the FIR data items were added as well as vehicle data items on the pane. Also added were the same context menus for their map counterparts (the right-click menus are shown in Figures CS2.18 and CS2.19).

- Problem 5: user did not find any keyboard shortcuts for frequently encountered tasks.

Solution: add keyboard shortcuts, maintaining consistency with the conventions and inform the user in some way or other.

A user who works with particular software for a long time becomes quite comfortable with it and also quite efficient at getting useful work out of it. To help him get through his tasks quicker keyboard shortcuts were provided so that he doesn't have to navigate through the menus every time something needs to be done.

Shortcuts were provided for common tasks and listed right next to the place where that task appears in the main menu (Figure CS2.20).

- Problem 6: user cannot find undo button to undo his accidental deletion of the entire description he or she just typed out.

Solution: add undo and redo mechanisms to help users recover from the errors.

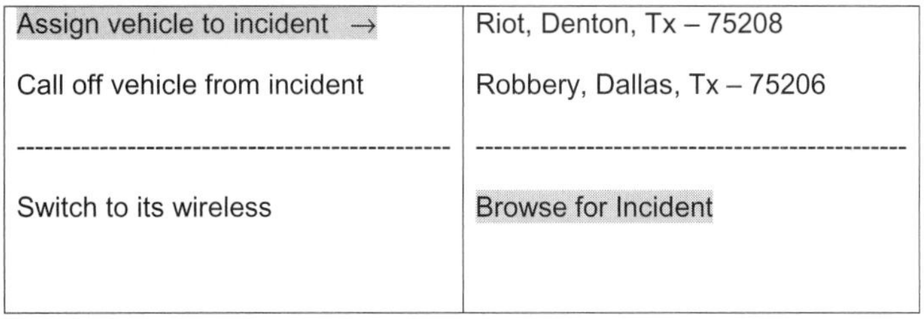

Assign vehicle to incident →	Riot, Denton, Tx – 75208
Call off vehicle from incident	Robbery, Dallas, Tx – 75206
--	--
Switch to its wireless	Browse for Incident

Figure CS2.18:
Low-fidelity prototype – second iteration for PC&CS – right-click pop-up menu for vehicle data item. Right-click menu for "Currently Active FIR" data item.

Edit FIR ...
Close & Archive FIR

Tune in to Incident Wireless

View vehicles assigned to only this ...

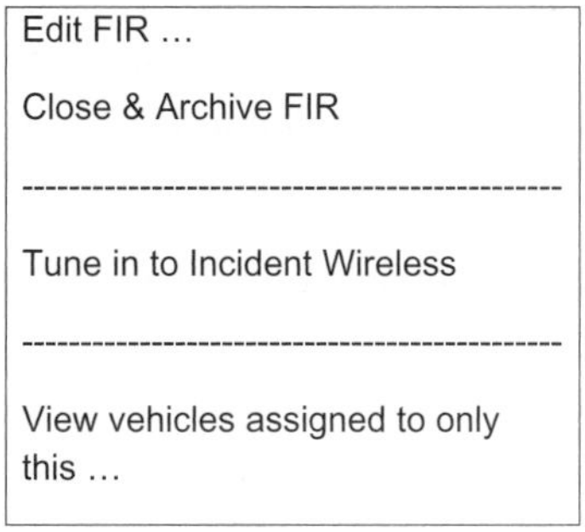

Figure CS2.19:
Low-fidelity prototype – second iteration for PC&CS – right-click pop-up menu for "Currently Active FIR" data item.

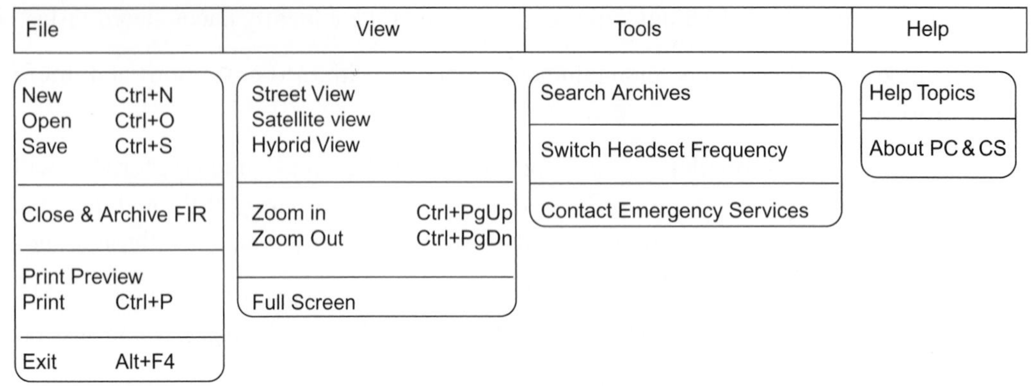

Figure CS2.20:
Low-fidelity prototype – second iteration for PC&CS – hierarchical menu bar.

File
Edit
View
Tools
Help
New Ctrl+N
Open Ctrl+O
Save Ctrl+S
Close & Archive FIR
Print Preview
Print Ctrl+P
Exit Alt+F4
Undo Ctrl+Z
Repeat Ctrl+Y
Cut Ctrl+X
Copy Ctrl+C
Paste Ctrl+V
Delete Del
Street View
Satellite View
Hybrid View
Zoom in Ctrl+PgUp
Zoom Out Ctrl+PgDn
Full Screen
Search Archives
Switch Headset Frequency
Contact Emergency Services
Help Topics
About PC & CS

Figure CS2.21:
Low-fidelity prototype – second iteration for PC&CS – hierarchical menu bar.

Very often users commit an act which deletes some of the data or information that is not yet saved, hence there should be mechanisms for the user to overcome such accidents. An "Edit" menu was added in the hierarchical menu at the top which has all the editing actions such cut, copy, paste, delete and, most important of these, undo.

Figure CS2.21 is the re-designed menu hierarchy for the same.

- Problem 7: user cannot find a taskbar for frequently used functions.

Solution: add a taskbar for frequently used functions.

The user doesn't want to navigate through the menus each and every time since mouse control can be slightly tricky and also for the novice who is not yet acquainted with the

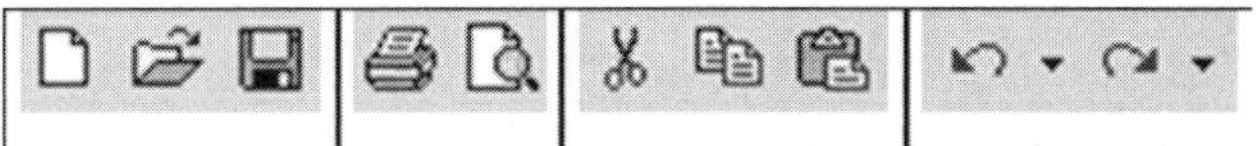

Figure CS2.22:
Low-fidelity prototype — second iteration for PC&CS — icons on the task bar.

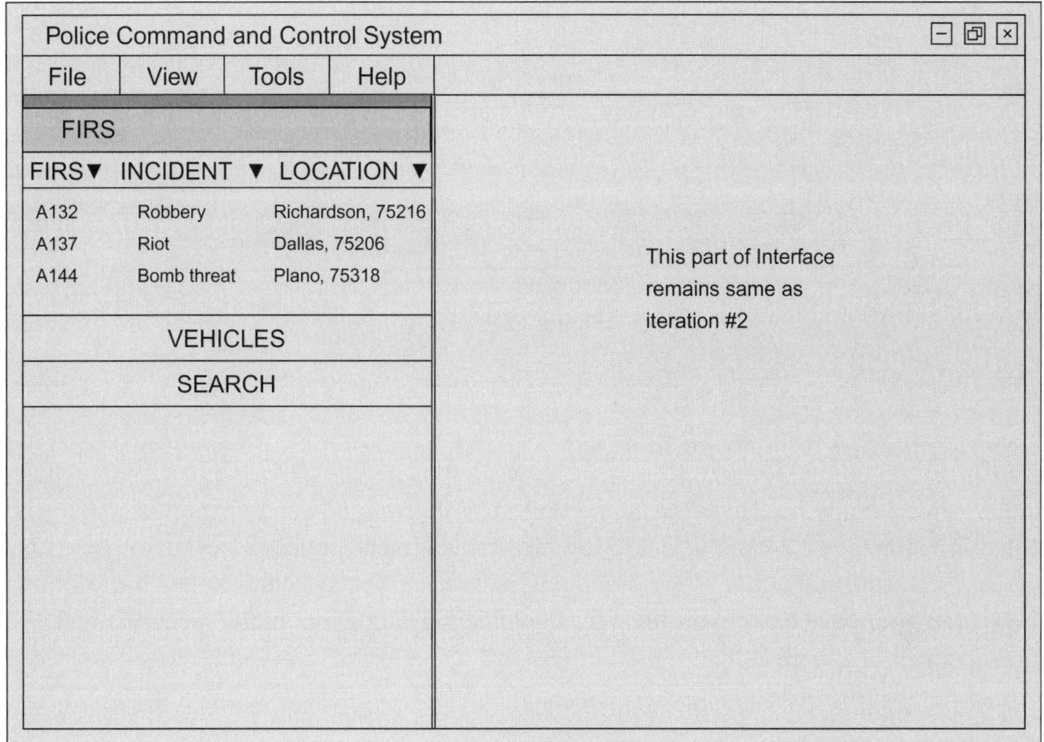

Figure CS2.23:
Finalized low-fidelity prototype — third iteration for PC&CS — entry screen.

keyboard shortcuts, so to speed up tasks by a small amount I provide the users with a task bar as shown in Figure CS2.22.

Final version of low-level prototypes

A final update to the low fidelity prototype is shown in Figure CS2.23.

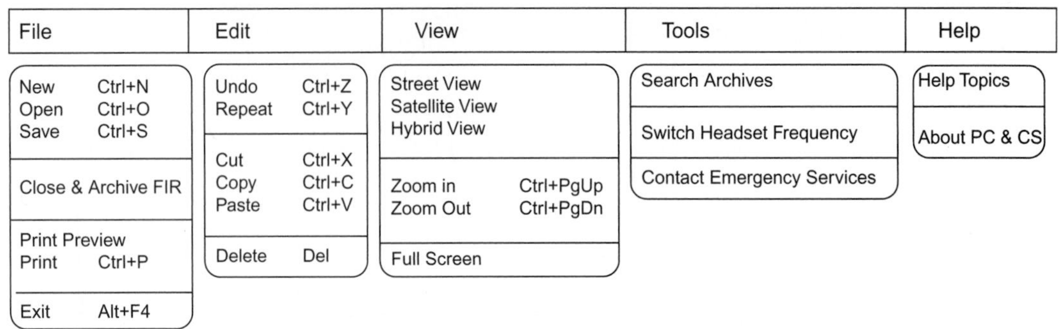

Figure CS2.24:
Low-fidelity prototype – second iteration for PC&CS – hierarchical menu bar.

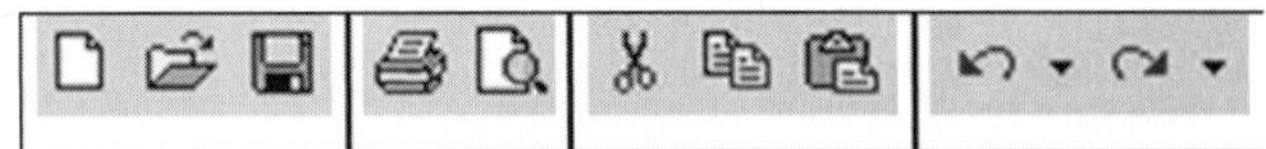

Figure CS2.25:
Low-fidelity prototype – second iteration for PC&CS – icons on the task bar.

Support transition from novice to expert

Additional capability was added to support a transition from novice to expert user. This is shown in Figures CS2.24 and CS2.25. The hierarchical menu supports keyboard shortcuts and uses standard shortcut keys for desktop applications. The system supports a transition of the user from novice to expert level by implementing shortcuts in the menu bar and quick icons on the toolbar.

High-fidelity prototype

The high fidelity prototype is as shown in Figures CS2.26, CS2.27, and CS2.28. This design was finalized after evaluation and feedback from an independent third person. Though there might still be certain flaws, the design process is an iterative process and there is plenty of scope for further exploration and subsequent improvement of the design, but within the stipulated time and scope of the project, this is the final functional prototype.

Quick-start guide

- Introduction to police command and control system (PC&CS):

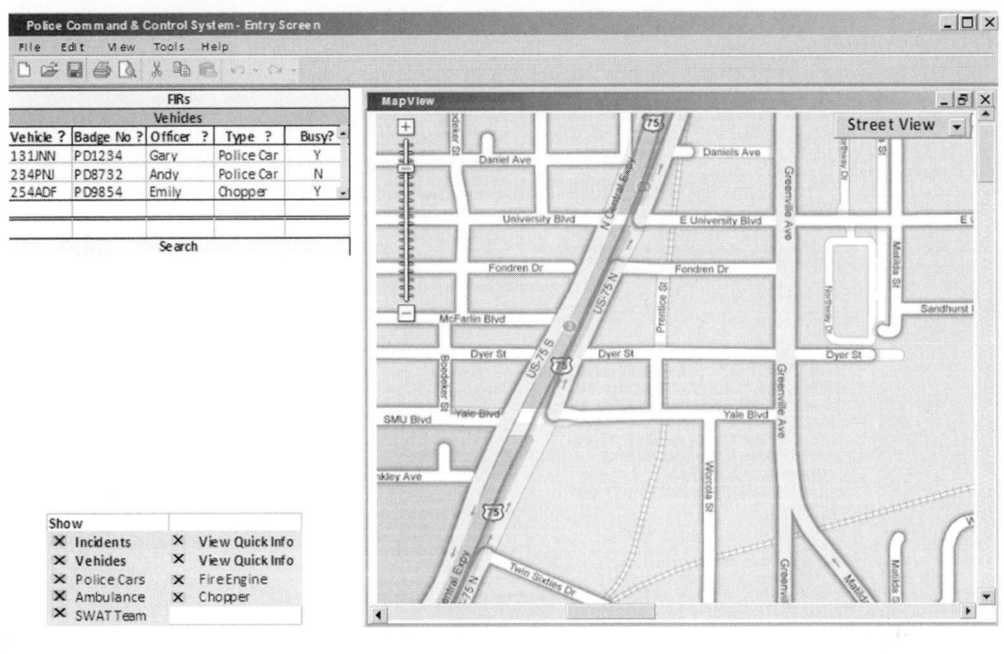

Figure CS2.26:
High-fidelity prototype — entry screen.

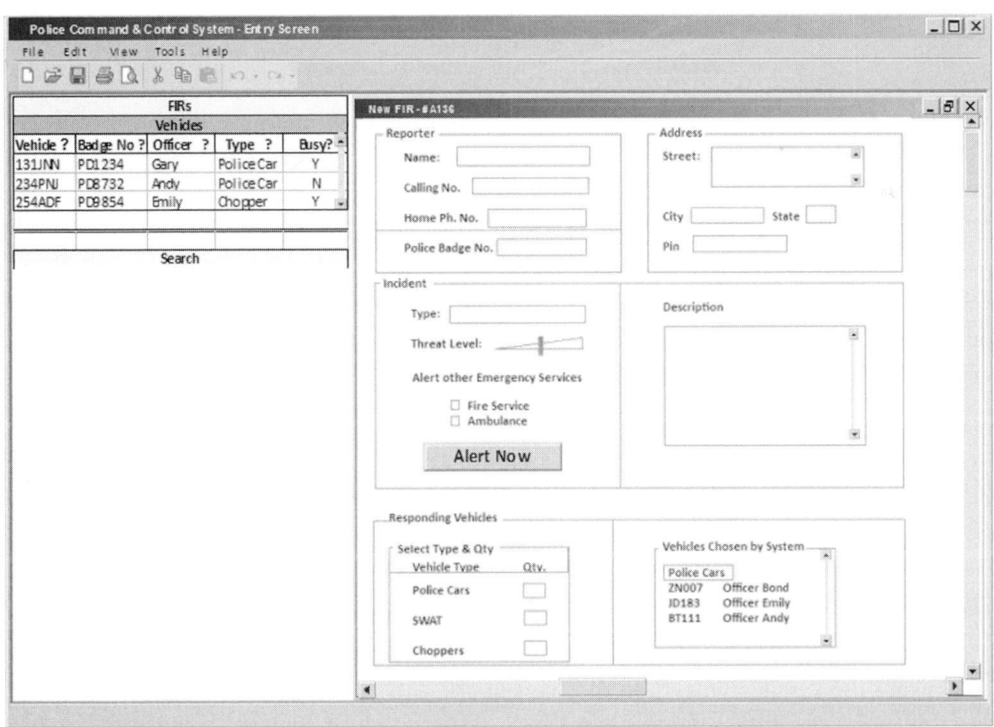

Figure CS2.27:
High-fidelity prototype — FIR screen.

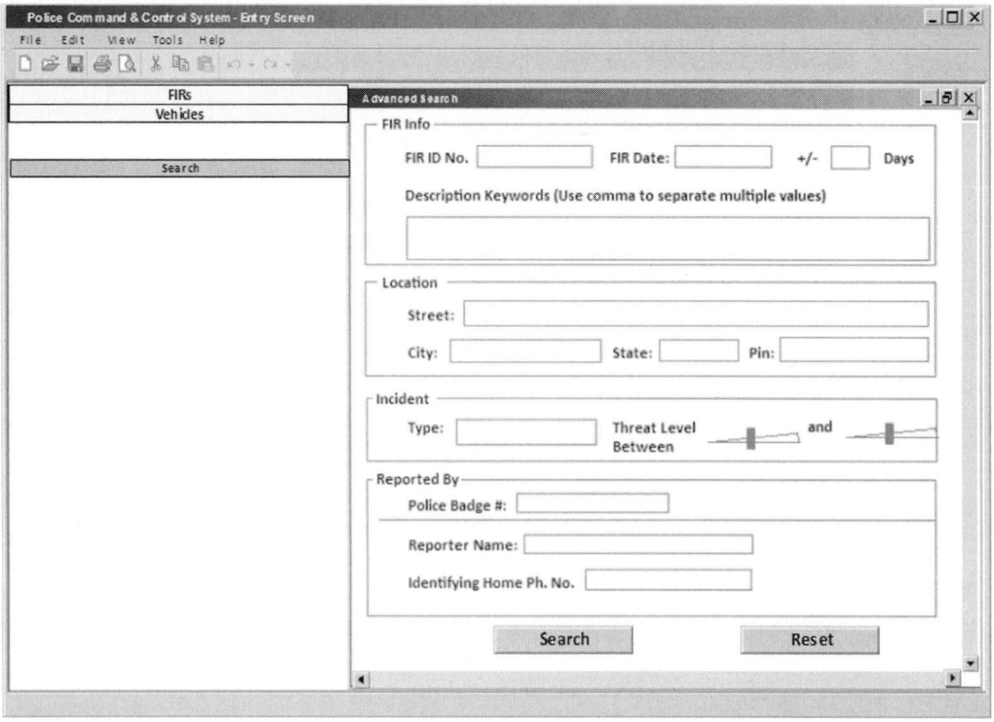

Figure CS2.28:
High-fidelity prototype — search screen.

PC&CS is a client-side police command and control application that can help a dispatcher to dispatch police services as quickly as possible to the reported incidents. The objective of PC&CS is to ensure that incidents are logged and routed quickly to the most appropriate vehicle. The PC&CS can act as a centralized control system since it can also alert emergency services in the case of special incidents.

- How to file an FIR.
  1. After login, go to Menu: File → New.
  2. The current FIR number is shown at the top of the input form.
  3. Enter the name of the reporter or the identification of the police agent who is reporting the incident.
  4. Enter the address of location where the incident is taking place.
  5. Enter the type of incident taking place at the location mentioned or select the type using the suggestive and predictive search.
  6. Assign a threat level to the incident

7. If other emergency services need to be alerted about the incident, select Other Emergency Services and press Alert now. Ensure that you have entered the address and the description of the incident.
8. Select the vehicle type and quantity from the responding vehicles sections. You can overview the selected vehicles in the "Vehicles chosen/suggested by the system" section.
9. Hit Ctrl + S or go to Menu: File → Save.
10. You can now monitor and update the current incident(s) saved in the current FIR on a map.
11. After the incident is resolved, you can update the status of the incident as closed and archive it. This incident can be searched using the search functionality for future reference.

CASE STUDY 3

Transitioning to Multicore

Shuai Wang and Robert Oshana

Typical Application Software Overview

The transition to multicore processing requires changing the software programming model, scheduling, partitioning, and optimization strategies. Software often requires modifications to divide the workload among cores and accelerators, thereby utilizing all the available processing in the system and maximizing performance.

Networking systems, for example, normally include "control-plane" software and "data-plane" software (Figure CS3.1). The control plane is responsible for the management and maintenance protocols (e.g., OSPF, SNMP, IPSec/IKE, etc.), and other special functions such as high-availability processing, hot plug and play, hot swap, and status backup. Control-plane functions include management, configuration, protocol hand-shaking, security, and exceptions. These functions are reliability-sensitive but not extremely time-sensitive. Normally, control-plane data packets/frames only occupy ~5% of the overall system load.

Data-plane functions focus on high-throughput data processing and forwarding. Once the required connections and links are established by the control plane, most traffic is data-plane packets. Normally ~95% of the overall system load will be for data-plane packets/frames. Therefore, overall system throughput and performance is primarily dependent on data-plane processing capacity, and any optimization in this area can increase system performance significantly. The data-plane software complexity is lower, primarily focusing on packet header analysis, table lookups, encapsulation/decapsulation, counting and statistics, quality of service (QoS) scheduling, etc.

A network router is a good example of the migration from single-core processing to multicore processing. The software architecture for these products has evolved over the last several years.

- Unit routers: all software runs on a single-core CPU, including all the control-plane modules and data-plane modules. These modules are standalone tasks/processes/threads running on a real-time operating system (e.g., VxWorks). Software integrators must carefully adjust the priorities of each task to achieve improved system performance.

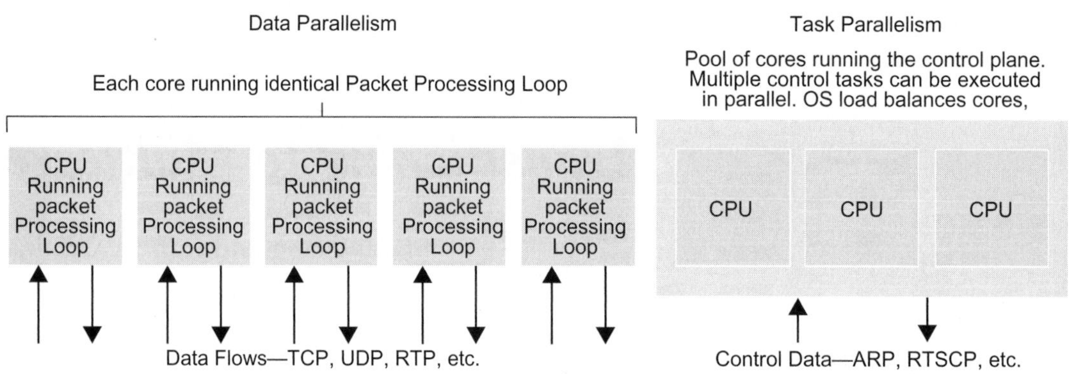

Figure CS3.1:
Data and task parallelism.

Certain high-performance functions such as table lookup actions (FIB, 5-tuple classify, NAT, etc.) are performed by software, often with the help of offline assistant engines such as Encryption/Decryption/Authentication running on a FPGA or ASIC or other acceleration device connected to the CPU for IPSec-related application use. This architecture is for ultra-low-end or low-end unit router products. System performance is lower due to centralized processing on the CPU core.

- Chassis routers: these products have a more distributed system architecture without significant support from an ASIC. The main processing unit (MPU) cards manage control-plane jobs. Line processing unit (LPU) cards manage data-plane jobs. Each MPU and LPU card contains one single-core CPU. These CPUs are connected through the backplane (normally FE/GE port switch) to each other. All user-end interfaces are provided on the LPU cards. The MPU cards only provide management interface and heartbeat/backup interfaces. The LPU cards may have optional acceleration engines (encrypt/decrypt etc. FPGA/ASICs) sitting beside the CPU. The master MPU will discover the routing topologies and generate the FIB entries to each LPU. The LPUs will do the forwarding etc. data-plane jobs for user data packets themselves. Both MPU and LPU run multiple tasks on top of a real-time operating system. Overall system performance is much better than unit routers due to the distributed processing and LPU scalability features.
- Chassis high-end routers: the software architecture is a distributed system architecture with ASIC/NP. Each LPU card contains additional acceleration (ASIC or NP chip) which is powerful enough to perform the data-plane jobs at very high speed. Normally, the backplane connecting all ASICs/NPs is composed of some specific crossbar or fabric. The general CPU on each LPU card will do the IPC (inter-processor communication) jobs and configure the ASIC/NP tables. There are some differences between the ASIC architecture and the NP architecture; the ASIC

can provide higher and steadier data-processing rates than the NP, while the NP can provide more flexible functionality. MPU and LPU will run multiple tasks over a real-time operating system.

For the three software architectures described above, the software running on each CPU is still a logical standalone system – the programming model is still single-core. Even for distributed systems, the key system resources (memory, ports, etc.) are still managed by each CPU, with limited IPC between the CPUs.

When porting to a multicore system, there are several key areas to focus on from a software programming model perspective;

- overall system partitioning (mainly cores, memory, and port resources)
- operating system consideration (control-plane OS section and migration, data-plane bare-board or lightweight run-time environment decisions)
- data-plane core working architecture (functionality bound to each core/core-group)
- decision of the mutex mechanism and implementation
- how to share data-plane tables among all data-plane cores (and the decision of the shared memory mechanism)
- decision on the inter-core communication mechanism
- decision on the use of system global variables, and CPU global variables
- migration of the Rx/Tx driver
- implementation of architecture-specific accelerators
- control-plane partition and data-plane partition communications.

Software system partition

The software system must be partitioned into two parts – control plane and data plane. The first decision is how many cores should be assigned for control-plane use and how many cores for data-plane use. Standard software performance engineering estimates can be used to determine how many cores are required for this purpose.

Control-plane software migration

The control-plane partition will normally run an operating system such as Linux or even a real-time operating system if required, to provide a multitasking environment for the user software components. This is fairly straightforward and most legacy control-plane software components will not require large changes for this migration. But there are a few key points that need attention:

- For the single-core architecture system, control-plane software shares all the data-plane tables inside the same CPU memory space. Updating these tables requires a direct write with a semaphore-like mutex protection. On a multicore platform, the table update actions are different – table updates are performed either by sending self-defined messages to data-plane cores for the update, or via a direct write to the shared table (memory shared between partitions/cores) with splinlock/RCU mutex protection.

- When using more than one core in the control-plane partition, the most common configuration is symmetric multiprocessing (SMP) mode. The legacy multitasking software should be checked to make sure it will run correctly and efficiently in an SMP environment, especially the inter-task communication (mutex or synchronization, etc.) mechanisms.

Data-plane software migration

Data-plane software migration to multicore is more difficult. The data-plane partition will typically perform the following functions;

- data-packet processing
- data communication with the control-plane partition
- management proxy processing.

The legacy data-plane software typically runs on an RTOS which supports a multitasking environment. Data-packet processing is a run-to-completion execution model, executing in one single task/process/kernel-thread. For example in VxWorks, the data-packet processing is done in the tNetTask environment. In Linux, the data-packet processing is done in the NET_RX_SOFTIRQ software interrupt environment. Whether using tNetTask or softirq, the priority must be high to prevent being preempted during processing, and keeping overall system performance as high as possible.

The management proxy component in legacy software is typically composed of one or more tasks running in parallel with the data-packet-processing task. The proxy component waits for management or configuration instructions from the control-plane modules to update the data tables or to perform other high-priority tasks. These tasks must have a priority as high as or even higher than the data-packet-processing task. Since the management proxy task does not execute often, the data-packet-processing task will not be preempted often, and impact on system performance is minor.

When migrating to a multicore environment, the most efficient way to configure the data-plane partition is to run in a "bare-metal" mode or a similar lightweight executive (LWE) mode. These are run-to-completion environments and are more efficient than a multitasking environment.

At first glance, it may seem relatively straightforward to migrate legacy data-packet-processing task code to a multicore environment. These tasks are run-to-completion written in standard C code. This is true only from a functional perspective. But on the data plane, performance is king, and the number one concern for the data-plane partition. To achieve the highest performance possible, some additional optimization is necessary.

Parallel processing of data packets

Consider the data-packet-processing routing function execution flow in Figure CS3.2.

```
/****************************
 * data processing task
 ****************************/

do {

  rxpkt_from_hw();      // get a packet from the hardware.
  l2_process();         // Link layer verification.
  classify();           // lookup classify-table with 5-Tuples to get the according Qos values.
  ip_table_lookup();    // lookup the FIB table with DIP to get the gateway-IP and egress port-id.
  arp_lookup();         // lookup the ARP table with gw-IP to get the gateway-MAC address.
  l2_modify();          // replace the original SMAC/DMAC with the proper ones.
  txpkt_to_hw();        // send packet out to the hardware.

} while (1);
```

This is a very simple routing process. The code can be easily ported to the data-plane cores to run in parallel as shown in Figure CS3.3.

Multicore processors allow each core to share traffic from a shared user port. For example the P4080 multicore device uses the frame manager (FMan) acceleration block which has

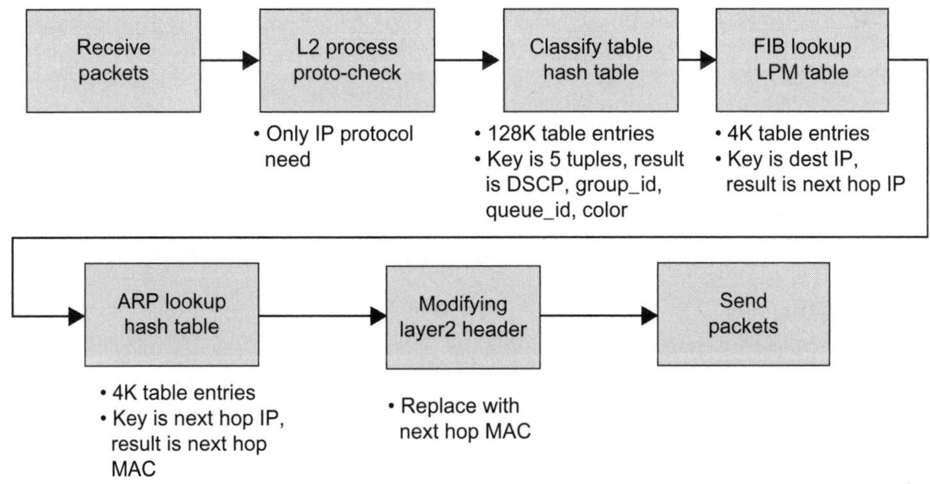

Figure CS3.2:
Network packet-processing routing function execution flow.

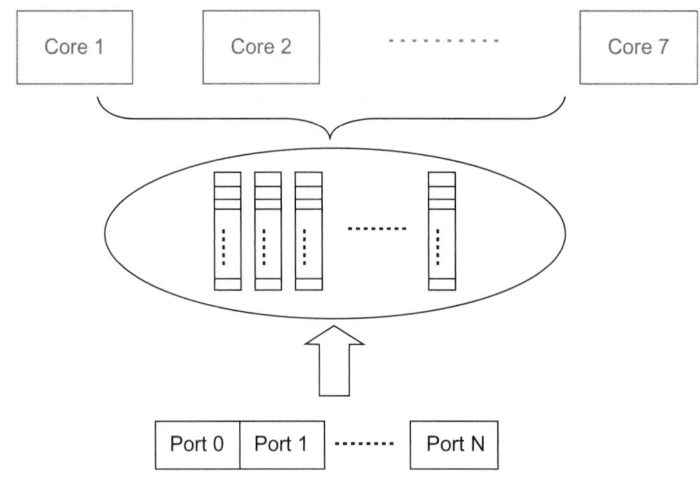

Figure CS3.3:
Multicore implementation of network packet-processing routing function.

the ability to load-balance traffic from one port to a group of frame queues (FQs). Any one of the data-plane cores can receive packets to process from any of these frame queues while the sequence number of each of the flows remains unchanged.

In the data-processing task pseudo code in Figure CS3.2, rxpkt_from_hw() and txpkt_to_hw() are architecture-specific driver code. On the P4080 platform, they draw packets from FQs and feed packets to FQs with the help of a queue manager (QMan). This is different from single-core devices, where the Ethernet controller's RxBD and TxBD are memory-mapped to CPU memory space for direct access, which prevents the Ethernet port from being shared by more than one core.

The classify(), ip_table_lookup() and arp_lookup() functions have one key difference between multicore platforms and single-core devices. The lookup tables are shared among all CPU cores.

As shown in Figure CS3.4, there are three types of memory on modern multicore platforms;

- core-private memory
- partition-global-memory-among-cores
- global-memory-among-partitions.

On a single-core system, lookup tables are protected by semaphores to provide mutual exclusion. On multicore systems, lookup tables are often protected by spinlocks.
But for lookup tables that are read by the data-plane cores more than they are written to by the control-plane cores, a better choice would be RCU (read copy update) locks.

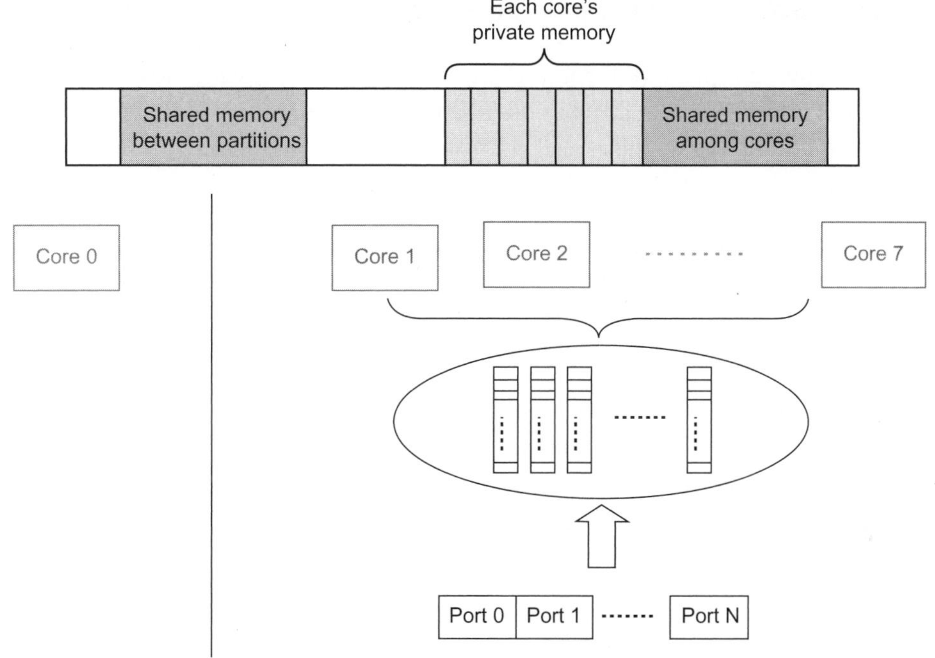

Figure CS3.4:
Multicore memory models.

Different memory areas have different allocation/free APIs for software use. For example, on the P4080 lightweight executive environment, the core private memory block is allocated by tlmalloc() while the partition global memory block is allocated by malloc(). This also needs to be considered when migrating.

In addition to memory blocks, global variables are also divided to multiple types;

- percpu global-variables
- partition-global-variables-among-cores
- global-variables-among-partitions.

As with memory blocks, global variables also have different uses. For example, the macro PERCPU is used for percpu global-vars definition.

In some applications, routing functions are pipelined. One core does the classify() operations and then delivers packets to downstream cores to do the ip_lookup() and other functions. However, a pipelined approach does not take advantage of warm caches. A parallel approach, as described above, should be able to provide better overall system performance than a pipelined approach due to warmed-cache effects.

Hybrid approaches (parallel plus pipeline)

Figure CS3.5 shows a typical QoS-routing process. As this processing flow shows, data packets will not be sent out directly but queued into a set of software queues. An additional scheduling task will de-queue these packets from the software queues and send them out in a given sequence.

On legacy single-core systems, this queue/de-queue operation requires two tasks to implement – one for the packet-processing task, and the other for the scheduling task. The software queues are shared between the two tasks and protected by semaphores as shown in the pseudocode in Figure CS3.6.

In multicore systems, it is more difficult to allocate these operations to data-plane cores in parallel because of the restriction of having only one QoS scheduler in the system. The ingress pipe (yellow blocks in Figure CS3.5) can be run in parallel on multiple cores while the egress pipe (brown blocks) must run on a single core.

Figure CS3.7 shows the partitioning of ingress and egress processing on a multicore device. The data-plane cores are configured in two groups – one group for the ingress pipe, the other group for the egress pipe. In this case, the egress pipe core group has only one core. The ingress pipe cores do the data-packet-processing tasks. The egress pipe core does the scheduling tasks. The shared soft-queues are protected with spinlocks.

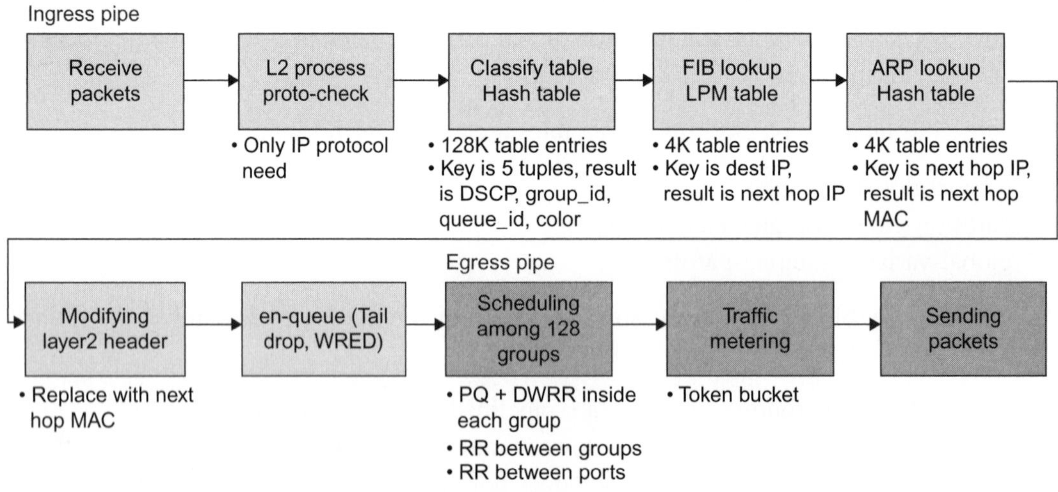

Figure CS3.5:
Typical networking quality-of-service algorithm processing flow.

```
/***************************
 * data processing task
 ***************************/
do {

  rxpkt_from_hw();      // get a packet from the hardware.
  l2_process();         // Link layer verification.
  classify();           // lookup classify-table with 5-Tuples to get the according Qos values.
  ip_table_lookup();    // lookup the FIB table with DIP to get the gateway-IP and egress port-id.
  arp_lookup();         // lookup the ARP table with gw-IP to get the gateway-MAC address.
  l2_modify();          // replace the original SMAC/DMAC with the proper ones.
  enque();              // enque the packet to the soft-queues.

} while (1);

/***************************
 * scheduling task
 ***************************/
do {

  deque();              // deque packet from the soft-queues according to rule.
  tbucket_meter();      // token bucket metering to each packet.
  txpkt_to_hw();        // send packet out to the hardware.

} while (1);
```

Figure CS3.6:
Queuing and de-queuing operations in a single-core system.

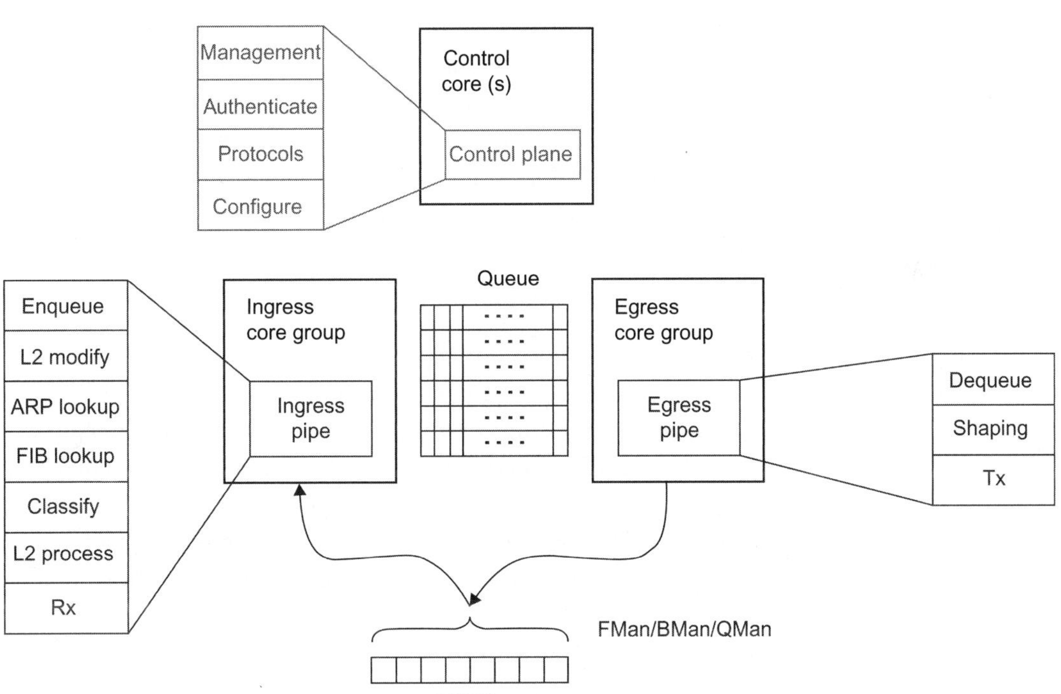

Figure CS3.7:
Ingress and egress processing on multicore.

Data communication with control-plane partition

On legacy single-core systems, control-plane packets (management, protocol handshaking, etc.) are branched to the corresponding control tasks at the IP stack level, according to the DIP address (local host, multicast, broadcast, etc.) or/and IP protocol values (OSPF, BGP, IGMP, etc.).

Multicore systems often incorporate hardware assistant mechanisms (in the P4080, this is called the parse-classify-distribute (PCD) hardware block) on the ingress side to exact-match control-plane packets. For matched packets, the control plane receive frame queues (Rx-FQs) will be selected. By default (exact match miss), the data-plane Rx-FQs will be chosen to enqueue. Thus, it's possible for data-plane cores to receive packets that belong to the control plane. Occasionally, packets that cannot be forwarded (due to no route) must be delivered to the control plane for ICMP report replies.

To port this software from a single-core system to a multicore system, a data channel between the control-plane partition and the data-plane partition must be established. For example, in the P4080, queue manager frame queues (QMan FQs) can be used as the data channel. This approach provides high efficiency (no spinlock needed) and a uniform interface. This provides a more efficient mechanism than the common shared memory (software message queues) approach.

An internal message communication system is also needed for efficient processing. In addition to the user data packet information, other control information (reason, actions, src_port, etc.) is needed for the control-plane partition for robust processing. For example, the scatter/gather buffer structure on the P4080 make it more efficient to pre-patch an additional message to the original data-packet before delivering to the control plane.

Management proxy

Management proxies also vary between single core and multicore systems. Multicore systems targeted for network processing have many management and configuration instructions supporting communication from the control plane to the data plane. Examples include table-update, IP-address/MAC-address configuration, statistics collection, core-state change, and core-regroup. Some of these management and configuration operations can be performed directly through global shared memory. Others cannot. A control channel and internal message system are needed to implement these if the global shared memory approach does not support this.

Rx/Tx drivers

Different device architectures have different receive/transmit drivers. Multicore devices often share Ethernet ports as a necessity. This requires a significantly different Ethernet driver implementation than the legacy memory-mapped BD-ring approach for most single-core devices.

For example, on the P4080 the Ethernet ports are virtualized. This brings some new concerns about congestion-avoidance issues.

An example of legacy Ethernet driver pseudocode is shown below for the "transmit packet to hardware" (txpkt_to_hw());

```
int txpkt_to_hw(void)
{
  ....

  if (enque_pkt_to_txbd() == OK) {
    /* TxPkt successfully */
  } else {
    /* dport in congestion */
    do_congestion_avoidance();
  }

  return 0;
}
```

In this example, the enque_pkt_to_txbd() function returns the congestion state directly in a synchronous operation. The legacy congestion-avoidance code can be executed immediately after the TxPkt call.

On a multicore device like the P4080 LWE, the txpkt_to_hw() is implemented differently:

```
int txpkt_to_hw(void)
{
  ....

again:
  if (qman_enqueue() == OK) {
    /* EQCR successfully but may be rejected by FQs */
  } else {
    /* EQCR in congestion but can't indicate which FQs are in congestion */
    // can't //do_congestion_avoidance();
    goto again;
  }

  return 0;
}
```

TxBDs in this case are virtualized by the queue manager frame queues. One QMan portal can access many QMan FQs, so the EQCR full status cannot indicate which FQ is in congestion mode (not the legacy synchronous mode in this case). The congestion-avoidance software must be changed to an asynchronous approach, which may or may not be desired.

CASE STUDY 4

Software Engineering for Embedded Systems Quality and Metrics Program

Robert Oshana

This case study will look at software development and system integration metrics for an embedded system. Actual industry data is used to reinforce many of the techniques discussed in the case study.

A femtocell is a low-power, short-range, self-contained base station. Femtocells are essentially mini base stations for the home and small offices. The key attributes of femtocells include IP backhaul (voice traffic is sent off the internet), self-optimization, low power consumption and ease of deployment.

Femtocells fall under the umbrella of "small cell", which is an umbrella term for low-powered radio access nodes operating in both licensed and unlicensed spectra with a range of 10 meters to several hundred meters (see Figure CS4.1).

Femtocell applications include residential, enterprise, hot spot, and metro.

The software architecture for a femtocell is shown in Figure CS4.2. This software architecture is composed of a Layer 1 software application which is primarily optimized signal-processing software written to run on a DSP, and a Layer 2 application which is control and scheduling software running on a general-purpose processor (GPP). A femto application programming interface (FAPI) is the interface between Layer 1 and Layer 2.

Development methodology

The software design process starts with algorithm implementation in floating point (Figure CS4.3). Matlab is used as the simulation tool. After initial floating-point simulation, data quantization on the function interfaces is introduced. This requires the inclusion of normalization and scaling and alignment operations. This emulation model allows a first level of validation of the performance, but is not bit exact with the final C implementation. The final Matlab model is based on DSP C code that was reintroduced into Matlab.

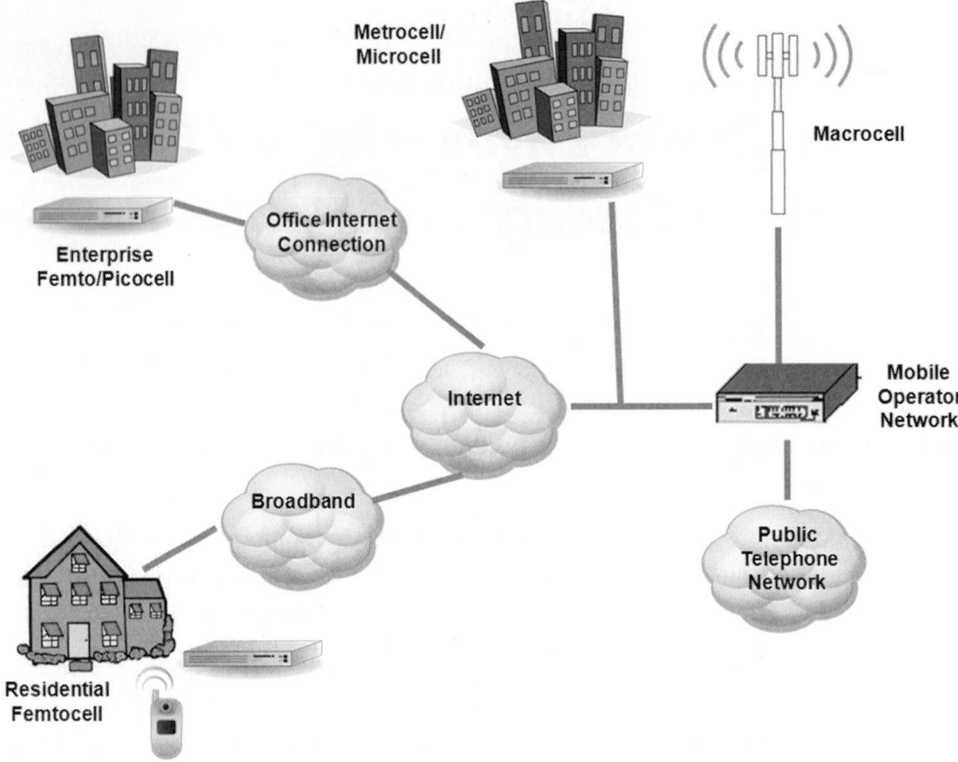

Figure CS4.1:
Femtocell technology.

This program involved the Layer 1 software being developed by the primary vendor. Layer 2 was contracted out to a software development partner and delivered into final system integration and test, which was managed by the primary vendor.

This program was an iterative development process, based loosely on the agile development model. The goal of an iterative development model is to develop a system through repeated cycles and in smaller portions at a time. This allows software developers to take advantage of what was learned during development of earlier versions of the system. This learning comes from both the development as well as the customer use of the system. Key steps in this process start with a simple implementation of a subset of the software requirements. That simple implementation is then iteratively enhanced in constantly evolving versions until the full system is implemented. At each iteration, design modifications are made (re-factoring) and new capabilities are added. Figure CS4.4 shows a diagram of the iterative development model used for this program.

The test program for the femtocell is based on the standard software testing "V" model which is shown in Figure CS4.5. Component testing is performed using a combination of

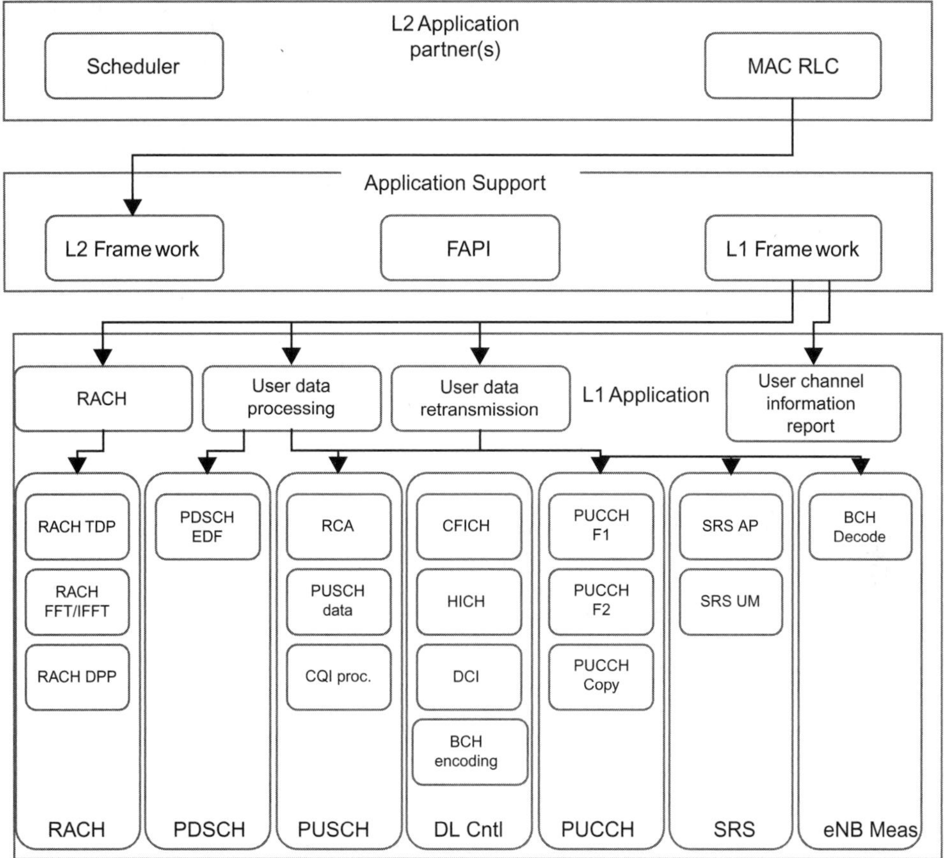

Figure CS4.2:
LTE Layer 1 application components.

static and dynamic analysis tools, unit testing, code reviews, cyclomatic complexity measures (and the necessary re-factoring), and statement coverage to assess overall software testing coverage and effectiveness.

Integration testing is based on testing the L1 layer (L1 is the primary software the vendor was responsible for delivering) through the FAPI interface. System integration testing was performed by the primary vendor and focused on use case/scenario-based testing of the entire system prior to shipping to the final customers. Some of these customers used their own L2 software instead of the L2 software integrated and tested with the final system. This required additional integration activities.

The overall component development flow is shown in Figure CS4.6. Initial Matlab models are validated and then converted into optimized DSP C software and unit-tested using the process shown in Figure CS4.5. These test results are then compared with the Matlab

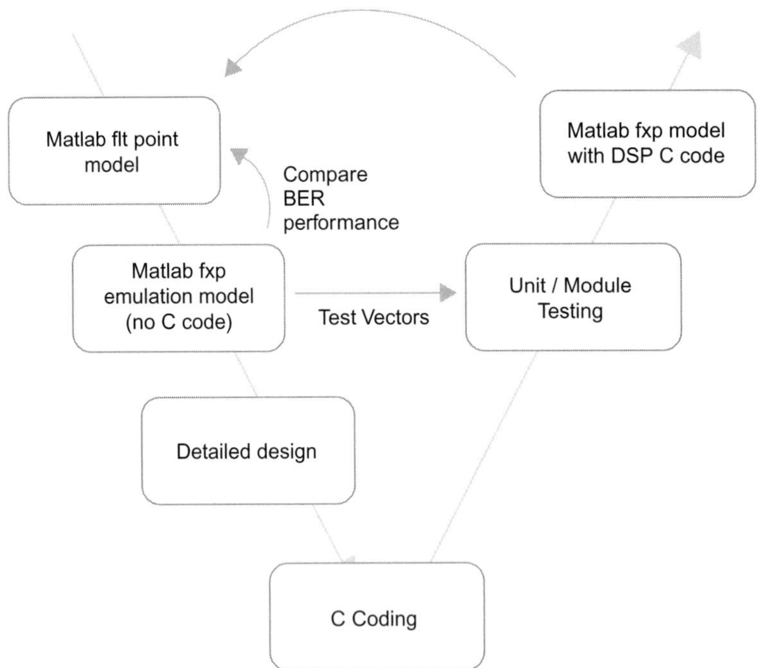

Figure CS4.3:
Femtocell development methodology.

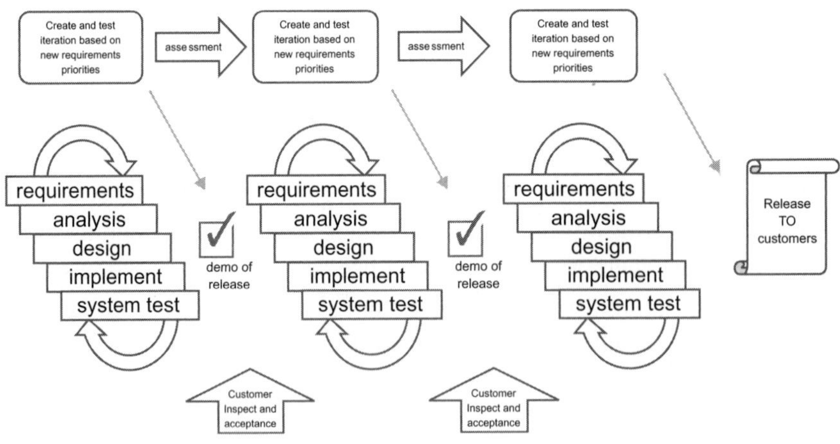

Figure CS4.4:
An iterative software development model.

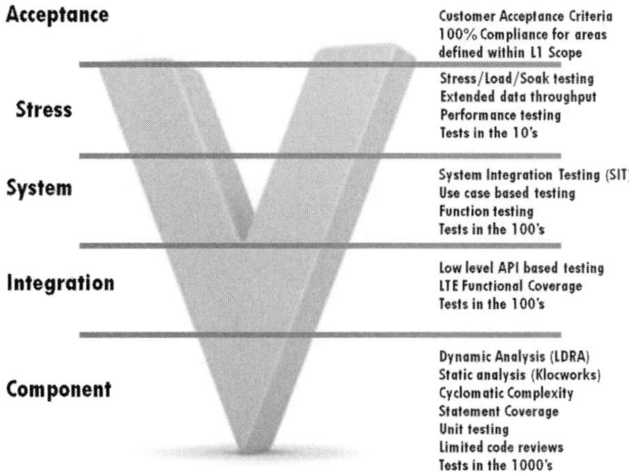

Figure CS4.5:
Layer 1 testing model.

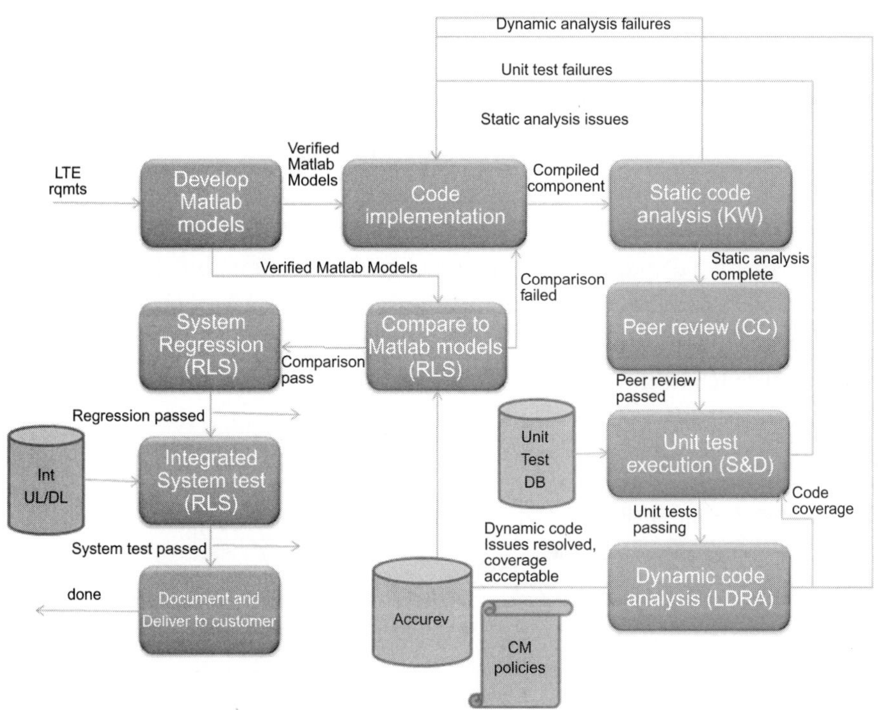

Figure CS4.6:
Development flow.

models to ensure bit accuracy of the implementations. These components are then integrated into subsystems and systems and tested in a controlled environment on a radio link simulator (RLS).

Before any software product or service can be recognized as having adequate quality, the appropriate standards must be put into place. Otherwise, it is impossible to judge the good from the bad. Only by determining exact measurements of quality is it possible to determine whether overall quality goals are being met.

Software metrics could be considered one of the single most important tools in software process improvement. Software metrics indicate to what extent desired characteristics are present and which ones may be missing. Efficiently improving factors such as reliability, volatility, errors and failure rates depends entirely on being able to measure all existing values.

Consistent measures are the only way to know that software development processes are improving. Repair, replacement and modification are only possible through the identification of present conditions. Precise formulas for monitoring functions like complexity and reliability provide benchmarks that enable consistent advancement. The intricate nature of software requires that it be quantified in a detailed and specific manner. Software metrics are the essential ingredients that allow software to be comprehensively analyzed and, over time, brought to its full potential and expectations.

A metrics program was initiated to manage and control the software development activities. The Goal Question Metric (GQM) model was used to drive this process (Figure CS4.7). The fundamental assumption for GQM is that for an organization to measure anything in a meaningful way it must first specify the goals for its projects, and then trace those goals to the specific data that is necessary to define those goals operationally. This data must also be interpreted with respect to the stated goals. Because of this, the key informational needs of the organization must be quantified and analyzed to determine whether or not the goals are achieved (see Figure CS4.8).

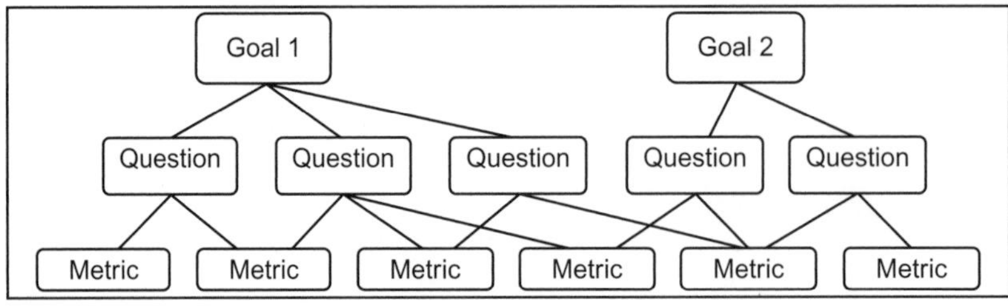

Figure CS4.7:
Goal question metric model.

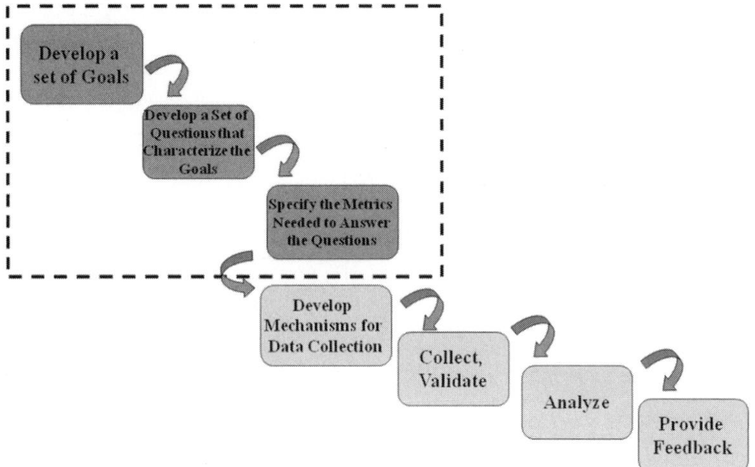

Figure CS4.8:
GQM development process.

The three levels of GQM shown in Figure CS4.7 are defined as;

1. Conceptual level (the Goal): a goal is defined based on a model of quality relative to a particular environment. These measurements can be based on products (an artifact or deliverable), a process (such as a software testing process), or resources (an example is personal on a project).
2. Operational level (the Questions): this is a set of questions that characterizes the way the assessment of the goal(s) is going to be performed. The questions selected need to characterize the object of whatever we are trying to measure (product, process, resource) as it relates to the quality goals being sought.
3. Quantitative level (the Metrics): this is the data associated with each question collected in such a way as to answer those questions in a quantitative way. The data can be objective (the number of versions of a software released or the size of a software program), or subjective (such as user satisfaction).

Metrics collection

This section summarizes some of the GQM-based metrics used for the system integration efforts for the femtocell program. This metrics program focuses primarily on L1-related measures but also includes some system performance-related measurements as well.

The GQM based metrics program for the Femtocell software system is shown in Figure CS4.9. Table CS4.1 summarizes these mapping for the GQM.

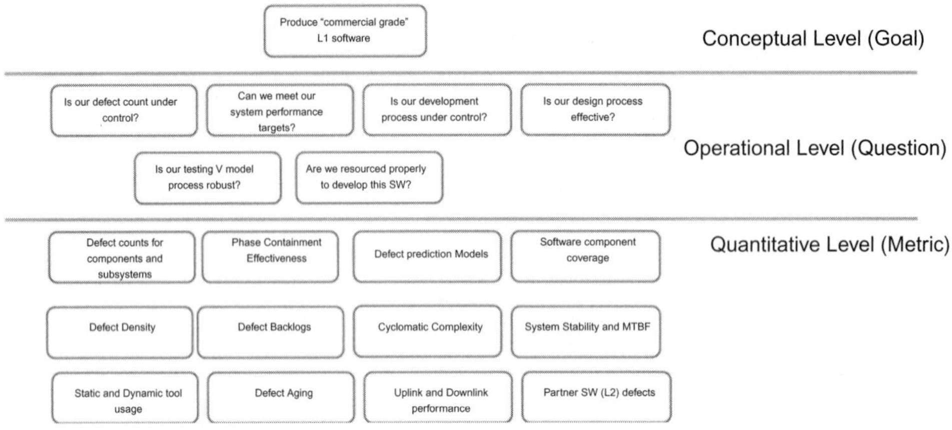

Figure CS4.9:
GQM model for the femtocell program.

Table CS4.1: GQM mappings for femto program.

Goal	Produce and deliver "Commercial Grade" Femto Software
Question	Is our defect count under control?
Metrics	Defect counts for each SW component
Question	Can we meet our system performance targets?
Metrics	Uplink and downlink performance
Question	Is our development process under control?
Metrics	Phase containment effectiveness
	Defect prediction models
	Defect density for each SW component
Question	Is our software design process effective?
Metrics	Partner defects
	System stability and MTBF
Question	Is our testing V model process robust?
Metrics	Software component coverage Static and dynamic tool usage
Question	Are we resourced properly to develop this SW?
	Defect backlog

Metric 1: total defects logged in system integration and test (SIT); this metric provides an indicator of system test stability. Once the cumulative count of defects begins to "flatten", this is an indicator of system stability. Figure CS4.10 shows a snapshot of this metric during the SIT phase. This shows a constant slope for this metric, an indicator that the system has not yet begun to stabilize. The defect backlog is also increasing, which is an indicator of on-going instability as outstanding bugs are not being addressed.

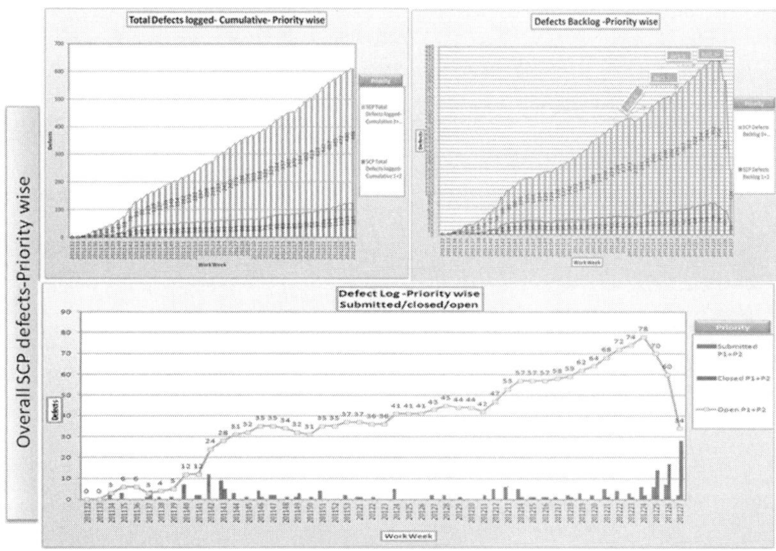

Figure CS4.10:
Defect metrics, total defects logged in system integration and test, total backlog defects, defect log by priority.

Metric 2: cumulative defects from partner-delivered software; this metric was used to provide visibility into the stability of the Layer 2 software deliveries from the third-party software provider (Figure CS4.11). The software development manager met weekly with the partner software provider to prioritize and manage this bug backlog and make decisions regarding potential design issues, performance issues, and API misinterpretations.

Metric 3: defect aging by priority and severity; this metric allows us to look at whether we have enough time and resource to burn off the outstanding defects being submitted by the SIT testing team. A growing backlog of defects is an indicator of a problem in resourcing, skill sets, and/or priorities in addressing these defects. Figure CS4.12 shows this metric for the femto program. As this metric shows, our priority 1 (P1) defects are being fixed in 4 days or less. The priority 3 (P3) defects are taking much longer, up to 2 weeks, to fix. Part of this was due to the fact that we resourced and prioritized the high-priority defects but a growing trend would still be of concern from an overall resourcing perspective.

Metric 4: phase-containment effectiveness; phase-containment effectiveness (PCE) is a technique used to measure the effectiveness of inspection and/or review conducted on software artifacts in the different phases of software development. Defects found in a later stage of the program will consume a relatively higher cost of correction. Therefore, it makes sense to promote an environment where the program team attempts to identify faults as early as possible and implement fixes within the phase in which the defect was found.

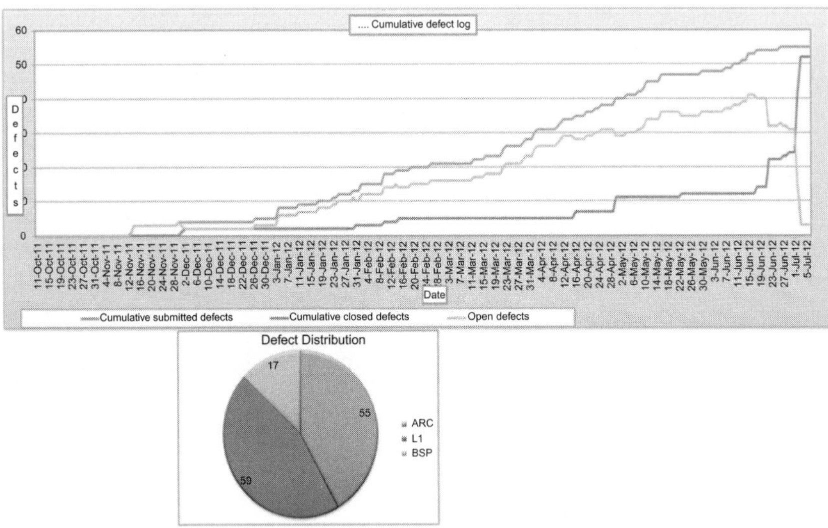

Figure CS4.11:
Cumulative defects of third-party software deliveries.

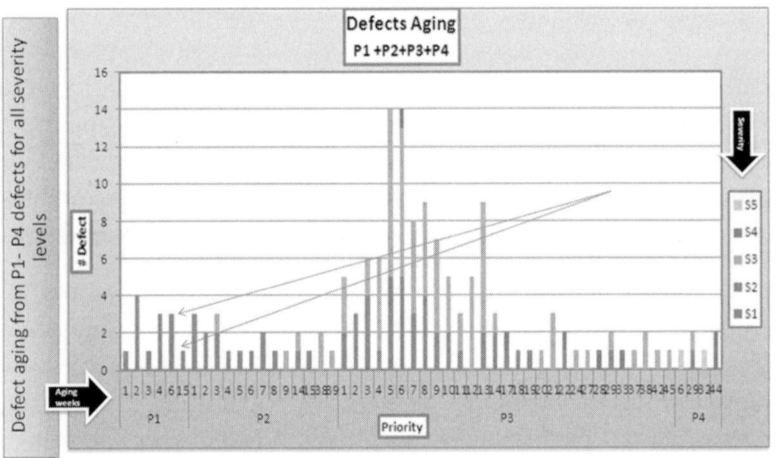

Figure CS4.12:
Defect aging by priority and severity.

PCE is a factor of the total number of errors and the total number of defects found from a software work product (see the rightmost column of Figure CS4.13). A value approaching 100% means that errors introduced are being identified in the same phase of review. The closer the value is to 100%, the more effective the review process is on a particular software work product.

S1+S2+S3		Phase Reported												
		Planning	Requirements	Archtecture	Design	Implementation/ Coding	System Integration	System Testing	Post-release	External	TotalErrors	Total Defects	Total Fauts	PCE
Phase Originated	Planning	0	0	0	0	2	0	1	0	0	0	3	3	0%
	Requirements		0	0	0	2	7	1	0	0	0	10	10	0%
	Archtecture			0	0	0	2	0	0	0	0	2	2	0%
	Design				4	6	11	5	1	0	4	23	27	15%
	Implementation/Coding					110	65	15	12	[illegible]	[illegible]	[illegible]	202	54%
	System Integration						52	16	6	[illegible]	[illegible]	22	74	70%
		0	0		4	120	137	38	19	0				

Figure CS4.13:
Overall phase containment effectiveness.

Figure CS4.13 is the overall PCE for this program. There are a couple of primary concerns with what this data is showing;

- Defects were not caught in the earlier phases of development (planning, requirements, architecture) but "escaped" to the customer. These become more expensive to fix.
- Many unit test defects escaped to system integration and test. This makes it very difficult during the SIT phase. Isolating and debugging a large number of defects that should have been caught in unit testing phases costs more time and effort and can cause program delays.

Table CS4.2 shows a summary of the key actions for improvement based on the data in the PCE. A majority of the focus on these actions for improvement involve additional code reviews, code coverage improvements, static and dynamic tool usage, and test case additions to prevent further defects from escaping into system test. Catching and resolving component defects in system test is more time-consuming and costly to fix so improvements in unit testing can improve this overall process.

Root cause analysis (RCA) was done periodically throughout the process. RCA is based on the fact that problems are best addressed by attempting to correct or eliminate root causes, as opposed to just addressing the obvious symptoms. It is more likely that problem recurrence will be prevented by directing corrective measures at root causes, even though complete prevention of recurrence by one corrective action is not always possible.

Categories of software defects were analyzed and several process improvements were put into place in order to reduce the numbers of defects in these categories.

Table CS4.2: Actions for improvement.

BIN Name	Action	Owner	Due Date	Status
LTE L1	Perform reviews consistently and log review comments/defects	L1	Ongoing	Work started. Evidence can be referenced •SRS design review completed review comments can be referenced •DL-CCH design review in progress for the new feature
LTE L1	Component owners to analyze the code coverage results and add test cases appropriately	L1	Q3'12	One run of dynamic analysis done with LDRA tool. Areas of improvement identified and are in progress.
QorIQ	Perform reviews consistently and log review comments/defects	BSP	Q3'12	All actions will be applicable for processor, review initiated for IPP - processor, review comments closed for IPP. Uboot test plan reviewed and comments incorporated. Review comments closed for Uboot test plan

Figure CS4.14 shows the root cause analysis that the software team used to drive this process. Figure CS4.15 shows some of the results from the RCA process. These changes were made to the development process over time.

The team analyzed the root cause data from these different collection metrics. A majority of the defects have been categorized as having one of the following root causes:

- change made without informing/checking
- failure to address all configurations or variants
- failure to complete required reviews or testing
- failure to consider dependencies or side effects
- failure to implement complete requirements
- inattention to detail (e.g., typo/logic error)
- incorrect handling of bad input or error cases
- incorrect handling of boundary or edge condition
- incorrect handling of memory or resources
- late or frequently changing requirements.

Some of the key actions taken by the development team after root cause analysis included:

- more automation required, hiring contract resources
- BB testing vendor to drive coverage
- more rigorous code reviews and Matlab modeling.

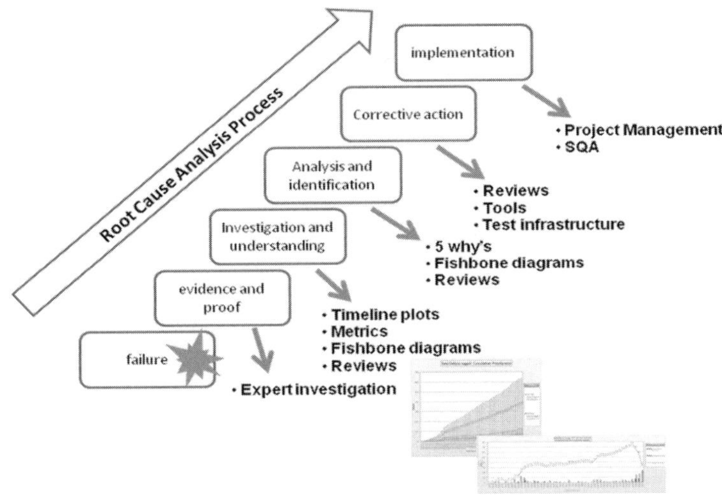

Figure CS4.14:
Root cause analysis process.

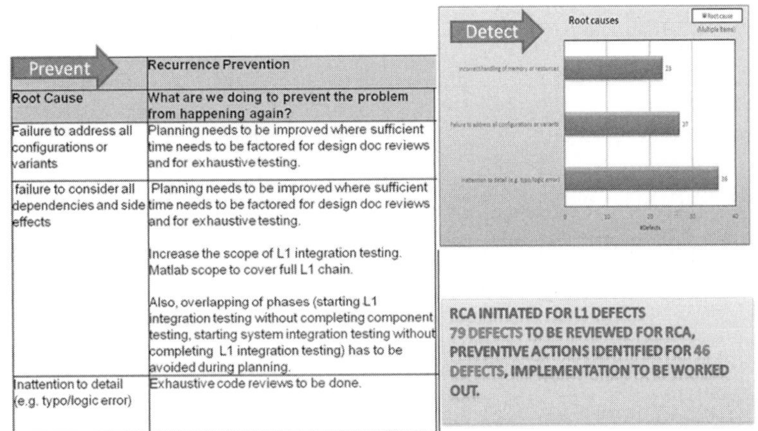

Prevent	Recurrence Prevention
Root Cause	What are we doing to prevent the problem from happening again?
Failure to address all configurations or variants	Planning needs to be improved where sufficient time needs to be factored for design doc reviews and for exhaustive testing.
failure to consider all dependencies and side effects	Planning needs to be improved where sufficient time needs to be factored for design doc reviews and for exhaustive testing. Increase the scope of L1 integration testing. Matlab scope to cover full L1 chain. Also, overlapping of phases (starting L1 integration testing without completing component testing, starting system integration testing without completing L1 integration testing) has to be avoided during planning.
Inattention to detail (e.g. typo/logic error)	Exhaustive code reviews to be done.

Figure CS4.15:
Root cause analysis preventive actions.

Metric 5: test progression for system integration and test; this metric is shown in Figure CS4.16. This proved to be an accurate measure of the progress of system testing for each of the incremental releases. The team as well as management was able to get a more accurate assessment of where we were in our testing plan by looking at total tests run and passed for each release of software. This eliminated the "almost done" mentality from skewing the actual reality of the testing progress. It also allowed us to see where we were

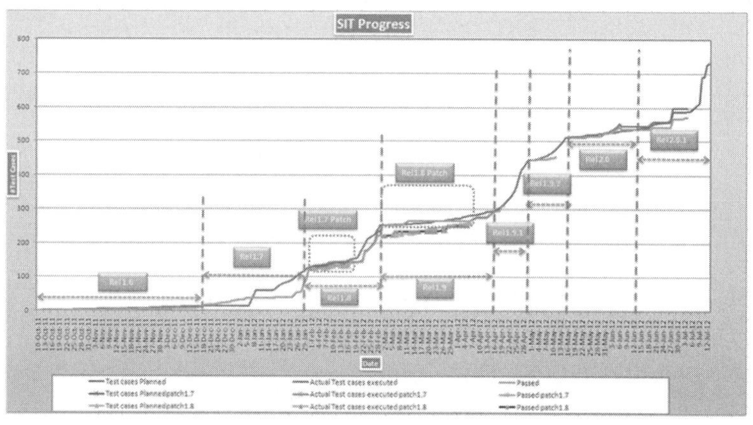

*The total count for each release includes cumulative regression test cases + new test cases

Figure CS4.16:
Weekly test progression for system integration and test.

Table CS4.3: Coverage analysis process by component.

Small Cell LTE L1	LDRA		
Module Name	**Statement coverage**	**Branch/ Decision**	**MC/DC [Modified Condition/Decision]**
Software Component 1	74%	66%	No BC
Software Component 2	81%	73%	No BC
Software Component 3	85%	70%	No BC
Software Component 4	79%	73%	No BC
Software Component 5	44%	39%	No BC
Software Component 6	44%	31%	7%
Software Component 7	47%	44%	8%
Software Component 8	91%	80%	60%
Software Component 9	89%	71%	10%
Software Component 10	* TBD-dependency-availability of coverage tool		
Software Component 11	* TBD-dependency-availability of coverage tool		
Software Component 12	70%	48%	2%
Software Component 13	* TBD-dependency-availability of coverage tool		
Software Component 14	* TBD-dependency-availability of coverage tool		
Software Component 15	* TBD-dependency-availability of coverage tool		

getting delayed by focusing attention on those parts of the graph where we were "flat-lined" for long periods of time.

Table CS4.3 shows a snapshot of coverage analysis by component. Each software component unit test suite was analyzed using a statement coverage tool. Each component was analyzed to branch coverage as well as branch/decision coverage. Branch/decision coverage answers the question; "Has every edge in the program been executed?" In other words, have the requirements of each branch of each control structure (such as in IF and CASE statements) been met as well as not met? The goal for the coverage measure was 90% for basic coverage and 85% for branch/decision coverage. This metric helped the team understand where we had gaps in our unit testing suite. The team added resources to those components where coverage was low in order to increase the overall component coverage.

Table CS4.4 shows a summary of the femtocell stability requirements and the mean time between failure (MTBF) goals. A commercial femtocell has a 99.5% availability, target which equates to 44 hours of downtime per year. The team developed a set of use-case-based tests in order to measure MTBF for the system under test. These use cases include simultaneous uplink (UL) and downlink (DL) configurations in both cabled and over the air (OTA) modes. Commercial user equipment (UE) was used in these stability tests and applications such Jperf and Iperf. Iperf is a commonly used network testing tool that can create TCP and UDP data streams and measure the throughput of a network that is carrying them. Iperf is a tool for network performance measurement written in C/C++. Jperf is a graphical front end for Iperf.

Figure CS4.17 shows a snapshot of the measurements for MTBF for single and multi-user configurations. These measurements show the progress in MTBF and system stability over time. These metrics give a system-level view of the overall stability of the system for different configurations and user types. The data is collected each week using the mainline software version.

Metric 6: performance is a key non-functional requirement for femto base stations. These systems have both throughput as well as latency requirements. Throughput requirements are important for both uplink and downlink channels. Femto stations also have a MIMO

Table CS4.4: Mean time between failures goals.

Level of Availability	Availabilty Target		Downtime Per Year
Commercial	99.5%-Femtocell		43.8 hours
Highly available	99.9%		8.8 hours
Fault resilient	99.99%		53 minutes
Fault tolerant	99.999% "Carrier Grade"-Pico/Metro/Macro		5 minutes
Continuous	100%		0
Acceptable Uptime (%)	**Downtime Per day**	**Downtime Per Month**	**Downtime Per Year**
95	72.00 minutes	36 hours	18.26 days
99	14.40 minutes	7 hours	3.65 days
99.9	86.40 seconds	43 minutes	8.77 hours
99.99	8.64 seconds	4 minutes	52.60 minutes
99 999	0.86 seconds	26 seconds	5.26 minutes

Table CS4.5: MTBF configurations.

MTBF Use Cases									
Sl. Num.	Chain	DL Antennae Cfg	Input Throughput	Cabled/ OTA	Target Duration	Type of UE	# of Ues	Application	Comments
1	DL-UL	Tx.Div	Max for given MCS	Cabled	> = 8	Commercial UE	1	Jperf/Iperf	
2	DL-UL	Tx.Div	Max for given MCS	OTA	> = 8	Commercial UE	1	Jperf/Iperf	Only one data point available
3	DL-UL	Tx.Div	Max for given MCS	Cabled	> = 8	Commercial UE	N(2 UE/ TTI)	Jperf/Iperf	Only one data point available
4	DL-UL	Tx.Div	Max for given MCS	Cabled	> = 8	Commercial UE	N(1 UE/ TTI)	Jperf/Iperf	
5	DL-UL	MIMO	Max for given MCS	Cabled	> = 8	Commercial UE	N(1 UE/ TTI)	Jperf/Iperf	

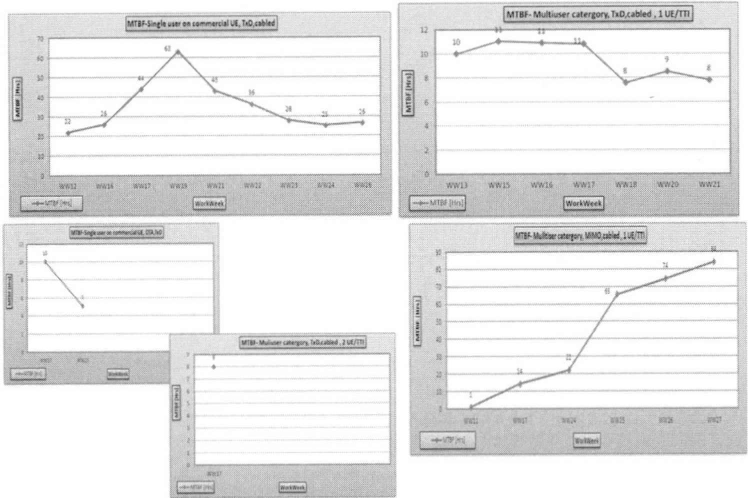

Figure CS4.17:
MTBF results.

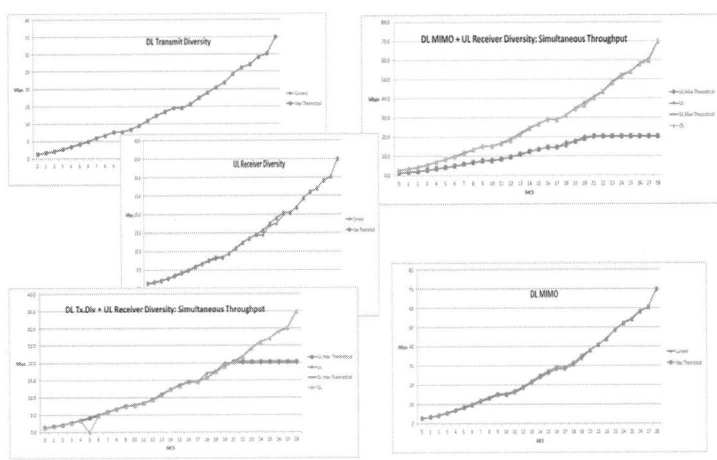

Figure CS4.18:
Throughput results.

(multiple input multiple output) capability (essentially multiple antennas) that creates multiple channels of data transmission.

Figure CS4.18 shows measured performance over a variety of module coding scheme (MCS) configurations. Femto quality coverage will vary with MCS. The expectation is that performance will increase with MCS and this is what the data is showing. Also Figure CS4.19 shows system-level uplink (UL) and downlink (DL) performance. The goal for UL and DL performance varies over time and the system is optimized further during

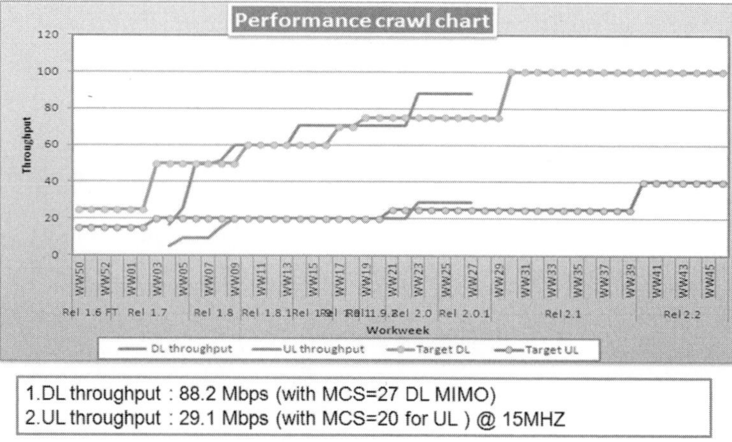

Figure CS4.19:
Uplink and downlink performance data.

later phases of integration. The use cases chosen for these measurements are MCS = 27, and MIMO mode for DL and MCS = 20 and 15 MHz. This current metric snapshot shows progress towards the 100 Mbps downlink performance and 40 Mbps uplink performance.

Static program analysis is the analysis of computer software performed without executing programs (analysis performed on executing programs is known as dynamic analysis). In many cases the analysis is performed on some version of the source code and in the other cases some form of the object code. Static analysis was used to offset human analysis techniques such as code reviews. The team used a commercial tool called Klocwork to perform this analysis.

This tool can also measure cyclomatic complexity of the software. This is used to indicate the complexity of a program. Cyclomatic complexity directly measures the number of linearly independent paths through a program's source code. Cyclomatic complexity is computed using the control flow graph of the computer software. The nodes of this graph correspond to indivisible groups of commands of a program, and a directed edge connects two nodes if the second command might be executed immediately after the first command. This allows an assessment of the overall complexity, and therefore difficulty to test, of a software component.

Table CS4.6 shows the summary of the static analysis for each of the major software components for Layer 1 software. The "Max complexity" column shows the measured cyclomatic complexity. Those components with a measured value greater than 20 were further analyzed for possible re-factoring. If the decision is made to not re-factor, this is summarized in the comments section.

The goal of the development team was to run the static analysis tool prior to each software component check in to the configuration management system.

Table CS4.6: Static analysis data

Project Name	Open Issues	Fixed Issues	No. of Complex Methods with Complexity > 20	Max Complexity	Comments from Component Owners for Complexity
Component 1	0	13	0	13	
Component 2	0	15	0	15	
Component 3	0	42	0	42	Complexity is due to error codes enabled by MACRO
Component 4	3	54	3	54	
Component 5	0	26	0	26	Complexity is due to error codes enabled by MACRO ERROR_CODE_ENABLED.
Component 6	0	111	0	111	Complexity can be reduced by re-designing the functions. More analysis is in progress.
Component 7	1	15	1	15	The reason for the high complexity report is due to extensive error testing and handling that is performed there. This code cannot be refactored or changed. In addition, this code is being performed only once in boot phase.
Component 8	0	290	0	290	
Component 9	1	0	1	0	
Component 10	0	17	0	17	
Component 11	0	148	0	148	Reducing complexity would impact cycle perfomance. More analysis is in progress.
Component 12	0	28	0	28	
Component 13	0	46	0	46	
Component 14	0	6	0	6	
Component 15	2	97	2	97	Code to be revisited in second phase if number of loops can be reduced. ■ Algorithmic constraints restrict any modification to the code structure.
Component 16	4	90	4	90	To reduce complexity more sub-functions will be required which will in-turn impact the cycle performance. Not planned due to BW issue.
Component 17	1	8	1	8	For RSP the complexity could probably be further reduced by introducing more sub functions. However impact on cycles should be further analyze and considered.
Component 18	0	23	0	23	

Metric 7: Figure CS4.20 shows defect density by component with associated cyclomatic complexity and number of test cases. This merged picture shows where testing investment may not be aligned with software complexity and overall number of test cases.

The components with highest defect density are analyzed further. Defect density is the number of confirmed defects detected in a software component during a defined period of development

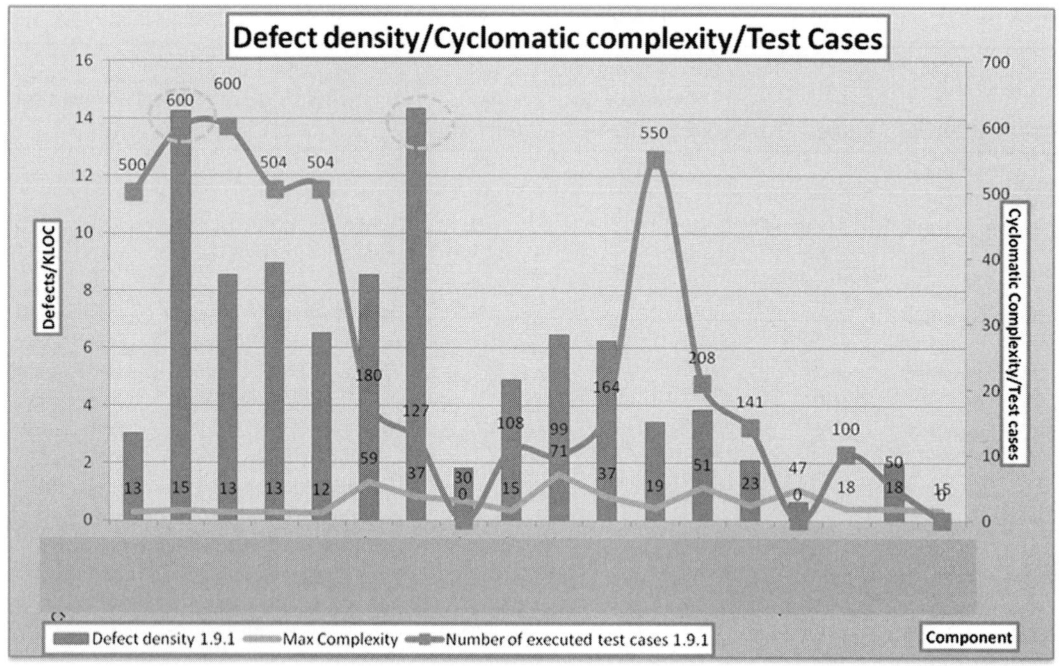

Figure CS4.20:
Defect density by component with associated cyclomatic complexity and number of test cases.

and operation divided by the size of the software component. Key components are highlighted as shown in Figure CS4.20 for further analysis. Defect density is used to compare the relative number of defects in various software components. This analysis helps to identify software component candidates for additional inspection or testing or for possible reengineering, re-factoring, or replacement. Identifying defect-prone components allows the concentration of limited resources into areas with the highest potential return on the investment.

Metric 8: Defect prediction models are used to provide a forecast of future defects escaping to the customer.

Using defect density and defect injection rates from upstream processes makes it is possible to estimate defect rates possible in downstream processes during the final stages of testing. These estimates are used to provide visibility into the software system before it is shipped.

The number of defects discovered and fixed during the life-cycle phases of a software project conforms to a numerical distribution. One popular distribution is a Rayleigh distribution. Estimation of overall defect density of the software project can be determined by performing a non-linear regression analysis using Rayleigh with observed defect data for design reviews and code reviews. Estimation for the number of defects for any stage (e.g., unit testing) can be obtained through a probability distribution function.

The nature of the Rayleigh curve indicates the overall pattern of the defect-removal rate in the life-cycle of the software. The steeper the slope, the less defect-prone the software is when delivered to the customer. If the slope is flat, it indicates an inefficient defect-removal rate which may indicate a larger number of defects escaping to the customer.

The Rayleigh model **is** one of a family of Weibull distributions. Rayleigh has been shown to be most suitable for predicting the reliability of software. This model predicts the expected value of defect density at different stages of the life-cycle of the project, once key parameters (such as the total number of defects or total cumulative defect rate and peak of the curve in terms of unit of time) for the curve are decided.

This approach is summarized in Figure CS4.21. The development team used a tool called Minitab to perform this estimation. The key input measures used were lines of code (LOC) for each software component along with the cumulative defects for those software components.

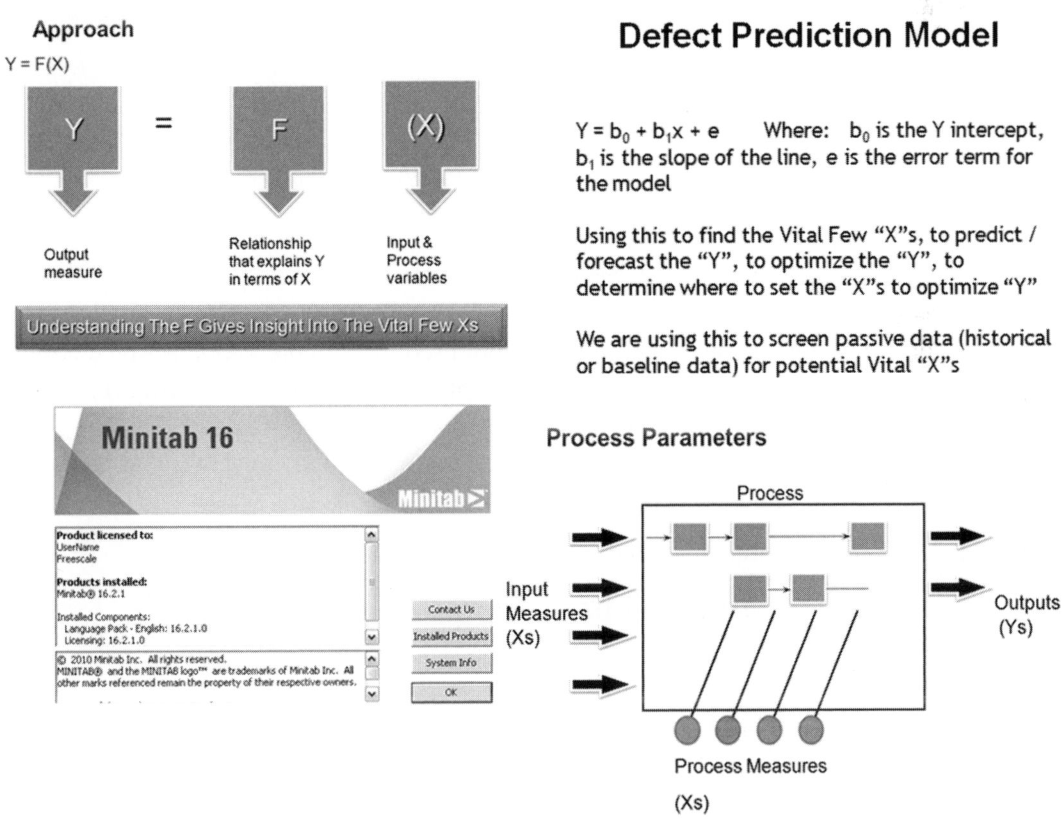

Figure CS4.21:
Defect prediction model.

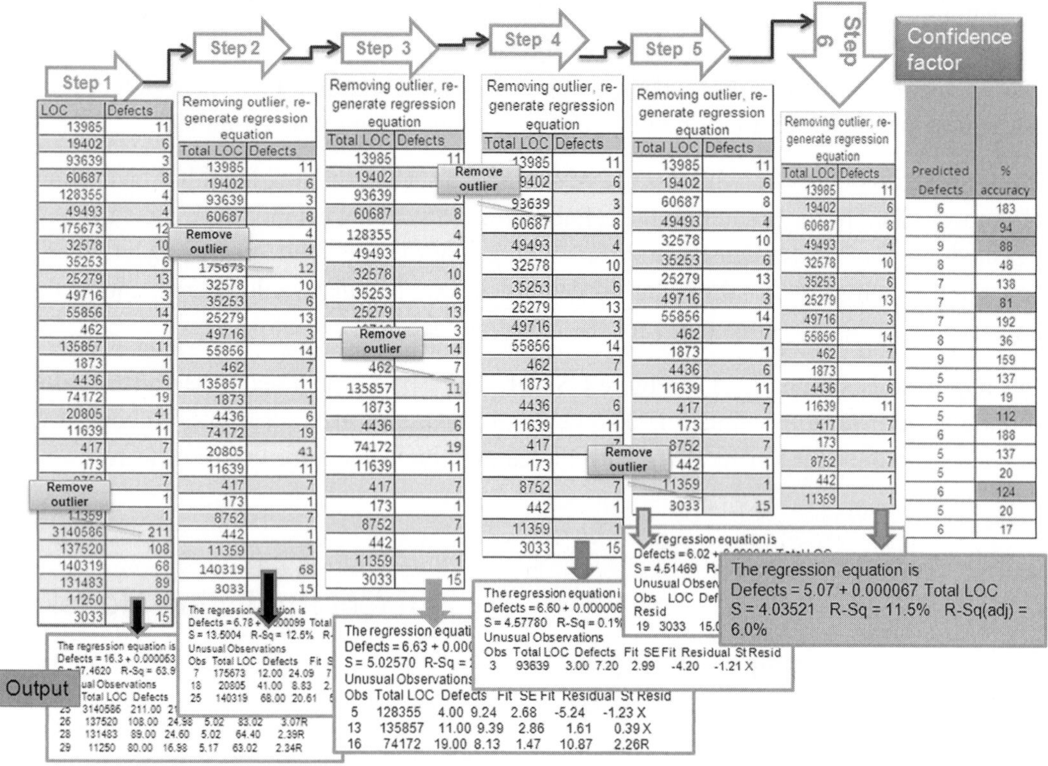

Figure CS4.22:
Defect prediction data.

Figure CS4.22 shows the iterative nature of the tool used to compute the defect prediction model. The tool uses the input data (software lines of code and defect information) to perform a regression equation. Outliers are discarded and the regression equation is re-computed without the outliers. This continues until the equation converges and then terminates with a final regression equation.

The final regression equation computed is;

$$\text{Defects} = 5.07 + 0.000067 \text{ Total LOC}$$

where $S = 4.03521$, $R^2 = 11.5\%$, $R^2(\text{adj}) = 6.0\%$.

Predictor	Coef	SE Coef	T	P
Constant	5.073	1.371	3.70	0.002

In this example (Figure CS4.23), there are only a few data points near the line, depicting 50% accuracy of the model. This would have to be improved in order to get a more accurate prediction of future defects.

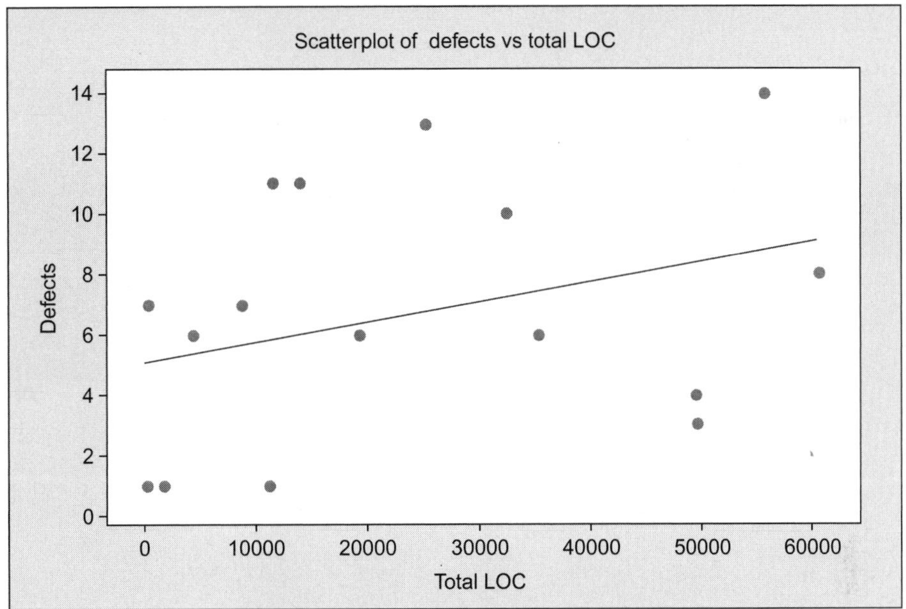

Figure CS4.23:
Scatterplot of defects versus total LOC.

R^2 is the percent of variation explained the model. R^2 (adjusted) is the percent of variation explained by the model, adjusted for the number of terms in the model and the number of data points. A good model should yield both a high R^2 and a high R^2 (adjusted). Since the P-value in the table is less than 0.01, there is a statistically significant relationship between the variables at the 95% confidence level. The R^2 statistic indicates that the model as fitted explains 95.8% of the variability in defects. The results show a high R^2 (adjusted) value $\sim$95.6% (practical significance) and a low P-value $<$ 0.05 (statistical significance).

Summary

Software metrics are measures of key attributes of software products and processes. Metrics play an increasingly central role in the planning and control of software development projects. The key to successful risk management is in the ability to measure. In order to increase quality and productivity, weaknesses must be identified in the methods currently used and steps taken to strengthen these areas of our software development process. In this femto software program, key metrics were identified and tracked in order to improve overall software quality.

Index

Note: Page numbers followed by "*f*" and "*t*" refer to figures and tables, respectively.

B

C

E

G

H

P

S

T